FACTS
ABOUT THE
STATES

OTHER BOOKS BY JOSEPH NATHAN KANE

Famous First Facts

Facts About the Presidents

FACTS
ABOUT THE
STATES

EDITORS

JOSEPH NATHAN KANE
STEVEN ANZOVIN
JANET PODELL

THE H. W. WILSON COMPANY
NEW YORK
1989

Library of Congress Cataloging in Publication Data

Kane, Joseph Nathan, 1899–
    Facts about the states / Joseph Nathan Kane, Steven Anzovin, Janet Podell.
        p. cm.
    Bibliography: p.
    ISBN 0-8242-0407-7 : $60.00
    1. United States—History, Local—Miscellanea.   2. State governments—
United States—Miscellanea.   3. United States—Administrative and political
divisions—Miscellanea.   I. Anzovin, Steven.   II. Podell, Janet.   III. Title.
E180.K4   1989   89-14829
973—dc20   CIP

PRINTED IN THE UNITED STATES OF AMERICA

CONTENTS

Comparative Tables

PREFACE

FACTS ABOUT THE STATES presents in convenient reference form the basic geographic, demographic, economic, political, and cultural facts about the fifty states of the Union, the District of Columbia, and Puerto Rico. Since the vast range of statistical information on the United States cannot be condensed into a single volume, the editors have selected information that not only provides concise portraits of individual states but also allows comparisons between states using identical standards of measurement. For this reason we have drawn our information primarily from the federal government sources listed on page ix rather than the numerous private, regional, and state organizations that analyze consumption, expenditure, and production in their fields of interest. The facts presented reflect the latest published government reports or official estimates.

Like FACTS ABOUT THE PRESIDENTS and FAMOUS FIRST FACTS, FACTS ABOUT THE STATES is organized to facilitate access to information. Within each state's chapter the facts are set out as follows: **basic information,** including the state seal, official symbols, location, population, motto, and capital city; **geography and climate,** including a topographic description, elevations, major rivers, lakes, and reservoirs, record temperatures, and land use statistics; **history,** a chronology of important events in the state's history from earliest European settlement to the present; **demography,** including population statistics and data on life expectancy, personal wealth, and birth, death, and crime rates; **government and politics,** including a list of all governors and their terms in office, salary levels and terms for elected and appointed officials, number of congressional representatives and electoral votes, and a record of how the state has voted in presidential elections since 1948; **finances,** listing revenues and expenditures; **economy,** listing production of major crops, livestock, and principal manufactures, along with employment and transportation figures and energy sources; **culture and education,** listing religions, ethnic groups, languages, major museums, libraries, art organizations, major league teams, and state holidays.

Each state's chapter concludes with three bibliographies: **the state in literature,** an annotated reading list including not only prose fiction but also journals, memoirs, collections of folklore, and examples of nature and travel writing—works that convey the character of a particular region or place at a particular time. These lists, which are far from exhaustive, are compiled from a wide range of general and specialized sources that includes BOOK REVIEW DIGEST, FICTION CATALOG, the Wilson Authors series, and studies and bibliographies of regional and state literature. **Guides to resources** brings together indexes, bibliographies, catalogs, surveys of historic sites, and other aids to research. **Selected nonfiction sources** lists important secondary sources for the study of the state's social, economic, political, and cultural history.

Finally, the **comparative tables** section of FACTS ABOUT THE STATES facilitates comparisons among the states in the following categories: area and population density, demography, order of settlement and admission to statehood, geographic characteristics, transportation, education, Defense Department expenditure, and the presidential vote.

FACTS ABOUT THE STATES is the inspiration of Joseph Nathan Kane, and to his original conception are owed the structure, scope, and flavor of the book. For the vast range of information from which we have selected our facts we are indebted to the many agencies and organizations named as our sources. During the lengthy collaborative process of selection, the aim of publishing a single, manageable volume has obliged us to omit many interesting facts. A first edition, however, is only a beginning, and it is our hope that future editions will allow more information to be included.

New York
July 1989

The Editors

Sources

U.S. Army Corps of Engineers: ports
U.S. Bureau of Economic Analysis: personal income
U.S. Bureau of Justice Statistics: federal and state prisoners
U.S. Bureau of Labor Statistics: employment and unemployment figures
U.S. Bureau of the Census: area, inland water, state population (including analyses of race, age, residence, education level, families below poverty line, and non-English-speakers), population of major cities, and state finances
U.S. Department of Agriculture: land use
U.S. Department of Commerce: temperatures
U.S. Department of Defense: military installations, civilian employees, military personnel, and contract awards
U.S. Department of Education: colleges and universities and enrollments; average teacher salary and pupil-teacher ratio in public schools
U.S. Department of the Interior: geographic centers, elevations, rivers, lakes, tribal lands, and reservations
U.S. Energy Information Administration: energy sources
U.S. Federal Aviation Administration: airports and hubs
U.S. Federal Bureau of Investigation: crime rate
U.S. Federal Highway Administration: motor vehicle registrations, miles of roadway
U.S. Fish and Wildlife Service: national wildlife refuges
U.S. Internal Revenue Service: millionaires
U.S. National Center for Health Statistics: average life expectancy, marriage, divorce, birth, and infant mortality rates; deaths from motor vehicle accidents
U.S. National Forest Service: national forest system
U.S. National Oceanic and Atmospheric Administration: tidal shoreline
U.S. National Park Service: national park system and national sites
U.S. Social Security Administration: public assistance recipients
National Association of State Park Directors: state park and recreation areas
National Center for State Courts: judiciary
National Education Association: expenditures per pupil
National Governors' Association: executive branch
American Association of Museums: museums
Association of American Railroads: railroad mileage
Council of State Governments: constitution and legislature
Alan S. Guttmacher Institute: abortion rate
Distilled Spirits Council of the United States, Inc.: alcohol consumption
NAACP Legal Defense Fund: capital punishment
People for the American Way: 1988 presidential primary elections

Information about state economies was derived from a variety of sources, including the U.S. Bureau of the Census, Bureau of Mines, Economic Research Service, Department of Agriculture, and Energy Information Administration.

Information about state insignia, symbols, governors, religions, ethnicities, Native American tribes, minimum ages, museums, arts organizations, sports teams, and holidays was derived from state publications.

FACTS
ABOUT THE
STATES

ALABAMA

Alabama is in the east south central part of the US. It is bordered on the north by Tennessee; on the east by Georgia and the Chattahoochie River; on the south by Florida and the Gulf of Mexico; and on the west by Mississippi.

FULL NAME State of Alabama
POSTAL ABBREVIATION AL
INHABITANT Alabamian
ADMITTED TO THE UNION Dec. 14, 1819.
  22d state
POPULATION (est. 1987) 4,083,000.
  Percent of US total: 1.68%. Rank: 22d

CAPITAL CITY Montgomery, in southeast central Alabama, on the Alabama River; population 185,000 (est. 1984). Founded in 1819, it was incorporated as a city in 1837 and became the state capital in 1847 (previous capitals were Huntsville, Cahaba, and Tuscaloosa). In 1861 it was made the first capital of the Confederacy.

STATE NAME AND NICKNAMES The name Alabama is probably derived from *alba* and *amo*, two Choctaw words meaning "plant gatherer." The term was applied to a tribe of Indians who gave their name to the Alabama River and thence to the state. The first European use of the term was in the records of the 1540 de Soto expedition. Alabama is also known as the Yellowhammer State, the Camellia State, and the Heart of Dixie.

STATE SEAL A map showing Alabama and parts of its neighbors, with the state in yellow, Mississippi in red, Tennessee in brown, Georgia in green, Florida in blue, and the Gulf of Mexico in a darker blue; the major rivers of Alabama are visible. A white border bears the legends "Alabama" and "Great Seal," with six stars.

MOTTO Audemus Jura Nostra Defendere (We dare maintain our rights)

SONG "Alabama," lyrics by Julia S. Tutwiler, music by Edna Gockel Gussen.

SYMBOLS
Flower camellia
Tree southern pine (longleaf yellow pine)
Bird yellowhammer
Mineral hematite
Rock marble
Freshwater fish largemouth bass
Saltwater fish tarpon
Horse rocking horse
Nut pecan
Dance square dance

LICENSE PLATE Blue on white, with two red hearts and red legend "Heart of Dixie."

FLAG A crimson cross of St. Andrew on a field of white.

GEOGRAPHY AND CLIMATE

The southern end of the Appalachian Mountains gives the northeastern half of Alabama a rugged character. A low-lying coastal plain with rich black soil covers the southern part of the state; the coastline itself is dotted with bayous and swamps. Breezes from the Gulf of Mexico moderate a generally hot, wet climate with a long growing season.

AREA 51,705 square miles. Rank: 29th
INLAND WATER 938 square miles
GEOGRAPHIC CENTER Chilton, 12 miles SW of Clanton
ELEVATIONS *Highest point:* Cheaha Mountain, in Cleburne County, 2,407 feet. *Lowest point:* Gulf of Mexico, sea level. *Mean elevation:* 500 feet

MAJOR RIVERS Mobile, Alabama, Tombigbee, Coosa

MAJOR LAKES AND RESERVOIRS Wheeler, Wilson, Mitchell, Guntersville, Martin, Weiss, Smith, Dannelly

TIDAL SHORELINE Gulf coast, 607 miles

LAND USE

	Thousands of acres
Urban (1982)	906
Rural (1982)	29,697
Cropland (1982)	4,510
Pastureland (1982)	3,817
Rangeland (1982)	0
Forestland (1982)	20,633
State parks and recreation areas (1983)	48
National park system (1984)	7
National forest system (1984)	1,274
Tribal lands (1984)	0

TEMPERATURES The highest recorded temperature was 112° F, on September 5, 1925, at Centerville. The lowest was -27° F, on January 30, 1966, at New Market.

NATIONAL SITES

NATIONAL HISTORIC SITE Tuskegee Institute
NATIONAL MONUMENT Russell Cave
NATIONAL MILITARY PARK Horseshoe Bend

NATIONAL WILDLIFE REFUGES Choctaw, Eufaula, Wheeler-Blowing Wind Cave

HISTORY

1507	Mobile Bay is shown on map by Austrian cartographer Martin Waldseemüller.
1519	Alonzo Alvárez de Piñeda is the first European to enter Mobile Bay.
1528	Panfílo de Narvez anchors in Mobile Bay.
1540	*July 2.* Spanish force led by Hernando de Soto reaches Mobile area from Florida. *July 26.* De Soto arrives at the Indian capital of Coosa near Talladega Creek. *October 18.* Spaniards defeat the Indians at the Battle of Mauvilla. Indian chief Tuscaloosa is killed. De Soto continues westward toward the Mississippi.
1559	Tristán de Luna establishes a settlement on Mobile Bay.
1561	Failing to find gold, the Spaniards abandon their settlement.
1629	English grant of the Carolinas to Sir Robert Heath, extending westward without boundaries, challenges Spanish claims.
1663	Second English grant, to Sir George Carteret, reinforces English claims.
1699	French force led by Pierre Le Moyne moves down the Mississippi and discovers Dauphin Island, claiming the region for France.
1702	*January 16.* Le Sieur de Bienville founds Fort Louis de la Mobile, first French settlement.
1704	Indians, incited by Spanish, attack the French settlement, but the French reinforce and *Le Pelican* lands a group of young women.
1711	Fort Louis is re-established at the healthier site of present-day Mobile.
1714	French build a second settlement, Fort Toulouse (near modern Wetumpka), to discourage English westward expansion.
1717	*March 19.* Crozat leads three more shiploads of settlers to Mobile.
1719	French land a shipload of black slaves on Dauphin Island.
1720	Second disembarkation of slaves at Mobile.
1722	French establishment of New Orleans consolidates their hold on the region.

1732	English grant Georgia to James Oglethorpe, renewing their territorial challenge.
1733	Hurricane and ensuing epidemic destroy Mobile.
1736	*May 20.* English and their Indian allies defeat the French.
1763	Treaty of Paris ends the Seven Years' War. French cede territory east of the Mississippi to Britain, so ending the period of French domination of Alabama. *October 20.* English force occupies Mobile.
1772	*August 30.* Second hurricane destroys Mobile.
1778	*March 7.* Abortive uprising in Mobile against the British.
1780	*March 4.* Britain declares war on France and Spain. Spanish seize Mobile.
1783	*September 3.* In Paris treaty Britain cedes to US all territory east of the Mississippi except Florida, leaving US and Spain to dispute possession of Alabama coast.
1786	*January 3.* US treaty with the Choctaw.
1787	Georgia/Alabama border established.
1802	Abram Mordecai builds the first cotton gin in the state at Coosada Bluff.
1803	*October 20.* Louisiana Purchase increases commerce and settlement in the region.
1806	Jefferson College, first educational institution in the state, founded. Migration from the Carolinas and Georgia increases.
1811	*Mobile Centinel*, the state's first newspaper, published.
1812	US declares war on Great Britain, thus legitimizing hostilities against Britain's ally, Spain.
1813	*April 15.* General James Wilkinson defeats the Spanish garrison of Mobile. *July 27.* Indian Wars begin with the battle of Burnt Corn. *August 30.* Indians led by William Weatherford attack Fort Mims.
1814	*March 27.* General Andrew Jackson defeats the Indians at the Battle of Horseshoe Bend. *August 9.* Jackson dictates a treaty compelling the Creeks to cede approximately half of the state.
1815	*February 12.* British occupy outer defenses of Mobile, but Treaty of Ghent ends the War of 1812.
1817	*March 3.* Congress passes an act creating Alabama Territory on the admission of Mississippi to statehood.
1818	*January 19.* First legislative assembly convenes. The first pig iron is made.
1819	*July 5.* First state convention convenes at Huntsville. *August 2.* Draft constitution signed. *December 14.* Alabama admitted to the Union as the 22d state.
1827	*October 21.* Fire destroys large part of Mobile.
1830	*September 27.* Choctaws cede their remaining lands in the Treaty of Rabbit Creek, and begin "the Great Removal" to Oklahoma.
1831	First railroad constructed near the Tennessee River.
1832	Creeks and Chickasaws cede remaining Indian lands.
1833	*November 13.* The day when "stars fell on Alabama."
1836	Cherokees begin their enforced migration to Oklahoma.
1848	*March 3.* Telegraph service begins.
1861	*January 11.* Delegates to secession convention vote to secede from the Union by a majority of 61 to 39. *February 4.* Provisional Congress of Confederate States meets in Montgomery and adopts constitution February 8. *May 21.* Congress votes to move the Confederate capital to Richmond, Virginia.
1864	*August 5.* Admiral David Farragut defeats Confederates at the Battle of Mobile Bay. *December 15.* Union forces invade from Tennessee and Georgia.
1865	*April 12.* Mobile and Montgomery surrender. *September 30.* New state constitution adopted.
1866	*January 16.* State legislature asks President Johnson to withdraw Federal troops.
1873	*December 9.* Normal school for blacks opens in Huntsville.
1876	*April 3.* Storm causes extensive damage. Federal troops withdraw from the state.
1881	*February 10.* Booker T. Washington opens the Tuskegee Institute.

1888	*March 8*. First Alabama steel produced at Birmingham.
1898	University of Alabama becomes completely coeducational.
1915	Liquor prohibition law goes into effect.
1918	Worker's compensation program begun.
1925	*May 18*. The state's first radio station, WBRC in Birmingham, begins broadcasting.
1931	*April*. In the Scottsboro Trial, eight of nine black youths are convicted and sentenced to death.
1932	*March 21*. Hurricane kills 315 people.
1953	NAACP obtains the admission of Autherine Lucy to the University of Alabama but harassment leads to her hasty withdrawal.
1954	Martin Luther King, Jr. becomes pastor of Dexter Avenue Baptist Church, Montgomery.
1955	*December 1*. Rosa Parks, a black seamstress, refuses to give up her seat on a Montgomery bus to a white person and is arrested. A 381-day black boycott of city buses follows.
1956	*November*. US Supreme Court declares state's bus segregation laws unconstitutional.
1958	First US satellite to be launched into orbit is developed at Huntsville.
1963	*January 14*. George C. Wallace becomes Governor, defying federal intervention in his inaugural speech.
	May 3. Racial conflicts climax in Birmingham when ousted Mayor Eugene "Bull" Connor orders firehoses and dogs turned on peaceful demonstrators. This nationally televised action spurs demonstrations from coast to coast.
1964	*June 11*. Two black students enroll at the University of Alabama in the face of local protest and the opposition of Governor Wallace.
1965	*March 23*. King marches 5 days with 25,000 followers from Montgomery to Selma gathering voter-registration support for blacks.
1967	*January 10*. Mrs. George C. (Lurleen) Wallace becomes governor.
1968	George Wallace runs for President.
1972	*May 15*. Governor Wallace is shot in Maryland while campaigning for President.
1982	9.8% unemployment is the second-highest rate in the country.

DEMOGRAPHY

Population (est. 1987) . . . 4,083,000
Population (1980) 3,893,978
Population density
   per square mile (1980) 75.3

POPULATION BY RACE (1980)
American Indian/Aleut/
   Eskimo 7,561
Asian/Pacific Islander 9,695
Black 995,623
Hispanic 33,100
White 2,869,688
Other 7,494

POPULATION CHARACTERISTICS (1980)
Percent of state population
Urban 47.3
Rural 52.7
Under 18 . . . . 29.8
65 or older 11.3
College-educated 12.6
Families below poverty line . . . 14.9
Public assistance recipients 8.1

Per capita personal
   income (1986) $11,115
Millionaires per 100,000
   residents (1982) 104.0
Average life expectancy (1980) . . . 72.53
Marriage rate per 1,000
   residents (1986) 11.5
Divorce rate per 1,000
   residents (1986) 6.2
Birth rate per 1,000
   residents (1985) 14.7
Infant mortality rate per
   1,000 births (1985) 13.0
Abortion rate per 1,000
   live births (1985) 333
Crime rate per 100,000
   residents (1986)
Violent 558.0
Property 3,730.3
Federal and state prisoners per
   100,000 residents (1984) 259
Alcohol consumption in gallons
   per capita (1985) 31.3
Deaths from motor vehicle accidents
   per 100,000 residents (1985) . . 22.0

MAJOR CITIES

	1984 population (est.)	Huntsville	149,527
Birmingham	279,813	Mobile	204,923
Dothan	52,052	Montgomery	184,963
		Tuscaloosa	73,151

GOVERNMENT AND POLITICS

Number of US Representatives 7
Electoral votes 9

POLITICAL PARTY NOMINEES FROM STATE
 * winner

William Smith (Whig faction)	1836 VP
William Rufus De Vane King*	
(D)	1852 VP
John Jackson Spackman (D)	1952 VP
John Geraerdt Crommelin	
(National States' Rights)	1960 VP
George Corley Wallace	
(American Independent/	
Courage/Patriotic)	1968 P

PRESIDENTIAL PRIMARY ELECTION In 1988, Alabama sent 61 Democratic delegates and 38 Republican delegates to the national conventions.

CONSTITUTION Alabama has had six constitutions: 1819, 1861, 1865, 1868, 1875, and the present one, adopted in 1901.

LEGISLATURE The Legislature is divided into the Senate (35 members, 4-year term, minimum age 25) and the House of Representatives (140 members, 4-year term, minimum age 21). In 1987, legislators were paid $10 per diem for a maximum of 105 days.

JUDICIARY The highest court is the Supreme Court, with 9 judges serving 6-year terms. In 1987, the annual salary was $77,420.

EXECUTIVE The governor serves a 4-year term; the minimum age for holding office is 30. In 1987, the annual salary was $70,223. There are 17 other elected officials.

PRESIDENTIAL VOTE 1948-1988 *(in percents)*

Year	State Winner	Democratic	Republican
1948	J. Strom Thurmond (States' Rights Democrat, 79.7)		19.0
1952	Stevenson (D)	64.6	35.0
1956	Stevenson (D)	56.4	39.5
1960	Kennedy (D)	56.8	42.1
1964	Goldwater (R)		69.5
1968	George C. Wallace (American Independent, 65.8)	18.8	14.0
1972	Nixon (R)	25.5	72.4
1976	Carter (D)	55.7	42.6
1980	Reagan (R)	47.5	48.8
1984	Reagan (R)	38.3	60.5
1988	Bush (R)	40.0	60.0

GOVERNORS

Governors of Mississippi Territory

Winthrop Sargent	1709-1801
William C.C. Claiborne	1801-1805
Robert Williams	1805-1809
David Holmes	1809-1817

Alabama Territorial Governor

William C. Bibb	1817-1819

State Governors

William W. Bibb (D)	1819-1820
Thomas Bibb (D)	1820-1821
Israel Pickens (D)	1821-1825
John Murphy (D)	1825-1829
Gabriel Moore (D)	1829-1831
Samuel B. Moore (D)	1831
John Gayle (D)	1831-1835
Clement C. Clay (D)	1835-1837
Hugh McVay (D)	1837
Arthur P. Bagby (D)	1837-1841
Benjamin Fitzpatrick (D)	1841-1845
Joshua L. Martin (D)	1845-1847
Reuben Chapman (D)	1847-1849
Henry W. Collier (D)	1849-1853
John A. Winston (D)	1853-1857
Andrew B. Moore (D)	1857-1861
John G. Shorter (D)	1861-1863
Thomas H. Watts (D)	1863-1865
Lewis E. Parsons (D/provisional governor)	1865

Robert M. Patton (R)   1865-1867
Wager Swayne (military governor)   1867-1868
William H. Smith (R)   1868-1870
Robert B. Lindsay (D)   1870-1872
David P. Lewis (R)   1872-1874
George S. Houston (D)   1874-1878
Rufus W. Cobb (D)   1878-1882
Edward A. O'Neal (D)   1882-1886
Thomas Seay (D)   1886-1890
Thomas G. Jones (D)   1890-1894
William C. Oates (D)   1894-1896
Joseph F. Johnston (D)   1896-1900
William J. Samford (D)   1900-1901
William D. Jelks (D)   1901-1904
Russell McW. Cunningham (D/acting)   1904-1905
Braxton B. Comer (D)   1907-1911
Emmett O'Neal (D)   1911-1915
Charles Henderson (D)   1915-1919
Thomas E. Kilby (D)   1919-1923
William W. Brandon (D)   1923-1927
Bibb Graves (D)   1927-1931
Benjamin M. Miller (D)   1931-1935
Bibb Graves (D)   1935-1939
Frank M. Dixon (D)   1939-1943
Chauncey M. Sparks (D)   1943-1947
James E. Folsom (D)   1947-1951
Gordon Persons (D)   1951-1955
James E. Folsom (D)   1955-1959
John Patterson (D)   1959-1963
George C. Wallace (D)   1963-1967
Lurleen Wallace (D)   1967-1968
Albert P. Brewer (D)   1968-1971
George C. Wallace (D)   1971-1979
Forrest James Jr. (D)   1979-1983
George C. Wallace (D)   1983-1987
Guy Hunt (R)   1987-

MINIMUM AGES

Majority	19
Marriage with parental consent	14
Marriage without parental consent	18
Making a will	19
Buying alcohol	21
Jury duty	19
Leaving school	16
Driver's license	16

CAPITAL PUNISHMENT
Number executed 1976-88: 3
On death row, Aug. 1, 1988: 95

MILITARY INSTALLATIONS
Total number: 34
Major bases:
  Army: 3
  Air Force: 1

FINANCES

Thousands of dollars

GENERAL REVENUE (1985)

Total general revenue	5,535,054
Total tax revenue	2,924,048
Sales and gross receipts	1,611,284
Individual income taxes	710,195
Corporate net income taxes	212,261

GENERAL EXPENDITURE (1985)

Total general expenditure	5,544,133
Education	2,247,464
Public welfare	659,853
Health	172,950
Hospitals	383,486
Natural resources	113,137
Highways	670,019
Police	43,631
Corrections	113,621

FEDERAL AID (1985)   1,719,040

ECONOMY

Cotton has been supplanted by soybeans as Alabama's main cash crop. Other major crops are peanuts and other legumes, pecans, fruits (especially melons), and tomatoes. Livestock and livestock products include chickens, eggs, beef, hogs, and dairy products. Alabama is an important primary metals manufacturing state, with steel fabrication supported by large deposits of iron ore, coal, and limestone. Other minerals include bauxite, natural gas, oil, manganese, copper, and asbestos. Steel, textiles, chemicals, wood products, and processed food are the major manufacturing industries.

EMPLOYMENT (1984)

Thousands of persons

Total number of employed workers	1,594
Construction	64.5
Finance, insurance, and real estate	62.6
Government	293.8
Mining	14.4
Manufacturing	358.4
Services	227.4
Transport, communications, and utilities	72.1
Wholesale and retail trade	290.3

Percent of civilian labor force unemployed (1984)	11.1

DEPARTMENT OF DEFENSE (1985)

Civilian workers employed . . 27,317
Military personnel 23,096
Contract awards . . . . $1.418 billion

ENERGY SOURCES FOR ELECTRIC UTILITIES (1983)

	Percent
Coal	52.2
Gas	0.1
Hydroelectric	14.6
Nuclear	33.0
Petroleum	0.1

TRANSPORTATION

Motor vehicles registered
in state (1986) 3,456,934
Miles of roads, streets
and highways (1986) 87,979
Miles of Class I railways
operated (1986) 3,650
Airports (1983) 169
Aviation hubs (1983) 4
Largest hub: Birmingham
Major ports, with gross tonnage in
thousands (1985):
Mobile 37,749

CULTURE AND EDUCATION

Native American tribes

Before the 19th century, Alabama was home to the Alabama, Apalachicola, Chatot, Cherokee, Chickasaw, Choctaw, Creek, Koasati, Mobile, Muklasa, Napochi, Natchez, Okmulgee, Pawokti, Sawokli, Shawnee, Taensa, Tohome, Tuskegee, and Yamasee. Some Creek communities remain.

Religions, ethnicities, and languages

Most Alabamians are descendants of the settlers and slaves who arrived in the 18th and 19th centuries. They are predominantly Protestant. In 1980, 1.9 percent of the population spoke a language other than English at home.

Major museums and libraries

Anniston Museum of Natural History
Birmingham Museum of Art
George Washington Carver Museum, Tuskegee Institute
Huntsville Museum of Art
Montgomery Museum of Fine Arts

Major arts organizations

Alabama Shakespeare Festival, Montgomery

Alabama Symphony Orchestra, Birmingham
Birmingham Opera Theater
Mobile Opera

Colleges and universities

Number public (1986-87) 53
Number private (1986-87) 26
Total enrollment, in full-time equivalent students (1985) 149,000

Public elementary and secondary schools

Expenditure per pupil in average daily attendance (1986-87) $2,610
Pupil-teacher ratio (1987) 19.8
Average teacher salary (1986-87) $24,480

Holidays

Robert E. Lee's Birthday. 3d Monday in January
Mardi Gras Day. Tuesday before Ash Wednesday
Confederate Memorial Day. Fourth Monday in April
Thomas Jefferson's Birthday. April 13
Jefferson Davis's Birthday. 1st Monday in June
State Fair, Birmingham. Early October

ALABAMA IN LITERATURE

James Agee and **Walker Evans** *Let Us Now Praise Famous Men* (1941)
Classic account of the lives of sharecroppers based on observations and interviews of 1936.

Byron Arnold *Folksongs of Alabama* (1950)
Anthology of music and lyrics.

Joseph J. Baldwin *The Flush Times of Alabama and Mississippi* (1853)
Classic memoir of the social life and customs of pioneers, with fictional accounts of rural characters.

Joe Barnes *Man on a Mountain* (1969)
An informal account of the Mountain Lakes region.

Philip D. Beidler (ed.) *The Art of Fiction in the Heart of Dixie: An Anthology of Alabama Writers* (1986)

Jack Bethea *Cotton* (1928)
Novel about the hardships of cotton farming. Bethea, editor of the *Birmingham Post*, also wrote the novels *Red Rock* (1924) and *Honor Bound* (1927), realistic accounts of convict life intended to reform the prison system.

Sara Brooks (ed. Thordis Simonsen) *You May Plow Here: The Narrative of Sara Brooks* (1987)
Oral history of a black domestic worker from a rural background.

Joe David Brown *Paper Moon* (1972)
Children's adventure set in rural Alabama during the Depression.

Ray B. Brown (ed.) *A Night with the Hants and Other Alabama Experiences* (1976)
Collection of local folklore.

Virginia P. Brown and **Laurella Owens** *Toting the Lead Row: Ruby Pickens Tartt, Alabama Folklorist* (1981)
Biography of a pioneer folklorist.

M. B. Bruson *Pea River Logic. Hand-Me-Downs from Grandfather's Trunk* (1987)
Collection of folktales.

Hortense Calisher *False Entry* (1961)
Novel about a white man who testifies against racists in a murder trial.

Nancy Callahan *The Freedom Quilting Bee* (1987)
History of a black woman's cooperative in Wilcox County, with an account of black rural life.

Truman Capote *A Christmas Memory* (1956)
Autobiographical story of the author's childhood.

Carl L. Carmer *Stars Fell on Alabama* (1934)
Account of customs and folklore in the 1920s.

Clarence Cason *90° in the Shade* (1935, rpt. 1983)
Memoir of life in the 1930s.

Frederick Carleton Chamberlin *In the Shoe String Country: A True Picture of Southern Life* (1906)
A study of Alabama politics and racial segregation.

Richard Chase *Jack Tales* (1943)
Collection of Mountain Country tales.

James Saxon Childers *In the Deep South* (1936, rpt. 1988)
Novel of social protest about the friendship between a white journalist and a black musician in 1930s Birmingham. Childers, who taught at Birmingham-Southern, used the college as a setting for his novel *Hilltop in the Rain* (1928).

Victoria Clayton *Black and White under the Old Regime* (1899, rpt. 1970)
Autobiography of a Barbour County woman who managed her plantation during her husband's service with the Confederate Army.

Sarah Johnson Cocke *Bypaths in Dixie: Folk Tales of the South* (1911, rpt. 1972)

Octavus Roy Cohen *Come Seven* (1920); *Highly Colored* (1921); *Assorted Chocolates* (1922); *Bigger and Blacker* (1925); *Black and Blue* (1926); *With Benefit of Clergy* (1935)
Humorous accounts of black life in Birmingham. Cohen was the organizer of the Loafers, a literary club.

William L. Coleman *Escape the Thunder* (1944)
Novel about black life in Montgomery, with realistic portrayals of local life and dialect.

Alexander Corkey *The Testing Fire* (1911)
Racial conflict in a black college town.

Harold Courlander *Negro Songs from Alabama* (rev. ed. 1963)

Kate Cumming *Gleanings from Southland* (1895)
Revised edition of *A Journal of Hospital Life in the Confederate Army of Tennessee.*

Mary Gordon Duffee (ed. V. P. Brown and J. P. Nabers) *Sketches of Alabama* (1970)
Social life of ante-bellum Jefferson County.

Fannie Flagg *Fried Green Tomatoes at the Whistle Stop Cafe* (1987, rpt. 1988)
Comic novel about two women who run a small-town restaurant in the 1930s.

Mitchell B. Garrett *Horse and Buggy Days on Hatchet Creek* (1982)
Memoir of rural life at the close of the 19th century.

Robert F. Gibbons *Bright Is the Morning* (1943)
Novel about a farm family.

William T. Going *Essays on Alabama Literature* (1975)

Philip H. Gosse *Letters from Alabama* (1859, rpt. 1983)
English naturalist's account of the fauna and planter society of the Black Belt in 1838.

Frances Nimmo Greene *The Right of the Strongest* (1913)
Novel about a schoolteacher set in the northern Alabama mountains.

Sara Haardt *The Making of a Lady* (1931); *Southern Album* (1936)
A novel, and a short-story collection, describing small-town life, by the wife of H. L. Mencken.

Parthenia A. V. Hague *A Blockaded Family: Life in Southern Alabama during the Civil War* (1888)
Autobiography of a Eufala, Barbour County, schoolteacher.

George Wylie Henderson *Ollie Miss* (1935, rpt. 1988)
Novel about black sharecroppers.

Marie S. Jemison and **Ellen Sullivan** (eds.) *An Alabama Scrapbook* (1988)
Thirty-two reminiscences of growing up in Alabama.

Johnson J. Hooper *Some Adventures of Captain Simon Suggs, Late of the Tallapoosa Volunteers* (1845); *The Widow Rugby's Husband, A Night at the Ugly Man's, and Other Tales of Alabama* (1851)
With George W. Harris of Tennessee and Augustus Langstreet of Georgia, Hooper was an originator of the humorous sketch of Southern character, portrayals of the folk wisdom and foibles of backwoods characters that were enjoyed by a national audience.

G. Ward Hubbs (ed.) *Rowdy Tales from Early Alabama* (1981)
Local humor of the 1850s from western Alabama, with a portrayal of ante-bellum Tuscaloosa.

Martin Luther King, Jr. *Stride toward Freedom: The Montgomery Story* (1964)
Account of the boycott King led against the Jim Crow buses of Montgomery.

Harper Lee *To Kill a Mockingbird* (1960)
A child's impressions of the injustices that come to light in a small Alabama town during the 1930s when her lawyer father defends a black man accused of raping a white woman.

Viola G. Liddell *With a Southern Accent* (1948, rpt. 1982)
Memoir of the Deep South before World War II.
————. *A Place of Springs* (1979, rpt. 1982)
Memoir of life in Camden, 1930–1970.

Andrew Lytle *The Long Night* (1936, rpt. 1988)
Historical novel set in the Black Belt in the 1850s concerning a man's revenge on his father's murderers.

William March (pseudonym of W.E.M. Campbell) *Trial Balance* (1945, rpt. 1987)
Collected short stories of an Alabama author whose portrayals of rural and small-town life have been compared with Faulkner.

Albert Murray *South to a Very Old Place* (1971)
Commentary on the culture of Southern towns, including Tuskegee and Mobile.
————. *Train Whistle Guitar* (1974)
Autobiographical novel about a black man coming of age in the 1920s.

George S. O'Neal *Weariest River* (1935)
Portrait of a mining town.

Mary White Ovington *Zeke* (1931)
A black farm boy wins a place at the Tuskegee Institute.

Samuel Mintern Peck *Alabama Sketches* (1902)
Local-color sketches.

Kate Mayhew Penney *Land Poor* (1928)
Stories of rural life.

Benjamin Faneuil Porter (ed. Sara Walls) *Reminiscences of Men and Things in Alabama* (1983)
Memoirs written c. 1829–1855.

Howell H. Raines *My Soul Is Rested: Movement Days in the Deep South Remembered* (1977)
Oral history of a civil rights campaigner covering the period 1955–1968.
————. *Whisky Man* (1977)
Novel set in Milo during the Depression.

Julian Lee Rayford *Cottonmouth* (1941)
Autobiographical novel about growing up in Mobile during World War II.

Anne Royall *Letters from Alabama on Various Subjects* (1830, rpt. 1975)
Classic memoir of social life and customs, 1820–1830.

Nate Shaw (ed. Theodore Rosengarten) *All God's Dangers: The Life of Nate Shaw* (1974)
  Edited transcription of recordings of a 90-year-old black tenant farmer, portraying the rural South during the twentieth century.

Scottie Fitzgerald Smith *An Alabama Journal* (1977)
  Local traditions, folkways, and customs.

Jack and **Olivia Solomon** *Zickary Zan: Childhood Folklore* (1980); *Ghosts and Goosebumps* (1981)
  Collections of local folklore.

Thomas S. Stribling *The Forge* (1931, rpt. 1985); *The Store* (1932, rpt. 1985); *Unfinished Cathedral* (1934, rpt. 1986)
  Trilogy of novels set in the Tennessee Valley region describing the fortunes of a family from a country town. *The Store* won the 1932 Pulitzer Prize.

Sue Turner *Bouquets, Brambles and Buena Vista, or "Down Home"* (1976)
  A collection of weekly columns about rural life written for the *Monroe Journal.*

Eugene Walter *The Untidy Pilgrim* (1954, rpt. 1987)
  Novel set in 1950s Mobile.

Lella Warren *Foundation Stone* (1940, rpt. 1986); *Whetstone Walls* (1952)
  Historical novels tracing the fortunes of a pioneer family from the 1820s through the Civil War.

Sarah W. Wiggins (comp.) *From Civil War to Civil Rights-Alabama, 1860–1960: An Anthology from the Alabama Review* (1987)

Benjamin B. Williams *A Literary History of Alabama: The Nineteenth Century* (1979)

Kathryn Tucker Windham *Alabama: One Big Front Porch* (1975)
  Collection of humorous tales and folklore.

Clement Wood *Nigger* (1922)
  Novel about several generations of a black family, from slavery to migration to Birmingham. Wood's novels set in the state also include *Folly* (1925), *The Mountain* (1927), *Deep River* (1934), and *If There Is a Hell* (1934).

GUIDES TO RESOURCES

Alabama Library Association *20th Century Alabama Authors: A Checklist* (1978)

Alabama, University of. Bureau of Public Administration. *Alabama Government Manual* (1959–)

Dodd, Donald B. *Historical Atlas of Alabama* (1974)

Federal Writers' Project *Alabama, A Guide to the Cotton State* (1949)
———. **Walker, Alyce Billings** (ed.) *Alabama: A Guide to the Deep South* (rev. ed. 1975)

Fuller, Willie J. *Blacks in Alabama, 1528–1865* (1976)

Gamble, Robert *The Alabama Catalog: Historic American Buildings Survey* (1987)

Lineback, Neal G. *Atlas of Alabama* (1973)

Marks, Henry S. *Who Was Who in Alabama* (1972)

Owen, Thomas M. *History of Alabama and Dictionary of Alabama Biography*, 4 vols. (1921)

Richardson, Jesse M. and **Herbert R. Padgett** (eds.) *Alabama Almanac and Book of Facts 1955–1956* (1955)

Waldrop, Ruth W. *Alabama Writers: Titles in Print* (1987)

SELECTED NONFICTION SOURCES

Abernethy, Thomas P. *The Formative Period in Alabama, 1815–1828* (1965)

Amos, Harriet E. *Cotton City: Urban Development in Antebellum Mobile* (1985)

Armes, Ethel *The Story of Coal and Iron in Alabama* (1910, rpt. 1972)

Badger, R. Reid and **Lawrence A. Clayton** *Alabama and the Borderlands; From Prehistory to Statehood* (1985)

Barnard, William D. *Dixiecrats and Democrats: Alabama Politics, 1942–1950* (1974)

Barney, William L. *The Secessionist Impulse: Alabama and Mississippi in 1860* (1974)

Bond, Horace M. *Negro Education in Alabama* (1939, rpt. 1969)

Boyd, Minnie C. *Alabama in the Fifties* (1966)

Brantley, William H. *Three Capitals: . . . St. Stephens, Huntsville, and Cahawba* (1947, rpt. 1976)

Brown, James S. (ed.) *Up before Daylight: Life Histories from the Alabama Writers' Project, 1938–1939* (1982)

Campbell, Thomas M. *The Movable School Goes to the Negro Farmer* (1936, rpt. 1969)

Carter, Dan T. *Scottsboro: A Tragedy of the American South* (rev. ed. 1979)

Couch, Ernie and **Jill** *Alabama Trivia* (1987)

Dalaney, Caldwell *Confederate Mobile; A Pictorial History* (1971)

Davis, Charles S. *The Cotton Kingdom of Alabama* (1939, rpt. 1974)

Denman, Clarence P. *The Secession Movement in Alabama* (1933, rpt. 1971)

Du Bose, Joel C. *Alabama History* (1908)

Elliot, Lawrence *George Washington Carver: The Man Who Overcame* (1966)

Fager, Charles E. *Selma, 1965: The March That Changed the South* (1974, rpt. 1985)

Fleming, Walter L. *Civil War and Reconstruction in Alabama* (1905, rpt. 1949)

Foley, Helen S. (comp.) *About People: Events from Newspapers from 1846–1890* (1970)

Frady, Marshall *Wallace* (1968)

Garrett, Mitchell B. *Horse and Buggy Days on Hatchet Creek* (1957)

Going, Allen J. *Bourbon Democracy in Alabama, 1874–1890* (1951)

Grafton, Carl and **Anne Permaloff** *Big Mules and Branchheads: James E. Folsom and Political Power in Alabama* (1985)

Griffith, Lucille B. *Alabama: A Documentary History to 1900* (rev. ed. 1972, rpt. 1987)

Haagen, Victor B. *Alabama: Portrait of a State* (1963)

Hackney, Sheldon *Populism to Progressivism in Alabama* (1969)

Hamilton, Peter *Colonial Mobile* (1910, rpt. 1976)

Hamilton, Virginia Van der Veer *Alabama: A Bicentennial History* (States and the Nation series) (1977)
———. *Hugo Black: The Alabama Years* (1982)
———. *Seeing Historic Alabama* (1982)

Hammond, Ralph *Ante Bellum Mansions of Alabama* (1951)

Harlan, Louis R. *Booker T. Washington: The Making of a Black Leader, 1856–1901* (1971)

Harris, W. Stuart *Dead Towns of Alabama* (1977)
———. *Alabama Place-Names* (1982)

Herskowitz, Mickey *The Legend of Bear Bryant* (1987)

Howard, Gene L. *Death at Cross Plains: An Alabama Reconstruction Tragedy* (1984)

Jones, James H. *Bad Blood: The Tuskegee Syphilis Experiment* (1981)

Jordan, Weymouth T. *Hugh Davis and His Alabama Plantation* (1948)
————. *Antebellum Alabama: Town and Country* (1957, rpt. 1986)

Kirby, James *Fumble: Bear Bryant, Wally Butts, and the Great College Football Scandal* (1986)

Kolchin, Peter *First Freedom: The Responses of Alabama's Blacks to Emancipation and Reconstruction* (1972)

Martin, Bessie *Desertion of Alabama Troops from the Confederate Army* (1966)

Martin, David L. *Alabama's State and Local Governments* (1975)

Mathis, Ray *John Horry Dent, South Carolina Aristocrat on the Alabama Frontier* (1979)

McLaurin, Melton and **Michael Thomason** *Mobile, the Life and Times of a Great Southern City: An Illustrated History* (1981)
————. *The Image of Progress: Alabama Photographs, 1872–1917* (1980)

McMillan, Malcolm C. *Constitutional Development in Alabama, 1798–1901* (1955)
————. *Yesterday's Birmingham* (1976)

Merritt, Raleigh H. *From Captivity to Fame: or The Life of Geo. Washington Carver* (1938)

Moore, Albert B. *History of Alabama* (1934)

Muskat, Beth T. and **Mary A. Neeley** *The Way It Was, 1850–1930; Photographs of Montgomery and Her Central Alabama Neighbors* (1985)

Nixon, Herman C. *Lower Piedmont Country* (1936, rpt. 1971)

Norrell, Robert J. *Reaping the Whirlwind: The Civil Rights Movement in Tuskegee* (1985)

Norris, Clarence *The Last of the Scottsboro Boys* (1979)

Owen, Marie Bankhead *Alabama: A Social and Economic History* (1938)

Rawick, George P. (ed.) *The American Slave: A Composite Autobiography* (vol. 6) *Alabama and Indiana Narratives* (1972)

Read, William A. *Indian Place Names in Alabama* (1937, rev. ed. 1984)

Robinson, Jo Ann Gibson *The Montgomery Bus Boycott and the Women Who Started It: The Memoir of Jo Ann Gibson Robinson* (1987)

Rogers, William Warren *The One-Gallused Rebellion; Agrarianism in Alabama, 1865–1896* (1970)
————. *August Reckoning: Jack Turner and Racism in Post–Civil War Alabama* (1973)

Schweninger, Loren *James T. Rapier and Reconstruction* (1978)

Sims, George E. *The Little Man's Big Friend* (1985)

Stevenson, Janet *The Montgomery Bus Boycott, December, 1955: American Blacks Demand an End to Segregation* (1971)

Stewart, John Craig *The Governors of Alabama* (1975)

Sulzby, James F. *Historic Alabama Hotels and Resorts* (1960)

Taft, Philip *Organizing Dixie: Alabama Workers in the Industrial Era* (rev. ed. 1981)

Thomason, Michael V. R. *Trying Times: Alabama Photographs, 1917–1945* (1985)

Thornton, J. Mills *Politics and Power in a Slave Society: Alabama, 1800–1860* (1977)

Underwood, John *Bear, the Hard Life and Good Times of Alabama's Coach Bryant* (1974)

Walker, Anne Kendrick *Tuskegee and the Black Belt* (1944)

Wallace, George *Stand Up for America* (1976)

Ward, Robert D. *Labor Revolt in Alabama: The Great Strike of 1894* (1965)

Washington, Booker T. *Up from Slavery* (1901)
————. *My Larger Education* (1911)

Watson, Elbert L. *Alabama United States Senators* (1982)

Wiener, Jonathan M. *Social Origins of the New South: Alabama, 1860–1885* (1978)

Wiggins, Sarah W. *The Scalawag in Alabama Politics, 1865–1881* (1977)
————. *From Civil War to Civil Rights. Alabama 1860–1960: An Anthology from the Alabama Review* (1987)

Wilson, Eugene M. *Alabama Folk Houses* (1975)

Windham, Kathryn T. *Exploring Alabama* (1970)

ALASKA

The Pacific state of Alaska is the largest state in the Union. It is bordered on the north by the Arctic Ocean; on the east by Canadian Yukon Territory and the province of British Columbia; on the south by British Columbia and by the Pacific Ocean; and on the west by the Bering Sea and the Arctic Ocean.

FULL NAME State of Alaska
POSTAL ABBREVIATION AK
INHABITANT Alaskan
ADMITTED TO THE UNION Jan. 3, 1959.
  49th state
POPULATION (est. 1987) 525,000.
  Percent of US total: 0.22%. Rank: 49th

CAPITAL CITY Juneau, on the Gastineau Channel, 90 miles northeast of Sitka; population 24,000 (est. 1984). Founded by gold miners in 1880, Juneau was made the capital of the new territory of Alaska in 1912 and became the state capital in 1959.

STATE NAME AND NICKNAMES From the Aleut word *alaxsxaq*, "the object toward which the action of the sea is directed" (e.g., the mainland), and the Eskimo word *alaska*, which has the same meaning. Also known as The Land of Midnight Sun, America's Last Frontier, and formerly as Seward's Folly and Seward's Ice Box (to ridicule the secretary of state who acquired the territory for the United States).

STATE SEAL A panorama of Alaskan life, with ships, railroads, forests, and icebergs, and above them the northern lights. The border bears the legend "The Seal of the State of Alaska."

MOTTO North to the Future

SONG "Alaska's Flag," lyrics by Marie Drake, music by Elinor Dusenbury.

SYMBOLS
Flower forget-me-not
Tree Sitka spruce
Bird Alaska willow ptarmigan
  (willow grouse)
Fish king salmon
Gem jade
Marine mammal bowhead whale
Mineral gold
Sport dog mushing

LICENSE PLATE Dark blue on gold, with state flag and legend "The Last Frontier."

FLAG Eight gold stars in a field of blue. Seven of the stars form the constellation Ursa Major; the eighth is the North Star, Polaris.

GEOGRAPHY AND CLIMATE

Alaska, the largest peninsula in the northern hemisphere, is also the least explored. Most of Alaska's sparse population lives in the temperate southern coastal areas, the archipelago of islands extending into the Gulf of Alaska and the Bering Sea, and fertile interior basins in the southern part of the state. Rugged mountains, including Denali (Mt. McKinley), the highest point in North America, encircle the central interior plains, home of vast numbers of wild animals. The North Slope, the one-third of Alaska that lies within the Arctic Circle, is permanently covered with tundra and permafrost. Volcanic activity and earthquakes are common along the southern rim.

AREA 591,004 square miles. Rank: 1st
INLAND WATER 20,171 square miles
GEOGRAPHIC CENTER 60 miles NW of Mt. McKinley, lat. 63° 50′N, long. 152° W
ELEVATIONS *Highest point:* Mt. McKinley, 20,230 feet. *Lowest point:* Pacific Ocean, sea level. *Mean elevation:* 1,900 feet

MAJOR RIVERS Yukon, Tanana, Kuskokwim
MAJOR LAKES AND RESERVOIRS Iliamna, Becharof, Tustumena, Teshekpuk, Naknek, Clark, Dall
TIDAL SHORELINE 31,383 miles, Pacific Ocean, Bering Sea, and Arctic Ocean

LAND USE

	Thousands of acres
Urban (1982)	not available
Rural (1982)	not available
Cropland (1982)	not available
Pastureland (1982)	not available
Rangeland (1982)	not available
Forestland (1982)	not available
State parks and recreation areas (1983)	3,030
National park system (1984)	52,106
National forest system (1984)	24,018
Tribal lands (1984)	90

TEMPERATURES The highest recorded temperature was 100° F on June 27, 1915, at Fort Yukon. The lowest was -80° F on January 23, 1971, at Prospect Creek.

NATIONAL SITES

NATIONAL HISTORICAL PARKS Klondike, Gold Rush, Sitka
NATIONAL MONUMENT Cape Krusenstern
NATIONAL MONUMENT AND PRESERVE Aniakchak
NATIONAL PARKS Kenai Fjords, Kobuk Valley
NATIONAL PARKS AND PRESERVES Denali, Gates of the Arctic, Glacier Bay, Katmai, Lake Clark, Wrangell-St. Elias
NATIONAL PRESERVES Bering Land Bridge, Noatak, Yukon-Charley Rivers

NATIONAL SCENIC RIVER Alagnak Wild River
NATIONAL SCENIC TRAIL Natchez Trace
NATIONAL WILDLIFE REFUGES Aleutian Islands–Bogoslof, Arctic National Wildlife Range, Clarence Rhode National Wildlife Range–Bering Sea/Cape Newenham/Chamisso/Hazen Bay/Nunivak, Forrester Island/Saint Lazaria/Hazy Islands, Izembek/Semidi/Simenof, Kenai National Moose Range, Kodiak

HISTORY

1728	*August 8*. Vitus Bering, a Dane in the employ of the Russian navy, discovers and names St. Lawrence Island but does not glimpse the Alaskan mainland because of fog.
1741	Bering's second expedition makes landfalls in southeastern Alaska. Survivors bring back sea-otter pelts, which become the basis of a lucrative trade conducted by Siberian merchants.
1784	First permanent white settlement is established on Kodiak Island by Gregory Shelikhov.
1799	Shelikhov's Russian-American Company wins an exclusive fur-trading charter and founds a station near Sitka.
1802	Tlingit Indians storm the company's fort and kill 408 of the 450 defenders.
1804	The Tlingit attack is avenged and New Archangel (present-day Sitka) is established as the new company headquarters.
1825	Great Britain and Russia define their boundaries in northwestern America; Russia's southern boundary is fixed at latitude 54°40′.

1835	American ships begin taking whales and walrus in Alaskan waters; the Russians are unable to halt these incursions.
1867	*March 30.* Secretary of State William H. Seward signs a treaty by which the United States purchases Alaska for $7.2 million; critics call it "Seward's Folly."
1870	The Alaska Commercial Company, formed by San Francisco businessmen, wins a 20-year lease allowing it exclusive exploitation of the lucrative fur-seal rookeries of the Pribilof Islands.
1876	First Protestant mission and school in Alaska founded at Wrangell.
1877	The Treasury Department assumes administration of Alaska, replacing the army. Two years later, the navy becomes the legal authority.
1880	Joe Juneau and Dick Harris make the first major gold strike in Alaska and establish the miners' camp named Juneau in 1882.
1884	Civil government is established, with the capital at Sitka. The laws of the state of Oregon are generally in force, as administered by federally appointed officials.
1891	Siberian reindeer are introduced to provide food for Eskimos, who are threatened with starvation by the near-extinction of whales and walrus.
1896–1897	In the wake of the discovery of gold in Canada's Yukon, along the Klondike River, almost 60,000 men pass through Alaska.
1898	Gold is found on Anvil Creek near present-day Nome.
1899	Alaska's salmon canneries turn out a million cases, outstripping those on Puget Sound in Washington. Congress replaces the prohibition of liquor with a licensing system.
1900	The population of Alaska has almost doubled since 1890, reaching 63,592, of whom 29,536 are Eskimos, Indians, or Aleuts. Juneau is made the capital of Alaska. Southeastern Alaska gold mines yield over $17 million.
1902	Alaska's most productive gold field is found in the Tanana river valley, and Fairbanks is founded at the site.
1903	The border between Canada and Alaska is established by arbitration.
1911	A 196-mile railway is completed between Cordova and copper mines in the Wrangell Mountains.
1912	*August 24.* Alaska becomes a US territory, giving the inhabitants limited self-rule.
1913	Women receive the right to vote.
1914	Anchorage is founded as a railroad construction camp.
1915	Alaska is the first US jurisdiction to provide for old-age pensions.
1916	Peak mining production, until recent years, of $48.6 million, including $29.5 million from copper and $17.2 million from gold. Almost 10,000 men are employed in mining.
1917	Establishment of Mt. McKinley National Park, now named Denali.
1918	Salmon production of 6,677,369 cases is worth $51 million.
1922	Opening of the Alaska Agricultural College and School of Mines, which in 1935 becomes the University of Alaska.
1923	Completion of the 470-mile, federally owned Alaska Railroad, linking Seward and Fairbanks.
1935	Hundreds of colonists are brought to Alaska by the federal government to farm the Matanuska Valley.
1936	Salmon production reaches an all-time high of 8.5 million cases.
1940	Pan American Airways establishes commercial air service to Alaska.
1941–1945	Well over $1 billion is spent in Alaska by the federal government during World War II. In 1943, the peak year, 152,000 troops are stationed there.
1942	*June 7.* Japanese forces land by sea on the Aleutian islands of Attu and Kiska. *November 20.* Opening of the 1,420-mile Alcan Highway from Great Falls, Montana, through Canada, to Fairbanks.
1943	*May 11.* US forces land on Attu, which is taken 18 days later. Kiska is evacuated by the Japanese, undetected, on July 23.
1945	Racial discrimination in public accommodations is made illegal.
1949	A territorial income tax is adopted.
1951	Alaska leads the 48 states in the production of platinum and tin.
1953	Heavy military spending in the post–World War II years peaks at $513 million.

1954	Opening of Alaska's first pulp and paper mill, at Ketchikan.
1957	Oil is discovered on the Kenai Peninsula.
1958	Following signing of a statehood bill on July 7, an August 26 referendum approves statehood by a 5-to-1 margin.
1959	*January 3.* Alaska is admitted to the union as the 49th state. It is given the right to select 103 million acres—over a quarter of Alaska—as state land.
1964	*March 27.* The most severe earthquake ever recorded in North America strikes south-central Alaska, leaving 115 dead and about $500 million in damage. Anchorage is hard hit, and Valdez is 80 percent destroyed.
1967	*August 14–15.* The Chena River floods Fairbanks, causing an estimated $176 million in damage and the evacuation of more than 18,000 people.
1968	Two oil wells are brought in on Alaska's Arctic Slope, near Prudhoe Bay; the field is estimated to contain between 5 billion and 10 billion barrels of recoverable oil.
1969	An oil-lease sale yields the state $900 million in revenue.
1971	A federal law grants to Eskimos, Indians, and Aleuts full title to 40 million acres and $962.5 million in cash.
1976	Voters approve the establishment of the Alaska Permanent Fund, setting aside 25 percent of mineral royalties and related income for cash dividends to every resident of the state.
1977	Completion of the $8-billion, 798-mile Trans-Alaska Pipeline allows oil to be shipped from Alaska's North Slope to the port of Valdez.
1978	An initiative calls for as much as 30 million acres of free land to be distributed to residents who pay the surveying costs.
1979	With output of 511.3 million barrels, Alaska becomes second among states in oil production, trailing only Texas.
1980	The personal income tax is repealed.
	Congress outrages many Alaskans by excluding more than 104 million acres of the state from commercial development.
	With a total of more than 1 billion pounds, Alaska is second among states in commercial landings of fish and shellfish.
1985	The state of Alaska assumes ownership of the Alaska Railroad, bought from the federal government for $22.3 million.
1987	Tanker involved with Alaska oil trade spills almost 40,000 barrels of petroleum into areas of rare beauty in North Pacific.
	March. Governor Steve Cowper begins program to end shooting of Alaskan wolves from helicopters.
1988	*July.* Fire chars over half-million acres.
1989	*March 24.* Oil tanker runs aground in Prince William Sound, creating the largest oil spill in US history.

DEMOGRAPHY

Population (est. 1987)	525,000
Population (1980)	401,851
Population density in persons per square mile (1980)	0.7

POPULATION BY RACE (1980)

American Indian/Aleut/ Eskimo	64,047
Asian/Pacific Islander	8,035
Black	13,619
Hispanic	9,497
White	308,455
Other	6,325

POPULATION CHARACTERISTICS (1980)

Percent of state population

Urban	64.3
Rural	35.7

Under 18	32.5
65 or older	2.9
College-educated	22.4
Families below poverty line	8.6
Public assistance recipients	4.6
Per capita personal income (1986)	$17,744
Millionaires per 100,000 residents	270.3
Average life expectancy in years (1980)	72.3
Marriage rate per 1,000 residents (1986)	11.1
Divorce rate per 1,000 residents (1986)	7.2
Birth rate per 1,000 residents (1985)	24.1

Infant mortality rate per
1,000 births (1985) 10.0
Abortion rate per 1,000
live births (1985) 283
Crime rate per 100,000
residents (1985)
Violent 570.4
Property 5675.5
Federal and state prisoners
per 100,000 residents (1984) . . 360
Alcohol consumption in gallons
per capita (1985) 53.8

Deaths from motor vehicle accidents
per 100,000 residents (1985) . . 24.0

MAJOR CITIES

	Population
Anchorage (est. 1984)	226,663
Fairbanks (1980)	22,500
Juneau (1980)	19,528
Kenia Peninsula (1980)	25,282

GOVERNMENT AND POLITICS

Number of US Representatives 1
Electoral votes 3

POLITICAL PARTY NOMINEES FROM STATE

Raymond L. Teague
(Theocratic) 1960 P

PRESIDENTIAL PRIMARY ELECTION In 1988, Alaska sent 17 Democratic delegates and 19 Republican delegates to the national conventions.
CONSTITUTION Alaska is using its original constitution, adopted in 1956.
LEGISLATURE The Legislature is divided into the Senate (20 members, 4-year term, minimum age 25) and the House of Representatives (40 members, 2-year term, minimum age 21). In 1987, the annual salary was $22,140.
JUDICIARY The highest court is the Supreme Court, with 5 judges serving 10-year terms. In 1987, the annual salary was $85,728.
EXECUTIVE The governor serves a 4-year term; the minimum age for holding office is 30. In 1987, the annual salary was $81,648. There is one other elected official.

PRESIDENTIAL VOTE 1960-1988 *(in percents)*

Year	State Winner	Democratic	Republican
1960	Nixon (R)	49.1	50.9
1964	Johnson (D)	65.9	34.1
1968	Nixon (R)	42.7	45.3
1972	Nixon (R)	34.6	58.1
1976	Ford (R)	35.7	57.9
1980	Reagan (R)	26.4	54.3
1984	Reagan (R)	29.9	66.6
1988	Bush (R)	38.0	62.0

GOVERNORS

District Governors
John H. Kinkead 1884-1885
A.P. Swineford 1885-1889
Lyman E. Knapp 1889-1893
James Sheakley 1893-1897
John G. Brady 1897-1906
Wilford B. Hoggatt 1906-1909
Walter E. Clark 1909-1913

Territorial Governors
John F.A. Strong 1913-1918
Thomas Riggs Jr. 1918-1921
Scott C. Bone 1921-1925
George A. Parks 1925-1933
John W. Troy 1933-1939
Ernest Gruening 1939-1953

B. Frank Heintzleman 1953-1957
Waino Hendrickson (acting) 1957
Michael A. Stepovich 1957-1958
Waino Hendrickson (acting) 1958-1959

State Governors
William A. Egan (D) 1959-1966
Walter J. Hickel (R) 1966-1969
Keith H. Miller (R) 1969-1970
William A. Egan (R) 1970–1974
Jay S. Hammond (R) 1974-1982
William Sheffield (D) 1982-1986
Steve Cowper (D) 1986-

MINIMUM AGES
Majority 18
Marriage with parental consent . . . 16

Marriage without parental consent . 18
Making a will 18
Buying alcohol 21
Jury duty 18
Leaving school 16
Driver's license 16

CAPITAL PUNISHMENT
None

MILITARY INSTALLATIONS
Total number: 47
Major bases:
   Army: 4
   Navy: 1
   Air Force: 2

FINANCES

Thousands of dollars

GENERAL REVENUE (1985)
Total general revenue . . . 5,453,073
Total tax revenue 1,885,811
Sales and gross receipts 112,908
Individual income taxes 1,268
Corporate net income taxes . . 204,600

GENERAL EXPENDITURE (1985)
Total general expenditure . 4,605,555
Education 1,143,566
Public welfare 200,154
Health 190,630
Hospitals 25,167
Natural resources 186,037
Highways 611,312
Police 61,257
Corrections 124,942

FEDERAL AID (1985) 639,871

ECONOMY

Agriculture has never played an important role in Alaska's economy, and food must be shipped in from out of state, with the exception of some dairy products and vegetables (primarily potatoes, cabbages, and carrots) grown in the Matanuska Valley near Anchorage and the Tanana Valley near Fairbanks. Total farm production is approximately $10 million per year. The state's true wealth is in its mineral resources, including gold, copper, and vast reserves of coal, oil, and natural gas; in sand and gravel mining; in timber and wood products (well over 500 million board feet of timber each year, much of it shipped to the Far East); and in fisheries, with the catch of salmon, crab, herring, and other species totaling more than $600 million in 1980. In heavy manufacturing and high-tech industries, Alaska is still relatively undeveloped. Tourism is increasingly a major industry, far larger than agriculture, and is helping to bring the trappings of a service economy to the state.

EMPLOYMENT (1984)
Thousands of persons
Total number of employed
  workers 220
Construction 20.1
Finance, insurance, and
  real estate 12.3
Government 65.9
Manufacturing 11.2
Mining 8.8
Services 43.2
Transportation, communications,
  and utilities 18.9
Wholesale and retail trade 44.6

Percent of civilian labor force
  unemployed (1984) 10.0

DEPARTMENT OF DEFENSE (1985)
Civilian workers employed . . . 5,005
Military personnel 20,375
Contract awards . . . . . $550 million

ENERGY SOURCES FOR ELECTRIC UTILITIES
Percent
Coal 9.0
Gas 62.9
Nuclear 0.0
Hydroelectric 15.8
Petroleum 12.3

TRANSPORTATION
Motor vehicles registered
  in state (1986) 362,679
Miles of roads, streets,
  and highways (1986) 13,639
Miles of Class I railway
  operated (1986) 0
Airports (1983) 615
Major aviation hubs (1983) 3
  Largest hub: Anchorage
Major ports, with gross tonnage in
  thousands (1985):
  Valdez Harbor 99,624

CULTURE AND EDUCATION

Native American tribes
Alaska was formerly home to the Ahtena, Eyak, Han, Ingalik, Koyukon, Kutchin, Tanaina, and Tanana tribes. Groups that continue to live in Alaska include the Aleut, Eskimo (Inuit), Haida, Tlingit, and Tsimshian. There are one federal reservation and 13 regional native corporations.

Religions, ethnicities, and languages
In addition to the indigenous peoples, Alaska's population includes people of American, Russian, Japanese, Chinese, Filipino, Scandinavian, and Balkan extraction. Protestant denominations predominate. In 1980, 12.5 percent of the population spoke a language other than English at home.

Major museums and libraries
Alaska Historical Library and Museum, Juneau
Anchorage Historical and Fine Arts Museum
Pratt Museum, Homer
University of Alaska Museum, Fairbanks

Major arts organizations
Alaska Repertory Theatre, Anchorage
Anchorage Opera Company
Anchorage Symphony Orchestra
Fairbanks Symphony Orchestra/Arctic Chamber Orchestra

Colleges and universities
Number public (1986-87) 12
Number private (1986-87) 3
Total enrollment, in full-time equivalent students (1985) 14,100

Public elementary and secondary schools
Expenditure per pupil in average daily attendance (1986-87) $8,842
Pupil-teacher ratio (1987) 16.7
Average teacher salary (1986-87) $46,082

Holidays
Seward's Day. Last Monday in March
Alaska Day. Third Monday in October
State Fair, Palmer. Late August to early September

ALASKA IN LITERATURE

David Bohn *Rambles through an Alaskan Wild: Katmai and the Valley of the Smokes* (1979)
A photographer's reaction to the wilderness.

Charles D. Brower *Fifty Years below Zero* (1942)
Reminiscences of Alaskan life, 1883–1940.

Sally Carrighar *Wild Voice of the North* (1959)
A naturalist's account of studying in Nome, and the habits of the Siberian husky.

Jim Christy *Rough Road to the North* (1980)
Narrative of a journey along the Alaska highway.

Horace S. Conger (ed. Carolyn J. Holeski) *in Search of Gold: The Alaska Journals of Horace Conger, 1898–1899* (1983)

David J. Cooper *Brooks Range Passage* (1982)
Account of wilderness adventures, including building a log raft.

Edna Ferber *Ice Palace* (1958)
Novel about attempts to achieve statehood.

John Hainas *Stories We Listened To* (1986)
Essays by an Alaskan poet.

Ernest Gruening (ed.) *An Alaska Reader, 1867–1967* (1967)
An anthology of traditional tales, folklore, and history gathered by a former Alaska governor.

Elyse Guttenberg and **Jean Anderson** *Inroads* (1988)
Anthology of writing by Alaskans, 1979–1987.

Robert Hedin and **Gary Holthaus** (eds.) *Alaska; Reflections on Land and Spirit* (1989)
Writing on the land and people by Jack London, Peter Matthiessen, Barry Lopez, John McPhee, and others.

John Hildebrand *Reading the River* (1988)
An account of an eighteen-hundred-mile journey from the headwaters of the Yukon to the Bering Sea.

Larry Kaniut *Alaska Bear Tales* (1983)

Lawrence D. Kaplan (ed.) *Ugiuvangmiut Quliapyuit: King Island Tales* (1989)
Eskimo history and legends from King Island in the Bering Strait, with photographs taken in 1937.

Rockwell Kent *Wilderness: A Journal of Quiet Adventure in Alaska* (1920)
The artist spent six months with his young son on Fox Island off the Kenai Peninsula in the winter of 1918–1919.

Jack London *Call of the Wild* (1903)
The adventures of a man and his dog in the Klondike.

Barry Lopez *Crossing Open Ground* (1988)
Collection of essays containing a description of the Alaska wolverine.

Curt Madison and **Yvonne Yarber** *Yukon-Koyukuk School District Biography Series* (1988)
Interviews with Eskimo and white residents who discuss history and folkways.

Robert Marshall *Arctic Wilderness* (1956, rpt. as *Alaska Wilderness*, 1970)
Account of expeditions to the Brooks Range.

Joe McGinnis *Going to Extremes* (1980)
Character sketches of Alaskans.

John McPhee *Coming into the Country* (1977)
A panoramic portrait of Alaskan people, landscape, and life.

Robert D. Mead *Journeys down the Line* (1978)
The building of the Alaska oil pipeline.

François Xavier Mercier (trans. Linda F. Yarborough) *Recollections of the Youkon: Memoires from the Years 1868–1885* (1986)

John P. Milton *Nameless Valleys, Shining Mountains: The Record of an Expedition into the Vanishing Wilderness of Alaska's Brooks Range* (1970)
Account of a 1967 expedition down the North Slope, taken just before the discovery of oil.

Lael Morgan *And the Land Provides* (1974)
Portraits of six Eskimo villagers.

John Muir *Travels in Alaska* (1917, rpt. 1979)
The great naturalist's account of an 800-mile journey through southeastern Alaska.

Margaret Murie *Two in the Far North* (1962)
The wife of the zoologist Olaus Murie records their early life together, including an expedition to the Sheenjek River.

Sigurd F. Olsen *Runes of the North* (1963)
Account of a journey to the Yukon and Alaska.

Richard Proenneke *One Man's Wilderness* (1973)
Journal of solitude in the wilderness.

David Roberts *The Mountain of My Fear* (1968)
A mountaineer describes the ascent of Mt. Huntington.

Ferdinand Schmitter *Upper Yukon Native Customs and Folklore* (1985)

Charles Sheldon *The Wilderness of Denali: Explorations of a Hunter-naturalist in Northern Alaska* (1930)

The author was the earliest advocate of granting national park status to Mt. McKinley.

Wessel Smitter *Another Morning* (1941)
Pioneering in the Matanuska Valley.

James Wickersham *A Bibliography of Alaskan Literature, 1724–1924* (1927)
———. *Old Yukon: Tales-Trails-and Trials* (1938)

Richard Wiley *Fools' Gold* (1988)
Novel about frontier society set in Nome during the Gold Rush.

Anthony C. Woodbury (ed.) *Eskimo Narratives and Tales from Chevak, Alaska* (1984)
Tales told by the Inuit elders of Chevak, 1977–78.

Billie Wright *Four Seasons North: a Journal of Life in the Alaskan Wilderness* (1973)
Account of living in the Brooks Range and the fragile ecology of Arctic life.

GUIDES TO RESOURCES

Alaska Department of Education *Alaska Blue Book* (biennial, 1977–)

Alaska Department of Labor *Alaska Population Overview* (annual)

Alaska Historical Commission *Publications, Research Reports and other Projects Supported by the Alaska Historical Commission, 1973–1985* (1985)

Alaska Northwest Publishing *Alaska Almanac* (annual)

Basque, Garnet *Yukon Ghost Town Atlas* (1981)

Bradbury, Connie, David A. Hales, and Nancy Lesh *Alaska People Index* (1986)

Evans, Henry H. *A Contribution toward a Check list of Bibliographies and Reference Material Relating to the History of the States and Territories of the American West, Including Alaska and Hawaii* (1950)

Falk, Marvin W. *Alaskan Maps: A Cartobibliography of Alaska to 1900* (1983)

Federal Writers' Project *A Guide to Alaska, Last American Frontier* (1939)

Graham, Roberta L. (Alaska Historical Commission) *A Sense of History: A Reference Guide to Alaska's Women, 1896–1985* (1985)

Haycox, Stephen W. and Betty J. *Melvin Ricks' Alaska Bibliography: An Introductory Guide to Alaskan Historical Literature* (1977)

Jones, Dorothy M. and John R. Wood *An Aleut Bibliography* (1975)

Kippler, Arthur E. and John R. Wood *The Alaska Eskimos: A Selected, Annotated Bibliography* (1977)

Lida-Mocarski, Valerian (ed.) *Bibliography of Books on Alaska Published before 1868* (1969)

Ricks, Melvin B. (ed. S. W. and B. J. Haycox) *Alaska Bibliography: An Introductory Guide to Alaskan Historical Literature* (1977)

Simmerman, Nancy L. *Alaska's Parklands: The Complete Guide* (1984)

Stirling, Dale A. (comp.) *The Alaska Records Survey: An Inventory of Archival Resources in Repositories of the US and Canada* (1986)

Tourville, Elsie A. (comp.) *Alaska, a Bibliography 1570–1970 with Subject Index* (1974)

Ulibarri, George S. *Documenting Alaskan History: Guide to Federal Archives Relating to Alaska* (1982)

University of Alaska, Anchorage (ed. Alden Rollins) *Census Alaska: Numbers of Inhabitants, 1792–1970* (1978)

University of Alaska, Fairbanks *Bibliography of Alaskana* (quarterly)

Woerner, R. K. *The Alaska Handbook* (1986)

SELECTED NONFICTION SOURCES

Adams, Ben *Last Frontier: Alaska* (1961)

Anchorage Daily News *The Village People* (1966)
———. *The Village People Revisited* (1981)

Andreev, A. I. *Russian Discoveries in the Pacific and in North America in the Eighteenth and Nineteenth Centuries: A Collection of Materials* (1952)

Andrews, C. L. *The Story of Alaska* (1938)

Antonson, Joan M. and William S. Hanable *Alaska's Heritage* (1985)

Bancroft, Hubert H. *History of Alaska 1730–1885* (1886)

Bandi, Hans-Georg *Eskimo Pre-History* (1969)

Barton, Pierre *The Klondike Fever* (1958)

Boeri, David *People of the Ice Whale: Eskimos, White Men, and the Whale* (1983)

Brebner, Phyllis L. *The Alaska Highway* (1986)

Brown, Emily I. *The Roots of Ticasuk: An Eskimo Woman's Family Story* (1981)

Caldwell, Francis E. *Land of the Ocean Mists: The Wild Ocean Coast West of Glacier Bay* (1986)

Campbell Hughes, Charles *An Eskimo Village in the Modern World* (1960)

Carlo, Poldine *Nulato: An Indian Life on the Yukon* (1978)

Case, David S. *Alaska Natives and American Laws* (1984)

Chance, Norman *The Eskimo of North Alaska* (1966)

Chevigny, Hector *Russian America: Alaskan Venture, 1741–1867* (1965)

Cole, Dermot *Frank Barr: Bush Pilot in Alaska and the Yukon* (1986)

Cole, Terrence (ed.) *The Sourdough Expedition: Stories of the Pioneer Alaskans Who Climbed Mt. McKinley in 1910* (1985)

Cooley, Richard A. *Alaska: A Challenge in Conservation* (1966)

Davidson, Art *Does One Way of Life Have to Die So Another Can Live?* (1974)

Davis, Neil *Alaska Science Nuggets* (1982)
———. *Energy/Alaska* (1984)

De Armond, Robert N. *The Founding of Juneau* (1967)

Dumond, Don E. *The Eskimos and Aleuts* (1977)

Farrar, Victor *Annexation of Russian America to the United States* (1937)

Fienup-Riordan, Ann *The Nelson Island Eskimo: Social Structure and Ritual Distribution* (1983)

Garfield, Brian *The Thousand Mile War* (1969)

Giddings, J. Louis *Ancient Men of the Arctic* (1985)

Gruening, Ernest *State of Alaska* (1954)
————. *The Battle for Alaska Statehood* (1967)
————. *The State of Alaska* (2d ed. 1968)

Gubser, Nicholas *The Nunamiut Eskimos: Hunters of Caribou* (1965)

Hanable, William S. *Alaska's Cooper River: the 18th and 19th Centuries* (1982)

Harris, Jana *Alaska* (1980)

Herbert, Belle (ed. Bill Pfisterer) *Shandaa: In My Lifetime* (1982)

Hinckley, Ted C. *The Americanization of Alaska, 1867–1897* (1973)

Hulley, Clarence C. *Alaska, 1741–1953* (1953)
————. *Alaska: Past and Present* (1981)

Hulse Brooks, Alfred *Blazing Alaska's Trails* (1953, rpt. 1973)

Hunt, William R. *North of 53 Degrees: The Wild Days of the Alaska-Yukon Mining Frontier, 1870–1914* (1974)
————. *Arctic Passage: The Turbulent History of the Land and People of the Bering Sea, 1697–1975* (1975)
————. *Alaska: A Bicentennial History* (1976)
————. *Distant Justice: Policing the Alaskan Frontier* (1987)

Janes, Dorothy *Aleuts in Transition: A Comparison of Two Villages* (1976)
————. *A Century of Servitude: Pribilof Aleuts Under U.S. Rule* (1980)

Jenness, Diamond *Eskimo Administration: Alaska* (1962)

Jensen, Billie B. *"Alaska's Pre-Klondike Mining: Men, Methods, and Minerals,"* Jour. of West 6 (1967)

Johnson, Hugh A. and Harold T. Jorgenson *Land Resources of Alaska* (1963)

Kresge, David T. et al. *Issues in Alaska Development* (1978)

Laughlin, William *Aleuts: Survivors of the Bering Land Bridge* (1980)

McMichael, Alfred G. *Klondike Letters: The Correspondence of a Gold Seeker in 1898* (1984)

Naske, Claus-M. *Interpretive History of Alaska Statehood* (1973)
————. *A History of Alaska Statehood* (1985)
———— and Herman E. Slotnick *Alaska: A History of the 49th State* (2d ed. 1987)

Nelson, Richard K. *Hunters of the Northern Ice* (1969)
————. *Hunters of the Northern Forests: Designs for Survival Among the Alaska Kutchin* (1973)
————. *Shadow of the Hunter* (1982)

Nichols, Jeannette P. *Alaska: A History of Its Administration, Exploitation and Industrial Development During Its First Half-Century Under the Rule of the United States* (1924, rpt. 1963)

Norris, Frank *North to Alaska: An Overview of Immigrants to Alaska, 1867–1945* (1984)
————. *Gawking at the Midnight Sun* (1985)

Okun, S. B. (trans. Carl Ginsburg) *The Russian American Company* (1951)

Orth, Donald *Dictionary of Alaska Place Names* US Geological Survey Professional Paper no. 567 (1967)

Oswalt, Wendell H. *Alaskan Eskimos* (1967)
————. *Eskimos and Explorers* (1979)

Ray, Dorothy J. *Eskimos of Bering Strait 1650–1898* (1975)
————. *Aleut and Eskimo Art: Tradition and Innovation in South Alaska* (1981)
————. *Ethnohistory in the Arctic: The Bering Strait Eskimo* (1983)

Rogers, George W. *Alaska in Transition: The Southeast Region* (1960)
————. *The Future of Alaska: Economic Consequences of Statehood* (1962)

Rowell, Galen *Alaska: Images of the Country* (1981)

Schoor, Alan E. *Alaska Place Names* 3d ed. (1986)

Senungetuk, Joseph E. *Give or Take a Century: An Eskimo Chronicle* (1971)

Sherwood, Morgan B. *Exploration of Alaska, 1865–1900* (1965)
———— (ed.) *Alaska and Its History* (1967)
————. *Big Game in Alaska: A History of Wildlife and People* (1981)

Simeone, William E. *A History of Alaskan Athapaskans* Alaska Historical Commission (1982)

Slwooko Carius, Helen *Sevukakmet: Ways of Life on St. Lawrence Island* (1979)

Smithsonian Institution *Handbook of North American Indians, Arctic* vol. 5, *SubArctic* vol. 6 (1984)

Spencer, Robert F. *The North Alaskan Eskimo: A Study in Ecology and Society* (1959, rpt. 1969)

Starr, S. Frederick *Russia's American Colony* (1987)

Sturtevart, William C. (ed.) *Subarctic* (1981)

Tompkins, Stewart R. *Alaska: Promyshlenik and Sourdough* (1945)

Van Stone, James *Eskimos of the Nushagak River: An Ethnographic History* (1967)
————. *Athapaskan Adaptations: Hunters and Fishermen of the Subarctic Forests* (1974)

Webb, Melody *The Last Frontier: A History of the Yukon Basin of Canada and Alaska* (1987)

Whitehead, John S. *Completing the Union: The Alaska and Hawaii Statehood Movement* (1986)

Williams, Terry T. and Ted Major *The Secret Language of Snow* (1984)

Wilson, William H. *Railroad in the Clouds: The Alaska Railroad in the Age of Steam, 1914–1945* (1977)

ARIZONA

Arizona is a southwestern mountain state. It is bordered on the north by Utah; on the east by New Mexico; on the south by the Mexican state of Senora; and on the west by Baja California in Mexico, and by California, Nevada, and the Colorado River.

FULL NAME State of Arizona
POSTAL ABBREVIATION AZ
INHABITANT Arizonan
ADMITTED TO THE UNION Feb. 14, 1912.
 48th state
POPULATION (est. 1987) 3,386,000.
 Percent of US total: 1.39%. Rank: 25th

CAPITAL CITY Phoenix, the largest city in the state, located on the Salt River in southwest central Arizona; population 853,266 (est. 1984). Founded in 1870 and incorporated as a city in 1881, it became the territorial capital in 1889 and the state capital in 1912.

STATE NAME AND NICKNAMES From *aleh-zon*, a Papago Indian term meaning "little spring," in reference to a spring in the southern part of the territory (now in Mexico). Also known as the Grand Canyon State, the Apache State, and the Copper State.

STATE SEAL On a field of azure, a shield showing a landscape beneath the rising sun, with mountains surrounding a green, cultivated valley, a dammed river, and grazing cattle; on the left is a miner near a quartz mill, symbolizing the state's mineral industry, and across the top of the shield is the state motto.

MOTTO Ditat Deus (God enriches)

SONG "Arizona March Song," lyrics by Margaret Rowe Clifford, music by Maurice Blumenthal.

SYMBOLS
Flower saguaro flower
Tree paloverde (green-barked acacia)
Bird cactus wren
Gem turquoise
Neckwear bola tie

LICENSE PLATES (1) White on red, with white border and legend "Grand Canyon State." (2) Blue on orange, with blue border and same legend.

FLAG The bottom half is a field of blue; the top half shows 13 rays (7 red, 6 yellow) emanating from a copper-colored, five-pointed star in the flag's center.

GEOGRAPHY AND CLIMATE

The Colorado Plateau extends over the northeastern two-thirds of Arizona, an area of canyons and mesas. This includes the Grand Canyon of the Colorado River, the largest canyon in the world. The remainder of the state, called the Basin and Range Province, is arid or semi-arid basin land punctuated by small mountain ranges. True deserts cover less than 1 percent of the state, but more than 40 percent is desert scrub.

AREA 114,000 square miles. Rank: 6th
INLAND WATER 492 square miles
GEOGRAPHIC CENTER Yavapai, 55 miles ESE of Prescott
ELEVATIONS *Highest point:* Humphreys Peak, Cocorino County, 12,633 feet. *Lowest point:* Colorado River, Yuma City, 70 feet. *Mean elevation:* 4,100 feet

MAJOR RIVERS Colorado, Little Colorado, Gila

MAJOR LAKES AND RESERVOIRS Mohave, Theodore Roosevelt, Mead, San Carlos

LAND USE

	Thousands of acres
Urban (1982)	711
Rural (1982)	39,582
Cropland (1982)	1,206
Pastureland (1982)	79
Rangeland (1982)	30,948
Forestland (1982)	4,760
State parks and recreation areas (1983)	34
National park system (1984)	2,667
National forest system (1984)	11,934
Tribal lands (1984)	19,695

TEMPERATURES The highest recorded temperature was 127°F on July 7, 1905, at Parker. The lowest was -40°F on January 7, 1971, at Hawley Lake.

NATIONAL SITES

NATIONAL HISTORIC SITES Fort Bowie, Hubbell Trading Post
NATIONAL MEMORIAL Coronado
NATIONAL MONUMENTS Canyon de Chelley, Casa Grande, Chiricajua, Montezuma Castle, Navajo, Organ Pipe Cactus, Pipe Spring, Saguaro, Sunset Crater, Tonto, Tumacacori, Tuzigoot, Walnut Canyon, Wupatki
NATIONAL PARKS Grand Canyon, Petrified Forest
NATIONAL RECREATION AREAS Glen Canyon, Lake Mead
NATIONAL WILDLIFE REFUGES Cabeza Prieta, Cibola, Havasu, Imperial, Kofa

HISTORY

1540	Francisco Vásquez de Coronado enters present-day southeastern Arizona from Mexico in search of the legendary Seven Cities of Cibola. A reconnaissance party of this expedition discovers the Grand Canyon, while another Spanish expedition discovers the Colorado River.
1629	Franciscan friars establish the first of several missions among the Hopi Indians of northeastern Arizona.
1680	Mission churches and buildings are destroyed in an uprising of Pueblo Indians.
1692	Father Eusebio Francisco Kino, a Jesuit priest, establishes the first of his seven missions among the Pima Indians of southeastern Arizona.
1700	Founding of San Xavier del Bac, the principal mission established by Kino.
1752	Following a revolt by Pima and Papago Indians, a military garrison is established at Tubac; the first permanent white settlement in Arizona grows around it.
1774–1776	Juan Bautista de Anza leads two expeditions through Arizona to the California coast.
1776	The Tubac presidio is moved to Tucson.
1780–1781	A mission and presidio in the Yuma area are abandoned after 50 men are massacred by Indians.
1821	Arizona passes from Spanish to Mexican rule.
1824–1832	Anglo-American mountain men, fanning out from the Santa Fe Trail, trap beaver along Arizona highland streams. Among them are Kit Carson and Jedediah Smith.

1846	Colonel Stephen Watts Kearny leads US troops across Arizona to occupy California in the Mexican War.
	December 17. The Mormon Battalion raises the Stars and Stripes over Tucson.
1848	By the Treaty of Guadalupe Hidalgo, northern and central Arizona are ceded to the United States by Mexico.
1853	The Gadsden Purchase adds southern Arizona to the United States.
1854	The first Arizona copper mine is opened at Ajo.
1858	The steamboat *General Jessup* ascends the Colorado to Black Canyon, just south of what is now Las Vegas, Nevada.
1858–1859	$2 million worth of gold is panned in Gila City.
1862	A Confederate company occupies Tucson on February 28 but abandons it on May 4; it is occupied by Union forces on May 20.
1863	Arizona is detached from New Mexico and made a territory.
	Henry Wickenburg discovers the Vulture gold mine near the town that bears his name. It yields over $3 million in the next 10 years.
1864–1871	Over 300 whites are killed by Apaches.
1868	Thousands of Navajo Indians transported to New Mexico are allowed to return to northeastern Arizona, where their lands form part of a reservation.
1870–1871	The White Mountain Reservation is established for Apache Indians.
1871	*April 30.* A total of 108 Apaches, almost all women and children, are massacred by whites at Camp Grant. A jury acquits the perpetrators.
1873	First cultivation of cotton by whites, near Phoenix.
	Discovery of the Silver King mine near Superior. It yields over $6 million by 1886.
1877	A silver strike is made at Tombstone. Production peaks in 1882 at over $5 million, and the population grows as high as 15,000.
1880	Southern Pacific Railroad reaches Tucson from Yuma. It continues eastward, reaching New Mexico in 1881.
1881	*October 26.* Wyatt Earp, two of his brothers, and Doc Holliday gun down three men in Tombstone in the Gunfight of the O.K. Corral.
1883	The Atlantic and Pacific Railroad crosses northern Arizona from east to west.
1885	At the height of the open-range ranching system, the Hashknife (owned by the Aztec Land and Cattle Company) has over 60,000 cattle on a 90-by-40-mile range between Holbrook and Flagstaff.
1886	Indian fighting ends with the surrender and exile of Geronimo and his band of Apache raiders.
1887–1892	The Pleasant Valley War between cattlemen and sheepmen kills 29.
1888	Copper passes gold and silver in amount of value.
1889	The territorial capital, previously at Prescott and Tucson, is moved to Phoenix.
1891	Arizona has a territorial peak of 720,940 cattle. About 5 million pounds of wool are clipped from 700,000 sheep.
1894	Establishment of Lowell Observatory (later the site of the discovery of the planet Pluto) in Flagstaff.
1907	Arizona leads the nation in copper production, a ranking it has held in every year to the present.
1911	Completion of the Roosevelt Dam impounds the water used to irrigate 245,940 acres of the Salt river valley.
1912	*February 14.* Arizona is admitted to the union as the 48th state.
1917	*July 13–14.* A miners' strike at Bisbee is crushed when 1,286 people are put into railroad boxcars and deposited in the New Mexico desert.
1919	Establishment of Grand Canyon National Park.
1931–1934	Nearly all Arizona copper mines are wholly or partly closed during the depths of the Great Depression.
1934	Parker Dam is constructed on the Colorado River.
1936	Completion of Boulder Dam (now Hoover Dam) on the Colorado, at the time the world's highest dam.
1942	Nearly 18,000 Japanese-Americans are interned in a camp at Poston.
1946	A right-to-work constitutional amendment prohibits contracts requiring union membership.

1947	Arizona is first among states in long-staple cotton and third in citrus fruit. The irrigated area is 750,000 acres.
1948	Arizona Indians win the right to vote.
1960	With a population of 1,302,161, Arizona has been the fastest growing state in the previous decade, increasing its population by 73.7 percent.
1962	The world's largest solar telescope is installed at Kitt Peak National Observatory, about 70 miles southwest of Tucson.
1964	Completion of the Glen Canyon Dam on the Colorado River. Manufacturing has become the chief source of income, tripling in volume since 1955 and employing some 60,000 people. The growth of the electronics industry is chiefly responsible for the gain. Senator Barry Goldwater of Arizona is the Republican party's presidential candidate.
1969	Senator Carl Hayden retires after a record 56 continuous years in Congress. First college on an Indian reservation, Navajo Community College, is opened in Tsaile.
1970	With a population of 580,275, Phoenix passes Denver as the most populous city in the Rocky Mountain area.
1977	Arizona is annually using 2.2 million acre-feet more water than can be replenished.
1985	Arizona accounts for 72 percent of national copper production. It is second among states in molybdenum, third in silver, and fourth in overall nonfuel mineral production. *November 15.* Dedication of the Central Arizona Project, intended to carry 2.8 million acre-feet of water annually from the Colorado River to urban centers by 1997.
1988	*April 4.* Governor Evan Mecham is convicted by the Arizona senate on two charges of misconduct and removed from office.

DEMOGRAPHY

Population (est. 1987) . . . 3,386,000
Population (1980) 2,718,425
Population density in persons
   per square mile (1980) 23.8

POPULATION BY RACE (1980)
American Indian/Aleut/
   Eskimo 152,857
Asian/Pacific Islander 22,098
Black 75,034
Hispanic 440,915
White 2,240,033
Other 227,844

POPULATION CHARACTERISTICS (1980)
Percent of state population
Urban 79.6
Rural 20.4
Under 18 . . . . 29.1
65 or older 11.3
College-educated 16.8
Families below poverty line 9.5
Public assistance recipients 3.0

Per capita personal income
   (1986) $13,220
Millionaires per 100,000
   residents (1982) 190.2

Average life expectancy
   in years (1980) 74.3
Marriage rate per 1,000
   residents (1986) 10.9
Divorce rate per 1,000
   residents (1986) 7.0
Birth rate per 1,000
   residents (1985) 18.5
Infant mortality rate per
   1,000 births (1985) 9.6
Abortion rate per 1,000
   live births (1985) 373
Crime rate per 100,000
   residents (1985)
   Violent 658.3
   Property 6,663.1
Federal and state prisoners per
   100,000 residents (1984) 252
Alcohol consumption in gallons
   per capita (1985) 50.9
Deaths from motor vehicle accidents
   per 100,000 residents (1985) . . 27.0

MAJOR CITIES
	1984 population (est.)
Mesa	193,931
Phoenix	853,266
Tempe	118,336
Tucson	365,422

23

GOVERNMENT AND POLITICS

Number of US Representatives 5
Electoral votes 7

POLITICAL PARTY NOMINEES FROM STATE

James Elmer Yates (Green-
back) 1940 VP
Barry Morris Goldwater
(Conservative Party of New
Jersey/declined) 1960 P
Barry Morris Goldwater (R) 1964 P
Ed Winn (Workers League) 1968 P

PRESIDENTIAL PRIMARY ELECTION In 1988, Arizona sent 40 Democratic delegates and 33 Republican delegates to the national conventions.

CONSTITUTION Arizona is using its original constitution of 1911.

LEGISLATURE The legislature is divided into the Senate (30 members, 2-year term, minimum age 25) and the House of Representatives (60 members, 2-year term, minimum age of 25). In 1987, the annual salary was $15,000.

JUDICIARY The highest court is the Supreme Court, with 5 judges serving 6-year terms. In 1987, the annual salary was $75,000.

EXECUTIVE The governor serves a 4-year term; the minimum age for holding office is 25. In 1987, the annual salary was $75,000. There are 8 other elected officials.

PRESIDENTIAL VOTE 1948-1988 *(in percents)*

Year	State Winner	Democratic	Republican
1948	Truman (D)	53.8	43.8
1952	Eisenhower (R)	41.7	58.4
1956	Eisenhower (R)	38.9	61.0
1960	Nixon (R)	44.4	55.5
1964	Goldwater (R)	49.5	50.5
1968	Nixon (R)	35.0	54.8
1972	Nixon (R)	30.4	61.6
1976	Ford (R)	39.8	56.4
1980	Reagan (R)	28.2	60.6
1984	Reagan (R)	32.5	66.4
1988	Bush (R)	39.0	61.0

GOVERNORS

Territorial Governors

John N. Goodwin (R)	1863-1866
Richard C. McCormick (R)	1866-1869
A.P.K. Safford (R)	1869-1877
John P. Joyt (R)	1877-1878
John C. Fremont (R)	1878-1881
Frederick A. Tritle (R)	1881-1885
C. Meyer Zulick (D)	1885-1889
Lewis Wolfley (R)	1889-1890
John N. Irwin (R)	1890-1892
Nathan O. Murphy (R)	1892-1893
Louis C. Hughes (D)	1893-1896
Benjamin J. Franklin (R)	1896-1897
Myron H. McCord (R)	1897-1898
Nathan O. Murphy (R)	1898-1902
Alexander O. Brodie (R)	1902-1905
Joseph H. Kibbey (R)	1905-1909
Richard E. Sloan (R)	1909-1911

State Governors

George W.P. Hunt (D)	1911-1919
Thomas E. Campbell (R)	1919-1923
George W.P. Hunt (D)	1923-1929
John C. Phillips (R)	1929-1931
George W.P. Hunt (D)	1931-1933
Benjamin B. Moeur (D)	1933-1938
Rawghlie C. Stanford (D)	1937-1939
Robert T. Jones (D)	1939-1941
Sidney P. Osborn (D)	1941-1948
Dan E. Garvey (D)	1948-1951
Howard Pyle (R)	1951-1955
Ernest W. McFarland (D)	1955-1959
Paul Fannin (R)	1959-1965
Samuel P. Goddard Jr. (D)	1965-1967
Jack Williams (R)	1967-1975
Raul H. Castro (D)	1975-1977
Wesley Bolin (D)	1977-1978
Bruce Babbitt (D)	1978-1987
Evan Mecham (D)	1987-1988
Rose Mofford (D)	1988-

MINIMUM AGES

Majority	18
Marriage with parental consent . . .	16
Marriage without parental consent .	18
Making a will	18
Buying alcohol	21
Jury duty	18

Leaving school . . . . after 10th grade
Driver's license 16

CAPITAL PUNISHMENT
Number executed 1976-88: 0
On death row, Aug. 1, 1988: 84

MILITARY INSTALLATIONS
Total number: 20
Major bases:
  Army: 2
  Air Force: 4
  Marine Corps: 1

FINANCES

Thousands of dollars

GENERAL REVENUE (1985)
Total general revenue . . . 4,292,969
Total tax revenue 2,945,422
Sales and gross receipts . . . 1,809,637
Individual income taxes 608,611
Corporate net income taxes . . 202,301

GENERAL EXPENDITURE (1985)
Total general expenditure . 4,251,280
Education 1,915,896
Public welfare 466,608
Health 97,618
Hospitals 57,052
Natural resources 56,132
Police 69,202
Corrections 141,411

FEDERAL AID (1985) 1,121,528

ECONOMY

Arizona's agriculture is based on feed-stocks and cotton farming, with cotton the largest cash crop, followed by feed crops, vegetables, and citrus. Beef and dairy products provide the main income from livestock. In minerals and mining, Arizona leads the US in copper production (more than 50 percent of the national total); sand, gravel, molybdenum, gold, zinc, uranium, diatomite, gypsum, and perlite asbestos are also important products. Electrical, electronic, and ceramic products and equipment are the notable manufactures. Tourism brings in well over $500 million to the state annually.

EMPLOYMENT (1984)
Thousands of persons
Total number of employed
  workers 1,361
Construction 96.2
Finance, insurance, and real
  estate 71.7
Government 206.1
Manufacturing 172.3
Mining 13.3
Services 274.1
Transportation, communications,
  and utilities 60.4
Wholesale and retail trade 286.6

Percent of civilian labor force
  unemployed (1984) 5.0

DEPARTMENT OF DEFENSE (1985)
Civilian workers employed . . . 10,365
Military personnel 20,704
Contract awards . . . . $2.006 billion

ENERGY SOURCES FOR ELECTRIC UTILITIES (1983)
Percent
Coal 52.2
Gas 0.0
Hydroelectric 14.6
Nuclear 33.0
Petroleum 0.1

TRANSPORTATION
Motor vehicles registered
  in state (1986) 2,345,521
Miles of roads, streets,
  and highways (1986) 77,314
Miles of Class I railway
  operated (1986) 1,698
Airports (1983) 240
Major aviation hubs (1983) 2
  Largest hub: Phoenix

CULTURE AND EDUCATION

Native American tribes
Arizona was formerly home to the Cocopa, Halchidhoma, Halyikwamai, Havasupai, Kohuana, Majove, Quechuan, Sobaipuri, and Yaqui tribes. Groups that continue to live in the state include the Apache, Hopi, Hualapai, Maricopa, Navajo, Papago, Pi-ma, Southern Paiute, and Yavapai. There are 200 federal reservations in Arizona.

Religions, ethnicities, and languages
Roman Catholicism, to which most of Arizona's large Mexican-American community belongs, is the single biggest denomination, followed by various Protestant groups. In 1980, 20.1 percent of Arizona's population spoke a language other than English (usually Spanish) at home.

Major museums and libraries
Amerind Foundation Museum, Dragoon
Arizona Historical Society Museum,
 Tucson
Arizona-Sonora Desert Museum, Tucson
Arizona State Museum, University of
 Arizona, Tucson
Desert Botanical Garden, Phoenix
Fort Huachuca Historical Museum
Heard Museum of Anthropology and
 Primitive Art, Phoenix
Museum of Northern Arizona, Flagstaff
Phoenix Art Museum
Tucson Museum of Art
University of Arizona Museum of Art,
 Tucson

Major arts organizations
Arizona Opera Company, Phoenix
Arizona Theatre Company, Tucson
Ballet Arizona, Phoenix
Phoenix Symphony Orchestra
Tucson Symphony Orchestra

Colleges and universities
Number public (1986-87)   19
Number private (1986-87)   13
Total enrollment, in full-time equivalent
 students (1985)   135,000

Public elementary and secondary schools
Expenditure per pupil in average daily
 attendance (1986-87) $2,784
Pupil-teacher ratio (1987)   18.4
Average teacher salary (1986-87)
 $28,971

Major league sports teams
Basketball: Phoenix Suns

Holidays
Admission Day. February 14
American Family Day. 1st Sunday in
 August
State Fair, Phoenix. Late October to early
 November

ARIZONA IN LITERATURE

Edward Abbey *Cactus Country* (1973)
 A paean to the Sonoran Desert.

Geoff Aggeler *Confessions of Johnny Ringo* (1987)
 Fictional autobiography of a famous outlaw, contemporary
 of the James brothers, and member of Quantrill's Raiders.
 Ray Hogan, *The Life and Death of Johnny Ringo* (1963), gives
 an account of the facts of Ringo's career.

Frank Guy Applegate *Indian Stories from the Pueblos* (1929)
 Retelling of Hopi legends.

Laura Armer *Waterless Mountain* (1931)
 Story of a Navajo boy.

Elliott Arnold *Blood Brother* (1947, rpt. 1979)
 A partly fictional history of the Southwest from the time of
 the Gadsden Purchase of 1856 until the end of the Indian
 Wars in 1870. Centers on the Apache chief Cochise and
 Indian agent Tom Jeffords.

Mary Austin *The Land of Little Rain* (1903, rpt. 1974)
 Classic evocation of desert landscape and folkways.

Amelia Bean *The Feud* (1960)
 Novel about a gun battle, based on an incident of the 1880s.

Charles Bowden *Blue Desert* (1986)
 Naturalist's essay on desert beauty and urban ugliness.

Mary Boyer *Arizona in Literature* (1934)

William Breakenridge *Helldorado; Bringing the Law to the
 Mesquite* (1928)
 An authentic memoir by a deputy sheriff of Tombstone.

Elliott Coues (ed. and trans.) *On the Trail of a Spanish Pioneer:
 The Diary of Francis Garces . . . 1775–1776* 2 vols. (1900)
 Garces, a Franciscan missionary, was among the earliest
 explorers of the Gila and Colorado Rivers.

Eulalia Bourne *Nine Months Is a Year at Baboquivari School*
 (1969); *Ranch Schoolteacher* (1974)
 Memoirs of a nun who taught for fifty years in rural schools.

J. Ross Browne (ed. Donald M. Powell) *Adventures in Apache
 Country* (1869, rpt. 1974)
 Record of the state in the 1860s.

Edwin Bryant *What I Saw in California* (1848, rpt. 1967,
 1985)
 The best-known trail guide for Forty-niners.

Abe and Mildred Chanin *This Land, These Voices: A Different
 View of Arizona History in the Words of Those Who Lived It*
 (1977)
 An oral history composed of thirty-three memoirs.

Grace Cooke *The Joy Bringer: A Tale of the Painted Desert*
 (1913)
 A romantic portrait of a Hopi reservation.

Harold Courlander *Hopi Voices: Recollections, Traditions, and
 Narratives of the Hopi Indians* (1982)

Thomas Cruse (ed. Eugene Cunningham) *Apache Days and
 After* (1987)
 Eyewitness account of the Indian Wars of 1879–1880 by an
 officer of the Sixth Cavalry.

William Decker *The Holdouts* (1979)
 Western novel about rustlers.

J. Frank Dobie *Apache Gold and Yaqui Silver* (1939)
 Tales of lost mines and Spanish colonial days.

Colin Fletcher *The Man Who Walked through Time* (1968)
 Naturalist's meditation on landscape inspired by a walk
 through the Grand Canyon.

Timothy Flint *Francis Bervain* (1826)
 Historical novel about a Yankee's involvement in the
 Mexican revolt of 1822, set on the southwestern frontier.

Earle Forrest *Arizona's Dark and Bloody Ground* (1936, rpt.
 1984)
 Story of the Pleasant Valley War, and the tragic feud
 between the Graham and Tewksbury clans.

Carol Fowler *Daisy Hooee Nampeyo* (1977)
 Biography of a Hopi Indian potter responsible for reviving
 the traditional arts of her people.

Frances Gillmor *Windsinger* (1930)
 Story of a Navajo prophet.
———. *Fruit Out of Rock* (1940)
 Novel about fruit farming evoking the Arizona landscape.

Zane Grey *The Call of the Canyon* (1924)
 Classic formulary western, with descriptions of Arizona
 landscape. Grey first visited the state where he set many of
 his novels in 1907, and was inspired to write his non-
 fictional study *The Last of the Plainsmen* (1908).

Frank Gruber *Gunsight* (1942)
 Western novel about law and order in a boomtown.

Oakley Hall *Warlock* (1958)
 Novel based on the Wyatt Earp legend.

Alberta Hannum *Spin a Silver Dollar* (1945); *Paint the Wind* (1958)
Biographical novels about a Navajo artist, set on the reservation.

Will Henry *MacKenna's Gold* (1963, rpt. 1985)
A Western melodrama set in 1897 centering on a prospector and a cache of gold.

Tony Hillerman *The Dark Wind* (1982)
Detective novel about a Navajo tribal policeman.

Paul Horgan *A Distant Trumpet* (1960, rpt. 1985)
Novel set at a cavalry outpost during the Indian Wars of the 1870s and 1880s.

Candace C. Kant *Zane Grey's Arizona* (1984)

Clarence Budington Kelland *Arizona* (1939)
Novel set in Civil War days.

Charles King *The Colonel's Daughter* (1910)
Romance of army life at Camp Verde during the Indian wars.

Joseph Wood Krutch *The Desert Year* (1952); *The Voice of the Desert* (1955); *Grand Canyon* (1958)
Philosophical essays on the flora, fauna, and landscape, by a literary scholar and conservationist.

Oliver La Farge *Laughing Boy* (1929, rpt. 1971); *The Enemy Gods* (1937)
Classic novels of Navajo life by a writer noted for his knowledge of native Americans.

Judy Nolte Lensink (ed.) *Old Southwest/New Southwest: Essays on a Region and Its Literature* (1986)

Frank C. Lockwood (intro. by John B. Harte) *Pioneer Portraits: Selected Vignettes* (1968)
Selected studies of early settlers drawn from the author's *Pioneer Days in Arizona* (1932).

Haniel Long *Piñon Country* (1941)
Folkways of the upper Sonora region.

Gary Paul Nabhan *The Desert Smells Like Rain* (1982); *Gathering the Desert* (1985)
Naturalist's observations of desert folkways.

Jack O'Connor *Boom Town* (1938)
Story of a silver town in the early '90s.

John Wesley Powell *Exploration of the Colorado River* . . . (1875, rpt. 1961); *Canyons of the Colorado* (1895)
Records by the first white man to travel the length of the Colorado.

Lawrence Clark Powell *Southwest Classics . . . Essays on Books and Their Writers* (1974)

Dan Quin (pseud. of Alfred Henry Lewis) *Wolfville* (1897)
First of a series of novels giving authentic accounts of ranching and mining c. 1900.

Mary Kidder Rak *A Cowman's Wife* (1934); *Mountain Cattle* (1936)
First-hand account of cattle ranching in Cochise County.

Rowland W. Rider (as told to D. M. Paulsen) *The Roll Away Saloon: Cowboy Tales of the Arizona Strip* (1988)
Humorous and part-factual stories of the Old West.

William H. Robinson *Thirsty Earth* (1937)
Novel set in the Choya valley in the 1890s.

Ross Santee *Cowboy* (1928); *Apache Land* (1947); *Lost Pony Tracks* (1953); *Dog Days* (1955)
Autobiographical tales of ranch life.

Dean and **Lucille Saxton** *O'othham Hoho'ok A'Agitha: Legends and Lore of the Papago and Pima Indians* (1973)

Martha Summerhayes *Vanished Arizona; Recollections of the Army Life of a New England Woman* (1908, enl. ed. 1911, rpt. 1960)
Classic memoir of Army life on the southwestern frontier c. 1870.

Godfrey Sykes *A Westerly Trend* (1944)
Autobiography of a Yorkshire man who came to Arizona in the 1880s and worked as a cowboy before becoming the architect of several observatories.

Ruth M. Underhill *Singing for Power: The Song Magic of the Papago Indians of Southern Arizona* (1938, rpt. 1973)

John Charles Van Dyke *The Grand Canyon of the Colorado* (1920)
Classic description of the sublimity of the Grand Canyon.

Frank Waters *The Book of the Hopi* (1964)
An oral history of the Hopi tribe dictated by their elders.

Helen C. White *Dust on the King's Highway* (1947)
Historical novel based on the life of Francisco Garces.

Stewart Edward White *Arizona Nights* (1907)
Fact, fiction, and folklore portraying ranch life.

Harold Bell Wright *The Mine with the Iron Door* (1923)
Novel about a gold mine in the Santa Catalinas.

GUIDES TO RESOURCES

Arizona Department of Education *Arizona History Resource Guide: A Resource Guide for Arizona Classroom Teachers* (1977)

Baker, Simon and **Thomas J. McCleneghan** *An Arizona Economic and Historic Atlas* (1966)

Beers, Henry P. *Spanish and Mexican Records of the American Southwest: A Bibliographic Guide to Archive and Manuscript Sources* (1979)

Federal Writers' Project (ed. Joseph Miller) *Arizona, The Grand Canyon State: A State Guide* (4th ed. 1966)

Granger, Byrd H. *Arizona's Names: X Marks the Place (1983)*

Hecht, Melvin E. and **Richard W. Reeves** *The Arizona Atlas* (1981)

Hinton, Richard J. *The Handbook to Arizona* (new ed. 1970)

Laird, W. David *Hopi Bibliography* (1977)

Martin, Douglas *Arizona Chronology* 2 vols. (1963–1966)

Polzer, Charles *A Kino Guide* (1972)

Spamer, Earle E. with **George H. Billingsley** et al. *Bibliography of the Grand Canyon and the Lower Colorado River, 1540–1980* (1981)

University of Arizona *Arizona: Its People and Resources* (1960, rpt. 1972)

Valley National Bank *Arizona Statistical Review* (34th ed. 1977)

Walker, Henry P. and **Don Bufkin** *Historical Atlas of Arizona* (2d ed. 1979)

Wallace, Andrew (ed.) *Sources and Readings in Arizona History* (1965)

Yates, Richard and **Mary Marshall** *The Lower Colorado River: A Bibliography* (1974)

SELECTED NONFICTION SOURCES

Altshuler, Constance W. *Chains of Command: Arizona and the Army, 1856–1875* (1981)
————. *Starting with Defiance: Nineteenth Century Arizona Military Posts* (1983)

Arizona and Its Heritage (University of Arizona General Bulletin No. 3) (1936)

Arnold, Oren *Arizona under the Sun* (1968)

Bailey, Lynn R. *Bisbee: Queen of the Copper Camps* (1983)

Bailey, Paul *City in the Sun: The Japanese Concentration Camp at Poston, Arizona* (1979)

BaKarich, Sarah G. *Gunsmoke–The True Story of Old Tombstone* (1954)

Baldwin, Gordon *The Warrior Apaches* (1966)

Bancroft, Hubert H. *History of Arizona and New Mexico* (rev. ed. 1962)

Barnes, Will Croft (rev. Byrd H. Granger) *Arizona Place Names* (1935, rpt. 1988)

Blaine, Peter, Sr. *Papagos and Politics* (1981)

Blair, Robert *Tales of the Superstitions: The Origins of the Lost Dutchman Legend* (1975)

Bourke, John G. *On the Border with Crook* (1962)

Bourne, Eulalia *Woman in Levis* (1967)

Bowers, Janice E. *A Sense of Place: The Life and Work of Forrest Shreve* (1988)

Brandes, Ray *Frontier Military Posts of Arizona* (1960)

Bret Harte, John *Tucson Portrait of a Desert Pueblo* (1980)

Brinkerhoff, Sidney B. and Rosalie Crowe (eds.) *Early Yuma* (1976)
—— and Odie B. Faulk *Lancers for the King* (1965)

Browne, J. Ross (ed. Donald M. Powell) *Adventures in Apache Country* (1869, rpt. 1974)

Burgess, Opie R. *Bisbee Not So Long Ago* (1967)

Byrkit, James W. *Forging the Copper Collar, Arizona's Labor Management War of 1901–1921* (1982)

Cline, Platt *They Came to the Mountain: The History of Flagstaff* (1976)

Comeaux, Malcolm L. *Arizona: A Geography* (1981)

Connor, Daniel E. *Joseph R. Walker and the Arizona Adventure* (1956)

Cookridge, E. H. *The Baron of Arizona* (1967)

Coolidge, Dane *Arizona Cowboys* (1984)

Corle, Edwin *The Gila: River of the Southwest* (Rivers of America series) (1951)

Cosulich, Bernice *Tucson, 1692–1900* (1953)

Dunbier, Roger *The Sonoran Desert: Its Geography, Economy, and People* (1968)

Dunlop, Richard *Goodfellow: Gunshot Surgeon of Tombstone* (1965)

Dunning, Charles *Arizona's Golden Road* (1961)
—— and Edward H. Peplow *Rock to Riches* (1959)

Faulk, Odie B. *Arizona, a Short History* (1970)
——. *Tombstone: Myth and Reality* (1972)

Fireman, Bert M. *Arizona Historic Land* (1982)

Forrest, Earle *Arizona's Dark and Bloody Ground* (1984)

Goldwater, Barry *Delightful Journey down the Green and Colorado Rivers* (1970)

Granger, Byrd *Grand Canyon Place Names* (1960)

Griffith, James S. *Southern Arizona Folk Arts* (1988)

Hamblin, W. Kenneth and Joseph R. Murphy *Grand Canyon Perspectives* (1969)

Haury, Emil W. *The Hohokam: Desert Farmers and Craftsmen* (1976)

Heatwole, Thelma *Ghost Towns and Historical Haunts in Arizona* (1981)

Hensen, Pauline *Founding a Wilderness Capital, Prescott, A.T., 1864* (1965)

Herne, Charles *The Arizona Rough Riders* (1970)

Hinton, R. *1,000 Old Arizona Mines* (1962)

Hodge, Hiram *Arizona As It Was in 1877* (1962)

Jennings, James R. *Arizona Was the West* (1970)

Johnson, Rich *The Central Arizona Project, 1918–1968* (1977)

Johnson, Wesley G., Jr. *Phoenix: Valley of the Sun* (1982)

Joseph, Alice, Jane Chesky, and Rosamond Spicer *The Desert People: A Study of the Papago Indians* (1974)

Kelly, George H. (comp.) *Legislative History: Arizona, 1864–1912* (1926)

Kerby, Robert L. *The Confederate Invasion of New Mexico and Arizona, 1861–62* (1958)

Kessell, John L. *Mission of Sorrows: Jesuit Guevavi and the Pimas, 1691–1767* (1970)

Lake, Stuart *Wyatt Earp: Frontier Marshal* (1931)

Lamar, Howard *The Far Southwest, 1846–1912: A Territorial History* (1966, rpt. 1970)

Leydet, François *Time and the River Flowing* (1968)

Lingenfelter, Richard E. *Steamboats on the Colorado River, 1852–1916* (1978)

Lockwood, Frank C. *The Apache Indians* (1912)
——. *Pioneer Days in Arizona* (1932)
——. *Life in Old Tucson* (1943)
——. *Pioneer Portraits; Selected Vignettes* (1968)

Lowe, Charles H. *Arizona's Natural Environment Landscapes and Habitats* (1964)

Luey, Beth and Noel J. Stowe (eds.) *Arizona at 75* (1988)

Mann, Dean E. *The Politics of Water in Arizona* (1963)

Martin, Douglas D. (ed.) *Tombstone's Epitaph* (1958)

Martin, Paul and Fred Plog *The Archeology of Arizona* (1973)

McClintock, James H. *Mormon Settlement in Arizona* (1921, rpt. 1985)

McElfresh, Patricia M. *Scottsdale: Jewel in the Desert* (1984)

McLaughlin, Herb and Dorothy (eds.) *Phoenix, 1870–1970, in Photographs* (1970)

Miller, Joseph *The Arizona Rangers* (1952)
—— (ed.) *Arizona Cavalcade* (1962)

Miller, Tom (ed.) *Arizona: The Land and the People* (1986)

Murphy, James M. *Laws, Courts, and Lawyers: Through the Years in Arizona* (1970)

Myers, John M. *The Last Chance: Tombstone's Early Years* (1950)
——. *Doc Holliday* (1955)

North, Diane M. T. *Samuel Peter Heintzelman and the Sonora Exploring and Mining Company* (1980)

O'Neal, Bill *The Arizona Rangers* (1987)

Officer, James E. *Hispanic Arizona, 1536–1856* (1987)

Paré, Madeline and Bert M. Fireman *Arizona Pageant, a Short History of the 48th State* (1970)

Paylore, Patricia, Ted de Grazia, and Donald M. Powell *Kino, a Commemoration* (1961)

Peplow, Edward H. *History of Arizona* 3 vols. (1958)

Peterson, Charles S. *Take Up Your Mission: Mormon Colonizing along the Little Colorado River, 1870–1900* (1973)

Powell, Donald M. *The Peralta Grant: James Addison Reavis and the Barony of Arizona* (1960)

Powell, Lawrence C. *Arizona: A Bicentennial History* (States and the Nation series) (1976)

Sack, Benjamin *Be It Enacted: The Creation of the Territory of Arizona* (1964)

Scharff, R. (ed.) *Grand Canyon National Park* (1967)

Schellie, Don *Vast Domain of Blood: The Story of the Camp Grant Massacre* (1968)

Sellers, William D. and Richard H. Hill (eds.) *Arizona Climate* (1974)

Sharp, Bob *Big Outfit: Ranching on the Baca Float* (1974)

Sheridan, Thomas E. *Los Tucsonenses: The Mexican Community in Tucson, 1854–1941* (1986)

Sherman, James E. and Barbara H. *Ghost Towns of Arizona* (1977)

Sikorsky, Robert *Fools' Gold: The Facts, Myths and Legends of the Lost Dutchman Mine and the Superstition Mountains* (1983)

Smalley, George *My Adventures in Arizona* (1966)

Smith, C. C. *William Sanders Oury: History Maker of the Southwest* (1967)

Smith, Fay, John Kessell, and Francis Fox *Father Kino in Arizona* (1966)

Sonnichsen, C. L. *Billy King's Tombstone; the Private Life of an Arizona Boom Town* (1942, rpt. 1972)
———. *Tucson: The Life and Times of an American City* (1982)

Southwest Mission Research Center *Tucson: A Short History* (1988)

Spicer, Edward H. *Cycles of Conquest; the Impact of Spain, Mexico and the United States on the Indians of the Southwest, 1530–1960* (1962)
———. *The Yaquis: A Cultural History* (1980)

Stegner, Wallace E. *Beyond the Hundredth Meridian: John Wesley Powell and the Second Opening of the West* (1954)

Stewart, Janet A. *Arizona Ranch Houses: Southern Territorial Styles, 1867–1900* (Arizona Historical Society Monograph No. 2) (1974, rpt. 1987)

Trimble, Marshall *Arizona: A Panoramic History of a Frontier State* (1977)

Tuck, Frank J. (comp.) *History of Mining in Arizona* (1955, 1963)

Udall, David K. and Pearl U. Nelson *Arizona Pioneer Mormon: David King Udall, His Story and His Family* (1959)

Underhill, Ruth M. *Singing for Power; the Song Magic of the Papago Indians of Southern Arizona* (1938, rpt. 1973)

University of Arizona *Arizona: Its People and Resources* (2d ed. 1972)

Wagoner, Jay J. *History of the Cattle Industry in Southern Arizona, 1540–1940* (University of Arizona Social Science Bulletin No. 20) (1952)
———. *Arizona Territory, 1863–1912: A Political History* (1970)
———. *Early Arizona: Prehistory to Civil War* (1975)
———. *Arizona's Heritage* (1977)

Walker, Dale L. *Death Was the Black Horse: The Story of Rough Rider Buckey O'Neill* (1975)

Waters, Frank *The Colorado* (Rivers of America series) (1946)
———. *The Earp Brothers of Tombstone: The Story of Mrs. Virgil Earp* (1960)

Weight, Harold O. *Lost Mines of Old Arizona* (1959)

Whitney, Stephen *A Field Guide to the Grand Canyon* (1982)

Woody, Clara T. and Milton L. Schwartz *Globe, Arizona* (1977)

Wyllys, Rufus K. *Arizona: The History of a Frontier State* (1950)

Young, Otis E. *How They Dug the Gold* (1967)

Zarbin, Earl A. *Roosevelt Dam: A History to 1911* (1984)

ARKANSAS

The west south central state of Arkansas is bounded on the north by Missouri; on the east by Missouri, Tennessee, and Mississippi, and the Mississippi River; on the south by Louisiana; and on the west by Oklahoma and Texas.

FULL NAME State of Arkansas
POSTAL ABBREVIATION AR
INHABITANT Arkansan
ADMITTED TO THE UNION June 15, 1836. 25th state
POPULATION (est. 1987) 2,388,000. Percent of US total: 0.98%. Rank: 32d

CAPITAL CITY Little Rock, the largest city in the state, on the south bank of the Arkansas River; population 170,388 (est. 1984). Founded in 1821 on the site of a Quapaw Indian settlement and made the territorial capital the same year, Little Rock was incorporated as a city in 1835. It became the state capital in 1836.

STATE NAME AND NICKNAMES "Arkansas" is derived from the French pronunciation of "Kansas," the name of one of the Indian tribes encountered by the French explorers Jacques Marquette and Louis Jolliet on their journey down the Mississippi River in 1673. The tribe called themselves the Quapaw; *Kansas* was the Algonkian name for them.

STATE SEAL An eagle with an olive branch and arrows in its talons, a ribbon bearing the state motto in its beak, and on its breast a shield showing a steamboat, a beehive, a plow, and a sheaf of wheat; to the left is an angel, inscribed "Mercy," and to the right a sword, inscribed "Justice"; above them is the Goddess of Liberty encircled by 13 stars and many rays. Around the border is the legend "Great Seal of the State of Arkansas."

MOTTO Regnat Populus (The people rule)

SONG "Arkansas," lyrics and music by Eva Ware Barnett.

SYMBOLS
Flower apple blossom
Tree pine
Bird mockingbird
Gem diamond
Mineral quartz crystal
Rock bauxite
Insect honeybee
Beverage milk
Musical instrument fiddle

LICENSE PLATE Red on white, with blue legend "Land of Opportunity."

FLAG On a field of red, a white diamond bearing the name "Arkansas," with one blue five-pointed star above the name and three below it. The white diamond is bordered by a blue diamond containing 25 stars.

GEOGRAPHY AND CLIMATE

The Ozark Plateau, an area of steep but low-lying hills and ridges, dominates the northwestern half of Arkansas. Extensive coal and natural gas deposits underlay the western highlands. To the southeast can be found fertile lowlands of the Mississippi Alluvial Plain and the West Gulf Coastal Plain, where forestry is one of the main industries.

AREA 53,187 square miles. Rank: 27th

INLAND WATER 1,159 square miles

GEOGRAPHIC CENTER Pulaski, 12 miles NW of Little Rock

ELEVATIONS *Highest point:* Magazine Mountain, Logan City, 2,753 feet. *Lowest point:* Ouachita River, Ashley/Union Counties, 55 feet. *Mean elevation:* 650 feet

MAJOR RIVERS Mississippi, Arkansas, Ouachita, White

MAJOR LAKES AND RESERVOIRS Bull Shoals, Ouachita, Beaver, Norfolk, Greers Ferry

LAND USE

	Thousands of acres
Urban (1982)	636
Rural (1982)	28,770
Cropland (1982)	8,102
Pastureland (1982)	5,794
Rangeland (1982)	162
Forestland (1982)	14,340
State parks and recreation areas (1983)	44
National park system (1984)	100
National forest system (1984)	3,502
Tribal lands (1984)	0

TEMPERATURES The highest recorded temperature was 120° F on August 10, 1936, at Ozark. The lowest was -29° F on February 13, 1905, at Pond.

NATIONAL SITES

NATIONAL HISTORIC SITE Fort Smith
NATIONAL MEMORIAL Arkansas Post
NATIONAL MILITARY PARK Pea Ridge
NATIONAL PARK Hot Springs
NATIONAL SCENIC RIVER Buffalo
NATIONAL WILDLIFE REFUGES Big Lake, Felsenthal, Holla Bend, Wapanocca, White River

HISTORY

1541	*June 18.* Spanish explorer Hernando de Soto crosses the Mississippi River, probably near Sunflower Landing, 20 miles south of Helena. He stays in Arkansas until spring 1542.
1673	*July.* French explorers Louis Jolliet and Father Jacques Marquette descend the Mississippi to the mouth of the Arkansas River. Warned by the Quapaw (Arkansas) Indians of hostile tribes farther south, they turn back.
1682	*March 13.* Robert Cavelier, Sieur de La Salle, reaches the Arkansas on his way to the mouth of the Mississippi. He visits a Quapaw village and claims the land in the name of King Louis XIV.
1686	French explorer Henri de Tonti leaves a garrison at Arkansas Post, the first permanent white settlement in the lower Mississippi Valley.
1721	A group of 1,300 half-starved colonists—whites and black slaves—abandons Arkansas Post after John Law's scheme to develop the Mississippi Valley collapses.
1762	France cedes the Louisiana Territory, including Arkansas, to Spain, but French soldiers continue to man Arkansas Post.
1803	The United States purchases the Louisiana Territory from France, to which it was returned from Spain in 1800.
1818	The Quapaw cede their lands between the Red and Arkansas rivers.
1819	*March 2.* Arkansas, which had been part of Missouri Territory since 1812, is detached and made a territory. *November 20.* Arkansas *Gazette*, the first newspaper in Arkansas, published.
1821	*October 25.* The capital moves from Arkansas Post to Little Rock.
1822	*March 16.* The *Eagle*, first steamboat to ascend the Arkansas River, arrives at Little Rock.
1830	*May 28.* Congress establishes the boundary separating Arkansas from Indian Territory to the west.

1832–1839	Removal of the "Five Civilized Tribes" of Indians from the Southeast through Arkansas to Indian Territory.
1836	*June 15.* Arkansas is admitted to the Union as the 25th state.
1846	Disillusioned by the collapse of two state-chartered banks, legislators ratify a constitutional amendment barring any banking institution from being established in the state.
1858	Edward Payson Washburn paints *The Arkansas Traveler.*
1859	*February 12.* Signing of legislation ordering all free Negroes out of Arkansas by the end of the year.
1860	On the eve of the Civil War, Arkansas has a population of 435,450, of whom 111,115 are black slaves and 11,481 are slaveowners.
1861	*May 6.* A convention votes to secede from the Union and join the Confederacy. The first of some 60,000 Arkansas residents join the Confederate troops, but some 9,000 whites and more than 5,000 blacks fight on the Union side during the war.
1862	*March 7–8.* Battle of Pea Ridge in northwest Arkansas. A Confederate advance north is rebuffed.
1863	*September 10.* Federal troops occupy Little Rock.
1864	A Unionist convention abolishes slavery in Arkansas and adopts a new constitution for the state.
1866	*August.* Ex-Confederates sweep control of the legislature and pass laws denying blacks the right to sit on juries, serve in the militia, or attend white public schools.
1867	*March 2.* Congress passes the Reconstruction Act, which voids the government of Arkansas and nine other Southern states.
1868	*March 13.* A new constitution adopted by referendum enfranchises Negroes and disenfranchises ex-Confederate soldiers.
	June 22. Arkansas is readmitted to the Union.
	November. Governor Powell Clayton declares martial law in much of the state; a mostly black militia battles the Ku Klux Klan.
1871	Completion of a railroad between Memphis and Little Rock.
1872	University of Arkansas opens in Fayetteville.
1874	*May 15.* Month-long "Brooks-Baxter War" between rival claimants to the governorship ends when President Ulysses S. Grant orders the forces of the former to disperse.
	October 13. Ratification of a new constitution restoring the franchise to all whites and guaranteeing full civil rights for blacks ends the Reconstruction era.
1887	Bauxite discovered southwest of Little Rock; peak output is reached in 1918, by which time almost all US bauxite is being mined in Arkansas.
1891	Jim Crow legislation segregates railroad coaches and waiting stations.
1892	Adoption of a constitutional amendment imposing a poll tax restricts the electorate.
1898	The Democratic party adopts whites-only primary elections.
1904	Near Ulm, William H. Fuller grows a 70-acre stand of rice, establishing one of the state's leading crops.
1906	*August 1.* Diamonds found near Murfreesboro, which becomes the site of the only diamond mine in the United States.
1909	Lumber production is the state's leading industry.
1920	Over 40 percent of land under cultivation is in cotton, the state's leading crop.
1921	*January 10.* Discovery of oil near El Dorado triggers a boom; Arkansas is fourth among states in oil in 1924, but production peaks in 1925.
	Establishment of Hot Springs National Park.
1927	The Mississippi River floods one-fifth of the state.
1928	A law prohibits the teaching of the theory of evolution in public schools. It is overturned by the US Supreme Court in 1968.
1929	A state personal income tax is adopted; however, per capita income is only 43 percent of the national average.
1931	Hattie W. Caraway becomes the first woman elected to the United States Senate.
1932	In the depths of the Great Depression, the lowest price is paid for cotton in a half-century.
1935	A state sales tax (two percent) is adopted.
1942	Arkansas ranks first among states in the production of strawberries, third in cotton and rice, and seventh in lumber.

1947	A right-to-work law bans the closed shop or union shop in Arkansas.
1957	Under orders from Governor Orval Faubus, the Arkansas National Guard turns away nine black students intending, under court order, to desegregate Little Rock's Central High School. On September 24, President Dwight David Eisenhower federalizes National Guard units and sends army paratroopers to the school to enforce desegregation.
1958	*September 30.* Little Rock's public high schools are closed by Faubus to prevent integration. They reopen in 1959 with eight blacks in two schools.
1960	With 1,786,272 people, Arkansas is one of only two states to have lost population for two successive decades. Per capita income of $1,341 is 49th among states.
1964	Voters adopt a constitutional amendment eliminating the poll tax as a requirement for voting. Arkansas ranks second among states in broiler and turkey production.
1966	Succeeding Faubus, who has served a record six terms, Winthrop Rockefeller becomes the first Republican elected governor since Reconstruction.
1967	Arkansas ranks third among states in soybean production and fourth in cotton.
1968	George Wallace of the American Independent party becomes the first non-Democratic presidential candidate ever to carry Arkansas.
1969	About half of the state's black pupils are attending integrated school systems.
1971	Completion of the Arkansas River Navigation System links the waterway westward from the Mississippi to Tulsa, Oklahoma.
1981	A state law requires public schools to give "balanced treatment" to "creation science" and evolution in courses dealing with the origins of life. A federal court invalidates the law.
1983	Arkansas becomes the first state to require teachers to pass basic-skills tests to keep their licenses. Ninety percent pass the first administration of tests in 1985.
1985	Reynolds Metals Company closes its two aluminum smelters in Arkansas.
1987	A Japanese-American consortium announces it will build a $175-million steel mill at Blytheville.

DEMOGRAPHY

Population (est. 1987) . . . 2,388,000
Population (1980) 2,286,419
Population density in persons
   per square mile (1980) 43.0

POPULATION BY RACE (1980)
American Indian/ Aleut/
   Eskimo 9,411
Asian/Pacific Islander 6,732
Black 373,192
Hispanic 17,873
White 1,890,002
Other 6,176

POPULATION CHARACTERISTICS (1980)
Percent of state population
Urban 51.6
Rural 48.4
Under 18 . . . . 29.4
65 or older 13.7
College-educated 9.7
Families below poverty line . . . 14.9
Public assistance recipients 7.2

Per capita personal income
   (1986) $10,773
Millionaires per 100,000
   residents (1982) 112.7

Average life expectancy in
   years (1980) 73.7
Marriage rate per 1,000
   residents (1986) 13.1
Divorce rate per 1,000
   residents (1986) 7.0
Birth rate per 1,000
   residents (1985) 14.9
Infant mortality rate per
   1,000 live births (1985) 10.9
Abortion rate per 1,000
   live births (1985) 159
Crime rate per 1,000
   residents (1985)
   Violent 394.8
   Property 3529.9
Federal and state prisoners per
   100,000 residents (1984) 185
Alcohol consumption in gallons
   per capita (1985) 29.6
Deaths from motor vehicle accidents
   per 100,0000 residents (1985) . 22.6

MAJOR CITIES
1984 population (est.)

Fort Smith	72,607
Little Rock	170,388
North Little Rock	65,025
Pine Bluff	55,860

GOVERNMENT AND POLITICS

Number of US Representatives 4
Electoral votes 6

POLITICAL PARTY NOMINEES FROM STATE

Charles E. Cunningham
  (Union Labor) 1888 VP
Joseph Taylor Robinson (D) 1928 VP
William Hope Harvey (Liberty) 1932 P
Orval Eugene Faubus (Nation-
  al States' Rights) 1960 P

PRESIDENTIAL PRIMARY ELECTION In 1988, Arkansas sent 44 Democratic delegates and 27 Republican delegates to the national conventions.

CONSTITUTION Arkansas has had five constitutions: 1836, 1861, 1864, 1868, and the present one, adopted in 1874.

LEGISLATURE The General Assembly is divided into the Senate (35 members, 4-year term, minimum age 25) and the House of Representatives (100 members, 2-year term, minimum age 21). In 1987, the annual salary was $7,500 plus $20 per day.

JUDICIARY The highest court is the Supreme Court, with 7 judges serving 8-year terms. In 1987, the annual salary was $66,010.

EXECUTIVE The governor serves a 4-year term; the minimum age for holding office is 25. In 1987, the annual salary was $35,000. There are 6 other elected officials.

PRESIDENTIAL VOTE 1948-1988 *(in percents)*

Year	State Winner	Democratic	Republican
1948	Truman (D)	61.7	21.0
1952	Stevenson (D)	55.9	43.8
1956	Stevenson (D)	52.5	45.8
1960	Kennedy (D)	50.2	43.1
1964	Johnson (D)	56.1	43.4
1968	George C. Wallace (American Independent, 38.9)	30.8	30.4
1972	Nixon (R)	30.7	68.9
1976	Carter (D)	65.0	34.9
1980	Reagan (R)	47.5	48.1
1984	Reagan (R)	38.3	60.5
1988	Bush (R)	43.0	57.0

GOVERNORS

Territorial Governors

James Miller	1819-1825
George Izard	1825-1829
John Pope	1829-1835
William S. Fulton	1835-1836

State Governors

James S. Conway (D)	1836-1840
Archibald Yell (D)	1840-1844
Samuel Adams (acting)	1844
Thomas S. Drew (D)	1844-1849
John S. Roane (D)	1849-1852
Elias N. Conway (D)	1852-1860
Henry M. Rector (D)	1860-1862
Harris Flanagin (D)	1862-1864
Isaac Murphy (Union)	1864-1868
Powell Clayton (R)	1868-1871
Ozra A. Hadley (R/acting)	1871-1873
Elisha Baxter (R)	1873-1874
Augustus H. Garland (D)	1874-1877
William R. Miller (D)	1877-1881
Thomas J. Churchill (D)	1881-1883
James H. Berry (D)	1883-1885
Simon P. Hughes (D)	1885-1889
James P. Eagle (D)	1889-1893
William M. Fishback (D)	1893-1895
James P. Clarke (D)	1895-1897
Daniel W. Jones (D)	1897-1901
Jeff Davis (D)	1901-1907
John S. Little (D)	1907
John I. Moore (D/acting)	1907
X.O. Pindall (D/acting)	1907-1909
George W. Donaghey (D)	1909-1913
Joseph T. Robinson (D)	1913
J.M. Futrell (D/acting)	1913
George W. Hays (D)	1913-1917
Charles H. Brough (D)	1917-1921
Thomas C. McRae (D)	1921-1925
Tom J. Terral (D)	1925-1927
John E. Martineau (D)	1927-1928
Harvey Parnell (D)	1928-1933
J.M. Futrell (D)	1933-1937
Carl E. Bailey (D)	1937-1941
Homer M. Adkins (D)	1941-1945
Ben T. Laney (D)	1945-1949
Sidney S. McMath (D)	1949-1953

Francis Cherry (D)	1953-1955
Orval E. Faubus (D)	1955-1967
Winthrop Rockefeller (R)	1967-1971
Dale Bumpers (D)	1971-1975
David Pryor (D)	1975-1979
William Clinton (D)	1979-1981
Frank D. White (R)	1981-1983
William Clinton (D)	1983-

MINIMUM AGES

Majority	18
Marriage with parental consent	16 female, 17 male
Marriage without parental consent	18
Making a will	18
Buying alcohol	21
Jury duty	18
Leaving school	15
Driver's license	16

CAPITAL PUNISHMENT
Number executed 1976-88: 3
On death row Aug. 1, 1988: 95

MILITARY INSTALLATIONS
Total number: 6
Major bases:
  Army: 1
  Air Force: 1

FINANCES

Thousands of dollars

GENERAL REVENUE (1985)

Total general revenue	2,924,952
Total tax revenue	1,744,945
Sales and gross receipts	989,532
Individual income taxes	471,448
Corporation net income taxes	130,231

GENERAL EXPENDITURE (1985)

Total general expenditure	2,797,251
Education	1,232,669
Public welfare	461,509
Health	91,230
Hospitals	125,027
Natural resources	83,098
Highways	363,441
Police	27,102
Corrections	53,182

FEDERAL AID (1985)   1,013,635

ECONOMY

Agriculture, once the state's main income-producing activity, now takes second place to manufacturing. Cotton, soybeans, and rice are the main cash crops; cattle and poultry are the primary livestock. The state's annual cash farm receipts exceeded $2 billion from 16.1 million acres of farmland in 1984. With some of the nation's best stands of southern pine, Arkansas has a flourishing timber industry, accounting for more than 20 percent of the total manufacturing payroll in 1982; it also has a growing chemical manufacturing industry. Arkansas has the nation's largest domestic supply of bauxite, a mineral necessary for aluminum manufacturing. Receipts from mining exceeded $1 billion in 1982. Thousands of small wells draw upon the state's large oil and natural gas reserves.

EMPLOYMENT (1984)

Thousands of persons

Total number of employed workers	951
Construction	34.3
Finance, insurance, and real estate	35.8
Government	140.4
Manufacturing	213.5
Mining	5.6
Services	134.1
Transport, communications, utilities	45.3
Wholesale and retail trade	173.5
Percent of civilian labor force unemployed	8.9

DEPARTMENT OF DEFENSE (1985)

Civilian workers employed	4,845
Military personnel	9,748
Contract awards	$810 million

ENERGY SOURCES FOR ELECTRIC UTILITIES

Percent

Coal	53.3
Gas	10.0
Hydroelectric	11.0
Nuclear	25.4
Petroleum	0.2

TRANSPORTATION

Motor vehicles registered in state (1986)	1,426,247
Miles of roads, streets, and highways (1986)	77,050
Miles of Class I railway operated (1986)	2,594
Airports (1983)	160
Major aviation hubs (1983)	1
Largest hub: Little Rock	

CULTURE AND EDUCATION

Native American tribes
Arkansas was the home of the Caddo, Cherokee, Chickasaw, Choctaw, Kaskinampo, Osage, Quapaw, Tunica, and Yazoo. All its indigenous peoples were removed by 1835.

Religions, ethnicities, and languages
Most Arkansans are descendants of the settlers (of English and Scotch-Irish stock) and slaves who came to the area after 1815. They are mainly Baptist and Methodist. In 1980, 1.8 percent of the population spoke a language other than English at home.

Major museums and libraries
Arkansas Arts Center, Little Rock
Arkansas State University Museum, Jonesboro
Arkansas Territorial Museum, Little Rock
Old State House State History Museum, Little Rock
University of Arkansas Museum, Fayetteville

Major arts organizations
Arkansas Art Center Children's Theatre, Little Rock
Arkansas Opera Theatre, Little Rock
Arkansas Repertory Theatre, Little Rock
Arkansas Symphony Orchestra, Little Rock

Colleges and universities
Number public (1986-87) 20
Number private (1986-87) 14
Total enrollment, in full-time equivalent students (1985) 63,200

Public elementary and secondary schools
Expenditure per pupil in average daily attendance (1986-87) $2,772
Pupil-teacher ratio (1987) 17.5
Average teacher salary (1986-87) $21,067

Holidays
Robert E. Lee's Birthday. January 19
General Douglas McArthur Day. January 26
World War II Memorial Day. August 14
State Fair, Little Rock. Late September to early October

ARKANSAS IN LITERATURE

Shirley Abbott *Womenfolks: Growing Up Down South* (1983)
An exploration of Southern culture through a memoir of an Arkansas upbringing.

Frederick W. Allsopp *Folklore of Romantic Arkansas* 2 vols. (1931)

Maya Angelou *I Know Why the Caged Bird Sings* (1970)
Classic black American autobiography depicting the author's early life in the segregated community of Stamps.

William M. Baker and **Ethel C. Simpson** *Arkansas in Short Fiction: Stories from 1841 to 1985* (1986)
A selection of classic regional fiction, including Thomas B. Thorpe's 1841 story "The Big Bear," examples of "local color" fiction of the 1880s, and early 20th-century writing by Thyra S. Winslow and David Thibault.

William Baxter *Pea Ridge and Prairie Grove; or, Scenes and Incidents of the War in Arkansas* (1864)

Margaret Bolsterli (ed.) *Vinegar Pie and Chicken Bread* (1983)
A farm woman's diary.

Clyde B. Davis *Something for Nothing* (1956)
Tales and legends of gamblers, with some stories set in Missouri and Arkansas.

Otis W. Coan *Rocktown, Arkansas: An Ozark Novel* (1953)
Small-town life in the northwest c.1920.

Marion Dickens *Ozark Odyssey* (1955)
Novel about Ozark life c.1900.

Richard M. Dorson *Negro Tales from Pine Bluff, Arkansas, and Calvin, Michigan* (1958)

Michael B. and **Carol W. Dougan** (eds.) *By the Cypress Swamp: The Arkansas Stories of Octave Thanet* (1980)
A selection of the regional stories of Alice French, who used the pseudonym Octave Thanet throughout her career (1887–1917).

Mary Dulton *Thorpe* (1967)
A small town in the 1930s, described by a child.

John B. Ellis *Arkinsaw Cousins: A Story of the Ozarks* (1908)
Stories of rural life.

Sarah Fountain (ed.) *Authentic Voices: Arkansas Culture, 1541–1860* (1986)
Writing by early explorers and residents.

Friedrich Gerstäcker *The Regulators of Arkansas, a Thrilling Tale of Border Adventure* (1857)
Lurid romantic tale of Perry County horse thieves, originally written in German by a pioneer of the backwoods during the 1830s and '40s.

Ellen Gilchrist *The Annunciation* (1983)
Biographical novel about a young woman, partly set in Fayetteville.

Janice Holt Giles *The Enduring Hills* (1950); *The Plum Thicket* (1954); *Johnny Osage* (1960)
Novels about Ozark customs and early Arkansas history.

Francis Irby Gwaltney *The Yeller-Headed Summer* (1954); *The Day the Century Ended* (1955); *A Moment of Warmth* (1957); *The Numbers of Our Day* (1959)
Novels about various aspects of regional culture.

Robert Herring *Hub* (1981)
Murder mystery set in the delta region.

Elizabeth P. Huckaby and **Ethel C. Simpson** (eds.) *Tulip Evermore: Emma Butler and William Paisley, Their Lives in Letters, 1857–1887* (1988)
Correspondence from the communities of Tulip and Dobyville written during the Civil War and Reconstruction.

Thomas W. Jackson (ed. W. K. McNeil) *On a Slow Train through Arkansaw* (1903, rpt. 1985)
Although this humorous, juvenile classic has no connection with the state other than its title, it did much to establish Arkansas' reputation as a backwoods, backward region. Jackson was an illiterate trainman who sold his material at local stations.

Douglas C. Jones *Elkhorn Tavern* (1980)
Historical novel about a farming family's struggle to pre-

serve their land during the Civil War and the Battle of Pea Ridge.

Virgil L. Jones and **Georgia H. Clark** *Arkansas Books and Writers* (University of Arkansas Library) (1952)

Bob Lancaster *Going Down for Gum Wrappers* (1986)
Comic memoir of adolescence by an Arkansas journalist.

Deirdre LaPin *Hogs in the Bottom: Family Folklore in Arkansas* (1982)

James W. Leslie *Saracen's Country: Some Southeast Arkansas History* (1974)
Essays relating to southeast Arkansas.
———. *Land of the Cypress and Pine: More Southeast Arkansas History* (1976)

James R. Masterson *Tall Tales of Arkansaw* (1943)
A study of local humor and folklore.

Phillip McMath *Native Ground* (1984)
Biographical novel of a rural south Arkansas boy who serves in Vietnam.

W. K. McNeil (comp.) *Ghost Stories from the American South* (1985); *Ozark Mountain Humor* (1988)
Collections by an Ozark folklorist.

Florence M. McRaven *Swift Current* (1954)
Memoir of folklore and local history.

Mary Medearis *Big Doc's Girl* (1942, rpt. 1985)
Classic regional juvenile novel based on the author's memories of her father, physician to the rural poor.

Franklin J. Meine *Tall Tales of the Southwest, 1830–1860* (1930)

Thomas Nuttall *Journals of Travel into the Arkansas Territory, During the Year 1819* (1821, rpt. 1905)
An English botanist's impressions of the Arkansas valley.

Charles Portis *True Grit* (1968)
A Yell County farm girl goes to Fort Smith and persuades a US marshal to help track down her father's killer.

William MacLeod Raine *Arkansas Guns* (1954)
Novel about western Arkansas life during Reconstruction.

Vance Randolph (ed.) *An Ozark Anthology* (1940)
Fiction by fourteen Ozark writers.
———. *Who Blowed Up the Church House? and Other Ozark tales* (1952)

Opie Read *I Remember* (1930)
Autobiography of a celebrated Chicago writer who was born in Tennessee but edited two Arkansas newspapers, including the *Traveler*, in the late 19th century and set several of his popular novels in the state. *Emmett Bonlore* (1891) depicts small towns in the 1880s, and *An Arkansas Planter* (1896) is set near Pine Bluff.

Roy Reed *Looking for Hogeye* (1986)
Life in the northern hills described by a journalist.

Maylon Rice (ed.) *The Best of the Arkansas Traveler, 1955–85* (1986)
A selection of historical and literary commentary.

Almeda Riddle (ed. Roger Abrahams) *A Singer and Her Songs: Almeda Riddle's Book of Ballads* (1970)

Mary Elsie Robertson *Jordan's Stormy Banks* (1962)
Stories of small town and rural communities.

Henry R. Schoolcraft (ed. Hugh Park) *Schoolcraft in the Ozarks: Reprint of a Journal of a Tour into the Interior of Missouri and Arkansas in 1818 and 1819* (1955)
Account of an exploratory canoe trip down the White River by a geologist who later became known for his studies of the American Indian.

Budd Schulberg *Some Faces in the Crowd* (1954)
Short stories about local characters.

Charlie May Simon *The Sharecropper* (1937)
Novel of rural life by the wife of J. G. Fletcher, best known for her children's books.

T. S. Stribling *Backwater* (1930)
Small-town life in the 1920s, with an account of the 1927 flood.

Ruth McEnery Stuart *In Simpkinsville: Character Tales* (1897)
Classic works of regional fiction, remarkable for their portrayal of rural dialects and folkways. Stuart lived near Washington, Arkansas, during the 1880s, where she set *Otto the Knight* (1893) and *By Inheritance* (1910), both studies of black characters.

Roy Swank *Trail to Marked Tree* (ed. Nolan Porterfield) (1968)
A narrative of early 20th-century life in the lowlands of northeast Arkansas.

Mark Twain *Life on the Mississippi* (1883)
Twain's memoir of his own years as a river pilot contains the celebrated speech "Change the Name of Arkansas," which he may have written, or recorded from an actual incident. This book, and the closely related masterpiece *The Adventures of Huckleberry Finn* (1884), were the first to record the dialect of poor whites and blacks of the region.

Constance Wagner *Sycamore* (1950)
Novel set in the Ozarks by a writer who lived in Eureka Springs.

Edward T. Wallace *Barington* (1945)
Tales of a small town in western Arkansas.

Don West *Broadside to the Sun* (1946)
Novel about farm life near Winslow.

Leonard Williams (ed.) *Cavorting on the Devil's Fork: The Pete Whetstone Letters of C. F. M. Noland* (1979)
Noland's rustic wit and practical commentary on pioneer customs, written shortly after the Civil War, are an early example of regional humor.

Charles Morrow Wilson *Acres of Sky* (1930)
Novel portraying a farmer's decision to remain on his land rather than move to the city.
———. *Backwoods America* (1934)
Essays on rural life.
———. *Rabble Rouser* (1936)
Novel about a local politician's contest with powerful business interests.
———. *A Man's Reach* (1944)
Novel based on the life of Archibald Yell, first federal judge west of the Mississippi.

John Quincy Wolf *Life in the Leatherwoods: An Ozark Boyhood Remembered* (1974, rev. ed. 1980, rpt. 1988)
Memoirs of a man who grew up in the Upper White River country in the 1870s and became a banker in Batesville.

GUIDES TO RESOURCES

Allen, Albert H. (ed.) *Arkansas Imprints, 1821–76* (1947)

Allsopp, Fred W. *The Romance of Books, with an Arkansas Bibliography* (1936)

Brimah, Farouk K. *Statistical Profile of Arkansas* (1983)

Brothers, Cassie M.C. *A Bibliography of Arkansas and Arkansas Authors' Materials* (1962)

Clark, Georgia H. and **R. Bruce Parham** (comps.) *Arkansas County and Local Histories: A Bibliography* (1976)

Compton, Lanelle and **Lorene** *Arkansas Books and Library Materials* (1967)

Dillard, Tom W. and **Valerie Thwing** *Researching Arkansas History: A Beginner's Guide* (1979)

Federal Writers' Project *Arkansas: A Guide to the Bluegrass State* (1941, rpt. 1980)
———. *The WPA Guide to 1930s Arkansas* (1987)

Ferguson, John Lewis *Arkansas Lives: The Opportunity Land Who's Who* (1964)

Hanson, Gerald T. and **Carl H. Moneyhon** *Historical Atlas of Arkansas* (1988)

Hodges, Norman L., Jr. *Thirty Years on Arkansas Government, 1945 to 1975: A Bibliographic Essay on the Political*

Science Literature on Arkansas State Government and Politics (1976)

Jones, Virgil L. and **Georgia H. Clark** *Arkansas Books and Writers* (1952)

Matthews, Jim P. and **Virgil L. Jones** *Arkansas Books* (1931)

Randolph, Vance *Ozark Folklore: An Annotated Bibliography* vol. I (1987)

Worley, Ted R. (comp.) *Books and Pamphlets Relating to Arkansas History and Biography* (1956)

SELECTED NONFICTION SOURCES

Alexander, Donald C. *The Arkansas Plantation, 1920–1942* (1943)

Allsopp, Fred W. *Albert Pike: A Biography* (1928)

Arkansas Commemorative Commission *Victorian Arkansas: How They Lived, Played and Worked* (1981)

Arkansas Gazette *Crisis in the South: The Little Rock Story* (1959)

Arkansas Press Women (eds.) *Horizons--100 Arkansas Women of Achievement* (1980)

Arnold, Morris S. *Unequal Laws Unto a Savage Race: European Legal Traditions in Arkansas* (1988)

Arsenault, Raymond *The Wild Ass of the Ozarks: Jeff Davis and the Social Bases of Southern Politics* (1984)

Ashmore, Harry S. *Arkansas: A Bicentennial History* (States and the Nation series) (1978)

Baird, David *The Quapaw Indians: A History of the Downstream People* (Civilization of the American Indian series) (1980)

Baskett, Tom (ed.) *Persistence of the Spirit: The Black Experience in Arkansas* (1986)

Bass, Sharon *For the Trees: An Illustrated History of the Ozark–St. Francis National Forests 1908–1978* (1981)

Bates, Daisy *The Long Shadow of Little Rock, a Memoir* (1962)

Bearss, Edwin C. and **Arrell M. Gibson** *Fort Smith: Little Gibraltar on the Arkansas* (1969, 2d ed. 1988)

Blossom, Virgil *It Has Happened Here* (1959)

Bolton, Charles, Cal Ledbetter, and **Gerald Hanson** *Arkansas Becomes a State* (1986)

Bradley, Matt *Arkansas, Its Land and People* (1980, rpt. 1984)

Brown, Walter L. *Albert Pike, Arkansan 1809–1847* (1950)
———. *Our Arkansas* (1958)

Cochran, Robert *Vance Randolph: An Ozark Life* (1985)

Collier, Calvin L. *"They'll Do to Tie to!" The Story of the Third Regiment, Arkansas Infantry C.S.A.* (1959)

Croy, Homer *Last of the Great Outlaws: The Story of Cole Younger* (1956)

Davis, Clyde B. *The Arkansas* (Rivers of America series) (1940)

Davis, Granville D. (comp.) *The Fighting Man of Arkansas* (1946)

DeBoer, Marvin E. *Dreams of Power and the Power of Dreams: Inaugural Addresses of Arkansas Governors* (1988)

Donaghey, George W. *Building a State Capitol* (1937)

Donovan, Timothy P. and **Willard B. Gatewood, Jr.** (eds.) *The Governors of Arkansas: Essays in Political Biography* (1981)

Dougan, Michael B. *Confederate Arkansas: The People and Policies of a Frontier State in Wartime* (1976)

Duvall, Leland (comp.) *Arkansas: Colony and State* (1973)

Faubus, Orval E. *Down from the Hills* (1980)

Ferguson, John L. *Arkansas and the Civil War* (1965)
——— and **J. H. Atkinson** *Historic Arkansas* (1966)

Fisher, George *Fisher's Comic Relief: Editorial Cartoons of the '80s* (1988)

Fletcher, John Gould *Arkansas* (1947)

Fountain, Sarah (ed.) *Authentic Voices: Arkansas Culture, 1541–1860* (1986)

Goodspeed Publishing Co. (eds.) *Biographical and Historical Memoirs of Arkansas* (1884, rpt. 1977)

Hall, Jessie H. and **William Franklin** *Arkansas 1836–1936* (1936)
———. *A Documentary History of Arkansas* (1984)

Hallum, John *Biographical and Pictorial History of Arkansas* (1887)

Harrell, John M. *The Brooks and Baxter War: A History of the Reconstruction Period in Arkansas* (1893)

Harrington, Donald *Let Us Build Us a City: Eleven Lost Towns* (1986)

Harrington, Fred Harvey *Hanging Judge* (1951)

Herndon, Dallas T. *Centennial History of Arkansas* 3 vols. (1922)
———. *Outline of Executive and Legislative History of Arkansas* (1922)
———. *Why Little Rock Was Born* (1933)
———. *Annals of Arkansas* 4 vols. (1947)

Huckaby, Elizabeth *Crisis at Central High: Little Rock, 1957–58* (1980)

Ingersoll, William H. *Arkansas in Retrospect* (1943)

Jackson, Bruce *Killing Time: Life in the Arkansas Penitentiary* (1977)

Jacobson, Charles *The Life Story of Jeff Davis: The Stormy Petrel of Arkansas Politics* (1925)

Johnson, Haynes and **Bernard M. Gwertzman** *Fulbright; the Dissenter* (1968)

Kennedy, Jon *Look Back and Laugh: 38 Years of Arkansas Political Cartoons* (1978)

Lecompte, Janet *Pueblo, Hardscrabble, Greenhorn: The Upper Arkansas, 1832–56* (1978, rpt. 1981)

Lester, Jim *A Man for Arkansas: Sid McMath and the Southern Reform Tradition* (1976)

Lyon, Marguerite *Hurrah for Arkansas! From Razorbacks to Diamonds* (1947)

MacArthur, Priscilla *Arkansas in the Gold Rush* (1986)

Mapes, Ruth B. *The Arkansas Waterway; People, Places, Events in the Valley, 1817–1971* (1972)

McDonough, Nancy *Garden Sass: A Catalog of Arkansas Folkways* (1975)

McGrimsey, Charles R., III *Indians of Arkansas* (1969)

McKnight, O. E. *A History of Development of Arkansas* (1939)

Medearis, Mary *Washington, Arkansas: History on the Southwest Trail* (1976)

Mills, William *The Arkansas: An American River* (1988)

Minick, Roger, Bob Minick, and **Leonard Sussman** *Hills of Home: The Rural Ozarks of Arkansas* (1975)

Moore, Waddy (ed.) *Arkansas in the Gilded Age, 1874–1900* (1976)

Patterson, Ruth P. *The Seed of Sally Good'n; a Black Family of Arkansas, 1833–1953* (1985)

Rhodes, Richard *The Ozarks* (1974)

Richards, Ira D. *Story of a Rivertown: Little Rock in the Nineteenth Century* (1969)

Roberts, Bobby and Carl Moneyhon *Portraits of Conflict: A Photographic History of Arkansas in the Civil War* (1987)

Ross, Margaret S. *Arkansas Gazette: The Early Years, 1819–66* (1969)

Sandford, Juanita *Poverty in the Land of Opportunity* (1978)

Shannon, Karr *On a Fast Train Through Arkansas* (1948)

Shirley, Glenn *Law West of Fort Smith* (1968)

Smith, C. Calvin *War and Wartime Changes: The Transformation of Arkansas, 1940–1945* (1986)

Smith, John I. *The Courage of a Southern Unionist: A Biography of Isaac Murphy* (1979)

Smith, Kenneth L. et al. *Arkansas's Natural Heritage* (1984)
———. *Sawmill* (1988)

Staples, Thomas S. *Reconstruction in Arkansas 1862–1874* (1923)

Stroud, Hubert B. and Gerald T. Hanson *Arkansas Geography: The Physical Landscape and the Cultural Setting* (1981)

Taylor, Orville W. *Negro Slavery in Arkansas* (1958)

Thomas, Charles E. *Jelly Roll: A Black Neighborhood in a Southern Mill Town* (1986)

Thomas, David Y. *Arkansas in War and Reconstruction, 1861–1874* (1926)

———. *Arkansas and Its People: A History, 1541–1930* 4 vols. (1930)

Thompson, George H. *Arkansas and Reconstruction: The Influence of Geography, Economics and Personality* (1976)

Tucker, David M. *Arkansas: A People and Their Reputation* (1985)

Tucker, S. C., Jr. *To Sell a Good Bull: A Story of the Arkansas River Valley* (1976)

Ward, John L. *The Arkansas Rockefeller* (1978)

White, Lonnie J. *Politics on the Southwestern Frontier: Arkansas Territory, 1819–1836* (1964)

Williams, C. Fred, S. Charles Bolton, et al. (eds.) *A Documentary History of Arkansas* (1984)

Wilson, Winston *Harvey Couch: The Master Builder* (1947)

Wolf, John Q. *Life in the Leatherwoods* (rev. ed. 1980)

Woodruff, William E. *The William E. Woodruff Papers, 1810–1882* (1955)
———. *Wilderness to Statehood with William E. Woodruff* (1961)

Woods, James M. *Rebellion and Realignment: Arkansas' Road to Secession* (1987)

Worley, Ted and Eugene Nolte *Pete Whetstone of Devil's Fork* (1957)

CALIFORNIA

California, the most populous state and the third largest in area, is located on the West Coast of the United States. It borders on the Pacific Ocean to the west; Oregon to the north; Nevada and Arizona and the Colorado River to the east; and the Mexican state of Baja California to the south.

FULL NAME State of California
POSTAL ABBREVIATION CA
INHABITANT Californian
ADMITTED TO THE UNION Sept. 9, 1850.
 31st state
POPULATION (est. 1987) 27,663,000.
 Percent of US total: 9.20%. Rank: 1st

CAPITAL CITY Sacramento, located in central California at the junction of the American and Sacramento rivers; population 304,131 (est. 1984). Founded as New Helvetia by Swiss settlers in 1839, it was laid out as the town of Sacramento in 1848 when the colony was overthrown by gold miners. It was incorporated as a city in 1850, and became the state capital in 1854.

STATE NAME AND NICKNAMES "California" was the name of a fictional island in *Las Sergas de Esplandián* (published 1510), a romance by the Spanish writer García Ordóñez de Montalvo. The name was given to the Baja California peninsula by the Spanish explorers Hernando Cortés and Fortún Ximenez early in the 16th century. The state's nickname "The Golden State" derives from its golden poppies as well as its gold deposits.

STATE SEAL A landscape showing the seated figure of the Roman goddess Minerva, a grizzly bear at her feet, gazing over a mountain-ringed bay dotted with sailing ships and a green peninsula where a miner is at work. In the sky, below a semicircle of 31 stars, is the state motto. The landscape is bordered by a gold circle bearing the legend "The Great Seal of the State of California."

MOTTO *Eureka!*, Greek for "I have found it!," from the cries of the gold prospectors.

SONG "I Love You, California," by F.B. Silverwood and A.F. Frankenstein.

SYMBOLS
Tree California redwood
Flower golden poppy
Bird California valley quail
Animal California grizzly bear
Marine mammal California gray whale
Reptile California desert tortoise
Fish golden trout
Insect California dog-face butterfly
Fossil saber-toothed cat
Mineral native gold
Rock serpentine

LICENSE PLATES (1) Dark blue on white, state name in red. (2) Dark blue on white with red stripe across top; across bottom, a blue stripe with the legend "1984 Olympics". (3) Blue on white, with gold legend "The Golden State" and state name displayed over background of a golden sunset. (4) Gold on medium blue. (5) Gold on black.

FLAG The California Bear Flag consists of a white field showing a grizzly bear walking on green earth above the legend "California Republic"; in the upper left corner is a red five-pointed star, and a red border runs across the bottom.

GEOGRAPHY AND CLIMATE

California encompasses extremes of physical diversity: a moderate climate in the heavily populated coastal region; the highest mountain range in the continental US, the Sierra Nevadas, astride the eastern half of the state; deserts to the south and northeast; temperate rain forest in the northwest; and a fertile agricultural heartland, the Central Valley, once the bed of a great inland sea.

AREA 158,706 square miles. Rank 3rd
INLAND WATER 2,407 square miles
GEOGRAPHIC CENTER In Madera county, 35 miles NE of Madera
ELEVATIONS *Highest point:* Mount Whitney, in Tulare county, 14,494 feet above sea level, the highest point in the continental United States. *Lowest point:* Death Valley, 282 feet below sea level, the lowest point in North America. *Mean elevation:* 2,900 feet

MAJOR RIVERS Sacramento, San Joaquin, Klamath

MAJOR LAKES AND RESERVOIRS Salton Sea, Tahoe, Goose, Clear, Eagle, Mono, Trinity, Shasta, Berryessa

TIDAL SHORELINE Pacific coast, 3,427 miles

LAND USE

	Thousands of acres
Urban (1982)	3,265
Rural (1982)	49,833
Cropland (1982)	10,518
Pastureland (1982)	1.393
Rangeland (1982)	18,125
Forestland (1982)	15,218
State parks and recreation areas (1983)	1,116
National park system (1984) . . .	4,511
National forest system (1984) . .	24,287
Tribal lands (1984)	501

TEMPERATURES The highest recorded temperature in the state was 134°F, recorded on July 10, 1913 at Greenland Ranch, Death Valley (this is the highest temperature ever recorded in the United States). The lowest recorded temperature was -45°F, on January 20, 1937, at Boca.

NATIONAL SITES

NATIONAL HISTORIC SITES Eugene O'Neill, Fort Point, John Muir
NATIONAL MONUMENTS Cabrillo, Death Valley, Devils Postpile, Joshua Tree, Lava Beds, Muir Woods, Pinnacles
NATIONAL PARKS Channel Islands, Kings Canyon, Lassen Volcanic, Redwood, Sequoia, Yosemite
NATIONAL RECREATION AREAS Golden Gate, Santa Monica Mountains, Whiskeytown-Shasta-Trinity
NATIONAL SEASHORE Point Reyes
NATIONAL TRAIL SYSTEM Pacific Crest Trail

NATIONAL WILD AND SCENIC RIVERS American River, North Fork, Eel River, Feather River, Middle Fork, Klamath River, Lower American River, Smith River, Trinity River
NATIONAL WILDLIFE REFUGES Cibola, Colusa, Delevan, Havasu, Imperial, Kern and Pixley, Klamath Basin Refuges–Tule Lake/ Clear Lake/Lower Klamath/Klamath Forest/Upper Klamath, Modoc, Sacramento, Salton Sea, San Francisco Bay– Farallon/Humboldt Bay/San Pablo Bay, San Luis–Kesterson/Merced, Sutter

HISTORY

1510	*Las Sergas de Esplandián,* a romance by Garcí Ordóñez de Montalvo written about 1500, mentions an island inhabited by Amazons named California.
1533	Fortún Jimenez discovers Baja California.
1535	Hernando Cortés visits Baja California and names it Santa Cruz.
1539	Cortés sends Francisco de Ulloa, leading a fleet of three ships, from Acapulco to explore the Gulf of California and find the legendary seven golden cities of Cibola.

1540	Hernando de Alarcón sails up the Colorado River, possibly reaching Alta California.
1541	Francisco de Bolanos explores Baja California.
1542	*June 27*. Portuguese-born navigator Juan Rodriguez Cabrillo, under orders from Viceroy Antonio de Mendoza, sets sail from Navidad on the west coast of Mexico in search of a northwest pasage. *September 28*. Cabrillo enters San Diego Bay .
1543	*January*. Cabrillo dies, but his pilot, Bartolomé Ferrelo, continues as far as Oregon before turning back on March 1.
1579	*June 17*. Sir Francis Drake lands at Drake's Bay, claiming the region for Queen Elizabeth I.
1587	Pedro de Unamuno enters Morro Bay.
1595	Sebastián Cermeño enters Drake's Bay.
1602	*December 16*. Sebastián Vizcaino explores the Monterey region.
1769	*January 9*. José de Galvez sends two land and three sea expeditions to secure Spanish control of San Diego and Monterey. One group reaches Monterey October 1, and discovers San Francisco Bay on the 21st. They return to San Diego January 21, 1770. *July 16*. Junípero Serra founds the San Diego mission.
1774	*January*. Juan Bautista de Anza's expedition leaves Tucson to find an overland route to Monterey. *March 22*. Anza reaches the San Gabriel mission.
1775	*August 5*. José Cañizares is the first Spaniard to sail through the Golden Gate.
1776	*March 29*. Anza's second overland expedition founds the San Francisco mission.
1777	San José, first secular community, is founded.
1781	*July 17*. Yuma Indians massacre Rivera's expedition at the Colorado River.
1797	Construction of the main church at San Juan Capistrano begins.
1809	Ivan Kuskof, Russian fur trader, founds a settlement near Bodega Bay.
1812	Russian merchants establish Fort Ross near Bodega Bay.
1814	John Gilroy jumps ship at Monterey and becomes the first non-Hispanic settler.
1821	Mexican revolution ends Spanish control of Alta California.
1824	*February*. Jedediah Smith leads a party of explorers through the Rocky Mountains in Wyoming to complete the first overland expedition to California.
1825	Mexico lays claim to California and sends José Maria de Echenedia to set up a territorial government.
1826	*November 27*. Jedediah Smith and a party of explorers arrive in San Diego, having travelled from the Great Salt Lake in 97 days,
1827	*May*. Jedediah Smith crosses the Sierra Nevada, reaching northern Utah on July 3.
1828	*July 9*. Smith makes the first overland journey from California to Oregon, but most of his party is killed by Umpqua Indians on July 14.
1829	*November 6*. Thirty-one men, including Antonio Armijo, last Mexican governor of California, leave Abiquiu in northern Mexico in search of a route to Southern California.
1831	*May 27*. Jedediah Smith killed by Comanches on the Santa Fe trail.
1832	Mexico promises California self-government if it will remain Mexican territory.
1834	Joseph R. Walker's expedition crosses the Sierra Nevada to the California coast and returns through Owen's Valley, becoming the first white men to see Yosemite.
1836	*November 7*. California declares independence from Mexico.
1839	August. John Augustus Sutter becomes the first settler in the upper Sacramento Valley.
1841	First wagon train of settlers reaches Sacramento via the Oregon Trail.
1842	*October 20*. Commander Thomas Jones seizes Monterey, capital of the Mexican province.
1843	*May 29*. John C. Frémont and Kit Carson begin their second journey.
1846	The Donner party attempts the crossing of the Sierras. *July 7*. Commodore John D. Sloat raises the American Flag in Monterey proclaiming US citizenship for the state.

1847	*January 13*. Mexican forces surrender.
1848	*January 24*. Gold discovered by James Wilson Marshall on the estate of John Sutter.
	February 2. Mexico cedes California to the US for $15 million.
1849	*February 28*. The first shipload of gold seekers arrives in San Francisco.
	September 1. California convention, meeting at Monterey, draws up a constitution prohibiting slavery and granting property rights to women, and requests admission to the Union.
1850	More than 42,000 people enter California to prospect for gold.
	September 9th. California admitted to the Union as a free state, thus giving free states the majority. State population approximately 96,000.
1852	San Quentin is founded.
1860	*April 3*. The Pony Express begins delivery of mail to Sacramento from St. Joseph, Missouri.
1892	Sierra Club founded.
1906	*April 18*. San Francisco earthquake.
1911	The first motion picture studio moves into Hollywood Hills.
1937	Golden Gate Bridge opens.
1949	Heavy snowfalls in Los Angeles, San Diego, and Palm Springs.
1951	*January*. A Los Angeles construction company holds a ground-breaking ceremony for a nuclear fallout shelter.
	April 17. A hero's welcome in San Francisco for General MacArthur.
1952	*April 17*. Supreme Court declares the state's alien land law unconstitutional.
1953	Ferlinghetti founds the City Lights bookstore in San Francisco.
1955	*June 17*. Disneyland opens in Anaheim.
1957	*October*. The New York Giants move to San Francisco, and the Brooklyn Dodgers to Los Angeles.
1959	*October*. The Dodgers win the World Series.
1962	*November*. Richard Nixon loses the gubernatorial election and tells reporters his political career is over.
	California becomes the most populous state.
1964	Four northern counties are declared disaster areas after heavy flooding.
	December 3. Over 800 free speech supporters are arrested during a sit-in at Berkeley.
1965	*August 11-16*. Race riots in Watts cause 34 deaths.
1966	*March 15*. Rioting breaks out again in Watts.
	December 15. Walt Disney dies in Los Angeles.
1967	*November 29*. Berkeley students protest the draft.
1968	*June 4*. Robert Kennedy wins the Democratic primary and is shot by Sirhan Sirhan.
	November 6. Richard Nixon wins the presidential election.
1969	*January-March*. Heavy rains cause more than 100 deaths and $60 million in property damage.
	May 10. Cesar Chavez leads a grapepickers strike.
	May 15. A demonstration in support of "People's Park" in Berkeley turns into a violent riot.
	November 20. Representatives of 20 Indian tribes seize Alcatraz.
1971	*February 9*. An earthquake causes 62 deaths in Southern California.
1972	*April 22*. Protests against the Vietnam War in San Francisco and Los Angeles.
1973	Thomas Bradley becomes the first black mayor of Los Angeles.
1974	*November 6*. Janet Hayes becomes mayor of San José, and second woman mayor of a major US city.
1975	*March*. UCLA defeats Kentucky to win its 10th NCAA Basketball Championship in 12 years—a national record.
1976	*June 8*. Voters reject proposition 15, permitting nuclear generating to continue.
1977	*May 4*. US Geological Survey reports water resources 87% below normal level.
1978	*June 28*. Bakke wins his case before the Supreme Court.
1981	Ronald Reagan elected president.
1984	*April 24*. A 6.2 earthquake, worst since 1911, hits San Francisco.

DEMOGRAPHY

Population (est. 1987) . . . 27,663,000
Population (1980) 23,667,837
Population density in persons
   per square mile (1980) 149.1

POPULATION BY RACE (1980)
American Indian/Aleut/
   Eskimo 201,311
Asian/Pacific Islander 1,253,987
Black 1,819,282
Hispanic 4,543,770
White 18,031,689
Other 2,362,293

POPULATION CHARACTERISTICS (1980)
Percent of state population
Urban 91.3
Rural 8.7
Under 18 . . . . 27.0
65 or older 10.2
College-educated 19.8
Families below poverty line . . . 8.7
Public assistance recipients 8.8

Per capita personal
   income (1986) $16,778
Millionaires per 100,000
   residents (1982) 261.2
Average life expectancy
   in years (1980) 74.6
Marriage rate per 1,000
   residents (1986) 8.1

Divorce rate per 1,000
   residents (1986) 5.0
Birth rate per 1,000
   residents (1985) 17.9
Infant mortality per 1,000
   births (1985) 9.5
Abortion rate per 1,000
   live births (1985) 640
Crime rate per 100,000
   residents (1986)
   Violent 920.5
   Property 5,842.3
Federal and state prisoners
   per 100,000 residents (1984) . . 163
Alcohol consumption in gallons
   per capita (1985) 44.3
Deaths from motor vehicle accidents
   per 100,000 residents (1985) . . 18.3

MAJOR CITIES
1984 population (est.)

Anaheim	233,516
Fresno	267,377
Los Angeles	3,096,668
Long Beach	378,894
Oakland	351,898
Riverside	182,245
Sacramento	304,131
San Diego	960,452
San Francisco	712,753
San Jose	686,178
Santa Ana	225,405
Stockton	171,6591

GOVERNMENT AND POLITICS

Number of US Representatives 45
Electoral votes 47

POLITICAL PARTY NOMINEES FROM STATE
  * winner

John Charles Fremont (R)	1856	P
John Charles Fremont (Independent)	1864	P
Marietta Lizzie Bell Stow (Equal Rights)	1884	VP
Peter Dinwiddie Wigginton (American)	1888	VP
John Bidwell (Prohibition)	1892	P
Job Harriman (Social-Democratic)	1900	VP
Hiram Warren Johnson (Progressive)	1912	VP
Marie Caroline Brehm (Prohibition)	1924	VP
Charles Hiram Randall (American)	1924	VP

Herbert Clark Hoover* (R)	1928	P
Frank Elbridge Webb (Farmer Labor)	1928	P
Herbert Clark Hoover (R)	1932	P
Claude A. Watson (Prohibition)	1936	VP
Earl Warren (R)	1938	VP
Claude A. Watson (Prohibition)	1944	P
Richard Milhous Nixon* (R)	1952	VP
Vincent William Hallinan (Progressive and American Labor)	1952	P
Stuart Hamblen (Prohibition)	1952	P
Daniel J. Murphy (American Vegetarian)	1952	P
Richard Milhous Nixon* (R)	1956	VP
Thomas Harold Werdel (States' Rights)	1956	VP
Edward M. Cooper (Prohibition)	1956	VP
Herbert M. Shelton (American Vegetarian)	1956	P
Richard Milhous Nixon (R)	1960	P

Whitney Hart Slocomb
(Greenback) 1960 P
Thomas H. Werdel (Indepen-
dent States' Rights Party) 1964 VP
Kirby James Hensley (Univer-
sal) 1964 P
Richard Milhous Nixon* (R) 1968 P
William Penn Patrick (Patriotic) 1968 VP
Kirby James Hensley (Univer-
sal) 1968 P
Richard Milhous Nixon* (R) 1972 P
John George Schmitz
(American) 1972 P
John Hospers (Libertarian) 1972 P
David Bergland (Libertarian) 1976 VP
Margaret Wright (People's) 1976 P
Ronald Wilson Reagan* (R) 1980 P
Ed Clark (Libertarian) 1980 P
Angela Y. Davis (Communist) 1980 VP
Eileen Shearer (American
Independent) 1980 VP
Maureen Smith (Peace and
Freedom) 1980 P
Elizabeth Cervantes Barron
(Peace and Freedom) 1980 VP
Frank Varnum (American) 1980 VP
Ronald Wilson Reagan* (R) 1984 P
Angela Y. Davis (Communist) 1984 VP

David Bergland (Libertarian) 1984 P
Mel Mason (Socialist Workers) 1984 P
Maureen Kennedy Salaman
(Populist) 1984 VP
Gloria La Riva (Workers
World) 1984 VP

PRESIDENTIAL PRIMARY ELECTION In 1988, California sent 336 Democratic delegates and 175 Republican delegates to the national conventions.

CONSTITUTION California adopted its first constitution in 1849 and its present one in 1879, with a major revision in 1966.

LEGISLATURE The Legislature is divided into the Senate (40 members, 4-year term, minimum age 18) and the Assembly (80 members, 2-year term, minimum age 18). In 1987, the annual salary was $37,195.

JUDICIARY The highest court is the Supreme Court, with 7 judges serving 12-year terms. In 1987, the annual salary was $103,469.

EXECUTIVE The governor serves a 4-year term; the minimum age for holding office is 18. In 1987, the annual salary was $85,000. There are 6 other elected officials.

PRESIDENTIAL VOTE 1948-1988 *(in percents)*

Year	State Winner	Democratic	Republican
1948	Truman (D)	47.6	47.1
1952	Eisenhower (R)	42.7	56.3
1956	Eisenhower (R)	44.3	55.4
1960	Nixon (R)	49.6	50.1
1964	Johnson (D)	59.1	40.8
1968	Nixon (R)	44.7	47.8
1972	Nixon (R)	41.5	55.0
1976	Ford (R)	47.6	49.3
1980	Reagan (R)	35.5	92.7
1984	Reagan (R)	41.3	57.5
1988	Bush (R)	48.0	52.0

GOVERNORS

Peter H. Burnett (D)	1849-1851
John McDougal (D/acting)	1851-1852
John Bigler (D)	1852-1856
John N. Johnson (Know-Nothing)	1856-1858
John B. Weller (D)	1858-1860
Milton S. Latham (D)	1860
John G. Downey (D/acting)	1860-1862
Leland Stanford (R)	1862-1863
Frederick F. Low (Union)	1863-1867
Henry H. Haight (D)	1867-1871
Newton Booth (R)	1871-1875
Romualdo Pacheco (R/acting)	1875
William Irwin (D)	1875-1880
George C. Perkins (R)	1880-1883
George Stoneman (D)	1883-1887
Washington Bartlett (D)	1887
Robert W. Waterman (R/acting)	1887-1891
Henry H. Markham (R)	1891-1895
James H. Budd (D)	1895-1899
Henry T. Gage (R)	1899-1903
George C. Pardee (R)	1903-1907
James N. Gillett (R)	1907-1911
Hiram W. Johnson (R)	1911-1917
William D. Stephens (R)	1917-1923

Friend W. Richardson (R)	1923-1927
Clement C. Young (R)	1927-1931
James Rolph, Jr. (R)	1931-1934
Frank F. Merriam (R)	1934-1939
Culburt L. Olson (D)	1939-1943
Earl Warren (R)	1943-1953
Goodwin J. Knight (R)	1953-1959
Edmund G. Brown (D)	1959-1967
Ronald Reagan (R)	1967-1975
Edmund G. Brown, Jr. (D)	1975-1983
George Deukmejian (R)	1983-

MINIMUM AGES

Majority 18
Marriage with parental consent
    . . . . no minimum with court order
Marriage without parental consent . 18
Making a will (lower
   if married) 18
Buying alcohol 21
Serving on a jury 18
Leaving school 18
Driver's license 16

CAPITAL PUNISHMENT

Number executed 1976-88: 0
On death row, Aug. 1, 1988: 226

MILITARY INSTALLATIONS

Total number: 104
Major bases:
  Army: 3
  Navy: 3
  Air Force: 9
  Marine Corps: 1

FINANCES

Thousands of dollars

GENERAL REVENUE (1985)

Total general revenue . . . 46,046,986
Total tax revenue 28,952,494
Sales and gross receipts . . 12,105,062
Individual income taxes . . 10,762,213
Corporate net income taxes . 3,658,093

GENERAL EXPENDITURE (1985)

Total general expenditure . 45,774,836
Education 17,904,476
Public welfare 11,000,955
Health 1,778,090
Hospitals 1,331,274
Natural resources 1,204,074
Highways 2,296,534
Police 500,247
Corrections 1,237,968

FEDERAL AID (1985) 10,558,790

ECONOMY

California leads the nation in cash value of all farm commodities, and in crop value as well. Principal crops and livestock include dairy products, citrus, grapes and wine, cotton, nursery products, hay, tomatoes, lettuce, eggs, almonds, wheat, strawberries, rice, cattle, hogs, sheep, and poultry. Crop marketing receipts topped $10 billion in 1982. (Unofficial estimates rate marijuana as the state's biggest cash crop, with annual revenues in excess of $2 billion.) California is also the leading state in fisheries (the catch in 1983 was 529 million pounds) and second in production of lumber.

The state's mineral wealth includes oil, natural gas, iron ore, cement, boron (the nation's only supply), diatomite, gypsum, potash, mercury, tungsten, sand and gravel, with 2,196 mining and quarrying operations active in 1982. Principal manufacturing industries are aerospace, construction, and electronics. Especially notable are Silicon Valley, regarded as the nation's center for development in computers and electronics, and Hollywood, the world's film and television capital. Among service industries, banking is dominant.

EMPLOYMENT (1984)

Thousands of persons
Total number of employed
  workers 11,532
Construction 442.8
Finance, insurance, and
  real estate 695.0
Government 1,729.8
Manufacturing 2,047,0
Mining 49.6
Services 2,527,9
Transportation, communications,
  and utilities 548.9
Wholesale and retail trade . . . 2,512.2

Percent of civilian labor force
  unemployed (1984) 7.8

DEPARTMENT OF DEFENSE (1985)

Civilian workers employed . . 137,935
Military personnel 204,822
Contract awards . . . . . $29.115 billion

ENERGY SOURCES FOR ELECTRIC UTILITIES (1983)

Percent
Coal 0.0
Gas 36.4

Hydroelectric 48.3
Nuclear 4.8
Petroleum 5.4

TRANSPORTATION
Motor vehicles registered
  in state (1986) 19,760,260
Miles of roads, streets,
  and highways (1986) 175,092

Miles of Class I railway
  operated (1986) 6,287
Airports (1983) 862
Major aviation hubs (1983) 8
  Largest hub: Los Angeles/Burbank/
  Long Beach
Major ports, with gross tonnage (1985):
  Long Beach 43,977l
  Los Angeles 36,374
  Richmond 17,178

CULTURE AND EDUCATION

Native American tribes
California was formerly the home of the Atsugewi, Bear River, Cahwilla, Chetco, Chilula, Chimariko, Chumash, Costano, Cupeno, Diegueno, Esselem, Fernandeno, Gabrieleno, Guiacura, Halchidhoma, Huchnom, Juaneno, Kamia, Kato, Kawaiisu, Kitanemuk, Klamath, Konomihu, Lassik, Luiseno, Mattole, Modoc, Nongatl, Okwanuchu, Panamint, Patwin, Quahatica, Salina, Serrano, Sinkyone, Tolowa, Tubatulabal, Vanyume, Wailaki, Yahi, Hana, and Yuma. Groups that continue to live in California include the Achomawi, Alliklik, Chemehuevi, Hupa, Karok, Maidu, Miwok, Mojave, Mono, Pomo, Quechan, Shashta, Wappo, Western Shoshone, Whilkut, Wintun, Wiyot, Yokut, Yuki, and Yurok. There are 78 federal reservations.

Religions, ethnicities, and languages
The recipient of enormous domestic and foreign immigration since the Gold Rush years, California has a highly diverse population, including the nation's largest communities of people of Chinese, Japanese, and Mexican descent. Its religious connections are equally diverse. In addition to strong Roman Catholic, Protestant, fundamentalist Christian, Mormon, Buddhist, and Jewish communities, California is home to hundreds of indigenous cults. In 1980, 22.6 of California's population spoke a language other than English at home.

Major museums and libraries
Asian Art Museum of San Francisco
California Academy of Sciences, San Francisco
California Museum of Science and Industry, Los Angeles
California Palace of the Legion of Honor, San Francisco
California State Library, Sacramento
Crocker Art Gallery, Sacramento
M.H. de Young Memorial Museum, San Francisco

Fine Arts Gallery, San Diego
J. Paul Getty Museum, Malibu
Hoover Library of War, Revolution, and Peace, Stanford
Henry E. Huntington Library, Art Gallery, and Botanical Gardens, San Marino
Los Angeles County Museum of Art
Los Angeles County Museum of Natural History
Norton Simon Museum, Pasadena
San Diego Natural History Museum
Southwest Museum, Los Angeles

Major arts organizations
American Conservatory Theatre, San Francisco
Los Angeles Theatre Center
Oakland Ballet
Old Globe Theater, San Diego
Los Angeles Music Center Opera
Los Angeles Philharmonic Orchestra
San Diego Symphony Orchestra
San Francisco Ballet
San Francisco Opera
San Francisco Symphony Orchestra
Mark Taper Forum, Los Angeles

Colleges and universities
Number public (1986-87) 138
Number private (1986-87) 161
Total enrollment, in full-time equivalent students (1985) 1,062,400

Public elementary and secondary schools
Expenditure per pupil in average daily attendance (1986-87) $3,887
Pupil-teacher ratio (1987) 23.0
Average teacher salary (1986-87) $32,230

Major league sports teams
Baseball: California Angels, Los Angeles Dodgers, Oakland Athletics, San Diego Padres, San Francisco Giants
Basketball: Golden State Warriors, Los Angeles Clippers, Los Angeles Lakers, Sacramento Kings

Football: Los Angeles Rams, Los Angeles Raiders, San Francisco 49ers, San Diego Chargers
Hockey: Los Angeles Kings

Holidays
State Fair, Sacramento. Late August to early September
Admission Day. September 9

CALIFORNIA IN LITERATURE

Ansel Adams *Autobiography* (1985)
Photographer's account of his San Francisco upbringing and life-long passion for Yosemite and the Sierras.

Gertrude Atherton *California: An Intimate History* (1914, rpt. 1983)
An account of the state by a member of the San Francisco literary community and author of several historical novels about Spanish colonial times: *The Doomswoman* (1892), *Before the Gringo Came* (1894), and *The Californians* (1898).

Mary Austin *The Land of Little Rain* (1903, rev. ed. 1950, rpt. 1974)
Essays written in Independence in appreciation of the landscape and people of the Western desert. Works by Austin with a California setting include *The Basket Woman* (1904), stories of the Paiute Indians; *Isidro* (1905), a romantic novel set in the days of Mexican rule; *The Flock* (1906), a story of desert shepherds; *California, the Land of the Sun* (1914); and *The Ford* (1917), a novel about real estate development.

Hubert H. Bancroft *California Pastoral* (1888); *California Inter Pocula* (1888, rpt. 1967)
Accounts of the Spanish colonial era and the Gold Rush.

James P. Beckwourth and **Thomas D. Bonner** *The Life and Adventures of James P. Beckwourth* (1972)
Autobiography of a black mountain man. A classic western adventure narrative.

Horace Bell *Reminiscences of a Ranger* (1881)
Memoirs of a Gold Rush adventurer, Union army scout, and lawyer.

John Bidwell *A Journey to California* (1843, rpt. 1907)
Bidwell organized the first overland trek from Missouri.

Ambrose Bierce *Can Such Things Be?* (1893)
A collection of frontier tales.

T. D. Bonner *Life and Adventures* (1856)
The reminiscences of James P. Beckwourth, a Virginian who discovered the northern Sierra Nevada Pass.

John David Borthwick *Three Years in California* (1857)
Illustrated memoir by a Scottish-born artist who lived in San Francisco during the Gold Rush.

T. Coraghessan Boyle *Budding Prospects* (1984)
A young man spends nine months cultivating marijuana in northern California.

J. Terwhitt Brooks (pseud. of Henry Vizetelly) *Four Months Among the Goldfinders in California* (1849)
One of the earliest accounts of the Gold Rush, narrated as autobiography, but actually based on reports.

Noah Brooks *The Boy Emigrants* (1876)
A journalist's record of his trip to California in 1859.

Joseph Goldsborough Bruff *Gold Rush* (1944)
Account of a journey to California from Washington, D.C., and a stay in the mining country 1849–1851.

Edward Gould Buffum *Six Months in the Gold Mines: From a Journal of Three Years in Upper and Lower California, 1847–1849* (1850)
Memoirs of a journalist who served with Stevenson's regiment and joined the Gold Rush in 1849.

Lafayette H. Bunnell *Discovery of the Yosemite* (1880)
An account by one of the valley's white discoverers.

Gelett Burgess *The Heart Line* (1907)
Novel about the craze for the occult in turn-of-the-century San Francisco.
———. *Bayside Bohemia* (1954); *Behind the Scenes* (1968)
Journalism written in San Francisco early in the century.

W. R. Burnett *High Sierra* (1940)
Novel about a gangster who flees into the mountains.

Herb Caen *Baghdad by the Bay* (1949); *Don't Call it Frisco* (1953); *Only in San Francisco* (1960); *One Man's San Francisco* (1976)
Essays by a San Francisco journalist.

Kit Carson *Kit Carson's Own Story of His Life* (1926)
Memoirs of the Indian fighter and mountain-man.

Raymond Chandler *The Big Sleep* (1939); *Farewell, My Lovely* (1940)
Classic hard-boiled detective fiction set in Los Angeles.

Daniel W. Coit *An Artist in El Dorado* (1937); *Digging Gold Without a Shovel* (ed. George P. Hammond) (1967)
Sketches and letters of a banker and amateur artist who joined the Gold Rush.

Clarkson Crane *The Western Shore* (1925)
Novel about campus life at the University of California.

Juan Crespí (trans. and ed. Herbert E. Bolton) *Juan Crespí* (1927)
Diaries of a Franciscan missionary and explorer who was a member of Portolá's expedition.

Dame Shirley (pseud. of Louise Clappe) *The Shirley Letters from the California Mines,* 1851–1852 (1854; rpt. 1970)
Gold Rush memoir. The author was the wife of a doctor at the Feather River settlement.

Richard Henry Dana Jr. *Two Years Before the Mast* (1840, rpt. 1964, 1984)
Journal of a Harvard student describing his enlistment in 1834 in the crew of a brig sailing to California, and his stay in the Laguna Beach area.

Marion Davies *The Times We Had* (1975)
Memoirs of the chorus girl and actress who was William Randolph Hearst's mistress.

William Heath Davis *Sixty Years in California* (1889)
The Gold Rush experiences of a Northerner who married into a wealthy California family.

Alonzo Delano *Across the Plains and Among the Diggings* (1854)
The diary of a New Yorker who joined the Gold Rush and became a journalist.
———. *Alonzo Delano's California Correspondence* (1952)
Letters to newspapers about the Feather River mines.

Frederick S. Dellenbaugh *A Canyon Voyage* (1908)
A New York artist's recollections of J. W. Powell's explorations of the Green and Colorado rivers (1871)
———. *Frémont and '49* (1914)
A history of early California explorations.

Joan Didion *Run River* (1963)
Changing ways of life in the Sacramento Valley.
———. *Slouching toward Bethlehem* (1968)
Essays on California culture.
———. *Play It As It Lays* (1970)
Fashionable Hollywood life.

John Gregory Dunne *Delano* (1967)
Cesar Chavez' union movement.
———. *The Studio* (1969)
The movie industry.

Job Francis Dye *Recollections of a Pioneer of California* (1869)
Memoirs of a Kentucky mountain man who travelled to California in 1832, ran a store in Santa Cruz, and took part in the Gold Rush.

Lee Early and **Aim Morhardt** *Western Men and Desert Gold: Stories, Songs and Poems of the Death Valley Region* (1954)

John Fante *Wait Until Spring, Bandini* (1938); *The Brotherhood of the Grape* (1977)
Novels of Italian family life.

Thomas J. Farnham *Life and Adventures in California* (1846)
Sensational account of San Francisco in the 1840s.

Francis P. Farquhar (ed.) *A Journey to California, 1841; The First Emigrant Party to California by Wagon Train: The Journal of John Bidwell* (1964)

Federal Writers' Program *The Old West: Pioneer Tales of San Bernardino County Compiled by Workers of the WPA* . . . (1940)

Joseph A. Filcher *Untold Tales of California: Short Stories Illustrating Phases of Life Peculiar to Early Days in the West* (1903)

F. Scott Fitzgerald *The Last Tycoon* (1941)
Fictional portrait of a movie producer.

Pedro Font (ed. H. E. Bolton) *Complete Diary* (1933)
A detailed memoir written in 1777 by the chaplain who served with Anza's second expedition (1776).

Arnold Genthe *As I Remember* (1936); *Pictures of Old Chinatown*
Memoirs by the photographer who recorded Chinatown and the San Francisco earthquake.

Allen Ginsberg *Journals* (1977)
The poet's account of the San Francisco literary circle centered on Lawrence Ferlinghetti's City Lights bookstore.

Ralph J. Gleason *The San Francisco Scene* (1968)
The first book to treat rock music as an art form.

Herbert Gold *The Great American Jackpot* (1970)
The San Francisco counter-cultural movement.

Margaret Collier Graham *Stories of the Foothills* (1895)
Local color stories of southern California.

Horace Greeley *An Overland Journey from New York to San Francisco in the Summer of 1859* (1860)
Account of an overland trek made by the famous journalist in the company of Hank Monk the stagecoach driver.

Oakley Hall *Corpus of Joe Barley* (1953); *Report from Beau Harbor* (1971)
Humorous descriptions of Californian manners.

Jerome A. Hart *A Vigilante Girl* (1910); *The Golconda Bonanza* (1923); *In Our Second Century* (1931)
Memoirs of San Francisco bohemian life.

Bret Harte *M'liss* (1860)
Novelette about the adventures of a girl in the Gold Rush.
———. *The Luck of Roaring Camp and Other Sketches* (1870)
Humorous tales of mining and frontier life regarded as the earliest examples of American "local color" fiction.

Gerald W. Haslam and **James D. Houston** (eds.) *California Heartland: Writing from the Great Central Valley* (1978)
An anthology.

J. S. Holliday (ed.) *The World Rushed In: The California Gold Rush Experience* (1981)
Anthology of diaries and other first-hand accounts.

John Clellon Holmes *Nothing More to Declare* (1952)
Memoir of the Beat Movement.

Aldous Huxley *After Many a Summer Dies the Swan* (1939)
Novel based on the life of William Randolph Hearst.

Will Irwin *Old Chinatown* (1908)
The San Francisco neighborhood before the earthquake.

Wallace A. Irwin *Seed of the Sun* (1921)
Novel about conflict between white and Japanese farmers.

Joseph H. Jackson *Continent's End: A Collection of California Writing* (1944)
———. *Bad Company* (1949)
Novelization of the careers of seven mid-nineteenth-century bandits.
———. *The Western Gate: A San Francisco Reader* (1952)

Helen Hunt Jackson *Ramona* (1884)
A romantic novel set on a southern California ranch.

Idwal Jones *China Boy* (1936)
Stories about California Chinese.
———. *The Vineyard* (1942)
Novel set in the Napa Valley.
———. *Vermillion* (1947)
Novel about a California mining family.

———. *Ark of Empire* (1951)
A non-fiction account of H. W. Halleck's Montgomery Block in San Francisco.

Edward Cleveland Kemble *A Kemble Reader* (1963)
Essays on history and society by a San Francisco journalist.

Jack Kerouac *The Subterraneans* (1958)
A romance set in San Francisco during the Beat movement.

Clarence King *Mountaineering in the Sierra Nevada* (1872, rpt. 1970)
A geological and geographical account including anecdotes of the author's climbing experiences and fiction about local people.

Maxine Hong Kingston *The Woman Warrior: Memoirs of a Girlhood Among Ghosts* (1976); *China Men* (1981)
A Cantonese-American upbringing in Stockton.

Hector Lee *Heroes, Villains, and Ghosts: Folklore of Old California* (1984); *The Bodega War, and Other Tales from Western Lore* (1988)

W. Storrs Lee (ed.) *California: A Literary Chronicle* (1969)
An anthology.

Zenas Leonard *Narrative of Zenas Leonard* (1839)
Leonard was a member of the group led by Joseph Walker who were the first white men to make a westward crossing of the Sierra Nevada (1833–34).

Oscar Lewis *Bay Window Bohemia: An Account of the Brilliant Artistic World of Gaslight San Francisco* (1956)
———. *I Remember Christine* (1942, rpt. 1989)
Novel about the life of a San Francisco entrepreneur.

Jack London *Martin Eden* (1909)
Novel about a sailor and laborer on the Oakland waterfront.

Alison Lurie *The Nowhere City* (1966)
Comic novel about an east-coast history professor who moves to Los Angeles.

Ross Macdonald *The Underground Man* (1971)
Classic detective mystery set in Southern California.

Cyra McFadden *The Serial* (1977)
A satiric portrait of life in the '70s in Marin County.

Frances Moffatt *Dancing on the Brink of the World* (1977)
A history of San Francisco society.

Dale L. Morgan *Overland in 1846: Diaries and Letters of the California-Oregon Trail* (1963)

Wright Morris *The Huge Season* (1954)
Novel set at Pomona College.

John Muir *The Mountains of California* (1894, rev. ed. 1911, rpt. 1961); *My First Summer in the Sierra* (1911); *The Yosemite* (1912); (ed. L. M. Wolfe) *The Wilderness World of John Muir* (1954)
Observations of the mountain wilderness by the naturalist and pioneer conservationist.

Barbara Myerhoff *Number Our Days* (1979)
Account of the Jewish community in Venice.

David Nevin *Dream West* (1984)
Biographical novel about Frémont.

Walter Nordhoff *The Journey of the Flame* (1933)
Historical novel purporting to be the autobiography of an old Spanish Californian of the 19th century.

Frank Norris *McTeague* (1899)
Life on Polk Street in San Francisco.
———. *Blix* (1899)
The courtship of a San Francisco society girl.
———. *The Octopus* (1901, rpt. 1986)
Novel depicting conflict between tenant farmers and developers, based on the Mussel Slough incident of 1880.

Lawrence Clark Powell *California Classics: The Creative Literature of the Golden State* (1971)
An anthology.

Ishmael Reed *The Last Days of Louisiana Red* (1974)
Novel set in Berkeley during the 1960s.

David Robertson *West of Eden: A History of the Art and Literature of Yosemite* (1984)

Josiah Royce *The Feud of Oakfield Creek* (1887)
A fictional treatment of the Mussel Slough incident.

Thomas Sanchez *The Zoot Suit Murders* (1978)
A fictional treatment of a notorious instance of racial prejudice against Chicanos that was instigated by the death of a Los Angeles man in 1942.

William Saroyan *The Human Comedy* (1943, rev. ed. 1971)
Central Valley farm life during World War I seen through the eyes of a fourteen-year-old boy.

Frank Soulé, Frank Gihon, and **James Nisbet** *Annals of San Francisco* (1855)
A narrative history from the earliest explorations to 1855, with essays and biographies.

Lincoln Steffens *The Autobiography of Lincoln Steffens* (1931)
Account of the author's upbringing in Sacramento.

Wallace Stegner *The Big Rock Candy Mountain* (1943)
A western family's search for prosperity c.1910.

John Steinbeck *The Pastures of Heaven* (1932)
Stories of a farm community.
———. *Tortilla Flat* (1935)
Mexican life in Monterey.
———. *In Dubious Battle* (1936)
Novel depicting conflicts between migratory farm laborers and landowners.
———. *The Grapes of Wrath* (1939)
Destitute Oklahoma farmers migrate to California but find only new hardship.
———. *Cannery Row* (1945)
A romantic evocation of the Monterey neighborhood.
———. *East of Eden* (1952)
Saga of a family of settlers in the Salinas Valley.

Robert Louis Stevenson *The Silverado Squatters* (1883)
Narrative of Stevenson's honeymoon in the abandoned cabin of a silver mine.
———. *The Wrecker* (1892)
A romantic account of San Francisco.

George R. Stewart *Ordeal by Hunger* (1936)
An account of the Donner party's Sierra crossing, based on the diary of a survivor, Patrick Breen.
———. *East of the Giants* (1938)
Historical novel set in the 1840s and '50s.

Charles Warren Stoddard *For the Pleasure of His Company: An Affair of the Misty City* (1903, rpt. 1987)
An autobiographical novel about homosexual love in turn-of-the-century San Francisco.

Irving Stone *Sailor on Horseback* (1938)
Fictionalized biography of Jack London.
———. *Immortal Wife* (1944)
Fictionalized biography of Jessie Frémont.
———. *Men to Match My Mountains* (1956)
Fictionalized biographies of California pioneers.

Maurice Sullivan (ed.) *The Journal of Jedediah Strang Smith* (1934)
Records of the trapper's journeys of 1826 and 1828.

John Alfred Swan *A Trip to the Gold Mines . . . in 1848* (1960)

Experiences in the Gold Rush related by an English-born sailor who settled in Monterey.

B. Taper (ed.) *Mark Twain's San Francisco* (1976)
Twain's California and Nevada journalism.

Ben C. Truman *Life, Adventures and Capture* (1874)
A biography of Tiburcio Vásquez, stagecoach robber and rustler, who was executed in Los Angeles in 1874.

Mark Twain *Roughing It* (1872)
A fictional treatment of Twain's journey from Carson City to San Francisco, where he worked as a journalist.

Franklin D. Walker *San Francisco's Literary Frontier* (1939); *A Literary History of Southern California* (1950); *The Seacoast of Bohemia: An Account of Early Carmel* (1966)

Samuel Ward *Sam Ward in the Gold Rush* (1949)
Reminiscences of a New Yorker who joined the Gold Rush to recover his fortunes.

Evelyn Waugh *The Loved One* (1948)
A satirical account of the funeral industry inspired by Forest Lawn Cemetery.

Dixon Wecter (ed.) *Literary Lodestone: One Hundred Years of California Writing* (1950)

Nathanael West (pseud. of Nathan Weinstein) *The Day of the Locust* (1939)
A surrealistic satire of Los Angeles and the film industry.

Jessamyn West *Cress Delahanty* (1953)
Novel about a girl's upbringing on a California ranch.
———. *South of the Angels* (1960)
Novel about real estate development near Los Angeles in the early 20th century.

Herman Whitaker (ed.) *West Winds: California's Book of Fiction, Written by California Authors* (1914)

Stewart Edward White *Story of California* (1927)
A trilogy of novels comprising *Gold* (1913), *The Gray Dawn* (1915), and *The Rose Dawn* (1920), about the Gold Rush, early San Francisco, and Southern California in the 1880s. His second trilogy, comprising *The Long Rifle* (1932), *Ranchero* (1933), and *Folded Hills* (1934), describes the life of a pioneer and successive generations of his family. These were gathered with a novelette, *Stampede* (1942) in *The Saga of Andy Burnett*.
———. *The Mountains* (1904); *The Pass* (1906); *The Cabin* (1911)
Sketches of life in the Sierras.

Laura Ingalls Wilder (ed. Roger L. MacBride) *West from Home: Letters of Laura Ingalls Wilder to Almanzo Wilder, San Francisco 1915* (1974)
Letters by the famous children's writer to her husband while visiting her married daughter at the time of the Panama Pacific International Exposition.

Edmund Wilson *The Boys in the Back Room* (1941)
Critical essays on California writers.

GUIDES TO RESOURCES

Andrews, Thomas F. " 'Ho! For Oregon and California!': An Annotated Bibliography of Published Advice to the Emigrant, 1841–1847." *Princeton University Library Chronicle* 30 (1971)

Beck, Warren A. and **Ynez D. Haase** *Historical Atlas of California* (1974)

Benet, James W. *A Guide to San Francisco and the Bay Region* (1963)

Bullock, Constance S. (comp.) *The UCLA Oral History Program: Catalog of the Collection* (1982)

California Historical Society *Index to California Historical Society Quarterly* vols 1–40 (1965); vols. 41–54 (1977)

Cowan, Robert E. and **Robert G.** *A Bibliography of the History of California, 1510–1930* 4 vols. (1933–1964)

———. *A Bibliography of the History of California and the Pacific Coast* (1952)

Coy, Owen C. *Guide to County Archives of California* (1919)

Fay, James, Anne G. Lipow and **Stephanie W. Fay** (eds.) *California Almanac* (1984–)

Federal Writers' Project *San Diego: A California City* (1937)
———. *California* (1939, rpt. 1984)
———. *Death Valley, A Guide* (1939)
———. *Los Angeles* (1939)
———. *San Francisco: The Bay and Its Cities* (1940, rev. eds. 1947, 1973)
———. *Santa Barbara: A Guide to the Channel City . . .* (1941, rpt. 1980)

Gaer, Joseph *Bibliography of California Literature: Fiction of the Gold Rush Period, Poetry of the Gold Rush Period* (1935, rpt. 1970)

————. *Bibliography of California Literature: Pre–Gold Rush Period* (1935, rpt. 1971)

Gudde, Erwin G. *California Gold Camps: A Geographical and Historical Dictionary of Camps and Localities…* (1975)

Hager, Anna M. and Everett G. (comps.) *Historical Society of Southern California Bibliography of Published Works, 1884–1957*

Hart, James D. *A Companion to California* (1987)

Heckman, Marlin L. *Overland on the California Trail, 1846–1859: A Bibliography of Manuscript and Printed Travel Narratives* (1984)

Hinkel, Edgar J., and William E. McCann *Bibliography of California Fiction, Poetry, Drama* (1938)

Morrison, Faye B. and Kathryn Cusick *Golden Poppies: California History and Contemporary Life in Books and Other Media for Young Readers: An Annotated Bibliography* (1987)

Riess, Suzanne and Willa K. Baum (eds.) *Catalogue of the Regional Oral History Office, 1954–1979* Bancroft Library, University of California (1980)

Rocq, Margaret M. (ed.) *California Local History: Bibliography and Union List of Library Holdings* 2nd ed. (1970)

San Luis Obispo County Oral History Organization *History Comes Alive: Catalog of Oral History Holdings in San Luis Obispo County* San Luis Obispo County Oral History Organization (1980)

Scheuring, Ann F. (ed.) *A Guidebook to California Agriculture* (1983)

Stephenson, Shirley S. (ed.) *Oral History Collections: California State University, Fullerton* (1985)

Trzyna T. C. (ed.) *The California Handbook* (1987)

Weber, Francis J. *A Bibliography of California Bibliographies* (1968)

SELECTED NONFICTION SOURCES

Asbury, Herbert *The Barbary Coast* (1933)

Baker, Laura N. *Ground Afire: The Story of Death Valley National Monument* (1971)

Bakker, Elna *An Island Called California* (1971)

Bancroft, Hubert H. *History of California* 7 vols. (1884–1890)

Bean, Walton *Boss Ruef's San Francisco* (1952, rpt. 1967)
————. *California: An Interpretive History* (1973)

Beasley, Delilah L. *The Negro Trail Blazers of California* (1919)

Beck, Warren A. and David A. Williams *California: A History of the Golden State* (1972)

Berger, Bennett M. *Hippie Country* (1981)

Billington, Ray A. *The Spanish Borderlands* (1921)

Birmingham, Stephen *California Rich* (1981)

Block, Eugene B. *Immortal San Franciscans: For Whom the Streets Were Named* (1971)

Bowman, Lynn *Los Angeles: Epic of a City* (1974)

Bronson, William *The Earth Shook, The Sky Burned* (1959, rpt. 1971)
————. *How to Kill a Golden State* (1968)

Browing, Peter *Yosemite Place Names* (1988)

Brown, Allen *Golden Gate: Biography of a Bridge* (1965)

Brownlow, Kevin *The War, the West and the Wilderness* (1979)

Caen, Herb *Baghdad-By-The-Bay* (1949)

Caughey, John W. *California: A Remarkable State's Life History* (1970)
————. and Laree (eds.) *California Heritage: An Anthology of History and Literature* (1962, rev. ed. 1971)

Chapman, Charles E. *The Founding of Spanish California, 1687–1783* (1916)
————. *A History of California: The Spanish Period* (1921)

Chartkoff, Joseph L. *The Archaeology of California* (1984)

Chu, Daniel and Samuel *Passage to the Golden Gate: A History of the Chinese in America to 1910* (1967)

Cleland, Robert G. *A History of California, the American Period* (1922)
————. *From Wilderness to Empire: California* (1944, rev. ed. 1959)
————. *California in Our Time* (1947)
————. *The Cattle on a Thousand Hills* (1951)

Conot, Robert *Rivers of Blood, Years of Darkness* (1967)

Conrat, Maisie and Richard *Executive Order 9066: The Internment of 110,000 Japanese Americans* (1972)

Cook, Bruce *The Beat Generation* (1971)

Cook, Sherburne F. *Conflict between California Indian and White Civilization* (1943)

Coolidge, Dane *Old California Cowboys* (1939)

Cowan, Robert E. *Forgotten Characters of Old San Francisco* (1964)

Dana, Julian *The Man Who Built San Francisco* (1936)

Dasmann, Raymond F. *The Destruction of California* (1965, rpt. 1969)

Davie, Michael *California: The Vanishing Dream* (1972)

De Voto, Bernard *Year of Decision: 1846* (1943)

Dickson, Samuel *Tales of San Francisco* (1965)

Dillon, Richard *Embarcadero* (1959)
————. *The Hatchet-men: The Story of the Tong Wars in San Francisco* (1962)

Dobie, Charles Caldwell *San Francisco, A Pageant* (1933)
————. *San Francisco's Chinatown* (1936)

Douglas, William O. *Muir of the Mountains* (1961)

Eldredge, Zoeth S. *The March of Portolá* (1909)
————. *The Beginnings of San Francisco* 2 vols. (1912)
————. (ed.) *History of California* 5 vols. (1915)

Ellison, Joseph *California and the Nation, 1850–1869: A Study of the Relations of a Frontier Community with the Federal Government* (1927)

Farquhar, Francis *History of the Sierra Nevada* (1965)

Fehrenbacher, Don E. *Basic History of California* (1964)
————. and Norman E. Tutorow *California: Illustrated History* (1968)

Ferlinghetti, Lawrence and Nancy J. Peters *Literary San Francisco: A Pictorial History from the Beginings to the Present Day* (1980)

Fogelson, Robert M. *Fragmented Metropolis: Los Angeles, 1850–1930* (1967)

Gagey, Edmond M. *San Francisco Stage: A History* (1950)

Gates, Paul W. (ed.) *California Ranchos and Farms, 1846–1862* (1967)

Geiger, Maynard J. *The Life and Times of Fray Junípero Serra* (1959)
————. *Mission Santa Barbara* (1965)
————. *Franciscan Missionaries in Hispanic California* (1969)

Gordon, Thomas *The San Francisco Earthquake* (1971)

Greever, William S. *Bonanza West: Western Mining Rushes, 1848–1900* (1963)

Griswold, Wesley S. *A Work of Giants: Building the First Transcontinental Railroad* (1962)

Gudde, Erwin G. *California Place Names* (1949, rev. ed. 1969)

Hannaford, Donald R. *Spanish Colonial or Adobe Architecture of California, 1800–1850* (1931)

Hart, Jerome *In Our Second Century* (1931)

Henstell, Bruce *Los Angeles: An Illustrated History* (1980)

Hittell, Theodore H. *History of California* 4 vols. (1885–1897)

Hutchinson, C. Alan, *Frontier Settlement in Mexican California* (1969)

Hutchinson, William H. *California* (1969)

Iacopi, Robert *Earthquake Country* (1964)

Kemble, John H. *San Francisco Bay* (1957)

Kennedy, John C. *The Great Earthquake and Fire* (1963)

Kinnaird, Lawrence *History of Greater San Francisco Bay Region* 3 vols. (1966)

Kirsch, Robert R., and William S. Murphy *West of the West: California Experience, 1542–1906* (1967)

Kroeber, Theodora *Ishi in Two Worlds: A Biography of the Last Wild Indian in North America* (1962, rpt. 1971)

Lasky, Jesse L. *Whatever Happened to Hollywood?* (1975)

Lavender, David S. *The Great Persuader: A Biography of Collis P. Huntington* (1970)
———. *California: Land of New Beginnings* (1972)
———. *Nothing Seemed Impossible: A Biography of William C. Ralston* (1975)
———. *California* (States and the Nation Series) (1976)
———. *The Overland Migration* (1980)

Lewis, Oscar *Big Four* (1938)
———. *Silver Kings* (1947)
———. *Sea Routes to the Gold Fields* (1949)
———. *San Francisco Mission to Metropolis* (1966)
——— and Carroll D. Hall *Bonanza Inn* (1939)

Lillard, Richard *Eden in Jeopardy, Man's Prodigal Meddling with His Environment: The Southern California Experience* (1966)

Lingenfelter, Richard E. *Death Valley and the Amargosa: A Land of Illusion* (1986)

Longstreet, Stephen *The Wilder Shore* (1968)

Lotchin, Roger W. *San Francisco, 1846–1856* (1974)

McGowan, Joseph A. *History of Sacramento Valley* 3 vols. (1961)

McWilliams, Carey *Factories in the Field* (1939, rev. ed. 1946)
———. *Southern California Country* (1946)
———. *California: The Great Exception* (1949)

Melendy, H. Brett, and Benjamin F. Gilbert *Governors of California: Peter H. Burnett to Edmund G. Brown* (1965)

Morgan, Neil *Westward Tilt* (1963)

Mowry, George *The California Progressives* (1951)

Myers, John M. *San Francisco's Reign of Terror* (1966)

Nadeau, Remi *The Water Seekers* (1950)
———. *California: The New Society* (1963, rpt. 1974)

Nash, Gerald D. *State Government and Economic Development: Administrative Policies in California 1849–1933* (1964)
———. *The American West in the Twentieth Century* (1973)

Paul, Rodman W. *California Gold* (1947)
———. *Mining Frontiers of the Far West* (1963)

Pitt, Leonard *The Decline of the Californias: A Social History of the Spanish-Speaking Californians, 1846–1900* (1966)

Pomeroy, Earl *The Pacific Slope* (1965)

Putnam, George P. *Death Valley and Its Country* (1946)

Richman, I. B. *California under Spain and Mexico, 1535–1847* (1911)

Robinson, Alfred *Life in California before the Conquest* 2nd ed. (1968)

Robinson, W. W. *Land in California* (1948)
———. *Los Angeles: From the Days of the Pueblo* (1959)

Rolle, Andrew F. *California* 2nd ed. (1969)

Roske, Ralph J. *Everyman's Eden: California* (1968)

Sanchez, Nellie V. *Spanish and Indian Place Names of California* (1930, rpt. 1976)

Saroyan, Aram *Genesis Angels: The Saga of Lew Welch and the Beat Generation* (1979)

Saxton, Alexander *The Indispensable Enemy: Labor and the Anti-Chinese Movement in California* (1971)

Scherer, James A. B. *The Lion of the Vigilantes* (1939)

Scott, Mellier G. *San Francisco Bay Area* (1959)

Seidenbaum, Art *This Is California: Please Keep Out!* (1975)
———. *Los Angeles 200: A Bicentennial Celebration* (1980)

Seidman, Laurence I. *The Fools of '49. The California Gold Rush 1848–1856* (1976)

Starr, Kevin *Americans and the California Dream* (1973)

Stewart, George R. *The California Trail: An Epic with Many Heroes* (1962)
———. *Committee of Vigilance: Revolution in San Francisco, 1851* (1964)
———. *Donner Pass: And Those Who Crossed It* (1964)

Stoughton, Gertrude K., *Books of California* (1968)

Swift, Hildegarde Hoyt *From the Eagle's Wing: A Biography of John Muir* (1962)

Syme, Ronald *John Charles Frémont: The Last American Explorer* (1974)

Taylor, Bayard *Eldorado, or Adventures in the Path of Empire* (1850, rpt. 1949)

Tytell, John *Naked Angels: The Lives and Literature of the Beat Generation* (1976)

Underhill, Ruth *Indians of Southern California* (1941)

Vail, Wesley D. *Victorians: An Account of Domestic Architecture in Victorian San Francisco 1870–1890* (1964)

Wagner, Walter *Beverley Hills: Inside the Golden Ghetto* (1976)

Walker, Franklin *San Francisco's Literary Frontier* (1969)

Watkins, T. H. *California: An Illustrated History* (1973)

Wellman, Paul I. *Gold in California* (1958)

Wierzbicki, Felix *California As It Is and As It May Be* (1849)

Williams, Mary Floyd *History of the San Francisco Committee of Vigilance of 1851* (1921)

Wright, Ralph B. (ed.) *California's Missions* (1950, rpt. 1978)

Young, J. P. *San Francisco, a History of the Pacific Coast Metropolis* 2 vols. (1913)

COLORADO

The mountain state of Colorado is bordered on the north by Wyoming and Nebraska; on the east by Nebraska and Kansas; on the south by Oklahoma and New Mexico; and on the west by Utah.

FULL NAME State of Colorado
POSTAL ABBREVIATION CO
INHABITANT Coloradan
ADMITTED TO THE UNION Aug. 1, 1876.
  38th state
POPULATION (est. 1987) 3,296,000.
  Percent of US total: 1.35%. Rank: 26th

CAPITAL CITY Denver, the largest city in the state, located on the South Platte River in northeast central Colorado; population 504,566 (est. 1984). Founded in 1860 on the site of a trading post and several gold rush towns, it was incorporated as a city in 1861 and became the state capital in 1867.

STATE NAME AND NICKNAMES *Colorado* is the Spanish word for "red," and describes the waters of the Colorado River, which gave its name to the territory and thence to the state. Also known as the Centennial State, the Highest State, and the Switzerland of America.

STATE SEAL A blue field bearing a heraldic shield, with miner's tools displayed on the lower part and snow-capped mountains on the upper; above the shield, the fasces, bound by a band of red, white, and blue with the legend "Union and Constitution"; above the fasces, the eye of God in a triangle, from which come golden rays; below the shield, the state motto on a white banner. The red border bears the legend "State of Colorado, 1876."

MOTTO Nil Sine Numine (Nothing without providence)

SONG "Where the Columbines Grow," lyrics and music by A.J. Flynn.

SYMBOLS
Flower white and lavender columbine
Tree blue spruce
Bird lark bunting
Gem aquamarine
Animal Rocky Mountain bighorn sheep

LICENSE PLATE White on forest green, with silhouette of a mountain range; white-and-green border.

FLAG Three horizontal stripes of blue, white, and blue, bearing the letter "C" in red with a yellow disk in its center.

GEOGRAPHY AND CLIMATE

Colorado's varied terrain can be divided into three zones: the dry, windy high plains to the east; the Colorado Piedmont, a hilly central area containing 80 percent of the state's population; and the Colorado Rocky Mountains to the west, a complex network of high ranges (up to 14,000 feet) and the main watershed of the western United States.

AREA 104,091 square miles. Rank: 8th
INLAND WATER 496 square miles
GEOGRAPHIC CENTER Park, 30 miles NW of Pikes Peak
ELEVATIONS *Highest point:* Mount Elbert, Lake County, 14,433 feet. *Lowest point:* Arkansas River, Prowers County, 3,350 feet. *Mean elevation:* 6,800 feet

MAJOR RIVERS Colorado, Arkansas, South Platte, Rio Grande

MAJOR LAKES AND RESERVOIRS Granby, Pueblo, John Martin, Lake Granby, Blue Mesa

LAND USE

	Thousands of acres
Urban (1982)	672
Rural (1982)	41,271
Cropland (1982)	10,603
Pastureland (1982)	1,260
Rangeland (1982)	24,223
Forestland (1982)	15,218
State parks and recreation areas (1983)	160
National park system (1984)	588
National forest system (1984) .	16,023
Tribal lands (1984)	784

TEMPERATURES The highest recorded temperature was 118°F on July 11, 1888, at Bennett. The lowest was -61°F on February 1, 1985, at Maybell.

NATIONAL SITES

NATIONAL HISTORIC SITE Bent's Old Fort
NATIONAL MONUMENTS Black Canyon of the Gunnison, Colorado Dinosaur, Florissant Fossil Beds, Great Sand Dunes, Hovenweep, Yucca House

NATIONAL PARKS Mesa Verde, Rocky Mountain National Recreation Areas, Curecanti
NATIONAL WILDLIFE REFUGES Alamosa–Monte Vista, Arapaho–Bamforth/Hutton Lake/Pathfinder, Browns Park

HISTORY

1700	French explorers reach the Rocky Mountains.
1706	Spanish soldiers and their Indian auxiliaries, led by Juan de Uribarri, visit Apache villages near present-day Pueblo.
1739	A party of French travelers led by the Mallet brothers passes through Colorado. Other French merchants follow.
1779	Spanish soldiers, led by Juan Bautista de Anza, subdue Comanche Indians near Pueblo.
1803	The fur trade lures the first American, James Purcell, into the region.
1806	Leading a party of 15 US soldiers from St. Louis, Lieutenant Zebulon Pike attempts to climb the peak that bears his name.
1819	The Adams–Onís Treaty acknowledges most of eastern Colorado as US territory; the rest is recognized as Spanish.
1820	Major Stephen H. Long leads a party exploring the region along the new boundary; Dr. Edwin James scales Pike's Peak.
1835	Bent's Old Fort is completed on the Arkansas River near La Junta, serving as a post and rendezvous point for fur trappers and traders.
1842–1853	John C. Frémont leads five expeditions through Colorado while exploring the West.
1848	The Treaty of Guadalupe Hidalgo, which concludes the Mexican War, cedes the entire Southwest, including Colorado, to the United States.
1851	San Luis, the first permanent non-Indian settlement, is founded in southern Colorado by six Hispanic families.
1858	*July 7–8.* Gold is found along Cherry Creek on the present site of Denver, touching off a stampede of prospectors hoping to strike it rich.
1859	*April 23. The Rocky Mountain News*, published in Auraria, is the first Colorado newspaper.

	May 6. More gold is struck along Clear Creek in what is now Central City. As many as 40,000 people flock to Colorado.
1861	*February 28*. Colorado Territory is created within the present state borders. The Cheyenne relinquish the greater part of their Colorado lands.
1864	*November 29*. Federal cavalry and volunteer militia massacre about 150 residents of a Cheyenne and Arapaho village. The incident revives Indian warfare in Colorado.
1865	Arapaho, Cheyenne, and Sioux kill 40 whites at Julesburg in northeastern Colorado.
1867	By the Treaty of Medicine Lodge, the Cheyenne and Arapaho agree to move to Indian Territory (Oklahoma).
1868–1869	Cheyenne and allied bands resisting removal are defeated at Beecher Island and Summit Springs. Most of western Colorado is reserved for Ute Indians.
1870	Rail connections link Denver to the transcontinental line at Cheyenne and to the east from Kansas City.
1872	The Denver and Rio Grande Railroad reaches Pueblo from Denver.
1873	A treaty detaches the mineral-rich San Juan district from the Ute reservation.
1876	*August 1*. Colorado is admitted to the Union as the 38th state.
1877	University of Colorado opens in Boulder.
1877–1880	Heyday of the silver boom at Leadville, which sports an opera house and swells to a population of at least 25,000. Silver production in the area reaches a peak value of $11.5 million in 1880.
1879	Twenty-six soldiers and Indian agents killed by Utes in "Meeker's massacre" in northwestern Colorado.
1880	Ute reservation is again reduced.
1884	Near the end of the open-range system, Colorado has more than a million cattle, many of them driven north from Texas.
1890	Irrigated land totals 890,735 acres, over half the state's improved farmland.
1891	Gold is discovered at Cripple Creek.
1892	Founding by merger of the Colorado Fuel & Iron Corporation, whose holdings include the only integrated steel plant in the West, at Pueblo. It passes under the control of Rockefeller interests in 1903.
1893	Demonetization of silver has a crippling effect on prices and production of the metal. *November 2*. Colorado gives women the right to vote.
1899	American Smelting and Refining Company, backed by Rockefeller (and, later, Guggenheim) money, absorbs six of Colorado's largest plants.
1903–1904	State and National Guard troops break strikes by the Western Federation of Miners.
1909	Colorado is first among states in irrigated area, which totals almost 3 million acres.
1912	Voters approve the adoption of the initiative and referendum.
1914	*April 20*. Twenty persons, including 12 children, die when National Guardsmen burn a tent colony of striking Colorado Fuel & Iron Corporation miners at Ludlow. More than a thousand miners then take up arms in a 10-day uprising that culminates in the dispatch of federal troops.
1915	Creation of Rocky Mountain National Park, which is to become a great tourist attraction.
1917	Two US Bureau of Reclamation projects since 1902 have doubled the irrigated land in western Colorado to 600,000 acres.
1924	Ku Klux Klan members in Colorado are elected to major state offices, and Klan-endorsed candidates are elected governor and senator.
1932–1937	Prolonged drought and high winds cause tremendous damage in southeastern Colorado through soil erosion.
1936	Voters approve a constitutional amendment promising $45 a month to retired Coloradans over the age of 60.
1942	A relocation center near Granada for West Coast Japanese-Americans has a peak population of 7,567.

1943	A Denver ordnance plant manufacturing small-arms ammunition is employing 19,500 persons in the World War II effort.
1955	Colorado is first among states in the production of uranium, molybdenum, and vanadium. More than 400 uranium mines are in operation.
1956	Martin Marietta Aerospace Corporation moves to Littleton to build Titan intercontinental ballistic missiles, employing as many as 17,000 persons. Completion of the Colorado–Big Thompson water-diversion system, providing water from western Colorado to populous eastern Colorado.
1957	Manufacturing replaces agriculture as Colorado's chief source of income. The North American Air Defense Command (NORAD) is established at Ent Air Force Base in Colorado Springs.
1958	The US Air Force Academy opens its Colorado Springs campus. Record oil production of 58 million barrels places Colorado ninth among states.
1964	Colorado receives a record 5.6 million visitors, many attracted by the growing number of skiing resorts.
1967	*April 25.* Colorado is the first state to approve liberalized abortion laws (i.e.: therapeutic abortions, rape or incest pregnancies).
1974	Six years of bitter resistance to racial integration end in the court-ordered busing of 18,000 schoolchildren.
1983	The Air Force announces plans to construct its Space Operations Center at Colorado Springs.

DEMOGRAPHY

Population (est. 1987)	3,296,000
Population (1980)	2,889,735
Population density per square mile (1980)	27.8

POPULATION BY RACE (1980)

American Indian/ Aleut/Eskimo	18,059
Asian/Pacific Islander	29,897
Black	101,702
Hispanic	339,300
White	2,570,615
Other	168,561

POPULATION CHARACTERISTICS (1980)

Percent of state population

Urban	80.6
Rural	19.4
Under 18	28.0
65 or older	8.6
College-educated	23.0
Families below poverty line	7.4
Public-assistance recipients	3.7

Per capita personal income (1986)	$15,113
Millionaires per 100,000 residents (1982)	224.8
Average life expectancy (1980)	75.3

Marriage rate per 1,000 residents (1986)	10.0
Divorce rate per 1,000 residents (1986)	6.0
Birth rate per 1,000 residents (1985)	17.1
Infant mortality rate per 1,000 births (1985)	10.6
Abortion rate per 1,000 live births (1985)	305
Crime rate per 100,000 residents (1986)	
Violent	523.6
Property	6,508.3
Federal and state prisoners per 100,000 residents (1984)	102
Alcohol consumption in gallons per capita (1985)	44.2
Deaths from motor vehicle accidents per 100,000 residents (1985)	17.8

MAJOR CITIES

	1984 population (est.)
Colorado Springs	247,739
Denver	504,566
Fort Collins	70,721
Greeley	54,758
Pueblo	99,967

GOVERNMENT AND POLITICS

Number of US Representatives	6
Electoral votes	8

POLITICAL PARTY NOMINEES FROM STATE

Theodore C. Billings (Constitution)	1964 VP
Earl F. Dodge (Prohibition)	1976 VP
Earl F. Dodge (National Statesman)	1980 VP
Earl F. Dodge (National Statesman)	1984 P

PRESIDENTIAL PRIMARY ELECTION In 1988, Colorado sent 51 Democratic delegates and 36 Republican delegates to the national conventions.

CONSTITUTION Colorado is using its original constitution of 1876.

LEGISLATURE The General Assembly is divided into the Senate (35 members, 4-year term, minimum age 25) and the House of Representatives (65 members, 2-year term, minimum age 25). In 1987, the annual salary was $17,500.

JUDICIARY The highest court is the Supreme Court, with seven judges serving 10-year terms. In 1987, the annual salary was $72,000.

EXECUTIVE The governor serves a 4-year term; the minimum age for holding office is 30. In 1987, the annual salary was $70,000. There are 6 other elected officials.

PRESIDENTIAL VOTE 1948-1988 *(in percents)*

Year	State Winner	Democratic	Republican
1948	Truman (D)	51.9	46.5
1952	Eisenhower (R)	39.0	60.3
1956	Eisenhower (R)	39.8	59.5
1960	Nixon (R)	44.9	54.6
1964	Johnson (D)	61.3	38.2
1968	Nixon (R)	41.3	50.5
1972	Nixon (R)	34.6	62.6
1976	Ford (R)	42.6	54.0
1980	Reagan (R)	31.1	55.1
1984	Reagan (R)	35.1	63.4
1988	Bush (R)	46.0	54.0

GOVERNORS

Territorial Governors

William Gilpin	1861-1862
John Evans	1862-1865
Alexander Cummings	1862-1867
A. Cameron Hunt	1867-1869
Edward M. McCook	1869-1873
Samuel H. Elbert	1873-1874
Edward M. McCook	1874-1875
John L. Routt	1875-1876

State Governors

John L. Routt (R)	1876-1879
Frederick W. Pitkin (R)	1879-1883
James B. Grant (D)	1883-1885
Benjamin H. Eaton (R)	1885-1887
Alva Adams (D)	1887-1889
Job A. Cooper (R)	1889-1891
John L. Routt (R)	1891-1893
Davis H. Waite (Populist)	1893-1895
Albert W. McIntire (R)	1895-1897
Alva Adams (D)	1897-1899
Charles S. Thomas (D)	1899-1901
James B. Orman (D)	1901-1903

James H. Peabody (R)	1903-1905
Alva Adams (D)	1905
James H. Peabody (R)	1905
Jesse F. McDonald (R)	1905-1907
Henry A. Buchtel (R)	1907-1909
John F. Shafroth (D)	1909-1913
Elias M. Ammons (D)	1913-1915
George A. Carlson (R)	1915-1917
Julius C. Gunter (D)	1917-1919
Oliver H. Shoup (R)	1919-1923
William E. Sweet (D)	1923-1925
Clarence J. Morley (R)	1925-1927
William H. Adams (D)	1927-1933
Edwin C. Johnson (D)	1933-1937
Ray H. Talbot (D)	1937
Teller Ammons (D)	1937-1939
Ralph L. Carr (R)	1939-1943
John C. Vivian (R)	1943-1947
William Lee Knous (D)	1947-1950
Walter W. Johnson (D)	1950-1951
Dan Thornton (R)	1951-1955
Edwin C. Johnson (D)	1955-1957
Stephen L.R. McNichols (D)	1957-1963
John A. Love (R)	1963-1973

John Vanderhoof (R)	1973-1975
Richard D. Lamm (D)	1975-1987
Roy Romer (D)	1987-

MINIMUM AGES

Majority	18
Marriage with parental consent . . .	16
Marriage without parental consent .	18
Making a will	18
Buying alcohol	21
Jury duty	18
Leaving school	16
Driver's license	18

CAPITAL PUNISHMENT
Number executed 1976-88: 0
On death row Aug. 1, 1988: 3

MILITARY INSTALLATIONS
Total number: 13
Major bases:
   Army: 1
   Air Force: 2

FINANCES

Thousands of dollars

GENERAL REVENUE (1985)

Total general revenue . . .	4,133,456
Total tax revenue	2,284,417
Sales and gross receipts . . .	1,081,766
Individual income taxes	907,619
Corporate net income taxes . .	101,654

GENERAL EXPENDITURES (1985)

Total general expenditure .	4,251,146
Education	1,833,724
Public welfare	675,957
Health	117,641
Hospital	231,662
Natural resources	107,358
Highways	473,537
Police	31,311
Corrections	81,895

FEDERAL AID (1985) 1,165,999

ECONOMY

About two-fifths of Colorado's land is devoted to agriculture. Cattle is the most valuable farm product; winter wheat is the most important crop, followed by potatoes, beans, onions, lettuce, and tomatoes. Net farm income in 1983 was $334 million.

Mineral and mining products include gold, silver, zinc, and copper (now mostly in low-grade ores), molybdenum, uranium, oil, gravel, sand, and stone. Though mining has decreased in economic importance since the turn of the century, mining equipment is still one of the state's main exports. The manufacturing sector is dominated by food processing, military equipment and defense research and development, aerospace, and electronics. The tourist industry is the third-largest in the state, bringing more than 7 million visitors to Colorado every year.

EMPLOYMENT (1984)

Thousands of persons

Total number of employed workers	1,610
Construction	88.3
Finance, insurance, and real estate	93.3
Government	243.8
Manufacturing	192.3
Mining	36.0
Services	305.4
Transportation, communications, and utilities	85.8
Wholesale and retail trade	340.0

Percent of civilian labor force
unemployed (1984) 5.6

DEPARTMENT OF DEFENSE (1985)

Civilian workers employed . . .	14,125
Military personnel	36,914
Contract awards	$1.563 billion

ENERGY SOURCES FOR ELECTRIC UTILITIES (1983)

Percent

Coal	88.2
Gas	1.2
Hydroelectric	7.4
Nuclear	3.0
Petroleum	0.2

TRANSPORTATION

Motor vehicles registered in state (1986)	2,762,952
Miles of roads, streets, and highways (1986)	76,318
Miles of Class I railway operated (1986)	3,369
Airports (1983)	321
Major aviation hubs (1983)	2
Largest hub: Denver	

CULTURE AND EDUCATION

Native American tribes
Colorado was formerly home to the Apache, Arapaho, Bannock, Cheyenne, Comanche, Kiowa, and Navajo. Groups that continue to live there include the Ute. There are 2 federal reservations in Colorado.

Religions, ethnicities, and languages
Half of the state's population was born in Colorado; immigration is mainly from Europe, Mexico, Canada, and Japan. In 1980, 10.6 percent of the population spoke a language other than English at home.

Major museums and libraries
Colorado Springs Fine Arts Center
Colorado State Museum, Denver
Denver Art Museum
Denver Museum of Natural History
Library and museums of the State Historical Society of Colorado

Major arts organizations
Central City Opera House, Denver
Colorado Ballet, Denver

Denver Center Theatre Company
Denver Symphony Orchestra
Opera Colorado, Denver

Colleges and universities
Number public (1986-87) 29
Number private (1986-87) 23
Total enrollment, in full-time equivalent students (1985) 121,800

Public elementary and secondary schools
Expenditure per pupil in average daily attendance (1986-87) $4,107
Pupil-teacher ratio (1987) 18.2
Average teacher salary (1986-87) $28,400

Major league sports teams
Basketball: Denver Nuggets
Football: Denver Broncos

Holidays
Colorado Day. First Monday in August
State Fair, Pueblo. Last week in August

COLORADO IN LITERATURE

William M. Anderson (ed. Dale L. Morgan and Eleanor T. Harris) *The Rocky Mountain Journals of William Marshall Anderson: The West in 1884* (1986)
Memoir of the fur trade.

Sanora Babb *An Owl on Every Post: A Personal Recollection of Life on the Plains* (1970, rpt. 1972)
Memoir of pioneer life c.1900 by an Oklahoma emigrant.

Harriet F. Backus *Tomboy Bride* (1969, rpt. 1977)
Autobiography of a woman who lived near the Tomboy mine during the boom years.

Edwin Lewis Bennett (ed. Agnes W. Spring) *Boom Town Boy* (1966)
Memoir of the gold camp of Creede in 1893.

Horace Bennett *Bright Yellow Gold* (1935)
Memoirs of the Cripple Creek gold strike.

Isabella Bird (Isabella L. Bird Bishop) *A Lady's Life in the Rocky Mountains* (1879, rpt. 1960)
The author, first woman to be elected fellow of the Royal Geographic Society, visited the Rockies in 1873 and climbed Long's Peak.

Hal C. Borland *Rocky Mountain Tipi Tales* (1924)
Collection of Indian tales.

———. *High, Wide and Lonesome* (1956); *Country Editor's Boy* (1970)
Autobiographies of growing up in the dryland town of Flagler.

Willa Cather *The Song of the Lark* (1915)
Novel about the musically gifted daughter of Swedish immigrants who grows up in a small town in the 1880s and leaves for Chicago to study.

Daniel E. Conner (ed. D. Berthrong and O. Davenport) *A Confederate in the Colorado Gold Fields* (1970)
The author was a member of a small force that attempted to surprise Union garrisons in Colorado and New Mexico in 1862. When the attempt failed, Conner joined the Gold Rush.

David J. Cook *Hands Up; or, Thirty-five Years of Detective Life in the Mountains and on the Plains* (1882, rpt. 1897, 1971)
The chief of police in Denver, and later major-general of militia, describes encounters with desperadoes.

Donald Danker (ed.) *Mollie: The Journal of Mollie Dorsey Sanford, 1857–1866* (1959, rpt. 1976)
Journal of the trek between Indianapolis and Denver, 1857–1865.

C. C. Davis *Olden Times in Colorado* (1916)
Reminiscences of the mining boom by the editor-owner of the Leadville *Chronicle*.

John L. Dyer *The Snow-Shoe Itinerant: An Autobiography* (1890, rpt. 1975, 1977)
Memoirs of an itinerant preacher.

Anne Ellis *The Life of an Ordinary Woman* (1929, rpt. 1980); *Plain Anne Ellis: More About the Life of an Ordinary Woman* (1984)
Detailed record of life in mining towns, c.1890–1920.

Aurelio M. Espinosa (ed. J. M. Espinosa) *The Folklore of Spain in the American Southwest: Traditional Spanish Folk Literature in Northern New Mexico and Southern Colorado* (1985)

John Fante *Dago Red* (1940)
Stories of Italian immigrant life in a small town.

Vardis Fisher *Mountain Man* (1965)
Novel about pioneers in the Rockies in the 1830s.

Mary Hallock Foote *Led Horse Claim* (1883)
Western variation on the Romeo and Juliet story set in a mining camp.

———. *Coeur d'Aléne* (1894)
Novel about the struggle between union and nonunion miners in the Coeur d'Alène region.

Gene Fowler *Salute to Yesterday* (1937)
Picaresque novel about early modern Denver.

Emily French (ed. Janet Lecompte) *Emily: The Diary of a Hard-Worked Woman* (1987)
Journal of a working-class Denver woman in the 1890s.

Dorothy Gardiner *Golden Lady* (1936); *Snow Water* (1939)
Romantic novels set in mining boom days.

———. *Great Betrayal* (1949)
Fictional account of the 1864 Sandy Creek Massacre.

Hamlin Garland *They of the High Trails* (1916)
Stories of western characters of the Rocky Mountains.

Joanne Greenberg *Simple Gifts* (1986)
Novel about the effect of social change on a family of ranchers.

Kent Haruf *The Tie That Binds* (1984)
Novel about a farming family set in northeastern Colorado, 1896–1977.

Alice Polk Hill *Tales of the Colorado Pioneers* (1884, rpt. 1976)

Irving Howbert *Memories of a Lifetime in the Pike's Peak Region* (1925, rpt. 1970)
The author came to Colorado in 1860, took part in the Battle of Sand Creek, and became El Paso County Clerk before his death in 1934.

David Lavender *One Man's West* (1977)
A Western historian's account of growing up in southwestern Colorado during the 1930s.

Mabel B. Lee *Cripple Creek Days* (1984)
Memoir of a settler of 1892.

William Storrs Lee (comp.) *Colorado; a Literary Chronicle* (1970)

Van Wyck Mason *End of the Track* (1943)
Western novel about the coming of the railroad to a small town.

James Michener *Centennial* (1974)
A saga, ranging from prehistoric time to the present, centering on a fictional town.

Joe Mills *A Mountain Boyhood* (1988)
Life in Estes Park c.1910.

Forbes Parkhill *The Wildest of the West* (1951)
Study of Denver's demimonde at the turn of the century.

Eugene Parsons "Colorado Literature" *History of Colorado* (ed. W.F. Stone) vol. 1 (1918)

Clarice E. Richards *A Tenderfoot Bride: Tales from an Old Ranch* (1988)
Pioneer memoir of Elbert County in 1900.

Lorene L. Scott *Colorado Winters* (1939)

Upton Sinclair *King Coal* (1917)
Novel closely based on the coalminers' strike of 1914–1915.

Jean Stafford *The Mountain Lion* (1947)
Novel depicting the unhappy youth of a brother and sister and their escape to a Colorado ranch.

Michael Straight *A Very Small Remnant* (1963)
Fictional account of the Sandy Creek Massacre of a Cheyenne village in 1864.

Richard B. Townshend *A Tenderfoot in Colorado* (1968)
Memoirs of an English immigrant who arrived in the state in 1869.

Frank Waters *Pike's Peak: A Family Saga* (1977)
Semi-autobiographical novel set during the mining boom.

William A. Weber and **Theodore Cockerell** *Letters from West Cliff, Colorado, 1887–1889* (1978)

Virginia L. Wilcox *Colorado: A Selected Bibliography of Its Literature, 1858–1952* (1954)

George F. Willison *Here They Dug the Gold* (1931)
Detailed chronicle of the Gold Rush.

Muriel S. Wolle *Timberline Tailings: Tales of Colorado's Ghost Towns and Mining Camps* (1977)

GUIDES TO RESOURCES

Allen, Gerald L. *Statistical Abstract of Colorado* (1987)

Ayer, Eleanor H. (comp.) *Colorado Chronicles Index* (1986)

Chamblin, Thomas S. (ed.) *The Historical Encyclopedia of Colorado* 2 vols. (rev. ed. 1975)

Colorado. Water Conservation Board *Basic Maps of Colorado and History of Changes in County Boundaries* (1939)

Colorado Legislative Council *A Directory of Colorado State Government* (1984)

Denver Atlas: A Sourcebook of Social and Economic Information Prepared by the Denver Planning Office and the Geography Department of the University of Denver. (1978)

Eichler, George R. *Colorado Place Names. Communities, Peaks, Passes; with Historical Lore and Facts, Plus a Pronunciation Guide* (1977)

Erickson, Kenneth A. and **Albert W. Smith** *Atlas of Colorado* (1985)

Federal Writers' Project *Colorado: A Guide to the Highest State* (1941, rpt. 1980)
————. *The WPA Guide to 1930s Colorado* (1987)

McTighe, James *Roadside History of Colorado* (1984)

Ormes, Robert M. (ed.) *Guide to the Colorado Mountains* (6th ed. 1970)

Tyler, Thomas G. (comp.) *Statistical Abstract of Colorado* (1977)

University of Colorado Business Research Division *What's Published about Colorado* (1978)

University of Colorado Libraries. Western Historical Collections *A Guide to Manuscript Collections* (1977)

Wagner, Henry R. *The Plains and the Rockies: A Bibliography of Original Narratives of Travel and Adventure, 1800–1865* (3rd ed. 1953)

Wynar, Bohdan S. and **Roberta J. Depp** (eds.) *Colorado Bibliography* (1980)

SELECTED NONFICTION SOURCES

Abbott, Carl *Colorado, a History of the Centennial State* (rev. ed. 1982)

Abbott, Morris W. *The Pike's Peak Cog Road* (1972)

Akers, Carl *Carl Akers' Colorado* (1975)

Arps, Louisa W. (ed.) *Faith on the Frontier* (1976)
————. *Denver in Slices* (2d ed. 1983)

Athearn, Frederic J. *An Isolated Empire: A History of Northwest Colorado* (1976, rpt. 1982)

Athearn, Robert G. *Rebel of the Rockies: A History of the Denver and Rio Grande Railroad* (1962)
————. *The Coloradans* (1976)

Baker, James H. and **LeRoy R. Hafen** (eds.) *History of Colorado* 5 vols. (1927)

Bancroft, Caroline *Silver Queen: The Fabulous Story of Baby Doe Tabor* (1950)

————. *Colorful Colorado: Its Dramatic History* (1959, rpt. 1966)
————. *The Unsinkable Molly Brown* (1963)
————. *The Brown Palace in Denver; Hotel of Plush, Power and Presidents* (1974)

Beshoar, Barron B. *Out of the Depths: The Story of John R. Lawson, a Labor Leader* (1942, rpt. 1980)
————. *Hippocrates in a Red Vest: The Biography of a Frontier Doctor* (1973)

Blair, Charles E. *Americans Speak Out* (1972)

Bluemel, Elinor *One Hundred Years of Colorado Women* (1973)

Bollinger, Edward T. (ed. William C. Jones) *Rails That Climb: A Narrative History of the Moffat Road* (1950, rpt. 1979)

Brettell, Richard R. *Historic Denver; the Architects and the Architecture, 1858–1893* (1973)

Brown, Robert L. *Ghost Towns of the Colorado Rockies* (1968)
———. *The Great Pikes Peak Gold Rush* (1985)

Buchholtz, C. W. *Rocky Mountain National Park: A History* (1983)

Bueler, Gladys R. *Colorado's Colorful Characters* (1974)

Bueler, William M. *Roof of the Rockies: A History of Colorado Mountaineering* (2d ed. 1986)

Burger, Rex *Colorado Trivia* (1986)

Busch, Paul *Colorado Sketchbook: A Graphic History of the Early Years* (1976)

Cafky, Morris *The Colorado Midland* (1965)

Casotti, Fred *The Golden Buffaloes: Colorado Football* (1980)

Clifford, Peggy *To Aspen and Back: An American Journey* (1980)

Crossen, Forest *The Switzerland Trail of America* (1962)

Dallas, Sandra *No More Than Five in a Bed: Colorado Hotels in the Old Days* (1967, rpt. 1977)
———. *Cherry Creek Gothic: Victorian Architecture in Denver* (1971)
———. *Yesterday's Denver* (1974)
———. *Gaslights and Gingerbread: Colorado's Historic Homes* (1984)
———. *Colorado Ghost Towns and Mining Camps* (1985)
———. *Colorado Homes* (1986)

Davidson, Levette J. (ed. Leroy R. Hafen) *Colorado and Its People* (1948)

Davis, Sally and Betty Baldwin *Denver Dwellings and Descendants* (1963)

Dempsey, Stanley and James E. Fell *Mining the Summit: Colorado's Ten Mile District, 1860–1960* (1986)

Denver Public Library *Nothing Is Long Ago: A Documentary History of Colorado, 1776–1976* (1975)

Dorset, Phyllis F. *The New Eldorado: The Story of Colorado's Gold and Silver Rushes* (1970)

Dorsett, Lyle W. *The Queen City: A History of Denver* (1977)

Echevarría, Evelio and José Otero *Hispanic Colorado, Four Centuries: History and Heritage* (1976)

Emmitt, Robert *The Last War Trail: The Utes and the Settlement of Colorado* (1954)

Etter, Don *Auraria, Where Denver Began* (1972)

Fossett, Frank *Colorado: Its Gold and Silver Mines, Farms and Stock Ranges, and Health and Pleasure Resorts* (2d ed. 1880, rpt. 1973)

Frink, Maurice *The Boulder Story; Historical Portrait of a Colorado Town* (1965)

Gjevre, John A. *Chili Line, the Narrow Rail Trail to Santa Fe: The Story of . . . Denver and Rio Grande Western's Santa Fe Branch, 1880–1941* (1984)

Goff, Richard and Robert H. McCaffree *Century in the Saddle* (1967)

Griffiths, Mel and Lynnell Rubright *Colorado: A Geography* (1983)

Griswold, Don Luverne and Jean H. *The Carbonate Camp Called Leadville* (1951)

Hafen, LeRoy R. *Colorado: The Story of a Western Commonwealth* (1933)
——— (ed.) *Colorado and Its People: A Narrative and Topical History of the Centennial State* 4 vols. (1948)

Hauck, Cornelius *Narrow Gauge to Central and Silver Plume* (1972)

Henderson, Junius et al. *Colorado: Short Studies of Its Past and Present* (1927)

Hession, Joseph and Michael Spence *Broncos: Three Decades of Football* (1987)

Hoig, Stan *The Sand Creek Massacre* (1961)

Holland, F. Ross *Rocky Mountain National Park; Historical Background Data* (1971)

Hollister, Ovando J. *The Mines of Colorado* (1867, rpt. 1974)

Hosokawa, Bill *Thunder in the Rockies: The Incredible Denver Post* (1976)

Hughes, J. Donald *American Indians in Colorado* (1960, 2d ed. 1987)

Hunt, Inez *To Colorado's Restless Ghosts* (1960)

Hyman, Sidney *The Aspen Idea* (1975)

Jackson, W. Turrentine *Wells Fargo in Colorado Territory* (1982)

Jessen, Kenneth *Railroads of North Colorado* (1982)
———. *Colorado Gunsmoke: True Stories of Outlaws and Lawmen on the Colorado Frontier* (1986)

Johnson, Charles A. *Denver's Mayor Speer* (1970)

Jones, William and Elizabeth *William Henry Jackson's Colorado* (1975)
——— and Kenton Forrest *Denver: A Pictorial History from Frontier Camp to Queen City of the Plains* (1985)

Kania, Alan J. *John Otto of Colorado National Monument* (1984)

Karnes, Thomas L. *William Gilpin, Western Nationalist* (1970)

Kelly, George V. *The Old Gray Mayors of Denver* (1974)

Kelsey, Harry E., Jr. *Frontier Capitalist: The Life of John Evans* (1969)

King, Joseph E. *A Mine to Make a Mine; Financing the Colorado Mining Industry, 1859–1902* (1977)

Knight, Harold V. *Working in Colorado: A Brief History of the Colorado Labor Movement* (1971)

Kohl, Edith E. *Denver's Historic Mansions: Citadels to the Empire Builders* (1957)

Larsen, Charles *The Good Fight: The Remarkable Life and Times of Judge Ben Lindsey, the Colorful American Reformer . . .* (1972)

Lavender, David *Bent's Fort* (1954, rpt. 1972)

Lee, Mabel B. *Cripple Creek Days* (1958)

Loe, Nancy E. *Life in the Altitudes: An Illustrated History of Colorado Springs* (1983)

Look, Al *1,000 Million Years on the Colorado Plateau* (1955)
———. *Unforgettable Characters of Western Colorado* (1966)

Mangan, Terry W. *Colorado on Glass: Colorado's First Half Century As Seen by the Camera; with a Directory of Early Colorado Photographers by Opal Murry Harber* (1975)

Martin, Mary Joy *Twilight Dwellers: Ghosts, Ghouls and Goblins of Colorado* (1985)

May, Stephen *Pilgrimage: A Journey through Colorado's History and Culture* (1987)

McCarthy, G. Michael *Hour of Trial: The Conservation Conflict in Colorado and the West, 1891–1907* (1977)

McClure, Grace *The Bassett Women* (1985)

McKay, Douglas R. *Asylum of the Gilded Pill: The Story of Cragmor Sanatorium* (1983)

McKeehan, Irene P. *Colorado: Short Studies of Its Past and Present* (1927)

Mehls, Steven F. *The New Empire of the Rockies: A History of Northeast Colorado* (1984)

Mills, Enos A. *The Rocky Mountain National Park* (1932)

Monnett, John H. and Michael McCarthy *Colorado Profiles: Men and Women Who Shaped the Centennial State* (1987)

Mumey, Nolie *Pioneer Denver* (1948)

Noel, Thomas J. *The City and the Saloon, Denver, 1858–1916* (1982)

O'Rourke, Paul M. *Frontier in Transition: A History of Southwestern Colorado* (1980)

Parkhill, Forbes *The Wildest of the West* (3d enl. ed. 1957)

Petler, John *The Pikes Peak People; the Story of America's Most Popular Mountain* (1966)

Propst, Nell Brown *Those Strenuous Dames of the Colorado Prairie* (1982)

Richardson, Robert W. and Gordon Chappell *The South Park Line* (1975)

Richmond, Jerry *Denver--America's Mile High Center of Enterprise* (1983)

Robertson, Frank C. and Beth K. Harris *Soapy Smith, King of the Frontier Con Men* (1961)

Rockwell, Wilson *The Utes: A Forgotten People* (1956)

Rohrbough, Malcolm J. *Aspen: The History of a Silver-Mining Town, 1879–1893* (1986)

Schmidt, Cynthia *Colorado: Grassroots* (1984)

Shikes, Robert H. *Rocky Mountain Medicine: Doctors, Drugs, and Disease in Early Colorado* (1986)

Siemer, Eugene *Colorado Climate* (1977)

Smiley, Jerome C. *History of Denver* (1901, rpt. 1971)

Smith, Duane A. *Horace Tabor: His Life and the Legend* (1973)
———. *Silver Saga; the Story of Caribou, Colorado* (1974)
———. *Colorado Mining: A Photographic History* (1977)

Sprague, Marshall *Newport in the Rockies; the Life and Good Times of Colorado Springs* (rev. ed. 1971)
———. *Colorado: A Bicentennial History* (States and the Nation series) (1976)

Stegner, Wallace E. (ed.) *This Is Dinosaur: Echo Park Country and Its Magic Rivers* (1955)

Tushar, Olibama Lopez *The People of "El Valle": A History of the Spanish Colonies in the San Luis Valley* (1976)

Ubbelohde, Carl et al. *A Colorado History* (3d ed. 1972)
——— et al. *A Colorado Reader* (rev. ed. 1982)

Uchill, Ida L. *Pioneers, Peddlers, and Tsadikim* (1957)

Vandenbusche, Duane *A Land Alone, Colorado's Western Slope* (1981)

Villard, Henry *The Past and Present of the Pike's Peak Gold Regions* (1860, rpt. 1972)

Walker, William and D. F. Baber *The Longest Rope: The Truth about the Johnson County Cattle War* (1959)

Walther, Lou *Old Names and Golden Splendors: A Handbook of Colorado Names and Their Origins* (1984)

Waters, Frank *The Colorado* (1985)

Wentworth, Frank L. *Aspen on the Roaring Fork; an Illustrated History of Colorado's "Greatest Silver Camp"* (3d ed. rev. 1976)

West, William A. (photographs by Don D. Etter) *Curtis Park, a Denver Neighborhood* (1980)

Wolle, Muriel S. *Stampede to Timberline: Ghost Towns and Mining Camps of Colorado* (rev. ed. 1974)

Wood, Myron *Colorado; Big Mountain Country* (rev. ed. 1972)

Wright, James E. *The Politics of Populism: Dissent in Colorado* (1974)

CONNECTICUT

Connecticut, one of the original 13 colonies, is the southernmost New England state. It is bordered on the north by Massachusetts; on the east by Rhode Island; on the south by Long Island Sound; and on the west by New York.

FULL NAME State of Connecticut
POSTAL ABBREVIATION CT
INHABITANT Nutmegger
ADMITTED TO THE UNION Jan. 9, 1788.
5th state
POPULATION (est. 1987) 3,211,000.
Percent of US total: 1.32%. Rank: 28th

CAPITAL CITY Hartford, the largest city in the state, located on the Connecticut River in north central Connecticut; population 135,720 (est. 1984). Founded by the Dutch as a fort in 1633, settled by Massachusetts Bay colonists in 1635, it was co-capital of Connecticut, along with New Haven, from 1701 to 1874. It was incorporated as town and city in 1784.

STATE NAME AND NICKNAMES From *quinnehtukqut*, an Indian word meaning "beside the long tidal river." Official nickname: The Constitution State. Also known as the Nutmeg State and the Land of Steady Habits.

STATE SEAL An ellipse, bordered by the legend "Sigillum Reipublicae Connecticutensis" (Seal of the Republic of Connecticut). In the center are three staked grapevines, symbolizing the transplant of Old World culture to the New World, with a streamer bearing the state motto.

MOTTO Qui Transtulit Sustinet (He who transplanted still sustains)

SONG "Yankee Doodle," lyrics from folk tradition, melody from an English tune, "The World Turned Upside Down."

SYMBOLS
Flower mountain laurel
Tree white oak
Bird American robin
Mineral garnet
Animal sperm whale
Insect praying mantis
Ship U.S.S. Nautilus

LICENSE PLATES (1) White on dark blue, with white border and state outline. (2) White on dark blue, with white border, some with legend "Constitution State." (3) Dark blue on white, with blue border, state outline, and legend "Combination." (4) Dark blue on white, with blue border and legend "Constitution State." (5) Medium blue on white, with blue border and legend "Combination."

FLAG A field of azure, bearing the state coat of arms, a white rococo shield bordered by gold and embroidered with three staked and fruited grapevines. Below the shield is a white streamer bordered by gold and brown and bearing the state motto in dark blue letters.

GEOGRAPHY AND CLIMATE

Connecticut's three main geographical regions are the Western Uplands, including the eastern end of the Berkshire Range; the Connecticut Valley, a narrow wedge of fertile land drained by the Connecticut River; and the Western Uplands, a hilly region of dairy farms. Stretches of beach and rocky coves line Connecticut's coast along Long Island Sound.

AREA 5,108 square miles. Rank: 48th
INLAND WATER 146 square miles
GEOGRAPHIC CENTER Hartford, at East Berlin
ELEVATIONS *Highest point:* Mount Frissell, Litchfield County, 2,380. *Lowest point:* Long Island Sound, sea level. *Mean elevation:* 500 feet

MAJOR RIVERS Connecticut, Housatonic, Thames

MAJOR LAKE Candlewood

TIDAL SHORELINE 618 miles, coast of Long Island Sound

LAND USE

	Thousands of acres
Urban (1982)	603
Rural (1982)	2,401
Cropland (1982)	245
Pastureland (1982)	114
Rangeland (1982)	0
Forestland (1982)	1,828
State parks and recreation areas (1983)	167
National park system (1984)	3
National forest system (1984)	0
Tribal lands (1984)	0

TEMPERATURES The highest recorded temperature was 105°F on July 22, 1926, at Waterbury. The lowest was -32°F on February 16, 1943, at Falls Village.

NATIONAL SITES

NATIONAL SCENIC TRAIL Appalachian
NATIONAL WILDLIFE REFUGE Salt Meadow

HISTORY

1614	Adriaen Block sails up the Connecticut River and claims the region for the Dutch. Between 6,000 and 7,000 Indians of the Algonkian family live in the area. Mohicans and Pequots are best known.
1632	*March 19.* The English secure a grant from Earl of Warwick that includes the Connecticut area.
1633	*June 6.* The Dutch purchase land from the Pequot Indians and erect a fort and a trading post at present site of Hartford.
1635	English settlers under John Winthrop, Jr. erect a fort at Saybrook.
1636	*Spring.* Thomas Hooker and his congregation settle at Hartford.
1637	Pequot Indians war against the colonists. *July 13.* Swamp fight near Fairfield breaks the Indians' power.
1638	*June.* Earthquake shakes southern Connecticut.
1639	*January 14.* First written constitution, The Fundamental Orders of Connecticut, is adopted.
1654	English colonists seize the Dutch fort and trading post at Hartford.
1657	Shipbuilding begins at Derby on the Housatonic River.
1665	*January 5.* New Haven is annexed.
1675–1676	King Philip's War. Colonist troops defeat the Wampanoag Indians ending the war in the Connecticut region.
1687	*October 31.* Sir Edmund Andros arrives in Hartford to seize Connecticut's charter in plan to incorporate all of New England under British Dominion.
1701	Collegiate School is founded. As Yale it becomes the nation's third-oldest university.
1717–1718	Collegiate School moves to New Haven from Saybrook and is renamed Yale College.
1740	First tinware in America is manufactured at Berlin in central Connecticut.
1744	Beginning of King George's War. Connecticut enlists 1,100 men to fight French and Indians.
1755	First Connecticut newspaper, *The Connecticut Gazette*, is published in New Haven.
1777	*April.* British raid supply depots at Danbury.

1779	New Haven is attacked and Fairfield and Norwalk burned.
1781	Connecticut-born Benedict Arnold leads British troops to raid and burn New London.
1784	America's first law school is founded at Litchfield.
1788	*January 8.* Connecticut ratifies the US Constitution.
1792	The first toll-gate turnpike is incorporated.
1795	The Mutual Assurance Company of Norwich is incorporated. Hartford becomes known as the insurance center of the US.
1798	Mass production is born when inventor Eli Whitney uses standard parts to produce muskets in Whitneyville.
1806	Noah Webster publishes first American dictionary at New Haven.
1812–1814	War of 1812. Connecticut contributes 3,000 men. Many Connecticut privateers run the British blockade.
1814	*August 9–13.* British bombard Stonington.
1825	*July 4.* Construction begins on the Farmington Canal. Connecticut hoped its canal system would compete with the great Erie Canal system.
1826	Boundary dispute with Massachusetts is finally settled.
1831	Wesleyan University, Middletown, is organized.
1833	Hartford and New Haven Railroad is incorporated.
1849	Teacher's College of Connecticut is founded at New Britain.
1861–1865	Civil War. Connecticut, which abolished slavery in 1784, furnishes over 57,000 men.
1878	*January 28.* The first commercial telephone exchange in the world is established in New Haven.
1881	Connecticut University is organized at Storrs in northeastern Connecticut.
1882	National organization of Knights of Columbus is founded at New Haven.
1888	*March 12–14.* A great blizzard devastates much of the state.
1893	*August 24.* Severe storm damages Connecticut Valley's tobacco crop.
1910	Coast Guard Academy moves to New London.
1915	Connecticut College for Women opens at New London.
1916	German submarine, *Deutschland*, docks at New London.
1917	A submarine base begins operation in Groton, Connecticut.
1917–1918	World War I. Connecticut becomes a munitions supply center. It contributes over 60,000 men to the armed forces.
1920	Brainard Field in Hartford becomes the country's first city-owned airport.
1922	WDRC, Connecticut's first radio station, begins broadcasting at Hartford.
1930	The Depression creates widespread unemployment. Connecticut recovers slowly since manufacturing is one of the hardest hit areas.
1932	The state's jobless number more than 150,000.
1934	*February 19–20.* Another disastrous blizzard strikes the state.
1935	*June 5. The Comet,* first streamlined train on the New Haven system, makes its initial run. State celebrates its tercentenary of first settlers coming to the area (1635).
1936	Connecticut's annual report lists 21 aviation fields, 765 licensed pilots, and 322 registered aircraft.
1937	Merit system is inaugurated in state departments.
1941–1945	World War II. Connecticut becomes an important supplier of war materials. Its many factories produce airplane engines and propellers, submarines, shell cases, small arms, and other supplies.
1954	*January. Nautilus,* first atomic-powered submarine, is launched at Groton.
1960s	New Haven and Hartford begin busing programs.
1963	*October.* Yale University selects a new president, Kingman Brewster, Jr.
1969	*September.* Race riots in black and Puerto Rican sections of Hartford are worst in city's history.
1973	A solid waste agency is created with bonding power of $250 million to establish statewide refuse disposal and recycling facilities.
1974	First woman governor elected without succeeding her husband is Connecticut's Ella Grasso.
1978	*February 6–7.* Up to 25 inches of snow fall on the state in less than 30 hours. All roads and highways are closed. Nine persons die.

1983	A major road-building program begins as one of the state's main endeavors to improve the nearly 20,000 miles of its highways.
1984	*November 13.* Ellen Ash Peters is named to the Connecticut Supreme Court by Governor O'Neill. She is the first woman so named.
1988	Yale students erect shanty on campus to protest University investments in South African firms. During alumni reunion, a Yale alumnus sets fire to the shanty. He is arrested and sentenced.

DEMOGRAPHY

Population (est. 1987) . . . 3,211,000
Population (1980) 3,107,576
Population density in persons
   per square mile (1980) 619.3

POPULATION BY RACE (1980)
American Indian/Aleut/
   Eskimo 4,533
Asian/Pacific Islander 18,970
Black 217,433
Hispanic 124,499
White 2,799,420
Other 67,220

POPULATION CHARACTERISTICS (1980)
Percent of state population
Urban 78.8
Rural 21.2
Under 18 . . . . 26.5
65 or older 11.7
College-educated 21.2
Families below poverty line 6.2
Public-assistance recipients 5.2

Per capita personal
   income (1986) $19,208
Millionaires per 100,000
   residents (1982) 300.7
Average life expectancy in
   years (1980) 75.1

Marriage rate per 1,000
   residents (1986) 8.2
Divorce rate per 1,000
   residents (1986) 2.9
Birth rate per 1,000
   residents (1985) 11.6
Infant mortality rate per 1,000
   births (1985) 11.2
Abortion rate per 1,000
   live births (1985) . . . . 550.
Crime rate per 100,000 residents (1985)
   Violent 425.8
   Property 4,403.0
Federal and state prisoners (1984) . 184
Alcohol consumption in gallons
   per capita (1985) 37.1
Deaths from motor vehicle accidents
   per 100,000 residents (1985) . . 14.0

MAJOR CITIES

	1984 population (est.)
Bridgeport	142,140
Bristol	58,068
Danbury	63,240
Hartford	135,720
Meriden	57,989
New Britain	72,537
New Haven	124,188
Norwalk	78,189
Stamford	101,917
Waterbury	102,861

GOVERNMENT AND POLITICS

Number of US Representatives   6
Electoral votes   8

POLITICAL PARTY NOMINEES FROM STATE
Sam Huntington	1789	P
John A. Conant (American		
Prohibition)	1884	VP
Jim Lewis (Libertarian)	1984	VP

PRESIDENTIAL PRIMARY ELECTION In 1988, Connecticut sent 59 Democratic delegates and 35 Republican delegates to the national conventions.

CONSTITUTION Connecticut has had two constitutions, 1818 and the present one, adopted in 1965.

LEGISLATURE The General Assembly is divided into the Senate (36 members, 2-year term, minimum age 18) and the House of Representatives (151 members, 2-year term, minimum age 18). In 1987, the annual salary was $15,200.

JUDICIARY The highest court is the Supreme Court, with seven judges serving 8-year terms. In 1987, the annual salary was $77,283.

EXECUTIVE The governor serves a 4-year term; the minimum age for holding office is 30. In 1987, the annual salary was $78,000. There are 5 other elected officials.

PRESIDENTIAL VOTE 1948-1988 *(in percents)*

Year	State Winner	Democratic	Republican
1948	Dewey (R)	47.9	49.6
1952	Eisenhower (R)	43.9	55.7
1956	Eisenhower (R)	36.3	63.7
1960	Nixon (R)	46.3	53.7
1964	Johnson (D)	67.8	32.1
1968	Humphrey (D)	49.5	44.3
1972	Nixon (R)	40.1	58.6
1976	Ford (R)	42.6	54.0
1980	Reagan (R)	38.5	48.2
1984	Reagan (R)	38.8	60.7
1988	Bush (R)	47.0	53.0

GOVERNORS

Governors of New Haven Colony
Theophilus Eaton	1639-1658
Francis Newman	1658-1660
William Leete	1661-1664

Governors of Connecticut Colony
John Haynes	1639-1640
Edward Hopkins	1640-1641
John Haynes	1641-1642
George Wyllys	1642-1643
John Haynes	1643-1644
Edward Hopkins	1644-1645
John Haynes	1645-1646
Edward Hopkins	1646-1647
John Haynes	1647-1648
Edward Hopkins	1648-1649
John Haynes	1649-1650
Edward Hopkins	1650-1651
John Haynes	1651-1652
Edward Hopkins	1652-1653
John Haynes	1653-1654
Edward Hopkins	1654-1655
Thomas Welles	1655-1656
John Webster	1656-1657
John Winthrop Jr.	1657-1658
Thomas Welles	1658-1659
John Winthrop Jr.	1659-1676
William Leete	1676-1683
Robert Treat	1683-1687
Sir Edmund Andros	1687-1689
Robert Treat	1689-1698
Fitz-John Winthrop	1698-1707
Gurdon Saltonstall	1707-1724
Joseph Talcott	1724-1741
Jonathan Law	1741-1750
Roger Wolcott	1750-1754
Thomas Fitch	1754-1766
William Pitkin	1766-1769
Jonathan Trumbull Sr.	1769-1776

State Governors
Jonathan Trumbull Sr.	1776-1784
Matthew Griswold	1784-1786
Samuel Huntington (Federalist)	1786-1796
Oliver Wolcott (Federalist)	1796-1797
Jonathan Trumbull Jr. (Federalist)	1797-1809
John Treadwell (Federalist)	1809-1811
Roger Griswold (Federalist)	1811-1812
John Cotton Smith (Federalist)	1812-1817
Oliver Wolcott (Toleration Party)	1817-1827
Gideon Tomlinson (Democratic-Republican)	1827-1831
John S. Peters (National Republican)	1831-1833
Henry W. Edwards (D)	1833-1834
Samuel A. Foot (Whig)	1834-1835
Henry W. Edwards (D)	1835-1838
William W. Ellsworth (Whig)	1838-1842
Chauncey F. Cleveland (D)	1842-1844
Roger S. Baldwin (Whig)	1844-1846
Isaac Toucey (D)	1846-1847
Clark Bissell (Whig)	1847-1849
Joseph Trumbull (Whig)	1849-1850
Thomas H. Seymour (D)	1850-1853
Charles H. Pond (D)	1853-1854
Henry Dutton (Whig)	1854-1855
William T. Minor (Know-Nothing)	1855-1857
Alexander H. Holley (Whig)	1857-1858
William A. Buckingham (R)	1858-1866
Joseph R. Hawley (R)	1866-1867
James E. English (D)	1867-1869
Marshall Jewell (R)	1869-1870
James E. English (D)	1870-1871
Marshall Jewell (R)	1871-1873
Charles R. Ingersoll (D)	1873-1877
Richard D. Hubbard (D)	1877-1879
Charles B. Andrews (R)	1879-1881
Hobart B. Bigelow (R)	1881-1883
Thomas M. Waller (D)	1883-1885
Henry B. Harrison (R)	1885-1887
Phineas C. Lounsbury (R)	1887-1889

Morgan G. Bulkeley (R)	1889-1893
Luzon B. Morris (D)	1893-1895
O. Vincent Coffin (R)	1895-1897
Lorrin A. Cooke (R)	1897-1899
George E. Lounsbury (R)	1899-1901
George P. McLean (R)	1901-1903
Abiram Chamberlain (R)	1903-1905
Henry Roberts (R)	1905-1907
Rollin S. Woodruff (R)	1907-1909
George L. Lilley (R)	1909
Frank B. Weeks (R)	1909-1911
Simeon E. Baldwin (D)	1911-1915
Marcus H. Holcomb (R)	1915-1921
Everett J. Lake (R)	1921-1923
Charles A. Templeton (R)	1923-1925
Hiram Bingham (R)	1925
John H. Trumbull (R)	1925-1931
Wilbur L. Cross (D)	1931-1939
Raymond E. Baldwin (R)	1939-1941
Robert A. Hurley (D)	1941-1943
Raymond E. Baldwin (R)	1943-1946
Wilbert Snow (D)	1946-1947
James L. McConaughy (R)	1947-1948
James C. Shannon (R)	1948-1949
Chester Bowles (D)	1949-1951
John Davis Lodge (R)	1951-1955
Abraham A. Ribicoff (D)	1955-1961
John N. Dempsey (D)	1961-1971
Thomas J. Meskill (R)	1971-1975
Ella T. Grasso (D)	1975-1980
William A. O'Neill (D)	1981-

MINIMUM AGES

Majority	18
Marriage with parental consent	16
Marriage without parental consent	18
Making a will	18
Buying alcohol	21
Jury duty	18
Leaving school	16
(if employed)	14
Driver's license	16

CAPITAL PUNISHMENT
Number executed 1976-88: 0.
On death row, Aug. 1, 1988: 1

MILITARY INSTALLATIONS
Total number: 6
Major bases:
  Navy: 1

FINANCES

Thousands of dollars

GENERAL REVENUE (1985)

Total general revenue	5,697,963
Total tax revenue	3,497,970
Sales and gross receipts	2,379,145
Individual income taxes	291,640
Corporate net income taxes	489,507

GENERAL EXPENDITURE (1985)

Total general expenditure	4,871,035
Education	1,279,610
Public welfare	953,287
Health	118,684
Hospitals	360,143
Natural resources	38,647
Highways	443,415
Police	53,903
Corrections	128,997

FEDERAL AID (1985) 1,377,388

ECONOMY

Agriculture has long been in decline in Connecticut as land values have risen, especially in the postwar period. Shade-grown wrapping tobacco—the best in the world is grown along the Connecticut River Valley—is the primary crop, yielding $66 million in revenue in 1982, followed by potatoes, truck vegetables, apples, strawberries, and ornamentals. Cattle, milk, and cheese are the main livestock products. Connecticut was an early center for the brass, firearms, rubber, and small machinery industries; today the manufacturing sector is dominated by high-tech and defense industries making jet engines, helicopters, and submarines. Mining products include traprock, sand and gravel, feldspar, and clay. Hartford is the center of the nation's insurance industry.

EMPLOYMENT (1984)

Thousands of persons

Total number of employed workers	1,595
Construction	61.0
Finance, insurance, and real estate	123.1
Government	185.8
Manufacturing	418.6
Mining	1.4
Services	335.5
Transportation, communications, and utilities	66.5
Wholesale and retail trade	333.8

Percent of civilian labor force unemployed (1984)	4.6

DEPARTMENT OF DEFENSE (1985)

Civilian workers employed	4,954
Military personnel	6,526
Contract awards	$5.543 billion

ENERGY SOURCES FOR ELECTRIC UTILITIES (1983)

Percent

Coal	0
Gas	0
Hydroelectric	1.6
Nuclear	48.5
Petroleum	50.0

TRANSPORTATION

Motor vehicles registered
in state (1986) 2,562,349

Miles of roads, streets,
and highways (1986) 19,688
Miles of Class I railway
operated (1986) 466
Airports (1983) 105
Major aviation hubs (1983) 1
Largest hub: Hartford
Major ports, with gross tonnage in
thousands (1985):
New Haven 9,349

CULTURE AND EDUCATION

Native American tribes

Connecticut was formerly home to the Mattabesec, Mohegan, Narragansett, Nipmuc, Pocomtuc, Podunk, and Quinnipiac tribes. Groups that continue to live in the state include the Mahican, Niantic, Pequawket, Pequot, and Wappinger.

Religions, ethnicities, and languages

Originally settled by the Dutch and English, Connecticut received most of its 19th-century immigrants from Ireland, French Canada, Italy, Russia, and central Europe; after World War II it received Black Americans and Puerto Ricans. In 1980, 14.3 percent of Connecticut's population spoke a language other than English at home. The majority of the state's residents are Protestant, but Roman Catholics constitute the single largest religious minority.

Major museums and libraries

Mystic Seaport Museum, Mystic
Peabody Museum of Natural History, New Haven
Wadsworth Atheneum, Hartford

Yale University Art Gallery, New Haven

Major arts organizations

American Shakespeare Festival Theatre, Stratford
Connecticut Opera Association, Hartford
Goodspeed Opera House, East Haddam
Hartford Stage Company
Hartford Symphony Orchestra
Long Wharf Theatre, New Haven
New Haven Symphony Orchestra
Yale Repertory Theatre, New Haven

Colleges and universities

Number public (1986-87) 24
Number private (1986-87) 25
Total enrollment, in full-time equivalent students (1985) 107,800

Public elementary and secondary schools

Expenditure per pupil in average daily attendance (1986-87) $5,552
Pupil-teacher ratio (1987) 13.7
Average teacher salary (1986-87) $30,193

Major league sports teams

Hockey: Hartford Whalers

CONNECTICUT IN LITERATURE

Bronson Alcott *New Connecticut* (1887)
Autobiography of the educational reformer and transcendentalist.

Hal Borland *This Hill, This Valley* (1957); *Beyond Your Doorstep: A Handbook to the Country* (1962)
Descriptions by a naturalist of life on his farm near Salisbury.

Rose Terry Cooke *Somebody's Neighbors* (1881); *The Sphinx's Children and Other People's* (1886); *Huckleberries Gathered from New England Hills* (1891)
Short stories of rural northwestern Connecticut portraying the decline of traditional Yankee virtues. Cooke was also the author of a historical novel of colonial days, *Steadfast* (1889)

James Gould Cozzens *The Last Adam* (1933)
Satiric novel of manners set in a farming town.

Wilbur L. Cross *Connecticut Yankee* (1943)
Autobiography of a Yale scholar and state governor.

John W. DeForest *History of the Indians of Connecticut* (1853)
Indian life to 1850, described by a novelist who lived in New Haven. *Seacliff, or the Mystery of the Westervelts* (1859), a lesser novel of the author's, is set in the state.

Peter De Vries *The Tunnel of Love* (1954); *Reuben, Reuben* (1964)
Comic novels of domestic intrigue set in southern Connecticut suburbs.

Edna Ferber *American Beauty* (1931)
Historical novel tracing many generations of a Connecticut family.

Hannah Webster Foster *The Coquette; or, The History of Eliza Wharton* (1797)
Epistolary novel of sexual intrigue and seduction, reputedly based on the lives of Hartford residents. Enormously popular in its time, the novel is now remembered as one of the earliest works of American fiction.

Lewis Gannett *Cream Hill* (1949)
Account of life on a northwest Connecticut farm.

Donald Grant Mitchell *Dr. Johns* (1866)
Novel about early-nineteenth-century village life by an essayist and lecturer who described the pleasures of a secluded life on his New London County farm in several volumes of essays, including *My Farm of Edgewood* (1863), and *Rural Studies* (1867).

Inge Morath and **Arthur Miller** *In the Country* (1977)
Photographs and text depict vanished pastoral scenes of rural Connecticut destroyed by development.

Ann Petry *Country Place* (1947); *The Narrows* (1953)
Novels set in the town of Lennox, and in the Monmouth ghetto, by a black writer brought up in Old Saybrook.

Christopher Rand *The Changing Landscape: Salisbury, Connecticut* (1968)
Essays portraying change in a small town, written 1952–1966.

Odell Shepard *Connecticut: Past and Present* (1939)
Observations on local history and landscape.

Max Shulman *Rally Round the Flag, Boys!* (1957)
Rival socio-economic groups struggle for dominance in a small town.

Harriet Beecher Stowe *Poganuc People* (1878)
Novel about small-town New England society, closely based on the author's childhood experiences of Litchfield.

Gladys Taber *Stillmeadow Sampler* (1959); (ed. Constance Taber Colby) *The Best of Stillmeadow: A Treasury of Country Living* (1976)
Essays on rural life and customs.

Edwin Way Teale *A Walk through the Year* (1978)
Observations of seasonal change on a Connecticut farm.

Charles Burr Todd *In Olde Connecticut* (1906)
Essays in regional history.

GUIDES TO RESOURCES

Clark, Rheta, David M. Roth, and **Arthur E. Soderlind** (comps.) *Connecticut Yesterday and Today: A Selected Bibliography for Connecticut Schools* (1974)

Federal Writers' Project *Connecticut: A Guide to Its Roads, Lore, and People* (1938, rpt. 1980)

Kemp, Thomas Jay *Connecticut Researcher's Handbook* (1981)

Parks, Roger (ed.) *Connecticut: A Bibliography of Its History* (Bibliographies of New England History, Vol. 6) (1986)

Schnare, Robert E. *Local Historical Resources in Connecticut: A Guide to Their Use* (1975)

SELECTED NONFICTION SOURCES

Allis, Marguerite *Connecticut Trilogy* (1934)
——. *Connecticut River* (1939)

Andersen, Ruth O. *From Yankee to American: Connecticut 1865 to 1914* (1975)

Andrews, Charles M. *Connecticut's Place in Colonial History* (1924)

Barrow, Thomas C. *Connecticut Joins the Revolution* (1973)

Bingham, Harold J. *History of Connecticut* 4 vols. (1962)

Black, Robert C., III *The Younger John Winthrop* (1966)

Blanchard, Fessenden S. *Long Island Sound* (1958)

Bollier, David *Crusaders and Criminals, Victims and Visionaries: Historic Encounters Between Connecticut Citizens and the United States Supreme Court* (1986)

Boutell, Lewis H. *The Life of Roger Sherman* (1896)

Buel, Richard, Jr. *Dear Liberty: Connecticut's Mobilization for the Revolutionary War* (1980)

Bushman, Richard L. *From Puritan to Yankee: Character and the Social Order in Connecticut, 1690–1765* (1967)

Callahan, North *Connecticut's Revolutionary War Leaders* (1973)

Cohen, Sheldon S. *Connecticut's Loyalist Gadfly: The Reverend Samuel Andrew Peters* (1976)

Collier, Christopher *Roger Sherman's Connecticut: Yankee Politics and the American Revolution* (1971)
——. *Connecticut in the Continental Congress* (1973)

Cowie, A. *John Trumbull: Connecticut Wit* (1936)

Cutler, Charles C. *Mystic; the Story of a Small New England Seaport* (1945)
——. *Connecticut's Revolutionary Press* (1975)

Daniels, Bruce C. *Connecticut's First Family: William Pitkin and His Connections* (1975)
——. *The Connecticut Town: Growth and Development, 1635–1790* (1979)

Day, Clive *The Rise of Manufacturing in Connecticut 1820–1850* (1935)

Decker, Robert O. *Whaling Industry of New London* (1973)
——. *The Whaling City: A History of New London* (1976)

Deming, Dorothy *The Settlement of Connecticut Towns* (1933)

Destler, Chester M. *Connecticut: The Provisions State* (1973)

East, Robert A. *Connecticut's Loyalists* (1974)

Feinstein, Estelle *Stamford in the Gilded Age: The Political Life of a Connecticut Town, 1868–1893* (1984)
—— and **Joyce S. Pendry** *Stamford: An Illustrated History* (1984)

Fennelly, Catherine *Connecticut Women in the Revolutionary Era* (1975)

Frost, J. William *Connecticut Education in the Revolutionary Era* (1974)

Garvan, Anthony *Architecture and Town Planning in Colonial Connecticut* (1951)

Gerlach, Larry R. *Connecticut Congressman: Samuel Huntington, 1731–1796* (1976)

Grant, Charles *Democracy in the Frontier Town of Kent* (1961)

Groff, William H. *The Population of Connecticut: A Decade of Change, 1970–1980* (1982)

Hart, Samuel (ed. K. W. Cameron) *Old Connecticut: Historical Papers on People, Places, Traditions, and Early Anglicanism* (1976)

Hayes, John T. *Connecticut's Revolutionary Cavalry: Sheldon's Horse* (1975)

Howard, L. *The Connecticut Wits* (1943)

Hoyt, Joseph *The Connecticut Story* (1961)

Hughes, Arthur H. and **Morse S. Allen** *Connecticut Place Names* (1976)

Ifkovic, John W. *Connecticut's Nationalist Revolutionary: Jonathan Trumbull, Junior* (1977)

Jacobus, Melancthon W. *The Connecticut River Steamboat Story* (1956)

Janick, Herbert F. *A Diverse People: Connecticut 1914 to the Present* (1975)

Jeffries, John W. *Testing the Roosevelt Coalition: Connecticut Society and Politics in the Era of World War II* (1978)

Koenig, Samuel *Immigrant Settlements in Connecticut: Their Growth and Characteristics* (1956)

Larned, Ellen D. *History of Windham County, Connecticut* 2 vols. (1874–1880, rpt. 1975)

Lee, W. Storrs *The Yankees of Connecticut* (1957)

Lewis, Thomas R. and **John E. Harmon** *Connecticut, a Geography* (1986)

Lieberman, Joseph I. *The Power Broker: A Biography of John M. Bailey, Modern Political Boss* (1966)

Lucas, Paul R. *Valley of Discord: Church and Society along the Connecticut River: 1636–1725* (1976)

Main, Jackson T. *Connecticut Society in the Era of the American Revolution* (1977)

McCaughey, Elizabeth P. *From Loyalist to Founding Father: The Political Odyssey of William Samuel Johnson* (1980)

McDevitt, Robert F. *Connecticut Attacked: A British Viewpoint, Tryon's Raid on Danbury* (1974)

Meyer, David R. *Urban Change in Central Connecticut* (1976)

Meyer, Freeman W. *Connecticut Congregationalism in the Revolutionary Era* (1977)

Miller, James W. *As We Were on the Valley Shore: An Informal History of Sixteen Connecticut Towns* (1976)

Morse, Jarvis M. *A Neglected Period of Connecticut's History, 1818–1850* (1933)

Niven, John *Connecticut for the Union: The Role of the State in the Civil War* (1965)
————. *Connecticut Hero: Israel Putnam* (1977)

Osterweis, Rollin G. *Three Centuries of New Haven, 1638–1938* (1953)

Parker, Wyman W. *Connecticut's Colonial and Continental Money* (1976)

Parrington, Vernon L. *The Connecticut Wits* (1927)

Purcell, Richard J. *Connecticut in Transition, 1775–1818* (1918)

Rolleston, Sara E. *Heritage Houses: The American Tradition in Connecticut, 1660–1910* (1979)

Rome, Adam W. *Connecticut's Cannon: The Salisbury Iron Furnace in the American Revolution* (1977)

Roth, David M. *Connecticut's War Governor: Jonathan Trumbull* (1974)
————. *Connecticut: A Bicentennial History* (States and the Nation series) (1979)

Sandler, Martin W. *This Was Connecticut: Images of a Vanished World* (1977)

Shelton, Jane DeForest *Salt Box House: Eighteenth-Century Life in a New England Hill Town* (1900)

Shepard, Odell *Connecticut Past and Present* (1939)

Stark, Bruce P. *Connecticut Signer: William Williams* (1975)

Strother, Horatio T. *The Underground Railroad in Connecticut* (1962)

Taylor, John M. *Roger Ludlow: The Colonial Lawmaker* (1900)
————. *The Witchcraft Delusion in Colonial Connecticut* (1908, rpt. 1969)

Taylor, Robert J. *Colonial Connecticut: A History* (1979)

Tedone, David (ed.) *A History of Connecticut's Coast* (1982)

Tolis, Peter *Elihu Burritt: Crusader for Brotherhood* (1968)

Trecker, Janice L. *Preachers, Rebels, and Traders: Connecticut 1818 to 1865* (1975)

Trowbridge, B. C. *Old Houses of Connecticut* (1923)

Tucker, Louis L. *Connecticut's Seminary of Sedition: Yale College* (1974)

Van Dusen, Albert E. *Connecticut* (1961)
————. *Puritans against the Wilderness: Connecticut History to 1973* (1975)

Wallace, Willard M. *Connecticut's Dark Star of the Revolution: General Benedict Arnold* (1978)

Warfel, Harry R. *Noah Webster: Schoolmaster to America* (1936)

Warren, William L. *Connecticut Art and Architecture: Looking Backwards Two Hundred Years* (1976)

Weaver, Glenn *Jonathan Trumbull: Connecticut's Merchant Magistrate (1710–1785)* (1956)

Welsh, Marvis O. *Prudence Crandall: A Biography* (1983)

White, David O. *Connecticut's Black Soldiers, 1775–1783* (1973)

Willingham, William F. *Connecticut Revolutionary: Eliphalet Dyer* (1976)

Wroth, Lawrence C. *Abel Buell of Connecticut: Silversmith, Type Founder and Engraver* (2d ed. 1958)

Zeichner, Oscar *Connecticut's Years of Controversy, 1750–1776* (1970)

Zunder, Theodore A. *The Early Days of Joel Barlow: A Connecticut Wit, Yale Graduate, Editor, Lawyer, and Poet Chaplain during the Revolutionary War. His Life and Works from 1754 to 1787* (1934, rpt. 1969)

DELAWARE

Delaware, one of the original 13 colonies, is on the South Atlantic coast of the US. It is bordered on the north by Pennsylvania; on the east by New Jersey, Delaware Bay, and the Atlantic Ocean; and on the south and west by Maryland.

FULL NAME State of Delaware
POSTAL ABBREVIATION DE
INHABITANT Delawarean
ADMITTED TO THE UNION Dec. 7, 1787.
1st state
POPULATION (est. 1987) 644,000.
Percent of US total: 0.26%. Rank: 47th

CAPITAL CITY Dover, located in central Delaware; population 23,512 (1980). Founded in 1717 by order of William Penn, it became the state capital in 1777 and was incorporated as a town in 1829 and as a city in 1929.

STATE NAME AND NICKNAMES Named after Sir Thomas West, Lord De La Warr, first colonial governor of Virginia. Also known as the First State, the Peach State, and the Diamond State.

STATE SEAL A farmer and a rifleman on either side of a shield, with the state motto on a streamer below them. On the upper part of the shield is a sheaf of wheat and an ear of maize; on the lower, a cow; above the shield is a ship in full sail. Around the border of this coat of arms is the legend "Great Seal of the State of Delaware, 1793, 1847, 1907."

MOTTO Liberty and Independence

SONG "Our Delaware," lyrics by George B. Hynson, music by Will M.S. Brown.

SYMBOLS
Flower peach blossom
Tree American holly
Bird blue hen chicken
Mineral sillimanite
Fish weakfish
Bug ladybug
Beverage milk

LICENSE PLATE Gold on dark blue with gold border and legend "The First State."

FLAG On a field of blue, a yellow diamond bearing the coat of arms from the state seal; below the diamond is the legend "December 7, 1787."

GEOGRAPHY AND CLIMATE

Delaware, the second smallest state in total area, is also the second lowest in average elevation. Lagoons, shallow bays, and long sandy beaches border Delaware's flatlands, part of the Atlantic Coastal Plain. The Delaware River feeds into Delaware Bay, the state's main inlet.

AREA 2,044 square miles. Rank: 49th

INLAND WATER 112 square miles

GEOGRAPHIC CENTER Kent, 11 miles S of Dover

ELEVATIONS *Highest point:* Ebright Road, Newcastle County, 442 feet. *Lowest point:* Atlantic Ocean, sea level. *Mean elevation:* 60 feet

MAJOR RIVERS Delaware, Nanticoke, Christina

MAJOR LAKE Lum's Pond

TIDAL SHORELINE 381 miles, Atlantic coast

LAND USE

	Thousands of acres
Urban (1982)	128
Rural (1982)	1,039
Cropland (1982)	519
Pastureland (1982)	35
Rangeland (1982)	0
Forestland (1982)	348
State parks and recreation areas (1983)	10
National park system (1984)	0
National forest system (1984)	0
Tribal lands (1984)	0

TEMPERATURES The highest recorded temperature was 110°F on July 21, 1930, at Millsboro. The lowest was -17°F on January 17, 1893, at Millsboro.

NATIONAL SITES

NATIONAL WILDLIFE REFUGES Bombay Hook, Prime Hook

HISTORY

1609	*August 28.* Henry Hudson, sailing for the Dutch East Indies, discovers Delaware Bay and establishes basis for Netherland territorial claims.
1610	Lord de la Warr, governor of the Virginia Colony, sends a ship to explore the bay and river, naming both for himself.
1629	Dutch East India Company agents begin negotiations with Lenni-Lenape Indians for purchase of land.
1631	*April.* Thirty Dutch citizens establish their first settlement, Zwaanendall, at the mouth of Delaware Bay near the present site of Lewes. Settlement wiped out by Indians in 1632.
1638	*March.* Swedish expedition, headed by Peter Minuit, establishes first permanent settlement, calling it New Sweden. A fort is built nearby at present-day Wilmington.
1655	Peter Stuyvesant leads force against Swedish Colony. Colony is captured, restoring the area to complete Dutch rule.
1664	English seize town of New Castle.
1682	Delaware counties are taken over by William Penn, beginning a territorial dispute with Maryland that does not end until 1776.
1698	Town of Lewes is sacked by pirates.
1700	Captain William Kidd sails into Delaware Bay and forces people of Lewes to sell him supplies.
1726	Trial courts of law and a single supreme appeals court established by Assembly.
1735	Quakers William and Elizabeth Shipley buy most of Willington (Wilmington). The city develops fast due to the Quaker energy for commerce.
1761	First printing press in Delaware operates in Wilmington.
1776	Revolutionary War. First naval battle of war occurs in Delaware Bay. Colonists drive away British ships. First state legislature meets at New Castle.
1777	*September 11.* Battle of the Brandywine. George Washington's troops fail to halt the British advance toward Philadelphia. About 300 American troops killed.
1779	Articles of Confederation are ratified by Delaware.
1787	*December 7.* Delaware becomes first state to ratify the Constitution of the United States, winning title, "The First State."

1800	Du Ponts migrate from France and construct gunpowder plant on Brandywine River, beginning great industrial empire.
1813	War of 1812 in progress. Lewes fired on for 22 hours by British fleet. Citizens report: one chicken killed and one pig wounded.
1824	"African School Society of Wilmington" is organized to provide educational opportunities for black families.
1829	*October 17.* Chesapeake and Delaware Canal opens.
1831	*July 4.* One and one-half miles of New Castle and Frenchtown Railroad opens, using horse-drawn cars.
1832	First steam locomotive is used on New Castle–Frenchtown Railroad. Isaac Reeves plants first peach orchard near Delaware City.
1846–1848	Mexican War. Delaware Regiment participates.
1855	Statewide prohibition law enacted. It is repealed two years later.
1861–1865	Civil War. Delaware, although a slave-holding state, does not secede from the Union. Slaves in Delaware are not freed until 13th Amendment goes into effect in December, 1865.
1878	*April.* First telephones are installed in Wilmington.
1885	*March 6.* Thomas Francis Bayard of Delaware appointed by President Grover Cleveland as Secretary of State.
1889	*February 26.* Law is enacted, forbidding punishment of women at whipping-post or pillory.
1897	Delaware adopts its present constitution.
1900	Howard Pyle, noted illustrator, opens school of art at Wilmington.
1905	*March 20.* Delaware becomes last state to abolish the use of the pillory.
1909	*March 18.* Legislature transfers title of Chesapeake and Delaware Canal to the US Government.
1916–1918	World War I. Delaware National Guardsmen sent to Deming, New Mexico, for war training. First Delaware troops ship out from Hoboken, N.J. for France (1918). Du Pont manufactures nearly 1.5 billion rounds of explosives for allies and employs over 100,000.
1921	Wilmington volunteer fire companies merge into paid fire department.
1937	Nylon is invented by Dr. W. H. Carothers of the Du Pont Company.
1939	E. Paul Burkholder, state senator, proposes establishment of "Delaware Day."
1941–1945	World War II. Delaware industries turn to war work. Dravo Shipyards, Wilmington, is state's largest wartime employer.
1946	President Harry S. Truman signs bill that authorizes construction of $25 million Delaware Bridge.
1948	Pea Patch Island, ceded to the US in 1813, is returned to Delaware and operated as a state health center.
1951	Delaware Memorial Bridge opens.
1954	Fort Delaware becomes a state park.
1955	Delaware City begins construction of $160 million oil refinery.
1957	State begins providing funds for needy students to attend the University of Delaware.
1962	General dock workers' strike on East Coast ties up virtually all shipping to and from US crippling the Delaware shipping industry.
1963	New national wildlife refuge is established at Prime Hook Neck.
1965	First major mosquito control project in 30 years is initiated.
1971	Coastal Zone Act adopted by state legislature. This act outlaws all new heavy industry "incompatible with the protection of the natural environment." Du Pont employs 11% of the state's work force.
1975	Wilmington teachers go on six-week strike for better pay. Wages are raised over three-year period.
1979	Tourism increases. Out-of-state visitors spend $385.5 million. Rehobeth Beach called "nation's summer capital."
1981	*January.* Pierre S. du Pont IV takes office as governor.
1983	University of Delaware observes a year-long celebration of the 150th anniversary of its founding. Honorary doctorate is awarded to Vice President Bush.

1985	Water supply is a major concern as drought develops over middle Atlantic states. Delaware adopts mandatory water restrictions.
1987	Delaware's Senator Joseph Biden withdraws from the Democratic race for presidential nomination due to charges of plagiarism.
	Charles J. Pederson, research chemist for E. I. du Pont de Nemours & Company of Wilmington, is one of the winners of the Nobel Chemistry Prize.
1988	*February 18.* Former Governor Pierre S. du Pont IV, earliest announced candidate in Republican presidential race, becomes one of the earliest dropouts.

DEMOGRAPHY

Population (est. 1987) 644,000
Population (1980) 594,317
Population density in persons per
  square mile (1980) 290.8

POPULATION BY RACE (1980)
American Indian/Aleut/
  Eskimo 1,330
Asian/Pacific Islander 4,132
Black 95,971
Hispanic 9,671
White 488,543
Other 5,249

POPULATION CHARACTERISTICS (1980)
Percent of state population
Urban 70.6
Rural 29.4
Under 18 . . . . 28.0
65 or older 10.0
College-educated 16.3
Families below poverty line . . . 8.9
Public assistance recipients . . . 6.6

Per capita personal
  income (1986) $15,010
Millionaires per 100,000
  residents (1982) 116.7

Average life expectancy
  in years (1980) 73.2
Marriage rate per 1,000
  residents (1986) 8.7
Divorce rate per 1,000
  residents (1986) 4.9
Birth rate per 1,000
  residents (1986) 15.9
Infant mortality rate per 1,000
  births (1985) 13.2
Abortion rate per 1,000
  live births (1985) 451
Crime rate per 100,000
  residents (1985)
  Violent 427.0
  Property 4,404.6
Federal and state prisoners per
  100,000 residents (1984) 361
Alcohol consumption in gallons
  per capita (1985) 45.0
Deaths from motor vehicle accidents
  per 100,00 residents (1985) . . . 9.6

MAJOR CITIES
	Population
Wilmington (est. 1984)	69,694
Dover (1980)	23,512
Elsmere (1980)	6,493
Newark (1980)	25,247

GOVERNMENT AND POLITICS

Number of US Representatives 1
Electoral votes 3

POLITICAL PARTY NOMINEES FROM STATE
Daniel Rodney 1820 VP
Traves Brownlee (American) 1984 VP

PRESIDENTIAL PRIMARY ELECTION In 1988, Delaware sent 1 Democratic delegate and 3 Republican delegates to the national conventions.
CONSTITUTION Delaware has had four constitutions: 1776, 1792, 1831, and the present one, adopted in 1897.

LEGISLATURE The General Assembly is divided into the Senate (21 members, 4-year term, minimum age 27) and the House of Representatives (41 members, 2-year term, minimum age 24). In 1987, the annual salary was $21,000.
JUDICIARY The highest court is the Supreme Court, with 5 judges serving 12-year terms. In 1987, the annual salary was $81,900.
EXECUTIVE The governor serves a 4-year term; the minimum age for holding office is 30. In 1987, the annual salary was $70,000. There are 5 other elected officials.

PRESIDENTIAL VOTE 1948-1988 *(in percents)*

Year	*State Winner*	*Democratic*	*Republican*
1948	Dewey (R)	48.8	50.0
1952	Eisenhower (R)	47.9	51.8
1956	Eisenhower (R)	44.6	55.1
1960	Kennedy (D)	50.6	49.0
1964	Johnson (D)	61.0	38.8
1968	Nixon (R)	41.6	45.1
1972	Nixon (R)	39.2	59.6
1976	Carter (D)	52.0	46.6
1980	Reagan (R)	44.8	47.2
1984	Reagan (R)	39.9	59.8
1988	Bush (R)	43.0	57.0

GOVERNORS (Delaware shared governors with Pennsylvania from 1638 to 1655, with New York from 1655 to 1682, and again with Pennsylvania from 1682 to 1776.)

State Presidents

John McKinly	1777
Thomas McKean (acting)	1777
George Read (acting)	1777-1778
Caesar Rodney	1778-1781
John Dickinson	1781-1782
John Cook (acting)	1782-1783
Nicholas Van Dyke	1783-1786
Thomas Collins	1786-1789
Jehu Davis (acting)	1789
Joshua Clayton	1789-1793

State Governors

Joshua Clayton (Federalist)	1793-1796
Gunning Bedford (Federalist)	1796-1797
Daniel Rogers (Federalist/acting)	1797-1799
Richard Bassett (Federalist)	1799-1801
James Sykes (Federalist/acting)	1801-1802
David Hall (Democratic-Republican)	1802-1805
Nathaniel Mitchell (Federalist)	1805-1808
George Truitt (Federalist)	1808-1811
Joseph Haslet (D-R)	1811-1814
Daniel Rodney (Federalist)	1814-1817
John Clark (Federalist)	1817-1820
Jacob Stout (Federalist/acting)	1820-1821
John Collins (D-R)	1821-1822
Caleb Rodney (D-R/acting)	1822-1823
Joseph Haslet (D-R)	1823
Charles Thomas (D-R/acting)	1823-1824
Samuel Paynter (Federalist)	1824-1827
Charles Polk (Federalist)	1827-1830
David Hazzard (American Republican)	1830-1833
Caleb P. Bennett (D)	1833-1836
Charles Polk (Whig/acting)	1836-1837
Cornelius P. Comegys (Whig)	1837-1841
William B. Cooper (Whig)	1841-1845
Thomas Stockton (Whig)	1845-1846
Joseph Maull (Whig/acting)	1846-1847
William Temple (Whig/acting)	1847
William Tharp (D)	1847-1851
William H. Ross (D)	1851-1855
Peter Causey (Know-Nothing)	1855-1859
William Burton (D)	1859-1863
William Cannon (Union)	1863-1865
Gove Saulsbury (D/acting)	1865-1867
Gove Saulsbury (D)	1867-1871
James Ponder (D)	1871-1875
John P. Cochran (D)	1875-1879
John W. Hall (D)	1879-1883
Charles C. Stockley (D)	1883-1887
Benjamin T. Biggs (D)	1887-1891
Robert J. Reynolds (D)	1891-1895
Joshua H. Marvel (R)	1895
William T. Watson (D/acting)	1895-1897
Ebe W. Tunnell (D)	1897-1901
John Hunn (R)	1901-1905
Preston Lea (R)	1905-1909
Simeon S. Pennewill (R)	1909-1913
Charles S. Miller (R)	1913-1917
John G. Townsend Jr. (R)	1917-1921
William D. Denney (R)	1921-1925
Robert P. Robinson (R)	1925-1929
C. Douglas Buck (R)	1929-1937
R.C. McMullen (D)	1937-1941
Walter W. Bacon (R)	1941-1949
Elbert N. Carvel (D)	1949-1953
James Caleb Boggs (R)	1953-1960
David N. Buckson (R/acting)	1960-1961

Elbert N. Carvel (D)	1961-1965
Charles L. Terry Jr. (D)	1965-1969
Russell W. Peterson (R)	1969-1973
Sherman W. Tribbitt (D)	1973-1977
Pierre S. du Pont (R)	1977-1985
Michael N. Castle (R)	1985-

MINIMUM AGES

Majority	18
Marriage with parental consent	
female	16
male	18
Marriage without parental consent	18
Making a will	18
Buying alcohol	21
Jury duty	18
Leaving school	16
Driver's license	16

CAPITAL PUNISHMENT
Number executed 1976-88: 0
On death row Aug. 1, 1988: 1

MILITARY INSTALLATIONS
Total number: 3
Major bases:
Air Force: 1

FINANCES

Thousands of dollars

GENERAL REVENUE (1985)

Total general revenue	1,541,758
Total tax revenue	816,238
Sales and gross receipts	98,240
Individual income taxes	365,589
Corporate net income taxes	77,060

GENERAL EXPENDITURE (1985)

Total general expenditure	1,251,097
Education	481,488
Public welfare	117,386
Health	40,347
Hospitals	40,697
Natural resources	23,154
Highways	124,316
Police	21,527
Corrections	40,140

FEDERAL AID (1985) 318,028

ECONOMY

Delaware is one of the nation's centers of chicken farming, with broilers produced in large automated hatcheries accounting for about half of the state's farm income. The sale of chickens and chicken products earned $404 million in 1982. Soybeans are the major cash crop, followed by truck vegetables and fruits. The manufacturing sector is led by chemicals, including nylon, other plastics, and petrochemicals. Several major chemical companies maintain headquarters in or near Wilmington. Fisheries, mining, and timber account for only a fraction of the state's annual income.

EMPLOYMENT (1984)
Thousands of persons

Total number of employed workers	289
Construction	16.9
Finance, insurance, and real estate	17.4
Government	43.4
Manufacturing	705.
Mining	0.1
Services	57.7
Transportation, communications, and utilities	12.1
Wholesale and retail trade	62.6
Percent of civilian labor force unemployed (1984)	6.2

DEPARTMENT OF DEFENSE (1985)

Civilian workers employed	1,796
Military personnel	4,662
Contract awards	$261 million

ENERGY SOURCES FOR ELECTRIC UTILITIES (1983)
Percent

Coal	69.0
Gas	5.5
Hydroelectric	0
Nuclear	0
Petroleum	25.5

TRANSPORTATION

Motor vehicles registered in state (1986)	479,665
Miles of roads, streets, and highways (1986)	5,332
Miles of Class I railway operated (1986)	212
Airports	37

CULTURE AND EDUCATION

Native American tribes
Delaware was formerly home to the Nanticoke tribe.

Religions, ethnicities, and languages
The first non-Indian settlers in Delaware were Swedes, Finns, Dutch, and Africans. During the 19th century, immigrants were mainly German, Irish, Italian, Polish, and Jewish; in the 20th, mainly Ukrainian, Russian, Scandinavian, and Greek. In 1980, 5.5 percent of Delaware's population spoke a language other than English at home.

Major museums and libraries
Delaware Art Museum, Wilmington
Delaware State Museum, Dover
Eleutherian Mills Historical Library, Greenville
Hagley Museum, Wilmington
Henry Francis du Pont Winterthur Museum, Wilmington

Major arts organizations
Delaware Symphony Orchestra, Wilmington
Opera Delaware, Wilmington
The Playhouse, Wilmington

Colleges and universities
Number public (1986-87) 5
Number private (1986-87) 5
Total enrollment, in full-time equivalent students (1985) 25,800

Public elementary and secondary schools
Expenditure per pupil in average daily attendance (1986-87) $4,776
Pupil-teacher ratio (1987) 16.0
Average teacher salary (1986-87) $28,440

Holidays
Delaware Day. December 7
Separation Day. June 15
State Fair, Harrington. Late July

DELAWARE IN LITERATURE

Daniel G. Brinton (ed.) *The Lenape and Their Legends* (1884, rpt. 1973)

Gilbert Byron *The Lord's Oysters* (1957, rpt. 1977)
The life of a fisherman on the Chester River at the turn of the century.

Henry Seidel Canby *The Age of Confidence: Life in the Nineties* (1934)
An account of Wilmington during the author's boyhood. Canby was the principal organizer of the Book of the Month Club.

Charles Heber Clark (pseudonym of Max Adeler) *Out of the Hurly-Burly; or, Life in an Old Corner* (1874)
Comic tales of Newcastle life.

Gertrude Crownfield *Where Glory Waits* (1934)
Romantic historical novel about Mary Vining and her love for General Anthony Wayne.

A.O.H. Grier *This Was Wilmington* (1945)
Collection of newspaper articles on regional history and social life in the early twentieth century by a veteran Wilmington journalist.

Elizabeth Montgomery *Reminiscences of Wilmington* (1851, rpt. 1872)
Classic account of early nineteenth-century social life and customs in Wilmington.

Anne Parrish *The Perennial Bachelor* (1925)
Historical novel depicting the decline of a great estate, 1860–1910. The setting was suggested by the author's childhood home near Claymont.

Walter A. Powell *Annals of a Village in Kent County, Delaware* (1934)
Reminiscences of the mid-nineteenth century.

George Alfred Townsend *Tales of the Chesapeake* (1880)
Collection of local-color stories.
———. *The Entailed Hat* (1884)
Novel about the kidnapping of free blacks before the Civil War.

Olum, Walam (trans. and ed. Daniel G. Briton) *The Lenope and Their Legends* (1884, rpt. 1973)

GUIDES TO RESOURCES

Coghlan, Gladys M. and **Dale Fields** (eds.) *Index to the History of Delaware, 1609–1888* 3 vols. (1976)

Delaware Data Book (annual)

Eberlein, Harold Donaldson and **Cortlandt V. D. Hubbard** *Historic Houses and Buildings of Delaware* (1962)

Federal Writers' Project (ed. Jeannette Eckman) *Delaware: A Guide to the First State* (rev. ed. 1955)
——— (ed. Anthony Higgins) *New Castle on the Delaware* (rev. ed. 1973)

J. M. Runk and Company *Biographical and Genealogical History of the State of Delaware* 2 vols. (1899)

Macdonald, Betty H. (ed. Jeannette Eckman) *Historic Landmarks of Delaware and the Eastern Shore* (rev. ed. 1976)

Munroe, John A. *Delaware: A Students' Guide to Localized History* (1965)

Porter, Frank W. *Indians in Maryland and Delaware: A Critical Bibliography* (The Newberry Library) (1979)
———. *In Pursuit of the Past: An Anthropological and Bibliographic Guide to Maryland and Delaware* (1986)

Reed, H. Clay and **Marion B. Reed** *A Bibliography of Delaware through 1960* (1966)

University of Delaware, Hugh M. Morris Library *Bibliography of Delaware, 1960–1974* (1976)

SELECTED NONFICTION SOURCES

Acrelius, Israel (trans. W. M. Reynolds) *A History of New Sweden: or, The Settlements on the River Delaware* (1874, rpt. 1972)

Bennett, George F. *Early Architects of Delaware* (1932)

Caldwell, Robert G. *The New Castle County Workhouse* (1940)
———. *Red Hannah: Delaware's Whipping Post* (1947)

Carr, William H. *The Du Ponts of Delaware: A Fantastic Dynasty* (1964)

Cawley, James and Margaret *Along the Delaware and Raritan Canal* (1970)

Chandler, Alfred D. and Stephen Salsbury *Pierre S. du Pont and the Making of the Modern Corporation* (1971)

Coleman, John M. *Thomas McKean: Forgotten Leader of the Revolution* (1975)

Conner, William H. and Leon de Valinger, Jr. *Delaware's Role in World War II* 2 vols. (1955)

Cooch, Edward W. *Battle of Cooch's Bridge* (1940)
———. *Delaware Historic Events* (1946)

Dolan, Paul and James R. Soles *Government of Delaware* (1976)

Dorian, Max *Du Ponts: From Gunpowder to Nylon* (1962)

Duke, Marc *The du Ponts: Portrait of a Dynasty* (1976)

Dunlap, Arthur Ray *Indian Place-Names in Delaware* (1950)
———. *Dutch and Swedish Place-Names in Delaware* (1956)

Eckman, Jeannette *Crane Hook on the Delaware, 1667–1699* (1958)

Elliott, Richard V. *Last of the Steamboats: The Saga of the Wilson Line* (1970)

Ferris, Benjamin *A History of the Original Settlements on the Delaware* (1846)

Gibson, George H. (comp.) *The Collected Essays of Richard S. Rodney on Early Delaware* (1975)

Gray, Ralph L. *The National Waterway* (1967)

Green, Charles E. *Delaware Heritage: The Story of the Diamond State in the Revolution* (1975)

Grier, A. O. H. *This Was Wilmington* (1945)

Hancock, Harold B. *Delaware during the Civil War* (1962)
———. *Liberty and Independence: The Delaware State during the American Revolution* (1976)
———. *The Loyalists of Revolutionary Delaware* (1977)
———. *Delaware Two Hundred Years Ago, 1780–1800* (1987)

Hoffecker, Carol E. (comp.) *Readings in Delaware History* (1973)
———. *Brandywine Village: The Story of a Milling Community* (1974)
———. *Delaware: A Bicentennial History* (States and the Nation series) (1977)
———. *Corporate Capital: Wilmington in the Twentieth Century* (1983)

Johnson, Amandus *The Swedish Settlements on the Delaware* 2 vols. (1911–1912)

Lincoln, Anna T. *Wilmington, Delaware: Three Centuries under Four Flags, 1609–1937* (1937)

Lunt, Dudley C. *The Farmer's Bank, 1807–1957* (1957)
———. *Taylor's Gut in the Delaware State* (1968)

Martin, Kenneth R. *Delaware Goes Whaling, 1833–1845* (1974)

Marvil, James *Sailing Rams* (1961, rpt. 1974)
———. *Pilots of the Bay and River Delaware and Lewes Lore* (1965)

Menzies, Elizabeth G. *Passage between Rivers: A Portfolio of Photographs with a History of the Delaware and Raritan Canal* (1976)

Munroe, John A. *Federalist Delaware, 1775–1815* (1954)
———. *Louis McLane: Federalist and Jacksonian* (1973)
———. *Colonial Delaware: A History* (1978)
———. *History of Delaware* (2d ed. 1984)

Passmore, Joanne et al. *History of the Delaware State Grange and the State's Agriculture, 1875–1976* (1975)

Pitz, Henry C. *The Brandywine Tradition* (1969)
———. *Howard Pyle: Writer, Illustrator, Founder of the Brandywine School* (1975)

Reed, H. Clay *Delaware, a History of the First State* . . . 3 vols. (1947)
———. *The Delaware Colony* (1970)

Reese, Charles L. *The Horse on Rodney Square* (1977)

Sarick, Ambrose *Pierre Samuel Du Pont de Nemours* (1965)

Scharf, John T. et al. *History of Delaware, 1609–1888* 2 vols. (1888, rpt. 1972)

Silliman, Charles *A Time to Remember, 1920–1960: Picture Story of Forty Years in the History of Northern New Castle County, Delaware* (1962)

Truitt, Charles J. *Breadbasket of the Revolution: Delmarva in the War for Independence* (1975)

Turner, C. H. B. *Rodney's Diary and Other Delaware Records* (1911)

Tyler, David B. *The Bay and River Delaware* (1955)
———. *The American Clyde* (1958)

Vallandigham, Edward N. *Delaware and the Eastern Shore* (1922, rpt. 1972)

Wade, William J. *Sixteen Miles from Anywhere, a History of Georgetown, Delaware* (1976)

Ward, Christopher *The Dutch and the Swedes on the Delaware, 1609–1664* (1930)
———. *The Delaware Continentals, 1776–1783* (1941)

Weslager, C. A. *Delaware's Forgotten River; the Story of the Christina* (1947)
———. *The Nanticoke Indians* (1948)
———. *Brandywine Springs; the Rise and Fall of a Delaware Resort* (1949)
———. *A Brief Account of the Indians of Delaware* (1953)
———. *Red Men on the Brandywine* (1953)
———. *The Richardsons of Delaware* (1957)
———. *Dutch Explorers, Traders and Settlers in the Delaware Valley, 1609–1664* (1961)
———. *The English on the Delaware, 1610–1682* (1967)
———. *Delaware's Buried Past, a Story of Archaeological Adventure* (rev. ed. 1968)
———. *The Delaware Indians* (1972)

Wildes, Harry E. *The Delaware* (Rivers of America series) (1940)

Wilkinson, Norman B. *The Brandywine Home Front during the Civil War* (1966)

Wilson, W. Emerson (ed.) *Delaware in the Civil War* (1962)
———. *Forgotten Heroes of Delaware* (1969)

Wuorinen, John H. *The Finns on the Delaware, 1667–1699* (1958)

FLORIDA

Florida, a South Atlantic state, juts from the southeastern corner of the US to divide the Atlantic Ocean from the Gulf of Mexico. It is bordered on the north by Alabama, Georgia, and St. Mary's River; on the east by the Atlantic Ocean; on the south by the Straits of Florida; and on the west by Alabama, the Gulf of Mexico, and the Perdido River.

FULL NAME State of Florida
POSTAL ABBREVIATION FL
INHABITANT Floridian
ADMITTED TO THE UNION Mar. 3, 1845. 27th state
POPULATION (est. 1987) 12,023,000. Percent of US total: 4.94%. Rank: 4th

CAPITAL CITY Tallahassee, located in the northwestern part of Florida; population 112,258 (est. 1984). Founded during the Spanish colonial era, near the site of an Indian village, it became the capital of the territory of Florida in 1823, was incorporated in 1825, and became the state capital in 1845.

STATE NAME AND NICKNAMES Named *La Florida* by Ponce de Leon on Easter Sunday 1513, to commemorate Pascua Florida ("Flowering Easter," the Spanish Easter holiday), the day on which the explorer first arrived on the peninsula. Also known as the Sunshine State, the Orange State, the Everglades State, the Alligator State, and the Southernmost State.

STATE SEAL A landscape showing an Indian woman scattering flowers, with a sabal palmetto tree and steam and sailing ships visible in the background, and the sun's rays shining on a highland in the distance. Around the border is the legend "Great Seal of the State of Florida" and the state motto.

MOTTO In God We Trust

SONG "Old Folks at Home" ("Swanee River"), lyrics and music by Stephen Foster.

SYMBOLS
Flower orange blossom
Tree sabal palmetto palm (cabbage palm)
Bird mockingbird
Gem moonstone
Stone agatized coral
Animal Florida panther
Marine mammal manatee
Saltwater mammal porpoise
Freshwater fish Florida largemouth bass
Saltwater fish Atlantic sailfish
Shell horse conch (giant band shell)
Beverage orange juice
Air fair Central Florida Air Fair
Festival Calle Ocho–Open House 8
Pageant "Indian River"
Play "Cross and Sword"
Litter control symbol "Glenn Glitter"

LICENSE PLATES (1) Blue on multicolored background showing shuttle liftoff from orange flames through white smoke to blue sky, with legend "Challenger." (2) Orange on white, with turquoise state map and legend "DMV" (3) Black on white, with gold state map and legend indicating county.

FLAG A red cross of St. Andrew on a field of white, with the state seal in the center.

GEOGRAPHY AND CLIMATE

Florida, the southernmost state in the continental US, is geographically one of the youngest regions in North America. The Floridian peninsula, a low-lying plain of sandstone and porous, waterbearing limestone, is crisscrossed by a network of streams, canals, and swamps draining into 39 basins and some 30,000 lakes. The northern panhandle is rural and hilly, with a temperate climate; the southern peninsula is truly tropical; while the Keys, an island crescent curving out into the Gulf of Mexico, are typically Caribbean in climate and geology.

AREA 58,664 square miles. Rank: 22nd
INLAND WATER 4,511 square miles
GEOGRAPHIC CENTER Hernando, 12 miles NNW of Brooksville
ELEVATIONS *Highest point:* Geological survey section 30, T6 north, R20 west, in Walton County, 345 feet. *Lowest point:* Atlantic Ocean, sea level. *Mean elevation:* 100 feet

MAJOR RIVERS St. Johns, Apalachicola, Suwanee

MAJOR LAKES AND RESERVOIRS Okeechobee, George, Kissimmee, Apopka, Istokpoga

TIDAL SHORELINE 3,331 miles, Atlantic coast; 5,095 miles, Gulf coast

LAND USE

	Thousands of acres
Urban (1982)	2,770
Rural (1982)	27,730
Cropland (1982)	3,557
Pastureland (1982)	4,273
Rangeland (1982)	3,804
Forestland (1982)	12,430
State parks and recreation areas (1983)	253
National park system (1984)	2,145
National forest system (1984)	1,225
Tribal lands (1984)	156

TEMPERATURES The highest recorded temperature was 109°F on June 29, 1931, at Monticello. The lowest was -2°F on February 13, 1899, at Tallahassee.

NATIONAL SITES

NATIONAL MEMORIALS DeSoto, Fort Caroline
NATIONAL MONUMENTS Castillo de San Marcos, Fort Jefferson, Fort Matanzas
NATIONAL PARKS Biscayne, Everglades
NATIONAL PRESERVE Big Cypress
NATIONAL SEASHORES Canaveral, Gulf Islands
NATIONAL WILDLIFE REFUGES Chassahowitzka –Cedar Keys/Lower Suwannee, Darling– Calloosahatchee/Egmont Key/Island Bay/ Ma Iacha Pass/Passage Key/Pine Island/ Pinellas, Lake Woodruff, Merritt Island– Pelican Island/St. Johns, Okefenokee, St. Marks, St. Vincent South Florida Refuges–Great White Heron/Hobe Sound/ Key West/Loxahatchee

HISTORY

1513	*April 3.* Ponce de León lands on the coast of Florida on Easter Sunday and claims the region for Spain. He names it Florida (*Pascua florida*), meaning flowery Easter.
1517	Led by Francis Hernandez de Cordova, Spaniards land in Florida but are forced by natives to flee.
1521	As governor, Juan Ponce de León establishes colony in Florida. Fatally wounded in an Indian encounter five months later, Ponce De Leon returns with colonists to Cuba where he dies.
1528	*April 14.* Panfilo de Narváez leads an ill-fated expedition of Spaniards into Florida. A few survivors reach Mexico in 1536.
1539	*May.* Hernando de Soto lands at Tampa Bay with large forces. Remnant of expedition reaches Mexico four years later with news of de Soto's death and burial in Mississippi River in 1542.
1549	Dominican Father Luis de Cancer dies leading a group of missionaries to Florida.
1559	Don Tristan de Luna arrives with colonists in Pensacola Bay. Starving survivors of colony are later taken to Mexico.
1562	*May 1.* French Huguenots land at mouth of St. Johns River.
1564	Huguenots erect Fort Caroline above St. Johns Bluff on the St. Johns River.
1565	*September 8.* Don Pedro Menéndez lands on shores of Matanzas River and founds St. Augustine, the oldest city in the US.

1573	Missionaries try to convert Indians. Eventually they plant a series of missions from Florida northward to present South Carolina.
1586	Sir Francis Drake burns town of St. Augustine but is unable to capture fort.
1638	Apalachee Indians are defeated by Spaniards and used as slave labor to strengthen St. Augustine fortifications.
1668	John Davis, English buccaneer, sacks St. Augustine.
'1698	Fort San Carlos is erected near Pensacola Bay because of French activity along the Gulf Coast.
1704	Repeated raids by English destroy many Spanish missions and enslave Indians.
1715	Spanish treasure fleet is wrecked off Cape Canaveral killing over 700 people. The $3.5 million treasure is discovered by a beachcomber in 1965.
1721	By terms of peace treaty of 1721 the Pensacola area is restored to Spain.
1750	Party of Creek Indians migrate from Georgia into Florida and become known as the Seminole Indians.
1763	Spain cedes Florida to England. This gives the English control of all the mainland to the Mississippi River.
1777	Revolutionary War. British launch attack from St. Augustine against Savannah, Ga.
1782	English Tories, refugees from Georgia and South Carolina, build St. Johns Town on St. Johns River.
1783	Florida's first newspaper, *East Florida Gazette*, is published at St. Augustine. Great Britain cedes Florida, East and West, back to Spain.
1811	*January 15.* US Congress authorizes President Madison "to seize West Florida if a foreign power tries to take it."
1812	War of 1812. Republic of Florida is organized by American 'patriots' who occupy Spanish fort at Fernandina.
1819–1821	United States buys Florida from Spain. No money is paid to Spain, however, as American indemnities equal purchase price of 5 million dollars.
1823	Key West is made US naval depot and station. *October 23.* Tallahassee is selected as site of capital of Florida.
1826	Floridians gain election rights for their territorial legislative council.
1831	Cigar industry comes to Florida with establishment of factory in Key West.
1835	*December 28.* Seven-year Seminole war begins.
1845	*March 3.* Florida admitted to the Union as the 27th state.
1846	Steam locomotives are used in state for first time.
1858	Law provides that free blacks who wish to become slaves can choose their own masters.
1861	*January 10.* Florida becomes the third state to secede from the Union.
1865	*October 28.* Ordinance of secession is annulled. *November.* New state constitution is adopted.
1867	*December 22.* Council of Ku Klux Klan is organized in Palatka.
1868	*July 4.* Florida formally readmitted to the Union.
1876	Florida is charged with the tampering of its electoral vote in the Tilden-Hayes presidential election.
1877	Reconstruction period generally considered to have ended.
1878	Statewide yellow-fever epidemic.
1883	First electric lights are installed in a hotel in Jacksonville.
1886	Fire destroys almost half of Key West. Cigar industry moves to Tampa.
1888	Yellow-fever epidemic again ravages state.
1889	*February.* State Board of Health created to fight epidemic of yellow fever.
1894	Orange groves are damaged by frost.
1898	Thousands of American soldiers embark from Florida ports for Spanish-American War duty.
1901	*May 3.* Flames destroy almost entire city of Jacksonville.
1903	Daytona Beach is scene of automobile speed tests. An R. E. Olds reaches speed of 68 miles per hour.
1905	Greeks establish sponge industry at Tarpon Springs.
1909	Hurricane destroys construction work on overseas railroad.

1912	*January 22*. Overseas railroad to Key West is finished after eight years of construction work.
1921	WQAM Miami becomes first radio broadcasting station in state.
1925	Peak of real estate boom.
	Florida passes a bill requiring daily Bible reading in all public schools.
1926	Real estate boom collapses.
1928	*April 25*. Tamiami Trail across Florida west to east is opened to public after years of construction.
1929	John Ringling selects winter quarters for circus at Sarasota.
1933	*February 15*. Miami. Would-be assassin of President Franklin Delano Roosevelt fatally wounds Mayor Anton Joseph Cermak of Chicago.
1935	*March 7*. Daytona Beach. Sir Malcolm Campbell sets automobile speed record of 276 miles per hour.
1940	January freeze causes damage to citrus farms estimated at 20 million dollars.
1941	World War II. Farm, mine, and factory production increases in war effort. Military and naval bases expanded.
1947	Everglades National Park is established.
1950	*July 24*. First rocket launching at Cape Canaveral takes place.
1958	NASA (National Aeronautics and Space Agency) begins administration of Cape Canaveral. Launching site called Kennedy Space Center in honor of President John F. Kennedy after his assassination in 1963.
1968	New state constitution is adopted.
1970	*September 26*. President Nixon authorizes $20 million to purchase and preserve privately held land within Everglades National Park.
1972	Disney World creates many new jobs.
1981	Great influx of Cuban and Haitian refugees creates welfare and housing problems. "Cocaine Cowboys" in south Florida cause increase in violence and crime.
1986	*January 28*. *Challenger* explodes just after lift off from Kennedy Space Center, killing entire crew.
1988	*September 29*. *Discovery* is launched at Kennedy Space Center.

DEMOGRAPHY

Population (est. 1987) 12,023,000
Population (1980) 9,746,342
Population density in persons
   per square mile (1980) 166.1

POPULATION BY RACE (1980)
American Indian/Aleut/
   Eskimo 19,316
Asian/Pacific Islander 56,756
Black 1,342,478
Hispanic 857,898
White 8,178,387
Other 143,055

POPULATION CHARACTERISTICS (1980)
Percent of state population
Urban 84.3
Rural 15.7
Under 18 . . . . 24.3
65 or older 17.3
College-educated 14.7
Families below poverty line 9.9
Public assistance recipients 4.4

Per capita personal
   income (1986) $14,281

Millionaires per 100,000
   residents (1982) 387.8
Average life expectancy
   in years (1980) 74.3
Marriage rate per 1,000
   residents (1986) 11.0
Divorce rate per 1,000
   residents (1986) 6.7
Birth rate per 1,000
   residents (1985) 14.4
Infant mortality rate per 1,000
   births (1985) 11.3
Abortion rate per 1,000
   live births (1985) 465
Crime rate per 100,000
   residents (1985)
     Violent 1,036.5
     Property 7,191.9
Federal and state prisoners
   per 100,000 residents (1984) . . 243
Alcohol consumption in gallons
   per capita (1985) 46.4
Deaths from motor vehicle accidents
   per 100,000 residents (1985) . . 24.2

MAJOR CITIES

	1984 population (est.)
Clearwater	96,276
Fort Lauderdale	149,872
Gainesville	83,099
Jacksonville	577,971

Miami	372,634
Miami Beach	95,799
Orlando	137,145
Tallahassee	112,258
Tampa	275,479
St. Petersburg	241,294

GOVERNMENT AND POLITICS

Number of US Representatives	19
Electoral votes	21

POLITICAL PARTY NOMINEES FROM STATE

Christopher Gian-Cursio (Vegetarian)	1960 VP
Rufus Shackleford (American)	1976 VP

PRESIDENTIAL PRIMARY ELECTION In 1988, Florida sent 146 Democratic delegates and 82 Republican delegates to the national conventions.

CONSTITUTION Florida has had six constitutions: 1839, 1861, 1865, 1866, 1868, and the present one, adopted in 1968.

LEGISLATURE The Legislature is divided into the Senate (40 members, 4-year term, minimum age 21) and the House of Representatives (120 members, 2-year term, minimum age 21). In 1987, the annual salary was $19,848.

JUDICIARY The highest court is the Supreme Court, with seven judges serving 6-year terms. In 1987, the annual salary was $88,825.

EXECUTIVE The governor serves a 4-year term; the minimum age for holding office is 30. In 1987, the annual salary was $96,646. There are 6 other elected officials.

PRESIDENTIAL VOTE 1948-1988 *(in percents)*

Year	*State Winner*	*Democratic*	*Republican*
1948	Truman (D)	48.8	33.6
1952	Eisenhower (R)	45.0	55.0
1956	Eisenhower (R)	42.7	57.2
1960	Nixon (R)	48.5	51.5
1964	Johnson (D)	51.2	48.9
1968	Nixon (R)	30.9	40.5
1972	Nixon (R)	27.8	71.9
1976	Carter (D)	51.9	46.6
1980	Reagan (R)	38.5	55.5
1984	Reagan (R)	34.7	65.3
1988	Bush (R)	39.0	61.0

GOVERNORS

Territorial Governors

Andrew Jackson	1821
William P. Duval	1822-1834
John H. Eaton	1834-1836
Richard K. Call	1836-1839
Robert R. Reid	1839-1841
Richard K. Call	1841-1844
John Branch	1844-1845

State Governors

William D. Moseley (D)	1845-1849
Thomas Brown (Whig)	1849-1853
James E. Broome (D)	1853-1857
Madison S. Perry (D)	1857-1861
John Milton (D)	1861-1865
Abraham K. Allison (acting)	1865
William Marvin (provisional)	1865

David Shelby Walker (D)	1865-1868
Harrison Reed (R)	1868-1873
Ossian B. Hart (R)	1873-1874
Marcellus L. Stearns (acting)	1874-1877
George F. Drew (D)	1877-1881
William D. Bloxham (D)	1881-1885
Edward A. Perry (D)	1885-1889
Francis P. Fleming (D)	1889-1893
Henry L. Mitchell (D)	1893-1897
William D. Bloxham (D)	1897-1901
William S. Jennings (D)	1901-1905
Naopleon B. Broward (D)	1905-1909
Albert W. Gilchrist (D)	1909-1913
Park Trammell (D)	1913-1917
Sidney J. Catts (D)	1917-1921
Cary A. Hardee (D)	1921-1925
John W. Martin (D)	1925-1929
Doyle E. Carlton (D)	1929-1933
David Sholtz (D)	1933-1937

Frederick P. Cone (D)	1937-1941
Spessard L. Holland (D)	1941-1945
Millad F. Caldwell Jr. (D)	1945-1949
Fuller Warren (D)	1949-1953
Daniel T. McCarthy (D)	1953
Charley E. Johns (D/acting)	1953-1955
LeRoy Collins (D)	1955-1961
C. Farris Bryant (D)	1961-1965
Haydon Burns (D)	1965-1967
Claude Kirk Jr. (R)	1967-1971
Reubin Askew (D)	1971-1979
Robert Graham (D)	1979-1987
Bob Martinez (R)	1987-

MINIMUM AGES
Majority 18
Marriage with parental consent . . . 16
Marriage without parental consent . 18
Making a will 18
Buying alcohol 21
Jury duty 18
Leaving school 16
Driver's license 16

CAPITAL PUNISHMENT
Number executed 1976-88: 18
On death row Aug. 1, 1988: 284

MILITARY INSTALLATIONS
Total number: 53
Major bases:
  Navy: 6
  Air Force: 7

FINANCES

Thousands of dollars

GENERAL REVENUE (1985)
Total general revenue 11,882,029
Total tax revenue 8,328,869
Sales and gross receipts 6,501,496
Individual income taxes 0
Corporate net income taxes . . . 454,088

GENERAL EXPENDITURE 1985)
Total general expenditure . 12,147,670
Education 4,976,742
Public welfare 1,546,774
Health 694,783
Hospitals 255,672
Natural resources 420,325
Highways 1,209,796
Police 151,094
Corrections 411,997

FEDERAL AID (1985) 3,121,681

ECONOMY

Citrus—primarily oranges—leads the state's agricultural economy, yielding over $4 billion in income in 1982. Other crops include corn, peanuts, soybeans, pecans, avocados, and flowers. Livestock, mainly horses, cows, and hogs, accounts for about a third of the total farm income. Total farm cash receipts were $4.3 billion in 1983. Softwoods, mostly southern pine, are the main forest product, feeding a thriving pulp and paper products industry. Florida mining yields one of the world's largest supplies of phosphate. Canned and frozen orange juice, cigars, clothing, and electronics (from the high-tech industries around Cape Canaveral) are the main manufactures. Tourism is perhaps the state's most important and fastest-growing industry, with more than 20 million visitors annually.

EMPLOYMENT (1984)
Thousands of persons
Total number of employed
  workers 4,777
Construction 319.4
Finance, insurance, and
  real estate 298.7
Government 652.6
Manufacturing 502.3
Mining 10.2
Services 1,068.4
Transportation, communications,
  and utilities 242.5
Wholesale and retail trade . . . 1,114.1

Percent of civilian labor force
  unemployed (1984) 6.3

DEPARTMENT OF DEFENSE (1985)
Civilian workers employed . . . 33,029
Military personnel 73,140
Contract awards . . . . $5.271 billion

ENERGY SOURCES FOR ELECTRIC UTILITIES (1983)
Percent
Coal 31.6
Gas 17.9
Hydroelectric 0.2
Nuclear 16.2
Petroleum 34.1

TRANSPORTATION
Motor vehicles registered
  in state (1986) 10,361,512
Miles of roads, streets,
  and highways (1986) 99,074
Miles of Class I railway
  operated (1986) 3,085

Airports (1983) 541
Major aviation hubs (1983) 11
   Largest hub: Miami

Major ports, with gross tonnage (1985):
   Tampa Harbor 46,905
   Port Everglades 11,649
   Jacksonville 11,332

CULTURE AND EDUCATION

Native American tribes

Florida was formerly home to the Acuera, Ais, Amacano, Apalachee, Apalachicola, Calusa, Caparaz, Chatot, Chiaha, Chilucan, Chine, Creek, Cusabo, Freshwater, Guacata, Guale, Hitchiti, Icafui, Jeaga, Koasati, Macapiras, Mobile, Mococo, Mosquito, Muklasa, Ocale, Oconee, Onatheaqua, Pawokti, Pensacola, Pohoy, Potano, Saturiwa, Sawokli, Surruque, Tacatacura, Tamathli, Tawasa, Tekesta, Timucua, Tocobaga, Yamasee, and Yui tribes. Groups that continue to live there include the Miccosukee and the Seminole. There are 3 federal reservations in Florida.

Religions, ethnicities, and languages

Florida has been receiving immigrants since 1790, when people of English and Scotch-Irish descent began to arrive from the southeastern states. There are substantial populations of American Blacks and of Cubans, as well as Spanish, Italian, Greek, Slovak, and Jewish communities. In 1980, 13.2 percent of Florida's population spoke a language other than English at home. The major religious groups are Baptists, Methodists, Presbyterians, Episcopalians, and Roman Catholics.

Major museums and libraries

Florida State Museum, Gainesville
Marine Library and Museum, Miami
John and Mabel Ringling Museum of Art, Sarasota
U.S. Naval Aviation Museum, Pensacola

Major arts organizations

Coconut Grove Playhouse, Miami
Florida Ballet, Jacksonville
Florida Symphony Orchestra, Orlando
Greater Miami Opera Association
Miami City Ballet
New World Symphony, Miami
Symphony orchestras of Fort Lauderdale, Jacksonville, Tampa

Colleges and universities

Number public (1986-87) 37
Number private (1986-87) 52
Total enrollment, in full-time equivalent students (1985) 308,300

Public elementary and secondary schools

Expenditure per pupil in average daily attendance (1986-87) $4,056
Pupil-teacher ratio (1987) 17.5
Average teacher salary (1986-87) $25,552

Major league sports teams

Football: Miami Dolphins, Tampa Bay Buccaneers

Holidays

Robert E. Lee's Birthday. January 19
Susan B. Anthony's Birthday. February 15
State Fair, Tampa. Early to mid-February
Gasparilla festival. February
Pascua Florida Day. April 2
Confederate Memorial Day. April 26
Jefferson Davis's Birthday. June 3.

FLORIDA IN LITERATURE

Edward C. Anderson (ed. W. Stanley Hoole) *Florida Territory in 1844: The Diary of Master Edward C. Anderson, United States Navy* (1977)

William Bartram *Travels Through North and South Carolina, Georgia, East and West Florida* . . . (1791, rpt. 1955, 1959) Influential travel writing by a prominent naturalist whose descriptions of Indian culture did much to form the Romantic concept of the "noble savage." This was the first book by an American to be widely read in Europe.

Nikki Beare *Pirates, Pineapples and People: A History, Tales, and Legends of the Upper Florida Keys* (1961)

Jack Beater *True Tales of the Florida West Coast* (1959)

Stephen Vincent Benet *Spanish Bayonets* (1926) Romantic historical novel set in the eighteenth century.

Wyatt Blassingame *Halo of Spears* (1962) Novel set in the turpentine forests c.1900.

Charles M. Brookfield and **Oliver T. Griswold** *They All Called It Tropical: True Tales of the Romantic Everglades National Park, Cape Sable, and the Florida Keys* (1949)

James Branch Cabell *The First Gentleman of America* (1942). Historical novel set in Spanish colonial times.
———. *There Were Two Pirates* (1946) Romantic novel based on the tale of the Spanish explorer Gasparilla.
———. *The Devil's Own Dear Son* (1949) Comic novel about the Hispanic owner of a St. Augustine motel.

Richard L. Campbell *Historical Sketches of Colonial Florida* (1892, rpt. 1975)

Henry Castor *The Year of the Spaniard* (1950) Romance set in Tampa during the Spanish-American War.

François Auguste Réné, Vicomte de Chateaubriand *Atala* (1801) A romantic tale of a Natchez Indian captured by the

Seminoles. It is doubtful whether the author, who travelled in the U.S. in 1791, visited Florida; his tale may be based on the writing of William Bartram.

Earl Conrad *Gulf Stream North* (1954)
Documentary novel about Menhaden fishing.

James Femimore Cooper *Jack Tier: or, The Florida Reef* (1848)
A historical romance of the U.S.-Mexican war.

Stephen Crane *The Open Boat and Other Stories* (1898)
Adventures at sea off the Florida coast based on Crane's expedition from Jacksonville to Cuba in 1896.

Harry Crews *Car* (1972)
A satiric comedy about a car wrecker in Jacksonville.
———. *The Gypsy's Curse* (1974)
Novel narrated by a deformed man living in a gymnasium in Jacksonville.
———. *Florida Frenzy* (1982)
Essays on regional topics.
———. *Naked in Garden Hills* (1969)
A novel in the Southern Gothic tradition depicting derelicts in a Polk County phosphate-mining area.

Elmer H. Davis *White Pants Willie* (1932)
Novel depicting the lives of the wealthy and fashionable in Palm Beach.

Mary Andrews Denison *Cracker Joe: A Story of Florida* (1887)
Novel about a north Florida cotton grower.

Jonathan Dickinson *God's Protecting Providence* (1699)
Dickinson's account of his shipwreck near Jupiter Island in September 1696, and journey to St. Augustine in company with some twenty other survivors, is one of the earliest books written and published in the New World.

Joan Didion *Miami* (1987)
Journalist's reflections on the city's political life.

Marjory Stoneman Douglas *The Everglades: River of Grass* (Rivers of America Series) (1947, rpt. 1987)
A classic study of the region, and a plea for its conservation.
———. *Road to the Sun* (1952)
A novel depicting the despoiling of the Everglades and the Miami real estate boom before World War I.
———. *Florida: The Long Frontier* (1967)
———. *Voice of the River: An Autobiography* (1987)

Ronald Foreman (ed.) *First Citizens and Other Florida Folks* (1984)
Tales from oral tradition.

Ernest Hemingway *To Have and Have Not* (1934)
Novel about a Key West boatman who becomes involved in crime through his efforts to support his family during the Depression.

Zora Neale Hurston *Jonah's Gourd Vine* (1934)
An Alabama cotton-picker becomes a preacher in a small Florida town. A novel based on the lives of Hurston's parents.
———. *Their Eyes Were Watching God* (1937)
The three marriages of an Eatonville woman.
———. *Dust Tracks on a Road* (1942)
Autobiography of the black anthropologist and novelist from Eatonville.
———. *Seraph on the Suwannee* (1948)
Novel about life in the turpentine camps of west Florida.
———. (ed. Alice Walker) *I Love Myself When I Am Laughing: A Zora Neale Hurston Reader* (1979)

Elia Kazan *Acts of Love* (1978)
Novel about life in a Greek immigrant community in Tarpon Springs.

Baynard Kendrick *Flames of Time* (1948)
Conflict among Indians and Spanish and American settlers in the early nineteenth century.

Sidney Lanier *Florida: Its Scenery, Climate, and History . . .* (1875)

Ring Lardner *Round Up* (1929)
A collection containing two stories set in Florida resorts during the 1920s: "The Golden Honeymoon," and "Sun Cured."

Elmore Leonard *LaBrava* (1983)
Detective novel set in Miami's South Beach area.

Ellen Call Long (ed. Margaret S. Chapman) *Florida Breezes: or, Florida New and Old* (1883, rpt. 1962)

Andrew Lytle *At the Moon's Inn* (1941)
Historical novel based on the life and travels of the Spanish explorer de Soto.

John D. MacDonald *The Deep Blue Goodbye* (1964)
The first of the author's detective mysteries centering on the waterfront character Travis McGee.

Walter S. Mason *The People of Florida as Portrayed in American Fiction* (1949)

Kevin McCarthy (ed.) *Florida Stories* (1988)
An anthology including writing from the Spanish conquest to the present.

John McPhee *Oranges* (1977)
A factual account of the citrus industry.

Alton C. Morris *Folksongs of Florida* (1950)

Robert Moss and **Arnaud de Borchgrave** *Monimbó* (1983)
A thriller set in Miami about a journalist's investigation of a third-world revolutionary plot.

Jacob Rhett Motte (ed. James F. Sunderman) *Journey Into Wilderness: An Army Surgeon's Account of Life in Camp and Field During the Creek and Seminole Wars, 1836–1838.* (1953)

Josephine Pinckney *Hilton Head* (1941)
Historical novel set in the late seventeenth century about an English traveller captured by the Spanish and imprisoned in St. Augustine.

Edith Pope *River in the Wind* (1954)
Novel set during the Seminole War.

Richard Pitts Powell *I Take This Land* (1962)
A novel depicting the development of southwest Florida 1895–1946.

Theodore Pratt *The Barefoot Mailman* (1939); *The Flame Tree* (1950); *The Big Bubble* (1951)
A trilogy of novels based on eastern Florida history 1880–1920 by a prolific Florida author who also wrote detective fiction set in the state under the pseudonym Timothy Brace. *Florida Roundabout* (1959) is a collection of regional tales.

Eugenia Price *Don Juan McQueen* (1974); *Maria* (1977); *Margaret's Story* (1980)
A family saga set against a background of eighteenth- and nineteenth-century history.

Kathryn Hall Proby *Audubon in Florida. With Selections from the Writings of John James Audubon* (1974)

Marjorie Kinnan Rawlings *The Yearling* (1938)
Classic novel of a farm boy's love for a deer set in central Florida in 1870. Rawlings, who owned a Cross Creek citrus farm from 1928 to 1947, also wrote *South Moon Under* (1933), *Golden Apples* (1935), *When the Whippoorwill* (1940), *Jacob's Ladder* (1950), and *The Secret River* (1955).
———. (ed. J. S. Bigham) *The Marjorie Rawlings Reader* (1956)
———. (ed. G. E. Bigelow and L. V. Monti) *Selected Letters of Marjorie Kinnan Rawlings* (1983)
Many letters in this selection describe life at Cross Creek.

J. Russell Reaver (ed.) *Florida Folktales* (1987)

Anne Rowe *The Idea of Florida in the American Literary Imagination* (1986)

Jack Rudloe *The Living Dock at Panacea* (1977)
A biologist's account of the marine life and the fishermen of the Gulf Coast.

Damon Runyon *Runyon à la Carte* (1949)
A collection containing four stories with Florida settings.

Charles Torrey Simpson *In Lower Florida Wilds* (1920); *Florida Wild Life* (1932)
Essays on wildlife and geology by a noted regional naturalist.

Frank G. Slaughter *Fort Everglades* (1951)
Historical novel set during the second Seminole War, one of several works by Slaughter with historical Florida settings.

Patrick Smith *Forever Island and Allapattah: A Patrick Smith Reader* (1972, 1979, rpt. 1980)
Novels about Indian life in the Everglades.

Harriet Beecher Stowe (ed. Mary B. Graff) *Palmetto Leaves* (1873, rpt. 1968)
The author of *Uncle Tom's Cabin* lived in Mandarin on the St. John's River during Reconstruction, and described the region in these sketches.

Maurice Thompson *A Tallahassee Girl* (1882)
Novel about a spring social season during Reconstruction.

Cornelius Vanderbilt, Jr. *Palm Beach* (1931)
An ironic account of social life in Palm Beach during Prohibition.

Robert Wilder *Bright Feather* (1948)
Romantic novel of the Seminole War.

Hugh Laussat Willoughby *Across the Everglades; a Canoe Journey of Exploration* (1898)

Constance Fenimore Woolson *Rodman the Keeper: Southern Sketches* (1886)
Short stories of society in St. Augustine c.1880.

José Yglesias *A Wake in Ybor City* (1963); *The Truth about Them* (1972)
Novels, the latter autobiographical, about Cuban-American society.

Delight Youngs *The Gladesman* (1955)
Novel depicting the exploitation of the Everglades.

GUIDE TO RESOURCES

De Wire, Elinor *Guide to Florida Lighthouses* (1988)

Federal Writers' Project *Florida: A Guide to the Southernmost State* (1939, rpt. 1976)
————. *The Spanish Missions of Florida* (1940)
————. *A Guide to Key West* (2d ed. 1949)

Fernald, Edward A. (ed.) *Atlas of Florida* (1981)

Florida Department of State *Florida Cultural Directory: A Guide to Florida's Cultural, Scientific, and Historical Resources* (1980)

Florida State Library (comp. Gill T. Bodziony) *Genealogy and Local History: A Bibliography* (rev. ed. 1978)

Gardner, Janette C. *An Annotated Bibliography of Florida Fiction, 1801–1980* (1983)

Harris, Michael H. (comp.) *Florida History: A Bibliography* (1972)

Marth, Del and **Martha** (eds.) *Florida Almanac: 1986–1987* (1987)

McRory, Mary O. *Florida in Fiction, a Bibliography* (1958)

Morris, Allen (ed.) *The Florida Handbook: 1987–88* (1987)

Ranson, Robert *Chronology of the Most Important Events Connected with Florida History During Four Hundred and Seventeen Years, 1513 to 1930* (2d ed. 1930)

Robie, Diane C. *Searching in Florida: A Reference Guide to Public and Private Records* (1982)

Terhune, Frances W. (ed.) *Florida Counties* (1984)

University of Florida. Bureau of Economic and Business Research (various eds.) *Florida Statistical Abstract* (annual)

SELECTED NONFICTION SOURCES

Abbey, Kathryn T. *Florida, Land of Change* (2d ed. 1948)

Allman, T. D. *Miami: City of the Future* (1987)

Andrews, Allen H. *A Yankee Pioneer in Florida. Recounting the Adventures of a City Chap Who Came to the Wilds of South Florida in the 1890's and Remained to Grow Up with the Country* (1950)

Archer, Jules *Indian Friend, Indian Foe: The Story of William S. Harney* (1969)

Arnade, Charles W. *The Siege of St. Augustine in 1702* (1959)

Ballinger, Kenneth *Miami Millions* (1936)

Barrientos, Bartolomé (trans. Anthony Kerrigan) *Pedro Menéndez de Aviles, Founder of Florida*. (Floridiana Facsimile and Reprint series) (1965)

Beach, Rex *The Miracle of Coral Gables* (1926)

Bennett, Charles E. *Florida's "French" Revolution, 1793–1795* (1981)

Bickel, Karl A. *The Mangrove Coast, the Story of the West Coast* (1942)

Blackman, Lucy W. *The Women of Florida* 2 vols. (1940)

Blassingame, Wyatt *Seminoles of Florida* (1959)

Bloodworth, Bertha E. and **Alton C. Morris** *Places in the Sun: The History and Romance of Florida Place-Names* (1978)

Bolton, Herbert E. *The Spanish Borderlands; a Chronicle of Old Florida and the Southwest* (1921)

Bothwell, Dick *Sunrise 200: A Lively Look at St. Petersburg's Past* (1975)

Bowe, Richard J. *Pictorial History of Florida* (1965)

Boyd, Mark F., Hale G. Smith, and **John W. Griffin** *Here They Once Stood: The Tragic End of the Apalachee Missions* (1951)

Brevard, Caroline (ed. James A. Robertson) *A History of Florida from the Treaty of 1763 to Our Own Times* 2 vols. (1924–1925)

Brinton, Daniel G. *Notes on the Floridian Peninsula, Its Literary History, Indian Tribes, and Antiquities* (1859)

Britt, Lora S. *My Gold Coast: South Florida in Earlier Years* (1984)

Brookfield, Charles M. and **Oliver Griswold** *They All Called It Tropical* (1977)

Browne, Jefferson B. *Key West, the Old and the New* (1912, rpt. 1973)

Buker, George E. *Swamp Sailors: Riverine Warfare in the Everglades, 1835–1842* (1975)

Burnett, Gene M. *Florida's Past: People and Events That Shaped the State* (1986)

Cabell, James B. and **A. J. Hanna** *The St. Johns: A Parade of Diversities* (1943)

Campbell, A. Stuart *The Cigar Industry of Tampa* (1939)

Campbell, George *Nature of Things on Sanibel* (rev. ed. 1988)

Cantrell, Elizabeth *When Kissimmee Was Young* (1948)

Carson, Ruby L. and **Charlton W. Tebeau** *Florida: From Indian Trail to Space Age* 3 vols. (1966)

Cash, Williams T. *The Story of Florida* 4 vols. (1938)

Caulfield, Patricia *Everglades* (1970)

Chandler, David L. *Henry Flagler: The Astonishing Life and Times of the Visionary Robber Baron Who Founded Florida* (1986)

Colburn, David R. *Racial Change and Community Crisis: St. Augustine, Florida, 1877–1980* (1985)

Covington, James W. (ed.) *Pirates, Indians, and Spaniards: Father Escobedo's "La Florida"* (1963)

Cox, Christopher *A Key West Companion* (1983)

Cox, Merlin G. and **J. E. Dovell** *Florida: From Secession to Space Age* (1974)

Damkohler, Elwin E. *Estero, Florida, 1882; Memoirs of the First Settler* (1967)

Dasmann, Raymond F. *No Further Retreat--the Fight to Save Florida* (1971)

Davis, William W. *The Civil War and Reconstruction in Florida* (1913)

Dovell, Junius E. *Florida: Historic, Dramatic, Contemporary* 4 vols. (1952)

Dunlop, Beth *Florida's Vanishing Architecture* (1988)

Dunn, Hampton *Florida Sketches* (1974)

Fairbanks, George R. *The Early History of Florida* (1857)
———. *The History and Antiquities of the City of St. Augustine, Florida, Founded A.D. 1565* (1858)
———. *History of Florida from Its Discovery by Ponce de Leon, in 1512, to the Close of the Florida War, in 1842* (1871)
———. *Florida, Its History and Romance* (1898)

Fernald, Edward A. *Florida: Its Problems and Prospects* (1972)

Fox, Charles D. *The Truth About Florida* (1925)

Frazure, Hoyt *Memories of Old Miami* (1969)

Frisbie, Louise K. *Peace River Pioneers* (1974)
———. *Yesterday's Polk County* (1976)

Fritz, Florence *Unknown Florida* (1963)

Fuller, Walter P. *St. Petersburg and Its People* (1972)

Gallagher, Patrick L. *The Cuban Exile: A Socio-Political Analysis* (1980)

Gannon, Michael V. *The Cross in the Sand: The Early Catholic Church in Florida, 1513–1870* (1965)

Glenn, James L. (ed. Harry A. Kersey, Jr.) *My Work Among the Florida Seminoles* (1982)

Graff, May B. *Mandarin on the St. Johns* (1953)

Griffin, John W. (ed.) *The Florida Indian and His Neighbors* (1949)

Grismer, Karl A. *The Story of St. Petersburg: The History of Lower Pinellas Peninsula and the Sunshine City* (1948)
———. *The Story of Fort Myers: The History of the Land of the Caloosahatchee and Southwest Florida* (1949)
———. *Tampa: A History of the City of Tampa and the Tampa Bay Region of Florida* (1950)

Groene, Bertram H. *Ante-Bellum Tallahassee* (1971)

Hann, John H. *Apalachee: The Land between the Rivers* (1988)

Hanna, Alfred J. and Kathryn Abbey *Lake Okeechobee--Wellspring of the Everglades* (1948)

Hanna, Kathryn T. *Florida: Land of Change* (2d rev. ed. 1948)

Harner, Charles E. *Florida's Promoters: The Men Who Made It Big* (1973)

Harvey, Karen *A Pictorial History of St. Augustine and St. John's County* (1980)

Harwood, Kathryn C. *The Lives of Vizcaya: Annals of a Great House* (1985)

Hatton, Hap *Tropical Splendor: An Architectural History of Florida* (1987)

Hawk, Robert *Florida's Army: Militia, State Troops and National Guard, 1565–1985* (1988)

Hepburn, Andrew *Florida* (1956)

Hoffstot, Barbara D. *Landmark Architecture of Palm Beach* (1974)

Hoole, William S. *Florida Territory in 1844* (1977)

Hopkins, James *Fifty Years of Citrus: The Florida Citrus Exchange, 1909–1959* (1960)

Howard, Clinton N. *The British Development of West Florida, 1763–1769* (1947)

Irving, Theodore (ed.) *The Conquest of Florida*, by Hernando de Soto (1869, rpt. 1971)

Jackson, W. R. *Early Florida through Spanish Eyes* (1954)

Jahoda, Gloria *The Other Florida* (1967)
———. *River of the Golden Ibis* (1973)
———. *Florida: A Bicentennial History* (States and the Nation series) (1976)

Johns, John E. *Florida during the Civil War* (1963)

Jones, Kenneth M. *War with the Seminoles, 1835–1842* (1975)

Joseph, Richard *Florida* (1958)

Kaufelt, Lynn *Key West Writers and Their Houses* (1986)

Kennedy, Stetson *Palmetto Country* (1942)

Kenny, Michael *The Romance of the Floridas* (1934)

Kersey, Harry A., Jr. *Pelts, Plumes and Hides: White Traders Among the Seminole Indians, 1870–1930* (1975)

Klingman, Peter D. *Josiah Walls: Florida's Black Congressman of Reconstruction* (1976)

Langley, Wright and Joan *Key West: Images of the Past* (1982)

Lanning, John T. *The St. Augustine Expedition of 1740* (1954)

Mahon, John K. *The Second Seminole War* (1968)

Martin, Richard A. and Daniel L. Schaefer *Jacksonville's Ordeal by Fire: A Civil War History* (1984)

Martin, Sidney W. *Florida During the Territorial Days* (1944)

Marx, Robert F. *Shipwrecks in Florida Waters* (1969)

McIver, Stuart *Yesterday's Palm Beach* (1976)

McKay, D. B. (ed.) *Pioneer Florida* 3 vols. (1959)

McNeer, May Y. *The Story of Florida* (1947)

McReynolds, Edwin C. *The Seminoles* (1957)
———. *Naples--Marco Island: An Illustrated History* (1981)

Morris, Allen *Florida Place Names* (1974)

Muir, Helen *Miami USA* (1953)

Nance, Elwood C. (ed.) *The East Coast of Florida: A History* (1962)

Neill, Wilfred T. *The Story of Florida's Seminole Indians* (1964)

Ney, John *Palm Beach: The Place, the People, Its Pleasures and Palaces* (1966)

Nolan, David *Fifty Feet in Paradise: The Booming of Florida* (1984)

Parks, Arva M. *Miami: The Magic City* (1981)

Patrick, Rembert W. *Florida Fiasco: Rampant Rebels on the Georgia-Florida Frontier, 1810–1815* (1954)
——— and Allen Morris *Florida under Five Flags* (4th ed. 1967)

Peters, Thelma *Lemon City: Pioneering on Biscayne Bay 1850–1925* (1976)

Peters, Virginia B. *The Florida Wars* (1979)

Pierce, Charles W. (ed. Donald W. Curl) *Pioneer Life in Southeast Florida* (1970)

Price, Hugh D. *The Negro and Southern Politics: A Chapter of Florida History* (1957)

Priestley, Herbert I. *Tristan de Luna, Conquistador of the Old South; a Study of Spanish Imperial Policy* (1936)

Proctor, Samuel (ed.) *Eighteenth Century Florida and Its Borderlands* (1975)
——— (ed.) *Eighteenth Century Florida and the Caribbean* (1976)
——— (ed.) *Eighteenth Century Florida Life on the Frontier* (1976)
——— (ed.) *Eighteenth Century Florida: The Impact of the American Revolution* (1978)

Rackleff, Robert B. *Close to Crisis: Florida's Environmental Problems* (1972)

"Rambler" *Guide to Florida* (1875, rpt. 1964)

Read, William A. *Florida Place-names of Indian Origin and Seminole Personal Names* (1934)

Rerick, Rowland H. *Memoirs of Florida; Embracing a General History of the Province, Territory and State* 2 vols. Edited by Francis P. Fleming (1902)

Richardson, Joseph M. *The Negro in the Reconstruction of Florida* (1965)

Rieff, David *Going to Miami* (1987)

Robertson, Fred L. *Soldiers of Florida in the Seminole Indian, Civil and Spanish American Wars* (1903)

Robertson, William B., Jr. *Everglades: the Park Story* (1959)

Rogers, William W. *Outposts on the Gulf: Saint George Island and Apalachicola from Early Exploration to World War II* (1986)

Sanger, Marjory B. *World of the Great White Heron: A Saga of the Florida Keys* (1967)

Schofield, Arthur C. *Yesterday's Bradenton* (1975)

Sewell, John *Memoirs and History of Miami* (1933)

Sherrill, Chris and Roger Aiella *Key West: The Last Resort* (1978)

Shipp, Barnard *The History of Hernando de Soto and Florida; or, Record of the Events of Fifty-six Years, From 1512 to 1568* (1881, rpt. 1971)

Shofner, Jerrell H. *Nor Is It Over Yet: Florida in the Era of Reconstruction, 1863–1877* (1974)

Shoumatoff, Alex *Florida Ramble* (1974)

Simpson, Charles T. *In Lower Florida Wilds* (1920)

Smith, Joseph B. *The Plot to Steal Florida: James Madison's Phony War* (1983)

Smith, Julia F. *Slavery and Plantation Growth in Ante-Bellum Florida, 1821–1860* (1968)

Tebeau, Charlton W. *Man in the Everglades: 2000 Years of Human History in the Everglades National Park* (rev. ed. 1968)
————. *Florida's Last Frontier--the History of Collier County* (rev. ed. 1970, rpt. 1985)
————. *A History of Florida* (1970, rpt. 1981, 1987)

Tepaske, John J. *The Governorship of Spanish Florida, 1700–1763* (1964)

Thompson, Arthur W. *Jacksonian Democracy on the Florida Frontier* (1961)

Van Campen, J. T. *The Story of St. Augustine, Florida's Colonial Capital* (1971)

Walton, George *Fearless and Free: The Seminole Indian War of 1835–1842* (1977)

Warner, Helen Garnie *Home Life in Florida* (1889)

Warnke, James R. *Ghost Towns of Florida* (1971)

Weidling, Philip and August Burghard *Checkered Sunshine: The Story of Fort Lauderdale, 1793–1955* (1966)

Westfall, L. Glenn *Key West: Cigar City U.S.A.* (1984)

Will, Lawrence E. *A Dredgeman of Cape Sable* (1967)
————. *Swamp to Sugar Bowl: Pioneer Days in Belle Glade* (1968)

Williamson, Edward C. *Florida in the Gilded Age, 1877–1893* (1976)

Willson, Minnie M. *The Seminoles of Florida* (1920)

Windhorn, Stan and Wright Langley *Yesterday's Florida Keys* (1974)

Wright, J. Leitch, Jr. *Florida in the American Revolution* (1975)

Ziegler, Louis W. and Herbert S. Wolfe *Citrus Growing in Florida* (1961)

GEORGIA

The South Atlantic state of Georgia is one of the original thirteen colonies. It is bordered on the north by Tennessee and North Carolina; on the east by South Carolina, the Savannah River, and the Atlantic Ocean; on the south by Florida and St. Marys River; and on the west by Florida, Alabama, and the Chattahoochee River.

FULL NAME State of Georgia
POSTAL ABBREVIATION GA
INHABITANT Georgian
ADMITTED TO THE UNION Jan. 2, 1788.
 4th state
POPULATION (est. 1987) 6,222,000.
 Percent of US total: 2.56%. Rank: 11th

CAPITAL CITY Atlanta, the largest city in the state, located on the Chattahoochee River in northwest central Georgia; population 426,090 (est. 1984). Founded as a railroad terminus in 1836, it was incorporated as the town of Marthasville in 1843 and as the city of Atlanta in 1847. It became the temporary state capital in 1868, replacing Milledgeville, and the permanent capital in 1887.

STATE NAME AND NICKNAMES Named after King George II of Britain by James Oglethorpe in fulfillment of the conditions of his charter. Also known as the Peach State, the Goober State, the Empire State of the South, the Cracker State, the Buzzard State, the Yankee-Land of the South.

STATE SEAL Georgia's seal has two faces. On one side is a landscape showing a ship at dockside taking on a load of tobacco and cotton; in the distance is a farmer plowing and a flock of sheep under a tree. The border bears the state motto, "Agriculture and Commerce, 1776." The other side shows the state coat of arms, consisting of three pillars, representing the three branches of government and bearing the

titles "Wisdom," "Justice," and "Moderation," holding up an arch with the legend "Constitution." Beneath the arch stands an armed man. The legend around the border reads "State of Georgia, 1776."

MOTTOES Agriculture and Commerce, 1776
 Wisdom, Justice, Moderation

SONGS "Georgia on My Mind," lyrics by Stuart Gorrell, music by Hoagy Carmichael, and state waltz, "Our Georgia," music by James B. Burch.

SYMBOLS
Flower Cherokee rose
Wildflower azalea
Tree live oak
Bird brown thrasher
Gem quartz
Mineral staurolite
Marine mammal right whale
Fish largemouth bass
Insect honeybee
Fossil shark tooth
Atlas The Atlas of Georgia

LICENSE PLATES (1) Dark green on white, with legend indicating county name. (2) Red on white with red border, bearing blue legend "Ga. 1776-1976."

FLAG One-third of the flag is a field of blue bearing the state coat of arms; the remaining two-thirds constitute the Confederate flag (a blue-and-white cross of St. Andrew, bearing 13 white stars, on a field of red).

GEOGRAPHY AND CLIMATE

Georgia, largest state east of the Mississippi, is bounded on the north by the Blue Ridge of the Appalachian Mountains, to the east by the marshy Atlantic coast, and to the south by lowlands and the Okefenokee Swamp. Notable among states for the unusual number of soil types (including "Georgia red clay"), Georgia has an ideal climate for cotton and rice agriculture.

AREA 58,910 square miles. Rank: 21st
INLAND WATER 854 square miles
GEOGRAPHIC CENTER Twiggs, 18 miles SE of Macon
ELEVATIONS *Highest point:* Brasstown Bald, Towns-Union County, 4,784 feet. *Lowest point:* Atlantic Ocean, sea level. *Mean elevation:* 600 feet

MAJOR RIVERS Altamaha, Chattahoochee, Savannah

MAJOR LAKES AND RESERVOIRS Sidney Lanier, Allatoona, Seminole, Eufaula, Sinclair, Clark Hill.

TIDAL SHORELINE 2,344 miles, Atlantic coast

LAND USE

	Thousands of acres
Urban (1982)	1,632
Rural (1982)	32,536
Cropland (1982)	6,568
Pastureland (1982)	2,977
Rangeland (1982)	0
Forestland (1982)	21,884
State parks and recreation areas (1983)	60
National park system (1984)	40
National forest system (1984)	1,911
Tribal lands (1984)	0

TEMPERATURES The highest recorded temperature was 113°F on March 27, 1978, at Greenville. The lowest was -17°F on January 27, 1940, at CCC Camp F-16.

NATIONAL SITES

NATIONAL BATTLEFIELD PARK Kennesaw Mountain
NATIONAL HISTORIC SITES Andersonville, Martin Luther King, Jr.
NATIONAL MILITARY PARKS Chickamauga and Chattanooga
NATIONAL MONUMENTS Fort Frederica, Fort Pulaski, Ocmulgee
NATIONAL RECREATION AREA Chattahoochee River

NATIONAL SCENIC TRAIL Appalachian, Natchez Trace
NATIONAL SEASHORE Cumberland Island
NATIONAL WILDLIFE REFUGES Eufaula, Okefenokee, Piedmont, Savannah–Blackbeard Island/Harris Neck/Pinckney Island/Tybee/Wassaw/Wolf Island

HISTORY

1540	Hernando de Soto, searching the Mississippi region for gold, passes through Georgia.
1566	Pedro Menendez de Aviles builds a fort on Santa Catalina (St. Catherine's) Island.
1573	Franciscan friars erect a mission on Cumberland Island.
1689	Spanish missions along the Georgia coast are abandoned due to English, Indian, and pirate attacks.
1721	Fort King George, the first English settlement in the territory, is built at the mouth of the Altamaha River.
1732	*June 9.* King George II signs a charter giving James Edward Oglethorpe and his English colleagues control over "The land lying between the Savannah and Altamaha Rivers."
1733	*February 12* Led by Oglethorpe, the first Georgia colonists arrive at Yamacraw Bluff (Savannah).
1735	Augusta is founded.
1740	The Reverend George Whitefield and James Habersham establish the Bethesda Orphan House.
1743	Oglethorpe returns to England permanently as the colony makes the transition from military to civil government.
1749	The ban on slaveholding is removed.

1754	Georgia becomes a royal province with Governor John Reynolds, a council, and an elected house of commons.
1757	*November 3.* British sign a treaty of peace and commerce with Creek and Cherokee as a strategy against the French.
1763	*April 7.* The *Georgia Gazette,* Georgia's first newspaper, begins publication in Savannah.
1766	*February.* Colonists riot in Savannah in opposition to the Stamp Act.
1774	Due to strong crown loyalty, Georgia declines to send delegates to First Continental Congress.
1776	*August 2.* Delegates sign the Declaration of Independence.
1777	*February 5.* Legislature adopts the state's first constitution.
1778	English capture Savannah during the Revolutionary War.
1779	*September.* Colonial troops aided by French fleet lay siege to Savannah.
1781	The Continental Army, under the command of Colonel "Light Horse Harry" Lee, recaptures Augusta, occupied by the British since 1779.
1782	*July 12.* The British surrender Savannah. Governor John Martin reestablishes state government.
1788	*January 2.* Georgia becomes the fourth state to ratify the federal constitution.
1793	*June 20.* Eli Whitney invents the cotton gin near Savannah.
1802	Sarah Porter Hillhouse becomes the first woman in the US to own and edit a newspaper; *The Washington Gazette.*
1816	*April.* Regular steamboat transportation begins on the Savannah River.
1819	*May 22.* The *S.S. Savannah,* first steamship to cross the Atlantic, leaves Savannah for Liverpool, England.
1825	*February 12.* Georgia extinguishes major Indian land titles when Creeks cede all remaining lands east of Flint River.
	April 30. Creek Indian chief William McIntosh is murdered by tribesmen for his involvement in the ceding of their lands.
1829	The gold rush in northern Georgia sends thousands of whites into Cherokee territory. State legislature claims legal authority over area.
1831	The US Supreme Court rejects Cherokee pleas against removal laws.
1832	The state arbitrarily divides the Cherokee territory in north Georgia into 10 counties and begins raffling land and gold lots off to homesteaders.
1835	*December.* Cherokee accept 5 million dollars and new lands in the West in exchange for their Georgia holdings.
1842	*March 30.* Dr. Crawford Long, a Georgian physician, becomes the first to administer ether for surgery.
1844	Dispute over the ownership of slaves by Bishop James Andrews brings about the division of the Methodist Church into northern and southern conferences.
1861	*January 19.* Georgia secedes from the Union.
1863	*September 20.* Confederate troops defeat Union troops in the Battle of Chickamauga.
1864	*November 15.* General Sherman leaves Atlanta and begins his march to the sea.
1865	*May 10.* Jefferson Davis, president of the Confederate States, is captured near Atlanta.
1867	*April 1.* Refusing to ratify the 14th Amendment, Georgia is placed under military rule.
	Ku Klux Klan makes first appearance in Georgia.
1868	*July 21.* Legislature ratifies the 14th Amendment and civil government is restored.
1869	*December.* Georgia is again placed under military rule for failure to comply with the Reconstruction Acts.
1886	John Styth Pemberton invents the concoction Coca-Cola.
1870	*July 15.* Dominated by Carpetbaggers, Georgia ratifies the 15th Amendment and is formally readmitted to the Union.
1881	*October.* International Cotton Exposition is held in Atlanta.
1900	In her book, *Georgia Land and People,* Francis Mitchell originates the idea of an annual celebration of the Oglethorpe party's arrival date.
1902	Martha Berry opens a school for poor mountain children.
1907	A statewide prohibition law is passed.

1912	Juliette Gordon Low of Savannah organizes the Girl Scouts of America.
1921	Boll weevil seriously damage the state's cotton crop.
1922	Rebecca Felton is the first woman senator.
1937	Margaret Mitchell of Atlanta receives the Pulitzer Prize for her novel, *Gone With the Wind*.
1938	*March*. Prohibition is repealed.
1947	*January 18*. The sudden death of Governor-elect Eugene Tallmadge results in outgoing Governor Ellis Arnall's refusal to vacate office.
1948	*November 17*. Herman Tallmadge, Eugene's son, wins special election for Governor. Tallmadge says he will preserve segregation at all costs.
1950	White Atlanta women establish Help Our Public Education (HOPE).
1960	Lester G. Maddox organizes Georgians Unwilling to Surrender (GUTS), boycotting any store that changes its segregation policies.
1961	*January*. Charlayne Hunter and Hamilton Holmes, with court orders, request permission to enter the University of Georgia. State officials briefly terminate school funds and mobs attack Hunter's dormitory.
1966	Race riots in Atlanta.
1968	*April 9*. The Reverend Martin Luther King, Jr. is buried in Atlanta. His remains are moved later to a crypt near Ebenezer Baptist Church.
1970	*January 15*. King's crypt is dedicated as part of a memorial for the Martin Luther King Center for Social Change.
1973	Maynard Jackson, Jr. becomes Atlanta's first black mayor.
1976-1980	During Jimmy Carter's presidency, Georgians become prominent on the national political scene. Tourism increases.
1986	Prolonged drought reaches crisis proportions.
1987	For the second consecutive year, Gwinnet County in metro Atlanta is the fastest-growing county in the nation.

DEMOGRAPHY

Population (est. 1987) . . . 6,222,000
Population (1980) 5,462,992
Population density in persons
per square mile (1980) 92.7

POPULATION BY RACE (1980)
American Indian/Aleut/
Eskimo 7,619
Asian/Pacific Islander 24,461
Black 1,465,457
Hispanic 61,261
White 3,948,007
Other 18,721

POPULATION CHARACTERISTICS (1980)
Percent of state population
Urban 62.4
Rural 37.6
Under 18 . . . . 30.1
65 or older 9.5
College-educated 15.3
Families below poverty line . . . 13.2
Public assistance recipients 6.9

Per capita personal income
(1980) $13,224
Millionaires per 100,000
residents (1982) 102.6
Average life expectancy
in years (1980) 72.2

Marriage rate per 1,000
residents (1986) 11.8
Divorce rate per 1,000
residents (1986) 5.4
Birth rate per 1,000
residents (1985) 16.7
Infant mortality rate per 1,000
births (1985) 10.8
Abortion rate per 1,000
live births (1985) 397
Crime rate per 100,000
residents (1985)
Violent 587.6
Property 4,867.8
Federal and state prisoners per
100,000 residents (1984) 266
Alcohol consumption in gallons
per capita (1985) 37.2
Deaths from motor vehicle accidents
per 100,000 residents (1985) . . 22.3

MAJOR CITIES
	1984 population (est.)
Albany	84,970
Atlanta	426,090
Columbus	174,824
Macon	120,226
Savannah	145,014

GOVERNMENT AND POLITICS

Number of US Representatives 10
Electoral votes 12

POLITICAL PARTY NOMINEES FROM STATE
* winner

John Milton	1789	P
Edward Telfair	1789	P
William Harris Crawford	1824	P
Herschel Vespasian Johnson (D)	1860	VP
Thomas Edward Watson (Populist)	1896	VP
Thomas Edward Watson (People's)	1904	P
Austin Holcomb (Continental)	1904	P
John Temple Graves (Independence)	1908	VP
Thomas Edward Watson (People's)	1908	P
Will Vereen (Farmer Labor)	1928	VP
James William Upshaw (Prohibition)	1932	P
Clennon King (Independent Afro-American)	1960	P
Reginald Carter (Independent Afro-American)	1960	VP
J.B. Stoner (National States' Rights)	1964	VP
Samuel Marvin Griffin (American Independent)	1968	VP
Linda Jenness (Socialist Worker)	1972	P
Jimmy Carter* (D, Social Democrat)	1976	P
Lester Garfield Maddox (American Independent)	1976	P
Jimmy Carter (D)	1980	P

PRESIDENTIAL PRIMARY ELECTION In 1988, Georgia sent 86 Democratic delegates and 48 Republican delegates to the national conventions.

CONSTITUTION Georgia has had ten constitutions: 1777, 1789, 1798, 1861, 1865, 1868, 1877, 1945, 1976, and the present one, adopted in 1982.

LEGISLATURE The General Assembly is divided into the Senate (56 members, 2-year term, minimum age 25) and the House of Representatives (180 members, 2-year term, minimum age 21). In 1987, the annual salary was $10,125.

JUDICIARY The highest court is the Supreme Court, with seven judges serving 6-year terms. In 1987, the annual salary was $75,564.

EXECUTIVE The governor serves a 4-year term; the minimum age for holding office is 30. In 1987, the annual salary was $84,594. There are 12 other elected officials.

PRESIDENTIAL VOTE 1948-1988 *(in percents)*

Year	State Winner	Democratic	Republican
1948	Truman (D)	60.8	18.3
1952	Stevenson (D)	69.7	30.3
1956	Stevenson (D)	66.4	33.3
1960	Nixon (R)	37.4	62.5
1964	Goldwater (R)	45.9	54.1
1968	George C. Wallace (American Independent, 42.8)	26.8	30.4
1972	Nixon (R)	24.7	75.3
1976	Carter (D)	66.7	33.0
1980	Carter (D)	55.8	41.0
1984	Reagan (R)	39.8	60.2
1988	Bush (R)	40.0	60.0

GOVERNORS

Colonial Governors under the Trustees

James Edward Oglethorpe	1733-1743
William Stephens, president	1743-1751
Henry Parker, president	1751-1753
Patrick Graham, president	1753-1754

Colonial Governors under the Crown

John Reynolds	1754-1757
Henry Ellis	1757-1760
Sir James Wright	1760-1782

State Governors

Archibald Bulloch	1776-1777
Button Gwinnett	1777
John A. Treutlen	1777-1778
John Houstoun	1778-1779
John Wereat (acting)	1779
George Walton	1779-1780

95

Richard Howley	1780	Hoke Smith (D)	1907-1909
Stephen Heard (acting)	1780-1781	Joseph M. Brown (D)	1909-1911
Myrick Davies (acting)	1781	Hoke Smith (D)	1911
Nathan Brownson	1781-1782	Joseph M. Brown (D)	1911-1913
John Martin	1782-1783	John M. Slaton (D)	1913-1915
Lyman Hall	1783-1784	Nathaniel E. Harris (D)	1915-1917
John Houstoun	1784-1785	Hugh M. Dorsey (D)	1917-1921
Samuel Elbert	1785-1786	Thomas W. Hardwick (D)	1921-1923
Edward Telfair	1786-1787	Clifford M. Walker (D)	1923-1927
George Matthews	1787-1788	Lamartine G. Hardman (D)	1927-1931
George Handley	1788-1789	Richard B. Russell (D)	1931-1933
George Walton (D-R)	1789-1790	Eugene Talmadge (D)	1933-1937
Edward Telfair (D-R)	1790-1793	Eurith D. Rivers (D)	1937-1941
George Matthews (D-R)	1793-1796	Eugene Talmadge (D)	1941-1943
Jared Irwin (D-R)	1796-1798	Ellis Arnall (D)	1943-1947
James Jackson (D-R)	1798-1801	Melvin E. Thompson (D/	
David Emanuel (D-R)	1801	acting)	1947-1949
Josian Tattnall (D-R)	1801-1802	Herman Talmadge (D)	1949-1955
John Milledge (D-R)	1802-1806	Marvin Griffin (D)	1955-1959
Jared Irwin (D-R)	1806-1809	S. Ernest Vandiver (D)	1959-1963
David B. Mitchell (D-R)	1809-1813	Carl E. Sanders (D)	1963-1967
Peter Early (D-R)	1813-1815	Lester G. Maddox (D)	1967-1971
David B. Mitchell (D-R)	1815-1817	Jimmy Carter (D)	1971-1975
William Rabun (D-R)	1817-1819	George Busbee (D)	1975-1983
Matthew Talbot (D-R)	1819	Joe Frank Harris (D)	1983-
John Clark (D-R)	1819-1823		
George M. Troup (D-R)	1823-1827		
John Forsyth (D-R)	1827-1829		
George R. Gilmer (National			
Republican)	1829-1831		
Wilson Lumpkin (Union			
Democrat)	1831-1835		
William Schley (Union			
Democrat)	1835-1837		
George R. Gilmer (Whig)	1837-1839		
Charles J. Macdonald (D)	1839-1843		
George W. Crawford (Whig)	1843-1847		
George W.B. Towns (D)	1847-1851		
Howell Cobb (D)	1851-1853		
Herschel V. Johnson (D)	1853-1857		
Joseph E. Brown (D)	1857-1865		
James Johnson (D/provi-			
sional)	1865		
Charles J. Jenkins (D)	1865-1868		
Thomas H. Ruger (military			
governor)	1868		
Rufus B. Bullock (R)	1868-1871		
Benjamin Conley (R/acting)	1871-1872		
James M. Smith (D)	1872-1877		
Alfred H. Colquit (D)	1877-1882		
Alexander H. Stephens (D)	1882-1883		
James S. Boynton (D/act-			
ing)	1883		
Henry D. McDaniel (D)	1883-1886		
John B. Gordon (D)	1886-1890		
William J. Northen (D)	1890-1894		
William Y. Atkinson (D)	1894-1898		
Allen D. Candler (D)	1898-1902		
Joseph M. Terrell (D)	1902-1907		

MINIMUM AGES

Majority	18
Marriage with parental consent . . .	16
Marriage without parental consent .	18
Making a will	18
Buying alcohol	21
Jury duty	18
Leaving school	16
Driver's license	16

CAPITAL PUNISHMENT
Number executed 1976-88: 13
On death row Aug. 1, 1988: 108

MILITARY INSTALLATIONS
Total number: 21
Major bases:
  Army: 4
  Air Force: 1

FINANCES

Thousands of dollars

GENERAL REVENUE (1985)

Total general revenue . . .	7,572,067
Total tax revenue	4,525,038
Sales and gross receipts . . .	2,207,367
Individual income taxes . .	1,718,326
Corporate net income taxes . .	418,251

GENERAL EXPENDITURE (1985)

Total general expenditure .	7,086,938
Education	3,034,575

Public welfare	1,135,368
Health	268,390
Hospitals	335,531
Natural resources	182,458
Highways	940,348
Police	71,815
Corrections	230,337

FEDERAL AID (1985) 2,371,486

ECONOMY

Cotton, peanuts, pecans, and peaches are the traditional Georgia crops, and account for the bulk of the state's agricultural output. Poultry farming is a rising industry. Total farm cash receipts were $3.3 billion in 1983 from about 50,000 farms. Manufacturing now dominates the state's economy, with Georgia a leading producer of textiles, paper and pulp, processed foods, lumber products, aircraft and other transportation equipment, clothing, gum resins, turpentine, and pine oil. The nation's primary source of kaolin and fuller's earth are mines near the Georgia coast. Marble, granite, bauxite, talc, soapstone, and small quantities of gold are other mineral products.

EMPLOYMENT (1984)

Thousands of persons

Total number of employed workers	2,594
Construction	132.4
Finance, insurance, and real estate	128.9

Government	439.9
Manufacturing	545.4
Mining	7.9
Services	440.0
Transportation, communications, and utilities	155.1
Wholesale and retail trade	608.2

Percent of civilian labor force unemployed (1984) 6.0

DEPARTMENT OF DEFENSE (1985)

Civilian workers employed	40,356
Military personnel	64,390
Contract awards	$3.250 billion

ENERGY SOURCES FOR ELECTRIC UTILITIES (1983)

Percent

Coal	81.8
Gas	0.2
Hydroelectric	6.1
Nuclear	11.7
Petroleum	0.2

TRANSPORTATION

Motor vehicles registered in state (1986)	4,840,848
Miles of roads, streets, and highways (1986)	106,607
Miles of Class I railway operated (1986)	5,031
Airports (1983)	302
Major aviation hubs (1983)	2
Largest hub: Atlanta	
Major ports, with gross tonnage in thousands (1985) Savannah	11,327

CULTURE AND EDUCATION

Native American tribes
Georgia was formerly home to the Apalachicola, Chatot, Cherokee, Chiaha, Chickasaw, Creek, Guale, Hitchiti, Icafui, Oconee, Okmulgee, Sawokli, Shawnee, Tamathli, Yamasee, Yuchi, and Yui tribes.

Religions, ethnicities, and languages
At the time of the Civil War, about 56 percent of the state's population was white–mainly of European Protestant descent–and 44 percent was black. The 19th-century mass immigrations from Europe and Asia barely affected Georgia. It remains overwhelmingly Protestant, with Baptists constituting about two-thirds of the population, followed by Methodists, Presbyterians, and Disciples of Christ. In 1980, 2.6 percent of Georgia's population

spoke a language other than English at home.

Major museums and libraries
Columbus Museum of Arts and Sciences
High Museum of Art, Atlanta
Telfair Academy of Arts and Sciences, Savannah

Major arts organizations
Alliance Theatre, Atlanta
Atlanta Ballet Company
Atlanta Opera
Atlanta Symphony Orchestra
Savannah Symphony Orchestra

Colleges and universities
Number public (1986-87) 36
Number private (1986-87) 45

Total enrollment, in full-time equivalent
  students (1985) 162,000

Public elementary and secondary schools
Expenditure per pupil in average daily
  attendance (1986-87) $3,167
Pupil-teacher ratio (1987) 18.9
Average teacher salary (1986-87) $25,600

Major league sports teams
Baseball: Atlanta Braves
Basketball: Atlanta Hawks
Football: Atlanta Falcons

Holidays
Georgia Day. February 12
Confederate Memorial Day. April 26

GEORGIA IN LITERATURE

Raymond Andrews *Appalachee Red* (1978); *Rosiebelle Lee Wildcat Tennessee* (1980); *Baby Sweet's* (1983)
Trilogy of novels about black life in Muskhogean County, 1910–1960.

John Brown (ed. F. N. Boney) *Slave Life in Georgia* (1855, rpt. 1972)
Narrative of a fugitive slave describing plantation life.

Olive Ann Burns *Cold Sassy Tree* (1984)
Novel of family life in a small town in 1906.

Erskine Caldwell *Tobacco Road* (1932); *God's Little Acre* (1933)
The best-known novels of this prolific Georgia-born writer are portrayals of impoverished sharecroppers and mountain folk. Their realistic portrayal of squalid lives, once found offensive by some readers, is still regarded as an accurate record of backwoods life. Other works by Caldwell with Georgia settings include *Tragic Ground* (1944), *Jenny by Nature* (1961), and *Georgia Boy* (1943), a collection of comic tales about a poor white family.

Brainard Cheney *River Rogue* (1942)
Historical novel about raftsmen on the Oconee and Altamaha rivers during the 1880s.

Lonnie Coleman *Beulah Land* (1973); *Look Away, Beulah Land* (1977); *The Legacy of Beulah Land* (1980)
Trilogy of novels about manners and customs of ante- and post-bellum Georgia.

Harry Crews *Childhood: The Biography of a Place* (1978)
Memoir of rural Bacon County where Crews was born and grew up on a farm before World War II. Rural Georgia is also the setting of *Gospel Singer* (1968), *This Thing Don't Lead to Heaven* (1970), and *Feast of Snakes* (1976).

John Richard Dennett *The South As It Is, 1865–1866* (1965, rpt. 1986)
Dennett, a journalist working for *The Nation*, began a nine-month tour of the South in 1865, sending these thirty-six dispatches home.

James Dickey *Deliverance* (1970)
Novel about four Atlanta businessmen on a weekend hunting trip that turns into a nightmare in the backwoods.

Augusta Jane Evans *St. Elmo* (1866)
Popular, sentimental novel expressing a Confederate point of view. Evans, the first best-selling Southern novelist, was visiting the Columbus mansion of her aunt and uncle when she began writing the book.

Betsy Fancher *The Lost Legacy of Georgia's Golden Isles* (1971)
Account of the landscape and history of the Atlantic islands.

Rebecca Latimer Felton *Country Life in Georgia in the Days of My Youth* (1919)
Felton was an abolitionist and suffragist who aggressively campaigned for a wide range of social reforms during the later nineteenth century. In *The Romantic Story of Georgia's Women* (1930) she included her own biography.

Glen Fleishman *While Rivers Flow* (1963)
Novel about the Cherokees' struggle for survival in the early nineteenth century.

Williams Forrest *Trail of Tears* (1958)
Novel about the Cherokees' expulsion to Oklahoma, centering on their leader, John Ross.

John Porter Fort *God in the Straw Pen* (1931)
Novel about the Methodist revival of 1830 and its effect on the rural poor.

Georgia Writers' Project *Drums and Shadows: Survival Studies among the Georgia Coastal Negroes* (1940, rpt. 1986)
Observations of folkways collected in the late 1930s.

Will N. Harben *Northern Georgia Sketches* (1900)
A collection of realistic sketches of poor white and black rural people. Harben, who grew up in Dalton in the 1860s, was a prolific writer whose Georgia novels include *Mam' Linda* (1907), about racial injustice, and *Gilbert Neal* (1908), about poor white mountain farmers.

Joel Chandler Harris *Uncle Remus: His Songs and His Sayings* (1880); *Nights with Uncle Remus* (1883)
Harris' tales, narrated by a fictitious old black slave, originated in a column in the Atlanta *Constitution* in 1879, and were based on the dialect tales he had heard on a plantation. In addition to his five Uncle Remus collections, Chandler published numerous stories and novels about Georgia life, including *Mingo and Other Sketches in Black and White* (1884), and *On the Plantation: A Story of a Georgia Boy's Adventures during the War* (1892, rpt. 1980), an autobiographical novel about his youth.

Mariella G. Hartsfield *Tall Betsy and Dunce Baby: South Georgia Folktales* (1987)
Stories collected from white residents of Grady County.

Richard M. Johnston *Dukesborough Tales* (1871, rpt. 1883)
Humorous dialect tales written in the 1850s in imitation of Longstreet. When, in the 1880s, regional humor enjoyed national popularity, he returned to the genre and produced several other works, including *Mr. Absalom Billingslea and Other Georgia Folk* (1888).

Patricia Jones-Jackson *When Roots Die: Endangered Traditions on the Sea Islands* (1987)
Study of Gullah language and culture.

MacKinlay Kantor *Arouse and Beware* (1936); *Andersonville* (1955)
Novels about Confederate prisons at Andersonville and Belle Island.

Fanny (Frances Ann) Kemble *Journal of a Residence on a Georgian Plantation* (1863, rpt. 1961, 1984)
The English actress toured America in the 1830s and married Pierce Butler, owner of a plantation with 700 slaves. She wrote the journal in 1839 but published it in 1863 to influence English opinion against the South, whose "peculiar institution" she despised.

John Oliver Killens *Youngblood* (1954, rpt. 1982)
Novel of a black rural family in the early years of this century.

Ronald G. Killion and **Charles T. Waller** (eds.) *A Treasury of Georgia Folklore* (1972)

Richard Kluger *Members of the Tribe* (1977)
Novel about Jews in the South; the first half describes Savannah, 1870–1914; the second is a fictional version of the Frank murder trial and lynching of 1913.

Mills Lane (ed.) *The Rambler in Georgia; Desultory Observations on the Situation, Extent, Climate, Population, Manners, Customs, Commerce, Constitution, Government, etc. of the State from the Revolution to the Civil War Recorded by Thirteen Travelers* (1973)
————. (ed.) *War Is Hell: William T. Sherman's Personal Narrative of His March through Georgia* (1974)
Narrative mainly drawn from Sherman's letters to his wife.

Jack Leigh *The Ogeechee: A River and Its People* (1986)
Portrait of a traditional rural way of life.

Augustus Baldwin Longstreet *Georgia Scenes, Characters, and Incidents* . . . (1835, rpt. 1970)
Longstreet's tall tales and portraits of regional characters and manners, which began to appear in Milledgeville and Augusta newspapers in the 1820s, are among the earliest examples of humorous regional writing, and influenced the style of Mark Twain. He also wrote *Master William Mitten* (1864), a partly autobiographical novel about growing up in Georgia.

Jane Maguire *On Shares: Ed Brown's Story* (1976)
Study of farmers' efforts to survive economic hardships and the ravages of the boll weevil.

Van Wyck Mason *Rivers of Glory* (1942)
Novel of the Revolution, with an account of the Siege of Savannah.

Carson McCullers *The Heart Is a Lonely Hunter* (1940)
Like that of Flannery O'Connor, McCullers' work is regarded as a part of the Southern literary tradition rather than as a product of a narrowly regional school, but owes some of its peculiarity to her Columbus upbringing.

Barbara McKenzie *Flannery O'Connor's Georgia* (1980)
An illustrated essay on the writer's milieu.

Caroline Miller *Lamb in His Bosom* (1933)
Pulitzer Prize–winning novel about backwoods life before the Civil War.
———. *Lebanon* (1944)
Historical novel about frontier life.

Margaret Mitchell *Gone with the Wind* (1936)
Classic romantic novel describing a plantation during the Civil War and Reconstruction.

Flannery O'Connor *Wise Blood* (1952); *The Violent Bear It Away* (1960); *The Complete Stories* (1972)
Novels and stories of religious quest and expiation set in realistically depicted small towns and backwoods.

Lydia Parrish *Slave Songs of the Georgia Sea Islands* (1942)

Eugenia Price *The Blood Invader* (1965); *New Moon Rising* (1969); *Lighthouse* (1971)
A trilogy of historical romances set on St. Simon's Island during the nineteenth century.

Art Rosenbaum *Folk Visions and Voices: Traditional Music and Song in North Georgia* (1983)

John Rozier (ed.) *The Granite Farm Letters: Civil War Correspondence of Edgeworth and Sallie Bird* (1988)
Edgeworth, who served with Toombs and Longstreet in the major campaigns of the war, exchanged letters with his wife, who wrote from their cotton plantation in middle Georgia, and from Richmond, where she travelled to be near her husband.

Elise Sanguinetti *The Last of the Whitfields* (1962, rev. ed. 1984)
Novel about agitation for civil rights in a small town.

Carroll Procter Scruggs *Georgia from Plum Orchard to Plum Nelly* (1971)

Descriptions of places and buildings in coastal and northwestern Georgia.

William Gilmore Simms *Guy Rivers* (1834)
Novel of northern Georgia outlaws during 1820s gold rush.

Charles Henry Smith *A Side Show of the Southern Side of the War by Bill Arp, So Called* (1866)
Smith, a Civil War veteran, state senator, and mayor of Rome, 1868–1869, contributed letters under the pseudonym Bill Arp to the Atlanta *Constitution* for more than thirty years. The letters had at first a satirical edge and a political tone, but later became essays in rustic Southern philosophy.

Lillian Smith *Strange Fruit* (1944)
Novel centering on the conflict between racial prejudices and personal affections in a small Georgia town.

John L. Spivak *Georgia Nigger* (1932)
Realistic novel about a black prisoner on a chain gang.

Patrick Tailfer *A True and Historical Narrative of the Colony of Georgia* (1741, rpt. 1842, 1971)
A satiric account of Georgia politics and history by a discontented former resident.

William Tappan Thompson *Major Jones's Courtship* (1843); *Major Jones's Chronicles of Pineville* (1845); *Major Jones's Sketches of Travel* (1848)
Thompson, a journalist and colleague of A. B. Longstreet, created one of the earliest representations of the Georgia cracker in these collections of humorous anecdotes and homespun philosophy.

Jean Toomer *Cane* (1923)
Collection of short stories and essays evoking black life in Georgia and Washington, D.C.

Alice Walker *The Third Life of Grange Copeland* (1970)
Novel about a black rural family. Walker has also written a collection of poems, *Revolutionary Petunia* (1973), evoking her childhood in Eatonton.

Margaret Walker *Jubilee* (1966)
Historical novel, written in part as a slave narrative, set before and after the Civil War.

Eliot Wigginton *The Foxfire Book: Hog Dressing, Log Cabin Building, Mountain Crafts and Foods, Planting by the Signs, Snake Lore, Hunting Tales, Faith Healing, Moonshining, and Other Affairs of Plain Living* (1972)
———. *Foxfire 2: Ghost Stories, Spring Wild Plant Foods, Spinning and Weaving, Midwifing, Burial Customs, Corn Shuckin's, Wagon Making and More Affairs of Plain Living* (1973)
Vernacular anthologies of Appalachian folkways preserving the folkways and dialect of the region.

Vinnie Williams *Walk Egypt* (1960); *Greenbones* (1967)
Novels set in Georgia depicting rural speech and folkways.

Constance Fenimore Woolson *Jupiter Lights* (1889)
Novel set in southern Georgia by a pioneer regional writer who was the great-niece of James Fenimore Cooper.

GUIDES TO RESOURCES

Bonner, John Wyatt, Jr. *Bibliography of Georgia Authors 1949–1965* (1966) followed by annual compilations 1966–69 in *Georgia Review.*

Candler, Allen D. (comp.) *The Revolutionary Records of the State of Georgia* (1908, rpt. 1972)

Coleman, Kenneth and **Charles S. Gurr** (eds.) *Dictionary of Georgia Biography* (1983)

Crutchfield, James *The Georgia Almanac and Book of Facts* (1988)

Dorsey, James E. *Bibliography of the Writings on Georgia History: A Supplement* (1983)
———. *Georgia Genealogy and Local History: A Bibliography* (1983)

Federal Writers' Project *Savannah* (1937)
———. *Savannah River Plantations* (1947, rpt. 1972)
———. *Augusta* (1938)
———. *Georgia: A Guide to Its Towns and Countryside* (1940)

Georgia Department of Archives and History *Georgia Heritage: Documents of Georgia History, 1730–1790* (1973)
———. *Directory of Georgia's Historical Organizations and Resources* (1987)

Lankevich, George J. (comp.) *Atlanta: A Chronological and Documentary History, 1813–1976* (1978)

Leckie, George G. *Georgia: A Guide to Its Towns and Countryside* (rev. ed. 1954)

Linley, John *The Georgia Catalog, Historic American Buildings Survey: A Guide to the Architecture of the State* (1982)

Murray, Malcolm A. *Atlas of Atlanta; the 1970's* (1974)

Purdie, Hazel (comp.) *Georgia Bibliography: County History* (2d ed. 1979)

Rowland, Arthur R. and James E. Dorsey *A Bibliography of the Writings on Georgia History 1900–1970* (rev. and enl. ed. 1978)

Sherwood, Adiel *Gazetteer of Georgia* (rev. ed. 1860, rpt. 1970)

————. *The Colonial Records of the State of Georgia* vol. 1– (1904–   )

Simpson, John Eddins (comp.) *Georgia History: A Bibliography* (1976)

University of Georgia. Graduate School of Administration. Bureau of Business and Economic Research *Georgia: Statistical Abstract* (1951–1972)

White, George (comp.) *Statistics of the State of Georgia* (1849)
———— (comp.) *Historical Collections of Georgia* (1854, rpt. 1968)

SELECTED NONFICTION SOURCES

Abbot, W. W. *The Royal Governors of Georgia, 1754–1775* (1959)

Anderson, Mary S., Elfrida D. Barrow, Elizabeth M. Screven, and Martha G. Waring *Georgia, a Pageant of Years* (1933)

Anderson, William *The Wild Man from Sugar Creek: The Political Career of Eugene Talmadge* (1975)

Andrews, Eliza F. *The War-Time Journal of a Georgia Girl: 1864–1865* (1908, rpt. 1960)

Arnett, Alex M. *The Populist Movement in Georgia* (1922)

Atlanta Historical Society *Atlanta in 1890: "The Gate City"* (1986)

Atlanta Journal-Constitution *Georgia Rivers* (1962)

Avery, Isaac W. *The History of the State of Georgia from 1850 to 1881, Embracing the Three Important Epochs* (1972)

Bailey, Ronald H. and the Editors of Time-Life Books *Battles for Atlanta: Sherman Moves East* (1985)

Barnard, George N. *Photographic Views of Sherman's Campaign* (1977)

Bartley, Numan V. *The Creation of Modern Georgia* (1983)
————. *From Thurmond to Wallace: Political Tendencies in Georgia, 1948–1968* (1970)

Belcher, John C. and Imogene Dean (eds.) *Georgia Today: Facts and Trends* (1960)
————. *The Dynamics of Georgia's Population* (1964)
———— and Carolyn N. Allman *The Non-White Population of Georgia* (1969)

Bickley, R. Bruce *Joel Chandler (ok?? ms unclear) Harris* (1987)

Blackburn, Joyce *James Edward Oglethorpe* (1970, rpt. 1983)

Bode, Frederick A. and Donald E. Ginter *Farm Tenancy and the Census in Antebellum Georgia* (1986)

Bonner, James C. and Lucien E. Roberts *Georgia History and Government* (1940, rpt. 1974)
————. *The Georgia Story* (1958)
————. *A History of Georgia Agriculture, 1732–1860* (1964)
————. *Georgia's Last Frontier: The Development of Carroll County* (1971)
————. *Milledgeville, Georgia's Antebellum Capital* (1977)

Boylston, Elise R. *Atlanta--Its Lore, Legends and Laughter* (1968)

Brantly, Rabun L. *Georgia Journalism of the Civil War Period* (1929)

Bridges, Edwin C. et al. *Georgia's Signers and the Declaration of Independence* (1981)

Brooks, Robert P. *History of Georgia* (1913, rpt. 1972)

Bryan, T. Conn *Confederate Georgia* (1953)

Burke, Emily P. *Reminiscences of Georgia* (1850)

Burns, Robert E. *I Am a Fugitive from a Georgia Chain Gang* (1932)

Butler, Addie Louise Joyner *The Distinctive Black College: Tailadega, Tuskegee, and Morehouse* (1977)

Byers, Tracy *Martha Berry, the Sunday Lady of Possum Trot* (1932, rpt. 1971)

Capps, Clifford S. *Colonial Georgia* (1972)

Carter, Samuel, III *The Siege of Atlanta, 1864* (1973)

Catledge, Oraien E. *Cabbagetown* (1985)

Cole, Margaret D. *Our Todays and Yesterdays; a Story of Brunswick and the Coastal Islands* (rev. ed. 1930, rpt. 1972)

Coleman, Kenneth *The American Revolution in Georgia, 1763–1789* (1958)
————. *Georgia History in Outline* (rev. ed. 1978)
————. *Colonial Georgia: A History* (1976)
———— (ed.) *A History of Georgia* (1977)

Conway, Alan *The Reconstruction of Georgia* (1966)

Cook, James F. *The Governors of Georgia* (1977)

Corley, Florence F. *Confederate City: Augusta, Georgia, 1860–1865* (1969)

Corry, John P. *Indian Affairs in Georgia, 1732–1756* (1936)

Corse, Clarita D. *The Key to the Golden Islands* (1931)

Coulter, E. Merton *Georgia: A Short History* (rev. ed. 1960)

Davis, Robert S., Jr. *Georgia Citizens and Soldiers of the American Revolution* (1979)

DeBolt, Margaret W. *Savannah: A Historical Portrait* (1977)

Dittmer, John *Black Georgia in the Progressive Era, 1900–1920* (1977)

Drago, Edmund L. *Black Politicians and Reconstruction in Georgia* (1982)

Duncan, Russell *Freedom's Shore: Tunis Campbell and the Georgia Freedmen* (1986)

Fallows, James M. *The Water Lords* (1971)

Fancher, Betsy *The Lost Legacy of Georgia's Golden Isles* (1971)
————. *Savannah: A Renaissance of the Heart* (1976)

Flanders, Ralph B. *Plantation Slavery in Georgia* (1933)

Floyd, Charles F. *The Georgia Regional Economies: The Challenge of Growth* (1974)

Flynn, Charles L., Jr. *White Land, Black Labor: Caste and Class in Late Nineteenth-Century Georgia* (1983)

Futch, Ovid L. *History of Andersonville Prison* (1968)

Galphin, Bruce *The Riddle of Lester Maddox* (1968)

Gamble, Thomas *Savannah Duels and Duellists, 1733–1877* (1923)

Garrett, Franklin M. *Atlanta and Environs* (1954, rpt. 1969)
————. *Yesterday's Atlanta* (1974)

Garrison, Webb B. *Oglethorpe's Folly: The Birth of Georgia* (1982)

Georgia Department of Archives and History *Vanishing Georgia* (1982)

Gleason, David K. *Antebellum Homes of Georgia* (1987)

Gosnell, Cullen B. *Government and Politics of Georgia* (1936)

Griffith, Louis T. and John E. Talmadge *Georgia Journalism, 1763–1950* (1951)

Hahn, Steven *The Roots of Southern Populism; Yeoman Farmers and the Transformation of the Georgia Upcountry, 1850–1890* (1985)

Harden, William *A History of Savannah and South Georgia* (1913, rpt. 1969)

Harper, Francis *Okefinokee Album* (1981)

Harris, J. William *Plain Folk and Gentry in a Slave Society: White Liberty and Black Slavery in Augusta's Hinterlands* (1986)

Harris, Julia C. *Joel Chandler Harris, Editor and Essayist* (1931)

Head, Sylvia and Elizabeth W. Ethridge *The Neighborhood Mint: Dahlonega in the Age of Jackson* (1986)

Henson, Allen L. *Red Galluses: A Story of Georgia Politics* (1945)

Hepburn, Lawrence R. *The Georgia History Book* (1982)

Hill, Louise B. *Joseph E. Brown and the Confederacy* (1939)

Hoehling, A. A. *Last Train from Atlanta* (1958)

Holmes, Michael S. *The New Deal in Georgia: An Administrative History* (1975)

Hough, Franklin B. (ed.) *The Siege of Savannah, by the Combined American and French Forces under the Command of Gen. Lincoln and the Count D'Estaing in the Autumn of 1779* (1866, rpt. 1974)

Hynds, Ernest C. *Antebellum Athens and Clarke County, Georgia* (1974)

Ivers, Larry E. *British Drums on the Southern Frontier; the Military Colonization of Georgia, 1733–1749* (1974)

Jackson, Harvey H. and Phinizy Spalding (eds.) *Forty Years of Diversity: Essays on Colonial Georgia* (1984)

Johnson, Amanda *Georgia as Colony and State* (1938, rpt. 1970)

Johnson, Michael P. *Toward a Partriarchal Republic: The Secession of Georgia* (1977)

Jones, Charles C. *The History of Georgia* (1883, rpt. 1969)

Jones, James P. *Yankee Blitzkrieg: Wilson's Raid through Alabama and Georgia* (1976)

Kane, Harnett T. *Miracle in the Mountains* (1956)

King, Spencer B., Jr. *Georgia Voices: A Documentary History to 1872* (1966)

Knight, Lucian L. *Standard History of Georgia and Georgians* 2 vols. (1917)

Krakow, Kenneth K. *Georgia Place-Names* (1975)

Kollock, John *These Gentle Hills* (1976)

Lamar, Clarinda P. *The Life of Joseph Rucker Lamar, 1857–1916* (1926)

Lamplugh, George R. *Politics on the Periphery; Factions and Parties in Georgia, 1783–1806* (1986)

Lane, Mills *Savannah Revisited: A Pictorial History* (2d ed. 1973)
———. *The People's Georgia: An Illustrated History* (1975)

Lanning, John Tate *The Spanish Missions of Georgia* (1935)
———. *The Diplomatic History of Georgia; a Study of the Epoch of Jenkins' Ear* (1936)

Lawrence, Alexander A. *Storm Over Savannah: The Story of Count d'Estaing and the Siege of the Town in 1779* (1951)
———. *James Johnston: Georgia's First Printer* (1956)

———. *A Present for Mr. Lincoln: The Story of Savannah from Secession to Sherman* (1961)

Lovell, Caroline C. *The Golden Isles of Georgia* (1932)

Lumpkin, Wilson *The Removal of the Cherokee Indians from Georgia* (1907, rpt. 1969)

Martin, Harold H. *Georgia: A Bicentennial History* (States and the Nation series) (1977)

Meadows, John C. *Modern Georgia* (rev. ed. 1954)

Mohr, Clarence L. *On the Threshold of Freedom: Masters and Slaves in Civil War Georgia* (1986)

Montgomery, Horace (ed.) *Georgians in Profile* (1958)
———. *Johnny Cobb; Confederate Aristocrat* (1964)

Myers, Robert M. (ed.) *The Children of Pride; a True Story of Georgia and the Civil War* (1972)

Nichols, Frederick D. and Frances B. Johnston *The Early Architecture of Georgia* (1957)

Nixon, Raymond B. *Henry W. Grady, Spokesman of the New South* (1943)

Orr, Dorothy *A History of Education in Georgia* (1950)

Parks, Joseph H. *Joseph E. Brown of Georgia* (1977)

Perkerson, Medora *White Columns in Georgia* (1952)

Preston, Howard L. *Automobile Age Atlanta: The Making of a Southern Metropolis, 1900–1935* (1979)

Quattlebaum, Julian K. *The Great Savannah Races* (1957, rpt. 1983)

Range, Willard *A Century of Georgia Agriculture, 1850–1950* (1954)

Rawick, George P. (ed.) *The American Slave: A Composite Autobiography* vols. 12 and 13, *Georgia* (1972)

Reese, Trevor R. *Colonial Georgia: A Study in British Imperial Policy in the Eighteenth Century* (1963)
——— (ed.) *The Most Delightful Country of the Universe* (1972)
——— (ed.) *The Clamorous Malcontents* (1973)

Rogers, George A. and R. Frank Saunders *Swamp Water and Wiregrass: Historical Sketches of Coastal Georgia* (1984)

Russell, Franklin and the Editors of Time-Life Books *The Okefenokee Swamp* (1973)

Saye, Albert B. *Georgia's Charter of 1732* (1942)
———. *New Viewpoints in Georgia History* (1943)
———. *A Constitutional History of Georgia* (rev. ed. 1970)

Schultz, Gladys *Lady from Savannah: The Life of Juliette Low* (1958)

Searcy, Martha C. *The Georgia-Florida Contest in the American Revolution, 1776–1778* (1985)

Shavin, Norman and Bruce Galpin *Atlanta, Triumph of a People: An Illustrated History* (rev. ed. 1985)

Shryock, Richard H. *Georgia and the Union in 1850* (1926, rpt. 1968)

Smith, Julia F. *Slavery and Rice Culture in Low Country Georgia, 1750–1860* (1985)

Spalding, Phinizy *Oglethorpe in America* (1977)

Standard, Diffie W. *Columbus, Georgia in the Confederacy: The Social and Industrial Life of the Chattahoochee River Port* (1954)

Stevens, William B. *A History of Georgia* 2 vols (1847, 1859, rpt. 1972)

Stokes, Thomas L. *The Savannah* (Rivers of America series) (1951)

Temple, Sarah B. G. and **Kenneth Coleman** *Georgia Journeys* (1961)

Thompson, Mildred *Reconstruction in Georgia: Economic, Social and Political, 1865–1872* (1915, rpt. 1974)

Todd, Helen *Mary Musgrove, Georgia Indian Princess* (1981)

Trillin, Calvin *An Education in Georgia: The Integration of Charlayne Hunter and Hamilton Holmes* (1964)

Tucker, Gleen *Chickamauga: Bloody Battle in the West* (1961)

Vanstory, Burnette *Georgia's Land of the Golden Isles* (1956)

Wade, John D. *Augustus Baldwin Longstreet* (1924)

Wagner, Kenneth C. and **M. Dale Henson** *Industrial Development in Georgia Since 1947: Progress, Problems and Goals* (1961)

Walker, Jack L. *Sit-ins in Atlanta* (1964)

Wallenstein, Peter *From Slave South to New South; Public Policy in Nineteenth-Century Georgia* (1987)

Ware, Ethel K. *A Constitutional History of Georgia* (1947, rpt. 1967)

Watkins, Floyd C. and **Charles H.** *Yesterday in the Hills* (1963)

Wiggins, Gene *Fiddlin' Georgia Crazy: Fiddlin' John Carson, His Real World, and the World of His Songs* (1987)

Wightman, Orrin S. and **Margaret D. Cake** *Early Days of Coastal Georgia* (1955)

Williford, William B. *Peachtree Street, Atlanta* (1962)

Wood, Betty *Slavery in Colonial Georgia, 1730–1775* (1984)

Woodward, C. Vann *Tom Watson, Agrarian Rebel* (1938, rpt. 1970)

Wooley, Edwin C. *The Reconstruction of Georgia* (1901)

Wynne, Lewis N. *The Continuity of Cotton: Planter Politics in Georgia, 1865–1892* (1986)

HAWAII

Hawaii, the newest state in the Union, is also the farthest from the 48 contiguous states. The geographic center of Hawaii's 132 islands is located approximately 2,400 miles west of San Francisco, in the mid-Pacific Ocean.

FULL NAME State of Hawaii
POSTAL ABBREVIATION HI
INHABITANT Hawaiian
ADMITTED TO THE UNION Aug. 21, 1959.
 50th state.
POPULATION (est. 1987) 1,083,000.
 Percent of US total: .45%. Rank: 39th

CAPITAL CITY Honolulu, located in the southeast part of Oahu Island; population 373,000 (est. 1984). Founded by Russian traders in 1816 on the site of an earlier settlement, it became the capital of the kingdom in 1850 and the state capital in 1959.

STATE NAME AND NICKNAMES Hawaii Loa, according to legend, was the name of the man who discovered the islands. The name may also be derived from *hawa*, meaning "homeland," and the suffix *ii* meaning "raging" or "small." Official nickname: The Aloha State. Also known as the Pineapple State, the Paradise of the Pacific, and the Youngest State.

STATE SEAL In the center is a heraldic shield, bearing in two quarters the tricolored stripes of the Hawaiian flag and in two quarters a symbol (a white ball on a black staff) in a yellow field, as well as a green

shield with a yellow star. To the right stands King Kamehameha I, to the left the Goddess of Liberty holding the Hawaiian flag; above is the rising sun and the legend "1959"; below is a multicolored phoenix arising from the flames, and representations of taro leaves, banana foliage, and maidenhair ferns. The border displays the legend "State of Hawaii" and the state motto.

MOTTO *Ua Mau ke Ea o ka Aina i ka Pono* (The life of the land is perpetuated in righteousness)

SONG "Hawaii Ponoi" (Our Hawaii)

SYMBOLS
Flower hibiscus
Tree kukui (candlenut)
Bird nene (Hawaiian goose)

LICENSE PLATE Dark red on white, with the legend "Aloha State" and an orange portrait of King Kamehameha I.

FLAG Eight stripes of alternating white, red, and blue, representing the eight Hawaiian islands; in the upper right corner, the Union Jack.

GEOGRAPHY AND CLIMATE

The only island state, Hawaii is an archipelago of eight major islands (Hawaii, Maui, Kahoolawe, Lanai, Molokai, Oahu, Kauai, Niihau) and 124 islets; in reality, these are the tips of submerged volcanic mountains standing tens of thousands of feet above the ocean floor. All the islands share a similar geology of volcanic rock, sand, ash, and sandy soil. Spectacular eruptions are still emitted from active volcanoes on the largest island, Hawaii, but most of the region is now dormant. Trade winds from the northeastern Pacific cool the state; although the climate is tropical, temperatures rarely rise above 90 degrees.

AREA 6,471 square miles. Rank: 47th
INLAND WATER 46 square miles
GEOGRAPHIC CENTER Hawaii, 20°15′, 156°20′, off Maui Island
ELEVATIONS *Highest point:* Mauna Kea, Hawaii Island, 13,796 feet. *Lowest point:* Pacific Ocean, sea level. *Mean elevation:* 3,030 feet

MAJOR RIVERS None

MAJOR LAKE Koloa Reservoir

TIDAL SHORELINE 1,052 miles, Pacific Ocean

LAND USE

	Thousands of acres
Urban (1982)	126
Rural (1982)	3,610
Cropland (1982)	333
Pastureland (1982)	974
Rangeland (1982)	0
Forestland (1982)	1,474
State parks and recreation areas (1983)	21
National park system (1984)	245
National forest system (1984)	0
Tribal lands (1984)	0

TEMPERATURES The highest recorded temperature was 100°F on April 27, 1931, at Pahala. The lowest was 12°F on May 17, 1979, at Mauna Kea.

NATIONAL SITES

NATIONAL HISTORIC SITE Puukohola Heiau
NATIONAL HISTORICAL PARKS Kaioko-Honokohau, Kalaupapa, Puuhonua o Honaunau
NATIONAL MEMORIAL USS Arizona
NATIONAL PARKS Haleakala, Hawaii Volcanoes

NATIONAL WILDLIFE REFUGES Hanalei, Hawaiian Islands–Baker/Howland/Huleia/James C. Campbell/Jarvis Island/Johnston Island/Kakahaia/Pearl Harbor/Rose Atoll

HISTORY

1778   *January 18.* A British naval squadron commanded by Captain James Cook discovers the Hawaiian Islands, which are named by Cook the Sandwich Islands. The men land on Kauai the following day.

1779   *February 13.* Cook is killed during an altercation with natives on the island of Hawaii.

1787   At least six vessels, all connected with the fur trade, are in Hawaiian waters. Others, mainly British or American, follow.

1791   Kamehameha, a warrior of high rank, unifies the island of Hawaii under his rule.

1796   Kamehameha becomes master of all the islands except Kauai and Niihau, which are eventually ceded without bloodshed.

1804   A great plague, probably cholera, takes a heavy toll on the population.

1811   An active trade begins in sandalwood, ending about 1830 with its depletion on the islands.

1819   Kamehameha II, succeeding on his father's death, renounces the native gods and taboos.

1820   New England missionaries arrive from Boston to disseminate Christianity in the islands.

1823   A survey commissioned by the missionaries finds that the population has fallen to 140,000, largely because of the introduction of diseases to which the Hawaiians have no immunity.

1826	Nearly 40 American whaling vessels stop at Honolulu, which has become an important refitting and supply port for the trade.
1835	The American firm of Ladd & Company begins the first extensive agricultural development by leasing land on Kauai to grow sugarcane.
1840	Kamehameha III promulgates the first written constitution for Hawaii; it creates a lower house of legislators elected by the people.
1846	Pacific whaling activity is nearing its peak, with almost 600 ships arriving in Hawaiʻan ports during this year.
1848	The feudal system of land tenure is abolished, and commoners are granted title to the lands they occupy and cultivate.
1864	Kamehameha V issues a new constitution that increases royal powers and limits the right to vote.
1867	Monthly steamship service begins between San Francisco and Honolulu.
1872	*June 11*. Kamehameha V proclaims this day to honor his grandfather, Kamehemeha I, who united the islands into one kingdom.
1876	A reciprocity treaty with the US allows most goods of the two countries to enter free of customs duties. This pact greatly stimulates the Hawaiian sugar industry.
1877–1890	More than 55,000 immigrant laborers are brought to the islands as contract workers; half are Chinese.
1886	A treaty provides for the introduction of Japanese contract workers; by 1908, 180,000 have arrived, although 126,000 have left the islands.
1893	*January 17*. Queen Liliuokalani is overthrown by an influential group of American residents and Hawaiian-born sons of American missionaries.
1894	*July 4*. A new constitution establishes the Republic of Hawaii and names Sanford B. Dole as president.
1898	*August 12*. Hawaii is annexed to the US by terms of a treaty passed and ratified the previous year.
1900	An act of Congress establishes a territorial government. The population of 154,001 includes 61,111 Japanese, 39,656 Hawaiians and part-Hawaiians, and 25,767 Chinese.
1901	James D. Dole organizes the Hawaiian Pineapple Company; by 1919, production has reached nearly six million cases of canned pineapple a year. A territorial income tax is adopted.
1902	Republicans dominate legislative elections, continuing to do so until 1954.
1907	"Gentleman's Agreement" between the US and Japan stops immigration to the US by Japanese laborers. Sugar planters recruit Filipino workers; by 1932, about 125,000 Filipinos have come to Hawaii.
1908	Opening in Honolulu of the College of Agriculture and Mechanical Arts, which becomes the University of Hawaii in 1920.
1909	Construction of a naval base at Pearl Harbor is begun; it is completed in 1919 and thereafter expanded.
1916	Establishment of Hawaii Volcanoes National Park, on Hawaii island, and Haleakala National Park, on Maui.
1917	Prince Kuhio establishes the Hawaiian Civic Club to preserve his people's culture.
1919	Sugar planters respond to a strike of Japanese and Filipino workers by evicting about 12,000. Passage of an act allotting 200,000 acres to those of at least one-half Hawaiian ancestry fails to stem migration to Honolulu.
1922	The Hawaiian Pineapple Company buys almost the entire island of Lanai.
1924	*September 9*. Twenty persons, including four policemen, are killed in a riot on Kauai stemming from a strike by Filipino sugar workers.
1928	*May 1*. Lei Day is initiated in celebration of the flower garland—honoring friendship and the aloha spirit.
1931	Racial tensions are aggravated when a Hawaiian accused of assaulting a white woman is murdered and the perpetrators, found guilty of manslaughter, have their sentence commuted by the governor.

1941	*December 7.* A Japanese attack severely damages the US Pacific Fleet anchored at Pearl Harbor; all eight battleships are put out of action, along with 10 other vessels, and 188 airplanes are destroyed. Martial law is declared, and military courts assume the right to try civilians.
1943–1945	Hawaiian-born Japanese-Americans win distinction in Europe during World War II in the 100th Infantry Battalion and 442nd Regimental Combat Team.
1944	*October 24.* President Roosevelt lifts martial law in Hawaii. In 1946, the US Supreme Court finds the imposition of martial law to have been unconstitutional.
1949	A 179-day dock strike closes Hawaiian ports and raises the number of jobless in the territory to 20,000—twice that in the Great Depression.
1950	A constitution, framed in preparation for statehood, is approved by the electorate by a 3-to-1 margin.
1958	A statehood bill is signed on March 18 and approved by the voters on June 27 by a 17-to-1 margin.
1959	*August 21.* Hawaii is admitted to the Union as the 50th state.
1960	*May 23.* Fifty-seven persons are dead and four missing as a 35-foot tidal wave hits Hilo, causing $50 million in property damage.
1961	Hawaii becomes the first state to adopt a statewide land-use program.
1966	Peak sugarcane production of 11.6 million tons. After 1975, Florida outstrips Hawaii in sugarcane production.
1967	With 47 percent of the land in Hawaii owned by only 72 private landowners, a land reform act allows the state to transfer ownership to estate tenants. Hawaii is the first state to institute an ombudsman. Founding of Mauna Kea Observatory, an astronomical research facility affiliated with the University of Hawaii.
1969	A new $28-million state capitol is dedicated, with a roof open to the sky and shaped to resemble a volcanic cone.
1978	Voters adopt more than 100 constitutional amendments proposed by a convention.
1980	According to the Census Bureau, Hawaii's population of 964,691 is 34 percent white, 25 percent Japanese, 14 percent Filipino, 12 percent Hawaiian, and 6 percent Chinese.
1983	A record 4.4 million tourists spend about $4 billion; tourism accounts for 25 percent of the gross state product and nearly 20 percent of the work force.
1983–1984	Department of Defense expenditure in Hawaii during fiscal 1984 is $2.3 billion; the per-capita expenditure of $2,237 is higher than in any other state.
1985	The marijuana crop is estimated to be worth $4 billion—about ten times the value of the sugar crop.
1987	Japanese investors are reported to have spent $3.3 billion for Hawaiian real estate during the year.

DEMOGRAPHY

Population (est. 1987) . . . 1,083,000
Population (1980) 964,691
Population density in persons
   per square mile (1980) 149.1

POPULATION BY RACE (1980)
American Indian/Aleut/
   Eskimo 2,778
Asian/Pacific Islander 583,660
Black 17,352
Hispanic 71,479
White 318,608
Other 42,602

POPULATION CHARACTERISTICS (1980)
          Percent of state population
Urban 86.5

Rural 15.5
Under 18 . . . . 28.6
65 or older 7.9
College-educated 20.3
Families below poverty line 7.8
Public assistance recipients 7.3

Per capita personal income
   (1980) $14,691
Millionaires per 100,000
   residents (1982) 80.2
Average life expectancy
   in years (1980) 77.0
Marriage rate per 1,000
   residents (1986) 15.3
Divorce rate per 1,000
   residents (1986) 4.3

Birth rate per 1,000
residents (1985) 17.3
Infant mortality rate per
1,000 births (1985) 9.1
Abortion rate per 1,000
live births (1985) 611
Crime rate per 100,000
residents (1985)
Violent 245.2
Property 5,426.2
Federal and state prisoners per
100,000 residents (1984) 163

Alcohol consumption in gallons
per capita (1985) 47.3
Deaths from motor vehicle accidents
per 100,000 residents (1985) . . 11.9

MAJOR CITIES (COUNTED AS COUNTY SUBDIVISIONS)

	Population
Ewa (1980)	190,037
Honolulu (est. 1984)	373,000
Koolaupoko (1980)	109,373
Wahaiwa (1980)	41,562

GOVERNMENT AND POLITICS

Number of US Representatives 2
Electoral votes 4

POLITICAL PARTY NOMINEES FROM STATE
None

PRESIDENTIAL PRIMARY ELECTION In 1988, Hawaii sent 25 Democratic delegates and 20 Republican delegates to the national conventions.
CONSTITUTION Hawaii is using its original constitution, adopted in 1950.
LEGISLATURE The Legislature is divided

into the Senate (25 members, 4-year term, minimum age 18) and the House of Representatives (51 members, 2-year term, minimum age 18). In 1987, the annual salary was $15,600.
JUDICIARY The highest court is the Supreme Court, with 5 judges serving 10-year terms. In 1987, the annual salary was $78,500.
EXECUTIVE The governor serves a 4-year term; the minimum age for holding office is 30. In 1987, the annual salary was $80,000. There are 14 other elected officials.

PRESIDENTIAL VOTE 1948-1988 *(in percents)*

Year	State Winner	Democratic	Republican
1960	Tie between Nixon (R)/Kennedy (D)	50.0	50.0
1964	Johnson (D)	78.8	21.2
1968	Humphrey (D)	59.8	38.7
1972	Nixon (R)	37.5	62.5
1976	Carter (D)	50.6	48.1
1980	Carter (D)	44.8	41.0
1984	Reagan (R)	43.8	55.1
1988	Dukakis (D)	55.0	45.0

GOVERNORS

Territorial Governors

Sanford B. Dole	1900-1903
George R. Carter	1903-1907
Walter D. Frear	1907-1913
Lucius E. Pinkham	1913-1918
Charles J. McCarthy	1918-1921
Wallace R. Farrington	1921-1929
Lawrence M. Judd	1929-1934
Joseph B. Poindexter	1934-1942
Ingram M. Stainback	1942-1951
Oren E. Long	1951-1953
Samuel Wilder King	1953-1957
William F. Quinn	1957-1959

State Governors

William F. Quinn (R)	1959-1962
John A. Burns (D)	1962-1974
George R. Ariyoshi (D)	1974-1986
John Waihee (D)	1986-

MINIMUM AGES

Majority	18
Marriage with parental consent . . .	16
Marriage without parental consent .	18
Making a will	18
Buying alcohol	21
Jury duty	18
Leaving school	18
(if employed)	15
Driver's license	15

CAPITAL PUNISHMENT
None

MILITARY INSTALLATIONS
Total number: 47
Major bases:
    Army: 2
    Navy: 4
    Air Force: 1
    Marine Corps: 1

FINANCES

Thousands of dollars

GENERAL REVENUE (1985)

Total general revenue	2,245,293
Total tax revenue	1,362,595
Sales and gross receipts	851,297
Individual income taxes	429,398
Corporate net income taxes	48,717

GENERAL EXPENDITURE (1985)

Total general expenditure	2,080,777
Education	729,962
Public welfare	287,048
Health	76,523
Hospitals	102,972
Natural resources	47,293
Highways	84,542
Police	2,452
Corrections	43,559

FEDERAL AID (1985) 435,570

ECONOMY

Sugarcane, pineapple, and floriculture, especially orchids, are Hawaii's main agricultural crops. The state economy is mainly driven by the Pentagon and defense industries, on the one hand, and tourism on the other (4 million visitors per year), yielding a combined income of $1 billion annually. Scientific research is also an important industry on the islands, which contain several important seismological and astronomical observatories and earth-space communications stations. Retail trade, serving the tourist industry, is a major employer. The growth of manufacturing has been inhibited partly by poor transportation services throughout the islands and the state's high cost of living.

EMPLOYMENT (1984)

Thousands of persons

Total number of employed workers	446
Construction	16.1
Finance, insurance, and real estate	31.9
Government	91.7
Manufacturing	21.8
Mining	N/A
Services	108.5
Transportation, communications, and utilities	31.9
Wholesale and retail trade	110.6

Percent of civilian labor
force unemployed (1984) 5.6

DEPARTMENT OF DEFENSE (1985)

Civilian workers employed	21,259
Military personnel	46,973
Contract awards	$626 million

ENERGY SOURCES FOR ELECTRIC UTILITIES (1983)

Percent

Coal	0
Gas	0
Hydroelectric	0.3
Nuclear	0
Petroleum	99.3

TRANSPORTATION

Motor vehicles registered in state (1986)	689,034
Miles of roads, streets, and highways (1986)	4,040
Miles of Class I railway operated (1986)	N/A
Airports (1983)	51
Major aviation hubs (1983)	5

Largest hub: Honolulu

CULTURE AND EDUCATION

Religions, ethnicities, and languages
The native population of Hawaii arrived from Polynesia between 400 and 800 A.D. Their descendants are a minority in contemporary Hawaii. Immigrants to Hawaii during the 19th century, in addition to European and American missionaries, came from Japan, China, Korea, and the Philippines, and in the 20th century from the American mainland and from Samoa and other Pacific islands. In 1980, 25.8 percent of Hawaii's population spoke a language other than English at home. By the mid-19th century, most of the surviving indigenous people had been converted to various denominations of Christianity; imported forms of Buddhism and Confucianism are also active.

Major museums and libraries
Bernice P. Bishop Museum, Honolulu
Honolulu Academy of Arts

Major arts organizations
Hawaii Opera Theatre, Honolulu
Hawaii State Ballet
Honolulu Symphony Orchestra
Honolulu Theatre for Youth

Colleges and universities
Number public (1986-87) 9
Number private (1986-87) 5
Total enrollment, in full-time equivalent
students (1985) 37,000

Public elementary and secondary schools
Expenditure per pupil in average daily
attendance (1986-87) $4,372
Pupil-teacher ratio (1987) 22.6
Average teacher salary (1986-87) $27,646

Holidays
Prince Jonah Kuhio Kalanianaole Day.
March 26
State Fair, Honolulu. Late May to mid-
June
King Kamehameha I Day. June 11
Admission Day. August 20 (third Friday
in August)

HAWAII IN LITERATURE

George Washington Bates *Sandwich Island Notes* (1854)
Bates toured the islands in 1853, when it seemed possible
that Hawaii would be annexed to the US, making detailed
observations on agricultural and social conditions.

Martha Beckwith *Hawaiian Mythology* (1940, rpt. 1970)
An anthropological study of Hawaiian culture.

Earl D. Biggers *The House without a Key* (1925)
The first of the many detective stories featuring Chinese
policeman Charlie Chan was set in Waikiki.

Hiram Bingham *Residence of Twenty–One Years in the Sandwich
Islands* (1847)
Memoirs of a Congregational clergyman, missionary to the
Hawaiian Islands.

Isabella Bird *The Hawaiian Archipelago: Six Months among the
Palm Groves, Coral Reefs, and Volcanoes of the Sandwich
Islands* (1875, rpt. 1974)
Observations of landscape and culture by the first woman
elected to the Royal Geographic Society.

Oswald A. Bushnell *The Return of Lono: A Novel of Captain
Cook's Last Voyage* (1956, rpt. 1971); *Molokai* (1963, rpt.
1975); *Ka'a'awa: A Novel about Hawaii in the 1850s* (1972)
Historical novels set respectively in 1779, 1884, and 1853,
portraying the death of Cook, the life of Father Joseph de
Veuster, and the adventures of a Yankee sailor.

Lord Byron (George Anson) *Voyage of H. M. S. "Blonde" to
the Sandwich Islands, 1824–25* (1826)
Lord Byron was commander of the vessel that brought back
the bodies of Kamehameha II and his wife from England.
The *Blonde* party explored the Hilo and volcano regions of
the Big Island in 1825.

Archibald Campbell *Voyage Round the World, from 1806 to
1812* (1816, rpt. 1967)
A classic narrative of the sea and a primary source of
information about life in early Hawaii before the coming of
the missionaries.

Tin-Yuke Char (ed.) *The Sandalwood Mountains: Readings
and Stories of the Early Chinese in Hawaii* (1975)

William Chickering *Within the Sound of These Waves* (1941,
rpt. 1971)
Popular history partly based on legend.

Padraic Colum *At the Gateways of the Day* (1924); *The Bright
Islands* (1925); *Legends of Hawaii* (1937, rpt. 1973, 1987)
A collection of stories from Hawaiian folklore, adapted for
children's reading.

A. Grove Day and **Carl Stroven** (eds.) *A Hawaiian Reader*
(1959); *The Spell of Hawaii* (1968)
Selections from Robert Louis Stevenson and Jack London
to Somerset Maugham and James Jones.

Constance F. Gordon-Cumming *Fire Fountains: The Kingdom of Hawaii, Its Volcanoes and the History of the Missions*
(1883)
English traveler's impressions of Hawaii in the 1870s.

Samuel B. Harrison *The White King* (1950)
Fictional biography of Dr. Gerrit P. Judd, the first medical
missionary to the islands, who arrived in 1828 and spent the
remainder of his life there. Judd's wife Laura kept a diary
of the years 1828–1861, published in 1880 as *Honolulu:
Sketches of the Life . . . in the Hawaiian Islands* (rpt. 1928)

John D. Holt (ed.) *An Account of the Sandwich Islands: The
Hawaiian Journal of John B. Whitman, 1813–1815* (1979)

James Jones *From Here to Eternity* (1951)
Novel about military life before the Japanese attack.

Laura Fish Judd *Honolulu: Sketches of Life, Social, Political
and Religious in the Hawaiian Islands, from 1828 to 1861*
(1880, rpt. 1928)

Norman Kalkov *Blood and Orchids* (1983)
A crime drama based on an actual case of the 1930s.

Alfons L. Korn *The Victorian Visitors* (1958)
Biographical study of Sophia Cracroft and Lady Jane
Franklin, who visited Hawaii in 1861, with quotations from
their letters and journals.

W. Storrs Lee *Hawaii: A Literary Chronicle* (1967)
Anthology of regional writing.

Amos P. Leib *Hawaiian Legends in English: An Annotated
Bibliography* (1949)
A study of Hawaiian legends and lore, with a critical history
of the translation of Hawaiian myths and legends.

Charmian K. London *Our Hawaii* (1917)
An account of Jack London's experiences by his wife.

Jack London *Stories of Hawaii* (1965)
Stories written while London was living in Hawaii, concerning local customs and superstitions, and evoking life
1915–1916.

Albertine Loomis *Grapes of Canaan: Hawaii 1820* (1951)
The author's great-grandparents were among the first group
of American missionaries to Hawaii in 1820. This account
of their first seven years in Hawaii is based in part on the
journals and letters of Elisha and Maria Loomis.

Katharine Luomala *Voices on the Wind: Polynesian Myths and
Chants* (1955)
A re-telling of legends of Maui, Tinirou, and Rata.

Chester S. Lyman *Around the Horn to the Sandwich Islands
and California, 1845–1850* (1924)
Memoir of a seaman's adventures.

Martha M. McGaw *Stevenson in Hawaii* (1950, rpt. 1978)

Ruth E. McKee *The Lord's Anointed* (1934)
Novel of Boston missionaries of the 1820s.

James Michener *Hawaii* (1959, rpt. 1987)
A saga of Hawaiian history from the days of Tahitian
colonizers to the present.

Susanna Moore *My Old Sweetheart* (1982)
A novel of family life set on a plantation during the 1950s and the present.

J. Munford (ed.) *John Ledyard's Journal of Captain Cook's Last Voyage* (1963)

Francis A. Olmsted *Incidents of a Whaling Voyage* . . . (1841, rpt. 1969)
Memoir of Hawaii by an early visitor.

Hiram Paulding *Journal of a Cruise of the United States Schooner"Dolphin"* . . . *in Pursuit of the Mutineers of the Whale Ship "Globe"* (1831, rpt. 1970)
An eyewitness account of the first visit by a US Navy vessel.

Mary Kawena Pukui *'Olelo No'eau: Hawaiian Proverbs and Poetical Sayings* (B. P. Bishop Museum Special Publication 71) (1983)

William Hyde Rice (comp. and tr.) *Hawaiian Legends* (1923, rpt. 1971)
Retellings of legends.

Marjorie Sinclair *Kona* (1947)
A saga of family life by the region's best-known post-war woman writer.

Robert Louis Stevenson (ed. A. Grove Day) *Travels in Hawaii* (1973)
A journal of the author's five-month stay in 1889.

Frank Stewart (ed.) *Passages to the Dream Shore: Short Stories of Contemporary Hawaii* (1987)

Charles Warren Stoddard *South Sea Idylls* (1873); *The Lepers of Molokai* (1885); *Hawaiian Life* (1894); *The Island of Tranquil Delights* (1904)
A friend of Stevenson, Twain, and Bret Harte, Stoddard was well-known for his idyllic sketches of the South Seas.

Darwin Teilhet *The Happy Island* (1950)
Popular mystery novel set on Maui.
———. *The Mission of Jeffery Tolamy* (1951)
Historical adventure novel of the 1816 Russian expedition.

Armine Von Tempski *Born in Paradise* (1940)
Memoir by an English-Polish woman born on a large cattle ranch in Hawaii at the beginning of the century.

Thomas G. Thrum *Hawaiian Folk Tales: A Collection of Native Legends* (1907)
Thrum published the *Hawaiian Almanac and Annual*, which began publication in 1875. He also edited and translated *The Fornander Collection of Hawaiian Antiquities and Folklore* (1916–1920), the greatest single repository of Hawaiian folklore.

Lucy Goodale Thurston *The Life and Times of Lucy G. Thurston* (1882, rpt. 1934)
Memoirs of the wife of an early missionary.

Mark Twain (ed. A. Grove Day) *Mark Twain's Letters from Hawaii* (1966, rpt. 1975)
Twenty-five travel letters written during a four-month visit in 1866. Also published in Samuel L. Clemens *Letters from the Sandwich Islands* (1938, rpt. 1972).

GUIDES TO RESOURCES

Alcantara, Ruben R. *The Filipinos in Hawaii: An Annotated Bibliography* (Hawaii series, no. 6) (1977)

Catalog of Oral History Collections in Hawaii University of Hawaii (1982)

Daws, Gavan and O. A. Bushnell *Illustrated Atlas of Hawaii* (1970)

Day, A. Grove *Books About Hawaii: Fifty Basic Authors* (1977)
———. *History Makers of Hawaii; a Biographical Dictionary* (1984)

Dictionary Catalog of the Hawaiian Collection, University of Hawaii 4 vols. (1963)

Grace, Jean McKean (ed.) *Marine Atlas of Hawaii: Bays and Harbors* (1974)

Hawaii Department of Planning and Economic Development *Directory of Hawaii Map Sources* (1976–)

Hawaii Department of Research and Development *County of Hawaii Data Book* (annual)

Hawaii Library Association *Official Publications of the Territory of Hawaii, 1909–1959* (1962)

Hawaii State Department of Planning and Economic Development *State of Hawaii Data Book: A Statistical Abstract* (1981)

Jackson, Frances, Agnes Conrad, and Nancy Bannick *Old Honolulu: A Guide to Oahu's Historic Buildings* (1969)

Kittelson, David J. *The Hawaiians: An Annotated Bibliography* (1984)

Leib, Amos P. and A. Grove Day *Hawaiian Legends in English: An Annotated Bibliography* (2d ed. 1979)

Matsuda, Mitsugu (rev. by Dennis M. Ogawa with Jerry Y. Fujioka) *The Japanese in Hawaii: An Annotated Bibliography of Japanese Americans* (1975)

Murdoch, Clare G. and Masae Gotanda *Basic Hawaiiana* (1969)

Pendleton, Edwin C. *Labor in Hawaii: A Bibliography* (2d ed. 1971)

Pukui, Mary Kawena and Samuel H. Elbert *Hawaiian Dictionary: Hawaiian-English, English-Hawaiian* (rev. and enl. ed. 1986)

Ronck, Ronn (comp. and ed.) *Ronck's Hawaii Almanac* (1984)

Rubano, Judith *Culture and Behavior in Hawaii: An Annotated Bibliography* (rpt. 1988)

Schmitt, Robert C. *Demographic Statistics of Hawaii 1778–1965* (1968)
———. *Historical Statistics of Hawaii* (1977)

Spriggs, Matthew J. T. and Patricia L. Tanaka *Na Mea 'Imi Ka Wa Kahiko: An Annotated Bibliography of Hawaiian Archaeology* (1988)

Stearns, Harold T. *Road Guide to Points of Geologic Interest in the Hawaiian Islands* (1978)

Stoneburner, Bryan C. *Hawaiian Music: An Annotated Bibliography* (1986)

University of Hawaii Department of Geography *Atlas of Hawaii* (2nd ed. 1983)

Whitney, Henry M. *The Hawaiian Guide Book* (1875, rpt. 1970)

Young, Nancy Foon *The Chinese in Hawaii: An Annotated Bibliography* (Hawaii series, no. 4) (1973)

SELECTED NONFICTION SOURCES

Adler, Jacob *Claus Spreckels: The Sugar King of Hawaii* (1966)

Allen, Helena G. *The Betrayal of Liliuokalani: Last Queen of Hawaii, 1838–1917* (1982)

Anderson, Bern *The Life and Voyages of Captain George Vancouver, Surveyor of the Sea* (1960)

Apple, Russell A. *The Hawaiian Thatched House* (1973)

Bailey, Paul *Those Kings and Queens of Old Hawaii: A Mele to Their Memory* (1975)
———. *Hawaii's Royal Prime Minister: The Life and Times of Walter Murray Gibson* (1980)

Baker, Ray Jerome (ed. Robert E. Van Dyke) *Hawaiian Yesterdays: Historical Photographs* (1982)

Barrow, Terence *Captain Cook in Hawaii* (1978)

Bauer, Helen *Hawaii: The Aloha State* (rev. ed. 1982)

Beechert, Edward D. *Working in Hawaii: A Labor History* (1985)

Beevers, John *A Man for Now; the Life of Damien de Veuster, Friend of Lepers* (1973)

Bell, Roger *Last Among Equals: Hawaiian Statehood and American Politics* (1984)

Bradley, Harold W. *The American Frontier in Hawaii: The Pioneers, 1789–1843* (1942)

Brennan, Joseph *The Parker Ranch of Hawaii; the Saga of a Ranch and a Dynasty* (1974)

Buck, Peter H. *Arts and Crafts of Hawaii* (1964)

Callies, David L. *Regulating Paradise: Land Use Controls in Hawaii* (1984)

Carlquist, Sherwin *Hawai'i: A Natural History* (2d ed. 1980)

Carr, Elizabeth B. *Da Kine Talk: From Pidgin to Standard English in Hawaii* (1972)

Chinen, John J. *The Great Mahele: Hawai'i's Land Division of 1848* (1958)

Clark, Blake *Remember Pearl Harbor!* (1942)
———. *Hawaii, the 49th State* (1947)

Conroy, Hilary *The Japanese Frontier in Hawaii* (1953)

Cooper, George *Land and Power in Hawaii: The Democratic Years* (1985)

Creighton, Thomas H. *The Lands of Hawai'i: Their Use and Misuse* (1978)

Culliney, John *Islands in a Far Sea: Nature and Man in Hawaii* (1988)

Davis, Eleanor H. *Abraham Fornander: a Biography* (1979)

Daws, Gavan *Shoal of Time: A History of the Hawaiian Islands* (1968)
———. *Holy Man: Father Damien of Molokai* (1973)

Day, A. Grove *Hawaii and Its People* (rev. ed. 1968)
———. *Kamehameha, First King of Hawaii* (1974)
——— and Carl Stroven (eds.) *A Hawaiian Reader* (1959, rpt. 1985)

Dudley, Walter C. and Minn Lee *Tsunami!* (1988)

Fairfax, Geoffrey W. *The Architecture of Honolulu* (1972)

Farrell, Bryan H. *Hawaii, the Legend That Sells* (1981)

Forbes, David *Queen Emma and Lawai* (1970)

Fornander, Abraham *An Account of the Polynesian Race, Its Origins and Migrations and the Ancient History of the Hawaiian People to the Times of Kamehameha I* (1980)

Fuchs, Lawrence H. *Hawaii Pono: A Social History* (1961)

Gallagher, Charles F. *Hawaii and Its Gods* (1975)

Glick, Clarence E. *Sojourners and Settlers, Chinese Migrants in Hawaii* (1980)

Goodman, Robert B. et al. *The Hawaiians* (1971)

Gray, Francine du Plessis *Hawai'i: The Sugar-Coated Fortress* (1972)

Greer, Richard A. (ed.) *Hawaii Historical Review: Selected Readings* (1969)

Handy, E. Craighill et al. *Ancient Hawaiian Civilization* (rev. ed. 1965)

Hemmings, Fred *Surfing: Hawaii's Gift to the World of Sports* (1977)

Holmes, Tommy *The Hawaiian Canoe* (1981)

Holt, John Dominis *On Being Hawaiian* (1964)
———. *Monarchy in Hawaii* (1971)

Horwitz, Robert H. and Norman Meller *Land and Politics in Hawaii* (1966)

Inouye, Daniel K. and Lawrence Elliott *Journey to Washington* (1967)

Joesting, Edward *Hawaii, an Uncommon History* (1972, rpt. 1978)
———. *Tides of Commerce* (1983)
———. *Kauai; the Separate Kingdom* (1984)
——— and Bushnell, O. A. (ed. Joseph Feher) *Hawaii: A Pictorial History* (1969)

Judd, Bernice *Voyages to Honolulu Before 1860* (rev. ed. 1973)

Judd, Gerrit Parmela *Hawaii: An Informal History* (1961)

Judd, Walter F. *Palaces and Forts of the Hawaiian Kingdom: From Thatch to American Florentine* (1975)

Kamakau, Samuel M. *Ruling Chiefs of Hawaii* (1961)

Kanahele, George S. *Hawaiian Music and Musicians: An Illustrated History* (1979)

Kent, Harold W. *Charles Reed Bishop, Man of Hawaii* (1965)

Kent, Noel J. *Hawaii, Islands under the Influence* (1983)

Kirch, Patrick V. *Feathered Gods and Fishhooks: An Introduction to Hawaiian Archaeology and Prehistory* (1985)

Kuykendall, Ralph S. *The Hawaiian Kingdom* 3 vols. (vol. 1 rev. ed. 1969, vol. 2 rev. ed. 1966, vol. 3 1967)
——— and A. Grove Day *Hawaii: A History from Polynesian Kingdom to American Commonwealth* (1948)

Layton, Edwin T., Roger Pineau, and John Costello *And I Was There; Pearl Harbor and Midway--Breaking the Secrets* (1987)

Liliuokalani *Hawaii's Story, by Hawaii's Queen* (1898, rpt. 1964)

Lind, Andrew W. *An Island Community: Ecological Succession in Hawaii* (1938)
———. *Hawaii's Japanese: An Experiment in Democracy* (1946)
———. *Hawaii's People* (4th ed. 1980)

Lindo, Cecilia Kapua and Nancy Alpert Mower *Polynesian Seafaring Heritage* (1980)

Lloyd, C. (ed.) *The Voyages of Captain Cook* (1949)

Loomis, Albertine *Grapes of Canaan: Hawaii 1820* (1951)
———. *For Whom the Stars?* (1976)

Lord, Walter *Day of Infamy* (1957)

Lyman, Chester S. (ed. Frederick J. Teggert) *Around the Horn to the Sandwich Islands and California 1845–1850; Being a Personal Record Kept by Chester S. Lyman* (1924, rpt. 1971)

MacDonald, Alexander *Revolt in Paradise* (1944)

Macdonald, George Andrew, Agatin Townsend Abbott, and Frank L. Peterson *Volcanoes in the Sea: The Geology of Hawaii* (2d ed. 1983)

Macdonald, Gordon A. and Douglass H. Hubbard *Volcanoes of the National Parks in Hawaii* (6th ed. rev. 1973)

Malo, David (trans. Nathaniel B. Emerson) *Hawaiian Antiquities (Mo'olelo Hawai'i)* (1987)

McBride, L. R. *The Kahuna; Versatile Mystics of Old Hawaii* (1972)

McDermott, John, Jr., Wen-Shing Tseng, and Thomas W. Maretzki (eds.) *People and Cultures of Hawaii: A Psychocultural Profile* (1980)

Mellen, Kathleen D. *The Lonely Warrior: Kamehameha the Great of Hawaii* (1949)
———. *The Gods Depart; a Saga of the Hawaiian Kingdom* (1956)
———. *An Island Kingdom Passes; Hawaii Becomes American* (1958)
———. *Hawaiian Heritage; a Brief Illustrated History* (1963)

Merrill, Sibley S. (ed.) *The Kahunas, Magicians of Hawaii* (1968)

Morgan, Joseph *Hawaii, a Geography* (Geographies of the United States series) (1983)

Nedbalek, Lani *Wahiawa: From Dream to Community* (1984)

Nordyke, Eleanor C. *The Peopling of Hawaii* (1977)

Ogawa, Dennis M. *Jan ken po: The World of Hawaii's Japanese Americans* (1973)

Oliver, Douglas *The Pacific Islands* (rev. ed. 1975)

Osborne, Thomas J. *"Empire Can Wait": American Opposition to Hawaiian Annexation, 1893–1898* (1981)

Peterson, Barbara B. (ed.) *Notable Women of Hawaii* (1984)

Porteus, Stanley D. *Calabashes and Kings: An Introduction to Hawaii* (1954, rpt. 1970)

Potter, Kasdon and Hazama *Hawaii: Our Island State* (rev. ed. 1979)

Prange, Gordon William, Donald M. Goldstein, and Katherine V. Dillon *Pearl Harbor: The Verdict of History* (1986)

Pukui, Mary Kawena, Samuel H. Elbert, and Esther T. Mookini *Place Names of Hawaii* (rev. and enl. ed. 1974)

Rapson, Richard C. *Fairly Lucky You Live Hawaii: Cultural Pluralism in the Fiftieth State* (1980)

Russ, William A. *The Hawaiian Revolution, 1893–94* (1959)
———. *The Hawaiian Republic, 1894–1898, and the Struggle to Win Annexation* (1961)

Samwell, D. *Captain Cook and Hawaii* (1957)

Scott, Edward B. *The Saga of the Sandwich Islands* (1968)

Simpich, Frederick, Jr. *Anatomy of Hawaii* (1971)

Sinclair, Marjorie *Nahienaena, Sacred Daughter of Hawaii* (1976)

Smith, Bradford *Yankees in Paradise; the New England Impact on Hawaii* (1956)

Stephan, John J. *Hawaii under the Rising Sun: Japan's Plans for Conquest after Pearl Harbor* (1984)

Tabrah, Ruth M. *Hawaii* (States and the Nation series) (1980)

Takaki, Ronald T. *Pau Hana; Plantation Life and Labor in Hawaii, 1835–1920* (1983)

Tate, Merze *The United States and the Hawaiian Kingdom; a Political History* (1965)

Toland, John *Infamy: Pearl Harbor and Its Aftermath* (1982)

White, Henry A. *James D. Dole: Industrial Pioneer of the Pacific, Founder of Hawaii's Pineapple Industry* (1957)

Whittaker, Elvi *The Mainland HAOLE: The White Experience in Hawaii* (1986)

Wright, Theon *The Disenchanted Isles; the Story of the Second Revolution in Hawaii* (1972)

Zambucka, Kristin *Princess Kaiulani: The Last Hope of Hawaii's Monarchy* (1976)

IDAHO

Idaho is a northern Mountain state. It is bordered on the north by the Canadian province of British Columbia; on the northeast and east by Montana and Wyoming; on the south by Nevada and Utah; and on the west by Oregon, Washington, and the Snake River.

FULL NAME STATE State of Idaho
POSTAL ABBREVIATION ID
INHABITANT Idahoan
ADMITTED TO THE UNION July 3, 1890.
43d state
POPULATION (est. 1987) 998,000.
Percent of US total: 0.41%. Rank: 42d

CAPITAL CITY Boise, the largest city in the state, located on the Boise River in southwestern Idaho; population 107,188 (est. 1984). Originally an army camp, it was founded as a mining settlement in 1863 and was incorporated as a city the following year, when it also became the territorial capital.

STATE NAME AND NICKNAMES The name "Idaho" is an artificial Indian word invented by George M. Willing. Also known as the Gem State and the Gem of the Mountains (the putative meaning of "Idaho").

STATE SEAL In the center is a shield showing a landscape, with the Snake River, mountains, a fir tree, and a farmer at the plow. Above the shield is an elk's head and the state motto on a scroll; below it is a sheaf of wheat; to the right is a miner; to the left a woman holding symbols of justice and liberty. Along the bottom are agricultural symbols, including two cornucopias, the state flower, and ripened wheat. The yellow border reads "Great Seal of the State of Idaho."

MOTTO Esto Perpetua (It is forever)

SONG "Here We Have Idaho," lyrics by McKinley Helm and Albert J. Tompkins, music by Sallie Hume Douglas.

SYMBOLS
Flower syringa
Tree white pine
Bird mountain bluebird
Gem star garnet
Horse Appaloosa

LICENSE PLATES (1) Brown on multicolored background showing landscape of trees and mountains silhoutted against pale and orange skies, with the legend "Centennial, 1890-1990." (2) Dark green on white, with stylized silhouette of mountains and the legend "Famous Potatoes."

FLAG A blue field with the state seal in the center and below it a red band bearing the legend "State of Idaho."

GEOGRAPHY AND CLIMATE

As a Rocky Mountain state, Idaho is dominated by mountain terrain, with the Continental Divide forming the eastern border. The state contains some of the largest stretches of unspoiled wilderness in the continental US, with a wide diversity of flora and game. Idaho also has more than 2,000 lakes and ten major rivers. Heavily irrigated farmland lines the Snake River valley, the state's major drainage; Hell's Canyon, along the western Snake River, is the deepest gorge—about one mile in depth—in North America.

AREA 83,564 square miles. Rank 13th
INLAND WATER 1,152 square miles
GEOGRAPHIC CENTER Custer, SW of Challis
ELEVATIONS *Highest point:* Borah Peak, Custer County, 12,662 feet. *Lowest point:* Snake River, Nez Perce County, 710 feet. *Mean elevation:* 5,000 feet

MAJOR RIVERS Snake, Salmon, Clearwater

MAJOR LAKES AND RESERVOIRS Pend Oreille, Coeur d'Alene, Priest, Bear, American Falls, Cascade, and Dworshak

LAND USE

	Thousands of acres
Urban (1982)	189
Rural (1982)	18,934
Cropland (1982)	6,390
Pastureland (1982)	1,274
Rangeland (1982)	6,733
Forestland (1982)	3,977
State parks and recreation areas (1983)	42
National park system (1984)	87
National forest system (1984)	21,703
Tribal lands (1984)	463

TEMPERATURES The highest recorded temperature was 118°F on July 28, 1934, at Orotino. The lowest was -60°F on January 18, 1943, at Island Park Dam.

NATIONAL SITES

NATIONAL HISTORIC TRAILS Lewis & Clark, Oregon
NATIONAL HISTORICAL PARK Nez Perce
NATIONAL MONUMENT Craters of the Moon
NATIONAL PARK Yellowstone
NATIONAL WILDLIFE REFUGES Bear Lake, Camas, Deer Flat, Grays Lake, Kootenai, Minidoka

HISTORY

1805	A US expedition led by Meriwether Lewis and William Clark crosses what is now the Idaho panhandle en route to the Pacific coast.
1809	David Thompson of the North West Company establishes a trading post on the eastern shore of Lake Pend Oreille.
1810	Andrew Henry of the Missouri Fur Company establishes a camp on a fork of the Snake River but abandons it the following year.
1818	The United States and Great Britain agree on joint occupancy of the Pacific Northwest, including what is now Idaho.
1834	Fort Hall and Fort Boise are constructed to aid fur traders; these posts become stops on the Oregon Trail, which by 1845 is a well-traveled road.
1836	Henry Spalding establishes a mission to the Nez Percé Indians at Lapwai.
1846	*June 15.* A treaty with Great Britain establishes the Pacific Northwest below the 49th parallel as US territory.
1848	*August 14.* Oregon Territory is created, including present-day Idaho.
1855	A treaty with the Koutenai, Pend Oreille, and Flathead Indians creates reservations for them in what is now Idaho and Montana. A treaty with the Nez Percé establishes for them a reserve in what is now Idaho, Oregon, and Washington.
1860	*June 15.* First permanent settlement in Idaho, at Franklin, by Mormons from Utah. In 1911 this day is proclaimed Pioneer Day. Gold is discovered in the Clearwater River country.
1862	The *Golden Age* is Idaho's first newspaper and is published in Lewiston.
1863	*March 4.* Creation of Idaho Territory. Some Nez Percé accept a smaller reservation replacing the 1855 area, overrun by gold prospectors.

1864	Peak year for gold production, valued at $12 million. During 1860–1866 total gold value is $53.4 million, of which $24 million is in the Boise Basin.
1867	Almost two million acres are set aside in southern Idaho as Fort Hall Reservation for Shoshone Indian groups. Bannocks join this reserve in 1869.
1870	Of a population of about 15,000 in Idaho, almost a third are Chinese, despite anti-Chinese violence in 1866–1867 that leaves over a hundred dead.
1874	The Utah Northern Railroad reaches Franklin from Ogden, Utah.
1877	Nontreaty Nez Percé led by Chief Joseph, expelled from northeastern Oregon, are pursued through Idaho by federal troops before surrendering in Montana.
1878	Forty whites and 78 Indians die in an uprising by Paiutes and Bannocks. Indian warfare in Idaho ends the following year.
1880	Silver is found in the Wood River region.
1882	The Northern Pacific Railroad links northern Idaho to the east and the Pacific Northwest seaports.
1884	Completion of the Oregon Short Line Railroad from Wyoming through southern Idaho to Oregon.
1885	Noah S. Kellogg finds silver in the Coeur d'Alene area. The Bunker Hill and Sullivan mines become the biggest in the chief lead-silver district in the US, which has yielded about $2 billion.
	Test Oath Act bars Mormons from voting, holding office, or serving on juries. These disabilities become part of the state constitution and remain in force until 1890 when Mormons renounce polygamy as an act of faith.
1890	*July 3.* Idaho is admitted to the Union as the 43d state. Its constitution establishes state control over water rights, provides for an eight-hour day on all public works, and prohibits child labor in the mines.
	Agriculture overtakes mining in total value of production.
1892	Martial law is declared in northern Idaho mining towns, where the dispatch of federal troops helps break a miners' strike. More than 600 union leaders and sympathizers are arrested.
1896–1902	Democrats, allied with Populists, control state politics. They also receive support from dissident Republicans who join in seeking the remonetization of silver.
1899	Dynamiting of Bunker Hill concentrator results in the reimposition of martial law and dispatch of US troops. The Western Federation of Miners is suppressed, and hundreds of miners are imprisoned for six months.
1905	Women receive the right to vote.
	December 30. Former governor Frank Steunenberg is assassinated.
1907	Clarence Darrow successfully defends "Big Bill" Haywood and two other Western Federation of Miners officials found not guilty of conspiracy in Steunenberg's murder. William Borah, the prosecutor, is elected to the US Senate; he serves until his death in 1940.
1912	Voters adopt constitutional amendments establishing the initiative, referendum, and recall.
1914	Moses Alexander is elected the first Jewish governor of any state.
1915	Arrowrock Dam, completed on the Boise River, is, at 354 feet, the highest dam in the world.
1922	Farmers are receiving less than one-third of 1919 prices for crops and livestock.
1927	The American Falls Dam, on the Snake River near Pocatello, provides irrigation water for one million acres.
	Completion of US Highway 95, the only land connection between northern and southern Idaho.
1931	Adoption of a state income tax and a tax on private-power combines.
1932	As a result of the Great Depression, average income has fallen 49 percent since 1929. Cash income of farmers has fallen by almost two-thirds.
1934	Idaho is first among states in silver and second in lead production. Shoshone County has the nation's largest silver mine (the Sunshine Mine) and the three largest lead producers. The state also ranks third in hay and fifth in wool.
1936	The Union Pacific Railroad creates Sun Valley as a ski resort.
1939	Per capita income has risen to $452 from $287 in 1933.

1942	Nearly 10,000 persons of Japanese ancestry are sent from the West Coast to an internment camp at Hunt.
1951	The Atomic Energy Commission's National Reactor Testing Station, near Arco, successfully uses atomic energy to produce electricity.
	Opening, at Lewiston, of Idaho's first pulp and paper plant.
1952	Completion of the Anderson Ranch Dam on the south fork of the Boise River.
1958	With 1,437 million board-feet cut, Idaho passes North Carolina to rank fourth among states in timber until 1982.
	Idaho is first among states in the mining of silver, lead, antimony, cobalt, and columbium-tantalum.
1959	Completion of the Brownlee Dam on the Hell's Canyon stretch of the Snake River.
	Idaho is fourth among states in irrigated acres—2,330,000—comprising 54 percent of the state's farmland.
1965	A state sales tax of three percent is adopted.
1972	*May 2.* A fire in the Sunshine Mine kills 91 miners.
1973	Completion of the Dworshak Dam on the Clearwater River.
1975	Lewiston becomes a seaport with the dedication of a $344-million deep-channel waterway linking the Snake and Columbia rivers to the Pacific Ocean.
1976	*June 5.* The Teton Dam on the Snake River collapses, killing 11 persons and causing at least $400 million in property damage.
1980	Creation of the 2.2-million-acre River of No Return Wilderness, the largest wilderness preserve in the United States outside of Alaska.
1982	The Sunshine Mine and Bunker Hill mine and smelter are closed because of low silver prices.
1985	Idaho accounts for 48 percent of national silver production. It also produces all the nation's antimony and ranks second among states in lead and vanadium production and third in phosphate rock and molybdenum.
	Record potato production of over 102 million hundredweight comprises one-fourth of all US potatoes.
1986	Idaho voters adopt a right-to-work constitutional amendment prohibiting the payment of union dues as a condition for employment.

DEMOGRAPHY

Population (est. 1987) 998,000
Population (1980) 944,038
Population density in persons
per square mile (1980) 11.3

POPULATION BY RACE (1980)
American Indian/Aleut/
  Eskimo 10,521
Asian/Pacific Islander 5,948
Black 2,716
Hispanic 36,615
White 901,641
Other 23,109

POPULATION CHARACTERISTICS (1980)
Percent of state population
Urban 54.0
Rural 46.0
Under 18 . . . . 32.5
65 or older 9.9
College-educated 16.1

Families below poverty line 9.6
Public assistance recipients 3.0

Per capita personal income
(1986) $11,432
Millionaires per 100,000
residents (1982) 102.4
Average life expectancy in
years (1980) 75.2
Marriage rate per 1,000
residents (1986) 10.5
Divorce rate per 1,000
residents (1986) 6.0
Birthrate per 1,000
residents (1985) 17.4
Infant mortality per 1,000
births (1985) 7.7
Abortion rate per 1,000
live births (1985) 155
Crime rate per 100,000
residents (1985)
Violent 222.5
Property 3,984.4

Federal and state prisoners per
100,000 residents (1984) 123
Alcohol consumption in gallons per
capita (1985) 40.5
Deaths from motor vehicle accidents
per 100,000 residents (1985) . . 25.5

MAJOR CITIES

	Population
Boise (est. 1984)	107,188
Idaho Falls (1980)	39,739
Pocatello (1980)	46,340
Twin Falls (1980)	26,209

GOVERNMENT AND POLITICS

Number of US Representatives   2
Electoral votes   4

POLITICAL PARTY NOMINEE FROM STATE
Glen Hearst Taylor
(Progressive)   1948 VP

PRESIDENTIAL PRIMARY ELECTION In 1988,
Idaho sent 23 Democratic delegates and 22
Republican delegates to the national conventions.
CONSTITUTION Idaho is using its original
constitution, adopted in 1889.
LEGISLATURE The Legislature is divided

into the Senate (42 members, 2-year term,
minimum age 18) and the House of Representatives (84 members, 2-year term,
minimum age 18). In 1987, the salary was
$30 per diem.
JUDICIARY The highest court is the Supreme
Court, with 7 judges serving 10-year terms.
In 1987, the annual salary was $59,750.
EXECUTIVE The governor serves a 4-year
term; the minimum age for holding office
is 30. In 1987, the annual salary was
$55,000. There are 6 other elected officials.

PRESIDENTIAL VOTE 1948-1988 *(in percents)*

Year	*State Winner*	*Democratic*	*Republican*
1948	Truman (D)	50.0	47.3
1952	Eisenhower (R)	34.4	65.4
1956	Eisenhower (R)	38.8	61.2
1960	Nixon (R)	46.2	53.8
1964	Johnson (D)	50.9	49.1
1968	Nixon (R)	30.7	56.8
1972	Nixon (R)	26.0	64.2
1976	Ford (R)	36.8	59.3
1980	Reagan (R)	25.2	66.5
1984	Reagan (R)	26.4	72.4
1988	Bush (R)	37.0	63.0

GOVERNORS

Territorial Governors

William H. Wallace	1863
William B. Daniels (acting)	1863-1864
Caleb Lyon	1864-1865
C. De Witt Smith (acting)	1865
Horace Gilson (acting)	1866
David Ballard	1866-1870
Edward J. Curtis (acting)	1870
Thomas M. Bowen	1871
Edward J. Curtis (acting)	1871
Thomas W. Bennett	1871-1875
Edward J. Curtis (acting)	1875
David P. Thompson	1875-1876
Mason Brayman	1876-1878
R.A. Sidebotham (acting)	1878-1880
John B. Neil	1880-1883
Edward J. Curtis (acting)	1883-1884
William M. Bunn	1884-1885
Edward A. Stevenson	1885-1889
George L. Shoup	1889-1890

State Governors

George L. Shoup (R)	1890
Norman B. Willey (R)	1890-1893
William J. McConnell (R)	1893-1897
Frank Steunenberg (D)	1897-1901
Frank W. Hunt (D)	1901-1903
John T. Morrison (R)	1903-1905
Frank R. Gooding (R)	1905-1909
James H. Brady (R)	1909-1911
James H. Hawley (D)	1911-1913
John M. Haines (R)	1913-1915
Moses Alexander (D)	1915-1919
David W. Davis (R)	1919-1923
Charles C. Moore (R)	1923-1927
H.C. Baldridge (R)	1927-1931

C. Ben Ross (D)	1931-1937
Barzilla W. Clark (D)	1937-1939
C.A. Bottolfsen (R)	1939-1941
Chase A. Clark (D)	1941-1943
C.A. Bottolfsen (R)	1943-1945
C.C. Gossett (D)	1945
Arnold Williams (D)	1945-1947
Charles A. Robins (R)	1947-1951
Len B. Jordan (R)	1951-1955
Robert E. Smylie (R)	1955-1967
Don Samuelson (R)	1967-1971
Cecil D. Andrus (D)	1971-1977
John V. Evans (D)	1977-1987
Cecil D. Andrus (D)	1987-

MINIMUM AGES

Majority	18
Marriage with parental consent	16
Marriage without parental consent	18
Making a will (lower if married)	18
Buying alcohol	21
Jury duty	18
Leaving school	16
Driver's license	16

CAPITAL PUNISHMENT
Number executed 1976-88: 0
On death row Aug. 1, 1988: 16

MILITARY INSTALLATIONS
Total number: 4
Major bases:
Air Force: 2

FINANCES

Thousands of dollars

GENERAL REVENUE (1985)

Total general revenue	1,298,527
Total tax revenue	733,575
Sales and gross receipts	361,870
Individual income taxes	258,230
Corporate net income taxes	42,682

GENERAL EXPENDITURE (1985)

Total general expenditure	1,258,047
Education	539,240
Public welfare	139,564
Health	44,049
Hospitals	22,312
Natural resources	61,289
Highways	206,299
Police	13,990
Corrections	21,006

FEDERAL AID (1985) 444,926

ECONOMY

The Idaho potato remains the state's most important cash crop, followed by wheat, sugar beets, alfalfa, beans, truck vegetables, and peas. Cattle are the main livestock. Total farm receipts were over $2 billion in 1983. Manufacturing in the state is centered around potato and beet-sugar processing, lumber products, and chemicals. Silver, lead, and zinc, sand, gravel, basalt, pumice, garnet, and phosphate are the principle mining products. As in many Western states, tourism is one of the fastest growing industries, as visitors flock to see Idaho's spectacular national and state parks.

EMPLOYMENT (1984)

Thousands of persons

Total number of employed workers	431
Construction	12.8
Finance, insurance, and real estate	23.5
Government	68.0
Manufacturing	54.2
Mining	4.0
Services	61.6
Transportation, communications, and utilities	19.0
Wholesale and retail trade	82.3

Percent of civilian labor force unemployed (1984)	7.2

DEPARTMENT OF DEFENSE (1985)

Civilian workers employed	1,271
Military personnel	5,647
Contract awards	$50 million

ENERGY SOURCES FOR ELECTRIC UTILITIES (1983)

Percent

Coal	0
Gas	0
Hydroelectric	100
Nuclear	0
Petroleum	0

TRANSPORTATION

Motor vehicles registered in state (1986)	857,326
Miles of roads, streets, and highways (1986)	71,544
Miles of Class I railway operated (1986)	2,256
Airports (1983)	196
Major aviation hubs (1983)	1
Largest hub: Boise	

CULTURE AND EDUCATION

Native American tribes
Idaho was formerly home to the Kalispel, Nehelem, Northern Paiute, Palouse, and Spokane tribes. Groups that continue to live there include the Bannock, Coeur d'Alene, Kootenay, Nez Perce, Northern Shoshoni, and Western Shoshoni. There are four federal reservations in Idaho.

Religions, ethnicities, and languages
More than half of Idaho's population was born in Idaho; the rest is drawn mainly from the western and north central states. There is also a large community of Basque descendants who continue their sheepherding tradition. In 1980, 5.6 percent of Idaho's population spoke a language other than English at home. Among churchgoers, Mormons are the biggest group, followed by Catholics and Methodists.

Major museums and libraries
Boise Gallery of Art
Idaho State Historical Museum, Boise

Major arts organizations
Boise Opera
Boise Philharmonic Association
Idaho Falls Symphony
Idaho Shakespeare Festival, Boise

Colleges and universities
Number public (1986-87) 6
Number private (1986-87) 4
Total enrollment, in full-time equivalent students (1985) 32,600

Public elementary and secondary schools
Expenditure per pupil in average daily attendance (1986-87) $2,555
Pupil-teacher ratio (1987) 20.4
Average teacher salary (1986-87) $22,299

Holidays
State Fair, Boise. Late August
State Fair, Blackfoot. Early September

IDAHO IN LITERATURE

Nancy Mae Anderson *Swede Homestead* . . . (1942)
Memoir of pioneer homesteading in the Lake Coeur d'Alene district from 1893.

Louie W. Attebery *Idaho Folklife* (1985)

John Baumann *Old Man Crow's Boy* (1948)
Memoir of rural life in central Idaho, 1880–1909.

George F. Brimlow (ed.) "Nez Percé War Diary" *Idaho State Historical Society* 17th Biennial Report (1940)
Cavalry trooper's account of Indian warfare in 1877.

Ella E. Clark *Indian Legends from the Northern Rockies* (1966, rpt. 1988)

William E. Davis (ed.) "George Forman, the Great Pedestrian" *Idaho Yesterdays* 10, no. 1 (1966)
Descriptions of gold prospecting and violent incidents in Idaho City and the Boise Basin, 1864–1865.

Nelle Davis *Stump Ranch Pioneer* (1943)
Novel about a pioneer woman farmer.

Federal Writers' Project *Idaho Lore* (1939)

Vardis Fisher *In Tragic Life* (1932)
The first volume in a tetralogy of autobiographical novels by the state's best-known writer that includes *Passions Spin the Plot* (1934), *We Are Betrayed* (1935), *No Villain Need Be* (1936). The sequence traces the development of a boy from a Mormon pioneer background. Fisher also edited the Federal Writers' Project *Idaho State Guide* during the 1930s. His early novels *Toilers of the Hills* (1928) and *Dark Bridwell* (1931) are set on an eastern Idaho farm and on the Snake River. *April, a Fable of Love* (1937) is a novel about a girl's upbringing on a ranch.

Annie Greenwood *We Sagebrush Folks* (1934)
Autobiographical account of farming in the sagebrush desert of southern Idaho.

Mike Hanley and **Omer Stanford** *Sage Brush and Axle Grease* (1976)
Collection of reminiscences of pioneer days.

Grace Jordan *Home below Hell's Canyon* (1954)
Memoir of a farm family's struggles during the Depression.
————. *Idaho Reader* (1963)
Anthology of accounts of Idaho life past and present.

Sarah Lockwood *Elbow of the Snake* (1958)
Novel about pioneer farmers in the early 1900s.

Harold Peterson *The Last of the Mountain Men* (1969)
Account of Sylvan Hart's attempt to live as a mountain man during the 1940s.

George R. Stewart *Reluctant Soil* (1936)
Novel about a pioneer woman farmer.

William Stoll *Silver Strike: The True Story of Silver Mining in the Coeur d'Alenes* (1932)
Autobiographical narrative of boom-town life during the 1883 silver rush.

Arthur S. Taylor and **William McKinney** (eds.) "An Accurate Observer: William Hoffman's View of Idaho in 1853" *Idaho Yesterdays* 8, no. 2 (1964)
Extracts describing landscape from an Oregon trail diary.

GUIDES TO RESOURCES

Birdsall, Douglas G. (ed.) *Dissertations and Theses about Idaho, 1900–1978, a Bibliography with a Checklist of Library Holdings* (1980)

Buckendorf, Madeline and **Elizabeth P. Jacox** (comps. and eds.) *Directory of Oral History Resources* Idaho State Historical Society (1982)

Caldwell, Harry H. (ed.) *Idaho Economic Atlas* (1970)

Etulain, Richard W. and **Merwin Swanson** *Idaho History: A Bibliography* (rev. ed. 1979)

Federal Writers' Project *Idaho State Guide* (1937)
————. *Idaho: A Guide in Word and Picture* (2d ed. rev. 1950)

Idaho. Department of Highways *Route of the Oregon Trail in Idaho* (1963)

Idaho Department of Commerce and Development *Idaho Almanac* (1963–)
Idaho Blue Book (1969/70–)

Federal Writers' Project *The Idaho Encyclopedia* (1938)

Lu, Joseph K. *Idaho Statistics: An Annotated Guide to Government Publications* (1984)

Nelson, Milo G. and Charles A. Webbert *Idaho Local History, a Bibliography with a Checklist of Library Holdings* (1976)

Rikoon, J. Sanford *An Annotated Bibliography of Materials on Idaho Folklife* (1985)

SELECTED NONFICTION SOURCES

Bachman, J. R. *Story of the Amalgamated Sugar Company, 1897–1961* (1962)

Bailey, Robert G. *River of No Return* . . . (rev. ed. 1947)

Barber, Floyd R. and Dan W. Martin *Idaho in the Pacific Northwest* (1961)

Barrett, Glen *J. Lynn Driscoll: Western Banker* (1974)

Beal, Merrill D. *A History of Southeastern Idaho; an Intimate Narrative of Peaceful Conquest by Empire Builders* . . . (1942)
—— and Merle William Wells *History of Idaho* 3 vols. (1959)

Beatty, Robert O. *Idaho* (1974)

Bird, Annie L. *Boise, the Peace Valley* (1934)
——. *Old Fort Boise* (1971)

Brooks, Charles E. *The Henry's Fork* (1986)

Brosnan, Cornelius J. *History of the State of Idaho* (rev. 5th ed. 1948)

Carrey, John *Sheepeater Indian Campaign* (1968)
—— and Cort Conley *The Middle Fork and the Sheepeater War* (1977)

Clements, Louis J. *Pioneering the Snake River Fork Country* (1972)

Curtis, Albert B. *White Pines and Fires: Cooperative Forestry in Idaho* (1983)

Davis, James W. and Nikki Balch *Aristocrat in Burlap: A History of the Potato in Idaho* (1975)

Donaldson, Thomas B. *Idaho of Yesterday* (1941, rpt. 1970)

Dubois, Fred T. *Fred T. Dubois's The Making of a State* (1971)

Elsensohn, Sister M. Alfreda *Pioneer Days in Idaho Country* (1947)
——. *Idaho Chinese Lore* (1970)

Fahey, John *The Ballyhoo Bonanza: Charles Sweeny and the Idaho Mines* (1971)
——. *The Days of the Hercules* (1978)

Gibbs, Rafe *Beckoning the Bold: Story of the Dawning of Idaho* (1976)

Gittins, H. Leigh *Pocatello Portrait: The Early Years, 1878 to 1928* (1983)

Greever, William S. *Bonanza West: The Story of the Western Mining Rushes* (1963)

Gulick, Bill *Snake River Country* (1971)

Hailey, John *The History of Idaho* (1910)

Hanley, Mike *Owyhee Trails; the West's Forgotten Corner* (1973)

Hart, Patricia and Ivar Nelson *Mining Town: The Photographic Record of T. N. Barnard and Nellie Stockbridge from the Coeur d'Alenes* (1984)

Hult, Ruby El *Steamboats in the Timber* (1952)

Jackson, W. Turrentine *Wells, Fargo & Co. in Idaho Territory* (1984)

Johnson, Claudius O. *Borah of Idaho* (1967)

Liljeblad, Sven *Indian Peoples of Idaho* (1957)

Madsen, Brigham D. *The Bannock of Idaho* (1958)
——. *Chief Pocatello, the White Plume* (1986)

Magnuson, Richard G. *Coeur d'Alene Diary: The First Ten Years of Hardrock Mining in North Idaho* (2d ed. 1983)

Malone, Michael P. *Ben Ross and the New Deal in Idaho* (1970)

McConnell, William J. and James S. Reynolds (ed. Joyce Lindstrom) *Idaho's Vigilantes* (1984)

McDermott, John D. *Forlorn Hope: A Study of the Battle of White Bird Canyon, Idaho, and the Beginning of the Nez Perce War* (1968)

Moser, Don and the Editors of Time-Life Books *The Snake River Country* (American Wilderness series) (1974)

Newell, Helen Marie *Idaho's Place in the Sun* (1975)

Norton, Boyd *Snake Wilderness* (1971)

Oppenheimer, Doug *Sun Valley: A Biography* (1976)

Peterson, F. Ross *Idaho: A Bicentennial History* (States and the Nation series) (1976)

Peterson, Harold *The Last of the Mountain Men* (1969)

Platt, Kenneth B. *Salmon River Saga* (1978)

Sappington, Roger E. *The Brethren along the Snake River* (1966)

Scott, Orland A. *Pioneer Days on the Shadowy St. Joe* (1967)

Simpson, Claude *North of the Narrows: Men and Women of the Upper Priest Lake Country, Idaho* (1981)

Siporin, Steve (ed.) *Folk Art in Idaho* (Idaho Commission on the Arts) (1984)

Space, Ralph *Lewis and Clark through Idaho* (1964)

Sparling, Wayne C. *Southern Idaho Ghost Towns* (1974)

Spencer, Layne G. *And Five Were Hanged and Other Historical Short Stories of Pierce and the Oro Fino Mining District* (1968)

Thompson, Erwinn N. *Fort Lapwai, Nez Perce National Historical Park, Idaho* (1973)

Walker, Deward E., Jr. *American Indians of Idaho* (1971)

Welch, Julia C. *Gold Town to Ghost Town: The Story of Silver City, Idaho* (1982)

Wright, Patricia and Lisa B. Reitzes *Tourtellotte and Hummel of Idaho: The Standard Practice of Architecture* (1988)

ILLINOIS

The east north central state of Illinois is bordered on the north by Wisconsin; on the east by Lake Michigan, Indiana, and the Wabash River; on the south by Kentucky and the Ohio River; and on the west by Missouri, Iowa, and the Mississippi River.

FULL NAME State of Illinois
POSTAL ABBREVIATION IL
INHABITANT Illinoisan
ADMITTED TO THE UNION Dec. 3, 1818. 21st state
POPULATION (est. 1987) 11,582,000. Percent of US total: 4.91%. Rank: 6th

CAPITAL CITY Springfield, located on the Sangamon River in central Illinois; population 101,570 (est. 1984). Settled in 1818 and incorporated as a town in 1832 and as a city in 1840, it became the state capital when it was transferred there from Vandalia in 1837.

STATE NAME AND NICKNAMES From an Illinois and Peoria Indian word, *ilini* (pl. *iliniwok*), meaning "man" or "warrior." La Salle applied a French version of the name to the river he explored in 1679. Official nickname: Land of Lincoln. Also known as the Prairie State and the Corn State.

STATE SEAL An eagle in a prairie, standing on a boulder inscribed "1868, 1818" and holding in its talons a shield with the Stars and Stripes decorated with an olive branch;

in its beak is a scroll bearing the state motto. The rising sun is visible across a blue river. Around the border is the legend "Seal of the State of Illinois, Aug. 26th, 1818."

MOTTO State Sovereignty, National Union

SONG "Illinois," lyrics by C.H. Chamberlain, music by Archibald Johnston.

SYMBOLS
Flower violet
Tree white oak
Bird cardinal
Mineral fluorite
Animal white-tailed deer
Insect monarch butterfly
Language English

LICENSE PLATE Dark blue on white, with legend "Land of Lincoln" underscored by three stripes.

FLAG The state seal, without its border, on a field of white, with the legend "Illinois" in blue below it.

GEOGRAPHY AND CLIMATE

The upper two-thirds of Illinois, one of the longest states east of the Mississippi, has the character of a heartland state, with black-soil prairie covering the porous rock of the northern, western, and central regions. The southern end is more Appalachian in terrain. Illinois is defined by water: the state's main waterways are the Mississippi River, which forms the state's western border; the Ohio, along the southern border; the Wabash, dividing southern Illinois from southern Indiana; and Lake Michigan to the northeast.

AREA 56,345 square miles. Rank: 25th
INLAND WATER 700 square miles
GEOGRAPHIC CENTER Logan, 28 miles NE of Springfield
ELEVATIONS *Highest point:* Charles Mound, Jo Daviess County, 1,235 feet. *Lowest point:* Mississippi River, Alexander County, 279 feet. *Mean elevation:* 600 feet

MAJOR RIVERS Mississippi, Illinois, Kaskaskia

MAJOR LAKES AND RESERVOIRS Crab Orchard, Michigan, Chain O'Lakes, Carlyle, Rend, Spring, Shelbyville

LAND USE

	Thousands of acres
Urban (1982)	1,846
Rural (1982)	32,076
Cropland (1982)	24,727
Pastureland (1982)	3,157
Rangeland (1982)	0
Forestland (1982)	3,429
State parks and recreation areas (1983)	273
National park system (1984)	0
National forest system (1984) . . .	640
Tribal lands (1984)	0

TEMPERATURES The highest recorded temperature was 117°F on July 14, 1954, at East St. Louis. The lowest was -35°F on January 22, 1930, at Mount Carroll.

NATIONAL SITES

NATIONAL HISTORIC SITES Chicago Portage, Lincoln Home
NATIONAL HISTORIC TRAILS Lewis & Clark, Mormon Pioneer
NATIONAL WILDLIFE REFUGES Batchtown and Calhoun Division, Clarence Cannon, Chautauqua–Meredosia, Crab Orchard, Louisa and Keithsburg Division, Mark Twain, Savanna District, Upper Mississippi River Wildlife and Fish Refuge

HISTORY

1673	*September.* Returning from their voyage down the Mississippi, French explorers Louis Jolliet and Father Jacques Marquette reach the site of Chicago.
1675	Marquette founds a Jesuit mission near present-day Ottawa.
1680	Robert Cavelier, Sieur de La Salle, erects Fort Crèvecoeur near present-day Peoria.
1682	On his return from the mouth of the Mississippi, La Salle builds Fort St. Louis on Starved Rock, overlooking the Illinois River near Ottawa.
1699	First permanent settlement in Illinois is a mission at Cahokia.
1703	Another mission is built at Kaskaskia.
1720	Fort de Chartres, on the Mississippi 15 miles upstream from Kaskaskia, becomes the seat of French civil and military power from the Great Lakes to Arkansas.
1763	*February 10.* France cedes to Great Britain all her North American continental possessions east of the Mississippi except New Orleans.
1765	*October 10.* The British flag replaces the French at Fort de Chartres.
1778	*July 4.* Virginia frontiersman George Rogers Clark, with a band of 175 men, captures Kaskaskia from the British.
c. 1779	Permanent settlement at Chicago begins with Jean Baptist Point du Sable, a West Indian black or mulatto.
1783	Illinois passes to the United States as a result of the Treaty of Paris, which ends the war for American independence.
1800	Illinois country has 2,458 non-Indian residents.
1801	*July 4.* Illinois becomes part of Indiana Territory.

1803	Fort Dearborn is established by federal infantry at the confluence of the Chicago River and Lake Michigan.
	Kaskaskian Indians cede the greater part of southern Illinois.
1809	*February 3.* Illinois Territory, including present-day Wisconsin, is established with Kaskaskia as its capital.
1812	*August 15.* About 75 whites are massacred by Indians on evacuating Fort Dearborn.
1818	*December 3.* Illinois becomes the 21st state. The state constitution forbids the introduction of slavery, but not slavery itself.
1820	*December 4.* The General Assembly holds its first session at Vandalia, the state's new capital.
1823	The first large-scale lead smelter is established at Galena.
1831–1832	Friction between white settlers and Indians in western Illinois leads to war in which the Sauk and Fox, under Black Hawk, are defeated and expelled.
1833	The Potawatomi, Ottawa, and Chippewa cede their lands in Illinois, removing all Indian tribes from the state.
1837	*February 23.* The legislature votes to move the state capital to Springfield.
	March 4. Chicago is incorporated as a city, with a population of 4,071.
	November 8. Abolitionist editor Elijah Lovejoy is murdered in Alton while defending his press from a pro-slavery mob.
	John Deere of Grand Detour perfects the steel plow, needed to break the prairie sod.
1840	State population has tripled in 10 years, to 476,183.
1844	*June 27.* Mormon leader Joseph Smith is murdered in Carthage; in 1846, the Mormons, led by Brigham Young, leave their settlement at Nauvoo to travel west to Utah.
1847	Cyrus McCormick builds a plant in Chicago to manufacture his mechanical reaper.
1848	*April 23.* Illinois and Michigan Canal is completed, linking Lake Michigan at Chicago with the Illinois River and therefore with the Mississippi.
1853	The legislature forbids free blacks to enter Illinois.
1856	Completion of the Illinois Central Railroad line between Chicago and Cairo at the Ohio-Mississippi confluence.
1858	Stephen Douglas and Abraham Lincoln hold a series of seven historic debates in Illinois cities.
1860	Lincoln, a resident of Springfield, receives the Republican party presidential nomination at the Wigwam in Chicago and is elected the 16th president.
	Illinois leads all states in corn and wheat production.
1861–1865	Illinois contributes 259,092 men to the Union cause, of whom 34,834 die.
1865	*February 1.* Illinois is the first state to ratify the 13th Amendment, abolishing slavery.
	Chicago becomes a meatpacking center with the establishment of the Union Stock Yards.
1871	*October 8.* The Great Chicago Fire levels most of the city, killing 300 people and causing property damage of $192 million.
1873	*November 1.* Joseph Glidden begins manufacturing barbed wire, making De Kalb for 64 years "barbed wire capital of the world."
1885	Erection in Chicago of the ten-story Home Insurance Building, prototype of all skyscraper design, with an all-metal skeleton to support the floor and walls.
1886	*May 4.* A bomb kills seven policemen during a rally at Chicago's Haymarket Square pressing for the eight-hour work day. Anarchists are blamed, and four men are later hanged.
1889	Jane Addams establishes Hull House to help Chicago's poor.
1890	Illinois is the third biggest state, and Chicago is the nation's second biggest city. Meatpacking is the chief state industry.
1893	The World Columbian Exposition is held in Chicago.
1894	President Grover Cleveland sends federal troops to Chicago to help crush the Pullman Car Company railroad strike.
1903	*December 30.* A fire in Chicago's Iroquois Theater results in 596 deaths.

1912	*Poetry* magazine is founded in Chicago; Illinois poets Carl Sandburg, Vachel Lindsay, and Edgar Lee Masters receive attention in its pages.
1915	*July 24.* The *Eastland,* a holiday steamer, capsizes in the Chicago River, drowning 812 people.
1916	Chicago's brief period as a moviemaking capital nears close as Charlie Chaplin moves to Hollywood.
1917	More than 100 blacks are killed in two East St. Louis race riots. Illinois is third among states in coal production, with 810 mines producing more than 86 million tons.
1918	Most Illinois National Guard units are amalgamated into the 33d or Prairie Division in World War I. This division served on the Western Front from July 4 to the armistice.
1919	In five days of July rioting in Chicago, 22 blacks and 16 whites are killed.
1920	*September 28.* Eight Chicago White Sox players are indicted for "throwing" the 1919 World Series.
1929	*February 14.* Seven killed in Chicago's St. Valentine's Day massacre as gangsters—dressed as policemen and presumably on orders from Al Capone—gun down rivals in a North Side garage.
1930	*February 10.* One of the nation's largest bootlegging operations is exposed in Chicago.
1933	State sales tax adopted to help provide for the 1.5 million residents who are unemployed in the Great Depression.
1942	*December 2.* First controlled release of nuclear energy, a self-sustaining chain reaction, at the University of Chicago.
1943	Over 800 Illinois plants are manufacturing aircraft and parts for the World War II effort.
1945	McLean County is the first in the nation in corn production; Henry County leads in hogs; and Champaign County is first in soybeans.
1955	Richard J. Daley wins the first of five consecutive terms as mayor of Chicago.
1959	*April 30.* The first oceangoing vessel to pass through the St. Lawrence Seaway arrives in Chicago.
1966	Dr. Martin Luther King campaigns in Chicago for housing, welfare, and education reforms.
1968	*April 5–7.* 11 blacks die in Chicago rioting following the King assassination. *August 28.* Anti–Vietnam War demonstrators protest the Democratic National Convention's nomination, in Chicago, of Hubert Humphrey for president.
1969	Illinois becomes the 39th state to adopt an income tax. *September 24.* Trial begins of the Chicago 8—Black Panther leaders who incited the 1968 convention riots.
1970	*November 18.* Voters ratify the fourth state constitution.
1974	Chicago's Sears Tower completed; at 109 stories and 1,469 feet, it is the tallest building in the world.
1980	Tampico-born Ronald Reagan becomes the first Illinois native elected president of the United States.
1983	Harold Washington is elected Chicago's first black mayor.
1986	James Thompson is elected to a fourth term as governor, a state record.

DEMOGRAPHY

Population (est. 1987) . . . 11,582,000
Population (1980) 11,427,414
Population density in persons
   per square mile (1980) 203.0

Black 1,675,525
Hispanic 635,525
White 9,225,575
Other 341,835

POPULATION BY RACE (1980)
American Indian/Aleut/
   Eskimo 16,271
Asian/Pacific Islander 159,551

POPULATION CHARACTERISTICS (1980)
Percent of state population
Urban 83.3
Rural 16.7
Under 18 . . . . 28.4

65 or older	11.0
College-educated	14.5
Families below poverty line	8.4
Public assistance recipients	7.0

Per capita personal income
(1986) $15,420
Millionaires per 100,000
residents (1982) 126.5
Average life expectancy
in years (1980) 73.4
Marriage rate per 1,000
residents (1986) 8.3
Divorce rate per 1,000
residents (1986) 4.0
Birth rate per 1,000
residents (1985) 15.4
Infant mortality per 1,000
births (1985) 11.2
Abortion rate per 1,000
live births (1985) 372
Crime rate per 1,000
residents (1985)
Violent 800.0
Property 4,746.0

Federal and state prisoners per
100,000 residents (1984) 146
Alcohol consumption in gallons per
capita (1985) 41.6
Deaths from motor vehicle accidents
per 100,000 residents (1985) .. 13.3

MAJOR CITIES

1984 population (est.)

Aurora	85,735
Chicago	2,992,472
Decatur	91,851
Elgin	7,595
Evanston	72,074
Joliet	76,488
Peoria	117,113
Rockford	136,531
Springfield	101,570
Waukegan	70,077

GOVERNMENT AND POLITICS

Number of US Representatives 22
Electoral votes 24

POLITICAL PARTY NOMINEES FROM STATE
 * winner

Abraham Lincoln* (R)	1860	P
Stephen Arnold Douglas (D)	1860	P
Abraham Lincoln* (R)	1864	P
Ulysses Simpson Grant* (R)	1868	P
Ulysses Simpson Grant* (R, National Working Men's Convention)	1872	P
David Davis (Labor Reform)	1872	P
James B. Walker (American National)	1876	P
John Alexander Logan (R)	1884	VP
Alson Jennes Streeter (Union Labor)	1888	P
Robert Hall Cowdery (United Labor)	1888	P
Adlai Ewing Stevenson* (D)	1892	VP
John McAuley Palmer (National Democratic)	1896	P
Hale Johnson (Prohibition)	1896	VP
Adlai Ewing Stevenson (D, People's, and Silver Republican)	1900	VP
John Granville Wooley (United Christian/declined)	1900	VP
John Granville Wooley (Prohibition)	1900	P
William Wesley Cox (Socialist Labor)	1904	VP
Eugene Wilder Chafin (Prohibition)	1908	P
Daniel Braxton Turner (United Christian)	1908	VP
Eugene Wilder Chafin (Prohibition)	1912	P
Caleb Harrison (Socialist Labor)	1916	VP
Seymour Stedman (Socialist)	1920	VP
Charles Gates Dawes* (R)	1924	VP
William Zebulon Foster (Workers)	1924	P
Duncan McDonald (Farmer Labor/withdrew)	1924	P
William Zebulon Foster (Workers)	1928	P
William Zebulon Foster (Communist)	1932	P
Frank Stewart Regan (Prohibition)	1932	VP
Frank Knox (R)	1936	VP
Maynard C. Krueger (Socialist)	1940	VP
Edgar V. Moorman (Prohibition)	1940	VP
John Maxwell (Vegetarian)	1948	P
Adlai Ewing Stevenson (D)	1952	P
Enoch Arden Holtwick (Prohibition)	1952	VP

Adlai Ewing Stevenson (D, Liberal)	1956	P
Enoch Arden Holtwick (Prohibition)	1956	P
Burr McCloskey (Pioneer)	1956	VP
Lar Daly (Tax Cut)	1960	P
Dick Gregory (Freedom and Peace)	1968	P
Andrew Pulley (American/disqualified)	1972	VP
Louis Fisher (Socialist Labor)	1972	P
Willie Mae Reid (Socialist Workers)	1976	VP
Quinn Brisben (Socialist)	1976	VP
John Bayard Anderson (independent candidate)	1980	P
Andrew Pulley (Socialist Workers/disqualified)	1980	P
John Bayard Anderson (National Unity Party of Kentucky)	1984	P

PRESIDENTIAL PRIMARY ELECTION In 1988, Illinois sent 187 Democratic delegates and 92 Republican delegates to the national conventions.

CONSTITUTION Illinois has had four constitutions: 1818, 1848, 1870, and the present one, adopted in 1970.

LEGISLATURE The General Assembly is divided into the Senate (59 members, a staggered system of 4-year and 2-year terms, minimum age 21) and the House of Representatives (118 members, 2-year term, minimum age 21). In 1987, the annual salary was $32,500.

JUDICIARY The highest court is the Supreme Court, with 7 judges serving 10-year terms. In 1987, the annual salary was $93,266.

EXECUTIVE The governor serves a 4-year term; the minimum age for holding office is 25. In 1987, the annual salary was $93,266. There are 14 other elected officials.

PRESIDENTIAL VOTE 1948-1988 *(in percents)*

Year	State Winner	Democratic	Republican
1948	Truman (D)	50.1	49.2
1952	Eisenhower (R)	44.9	54.8
1956	Eisenhower (R)	40.3	59.5
1960	Kennedy (D)	50.0	49.8
1964	Johnson (D)	59.5	40.5
1968	Nixon (R)	44.2	47.1
1972	Nixon (R)	40.5	59.0
1976	Ford (R)	48.1	50.1
1980	Reagan (R)	41.7	49.6
1984	Reagan (R)	43.3	56.2
1988	Bush (R)	37.0	63.0

GOVERNORS

Territorial Governors

Ninian Edwards	1809-1818

State Governors

Shadrach Bond (D-R)	1818-1822
Edward Coles (D-R)	1822-1826
Ninian Edwards (D-R)	1826-1830
John Reynolds (D)	1830-1834
William L.D. Ewing (D)	1834
Joseph Duncan (D)	1834-1838
Thomas Carlin (D)	1838-1842
Thomas Ford (D)	1842-1846
Augustus C. French (D)	1846-1853
Joel A. Matteson (D)	1853-1857
William H. Bissell (R)	1857-1860
John Wood (R)	1860-1861
Richard Yates (R)	1861-1865
Richard J. Oglesby (R)	1865-1869
John M. Palmer (R)	1869-1873

Richard J. Oglesby (R)	1873
John L. Beveridge (R)	1873-1877
Shelby M. Cullom (R)	1877-1883
John M. Hamilton (R)	1883-1885
Richard J. Oglesby (R)	1885-1889
Joseph W. Fifer (R)	1889-1893
John Peter Altgeld (D)	1893-1897
John Riley Tanner (R)	1897-1901
Richard Yates (R)	1901-1905
Charles S. Deneen (R)	1905-1913
Edward F. Dunne (D)	1913-1917
Frank O. Lowden (R)	1917-1921
Len Small (R)	1921-1929
Louis L. Emmerson (R)	1929-1933
Henry Horner (D)	1933-1940
John Stelle (D)	1940-1941
Dwight H. Green (R)	1941-1949
Adlai E. Stevenson (D)	1949-1953
William G. Stratton (R)	1953-1961
Otto Kerner Jr. (D)	1961-1968
Samuel H. Shapiro (D)	1968-1969
Richard B. Ogilvie (R)	1969-1973

Daniel Walker (D)   1973-1977
James R. Thompson (R)   1977-

MINIMUM AGES

Majority 18
Marriage with parental consent 16
Marriage without parental consent . . 18
Making a will 18
Buying alcohol 21
Jury duty 18
Leaving school 16
Driver's license 16

CAPITAL PUNISHMENT
Number executed 1976-88: 0
On death row Aug. 1, 1988: 116

MILITARY INSTALLATIONS
Total number: 15
Major bases:
   Army: 2
   Navy: 1
   Air Force: 1

FINANCES

Thousands of dollars

GENERAL REVENUE (1985)
Total general revenue . . . 15,377,208
Total tax revenue 9,227,777
Sales and gross receipts . . . 4,950,229
Individual income taxes . . 2,600,864
Corporate net income taxes . . 706,009

GENERAL EXPENDITURE (1985)
Total general expenditure . 14,781,436
Education 4,916,620
Public welfare 3,489,101
Health 430,006
Hospitals 495,376
Natural resources 168,201
Highways 1,850,702
Police 144,460
Corrections 401,045

FEDERAL AID (1985) 4,688,411

ECONOMY

As one of the three top-ranking states in total exports, Illinois plays a crucial part in the nation's economy. Leading the nation in soybean and corn production, Illinois is also a top producer of hogs, cattle, sheep, and poultry. In 1982, 71% of the state was farmland; total farm cash receipts reached

$8.1 billion in 1983. Soft coal and petroleum are the main mining products, along with fluorspar, sandstone, limestone, gravel, and silica sand. The total value of mineral production in 1982 was over $3 billion. Illinois also has a large and varied manufacturing sector, centered mainly around Chicago and Peoria; items manufactured include steel stock, agricultural machinery, diesel engines, trains and train equipment, television sets and telephone equipment, farm implements, machine tools, soap, feedstocks, and processed foods.

EMPLOYMENT (1984)
Thousands of persons
Total number of employed
  workers 5,093
Construction 149.9
Finance, insurance, and
  real estate 317.8
Government 691.3
Manufacturing 985.5
Mining 24.9
Services 1,048.4
Transportation, communications,
  and utilities 274.2
Wholesale and retail trade . . . 1,144.4

Percent of civilian labor force
  unemployed (1984) 9.1

DEPARTMENT OF DEFENSE (1985)
Civilian workers employed . . . 22,664
Military personnel 40,874
Contract awards . . . . $1.693 billion

ENERGY SOURCES FOR ELECTRIC UTILITIES (1983)
Percent
Coal 67.5
Gas 1.0
Hydroelectric 0.1
Nuclear 28.3
Petroleum 3.2

TRANSPORTATION
Motor vehicles registered
  in state (1986) 7,419,535
Miles of roads, streets,
  and highways (1986) 134,778
Miles of Class I railway
  operated (1986) 7,960
Airports (1983) 909
Major aviation hubs (1983) 1
  Largest hub: Chicago
Major ports, with gross tonnage (1985)
  Chicago 22,574

CULTURE AND EDUCATION

Native American tribes
Illinois was formerly home to the Fox, Illinois, Miami, Ojibway, Ottawa, Peora, Piankashaw, Potawatomi, Sauk, Shawnee, Wea, Winnebago, and Wyandot tribes.

Religions, ethnicities, and languages
Illinois is known for its ethnic diversity. The first settlers, from the eastern and southern states, were of English and Scotch-Irish descent. In the 19th century, Illinois absorbed thousands of German, Irish, Polish, Italian, Norwegian, Swedish, Russian, Austrian, Hungarian, and Jewish immigrants, as well as Blacks from the American South; in the 20th century, immigrants were predominantly Greek, Iranian, Czech, Japanese, Chinese, Filipino, Puerto Rican, and Mexican. In 1980, 11.5 percent of Illinois's population spoke a language other than English at home. The major Christian denominations are Methodist, Baptist, Presbyterian, and United Church of Christ; in the cities, there are large communities of Roman Catholics, Jews, and Eastern Orthodox.

Major museums and libraries
Adler Planetarium, Chicago
Art Institute of Chicago
Field Museum of Natural History, Chicago
Illinois State Library, Springfield
Illinois State Museum, Springfield
Spertus Museum of Judaica, Chicago
Museum of Contemporary Art, Chicago
Museum of Science and Industry, Chicago

Major arts organizations
Chicago City Ballet
Chicago Symphony Orchestra
Chicago Symphony Wind Ensemble
Civic Orchestra of Chicago
Goodman Theatre, Chicago
Hubbard Street Dance Company, Chicago
Lyric Opera of Chicago
Second City, Chicago
Steppenwolf Theatre Company, Chicago

Colleges and universities
Number public (1986-87) 59
Number private (1986-87) 104
Total enrollment, in full-time equivalent students (1985) 450,500

Public elementary and secondary schools
Expenditure per pupil in average daily attendance (1986-87) $3,980
Pupil-teacher ratio (1987) 17.4
Average teacher salary (1986-87) $29,399

Major league sports teams
Baseball: Chicago Cubs, Chicago White Sox
Basketball: Chicago Bulls
Football: Chicago Bears
Hockey: Chicago Black Hawks

Holidays
General Casimir Pulaski's Birthday. 1st Monday of March
State Fair, Springfield. Early August

ILLINOIS IN LITERATURE

Jane Addams *Twenty Years at Hull House* (1910, rpt. 1981); *The Second Twenty Years at Hull House* (1930)
Autobiographies of the Chicago social reformer.

Nelson Algren *Never Come Morning* (1942)
Novel about a Polish boxer set on the South Side.
———. *The Neon Wilderness* (1947, rpt. 1960)
Short stories set in the Chicago slums.
———. *The Man with the Golden Arm* (1949)
A young hustler's fate in the Chicago slums.
———. *Chicago: City on the Make* (1951, rpt. 1961)
Portrait of Chicago as an urban wilderness.

Sherwood Anderson *Windy McPherson's Son* (1916, rpt. 1965)
A young man from Iowa succeeds in Chicago.
———. *Marching Men* (1917)
Novel about union politics in Chicago.
———. *Horses and Men* (1923)
Four naturalistic stories set in Illinois and Chicago.

Clarence Andrews *Chicago in Story: A Literary History* (1982)

Paul M. Angle (ed.) *Prairie State: Impressions of Illinois, 1637–1967 by Travelers and Other Observers* (1968)

Saul Bellow *The Adventures of Augie March* (1953, rpt. 1984)
Classic novel of a young man's upbringing in 1930s Chicago. Other novels and stories by Bellow with Chicago settings include *Dangling Man* (1944), *Mosby's Memoirs and Other Stories* (1968, rpt. 1984), *Humboldt's Gift* (1975, rpt. 1984), and *The Dean's December* (1982).

Morris Birkbeck *Notes on a Journey in America* (1817); *Letters from Illinois* (1818, rpt. 1970)
Memoirs of the English pioneer and co-founder of the Wabash River settlement.

Chief Black Hawk (ed. Donald H. Jackson) *Black Hawk: An Autobiography* (1833, 1955)
Autobiography, first by a native American, of the chief defeated in the Black Hawk war.

Edward Bonney (ed. Philip D. Jordan) *The Banditti of the Prairies, or, The Murderer's Doom* (1856, rpt. 1963)
Accounts of sensational crimes on the Illinois frontier, sometimes regarded as fiction.

Ray Bradbury *Dandelion Wine* (1957, rpt. 1969)
Novel of small town life.

Robert Bray *Rediscoveries: Literature and Place in Illinois* (1982)
——— (ed.) *A Reader's Guide to Illinois Literature* (1987)

Gwendolyn Brooks *Maud Martha* (1953, rpt. 1974)
Novel about a young black woman growing up in 1930s and '40s Chicago.

Baker Brownell *Earth Is Enough* (1933)
Evocations of Chicago and Vandalia.
————. *The Other Illinois* (1958)
Description of rural southern Illinois.

Robert Burdette *The Drums of the 47th* (1914)
Memoirs of a Civil War soldier.

Rebecca Burlend *A True Picture of Emigration* (1848, rpt. 1936, 1987)
Yorkshire emigrant's harsh experience of the frontier in Pike County.

W. R. Burnett *Little Caesar* (1929)
Classic Chicago gangster novel.

Peter Cartwright *Autobiography of Peter Cartwright* (1856, rpt. 1956)
Memoir of a Methodist circuit rider.

Cyrus Colter *The Beach Umbrella* (1970)
Short stories about black life in Chicago.

Robert Coover *The Origin of the Brunists* (1966, rpt. 1978)
Novel based on a 1951 mining accident at West Frankfort.

Mark Costello *The Murphy Stories* (1973)
Tales set in Decatur.

Dale Cramer *Chicago Renaissance* (1966)

Floyd Dell *Moon-Calf* (1920); *The Briary Bush* (1921)
Autobiographical novels about a young artist's social rebellion.

Theodore Dreiser *Jennie Gerhardt* (1911, rpt. 1982)
Novel about the lonely, despairing life of the daughter of German immigrants in late-nineteenth-century Chicago.
————. *The Titan* (1914)
Novel about a successful financier based on the life of the industrialist Charles Yerkes.

Leonard Dubkin *Enchanted Streets: The Unlikely Adventures of an Urban Nature Lover* (1947)
Essays on the natural life of Chicago parks and neighborhoods.
————. *The Natural History of a Yard* (1955)
Essay on the natural life of an apartment building yard on Chicago's north side. The gradual destruction of Chicago as Dubkin knew it is traced in his *My Secret Places* (1972).

Bernhard Duffy *The Chicago Renaissance in American Letters* (1954)

Hugh Duncan *The Rise of Chicago as a Literary Center* (1964)

Finley Peter Dunne *Dissertations by Mr. Dooley* (1906, rpt. 1977); *Mr. Dooley in Peace and War* (1988)
The opinions of Dooley, a fictional Irish barman, originally appeared in the Chicago *Post*, and reflect conditions in Chicago during the 1890s.

Stuart Dybek *Childhood and Other Neighborhoods* (1980)
Stories of Slavic Chicago neighborhoods.

Marie Hall Ets *Rosa: The Life of an Italian Immigrant* (1970)
Autobiography of an Italian woman who settled in Chicago in the 1890s.

Ronald Fair *Hog Butcher* (1966); *We Can't Breathe* (1972); *World of Nothing* (1970)
Tales of life in the black ghettos of Chicago.

Eliza Farnham *Life in Prairie Land* (1846, rpt. 1972)
New York emigrant's account of the frontier in Tazewell and Lee Counties, 1835–1840.

James T. Farrell *Studs Lonigan: A Trilogy* (1935, rpt. 1976, 1979)
Classic naturalistic novel of a Chicago man's boyhood and early death, comprising *Young Lonigan* (1933), *The Young Manhood of Studs Lonigan* (1934), and *Judgment Day* (1935). Farrell also wrote five autobiographical novels tracing the life of Danny O'Neill, a lower-middle-class Irish American from the South Side.

Edna Ferber *So Big!* (1924, rpt. 1978)
Pulitzer prize–winning novel about a determined woman farmer.
————. *A Peculiar Treasure* (1939, rpt. 1971)
Autobiography that includes an account of life in the Chicago Jewish community, which Ferber also described in the stories *Fanny Herself* (1917, rpt. 1975).
————. *One Basket* (1947, rpt. 1957)
Stories of working people in Chicago during the early years of the century.

Jack Finney *I Love Galesburg in the Springtime* (1963)
Short stories set in small Illinois towns.

Edmund Flagg *The Far West* (1838)
The Illinois frontier romantically described in articles written for the Louisville *Journal*.

Leon Forrest *There Is a Tree More Ancient Than Eden* (1973)
Novel about black community life in Chicago.

Edith Freund *Chicago Girls* (1985)
Comic novel set in contemporary Chicago.

Henry Blake Fuller *With the Procession* (1895, rpt. 1967); *The Cliff-Dwellers* (1893, rpt. 1981)
Novels set in the Chicago society of the 1890s.

Hamlin Garland *Rose of Dutcher's Coolly* (1905, rpt. 1969)
Young woman from Wisconsin makes a literary career in Chicago.

Charles Gerard *Illinois River Hokeypokey* (1969)
Comic novel about Illinois bootlegging.

Ruby B. Goodwin *It's Good to Be Black* (1954)
Black society in Du Quoin, 1905–1915.

Francis Grierson *The Valley of the Shadows* (1909, rpt. 1970)
The Illinois frontier before the Civil War, and an account of the Underground Railroad during the 1850s.

Albert Halper (ed.) *This Is Chicago: An Anthology* (1952)

Harry Hansen *Midwest Portraits* (1923)
An account of Sandburg, Anderson, Hecht, and other writers of the Chicago Renaissance.

Ben Hecht *Erik Dorn* (1921)
Novel about a Chicago journalist during World War I.
————. *1001 Afternoons in Chicago* (1923)
Collected journalism.
————. *A Child of the Century* (1954)
Autobiography of the Chicago novelist, journalist, and playwright.

Robert Herrick *Memoirs of an American Citizen* (1905, rpt. 1963)
An Indiana boy prospers in the Chicago meatpacking industry, 1880–1900.

Betty Howland *Blue in Chicago* (1978)
Autobiographical stories of contemporary Chicago.

Isabel Jamison "Literature and Literary People of Early Illinois" *Transactions of the Illinois State Historical Society* 13 (1908)

Thomas L. Kilpatrick and **Patsy-Rose Hoshiko** *Illinois! Illinois! An Annotated Bibliography of Fiction* (1979)

Juliette Kinzie *Narrative of the Massacre at Chicago* (1844); *Wau-Bun, the "Early Day" in the Northwest* (1856, rpt. 1901, 1932)
Account of an 1830 trek to Chicago and of the Fort Dearborn massacre.

Joseph Kirkland *Zury: The Meanest Man in Spring County* (1887, rpt. 1956)
Novel of rural life depicting a pioneer community c.1920.

Jerry Klein *Played in Peoria* (1980)
Feature articles on central Illinois towns.
————. *Fathersday* (1981)
Novel about family life set in Peoria.

Ring Lardner *Best Short Stories of Ring Lardner* (1957)
Some of these humorous, satirical stories date from Lardner's early years as a Chicago journalist.

Meyer Levin *Citizens* (1940); *Compulsion* (1956, rpt. 1984); *The Old Bunch* (1937, rpt. 1985)
Novels about Chicago life in the 1930s. The latter is regarded as a classic description of Chicago Jewish society.

Norman Mailer *Miami and the Siege of Chicago* (1968)
The political conventions of 1968.

David Martin *The Crying Heart Tattoo* (1982); *Tethered* (1979)
Comic novels set in southern Illinois.

Edgar Lee Masters *Mitch Miller* (1920)
Novel about boyhood in a small town, reminiscent of *Tom Sawyer*.
———. *Across Spoon River* (1936)
Poet's memoirs of Petersburg, Lewistown, and Chicago.

William Maxwell *So Long, See You Tomorrow* (1980, rpt. 1981)
An elderly man remembers events on an Illinois farm during his childhood. Maxwell's other fiction, some of which is set in Lincoln, also includes *The Folded Leaf* (1945, rpt. 1981), *Over by the River, and Other Stories* (1977), and *Time Will Darken It* (1948, rpt. 1983).

Isabella M. Mayne *Maud* (1939)
Journal of a woman's life in Cairo, 1881–1895.

Harriet Monroe *A Poet's Life* (1938)
Autobiographical account of literary Chicago.

Willard Motley *Knock on Any Door* (1947)
Novel about an Italian Chicago boy turned gangster.

Frank Norris *The Pit: A Story of Chicago* (1903)
Novel about the fortunes of a Chicago businessman.

William Oliver *Eight Months in Illinois* (1843)
Descriptions of the frontier by an English immigrant.

Donald Culross Peattie *An Almanac for Moderns* (1935, rpt. 1980)
Observations of nature, chiefly in Kennicott's Grove, Chicago.

Harry Mark Petrakis *Stelmark* (1970)
Autobiography of the Chicago Greek writer, depicting his Depression childhood and the life of the immigrant Greek community.
———. *Nick the Greek* (1979, rpt. 1984); *Pericles on 31st Street* (1965)
A novel and a collection of stories set in the Chicago Greek community.

David Pichaske *The Jubilee Diary* (1982)
A naturalist's account of weekly visits to Jubilee College State Park, 1980–1981.

John R. Powers *The Last Catholic in America* (1973, rpt. 1981); *Do Patent Leather Shoes Really Reflect Up?* (1975, rpt. 1982)
Comic novels about a Chicago Irish schoolboy during the 1950s and '60s.

John Regan *The Emigrant's Guide to the Western States of America* (1852)
Landscape and people of the Western frontier by a Scottish emigrant.

John Roeburt *Al Capone* (1959)
Fictional biography of Al Capone.

Sam Ross *The Sidewalks Are Free* (1950, rpt. 1984)
Novel set in the Chicago Russian-Jewish community in 1918.

Philip Roth *Letting Go* (1962)
Novel chiefly set in the Hyde Park neighborhood of the University of Chicago, about the life of a professor.

Ralph L. Rusk *The Literature of the Middle Western Frontier* 2 vols. (1926)

Ruth Russell *Lake Front* (1931)
Novel about two generations of an immigrant Irish family in Chicago, 1835–1894.

Carl Sandburg *Always the Young Strangers* (1953)
The poet's years in Galesburg, 1878–1898.

Harold Sinclair *American Years* (1938); *The Years of Growth* (1940); *Years of Illusion* (1941)
A trilogy of novels relating the history of a small town (1830–1914), closely based on Bloomington.

Upton Sinclair *The Jungle* (1906, rpt. 1981)
Classic muckraking novel written to expose conditions in the Chicago meatpacking industry.

Carl Smith *Chicago and the American Literary Imagination, 1880–1920* (1984)

Julian Street *Abroad at Home* (1914)
Description of Chicago c.1920.

Studs Terkel *Division Street: America* (1967, rpt. 1982)
Interviews with Chicagoans.

Christiana H. Tillson *A Woman's Story of Pioneer Illinois* (1919)
Account of pioneer experiences, 1870–1871.

Waters E. Turpin *O Canaan!* (1939)
Novel about a black Southern family that immigrates to Chicago during World War I.

Melvin Van Peebles *A Bear for the FBI* (1968)
Novel about black middle-class family life in Chicago during the 1940s.

Howard W. Webb, Jr. (ed.) *Illinois Prose Writers: A Selection* (1968)

Kenny J. Williams *Prairie Voices: A Literary History of Chicago from the Frontier to 1893* (1980)
——— and **Bernard Duffey** (eds.) *Chicago's Public Wits* (1983)
A collection of humorous writing from Chicago newspapers, 1840–1980.

Harry Wilson *The Boss of Little Arcady* (1905)
Small town life after the Civil War.

Larry Woiwode *Beyond the Bedroom Wall: A Family Album* (1975)
Novel about four generations of a German Catholic family who settle near Pekin.

Richard Wright *Native Son* (1940, rpt. 1969)
Classic novel of black experience, depicting the struggles of its hero, Bigger Thomas, against racial prejudice.

GUIDES TO RESOURCES

Angle, Paul M. and **Richard L. Beyer** *A Handbook of Illinois History* (1943)

Beckstead, Gayle and **Mary L. Kozub** *Searching in Illinois: A Reference Guide to Public and Private Records* (1984)

Bennett, Gwen P. *A Bibliography of Illinois Archaeology* Illinois State Museum Scientific Papers, vol. 21 (1985)

Bridges, Roger and **Rodney Davis** (eds.) *Illinois: Its History and Legacy* (1984)

Chicago Fact Book Consortium *Local Community Fact Book: Chicago Metropolitan Area* (1984)

Federal Writers' Project *Selected Bibliography. Illinois, Chicago and Its Environs* (1937)
———. *Final Narrative Report . . . Bibliography of Illinois Writers* (1940)
———. *Illinois: Galena Guide* (1937, rpt. 1986)

———. *Illinois: A Descriptive and Historical Guide* (1947, rpt. 1971)

Gove, Samuel (ed.) *State and Local Government in Illinois: A Bibliography* (1953)
——— and **Alvin D. Sokolow** *Supplement to State and Local Government in Illinois: A Bibliography* (1958)

Hochstetter, Nancy (ed.) *Travel Historic Illinois: A Guide to Historic Sites and Markers* (1986)

Holt, Glen E. and **Dominic A. Pacyga** *Chicago: A Historical Guide to the Neighborhoods, the Loop and South Side* (1979)

Howard, Vivian H., Alma Lunsden, and **Agatha Shay** (comps.) *Illinois: A Bibliography* (1952, rev. ed. in *Illinois Libraries* September 1960)

Illinois Historical Library *Illinois Historical Collections* 31 vols. (1907–1950)

Illinois Secretary of State *Illinois Blue Book* (biennial)

Illinois State Historical Library (various compilers) *Cumulative Index to the Journal of the Illinois State Historical Society* (1949, 1968, 1971)

Local Community Fact Book: Chicago Metropolitan Area, Based on the 1970 and 1980 Censuses (1984)

National Park Service (ed. J. William Rudd) *Historic American Buildings Survey: Chicago and Nearby Illinois Areas* (1965)

Plucker, Lina S. and Kaye L. Roerick (eds.) *Breuet's Illinois Historical Markers and Sites* (1976)

Scott, Franklin W. *Newspapers and Periodicals of Illinois, 1814–1879* (Illinois Historical Collections, Vol. 6) (1910)

Szucs, Loretta D. *Chicago and Cook County Sources: A Genealogical and Historical Guide* (1986)

Wood, W. Raymond (ed.) *An Atlas of Early Maps of the American Midwest* Illinois State Museum Scientific Papers, vol. 18 (1983)

Wrigley, Kathryn *Directory of Illinois Oral History Resources* Sangamon State University (1981)

SELECTED NONFICTION SOURCES

Allen, John W. *Legends and Lore of Southern Illinois* (1963)
———. *It Happened in Southern Illinois* (1968)

Alvord, Clarence W. *The Illinois Country, 1673–1818* (*Centennial History of Illinois* Vol. I) (1917–1920)
———. (ed.) *The Centennial History of Illinois, 1673–1918* 5 vols. (1919–1920)

Anderson, David D. *Abraham Lincoln* (1970)
———. *Robert Ingersoll* (1972)

Andrews, Wayne *Architecture in Chicago and Mid-America: A Photographic History* (1968)

Angle, Paul M. *Suggested Readings in Illinois History: with a Selected List of Historical Fiction* (1935)
———. *"Here I Have Lived": A History of Lincoln's Springfield* (1935, rpt. 1971)
———. *Bloody Williamson: A Chapter in American Lawlessness* (1952)
———. (ed.) *Prairie State: Impressions of Illinois, 1673–1967, by Travelers and Other Observers* (1968)

Asbury, Herbert *Gem of the Prairie: An Informal History of the Chicago Underworld* (also published under the title *Chicago Underworld*) (1940)

Aschenbrenner, Joyce *Lifelines: Black Families in Chicago* (1975)

Atherton, Lewis *Main Street on the Middle Border* (1954)

Bateman, Newton and Paul Selby (eds.) *Historical Encyclopedia of Illinois* (1899) Reissued in combination with some 34 county histories and biographical collections, 1899–1913. *Historical Encyclopedia with Commemorative Biographies* (with J. Seymour Currey et al.) 3 vols. (1926–1943)

Beadle, Muriel et al. *The Fortnightly of Chicago* (1973)

Becker, Stephen D. *Marshall Field III* (1964)

Beveridge, Albert J. *Abraham Lincoln, 1809–1858* 2 vols. (1928)

Boewe, Charles E. *Prairie Albion: An English Settlement in Pioneer Illinois* (1962)

Bogart, Ernest L. and John M. Mathews *The Modern Commonwealth, 1893–1918* (*Centennial History of Illinois* Vol. V) (1917–1920)
——— and Charles Manfred Thompson *The Industrial State, 1870–1893* (1920)

Bonnell, Clarence *The Illinois Ozarks* (1946)

Bridges, Roger D. and Rodney O. Davis (eds.) *Illinois: Its History and Legacy* (1984)

Bright, John *Hizzoner Big Bill Thompson: An Idyll of Chicago* (1930)

Buck, Solon J. *Illinois in 1818* (1918, rpt. 1967)

Buley, R. Carlyle *The Old Northwest: Pioneer Period, 1815–1840* (1950)

Calkins, Earnest E. *They Broke the Prairie* (1937)

Carter, William *Middle West Country* (1975)

Clark, George Rogers (ed. Milo M. Quaife) *The Conquest of Illinois* (1920)

Clemen, R. A. *The American Livestock and Meat Industry* (1923)

Cole, Arthur C. *The Era of the Civil War, 1848–1870* (*Centennial History of Illinois* Vol. III) (1917–1920)

Condit, Carl W. *Chicago, 1910–1929: Building, Planning, and Urban Technology* (1973)
———. *Chicago, 1930–1970* (1975)

Cramer, C. H. *Royal Bob: The Life of Robert G. Ingersoll* (1952)

Cromie, Robert A. *The Great Chicago Fire* (1958)

David, Henry *The History of the Haymarket Affair* (2d ed. 1958)

Davis, Allen F. *American Heroine: The Life and Legend of Jane Addams* (1973)
——— and Mary L. McCree *Eighty Years at Hull House* (1969)

Dedmon, Emmett *Fabulous Chicago* (1953)

Dillon, Merton L. *Elijah P. Lovejoy: Abolitionist Editor* (1961)

Drake, St. Clair and Horace R. Cayton *Black Metropolis: A Study of Negro Life in a Northern City* (1945)

Drury, John *Old Illinois Houses* (1977)

Duis, Perry *Chicago: Creating New Traditions* (1976)

Duncan, Hugh D. *Culture and Democracy: The Struggle for Form and Architecture in Chicago and the Middle West during the Life and Times of Louis H. Sullivan* (1965)

Ebner, Michael H. *Creating Chicago's North Shore: A Suburban History* (1988)

Eby, Cecil *"That Disgraceful Affair": The Black Hawk War* (1973)

Elazar, Daniel *Cities of the Prairie* (1969)

Faragher, John M. *Sugar Creek: Life on the Illinois Prairie* (1986)

Flanders, Robert B. *Nauvoo: Kingdom on the Mississippi* (1965, rpt. 1975)

Ford, Thomas *A History of Illinois* (1854)

Gilbert, Paul and Charles Lee *Chicago and Its Makers* (1929)

Gitlin, Todd and Nanci Hollander *Uptown: Poor Whites in Chicago* (1970)

Gleason, Bill *Daley of Chicago* (1970)

Golden, Harry *Carl Sandburg* (1988)

Grant, Bruce *Right for a City: The Story of the Union League of Chicago and Its Times, 1880–1955* (1955)

Gray, James *The Illinois* (Rivers of America series) (1940)

Hansen, Harry *The Chicago* (Rivers of America series) (1942)

Hicken, Victor *Illinois in the Civil War* (1966)

Horrell, C. William et al. *Land Between the Rivers: The Southern Illinois Country* (1973, rpt. 1982)

Howard, Robert P. *Illinois: A History of the Prairie State* (1972)

Hutchinson, William T. *Cyrus Hall McCormick* 2 vols. (1930–1935)

Jensen, Richard J. *The Winning of the Midwest: Social and Political Conflict, 1888–1896* (1971)
———. *Illinois: A History* (States and the Nation series) (1978)

Kennedy, Eugene *Himself: The Life and Times of Richard J. Daley* (1978)

Koeper, Frederick *Illinois Architecture from Territorial Times to the Present* (1968)

Kogan, Herman and Robert Cromie *The Great Fire: Chicago 1871* (1971)
——— and Lloyd Wendt *John and Hinky Dink* (1943, rpt. 1952, 1967 as *Bosses in Lusty Chicago*)
——— and Lloyd Wendt *Give the Lady What She Wants!* (1952)
——— and Lloyd Wendt *Big Bill of Chicago* (1953)

Kupcinet, Irv *Kup's Chicago* (1962)

Langstreet, Stephen *Chicago, 1860–1919* (1973)

Leech, Harper and John C. Carroll *Armour and His Times* (1938)

Lindsey, Almont *The Pullman Strike* (1942)

Magdol, Edward *Owen Lovejoy: Abolitionist in Congress* (1967)

Martin, John B. *Adlai Stevenson of Illinois* (1976)

Masters, Edgar Lee *The Tale of Chicago* (1933)
———. *The Sangamon* (Rivers of America series) (1942, rpt. 1988)

Mayer, Harold M. and Richard C. Wade *Chicago: The Growth of a Metropolis* (1969)

McDonald, Forrest *Insull* (1962)

Milton, George Fort *The Eve of Conflict* (1934)

Monaghan, Jay *This Is Illinois: A Pictorial History* (1949)

Moore, Edward C. *Forty Years of Opera in Chicago* (1930)

Morrison, Olin D. *Illinois "Prairie State": A History, Social, Political, Economic* 3 vols. (1960–1964)

Murray, George *The Madhouse on Madison Street* (1965)

Nelli, Hubert *Italians of Chicago, 1880–1930* (1970)

Nevins, Allan *Illinois* (1917)

Pacyga, Dominic A. and Ellen Skerrett *Chicago: City of Neighborhoods* (1986)

Pasley, Fred D. *Al Capone* (1930)

Pease, Theodore C. *The Frontier State, 1818–1848* (Centennial History of Illinois Vol. II) (1917–1920)
——— and Marguerite J. *George Rogers Clark and Revolution in Illinois, 1763–1787* (1929)
——— and Marguerite J. *The Story of Illinois* (3d ed. 1965)

Peisch, Mark L. *The Chicago School of Architecture: Early Followers of Sullivan and Wright* (1964)

Pierce, Bessie L. (ed.) *As Others See Chicago: Impressions of Visitors, 1673–1933* (1933)
——— (ed.) *A History of Chicago* 3 vols.: *The Beginnings of a City, 1673–1848* (1937), *From Town to City, 1848–1871* (1940), *The Rise of a Modern City, 1871–1893* (1957)

Poole, Ernest *Giants Gone: Men Who Made Chicago* (1943)

Putnam, James W. *The Illinois and Michigan Canal* (1918)

Quaife, Milo M. *Chicago and the Old Northwest, 1673–1835* (1913)
——— (ed.) *Pictures of Illinois One Hundred Years Ago* (1918)
———. *Chicago's Highways Old and New* (1923)
———. *Checagou, from Indian Wigwam to Modern City, 1673–1833* (1933)
———. *Lake Michigan* (American Lakes series) (1944)

Rakove, Milton *Don't Make No Waves: An Insider's Analysis of the Daley Machine* (1975)

Rayko, Mike *Boss* (1971)

Reid, Robert L. and Larry A. Viskochil (eds.) *Chicago and Downstate: Illinois as Seen by the Farm Security Administration Photographers, 1936–1943* (1989)

Reynolds, Barbara *Jesse Jackson* (1975)

Ridgley, Douglas C. *The Geography of Illinois* (1921)

Rosenblum, Walter (ed.) *Changing Chicago: A Photodocumentary* (1989)

Sandburg, Carl *The Chicago Race Riots* (1919, rpt. 1969)
———. *Abraham Lincoln: The Prairie Years* 2 vols. (1926)

Scott, Roy V. *The Agrarian Movement in Illinois, 1880–1896* (1962)

Smith, Alson J. *Chicago's Left Bank* (1953)

Smith, Henry Justin *Chicago, a Portrait* (1931)

Sutton, Robert P. (ed.) *The Prairie State: A Documentary History of Illinois* 2 vols. (1976)

Tallmadge, Thomas *Architecture in Old Chicago* (1941)

Tebbel, John W. *The Marshall Fields: A Study in Wealth* (1947)
———. *American Dynasty: Story of the McCormicks, Medills, and Pattersons* (1968)

Thomas, Benjamin P. *Lincoln's New Salem* (1934)

Thomson, Gladys Scott *A Pioneer Family: The Birkbecks in Illinois, 1818–1827* (1953)

Waldrop, Frank C. *McCormick of Chicago* (1966)

Walters, Mary *Illinois in the Second World War* 2 vols. (1951, 1952)

Walton, Clyde C. (ed.) *An Illinois Reader* (1970)

Washburn, Charles *Come into My Parlor: A Biography of the Aristocratic Everleigh Sisters of Chicago* (1936)

Whitney, Ellen M. (ed.) *The Black Hawk War, 1831–1832* (1970)

Wille, Lois *Forever Open, Clear and Free: The Historic Struggle for Chicago's Lakefront* (1972)

Williams, Kenny J. *In the City of Men: Another Story of Chicago* (1974)

INDIANA

Indiana, an east north central state, is bordered on the north by Lake Michigan and the state of Michigan; on the east by Ohio; on the south by the Ohio River and Kentucky; and on the west by the Wabash River and Illinois.

FULL NAME State of Indiana
POSTAL ABBREVIATION IN
INHABITANT Hoosier
ADMITTED TO THE UNION Dec. 11, 1816. 19th state
POPULATION (est. 1987) 5,531,000. Percent of US total: 2.27%. Rank: 14th

CAPITAL CITY Indianapolis, the largest city in the state, located on the White River in central Indiana; population 710,280 (est. 1984). It was founded in 1821 on a site previously selected for the state capital and was laid out on a radical plan similar to that of the nation's capital. The city formally became the seat of government in 1825.

STATE NAME AND NICKNAMES The name "Indiana," meaning "Land of the Indians," was coined by Congress in 1800 when it established the new territory. Also known as the Hoosier State. The word Hoosier is variously said to have been derived from the name of a contractor, Sam Hoosier; from "husher," a riverboat worker; or from the question "Who's here?"

STATE SEAL A pioneer scene showing a green field with the sun setting behind distant hills. In the left foreground is a buffalo jumping over a log; in the right, a woodsman felling a sycamore tree. The light blue border bears the legend, in white letters, "Seal of the State of Indiana, 1816."

MOTTO The Crossroads of America

SONG "On the Banks of the Wabash, Far Away," lyrics and music by Paul Dresser.

SYMBOLS
Flower peony
Tree tulip tree
Bird cardinal
Stone limestone
Language English
Poem "Indiana" by Arthur Franklin Mapes

LICENSE PLATE Blue on white, with horizontal blue bars top and bottom and the legend "Back Home Again," and on the white background the gold torch-and-stars design of the state flag.

FLAG On a blue field, a gold torch surrounded by a circle of 13 stars and an inner half-circle of five stars, and above it a larger star under the legend "Indiana."

GEOGRAPHY AND CLIMATE

As a typical state of the Central Lowlands, Indiana is primarily flat, fertile agricultural land, with some highlands along the Ohio River, which forms the state's southern border. Northern Indiana contains large deposits of sandy gravel from heavy glaciation during the last Ice Age; much of the state also sits on a bed of porous limestone and sandstone. Early summer tornadoes are a regular feature of what is otherwise a temperate climate.

AREA 36,185 square miles. Rank: 38th
INLAND WATER 253 square miles
GEOGRAPHIC CENTER Boone, 14 miles NNW of Indianapolis
ELEVATIONS *Highest point:* Franklin Township, Wayne County, 1,257 feet. *Lowest point:* Ohio River, Posey County, 320 feet. *Mean elevation:* 700 feet

MAJOR RIVERS Wabash, Ohio, White

MAJOR LAKES AND RESERVOIRS Michigan, Wawasee, Monroe, Patoka, Salamonie, Mississinewa

LAND USE

	Thousands of acres
Urban (1982)	1,192
Rural (1982)	20,597
Cropland (1982)	13,781
Pastureland (1982)	2,212
Rangeland (1982)	0
Forestland (1982)	3,640
State parks and recreation areas (1983)	54
National park system (1984)	10
National forest system (1984)	645
Tribal lands (1984)	0

TEMPERATURES The highest recorded temperature was 116°F on July 14, 1936, at Collegeville. The lowest was -35°F on February 2, 1951, at Greensburg.

NATIONAL SITES

NATIONAL HISTORICAL PARK George Rogers Clark
NATIONAL MEMORIAL Lincoln Boyhood
NATIONAL LAKESHORE Indiana Dunes
NATIONAL WILDLIFE REFUGE Muscatatuck

HISTORY

1679	*December 5.* Robert Cavelier, Sieur de La Salle, reaches the approximate site of South Bend, on his way to the Illinois River.
1681	*May.* On a second trip, La Salle holds a council with Miami and Illinois Indians at the same site.
1708	Possible founding date of Vincennes, the center of French settlement in present-day Indiana.
1720	A fort is built at Ouiatenon, near present-day Lafayette.
1722	The French build Fort Miami at the site of present-day Fort Wayne.
1763	By the terms of the Treaty of Paris, ending the French and Indian War, France cedes to Great Britain the territory that includes present-day Indiana. Indians capture the fort at Ouiatenon and Fort Miami.
1778	Aided by disaffected French settlers, George Rogers Clark, a Virginian, and his band of frontiersmen take Vincennes from the British. It is recaptured on December 17.
1779	*February 25.* British troops at Vincennes surrender to 170 American and French volunteers serving under Clark.
1791	*November 4.* Miami war chief Little Turtle defeats federal troops and militia near Fort Miami; close to 1,000 are killed or wounded.
1794	*August 20.* The defeat of the Miami in the Battle of Fallen Timbers, near present-day Toledo, Oh., opens the way for white settlement in Indiana.
1795	*August 3.* By the Treaty of Greenville, Indians cede lands that include a portion of what is now east-southeast Indiana.
1800	*May 7.* Indiana Territory created, with Vincennes as its capital. Territory population is 5,641.
1805	*January 11.* Michigan is detached from Indiana Territory.
1807	First federal land sale in Indiana, at Vincennes.
1809	*February 9.* Illinois Territory organized, reducing Indiana to its present borders. Governor William Henry Harrison buys 3 million acres from the Miami, Wea, and Delaware for $10,000 and a small annuity.

1811	*November 7*. Harrison defeats the Shawnee confederacy at the Battle of Tippecanoe.
1812	*September 3*. Twenty-four white settlers in Scott County are killed by Indians in the Pigeon Roost Massacre.
	December 17–18. Miami Indians defeated near Peru in the last battle fought in Indiana.
1816	*December 11*. Indiana admitted to the Union as the 19th state. The constitution excludes slavery.
1818	Most of central Indiana is bought from Indian tribes.
1820	*June*. Indianapolis replaces Corydon as the permanent state capital.
1825	The utopian colony of New Harmony is founded by Robert Owen.
1826	Indians cede most of their lands north and west of the Wabash River.
1838	A group of 859 Potawatomi is forcibly expelled from Indiana, virtually clearing the state of Indians.
1851	The new constitution contains a provision that no blacks be allowed to settle in the state.
1853	Opening of the Wabash and Erie Canal, linking Toledo, Ohio, on Lake Erie, with Evansville on the Ohio River.
1855	Eight rail lines are using Union Depot in Indianapolis; rail mileage rises from 212 in 1850 to 2,163 in 1860.
1860	Indiana is first among states in hogs raised, second in wheat production, fourth in corn production.
	The state ranks sixth in population, with 1,350,428.
1861–1865	Indiana contributes 196,363 men to the Union cause in the Civil War, of whom 25,028 die. Indiana troops take part in 308 engagements.
1863	*July 8–13*. Confederate cavalrymen under General John Hunt Morgan raid southern Indiana.
1869	Eighteen percent of all US lumber comes from Indiana.
1877	James Whitcomb Riley becomes a regular contributor of verse to the Indianapolis *Journal*, establishing a career as the state's virtual poet laureate.
1888	Indianapolis resident Benjamin Harrison, a former senator, is elected president of the United States.
1889	The Standard Oil Company builds one of the world's largest oil refineries in Whiting.
1894	*July 4*. Early auto pioneer Elwood Haynes successfully tests his horseless carriage in Kokomo.
1900	Peak number of farms in Indiana—221,897.
1901	The Socialist party is founded in Indianapolis, with Hoosier native Eugene V. Debs as its president.
1905	Gary is founded as the site of the US Steel Corporation's largest plant.
1911	*May 30*. First Indianapolis 500 Memorial Day weekend auto race.
1919	Indiana ranks third among states in iron and steel production.
1923	The Ku Klux Klan has 300,000 members in Indiana. Its political power wanes after 1924.
1933	To finance the needy of the Great Depression, the state legislature adopts a gross income tax—a combination of income tax and sales tax.
1934	*July 23*. Shooting of John Dillinger outside Chicago's Biograph Theater ends his gang's string of Indiana bank robberies.
1937	*January 31*. The Ohio River reaches its highest level ever recorded in Indiana. Entire cities are inundated, hundreds drown.
1948	Indiana University biologist Alfred Kinsey stirs controversy with the publication of the first of his two surveys on human sexual behavior.
1949	Indiana's schools are fully desegregated.
1957	A state right-to-work law abolishes the closed and union shops.
1965	The Studebaker auto plant in South Bend shuts its doors after 63 years of producing automobiles.

1967	Richard D. Hatcher of Gary becomes the first black mayor of an Indiana city.
1970	A constitutional amendment establishes annual General Assembly sessions. Consolidation of Indianapolis and its suburbs raises the city's population to 736,856.
1974	*April 3.* Tornadoes kill about 48 people and cause property damage of over $200 million.
1984	Professional football's Baltimore Colts move to Indianapolis to play in that city's Hoosier Dome.

DEMOGRAPHY

Population (est. 1987) . . . 5,531,000
Population (1980) 5,490,260
Population density in persons
   per square mile (1980) . . . 151.7

POPULATION BY RACE (1980)
American Indian/Aleut/
   Eskimo 7,835
Asian/Pacific Islander 21,488
Black 414,732
Hispanic 87,000
White 5,004,567
Other 42,557

POPULATION CHARACTERISTICS (1980)
Percent of state population
Urban 64.2
Rural 35.8
Under 18 . . . . 29.4
65 or older 10.7
College-educated 12.4
Families below poverty line . . . 7.3
Public assistance recipients 3.7

Per capita personal
   income (1986) $12,944
Millionaires per 100,000
   residents (1982) 82.1
Average life expectancy
   in years (1980) 73.8
Marriage rate per 1,000
   residents (1986) 9.2

Divorce rate per 1,000
   residents 7.7
Birth rate per 1,000
   residents (1985) 14.7
Infant mortality rate per 1,000
   births (1985) 10.3
Abortion rate per 1,000
   live births (1985) 202
Crime rate per 100,000
   residents (1985)
   Violent 307.7
   Property 3,547.1
Federal and state prisoners per
   100,000 residents (1984) 170
Alcohol consumption in gallons
   per capita (1985) 36.5
Deaths from motor vehicle accidents
   per 100,000 residents (1985) . 17.7

MAJOR CITIES

	1984 population (est.)
Anderson	61,771
Bloomington	52,219
Evansville	130,333
Fort Wayne	165,415
Gary	143,096
Hammond	89,364
Indianapolis	710,280
Muncie	74,190
South Bend	107,117
Terre Haute	58,767

GOVERNMENT AND POLITICS

Number of US Representatives   10
Electoral votes   12

POLITICAL PARTY NOMINEES FROM STATE
  * winner

George Washington Julian
  (Free Soil)   1852 VP
Schuyler Colfax* (R)   1868 VP
Thomas Andrews Hendricks
  (D)   1876 VP
William Hayden English (D)   1880 VP
Thomas Andrews Hendricks*
  (D)   1884 VP

Benjamin Harrison* (R)   1888   P
Benjamin Harrison (R)   1892   P
Eugene Victor Debs (Social-
  Democratic)   1900   P
Charles Warren Fairbanks* (R) 1904 VP
Eugene Victor Debs (Socialist) 1904   P
John Worth Kern (D)   1908 VP
Eugene Victor Debs (Socialist) 1908   P
Samuel Williams (People's)   1908 VP
Thomas Riley Marshall* (D)   1912 VP
Eugene Victor Debs (Socialist) 1912   P
Thomas Riley Marshall* (D)   1916 VP
Charles Warren Fairbanks (R) 1916 VP

James Franklin Hanley (Prohibition) 1916 P
Eugene Victor Debs (Socialist) 1920 P
John Zahnd (Greenback) 1924 P
John Zahnd (Greenback) 1928 P
John Zahnd (National Greenback) 1936 P
John Zahnd (Greenback) 1940 P
Granville B. Leeke (Greenback) 1948 VP
Edward J. Bedell (Greenback) 1952 VP
William Ezra Jenner (Texas Constitutional) 1956 P
William Ezra Jenner (States' Rights Party of Kentucky) 1956 VP

PRESIDENTIAL PRIMARY ELECTION In 1988, Indiana sent 85 Democratic delegates and 51 Republican delegates to the national conventions.

CONSTITUTION Indiana has had two constitutions: 1816 and the present one, adopted in 1851.

LEGISLATURE The General Assembly is divided into the Senate (50 members, 4-year term, minimum age 25) and the House of Representatives (100 members, 2-year term, minimum age 21). In 1987, the salary was $80 per diem.

JUDICIARY The highest court is the Supreme Court, with 5 judges serving terms of two years initially and ten years upon retention. In 1987, the annual salary was $66,000.

EXECUTIVE The governor serves a 4-year term; the minimum age for holding office is 30. In 1987, the annual salary was $77,200. There are 6 other elected officials.

PRESIDENTIAL VOTE 1948-1988 *(in percents)*

Year	State Winner	Democratic	Republican
1948	Dewey (R)	48.8	49.6
1952	Eisenhower (R)	41.0	58.1
1956	Eisenhower (R)	39.7	59.9
1960	Nixon (R)	44.6	55.0
1964	Johnson (D)	56.0	43.6
1968	Nixon (R)	38.0	50.3
1972	Nixon (R)	33.3	66.1
1976	Ford (R)	45.7	53.3
1980	Reagan (R)	37.7	56.0
1984	Reagan (R)	37.7	61.7
1988	Bush (R)	40.0	60.0

GOVERNORS

Territorial Governors
John Gibson (acting) 1800-1801
William Henry Harrison 1801-1812
John Gibson (acting) 1812-1813
Thomas Posey 1813-1816

State Governors
Jonathan Jennings (Jeffersonian-Republican) 1816-1822
Ratliff Boon (Jeffersonian-Republican) 1822
William Hendricks (Jeffersonian-Republican) 1822-1825
James B. Ray (Independent) 1825-1831
Noah Noble (National Republican-Whig) 1831-1837
David Wallace (Whig) 1837-1840
Samuel Bigger (Whig) 1840-1843
James Whitcomb (D) 1843-1848
Paris C. Dunning (D) 1848-1849
Joseph A. Wright (D) 1849-1857
Ashbel P. Willard (D) 1857-1860

Abram A. Hammond (D) 1860-1861
Henry S. Lane (R) 1861
Oliver P. Morton (R) 1861-1867
Conrad Baker (R) 1867-1873
Thomas A. Hendricks (D) 1873-1877
James D. Williams (D) 1877-1880
Isaac P. Gray (D) 1880-1881
Albert G. Porter (R) 1881-1885
Isaac P. Gray (D) 1885-1889
Alvin P. Hovey (R) 1889-1891
Ira J. Chase (R) 1891-1893
Claude Matthews (D) 1893-1897
James A. Mount (R) 1897-1901
Winfield T. Durbin (R) 1901-1905
J. Frank Hanly (R) 1905-1909
Thomas R. Marshall (D) 1909-1913
Samuel M. Ralston (D) 1913-1917
James P. Goodrich (R) 1917-1921
Warren T. McCray (R) 1921-1924
Emmett F. Branch (R) 1924-1925
Ed Jackson (R) 1925-1929
Harry G. Leslie (R) 1929-1933
Paul V. McNutt (D) 1933-1937
M. Clifford Townsend (D) 1937-1941

Henry F. Schricker (D)	1941-1945
Ralph F. Gates (R)	1945-1949
Henry F. Schricker (D)	1949-1953
George N. Craig (R)	1953-1957
Harold W. Handley (R)	1957-1961
Matthew E. Welsh (D)	1961-1965
Roger D. Branigin (D)	1965-1969
Edgar D. Whitcomb (R)	1969-1973
Otis R. Bowen (R)	1973-1981
Robert D. Orr (R)	1981-1989
Evan Bayh (D)	1989-

MINIMUM AGES

Majority	18
Marriage with parental consent	17
Marriage without parental consent	18
Making a will	18
Buying alcohol	21
Jury duty	18
Leaving school	16
Driver's license	16

CAPITAL PUNISHMENT
Number executed 1976-88: 2
On death row Aug. 1, 1988: 48

MILITARY INSTALLATIONS
Total number: 11
Major bases:
   Army: 2
   Navy: 1

FINANCES

Thousands of dollars

GENERAL REVENUE (1985)

Total general revenue	7,102,450
Total tax revenue	4,336,068
Sales and gross receipts	2,632,614
Individual income taxes	1,287,050
Corporate net income taxes	178,345

GENERAL EXPENDITURE (1985)

Total general expenditure	6,624,083
Education	2,908,024
Public welfare	1,009,370
Health	182,607
Hospitals	263,390
Natural resources	119,493
Highways	769,020
Police	60,271
Corrections	145,760

FEDERAL AID (1985) 1,825,318

ECONOMY

The traditional mainstays of Indiana's agricultural economy, corn and hogs, are still the biggest cash producers, along with soybeans, wheat, and cattle. Other crops include oats, rye, hay, barley, tobacco, truck vegetables, and varieties of mint. Farm cash receipts were $5.4 billion in 1983. Mining yields bituminous coal, oil, granite, marble, sandstone, limestone, peat, clay, sand, and gravel. Manufactured products include steel, auto parts, ceramic and glass items, food processing (primarily meat packing), and electrical machinery. The total value added by manufacture for the state was $26 billion in 1982.

EMPLOYMENT (1984)

Thousands of persons

Total number of employed workers	2,400
Construction	80.7
Finance, insurance, and real estate	103.6
Government	330.3
Manufacturing	621.1
Mining	10.2
Services	387.3
Transportation, communications, and utilities	105.5
Wholesale and retail trade	492.7

Percent of civilian labor force unemployed (1984)	8.6

DEPARTMENT OF DEFENSE (1985)

Civilian workers employed	15,436
Military personnel	6,576
Contract awards	$3.177 billion

ENERGY SOURCES FOR ELECTRIC UTILITIES (1983)

Percent

Coal	98.8
Gas	0.4
Hydroelectric	0.6
Nuclear	0.0
Petroleum	0.3

TRANSPORTATION

Motor vehicles registered in state (1986)	4,173,614
Miles of roads, streets, and highways (1986)	91.462
Miles of Class I railway operated (1986)	4,813
Airports (1983)	498
Major aviation hubs (1983)	2

Largest hub: Indianapolis
Major ports, with gross tonnage in thousands (1985):
   Indiana Harbor 13,549

CULTURE AND EDUCATION

Native American tribes
Indiana was formerly home to the Delaware, Erie, Illinois, Neutral, Ofo, Ojibway, Ottawa, Peoria, Piankashaw, Potawatomi, Seneca, Shawnee, Wea, and Wyandot tribes. Groups that continue to live in the state include the Miami.

Religions, ethnicities, and languages
About 95 percent of Indiana's population was born in the state; for the most part, they are descended from the early settlers, of English, Scotch-Irish, and German stock. The cities have large Black, Polish, Hungarian, Italian, Polish, and Mexican populations. In 1980, 4.1 percent of Indiana's population spoke a language other than English at home. The majority are Protestant, with a concentration of Catholics in the urban areas; there are rural communities of Amish and Mennonites.

Major museums and libraries
Children's Museum of Indianapolis
Evansville Museum of Arts and Science
Fort Wayne Museum of Art
Herron Museum of Art, Indianapolis
Indiana State Library, Indianapolis
Indiana State Museum, Indianapolis
Indianapolis Museum of Art

Snite Museum of Art, University of Notre Dame, Notre Dame

Major arts organizations
Fort Wayne Ballet
Fort Wayne Philharmonic Orchestra
Indianapolis Ballet Theatre
Indianapolis Opera
Indiana Repertory Theatre, Indianapolis
Indianapolis Symphony Orchestra

Colleges and universities
Number public (1986-87) 29
Number private (1986-87) 47
Total enrollment, in full-time equivalent students (1985) 195,600

Public elementary and secondary schools
Expenditure per pupil in average daily attendance (1986-87) $3,310
Pupil-teacher ratio (1987) 18.3
Average teacher salary (1986-87) $26,557

Major league sports teams
Basketball: Indiana Pacers
Football: Indianapolis Colts

Holidays
State Fair, Indianapolis. Mid-August

INDIANA IN LITERATURE

Ronald L. Baker *Jokelore: Humorous Folktales from Indiana* (1986)

Richard E. Banta (comp.) *Indiana Authors and Their Books, 1816–1916* . . . (1949)
———. (ed.) *Hoosier Caravan: A Treasury of Indiana Life and Lore* (2d ed. 1975)

J. Richard Beste *The Wabash; or, Adventures of an English Gentleman's Family in the Interior of America* 2 vols. (1855)

Jan H. Brunvand (comp.) *A Dictionary of Proverbs and Proverbial Phrases from Books Published by Indiana Authors Before 1890* (1961)

Carol Burke (ed.) *Plain Talk* (1983)
Humorous anecdotes and rural folklore.

Linda Dean (ed.) *Indiana Folklore: A Reader* (1980)

Theodore Dreiser *A Hoosier Holiday* (1916)
A jaundiced account of the writer's youth that caused offense in Dreiser's home state by its portraits of his contemporaries. Includes a sketch of Dreiser's brother Paul Dresser, composer of the state song.

Jacob P. Dunn *True Indian Stories* (1908)

Edward Eggleston *The Hoosier Schoolmaster* (1871); *The Hoosier Schoolboy* (1883)
Sentimental but realistic accounts of pioneer community life, noted for their portrayal of Scottish and Irish dialect and manners.

Logan Esarey *The Indiana Home* (2d ed. 1953)
Essays on pioneer life in the state.

Edward Fischer *Notre Dame Remembered: An Autobiography* (1987)

William H. Gass *In the Heart of the Heart of the Country* (1968)
The title story of this collection consists of sketches of life in a small Indiana town.

Millard F. Kennedy *Schoolmaster of Yesterday: A Three-Generation Story* (1940)
Detailed memoir by a Johnson County teacher, covering the years 1820–1919.

Harlow Lindley (ed.) *Indiana as Seen by Early Travelers* (1916)

Ross Lockridge, Jr. *Raintree County* (1948)
A lengthy historical novel describing the life of a schoolteacher and Civil War veteran from a small town.

Robert Lynd *Middletown: A Study in Contemporary American Culture* (1929); *Middletown in Transition* (1937)
Lynd's two studies of Muncie, written in collaboration with his wife Helen, were landmarks in American sociology. Their methods of observation had hitherto been used only in studies of primitive peoples.

Charles Major *The Bears of Blue River* (1901); *A Forest Hearth: A Romance of Indiana in the Thirties* (1903)
A successful writer of romances with European settings, Major also applied his unrealistic style to the pioneer life of his home state.

Thomas Riley Marshall *Recollections . . . a Hoosier Salad* (1925)
Memoirs of the Indiana lawyer who twice served as Vice-President.

Shirley S. McCord *Travel Accounts of Indiana, 1679–1961* (1970)

Meredith Nicholson *The Hoosiers* (1900); *A Hoosier Chronicle* (1912)
Although famous in his day for his Indiana romances, of which *The House of a Thousand Candles* (1905) was the best known, Nicholson is now valued for his historical essays on the state.

Robert Owen *The Life of Robert Owen, by Himself* (1920)
Autobiography of the leader of the Harmony group.

Howard H. Peckham and **Shirley Snyder** (eds.) *Letters from Fighting Hoosiers* (1948)

Rachel Peden *Speak to the Earth: Pages from a Farmwife's Journal* (1974)

Gene Stratton Porter *Girl of the Limberlost* (1909)
Much despised, even at the height of her popularity, for trite sentimentality, this writer's accounts of wildlife in Indiana cannot be faulted for accuracy.

Jean Shepherd *In God We Trust: All Others Pay Cash* (1966); *Wanda Hickey's Night of Golden Memories, and Other Disasters* (1971)
Short stories of adolescence in a small town during the late 1930s.

Arthur W. Shumaker *A History of Indiana Literature: With Emphasis on the Authors . . . Writing Prior to World War II* (1962)

O. H. Smith *Early Indiana Trials and Sketches* (1858)

Caroline Snedeker *Seth Way: A Romance of the New Harmony Community* (1917)
Historical novel chiefly interesting for its use of the utopian community as a setting.

Irving Stone *Adversary in the House* (1947)
A biographical novel of socialist reformer Eugene Debs, who spent much of his life in Terre Haute.

Booth Tarkington *The Gentleman from Indiana* (1899)
The first of Tarkington's forty novels deals with a rural newspaper editor's political career, but he is chiefly remembered for deft social comedies of the prosperous middle class such as *The Magnificent Ambersons* (1918) and *Alice Adams* (1921). Almost all his work was set in a generalized Midwest, and draws upon his experience of growing up in Indianapolis. *The Conquest of Canaan* (1905) depicts a socially ambitious lawyer in a small town, and *Growth* (1927), a trilogy that includes *The Magnificent Ambersons*, attempts a panoramic view of Indiana urban life. His popular tale of adolescence, *Penrod* (1914), was once regarded as a Midwestern rival to *Tom Sawyer*.

Edwin Way Teale *The Lost Woods: Adventures of a Naturalist* (1945)
Meditation on the value of natural life inspired by Teale's recollection of his grandfather's Indiana farm.

Steve Tesich *Summer Crossing* (1982)
Novel about unhappy adolescence set in an industrial town, by the author of the screenplay of *Breaking Away* (1979), Peter Yates' film about a Bloomington boyhood.

Donald E. Thompson (comp.) *Indiana Authors and Their Books* 3 vols. (1981)

Maurice Thompson *Alice of Old Vincennes* (1900)
Historical novel depicting General George Clark's capture of the former French settlement and his rule of the Northwest Territory. His first book, *Hoosier Mosaics* (1875), is an amusing portrait of small-town life.

Jessamyn West *The Friendly Persuasion* (1945); *Except for Me and Thee* (1969)
Historical novels about a Quaker family during Reconstruction.

———. *The Massacre at Fall Creek* (1975)
Fictional rendering of an incident that took place on the Indiana frontier in 1824.

GUIDES TO RESOURCES

Black, Harry G. *Trails to Hoosier Heritage* (1981)

Carty, Mickey D. *Searching in Indiana: A Reference Guide to Public and Private Records* (1985)

Federal Writers' Project *The Calumet Region Historical Guide* (1939)
———. *Indiana: A Guide to the Hoosier State* (1941)

Hedge, Christine *Indiana: A Guide to State Forests, State Parks, Reservoirs* (1987)

Jonsson, Ingrid E. *Reference Guide to Indiana* (1977)

Pumroy, Eric and **Paul Brockman** *A Guide to the Manuscript Collections of the Indiana State Historical Society* (1986)

Rudolph, L. C. and **Judith E. Endelman** *Religion in Indiana: A Guide to Historical Resources* (1986)

SELECTED NONFICTION SOURCES

Baker, Ronald L. and **Marvin Carmony** *Indiana Place Names* (1975)

Ball, T. H. *Northwestern Indiana from 1800 to 1900* (1900)

Barce, Elmore *The Land of the Miamis* (1922)

Barnhart, John D. and **Donald F. Carmony** *Indiana: From Frontier to Industrial Commonwealth* 4 vols. (1954)

Benton, E. J. *The Wabash Trade Route in the Development of the Old Northwest* (1903)

Beveridge, Albert J. *Abraham Lincoln, 1809–1858* 2 vols. (1928)

Black, Glenn A. *Angel Site: An Archeological, Historical, and Ethnological Study* 2 vols. (1967)

Bloemker, Al *500 Miles to Go: The Story of the Indianapolis Speedway* (1961)

Bole, John Archibald *The Harmony Society* (1904)

Bowman, Heath *Hoosier* (1944)

Boyd, Thomas *Mad Anthony Wayne* (1929)

Burnet, Mary Q. *Arts and Artists of Indiana* (1921)

Burns, Lee *Early Architects and Builders of Indiana* (1935)

Carmony, Donald F. (ed.) *Indiana: A Self-Appraisal* (1966)

Cathcart, Charlotte *Indianapolis from Our Old Corner* (1965)

Cauthorn, Henry S. *History of the City of Vincennes* (1902)

Cavinder, Fred D. *The Indiana Book of Records, Firsts, and Fascinating Facts* (1985)

Cleaves, Freeman *Old Tippecanoe: William Henry Harrison and His Times* (1939)

Cockrum, William M. *Pioneer History of Indiana: Including Stories, Incidents, and Customs of the Early Settlers* (1907, rpt. 1980)

Cottman, George S. *Centennial History and Handbook of Indiana* (1915)

Cummins, Cedric C. *Indiana Public Opinion and the World War, 1914–1917* (1945)

Dillon, John B. *The History of Indiana from Its Earliest Exploration by Europeans to . . . 1816 . . .* (1859, rpt. 1971)

Duke, Basil W. *A History of Morgan's Cavalry* (1961)

Dunn, Jacob P. *Indiana: A Redemption from Slavery* (new and enl. ed. 1905, rpt. 1973)

Engel, J. Ronald *Sacred Sands: The Struggle for Community in the Indiana Dunes* (1983)

Evans, Madison *Biographical Sketches of the Pioneer Preachers of Indiana* (1864)

Ewbank, Louis B. *Morgan's Raid in Indiana* (1923)

Fatout, Paul *Indiana Canals* (1972)

Feinstein, John *A Season on the Brink: A Year with Bob Knight and the Hoosiers* (1986)

Funk, Arville L. *A Sketchbook of Indiana History* (1969)

Furlong, Patrick J. *Indiana: An Illustrated History* (1985)

Goodrich, Dewitt C. and Charles R. Tuttle *An Illustrated History of the State of Indiana* (1875)

Gray, Ralph D. (ed.) *Gentlemen from Indiana: National Party Candidates, 1836–1940* (1977)
—— (ed.) *The Hoosier State: Readings in Indiana History* 2 vols. (1980)

Hawkins, Hubert H. (ed.) *Indiana's Road to Statehood: A Documentary Record* (1964)

Hernandez, Ernie *Ethnics in Northwest Indiana* (1984)

Hyman, Max R. *Handbook of Indianapolis* (1897)

Julian, George W. *Political Recollections, 1840–1872* (1884)

Kellar, James H. *An Introduction to the Prehistory of Indiana* (1983)

Keller, Allan *Morgan's Raid* (1961)

Lane, James B. *"City of the Century": A History of Gary, Indiana* (1978)

Latta, William C. *Outline History of Indiana Agriculture* (1938)

Leary, Edward A. *Indianapolis, Story of a City* (1971)

Leibowitz, Irving *My Indiana* (1964)

Levering, Julia H. *Historic Indiana* (1909)

Lilly, Eli *Prehistoric Antiquities of Indiana* (1937)

Madison, James H. *Indiana through Tradition and Change: A History of the Hoosier State and Its People, 1920–1945* (The History of Indiana, Vol. V) (1982)
——. *The Indiana Way: A State History* (1986)

Martin, John Bartlow *Indiana, an Interpretation* (1947)

Moore, Powell A. *The Calumet Region: Indiana's Last Frontier* (1959)

Nolan, Alan T. *The Iron Brigade: A Military History* (1961)

Noland, Jeannette C. *Hoosier City, the Story of Indianapolis* (1943)

Oskinson, John M. *Tecumseh and His Times* (1938)

Peat, Wilbur D. *Pioneer Painters of Indiana* (1954)
——. *Indiana Houses of the Nineteenth Century* (1962)

Peckham, Howard H. *Indiana: A Bicentennial History* (States and the Nation series) (1978)

Pence, George and Nellie C. Armstrong *Indiana Boundaries: Territory, State, and County* (1933)

Phillips, Clifton J. *Indiana in Transition: The Emergence of an Industrial Commonwealth, 1880–1920* (The History of Indiana, Vol. IV) (1968)

Pirtle, Alfred *The Battle of Tippecanoe* (1900)

Price, Robert *Johnny Appleseed, Man and Myth* (1954)

Quaife, Milo M. *The Capture of Old Vincennes* (1927)

Rowell, John W. *Yankee Artillerymen: Through the Civil War with Eli Lilly's Indiana Battery* (1975)

Sandburg, Carl *Abraham Lincoln, the Prairie Years* 2 vols. (1926)

Sanders, Scott R. *Stone Country* (1985)

Schiereth, Thomas J. *US 40: A Roadscape of the American Experience* (1985)

Schwomeyer, Herb *Hoosier Hysteria* (1975)

Simons, Richard S. *The Rivers of Indiana* (1985)

Stampp, Kenneth *Indiana Politics during the Civil War* (1949, rpt. 1978)

Starr, George W. *Industrial Development of Indiana* (1937)

Stuart, Ben F. *History of the Wabash and Valley* (1924)

Sweet, William Warren *Circuit-Rider Days in Indiana* (1916)

Thornbrough, Emma Lou *Indiana in the Civil War Era, 1850–1880* (The History of Indiana, Vol. III) (1965)

Thornbrough, Gayle and Dorothy Riker (eds.) *Readings in Indiana History* (1956)

Trissal, Francis M. *Public Men of Indiana* (1922)

Troyer, Byron L. *Yesterday's Indiana* (1975)

Truesdell, Mary Van Hogel *Tippecanoe: A Legend of the Border* (1840)

VanderMeer, Philip R. *The Hoosier Politician: Officeholding and Political Culture in Indiana, 1896–1920* (1985)

Visher, Stephen S. *Economic Geography of Indiana* (1923)
——. *Climate of Indiana* (1944)

Warren, Louis A. *Lincoln's Youth: Indiana Years, Seven to Twenty-one, 1816–1830* (1959)

Wilson, William E. *The Wabash* (The Rivers of America series) (1940)
——. *Shooting Star: The Story of Tecumseh* (1942)
——. *The Angel and the Serpent: The Story of New Harmony* (1964)
——. *Indiana, a History* (1966)

Wood, Mary E. *French Imprint on the Heart of America: Historical Vignettes of 110 French-related Localities in Indiana and the Ohio Valley* (1977)

IOWA

Iowa is a west north central state. It is bordered on the north by Minnesota; on the east by the Mississippi River, Wisconsin, and Illinois; on the south by Missouri; and on the west by Nebraska, South Dakota, and the Missouri and Big Sioux rivers.

FULL NAME State of Iowa
POSTAL ABBREVIATION IA
INHABITANT Iowan
ADMITTED TO THE UNION Dec. 28, 1846. 29th state
POPULATION (est. 1987) 2,834,000. Percent of US total: 1.16%. Rank: 29th

CAPITAL CITY Des Moines, the largest city in the state, located at the confluence of the Des Moines and Raccoon rivers in south central Iowa; population 190,832 (est. 1984). Originally the site of a fort built in 1843, it was incorporated as the settlement of Fort Des Moines in 1851 and chartered as a city in 1857, the same year it became the state capital.

STATE NAME AND NICKNAMES From the Iowa Indian tribal name *ayuxwa*, "one who puts to sleep," misspelled Ioway by English settlers and Ayoua by the French. Also known as the Hawkeye State, probably from the Sauk chief Black Hawk, and as the Land Where the Tall Corn Grows, the Nation's Breadbasket, and the Corn State.

STATE SEAL A landscape showing on the left side a field of standing wheat with a scythe and farming tools, and on the right side a lead furnace and a pile of pig lead; in the background, the Mississippi River, carrying a steamboat, and hills beyond it. In the foreground is a soldier standing in front of a plow and holding an American flag topped by the Phrygian cap of liberty. At the top is an eagle holding in its beak a streamer bearing the state motto. Around the border, in red letters on gold, is the legend "The Great Seal of the State of Iowa."

MOTTO Our Liberties We Prize, and Our Rights We Will Maintain

SONG "The Song of Iowa," lyrics by S.H.M. Byers, melody from the folk tune "O Tannenbaum" (to protest its use in the Confederate song "My Maryland").

SYMBOLS
Flower wild rose
Tree oak
Bird eastern goldfinch
Rock geode

LICENSE PLATE White on dark blue.

FLAG Three vertical stripes of blue, white, and red; the white stripe bears the eagle-and-streamer design of the state seal, and below it in red is the legend "Iowa."

GEOGRAPHY AND CLIMATE

Rising gently from the Mississippi River along the state's eastern border, Iowa's flat terrain changes gradually from that of a Central Lowlands state to that of a prairie state. Rich glacial soils cover nearly all of Iowa, making 95 percent of the land suitable for agriculture. With cold winters and hot, humid summers, Iowa has the climate of a typical heartland state.

AREA 56,275 square miles. Rank: 24th
INLAND WATER 310 square miles
GEOGRAPHIC CENTER Story, 5 miles NE of Ames
ELEVATIONS *Highest point:* Geographical survey section 29, 100N, R41W, Osceola County, 1,670 feet. *Lowest point:* Mississippi River, Lee County, 480 feet. *Mean elevation:* 1,100 feet

MAJOR RIVERS Des Moines, Mississippi, Missouri, Big Sioux

MAJOR LAKES AND RESERVOIRS Rathbun, Clear, Storm, Spirit

LAND USE

	Thousands of acres
Urban (1982)	623
Rural (1982)	33,709
Cropland (1982)	26,441
Pastureland (1982)	4,536
Rangeland (1982)	0
Forestland (1982)	1,756
State parks and recreation areas (1983)	161
National park system (1984)	2
National forest system (1984)	0
Tribal lands (1984)	4

TEMPERATURES The highest recorded temperature was 118°F on July 20, 1934, at Keokuk. The lowest was -47°F on January 12, 1912, at Washta.

NATIONAL SITES

NATIONAL HISTORIC SITE Herbert Hoover
NATIONAL HISTORIC TRAILS Lewis & Clark, Mormon Pioneer
NATIONAL MONUMENT Effigy Mounds
NATIONAL WILDLIFE REFUGES De Soto, Lansing District, Louisa and Keithsburg Division, Mark Twain, Union Slough, Upper Mississippi River Wildlife and Fish Refuge

HISTORY

1673	*June 25.* Louis Jolliet and Father Jacques Marquette are the first white men to visit Iowa. They land on the west bank of the Mississippi River, near present-day McGregor, and spend two days in an Illinois Indian village.
1680	Flemish missionary Father Louis Hennepin explores parts of Iowa.
1735	*April 19.* Pitched battle at Raccoon Fork of the Des Moines River between the Sauk (or Sac) and Fox and 80 French with their Indian allies.
1762	By a secret treaty France transfers its lands west of the Mississippi to Spain.
1788	Julien Dubuque, a French Canadian, becomes the first white man to settle permanently in the Iowa region, making his home just south of the present city that bears his name and working the lead deposits in the area.
1803	A month after French control of the Louisiana Territory is reestablished, Napoleon sells it to the United States.
1805	An estimated 8,000 Indians are resident in Iowa, including Sauk and Fox, Winnebago, Iowa, Sioux, Omaha, Oto, and Missouri.
1808	Fort Madison is established as a government trading post for the Indian trade.
1809	Iowa annual fur trade is valued at $60,000.
1812	Iowa country is attached to the Territory of Missouri.
1813	Fort Madison is abandoned during the War of 1812, after several Indian attacks led by Sauk and Fox leader Black Hawk.
1814	*September.* A force of 30 to 60 British soldiers and about 1,000 Indian allies defeat 334 US soldiers under Major Zachary Taylor on Credit Island in the Mississippi.
1821	Admission of Missouri as a state leaves Iowa unorganized for 13 years.
1824	Sauk and Fox make their first cession in the Iowa region, a small area in the southeast called Half-Breed Tract.
1829	*November 22.* First white child born in Iowa, near present-day Keokuk.
1830	*October 4.* Isaac Galland organizes the first school near the town that bears his name.

1832	Defeat of Black Hawk results in a treaty pushing Indians 50 miles west of the Mississippi.
1833	Dubuque, Burlington, Fort Madison, Peru, and Bellevue are founded.
1834	Three companies of dragoons, led by Lieutenant Colonel Stephen Watts Kearny, establish Fort Des Moines.
1836	*May 11*. First newspaper in Iowa, the *Du Buque Visitor*, is published by John King.
1838	*June 12*. Territory of Wisconsin divided to create a separate Territory of Iowa, which also includes most of Minnesota and part of the Dakotas.
	First federal land offices in Iowa are established at Burlington and Dubuque; eventually 36 million acres are disposed of.
1840	*July 4*. Cornerstone of capitol laid, at Iowa City.
1842	*October 11*. Sauk and Fox agree to evacuate Iowa within three years.
1846	*December 28*. Iowa admitted to the Union as the 29th state.
1847	*February 25*. State University of Iowa established at Iowa City; classes begin in 1855.
1851	Sioux sell their lands in northern Iowa; this is the last Indian cession in the state.
1855	Establishment of Iowa settlement by the Amana Society, a German religious commune.
1856	*April 14*. Train crosses, at Davenport, first bridge across the Mississippi.
1857	Capital moved from Iowa City to Des Moines.
	March 7–13. Forty-two whites killed by Sioux in the Spirit Lake Massacre in northwestern Iowa.
1861–1865	Iowa provides the Union Army with nearly 80,000 men. Death toll is 13,001.
1862	Iowa is the first state to accept the terms of the Morrill Land-Grant College Act, making federal lands available to endow colleges. The state's grant is awarded to Iowa Agricultural College (later Iowa State University).
1868	State constitution amended to give blacks the right to vote and hold office.
1869	Trans-state railway completed, from Davenport to Council Bluffs.
1872	Over half of all local Granges in the country are in Iowa; these groups foster cooperative buying and selling by farmers.
1880	Last of discriminatory laws against blacks is abolished when "white" is removed from the qualifications for legislative office.
1884	*July 4*. Statewide prohibition of alcoholic beverages becomes law.
1890	Iowa leads all states in corn production.
1910	With 2,210,050 people, Iowa is the only state to have lost population in the first decade of the 20th century. Mechanization of agriculture and the lure of cheaper lands farther west are believed to be responsible.
1915	Prohibition readopted, lasts until 1933.
1926	A constitutional amendment admits women to the General Assembly.
1929	*March 4*. Iowa-born Herbert Hoover inaugurated president of the United States.
1931	Iowa artist Grant Wood paints *American Gothic*.
1936	Creation of University of Iowa's Writing Workshop.
1948	Iowa leads all states in the production of corn, hogs, oats, poultry, eggs, and finished cattle for market.
1957	The Aluminum Company of America's Davenport Works becomes the world's largest integrated aluminum plate and sheet mill.
1959	*September 22–23*. Soviet leader Nikita Khrushchev tours Iowa, visiting the model Roswell Garst farm at Coon Rapids.
1965	Capital punishment is abolished.
	For the first time in eight years, Illinois tops Iowa in corn production.
1966	Iowa has an unemployment rate of 1.6 percent, the lowest in state history.
1970	Sex discrimination banned in housing, employment, and public accommodations.
	Seventy-four of Iowa's counties, all in rural areas, lose population in the 1960s.
	Iowa-born Norman Borlaug wins the Nobel Peace Prize for developing an improved variety of wheat.
1976	Criminal code is rewritten for the first time in 125 years.
1982	Unemployment rate of 8.3 percent in October is the highest in the state since the Great Depression but still lower than the national average.

1985   An executive order imposes a one-year moratorium on the foreclosure of farmland.
1986   The 52-year state monopoly on liquor sales is ended, and 212 state-owned liquor stores are sold.

DEMOGRAPHY

Population (est. 1987) . . . 2,834,000
Population (1980) 2,913,808
Population density in persons
    per square mile (1980) 51.8

POPULATION BY RACE (1980)
American Indian/Aleut/
    Eskimo 5,453
Asian/Pacific Islander 11,577
Black 41,700
Hispanic 25,536
White 2,838,805
Other 15,852

POPULATION CHARACTERISTICS (1980)
Percent of state population
Urban 58.6
Rural 41.4
Under 18 . . . . 28.3
65 or older 13.3
College-educated 14.1
Families below poverty line 7.0
Public assistance recipients 4.6

Per capita personal income
    (1986) $13,222
Millionaires per 100,000
    residents (1982) 113.5
Average life expectancy in
    years (1980) 75.8

Marriage rate per 1,000
    residents (1986) 8.2
Divorce rate per 1,000
    residents (1986) 3.5
Birth rate per 1,000
    residents (1985) 14.6
Infant mortality rate per 1,000
    residents (1985) 8.5
Abortion rate per 1,000
    live births (1985) 248
Crime rate per 100,000
    residents (1985)
    Violent 235.1
    Property 3,915.6
Federal and state prisoners per
    100,000 residents (1984) 96
Alcohol consumption in gallons
    per capita (1985) 36.9
Deaths from motor vehicle accidents
    per 100,000 residents (1985) . . 16.6

MAJOR CITIES

	1984 population (est.)
Cedar Rapids	108,669
Council Bluffs	56,943
Davenport	102,129
Des Moines	190,832
Dubuque	60,228
Iowa City	50,984
Sioux City	81,767
Waterloo	75,661

GOVERNMENT AND POLITICS

Number of US Representatives   6
Electoral votes   8

POLITICAL PARTY NOMINEES FROM STATE
* winner

James Baird Weaver (Green-back Labor)	1880	P
James Baird Weaver (People's)	1892	P
Jonah Fitz Randolph Leonard (United Christian)	1900	P
Lorenzo S. Coffin (United Christian)	1908	VP
Henry Agard Wallace* (D)	1940	VP
Henry Agard Wallace (Progressive)	1948	P
John O. Hopkins (Universal)	1964	VP
Merle Thayer (Constitution)	1968	VP

PRESIDENTIAL PRIMARY ELECTION In 1988, 58 Democratic delegates and 37 Republican delegates to the national conventions.

CONSTITUTION Iowa has had two constitutions: 1846 and the present one, adopted in 1857.

LEGISLATURE The General Assembly is divided into the Senate (50 members, 4-year term, minimum age 25) and the House of Representatives (100 members, 2-year term, minimum age 21). In 1987, the annual salary was $14,600.

JUDICIARY The highest court is the Supreme Court, with 9 judges serving 8-year terms. In 1987, the annual salary was $65,200.

EXECUTIVE The governor serves a 4-year term; the minimum age for holding office is 30. In 1987, the annual salary was $70,000. There are 6 other elected officials.

PRESIDENTIAL VOTE 1948-1988 *(in percents)*

Year	State Winner	Democratic	Republican
1948	Truman (D)	50.3	47.6
1952	Eisenhower (R)	35.6	63.8
1956	Eisenhower (R)	40.7	59.1
1960	Nixon (R)	43.2	56.7
1964	Johnson (D)	61.9	37.9
1968	Nixon (R)	40.8	53.0
1972	Nixon (R)	40.5	57.6
1976	Ford (R)	48.5	49.5
1980	Reagan (R)	38.6	51.3
1984	Reagan (R)	45.9	53.3
1988	Dukakis (D)	55.0	45.0

GOVERNORS

Territorial Governors

Robert Lucas	1838-1841
John Chambers	1841-1845
James Clark	1845-1846

State Governors

Ansel Briggs (D)	1846-1850
Stephen Hempstead (D)	1850-1854
James Wilson Grimes (Whig and Free Soil Democrat)	1854-1858
Ralph P. Lowe (R)	1858-1860
Samuel J. Kirkwood (R)	1860-1864
William M. Stone (R)	1864-1868
Samuel Merrill (R)	1868-1872
Cyrus C. Carpenter (R)	1872-1876
Samuel J. Kirkwood (R)	1876-1877
Joshua G. Newbold (R)	1877-1878
John H. Gear (R)	1878-1882
Buren R. Sherman (R)	1882-1886
William Larrabee (R)	1886-1890
Horace Boies (D)	1890-1894
Frank Dorr Jackson (R)	1894-1896
Francis M. Drake (R)	1896-1898
Leslie M. Shaw (R)	1898-1902
Albert B. Cummins (R)	1902-1908
Warren Garst (R)	1908-1909
Beryl F. Carroll (R)	1909-1913
George W. Clarke (R)	1913-1917
William L. Harding (R)	1917-1921
Nathan E. Kendell (R)	1921-1925
John Hammill (R)	1925-1929
Daniel W. Turner (R)	1929-1933
Clyde L. Herring (D)	1933-1937
Nelson G. Kraschel (D)	1937-1939
George A. Wilson (R)	1939-1943
Bourke B. Hickenlooper (R)	1943-1945
Robert D. Blue (R)	1945-1949
William S. Beardsley (R)	1949-1954
Leo Elthon (R)	1954-1955
Leo A. Hoegh (R)	1955-1957
Herschel C. Loveless (D)	1957-1961
Norman A. Erbe (R)	1961-1963
Harold E. Hughes (D)	1963-1969
Robert Ray (R)	1969-1983
Terry Branstad (R)	1983-

MINIMUM AGES

Majority	18
Marriage with parental consent	16
Marriage without parental consent	18
Making a will	18
Buying alcohol	21
Jury duty	18
Leaving school	16
(if employed)	14
Driver's license	16

CAPITAL PUNISHMENT

None

MILITARY INSTALLATIONS

Total number: 5

FINANCES

Thousands of dollars

GENERAL REVENUE (1985)

Total general revenue	4,004,037
Total tax revenue	2,307,406
Sales and gross receipts	1,071,146
Individual income taxes	824,551
Corporate net income taxes	154,412

GENERAL EXPENDITURE (1985)

Total general expenditure	4,228,661
Education	1,789,860
Public welfare	734,993
Health	57,501
Hospitals	265,293
Natural resources	74,791
Highways	693,689
Police	30,409
Corrections	84,181

FEDERAL AID (1985) 1,163,730

ECONOMY

As the number of farms and farmers has decreased over the last few years in Iowa, farm receipts have fallen, bucking the national trend. Farm cash receipts were $9.3 billion in 1983, down 10 percent from one of the top agricultural producers in the nation. Livestock accounts for up to two-thirds of Iowa's farm income, with cattle and hogs the major products. The main cash crops are corn and soybeans. Processed foods are the chief manufactured products, along with farm implements and machinery, and home appliances. The value added by manufacture in 1982 was more than $12 billion. Limestone, shale, gravel, clays, and gypsum are the state's chief minerals.

EMPLOYMENT (1984)

Thousands of persons

Total number of employed
workers 1,318
Construction 37.1
Finance, insurance, and
real estate 61.5
Government 205.1
Manufacturing 210.9
Mining 2.0
Services 224.6
Transportation, communications,
and utilities 50.7
Wholesale and retail trade 270.5

Percent of civilian labor force
unemployed (1984) 7.0

DEPARTMENT OF DEFENSE (1985)
Civilian workers employed . . . 1,545
Military personnel 399
Contract awards . . . . . $590 million

ENERGY SOURCES FOR ELECTRIC UTILITIES (1983)

Percent
Coal 84.2
Gas 0.8
Hydroelectric 4.1
Nuclear 10.4
Petroleum 0.3

TRANSPORTATION
Motor vehicles registered
in state (1986) 2,638,176
Miles of roads, streets,
and highways (1986) . . . 112,498
Miles of Class I railway
operated (1986) 3,503
Airports (1983) 280
Major aviation hubs (1983) 1
Largest hub: Des Moines

CULTURE AND EDUCATION

Native American tribes
Iowa was formerly home to the Illinois, Iowa, Missouri, Ojibway, Omaha, Oto, Peoria, Potawatomi, Sioux, and Winnebago tribes. Groups that continue to live in the state include the Fox and Sauk. There is one federal reservation in Iowa.

Religions, ethnicities, and languages
Iowa's early settlers, from states to the east and south, were followed by newcomers from Germany, Ireland, Scotland, Scandinavia, Holland, Bohemia, Austria, and Hungary. In 1980, 3.4 percent of Iowa's population spoke a language other than English at home. About one quarter of churchgoers are Roman Catholic, followed by Methodists, Lutherans, and other Protestant denominations. There are also communities of Amish, Mormons, and Quakers, and one of the few survivors of

the Midwest's utopian communities, Amana.

Major museums and libraries
Herbert Hoover Library, West Branch
Iowa State Museum, Des Moines
Museum of Art, University of Iowa, Iowa City
Museum of Natural History, University of Iowa, Iowa City

Major arts organizations
Cedar Rapids Symphony Orchestra
Des Moines Metropolitan Opera
Des Moines Symphony
Symphony orchestras of Quad City, Sioux City, and Waterloo-Cedar Falls

Colleges and universities
Number public (1986-87) 21
Number private (1986-87) 40
Total enrollment, in full-time equivalent students (1985) 128,500

Public elementary and secondary schools
Expenditure per pupil in average daily
  attendance (1986-87) $3,740
Pupil-teacher ratio (1987) 15.5
Average teacher salary (1986-87) $23,434

Holidays
Bird Day. March 21
State Fair, Des Moines.
  Mid- to late August
Youth Honor Day. October 31

IOWA IN LITERATURE

Bess Aldrich *Miss Bishop* (1933)
Novel about a college teacher, 1880–1930.
———. *Song of Years* (1939)
Novel of pioneer life, 1854–1865.

Clarence Andrews *A Literary History of Iowa* (1972)
———. (ed.) *Growing Up in Iowa* (1988)
Anthology of memoirs by prominent local writers.

Douglas Bauer *Prairie City, Iowa: Three Seasons at Home* (1979, rpt. 1982)

Richard Bissell *7½ cents* (1953)
Comic novel about labor unrest in the author's native Dubuque.

Black Hawk (trans. Antoine Le Claire) *Autobiography* (1834, rpt. 1932)
The Sauk chief's autobiography, dictated to Le Claire in 1833, can be regarded as the earliest work of Iowa literature, although much that he relates took place in Wisconsin and Illinois. Black Hawk recalls his early life in the villages and hunting grounds on the Iowa prairies, his tribe's customs, the war of 1812, the Battle of Wisconsin Heights, and the massacre at Bad Axe.

Johnson Brigham (ed.) *A Book of Iowa Authors by Iowa Authors* (1930)

H. Clark Brown *Songs of the Iowa Prairie* (1921)

Harriet Connor Brown *Grandmother Brown's Hundred Years* (1929)
Biography of an Iowa pioneer.

Thomas P. Christensen (ed.) *Sagas of the Hawkeyes: Being Stories and Incidents of Early Iowa* (1945)

Cyrenus Cole *I Remember, I Remember* (1936)
Autobiography of an Iowa historian.

Paul Corey *Three Miles Square* (1939); *The Road Returns* (1940); *County Seat* (1941)
Trilogy of novels about an Iowa community, centering on the fortunes of a farming family, 1910–1930.

Leroy Judson Daniels (ed. Helen S. Herrick) *Tales of an Old Horsetrader* (1987)
Memoir of a man who ran away from home at sixteen to become an itinerant rural worker.

Floyd Dell *Moon-Calf* (1921)
Novel about growing up in an Iowa town, based on the author's life in Davenport.

J. Hyatt Downing *Sioux City* (1940); *Anthony Trant* (1941)
Novels focusing on the Sioux City boom, 1880–1930.

Paul Engle *Always the Land* (1941)
Novel about conflicts between two generations of Iowa farmers.
——— and **Rowena Torrevillas** (eds.) *The World Comes to Iowa* (1988)
Anthology of writing about the state by participants in the University of Iowa International Writing Program.

Feike Frederick Feikema (pseud. of Frederick Manfred) *This Is the Year* (1947)
Novel about the hardships of a Frisian farmer.

Alice French (pseud. Octave Thanet) *Stories of a Western Town* (1893)
"Octave Thanet," who did much to popularize local-color writing at the turn of the century, is best known for her tales of Arkansas, but set these sketches in Davenport, Iowa, where she lived for a time.

Hamlin Garland *Boy Life on the Prairies* (1899)
Autobiographical account of growing up in rural northeast-ern Iowa in the years following the Civil War. Garland also described his background in *O Iowa* (1935, rpt. 1979).

H. Roger Grant and **L. Edward Purcell** (eds.) *Years of Struggle: The Farm Diary of Elmer G. Powers, 1931–1936* (1988)
Journal of a farmer's hardships during the Depression.

Carl Hamilton *In No Time at All* (1975)
Farm life in Iowa.
——— (ed.) *Pure Nostalgia: Memories of Early Iowa* (1988)
Seven native Iowans recall life from 1850–1940.

Curtis Harnack *The Work of an Ancient Hand* (1960); *Love and Be Silent* (1962)
Novels of small town and rural life. *We Have All Gone Away* (1973, rpt. 1988) is an autobiography of farm life in the 1930s and '40s.

Nan Heacock *Crinoline to Calico* (1988)
Fictional biography of the author's grandparents, pioneers in the 1850s.

Rupert Hughes *In a Little Town* (1917)

Iowa Authors and Artists *Prairie Gold* (1917)

MacKinlay Kantor *The Jaybird* (1932); *Valedictory* (1939); *Happy Land* (1943); *God and My Country* (1954)
Novels and short stories of small town communities.

Alice Marple "Iowa Authors and Their Works" *Annals of Iowa* (1918)

Cornelia Meigs *As the Crow Flies* (1927)

Frank Mott *Literature of Pioneer Life in Iowa* (1923)

J. B. Newhall *A Glimpse of Iowa in 1846* (1846, rpt. 1957)

Chuck Offenburger *Iowa Boy* (1988)
Popular Des Moines journalist portrays Iowans in a collection of articles.

Hugh A. Orchard *Old Orchard Farm* (1952)
Anecdotal autobiography of a farmer and clergyman from Des Moines who grew up on a farm in the 1880s.

Frank Paluka *Iowa Authors: A Bio-Bibliography of Sixty Native Writers* (1967)

Beulah Meier Pelton *We Belong to the Land: Memories of a Midwesterner* (1984)

John Plumbe *Sketches of Iowa and Wisconsin* (1839, rpt. 1948)

Susan Puckett *A Cook's Tour of Iowa* (1988)
Folkways and ethnic customs of the state revealed by its cuisine.

Herbert Quick *Vandemark's Folly* (1922, rpt. 1987); *The Hawkeye* (1923); *The Invisible Woman* (1924)
Trilogy of novels describing Iowa history from pioneer days through the 1890s. *One Man's Life* (1925), an autobiography, contains an account of post–Civil War Iowa. Quick grew up on a farm in Grundy County in the 1860s.

James Sanders (ed.) "Times Hard but Grit Good" *Annals of Iowa* 47 (1984)
Farm woman's journal of domestic life near Grinnell.

Ross Santee *Dog Days* (1955)
Reminiscences of the author's boyhood at the beginning of the century.

Jay G. Sigmund *Wapsipinicon Tales* (1927)

Wallace Stegner *Remembering Laughter* (1937)
Short tragic novel about life on a remote farm.

Philip D. (Phil) Stong *State Fair* (1932)
Novel about domestic events set at the Des Moines fair. Other novels by Stong with rural and small-town Iowa settings include *Village Tale* (1934), *Career* (1936), *The Long Land* (1939). *Buckskin Breeches* (1937) is a novel of pioneer life c.1930.

Earl J. Stout (ed.) *Folklore from Iowa* (1936)

Ruth Suckow *Country People* (1924); *The Odyssey of a Nice Girl* (1925); *Iowa Interiors* (1926); *The Bonney Family* (1928); *Cora* (1929); *Children and Older People* (1931); *The Folks* (1934); *A Ruth Suckow Omnibus* (1988)
Novels and short stories of small town and rural life.

Susan Allen Toth *Blooming: A Small-Town Girlhood* (1981)

Carl Van Vechten *The Tattooed Countess* (1924, rpt. 1987)
Autobiographical novel set in the 1890s by a Cedar Rapids–born writer about a cosmopolitan woman who scandalized midwestern small-town society.

Margaret Wilson *The Able McLaughlins* (1923)
Pulitzer Prize–winning novel about pioneer Scots, c.1860.

GUIDES TO RESOURCES

Aitchison, Alison E. *Iowa State Geography* (1921)

Alex, Lynn M. *Exploring Iowa's Past: A Guide to Prehistoric Archaeology* (1980)

Andreas, Alfred T. *Illustrated Historical Atlas of the State of Iowa, 1875* (1875, rpt. 1970)

Federal Writers' Project *Iowa: A Guide to the Hawkeye State* (1938)
————. *The WPA Guide to 1930s Iowa* (1986)

Frankland, Philip and **Stephen Airola** *Atlas of Selected Iowa Services* (1978)

Historic American Buildings Survey (comp. Wesley I. Shank) *The Iowa Catalog* (1979)

Hochstetter, Nancy (ed.) *Travel Historic Iowa: A Guide to Historic Sites and Markers* (1987)

Hudson, David and **Patricia Dawson** *Iowa History and Culture: A Bibliography of Materials Published between 1952 and 1986* (1988)

Iowa State Historical Society (ed. B. F. Shambaugh) *Documentary Material Relating to the History of Iowa* 3 vols. (1901, rpt. 1986)

Morford, Charles *Biographical Index to the County Histories of Iowa* vol. 1– (1979–)

Petersen, William J. *Iowa History Reference Guide* (1952)

Pratt, LeRoy G. *Discovering Historic Iowa* (1972)

Wilson, D. Ray *Iowa Historical Tour Guide* (1986)

SELECTED NONFICTION SOURCES

Allen, Arthur F. (ed.) *Northwestern Iowa; Its History and Traditions, 1804–1926* . . . 3 vols. (1927)

Anderson, Duane *Western Iowa Prehistory* (1975)
————. *Eastern Iowa Prehistory* (1981)

Bogue, Allan G. *From Prairie to Cornbelt: Farming on the Illinois and Iowa Prairies in the Nineteenth Century* (1963)

Briggs, John E. *Iowa, Old and New* (1939)

Brigham, Johnson *Iowa, Its History and Its Foremost Citizens* 3 vols. (1915)
————. *The Sinclairs of Old Fort Des Moines* (1927)

Bright, Chuck *University of Iowa Football: The Hawkeyes* (1982)

Brown, Hazel E. *Grant Wood and Marvin Cone: Artists of an Era* (1987)

Childs, Chandler C. (ed. Robert F. Klein) *Dubuque: Frontier River City* (1984)

Clarke, S. J. *Prominent Iowans* (1915)

Cole, Cyrenus *A History of the People of Iowa* (1921)
————. *I Am a Man—the Indian Black Hawk* (1938)
————. *Iowa Through the Years* (1940)

Gue, Benjamin F. *History of Iowa* 4 vols. (1903)

Hake, Herbert V. *Iowa Inside Out* (1968)

Hamilton, Carl (ed.) *Pure Nostalgia: Memories of Early Iowa* (1979)

Harlan, Edgar R. *A Narrative History of the People of Iowa* 5 vols. (1931)

Haynes, Fred E. *History of Third Party Movements since the Civil War, with Special Reference to Iowa* (1916)

Hoffman, M. M. *Julien Dubuque, His Life and Adventures* (1933)

Houlette, William *Iowa, the Pioneer Heritage* (1970)

James, James A. *Constitution and Admission of Iowa into the Union* (1900, rpt. 1987)

Jones, Louis T. *The Quakers of Iowa* (1914)

Keyes, Margaret N. *Old Capitol: Portrait of an Iowa Landmark* (1988)

Lafore, Laurence *American Classic* (1975)

Macbridge, Thomas H. *In Cabins and Sod-houses* (1928)

McFarland, Julian E. *A History of the Pioneer Era on the Iowa Prairies* (1969)

Mills, George S. *Rogues and Heroes from Iowa's Amazing Past* (1972, rpt. 1986)
————. (ed. Joan Bunke) *Harvey Ingham and Gardner Cowles, Sr.: Things Don't Just Happen* (1977)

Morain, Thomas J. *Prairie Grass Roots: An Iowa Town in the Early Twentieth Century* (1988)

Nieuwenhuis, G. Nelson *Siouxland, a History of Sioux County, Iowa* (1983)

Noun, Louise R. *Strong Minded Women: The Emergence of the Woman Suffrage Movement in Iowa* (1969)

Perkins, Jacob R. *Trails, Rails, and War: Life of General G. M. Dodge* (1929)

Petersen, William J. *Iowa: The Rivers of Her Valleys* (1941)
————. *The Story of Iowa* 4 vols. (1952)

Richman, Irving B. *Ioway to Iowa* (1931)

Riley, Glenda *Frontierswomen, the Iowa Experience* (1981)

Roberts, Ronald E. *Ordinary Ghosts and Everyday People in an Iowa Coal Town* (1986)

Rosenberg, Morton M. *Iowa on the Eve of the Civil War; a Decade of Frontier Politics* (1972)

Ross, Earle D. *Iowa Agriculture* (1951)

Sabin, Henry and **Edwin L.** *The Making of Iowa* (1916)

Sage, Leland L. *A History of Iowa* (1974, rpt. 1987)

Salter, William *Iowa, the First Free State in the Louisiana Purchase* (1905)

Schmidt, John F. *A Historical Profile of Sioux City* (1969)

Schwieder, Elmer and **Dorothy** *A Peculiar People: Iowa's Old Order Amish* (1975, rpt. 1987)

Shambaugh, Benjamin F. *Documentary Material Relating to the History of Iowa* 3 vols. (1897–1901)

Shambaugh, Bertha M. H. *Amana That Was and Amana That Is* (1932)

Sharp, Abigail G. *History of the Spirit Lake Massacre and Captivity of Miss Abbie Gardner* (5th ed. 1902)

Shetrone, Henry C. *The Mound-Builders* (1930)

Stanford, John L. *Toronado: Accounts of Tornadoes in Iowa* (1977)

Stong, Philip D. *Hawkeyes: A Biography of the State of Iowa* (1940)

Swierenga, Robert P. *Pioneers and Profits* (1968)

Swisher, Jacob A. *Iowa—Land of Many Mills* (1940)
—— and Carl H. Erbe *Iowa History as Told in Biography* (1932)

Talbot, Ross B. *Iowa in the World Economy* (1985)

Taylor, Henry C. *Tarpleywick: A Century of Iowa Farming* (1970)

Teakle, Thomas *The Spirit Lake Massacre* (1918)

Throne, Mildred *Cyrus Clay Carpenter and Iowa Politics, 1854–1898* (1974)

Van de Zee, Jacob *The British in Iowa* (1922)

Vogel, Virgil J. *Iowa Place Names of Indian Origin* (1983)

Wall, Joseph F. *Iowa: A Bicentennial History* (States and the Nation series) (1978)

Wilson, Richard G. *The Prairie School in Iowa* (1977)

Winebrenner, Hugh *The Iowa Precinct Caucuses: The Making of a Media Event* (1988)

Winters, Donald L. *Farmers without Farms: Agricultural Tenancy in Nineteenth-Century Iowa* (1978)

Wubben, Hubert H. *Civil War Iowa and the Copperhead Movement* (1980)

KANSAS

Kansas is a west north central state, bordered by Nebraska on the north, Missouri on the east, Oklahoma on the south, and Colorado on the west.

FULL NAME State of Kansas
POSTAL ABBREVIATION KS
INHABITANT Kansan
ADMITTED TO THE UNION Jan. 29, 1861. 34th state
POPULATION (est. 1987) 2,376,000. Percent of US total: 1.02%. Rank: 33d

CAPITAL CITY Topeka, located on the Kansas River in northeast Kansas; population 118,945 (est. 1984). It was founded in 1854 by settlers opposed to the introduction of slavery into new territories and became the capital when Kansas was admitted to statehood in 1861.

STATE NAME AND NICKNAMES From the Kansas Indian word *kanze,* "south wind." Also known as the Squatter State, the Cyclone State, the Sunflower State, the Jayhawk State; during the conflict between free and slave states prior to the Civil War, known as Bleeding Kansas.

STATE SEAL A landscape showing a panorama of pioneer life, with a farmer plowing a field in the foreground and behind him a wagon train, a settler's cabin, mounted Indians chasing buffalo, and a steamboat on a river; in the distance, the sun is rising behind purple hills. In the sky,

above 34 stars, is a banner bearing the state motto. The white border bears the legend "Great Seal of the State of Kansas, January 29, 1861."

MOTTO Ad Astra per Aspera (To the stars through difficulties)

SONGS "Home on the Range," lyrics by Brewster Higley, music by Dan Kelley. State march: "The Kansas March" by Duff E. Middleton.

SYMBOLS
Flower wild sunflower
Tree cottonwood
Bird western meadowlark
Animal American buffalo
Insect Honeybee

LICENSE PLATES (1) Dark blue on white, with gold sheaf of wheat in center and blue stripes across top. (2) Medium blue on white, with gold sunburst. (3) White in medium blue, with gold sheaf of wheat.

FLAG On a blue field, the state seal without its border, with the state flower above it on a bar of blue and gold, and the legend "Kansas" in yellow below it.

GEOGRAPHY AND CLIMATE

Kansas, containing both the geographic and geodetic (magnetic) centers of the continental US, has a flat terrain of prairies and high plains. The deep soils of the central regions, built on a foundation of sediment laid down in the Cretaceous Period when Kansas lay under a great inland sea, are among the world's most fertile. To the west are treeless high plains, rising toward Colorado and the Continental Divide.

AREA 82,277 square miles. Rank: 14th
INLAND WATER 499 square miles
GEOGRAPHIC CENTER Barton, 15 miles NE of Great Bend
ELEVATIONS *Highest point:* Mount Sunflower, Wallace County, 4,039 feet. *Lowest point:* Verdigris River, Montgomery County, 680 feet. *Mean elevation:* 2,000 feet

MAJOR RIVERS Arkansas, Missouri, Kansas

MAJOR LAKES AND RESERVOIRS Milford, Waconda, Perry, Tuttle Creek, Cheney

LAND USE

	Thousands of acres
Urban (1982)	721
Rural (1982)	49,655
Cropland (1982)	29,118
Pastureland (1982)	2,241
Rangeland (1982)	16,909
Forestland (1982)	626
State parks and recreation areas (1983)	31
National park system (1984)	1
National forest system (1984)	117
Tribal lands (1984)	7

TEMPERATURES The highest recorded temperature was 121°F on July 24, 1936, near Alton. The lowest was -40°F on February 13, 1905, at Lebanon.

NATIONAL SITES

NATIONAL HISTORIC SITES Fort Larned, Fort Scott
NATIONAL HISTORIC TRAIL Lewis & Clark, Oregon
NATIONAL WILDLIFE REFUGES Flint Hills, Kirwin, Quivira

HISTORY

1541	Spanish explorer, Captain-General Francisco Vásquez de Coronado, searching for gold, enters Kansas area near present site of Liberal. Franciscan priest, Juan de Padilla, is slain by Indians in central Kansas—first Christian martyr in Mid-America.
1601	Spanish expeditions confirm Coronado's impression that area is of potential value to Spain.
1682	French explorer Robert Cavelier, Sieur de la Salle, claims region for France based on earlier explorations of the French.
1682–1704	French establish trading posts in Kansas area. Indians resist Spanish control.
1719	Charles Claude du Tisné strengthens French claims via exploration.
1720	French–Spanish rivalry in the area increases.
1722	French erect Fort Orléans near mouth of Osage River.
1724	Etienne Veniard de Bourgmont heads expedition through Kansas from east to west.
1728	Fort Orléans abandoned by French due to Indian uprising.
1762	France grants Louisiana Territory, which includes Kansas, to Spain at end of Seven Years War in Europe and French and Indian War in America.
1763	Flag of Charles III of Spain flies over Kansas territory.
1764	French fur trappers become increasingly active in territory.
1800	Spain, weakened by wars, returns Louisiana Territory to France.
1803	Kansas area becomes a US possession when Napoleon sells Louisiana Territory for approximately $15 million.
1804	Lewis and Clark expedition enters area now known as Kansas.
1806	Other explorers, including Zebulon Pike, discoverer of Pike's Peak, travel through Kansas.

1812	*June 4*. Kansas becomes part of newly created Territory of Missouri.
	American Fur Company establishes headquarters in Kansas.
1818	First US military post in Kansas.
1819	*August 10*. Scientific expedition, headed by Major Stephen Long, introduces first steamboat to Kansas waters.
1820	Two Presbyterian missions founded for Osage Indians.
1821	Captain William Becknill chooses Santa Fe Trail as route to cross Kansas.
	Colonel Henry Leavenworth selects site of Fort Leavenworth.
	Spain ends its claim to southwestern portion of the state.
1824	Presbyterians found the first Kansas mission.
1827	Daniel Morgan Boone, son of the famous pioneer, sent to teach farming to Kansas Indians.
1828	*August 22*. Napoleon Boone is first white child born in Kansas region.
1833	First printing press in Kansas is brought to Shawnee Baptist Mission.
1834	*June 20*. Due to forced migration of many eastern Indian Tribes, Kansas area is designated as Indian Country by Congress.
1842	More forts built in area, including Fort Riley, first named Fort Center, and Fort Scott.
1846	Mormons traveling to Salt Lake area cross Kansas plains.
1849	More than 90,000 people travel across Kansas in the California Gold Rush.
1854	*May 30*. The Territory of Kansas is established by the Kansas-Nebraska Act. Increase of pro-slavery groups crossing Missouri border into Kansas and anti-slavery groups coming in from eastern states.
	December 5. Topeka founded.
	More than 2 million acres of Indian lands made available to whites.
1855	Population of Kansas estimated at 8,500.
	July 2. First territorial legislature meets at Pawnee, and is dominated by pro-slavery majority.
	October 23–November 11. Anti-slavery convention meets at Topeka and adopts a constitution prohibiting slavery.
1856	*May 21*. Town of Lawrence, center of Free State activities, attacked by pro-slavery groups.
	May 23–24. John Brown retaliates with a raid on pro-slavery groups in Pottawatomie.
	The state becomes known as "bleeding Kansas."
1858	*January*. Kansas state library founded.
1859	*October 4*. Kansas voters approve the Wyandotte Constitution prohibiting slavery.
1860	The first railroad reaches Kansas.
	April. The Pony Express is established.
1861	*January 29*. Congress admits Kansas to the Union as the 34th State.
	May 21. Great Seal of Kansas is adopted.
	November 5. Topeka chosen as permanent state capital.
1862	Congress grants Kansas 90,000 acres for a college of agriculture.
1863	Congress provides for removal of all Indians from Kansas.
	Confederate guerrillas under William Quantrill sack and burn Lawrence.
1865	Civil War ends. Kansas supplied 20,000 men to Union Army.
1866	*January*. To promote railroad construction, 500,000 acres of state land are sold.
	September. Grasshoppers plague northern Kansas.
1867	Lucy Stone and Susan B. Anthony work for right of women to vote.
1870	Kansas population exceeds 364,000.
	July. Wichita incorporated as a village.
1874	Mennonite immigration from Russia begins. They introduce "Turkey Red" wheat to America.
1877	First telephone is installed in Topeka.
	January 29. L.G.A. Copley, a Paola teacher, originates Kansas Day observances.
1878	Blacks from former slave states begin arriving in great numbers.
1879	Prohibition amendment passed by state legislature. Ratified by voters one year later.
1882	Well near Paola produces large amounts of natural gas.

1886	Great blizzard destroys cattle herds and impoverishes farmers.
1887	Severe drought causes end of agricultural boom.
1889	First county high school in US is founded at Chapman.
1890	Menninger Clinic, noted for psychiatric research, is established in Topeka.
1892	Oil is discovered near Neodesha.
	October 5. Dalton gang raids Coffeyville.
1894	Many companies formed to develop gas and oil fields.
	Board of irrigation is created.
1896	*August.* William Allen White writes the Emporia *Gazette* editorial "What's the Matter with Kansas"
1898	Kansas sends four regiments to fight in Spanish-American War.
1900	Carry Nation begins crusade against saloons.
1901	Dial telephone system makes first appearance in Kansas.
1903	First helium in US is discovered in Dexter.
1912	Kansas votes complete suffrage for women.
1915	*January 11.* Arthur Capper is first Kansas native to become governor.
	Oil discovered near El Dorado.
1917	World War I. The Kansas National Guard is drafted into the US Army.
1918	World War I ends. Eighty thousand Kansans engaged in war service.
1919	Wichita is the site of the first airplane factory in Kansas. It eventually becomes nation's leading plane manufacturing facility.
1922	The state's first radio station, KFH, opens in Wichita.
1924	Ku Klux Klan becomes important issue in state. W. A. White runs for governor on anti-Klan platform. He loses, but his influence dispels support for Klan.
1928	US Senator Charles Curtis is elected vice president on ticket with Herbert Hoover.
1931	Kansas has record 240 million bushel wheat crop.
1932	Alfred Landon is elected governor.
	First serious dust storms that will last for seven years begin. Southwestern Kansas becomes known as the Dust Bowl.
1934	*November 8.* Landon is nation's only Republican governor to be reelected.
1936	New oil fields developed in western Kansas.
	Governor Landon is unsuccessful Republican presidential candidate, winning only eight electoral votes.
1937	State legalizes manufacture and sale of 3.2 percent beer.
	Two percent sales tax begins.
1938	*March 30.* Tornado at Columbus causes great property damage and injures 12 people.
1942	*June.* Dwight D. Eisenhower, who grew up in Abilene, is named commanding general of American forces in Europe. During World War II 215,000 Kansans serve in the armed forces.
1948	Kansans vote to repeal state Prohibition. Glenn Cunningham, noted Kansas athlete, leads in fight against the repeal.
1953	KTUH, the state's first commercial television station, begins telecasting from Hutchinson.
1954	The Dwight D. Eisenhower Memorial Museum opens in Abilene.
1955	*April 2–3.* Tornadoes sweep through various parts of Kansas.
1956	The 236-mile Kansas turnpike opens.
1965	*June 17–26.* Heavy rains along South Platte and Arkansas Rivers result in floods. Two people are killed.
1972	Terms for governor and other top officials are increased from two to four years. New terms become effective in 1974.
1976	*August 19.* Senator Robert J. Dole is nominated for vice president by Republican Party.
1977	*March 10–12.* Severe blizzard kills many farm animals and two people.
1982	The annual net income per Kansas farm is listed at $12,000 by the US Department of Agriculture.
1985	The Wolf Creek nuclear power plant goes into operation.
	Governor John Carlin vetoes the capital punishment bill for the fourth time.

1986   Voters approve liquor by the drink, paramutual wagering, and a state lottery. All three items are implemented in 1987.

1987   State legislature rejects 1.7 million dollar bill for highway construction, proposed by Governor Hayden.

DEMOGRAPHY

Population (est. 1987) . . . 2,476,000
Population (1980) 2,364,236
Population density in persons
  per square mile (1980) 28.7

POPULATION BY RACE (1980)
American Indian/Aleut/
  Eskimo 15,371
Asian/Pacific Islander 15,078
Black 126,127
Hispanic 63,333
White 2,167,752
Other 38,880

POPULATION CHARACTERISTICS (1980)
Percent of state population
Urban 66.7
Rural 33.3
Under 18 . . . . 27.5
65 or older 13.0
College-educated 15.7
Families below poverty line 7.4
Public assistance recipients 3.8

Per capita personal income
  (1986) $14,379
Millionaires per 100,000
  residents (1982) 132.9

Average life expectancy
  in years (1980) 75.3
Marriage rate per 1,000
  residents (1986) 9.2
Divorce rate per 1,000
  residents (1986) 3.3
Birth rate per 1,000
  residents (1985) 16.0
Infant mortality rate per
  1,000 births (1985) 8.7
Abortion rate per 1,000
  live births (1985) 264
Crime rate per 100,000
  residents (1985)
  Violent 368.8
  Property 4,453.8
Federal and state prisoners per
  100,000 residents (1984) 166
Alcohol consumption in gallons
  per capita (1985) 33.1
Deaths from motor vehicle accidents
  per 100,000 residents (1985) . . 19.8

MAJOR CITIES
	1984 population (est.)
Kansas City	160,468
Lawrence	54,197
Topeka	118,945
Wichita	283,496

GOVERNMENT AND POLITICS

Number of US Representatives   6
Electoral votes   8

POLITICAL PARTY NOMINEES FROM STATE
  * winner

Samuel Clarke Pomeroy
  (American)   1880 VP
Samuel Clarke Pomeroy (American Prohibition)   1884 P
John Pierce St. John (Prohibition)   1884 P
William H.T. Wakefield (United Labor)   1888 VP
John Colvin (Industrial Reform)   1888 VP
Charles Curtis* (R)   1928 VP
Charles Curtis (R)   1932 VP

Alfred Mossman Landon (R)   1936 P
Earl Russell Browder (Communist)   1936 P
Earl Russell Browder (Communist)   1940 P
Rolland E. Fisher (Prohibition) 1968 VP
Robert Joseph Dole (R)   1976 VP

PRESIDENTIAL PRIMARY ELECTION In 1988, Kansas sent 43 Democratic delegates and 34 Republican delegates to the national conventions.

CONSTITUTION Kansas is using its original constitution, adopted in 1859.

LEGISLATURE The Legislature is divided into the Senate (40 members, 4-year term, minimum age 18) and the House of Representatives (125 members, 2-year term, minimum age 18). In 1987, the salary was $55 per diem.

JUDICIARY The highest court is the Supreme Court, with 7 judges serving 6-year terms. In 1987, the annual salary was $65,553.

EXECUTIVE The governor serves a 4-year term; there is no minimum age for holding office. In 1987, the annual salary was $65,693. There are 15 other elected officials.

PRESIDENTIAL VOTE 1948-1988 *(in percents)*

Year	State Winner	Democratic	Republican
1948	Dewey (R)	44.6	53.6
1952	Eisenhower (R)	30.5	68.8
1956	Eisenhower (R)	34.2	65.4
1960	Nixon (R)	39.1	60.5
1964	Johnson (D)	54.1	45.1
1968	Nixon (R)	34.7	54.8
1972	Nixon (R)	29.5	67.0
1976	Ford (R)	44.9	52.5
1980	Reagan (R)	33.3	57.9
1984	Reagan (R)	32.6	66.3
1988	Bush (R)	43.0	57.0

GOVERNORS

Territorial Governors

Andrew H. Reeder	1854-1855
Wilson Shannon	1855-1856
John W. Geary	1856-1857
Robert J. Walker	1857
James W. Denver	1857-1858
Samuel Medary	1858-1860
George M. Beebe (acting)	1860-1861

State Governors

Charles Robinson (R)	1861-1863
Thomas Carney (R)	1863-1865
Samuel J. Crawford (R)	1865-1868
Nehemiah Green (R/acting)	1868-1869
James M. Harvey (R)	1869-1873
Thomas A. Osborn (R)	1873-1877
George T. Anthony (R)	1877-1879
John P. St. John (R)	1879-1883
George W. Glick (D)	1883-1885
John A. Martin (R)	1885-1889
Lyman U. Humphrey (R)	1889-1893
Lorenzo D. Lewelling (Populist-Democrat)	1893-1895
Edmund N. Morrill (R)	1895-1897
John W. Leedy (D)	1897-1899
William E. Stanley (R)	1899-1903
Willis J. Bailey (R)	1903-1905
Edward W. Hoch (R)	1905-1909
Walter R. Stubbs (R)	1909-1913
George H. Hodges (D)	1913-1915
Arthur Capper (R)	1915-1919
Henry J. Allen (R)	1919-1923
Jonathan M. Davis (D)	1923-1925
Ben S. Paulen (R)	1925-1929
Clyde M. Reed (R)	1929-1931
Harry H. Woodring (D)	1931-1933

Alfred M. Landon (R)	1933-1937
Walter A. Huxman (D)	1937-1939
Payne H. Ratner (R)	1939-1943
Andrew F. Schoeppel (R)	1943-1947
Frank Carlson (R)	1947-1950
Frank L. Hagaman (R)	1950-1951
Edward F. Arn (R)	1951-1955
Fred Hall (R)	1955-1957
John McCuish (R)	1957
George Docking (D)	1957-1961
John A. Anderson, Jr. (R)	1961-1965
William H. Avery (R)	1965-1967
Robert Docking (D)	1967-1975
Robert F. Bennett (R)	1975-1979
John W. Carlin (D)	1979-1987
Mike Hayden (R)	1987-

MINIMUM AGES

Majority	18
Marriage with parental consent	no minimum with court order
Marriage without parental consent	18
Making a will	18
Buying alcohol	21
Jury duty	18
Leaving school	16
Driver's license	16

CAPITAL PUNISHMENT
None

MILITARY INSTALLATIONS
Total number: 8
Major bases:
  Army: 2
  Air Force: 1

FINANCES

Thousands of dollars

GENERAL REVENUE
Total general revenue   . . . 3,141,972
Total tax revenue 1,915,199
Sales and gross receipts 862,879
Individual income taxes 603,459
Corporate income taxes 159,670

GENERAL EXPENDITURE (1985)
Total general expenditure   . 3,001,923
Education 1,351,679
Public welfare 457,307
Health 53,378
Hospitals 187,866
Natural resources 82,201
Highways 461,377
Police 18,074
Corrections 72,278

FEDERAL AID (1985) 855,394

ECONOMY

The flatlands of Kansas lead the nation in wheat production. Sorghum, alfalfa, rye, oats, barley, and popcorn are other important crops, while cattle and hogs are the main livestock. Total farm cash receipts in 1983 were $5.4 billion, of which cattle and hogs were the chief source. Principal mining products are oil, natural gas, coal, salt, lead, helium, and zinc. In manufacturing, processed foods (primarily packed meat and milled grain), and aircraft are the chief products, followed by small machinery, plastics and rubber, petrochemical products, and chemicals. Value added by manufacture in the state was $8.4 billion in 1982.

EMPLOYMENT (1984)

Thousands of persons
Total number of employed
  workers 1,135
Construction 42.2
Finance, insurance, and
  real estate 51.5
Government 186.4
Manufacturing 176.5
Mining 17.8
Services 183.7
Transportation, communications,
  and utilities 64.1
Wholesale and retail trade 238.3

Percent of civilian labor force
  unemployed (1984) 5.2

DEPARTMENT OF DEFENSE (1985)
Civilian workers employed . . . 7,028
Military personnel 23,627
Contract awards . . . . $2.139 billion

ENERGY SOURCES FOR ELECTRIC UTILITIES (1983)
Percent
Coal 82.4
Gas 16.5
Hydroelectric 0.0
Nuclear 0.0
Petroleum 1.1

TRANSPORTATION
Motor vehicles registered
  in state (1986) 2,176,023
Miles of roads, streets,
  and highways (1986) 132,642
Miles of Class I railway
  operated (1986) 7,376
Airports (1983) 380
Major aviation hubs (1983) · 1
  Largest hub: Wichita

CULTURE AND EDUCATION

Native American tribes
Kansas was formerly the home of the Arapaho, Cherokee, Cheyenne, Comanche, Delaware, Flathead, Illinois, Kansa, Kiowa, Miami, Osage, Oto, Pawnee, Peoria, Piankashaw, Quapaw, Wea, Wichita, and Yskani tribes. Groups that continue to live in the state include the Fox, Iowa, Kickapoo, Ottawa, Potawatomi, Sauk, Shawnee, and Wyandot. There are 4 federal reservations in Kansas.

Religions, ethnicities, and languages
The early settlers of Kansas, many of whom were opponents of slavery from the northeastern states, were augmented after the Civil War by immigrants from central Europe. Swedish, Bohemian, German, and Russian communities remain. In 1980, 4.7 percent of Kansas's population spoke a language other than English at home. Protestants, especially Methodists and Disciples of Christ, predominate; there is a large Catholic population also, and communities of Quakers, Amish, Mennonites, Dunkard Brethren, and Eastern Orthodox.

Major museums and libraries
Dyche Museum of Natural History, University of Kansas, Lawrence
Dwight E. Eisenhower Library, Abilene

Mid-American All-Indian Center,
 Wichita
Spencer Museum of Art, Lawrence
Wichita Art Museum

Major arts organizations
Music Theatre of Wichita
Wichita Symphony Orchestra

Colleges and universities
Number public (1986-87) 29
Number private (1986-87) 23

Total enrollment, in full-time equivalent
 students (1985) 100,800

Public elementary and secondary schools
Expenditure per pupil in average daily
 attendance (1986-87) $4,150
Pupil-teacher ratio (1987) 15.4
Average teacher salary (1986-87) $25,297

Holidays
State Fair, Hutchinson. 2d week of
 September

KANSAS IN LITERATURE

Marguerite Allis *Free Soil* (1957)
The Kansas frontier during the 1850s.

Albert Barnitz (ed. by Robert M. Utley) *Life in Custer's Cavalry: Diaries and Letters of Albert and Jennie Barnitz, 1867–1868* (1987)
A detailed account of army life on the frontier during the 1868 Washita campaign.

Louise Barry *The Beginning of the West: Annals of the Kansas Gateway to the American West, 1540–1854* (1972)

Truman Capote *In Cold Blood* (1966)
Nonfiction account of the murder of a farming family by two psychopaths.

Josephine Carson *Drives My Green Age* (1957)
Novel about a girl growing up in a small town.

Grace Stone Coates *Black Cherries* (1931)
Family life on a farm as seen through the eyes of a child.

David Dary *True Tales of Old-Time Kansas* (1984); *More True Tales of Old-Time Kansas* (1987)
Episodes and anecdotes from state history.

Kenneth Davis *Morning in Kansas* (1952)
Detailed chronicle of a family in a small town.

Leonard Ehrlich *God's Angry Man* (1932)
Historical novel about John Brown, abolitionist martyr.

Martha Farnsworth (ed. Marline and Haskell Springer) *Plains Woman: The Diary of Martha Farnsworth, 1882–1922.* (1986)
Journal of frontier life and customs, with an account of the campaign for women's suffrage.

T. H. Gladstone *The Englishman in Kansas; or, Squatter Life and Border Warfare* (1971)
Report on "bleeding Kansas" written in 1856 by a London journalist.

Frank Gruber *Buffalo Grass* (1956)
Novel about the founding and growth of a trail town in the late 1860s.

Emanuel and Marcet Haldeman-Julius *Dust* (1921)
Realistic moral tale of a pioneer and his wife.

Charles E. Hayes *The Four Winds* (1942)
Realistic novel about the decline of a Catholic farm family in northeastern Kansas during the Depression.

Arthur E. Hertzler *The Horse and Buggy Doctor* (1938)
Experiences of a country doctor.

Edgar Watson Howe *The Story of a Country Town* (1883, rpt. 1962)
This grimly realistic novel about a farming community is often regarded as the earliest American work of naturalistic fiction. Howe, editor of the Atchison *Globe*, was the most famous midwestern journalist of his time.

Langston Hughes *Not without Laughter* (1930)
A novel, related in dialect, about the education of a mulatto boy by his grandmother in a small Kansas town.

William E. Koch *Folklore from Kansas: Customs, Beliefs, and Superstitions* (1980)

Margaret Lynn *Free Soil* (1920); *The Land of Promise* (1927)
Historical novels set during the 1850s, at the time of debate over the slavery question.

John Joseph Mathews *Talking to the Moon* (1945)
Naturalist's observations of life on the prairie.

J. W. McManigal (ed. Grant Heilman) *Farm Town: A Memoir of the 1930's* (1987)

Truman Nelson *The Surveyor* (1960)
Historical novel about John Brown's abolition campaign.

Gordon Parks *The Learning Tree* (1963)
A novel about a black child growing up in a small town in the '20s.

Joseph Stanley Pennell *The History of Nora Beckham* (1948)
Novel about small-town life at the end of the nineteenth century.

Gilbert Rees *Respectable Women* (1954)
Novel about a puritanical family of Kansas women in the 1890s.

Sara Robinson *Kansas . . .* (1856)
Impressions of the state in the 1850s.

Howard Ruede (ed. John Ise) *Sod-House Days: Letters from a Kansas Homesteader, 1877–78* (1983)
Ruede left Pennsylvania with $75 to take up a claim on the frontier.

John Sedges *The Townsman* (1945)
Novel about an English immigrant's efforts to build a prairie community.

Julia Siebel *Narrow Covering* (1956); *For the Time Being* (1962)
Naturalistic novels about prairie life.

Donald Clifford Snow *The Justicer* (1960)
Historical novel about law and order on the prairie in 1889.

Gordon H. Soles *Cornbread and Milk; a Family Gathering* (1960)
Episodes of family life on a Kansas farm.

Joanna L. Stratton (ed.) *Pioneer Women: Voices from the Kansas Frontier* (1981)
Anthology selected from pioneer journals.

Lawrence Svobida *Farming the Dust Bowl: A First-Hand Account from Kansas* (1986)

Calvin Trillin "U.S. Journal: Kansas" *New Yorker* (August 7, 1978)

Paul I. Wellman *Bowl of Brass* (1944)
First in a series of four novels tracing the history of a Kansas town from 1889.

William Allen White *Forty Years on Main Street* (1937)
Collection of editorials from the Emporia *Gazette* portraying

the opinions of a liberal Republican whose pronouncements earned him fame as "the sage of Emporia." White also wrote three novels and five collections of stories with Kansas settings.

W. E. Youngman *Gleanings from Western Prairies* (1882, rpt. 1971)
Accounts of frontier life.

GUIDES TO RESOURCES

Baughman, Robert W. *Kansas in Maps* (1961)

Blackmar, Frank W. *Kansas: A Cyclopedia of State History, Embracing Events, Institutions, Counties, Cities, Towns, Prominent Persons, Etc.* 2 vols. (1912)

Buchanan, Rex and James R. McCauley *Roadside Kansas: A Traveler's Guide to Its Geology and Landmarks* (1987)

Cochran, Mary E. *A Bibliography of Kansas History, Biography, and Fiction* (1965)

Federal Writers' Project *Kansas: A Guide to the Sunflower State* (1939, rpt. 1984)

Heaston, Michael D. (comp.) *Trails of Kansas, a Bibliography* (1969)

Hochstetter, Nancy (ed.) *Travel Historic Kansas: A Guide to Historic Sites and Markers* (1986)

Kansas State Historical Society *Comprehensive Index to Publications: 1875–1930* (1959)

Mechem, Kirke (ed.) and Jennie S. Owen *Annals of Kansas, 1886–1925* 2 vols. (1954, 1956)

O'Brien, Patricia J. *Archeology in Kansas* (1984)

Owen, Jennie S. *The Annals of Kansas, 1886–1925* 2 vols. (1954, 1956)

Self, Huber *Geography of Kansas, Syllabus and Atlas* (1967)
———. *Environment and Man in Kansas: A Geographical Analysis* (1978)

Shortridge, James R. *Kaw Valley Landscapes: A Traveler's Guide to Northeastern Kansas* (1988)

Socolofsky, Homer and Huber Self *Historical Atlas of Kansas* (1978)

Unrau, William E. *The Emigrant Indians of Kansas: A Critical Bibliography* (1979)

SELECTED NONFICTION SOURCES

Andreas, A. T. *History of the State of Kansas* (1883)

Athearn, Robert G. *In Search of Canaan: Black Migration to Kansas 1879–80* (1978)

Bader, Robert S. *The Great Kansas Bond Scandal* (1982)
———. *Prohibition in Kansas: A History* (1986)
———. *Hayseeds, Moralizers, and Methodists: The Twentieth-Century Image of Kansas* (1988)

Barry, Louise *The Beginnings of the West, Annals of the Kansas Gateway to the American West, 1540–1854* (1972)

Blackmar, Frank W. *The Life of Charles Robinson, the First State Governor of Kansas* (1902)

Blanchard, Leola H. *Conquest of Southwest Kansas* (1931)

Boyer, Richard O. *The Legend of John Brown* (1971)

Brewerton, George D. *The War in Kansas* (1856, rpt. 1971)

Bright, John D. et al. (eds.) *Kansas: The First Century* 4 vols. (1956)

Brownlee, Richard S. *Gray Ghosts of the Confederacy: Guerrilla Warfare in the West, 1861–1865* (1984)

Bruce, Janet *The Kansas City Monarchs: Champions of Black Baseball* (1985)

Byers, William N. and J. H. Kellom *Hand Book to the Gold Fields of Nebraska and Kansas* (1859, rpt. 1973)

Castel, Albert *A Frontier State at War: Kansas, 1861–1865* (1958)

Clark, Carroll D. and Roy L. Roberts *People of Kansas: A Demographic and Sociological Study* (1936)

Clugston, William G. *Rascals in Democracy* (1940)

Cox, Thomas C. *Blacks in Topeka, Kansas, 1865–1915: A Social History* (1982)

Crimmins, Harold *A History of the Kansas Central R.R. 1877–1935* (1954)

Dancer, Daniel D. *The Four Seasons of Kansas* (1988)

Davis, Kenneth S. *Soldier of Democracy: A Biography of Dwight Eisenhower* (1945, 1952)
———. *River on the Rampage* (1953)
———. *Kansas: A Bicentennial History* (States and the Nation series) (1976)

Diggs, Annie L. *The Story of Jerry Simpson* (1920)

Dykstra, Robert R. *Cattle Towns* (1968)

Ebbutt, Percy G. *Emigrant Life in Kansas* (1886, rpt. 1975)

Evans, Terry *Prairie: Images of Ground and Sky* (1986)

Fitzgerald, Daniel *Ghost Towns of Kansas* 2 vols. (1976–1979)

Fowler, Richard B. *Alfred M. Landon* (1936)

Freeman, G. D. *Midnight and Noonday, or, The Incidental History of Southern Kansas and the Indian Territory, 1871–1890* (1984)

Gaeddert, Gustave R. *The Birth of Kansas* (1940)

Garwood, Darrell *Crossroads of America: The Story of Kansas City* (1948)

Gates, Frye W. *Thirty Years in Topeka: A Historical Sketch* (1886)

Griffith, Sally Foreman *Home-Town News: William Allen White and the Emporia Gazette* (1989)

Haywood, C. Robert *Trails South: The Wagon-road Economy in the Dodge City–Panhandle Region* (1986)

Hope, Holly *Garden City: Dreams in a Kansas Town* (1988)

Howes, Charles C. *This Place Called Kansas* (1952)

Hunt, Elvid *History of Fort Leavenworth, 1827–1927* (1926)

Ise, John *Sod and Stubble: The Story of a Kansas Homestead* (1936)

Langsdorf, Edgar et al. *Kansas: A Pictorial History* (1961)

Lowman, H. E. *Narrative of the Lawrence Massacre* (1864)

Lyle, Wes and James Fisher (eds.) *Kansas Impressions: Photographs and Words* (1972)

Malin, James C. *John Brown and the Legend of Fifty-Six* 2 vols. (1942, rpt. 1970)
———. (ed. Robert P. Swierenga) *History and Ecology: Studies of the Grassland* (1984)

McCoy, Joseph *Historic Sketches of the Cattle Trade of the West and Southwest* (1874)

McCoy, Sondra V. M. and Jan Hults *1001 Kansas Place Names* (1988)

Mead, James R. (ed. Schuyler Jones) *Hunting and Trading on the Great Plains, 1859–1875* (1986)

Miller, Nyle H. and Joseph W. Snell *Why the West Was Wild* (1963)
———. *Great Gunfighters of the Kansas Cowtowns, 1867–1886* (1967)

———. *Kansas—The 34th Star: A Photographic Treasury of Kansas Issued in Commemoration of the American Bicentennial* (1976)

Miller, Wallace E. *Peopling of Kansas* (1906)

Miner, H. Craig *Wichita: The Early Years, 1865–1880* (1982)
———. *West of Wichita: Settling the High Plains of Kansas, 1865–1890* (1986)
——— and William E. Unrau *The End of Indian Kansas: A Study of Cultural Revolution, 1854–1871* (1978)

Nevins, Allan *Kansas and the Stream of American Destiny* (1954)

Nichols, Alice *Bleeding Kansas* (1954)

Noble, Glenn *John Brown and the Jim Lane Trail* (1977)

Nugent, Walter T. K. *The Tolerant Populist: Kansas Populism and Nativism* (1963)

O'Neal, Bill *Henry Brown, the Outlaw-Marshal* (1980)

Oliva, Leo *Fort Hays* (1980)
———. *Fort Larned* (1982)
———. *Ash Rock and the Stone Church: The History of a Kansas Rural Community* (1983)

Painter, Nell Irvin *Exodusters: Black Migration to Kansas After Reconstruction* (1977)

Phillips, William A. *The Conquest of Kansas* (1856, rpt. 1971)

Potter, Don *1854–1954: Lawrence—100 Years of History Significant to Kansas* (1954)

Rawley, James A. *Race and Politics; "Bleeding Kansas" and the Coming of the Civil War* (1969)

Reimer, Gustav E. and G. R. Gaeddert *Exiled by the Czar: Cornelius Jansen and the Great Mennonite Migration, 1874* (1956)

Reinbach, Edna *Music and Musicians in Kansas* (1930)

Rich, Everett (ed.) *The Heritage of Kansas: Selected Commentaries on Past Times* (1960)

Richmond, Robert W. *Kansas; a Land of Contrasts* (1974)

Rosa, Joseph G. *They Called Him Wild Bill* (1964, rpt. 1974)

Rydjord, John *Kansas Place-Names* (1972)

Schruben, Francis W. *Wea Creek to El Dorado; Oil in Kansas, 1860–1920* (1972)

Scott, Otto J. *The Secret Six: John Brown and the Abolitionist Movement* (1979)

Snell, Jessie K. *Lore of the Great Plains* (1970)

Snyder, Ralph *We Kansas Farmers* (1953)

Spring, Leverett W. *Kansas: The Prelude to the War for the Union* (1907, rpt. 1973)

Starr, Stephen Z. *Jennison's Jayhawkers; a Civil War Cavalry Regiment and its Commander* (1974)

Streeter, Floyd B. *Prairie Trails and Cow Towns* (1936)
———. *The Kaw* (Rivers of America series) (1941)

Thornton, W. *Life of Alfred M. Landon* (1936)

University of Kansas *Territorial Kansas: Studies Commemorating the Centennial* (1954)

Vandergriff, James H. (comp.) *The Indians of Kansas* (1973)

Vestal, Stanley *Dodge City: Queen of Cow Towns* (1952)

Villard, Oswald Garrison *John Brown, Eighteen Hundred to Eighteen Fifty-Nine: A Biography Fifty Years After* (1910)

White, William A. *Autobiography of William Allen White* (1946)

Whittemore, Margaret *Historic Kansas: A Centenary Sketchbook* (1954)

Williams, Burton J. (ed.) *Essays on Kansas History: In Memoriam George L. Anderson, Jayhawker, Historian* (1977)

Wood, Charles L. *The Kansas Beef Industry* (1980)

Woodling, Chuck *Against All Odds: How Kansas Won the 1988 NCAA Championship* (1989)

Woods, Randall B. *A Black Odyssey: John Lewis Waller and the Promise of American Life, 1878–1900* (1981)

Wright, Robert *Dodge City, Cowboy Capital* (1913)

Zornow, William F. *Kansas: A History of the Jayhawk State* (1957)

KENTUCKY

Kentucky is an east south central state with an irregular border. It is bounded on the north by the Ohio River, Indiana, and Ohio; on the northeast by the Big Sandy and Tug rivers and West Virginia; on the southeast by Virginia; on the south by Tennessee; and on the west by the Mississippi and Ohio rivers and by Missouri and Illinois.

FULL NAME Commonwealth of Kentucky
POSTAL ABBREVIATION KY
INHABITANT Kentuckian
ADMITTED TO THE UNION June 1, 1792.
15th state
POPULATION (est. 1987) 3,727,000.
Percent of US total: 1.53%. Rank: 23d

CAPITAL CITY Frankfort, located on the Kentucky River in north central Kentucky; population 27,000 (est. 1984). It was founded in 1786 and was named the capital when Kentucky was admitted to statehood in 1792.

STATE NAME AND NICKNAMES From the Wyandot Indian word for "plain." Also known as the Bluegrass State, the Hemp State, the Tobacco State, and the Dark and Bloody Ground, in reference to the struggles between native tribes and white settlers.

STATE SEAL On a copper-colored field, a relief of two men — a frontiersman and a statesman — greeting each other, with the state motto above and below them, and around the border the legend "Commonwealth of Kentucky" decorated by sprigs of the state flower.

MOTTO United We Stand, Divided We Fall

SONG "My Old Kentucky Home," lyrics and music by Stephen Foster.

SYMBOLS
Flower goldenrod
Tree coffee tree
Bird Kentucky cardinal
Wild animal game species gray squirrel
Language English
Shakespeare festival Shakespeare in Central Park, Louisville
Tug-of-war championship Nelson County Fair Tug-of-War Championship Contest

LICENSE PLATES (1) Dark blue on white, with blue spires and roof bearing the county name, blue trotting horses, and the legend "Bluegrass State." (2) White in dark blue, with the county name.

FLAG On a field of blue, the state seal in white, without its border, with green and yellow flowering goldenrod sprigs below it and the legend "Commonwealth of Kentucky" in yellow above it.

<table>
<tr><td colspan="2" align="center">**GEOGRAPHY AND CLIMATE**</td></tr>
</table>

Three of Kentucky's borders are defined by rivers. The eastern part of the state is a maze of steep mountains, narrow ridges, and coal valleys; coal is mined in the western area as well. The Bluegrass region of central Kentucky, renowned for its superior pasturage, rests on a foundation of phosphate-rich limestone.

AREA 40,909 square miles. Rank: 37th

INLAND WATER 740 square miles

GEOGRAPHIC CENTER Marion, 3 miles NNW of Lebanon

ELEVATIONS *Highest point:* Black Mountain, Harlan County, 4,145 feet. *Lowest point:* Mississippi River, Fulton County, 257 feet. *Mean elevation:* 7 feet

MAJOR RIVERS Ohio, Kentucky

MAJOR LAKES AND RESERVOIRS Kentucky, Barkley, Cumberland

LAND USE

	Thousands of acres
Urban (1982)	636
Rural (1982)	22,866
Cropland (1982)	5,934
Pastureland (1982)	5,880
Rangeland (1982)	0
Forestland (1982)	10,158
State parks and recreation areas (1983)	43
National park system (1984)	79
National forest system (1984)	2,102
Tribal lands (1984)	0

TEMPERATURES The highest recorded temperature was 114°F on July 28, 1930, at Greensburg. The lowest was -34°F on January 28, 1963, at Cynthiana.

<table>
<tr><td align="center">**NATIONAL SITES**</td></tr>
</table>

NATIONAL HISTORIC SITE Abraham Lincoln Birthplace

NATIONAL HISTORICAL PARK Cumberland Gap

NATIONAL PARK Mammoth Cave

NATIONAL SCENIC RIVER AND RIVERWAY Big South Fork National River and Recreation Area

NATIONAL WILDLIFE REFUGE Reelfoot

<table>
<tr><td align="center">**HISTORY**</td></tr>
</table>

1654	Colonel Abraham Wood and fellow travellers chart a large portion of what is now Kentucky.
1673	Gabriel Arthur travels through northeast Kentucky as a prisoner of the Indians.
1682	Robert Cavelier, Sieur de La Salle, claims Louisiana Territory, which includes Kentucky, for King Louis XIV.
1736	The first village in Kentucky is established on the Ohio River by French traders.
1750	*April-June.* Virginian Dr. Thomas Walker and companions discover the Cumberland Gap. They spend several weeks exploring the eastern mountain range of Kentucky on behalf of the Loyal Land Company.
1752	Lewis Evans issues the first map of the region that includes Kentucky.
1769	Daniel Boone explores Kentucky wilderness for white settlement.
1774	James Harrod and a party from Pennsylvania arrive and establish Harrodsburg, the first permanent settlement.
1775	Daniel Boone marks the Wilderness Road and constructs Fort Boonesborough on the Kentucky River.
	Transylvania Company, headed by Colonel Richard Henderson, illegally purchases most of Kentucky from Cherokee in the Treaty of the Sycamore Shoals.
1776	*December 6.* Kentucky County is created.
	The Revolutionary War. Pioneers such as Daniel Boone and George Rogers Clark defend Kentucky from British-supported Indian attacks.
1777	Kentucky County sends representatives to the Virginia House of Burgesses.
	Saltmaking becomes Kentucky's earliest industry.
	Indian attacks on settlers are devastating.
1778	*September.* Shawnee and French lay siege to Boonesboro.
1779	Virginia legislature permits unsupervised surveys of Kentucky land. Badly marked claims lead to bitter feuds and lawsuits.
1780	*Spring.* Three hundred large boats full of pioneer families arrive at the Falls of the Ohio.

1782	*August 19.* Kentucky force is quickly defeated in the Battle of Blue Licks.
1783	The first horse race in Kentucky is run at Humble's Race Path.
	Evan Williams establishes a distillery, producing the first whiskey in Louisville, possibly the first in Kentucky.
1786	The General Assembly of Virginia consents to the separation of Kentucky.
1787	The *Kentucky Gazette* is established by John Bradford.
1791	*February.* Congress agrees to admit Kentucky as a state and authorizes the framing of a constitution.
1792	*June 1.* Kentucky joins the Union as the 15th state.
	June 4. The Kentucky legislature assembles at Lexington.
1798	*November 16.* The Kentucky Resolutions are passed.
1801	*August.* The Great Religious Revival along the frontier is sparked by a camp meeting at Cane Ridge attended by 20,000.
1805	The state legislature charters a company to build a canal around the Falls of the Ohio River at Louisville.
1812-1815	After the War of 1812 Kentuckians turn to farming. Tobacco production increases rapidly.
1815	The first steamboat reaches Louisville from New Orleans.
1819	Petroleum is found in southern Cumberland River by Martin Beatty, who was drilling for salt.
1828	Thomas Rice, known as "Daddy" Rice, introduces the minstrel character, "Jim Crow," in Louisville.
1830	*October 22.* The first rail of the Lexington and Ohio railroad is laid.
1833	*February.* A non-importation law is passed, aimed at the interstate slave trade.
1845	*August 14. The True American*, an emancipationist weekly, is closed down by a mob.
1847	*December.* Telegraph lines connect larger Kentucky cities with Nashville, TN and Cincinnati, OH.
1851	*March.* Emancipated slaves are compelled to leave the state.
1855	*August 6.* Twenty-two people die during "Bloody Monday" riots.
1861	*April 15.* The Civil War. Governor Beriah Magoffin refuses to furnish militia to Union. State's neutrality is guaranteed by President Lincoln.
	September 3. Confederates invade the state at bluffs overlooking the Mississippi.
	September 21 Louisville is secured as headquarters and a supply depot for Union forces. No longer neutral ground, the state is further divided as Kentuckians fight for North and South.
1862	*April.* The Battle of Shiloh.
	July. John Hunt Morgan and his men conduct raids behind Union lines into central Kentucky.
	October 4. Inaugural ceremonies of Provisional (Confederate) Government of Kentucky held at Frankfort. Four hours later this government flees, never to return.
	October 8. General Braxton Bragg attempts to invade Kentucky and recruit Southern sympathizers.
1863	*December 24.* Sugar and molasses reach Louisville for the first time since the Confederate blockade of the Mississippi was established in 1861.
1864	*January 4.* Governor Thomas E. Bramlette issues a proclamation indicating that he will hold southern sympathizers responsible for damage caused by guerilla raids.
	July. President Lincoln places Kentucky under martial law.
1865	*March 12.* Sue Manday (Marcellus Jerome Clark), notorious guerilla, is hanged in Louisville.
	December. The legislature repeals drastic wartime acts.
1868	*March 20.* Jesse James and gang rob Russellville bank.
1872	*April 27.* The Louisville Public Library opens with 20,000 books and 100,000 museum specimens.
1875	*May 17.* The first Kentucky Derby, held in Louisville and inspired by Colonel Meriwether Lewis Clark, Jr., is won by Aristides.
1879	The first telephone exchange in Louisville is opened.
1882	McCoy-Hatfield feud erupts.

1883	*August.* The Southern Exposition opens at Louisville.
1888	James William "Honorable Dick" Tate, state treasurer for 20 years, disappears with one-quarter of a million dollars in state funds.
1890	Tobacco replaces hemp as Kentucky's leading crop.
1897-1898	In a violent grassroots movement, "tollgate riders" attack gatekeepers employed by private road companies.
1902	In "Bloody Breathitt" County, the murder of Ben Hargis brings the Hargis-Cockrill feud into the open. Eventually, 37 people die.
1905-1908	In the "Black Patch War," night riders burn tobacco warehouses in organized resistance against prevailing market conditions in the tobacco industry.
1912	*May 4.* Ed Callahan is killed, bringing to an end the Breathitt County feuds. Soldiers train at camps Knox, Thomas, Zachary Taylor, and Stanley.
1918	Construction of modern road system is begun.
1921	Tobacco industry is hit hard by the Depression.
1924	*March 18.* Tornado destroys several towns.
1925	The *Louisville Courier Journal* originates the National Spelling Bee.
1926	Mammoth Cave National Park is established with 52,129 acres.
1932	Camp Knox becomes a permanent military post known as Fort Knox.
1937	The US Government establishes its gold vault at Fort Knox.
1941-45	World War II. About 325,000 Kentuckians are in the armed forces.
1948	The case of *Johnson vs. the University of Kentucky* forces the school to admit qualified black students.
1953	An atomic energy plant is completed near Paducah.
1963	*November 13.* President John F. Kennedy announces plans for aid to the coal-mining industry in the Appalachian area.
1964	The Tennessee Valley Authority opens the Land Between the Lakes recreation area in western Kentucky.
1966	*January.* The "Dixie Flyer" makes the last run on the Louisville and Nashville Railroad.
1970	Coal mine explosion near Wooton kills 36.
1973	Farmers plant over one million acres of soybeans.
1976	*March 9-11.* Twenty-six are killed in two methane gas explosions in the Scotia Coal Company's Black Mountain Mine.
1977	*August 30.* Louisville public schools open quietly after several years of controversy over court-ordered busing.
1986	Governor Martha Collins' political position is strengthened when she is successful in attracting Toyota Motors of Japan to construct an $800 million car assembly plant near Lexington.

DEMOGRAPHY

Population (est. 1987) . . . 3,727,000
Population (1980) 3,726,000
Population density in persons
  per square mile (1980) 90.6

POPULATION BY RACE (1980)
American Indian/Aleut/
  Eskimo 3,610
Asian/Pacific Islander 9,971
Black 259,490
Hispanic 27,403
White 3,379,648
Other 8,714

POPULATION CHARACTERISTICS (1980)
              Percent of state population
Urban 50.9
Rural 49.1
Under 18 . . . . 29.6

65 or older 11.2
College-educated 11.0
Families below poverty line . . . 14.6
Public assistance recipients 7.2

Per capita personal income
  (1986) $11,129
Millionaires per 100,000
  residents (1982) 94.7
Average life expectancy in
  years (1980) 73.1
Marriage rate per 1,000
  residents (1986) 12.7
Divorce rate per 1,000
  residents (1986) 5.2
Birth rate per 1,000
  residents (1985) 13.9
Infant mortality rate per 1,000
  births (1985) 10.8

Abortion rate per 1,000
live births (1985) 189
Crime rate per 100,000
residents (1985)
Violent 334.4
Property 2,757.8
Federal and state prisoners per
100,000 residents (1984) 128
Alcohol consumption in gallons per
capita (1985) 31.1
Deaths from motor vehicle accidents
per 100,000 residents (1985) . . 19.1

MAJOR CITIES

	Population
Covington (1980)	49,585
Lexington-Fayette (est. 1984)	210,150
Louisville (est. 1984)	289,843
Owensboro (est. 1984)	55,723

GOVERNMENT AND POLITICS

Number of US Representatives 7
Electoral votes 9

POLITICAL PARTY NOMINEES FROM STATE
*winner

Henry Clay (Democratic-Republican)	1824	P
Henry Clay (Whig faction)	1824	VP
Henry Clay (Republican)	1832	P
Richard Mentor Johnson* (Democratic-Republican)	1836	VP
Richard Mentor Johnson (Democratic-Republican-faction)	1840	VP
Henry Clay (Whig)	1844	P
William Orlando Butler (D)	1848	VP
John Cabell Breckinridge* (D)	1856	VP
John Cabell Breckinridge (National Democratic, Social Democratic)	1860	P
Green Clay Smith (Prohibition)	1876	P
Simon Bolivar Buckner (National Democratic)	1896	VP

Andrew Johnson (Prohibition)	1944 VP
Alben William Barkley* (D)	1948 VP

PRESIDENTIAL PRIMARY ELECTION In 1988, Kentucky sent 60 Democratic delegates and 38 Republican delegates to the national conventions.

CONSTITUTION Kentucky has had four constitutions: 1792, 1799, 1850, and the present one, adopted in 1891.

LEGISLATURE The General Assembly is divided into the Senate (38 members, 4-year term, minimum age 30) and the House of Representatives (100 members, 2-year term, minimum age 24). In 1987, the salary was $100 per day.

JUDICIARY The highest court is the Supreme Court, with 7 judges serving 8-year terms. In 1987, the annual salary was $65,633.

EXECUTIVE The governor serves a 4-year term; the minimum age for holding office is 30. In 1987, the annual salary was $68,364. There are 7 other elected officials.

PRESIDENTIAL VOTE 1948-1988 *(in percents)*

Year	State Winner	Democratic	Republican
1948	Truman (D)	56.7	41.5
1852	Stevenson (D)	49.9	49.8
1956	Eisenhower (R)	45.2	54.3
1960	Nixon (R)	46.4	53.6
1964	Johnson (D)	64.0	35.7
1968	Nixon (R)	37.7	43.8
1972	Nixon (R)	34.8	63.4
1976	Carter (D)	52.8	45.6
1980	Reagan (R)	47.6	49.1
1984	Reagan (R)	39.4	60.0
1988	Bush (R)	44.0	56.0

GOVERNORS

Isaac Shelby (Democratic-Republican)	1791-1796
James Garrard (D-R)	1796-1804

Christopher Greenup (D-R)	1804-1808
Charles Scott (D-R)	1808-1812
Isaac Shelby (D-R)	1812-1816
George Madison (D-R)	1816
Gabriel Slaughter (D-R)	1816-1820

John Adair (D-R)	1820-1824
Joseph Desha (D-R)	1824-1828
Thomas Metcalfe (National Republican)	1828-1832
John Breathitt (D)	1832-1834
James T. Morehead (National Republican)	1834-1836
James Clark (Whig)	1836-1839
Charles A. Wickliffe (Whig)	1839-1840
Robert P. Letcher (Whig)	1840-1844
William Owsley (Whig)	1844-1848
John J. Crittenden (Whig)	1848-1850
John L. Helm (Whig)	1850-1851
Lazarus W. Powell (D)	1851-1855
Charles S. Morehead (Know-Nothing)	1855-1859
Beriah Magoffin (D)	1859-1862
James F. Robinson (Union)	1862-1863
Thomas E. Bramlete (Union)	1863-1867
John L. Helm (D)	1867
John W. Stevenson (D)	1867-1871
Preston H. Leslie (D)	1871-1875
James B. McCreary (D)	1875-1879
Luke P. Blackburn (D)	1879-1883
J. Proctor Knott (D)	1883-1887
Simon B. Buckner (D)	1887-1891
John Young Brown (D)	1891-1895
William O. Bradley (R)	1895-1899
William S. Taylor (R)	1899-1900
William Goebel (D)	1900
J.C.W. Beckham (D)	1900-1907
Augustus E. Willson (R)	1907-1911
James B. McCreary (D)	1911-1915
Augustus O. Stanley (D)	1915-1919
Edwin P. Morrow (R)	1919-1924
William J. Fields (D)	1924-1927
Flem D. Sampson (R)	1927-1931
Ruby Laffoon (D)	1931-1935
A.B. Chandler (D)	1935-1939
Keen Johnson (D)	1939-1943
Simeon S. Willis (R)	1943-1947
Earle C. Clements (D)	1947-1951
Lawrence W. Wetherby (D)	1951-1955
A.B. Chandler (D)	1955-1959
Bert T. Combs (D)	1959-1963
Edward T. Breathitt (D)	1963-1967
Louie B. Nunn (R)	1967-1971
Wendell Ford (D)	1971-1974
Julian M. Carroll (D)	1974-1980
John Y. Brown Jr. (D)	1980-1984
Martha Layne Collins (D)	1984-

MINIMUM AGES

Majority	18
Marriage with parental consent	
. . . no minimum with court order	
Marriage without parental consent	18
Making a will	18
Buying alcohol	21
Jury duty	18
Leaving school	16
Driver's license	16

CAPITAL PUNISHMENT
Number executed 1976-88: 0
On death row Aug. 1, 1988: 33

MILITARY INSTALLATIONS
Total number: 7
Major bases:
  Army: 2

FINANCES

Thousands of dollars

GENERAL REVENUE (1985)

Total general revenue	5,396,063
Total tax revenue	3,012,713
Sales and gross receipts	1,351,422
Individual income taxes	776,569
Corporate net income taxes	211,284

GENERAL EXPENDITURE (1985)

Total general expenditure	4,982,194
Education	2,015,844
Public welfare	862,512
Health	134,944
Hospitals	153,233
Natural resources	149,853
Highways	629,412
Police	64,427
Corrections	97,498

FEDERAL AID (1985) 1,763,550

ECONOMY

Kentucky's chief crops include tobacco, soybeans, wheat, corn, oats, barley, rye, and bluegrass seed. Horses, especially thoroughbreds, are popular livestock, but cattle and calves are the main cash stock. Cash farm receipts were $2.8 billion in 1983. The chief mineral product is bituminous coal, mined in the eastern part of the state, along with oil, natural gas, clay, zinc, sand, and gravel. Timber production is about 500 million board feet per year, mostly of softwoods such as Southern pine. Kentucky's manufactures include bourbon whiskey, cigarettes, feed products, farm implements, plumbing and heating fixtures, trucks, and chemicals. In 1982, value added from manufacture was $11.8 billion.

EMPLOYMENT (1984)

Thousands of persons

Total number of employed workers	1,156
Construction	49.7
Finance, insurance, and real estate	55.1
Government	220.8
Manufacturing	257.8
Mining	45.3
Services	232.3
Transportation, communications, and utilities	64.9
Wholesale and retail trade	280.2
Percent of civilian work force unemployed (1984)	9.3

DEPARTMENT OF DEFENSE (1985)

Civilian workers employed	14,793
Military personnel	40,782
Contract awards	$506 million

ENERGY SOURCES FOR ELECTRIC UTILITIES (1983)

Percent

Coal	93.9
Gas	0.2
Hydroelectric	5.6
Nuclear	0.0
Petroleum	0.3

TRANSPORTATION

Motor vehicles registered in state (1986)	2,685,262
Miles of roads, streets, and highways (1986)	69,596
Miles of Class I railway operated (1986)	2,846
Airports	127
Major aviation hubs	2

Largest hub: Louisville

CULTURE AND EDUCATION

Native American tribes

Kentucky was formerly home to the Chickasaw, Ofo, and Shawnee tribes.

Religions, ethnicities, and languages

The vast majority of Kentucky's population — 99 percent — were born in the US, almost three quarters of them in Kentucky. Most are descended from the English and Scotch-Irish settlers who came from the eastern states and from the Germans, French, and Blacks who arrived by the mid-19th century. In 1980, 1.8 percent of Kentucky's population spoke a language other than English at home. Protestants predominate.

Major museums and libraries

Audubon Museum, Henderson
Kentucky Historical Collection, Frankfort
J.B. Speed Art Museum, Lousiville

Major arts organizations

Actors Theatre of Louisville
Kentucky Opera, Louisville
Louisville Ballet
Louisville Orchestra
Stage One: The Louisville Children's Theatre

Colleges and universities

Number public (1986-87) 21
Number private (1986-87) 35
Total enrollment, in full-time equivalent students (1985) 110,500

Public elementary and secondary schools

Expenditure per pupil in average daily attendance (1986-87) $3,107
Pupil-teacher ratio (1987) 18.6
Average teacher salary (1986-87) $23,560

Holidays

Robert E. Lee's Birthday. January 19
Franklin Delano Roosevelt's Birthday. January 30
Jefferson Davis's Birthday and Confederate Memorial Day. June 3
State Fair, Louisville. No fixed date

KENTUCKY IN LITERATURE

James Lane Allen *The Choir Invisible* (1897)
Historical novel set in Fayette County in 1795, but chiefly concerned with moral and social values.

Harriette Simpson Arnow *Hunter's Horn* (1944)
A poor white hill farmer's struggle to support his family. Arnow's second novel, which was admired for its realism, draws on her own experience of the Cumberland region, as does *Mountain Path* (1936), a semi-autobiographical story of a rural teacher. *The Kentucky Trace* (1974) is a historical novel of the revolutionary war. She also wrote *The Dollmaker* (1954), a novel about a Kentucky woman in wartime Detroit, and three works of social history: *Seedtime on the Cumberland* (1960), *The Flowering of the Cumberland* (1963), and *Old Burnside* (1977), a portrait of small-town life in the early 1900s.

Wendell Berry *Nathan Coulter* (1960); *A Place on Earth* (1967); *The Memory of Old Jack* (1974); *The Wild Birds: Six Stories of the Port William Membership* (1986)
The author, a native of Henry County, has described his upbringing and attachment to agrarian values in a sequence of novels, essays, and poems.

Henry Bibb *Narrative of the Life and Adventures of Henry Bibb, an American Slave* (1849)

Robert Montgomery Bird *Nick of the Woods; or, The Jibbenainosey* (1837)
Classic romance set in 1782.

Charles Neville Buck *The Call of the Cumberlands* (1913)
Love story set against the background of a family feud in a mountain community. One of the author's six novels set in rural Kentucky published between 1913 and 1935.

Ben L. Burman *Four Lives of Mundy Tolliver* (1953)
Novel about a World War II veteran who returns to Coal Creek.

Lorine Letcher Butler *My Old Kentucky Home* (1930)
Essays on regional topics.

James M. Cain *The Butterfly* (1947)
Life in a coal mining town on the West Virginia border.

Marie Campbell *Cloud-Walking* (1942, 2d ed. 1971)
Tales of mountain people.

Harry M. Caudill *Dark Hills to Westward: The Saga of Jennie Wiley* (1969)
Fictionalized version of a historical incident of 1789 in which an eastern Kentucky woman was abducted by Indians. Caudill is best known for his social history of Appalachia, *Night Comes to the Cumberlands* (1963), and has also written a novel about the ravages of mining, *The Senator from Slaughter County* (1973).

Rebecca Caudill *My Appalachia* (1966)
Memories of rural regions before the coming of the mines.

Winston Churchill *The Crossing* (1904)
Historical romance of the frontier.

Billy C. Clark *A Long Row to Hoe* (1960)
Autobiographical account of a rural childhood by a popular Appalachian writer from the Catlettsburg region.

Irvin S. Cobb *Old Judge Priest* (1916)
Sketches of rural and small-town life c.1900.

Olive Tilford Dargan *Highland Annals* (1925)
Stories of a mountain farm in the Unakas.

Gwen Davenport *Family Fortunes* (1949)
Family life in rural Kentucky.

Daniel Drake *Pioneer Life in Kentucky* (1870)
Letters recalling pioneer days, addressed to the author's children.

Allan W. Eckert *The Court-Martial of Daniel Boone* (1973)
Novel based on events of 1778.

John Fetterman *Stinking Creek* (1967)
Study of a Knox County community.

John Filson *The Discovery, Settlement, and Present State of Kentucke* (1784, rpt. 1962)

The first history of the state and the earliest account of the adventures of Daniel Boone.

Clark B. Firestone *Bubbling Waters* (1938)
Account of a walking tour of the Kentucky and Tennessee mountains.

Mary Donna Foley *Kentucky in Fiction: An Annotated Bibliography 1951–1980* (1981)

John William Fox, Jr. *Hell-fer-Sartain and Other Stories* (1897); *The Kentuckians* (1898); *The Little Shepherd of Kingdom Come* (1903); *The Trail of the Lonesome Pine* (1908); *Heart of the Hills* (1913)
Fox's tales and novels of mountain people exploited a vogue for regional fiction and contributed to the myth of wild, romantic Appalachia.

Lucy Furman *The Quare Women: A Story of the Kentucky Hills* (1923)
Novel about the founding of a settlement school. One of the author's five Kentucky novels about rural life. Furman also wrote an autobiography of her days as a mountain schoolteacher, *Mothering on Perilous* (1913).

Janice Holt Giles *The Enduring Hills* (1950, rpt. 1988)
Novel about a farm boy's reluctant affection for his birthplace. Giles, who lived in Knifley from 1945 to 1979, wrote several novels with Kentucky settings, including *The Kentuckians* (1953), *Hannah Fowler* (1956), and *The Land beyond the Mountains* (1958), a trilogy about pioneer tales. In *The Believers* (1957) Giles deals with the Shaker movement of the early nineteenth century.

Caroline Gordon *Penhally* (1931); *The Captive* (1932); *Aleck Maury, Sportsman* (1934); *The Garden of Adonis* (1937); *None Shall Look Back* (1937); *Green Centuries* (1941)
A related series of novels dealing with the fortunes of Kentucky families.

Harlan H. Hatcher *Tunnel Hill* (1931); *Patterns of Wolfpen* (1934)
Novels set in rural Kentucky depicting social changes brought by the advent of the lumber industry.

Joseph Hergesheimer *The Limestone Tree* (1931)
Historical novel about pioneers and their descendants.

Felix Holt *The Gabriel Horn* (1951); *Dan'l Boone Kissed Me* (1954)
Popular historical romances set in pioneer times, and in 1845.

Henry H. Hornsby *Lonesome Valley* (1949)
Novel about a mountain boy's growth to maturity.

Gilbert Imlay *The Emigrants* 3 vols. (1793)
This sentimental romance of pioneer days is the first novel written in Kentucky.

Willard R. Jillson *Tales of the Dark and Bloody Ground* (1930)
———. *Early Kentucky Literature, 1750–1849* (1932)
———. *Pioneer Kentucky* (1934)

Elmore Leonard *The Moonshine War* (1969)
A violent thriller about a mountain moonshiner.

John Uri Lloyd *Stringtown on the Pike* (1900)
First in a series of collections of regional tales set in Boone County.

Percy Mackaye *Tall Tales of the Kentucky Mountains* (1926)
Twelve tales told in the mountain vernacular by the legendary figure of Solomon Skell.

Gene Markey *Kentucky Pride* (1956)
Romantic novel set during Reconstruction.

Bobbie Ann Mason *Shiloh and Other Stories* (1982); *Love Life* (1989)
Stories set in contemporary western Kentucky, often depicting the collapse of a social order based on agriculture.

Bettye L. Mastin *Lexington, 1779: Pioneer Kentucky, as Described by Early Settlers* (1979)

Ed McClanahan *The Natural Man* (1983)
Comic novel about a boy's adolescence in a small town.

Josephine McGill *Folksongs of the Kentucky Mountains* (1917)

Gurney Norman *Kinfolks* (1977)
Stories of an eastern Kentucky family.

Ernest Poole *Nurses on Horseback* (1932)
Account of the frontier nursing service in the Kentucky mountains.

Joe Ashby Porter *The Kentucky Stories* (1983)
Tales of contemporary Kentucky people.

Alice Hegan Rice *Mrs. Wiggs of the Cabbage Patch* (1901)
A portrait of life in Louisville at the turn of the century, based on the author's experience as a social worker. Rice wrote eight novels about simple Kentucky folk but none equalled the success of her first publication, which is notable for its accurate portrayal of slum children. Alice Rice was the wife of the poet Cale Young Rice, author of *Early Reaping* (1929), a saga of a Kentucky family.

Jean Ritchie *Singing Family of the Cumberlands* (1955, rpt. 1963, 1980)
Memoir of a folk musician born in the Cumberlands in 1922, containing traditional songs and illustrations by Maurice Sendak.

Elizabeth Madox Roberts *The Time of Man* (1926)
This novel about the wife of a poor tenant mountain farmer is the best-known of the author's five works set in rural Kentucky, which include *The Haunted Mirror* (1932), a volume of short stories, and *The Great Meadow* (1930), a historical novel about pioneers.

Leonard W. Roberts *South from Hell-fer-Sartin: Kentucky Mountain Folk Tales* (1955, rpt. 1988)
Folk tales collected in Leslie and Perry Counties in the 1950s.
————. *Up Cutshin and Down Greasy: Folkways of a Kentucky Mountain Family* (1959, rpt. 1988)
An account of the folkways of the Couch family, long-time residents of the mountains at the headwaters of the Kentucky river, with descriptions of their farming methods, lumbering and mining work, musical tradition, and bootlegging activities.

James Sherburne *Hacey Miller* (1971); *The Way to Fort Pillow* (1972); *Stand Like Men* (1973)
Historical novels dealing with the abolition movement, the Civil War period, and the coal war of 1931 in Harlan County.

William Gilmore Simms *Beauchampe, or, the Kentucky Tragedy* (1842)
The best-known of Simms' "border romances," sensational accounts of Southern pioneer life. This novel is based on an actual crime of passion that occurred in 1825, and also inspired Mary E. MacMichael's *The Kentucky Tragedy* (1838) and Charles Fenno Hoffman's romance *Greyslaer* (1849).

The violent story was used again in Robert Penn Warren's *World Enough and Time* (1950) and Joseph Shearing's *To Bed at Noon* (1951).

James Still *River of Earth* (1940); *On Troublesome Creek* (1941); *Pattern of a Man and Other Stories* (1976)
A novel and a collection of short stories about Knott County mountain people. Still has also collected regional folklore in four works for children, including *Way Down Yonder on Troublesome Creek: Appalachian Riddles and Rusties* (1974).

Jesse Stuart *Head o' W-Hollow* (1936); *Men of the Mountains* (1941)
Realistic short stories about the author's birthplace near Riverton. Stuart wrote eighteen volumes of stories and nine novels about mountain people while working as a schoolteacher and superintendent of Greenup County schools. His first novel, *Cradle of the Copperheads*, which is largely an autobiographical account of Depression hardships in the mountains, was not published until 1988. *Taps for Private Tussie* (1943) is a comic folk tale.

Jean Thomas *The Traipsin' Woman* (1933)
One of numerous collections of reminiscences, folkways, and ballads by a celebrated local folklorist and musician.

Lawrence S. and **Algernon D. Thompson** *The Kentucky Novel* (1953)

John W. Townsend *Lore of the Meadowland: Short Studies in Kentuckiana* (1911, rpt. 1974)
————. and **Dorothy E. Townsend** *Kentucky in American Letters* vols. 1–2 1784–1912, vol. 3 1913–1975 (n.d.)

Daniel Trabue (ed. Chester Raymond Young) *Westward into Kentucky: The Narrative of Daniel Trabue* (1981)

William S. Ward *A Literary History of Kentucky* (1988)

Robert Penn Warren *Night Rider* (1939)
Novel about conflict between tobacco growers and manufacturers in the early twentieth century.
————. *Band of Angels* (1955)
Civil War story about a Kentucky plantation owner's daughter sold into slavery.
————. *Jefferson Davis Gets His Citizenship Back* (1980)
Essay on Southern history inspired by the 1879 Todd County ceremonies in honor of Davis.

Henry Watterson *Marse Henry* 2 vols. (1920)
Autobiography of a famous Kentucky journalist of the nineteenth century.

William C. Watts *The Chronicles of a Kentucky Settlement* (1897)
Romantic novel of pioneer life.

GUIDES TO RESOURCES

Channing, Steven A. *The Encyclopedia of Kentucky* (1985)

Coleman, J. Winston, Jr. (comp.) *Bibliography of Kentucky History* (1949)

Cook, Michael L. *Kentucky Index of Biographical Sketches in State, Regional and County Histories* (1986)

Federal Writers' Project *Lexington and the Bluegrass Country* (1938)
————. *Henderson, a Guide to Audubon's Home Town in Kentucky* (1941)
————. *Kentucky: A Guide to the Bluegrass State* (1942, rpt. 1969)

Feintuch, Burt *Kentucky Folkmusic: An Annotated Bibliography* (1985)

Jillson, Willard Rouse *An Historical Bibliography of Frankfort, Kentucky, 1751–1941* (1942)
————. *A Bibliography of Early Western Travel in Kentucky, 1674–1824* (1944)
————. *An Historical Bibliography of Lexington, Kentucky, 1774–1946* (1947)

Karan, P. P. and **Cotton Mather** (eds.) *Atlas of Kentucky* (1977)

Rone, Wendell H. *An Historical Atlas of Kentucky and Her Counties* (1965)

Sames, James W., III *Index of Kentucky and Virginia Maps, 1562 to 1900.* Ed. Lewis C. Woods, Jr. (1976)

Wells, Dianne and **Mary Lou S. Madigan** (comps.) *Update: Guide to Kentucky Historical Highway Markers* (1983)

SELECTED NONFICTION SOURCES

Allen, Hall *Center of Conflict: A Factual Story of the War Between the States in Western Kentucky and Tennessee* (1961)

Altsheler, Joseph A. *Kentucky Frontiersmen* (1988)

Axton, William F. *Tobacco and Kentucky* (The Kentucky Bicentennial Bookshelf) (1975)

Baird, Nancy Disher *David Wendel Yandell: Physician of Old Louisville* (1978)
———. *Luke Pryor Blackburn: Physician, Governor, Reformer* (The Kentucky Bicentennial Bookshelf) (1979)

Baylor, Orval W. *J. Dan Talbott* (1942)
———. *John Pope, Kentuckian; His Life and Times, 1770–1845: A Saga of Kentucky Politics from 1792 to 1850* (1943)

Bethell, Thomas N. *The Hurricane Creek Massacre: An Inquiry into the Circumstances Surrounding the Deaths of Thirty-eight Men in a Coal Mine Explosion* (1972)

Blakey, George T. *Hard Times and New Deal in Kentucky, 1929–1939* (1986)

Bodley, Temple *History of Kentucky* 4 vols. (1928)

Boles, John B. *Religion in Antebellum Kentucky* (1976)

Bolus, Jim *Run for the Roses; 100 Years at the Kentucky Derby* (1974)

Brannan, Beverley W. and **David Horvath** *A Kentucky Album: Farm Security Administration Photographs, 1935–1943* (1986)

Breckinridge, Mary *Wide Neighborhoods: A Story of the Frontier Nursing Service* (1981)

Breckinridge, Sophinisba *Madeline McDowell Breckinridge; a Leader in the New South* (1921)

Butler, Mann *A History of the Commonwealth of Kentucky* (2d ed. 1836)

Carson, Gerald *The Social History of Bourbon: An Unhurried Account of Our Star-Spangled American Drink* (1963, rpt. 1984)

Caudill, Harry M. *Night Comes to the Cumberlands: A Biography of a Depressed Area* (1962)
———. *A Darkness at Dawn: Appalachian Kentucky and the Future* (The Kentucky Bicentennial Bookshelf) (1976)
———. *Theirs Be the Power: The Moguls of Eastern Kentucky* (1983)

Channing, Steven A. *Kentucky; a Bicentennial History* (States and the Nation series) (1977)

Clark, Thomas D. *The Kentucky* (Rivers of America series) (1942)
———. *Kentucky, Land of Contrast* (1968)
———. *Agrarian Kentucky* (The Kentucky Bicentennial Bookshelf) (1977)
———. *A History of Kentucky* (rev. ed. 1977)
———. *Historic Maps of Kentucky* (1979)

Clarke, Mary Washington *Kentucky Quilts and Their Makers* (Kentucky Bicentennial Bookshelf) (1976)

Clift, G. Glenn *Governors of Kentucky, 1792 to 1942* (1942)

Coleman, J. Winston, Jr. *Stage-Coach Days in the Bluegrass; Being an Account of Stage-Coach Travel and Tavern Days in Lexington and Central Kentucky, 1800–1900* (1935)
———. *Slavery Times in Kentucky* (1940)
———. *Old Homes of the Blue Grass* (1950)
———. *Historic Kentucky* (1967)
——— (ed.) *Kentucky: A Pictorial History* (1971)
———. *Sketches of Kentucky's Past; a Series of Essays Concerning the State's History* (1979)

Collins, Lewis *History of Kentucky* (1968)

Connelly, William E. *The Founding of Harman's Station and the Wiley Captivity* (1910, rpt. 1966)
——— and **Ellis Merton Coulter** *History of Kentucky*, 5 vols. (1922)

Coulter, E. Merton *The Civil War and Readjustment in Kentucky* (1926, rpt. 1966)

Couto, Richard A. *Poverty, Politics, and Health Care: An Appalachian Experience* (1975)

Coward, Joan W. *Kentucky in the New Republic: The Process of Constitution Making* (1979)

Crocker, Helen B. *The Green River of Kentucky* (Kentucky Bicentennial Bookshelf) (1976)

Crowe-Carraco, Carol *The Big Sandy* (Kentucky Bicentennial Bookshelf) (1979)

Crowgey, Henry G. *Kentucky Bourbon: The Early Years of Whiskeymaking* (1971)

Curry, Leonard P. *Rail Routes South: Louisville's Fight for the Southern Market* (1969)

Davenport, F. Garvin *Ante-bellum Kentucky: A Social History, 1800–1860* (1943, rpt. 1983)

Davis, William C. *Breckinridge: Statesman, Soldier, Symbol* (1974)
———. *The Orphan Brigade: The Kentucky Confederates Who Couldn't Go Home* (1980)

Day, John *Bloody Ground* (1941, rpt. 1981)

DeLatte, Carolyn E. *Lucy Audubon, a Biography* (1982)

DePree, Gladis L. *The Self-Anointed* (1978)

Drake, Louise Carson *Kentucky in Retrospect: Noteworthy Personages and Events in Kentucky History, 1792–1967* (1967)

Dunnigan, Alice Allison *The Fascinating Story of Black Kentuckians; Their Heritage and Traditions* (1982)

Fuller, Paul E. *Laura Clay and the Women's Rights Movement* (1975)

Goldstein, Joel (ed.) *Kentucky Government and Politics* (1984)

Gore, J. Rogers *The Boyhood of Abraham Lincoln* (1921, rpt. 1935)

Gresham, John M. (ed.) *Biographical Cyclopedia of the Commonwealth of Kentucky* (1896)

Hall, Wade H. (comp. and ed.) *The Kentucky Book* (1979)

Hamilton, Holman *The Three Kentucky Presidents—Lincoln, Taylor, Davis* (1978)

Hammack, James W., Jr. *Kentucky and the Second American Revolution: The War of 1812* (1976)

Harrison, Lowell H. *The Civil War in Kentucky* (The Kentucky Bicentennial Bookshelf) (1975)
——— and **Nelson L. Dawson** (eds.) *A Kentucky Sampler: Essays from the Filson Club History Quarterly, 1926–1976* (1977)
———. *The Antislavery Movement in Kentucky* (The Kentucky Bicentennial Bookshelf) (1978)

Heck, Frank H. *Proud Kentuckian: John C. Breckinridge* (Kentucky Bicentennial Bookshelf) (1976)

Henry, Ruby A. *The First West* (1972)

Hevener, John W. *Which Side Are You On? The Harlan County Coal Miners, 1931–39* (1978)

Hollingsworth, Kent *The Kentucky Thoroughbred* (rev. ed. 1985)

Hood, Fred J. (comp.) *Kentucky, Its History and Heritage* (1978)

Howard, John Tasker *Stephen Foster, America's Troubadour* (1934)

Howard, Victor B. *Black Liberation in Kentucky: Emancipation and Freedom, 1861–1884* (1983)

Ireland, Robert M. *The County in Kentucky History* (1976)
———. *Little Kingdoms: The Counties of Kentucky, 1850–1891* (1977)

Irvin, Helen D. *Women in Kentucky* (The Kentucky Bicentennial Bookshelf) (1979)

Jewell, Malcolm E. and Everett W. Cunningham *Kentucky Politics* (1968)

Jillson, Willard R. *Tales of the Dark and Bloody Ground* (1930)
———. *Pioneer Kentucky* (1934) · ·

Johnston, L. F. *Famous Kentucky Tragedies and Trials; a Collection of Important and Interesting Tragedies and Criminal Trials Which Have Taken Place in Kentucky* (1912)

Jones, G. C. *Growing Up Hard in Harlan County* (1985)

Jones, Michael Owen *Craftsman of the Cumberlands* (1988)

Jones, Virgil C. *The Hatfields and the McCoys* (1948)

Karem, Anne S. *The Cherokee Area: A History* (2d ed. 1975)

Keating, L. Clark *Audubon: The Kentucky Years* (Kentucky Bicentennial Bookshelf) (1976)

Kentucky Commission on Human Rights *Kentucky's Black Heritage: The Role of the Black People in the History of Kentucky from Pioneer Days to the Present* (1971)

Kerr, Charles (ed.) *History of Kentucky* 5 vols. (1922)

Klotter, James C. *William Goebel: The Politics of Wrath* (1977)
——— and Peter J. Sehlinger (eds.) *Kentucky Profiles; Biographical Essays in Honor of Holman Hamilton* (1982)
———. *The Breckinridges of Kentucky, 1760–1981* (1986)

Lancaster, Clay *Ante Bellum Houses of the Bluegrass* (1961)
———. *Vestiges of the Venerable City: A Chronicle of Lexington, Kentucky, Its Architectural Development and Survey of Its Early Streets and Its Antiquities* (1978)

Langman, R. C. *Appalachian Kentucky, an Exploited Region* (1971)

Laudeman, Tev *The Rupp Years; the University of Kentucky's Golden Era of Basketball* (1972)

Lee, Lloyd G. *A Brief History of Kentucky and Its Counties* (1981)

Lester, William S. *The Transylvania Colony* (1935)

Libbey, James K. *Dear Alben: Mr. Barkley of Kentucky* (1979)

Ligon, Moses E. *A History of Public Education in Kentucky* (1942)

Lofaro, Michael A. *The Life and Adventures of Daniel Boone* (1986)

Mauer, David W. *Kentucky Moonshine* (1974)

McMurtry, Richard K. *John McMurtry and the American Indian; a Frontiersman in the Struggle for the Ohio Valley* (1980)

McVey, Frank L. *The Gates Open Slowly: A History of Education in Kentucky* (1949)

Meacham, Charles M. *A History of Christian County, Kentucky* (1930)

Merrill, Boynton, Jr. *Jefferson's Nephews: A Frontier Tragedy* (1976)

Meyer, Leland Winfield *The Life and Times of Colonel Richard M. Johnson of Kentucky* (1967)

Montell, William L. and Michael L. Morse *Kentucky Folk Architecture* (The Kentucky Bicentennial Bookshelf) (1976)
———. *Killings; Folk Justice in the Upper South* (1986)

Moore, Arthur K. *The Frontier Mind: A Cultural Analysis of the Kentucky Frontiersman* (1957)

Mutzenberg, Charles G. *Kentucky's Famous Feuds and Tragedies; Authentic History of the World Renowned Vendettas of the Dark and Bloody Ground* (1917)

National Committee for the Defense of Political Prisoners *Harlan Miners Speak; Report on Terrorism in the Kentucky Coal Fields* (Civil Liberties in American History series) (1932, rpt. 1970)

Neal, Julia *By Their Fruits: The Story of Shakerism in South Union, Kentucky* (1947, rpt. 1975)
———. *The Kentucky Shakers* (The Kentucky Bicentennial Bookshelf) (1982)

Nelli, Humbert S. *The Winning Tradition: A History of Kentucky Wildcat Basketball* (1984)

Newcomb, Rexford *Architecture in Old Kentucky* (1953)

Parks, Joseph H. *Felix Grundy* (1940)

Pearce, John E. *The Colonel: The Captivating Biography of the Dynamic Founder of a Fast-Food Empire* (1982)
———. *Divide and Dissent: Kentucky Politics, 1930–1963* (1987)

Perrin, William H. (ed.) *History of Bourbon, Scott, Harrison, and Nicholas Counties, Kentucky* (1882, rpt. 1979)
———, J. H. Battle, and G. C. Kniffin *Kentucky, a History of the State, Embracing a Concise Account of the Origin and Development of the Virginia Colony* (1887, rpt. 1979)

Peterson, Bill *Coaltown Revisited: An Appalachian Notebook* (1972)

Plunkett, H. Dudley and Mary J. Bowman *Elites and Change in the Kentucky Mountains* (1973)

Preston, John D. *The Civil War in the Big Sandy Valley of Kentucky* (1984)

Ramage, James A. *Rebel Raider: The Life of General John Hunt Morgan* (1986)

Reid, Richard *Historical Sketches of Montgomery County* (1882, rpt. 1926)

Rennick, Robert M. *Kentucky Place Names* (1984)

Rice, Otis K. *Frontier Kentucky* (Kentucky Bicentennial Bookshelf) (1975)

Rice, Russell *The Wildcats: A Story of Kentucky Football* (1975)

Richardson, Harold E. *Cassius Marcellus Clay* (1976)

Robertson, James Rood *Petitions of the Early Inhabitants of Kentucky to the General Assembly of Virginia, 1769 to 1792* (1981)

Sandburg, Carl and Paul M. Angle *Mary Lincoln, Wife and Widow* (1932)

Sears, Richard D. *The Day of Small Things: Abolitionism in the Midst of Slavery, Berea, Kentucky, 1854–1864* (1985)

Shackelford, Laurel and Bill Weinberg (eds.) *Our Appalachia: An Oral History* (1988)

Shannon, Jasper B. et al. *A Decade of Change in Kentucky Government and Politics* (1943)

Share, Allen J. *Cities in the Commonwealth: Two Centuries of Urban Life in Kentucky* (1982)

Simpson, Elizabeth M. *Bluegrass Homes and Their Traditions* (1932)
———. *The Enchanted Bluegrass* (1938)

Simpson, George B. *Biography of Judge Peter Casey, His Court, and Contemporaries, 1811–1812* (1981)

Slade, J. W. *The Possum Hunters: A Story of the Tobacco War in Kentucky* (1920)

Smith, Frank E. *Land Between the Lakes: Experiment in Recreation* (1971)

Smith, Zachariah F. *History of Kentucky, From Its Earliest Discovery and Settlement, to the Present Date* (1895)

Sprague, Stuart (ed.) *Eastern Kentucky: A Pictorial History* (1986)

Staples, Charles R. *The History of Pioneer Lexington, 1779–1806* (1939)

Steed, Virgil *Kentucky Tobacco Patch* (1947)

Stickles, Arndt M. *Simon Bolivar Buckner: Borderland Knight* (1940)

Stillwell, Lucille *John Cabell Breckinridge* (1936)

Stone, Richard G. *A Brittle Sword; the Kentucky Militia, 1776–1912* (Kentucky Bicentennial Bookshelf) (1977)
———. *Kentucky Fighting Men, 1861–1945* (Kentucky Bicentennial Bookshelf) (1982)

Sugrue, Thomas *There Is a River: The Story of Edgar Cayce* (1942)

Surface, Bill *The Hollow* (1971)

Tachau, Mary K. Bonsteel *Federal Courts in the Early Republic: Kentucky, 1786–1816* (1978)

Tapp, Hambleton *Kentucky: Decades of Discord, 1865–1900* (1977)

Thomas, Daniel Lindsey and Lucy B. Lindsey *Kentucky Superstitions* (1920)

Thomas, Elizabeth Patterson *Old Kentucky Homes and Gardens* (1939)

Thomas, Jean *The Singin' Fiddler of Lost Hope Hollow* (1938)
———. *Ballad Making' in the Mountains of Kentucky* (1939)

Thomas, William Roscoe *Life Among the Hills and Mountains of Kentucky* (1926)

Van Deusen, Glyndon G. *The Life of Henry Clay* (1937, rpt. 1979)

Walker, Juliet E. K. *Free Frank: A Black Pioneer on the Antebellum Frontier* (1983)

Wall, Joseph F. *Henry Watterson: Reconstructed Rebel* (1956)

Wallis, Frederick A. and Hambleton Tapp *A Sesqui-Centennial History of Kentucky* 4 vols. (1945)

Warfield, Ethelbert Dudley *The Kentucky Resolutions of 1798; an Historical Study* (2d ed. 1894, rpt. 1969)

Warren, Raymond *Abe Lincoln, Kentucky Boy* (1931)

Watlington, Patricia *The Partisan Spirit; Kentucky Politics, 1779–1792* (1972)

Watson, Thomas S. *Kentucky Pioneers* (1977)

Webb, Ross A. *Benjamin Helm Bristow: Border State Politician* (1969)
———. *Kentucky in the Reconstruction Era* (The Kentucky Bicentennial Bookshelf) (1979)

Withington, William A. *Kentucky in Maps* (1980)

Wolfe, Charles K. *Kentucky Country: Folk and Country Music of Kentucky* (1982)

Wootton, Clara *They Have Topped the Mountain* (1960)

Wright, George C. *Life Behind a Veil: Blacks in Louisville, Kentucky, 1865–1930* (1985)

Wrobel, Sylvia *Isaac Shelby: Kentucky's First Governor and Hero of Three Wars* (1974)

Wyatt, Wilson W., Sr. *Whistle Stops: Adventures in Public Life* (1985)

LOUISIANA

The west south central state of Louisiana is roughly L-shaped, with the Gulf of Mexico to the south; Texas and the Sabine River to the west; Arkansas to the north; and Mississippi to the east. The northeastern border is formed by the Mississippi River, the southeastern border by the Pearl River.

FULL NAME State of Louisiana
POSTAL ABBREVIATION LA
INHABITANT Louisianian
ADMITTED TO THE UNION April 30, 1812. 18th state
POPULATION (est. 1987) 4,461,000. Percent of US total: 1.83%. Rank: 20th

CAPITAL CITY Baton Rouge, the third largest city in the state, located on the Mississippi River in southeast central Louisiana; population 238,900 (est. 1984). Founded during the French colonial era and held successively by Britain, Spain, and France, it declared itself an independent county called Feliciana in 1810 and was incorporated as a town in 1817. It served as the state capital from 1849 to 1861 and again since 1882.

STATE NAME AND NICKNAMES The explorer La Salle gave the name La Louisianne to the area at the mouth of the Mississippi River, to honor King Louis XIV of France. Also known as the Bayou State, the Sugar State, the Pelican State, and the Child of the Mississippi.

STATE SEAL On a gold field, a relief of a pelican tearing its breast to feed the three young in the nest before it, encircled by the state motto. The blue border bears the legend "State of Louisiana."

MOTTO Union, Justice and Confidence

SONGS "Give Me Louisiana," lyrics and music by Doralice Fontane, arranged by John W. Schaum. Also "You Are My Sunshine," lyrics and music by Jimmy H. Davis and Charles Mitchell.

SYMBOLS
Flower magnolia
Tree bald cypress
Bird brown pelican
Gem agate
Dog Louisiana Catahoula leopard dog
Reptile alligator
Insect honeybee
Crustacean crawfish
Fossil petrified palmwood
Drink milk

LICENSE PLATES (1) Dark blue on white, with a blue border and the legend "Sportsman's Paradise." (2) Dark blue on white, with the legend "World's Fair" and the fair's logo. (3) Dark blue on white, with a blue border and the legend "Bayou State."

FLAG On a field of blue, the design from the state seal, with the pelicans white and the nest brown, and below them the state motto on a streamer.

GEOGRAPHY AND CLIMATE

Louisiana's physiography is dominated by the Mississippi River. The Mississippi flood plain and the Delta area form much of the lower state. These fertile regions, rich in alluvial soils, are well-suited to agriculture. The state's beachless coast contains an extensive system of bayous and marshes; along the Red River, in the northwest, are hills rising about 500 feet above sea level, the highest elevations in the state. Louisiana's climate is humid and subtropical, with regular tropical storms and a hurricane season extending for half the year.

AREA 47,751 square miles. Rank: 31st
INLAND WATER 3,230 square miles
GEOGRAPHIC CENTER Avogelles, 3 miles SE of Marksville
ELEVATIONS *Highest point:* Driskill Mountain, Bienville Parish, 535 feet. *Lowest point:* New Orleans, Orleans Parish, -5 feet. *Mean elevation:* 100 feet

MAJOR RIVERS Mississippi, Atchafalaya, Red, Ouachita

MAJOR LAKES AND RESERVOIRS Pontchartrain, Grand, White, Caddo, Salvador, Maurepas

TIDAL SHORELINE 7,721 miles, Gulf coast

LAND USE

	Thousands of acres
Urban (1982)	823
Rural (1982)	25,256
Cropland (1982)	6,409
Pastureland (1982)	2,369
Rangeland (1982)	241
Forestland (1982)	12,895
State parks and recreation areas (1983)	37
National park system (1984)	6
National forest system (1984)	1,023
Tribal lands (1984)	0.5

TEMPERATURES The highest recorded temperature was 114°F on August 10, 1936, at Plain Dealing. The lowest was -16°F on February 13, 1899, at Minden.

NATIONAL SITES

NATIONAL HISTORICAL PARK Jean Lafitte
NATIONAL WILDLIFE REFUGES Catahoula, D'Arbonne/Upper Ouachita, Delta-Breton, Lacassine/Shell Keys, Sabine

HISTORY

1519	Alonso Alvarez de Piñeda explores the Mississippi.
1541	Hernando de Soto scouts northern Louisiana and claims the Mississippi River for Spain.
1542	*May 21.* De Soto is buried in the Mississippi near where it meets the Red River.
1543	Survivors of de Soto's expedition are the first Europeans to descend the Mississippi to the Gulf of Mexico.
1682	*April 9.* Robert Cavelier, Sieur de La Salle, claims the territory watered by the Mississippi for King Louis XIV, for whom it is named.
1700	*Spring.* Father Paul Du Ru founds the first Catholic church in Louisiana.
1714	Louis Juchereau de St. Denis establishes a fort at Natchitoches; the first permanent settlement in Louisiana.
1717	John Law is granted proprietorship of the territory to promote development.
1718	New Orleans is founded.
1723	New Orleans becomes the capital of Louisiana superceding Biloxi.
1727	*August 7.* Ursuline nuns arrive in New Orleans to create a school for girls.
1731	Louisiana becomes a crown colony.
1762	*November 3.* In the Treaty of Fontainebleau, France cedes New Orleans and the Territory of Louisiana west of the Mississippi to Spain.
1763	Acadians ("Cajuns") begin migrating to area of Saint Martinville.
1764	French colonists petition Louis XV to rescind the cession to Spain.
1766	*March 5.* Spanish commissioner Don Antonio de Ulloa is coldly received in New Orleans as governor of the territory.
1768	*October 27-29.* Insurgents riot against Spanish rule and Ulloa sails for Cuba. For 10 months Louisiana enjoys freedom from foreign rule.
1769	*August 17.* Spanish authority is reinstated.

1776	Revolutionary War. Wartime supplies are sent to George Rogers Clark and other patriots. New Orleans is used as a base to pillage Loyalists in West Florida.
1779	Spanish Governor Bernardo de Galvez captures Baton Rouge and Natchez from British forces.
1788	Caterpillars destroy the indigo crop.
	March 21. New Orleans is almost completely destroyed by fire.
1794	*Moniteur de la Louisiane,* published by Louis Duclot, is the state's first newspaper.
	December 23. The Church St. Louis is dedicated as a cathedral.
1796	Étienne de Boré develops a process of crystallizing sugar from cane grown on his plantation.
1800	*October 1.* Spain returns Louisiana territory to France in the Treaty of San Idelfonso.
1803	*December 30.* US takes formal possession of Louisiana territory, which consists of 828,000 square miles of land between the Mississippi River and the Rocky Mountains.
1804	*March 26.* Louisiana is divided by Congress into the Territory of Orleans, covering about the same area as the present state, and the remaining part extending westward becomes the District of Louisiana, which comes under the jurisdiction of the Indiana Territory. The Territory of Orleans is established with a separate government.
1805	*December.* Aaron Burr's dubious conspiracy to join Louisiana and western territories with Mexico is broken up near Natchez.
1812	*January 10.* The steamboat *New Orleans* arrives in New Orleans from Pittsburgh.
	April 30. Louisiana (Territory of Orleans) enters the Union as the 18th state.
1815	*January 8.* The last battle of the War of 1812 is won by General Andrew Jackson at New Orleans. Jackson Day is made a legal holiday.
1821	John J. Audubon, one of the first to study and paint the birds of the United States, sets up his studio in New Orleans.
1823	Gas is discovered near Natchitoches, the first of many gas and oil wells found throughout the state.
1823-33	Yellow fever and cholera kill 10,000 in New Orleans.
1838	*Shrove Tuesday.* First Mardi Gras parade is held in New Orleans.
1850	Baton Rouge becomes the capital.
1853	Yellow fever kills 11,000 in New Orleans and wipes out many smaller towns.
1859	*September.* Four thousand vigilantes break up a gang of cattle thieves near Lafayette.
	December 1. French Opera House in New Orleans opens.
1861	*January 26.* Louisiana secedes from the Union.
	March 21. Louisiana joins the Confederacy.
1862	*April 25.* New Orleans is captured by a Federal fleet led by Admiral David G. Farragut.
1864	*May 13.* Alexandria is fired on by Federal troops and almost completely destroyed.
	June 23. A Republican convention revises the state constitution, abolishing slavery.
1865	Louisiana comes under complete Federal control.
1866-1867	Floods and worms destroy much of the state's cotton crop.
1868	*March 11.* The constitution is revised, granting blacks full social and civil rights.
	June 25. Louisiana is readmitted to the Union.
1872	*Shrove Tuesday.* Rex, King of the Carnival, parades for the first time.
1874	Thirty-one parishes (counties) are inundated by flooding.
	August 29-30. A black uprising at Coushatta is quelled by the White League, "protectors of white supremacy."
	September 14. The White League defeats the New Orleans metropolitan police in a bloody insurrection and gains brief control of the city government.
1877	Home rule is restored under Governor Francis Nicholls.
1879	New Orleans is made an ocean port.
1883	Train service between New Orleans and California is established.
	States concerned about flood control pool resources for curbing the Mississippi.

1890	Charles ("Buddy") Bolden, cornetist and pioneer of instrumental jazz, forms his own band in New Orleans.
1896	*November 1.* Free rural mail delivery is established.
1898	*May 12.* The state's new voting qualifications disinfranchise most blacks.
1910	*June 15.* Evangeline County is founded and named for Evangeline, the heroine of Henry Wadsworth Longfellow's poem.
1912	*April 10.* George Mestach, flying mail from New Orleans to Baton Rouge, makes second US airmail trip.
1915	*September 29.* Hurricane and attendant floodwaters injure many in New Orleans.
1919	*December 4.* The French Opera House is destroyed by fire.
1923	The Inner Harbor Navigation Canal is opened.
1927	The Mississippi reaches unprecedented heights.
1928-1932	Huey P. Long is governor, ruling with dictatorial methods though his programs are directed at the poor. He provides free textbooks for public schools.
1929	*May 16.* An attempt to impeach Governor Long is defeated.
1934	*August.* A barge tow makes the initial run on the Intracoastal Waterway.
1935	*September 8.* Long, a candidate for the Democratic presidential nomination, is assassinated.
1940-1944	Administration of Governor Jimmy Davis, country music singer and composer, contributes to the war effort but reforms are few.
1948	Governor Earl Long takes steps toward making Louisiana a welfare state.
1956	The world's longest overwater highway bridge (23.8 miles) is completed over Lake Pontchartrain.
	July 16. Governor Earl Long signs a bill that bans inter-racial athletic contests and social events.
1957	Louisiana begins construction of the Mississippi–Gulf Canal, a 76-mile short cut to the sea from New Orleans.
1958	State legislature passes an act authorizing the closing of desegregated schools.
1960	*November 17.* Anti-integration riots in New Orleans.
1963	*September.* In Baton Rouge, 27 blacks begin attending classes at four previously all-white schools. This is the first high school integration in the state.
1965	*September 9.* Hurricane Betsy strikes southeastern Louisiana causing 81 deaths and nearly $400 million in property damage.
1973	Louisiana gains almost $300 million in new annual income by changing the tax on petroleum products.
1976	*August 12.* Twelve die in an explosion at the Tenneco Oil Company in Chalmette.
1977	Hotel chains Hilton, Marriott, and Hyatt expand facilities in New Orleans and with the new Superdome, officials claim that New Orleans is now an ideal convention city.
1986	Declines in state revenues cause reductions in jobs among state employees and large cuts in spending in education, health, social and public services, and highway programs.
1987	*November 20.* Cuban inmates seize the federal detention center in Oakdale protesting plans to return them to Cuba.
	November 29. Government agrees to give individual hearings to detainees.

DEMOGRAPHY

Population (est. 1987) . . . 4,461,000
Population (1980) 4,206,098
Population density in persons
  per square mile (1980) 88.1

POPULATION BY RACE (1980)
American Indian/Aleut/
  Eskimo 12,064
Asian/Pacific Islander 23,771
Black 1,237,263
Hispanic 99,105
White 2,911,243
Other 19,631

POPULATION CHARACTERISTICS (1980)
Percent of state population
Urban 68.6
Rural 31.4
Under 18 . . . . 31.6
65 or older 9.6
College-educated 13.4

Families below poverty line . . . 15.1
Public assistance recipients 8.3

Per capita personal
income (1986) $11,227
Millionaires per 100,000
residents (1982) 141.5
Average life expectancy
in years (1980) 71.7
Marriage rate per 1,000
residents (1986) 8.2
Divorce rate per 1,000
residents (1986) 3.8
Birth rate per 1,000
residents (1985) 18.1
Infant mortality rate per
1,000 births (1985) 12.0
Abortion rate per 1,000
live births (1985) 240

Crime rate per 100,000
residents (1985)
Violent 758.2
Property 5,319.8
Federal and state prisoners per
100,000 residents (1984) 297
Alcohol consumption in
gallons per capita (1985) 40.6
Deaths from motor vehicle accidents
per 100,000 residents (1985) . . 20.7

MAJOR CITIES

	1984 population (est.)
Alexandria	52,532
Baton Rouge	238,900
Lafayette	82,608
Lake Charles	75,080
Monroe	55,968
New Orleans	559,101
Shreveport	219,996

GOVERNMENT AND POLITICS

Number of US Representatives 8
Electoral votes 10

POLITICAL PARTY NOMINEES FROM STATE
* winner

Zachary Taylor* (Whig) 1848 P
Donelson Caffery (National/
declined) 1900 P
John Milliken Parker (Progressive) 1916 VP
Kent H. Courtney (Conservative Party of NJ) 1960 VP
John R. Rarick (American Independent) 1980 VP

PRESIDENTIAL PRIMARY ELECTION In 1988, Louisiana sent 71 Democratic delegates and 41 Republican delegates to the national conventions.

CONSTITUTION Louisiana has had 11 constitutions: 1812, 1845, 1852, 1861, 1864, 1868, 1879, 1898, 1913, 1921, and the present one, adopted in 1974.
LEGISLATURE The Legislature is divided into the Senate (39 members, 4-year term, minimum age 18) and the House of Representatives (105 members, 4-year term, minimum age 18). In 1987, the annual salary was $16,800.
JUDICIARY The highest court is the Supreme Court, with 7 judges serving 10-year terms. In 1987, the annual salary was $76,166.
EXECUTIVE The governor serves a 4-year term; the minimum age for holding office is 30. In 1987, the annual salary was $68,364. There are 21 other elected officials.

PRESIDENTIAL VOTE 1948-1988 *(in percents)*

Year	State Winner	Democratic	Republican
1948	J. Strom Thurmond (States' Rights, 49.1)	32.8	17.5
1952	Stevenson (D)	52.9	47.1
1956	Eisenhower (R)	39.5	53.3
1960	Kennedy (D)	50.4	28.6
1964	Goldwater (R)	43.2	56.8
1968	George C. Wallace (American Independent, 48.3)	28.2	23.5
1972	Nixon (R)	28.6	66.0
1976	Carter (D)	51.7	46.0
1980	Reagan (R)	45.7	51.2
1984	Reagan (R)	38.2	60.8
1988	Bush (R)	45.0	55.0

GOVERNORS

William Charles Coles Claiborne	1812-1816
Jacques Philippe Villere	1816-1820
Thomas Bolling Robertson	1820-1824
Henry Schuyler Thibodaux (acting)	1824
Henry Johnson	1824-1828
Pierre Auguste Charles Bourguignon Derbigny	1828-1829
Armand Beauvais (acting)	1829-1830
Jacques Dupre	1830-1831
Andre Bienvenu Roman	1831-1835
Edward Douglas White	1835-1839
Andre Bienvenu Roman	1839-1843
Alexander Mouton	1843-1846
Isaac Johnson	1846-1850
Joseph Marshall Walker	1850-1853
Paul Octave Hebert	1853-1856
Robert Charles Wickliffe	1856-1860
Thomas Overton Moore	1860-1864
Henry Watkins Allen (Confederate governor)	1864-1865
George F. Shepley (military governor)	1862-1864
Georg Michael Hahn	1864-1865
James Madison Wells	1865-1867
Benjamin Flanders (military governor)	1867
Joshua Baker (military governor)	1867-1868
Henry Clay Warmoth	1868-1873
John McEnery	1873
William Pitt Kellogg	1873-1877
Francis Tillou Nicholls	1877-1880
Louis Alfred Wiltz	1880-1881
Samuel Douglas McEnery	1881-1888
Francis Tillou Nicholls	1888-1892
Murphy James Foster	1892-1900
William Wright Heard	1900-1904
Newton Crain Blanchard	1904-1908
Jared Young Sanders	1908-1912
Luther Egbert Hall	1912-1916
Ruffin Galson Pleasant	1916-1920
John Milliken Parker	1920-1924
Henry Fuqua	1924-1926
Oramel Hinckley Simpson (acting)	1926-1928
Huey Pierce Long Jr.	1928-1932
Alvin Olin King (acting)	1932
Oscar Kelly Allen	1932-1936
James Albert Noe (acting)	1936
Richad Webster Leche	1936-1939
Earl Kemp Long (acting)	1939-1940
Sam Houston Jones	1940-1944
James Houston Davis	1944-1948
Earl Kemp Long	1948-1952
Robert Floyd Kennon	1952-1956
Earl Kemp Long	1956-1960
James Houston Davis	1960-1964
John J. McKeithen	1964-1972
Edwin W. Edwards	1972-1976
Edwin W. Edwards	1976-1980
David C. Treen	1980-1984
Edwin W. Edwards	1984-1988
Charles E. Roemer 3d (D)	1988-

MINIMUM AGES

Majority	18
Marriage with parental consent female	16
male	18
Marriage without parental consent	18
Making a will (lower if married)	16
Buying alcohol	21
Jury duty	18
Leaving school	17
Driver's license	15

CAPITAL PUNISHMENT
Number executed 1976-88: 18
On death row Aug. 1, 1988: 42

MILITARY INSTALLATIONS
Total number: 11
Major bases:
Army: 1
Navy: 1
Air Force: 1

FINANCES

Thousands of dollars

GENERAL REVENUE (1985)

Total general revenue	6,961,177
Total tax revenue	3,855,780
Sales and gross receipts	1,946,644
Individual income taxes	526,684
Corporate net income taxes	293,598

GENERAL EXPENDITURE (1985)

Total general expenditure	6,562,216
Education	2,361,362
Public welfare	1,098,273
Health	167,710
Hospitals	534,317
Natural resources	167,868
Highways	681,750
Police	96,547
Corrections	175,522

FEDERAL AID (1985) 1,785,154

ECONOMY

Louisiana remains an important agricultural state despite postwar gains in manufacturing and mining. The state's sweet potato crop is the largest in the nation; other important cash crops are rice (including gourmet rices), soybeans, cotton, sugarcane, nuts, corn, wheat, hay, hot peppers, and strawberries. Cattle are the main livestock. Farm cash receipts were over $1.8 billion in 1983. Louisiana's fisheries produced 1.8 billion pounds of fish, shrimp, and other shellfish in 1983; timber is also a major source of income. Louisiana's great reservoirs of petroleum make it one of the nation's leaders in oil and natural gas; sulfur, clays, gypsum, salt, lime, stone, gravel, and sand are other important mining products. Manufactures include chemicals, petroleum products, lumber products and wood pulp, processed food, and ceramics. Tourism is an important industry, with New Orleans the major attraction.

EMPLOYMENT (1984)

Thousands of persons

Total number of employed workers	1,745
Construction	118.8
Finance, insurance, and real estate	83.1
Government	320.6
Manufacturing	181.9
Mining	81.1
Services	312.1
Transportation, communications, and utilities	118.1
Wholesale and retail trade	380.9
Percent of civilian labor force unemployed (1984)	10.0

DEPARTMENT OF DEFENSE (1985)

Civilian workers employed	9,306
Military personnel	25,710
Contract awards	$2.175 billion

ENERGY SOURCES FOR ELECTRIC UTILITIES (1983)

	Percent
Coal	22.6
Gas	76.4
Hydroelectric	0.0
Nuclear	0.0
Petroleum	1.0

TRANSPORTATION

Motor vehicles registered in state (1986)	2,889,658
Miles of roads, streets, and highways (1986)	58,229
Miles of Class I railway operated (1986)	2,785
Airports (1983)	311
Major aviation hubs (1983)	3
Largest hub: New Orleans	
Major ports, with gross tonnage in thousands (1985)	
New Orleans	152,054
Baton Rouge	90,669
Lake Charles	25,494

CULTURE AND EDUCATION

Native American tribes

Louisiana was formerly home to the Acolapissa, Adai, Apalachee, Atakapa, Avogel, Bayogoula, Biloxi, Caddo, Chatot, Chawasha, Choctaw, Creek, Koasati, Koroa, Natchez, Okelousa, Opelousa, Pascagoula, Quapaw, Quinipissa, Socatino, Taensa, Tangipahoa, Tawasa, Washa, and Yazoo tribes. Groups that continue to live there include the Alabama, Chitimacha, and Houma. There are two federal reservations in Louisiana.

Religions, ethnicities, and languages

Louisiana has a more varied population than any other state in the Deep South. The northern part is populated mainly by the descendants of white Protestant (particulary Baptist) settlers. The southern part is strongly Roman Catholic, with a large part of the population drawn from the the Creoles, the descendants of the early French and Spanish colonists; the Acadians (French Canadians), who arrived from Nova Scotia in the 18th century; enslaved Blacks who worked the state's plantations; and free Blacks from the West Indies. There are communities of Spanish (Canary Islanders), Irish, Hungarians, Germans, Dalmatians, Belgians, and Italians. In 1980, 10.0 percent of Louisiana's population spoke a language other than English at home; French is still widely heard in the south, as is Gumbo, a part-African language spoken by some Blacks and Creoles. Louisiana's culture is strongly influenced by its French and Spanish colonial past; its legal system is drawn from Roman law. Indigenous musical forms include jazz, Dixieland, and Cajun music.

Major museums and libraries

Louisiana Arts and Science Center, Baton Rouge
Louisiana State Museum, New Orleans
New Orleans Museum of Art

Vieux Carre Historic District, New Orleans

Major arts organizations
New Orleans City Ballet
New Orleans Opera Association
New Orleans Symphony Orchestra

Colleges and universities
Number public (1986-87) 20
Number private (1986-87) 12
Total enrollment, in full-time equivalent students (1985) 149,000

Public elementary and secondary schools
Expenditure per pupil in average daily attendance (1986-87) $3,008

Pupil-teacher ratio (1987) 18.5
Average teacher salary (1986-87) $21,736

Major league sports teams
Football: New Orleans Saints

Holidays
Battle of New Orleans Day. January 8
Robert E. Lee's Birthday. January 19
Mardi Gras. January or February
Confederate Memorial Day. June 3
Huey P. Long Day. August 30
State Fair, Shreveport. October

LOUISIANA IN LITERATURE

Nelson Algren *A Walk on the Wild Side* (1956, rpt. 1977)
Novel about life in the New Orleans slums during the Depression, seen by an innocent country boy.

Hewitt L. Ballowe *Lawd Sayin' the Same; Negro Folk Tales of the Creole Country* (1947); *Creole Folk Tales* (1948)
Collections of Delta folklore.

Hamilton Basso *Sun in Capricorn* (1942)
Novel based on the career of Huey Long by a New Orleans–born author who also wrote *Days before Lent* (1939), a psychological drama set during Mardi Gras, and a biography, *Beauregard: The Great Creole* (1933).

Henry Bibb *Narrative of the Life of Henry Bibb, an American Slave* (1849)

Gwen Bristow *Deep Summer* (1937); *The Handsome Road* (1939); *This Side of Glory* (1940)
Trilogy of novels about plantation life.

James Lee Burke *Heaven's Prisoners* (1988)
Novel about violent contemporary life in the bayous.

Ben Lucien Burman *Children of Noah* (1951)
Folklore and anecdotes from the Mississippi Valley.

George Washington Cable *Old Creole Days* (1879); *The Grandissimes: A Story of Creole Life* (1880)
The best-known of Cable's romantic portrayals of Creole life in New Orleans during the early nineteenth century. His other works include a history, *The Creoles of Louisiana* (1884); *Dr. Sevier* (1884), a novel about New Orleans before the Civil War; *Bonaventure* (1888), a sentimental account of Acadian life; and *Strange True Stories of Louisiana* (1889).

James Cain *Mignon* (1962)
Romance set in New Orleans during the Civil War.

Truman Capote *Other Voices, Other Rooms* (1941)
Novel about an adolescent's self-discovery, set on an old plantation.

John Dickson Carr *Papa Là-bas* (1968)
A mystery novel set in New Orleans in 1858, containing a portrait of Judah P. Benjamin.

Ruby Van A. Caulfield *The French Literature of Louisiana* (1929)

Kate O'Flaherty Chopin *Bayou Folk* (1894); *A Night in Acadie* (1897)
Stories of plantation and small-town life.
————. *The Awakening* (1899)
Tragic novella, set in New Orleans and Grand Isle, about a young woman's attempts to shake off the constraints of family life and find spiritual fulfilment.

Reverend Theodore Clapp *Autobiographical Sketches and Recollections During a Thirty-Five Years Residence in New Orleans* (1857)

John William Corrington *And Wait for the Night* (1964)
Historical novel set in Shreveport during the Union occupation of 1865.

————. *The Southern Reporter* (1981)
Collection of stories set in contemporary Louisiana.

Edwin D. Davis (ed.) *Plantation Life in the Florida Parishes of Louisiana, 1836–1846: As Reflected in the Diary of Bennett H. Barrow* (1943)
Account of life on a cotton plantation.

John William De Forest *Miss Ravenel's Conversion from Secession to Loyalty* (1867)
Naturalistic novel about two suitors of a New Orleans woman, partly set in the city during the Union occupation.

Federal Writers' Project (Lyle Saxon and Edward Dreyer, comps.) *Gumbo Ya-Ya: A Collection of Louisiana Folktales* (1945)

Alcée Fortier *Louisiana Folk-Tales in French Dialect and English Translation* (1895)

Ernest J. Gaines *The Autobiography of Miss Jane Pittman* (1971)
Gaines' best-known novel, the fictional autobiography of a 110-year-old black woman, exemplifies his consistent interest in the social history of the black community since Reconstruction. His novels include: *Catherine Carmier* (1964), *Of Love and Dust* (1968), *In My Father's House* (1978), and *A Gathering of Old Men* (1983).

Shirley Ann Grau *The Hard Blue Sky* (1958)
Novel about the descendants of French and Spanish immigrants living on the Isle aux Chiens.

Christopher Hallowell *People of the Bayou: Cajun Life in Lost America* (1979)
Anecdotal social history of the marshland people of the Gulf of Mexico.

Lafcadio Hearn *Chita: A Story of Last Island* (1889)
Hearn's fantastic tale of the destruction of a coastal resort was inspired by his experience of a tidal wave in 1884.

Idwal Jones *Black Bayou* (1941)
Novel of the hunters and trappers of the Louisiana swamps.

Robert Emmet Kennedy *Black Cameos* (1924); *Gritny People* (1927)
Stories of the daily lives of blacks in the early years of the century, with descriptions of black folklore and music.

Grace King *The Pleasant Ways of St. Médard* (1916)
Novel about the fortunes of a New Orleans family during and after the Civil War, closely based on King's own experience. The New Orleans–born writer also wrote, supposedly in hostile reaction to the fiction of George Washington Cable, several collections of stories about Creole life: *Monsieur Motte* (1888), *Tales of a Time and Place* (1892), and *Balcony Stories* (1892). Her autobiography, *Memories of a Southern Woman of Letters* (1932), contains a detailed account of Reconstruction in Louisiana.

Lizzie C. McVoy (ed.) *Louisiana in the Short Story* (1940)

Solomon Northup (ed. Sue Eakin and Joseph Logsdon) *Twelve Years a Slave* (1968)
Slave's narrative containing details of plantation life.

Michael Ondaatje *Coming through Slaughter* (1977)
Novel based on the life of black jazz cornet player Buddy Bolden and set in the heyday of Storyville.

André Pénicaut (trans. and ed. R. C. McWilliams) *Fleur de Lys and Calumet* (1988)
Narrative of a French carpenter who sailed to Louisiana in 1699 with Iberville and returned to France in 1721.

Walker Percy *The Moviegoer* (1961)
Novel about the scion of a New Orleans Garden District family who finds his true home among bohemians and misfits.

Lauren C. Post *Cajun Sketches* (1962)

Eliza Ripley *Social Life in Old New Orleans* (1912)
Recollections of a nineteenth-century upbringing.

Corinne Saucier *Folk Tales from French Louisiana* (1962)

Lyle Saxon *Father Mississippi* (1927)
Chronicle of the river's history.
———. *The Friends of Joe Gilmore* (1948)
Anecdotes of New Orleans bohemian life.

Kate Stone (ed. John Q. Anderson) *Brokenburn: The Journal of Kate Stone, 1861–1868* (1955)
Diary of the Civil War written by a young woman from a cotton plantation near Vicksburg whose family fled to Texas but returned to rebuild during Reconstruction.

Robert Stone *A Hall of Mirrors* (1967, rpt. 1987)
Novel about bohemian life in the New Orleans French Quarter during the 1960s.

Charles T. Jackson *Captain Sazarac* (1922)
Historical romance set in New Orleans in 1821.

Edward Larocque Tinker *Toucoutou* (1928)
A tragic tale of racial prejudice set in New Orleans in the 1850s.

John Kennedy Toole *A Confederacy of Dunces* (1980)
A comic novel centering on the exploits of a gargantuan eccentric living in the New Orleans French Quarter.

Felix Voorhies *Acadian Reminiscences* (1907, rpt. 1960)

Robert Penn Warren *All the King's Men* (1946)
Novel about politics in a southern state, loosely based on the career of Huey Long.

Irene T. Whitfield *Louisiana French Folk Songs* (1939)
Collection of French, Cajun, and Creole music.

James Wilcox *Modern Baptists* (1984); *North Gladiola* (1985); *Miss Undine's Living Room* (1988); *Sort of Rich* (1989)
Day-to-day incidents of ordinary life in the fictional town of Tula Springs, treated in a comic style that juxtaposes the characters' aspirations with the mundanity of everyday life.

Ben Ames Williams *The Unconquered* (1952)
Politics during Reconstruction.

Frank Yerby *The Vixens* (1947)
Sensational historical novel about Reconstruction society and politics in New Orleans.

Stark Young *Heaven Trees* (1926)
An idyllic, sentimental portrayal of plantation life before the Civil War.

GUIDES TO RESOURCES

Calhoun, Milburn and **Susan Cole Doré** (eds.) *The Louisiana Almanac 1988–89* (1988)

Conrad, Glenn R. *A Selected Bibliography of Scholarly Literature on Colonial Louisiana and New France* (1982)

Cruise, Boyd *Index of the Louisiana Historical Quarterly* (1956)

Cummings, Light T. and **Glen Jeansonne** (eds.) *A Guide to the History of Louisiana* (1982)

Federal Writers' Project *New Orleans City Guide* (1938, rpt. 1983)
———. *Louisiana: A Guide to the State* (1941, rpt. 1979)
———. (ed. H. Hansen) *Louisiana: A State Guide* (1971)

Foote, L. B. (comp.) *Bibliography of the Official Publications of Louisiana 1803–1934* (1942)

Holmes, Jack D. L. *A Guide to Spanish Louisiana* (1970)

Humphreys, Hubert *Louisiana Oral History Collections: A Directory* Louisiana State University (1980)

Lane, Mary Jane *Bibliographies of Louisiana State University Theses Pertaining to Louisiana, 1955–1980* Louisiana Library Assoc. (1986)

Noggle, Burl *Working with History: The Historical Records Survey in Louisiana and the Nation, 1936–1942* (1981)

Siegel, Martin (comp.) *New Orleans: A Chronological and Documentary History, 1539–1970* (1975)

SELECTED NONFICTION SOURCES

Adams, William H. *The Whig Party of Louisiana* (1973)

Arceneaux, George *Youth in Acadie: Reflections on Acadian Life and Culture in Southwest Louisiana* (1974)

Arsenault, Bona (trans. and ed. with Brian M. Upton and John G. McLaughlin) *History of the Acadians* (1966)

Arthur, Stanley C. *Jean Laffite, Gentleman Rover* (1952)

Asbury, Herbert *The French Quarter: An Informal History of the New Orleans Underworld* (1936)

Baiamonte, John V., Jr. *Spirit of Vengeance: Nativism and Louisiana Justice, 1921–1924* (1986)

Bannon, Lois E., Martha Y. Carr, and **Gwen A. Edward** *Magnolia Mound: A Louisiana River Plantation* (1984)

Baudier, Roger *The Catholic Church in Louisiana* 2 vols. (1939)

Beals, Carleton *The Story of Huey P. Long* (1935, rpt. 1971)

Becnel, Thomas *Labor, Church, and the Sugar Establishment: Louisiana, 1887–1976* (1980)

Benard de La Harpe, Jean Baptiste *Historical Journal of the Settlement of the French in Louisiana* trans. by Virginia

Koenig and Joan Cain, ed. and annotated by Glenn R. Conrad. (1971)

Bergerie, Maurine *They Tasted Bayou Water: A Brief History of Iberia Parish* (1962)

Berry, Jason, Jonathan Foose, and **Tad Jones** *Up from the Cradle of Jazz: New Orleans Music Since World War II* (1986)

Bethell, Tom *George Lewis: A Jazzman from New Orleans* (1977)

Bezou, Monsignor Henry C. *Metairie: A Tongue of Land to Pasture . . .* (1973)

Blassingame, John W. *Black New Orleans, 1860–1880* (1963)

Bourgeois, Lillian *Cabanocey, the History, Customs and Folklore of St. James Parish* (1957)

Boyle, James E. *Cotton and the New Orleans Cotton Exchange* (1934)

Bragg, Jefferson Davis *Louisiana in the Confederacy* (1941)

Brasseaux, Carl A. *The Founding of New Acadia: The Beginnings of Acadian Life in Louisiana, 1765–1803* (1987)

Brooks, Charles B. *The Siege of New Orleans* (1961)

Broven, John *South to Louisiana: The Music of the Cajun Bayous* (1983)

Brown, Wilbur S. *The Amphibious Campaign for New Orleans, 1814–1815* (1969)

Bruce, Curt *The Great Houses of New Orleans* (1977)

Bumstead, Gladys *Louisiana Composers* (1935)

Butler, W. E. *Down Among the Sugar Cane: The Story of Louisiana Sugar Plantations and Their Railroads* (1980)

Cable, George W. *The Creoles of Louisiana* (1884)
———. *Old Creole Days* (1897)

Capers, Gerald M. *Occupied City: New Orleans under the Federals 1862–1865* (1965)

Carleton, Mark T., Perry H. Howard, and Joseph B. Parker (eds.) *Readings in Louisiana Politics* (1975)

Carruth, Viola *Caddo: 1,000. A History of the Shreveport Area from the Time of the Caddo Indians to the 1970's* (1970)

Carter, Hodding (ed.) *The Past as Prelude: New Orleans 1718–1968* (1968)

Case, Gladys C. *Après la Roulaison: The Story of Sugar* (1970)

Casey, Powell A. *Louisiana in the War of 1812* (1963)
———. *Louisiana at the Battle of New Orleans* (1965)

Castellanos, Henry C. *New Orleans as It Was* (1895, rpt. 1978)

Chambers, Henry E. *A History of Louisiana* 3 vols. (1925)

Charters, Samuel B., IV *Jazz, New Orleans, 1885–1957: An Index to the Negro Musicians of New Orleans* (1958)

Chase, John C. *Frenchmen Desire Good Children and Other Streets of New Orleans* (1949, rpt. 1979)
———. *Louisiana Purchase: An American Story Told in That Most American Form of Expression . . . the Comic Strip* (1954)

Chidsey, Donald Barr *Louisiana Purchase* (1972)

Christian, Marcus *Negro Soldiers in the Battle of New Orleans* (1965)
———. *Negro Ironworkers in Louisiana 1718–1900* (1972)

Clark, John G. *New Orleans, 1718–1812: An Economic History* (1970)

Clement, William E. and Stuart O. Landry *Plantation Life on the Mississippi* (1952)

Cline, Rodney *Education in Louisiana: History and Development* (1974)

Conaway, James *Judge: The Life and Times of Leander Perez* (1973)

Conrad, Glenn R. (ed.) *The Cajuns: Essays on Their History and Culture* (1978)
———. (ed.) *Readings in Louisiana History* (1978)

Cook, Bernard A. and James R. Watson *Louisiana Labor from Slavery to "Right-to-Work"* (1985)

Craven, Avery O. *Rachel of Old Louisiana* (1975)

Crete, Liliane *Daily Life in Louisiana, 1815–1830* (1981)

Crouse, Nellis M. *Lemoyne d'Iberville: Soldier of New France* (1954)

Curtis, Nathaniel C. *New Orleans: Its Old Houses, Shops and Public Buildings* (1933)

Davis, Edwin A. *Louisiana: The Pelican State* (1959)
———. *The Story of Louisiana* (1960)
———. *Louisiana: A Narrative History* (1961)
——— (ed.) *Louisiana: A Narrative History* (1965)
——— (ed.) *The Rivers and Bayous of Louisiana* (1968)

Davis, William Hardy *Aiming for the Jugular in New Orleans* (1976)

Dawson, Joseph G., III *Army Generals and Reconstruction: Louisiana, 1862–1877* (1982)

DeGrummond, Jane L. *The Baratarians and the Battle of New Orleans* (1961)

Desmond, John *Louisiana's Antebellum Architecture* (1970)

Dethloff, Henry C. *Huey P. Long: Southern Demagogue or American Democrat?* (1976)

Deutsch, Herrmann B. *The Huey Long Murder Case* (1963)

Dominguez, Virginia R. *White by Definition: Social Classification in Creole Louisiana* (1986)

Dormon, James H. *The People Called Cajuns: An Introduction to an Ethnohistory* (1983)

Douglas, Walter B. *Encyclopaedia of New Orleans Artists, 1718–1918* (1987)

Du Pratz, Antoine Simon Le Page *The History of Louisiana* 3 vols. (1758)

Duffy, John *Sword of Pestilence: The New Orleans Yellow Fever Epidemic of 1853* (1966)

Dufour, Charles L. (ed.) *St. Patrick's of New Orleans 1833–1958: Commemorative Essays for the 125th Anniversary* (1958)
———. *The Night the War Was Lost* (1960)
———. *Ten Flags in the Wind: The Story of Louisiana* (1967)

Eckert, Allan W. *Bayou Backwaters* (1968)

Evans, Oliver Wendell *New Orleans* (1959)

Feibleman, Peter S. *The Bayous* (1973)

Fitzpatrick, John (ed. Margaret F. Dalrymple) *The Merchant of Manchac: The Letterbooks of John Fitzpatrick, 1768–1790* (1978)

Fontenot, Mary A. *The Louisiana Experience: An Introduction to the Culture of the Bayou State* (1983)

Forstall, Edmond J. *Agricultural Productions of Louisiana* (1845)

Fortier, Alcée *A History of Louisiana* 4 vols. (1904)

Fossier, Albert E. *New Orleans: The Glamour Period, 1800–1840* (1957)

Franks, Kenney A. and Paul F. Lambert *Early Louisiana and Arkansas Oil: A Photographic History, 1901–1946* (1982)

Gayarré, Charles *History of Louisiana* 4 vols. (1885)

Giraud, Marcel (trans. by Joseph C. Lambert) *A History of French Louisiana* (1974)

Gleig, George R. *The Campaign of the British Army at Washington and New Orleans in the Years 1814–1815* (1836)

Graham, Hugh D. *Huey Long* (1970)

Green, George D. *Finance and Economic Development in the South: Louisiana Banking, 1804–1861* (1972)

Haas, Edward F. *DeLesseps S. Morrison and the Image of Reform: New Orleans Politics, 1946–1961* (1974)

Hair, William I. *Bourbonism and Agrarian Protest in Louisiana, 1877–1900* (1965)

Hall-Quest, Olga *Old New Orleans, the Creole City: Its Role in American History, 1718–1803* (1968)

Hallowell, Christopher L. *People of the Bayou: Cajun Life in Lost America* (1979)

Hammond, Hilda P. *Let Freedom Ring* (1936)

Hardin, J. Fair *Northwestern Louisiana: A History of the Watershed of the Red River, 1714–1937* (1939)

Harris, Thomas O. *The Kingfish: Huey P. Long, Dictator* (1938)

Haskins, James *Pinckney Benton Stewart Pinchback* (1973)
———. *The Creoles of Color of New Orleans* (1975)

Henrici, Holice H. *Shreveport, the Beginnings* (1985)

Hepworth, George H. *The Whip, Hoe and Sword* (1979)

Hermann, Bernard M. *New Orleans* (1980)

Higginbotham, Jay *Fort Maurepas: The Birth of Louisiana* (1968)
——— (trans. and ed.) *The Journal of Sauvole, Historical Journal of the Establishment of the French in Louisiana* (1969)

Howard, Perry H. *Political Tendencies in Louisiana* (1971)

Huber, Leonard Victor, Samuel Wilson, Jr., and Garland F. Taylor *Louisiana Purchase* (1953)

—— and **Albert R. Huber** *The New Orleans Tomb* (1956)
—— and **Guy F. Bernard** *To Glorious Immortality: The Rise and Fall of the Girod Street Cemetery* (1961)
—— and **Samuel Wilson, Jr.** *Baroness Pontalba's Buildings, Their Site and the Remarkable Woman Who Built Them* (1964)
——. *New Orleans As It Was in 1814–1815* (1965)
——. *Notable New Orleans Landmarks* (1974)
——. *Louisiana: A Pictorial History* (1975)
——. *Mardi Gras: A Pictorial History of Carnival in New Orleans* (1977)

Jackson, Joy *New Orleans in the Gilded Age: Politics and Urban Progress, 1880–1896* (1969)

Jeansonne, Glen *Leander Perez: Boss of the Delta* (1977)

Jolly, Ellen R. and **James Calhoun** *The Pelican Guide to the Louisiana Capitol* (1980)

Jones, Terry L. *Lee's Tigers: The Louisiana Infantry in the Army of Northern Virginia* (1987)

Kane, Harnett T. *Louisiana Hayride: The American Rehearsal for Dictatorship, 1928–1940* (1941, rpt. 1971)
——. *Deep Delta Country* (1944)
——. *Plantation Parade; the Grand Manner in Louisiana* (1945)

Kendall, John S. *History of New Orleans* 3 vols. (1922)
——. *Golden Age of the New Orleans Theatre* (1952)

Keyes, Frances P. *All This Is Louisiana* (1950)

King, Grace E. *New Orleans: The Place and the People* (1904)
—— and **John R. Ficklen** *A History of Louisiana* 4 vols. (1904)
—— and **John R. Ficklen** *Stories from Louisiana History* (1905)
——. *Creole Families of New Orleans* (1921, rpt. 1971)

Kmen, Henry A. *Music in New Orleans: The Formative Years, 1791–1841* (1966)

Kniffen, Fred B. *Louisiana: Its Land and People* (1968)

Korn, Bertram Wallace *The Early Jews of New Orleans* (1969)

Kubly, Vincent L. *The Louisiana Capitol: Its Art and Architecture* (1977)

LaCour, Arthur B. and **Stuart L. Omer** *New Orleans Masquerade* (1952)

Landry, Stuart O. *The Battle of Liberty Place: The Overthrow of Carpet-Bag Rule in New Orleans—September 14, 1874* (1955)

Laughlin, Clarence J. and **David L. Cohn** *New Orleans and Its Living Past* (1941)
——. *Ghosts Along the Mississippi: An Essay in the Poetic Interpretation of Louisiana's Plantation Architecture* (1961)

LeBlanc, Dudley J. *The True Story of the Acadians* (1932)

LeBreton, Dagmar *Chahta-Ima: The Life of Adrien-Emmanuel Rouquette* (1974)

Leeper, Clare D'Artois *Louisiana Places: A Collection of the Columns from the Baton Sunday Advocate, 1960–1974* (1976); *1975 Supplement* (1976)

LeGardeur, René J., Jr. *The First New Orleans Theatre: 1792–1803* (1963)

Liebling, A. J. *The Earl of Louisiana* (2d ed. 1970)

Lindig, Carmen *The Path from the Parlor: Louisiana Women, 1879–1920* (1986)

Lockwood, C. C. *Atchafalaya: America's Largest River Basin Swamp* (1981)
——. *Discovering Louisiana* (1986)

Long, Huey P. *Every Man a King—the Autobiography of Huey* (1933)
——. *My First Days in the White House* (1935)

Looney, Ben E. *Cajun Country* (1974)

Lyon, E. Wilson *The Man Who Sold Louisiana* (1942)

Marquis, Donald M. *In Search of Buddy Bolden, First Man of Jazz* (1978)

Martin, François-Xavier *The History of Louisiana from the Earliest Times* 2 vols. (1827–29)

Martin, Thomas *Dynasty: The Longs of Louisiana* (1960)

Mason, F. van Wyck *The Battles for New Orleans* (1962)

McConnell, Roland C. *Negro Troops of Antebellum Louisiana: A History of the Battalion of Free Men of Color* (1968)

McGinty, Garnie W. *A History of Louisiana* (1949)

McLaughlin, James J. *The Jack Lafaience Book* (1922)

McWilliams, Richebourg G. *Fleur de Lys and Calumet* (1953)

Mignon, François *Plantation Memo: Plantation Life in Louisiana 1750–1970, and Other Matter* (1973)

Mills, Gary B. *The Forgotten People: Cane River's Creoles of Color* (1977)

Moore, Diane M. *Their Adventurous Will: Profiles of Memorable Louisiana Women* (1984)

Moore, John Preston *Revolt in Louisiana: The Spanish Occupation, 1766–1770* (1976)

Morgan, Elemore *The Face of Louisiana* (1969)

Mule, Marty *Sugar Bowl: The First Fifty Years* (1983)

Myers, Rose *A History of Baton Rouge* (1976)

Newton, Lewis W. *The Americanization of French Louisiana: A Study of the Process of Adjustment between the French and the Anglo-American Populations of Louisiana, 1803–1860* (1980)

Niehaus, Earl F. *The Irish in New Orleans, 1800–1860* (1965)

O'Neill, Charles Edwards, S.J. *Church and State in French Colonial Louisiana: Policy and Politics* (1966)

Opotowsky, Stan *The Longs of Louisiana* (1960)

Oudard, Georges *Four Cents an Acre: The Story of Louisiana under the French* (1931)

Overdyke, William Darrell *Louisiana Plantation Homes* (1965)

Panzeri, Louis *Louisiana Composers* (1972)

Phares, Ross *Cavalier in the Wilderness: The Story of the Explorer and Trader, Louis Juchereau de St. Denis* (1953)

Pinney, Edward L. and **Robert S. Freedman** *Political Leadership and the School Desegregation Crisis in Louisiana* (1963)

Poesch, Jessie J. *Early Furniture of Louisiana, 1750–1830* (1972)

Ramsey, Carolyn *Cajuns on the Bayous* (1957)

Read, William A. *Louisiana-French* (rev. ed. 1963)

Reed, Merl E. *New Orleans and the Railroads: The Struggle for Commercial Empire 1830–1860* (1966)
——. *The Governors of Louisiana* (1972)

Reeves, Miriam G. *The Governors of Louisiana* (1972)

Reilly, Robin *The British at the Gates: The New Orleans Campaign in the War of 1812* (1974)

Reinders, Robert C. *End of an Era: New Orleans, 1850–1860* (1964)

Ripley, C. Peter *Slaves and Freedmen in Civil War Louisiana* (1976)

Ripley, Eliza *Social Life in Old New Orleans* (1975)

Roberts, W. Adolphe *Lake Pontchartrain* (1946)

Roland, Charles P. *Louisiana Sugar Plantations during the American Civil War* (1957)

Rose, Al *Storyville New Orleans, Being an Authentic, Illustrated Account of the Notorious Red-Light District* (1974)

Rousseve, Charles B. *The Negro in New Orleans* (1969)

Rushton, William F. *The Cajuns: From Acadia to Louisiana* (1979)

Samuel, Ray . . . *to a Point Called Chef Menteur* (1959)
———. *The Great Days of the Garden District and the Old City of Lafayette* (1961)
——— and **Martha Ann Samuel** *The Uptown River Corner: The Story of Royal and Bienville* (1964)
——— and **Martha Ann Samuel** *Shreveport, a Photographic Remembrance, 1873–1949* (1968)

Saxon, Lyle *Fabulous New Orleans* (1928, rpt. 1988)
———. *Old Louisiana* (1929, rpt. 1988)

Shugg, Roger W. *Origins of Class Struggle in Louisiana: A Social History of White Farmers and Laborers during Slavery and After, 1840–1875* (1939)

Sinclair, Harold *The Port of New Orleans* (1942)

Sindler, Allan P. *Huey Long's Louisiana: State Politics, 1920–1952* (1956)

Sitterson, J. Carlyle *Sugar Country: The Cane Sugar Industry in the South, 1753–1950* (1953)

Skipper, Otis C. *J. D. B. DeBow, Magazinist of the Old South* (1958)

Somers, Dale A. *The Rise of Sports in New Orleans: 1850–1900* (1972)

Sothern, James M. *Last Island* (1980)

Sparks, W. H. *The Memories of Fifty Years* (1870)

Spedale, Rhodes, Jr. *A Guide to Jazz in New Orleans* (1984)

Stanforth, Dierdre *Romantic New Orleans* (1977)

Stephenson, Wendell H. *Alexander Porter, Whig Planter of Old Louisiana* (1969)

Stoddard, Amos *Sketches, Historical and Descriptive, of Louisiana* (1812)

Surrey, Nancy Maria *The Commerce of Louisiana During the French Régime, 1699–1763* (1968)

Swanson, Betsy *Historic Jefferson Parish: From Shore to Shore* (1975)

Tallant, Robert *Voodoo in New Orleans* (1946)
———. *Mardi Gras* (1976)

Taylor, Joe Gray *Negro Slavery in Louisiana* (1963)
———. *Louisiana Reconstructed, 1863–1877* (1974)
———. *Louisiana, a Bicentennial History* (States and the Nation series) (1976)

Texade, David Ker *Alejandro O'Reilly and the New Orleans Rebels* (1970)

Thomas, Maurice *The Story of Louisiana* (1888)

Tinker, Edward L. *Lafcadio Hearn's American Days* (1924)
———. *Louisiana's Earliest Poet* (1933)
———. *Creole City: Its Past and Its People* (1953)

Tunnell, Ted *Crucible of Reconstruction: War, Radicalism, and Race in Louisiana, 1862–1877* (1984)

Turner, Frederick W. *Remembering Song: Encounters with the New Orleans Jazz Tradition* (1982)

Val-Denuzière, Jacqueline P. *The Homes of the Planters* (1984)

Vandal, Giles *The New Orleans Riot of 1866; Anatomy of a Tragedy* (1983)

Vogt, Lloyd *New Orleans Houses: A House-Watcher's Guide* (1985)

Voorhies, Felix *Acadian Reminiscences with the True Story of Evangeline* (1907)

Voss, Reverend Louis *Presbyterianism in New Orleans and Adjacent Points* (1931)

Waldo, J. Curtis *History of the Carnival in New Orleans from 1857 to 1882* (1882)

Wallace, Joseph *The History of Illinois and Louisiana under the French Rule* . . . (1893)

Warmoth, Henry Clay *War, Politics and Reconstruction: Stormy Days in Louisiana* (1930)

Wells, Carol *Cane River Country Louisiana* (1979)

Wiesendanger, Martin and **Margaret** *19th Century Louisiana Painters and Painting* (1971)

Williams, T. Harry *P. G. T. Beauregard: Napoleon in Gray* (1954)
———. *Huey Long* (1969)

Wilson, Samuel, Jr. *A Guide to Architecture of New Orleans, 1699–1959* (1959)
———. *The Capuchin School in New Orleans, 1725* (1961)
———. *Plantation Houses on the Battlefield of New Orleans* (1965)
———. *The Vieux Carre, New Orleans: Its Plan, Its Growth, Its Architecture* (1968)
———, **Leonard V. Huber,** and **Abbey A. Gor** *The St. Louis Cemeteries of New Orleans* (1963)
——— and **Leonard V. Huber** *The Basilica on Jackson Square and Its Predecessors 1727–1965* (1965)
——— and **Leonard V. Huber** *The Cabildo on Jackson Square: The Colonial Period, 1723–1803, by Samuel Wilson, Jr., the American Period, 1803 to the Present, by Leonard V. Huber* (1970)

Winters, John D. *The Civil War in Louisiana* (1963)

Winzerling, Oscar *Acadian Odyssey* (1965)

Young, Perry *The Mistick Krewe: Chronicles of Comus and His Kin* (1931, rpt. 1969)

MAINE

Maine is a northern New England state, bordered on the north and east by the Canadian province of New Brunswick; on the south by the Atlantic Ocean; and on the west by New Hampshire and the Canadian province of Quebec.

FULL NAME State of Maine
POSTAL ABBREVIATION ME
INHABITANT Mainer
ADMITTED TO THE UNION March 14, 1820. 23d state
POPULATION (est. 1987) 1,187,000. Percent of US total: 0.49%. Rank: 38th

CAPITAL CITY Augusta, located on the Kennebec River in southwest Maine; population 21,819 (1980). It is built on the site of a 17th-century trading post and 18th-century fort. Incorporated as a town in 1797 and as a city in 1849, it became the capital of Maine in 1831.

STATE NAME AND NICKNAMES Possibly named for the French province of Mayne by French settlers, or after the explorers' term for a mainland. Official nickname: the Pine Tree State. Also known as the Lumber State, the Border State, and the Old Dirigo State.

STATE SEAL The seal shows the state coat of arms. In the center is a heraldic shield showing a moose in front of a forest of mast pines. To the left of the shield is a farmer, to the right a sailor; above it is the North Star in red and the state motto on a red scroll; below it, on a blue scroll, the legend "Maine."

MOTTO Dirigo (I direct)

SONG "State of Maine Song" by Roger Vinton Snow

SYMBOLS
Flower pine cone and tassel
Tree white pine
Bird chickadee
Mineral tourmaline
Animal moose
Cat Maine coon cat
Fish landlocked salmon
Insect honeybee
Fossil Pertica quadrifaria

LICENSE PLATE Dark blue on white with blue border, showing a red lobster and the red legend "Vacationland."

FLAG The coat of arms from the state seal on a blue field.

GEOGRAPHY AND CLIMATE

The largest of the New England states, Maine is also the wildest. Mountains and dense forests, fed by a network of scenic lakes and streams, cover the sparsely populated northern and western parts of the state, where annual snowfall often exceeds nine feet per year. The state's glacial soils make agriculture difficult, even in the river valleys of southern and eastern Maine. Maine's long, rocky coast is punctuated by numerous peninsulas, fjords, inlets, and more than 1,000 islands.

AREA 33,265 square miles. Rank: 39th

INLAND WATER 2,270 square miles

GEOGRAPHIC CENTER Piscataquis, 18 miles N of Dover

ELEVATIONS *Highest point:* Mount Katahdin, Piscataquis County, 5,268 feet. *Lowest point:* Atlantic Ocean, sea level. *Mean elevation:* 600 feet

MAJOR RIVERS Androscoggin, Kennebec, Penobscot, St. Croix

MAJOR LAKES AND RESERVOIRS Moosehead, Chesuncook, Sebago, Rangely, Mooselookmeguntic

TIDAL SHORELINE 3,478 miles, Atlantic coast

LAND USE

	Thousands of acres
Urban (1982)	212
Rural (1982)	19,066
Cropland (1982)	953
Pastureland (1982)	569
Rangeland (1982)	0
Forestland (1982)	16,770
State parks and recreation areas (1983)	66
National park system (1984)	41
National forest system (1984)	94
Tribal lands (1984)	222

TEMPERATURES The highest recorded temperature was 105°F on July 10, 1911, at North Bridgton. The lowest was -48°F on January 19, 1925, at Van Buren.

NATIONAL SITES

NATIONAL MONUMENT St. Croix Island

NATIONAL PARK Acadia

NATIONAL SCENIC TRAIL Appalachian

NATIONAL WILDLIFE REFUGES Moosehorn–Carlton Pond Waterfowl Production Area/Franklin, Island/Petit Manan, Pond Island, Rachel Carson, Seal Island

HISTORY

1000	Norsemen (Leif Ericson) touch the coast of Maine.
1497–1499	John Cabot, sent by Henry VII, explores coastal areas and thus establishes first claim to Maine territory for England.
1524	French employ Giovanni da Verrazano to explore Maine coast, thereby securing a claim for France.
1602	English ship, the *Concord,* returns from Maine with furs, cedar and sassafras.
1604	Group of Frenchmen settle on island in the St. Croix River, but after a Maine winter move their colony to Nova Scotia.
1605	Captain George Weymouth kidnaps five Indians and takes them to England.
1609	Henry Hudson sails his *Half Moon* into Casco Bay.
1615	Captain John Smith, writing about the Maine coast, says, "Of all the four parts of the world that I have seen not inhabited, I would rather live here than anywhere."
1628	The Plymouth Pilgrims establish several fur-trading posts in Maine territory.
1634	The first sawmill begins operation in the province of Maine.
1640s	French establish missions and convert many Indians.
1649	The government of Maine passes an act which grants all Christians the right to form churches.
1652	The Massachusetts General Court rules that Maine is part of the Massachusetts Bay Colony and annexes the province.
1675	Indians and French attack and burn a number of English settlements in Maine. Indian wars continue intermittently for nearly a century.
1677	Province of Maine purchased by Massachusetts for about $6,000.
1690	French and Indians from Canada pillage Maine until only four English settlements remain inhabited.

1754	Sixth Indian War. Maine Indians now struggle against complete extermination.
1760	Peace made with remnants of Maine Indians.
1763	The Treaty of Paris ends French efforts to control Maine territory.
1775	*May 12*. First naval action of the Revolutionary War occurs when patriots capture British ship off the coast of Maine.
	September 9. Benedict Arnold and his troops sail up the Kennebec River on their way to Quebec.
1778	The Continental Congress divides Massachusetts into three districts, one being called the District of Maine.
1785	*The Falmouth Gazette* is Maine's first newspaper.
1791	Portland Head Lighthouse begins operating. Oldest lighthouse on Atlantic Coast, its first keeper is appointed by George Washington.
1801	Maine's first free public library is founded at Castine.
1802	Bowdoin college at Brunswick opens.
1812	War of 1812 between US and Great Britain seriously affects Maine's shipping industry. Smuggling between Maine and Canada is large-scale.
1815	The first total abstinence society is founded in Portland.
1816	Record cold wave, known as "1800-and-froze-to-death," occurs.
1819	Maine votes to separate from Massachusetts and adopts a state constitution.
1820	*March 15*. Maine is admitted to the Union as the 23d state and as a free state.
1832	State capital moves from Portland to Augusta.
1834	State Anti-Slavery Society is formed.
1838	Earthquake, with vibrations lasting for 20 days, damages homes and lighthouses.
1846	*July 4*. Construction begins on the Atlantic and St. Lawrence Railroad linking Portland to Montreal, Canada.
1851	The state legislature passes the Maine law prohibiting the sale of liquor in any part of the state.
1861	Hannibal Hamlin of Maine is elected vice president of the United States on the ticket with Abraham Lincoln.
	During the Civil War (1861–1865) Maine contributes 73,000 men to the Union Army.
1870	Maine's popularity as a summer resort gives rise to an important industry.
1898	Battleship *Maine* is blown up in Havana Harbor. Spanish-American War follows. Maine furnishes a volunteer regiment.
1911	The state passes a direct primary voting law. Initiative and referendum law is also passed.
1914	Maine leads the nation in production of wood pulp.
1917–1919	Maine shipyards are busy supplying ships to the US in World War I. The state contributes 35,000 men and $116 million to the war effort.
1919	*January*. Maine legislature ratifies the 18th Amendment prohibiting alcohol. *November*. The 19th Amendment, giving nationwide suffrage to women, is ratified.
1924	Maine's first radio station, WABI, begins broadcasting from Bangor.
1933	Bank failures across the nation cause suffering in Maine's rural areas. Ninety-eight of Maine's 109 banks reopen after moratorium.
	Maine ratifies repeal of 18th Amendment.
1934	State prohibition amendment repealed.
1936	Maine experiences worst floods in its history, resulting in a $25 million loss.
1941–1945	Mills and factories in Maine supply shoes and uniforms for Allied soldiers in World War II. Maine men and women serving in the war number about 50,000.
1947	Many buildings in the Bar Harbor area are destroyed when a huge fire rages on Mount Desert Island.
1953	Maine's first television station, WABI-TV, begins telecasting from Bangor.
1954	Hurricane Edna sweeps across Maine, inflicting great damage.
1957	*November*. Governor Edmund S. Muskie becomes the first Democrat elected by the state to the US Senate.
1963	Local school districts are ordered to stop public school prayers throughout the state.

1969	Personal and corporate income taxes are adopted.
1971	*April 9.* The state legislature ratifies the 26th Amendment, lowering the voting age to 18.
1972	*October 23.* The Maine Yankee Atomic Power plant begins operating.
1973	*November 19.* The Maine law that licenses industries involved in the handling of oil and imposes liability for any damages caused by oil spills is upheld by the US Supreme Court.
1976	*May 25.* New York Mercantile speculators default on various futures contracts involving the delivery of nearly 50 million pounds of Maine potatoes—an economic blow to Maine farmers.
1977	*February 28.* The United States Justice Department indicates it will support the Passamaquoddy and Penobscot Indian tribes in their suit against Maine for the recovery of their aboriginal lands.
1979	The US Bureau of Indian Affairs lists Maine as having three Indian reservations with a total population of 1,247.
1981	Tourism continues to lead all industries of the state. Over $500 million spent by out-of-state visitors during the year.
1987	Kennebec River floods Augusta area. Lewiston, on the Androscoggin River, also hit by floods.
1988	*March.* Retired executive James Bryan heads drive to protect wild lands of Maine from development.

DEMOGRAPHY

Population (est. 1987) . . . 1,187,000
Population (1980) 1,125.030
Population density in persons per
   square mile (1980) 33.8

POPULATION BY RACE (1980)
American Indian/Aleut/
   Eskimo 4,087
Asian/Pacific Islander 2,947
Black 3,128
Hispanic 5,005
White 1,109,850
Other 4,648

POPULATION CHARACTERISTICS (1980)
Percent of state population
Urban 47.5
Rural 52.5
Under 18 . . . . 26.6
65 or older 13.1
College-educated 14.0
Families below poverty line 9.8
Public-assistance recipients 7.4

Per capita personal income
   (1986) $12,709
Millionaires per 100,000
   residents (1982) 70.4

Average life expectancy in
   years (1980) 74.6
Marriage rate per 1,000
   residents (1986) 10.3
Divorce rate per 1,000
   residents (1986) 4.8
Birth rate per 1,000
   residents (1985) 13.9
Infant mortality rate per 1,000
   births (1985) 8.8
Abortion rate per 1,000
   live births (1985) 308
Crime rate per 100,000
   residents (1985)
   Violent 147.0
   Property 3,314.0
Federal and state prisoners per
   100,000 residents (1984) 89
Alcohol consumption in gallons per
   capita (1985) 38.0
Deaths from motor vehicle accidents
   per 100,000 residents (1985) . . 17.6

MAJOR CITIES
	1984 population (est.)
Auburn	22,952
Bangor	30,827
Lewiston	39,405
Portland	61,803

GOVERNMENT AND POLITICS

Number of US Representatives 2
Electoral votes 4

POLITICAL PARTY NOMINEES FROM STATE
 * winner

Hannibal Hamlin* (R)	1860	VP
Neal Dow (Prohibition)	1880	P
James Gillespie Blaine (R)	1884	P
Arthur Sewall (D, National Silver)	1896	VP
Edmund Sixtus Muskie (D, Liberal)	1968	VP
Benjamin C. Bubar (Prohibition)	1976	P
Benjamin C. Bubar (National Statesman)	1980	P

PRESIDENTIAL PRIMARY ELECTION In 1988, Maine sent 27 Democratic delegates and 22 Republican delegates to the national conventions.

CONSTITUTION Maine is using its original constitution, adopted in 1819.

LEGISLATURE The Legislature is divided into the Senate (35 members, 2-year term, minimum age 25) and the House of Representatives (151 members, 2-year term, minimum age 21). In 1987, the salary was $9,000 for the first regular session, $6,000 for the second.

JUDICIARY The highest court is the Supreme Judicial Court, with 7 judges serving 7-year terms. In 1987, the annual salary was $71,746.

EXECUTIVE The governor serves a 4-year term; the minimum age for holding office is 30. In 1987, the annual salary was $70,000. There are no other elected officials.

PRESIDENTIAL VOTE 1948-1988 *(in percents)*

Year	State Winner	Democratic	Republican
1948	Dewey (R)	42.4	56.9
1952	Eisenhower (R)	33.8	66.2
1956	Eisenhower (R)	29.1	70.9
1960	Nixon (R)	43.0	57.1
1964	Johnson (D)	68.8	31.2
1968	Humphrey (D)	55.3	43.1
1972	Nixon (R)	38.5	61.5
1976	Ford (R)	48.1	48.9
1980	Reagan (R)	42.3	45.6
1984	Reagan (R)	38.8	60.8
1988	Bush	44.0	56.0

GOVERNORS

William King (D)	1820-1821
William D. Williamson (D/acting)	1821
Benjam Ames (D/acting)	1821
Albion K. Parris (D)	1822-1827
Enoch Lincoln (D)	1827-1829
Nathan Cutler (D/acting)	1829-1830
Joshua Hall (D/acting)	1830
Jonathan G. Hunton (D)	1830-1831
Samuel E. Smith (D)	1831-1834
Robert P. Dunlap (D)	1834-1838
Edward Kent (Whig)	1838-1839
John Fairfield (D)	1839-1840
Edward Kent (Whig)	1840-1841
John Fairfield (D)	1841-1843
Edward Kavanagh (D/acting)	1843-1844
Hugh J. Anderson (D)	1844-1847
John W. Dana (D)	1847-1850
John Hubbard (D)	1850-1853
William G. Crosby (Whig and Free Soil)	1853-1855
Anson P. Morrill (R)	1855-1856
Samuel Wells (D)	1856-1857
Hannibal Hamlin (R)	1857
Joseph H. William (R/acting)	1857-1858
Lot M. Morrill (R)	1858-1861
Israel Washburn (R)	1861-1863
Abner Coburn (R)	1863-1864
Samuel Cony (War Democrat)	1864-1867
Joshua L. Chamberlain (R)	1867-1871
Sidney Perham (R)	1871-1874
Nelson Dingley (R)	1874-1876
Selden Connor (R)	1876-1879
Alonzo Garcelon (D and Greenback)	1879-1880
Daniel F. Davis (R)	1880-1881
Harris M. Plaisted (D and Greenback)	1881-1883
Frederick Robie (R)	1883-1887

Joseph R. Bodwell (R)	1887
Sebastian S. Marble (R/act-	
ing)	1887-1889
Edwin C. Burleigh (R)	1889-1893
Henry B. Cleaves (R)	1893-1897
Llewellyn Powers (R)	1897-1901
John F. Hill (R)	1901-1905
William T. Cobb (R)	1905-1909
Bert M. Fernald (R)	1909-1911
Frederick W. Plaisted (D)	1911-1913
William T. Haines (R)	1913-1915
Oakley C. Curtis (D)	1915-1917
Carl E. Milliken (R)	1917-1921
Frederic H. Parkhurst (R)	1921
Percival P. Baxter (R)	1921-1925
Owen Brewster (R)	1925-1929
William T. Gardiner (R)	1929-1933
Louis J. Brann (D)	1933-1937
Lewis O. Barrows (R)	1937-1941
Sumner Sewall (R)	1941-1945
Horace A. Hildreth (R)	1945-1949
Frederick G. Payne (R)	1949-1952
Burton M. Cross (R)	1952-1955
Edmund S. Muskie (D)	1955-1959
Clinton A. Clauson (D)	1959
John H. Reed (R)	1959-1967
Kenneth M. Curtis (D)	1967-1975
James B. Longley (Indepen-	
dent)	1975-1979
Joseph E. Brennan (D)	1979-1987
John R. McKernan Jr. (R)	1987-

MINIMUM AGES

Majority	18
Marriage with parental consent	16
Marriage without parental consent	18
Making a will	18
Buying alcohol	21
Jury duty	18
Leaving school	17 or 9th grade or with permission
Driver's license	15

CAPITAL PUNISHMENT
None

MILITARY INSTALLATIONS
Total number: 9

FINANCES

Thousands of dollars

GENERAL REVENUE (1985)

Total general revenue	1,847,770
Total tax revenue	1,005,216
Sales and gross receipts	550,555
Individual income taxes	297,233
Corporate net income taxes	53,537

GENERAL EXPENDITURE (1985)

Total general expenditure	1,705,482
Education	547,113
Public welfare	436,295
Health	50,249
Hospitals	41,160
Natural resources	49,869
Highways	185,498
Police	17,001
Corrections	27,136

FEDERAL AID (1985) 659,419

ECONOMY

Maine is one of the three main producers of potatoes in the nation. Apples and berries are the other main cash crops, poultry and eggs the main stock products. Total farm cash receipts were $413 million in 1983. Maine's more than 16 million acres of well-managed forestland make lumber, pulp, paper, and wood products the mainstays of the state economy; other manufactures include rubber and plastics, leather goods, processed foods, textiles and clothing. Fish and shellfish are important exports, with lobsters accounting for about half the fisheries cash receipts. A significant proportion of the state's income — about 7 percent — comes from tourism.

EMPLOYMENT (1984)

Thousands of persons

Total number of employed workers	518
Construction	19.4
Finance, insurance, and real estate	19.6
Government	84.0
Manufacturing	110.4
Mining	0.2
Services	90.5
Transportation, communications, and utilities	19.3
Wholesale and retail trade	102.1

Percent of civilian labor force unemployed (1984)	6.1

DEPARTMENT OF DEFENSE (1985)

Civilian workers employed	10,601
Military personnel	5,382
Contract awards	$957 million

ENERGY SOURCES FOR ELECTRIC UTILITIES (1983)

Percents

Coal	0
Gas	0

Hydroelectric 20.2	
Nuclear 58.8	
Petroleum 21.0	

TRANSPORTATION
Motor vehicles registered
  in state (1986) 872,430

Miles of roads, streets,
  and highways (1986) 21,968
Miles of Class I railway
  operated (1986) 46
Airports (1983) 146
Major aviation hubs (1983) 1
  Largest hub: Portland

CULTURE AND EDUCATION

Native American tribes
Maine was formerly home to the Penna-cook. Groups that continue to live in the state include the Abnaki, Malecite, Passa-maquoddy, and Penobscot. Groups that were relocated to Maine include the Mic-mac. There are three federal reservations in Maine.

Religions, ethnicities, and languages
Most Mainers are descended from the English and Scotch-Irish settlers who ar-rived from western England, Massachu-setts, and New Hampshire in the 18th century. Protestant groups predominate, especially Baptist, Congregationalist, and Methodist. Almost a third of the popula-tion is Roman Catholic; the majority trace their origins to the forced migration from Acadia (Nova Scotia) in the 1760s and to later immigration from Quebec. Other im-migrant communities came from Ireland, Germany, Sweden, and France (the Hu-guenots). In 1980, 10.8 percent of Maine's population spoke a language other than English at home; French is the principal language in the St. John Valley.

Major museums and libraries
Bath Marine Museum
William A. Farnsworth Library and Mu-seum, Rockland
Maine State Museum, Augusta
Portland Museum of Art

Major arts organizations
Portland Stage Company
Portland Symphony

Colleges and universities
Number public (1986-87) 13
Number private (1986-87) 18
Total enrollment, in full-time equivalent students (1985) 38,000

Public elementary and secondary schools
Expenditure per pupil in average daily attendance (1986-87) $3,650
Pupil-teacher ratio (1987) 15.5
Average teacher salary (1986-87) $21,943

Holidays
Patriots Day. 3rd Monday in April

MAINE IN LITERATURE

James Acheson *The Lobster Gangs of Maine* (1988)
  A study of the working lives of lobstermen.

Roy Barrette *Countryman's Journal: Views of Life and Nature from a Maine Coastal Farm* (1986)

Horace P. Beck *Folklore and the Sea* (1973)
  Maritime legends, including many from Maine.

Henry Beston *Northern Farm: A Chronicle of Maine* (1948)
  Naturalist's account of a year on a Kennebec farm.
———— (ed.) *White Pine and Blue Water: A State of Maine Reader* (1950, rpt. 1976)
  Anthology of fiction and non-fiction.
————. *Especially Maine: The Natural World of Henry Beston* (1970)

Gerald Warner Brace *The Islands* (1936)
  Novel set on the Penobscot Islands.
————. *The World of Carrick's Cove* (1957)
  Fictional autobiography of an old islander.
————. *Between Wind and Water* (1966)
  An account of Maine summer resort life.

Gladys Hasty Carroll *As the Earth Turns* (1933); *A Few Foolish Ones* (1935); *Sing Out the Glory* (1957)
  Novels of rural life.

Mary Ellen Chase *Mary Peters* (1934); *Silas Crockett* (1935); *Windswept* (1941); *The Edge of Darkness* (1957)
  Historical novels set in coastal communities. Chase, a

descendant of an old maritime Maine family, described her childhood in Blue Hill in *A Goodly Heritage* (1932).

Carolyn Chute *The Beans of Egypt, Maine* (1985)
  Realistic novel of domestic life among the rural poor.

Elizabeth Coatsworth *Country Neighborhood* (1944)
  Sketches of rural life.

Robert P. T. Coffin *Lost Paradise: A Boyhood on a Maine Coast Farm* (1934)
  Maine poet's memoir of his childhood. Coffin's prose works about the state include *Yankee Coast* (1947), *Maine Doings* (1950), and *Kennebec* (1937).

Fannie Eckstrom and **Mary Winslow Smyth** (comps.) *Minstrelsy of Maine; Folk-Songs and Ballads of the Woods and the Coast* (1927)

Margaret Flint *Old Ashburne Place* (1936); *Down the Road Apiece* (1941)
  Realistic novels of rural life.

John Gould *And One to Grow On: Recollections of a Maine Boyhood* (1949); *Last One In: Tales of a New England Boyhood* (1966)
  Journalist's account of growing up in Freeport in the 1920s. Gould also published a collection of regional folklore, *The Jonesport Raffle, and Numerous Other Maine Veracities* (1969), and *No Other Place* (1984), a historical novel set in Penobscot in 1611.

Roland Palmer Gray (ed.) *Songs and Ballads of the Maine Lumberjacks, with Other Songs from Maine* (1924)

Sarah Orne Jewett *The Country of the Painted Firs* (1896)
This collection of inter-connected tales set in a small town not unlike the author's native Berwick, where her father practiced medicine, is regarded as the most successful of her writings. Her most popular work was a historical novel, *The Tory Lover* (1901). *See also* Willa Cather (selected and ed.) *The Best Stories of Sarah Orne Jewett* (1965).

Dudley C. Lunt *The Woods and the Sea: Wilderness and Seacoast Adventures in the State of Maine* (1965)
Essays on natural history and outdoor life.

John Neal *The Down-Easters* (1833)
Melodramatic novel of domestic tragedy containing regional character sketches by a pioneer Maine editor, businessman, and man of letters.

Charles Pratt *Here on the Island: Being an Account of a Way of Life Several Miles off the Coast of Maine* (1974)
A conservationist's account of a traditional way of island life.

Louise Dickinson Rich *The Peninsula* (1958)
Illustrated description of the Gouldsboro Peninsula by a naturalist who also wrote informal histories and guides: *My Neck of the Woods* (1950); *State O'Maine* (1964); and *The Coast of Maine* (rev. ed. 1975).

Kenneth L. Roberts *Arundel* (1930)
Historical novel of the Revolution set in southern Maine and describing Benedict Arnold's expedition against Quebec. *Rabble in Arms* (1933), relating the fortunes of soldiers from Maine, is the sequel. Roberts celebrated his state in *Trending into Maine* (1938, rev. ed. 1944) and *Don't Say That about Maine* (1950).

Richard Saltonstall Jr. *Maine Pilgrimage: The Search for an American Way of Life* (1974)
Interviews with Maine residents.

Dorothy Simpson and the **Maine Writers Research Club** *The Maine Islands in Story and Legend* (1960, rpt. 1987)
Collection of history and folklore.

Edmund Ware Smith *Upriver and Down; Stories from the Maine Woods* (1965)
Essays by a fisherman and naturalist.

Seba Smith *'Way Down East* (1854)
Realistic regional tales by a pioneer journalist whose fictional creation "Mayor John Downing" commented satirically on the political affairs of the 1820s and '30s.

Lee W. Storrs *Maine: A Literary Chronicle* (1968)
Anthology of descriptions of Maine.

Harriet Beecher Stowe *The Pearl of Orr's Island* (1862)
Novel set in coastal Maine, written while the author was living in Brunswick.

Helen V. Taylor *A Time to Recall; the Delights of a Maine Childhood* (1963)
Recollections of summers at grandfather's farm in Waterboro Center.

Henry David Thoreau *The Maine Woods* (1864)
Account of trips to Mount Katahdin, Moosehead Lake, the West Branch of the Penobscot, Lake Chesunesok, the Allegash River, and the East Branch.

Calvin Trillin *Runestruck* (1977)
Comic novel about two boys' discovery of a Viking artifact.

E. B. White *One Man's Meat* (1942)
Collection of monthly columns written for *Harper's* and the *New Yorker* during White's five-year stay on a salt-water farm.

Ben Ames Williams *Come Spring* (1940)
Historical novel of a frontier settlement during the Revolution, based on the records of the town of Union.

GUIDES TO RESOURCES

Balder, A. P. *Mariner's Atlas: Maine* (1986)

Bangor Public Library *Bibliography of the State of Maine* (1962)

Cayford, John E. *All about Maine: Historical Facts about People, Places and Events* (1981)

Courier-Gazette, Rockland, Maine *State O'Maine Facts* (1984)

Federal Writers' Project *Maine: A Guide 'Down East'* (1970)

Fishery Research and Management Division *Maine Lakes: A Sportsman's Inventory* (1953–1964)

Haskell, John D., Jr. (ed.) *Maine: A Bibliography of Its History* (Bibliographies of New England History, Vol. 2) (1977)

Department of Commerce and Industry *Maine Economic Data Book* (1973)

Maine. Department of Education *Through Maine on Printed Paths: A List of Maine Books for Teachers and Pupils* (1956)

Maine Historical Society *Documentary History of Maine* (1869–1916)
————. (Robert B. Rey, comp.) *The Indians of Maine: A Bibliographical Guide* (1972)
————. (Elizabeth Ring, comp.) *Maine Bibliographies: A Bibliographical Guide* (1973)
————. (Charles E. Clarke, comp.) *Maine during the Colonial Period: A Bibliographical Guide* (1974)

————. (Ronald F. Banks, comp.) *Maine during the Federal and Jeffersonian Period, a Bibliographical Guide* (1974)
————. (William A. Baker, comp.) *Maine Shipbuilding: A Bibliographical Guide* (1974)
————. *Maine Bicentennial Atlas: An Historical Survey* (1976)
————. (William B. Jordan, Jr., comp.) *Maine in the Civil War: A Bibliographical Guide* (1976)
————. (Edwin A. Churchill and James S. Leamon, comps.) *Maine in the Revolution, a Reader's Guide* (1976)

Maine League of Historical Societies and Museums *Adventures in Maine History: A Guide to Period Houses, Museums and Collections of Maine's Historical Societies* (1976)

Maine Library Association Bicentennial Committee *Bibliography of Maine, 1960–1975* (1976)

Maine Register: State Year-Book and Legislative Manual (annual)

Myers, Denys P. *Maine Catalog; Historic Buildings Survey* (1974)

Noyes, Sybil et al. *Genealogical Dictionary of Maine and New Hampshire* (1939, rpt. 1983)

Smith, David C. *Lumbering and the Maine Woods: A Bibliographical Guide* (1971)

Taranko, Walter J. and **Dorothy A. Gregory** *Maine Resources: Print and Non-Print* (1977)

SELECTED NONFICTION SOURCES

Abbott, Berenice *A Portrait of Maine* (1968)

Ahlin, John H. *Maine Rubicon, Downeast Settlers during the American Revolution* (1966)

Attwood, Stanley B. *The Length and Breadth of Maine* (1973)

Baker, George W. and Marjorie L. *Munsungun to the Sea* (1972)

Baker, William A. *A Maritime History of Bath, Maine and the Kennebec Region* 2 vols. (1973)

Banks, Ronald F. *Maine Becomes a State: the Movement to Separate Maine from Massachusetts* (2d ed. 1970)
——— (ed.) *A History of Maine; a Collection of Readings on the History of Maine, 1600–1971* (1971)

Barrington, Richard E. *A Maine Manifest* (1972)

Beam, Philip C. *Winslow Homer at Prout's Neck* (1966)

Berchen, William *Maine* (1973)

Bishop, William H. *Fish and Men in the Maine Islands* (1975)
———. *Lobster at Home in the Maine Waters* (1975)

Bradford, Peter A. *Fragile Structures: A Story of Oil Refineries, National Security, and the Coast of Maine* (1975)

Burrage, Henry S. *Beginnings of Colonial Maine* (1914)

Butcher, Russell D. *Maine Paradise: Mount Desert Island and Acadia National Park* (1973)

Butler, Joyce *Wildfire Loose: The Week Maine Burned* (1978)

Caldwell, Bill *Islands of Maine: Where America Really Began* (1981)
———. *Rivers of Fortune: Where Maine Tides and Money Flowed* (1983)

Calef, John *The Siege of Penobscot* (1971)

Chadbourne, Ava H. *Maine Place Names and the Peopling of Its Towns* (1955)

Clarke, Charles E. *Maine: A Bicentennial History* (States and the Nation series) (1977)

Clifford, Harold B. *The Boothbay Region, 1906–1960* (1961)
———. *Maine and Her People* (1968)

Coffin, Robert P. T. *Kennebec: Cradle of Americans* (Rivers of America series) (1937)

Collier, Sargent F. and Thomas Patrick Horgan *Mount Desert, the Most Beautiful Island in the World* (1952)

Conkling, Philip W. *Islands in Time: A Natural and Human History of the Islands of Maine* (1981)

Coolidge, Philip T. *History of the Maine Woods* (1963)

Day, Clarence A. *A History of Maine Agriculture* (1954)
———. *Farming in Maine, 1860–1940* (1963)
———. *Ezekiel Holmes, Father of Maine Agriculture* (1968)

Dibner, Martin *Seacoast Maine: People and Places* (1973)

Dietz, Lew *The Allagash* (1968)

Dow, Sterling T. *Maine Postal History and Postmarks* (rev. ed. 1976)

Eckstorm, Fannie H. *Indian Place Names of the Penobscot Valley and the Maine Coast* (1941, rpt. 1974)

Edwards, George T. *Music and Musicians of Maine* (1928, rpt. 1970)

Elkins, L. Whitney *The Story of Maine* (1924)

Elwell, Edward H. *Portland and Vicinity* (1975)

Everson, Jennie G. *Tidewater Ice of the Kennebec River* (1970)

Fairchild, Byron *Messrs. William Pepperrell: Merchants at Piscataqua* (1954)

Foster, Elizabeth *The Islanders* (1946)

Gilman, Stanwood and Margaret C. *Land of the Kennebec* (1966)

Gilpatrick, Gil *Allagash, the Story of Maine's Legendary Wilderness Waterway* (1983)

Griffiths, Thomas M. *Major General Henry Knox and the Last Heirs to Montpelier* (1965)

Grindle, Roger L. *Quarry and Kiln: The Story of Maine's Lime Industry* (1971)

Hamilton, Helen *Pine, Potatoes and People: The Story of Aroostook* (1948)

Hempstead, Alfred G. *The Penobscot Boom* (1931, rpt. 1975)

Horan, James F. *Downeast Politics: The Government of Maine* (1975)

Hubbard, Lucius L. *Woods and Lakes of Maine* (1971)

Hunt, Harry D. *The Blaine House: Home of Maine's Governors* (1974)

Hutchinson, Vernal *A Maine Town in the Civil War* (1967)
———. *When Revolution Came; the Story of Old Deer Isle in the Province of Maine during the War for American Independence* (1972)

Jones, Page H. *Evolution of a Valley: The Androscoggin Story* (1975)

Joy, Kenneth *The Kennebunks; Out of the Past* (1967)

Kershaw, Gordon E. *The Kennebeck Proprietors, 1749–1775: "Gentlemen of Large Property and Judicious Men"* (1975)

Kidder, Frederic *Military Operations in Eastern Maine and Nova Scotia during the Revolution* (1867, rpt. 1973)

Knowles, Katharine *Along the Maine Coast* (1973)

Lang, Constance R. *Kennebec, Boothbay Harbor Steamboat Album, Including Monhegan Island, Sheepscot and Damariscotta Rivers* (1971)

Laverty, Dorothy B. *Millinocket; Magic City of Maine's Wilderness* (1973)

Lund, Morten *Cruising the Maine Coast* (1967)

Martin, Kenneth R. *Whalemen and Whaleships of Maine* (1976)

Maunson, Gorham *Penobscot: Down East Paradise* (1959)

McLane, Charles B. *Blue Hill Bay: Islands of the Mid-Maine Coast* (1985)

Mellon, Gertrud A. and Elizabeth F. Wilder (eds.) *Maine and Its Role in American Art* (1963)

Merrill, Daphne W. *The Lakes of Maine; a Compilation of Fact and Legend* (1973)

Merrill, John and Suzanne (eds.) *Squirrel Island, Maine: The First Hundred Years* (1974)

Milliken, Roger *Forest for the Trees: A History of the Bakahegan Company* (1983)

Morison, Samuel E. *The Story of Mount Desert Island* (1960)

Murchie, Guy *Saint Croix, the Sentinel River* (1947)

Osborn, William C. *The Paper Plantation: Ralph Nader's Study Group on the Pulp and Paper Industry in Maine* (1974)

Porter, Eliot *Summer Colony: Penobscot Country* (1966)

Pratson, Frederick J. *The Sea in Their Blood* (1972)

Proper, Ida S. *Monhegan, the Cradle of New England* (1930)

Rich, Louise D. *The Peninsula* (1958, rpt. 1971)
———. *State O'Maine* (1964)
———. *The Coast of Maine: An Informal History and Guide* (1975)

Richardson, John M. *Steamboat Lore of the Penobscot: An Informal Story of Steamboating in Maine's Penobscot Region* (1941)

Ring, Elizabeth *Maine in the Making of the Nation, 1783–1870* (1987)

Rowe, William H. *The Maritime History of Maine, Three Centuries of Shipbuilding and Seafaring* (1966)

Rutherford, Phillip R. *The Dictionary of Maine Place-names* (1970, rpt. 1982)

Silber, Mark *Rural Maine* (1972)

Smith, David C. *A History of Lumbering in Maine, 1861–1960* (1972)

Smith, Mason P. *Confederates Downeast: Confederate Operations in and around Maine* (1985)

Smith, W. B. *The Lost Red Paint People of Maine* (1930)

Snell, Katherine *Historic Hallowell* (1962)

Speck, Frank G. *Penobscot Man: The Life History of a Forest Tribe in Maine* (1940)

Starbird, Charles M. *The Indians of the Androscoggin Valley* (1928)

Sterling, Robert T. *Lighthouses of the Maine Coast and the Men Who Keep Them* (1935)

Street, George E. (ed. Samuel A. Eliot) *Mount Desert: A History* (1905, rev. ed. 1926)

Sullivan, James *History of the District of Maine* (1795, rpt. 1970)

Swain, Raymond C. *A Breath of Maine; a Portrait of Robert P. Tristram Coffin* (1967)

Thompson, Deborah (ed.) *Maine Forms of American Architecture* (1976)

Van Winkle, Ted *Fred Boynton: Lobsterman, New Harbor, Maine* (1975)

Verrill, A. Hyatt *Romantic and Historic Maine* (1937)

Wasson, George S. *Sailing Days on the Penobscot: The Story of the River and the Bay in the Old Days* (1932, rev. ed. 1949)

Wilkins, Austin H. *Forests of Maine* (1932)

Willis, William P. *The History of Portland* (1972)

Wilson, Charles Morrow *Aroostook, Our Last Frontier: Maine's Picturesque Potato Empire* (1937)

Wood, Richard G. *A History of Lumbering in Maine, 1820–1861* (Maine Studies No. 33) (1935, rpt. 1961)

MARYLAND

Maryland is a south Atlantic state. It is bordered on the north by Pennsylvania; on the east by Delaware and the Atlantic Ocean; on the south by Virginia, the Potomac River, Chesapeake Bay, and West Virginia; and on the west by Virginia and West Virginia.

FULL NAME State of Maryland
POSTAL ABBREVIATION MD
INHABITANT Marylander
ADMITTED TO THE UNION April 28, 1788.
7th state
POPULATION (est. 1987) 4,535,000.
Percent of US total: 1.86%. Rank: 19th

CAPITAL CITY Annapolis, located on the Severn River and Chesapeake Bay in central Maryland; population 31,898 (est. 1984). Founded by Virginia colonists in 1649 as Providence, it was renamed Annapolis in honor of Princess Anne of England. The capital of Maryland since 1694, it became a city in 1708.

STATE NAME AND NICKNAMES Named by Lord Baltimore in honor of Queen Henrietta Maria (known as Queen Mary), the wife of King Charles I of England. Also known as the Free State and the Old Line State.

STATE SEAL The front of the seal shows the Lord Proprietary of colonial Maryland, Cecil Calvert, Lord Baltimore, riding in full armor on a horse along the seashore, silhouetted against the sky. The border reads "Caecilius Absolutus Dominus Terrae Mariae et Avaloniae Baro de Baltemore" (Cecil Absolute Lord of Maryland and Avalon Baron of Baltimore). The reverse side shows a heraldic shield, quartered, bearing the family arms of the Calvert and Crossland families. To the left of the shield is a farmer, to the right a fisherman; above it is a crown and banners from which flow

an ermine robe. One of the state mottoes, "Fatti Maschii Parole Femine," appears on a streamer below. The other state motto, and the date 1632, appears on the border.

MOTTOES Fatti Maschii Parole Femine (Manly deeds, womanly words; the Calvert family motto) Scuto Bonae Voluntatis Tuae Coronasti Nos (With favor wilt thou compass us as with a shield)

SONG "Maryland! My Maryland!," lyrics by James Ryder Randall, to the tune of "Lauriger Horatius."

SYMBOLS
Flower black-eyed Susan (yellow daisy)
Tree white oak
Bird Baltimore oriole
Dog Chesapeake Bay retriever
Fish striped bass
Insect Baltimore checkerspot butterfly
Fossil shell Ecphora quadricostata
Sport jousting
Theater Center Stage in Baltimore
Summer theater Olney Theatre in Montgomery County

LICENSE PLATE Black on white, with the state coat of arms (black, gold, white, and red).

FLAG Quartered, with the first and fourth quarters bearing the arms of the Calvert family, in gold and black, and the second and third bearing the arms of the Crossland family, in red and white.

GEOGRAPHY AND CLIMATE

Maryland is both a Coastal Plain state and an Appalachian one. Eastern Maryland, divided nearly in two by Chesapeake Bay (the largest estuary in the nation) and bounded along the south by the Potomac River and along the east by the Atlantic Ocean, is flat and fertile; the climate is warm and notoriously humid. The Maryland Piedmont, higher and drier ground, occupies the central part of the state. The hilly western end of Maryland, called "the Gateway of the Appalachians," is connected to the rest of the state by a panhandle only 1.5 miles in width.

AREA 10,460 square miles. Rank: 42d
INLAND WATER 623 square miles
GEOGRAPHIC CENTER Prince Georges, 4.5 miles NW of Davidsonville
ELEVATIONS *Highest point:* Backbone Mountain, Garrett County, 3,360 feet. *Lowest point:* Atlantic Ocean, sea level. *Mean elevation:* 3,190 feet

MAJOR RIVERS Potomac, Susquehanna, Patuxent

MAJOR LAKE Deep Creek

TIDAL SHORELINE 3,190 miles, Atlantic coast

LAND USE

	Thousands of acres
Urban (1982)	763
Rural (1982)	5,173
Cropland (1982)	1,794
Pastureland (1982)	534
Rangeland (1982)	0
Forestland (1982)	2,425
State parks and recreation areas (1983)	217
National park system (1984)	40
National forest system (1984)	0
Tribal lands (1984)	0

TEMPERATURES The highest recorded temperature was 109°F on July 10, 1936, at Cumberland and Frederick. The lowest was -40°F on January 13, 1912, at Oakland.

NATIONAL SITES

NATIONAL BATTLEFIELDS Antietam, Monocacy
NATIONAL CAPITAL PARKS National Capital Parks
NATIONAL CEMETERY Antietam
NATIONAL HISTORIC SITES Clara Barton, Hampton, Thomas Stone
NATIONAL HISTORICAL PARKS Chesapeake and Ohio Canal, Harpers Ferry
NATIONAL MONUMENT Fort McHenry
NATIONAL PARKWAY George Washington Memorial

NATIONAL SCENIC TRAILS Potomac Heritage, Appalachian
NATIONAL SEASHORE Assateague Island
OTHER PARKS Catoctin Mountain, Fort Washington Park, Greenbelt Park, Piscataway
NATIONAL WILDLIFE REFUGES Blackwater–Martin/Susquehanna, Chincoteague, Eastern Neck

HISTORY

1500s	Nanticoke and Piscataway Indian tribes dominate the region.
1526	Spanish explorers sail into Chesapeake Bay and call it Santa Maria.
1608	English captain John Smith investigates the Chesapeake Bay.
1631	Virginia councilman William Claiborne establishes a trading post on Kent Island.
1632	*June 20.* Charles I grants second Lord Baltimore Cecilius Calvert a charter for land north of the Potomac River.
1634	*February 27.* The *Ark* and *Dove* arrive at Chesapeake Bay with 200 colonists led by Governor Leonard Calvert.
	March 25. The colonists erect a cross on Saint Clements Island (Blakiston Island) and celebrate the Feast of Anunciation.
	St. Mary's is first city established.
1638	Cecilius Calvert surrenders his claim to have sole right of initiating legislation.
1644	Puritan captain Richard Ingle leads a rebellion against proprietary rule and captures St. Mary's.
1646	Governor Calvert defeats rebels at St. Mary's with a small army.

1649	*April 21*. Lord Baltimore instructs Governor William Stone to pass the Toleration Act thereby granting religious freedom to all Christians.
1654	Puritan colonists led by Claiborne revolt and win control of Maryland's government to end toleration until 1657.
1664	The colony's assembly rules for lifelong servitude for black slaves.
1689	*August 23*. The Protestant Association, formed by leader John Goode, demands the resignation of the Proprietorship.
1691	William and Mary declare Maryland a royal colony.
1695	The capital moves from St. Mary's to Annapolis.
1696	King Williams School (St. John's College) is founded.
1727	The *Maryland Gazette*, the state's first newspaper, is published in Annapolis.
1729	Baltimore Town is founded.
1744	The last Indian land claims in the state are purchased by the assembly.
1747	To ease the glutted market, the Tobacco Inspection Act is passed, whereby superior leaves are graded and "trash" leaves burned.
1756	French from Acadia, Canada seek refuge in Baltimore Town when exiled by British.
1765	*August 29*. A mob of 300 tear down the warehouse of stamp collector Zachariah Hood.
1767	The Mason Dixon survey establishes the boundaries between Maryland, Pennsylvania, and Delaware.
1774	*October 19*. The tea-loaded brig *Peggy Stewart* is burned.
1776	*November 9*. First state constitution is adopted.
1784	*January 14*. United States Congress meets at Annapolis capitol to sign the 1783 Treaty of Paris.
1788	*April 28*. Maryland becomes the seventh state to ratify the Constitution.
1791	Maryland cedes land along Potomac for construction of the District of Columbia.
1812	A charter is granted for the University of Maryland.
1814	*August 24*. Americans lose Battle of Bladensburg.
	September 12. British unsuccessfully attack North Point.
	September 14. Twenty-five hours of bombardment by the British on Fort McHenry inspires Francis Scott Key to write *The Star Spangled Banner*. (It becomes the US national anthem in March, 1931).
1828	*July*. Construction begins on both the Baltimore and Ohio Railroad and the Chesapeake and Ohio Canal.
1829	Chesapeake and Delaware Canal opens.
1834	*January*. Irish laborers for the C&O Canal revolt against working conditions.
1840	The Washington Temperance Society is formed.
1844	*May 24*. The first telegraph line opens between Baltimore and Washington, D.C.
1845	*October 10*. The Naval School (renamed the US Naval Academy in 1950) opens at Annapolis.
1861	*April 19*. Sixteen are killed when a Baltimore mob of southern sympathizers attacks the Sixth Massachusetts Regiment en route to Washington. Such acts typify the splitting political factions within the state.
	April 29. The Maryland House of Delegates rejects a bill of secession.
1862	*September 16-17* The Battle of Sharpesburg or Antietam results in over 23,000 casualties. Union armies keep confederates from moving further north.
1863	Confederate armies invade Maryland as General Robert E. Lee and troops move towards Gettysburg.
1864	Lieutenant General Jubal Early ravages Hagerstown.
1870	Pimlico Race Track opens near Baltimore.
1876	Johns Hopkins University opens.
1877	*July 20-22*. B&O workers strike and riot.
1882	Enoch Pratt Free Public Library is established.
1889	Steel plant opens at Sparrow's Point, becoming Maryland's largest manufacturing institution.
	May 7. Johns Hopkins Hospital opens.
1894	Maryland Women's Suffrage Association is founded.
1904	Downtown Baltimore is destroyed by fire.

1905	The influential critic, Henry Louis Mencken, joins the *Baltimore Sun*.
1910	The nation's first law requiring compensation for work-related injuries and death passes.
1914	George Herman (Babe) Ruth is sold to the Boston Red Sox for $6,900.
1919	Although it is a national law, Governor Albert Ritchie refuses to enforce prohibition.
1922	WCACO and WFBR begin broadcasting from Baltimore.
	United Mine Workers strike in western Maryland.
1924	The Potomac River floods and destroys the C&O Canal.
1931	*September*. Baltimore Trust Company, with holdings of $100 million, closes following the stock market crash.
1935	*October 8*. Federal government grants $9,180,000 additional for relief of destitute.
1936	*March 17-19*. Potomac River Valley floods, leaving thousands homeless.
1938	A $15 million federal housing project and the first state income tax law pass.
1941	Greenbelt, a New Deal designed and funded city, is completed.
1945	*May 23*. Maryland's Board of Censors bans the 1915 film *Birth of a Nation*.
1954	*September*. Baltimore's public schools are desegregated.
	July. The Chesapeake Bay Bridge is completed, paving the way for a shoreline boom in tourism and real estate.
1958	Baltimore Colts become the National Football League champions, defeating the New York Giants.
1962	Sixty Freedom Riders are arrested for sit-in demonstrations at various segregated restaurants in Cambridge, College Park, and Beltsville.
1966	Garrison Dam is completed.
	Orioles defeat Los Angeles Dodgers to win their first World Series.
	Spiro T. Agnew is elected governor.
1968	*April*. Rioting lasts four days following Martin Luther King's assassination.
1970	Baltimore's port ranks fourth in US foreign trade.
1972	*June 23*. Hurricane Agnes causes heavy flooding.
1973	Prince George's County begins busing program to achieve racial balance in schools.
	Vice President Agnew resigns following charges of tax evasion.
1974	Calvert Cliffs nuclear power plant begins operating.
1977	Baltimore's World Trade Center opens.
	August 23. Governor Marvin Mandell is found guilty of mail fraud and bribery.
1978	The state has 172 seafood-processing plants with an output worth $117,823,000.
1980	Harborplace, an $18 million complex, rejuvenates Baltimore's Inner Harbor.
1986	*May 14*. Maryland's promoter of world trade, the *Pride of Baltimore*, sinks off Puerto Rico, killing its captain and three crewmen.

DEMOGRAPHY

Population (est. 1987) . . .	4,535,000
Population (1980)	4,216,941
Population density in persons per square mile (1980)	403.2

POPULATION BY RACE (1980)

American Indian/Aleut/ Eskimo	8,021
Asian/Pacific Islander	164,276
Black	958,050
Hispanic	64,740
White	3,158,412
Other	27,687

POPULATION CHARACTERISTICS (1980)

	Percent of state population
Urban	80.3
Rural	19.7

Under 18	27.7
65 or older	9.4
College-educated	19.8
Families below poverty line	7.5
Public-assistance recipients	6.1

Per capita personal income (1986)	$16,588
Millionaires per 100,000 residents (1982; includes District of Columbia)	178.1
Average life expectancy in years (1980)	73.3
Marriage rate per 1,000 residents (1986)	10.3
Divorce rate per 1,000 residents (1986)	3.5

Birth rate per 1,000
residents (1985) 13.7
Infant mortality rate per 1,000
births (1985) 9.6
Abortion rate per 1,000 live
births (1985) 480
Crime rate per 100,000
residents (1985)
Violent 833.0
Property 4,768.8
Federal and state prisoners per
100,000 residents (1984) 301

Alcohol consumption in gallons
per capita (1985) 40.8
Deaths from motor vehicle accidents
per 100,000 residents (1985) . . 16.3

MAJOR CITIES

	1984 population (est.)
Annapolis	31,898
Baltimore	763,570
Frederick	31,943
Hagerstown	33,036

GOVERNMENT AND POLITICS

Number of US Representatives 8
Electoral votes 10

POLITICAL PARTY NOMINEES FROM STATE
  * winner

Robert Hanson Harrison	1789	P
John Henry	1796	P
John Eager Howard (Federalist)	1816	VP
Robert Goodloe Hooper (Federalist)	1816	VP
Robert Goodloe Hooper (Whig faction)	1820	VP
William Wirt (Anti-Masonic)	1832	P
William Daniel (Prohibition)	1884	VP
Joshua Levering (Prohibition)	1896	VP
F.C. Carrer (Prohibition/declined)	1944	P
Spiro Theodore Agnew* (R)	1968	VP
Robert Sargent Shriver (D)	1972	VP

PRESIDENTIAL PRIMARY ELECTION In 1988, Maryland sent 78 Democratic delegates and 41 Republican delegates to the national conventions.

CONSTITUTION Maryland has had 4 constitutions: 1776, 1851, 1864, and the present one, adopted in 1867.

LEGISLATURE The General Assembly is divided into the Senate (47 members, 4-year term, minimum age 25) and the House of Representatives (141 members, 4-year term, minimum age 21). In 1987, the annual salary was $22,000.

JUDICIARY The highest court is the Court of Appeals, with 7 judges serving 10-year terms. In 1987, the annual salary was $78,500.

EXECUTIVE The governor serves a 4-year term; the minimum age for holding office is 30. In 1987, the annual salary was $85,000. There are 3 other elected officials.

PRESIDENTIAL VOTE 1948-1988 *(in percents)*

Year	State Winner	Democratic	Republican
1948	Dewey (R)	47.8	49.2
1952	Eisenhower (R)	43.8	55.4
1956	Eisenhower (R)	40.0	60.0
1960	Kennedy (D)	53.6	46.4
1964	Johnson (D)	65.5	34.5
1968	Humphrey (D)	43.6	41.9
1972	Nixon (R)	37.4	61.3
1976	Carter (D)	52.8	46.7
1980	Carter (D)	47.1	44.2
1984	Reagan (R)	47.0	52.5
1988	Bush (R)	49.0	51.0

GOVERNORS

Lords Proprietary

Cecilius Calvert, 2nd Lord Baltimore	1632-1675
Charles Calvert, 3rd Lord Baltimore	1675-1715
Benedict Leonard Calvert, 4th Lord Baltimore	1715
Charles Calvert, 5th Lord Baltimore	1715-1751
Frederick Calvert, 6th Lord Baltimore	1751-1771
Henry Harford	1771-1776

Proprietary Governors

Leonard Calvert	1634-1647
Thomas Greene	1647-1649
William Stone	1649-1654
Commissioners	1654-1658
Josias Fendall	1658-1660
Philip Calvert	1660-1661
Charles Calvert	1661-1676
Cecilius Calvert	1676
Thomas Notley	1676-1679
Charles Calvert, 3rd Lord Baltimore	1679-1684
Benedict Leonard Calvert	1684-1688
William Joseph	1688-1692

Interval of Puritan Control

Protestant Associators	1689
Convention of Freemen and John Goode, commander in chief	1689-1690
Nehemiah Blakistone	1690-1692

Royal Governors

Sir Lionel Copley	1692-1693
Sir Thomas Lawrence	1693
Sir Edmund Andros	1693-1694
Colonel Nicholas Greenbury	1694
Sir Thomas Lawrence	1694
Francis Nicholson	1694-1699
Nathaniel Blakistone	1699-1702
Thomas Tench	1702-1704
John Seymour	1704-1709
Edward Lloyd	1709-1714

Proprietary Governors

John Hart	1715-1720
Charles Calvert	1720-1727
Benedict Leonard Calvert	1727-1731
Samuel Ogle	1731-1732
Charles, 5th Lord Baltimore	1732-1733
Samuel Ogle	1733-1742
Thomas Bladen	1742-1747
Samuel Ogle	1747-1752
Benjamin Tasker	1752-1753
Horatio Sharpe	1753-1769
Robert Eden	1769-1776
The Convention and Council of Safety	1776-1777

State Governors

Thomas Johnson	1777-1779
Thomas Sim Lee	1779-1782
William Paca	1782-1785
William Smallwood	1785-1788
John Eager Howard (Federalist)	1788-1791
George Plater (Federalist)	1791-1792
James Brice (Federalist)	1792
Thomas Sim Lee (Federalist)	1792-1794
John H. Stone (Federalist)	1794-1797

John Henry (Federalist)	1797-1798
Benjamin Ogle (Federalist)	1798-1801
John F. Mercer (R)	1801-1803
Robert Bowie (R)	1803-1806
Robert Wright (R)	1806-1809
Edward Lloyd (R)	1809-1811
Robert Bowie (R)	1811-1812
Levin Winder (Federalist)	1812-1815
Charles Ridgely of Hampton (Federalist)	1815-1818
Charles Goldsborough (Federalist)	1818-1819
Samuel Sprigg (R)	1819-1822
Samuel Stevens Jr. (R)	1822-1825
Joseph Kent (R)	1825-1828
Daniel Martin (Anti-Jackson)	1828-1829
Thomas K. Carroll (Jackson-Democrat)	1829-1830
Daniel Martin (Anti-Jackson)	1830-1831
George Howard (Whig)	1831-1833
James Thomas (Whig)	1833-1835
Thomas W. Veazey (Whig)	1835-1838
William Grason (D)	1838-1841
Francis Thomas (D)	1841-1844
Thomas G. Pratt (Whig)	1844-1846
Philip Francis Thomas (D)	1847-1850
Enoch Louis Lowe (D)	1850-1853
Thomas Watkins Ligon (D)	1853-1858
Thomas Holliday Hicks (American)	1858-1862
Augustus W. Bradford (Unionist)	1862-1865
Thomas Swann (Unionist, then Democrat)	1865-1868
Oden Bowie (D)	1868-1872
William Pinkney Whyte (D)	1872-1874
James Black Broome (D)	1874-1876
John Lee Carroll (D)	1876-1879
William T. Hamilton (D)	1880-1884
Robert M. McLane (D)	1884-1885
Henry Lloyd (D)	1885-1888
Elihu E. Jackson (D)	1888-1892
Frank Brown (D)	1892-1896
Lloyd Lowndes (R)	1896-1900
John W. Smith (D)	1900-1904
Edwin Warfield (D)	1904-1908
Austin L. Crothers (D)	1908-1912
Phillips L. Goldsborough (R)	1912-1916
Emerson C. Harrington (D)	1916-1920
Albert C. Ritchie (D)	1920-1935
Harry W. Nice (R)	1935-1939
Herbert R. O'Conor (D)	1939-1947
William Preston Lane (D)	1947-1951
Theodore R. McKeldin (R)	1951-1959
J. Millad Tawes (D)	1959-1967
Spiro T. Agnew (R)	1967-1969
Marvin Mandel (D)	1969-1977
Blair Lee III (D)	1977-1979

Harry R. Hughes (D)   1979-1987
William Donald Schaefer
  (D)   1987-

MINIMUM AGES

Majority 18
Marriage with parental consent . . 16
Marriage without parental consent . 18
Making a will 18
Buying alcohol 21
Jury duty 18
Leaving school 16
Driver's license 16

CAPITAL PUNISHMENT
Number executed 1976-88: 0
On death row, Aug. 1, 1988: 19

MILITARY INSTALLATIONS
Total number: 26
Major bases:
  Army: 2
  Navy: 3
  Air Force: 1

FINANCES

Thousands of dollars

GENERAL REVENUE (1985)
Total general revenue . . . 7,093,148
Total tax revenue 4,321,772
Sales and gross receipts . . . 1,949,496
Individual income taxes . . 1,768,256
Corporate net income taxes . . 246,123

GENERAL EXPENDITURE (1985)
Total general expenditure . 6,380,869
Education 1,964,693
Public welfare 1,199,007
Health 264,204
Hospitals 242,991
Natural resources 133,499
Highways 809,306
Police 158,439
Corrections 270,381

FEDERAL AID (1985) 1,811,665

ECONOMY

Dairy and poultry products yield the greatest part of Maryland's farm income, which produced $1 billion in cash receipts in 1983. Crops include corn, soybeans, tobacco, melons, vegetables, and fruits. Despite serious pollution of the coastal waters, fishing and seafood processing is still a major industry, with most of the value from shellfish such as Chesapeake Bay crabs and oysters. The 90-million-pound catch was worth $45 million in 1983. Bituminous coal is the main mining product; it is strip-mined in the western part of the state. Leading manufactures are steel, processed food, small machinery, chemicals, and transportation machinery; Maryland has excellent deepwater port facilities to handle volume imports and exports. Another important part of the state's economy is the provision of services to the Federal government in Washington, D.C.

EMPLOYMENT (1984)
Thousands of persons
Total number of employed
  workers 2,123
Construction 114.5
Finance, insurance, and
  real estate 103.8
Government 383.9
Manufacturing 218.1
Mining 1.6
Services 440.5
Transportation, communications,
  and utilities 90.1
Wholesale and retail trade . . . 449.2

Percent of civilian labor force
  unemployed (1984) 5.4

DEPARTMENT OF DEFENSE (1985)
Civilian workers employed . . . 43,292
Military personnel 35,687
Contract awards . . . . $4.608 billion

ENERGY SOURCES FOR ELECTRIC UTILITIES (1983)
Percent
Coal 47.5
Gas 0.4
Hydroelectric 5.4
Nuclear 35.8
Petroleum 10.9

TRANSPORTATION
Motor vehicles registered
  in state (1986) 3,683,394
Miles of roads, streets,
  and highways (1986) 27,738
Miles of Class I railway
  operated (1986) 849
Airports (1983) 147
Major aviation hubs (1983) 1
  Largest hub: Baltimore
Major ports, with gross tonnage
  in thousands (1985):
  Baltimore Harbor 36,425

Native American tribes

Before 1700, Maryland was home to the Conoy, Nanticoke, Powhatan Confederacy, Shawnee, and Susquehannock tribes, all of whom were destroyed or pushed westward.

Religions, ethnicities, and languages

Maryland's earliest colonists were English; they were joined in the 18th century by Scotch-Irish and German immigrants, including Mennonites and Moravians, whose descendants still live in the state's western parts. Baltimore, a haven for free Blacks prior to the Civil War, in the 19th-century absorbed many thousands of immigrants, including many Jews, from Germany, Russia, Poland, Czechoslovakia, Italy, and Greece; more recent immigration has been from China, Japan, the Philippines, and Southeast Asia. In 1980, 6.2 percent of Maryland's population spoke a language other than English at home.

Major museums and libraries

Baltimore Museum of Art
Municipal Museum of the City of
   Baltimore (Peale Museum)
Enoch Pratt Free Library, Baltimore
Walters Art Gallery, Baltimore

Major arts organizations

Baltimore Opera Company
Baltimore Symphony Orchestra
Center Stage, Baltimore
Maryland Ballet

Colleges and universities

Number public (1986-87) 32
Number private (1986-87) 24
Total enrollment, in full-time equivalent
   students (1985) 148,100

Public elementary and secondary schools

Expenditure per pupil in average daily
   attendance (1986-87) $4,660
Pupil-teacher ratio (1987) 17.1
Average teacher salary (1986-87) $29,940

Major league sports teams

Baseball: Baltimore Orioles

Holidays

Maryland Day. March 25
Defenders' Day. September 12
State Fair, Timonium. Late August or
   early September

MARYLAND IN LITERATURE

George Alsop *A Character of the Province of Mary-Land* (1666)
Sketches of early colonial society in prose and verse.

Donald L. Ball *Eastern Shore of Maryland Literature: A Bibliography* (1949)

John Barth *The Sot-weed Factor* (1960)
Historical novel set among the tobacco planters of seventeenth-century Maryland.

Silva Bedini *Benjamin Banneker* (1972)
Biography of a free black man, born in colonial Maryland, who instructed himself in mathematics and astronomy and helped survey the site of Washington, D.C.

Arthur Beverley-Giddings *Rival Shores* (1956)
Romance set on the Eastern Shore during Revolutionary times.

Robert H. Burgess *This Was Chesapeake Bay* (1963)
Stories about 300 years of shore life.

George G. Carey *Maryland Folklore and Folklife* (1970)
A comprehensive study of the state's folkways.
———. *A Faraway Time and Place: Lore of the Eastern Shore* (1971, rpt. 1977)
The folklore of fishing communities on the Eastern Shore.

Winston Churchill *Richard Carvel* (1900)
Historical novel of the Revolution, set in Maryland and London and containing a portrait of John Paul Jones.

William Eddis (ed. Aubrey C. Land) *Letters from America* (1969)
Descriptions of social life in Annapolis before the Revolution.

Clayton C. Hall (ed.) *Narratives of Early Maryland, 1633–1684* (1910)

Peggy Hoffman *My Dear Cousin* (1970)
Novel about Baltimore society before and during the War of 1812.

Tom Horton *Bay Country* (1988)
A naturalist's account of the Chesapeake region.

Harold D. Jopp and **R. H. Ingersoll** (eds.) *Shoremen: An Anthology of Eastern Shore Verse and Prose* (1974)
An anthology representing 300 years of literary history.

John Pendleton Kennedy *Swallow Barn* (1832)
A romance of plantation life.
———. *Rob of the Bowl* (1838)
Romantic historical novel based on events of 1677–1686.

Sophie Kerr *One Thing Is Certain* (1922)
Novel about a domestic tragedy set in a small town based on the author's native Denton.

Gilbert C. Klingel *The Bay: A Naturalist Discovers a Universe of Life above and below the Chesapeake* (1951)
Essays on marine and shore life.

H. L. Mencken *Prejudices* (1926)
A collection of essays in which Mencken explains and defends his preference for Baltimore over New York.
———. *Happy Days, 1880–1892* (1940)
Reminiscences of the author's childhood in Baltimore.

James A. Michener *Chesapeake* (1978)
Chronicle of 400 years of life on the Eastern Shore.

Conrad Richter *The Grandfathers* (1964)
Comic novel of western Maryland mountain people.

Don Robertson *By Antietam Creek* (1960)
Fictional account of the Civil War battle.

Frank R. Shivers, Jr. *Maryland Wits and Baltimore Bards* (1985)
Study of literary society in colonial and post-revolutionary Maryland.

George A. Townsend *Tales of the Chesapeake* (1880, rpt. 1968)
Humorous accounts of local folklore.

Waters Edward Turpin *These Low Grounds* (1937)
Novel about four generations of a black family on the Eastern Shore from slavery to 1930.

Anne Tyler *Celestial Navigation* (1974)
Novel about the life of an agoraphobic artist in a poor Baltimore neighborhood. Tyler has set many of her novels in the city.

GUIDES TO RESOURCES

Baer, Elizabeth *Seventeenth Century Maryland: A Bibliography* (1949)

Baltimore Council for International Visitors *Maryland, Our Maryland: An Ethnic and Cultural Directory* (1978)

Baltimore State Planning Department *The Counties of Maryland and Baltimore City: Their Origin, Growth and Development, 1634–1967* (1968)

Brown, Dorothy M. and **Richard R. Duncan** *Master's Theses and Doctoral Dissertations on Maryland History* (1970)

Cox, Richard J. *Tracing the History of the Baltimore Structure: A Guide to the Primary and Secondary Sources* (1980)
——— and **Larry E. Sullivan** (eds.) *Guide to the Research Collections of the Maryland Historical Society; Historical and Genealogical Manuscripts and Oral History Interviews* (1981)

Federal Writers' Project *Maryland, a Guide to the Old Line State* (1940, rpt. 1973)

Guertler, John T. (ed.) *The Records of Baltimore's Private Organizations: A Guide to Archival Resources* (1981)

Hall of Records Commission *Maryland Manual* (biennial)

Kaminkow, Marion J. *Maryland A to Z: A Topographical Dictionary* (1985)

Key, Betty M. (comp.) *Oral History in Maryland: A Directory* (1981)

Lawton, Elizabeth and **Raymond S. Sweeney** *Maryland History: A Selective Bibliography* (1975)

Maryland. Department of Economic and Community Development *The State of Maryland Historical Atlas* (1973)

Maryland Almanac (annual)

Meyer, Mary K. *Genealogical Research in Maryland: A Guide* (3d ed. 1983)

Papenfuse, Edward C. et al. (comps.) *An Inventory of Maryland State Papers* (1977–)
——— and **Joseph M. Coale III** (eds.) *The Hammond-Harwood Atlas of Historical Maps of Maryland, 1608–1908* (1982)

Pedley, Avril J. M. (ed.) *The Manuscript Collections of the Maryland Historical Society* (1968)

Porter, Frank W., III *In Pursuit of the Past: An Anthropological and Bibliographic Guide to Maryland and Delaware* (1986)

Reynolds, Michael M. *Maryland: A Guide to Information and Reference Sources* (1976)

Scarpaci, Jean *The Ethnic Experience in Maryland: A Bibliography* (1978)

Simpson, George A. "Bibliography of Maryland Folklore and Folklife" *Free State Folklore* (Spring 1975)

Thompson, Derek et al. *Atlas of Maryland* (1977)

SELECTED NONFICTION SOURCES

Agle, Nan H. *The Lords Baltimore* (1962)

Albright, Joseph *What Makes Spiro Run* (1972)

Anderson, Alan D. *The Origin and Resolution of an Urban Crisis: Baltimore, 1890–1930* (1977)

Andrews, Matthew P. *History of Maryland: Province and State* (1929, rpt. 1976)
———. *The Founding of Maryland* (1933)

Bailey, Kenneth *Thomas Cresap: Maryland Frontiersman* (1944)

Baker, Henry S., Jr. *Maryland Tobacco: Certain Aspects of a 300-Year-Old Enterprise* (1957)

Bard, Harry *Maryland, State and Government: Its New Dynamic* (1974)

Barker, Charles *The Background of the Revolution in Maryland* (1940, rpt. 1967)

Beirne, Francis *The Amiable Baltimoreans* (1951)
———. *Baltimore: A Picture History* (1958)

Blair, Carvel Hall and **Dyer Ansel Willits** *Chesapeake Bay: Notes and Sketches* (1970)

Blood, Pearl *The Geography of Maryland* (1961)

Bode, Carl *Mencken* (1969)
———. *Maryland: A Bicentennial History* (States and the Nation series) (1978)

Bodine, Aubrey *The Face of Maryland* (3d ed. 1970)

Brewington, Marion V. *Chesapeake Bay: A Pictorial Maritime History* (1956)

Brooks, Neal A. and **Eric G. Rockel** *A History of Baltimore County* (1979)

Browne, William Hand *Maryland: The History of a Palatinate* (rev. and enl. ed 1904, rpt. 1973)

Brugger, Robert J. *Maryland: A Middle Temperament, 1634–1980* (1988)

Capper, John, Garrett Power, and **Frank R. Shivers, Jr.** *Chesapeake Waters: Pollution, Public Health, and Public Opinion, 1602–1972* (1983)

Carr, Lois G. and **David W. Jordan** *Maryland's Revolution of Government, 1689–1692* (1973)
———, **Philip D. Morgan,** and **Jean B. Russo** (eds) *Colonial Chesapeake Society* (1988)

Cassell, Frank A. *Merchant Congressman in the Young Republic: Samuel Smith of Maryland* (1971)

Crooks, James B. *Politics and Progress: The Rise of Urban Progressivism in Baltimore, 1895–1911* (1966)

Crowl, Philip A. *Maryland during and after the Revolution: A Political and Economic Study* (1943)

Cunz, Dieter *The Maryland Germans, a History* (1948, rpt. 1972)

DiLisio, James E. *Maryland: A Geography* (1983)

Dozer, Donald M. *Portrait of a Free State: A History of Maryland* (1976)

Earle, Swepson *The Chesapeake Bay Country . . .* (3d ed. rev. 1929)

Eller, Ernest M. (ed.) *Chesapeake Bay in the American Revolution* (1981)

Ellis, Carolyn *Fisher Folk: Two Communities on Chesapeake Bay* (1986)

Evitts, William J. *A Matter of Allegiances: Maryland from 1850 to 1861* (1974)

Footner, Hulbert *Maryland Main and the Eastern Shore* (1942, rpt. 1967)

———. *Rivers of the Eastern Shore: Seventeen Maryland Rivers* (Rivers of America series) (1944)

Forman, H. C. *Old Buildings, Gardens, and Furniture in Tidewater Maryland* (1967)
———. *Maryland Architecture: A Short History from 1634 through the Civil War* (1968)

Garitte, Jerome R. *The Republic's Private Navy: The American Privateering Business as Practiced by Baltimore during the War of 1812* (1977)

Gibbons, Boyd *Wye Island: The True Story of an American Community's Struggle to Preserve Its Way of Life* (1977)

Goldsborough, William W. *The Maryland Line in the Confederate Army, 1861–1865* (2d ed. 1972)

Hall, Clayton C. *The Lords Baltimore and Their Maryland Palatinate* (1904)
———. (ed.) *Narratives of Early Maryland, 1633–1684* (1910)

Hamill, Kenny *The Placenames of Maryland, Their Origin and Meaning* (1984)

Hammond, John M. *Colonial Mansions of Maryland and Delaware* (1914, rpt. 1972)

Hart, Richard *Enoch Pratt: The Story of a Plain Man* (1935)

Harvey, Katherine A. *The Best Dressed Miners: Life and Labor in the Maryland Coal Region, 1835–1910* (1969)

Hill, Robert W. *The Chesapeake Bay Bridge-Tunnel; the Eighth Wonder of the World* (1972)

Hoffman, Ronald *A Spirit of Dissention: Economics, Politics, and the Revolution in Maryland* (1973)

Hungerford, Edward *The Story of the Baltimore and Ohio Railroad, 1827–1927* 2 vols. (1928)

Johnson, Paula J. (ed.) *Working the Water: The Commercial Fisheries of Maryland's Patuxent River* (1988)

Johnston, David E. *A History of the Middle New River Settlements* (1988)

Kent, Frank *The Story of Maryland Politics: An Outline History of the Big Political Battles of the State from 1864 to 1910* (1911)

Lambert, John R. *Arthur Pue Gorman* (1953)

Land, Aubrey C. *The Dulanys of Maryland* (rev. ed. 1968)
———. *Colonial Maryland: A History* (1981)

Lemay, J. A. Leo *Men of Letters in Colonial Maryland* (1972)

Levin, Alexandra L. *The Szolds of Lombard Street: A Baltimore Family, 1859–1909* (1909)

Lippman, Theo, Jr. *Spiro Agnew's America* (1972)

Main, Gloria L. *Tobacco Colony: Life in Early Maryland, 1650–1720* (1982)

McCauley, Lois B. (ed.) *Maryland Historical Prints, 1752 to 1889* (1975)

McConnell, Roland C. *Three Hundred and Fifty Years: Chronology of the Afro-American in Maryland, 1634–1984* (1985)

McSherry, James (ed. Bartlett B. James) *History of Maryland* (1904, rpt. 1968)

Meyer, Eugene L. *Maryland Lost and Found: People and Places from Chesapeake to Appalachia* (1986)

Middleton, Arthur P. *Tobacco Coast: A Maritime History of Chesapeake Bay in the Colonial Era* (1953)

Moore, Clay L. *You Take the High Road; a Guide to the Place Names of the Colonial Eastern Shore of Maryland* (1970)

Norris, Walter B. *Annapolis, Its Colonial and Naval Story* (1925)

Olson, Sherry H. *Baltimore: The Building of an American City* (1980)

Papenfuse, Edward C. *In Pursuit of Profit: The Annapolis Merchant in the Era of the Revolution, 1763–1805* (1975)

———, Gregory A. Stiverson, et al. (eds.) *Maryland: A New Guide to the Old Line State* (1976)

Parker, Franklin *George Peabody: A Biography* (1971)

Peffer, Randall S. *Watermen* (1979)

Quinn, David B. (ed.) *Early Maryland in a Wider World* (1982)

Radoff, Morris L. *Buildings of the State of Maryland at Annapolis* (1954)

Reps, John W. *Tidewater Towns: City Planning in Colonial Virginia and Maryland* (1972)

Risjord, Norman K. *Chesapeake Politics, 1781–1800* (1978)

Rollo, Vera F. *The Black Experience in Maryland* (1980)

Rouse, Parke *Roll, Chesapeake, Roll; Chronicles of the Great Bay* (1972)

Scharf, John T. *The Chronicles of Baltimore; Being a Complete History of "Baltimore Town" and Baltimore City from the Earliest Time to the Present Time* (1874, rpt. 1972)
———. *History of Maryland from Earliest Times to the Present Day* 3 vols. (1879)

Semmes, Raphael *Crime and Punishment in Early Maryland* (1938)

Sherwood, Arthur W. *Understanding the Chesapeake, a Layman's Guide* (1973)

Shomette, Donald G. *Shipwrecks on the Chesapeake; Maritime Disasters on Chesapeake Bay and Its Tributaries, 1608–1978* (1982)

Skaggs, David C. *Roots of Maryland Democracy 1753–1776* (1973)

Smith, Daniel B. *Inside the Great House: Planter Family Life in Eighteenth-Century Chesapeake Society* (1980)

Stenerson, Douglas C. *H. L. Mencken: Iconoclast from Baltimore* (1971)

Stevens, William Oliver *Annapolis; Anne Arundel's Town* (1971)

Stiverson, Gregory *Poverty in a Land of Plenty: Tenancy in Eighteenth Century Maryland* (1977)

Stone, William T. and Fessenden S. Blanchard *A Cruising Guide to the Chesapeake, Including the Passages from Long Island Sound along the New Jersey Coast and Inland Waterway* (rev. ed. 1973)

Titus, Charles *The Old Line State: Her Heritage* (1971)

Van Devanter, Ann C. *Anywhere So Long as There Be Freedom: Charles Carroll of Carrollton, His Family and His Maryland* (1975)

Walsh, Richard and William Lloyd Fox (eds.) *Maryland: A History 1632–1974* (1974)

Warner, William *Beautiful Swimmers: Watermen, Crabs, and the Chesapeake Bay* (1976)

Warren, Mame and Marion E. *Maryland Time Exposures, 1840–1940* (1984)

Wennersten, John R. *The Oyster Wars of Chesapeake Bay* (1981)

White, Frank, Jr. *The Governors of Maryland* (1970)

Willis, John T. *Presidential Elections in Maryland* (1984)

Wilstach, Paul *Potomac Landings* (1921)
———. *Tidewater Maryland* (1931)

Wolfe, George Hooper *I Drove Mules on the C & O Canal* (1969)

Wright, James *The Free Negro in Maryland, 1634–1860* (1921)

Wroten, William H., Jr. *Assateague* (2d ed. rev. and enl. 1972)

MASSACHUSETTS

Massachusetts is a New England state, bordered on the north by Vermont and New Hampshire; on the east by the Atlantic Ocean; on the south by the Atlantic Ocean, Rhode Island, and Connecticut; and on the west by New York.

FULL NAME Commonwealth of Massachusetts

POSTAL ABBREVIATION MA

INHABITANT Bay Stater

ADMITTED TO THE UNION Feb. 6, 1788. 6th state

POPULATION (est. 1987) 5,855,000. Percent of US total: 2.41%. Rank: 13th

CAPITAL CITY Boston, the largest city in the state, located on Massachusetts Bay at the mouths of the Charles and Mystic rivers; population 570,719 (est. 1984). Founded in 1630 by Puritan settlers, it became the capital of Massachusetts Bay Colony in 1632 and was incorporated as a city in 1822.

STATE NAME AND NICKNAMES From the Massachuset Indian term meaning "large hill place," in reference to the Great Blue Hill, south of the town of Milton. Also known as the Bay State, the Old Bay State, the Old Colony State, and the Baked Bean State.

STATE SEAL The seal shows the state coat of arms, a blue shield bearing the image of an Indian holding a bow and arrow, under a five-pointed star. Above the shield is a raised right arm holding a sword; below it, in gold letters on a blue streamer, is the state motto. Around the white border is the blue legend "Sigillum Reipublicae Massachusettensis" (Seal of the Republic of Massachusetts).

MOTTO Ense Petit Placidam Sub Libertate Quietem (By the sword we seek peace, but peace only under liberty)

SONGS "All Hail to Massachusetts," lyrics and music by Arthur J. Marsh. Official folk song is "Massachusetts," lyrics and music by Arlo Guthrie.

SYMBOLS
Flower mayflower (ground laurel)
Tree American elm
Bird chickadee
Gem rhodonite
Mineral Babingtonite
Rock Roxbury pudding stone
Building and monument stone granite
Dog Boston terrier
Horse Morgan horse
Marine mammal right whale
Fish cod
Insect ladybug
Fossil dinosaur track
Heroine Deborah Samson
Beverage cranberry juice
Explorer rock Dighton Rock
Historical rock Plymouth Rock
Poem "Blue Hills of Massachusetts" by Katherine E. Mullen

LICENSE PLATES (1) Dark green on white, with green border. (2) Red on white.

FLAG The state coat of arms, in blue and yellow, on a white field.

GEOGRAPHY AND CLIMATE

Typically New England soil—rocky, hard-packed, and poor for agriculture—covers Massachusetts's eastern half, which still exhibits the scouring of the last Ice Age. The jagged coastline forms many fine harbors, and one unique feature, the hook-shaped peninsula of Cape Cod. From the Connecticut Valley west the rolling hills are more fertile; the low mountains of the Berkshires and Taconic Range rise from the western state.

AREA 8,284 square miles. Rank: 45th

INLAND WATER 460 square miles

GEOGRAPHIC CENTER Worcester, in northern part of city

ELEVATIONS *Highest point:* Mount Greylock, Berkshire County, 3,491 feet. *Lowest point:* Atlantic Ocean, sea level. *Mean elevation:* 500 feet

MAJOR RIVERS Connecticut, Merrimack, Charles, Housatonic

MAJOR LAKES AND RESERVOIRS Quabbin, Wachusett, Assawompset Pond

TIDAL SHORELINE 1,519 miles, Atlantic coast

LAND USE

	Thousands of acres
Urban (1982)	883
Rural (1982)	3,839
Cropland (1982)	297
Pastureland (1982)	202
Rangeland (1982)	0
Forestland (1982)	2,970
State parks and recreation areas (1983)	261
National park system (1984)	31
National forest system (1984)	0
Tribal lands (1984)	0

TEMPERATURES The highest recorded temperature was 107°F on August 2, 1975, at New Bedford and Chester. The lowest was -35°F on January 12, 1981, at Chester.

NATIONAL SITES

NATIONAL HISTORIC SITES Adams, Boston African American, John F. Kennedy, Longfellow, Frederick Law Olmsted, Salem Maritime, Saugus Iron Works, Springfield Armory

NATIONAL HISTORICAL PARKS Boston, Lowell, Minute Man

NATIONAL SCENIC TRAIL Appalachian

NATIONAL WILDLIFE REFUGES Great Meadows–Monomoy/Oxbow, Nantucket, Parker River–John Hay/Pond Island/Thatcher Island/Wapack, Rachel Carson

HISTORY

1000	Vikings probably visit the Massachusetts shore. At this time seven tribes of Algonkian Indians are living along the coast.
1400s	French and Spanish fishermen sail along the Massachusetts shoreline.
1498	John Cabot, an Italian navigator employed by England, is believed to have explored the coast of Massachusetts.
1602	An English adventurer, Bartholomew Gosnold, lands on Cuttyhunk Island in the Elizabeth Islands. He gives Cape Cod its name.
1614	Captain John Smith sails along the Massachusetts seacoast. He draws maps that sailors use for many years.
1620	*December 11.* (December 20, according to the calendar now in use.) The *Mayflower* arrives and the Pilgrims disembark at Plymouth Rock. They had dropped anchor in Provincetown Harbor in November.
1621	Friendly Indians teach the Pilgrims how to plant corn and beans.
1623	*July 30.* Governor William Bradford sets aside a special day for the purpose of thankful prayer and celebration—the first Thanksgiving.
1628	Settlers establish a permanent colony in Salem. A year later a group called the Puritans join them. Their leader is John Winthrop, a London lawyer.
1630	Many Puritans migrate from Salem and establish Boston as their main colony.
1636	Harvard, the first college in the colonies, is founded at Cambridge.
1641	Massachusetts adopts its first code of law, the Body of Liberties.
1648	Margaret Jones of Charlestown is the first witch executed in America.
1651	Baptist ministers John Clarke and Obediah Holmes are arrested during religious observance in a private home.

1672	The Boston Post Road, a mail route, is completed.
1675–1676	King Philip's War. Indians kill about a tenth of the white male population. The war ends in eastern Massachusetts with the defeat of King Philip.
1682	Charles II, King of England, cancels the Massachusetts charter because the colonists have been trading with other countries.
1689	The colonists rebel and set up their own provisional government.
1692	Nineteen villagers are condemned as witches and executed in Salem.
1704	*February*. French and Indian War. The French and their Indian allies take the town of Deerfield.
1713	A peace treaty between the English and the French ends French competition along the Massachusetts coast. A 50-year era of prosperity begins.
1764–1765	Increasingly heavy taxes are placed on the colonists by the British, including the Sugar and the Stamp acts.
1770	*March 5*. Bitter feuding between the colonists and the British results in the Boston Massacre. Several colonists are killed including patriot Crispus Attucks.
1773	*December 16*. The Boston Tea Party. Enraged colonists disguised as Indians dump 342 chests of tea from a British ship in a protest against high taxes.
1775	*April 19*. The Revolutionary War begins. Minutemen, colonist patriots, fire the first shots against the British at Lexington and Concord. *June 17*. The Battle of Bunker Hill.
1780	Massachusetts adopts its constitution.
1787	*January 25*. Daniel Shays leads 1,100 men in an attempt to capture Springfield to protest treatment of poor farmers. Shays' Rebellion is put down by an army raised by the governor.
1788	*February 6*. Massachusetts becomes the sixth state of the US.
1797	*March 4*. John Adams, born in Quincy, becomes the second president of the US.
1807–1815	Thomas Jefferson's Embargo Act, shutting off all trade with England, brings great economic distress to Massachusetts that continues until the conclusion of the War of 1812 in 1814.
1825	*March 4*. John Quincy Adams, son of former president, John Adams, becomes the sixth president of the US.
1831	William Lloyd Garrison begins publishing his antislavery newspaper, *The Liberator*, and Massachusetts becomes the birthplace of the abolition movement.
1833	Massachusetts is the last state to separate church and state.
1846–1848	The Mexican War is unpopular in the state because the people regard it as a way to gain more slave territory in the US.
1852	Massachusetts makes school attendance mandatory for children between ages eight and 14.
1861–1865	The Civil War. Massachusetts provides almost 160,000 men to the Union Army and 30,000 men to the Navy. It builds and equips many ships.
1876	Alexander Graham Bell invents the telephone in Boston.
1912	A textile strike in Lawrence attracts nationwide attention to the working conditions of textile laborers. Some improvements follow.
1917–1918	World War I. The Yankee Division of Massachusetts is the first national guard division to reach the battlefields of France.
1920	*November 2*. Governor Calvin Coolidge of Massachusetts, nominated for Vice President, is elected with Warren Harding as president.
1923	*August 3*. Harding dies and Coolidge becomes president.
1924	*November 4*. Coolidge is elected for another term as president by a landslide vote.
1926–1928	Massachusetts textile and shoe industries are hard-hit by the competition from southern and western states.
1927	*August 23*. Immigrant anarchists Nicola Sacco and Bartolomeo Vanzetti are executed for the Braintree robbery.
1929–1932	The state carries out its own unemployment program during the Depression until the federal government steps in with nationwide relief programs.
1938	The first hurricane to hit the state in more than a hundred years causes millions of dollars in damage.

1941–1945   World War II. Many new factories are built to produce war materials. Boston shipyards build battleships and cargo ships.

1953   The state government organizes a new department of commerce to promote business and industry.
June 9. A tornado kills 86 people.

1950s   Many of the state's manufacturing plants change from making nondurable products such as textiles to durable products such as electronics.

1959   The US Navy launches the carrier *Long Beach* at Quincy. It is the first nuclear-powered surface ship.

1960   *November 8.* Brookline-born John F. Kennedy is elected president.

1962   Boston experiences an economic boom. The city's urban renewal program—the first in the nation—is a tremendous success.

1963   Notable laws are enacted in the field of social welfare.

1964   Edward Kennedy is elected to his first term in the US Senate.

1965   The University of Massachusetts decides to build a new medical school in Worcester.

1967   *May 23.* Three masked gunmen steal a Brink's armored truck carrying more than $600,000 at a Brockton shopping plaza.

1971   Unemployment reaches new high levels early in the year.

1973   *October 14.* Fire breaks out in Chelsea, northeast of Boston, and spreads over an 18-block section of this city of 30,000. It is one of the worst fires in recent urban US history.

1976   *December.* Governor Michael Dukakis appoints committee to make proposals for reform in the state court system.

1983   *January.* Michael Dukakis takes office.

1985   The state's financial community is startled when the Bank of Boston, largest in New England, pleads guilty to violation of federal currency regulations because of failure to report large cash transactions.

1988   *November 8.* Democratic presidential candidate Michael Dukakis loses election to Republican George Bush.

DEMOGRAPHY

Population (est. 1987) . . . 5,855,000
Population (1980) 5,737,081
Population density in persons
  per square mile (1980) 692.5

POPULATION BY RACE (1980)
American Indian/Aleut/
  Eskimo 7,743
Asian/Pacific Islander 49,501
Black 221,279
Hispanic 141,043
White 5,362,836
Other 95,678

POPULATION CHARACTERISTICS (1980)
Percent of state population
Urban 83.8
Rural 16.2
Under 18 . . . . 26.0
65 or older 12.7
College-educated 20.0
Families below poverty line 7.6
Public-assistance recipients 8.3

Per capita personal income
  (1986) $17,516
Millionaires per 100,000
  residents (1982) 132.3
Average life expectancy in
  years (1980) 75.0
Marriage rate per 1,000
  residents (1986) 7.0
Divorce rate per 1,000
  residents (1986) 3.4
Birth rate per 1,000
  residents (1985) 14.2
Infant mortality rate per 1,000
  births (1985) 9.1
Abortion rate per 1,000
  live births (1985) 533
Crime rate per 100,000
  residents (1985)
    Violent 556.9
    Property 4,166.5
Federal and state prisoners per
  100,000 residents (1984) 83
Alcohol consumption in gallons
  per capita (1985) 42.0

Deaths from motor vehicle accidents
  per 100,000 residents (1985) . . 12.7

Framingham	64,844
Lowell	93,473
Lynn	79,264
New Bedford	97,738
Springfield	150,454
Waltham	57,713
Worcester	159,843

MAJOR CITIES

1984 population (est.)

Boston	570,719
Brockton	95,892
Fall River	92,038

GOVERNMENT AND POLITICS

Number of US Representatives	11
Electoral votes	13

POLITICAL PARTY NOMINEES FROM STATE
  * winner

John Adams* (Federalist)	1789	P/VP
John Hancock	1789	P
Benjamin Lincoln	1789	P
John Adams* (Federalist)	1792	P/VP
John Adams* (Federalist)	1796	P
Samuel Adams	1796	P
John Adams (Federalist)	1800	P
Elbridge Gerry* (Democratic-Republican)	1812	VP
John Quincy Adams* (D-R)	1824	P
John Quincy Adams (Federalist/National Republican)	1828	P
Henry Lee (Independent)	1832	VP
Daniel Webster (Whig faction)	1836	P
Charles Francis Adams (Free-Soil Democratic)	1848	VP
Nathaniel Prentice Banks (North American Party)	1856	P
Edward Everett (Constitutional Union)	1860	VP
Henry Wilson* (R/National Working Men's Convention)	1872	VP
Charles Francis Adams (Straight-Out Democratic)	1872	VP
Frederick Douglas (People's Party)	1872	VP
Benjamin Frank Butler (Anti-Monopoly/Greenback)	1884	P
Simon Wing (Socialist Labor)	1892	P
Joseph Francis Maloney (Socialist Labor)	1900	P
Archibald Murray Howe (National/declined)	1900	P
Thomas Louis Hisgen (Independence)	1908	P
Arthur Elmer Reimer (Socialist Labor)	1912	P
Arthur Elmer Reimer (Socialist Labor)	1916	P
Calvin Coolidge* (R)	1920	VP
Calvin Coolidge* (R)	1924	P
John W. Aiken (Socialist Labor)	1932	VP
Seymour E. Allen (National/declined)	1932	P
John W. Aiken (Socialist Labor)	1936	P
Thomas Charles O'Brien (Union)	1936	VP
Roger Ward Babson (Prohibition)	1940	P
John W. Aiken (Socialist Labor)	1940	P
Edward Kirby Meador (Greenback)	1956	VP
John F. Kennedy* (D)	1960	P
Henry Cabot Lodge (R)	1960	VP
Edward Kirby Meador (Greenback)	1960	VP
Henning A. Blomen (Socialist Labor)	1964	VP
Mark Shaw (Prohibition)	1964	VP
Henning A. Blomen (Socialist Labor)	1968	P
Connie Blomen (Socialist Labor)	1976	VP
Michael S. Dukakis (D)	1988	P

PRESIDENTIAL PRIMARY ELECTION In 1988, Massachusetts sent 109 Democratic delegates and 52 Republican delegates to the national conventions.

CONSTITUTION Massachusetts is using its original constitution, adopted in 1780.

LEGISLATURE The General Court is divided into the Senate (40 members, 2-year term, minimum age 18) and the House of Representatives (160 members, 2-year term, minimum age 18). In 1987, the annual salary was $39,040.

JUDICIARY The highest court is the Supreme Judicial Court, with 7 judges serving until they reach the age of 70. In 1987, the annual salary was $80,500.

EXECUTIVE The governor serves a 4-year term; there is no minimum age for holding office. In 1987, the annual salary was $85,000. There are 5 other elected officials.

PRESIDENTIAL VOTE 1948-1988 *(in percents)*

Year	State Winner	Democratic	Republican
1948	Truman (D)	54.7	43.2
1952	Eisenhower (R)	45.5	54.2
1956	Eisenhower (R)	40.4	59.3
1960	Kennedy (D)	60.2	39.6
1964	Johnson (D)	76.2	23.4
1968	Humphrey (D)	63.0	32.9
1972	McGovern (D)	54.2	45.2
1976	Carter (D)	56.1	40.4
1980	Reagan (R)	41.7	41.9
1984	Reagan (R)	48.4	51.2
1988	Dukakis (D)	54.0	46.0

GOVERNORS

Governors of Plymouth Colony

John Carver	1620-1621
William Bradford	1621-1633
Edward Winslow	1633-1634
Thomas Prence	1634-1635
William Bradford	1635-1636
Edward Winslow	1636-1637
William Bradford	1637-1638
Thomas Prence	1638-1639
William Bradford	1639-1644
Edward Winslow	1644-1645
William Bradford	1645-1657
Thomas Prence	1657-1673
Josiah Winslow	1673-1680
Thomas Hinckley	1680-1692

Governors of Massachusetts Bay Colony

Matthew Cradock	1629
John Endecott (acting)	1629
John Winthrop	1629-1634
Thomas Dudley	1634-1635
John Haynes	1635-1636
Henry Vane	1636-1637
John Winthrop	1637-1640
Thomas Dudley	1640-1641
Richard Bellingham	1641-1642
John Winthrop	1642-1644
John Endecott	1644-1645
Thomas Dudley	1645-1646
John Winthrop	1646-1649
John Endecott	1649-1650
Thomas Dudley	1650-1651
John Endecott	1651-1654
Richard Bellingham	1654-1655
John Endecott	1655-1665
Richard Bellingham	1665-1672
John Leverett	1672-1679
Simon Bradstreet	1679-1686
Simon Bradstreet	1689-1692

Inter-Charter Period

Joseph Dudley (president of New England)	1686
Sir Edmund Andros (governor of New England)	1686-1689

Provincial Governors Appointed by the King

Sir William Phips	1692-1694
William Stoughton (acting)	1694-1699
Richard Coote	1699-1700
William Stoughton (acting)	1700-1701
The Council	1701-1702
Joseph Dudley	1702-1715
The Council	1715
Joseph Dudley	1715
William Tailer (acting)	1715-1716
Samuel Shute	1716-1723
William Dummer (acting)	1723-1728
William Burnet	1728-1729
William Dummer (acting)	1729-1730
William Tailer (acting)	1730
Jonathan Belcher	1730-1741
William Shirley	1753-1756
Spencer Phips (acting)	1756-1757
The Council	1757
Thomas Pownall	1757-1760
Thomas Hutchinson (acting)	1760
Francis Bernard	1760-1769
Thomas Hutchinson (acting)	1769-1771
Thomas Hutchinson	1771-1774
Thomas Gage	1774-1775

Revolutionary Governors

Provincial Congress	1774-1775
The Council	1775-1780

State Governors

John Hancock	1780-1785
James Bowdoin	1785-1787
John Hancock	1787-1793
Samuel Adams	1793-1797
Increase Sumner (Federalist)	1797-1799
Moses Gill (Federalist/acting)	1799-1800
Caleb Strong (Federalist)	1800-1807
James Sullivan (Democratic-Republican)	1807-1808

Levi Lincoln (D-R/acting)	1808-1809
Christopher Gore (Federalist)	1809-1810
Elbridge Gerry (D-R)	1810-1812
Caleb Strong (Federalist)	1812-1816
John Brooks (Federalist)	1816-1823
William Eustis (D-R)	1823-1825
Marcus Morton (D-R/acting)	1825
Levi Lincoln Jr. (D-R)	1825-1834
John Davis (Whig)	1834-1835
Samuel T. Armstrong (Whig/acting)	1835-1836
Edward Everett (Whig)	1836-1840
Marcus Morton (D)	1840-1841
John Davis (Whig)	1841-1843
Marcus Morton (D)	1843-1844
George N. Briggs (Whig)	1844-1851
George S. Boutwell (D and Free Soil)	1851-1853
John H. Clifford (Whig)	1853-1854
Emory Washburn (Whig)	1854-1855
Henry J. Gardner (American)	1855-1858
Nathaniel P. Banks (R)	1858-1861
John A. Andrew (R)	1861-1866
Alex H. Bullock (R)	1866-1869
William Claflin (R)	1869-1872
William B. Washburn (R)	1872-1874
Thomas Talbot (R/acting)	1874-1875
William Gaston (D)	1875-1876
Alex H. Rice (R)	1876-1879
Thomas Talbot (R)	1879-1880
John D. Long (R)	1880-1883
Benjamin F. Butler (D and Independent)	1883-1884
George D. Robinson (R)	1884-1887
Oliver Ames (R)	1887-1890
John Q.A. Brackett (R)	1890-1891
William E. Russell (D)	1891-1894
Frederick T. Greenhalge (R)	1894-1896
Roger Wolcott (R)	1896-1900
W. Murray Crane (R)	1900-1903
John L. Bates (R)	1903-1905
William L. Douglas (D)	1905-1906
Curtis Guild Jr. (R)	1906-1909
Eben S. Draper (R)	1909-1911
Eugene N. Foss (Progressive-Democrat)	1911-1914
David I. WAlsh (D)	1914-1916
Samuel W. McCall (R)	1916-1918
Calvin Coolidge (R)	1919-1921
Channing H. Cox (R)	1921-1925
Alvan T. Fuller (R)	1925-1929
Frank G. Allen (R)	1929-1931
Joseph B. Ely (D)	1931-1935
James M. Curley (D)	1935-1937
Charles F. Hurley (D)	1937-1939
Leverett Saltonstall (R)	1939-1945
Maurice J. Tobin (D)	1945-1947
Robert F. Bradford (R)	1947-1949
Paul A. Dever (D)	1949-1953
Christian A. Herter (R)	1953-1957
Foster Furcolo (D)	1957-1961
John A. Volpe (R)	1961-1963
Endicott Peabody (D)	1963-1965
John A. Volpe (R)	1965-1969
Francis W. Sargent (R)	1969-1975
Michael S. Dukakis (D)	1975-1979
Edward J. King (D)	1979-1983
Michael S. Dukakis (D)	1983-

MINIMUM AGES

Majority	18
Marriage with parental consent	. . . no minimum with court order
Marriage without parental consent	18
Making a will	18
Buying alcohol	21
Jury duty	18
Leaving school	16
Driver's license	17

CAPITAL PUNISHMENT
None

MILITARY INSTALLATIONS
Total number: 22
Major bases:
  Army: 1
  Air Force: 1

FINANCES

Thousands of dollars

GENERAL REVENUE (1985)

Total general revenue	10,417,026
Total tax revenue	6,620,595
Sales and gross receipts	2,225,515
Individual income taxes	3,158,971
Corporate net income taxes	851,283

GENERAL EXPENDITURE (1985)

Total general expenditure	10,171,442
Education	2,546,465
Public welfare	2,459,568
Health	424,446
Hospitals	552,842
Natural resources	71,374
Highways	469,112
Police	59,746
Corrections	220,147

FEDERAL AID (1985) 2,842,210

ECONOMY

In Massachusetts, agriculture is a minor part of the state's economy; farms are small and specialized, growing truck vegetables, apples, broadleaf tobacco, ornamentals, and cranberries, among other crops. Farm cash receipts were $387 million in 1983. Dairy products, eggs, and poultry are also important farm products; the state's fisheries bring in flounder, haddock, cod, whiting, ocean perch, lobsters, scallops, and shrimp. Electrical machinery, computers, aerospace components, textiles, shoes, processed foods, paper and paper products, tools, and plastics are among Massachusetts's principal manufactures. Value added by manufacture was $26 billion in 1982, among the highest values per worker in the nation. Service industries, including banking, data management, law, and insurance, are also important. The state's institutions of higher education have proved to be a vital economic asset; high-tech industries along Route 128 near Boston thrive on the outflow of basic research and researchers from MIT, Harvard, and other universities.

EMPLOYMENT (1984)

Thousands of persons

Total number of employed workers	2,906
Construction	96.1
Finance, insurance, and real estate	177.4
Government	369.7
Manufacturing	675.9
Mining	1.1
Services	750.7
Transportation, communications, and utilities	122.9
Wholesale and retail trade	657.9
Percent of civilian labor force unemployed (1984)	4.8

DEPARTMENT OF DEFENSE (1985)

Civilian workers employed	12,332
Military personnel	9,417
Contract awards	$7.714 billion

ENERGY SOURCES FOR ELECTRIC UTILITIES (1985)

	Percent
Coal	26.6
Gas	6.7
Hydroelectric	0.6
Nuclear	17.5
Petroleum	48.7

TRANSPORTATION

Motor vehicles registered in state (1986)	3,840,977
Miles of roads, streets, and highways (1986)	33,803
Miles of Class I railway operated (1986)	1,079
Airports (1983)	130
Major aviation hubs (1983)	1
Largest hub: Boston	
Major ports, with gross tonnage in thousands (1985):	
Boston	17,269

CULTURE AND EDUCATION

Native American tribes
Massachusetts was formerly home to the Mahican, Massachuset, Narragansett, Nashua, Nauset, Pennacook, and Pocomtuc tribes. Groups that continue to live in the state include the Nipmuc and Wampanoag.

Religions, ethnicities, and languages
Although the descendants of the English colonists are found throughout Massachusetts, Boston has been a center of immigration since the 1840s, taking in hundreds of thousands of Irish, Italian, French Canadian, Slovak, Polish, Russian Jewish, Greek, Scandinavian, Cuban, and Puerto Rican immigrants. There are Portuguese and Cape Verde communities along the coast, and an urban Black population. In 1980, 13.0 percent of Massachusetts's population spoke a language other than English at home. Despite the state's Protestant foundation, Roman Catholics are in the majority.

Major museums and libraries
Berkshire County Historical Society Museum, Pittsfield
Boston Athenaeum, Boston
Children's Museum, Boston
De Cordova and Dana Museum and Park, Lincoln
Fogg Art Museum, Harvard University, Cambridge
Isabella Stewart Gardner Museum, Boston
Museum of Science, Boston
Peabody Museum of Archaeology and Ethnology, Harvard University, Cambridge

Widener Library, Harvard University,
Cambridge

Major arts organizations
American Repertory Theatre, Cambridge
Berkshire Music Festival, Tanglewood
Berkshire Theatre Festival, Stockbridge
Boston Ballet
Boston Pops Orchestra
Boston Symphony Orchestra
Handel and Haydn Society, Boston
Huntington Theatre Company, Boston
Jacob's Pillow Dance Festival, Lee
Opera Company of Boston
Shakespeare and Company, Lenox
Stage West, Springfield
Williamstown Theatre Festival

Colleges and universities
Number public (1986-87) 31
Number private (1986-87) 90

Total enrollment, in full-time equivalent
students (1985) 321,000

Public elementary and secondary schools
Expenditure per pupil in average daily
attendance (1986-87) $4,856
Pupil-teacher ratio (1987) 14.4
Average teacher salary (1986-87) $30,810

Major league sports teams
Baseball: Boston Red Sox
Basketball: Boston Celtics
Football: New England Patriots
Hockey: Boston Bruins

Holidays
Evacuation Day, Boston. March 17
Patriots' Day. 3d Monday in April
Bunker Hill Day, Boston. June 17

MASSACHUSETTS IN LITERATURE

Abigail Adams (ed. Charles Francis Adams) *Letters, 1850–1860* (1840, rpt. 1913)
The wife of the second President comments widely on domestic issues and national affairs, giving an analytic view of contemporary society.

Thomas Bailey Aldrich *Ponnkapog Papers* (1903)
Essays and historical notes from a small village by the poet and sometime editor of the *Atlantic*.

Arlo Bates *The Philistines* (1889)
Satiric novel about Boston society.

Edward Bellamy *The Duke of Stockbridge* (1879, rpt. 1900)
This historical novel, set in Stockbridge during the time of Shays' Rebellion, was inspired by Bellamy's interest in post-Revolution society. The New England historian Samuel E. Morison regarded it as "one of the greatest historical novels."

Henry Beston *The Outermost House: A Year of Life on the Great Beach of Cape Cod* (1928)
Record of a naturalist's year spent in a two-room beach cabin.

William Bradford *Of Plimmouth Plantation* (1856, rpt. 1912)
The Yorkshire-born, self-educated Bradford had emigrated to Holland in 1609 to seek freedom of religion, and was one of the leaders of the "Pilgrim Fathers" who landed in Plymouth in 1620. He remained elected governor of the colony almost continuously from 1621 to 1656. Written between 1630 and 1651, his journal, intended for his descendants, relates the history of the colony to 1646.

Louis Bromfield *Early Autumn: A Story of a Lady* (1926)
Psychological novel about a woman's choice between love and the Puritan traditions of an old New England family.

William Hill Brown *The Power of Sympathy* (1789)
An epistolary novel of sexual intrigue by a Boston writer, portraying the mores of early New England society. Regarded as the first novel written in the US.

James Carroll *Mortal Friends* (1978)
Novel of Boston Irish life.

John Cheever *The Wapshot Chronicle* (1957); *The Wapshot Scandal* (1965)
Comic novels about the decline of an old New England family, descendants of 1630 settlers, and the social life of the fictional coastal town of St. Botolphs.

Lydia Maria Child *The Rebels* (1825)
Early historical novel depicting Boston before the Revolution. Child was a pioneer in women's suffrage and education, and in advocating abolition of slavery, and was the

author of one of the first household-management books for women.

James Fenimore Cooper *Lionel Lincoln; or, The Leaguer of Boston* (1825)
Historical romance of the Revolution, with accounts of the battles of Lexington and Bunker Hill.

William S. Davis *Gilman of Redford* (1927)
Novel set in Boston during the Revolution.

M. A. DeWolfe *A Venture in Remembrance* (1941)
Memoir of early twentieth-century Boston society.

André Dubus *Selected Stories* (1988)
Tales of contemporary life in the declining manufacturing towns of the northeastern corner of the state.

Marianne Dwight *Letters from Brook Farm, 1844–1847* (1928)
Descriptions of daily life at the utopian community.

Howard Fast *Citizen Tom Paine* (1943)
A fictional biography.
———. *April Morning* (1961)
The British raid on Lexington and Concord seen through the eyes of a boy.

Robert Finch *Common Ground; a Naturalist's Cape Cod* (1981)
Essays in natural history.

Esther Forbes *Mirror for Witches* (1928); *The Running of the Tide* (1948)
Historical novels set in Salem during the witchcraft trials, and during the nineteenth-century period of maritime prosperity.

Mary Wilkins Freeman *A New England Nun, and Other Stories* (1891)
Classic local color stories of the lives of eastern Massachusetts villagers, comparable with the genre writing of Sarah Orne Jewett. In addition to several collections of stories Freeman wrote novels and a play, *Giles Corey* (1893), based on an incident that took place in Salem during the witchcraft trials.

Ernest Gebler *Plymouth Adventure* (1950)
Historical novel about the settlers' first Plymouth winter.

Robert Grant *Fourscore* (1934)
Autobiography of a judge and writer who, in 1927, served on the committee investigating the Sacco-Vanzetti case. Grant was also well-known for two novels about Boston society: *The Chippendales* (1909), and *Dark Horse: A Story of the Younger Chippendales* (1931).

Edward Everett Hale *A New England Boyhood* (1893)
The Boston clergyman and writer recalls his upbringing in the 1820s and '30s. Nancy Hale, his grand-daughter, also recalled her Boston youth in the 1920s and '30s in *A New England Girlhood* (1958).

Joseph C. Hart *Miriam Coffin; or, The Whale-Fishermen* (1834)
The first American novel about whaling, set in Nantucket and New Bedford.

Nathaniel Hawthorne *Mosses from an Old Manse* (1846)
Tales and sketches of local customs and history written during Hawthorne's residence (1842–1846) at the Old Manse in Concord.
———. *The Scarlet Letter* (1850)
Classic novel of Puritan spiritual and emotional life, set in early Bay Colony society.
———. *The House of the Seven Gables* (1851)
Novel tracing the fortunes of a New England family, partly based on the legend that Hawthorne's own family was visited by a curse resulting from his great-grandfather's participation in the Salem witch trials.
———. *The Blithedale Romance* (1852)
Romantic novel set in a socialized community based on Hawthorne's experience of Brook Farm.

John Hay *The Great Beach* (1963)
Essays on the natural beauty of the Cape.

Joseph Hergesheimer *Java Head* (1919)
Historical novel of Salem seafaring in the early nineteenth century.

George V. Higgins *The Friends of Eddie Coyle* (1972)
Grimly realistic crime novel of Boston's underworld, one of the author's many crime stories set in Massachusetts.

Oliver Wendell Holmes *Elsie Venner: A Romance of Destiny* (1861)
Novel about a young schoolteacher of the Brahmin class and his woman pupil, set in Pittsfield.

Henry Beetle Hough *Mostly on Martha's Vineyard: A Personal Record* (1975)
Memoir by the editor of the *Vineyard Gazette*.

William Dean Howells *A Modern Instance* (1882)
Novel about a Maine journalist who moves to Boston.
———. *The Rise of Silas Lapham* (1885)
Novel about an uncultivated businessman's rise and fall in Boston society after the Civil War.

Henry James *The Bostonians* (1886)
Novel about reformist, blue-stocking society in late-nineteenth-century Boston, and a young man's struggle against political causes for the hand of a young feminist campaigner.

Howard Mumford Jones and **Bessie Zaban Jones** (eds.) *The Many Voices of Boston: A Historical Anthology, 1630–1975* (1975)

Sarah Kemble Knight *The Private Journal . . . Kept on a Journey from Boston to New York* (1825, rpt. 1920)
Diary of a colonist covering the years 1666–1727, remarkable for its plain and effective style.

Lucy Larcom *A New England Girlhood, Outlined from Memory* (1892)
Account of life in the Lowell mills and homes by a woman who became a well-known poet and children's writer.

Joseph Crosby Lincoln and **Freeman Lincoln** *The New Hope* (1941)
Historical novel of maritime adventure during the War of 1812.

Henry Cabot Lodge *Early Memories* (1913)
Statesman's memories of the state during the Civil War.

John P. Marquand *The Late George Apley* (1937)
A gentle satire of conservative Boston of the 1860s seen through the eyes of a cultivated man adapting his impulses to the constraints of inheritance and convention.

Herman Melville *Moby Dick* (1851)
Earlier chapters of Melville's classic mystical account of the whaling industry are a realistic record of early nineteenth-century New Bedford and Nantucket.

Samuel Eliot Morison *One Boy's Boston* (1962)
Eminent historian recalls his youth in the 1890s. This period was also described by the socialite Marion L. Peabody, *To Be Young Was Very Heaven* (1967), and by John Jay Chapman, in *Memories and Milestones* (1915).

Truman Nelson *The Passion by the Brook* (1953)
Historical novel about George Ripley and the utopian experiment at Brook Farm.

Elizabeth Phelps *A Peep at Number Five, or, A Chapter in the Life of a City Pastor* (1852)
Semi-autobiographical, closely observed account of the domestic life of a minister's wife. Phelps was one of the earliest exponents of realistic portrayal of ordinary New England lives.

Mary Rowlandson *A Narrative of the Captivity and Restoration . . .* (1682)
The author was held captive by the Indians in 1676, during King Philip's War. Her record of eleven weeks' hardship presents a graphic, and not unsympathetic, portrait of her Indian captors.

George Santayana *The Last Puritan: A Memoir in the Form of a Novel* (1936)
Satirical and philosophical novel about the conflict between a New England gentleman and a Latin hedonist, containing comic caricatures of Boston and Harvard "types."

Catharine Maria Sedwick *A New-England Tale; or, Sketches of New-England Character and Manners* (1822); *Redwood: A Tale* (1824); *Hope Leslie; or, Early Times in Massachusetts* (1827); *Home* (1835)
Sedgwick's novels represent the earliest successful attempt to portray New England as a region with a distinct culture. *A New-England Tale* and *Home* are set in Stockbridge, *Redwood* on a Vermont farm, and *Hope Leslie* is a romantic historical fiction set in western Massachusetts.

Anya Seton *The Winthrop Woman* (1958)
Historical novel based on the life of the niece of the governor of the Bay Colony.

Samuel Sewall *Diary* (1878–1882)
The author was appointed a judge at the Salem witchcraft trials in 1692 but became convinced of the innocence of the 19 victims by 1697. A preacher and businessman, he offers a detailed record of Puritan life and customs.

Upton Sinclair *Boston* (1928)
Novel about the city's political and social milieu based on the historical events of the Sacco and Vanzetti case.

Elizabeth Speare *The Prospering* (1967)
Historical novel set in eighteenth-century Stockbridge.

Harriet Beecher Stowe *Oldtown Folks* (1967)
Historical novel about village life and the Revolution. "Oldtown" was modelled on Natick, home town of the author's husband, but Stowe intended it to represent the "spirit and body of New England."

Phoebe Atwood Taylor *The Cape Cod Mystery* (1931)
First in a series of detective novels with realistic Cape Cod settings featuring the commonsense Yankee hero Asey Mayo.

Henry David Thoreau *Walden; or, Life in the Woods* (1854)
———. *Cape Cod* (1864, rpt. 1984)
Classic works of Transcendentalism based on observations of the Massachusetts landscape.

Mary M. Vorse *Time and the Town: A Provincetown Chronicle* (1942)
Autobiography and local history.

Mercy Warren *History of the Rise, Progress, and Termination of the American Revolution* (1805)
Classic narrative of the Revolution by an early sympathizer with the Colonial cause who was a close friend of John and Abigail Adams.

Edith Wharton *Ethan Frome* (1911); *Summer* (1917)
These novels were inspired by the author's wish "to draw life as it really was in the derelict mountain villages of New England." Both draw on her experiences of the Berkshires,

which she describes in her autobiography, *A Backward Glance* (1934)

Edward Winslow *A Relation or Journal . . . of the English Plantation* (1622); *Good News from New England . . .* (1624) The earliest narratives of the colony by one of its principal figures.

John Winthrop *A Journal of the Transactions . . . in the Settlement of Massachusettts . . .* (1790) Begun during his 1630 voyage on the *Arabella*, Winthrop's informal history is an important source of information on the religious and political life of the colony.

GUIDES TO RESOURCES

Brownlow, Arthur H. (ed.) *The Cape Cod Environmental Atlas* (1979)

Davis, Charlotte Pease (comp.) *Directory of Massachusetts Place Names: Current and Obsolete Counties, Cities, Towns, Sections or Villages, Early Names* (1987)

Elliott, Clark A. *A Descriptive Guide to the Harvard University Archives* (1974)

Federal Writers' Project *Massachusetts: A Guide to Its Places and People* (1937, rpt. 1971, 1983)

Forbes, H. M. *New England Diaries, 1602–1800* (1923)

Handbook of the Massachusetts Historical Society, 1791–1948 (1949)

Haskell, John D., Jr. (ed.) *Massachusetts: A Bibliography of Its History* (1976)

Kaufman, Martin, John W. Ifkovic, and **Joseph Carvalho III** *A Guide to the History of Massachusetts* (Reference Guides to State History and Research) (1988)

Massachusetts Historical Commission *Historical and Archaeological Resources of Cape Cod and the Islands . . .* (1987)

Massachusetts Historical Commission *Historical and Archaeological Resources of Southeast Massachusetts* (1982)

——. *Historical and Archaeological Resources of the Boston Area* (1982)

——. *Historical and Archaeological Resources of Central Massachusetts* (1948)

——. *Historical and Archaeological Resources of the Connecticut Valley* (1984)

——. *Historical and Archaeological Resources of Cape Cod and the Islands* (1987)

McManus, Douglas R. *Colonial New England: An Historical Geography* (1975)

Young, Alexander *Chronicles of the First Planters of the Colony of Massachusetts Bay, 1623–1636* (1846, rpt. 1975)

SELECTED NONFICTION SOURCES

Abrams, Richard *Conservatism in a Progressive Era: Massachusetts politics, 1900–1912* (1964)

Ackerman, Edward A. *New England's Fishing Industry* (1941)

Adams, Brooks *Emancipation of Massachusetts* (1887)

Adams, Charles F. *Three Episodes of Massachusetts History* 2 vols. (1896)

Adams, James T. *The Adams Family* (1930)

Amory, Cleveland *The Proper Bostonians* (1947)

Andrews, Charles M. *The Boston Merchants* (1917)
——. *The Colonial Period of American History* 4 vols. (1934)

Ashburn, Frank *Peabody of Groton* (1944)

Augur, Helen *An American Jezebel: The Life of Anne Hutchinson* (1930)

Bailyn, Bernard *The Ordeal of Thomas Hutchinson* (1974)

Banks, C. E. *The History of Martha's Vineyard* 3 vols. (1911–1925)

Banner, James M., Jr. *To the Hartford Convention: The Federalists and the Origin of Party Politics in Massachusetts* (1970)

Bartlett, Irving H. *Wendell Philips, Brahmin Radical* (1961)

Battis, Emery *Saints and Sectaries: Anne Hutchinson and the Antinomian Controversy in the Massachusetts Bay Colony* (1962)

Baum, Dale *The Civil War Party System: The Case of Massachusetts, 1848–1876* (1984)

Berry, Henry *Boston Red Sox* (1975)

Binford, Henry C. *The First Suburbs: Residential Communities on the Boston Periphery, 1815–1860* (1985)

Blodgett, Geoffrey *The Gentle Reformers: Massachusetts Democrats in the Cleveland Era* (1966)

Blouin, Francis X., Jr. *The Boston Region, 1810–1850: A Study of Urbanization* (1980)

Bowen, Catherine Drinker *John Adams and the American Revolution* (1950)

Boyer, Paul and **Stephen Nissenbaum** *Salem Possessed: The Social Origins of Witchcraft* (1974)

Bradford, William (ed. Samuel Morison) *Of Plymouth Plantation* (1647, rpt. 1952)

Briggs, L. Vernon *History of Shipbuilding on North River: 1640–1872* (1889)

Brooks, Van Wyck *The Flowering of New England, 1815–1865* (1936)
——. *New England Indian Summer* (1940)

Brown, Richard D. *Massachusetts: A History* (States and the Nation series) (1978)

Brown, Robert E. *Middle-Class Democracy and the Revolution in Massachusetts 1691–1780* (1955)

Campbell, Helen S. *Anne Bradstreet and Her Time* (1891)

Chinard, Gilbert *Honest John Adams* (1933)

Clark, George F. *History of Temperance Reform in Massachusetts, 1813–1883* (1888)

Colonial Society of Massachusetts *Seafaring in Colonial Massachusetts* (1980)

Conzen, Michael and **George K. Lewis** *Boston: A Geographical Portrait* (1976)

Corbett, Scott *We Chose Cape Cod* (1953)

Crawford, Mary C. *Romantic Days in Old Boston* (1922)
——. *Famous Families of Massachusetts* (1930)

Cronon, William *Changes in the Land: Indians, Colonists, and the Ecology of New England* (1983)

Curley, James Michael *I'd Do It Again: A Record of All My Uproarious Years* (1957)

Demos, John *A Little Commonwealth: Family Life in Plymouth Colony* (1970)

Dentler, Robert A. and **Marvin B. Scott** *Schools on Trial: An Inside Account of the Boston Desegregation Case* (1981)

Dewar, Margaret E. *Industry in Trouble. The Federal Government and the New England Fisheries* (1983)

Dineen, J. F. *The Purple Shamrock: The Honorable James Michael Curley of Boston* (1949)
——. *The Kennedy Family* (1959)

Dow, George F. *Everyday Life in the Massachusetts Bay Colony* (1935)

Dublin, Thomas *Women at Work: The Transformation of Work and Community in Lowell, Massachusetts, 1826–1860* (1979)

Dunn, Richard *Puritans and Yankees: The Winthrop Dynasty of New England* (1962)

Early, Eleanor *And This Is Boston* (1938)

Eaton, C. *Boston Opera* (1965)

Falls, Joe *Boston Marathon* (1977)

Federal Writers' Project *Boston Looks Seaward: The Story of the Port, 1630–1940* (1941)

Foote, Henry W. *Musical Life in Boston in the Eighteenth Century* (1940)

Forbes, Esther *Paul Revere and the World He Lived In* (1942)

Formisano, Ronald P. *The Transformation of Political Culture: Massachusetts Parties, 1790s–1840s* (1983)

Foster, Stephen *Their Solitary Way: The Puritan Social Ethic in the First Century of Settlement in New England* (1971)

Frank, Gerold *The Boston Strangler* (1966)

Frankfurter, Felix *The Case of Sacco-Vanzetti* (1927)

French, Allen *Day of Lexington and Concord* (1925)

Frothingham, O. B. *Boston Unitarianism* (1890)

Fuess, Claude M. *Daniel Webster* (1930)

Gibb, George S. *The Saco-Lowell Shops: Textile Machinery Building in New England, 1813–1949* (1950)

Goodman, Paul *The Democratic-Republicans of Massachusetts* (1964)

Green, Eugene and William L. Sachse *Names of the Land: Cape Cod, Nantucket, Martha's Vineyard, and the Elizabeth Islands* (1983)

Green, James and Hugh C. Donahue *Boston's Workers: A Labor History* (1944)

Greenslet, Ferris *The Lowells and Their Seven Worlds* (1946)

Griffin, Solomon B. *People and Politics Observed by a Massachusetts Editor* (1923)

Gross, Robert *The Minutemen and Their World* (1976)

Handlin, Oscar *Boston's Immigrants, 1790–1880: A Study in Acculturation* (rev. enl. ed. 1972)
—— and Mary F. *Commonwealth, a Study of the Role of Government in the American Economy: Massachusetts, 1774–1861* (1947)

Hansen, Chadwick *Witchcraft at Salem* (1969)

Hardy, Stephen *How Boston Played: Sport, Recreation, and Community, 1865–1915* (1982)

Hart, Albert B. (ed.) *Commonwealth History of Massachusetts, Colony, Province, and State* (1927–1930)

Hatch, Alden *The Lodges of Massachusetts* (1973)

Hennessy, Michael E. *Four Decades of Massachusetts Politics, 1890–1935* (1917)
——. *Twenty-Five Years of Massachusetts Politics, 1890–1915* (1917)

Hohman, Elmo P. *The American Whaleman. A Study of Life and Labor in the Whaling Industry* (1928)

Horton, James O. and Lois E. *Black Bostonians: Family and Community Struggle in the Antebellum North* (1979)

Hough, Henry B. *Martha's Vineyard, Summer Resort, 1835–1935* (1936)

Howe, Daniel W. *The Puritan Republic of Massachusetts Bay in New England* (1899)

Howe, Henry F. *Salt Rivers of the Massachusetts Shore* (Rivers of America series) (1951)

Howe, M. A. DeWolfe *Boston, the Place and the People* (1903)
——. *Later Years of the Saturday Club* (1921)

——. *The Boston Symphony Orchestra* (1931)
——. *A Venture in Remembrance* (1941)

Hoyt, Edwin P. *Nantucket, the Life of an Island* (1978)

Hutchinson, Thomas *History of the Colony and Province of Massachusetts Bay* (1767)

Huthmacher, J. Joseph *Massachusetts People and Politics, 1919–1933* (1959)

Jones, E. Alfred *The Loyalists of Massachusetts: Their Memorials, Petitions, and Claims* (1930)

Jones, Lamar *Village and Seaport: Migration and Society in Eighteenth-Century Massachusetts* (1981)

Keyssar, Alexander *Out of Work: The First Century of Unemployment in Massachusetts* (1986)

Kittredge, Henry C. *Shipmasters of Cape Cod* (1935)
——. *Cape Cod, Its People and Their History* (2d ed. 1968)

Knight, Peter *The Plain People of Boston, 1830–1860* (1971)

Krutch, Joseph Wood *Henry David Thoreau* (1948)

Labaree, Benjamin W. *The Boston Tea Party* (1964)
——. *Colonial Massachusetts* (1979)

Levin, David *Cotton Mather: The Young Life of the Lord's Remembrancer, 1663–1703* (1978)

Litt, Edgar *The Political Cultures of Massachusetts* (1965)

Lockridge, Kenneth A. *A New England Town, the First Hundred Years: Dedham, Massachusetts, 1636–1736* (expanded and enl. ed. 1985)

Lockwood, John *Western Massachusetts, a History, 1636–1925* (1926)

Lovejoy, David *The Glorious Revolution in America* (1972)

Lupo, Alan *Liberty's Chosen Home: The Politics of Violence in Boston* (1977)

Mann, Arthur *Yankee Reformers in the Urban Age: Social Reform in Boston, 1880–1900* (1954)

McFarland, Gerald W. *Mugwumps, Morals, and Politics, 1884–1920* (1975)

Middlekauff, Robert *The Mathers: Three Generations of Puritan Intellectuals, 1596–1728* (1971)

Miller, John C. *Sam Adams, Pioneer in Propaganda* (1936)

Miller, Perry *The New England Mind: The Seventeenth Century* (1939)
——. *The New England Mind: From Colony to Province* (1953)
—— and Thomas Johnson (eds.) *The Puritans: A Sourcebook of Their Writings* 2 vols. (1963)

Morgan, Edmund S. *The Puritan Dilemma* (1958)

Morison, Samuel Eliot *The Maritime History of Massachusetts, 1783–1860* (1921)
——. *Builders of the Bay Colony* (1930, rpt. 1964)
——. *Three Centuries of Harvard, 1636–1936* (1936)
——. *History of the Plymouth Plantation* (1952)

Murdock, Kenneth *Increase Mather: The Foremost American Puritan* (1925)

Newcomer, Lee N. *The Embattled Farmers: A Massachusetts Countryside in the American Revolution* (1953)

Poor, Alfred E. *Colonial Architecture of Cape Cod, Nantucket, and Martha's Vineyard* (1932, rpt. 1970)

Prudge, Jonathan *The Coming of Industrial Order: Town and Factory Life in Rural Massachusetts, 1810–1860* (1983)

Riley, Stephen T. *Dr. William Whiting and Shays' Rebellion* (1957)

Rosenzweig, Roy *Eight Hours for What We Will: Workers and Leisure in an Industrial City, 1870–1920* (1983)

Rose-Troup, Frances *John White, the Patriarch of Dorchester (Dorset) and the Founder of Massachusetts 1575–1648 with an*

Account of the Early Settlements in Massachusetts 1620–30 (1930)

Rossiter, William S. *Days and Ways in Old Boston* (1915)

Russell, Francis *Tragedy in Dedham: The Story of the Sacco-Vanzetti Case* (1971)
———. *A City in Terror: 1919, the Boston Police Strike* (1975)

Russell, Howard S. *A Long Deep Furrow. Three Centuries of Farming in New England* (1976)

Rutman, Darrett *Winthrop's Boston: Portrait of a Puritan Town* (1969)

Ryan, Dennis P. *Beyond the Ballot Box: A Social History of the Boston Irish, 1845–1917* (1983)

Schriftgiesser, Karl *The Gentleman from Massachusetts* (1944)

Schultz, Stanley *The Culture Factory: Boston Public Schools, 1789–1860* (1973)

Scully, Vincent *The Shingle Style and the Stick Style* (rev. ed. 1971)

Shand-Tucci, Douglass *Built in Boston: City and Suburb, 1800–1950* (1978, rpt. 1988)

Shipton, Clifford K. *Roger Conant, a Founder of Massachusetts* (1944)

Silverman, Kenneth *The Life and Times of Cotton Mather* (1984)

Sinnott, Edmund W. *Meetinghouse and Church in Early New England* (1963)

Smith, Bradford *Bradford of Plymouth* (1951)

Smith, Chard P. *The Housatonic, Puritan River* (Rivers of America series) (1947)

Snow, Edward Rowe *The Romance of Boston Bay* (1944)

Spring, James W. *Boston and the Parker House* (1927)

Starbuck, Alexander *History of the American Whale Fishery* (1878, rpt. 1964)
———. *History of Nantucket, County, Island, and Town* (1924)

Starkey, Marion L. *The Devil in Massachusetts: A Modern Inquiry into the Salem Witch Trials* (1949)

Stewart, James B. *Wendell Phillips: Liberty's Hero* (1986)

Stone, Orra L. *History of Massachusetts Industries* 4 vols. (1930)

Straler, Arthur N. *A Geologist's View of Cape Cod* (1966)

Sylvester, N. B. et al. *History of the Connecticut Valley in Massachusetts* (1829)

Tager, Jack and John W. Ifkovic (eds.) *Massachusetts in the Gilded Age: Selected Essays* (1985)

Taylor, Robert J. *Western Massachusetts in the Revolution* (1954)

Tharp, Louise H. *The Peabody Sisters of Salem* (1950)

Thernstrom, Stephan *Poverty and Progress: Social Mobility in a Nineteenth-Century City* (1964)

Thwing, Anne H. *The Crooked and Narrow Streets of Boston* (1920)

Todisco, Paula J. *Boston's First Neighborhood: The North End* (1976)

Tourtellot, Arthur Bernon *The Charles* (1941)

Trout, Charles H. *Boston, the Great Depression, and the New Deal* (1977)

Vanderbilt, Arthur T. *Treasure Wreck: The Fortunes and Fate of the Pirate Ship Whydah* (1986)

Warden, G. B. *Boston, 1689–1776* (1970)

Ware, Edith E. (comp.) *Political Opinion in Massachusetts during the Civil War and Reconstruction* (1916)

Warner, Sam B., Jr. *Streetcar Suburbs: The Process of Growth in Boston, 1870–1900* (1962)
———. *The Way We Really Live: Social Change in Metropolitan Boston since 1920* (1977)

Washburn, Frederick A. *The Massachusetts General Hospital* (1939)

Weisman, Richard *Witchcraft, Magic, and Religion in 17th-Century Massachusetts* (1984)

Whitehill, Walter M. *Boston: A Topographical History* (2d enl. ed. 1968)

Winslow, Ola *Samuel Sewall of Boston* (1964)

Withey, Lynne *Dearest Friend: A Life of Abigail Adams* (1981)

Wood, James P. *The People of Concord* (1970)

Wroth, L. Kinvin et al. *Province in Rebellion: A Documentary History of the Founding of the Commonwealth of Massachusetts* (1975)

Zobel, Hiller B. *The Boston Massacre* (1970)

MICHIGAN

Michigan is an east central state and consists of two peninsulas in the midst of the Great Lakes. The Upper Peninsula is bordered on the north by Lake Superior; on the east by Whitefish Bay and St. Mary's River; on the south by Lake Huron and Lake Michigan; and on the southwest and west by Wisconsin. The Lower Peninsula is bordered on the north by Lake Michigan and Lake Huron; on the east by Lake Huron, the Canadian province of Ontario, and Lake Erie; on the south by Ohio and Indiana; and on the west by Lake Michigan.

FULL NAME Michigan
POSTAL ABBREVIATION MI
INHABITANT Michiganian
ADMITTED TO THE UNION Jan. 26, 1837.
 26th state
POPULATION (est. 1987) 9,200,000.
 Percent of US total: 3.78%. Rank: 8th

CAPITAL CITY Lansing, located in the south central part of the lower peninsula; population 127,972 (est. 1984). It was founded about 1820 and became the capital in 1847.

STATE NAME AND NICKNAMES From the Chippewa Indian word *majigan*, "clearing," in reference to a location on the west side of the lower peninsula. Also known as the Wolverine State, the Lake State, the Auto State, the Great Lake State, and the Lady of the Lake.

STATE SEAL In the center is a shield showing a man on a grassy peninsula at lakeside, his right arm raised in greeting, a rifle in his left, and behind him the rising sun, with the legend "Tuebor" (I Will Defend). To the left of the shield is an elk, to the right a moose; above it is an eagle with olive branches and arrows in its talons and a red streamer bearing the legend "E Pluribus Unum" (From Many, One); below it is a streamer with the state motto. Around this coat of arms is an orange border with the legend "The Great Seal of the State of Michigan, A.D. MDCCCXXXV."

MOTTO Si Quaeris Peninsulam Amoenam Circumspice (If you seek a pleasant peninsula, look about you)

SONG "My Michigan," lyrics by Giles Kavanagh, music by H. J. O'Reilly Clint.

SYMBOLS
Flower apple blossom
Tree white pine
Bird robin
Gem chlorastrolite (greenstone)
Stone Petoskey stone
Fish trout

LICENSE PLATE White on dark blue, with legend "Great Lakes."

FLAG The state coat of arms on a field of blue.

GEOGRAPHY AND CLIMATE

Michigan is divided into two parts, the Upper Peninsula and the Lower Peninsula, by the Straits of Mackinac between Lake Huron and Lake Michigan. The Lower Peninsula is typically midwestern in terrain and climate, while the Upper Peninsula is upland terrain, heavily forested and rich in mineral deposits. Bordering four of the five Great Lakes, Michigan also contains more than 10,000 interior lakes and numerous small rivers.

AREA 58,527 square miles. Rank: 23d
INLAND WATER 1,573 square miles
GEOGRAPHIC CENTER Wexford, 5 miles NNW of Cadillac
ELEVATIONS *Highest point:* Mount Curwood, Baraga County, 1,980 feet. *Lowest point:* Lake Erie, Monroe County, 572 feet. *Mean elevation:* 900 feet

MAJOR RIVERS Grand, Kalamazoo, Escanaba, Saginaw

MAJOR LAKES AND RESERVOIRS Superior, St. Clair, Houghton, Torch, Charlevoix, Burt, Mullett, Manistique

LAND USE

	Thousands of acres
Urban (1982)	1,966
Rural (1982)	30,265
Cropland (1982)	9,443
Pastureland (1982)	2,911
Rangeland (1982)	0
Forestland (1982)	15,360
State parks and recreation areas (1983)	248
National park system (1984)	630
National forest system (1984)	4,873
Tribal lands (1984)	12

TEMPERATURES The highest recorded temperature was 112°F on July 13, 1936, at Mio. The lowest was -51°F on February 9, 1934, at Vanderbilt.

NATIONAL SITES

NATIONAL HISTORIC SITE Father Marquette
NATIONAL LAKESHORES Pictured Rocks, Sleeping Bear Dunes
NATIONAL PARK Isle Royale
NATIONAL SCENIC TRAIL North Country
NATIONAL WILDLIFE REFUGES Seney–Huron, Shiawassee–Michigan Islands/Wyandotte

HISTORY

c.1618–1620 French explorer Étienne Brulé becomes the first European in Michigan when he lands at the site of Sault Sainte Marie.

1634 Jean Nicolet, seeking a northwest passage to Asia, passes through the Straits of Mackinac, which link Lake Huron and Lake Michigan.

1659–1660 Médard Chouart, Sieur des Groseilliers, and Pierre Ésprit Radisson visit the Upper Peninsula of Michigan.

1668 Father Jacques Marquette founds the first settlement in the Middle West at Sault Sainte Marie as a Jesuit mission.

1671 Marquette establishes a mission chapel and military outpost at St. Ignace, commanding the Straits of Mackinac.

1673 Marquette and Louis Jolliet leave on a trip that takes them to the Mississippi a month later.

1679 Robert Cavelier, Sieur de La Salle, arrives at St. Ignace aboard the *Griffon*—the first sailing vessel on the upper Great Lakes.
November 1. Cavelier arrives at the site of St. Joseph, where he erects Fort Miami.

1680 La Salle crosses the lower peninsula from Fort Miami, reaching the Detroit River in ten days.

1691 Fort St. Joseph is built near what is now Niles; a Jesuit mission has already been established there.

1701 *July 24.* Antoine de la Mothe Cadillac founds Fort Pontchartrain on the site of present-day Detroit, which soon flourishes as a trading post.

1760 *November 29.* Detroit surrenders to Major Robert Rogers, leaving Rangers serving the British in the French and Indian War.
The British occupy abandoned Fort Michilimackinac the next year.

1763 Fort Michilimackinac, at present-day Mackinaw City, is captured by Chippewa Indians and Fort St. Joseph is taken by the Potawatomi, but Detroit survives a five-week siege by Ottawa Indians led by Pontiac. Michilimackinac is reoccupied in 1764.

1781   *February 12*. Ungarrisoned Fort St. Joseph is occupied by French and Spanish forces during the Revolutionary War for 24 hours.
Fort Michilimackinac is moved to Mackinac Island.

1783   *September 3*. The Treaty of Paris, ending the American Revolution, requires the British to leave Michigan, but they remain until 1796.

1785   The value of the fur trade at Detroit in this year is estimated at £180,000.

1795   First cession of Indian lands in Michigan to the United States, by the Treaty of Greenville.

1796   *July 11*. Following the ratification of Jay's Treaty, the American flag is raised in Michigan for the first time as the British evacuate Detroit.

1805   *January 11*. The Territory of Michigan is created, with Detroit as its capital.

1812   *July 17*. Fort Mackinac on Mackinac Island falls to the British in the War of 1812.
August 16. Detroit surrenders.

1813   *September 26*. Two weeks after Lieutenant Oliver Perry's naval victory over the British on Lake Erie (September 10), the British evacuate Detroit, after burning the public buildings.

1814   *December 24*. The Treaty of Ghent ends the War of 1812 without territorial changes, thereby returning Mackinac Island to the US.

1817   John Jacob Astor's American Fur Company establishes a trading post on Mackinac Island.

1818   *July 6*. Public land sales at auction begin at Detroit; average price bid is $4 an acre.
August 27. The *Walk-in-the-Water*, first steamboat on the upper Great Lakes, arrives at Detroit from Buffalo.

1825   Completion of the Erie Canal across New York stimulates trade and settlement in Michigan.

1836   Peak of the land boom, with about one-ninth of the state's land area sold in that year, for more than $5.2 million.

1837   *January 26*. Michigan is admitted to the Union as the 26th state. In return for accepting Ohio's boundary claim to the "Toledo strip," the state is awarded the remaining western three-quarters of the Upper Peninsula.

1841   University of Michigan opens at Ann Arbor.

1842   *October 4*. Indians cede virtually their last holdings in the state.

1846   *May 18*. Michigan is first state to abolish death penalty.

1847   *March 17*. Legislature meets for the last time in Detroit as state capital is moved to Lansing.
First of 41 consecutive years in which Michigan leads the nation in copper production (from the Upper Peninsula).

1849   *April 23*. A trans-state lower peninsula railway is completed from Detroit to New Buffalo.

1855   *May 31*. Opening of the Soo Canal, linking Lake Superior and Lake Huron, at Sault Sainte Marie.

1861–1865 *May 16*. Michigan supplies the first western Civil War regiment to reach Washington. Almost 90,000 Michigan soldiers see service; of whom nearly 15,000 die.

1863   Michigan Cavalry Brigade under George Armstrong Custer turns back Jeb Stuart's Confederate cavalry at Gettysburg.

1888   Michigan is producing about one-fourth of the nation's lumber.

1890   Michigan leads all states in iron-ore production, from Upper Peninsula mines.

1900   Completion of Olds Motor Works, the first US auto factory, in Detroit.

1903   *June 12*. The Ford Motor Company is organized in Detroit.

1908   Henry Ford introduces the Model T, selling for $850.

1914   Auto industry accounts for 37 percent of the state's manufacturing output. Henry Ford announces a $5 daily wage for an eight-hour day.

1920   Total farm acreage reaches a peak of 19,032,961.

1932   In the wake of the Great Depression, 43 percent of the state's nonagricultural labor force are reported out of work.

1935   State population has dropped 28 percent since 1930.

1936	*December 30*. A spontaneous sit-down strike at the General Motors auto plant in Flint begins, soon spreading to other plants and resulting in collective bargaining union agreements with GM and Chrysler.
1941	*April 19*. Construction begins of the Ford Willow Run airplane bomber factory, the world's largest assembly plant.
1943	*June 20–21*. A Detroit race riot leaves 34 dead and hundreds injured.
1958	G. Mennen Williams, Democrat, elected to an unprecedented sixth term as governor.
	June 28. Dedication of the Mackinac Island Bridge, one of the world's longest suspension spans, linking the lower and upper peninsulas.
1963	*April 1*. Voters narrowly approve a new constitution, the state's fourth.
1967	*July 21–23*. A two-day riot in Detroit's black ghetto results in at least 43 dead and $50 million in property damage.
1972	*January 1*. A no-fault divorce law, called the nation's most liberal, becomes effective.
1974	*August 9*. Vice President Gerald R. Ford of Grand Rapids becomes the nation's first president from Michigan.
1977	*March 1*. Opening of the 73-story Plaza Hotel, the keystone of the $350-million Renaissance Center in Detroit.
1980	*June 24*. The Chrysler Corporation receives the first installment of $1.5 billion in federal aid intended to save the auto manufacturer from bankruptcy.
1982	*December*. State unemployment reaches 17.3 percent, highest since the Great Depression. A total of 237,150 auto workers are on indefinite layoff.
1987	A monorail opens in downtown Detroit, 2.9 miles in length.

DEMOGRAPHY

Population (est. 1987) . . . 9,200,000
Population (1980) 9,262,070
Population density in persons
  per square mile (1980) 158.3

POPULATION BY RACE (1980)
American Indian/Aleut/
  Eskimo 40,038
Asian/Pacific Islander 56,731
Black 1,198,710
Hispanic 162,388
White 7,868,956
Other 93,909

POPULATION CHARACTERISTICS (1980)
Percent of state population
Urban 70.7
Rural 29.3
Under 18 . . . . 29.7
65 or older 9.8
College-educated 15.2
Families below poverty line 8.2
Public-assistance recipients 8.9

Per capita personal income
  (1986) $14,064
Millionaires per 100,000
  residents (1982) 80.1
Average life expectancy in
  years (1980) 73.4
Marriage rate per 1,000
  residents (1986) 8.6

Divorce rate per 1,000
  residents (1986) 4.1
Birth rate per 1,000
  residents (1985) 4.8
Infant mortality rate per 1,000
  births (1985) 11.0
Abortion rate per 1,000
  live births (1985) 486
Crime rate per 100,000
  residents (1985)
  Violent 803.9
  Property 5,687.6
Federal and state prisoners per
  100,000 residents (1984) 159
Alcohol consumption in gallons
  per capita (1985) 39.8
Deaths from motor vehicle accidents
  per 100,000 residents (1985) . . 16.9

MAJOR CITIES
	1984 population (est.)
Ann Arbor	107,673
Battle Creek	54,349
Dearborn	86,960
Detroit	1,088,973
Flint	149,007
Grand Rapids	183,000
Kalamazoo	77,226
Lansing	127,972
Pontiac	70,973
Saginaw	73,694

GOVERNMENT AND POLITICS

Number of US Representatives	9
Electoral votes	11

* winner

Lewis Cass (D)	1848	P
Charles C. Foote (National Liberal)	1848	VP
John Russell (Prohibition)	1872	VP
Verne L. Reynolds (Socialist Labor)	1928	P
Verne L. Reynolds (Socialist Labor)	1932	P
Gerald Lyman Kenneth Smith (America First)	1944	P
Tucker Powell Smith (Socialist)	1948	VP
Earle Harold Munn Sr. (Prohibition)	1960	VP
Earle Harold Munn Sr. (Prohibition)	1964	P
Earle Harold Munn Sr. (Prohibition)	1968	P
Earle Harold Munn Sr. (Prohibition)	1972	P
Gerald Rudolph Ford (R)	1976	P
R. Wayne Evans (US Labor)	1976	VP

PRESIDENTIAL PRIMARY ELECTION In 1988, Michigan sent 151 Democratic delegates and 77 Republican delegates to the national conventions.

CONSTITUTION Michigan has had four constitutions: 1835, 1850, 1908, and the present one, adopted in 1963.

LEGISLATURE The Legislature is divided into the Senate (38 members, 4-year term, minimum age 21) and the House of Representatives (110 members, 2-year term, minimum age 21). In 1987, the annual salary was $39,881.

JUDICIARY The highest court is the Supreme Court, with 7 judges serving 8-year terms. In 1987, the annual salary was $100,000.

EXECUTIVE The governor serves a 4-year term; the minimum age for holding office is 30. In 1987, the annual salary was $100,077. There are 35 other elected officials.

PRESIDENTIAL VOTE 1948-1988 *(in percents)*

Year	State Winner	Democratic	Republican
1948	Dewey (R)	47.6	49.2
1952	Eisenhower (R)	44.0	55.4
1956	Eisenhower (R)	44.2	55.6
1960	Kennedy (D)	50.9	48.8
1964	Johnson (D)	66.7	33.1
1968	Humphrey (D)	48.2	41.5
1972	Nixon (R)	41.8	56.2
1976	Ford (R)	42.0	54.9
1980	Reagan (R)	42.5	49.0
1984	Reagan (R)	40.2	59.2
1988	Bush (R)	46.0	54.0

GOVERNORS

Territorial Governors

William Hull	1805-1813
Lewis Cass	1813-1831
John T. Mason (acting)	1831
George P. Porter	1831-1834
Stevens T. Mason (ex officio)	1834-1835

State Governors

Stevens T. Mason (D)	1835-1840
William Woodbridge (Whig)	1840-1841
James W. Gordon (Whig/acting)	1841
John S. Barry (D)	1842-1846
Alpheus Felch (D)	1846-1847
William L. Greenly (D/acting)	1847
Epaphroditus Ransom (D)	1848-1850
John S. Barry (D)	1850-1851
Robert McClelland (D)	1852-1853
Andrew Parsons (D/acting)	1853-1854
Kinsley S. Bingham (R)	1855-1858
Moses Wisner (R)	1859-1860
Austin Blair (R)	1861-1864
Henry H. Crapo (R)	1865-1868
Henry P. Baldwin (R)	1869-1872
John J. Bagley (R)	1873-1876
Charles M. Croswell (R)	1877-1880
David H. Jerome (R)	1881-1882

Josiah W. Begole (D and Greenback)	1883-1884
Russell A. Alger (R)	1885-1886
Cyrus G. Luce (R)	1887-1890
Edwin B. Winans (D)	1891-1892
John T. Rich (R)	1893-1896
Hazen S. Pingree (R)	1897-1900
Aaron T. Bliss (R)	1901-1904
Fred M. Warner (R)	1905-1910
Chase S. Osborn (R)	1911-1912
Woodbridge N. Ferris (D)	1913-1916
Albert E. Sleeper (R)	1917-1920
Alexander J. Groesbeck (R)	1921-1926
Fred W. Green (R)	1927-1930
Wilber M. Brucker (R)	1931-1932
William A. Comstock (D)	1933-1934
Frank D. Fitzgerald (R)	1935-1936
Frank Murphy (D)	1937-1938
Frank D. Fitzgerald (R)	1939
Luren D. Dickinson (R)	1939-1940
Murray D. Van Wagoner (D)	1941-1942
Harry F. Kelly (R)	1943-1946
Kim Sigler (R)	1947-1948
G. Mennen Williams (D)	1949-1960
John B. Swainson (D)	1961-1962
George W. Romney (R)	1963-1969
William G. Milliken (R)	1969-1983
James J. Blanchard (D)	1983-

MINIMUM AGES

Majority	18
Marriage with parental consent	16
Marriage without parental consent	18
Making a will	18
Buying alcohol	21
Jury duty	18
Leaving school	16
Driver's license	16

CAPITAL PUNISHMENT
None

MILITARY INSTALLATIONS
Total number: 13
Major bases:
Army: 1

FINANCES

Thousands of dollars

GENERAL REVENUE (1985)

Total general revenue	15,164,596
Total tax revenue	8,684,163
Sales and gross receipts	3,519,875
Individual income taxes	3,048,512
Corporate net income taxes	1,391,863

GENERAL EXPENDITURE (1985)

Total general expenditure	14,063,002
Education	4,185,009
Public welfare	3,885,099
Health	917,373
Hospitals	703,333
Natural resources	185,486
Highways	1,114,350
Police	135,131
Corrections	366,695

FEDERAL AID (1985) 3,961,474

ECONOMY

Agriculture accounts for a small percentage of Michigan's income. Hay, corn, and dairy are the principal farm products. Soybeans, pole beans, sugar beets, apples, and fruits are also important crops; beef cattle and hogs are the main livestock. Mining products include iron and copper from the Upper Peninsula, oil, natural gas, salt, peat, limestone, gypsum, sand, and gravel in the Lower Peninsula. In manufacturing, where the state is a leader in value added to manufacture, motor vehicles are the dominant and best-known product, followed by metal and steel products, machine tools, appliances, pharmaceuticals, light machinery, plastics, apparel, furniture, processed foods, chemicals, and paper products. Michigan also has a thriving publishing industry, and tourism brings in over $1 billion in income to the state each year.

EMPLOYMENT (1984)

Thousands of persons

Total number of employed workers	3,871
Construction	89.2
Finance, insurance, and real estate	153.8
Government	566.5
Manufacturing	945.8
Mining	9.4
Services	696.5
Transportation, communications, and utilities	138.5
Wholesale and retail trade	743.6
Percent of civilian labor force unemployed (1984)	11.2

DEPARTMENT OF DEFENSE (1985)

Civilian workers employed	12,198
Military personnel	8,773
Contract awards	$2.789 billion

ENERGY SOURCES FOR ELECTRIC UTILITIES (1983)

	Percent
Coal	73.4
Gas	1.0
Hydroelectric	1.6
Nuclear	23.1
Petroleum	0.9

TRANSPORTATION

Motor vehicles registered
in state (1986) 6,831,762

Miles of roads, streets,
and highways (1986) 117,664
Miles of Class I railway
operated (1986) 3,451
Airports (1983) 422
Major aviation hubs (1983) 3
Largest hub: Detroit/Ann Arbor
Major ports, with gross tonnage in
thousands (1985):
Detroit 15,612

CULTURE AND EDUCATION

Native American tribes
Michigan was formerly home to the Fox, Kickapoo, Menominee, Miami, Neutral, Noquet, Piankashaw, Sauk, and Wyandot tribes. Groups that continue to live in the state include the Ojibway, Ottawa, and Potawatomi. There are five federal reservations in Michigan.

Religions, ethnicities, and languages
Roman Catholicism is the largest denomination in the state. The French settlers who founded Detroit in the 18th century were Catholic; since then, the city has attracted many Catholic immigrants from Ireland, Poland, Italy, and Canada. Detroit also has large Jewish and Black populations. Of the approximately 200 Protestant denominations active in Michigan, the largest are the Lutheran (brought by German, Finnish, and Scandinavian immigrants), Methodist, and Baptist churches. Dutch immigrants joined the Christian Reformed Church. The Seventh-Day Adventist Church was founded in Michigan in the early 1800s, the Black Muslim group in Detroit in 1930. In 1980, 6.5 percent of Michigan's population spoke a language other than English at home.

Major museums and libraries
Cranbrook Academy of Art Museum, Bloomfield Hills
Cranbrook Institute of Science, Bloomfield Hills
Detroit Institute of Arts

Henry Ford Museum and Greenfield Village, Dearborn
Grand Rapids Art Museum
International Afro-American Museum, Detroit
Kalamazoo Institute of Arts
Michigan Historical Museum, Lansing

Major arts organizations
Actors Alliance Theatre Company, Southfield
Detroit Symphony Orchestra
Michigan Opera Theatre

Colleges and universities
Number public (1986-87) 44
Number private (1986-87) 47
Total enrollment, in full-time equivalent students (1985) 354,700

Public elementary and secondary schools
Expenditure per pupil in average daily attendance (1986-87) $3,967
Pupil-teacher ratio (1987) 20.2
Average teacher salary (1986-87) $32,800

Major league sports teams
Baseball: Detroit Tigers
Basketball: Detroit Pistons
Football: Detroit Lions
Hockey: Detroit Red Wings

Holidays
State Fair, Detroit. Late August or early September
State Fair, Escanaba. Mid-August

MICHIGAN IN LITERATURE

Louise V. Armstrong *We Too Are the People* (1938)
Tales of the government effort of the 1930s to assist rural families in a lumbering region of northern Michigan.

Harriet Arnow *The Dollmaker* (1954)
Novel about the effect of city life on Gertie Nevels and her family, who migrate to Detroit from the Kentucky hills.

Al Barnes *Vinegar Pie and Other Tales of the Grand Traverse Region* (1959)
Folk history collected by a Traverse City journalist.

Earl C. Beck *Lore of the Lumber Camps* (rev. and enl. ed. (1948)
The first edition (1941) was entitled *Songs of the Michigan Lumberjacks.*
———. *They Knew Paul Bunyan* (1956)
Lumberjack legends.

Albert G. Black *Michigan Novels: An Annotated Bibliography* (1963)

Eleanor Blake *Seedtime and Harvest* (1935)
Novel set on a farm at the turn of the century.

James Cloyd Bowman *The Adventures of Paul Bunyan* (1927)
Tales of the legendary lumberjack.

Raymond D. Burroughs *Peninsular Country* (1965)
Sketches of Michigan life and lore by a naturalist and ecologist.

Bruce Catton *Waiting for the Morning Train* (1972)
Memoir of growing up in a small town at the turn of the century by a journalist and historian.

James Fenimore Cooper *Oak Openings* (1848)
Historical novel centering on the flight of a pioneer family from the pro-British Potawatomies after the fall of the Mackinac during the War of 1812.

David C. DeJong *Belly Fulla Straw* (1934); *Light Sons and Dark* (1940)
Novels about the farming life of Dutch ethnic communities.

Richard Dorson *Bloodstoppers and Bearwalkers; Folk Traditions of the Upper Peninsula* (1952)
A collection of folklore gathered in 1946.
———. *Negro Folktales in Michigan* (1956)
Collection of black folklore.

G. D. Eaton *Backfurrow* (1925)
Realistic, somber novel about farm life, regarded as a landmark of literary naturalism.

Richard B. Erno *The Catwalk* (1955) *My Old Man* (1955); *The Hunt* (1960)
Novels about simple, rural people set in small towns and villages.

Pauline Benedict Fischer *Clay Acres* (1938)
Novel about the rise and fall of a family in an agricultural community from 1860.

Richard C. Ford *Heroes and Hero Tales of Michigan* (1930)

Iola Fuller *The Loon Feather* (1940)
Historical novel about Indian life during fur trading days on Mackinac Island.

Emelyn E. Gardner and **Geraldine J. Chickering** (eds.) *Ballads and Songs of Southern Michigan* (1939)

Margaret Gay *Hatchet in the Sky* (1954)
Historical novel about the French and Indian War and Pontiac's conspiracy.

Joe Grimm (ed.) *Michigan Voices: Our State's History in the Words of People Who Lived It* (1987)

Marie C. W. Hamlin *Legends of Le Detroit* (1884, rpt. 1977)
Tales of early French settlement.

Jim Harrison *Farmer* (1976)
Novel about a Swedish-American schoolteacher-farmer in Upper Michigan.

Ulysses P. Hedrick *The Land of the Crooked Tree* (1948)
An account of pioneer life in the L'Arbe Croche region by a settler whose family migrated in 1874.

Ernest Hemingway *The Nick Adams Stories* (1972)
Semi-autobiographical stories, many set in northern Michigan.

Caroline M. Kirkland (pseud., Mrs. Mary Clavers) *A New Home--Who'll Follow? or, Glimpses of Western Life* (1839; reissued 1874 as *Our New Home, in the West: or, Glimpses of Life among Early Settlers*)
An unfavorable account of life among the pioneers of Pinckney in the 1820s and '30s. *Forest Life* (1842) and *Western Clearings* (1845) were in a similar vein.

Janet Lewis *The Invasion* (1932)
Historical novel tracing the fortunes of an Upper Michigan family from 1800 to the early twentieth century.

Leo E. Litwak *Waiting for the News* (1970)
Realistic novel about labor unrest in Detroit during the 1930s.

Della Lutes *Gabriel's Search* (1940)
Chronicle of farm life in southern Michigan.
———. *Country Schoolma'am* (1941)
Autobiographical memoir of rural life in the 1880s.

Malcolm X [Malcolm Little] *The Autobiography of Malcolm X* (1965)
The Black Muslim leader recounts his small-town Michigan boyhood.

John Bartlow Martin *Call It North Country: The Story of Upper Michigan* (1944, rpt. 1986)
The people, landscape, and history of the Upper Peninsula.

Arnold Mulder *The Dominie of Harlem* (1913); *The Outbound Road* (1919)
Realistic novels about Dutch immigrant life.

William Nowlin *The Bark Covered House* . . . (1876)
Pioneer's memoir.

Myron Orr *Mission to Mackinac* (1956)
Novel depicting French-British rivalries in northern Michigan before the War of 1812.

Earl H. Reed *The Dune Country* (1916); *Sketches in Duneland* (1918); *Sketches in Jacobia* (1919)
Accounts of landscape and customs in the dunes region at the southern end of Lake Michigan.

Henry H. Riley *Puddleford and Its People* (1854); *The Puddleford Papers* (1857)
Humorous memoir of the author's life as a frontier lawyer.

Henry Rowe Schoolcraft *Algic Researches* 2 vols. (1839)
A pioneer recorder of Indian lore and legend, Henry Rowe Schoolcraft (1793–1864), first Indian agent for the Lake Superior tribes at Sault Ste. Marie, provided in this book the source of Longfellow's *The Song of Hiawatha*, which is set in Michigan's Upper Peninsula.

Larry Smith *The Original* (1972)
Novel about rural life, 1890–1920.

Wessel Smitter *F.O.B. Detroit* (1938)
Novel about a 1930s auto worker, depicting the dehumanizing effects of work on an assembly line.

Curtis K. Stadtfeld *From the Land and Back* (1972)
Autobiographical memoir of the author's farming forbears and the destruction of their way of life by mechanization.

James Steele *The Conveyor* (1935)
Novel about the lives of auto workers.

James Floyd Stevens *Paul Bunyan* (1925); *The Saginaw Paul Bunyan* (1932); *Timber! The Way of Life in the Lumber Camps* (1942); *Paul Bunyan's Bears* (1947)
Folktales centering on the legendary lumberjack.

Neil Swanson *Judas Tree* (1933)
Romantic account of the defense of Fort Pitt during Pontiac's rebellion.

Newton G. Thomas *The Long Winter Ends* (1941)
Novel about a Cornish miner who emigrates to northern Michigan.

Margaret Walker *Fireweed* (1934)
Novel about the Scandinavians of a small lumbering town during the depression.

Gordon Webber *Years of Eden* (1951)
Novel describing a farm boy's life.

Georgia White *Free as the Wind* (1942)
Chronicle novel about a Dutch family that emigrates in the mid-nineteenth century.

Stewart Edward White *The Blazed Trail* (1902)
Realistic novel about lumbering at the turn of the century.

Constance Fenimore Woolson *Castle Nowhere: Lake-Country Sketches* (1875)
Stories based on the author's observations of Mackinac Island.

GUIDES TO RESOURCES

Blois, John T. *Gazeteer of the State of Michigan* (1839)

Bullock, Penelope L. *Michigan Bibliographies and Indexes* (1960)

Conway, James E. (comp. and ed.) *Historic Places around Detroit: A Guide to 330 Historic Sites in Wayne, Oakland, and Macomb Counties* (1977)

Federal Writers' Project *Michigan: A Guide to the Wolverine State* (1941, rpt. 1973)

Hindsdale, Wilbert A. *Archaeological Atlas of Michigan* (1931)

Karpinski, Louis C. *Bibliography of the Printed Maps of Michigan, 1804–1880* (1931)
———. *Historical Atlas of the Great Lakes and Michigan* (1931)

Library of Michigan *Sourcebook of Michigan Census, County Histories and Vital Records* (1986)

Michigan Department of Commerce *Michigan Economic and Population Statistics* (annual)

Michigan State University, East Lansing *Michigan Statistical Abstract* (1955–)

Romig, Walter *Michigan Place Names: The History of the Founding and the Naming of More Than Five Thousand Past and Present Michigan Communities* (1973, rpt. 1986)

Senninger, Earl J., Jr. *Atlas of Michigan* (3d ed. 1970)

Sommers, Lawrence M. (ed.) *Atlas of Michigan* (1977)

Stevens, Wystan *Directory of Historical Collections and Societies in Michigan* (1973)

Vexler, Robert I. (comp. and ed.) *Detroit: A Chronological and Documentary History, 1701–1976* (American Cities Chronology series) (1977)

Vogel, Virgil J. *Indian Names in Michigan* (1986)

Wood, L. H. *Geography of Michigan: Physical, Industrial, and Sectional* (1914)

SELECTED NONFICTION SOURCES

Angelo, Frank *Yesterday's Detroit* (1974)

Armstrong, Louise *We Too Are the People* (1938)

Babson, Steve *Working Detroit: The Making of a Union Town* (1984)

Babst, Earl D. and **Lewis G. Vander Velde** (eds.) *Michigan and the Cleveland Era* (1948)

Bald, F. Clever *Detroit's First American Decade, 1769 to 1805* (1948)
———. *The Sault Canal through 100 Years* (1954)
———. *Michigan in Four Centuries* (rev. ed. 1961)

Beasley, Norman and **George W. Stark** *Made in Detroit* (1957)

Brough, James *The Ford Dynasty: An American Story* (1977)

Brown, Prentiss *The Mackinac Bridge Story* (1956)

Burlingame, Roger *Henry Ford, a Great Life in Brief* (1955)

Burton, Clarence M. *City of Detroit, Michigan* 5 vols. (1922)

Catlin, George B. *The Story of Detroit* (1923)

Catton, Bruce *Michigan's Past and the Nation's Future* (1960)
———. *Michigan: A Bicentennial History* (States and the Nation series) (1976)

Chase, Lew Allen *Rural Michigan* (1922)

Cleveland, Reginald and **Samuel T. Williamson** *The Road Is Yours: The Story of the Automobile and the Men Behind It* (1951)

Clymer, Floyd *Henry Ford's Wonderful Model T, 1908–1927* (1955)

Cohn, David *Combustion on Wheels* (1944)

Cooley, Thomas M. *Michigan: A History of Governments* (rev. ed. 1905, rpt. 1973)

Dain, Floyd R. *Detroit and the Westward Movement* (1951)

Danforth, Mildred M. *A Quaker Pioneer: Laura Haviland, Superintendent of the Underground* (1961)

Darling, Birt *City in the Forest: The Story of Lansing* (1950)

Davis, Charles M. *Readings in the Geography of Michigan* (1964)

Delanglez, Jean *Life and Voyages of Louis Jolliet, 1645–1700* (1948)

Denison, Merrill *The Power to Go: The Story of the Automobile Industry* (1956)

Dorr, John A. and **Donald F. Eschman** *Geology of Michigan* (1970)

Dunbar, Willis F. *Michigan through the Centuries* 4 vols. (1955)
———. (rev. ed. **George S. May**) *Michigan: A History of the Wolverine State* (1980)

Ferry, W. Hawkins *The Buildings of Detroit* (rev. ed. 1980)

Fine, Benjamin *Sit-Down: The General Motors Strike of 1936–1937* (1969)

Fine, Sidney *Frank Murphy: The Detroit Years* (1975)

Formisano, Ronald P. *The Birth of Mass Political Parties, Michigan, 1827–1861* (1971)

Forster, Edith C. *Yesterday's Highlights: Traveling around Early Detroit* (1951)

Fowle, Otto *Sault Ste. Marie and Its Great Waterway* (1925)

Fuller, George N. *Economic and Social Beginnings of Michigan, 1805–1837* (1916)
———.*Michigan, a Centennial History of the State and Its People* (1939)

Gates, William B. *Michigan Copper and Boston Dollars* (1950)

Gibson, Arthur H. (comp.) *Artists of Early Michigan: A Biographical Dictionary of Artists Native to or Active in Michigan, 1701–1900* (1975)

Gilbert, Helen F. *Tonquish Tales: A Story of Early d'Etroit, Pioneers, and Michigan Indians* (1984)

Gillard, Kathleen I. *Our Michigan Heritage* (1955)

Gilpin, Alex R. *The Territory of Michigan (1805–1837)* (1970)

Glazer, Sidney *Detroit: A Study of Urban Development* (1965)

Goodrich, Calvin *The First Michigan Frontier* (1940)

Hanna, Frances C. *Sand, Sawdust, and Saw Logs; Lumber Days in Ludington* (1955)

Hartman, David (ed.) *Immigrants and Migrants: The Detroit Ethnic Experience* (1974)

Havighurst, Walter *Three Flags at the Straits: The Forts of Mackinac* (1966)

Hayne, Coe *Baptist Trail Makers in Michigan* (1936)

Hedrick, Ulysses P. *The Land of the Crooked Tree* (1948)

Henrickson, Wilma (ed.) *Detroit Perspectives: Crossroads and Turning Points* (1988)

Hindsdale, Wilbert B. *The First People of Michigan* (1930)

Holbrook, Stewart *Holy Old Mackinaw, a Natural History of the American Lumberjack* (1938)

Hough, John T., Jr. *A Peck of Salt; a Year in the Ghetto* (1970)

Hudgins, Bert *Michigan: Geographic Backgrounds in the Development of the Commonwealth* (4th ed. 1961)

Hulbert, William D. *White Pine Days on the Taquamenon* (1949)

Johnson, Ida A. *The Michigan Fur Trade* (1919)

Judson, Clara *The Mighty Soo; Five Hundred Years at Sault Ste. Marie* (1955)

Katzman, David M. *Before the Ghetto: Black Detroit in the Nineteenth Century* (1973)

Kuhn, Madison *Michigan State: The First Hundred Years* (1955)

Larson, Herbert F., Sr. *Be-wa-bic Country; the Story of the Menominee Iron Range in the Upper Peninsula of Michigan* (1963)

Laut, Agnes C. *Cadillac, Knight Errant of the Wilderness, Founder of Detroit, Governor of Louisiana from the Great Lakes to the Gulf* (1931)

Lewis, Ferris E. *Detroit; a Wilderness Outpost of Old France* (1951)

Locke, Hubert G. *The Detroit Riot of 1967* (1969)

Lovett, William P. *Detroit Rules Itself* (1930)

Manassah, Sallie M., David A. Thomas, and James F. Wallington *Lansing: Capital, Campus, and Cars* (1988)

May, George S. *A Michigan Reader: 11,000 B.C. to A.D. 1865* (1974)
———. *A Most Unique Machine; the Michigan Origins of the American Automobile Industry* (1974)

Maybee, Rolland H. *Michigan's White Pine Era, 1840–1900* (1960)

McCoy, Raymond *The Massacre of Old Fort Mackinac* (6th ed. 1946)

McLaughlin, Doris B. *Michigan Labor: A Brief History from 1818 to the Present* (1970)

Metcalf, Kenneth N. *Fun and Frolic in Early Detroit* (1951)

Milio, Nancy *9226 Kercheval: The Storefront That Did Not Burn* (1970)

Millspaugh, Arthur *Party Organization and Machinery in Michigan since 1890* (1917)

Nevins, Allan and Frank E. Hill *Ford: The Times, the Man, the Company* (1954)
——— and Frank E. Hill *Ford, Expansion and Challenge 1915–1933* (1957)

Niemeyer, Glenn *The Automotive Career of Ransom E. Olds* (1964)

Olson, David C. B. *Life on the Upper Michigan Frontier* (1974)

Parkman, Francis *Conspiracy of Pontiac* (1851)

Peckham, Howard *Pontiac and the Indian Uprising* (rev. ed. 1961)

Petersen, Eugene T. *Mackinac Island: Its History in Pictures* (1973)

Porter, K. W. *John Jacob Astor, Businessman* 2 vols. (1931)

Pound, Arthur *The Turning Wheel: The Story of General Motors through Twenty-Five Years* (1934)
———. *Detroit: Dynamic City* (1940)
———. *The Automobile and an American City* (1962)

Powell, Horace B. *The Original Has This Signature--W. K. Kellogg* (1956)

Powers, Perry F. *History of Northern Michigan* (1912)

Praus, Alexis (ed.) *The Cholera in Kalamazoo* (1961)

Quaife, Milo M. *Lake Michigan* (1944)
——— and Sidney Glazer *Michigan: From Primitive Wilderness to Industrial Commonwealth* (1948)
———. *This Is Detroit, 1701–1951* (1951)
——— and Joseph and Estelle Bayliss *River of Destiny: The St. Marys* (1955)

Richards, William C. *The Last Billionaire, Henry Ford* (1948)

Rubenstein, Bruce A. *Michigan, a History of the Great Lakes State* (1981)

Russell, Nelson V. *The British Regime in Michigan and the Old Northwest, 1760–1796* (1939)

Santer, Richard A. *Michigan: Heart of the Great Lakes* (1977)

Sawyer, Alvah L. *A History of the Northern Peninsula and Its People: Its Mining, Lumber and Agriculture Industries* 3 vols. (1911)

Shogan, Robert and Tom Craig *The Detroit Race Riot; a Study in Violence* (1964)

Simonds, William A. *Henry Ford, Motor Genius* (1929)
———. *Henry Ford and Greenfield Village* (1938)

Smith, Alexander H. and Harry D. Thiers *The Boletes of Michigan* (1970)

Sommers, Lawrence M. *Michigan: A Geography* (1984)

Sorenson, Charles E. *My Forty Years with Ford* (1962)

Stark, George W. *In Old Detroit* (1939)

Steinman, David B. (in collaboration with John T. Nevill) *Miracle Bridge at Mackinac* (1988)

Stern, Philip V. *Tin Lizzie: The Story of the Fabulous Model T Ford* (1955)

Sweeney, J. Gray *Artists of Michigan from the Nineteenth Century* (1988)

Utley, Henry M. and Byron M. Cutcheon *Michigan as a Province, Territory, and State* 4 vols. (1906)

Vanderhill, C. W. *Settling the Great Lakes Frontier: Immigration to Michigan 1857–1924* (1970)

Wahlgren, E. *The Kensington Stone, a Mystery Solved* (1958)

Warner, Robert and C. Warren Vanderhill (eds.) *A Michigan Reader: 1865 to the Present* (1974)

Wilder, Keith R. *Reveille Till Taps: Soldier Life at Fort Mackinac, 1780–1895* (1973)

Williams, Meade C. *Early Mackinac. A Sketch, Historical and Descriptive* (rev. ed. 1912)

Wood, Edwin O. *Historic Mackinac* 2 vols. (1918)

Woodford, Frank B. *Lewis Cass, the Last Jeffersonian* (1950)
———. *Mr. Jefferson's Disciple: A Life of Justice Woodward* (1953)
——— and Arthur M. *All Our Yesterdays; a Brief History of Detroit* (1969)
——— and Arthur M. *Detroit, American Urban Renaissance: A Pictorial and Entertaining Commentary on the Growth and Development of Detroit, Michigan* (1979)

Yarnell, Duane *Auto Pioneering, the Remarkable Story of Ransom E. Olds, Father of Oldsmobile and Reo* (1949)

MINNESOTA

Minnesota is a west north central state. It is bordered on the north by the Canadian provinces of Manitoba and Ontario and by the Rainy River; on the east by Lake Superior and Wisconsin, and by the St. Croix and Mississippi rivers; on the south by Iowa; and on the west by South Dakota, North Dakota, and the Red River of the North and Bois de Sioux rivers.

FULL NAME State of Minnesota
POSTAL ABBREVIATION MN
INHABITANT Minnesotan
ADMITTED TO THE UNION May 11, 1858.
32d state
POPULATION (est. 1987) 4,246,000.
Percent of US total: 1.75%. Rank: 21st

CAPITAL CITY St. Paul, located on the Mississippi River in eastern Minnesota; population 265,903 (est. 1984). Founded in 1838 (and known as Pig's Eye until 1841) and incorporated in 1854, St. Paul became the territorial capital in 1849.

STATE NAME AND NICKNAMES From the Dakota Indian word *mnishota*, "cloudy" or "milky water," in reference to the Minnesota River. Also known as the North Star State, the Land of Ten Thousand Lakes, the Gopher State, and the Bread and Butter State.

STATE SEAL The seal shows a scene from 1858. In the foreground, in front of the St. Anthony Falls, is a farmer at the plow, his rifle propped nearby. In the background is an Indian riding west on horseback into the setting sun. The two figures are looking at each other. Above them is a scroll with the legend "L'Etoile Du Nord" (The Star of the North). The border reads "The Great Seal of the State of Minnesota, 1858."

MOTTO L'Etoile du Nord (The star of the north)

SONG "Hail! Minnesota," first verse and music by Truman E. Rickard, second verse by Arthur E. Upson.

SYMBOLS
Flower pink and white lady slipper
Tree red pine (Norway pine)
Bird loon
Gem Lake Superior agate
Fish walleye
Grain wild rice
Mushroom morel
Drink milk

LICENSE PLATES (1) Dark blue and green on a white background, with pine trees pictured and the legend "10,000 Lakes"; some also have the legend "Explore Minnesota." (2) Dark blue on white, with blue border and legend "10,000 Lakes."

FLAG On a blue field, a circular emblem showing the 1858 scene from the state seal surrounded by a border of intertwined blossoms of the state flower and the dates 1819, 1858, and 1893; around it is a white border with the red legend "Minnesota" at the bottom and five groupings of gold stars, 19 in all.

GEOGRAPHY AND CLIMATE

Minnesota, near the center of North America, is comprised of subarctic forest to the north and west-central prairie to the south. The state's thousands of lakes (more than 10,000 of them over 25 acres in size) are the product of the last Ice Age, which flattened and scoured the terrain. The headwaters of the Mississippi River are in Minnesota, at Lake Itasca. A small projection up from the northern border (at Lake of the Woods) makes Minnesota the most northerly of the 48 contiguous states; it is also one of the coldest, with record low temperatures recorded regularly at International Falls.

AREA 84,402 square miles. Rank: 12th
INLAND WATER 4,854 square miles
GEOGRAPHIC CENTER Crow Wing, 10 miles SW of Brainerd
ELEVATIONS *Highest point:* Eagle Mountain, Cook County, 2,301 feet. *Lowest point:* Lake Superior, 602 feet. *Mean elevation:* 1,200 feet

MAJOR RIVERS Mississippi, Red River of the North, Minnesota

MAJOR LAKES AND RESERVOIRS Superior, Red, Lake of the Woods, Rainy, Mille Lacs, Leech, Winnibigoshish

LAND USE

	Thousands of acres
Urban (1982)	904
Rural (1982)	45,036
Cropland (1982)	23,024
Pastureland (1982)	3,590
Rangeland (1982)	199
Forestland (1982)	13,956
State parks and recreation areas (1983)	182
National park system (1984)	138
National forest system (1984)	5,467
Tribal lands (1984)	714

TEMPERATURES The highest recorded temperature was 114°F on July 6, 1936, at Moorhead. The lowest was -59°F on February 16, 1903, at Pokegama Dam.

NATIONAL SITES

NATIONAL MONUMENTS Grand Portage, Pipestone
NATIONAL PARK Voyageurs
NATIONAL SCENIC RIVERS AND RIVERWAYS Lower St. Croix, St. Croix
NATIONAL SCENIC TRAIL North Country
NATIONAL WILDLIFE REFUGES Agassiz, Big Stone, Benson Wetland Management District, Detroit Lakes Wetland Management District, Fergus Falls Wetland Management District, Litchfield Wetland, Minnesota Valley, Minnesota Wetland Complex, Rice Lake–Mille Lacs/Sandstone, Sherburn, Tamarac, Upper Mississippi River Wild Life and Fish Refuge–Cassville District/La Crosse District/Lansing District, Savanna District, Trempealeau

HISTORY

1660	French explorers Pierre Espirit Radisson and Médard Chouart, Sieur des Grosseilliers, probably canoe along the Minnesota shore of Lake Superior.
1679	Daniel Greysolon, Sieur du Luth (or Lhut), lands near present-day Duluth, then penetrates inland to a Minnesota Sioux (Dakota) village on the shores of Mille Lacs Lake.
1680	*July 25.* Du Luth rescues three white captives of the Sioux; one is Father Louis Hennepin, who has seen and named the Falls of St. Anthony on the Mississippi—the future site of Minneapolis.
1732	Pierre Gaultier de Varennes, Sieur de La Vérendrye, seeking a northwest passage to the Pacific, canoes and portages to Lake of the Woods, building Fort St. Charles on its shores.
1762–1763	France cedes the eastern part of what is now Minnesota to Great Britain and the rest to Spain.
1778	A British fort and fur-trading post at Grand Portage on Lake Superior—the largest of more than 20 in Minnesota—employs 500 and does £40,000 worth of business.
1783	Minnesota east of the Mississippi passes to the newly born United States of America.
1803	The Louisiana Purchase includes Minnesota west of the Mississippi in the United States.

1818	A British-American agreement establishes the western part of Minnesota's northern border.
1819	Fort St. Anthony (later Fort Snelling) is established at the confluence of the Mississippi and Minnesota rivers.
1823	The steamboat *Virginia* reaches Fort Snelling from St. Louis.
1832	*July 13*. Henry Rowe Schoolcraft establishes the source of the Mississippi as Lake Itasca in north-central Minnesota.
1836	Artist George Catlin visits the sacred pipestone quarry of the Indians at Fort Snelling and continues his work of painting the Indians' world.
1837	Sioux cede east-central Minnesota to the US.
1842	An agreement resolves the border between Canada and the eastern part of Minnesota.
1847	Regular Mississippi steamboat service begins at St. Paul.
1849	*March 3*. Minnesota, with fewer than 4,000 whites, becomes a territory extending to the Missouri River. St. Paul is the capital.
1851	Sioux cede most of southern Minnesota. University of Minnesota chartered.
1854–1866	Most of northern Minnesota is ceded by the Chippewa (Ojibway) in four treaties.
1856	Federal land sales, which began in 1848, reach peak, with over two million acres sold at six Minnesota offices.
1858	*May 11*. Minnesota becomes the 32d state admitted to the Union.
1861–1865	A total of 21,982 Minnesotans see Civil War service; the First Minnesota Regiment distinguishes itself at Gettysburg.
1862	Militant Sioux, frustrated by land treaties and the white man's policies, revolt and kill 486 whites, almost overwhelm Fort Ridgely and the settlement of New Ulm.
1863	Sioux and Winnebago reservations are abrogated and the Sioux expelled from Minnesota.
1867	St. Paul and Minneapolis are linked to Chicago by rail.
1869	Forty of the first 49 Granges are in Minnesota; this organization seeks to regulate railroads and grain dealers.
1873–1877	Grasshopper plagues cause major damage to crops.
1880	State population is 780,773, of whom 267,676 are foreign born; of these Germans number 66,592 and Norwegians 62,521.
1882	With nearly 70 percent of Minnesota farmland in wheat, Minneapolis is the nation's leading flour-milling center.
1883	The Northern Pacific Railroad line from Duluth to the Pacific at Portland, Ore., is completed.
1889	Opening of the hospital in Rochester that becomes world famous as the Mayo Clinic.
1890	Minnesota leads all states in wheat production. *November 16*. Discovery of the iron-ore potential of the Mesabi Range in northern Minnesota.
1893	James J. Hill's Great Northern Railway stretches to the Pacific, from St. Paul to Seattle.
1894	September forest fires sweep 400 square miles and kill 413, including 197 in Hinckley.
1896	Three-quarters of the Red Lake Chippewa Reservation is opened to whites.
1899	Peak lumber production of over two billion board feet.
1903	*November 5*. The Minneapolis Symphony Orchestra gives its first concert.
1908	Capital punishment is abolished in Minnesota.
1918	*October 12*. About 2,000 square miles in northeastern Minnesota are devastated by fire; 432 people lose their lives and property damage is about $25 million.
1930	Floyd Olson becomes the first governor elected from a third party—the Farmer-Labor party.
1933	A graduated state income tax is adopted.
1934	Teamsters's victory in a sometimes violent Minneapolis trucking strike ushers in a period of major union gains.
1936	Minnesota leads all states in butter production.
1944	The Democratic and Farmer-Labor parties merge.

1948	For the first time the dollar value of manufactured goods in Minnesota exceeds the total of cash farm receipts.
1950	Minnesota ranks second among states in oat production, third in barley, fourth in rye, fifth in corn, and sixth in soybeans.
1951	Record iron-ore production of nearly 90 million tons—82 percent of the nation's output.
1959	Opening of the St. Lawrence Seaway makes Duluth the westernmost Atlantic port.
1963	*May* 7. Opening of Tyrone Guthrie Theater in Minneapolis to house the Guthrie professional repertory company.
1967	A 3 percent state sales tax is imposed on most goods. Taconite passes high-grade iron-ore shipments in volume for the first time.
1968	Two Minnesotans, Vice President Hubert Humphrey and Senator Eugene McCarthy, seek the Democratic party presidential nomination.
1969	Warren E. Burger of St. Paul is appointed chief justice of the U.S. Supreme Court.
1984	Vice President Walter Mondale runs for president as the Democratic party candidate losing every state but Minnesota.
1987	First state unisex parental-leave law allows parents up to six weeks of unpaid leave from work.

DEMOGRAPHY

Population (est. 1987) . . . 4,246,000
Population (1980) 4,075,970
Population density in persons per
square mile (1980) 48.3

POPULATION BY RACE (1980)
American Indian/Aleut/
Eskimo 35,026
Asian/Pacific Islander 26,533
Black 53,342
Hispanic 32,124
White 3,936,948
Other 25,299

POPULATION CHARACTERISTICS (1980)
Percent of state population
Urban 66.9
Rural 33.1
Under 18 . . . . 28.7
65 or older 11.8
College-educated 16.7
Families below poverty line 7.0
Public-assistance recipients 4.2

Per capita personal income
(1986) $14,737
Millionaires per 100,000
residents (1982) 425.9

Average life expectancy in
years (1980) 76.2
Marriage rate per 1,000
residents (1986) 8.3
Divorce rate per 1,000
residents (1986) 3.3
Birth rate per 1,000
residents (1985) 15.9
Infant mortality rate per 1,000
births (1985) 9.6
Abortion rate per 1,000
live births (1985) 257
Crime rate per 100,000
residents (1985)
Violent 284.6
Property 4,077.6
Federal and state prisoners
per 100,000 residents (1984) . . . 52
Alcohol consumption in gallons
per capita (1985) 39.6
Deaths from motor vehicle accidents
per 100,000 residents (1985) . . 14.5

MAJOR CITIES
1984 population (est.)
Bloomington 84,127
Duluth 85,612
Minneapolis 358,335
Rochester 58,151
St. Paul 265,903

GOVERNMENT AND POLITICS

Number of US Representatives 2
Electoral votes 4

POLITICAL PARTY NOMINEES FROM STATE
  * winner

Ignatius Donnelly (People's)	1900	VP
Julius J. Reiter (Farm Labor)	1932	VP
Grace Carlson (Socialist Workers)	1948	VP
Hubert Horatio Humphrey* (D/Liberal)	1964	VP
Hubert Horatio Humphrey (D/ Liberal)	1968	P
Genevieve Gunderson (Socialist Labor)	1972	VP
Walter Frederick Mondale* (D/ Social Democrats)	1976	VP
Walter Frederick Mondale (D)	1980	VP
Walter Frederick Mondale (D)	1984	P

PRESIDENTIAL PRIMARY ELECTION In 1988, Minnesota sent 87 Democratic delegates and 31 Republican delegates to the national conventions.

CONSTITUTION Minnesota is using its original constitution, adopted in 1857.

LEGISLATURE The Legislature is divided into the Senate (67 members, 4-year term, minimum age 21) and the House of Representatives (134 members, 2-year term, minimum age 21). In 1987, the annual salary was $24,174.

JUDICIARY The highest court is the Supreme Court, with 7 judges serving 6-year terms. In 1987, the annual salary was $73,981.

EXECUTIVE The governor serves a 4-year term; the minimum age for holding office is 25. In 1987, the annual salary was $94,204. There are 5 other elected officials.

PRESIDENTIAL VOTE 1948-1988 *(in percents)*

Year	State Winner	Democratic	Republican
1948	Truman (D)	57.2	39.9
1952	Eisenhower (R)	44.1	55.3
1956	Eisenhower (R)	46.1	53.7
1960	Kennedy (D)	50.6	49.2
1964	Johnson (D)	63.8	36.0
1968	Humphrey (D)	54.0	41.5
1972	Nixon (R)	46.1	51.6
1976	Carter (D)	54.9	42.0
1980	Carter (D)	46.5	42.6
1984	Mondale (D)	49.7	49.5
1988	Dukakis (D)	54.0	46.0

GOVERNORS

Territorial Governors

Alexander Ramsey	1849-1853
Willis A. Gorman	1853-1857
Samuel Medary	1857-1858

State Governors

Henry H. Sibley (D)	1858-1860
Alexander Ramsey (R)	1860-1863
Henry A. Swift (R)	1863-1864
Stephen Miller (R)	1864-1866
William R. Marshall (R)	1866-1870
Horace Austin (R)	1870-1874
Cushman K. Davis (R)	1874-1876
John S. Pillsbury (R)	1876-1882
Lucius F. Hubbard (R)	1882-1887
Andrew R. McGill (R)	1887-1889
William R. Merriam (R)	1889-1893
Knute Nelson (R)	1893-1895
David M. Clough (R)	1895-1899
John Lind (D)	1899-1901
Samuel R. Van Sant (R)	1901-1905
John A. Johnson (D)	1905-1909
Adolph O. Eberhart (R)	1909-1915
Winfield S. Hammond (D)	1915
Joseph A.A. Burnquist (R)	1915-1921
Jacob A.O. Preus (R)	1921-1925
Theodore Christianson (R)	1925-1931
Floyd B. Olson (Farmer-Labor)	1931-1936
Hjalmar Petersen (Farmer-Labor)	1936-1937
Elmer A. Benson (Farmer-Labor)	1937-1939
Harold E. Stassen (R)	1939-1943
Edward J. Thye (R)	1943-1947
Luther W. Youngdahl (R)	1947-1951
C. Elmer Anderson (R)	1951-1955
Orville L. Freeman (Democrat-Farmer Labor)	1955-1961
Elmer L. Andersen (R)	1961-1963

Karl Rolvaag (D)	1963-1967
Harold LeVander (R)	1967-1971
Wendell R. Anderson (D)	1971-1976
Rudolph Perpich (Democrat-Farmer Labor)	1976-1979
Albert H. Quie (R)	1979-1983
Rudolph Perpich (Democrat-Farmer Labor)	1983-

MINIMUM AGES

Majority	18
Marriage with parental and judicial consent	16
Marriage without parental consent	18
Making a will	18
Buying alcohol	21
Jury duty	18
Leaving school	16
Driver's license	16

CAPITAL PUNISHMENT
None

MILITARY INSTALLATIONS
Total number: 5

FINANCES

Thousands of dollars

GENERAL REVENUE (1985)

Total general revenue . . .	8,260,655
Total tax revenue	5,228,004
Sales and gross receipts . . .	2,163,282
Individual income taxes . .	2,233,467
Corporate net income taxes . .	383,264

GENERAL EXPENDITURE (1985)

Total general expenditure .	7,492,284
Education	2,695,769
Public welfare	1,479,501
Health	130,332
Hospitals	381,181
Natural resources	197,356
Highways	713,899
Police	53,890
Corrections	101,250

FEDERAL AID (1985) 1,982,655

ECONOMY

The largest share of Minnesota's farm income derives from dairy products, cattle, hogs, poultry, and sheep. Principal crops are oats, corn, soybeans, sugar beets, hay, wheat, legumes, flaxseed, potatoes, rye, barley, and apples. Farm cash receipts totaled $6.7 million in 1983. Among mining products, iron ore, in the form of taconite, is the most important, followed by granite, limestone, and other building stones, sand, and gravel. Industrial goods produced include processed foods, electronic instruments and computers, office equipment, metal goods, petroleum products, printed materials, and paper products. High-tech industries center around the Twin Cities area.

EMPLOYMENT (1984)

Thousands of persons

Total number of employed workers	2,088
Construction	68.4
Finance, insurance, and real estate	106.1
Government	292.0
Manufacturing	373.9
Mining	9.4
Services	417.8
Transportation, communications, and utilities	97.0
Wholesale and retail trade	459.5

Percent of civilian labor force
unemployed (1984) 6.3

DEPARTMENT OF DEFENSE (1985)

Civilian workers employed . . .	2,840
Military personnel	859
Contract awards	$2.298 billion

ENERGY SOURCES FOR ELECTRIC UTILITIES (1983)

Percent

Coal	56.9
Gas	0.7
Hydroelectric	3.1
Nuclear	39.2
Petroleum	0.1

TRANSPORTATION

Motor vehicles registered in state (1986)	3,086,980
Miles of roads, streets, and highways (1986)	132,644
Miles of Class I railway operated (1986)	5,092
Airports (1983)	492
Major aviation hubs (1983)	1
Largest hub: Minneapolis/St. Paul	
Major ports, with gross tonnage in thousands (1985):	
Duluth-Superior	28,817
St. Paul	9,986

CULTURE AND EDUCATION

Native American tribes
Minnesota was formerly the home of the Arapaho, Cheyenne, Fox, Iowa, Missouri, Omaha, Oto, Ottawa, Sauk, and Wyandot tribes. Groups that continue to live in the state include the Ojibway, Sioux, and Winnebago. There are 14 federal reservations in Minnesota.

Religions, ethnicities, and languages
The early settlers of Minnesota were mainly Yankees from New England. Most Minnesotans are descended from 19th-century immigrants from northern Europe, particularly Norwegians (Evangelical Lutherans), Swedes (Augustana Lutherans), and Germans (evenly divided between Lutherans and Roman Catholics). Other immigrant groups include the Finns, Poles, Bohemians, Ukrainians, Irish, Croatians, and Italians. Some 97 percent of all Minnesotans are native-born. In 1980, 5.6 percent of the population spoke a language other than English at home.

Major museums and libraries
American Swedish Institute, Minneapolis
Minneapolis Institute of Arts
Minnesota Museum of Art, St. Paul
St. Paul Arts and Science Center
Walker Art Center, Minneapolis

Major arts organizations
Children's Theatre Company, Minneapolis

Duluth Symphony
Tyrone Guthrie Theater Company, Minneapolis
Minnesota Dance Theatre, Twin Cities
Minnesota Opera, St. Paul
Minnesota Orchestra, Minneapolis
Northern Theatre Ballet Company, Twin Cities
St. Paul Chamber Orchestra

Colleges and universities
Number public (1986-87) 33
Number private (1986-87) 40
Total enrollment, in full-time equivalent students (1985) 171,000

Public elementary and secondary schools
Expenditure per pupil in average daily attendance (1986-87) $4,239
Pupil-teacher ratio (1987) 17.4
Average teacher salary (1986-87) $30,190

Major league sports teams
Baseball: Minnesota Twins
Football: Minnesota Vikings
Hockey: Minnesota North Stars

Holidays
Susan B. Anthony's Birthday. February 15
Minnesota Day. May 11
State Fair, St. Paul. Before Labor Day
Leif Erikson Day. October 10

MINNESOTA IN LITERATURE

Chester Anderson (ed.) *Growing Up in Minnesota: Ten Writers Remember Their Childhoods* (1976)
Anderson, Meridel Le Sueur, Harrison Salisbury, Gerald Vizenor, Keith Gunderson, Shirley Schoonover, Toyse Kyle, Robert Bly, Edna and Howard Hong, and Mary Hong Loe.

Gary Anderson and **Alan R. Woolworth** (eds.) *Through Dakota Eyes: Narrative Accounts of the Minnesota Indian War of 1862* (1988)
Material gathered from newspapers, court testimony, and written memoirs, 1862–1920.

Christopher C. Andrews *Minnesota and Dacotah: In Letters Descriptive of a Tour through the North-West, in the Autumn of 1856* (1857, rpt. 1975)

Theodore C. Blegen and **Martin Ruud** (eds.) *Norwegian Emigrant Songs and Ballads* (1936)
Original texts with prose translations.

Carol Bly *Letters from the Country* (1981)
Essays from an isolated community in western Minnesota.

Theodore Bost and **Sophie Bost** (ed. and trans. Ralph H. Bowen) *A Frontier Family in Minnesota: Letters of Theodore and Sophie Bost, 1851–1920* (1981)
Swiss-French pioneers write about the hardships of farm life.

Cornelia James Cannon *Red Rust* (1928)
Novel about a Swedish wheat farmer's lifelong battle with the land.

Mary H. Eastman *Dahcotah; or, Life and Legends of the Sioux around Fort Snelling* (1849, rpt. 1962, 1975)
First-hand account of Indian life.

Edward Eggleston *The Mystery of Metropolisville* (1873)
Melodramatic novel about a real-estate boom of the 1850s and '60s by the author of an Indiana classic, *Hoosier Schoolmaster* (1871).

Dana Faralla *Circle of Trees* (1955)
Novel about Danish pioneer farmers.

F. Scott Fitzgerald *All the Sad Young Men* (1926)
Collection of short stories, some set in Minnesota.

Grace Flandrau *Indeed This Flesh* (1934)
Novel about the moral scruples of a young man in nineteenth-century Minnesota.

Melvin R. Gilmore *Prairie Smoke* (1929, rpt. 1987)
Folklore of the Plains Indians.

Edward Havill *Big Ember* (1947)
Novel about Norwegian settlers' daily life on the southern Minnesota frontier.

Helen Hoover *The Long-Shadowed Forest* (1964); *The Years of the Forest* (1973)
Autobiographical accounts of life in a wilderness cabin.

Lois Phillips Hudson *Reapers of the Dust: A Prairie Chronicle* (1984)
Autobiographical tales of a Depression childhood.

Garrison Keillor *Lake Wobegon Days* (1985); *Leaving Home* (1987)
Chronicle of the author's imaginary hometown in northwestern Minnesota, and 36 anecdotes of adolescence and departure from the Midwest.

John J. Koblas *F. Scott Fitzgerald: His Homes and Haunts* (Minnesota Historic Sites Pamphlet No. 18) (1978)

Herbert Arthur Krause *Wind without Rain* (1939); *The Thresher* (1947)
Novels of rural life. Krause also wrote a historical novel, *Oxcart Trail* (1954), about an immigrant to the Red River settlements in the 1850s.

Sinclair Lewis *Main Street* (1920); *Babbitt* (1922)
Classic novels satirizing small-town narrow-mindedness based on the Nobel prize–winning novelist's upbringing in Sauk Center. Lewis' fictional town of Gopher Prairie has become a symbol of provincial values.

Frank B. Mayer (ed. Bertha L. Heilbron) *With Pen and Pencil on the Frontier in 1851: The Diary and Sketches of Frank Blackwell Mayer* (1932)
Diary of a young Baltimore artist.

William McNally *The House of Vanished Splendor* (1932); *The Roofs of Elm Street* (1936)
Novels chronicling three Minnesota families during the period 1870–1920.

Peg Meier and **Dave Wood** *The Pie Lady of Winthrop, and Other Minnesota Tales* (1985)

Vilhelm Moberg *The Emigrants* (1951); *Unto a Good Land* (1954); *The Last Letter Home* (1961)
Trilogy of novels comprising a saga of Swedish immigrant farm life in the St. Croix valley.

Lucy Leavenworth Morris (ed.) *Old Rail Fence Corners: Frontier Tales Told by Minnesota Pioneers* (1914, rpt. 1976)
Reminiscences by 154 early settlers.

Sigurd F. Olson *Singing Wilderness* (1956)
The first of a naturalist's four books about the wildlife of the "canoe country" of the Quetico-Superior region.

Walter O'Meara *Trees Went Forth* (1947)
Novel about a Minnesota lumber camp in 1906.
———. *We Made It through the Winter: A Memoir of Northern Minnesota Boyhood* (1974)
The author grew up in Cloquet at the turn of the century.

Martha Ostenso *Wild Geese* (1925)
Melodramatic but realistic novel about farm life, one of several works by this author with northwestern rural settings.

Gordon Parks *Choice of Weapons* (1966, rpt. 1986)
A black photographer's memoir of growing up in St. Paul in the '20s.

Carmen N. Richards (ed.) *Minnesota Writers: A Collection of Autobiographical Stories by Minnesota Prose Writers* (1961)
——— and **Genevieve R. Breen** (eds.) *Minnesota Writers: A Collection of Autobiographical Stories by Minnesota Prose Writers* (1945)

Ole Edvart Rølvaag *Giants in the Earth* (1927); *Peder Victorious* (1929); *Their Fathers' God* (1931)
Trilogy of novels realistically depicting the life of Norwegian immigrant farmers on the northwestern frontier, and the psychological effect of the hard life on people whose labors are a constant struggle against the impersonal forces of nature. All Rølvaag's novels were written in his native Norwegian.

William Joseph Snelling *Tales of the Northwest; or, Sketches of Indian Life and Character* (1830, rpt. 1936)
As a young man Snelling, son of the colonel for whom the fort was named, lived among the Dakota Indians near St. Paul, where he gathered information for this book.

James Stevens *Paul Bunyan* (1925)
The exploits of this legendary lumberjack may have taken place in Michigan.

Gerald Vizenor (ed.) *Touchwood: A Collection of Ojibway Prose* (1987)
Examples of nineteenth-century and contemporary Ojibway writing.

Evelyn Wise *The Long Tomorrow* (1938)
Affecting, sentimental novel about a priest's work in an isolated rural settlement during the 1880s.

Carl A. Zapffe (ed. Louis Hoglund) *Oldtimers: Stories of Our Pioneers in the Cass and Crow Wing Lake Region* (1987)

GUIDES TO RESOURCES

Andreas, A. T. *An Illustrated Historical Atlas of the State of Minnesota* (1874, rpt. 1979)

Blegen, Theodore C. and **Theodore L. Nydahl** *Minnesota History: A Guide to Reading and Study* (1960)

Bogue, Margaret B. and **Virginia A. Palmer** *Around the Shores of Lake Superior: A Guide to Historic Sites, Including a Color Tour Map Showing Lake Superior's Sites* (1979)

Borchert, John R. and **Donald P. Yaeger** *Atlas of Minnesota Resources and Settlement* (rev. ed. 1969)

Breining, Greg and **Linda Watson** *A Gathering of Waters: A Guide to Minnesota's Rivers* (Minnesota Department of Natural Resources) (1977)

Brook, Michael (comp.) *Reference Guide to Minnesota History: A Subject Bibliography of Books, Pamphlets, and Articles in English* (1974)
——— and **Sarah P. Rubinstein** (comps.) *A Supplement to Reference Guide to Minnesota History: A Subject Bibliography, 1970–80* (1983)

Coleman, Patrick K. and **Charles R. Lamb** (comps.) *The Nonpartisan League, 1915–22: An Annotated Bibliography* (1985)

Federal Writers' Project *The WPA Guide to Minnesota* (1938, rpt. 1985)
———. *The Bohemian Flats* (1941, rpt. 1986)
———. *The WPA Guide to the Minnesota Arrowhead Country* (1941, rpt. 1988)

Gebhard, David and **Tom Martinson** *A Guide to the Architecture of Minnesota* (1977)

Gjelten, Dan (ed.) *Business Conditions in Minnesota, 1939–1984* (1984)

Goff, Lila J. and **James E. Fogerty** (eds.) *The Oral History Collection of the Minnesota Historical Society* (1984)

Holbert, Sue and **June D. Holmquist** *A History Tour of 50 Twin City Landmarks* (1966)

Holmquist, June D. et al. *History along the Highways: An Official Guide to Minnesota State Markers and Monuments* (Minnesota Historic Sites Pamphlet Series 3) (1967)
———. and **Jean A. Brookins** *Minnesota's Major Historical Sites: A Guide* (rev. 2d ed. 1972)

Jerabek, Esther A. (comp.) *Bibliography of Minnesota Territorial Documents* (1936)
———. (comp.) *Checklist of Minnesota State Documents, 1858–1923* (1972)

Katz, Helen T. (ed.) *Consolidated Index to Minnesota History, 1930–1967* vols. 11–40 (1983)

Kidder, Dorothy P. and **Cynthia A. Matson** (comps.) *A Supplement to History along the Highways: An Official Guide to Minnesota Markers and Monuments, 1967–1972* (Minnesota Historic Sites Pamphlet Series 6) (1973)

Kinney, Gregory and **Lydia Lucas** (comps.) *A Guide to the Records of Minnesota's Public Lands* (1985)

Lucas, Lydia A. (comp.) *Manuscript Collections of the Minnesota Historical Society* (1977)

Minnesota Department of Administration. Documents Section *Minnesota State Publications* (1976–   )

Minnesota Department of Economic Development. Research Division *Minnesota Statistical Profile* (n.d.)

Minnesota Historical Society *Chippewa and Dakota Indians: A Subject Catalog of Books, Pamphlets, Periodical Articles and Manuscripts in the Minnesota Historical Society* (1969)
———. *Directory of Historical Organizations* (1979)
———. *Historic Resources in Minnesota: A Report on Their Extent, Location, and Need for Preservation, Submitted to the Minnesota Legislature* (1979)

Mittlefehdt, Pamela J. (comp.) *Minnesota Folklife: An Annotated Bibliography* (1979)

Parker, Nathan H. *The Minnesota Handbook for 1856–7* (1857, rpt. 1975)

Pope, Wiley R. and **Alissa L. Wiener** *Tracing Your Ancestors in Minnesota: A Guide to the Sources* (rev. 2d ed. 1980)

Rowan, Thomas J. (ed.) *The Minnesota Almanac, 1977* (1976)

Saucedo, Ramedo J. (comp.) *Mexican Americans in Minnesota: An Introduction to Historical Sources* (1977)

Singley, Grover *Tracing Minnesota's Old Government Roads* (1974)

Spadaccini, Victor M. *Minnesota Data Book: 1985–1986* (1986)

Swanson, Roy *The Minnesota Book of Days* (1949)

Taylor, David V. (comp.) *Blacks in Minnesota: A Preliminary Guide to Historical Sources* (1976)

Treude, Mai *Windows to the Past: A Bibliography of Minnesota County Atlases* (1980)

U.S. Government Printing Office *State Statistical and Economic Abstract Series: Minnesota* (1987)

White, Bruce M (comp.) *The Fur Trade in Minnesota: An Introductory Guide to Manuscript Sources* (1977)

SELECTED NONFICTION SOURCES

Anderson, Gary C. *Little Crow, Spokesman for the Sioux* (1986)

Atkins, Annette *Harvest of Grief: Grasshopper Plagues and Public Assistance in Minnesota, 1873–78* (1984)

Beecher, John *Tomorrow Is a Day: A Story of the People in Politics* (1980)

Bjornson, Valdimar *The History of Minnesota* 4 vols. (1969)

Blegen, Theodore C. *Grass Roots History* (1947)
———. *The Land Lies Open* (1949)
———. *The Kensington Rune Stone: New Light on an Old Riddle* (1968)
———. *Minnesota: A History of the State* (1975)
——— and **Philip D. Jordan** (eds.) *With Various Voices: Recordings of North Star Life* (1949)

Bray, Edmund C. *Billions of Years in Minnesota: The Geological Story of the State* (1977)

Bridges, Hal *Iron Millionaire: Life of Charlemagne Tower* (1952)

Brill, Charles *Indian and Free: A Contemporary Portrait of Life on a Chippewa Reservation* (1974)

Brink, Carol R. *The Twin Cities* (1961)

Cantrell, Dallas *Youngers' Fatal Blunder: Northfield, Minnesota* (1973)

Carley, Kenneth *The Sioux Uprising of 1862* (2d ed. 1976)

Castle, Henry A. *Minnesota: Its Story and Biography* 3 vols. (1915)

Chrislock, Carl H. *The Progressive Era in Minnesota, 1899–1918* (1971)

Christianson, Theodore *Minnesota, the Land of Sky-Tinted Waters: A History of the State and Its People* 5 vols. (1935)

Connor, William Van (ed.) *A History of the Arts in Minnesota* (1958)

Crouse, Nellis M. *La Vérerendrye: Fur Trader and Explorer* (1956, rpt. 1972)

Dana, Samuel T., John H. Allison, and **R. N. Cunningham** *Minnesota Lands* (1960)

Davis, E. W. *Pioneering with Taconite* (1964)

Densmore, Frances *Dakota and Ojibwe People in Minnesota* (1977)

Dobbs, Farrell *Teamster Rebellion* (1972)

Dobie, John G. *The Itasca Story* (1959)

Drache, Hiram M. *The Challenge of the Prairie: Life and Times of the Red River Pioneers* (1970)

Dunn, James T. *The St. Croix: Midwest Border River* (Rivers of America series) (1965, rpt. 1979)

Ebbott, Elizabeth *Indians in Minnesota* (4th ed. 1985)

Engelmayer, Sheldon D. and **Robert J. Wagman** *Lord's Justice* (1985)

Ervin, Jean A. *The Twin Cities Perceived: A Study in Words and Drawings* (1976)

Flanagan, Barbara *Minneapolis* (1976)

Flandrau, Charles E. *The History of Minnesota and Tales of the Frontier* (1900)

Folwell, William W. *Minnesota, the North Star State* (1908, rpt. 1973)
———. *A History of Minnesota* 4 vols. (rev. ed. 1956–1969)

Forsyth, James *Tyrone Guthrie: A Biography* (1976)

Frame, Robert M., III *Millers to the World: Minnesota's Nineteenth Century Water Power Flour Mills* (1977)

Gates, Charles M. (ed.) *Five Fur Traders of the Northwest: Being the Narrative of Peter Pond and the Diaries of John Macdonell, Archibald N. McLeod, Hugh Faries and Thomas Connor* (1933, rpt. 1965)

Gilman, Rhoda R. and **June D. Holmquist** (eds.) *Selections from "Minnesota History": A Fiftieth Anniversary Anthology* (1965)

Gluek, Alvin M., Jr. *Minnesota and the Manifest Destiny of the Canadian Northwest: A Study in Canadian-American Relations* (1965)

Gray, James *Pine, Stream and Prairie: Wisconsin and Minnesota in Profile* (1945)
———. *Business without Boundary* (1954)

Haines, Lynn and **Dora B.** *The Lindberghs* (1931)

Hall, Steve *Fort Snelling: Colossus of the Wilderness* (1987)

Hansen, Marcus L. *Old Fort Snelling, 1819–1858* (1918, rpt. 1958)

Haynes, John E. *Dubious Alliance: The Making of Minnesota's DFL Party* (1984)

Heck, Frank H. *The Civil War Veteran in Minnesota Life and Politics* (1941)

Heillbron, Bertha L. *The Thirty-Second State: A Pictorial History of Minnesota* (2d ed. 1966)

Holmquist, June D. *They Chose Minnesota: A Survey of the State's Ethnic Groups* (1981)

Huck, Virginia *Brand of the Tartan: The 3M Story* (1955)

Hughs, Thomas *Indian Chiefs of Southern Minnesota* (1927)

Jarchow, Merrill E. *The Earth Brought Forth* (1949)

Johnson, Elden *Prehistoric Peoples of Minnesota* (1969)

Jones, Evan *The Minnesota: Forgotten River* (Rivers of America series) (1962)
———. *Citadel in the Wilderness: The Story of Fort Snelling and the Old Northwest Frontier* (1966)

Kane, Lucile M. *The Falls of St. Anthony: The Waterfall That Built Minneapolis* (1987)
——— and **Alan Ominsky** *Twin Cities: A Pictorial History of Saint Paul and Minneapolis* (1983)

Kennedy, Roger G. *Minnesota Houses: An Architectural and Historical View* (1967)

King, Frank A. *Minnesota Logging Railroads: A Pictorial History of the Era When White Pine and the Logging Railroads Reigned Supreme* (1981)

Kunz, Virginia B. *Muskets to Missiles: A Military History of Minnesota* (1958)
———. *St. Paul, Saga of an American City* (1977)

Larsen, Erling *Minnesota Trails: A Sentimental History* (1958)

Larsen, Lawrence H. *Wall of Flames: The Minnesota Forest Fire of 1894* (1984)

Larson, Agnes *History of the White Pine Industry in Minnesota* (1949)

Larson, Don W. *Land of the Giants: A History of Minnesota Business* (1979)

Lass, William E. *Minnesota: A Bicentennial History* (States and the Nation series) (1977)

Le Sueur, Meridel *North Star Country* (1945, rpt. 1984)

Lettermann, Edward J. *From Whole Log to No Log: A History of the Indians Where the Mississippi and Minnesota Rivers Meet* (1969)

Loehr, Rodney C. *Minnesota Farmers' Diaries* (1939)

Lydecker, Ryck and **Lawrence J. Sommer** (eds.) *Duluth Sketches of the Past: A Bicentennial Collection* (1976)

Malcolm, Andrew H. *Final Harvest: An American Tragedy* (1986)

Mayo, Charles W. *Mayo: The Story of My Family and My Career* (1968)

McGrane, Bill *Bud, the Other Side of the Glacier* (1986)

Mitau, G. Theodore *Politics in Minnesota* (2d rev. ed. 1970)

Morgan, Dan *Merchants of Grain* (1979)

Morlock, Bill and **Rick Little** *Split Doubleheader: An Unauthorized History of the Minnesota Twins* (1979)

Nelson, Lowry *The Minnesota Community: County and Town in Transition* (1960)

Nordstrom, Byron J. (ed.) *The Swedes in Minnesota* (1976)

Nourse, Alan E. *Inside the Mayo Clinic* (1979)

Nute, Grace L. *The Voyageur* (1931)
———. *The Voyageur's Highway: Minnesota's Border Lake Land* (1941)
———. *Rainy River Country: A Brief History of the Region Bordering Minnesota and Ontario* (1950)

Pond, Samuel W. *The Dakota or Sioux in Minnesota As They Were in 1834* (1986)

Pritchett, John P. *The Red River Valley, 1811–1849: A Regional Study* (1942)

Roddis, Louis H. *The Indian Wars of Minnesota* (1956)

Russell, Carol (ed.) *In Our Own Back Yard: A Look at Beltrami, Cass and Itasca Counties at the Turn of the Century* (1979)

Schwartz, George M. and **George A. Thiel** *Minnesota's Rocks and Waters: A Geological Story* (1954)

Searle, R. Newell *Saving Quetico-Superior: A Land Set Apart* (1979)

Seitz, Peter *A Minnesota Mosaic: The Bicentennial in Photographs* (1977)

Sherman, John K. *Art and Culture in Minneapolis* (1964)

Shutter, Marion D. (ed.) *History of Minneapolis* 3 vols. (1923)

Singley, Grover *Tracing Minnesota's Old Government Roads* (1974)

Stuhler, Barbara *Ten Men of Minnesota and American Foreign Policy, 1898–1968* (1973)
——— and **Gretchen Kreuter** (eds.) *Women of Minnesota: Selected Biographical Essays* (1977)

Suprey, Leslie V. *Steam Trains of the Soo* (rev. ed. 1962)

Thompson, Neil B. *Minnesota's State Capitol: The Art and Politics of a Public Building* (Minnesota Historic Sites Pamphlet series 9) (1974)

Thompson, Pamela M. et al. *Iron Range Country: A Historical Travelogue of Minnesota's Iron Ranges* (1979)

Trenerry, Walter N. *Murder in Minnesota: A Collection of True Cases* (1962, rpt. 1985)

Treuer, Robert *Voyageur Country: A Park in the Wilderness* (1979)

Upham, Warren *Minnesota Geographic Names: Their Origin and Historic Significance* (2d rev. ed. 1969)

Wahlgren, Erick *The Kensington Stone: A Mystery Solved* (1958)

Wakefield, Sarah F. *Six Weeks in the Sioux Tepees* (1863, rpt. 1985)

Walker, Charles R. *American City: A Rank-and-File History* (1937, rpt. 1971)

Walker, David A. *Iron Frontier: The Discovery and Early Development of Minnesota's Three Ranges* (1979)

Wanlass, Dorothy L. (comp. and ed.) *Century Farms of Minnesota: One Hundred Years of Changing Life Styles on the Farm* (1985)

Waters, Thomas F. *The Streams and Rivers of Minnesota* (1977)
———. *The Superior North Shore* (1987)

Williams, J. Fletcher *The History of the City of Saint Paul to 1875* (1983)

Wirth, Fremont P. *Discovery and Exploitation of the Minnesota, Sleeping Giant of the Mesabi* (1948)

Ziebarth, Marilyn and **Alan Ominsky** *Fort Snelling, Anchor Post of the Northwest* (1970)

Zumberge, James H. *The Lakes of Minnesota* (1952)

MISSISSIPPI

Mississippi is an east south central state, bordered on the north by Tennessee; on the east by Alabama; on the south by the Gulf of Mexico, the Pearl River, and Lousiana; and on the west by the Mississippi River, Louisiana, and Arkansas.

FULL NAME State of Mississippi
POSTAL ABBREVIATION MS
INHABITANT Mississippian
ADMITTED TO THE UNION Dec. 10, 1817.
20th state
POPULATION (est. 1987) 2,625,000.
Percent of US total: 1.08%. Rank: 31st

CAPITAL CITY Jackson, located on the Pearl River in southwest central Mississippi; population 208,810 (est. 1984). It was originally the site of a trading post, Le Fleur's Bluff, founded in 1792. It was chosen as the state capital in 1821, renamed in 1822, and laid out on a plan designed by Thomas Jefferson.

STATE NAME AND NICKNAMES From the Chippewa Indian word meaning "large river," in reference to the Mississippi River. Also known as the Magnolia State, the Eagle State, the Border-Eagle State, the Bayou State, and the Mud-cat State.

STATE SEAL The Federal eagle, with olive branch and arrows in its talons and the shield of the Stars and Stripes on its breast;

around it is a border reading "The Great Seal of the State of Mississippi."

MOTTO Virtute et Armis (By valor and arms)

SONG "Go, Mississippi," lyrics and music by Houston Davis

SYMBOLS
Flower evergreen magnolia
Tree evergreen magnolia
Bird mockingbird
Land mammal white-tailed deer
Water mammal bottlenosed dolphin
Waterfowl wild duck
Fish largemouth bass
Insect honeybee
Shell oyster shell
Fossil prehistoric whale
Beverage milk

LICENSE PLATE Dark blue on white, with state name in red.

FLAG One half red, with the Confederate flag in the upper part; the other half filled by three horizontal stripes of blue, white, and red.

GEOGRAPHY AND CLIMATE

The Delta region of Mississippi, a strip about 65 miles wide bordering the western side of the state, is covered with deep black alluvium deposited by the Mississippi, Yazoo, and other rivers. The hills of central Mississippi are also fertile. South of Jackson is the Piney Woods, shading into meadowlands and coastal plains along the Gulf of Mexico. Forests cover more than half the state. In climate, Mississippi is warm and wet, with nearly a year-round growing season.

AREA 47,689 square miles. Rank: 32d
INLAND WATER 456 square miles
GEOGRAPHIC CENTER Leake, 9 miles WNW of Carthage
ELEVATIONS *Highest point:* Woodall Mountain, Tishomingo County, 806 feet. *Lowest point:* Gulf of Mexico, sea level. *Mean elevation:* 300 feet

MAJOR RIVERS Mississippi, Yazoo, Pearl, Big Black

MAJOR LAKES AND RESERVOIRS Grenada, Sardis, Enid, Columbus, Okatibbee, Ross Barnett

TIDAL SHORELINE 359 miles, Gulf coast

LAND USE

	Thousands of acres
Urban (1982)	582
Rural (1982)	27,063
Cropland (1982)	7,415
Pastureland (1982)	3,975
Forestland (1982)	0
State parks and recreation areas (1983)	21
National park system (1984)	108
National forest system (1984)	2,310
Tribal lands (1984)	18

TEMPERATURES The highest recorded temperature was 115°F on July 29, 1930, at Holly Springs. The lowest was -19°F on January 30, 1966, at Corinth.

NATIONAL SITES

NATIONAL BATTLEFIELD Tupelo
NATIONAL BATTLEFIELD SITE Brices Crossroads
NATIONAL CEMETERY Vicksburg
NATIONAL MILITARY PARK Vicksburg
NATIONAL PARKWAY Natchez Trace
NATIONAL SEASHORE Gulf Islands
NATIONAL WILDLIFE REFUGES Hillside, Mississippi Sandhill Crane–Morgan Brake, Noxubee, Yazoo

HISTORY

1528	Panfilo de Narvaez explores the Mississippi region. At this time between 25,000 and 30,000 Indians live in the area—mainly Chickasaw, Choctaw, and Natchez.
1541	*May.* Hernando de Soto discovers the Mississippi River.
1542	*May 21.* De Soto dies and is buried in the river.
1673	Father Jacques Marquette and Louis Joliet descend the river.
1682	René Robert Cavelier, Sieur de La Salle, explores the Mississippi River and claims the valley for France.
1699	Pierre Le Moyne, Sieur d'Iberville, establishes the first French colony at Old Biloxi.
1704	Poor young French women known as "casket girls," are brought into the region as wives for settlers.
1717	*August.* The Mississippi Company is chartered by the King of France.
1720	Three hundred settlers locate at Natchez.
1729	French settlers and soldiers are massacred at Fort Rosalie.
1732	The Mississippi Company surrenders its charter.
1763	Mississippi becomes English territory after the French and Indian War.
1764	The boundaries of British West Florida are extended to include the Mississippi settlements.
1775	The Revolution of the American Colonies begins. The Mississippi area, which is a part of West Florida, remains loyal to the Crown. Many loyalists settle there.
1779	*September 21.* West Florida, including Mississippi, is surrendered to Spain.
1798	*April 7.* Mississippi becomes an American territory.
1800	Benjamin F. Stokes publishes the *Mississippi Gazette*.
1801	*October 24.* The Treaty of Chickasaw Bluffs opens the Natchez Trace.

1806	"Great Cotton Era" begins with the introduction of Petit Gulf, a Mexican seed cotton.
1809	*January 9.* Congress extends the right of suffrage to the Mississippi Territory. *December 23.* The Bank of Mississippi is established at Natchez.
1812	During the War of 1812 the Choctaw Indians remain friendly to the Americans and help them defeat the British in the Battle of New Orleans.
1814	*December.* The Battle of Pass Christian, last naval battle of the war, is fought near St. Louis Bay.
1817	*December 10.* Mississippi becomes the 20th state of the Union.
1822	*January 23.* Legislature convenes at Jackson—the first session in the new capital.
1831	The first Mississippi charter is granted for a railroad to run from Woodville to St. Francisville, Louisiana.
1832	*November.* A new state constitution is ratified.
1836	*February 26.* Construction of a state penitentiary authorized.
1839	*February 15.* Legislative act defines married women's right to property.
1846	*March 4.* The State is divided into congressional districts. Common schools are established by law.
1848	*February 7.* Chickasaw school lands are opened for leasing for 99 years.
1861	*January 9.* The Civil War. Mississippi is the second state to secede from the Union.
1862	*February 22.* Jefferson Davis, former US Senator from Mississippi, is inaugurated President of the Confederacy.
1863	*July 4.* Union forces capture Vicksburg after a 47-day siege.
1865	Once ranked fifth in per capita wealth, the state drops to last place status.
1867	Mississippi comes under Union military rule.
1870	*February 23.* Mississippi is readmitted to the Union.
1871	First Mississippi monument to the Confederate dead is dedicated at Liberty.
1874	*December 7.* Race riots near Vicksburg. Seventy blacks are killed.
1878	*August–November.* Yellow fever epidemic claims many lives.
1886	*March 11.* General local option (liquor) law is passed.
1898	Spanish-American War. Mississippi raises three regiments for service.
1904	Separate but equal accommodation for whites and blacks on streetcars is legislated.
1908	Statewide prohibition is effected.
1917	World War I. Mississippi ratifies President Wilson's Declaration of War on Germany. Payne Field is established at West Point, Mississippi, as a training base for army pilots.
1922	*March 25.* A law is passed permitting women to vote.
1926	The teaching of evolution in state-supported schools is prohibited.
1927	*April 21.* Mississippi floods the Mississippi-Yazoo Delta.
1932	Widespread economic suffering due to the Depression. Relief work organizations are set up.
1933	Twelve Civilian Conservation Corps camps (CCC) are established.
1936	*March 23.* Old–age pension, teachers' pensions, and unemployment compensation acts are passed.
1941–1945	World War II. Many war plants are opened in the state. The port of Pascagoula becomes an assembly point for war convoys.
1953	The state begins a program for separate but equal schools.
1954	State legislature passes an open shop law.
1958	Clennon King, a black, is committed to the state mental hospital after trying to enroll in Ole Miss University.
1962	*September 30.* Black student James Meredith enters the University of Mississippi as 3,000 federal soldiers restrain violent mobs in which 2 men are killed.
1963	*June 12.* Medgar Evers, field secretary for the NAACP, is murdered at his home in Jackson.
1964	*June.* Three young civil rights workers are murdered in Neshola County.
1965	Manufacturing employment exceeds agricultural employment for the first time. *June 18.* More than 850 people are arrested in Jackson following five days of demonstrations.

1967	Continued outbreaks of violence occur due to state's efforts to adjust to integration.
	October 30. Violent tornado hits Gulfport coastal area killing three persons and causing property damage of more than $7 million.
1968	Major victory for black and white liberal communities when their delegation to the National Democratic Convention is recognized.
1969	*May 13.* Charles Evers is elected mayor of Fayette; the first black mayor in the state's history.
1973	Of Mississippi's 82 counties, 52 are overrun by flooding rivers and backwater.
1976	Industry employs 80% of the labor force.
1977	Early in year unusually cold weather causes serious shortages of natural gas.
1979	Hurricane Frederic slams into coastal area and causes property damage of more than $500 million.
1983	*June.* Unemployment climbs to a record 13.8%. For Mississippians it is a year marked by continued economic distress.
1985	*June.* The $2 billion Tennessee-Tombigbee Waterway is officially dedicated.
1987	*October–November.* A prolonged drought leads to wildfires that destroy thousands of acres of public and private lands.
1988	*May 13.* Three southern governors, including Roy Mabus of Mississippi, sign an agreement to coordinate efforts to improve conditions in the Mississippi Delta area, which has one of the highest poverty rates in the nation.

DEMOGRAPHY

Population (est. 1987) . . . 2,625,000
Population (1980) 2,520,631
Population density in persons per
square mile (1980) 52.9

POPULATION BY RACE (1980)

American Indian/Aleut/
Eskimo 6,180
Asian/Pacific Islander 7,142
Black 887,206
Hispanic 24,731
White 1,615,190
Other 4,650

POPULATION CHARACTERISTICS (1980)
Percent of state population

Urban 47.3
Rural 52.7
Under 18 . . . . 32.3
65 or older 11.5
College-educated 13.0
Families below poverty line . . . 18.7
Public-assistance recipients 11.4

Per capita personal income
(1986) $9,552
Millionaires per 100,000
residents (1982) 77.9

Average life expectancy
in years (1980) 72.0
Marriage rate per 1,000
residents (1986) 9.2
Divorce rate per 1,000
residents (1986) 5.4
Birth rate per 1,000
residents (1985) 16.2
Infant mortality rate per 1,000
births (1985) 13.3
Abortion rate per 1,000
live births (1985) 142
Crime rate per 100,000
residents (1985)
Violent 274.1
Property 3,070.9
Federal and state prisoners
per 100,000 residents (1984) . . 222
Alcohol consumption in gallons
per capita (1985) 35.0
Deaths from motor vehicle accidents
per 100,000 residents (1985) . . 25.3

MAJOR CITIES
1984 population (est.)

Biloxi	48,685
Gulfport	41,232
Jackson	208,810
Pascagoula	30,085

GOVERNMENT AND POLITICS

Number of US Representatives 18
Electoral votes 20

POLITICAL PARTY NOMINEES FROM STATE

Absolom Madden West (Anti-
Monopoly/Greenback) 1884 VP
Fielding Lewis Wright (States'
Rights) 1948 VP
Charles Loten Sullivan (Consti-
tutional Party of TX) 1960 P
Billy Davis (Independent
Democrat) 1984 VP

PRESIDENTIAL PRIMARY ELECTION In 1988, Mississippi sent 45 Democratic delegates and 31 Republican delegates to the national conventions.

CONSTITUTION Mississippi has had four constitutions: 1817, 1832, 1869, and the present one, adopted in 1890.

LEGISLATURE The Legislature is divided into the Senate (52 members, 4-year term, minimum age 25) and the House of Representatives (122 members, 4-year term, minimum age 21). In 1987, the annual salary was $10,000.

JUDICIARY The highest court is the Supreme Court, with 9 judges serving 8-year terms. In 1987, the annual salary was $59,000.

EXECUTIVE The governor serves a 4-year term; the minimum age for holding office is 30. In 1987, the annual salary was $63,000. There are 13 other elected officials.

PRESIDENTIAL VOTE 1948-1988 *(in percents)*

Year	State Winner	Democratic	Republican
1948	J. Strom Thurmond (States' Rights), 87.2	10.1	2.5
1952	Stevenson (D)	60.4	39.6
1956	Stevenson (D)	58.2	24.5
1960	Unpledged electors for Harry F. Byrd, 39.0	36.3	24.7
1964	Goldwater (R)	12.9	87.1
1968	George C. Wallace (American Independent), 63.5	23.0	13.5
1972	Nixon (R)	19.6	78.2
1976	Carter (D)	49.6	47.7
1980	Reagan (R)	48.1	49.4
1984	Reagan (R)	37.4	61.9
1988	Bush (R)	40.0	60.0

GOVERNORS

Territorial Governors
Winthrop Sargent 1798-1801
William C.C. Claiborne 1801-1805
Robert Williams 1805-1809
David Holmes 1809-1817

State Governors
David Holmes (Democratic-
Republican) 1817-1820
George Poindexter (D-R) 1820-1822
Walter Leake (D-R) 1822-1825
Gerard C. Brandon (D-R) 1825-1826
David Holmes (D-R) 1826
Gerard C. Brandon (D-R) 1826-1832
Abram M. Scott (D) 1832-1833
Charles Lynch (D) 1833
Hiram G. Runnels (D) 1833-1835
John A. Quitman (Whig) 1835-1836
Charles Lynch (D) 1836-1838
Alexander G. McNutt (D) 1838-1842
Tilghman M. Tucker (D) 1842-1844

Albert G. Brown (D) 1844-1848
Joseph M. Matthews (D) 1848-1850
John A. Quitman (D) 1850-1851
John I. Guion (D) 1851
James Whitfield (D) 1851-1852
Henry S. Foote (Union
Democrat) 1852-1854
John J. Pettus (D) 1854
John H. McRae (D) 1854-1857
William McWillie (D) 1857-1859
John J. Pettus (D) 1859-1863
Charles Clark (D) 1863-1865
William L. Sharkey (provi-
sional) 1865
Benjamin G. Humphreys
(D) 1865-1868
Adelbert Ames (provisional
military governor) 1868-1870
James L. Alcorn (R) 1870-1871
Ridgley C. Powers (R) 1871-1874
Adelbert Ames (R) 1874-1876
John M. Stone (D) 1876-1882
Robert Lowry (D) 1882-1890

John M. Stone (D)	1890-1896
Anselm J. McLaurin (D)	1896-1900
Andrew H. Longino (D)	1900-1904
James K. Vardaman (D)	1904-1908
Edmund F. Noel (D)	1908-1912
Earl L. Brewer (D)	1912-1916
Theodore G. Bilbo (D)	1916-1920
Lee M. Russell (D)	1920-1924
Henry L. Whitfield (D)	1924-1927
Dennis Murphree (D)	1927-1928
Theodore G. Bilbo (D)	1928-1932
Martin Sennett Conner (D)	1932-1936
Hugh L. White (D)	1936-1940
Paul B. Johnson (D)	1940-1943
Dennis Murphree (D)	1943-1944
Thomas L. Bailey (D)	1944-1946
Fielding L. Wright (D)	1946-1952
Hugh L. White (D)	1952-1956
James P. Coleman (D)	1956-1960
Ross R. Barnett (D)	1960-1964
Paul B. Johnson Jr. (D)	1964-1968
John Bell Williams (D)	1968-1972
William Waller (D)	1972-1976
Cliff Finch (D)	1976-1980
William Winter (D)	1980-1984
Bill Allain (D)	1984-1988
Ray Mabus (D)	1988-

MINIMUM AGES

Majority	18
Marriage with parental consent	
female	15
male	17
Marriage without parental consent	21
Making a will	18
Buying alcohol	21
Jury duty	21
Leaving school	17
Driver's license	15

CAPITAL PUNISHMENT
Number executed 1976-88: 3
On death row Aug. 1, 1988: 48

MILITARY INSTALLATIONS
Total number: 13
Major bases:
Navy: 1
Air Force: 1

FINANCES

Thousands of dollars
GENERAL REVENUE (1985)

Total general revenue	3,303,269
Total tax revenue	1,811,598
Sales and gross receipts	1,190,037
Individual income taxes	259,447
Corporate net income taxes	106,484

GENERAL EXPENDITURE (1985)

Total general expenditure	3,203,645
Education	1,285,217
Public welfare	482,160
Health	98,578
Hospitals	167,487
Natural resources	104,814
Highways	410,301
Police	35,268
Corrections	62,977

FEDERAL AID (1985) 188,296

ECONOMY

Cotton brings in the most income of any of Mississippi's agricultural products. Soybeans and rice are also important crops; cattle and poultry are the main livestock. Farm cash receipts in 1983 were $2.3 billion. Oil and natural gas are the main mineral resources, along with cement, sand, gravel, and clay. The state's timber industry accounts for about 20 percent of the total manufacturing payroll, feeding Mississippi's extensive capability for producing lumber, wood products, furniture, paper, and pulp. Other manufactured goods include clothes, transportation equipment, processed food, and electrical goods.

EMPLOYMENT (1984)
Thousands of persons

Total number of employed workers	958
Construction	37.6
Finance, insurance, and real estate	34.2
Government	183.5
Manufacturing	218.6
Mining	9.2
Services	125.5
Transportation, communications, and utilities	39.1
Wholesale and retail trade	175.5
Percent of civilian labor force unemployed (1984)	10.8

DEPARTMENT OF DEFENSE (1985)

Civilian workers employed	11,558
Military personnel	16,029
Contract awards	$1.310 billion

ENERGY SOURCES FOR ELECTRIC UTILITIES (1983)
Percent

Coal	66.5
Gas	32.9

Hydroelectric 0.0
Nuclear 0.0
Petroleum 0.6

TRANSPORTATION
Motor vehicles registered
in state (1986) 1,769,773
Miles of roads, streets,
and highways (1986) 71,818

Miles of Class I railway
operated (1986) 1,510
Airports (1983) 181
Major aviation hubs (1983) 1
Largest hub: Jackson/Vicksburg
Major ports, with gross tonnage in
thousands (1985):
Pascagoula 20,006

CULTURE AND EDUCATION

Native American tribes
Mississippi was formerly home to the Acolapissa, Biloxi, Chakchiuma, Chickasaw, Choula, Griga, Houma, Ibitoupa, Koasati, Koroa, Moctobi, Natchez, Ofo, Okelousa, Pascagoula, Quapaw, Taposa, Tiou, Tunica, and Yazoo tribes. Groups that continue to live there include the Choctaw. There is one federal reservation in Mississippi.

Religions, ethnicities, and languages
For a century prior to 1940, when the Black emigration to other states began, Black people were the majority in Mississippi. Most Blacks in the state are the descendants of slaves. The white population is mainly descended from the settlers (of Scotch-Irish, English, and northern European descent) who arrived from the eastern and northern states. Some four-fifths of Mississippi's population was born in the state. In 1980, 1.9 percent of Mississippi's population spoke a language other than English at home.

Major museums and libraries
Mississippi Museum of Natural History, Jackson
Mississippi State Historical Museum, Jackson

Lauren Rogers Library and Museum of Art, Laurel

Major arts organizations
Jackson Symphony Orchestra
Mississippi Opera, Jackson
New Stage Theatre, Jackson
Opera/South, Jackson

Colleges and universities
Number public (1986-87) 25
Number private (1986-87) 17
Total enrollment, in full-time equivalent students (1985) 86,800

Public elementary and secondary schools
Expenditure per pupil in average daily attendance (1986-87) $2,534
Pupil-teacher ratio (1987) 19.0
Average teacher salary (1986-87) $20,050

Holidays
Robert E. Lee's Birthday. 3d Monday in January
Confederate Memorial Day. 4th Monday in April
Jefferson Davis's Birthday. 1st Monday in June
State Fair, Jackson. Fall

MISSISSIPPI IN LITERATURE

Dorothy R. Abbott *Mississippi Writers: Reflections of Childhood and Youth* 2 vols. (1985, 1986)
Anthology of fiction and autobiographical essays.

Terry Alford *Prince among Slaves* (1986)
Biography of Ibrahima, slave of a Natchez farmer, who returned to Africa after twenty years.

Richard Bissell *A Stretch on the River* (1987)
Novel of adventure on a Mississippi River towboat.

Walter Blair and **Franklin J. Meine** *Half Horse, Half Alligator: The Growth of the Mike Fink Legend* (1956); *Mike Fink: King of the Mississippi Keelboatmen* (1971)
Studies of the historical figure, and of the legends that grew around him.

B. A. Botkin *A Treasury of Mississippi Folklore* (1955)

Charlotte Capers *The Capers Papers* (1982)
Informal essays on regional topics.

Hodding Carter *Where Main Street Meets the River* (1953)
Autobiography of a newspaperman who opposed Senator Bilbo and Huey Long.

Carroll Case *Youth: A Memory* (1979)
Reminiscences of growing up in the 1940s and '50s.

William M. Cash and **Lucy Somerville Howorth** (eds.) *My Dear Nellie: The Civil War Letters of William L. Nugent to Eleanor Smith Nugent* (1977)
Letters written by a cavalryman to his wife.

Jane Curry (ed.) *The River's in My Blood: Riverboat Pilots Tell Their Story* (1983)
Oral history of the steamboatmen.

Ellen Douglas *The Rock Cried Out* (1979)
Novel set against a background of social turmoil arising from the civil rights movement. Douglas' novels and stories, which include *A Family's Affairs* (1962), and *A Lifetime Burning* (1982), are set in the fictional Homochito

County, which, like Faulkner, she employs as her characters' domain.

Charles Lawrence Dyer *Along the Gulf* (1894, rpt. 1983)
The resorts and cities of the Gulf at the turn of the century.

James Faulkner *Across the Creek: Faulkner Family Stories* (1986)

John Faulkner *Dollar Cotton* (1942)
Realistic novel of cotton raising in the Delta.

William Faulkner *Sartoris* (1929)
The tale of Bayard Sartoris is the first of seven novels that constitute the Yoknapatawpha saga, a fictional realm closely resembling Lafayette County and Oxford, Mississippi, which Faulkner populated with members of the Sartoris and Snopes families and a diverse group of Southerners. A major concern of Faulkner's fiction is the relation between Southern values of the past, embodied in the history of the Sartoris family, and the less noble, more complex, demands of the twentieth century.

Fannie Flagg *Coming Attractions: A Wonderful Novel* (1981)
Comic novel, in the form of a beauty queen's journal, about growing up in the 1950s.

Shelby Foote *Tournament* (1949); *Follow Me Down* (1950); *Love in a Dry Season* (1951); *Jordan County* (1954)
Novels with realistic Delta settings, 1890–1940.

William Lovelace Foster (ed. K. T. Urquhart) *Vicksburg: Southern City under Siege* (1980)
Eyewitness account of the siege, June 20–July 4, 1863, sent to the author's wife as a letter.

Emerson Gould *Fifty Years on the Mississippi* (1889)
Autobiography of a flatboatman.

Minrose Gwin (ed.) *Olden Times Revisited* (1982)
Articles by Washington L. Clayton about frontier life 1840–1870, originally published in the Tupelo *Journal* in 1905–1906.

Annie Harper (ed. Jeannie M. Deen) *Annie Harper's Journal: A Southern Mother's Legacy* (1983)
Journal of the Civil War and Reconstruction written in Natchez.

Arthur Palmer Hudson *Folksongs of Mississippi and Their Background* (1936)
—— (ed.) *Humor of the Old Deep South* (1936)
—— and **George Herzog** *Folk Tunes from Mississippi* (1937)

John G. Jones (ed.) *Mississippi Writers Talking* 2 vols. (1982)
Conversations with contemporary authors.

Harnett Thomas Kane *Bride of Fortune* (1948)
Fictional account of Jefferson Davis' courtship and marriage.

Anna Knight *Mississippi Girl: An Autobiography* (1952)
Story of a black missionary.

James B. Lloyd (ed.) *Lives of Mississippi Authors, 1817–1967* (1981)

Beverly Lowry *Come Back, Lolly Ray* (1977)
Satirical novel of a Delta town in the 1970s.

John Roy Lynch *Reminiscences of an Active Life* (1970)
Memoirs of black politician, attorney, and author.

James Meredith *Three Years in Mississippi* (1965)
Personal account of the first black student to enter the University of Mississippi.

Berry Morgan *The Mystic Adventures of Roxie Stoner* (1974)
Stories of social change in a small town, told from the point of view of an uneducated black woman.

Willie Morris *North toward Home* (1967); *Yazoo: Integration in a Deep Southern Town* (1975)
Non-fiction accounts of contemporary events in the town of Yazoo.

William A. Percy *Lanterns on the Levee: Recollections of a Planter's Son* (1941)
Life on the Delta during the early twentieth century.

Noel E. Polk and **James R. Scafidel** (eds.) *An Anthology of Mississippi Writers* (1979)

Peggy W. Prenshaw (ed.) *Conversations with Eudora Welty* (1984)

Louise Clarke Pyrnelle *Diddie, Dumps, and Tot, or, Plantation Child-Life* (1980)
Reminiscence of growing up on a plantation before the Civil War, containing details of legends and folkways.

Shirley Seifert *Proud Way* (1948)
Historical novel based on two years in the life of Varina Howell, first lady of the Confederacy.

Harold Sinclair *Horse Soldiers* (1955)
A fictional account of the daring Civil War exploit known as Grierson's Raid.

Pat Smith *River Is Home* (1953)
Story of a boy's life on a bayou.

Elizabeth Spencer *Fire in the Morning* (1948); *This Crooked Way* (1952); *The Voice at the Back Door* (1956); *Salt Line* (1984)
Novels portraying life in Mississippi since World War II.

Mildred S. Topp *Smile Please* (1948); *In the Pink* (1951)
Two-volume autobiography portraying social life and customs of the Delta in the early 1900s.

Mark Twain *Life on the Mississippi* (1883, rpt. 1960)
Classic account of the customs and speech of the raftsmen and flatboatmen.

Robert Weekley *House in Ruins* (1958)
Novel about guerilla warfare during Reconstruction.

Eudora Welty *Collected Stories* (1980)
Classic stories of small town and rural life by the Jackson-born writer who, with Faulkner, is regarded as the state's finest author. Welty published a partial account of her life in *One Time, One Place: Mississippi in the Depression, a Snapshot Album* (1971).

Richard Wright *Black Boy: A Record of Childhood and Youth* (1945)
Classic autobiography of a black youth. Wright also wrote the Mississippi novel *Long Dream* (1958), about racial prejudice and political corruption in a small town.

Stark Young *Heaven Trees* (1926); *So Red the Rose* (1934)
Romantic historical novels portraying plantation life in Natchez before and during the Civil War.

GUIDES TO RESOURCES

Capers, Charlotte (ed.) *Guide to Civil War Source Material in the Mississippi Department of Archives and History* (1962)

Dennis, Frank A. *Index to the Journal of Mississippi History, 1939–1958* (1984)

Federal Writers' Project *Mississippi: A Guide to the Magnolia State* (1938, rpt. 1988)
——. *Mississippi Gulf Coast: Yesterday and Today, 1699–1939* (1939)

Kempe, Helen *Pelican Guide to Old Homes of Mississippi* 2 vols. (1977)

McCain, William D. *Mississippiana for Public, High School, and Junior College Libraries* (1941)

Mississippi Department of Archives and History (comp. Thomas W. Henderson and Ronald E. Tomlin) *Guide to Official Records in the Mississippi Department of Archives and History* (1975)

Mississippi Research and Development Center. Information Services Division *Handbook of Selected Data for Mississippi* (1983)

Moore, John H. and **Margaret D.** *Mississippi: A Guide to Localized History* (1969)

State of Mississippi *Historic Properties: State-owned Buildings of Historic and Architectural Significance* (1982)

SELECTED NONFICTION SOURCES

Alford, Terry *Prince Among Slaves* (1977)

Ames, Blanche A. *Adelbert Ames, 1835–1933* (1964)

Barrett, Russell H. *Integration at Ole Miss* (1965)

Belfrage, Sally *Freedom Summer* (1965)

Berry, Jason *Amazing Grace: With Charles Evers in Mississippi* (1973)

Bettersworth, John K. *Confederate Mississippi: The People and Politics of a Cotton State in Wartime* (1943)
———. (ed.) *Mississippi in the Confederacy: As They Saw It* (1961)
———. *Mississippi: The Land and the People* (1981)

Blake, Edward L. *Farm Bureau in Mississippi: A History of the Mississippi Farm Bureau Federation* (1971)

Bond, Willard F. *I Had a Friend: An Autobiography* (1958)

Brandfon, Robert L. *Cotton Kingdom of the New South: A History of the Yazoo-Mississippi Delta from Reconstruction to the Twentieth Century* (1967)

Brown, Calvin S. *Archeology of Mississippi* (1926)

Bruynoghe, Yannick *Big Bill Blues: William Broonzy's Story* (1964)

Butler, Pierce *The Unhurried Years* (1948)

Cain, Helen and Anne D. Czarniecki *An Illustrated Guide to the Mississippi Governor's Mansion* (1984)

Canfield, Cass *The Iron Will of Jefferson Davis* (1978)

Claiborne, John F. H. *Life and Correspondence of John A. Quitman, Major-General, U.S.A., and Governor of the State of Mississippi* 2 vols. (1860)
———. *Life and Times of Gen. Sam Dale, the Mississippi Partisan* (1860)
———. *Mississippi as a Province, Territory and State* (1880, rpt. 1964)

Coastes, Robert M. *The Outlaw Years: The History of the Land Pirates of the Natchez Trace* (1930)

Cohn, David L. *God Shakes Creation* (1935)

Conner, Douglas L. *A Black Physician's Story: Bringing Hope in Mississippi* (1985)

Cooper, J. Wesley *Ante-Bellum Houses of Natchez* (1970)

Crocker, Mary W. *Historic Architecture in Mississippi* (1973)

Cunningham, W. J. *Agony at Galloway: One Church's Struggle with Social Change* (1980)

Currie, James T. *Enclave: Vicksburg and Her Plantations, 1863–1870* (1980)

Cushman, H. B. *History of the Choctaw, Chickasaw, and Natchez Indians* (1972)

Daniel, Peter *Deep'n As It Come: The 1927 Mississippi River Flood* (1977)

Daniels, Jonathan *The Devil's Backbone; the Story of the Natchez Trace* (1962)

Davis, Edwin A. and William R. Hogan *The Barber of Natchez* (1954)

Debo, Angie *The Rise and Fall of the Choctaw Republic* (1982)

Everett, Frank E., Jr. *Brierfield: Plantation Home of Jefferson Davis* (1971)

Everhart, William C. *Vicksburg, National Military Park, Mississippi* (1954)

Evers, Charles *Evers* (1971)

Farm Security Administration (ed. Patti C. Black) *Documentary portrait of Mississippi: The Thirties* (1982)

Faulkner, John *My Brother Bill: An Affectionate Reminiscence* (1975)

Ferris, William R. *Blues from the Delta* (1978, rpt. 1984)

Fulkerson, Howard S. *Random Recollections of Early Days in Mississippi* (1885)

Galloway, Patricia (ed.) *Anthology of Mississippi Archaeology, 1966–1979* (1985)

Gandy, Joan W. and Thomas H. *Norman's Natchez: An Early Photographer and His Town* (1979)

Garner, James W. *Reconstruction in Mississippi* (1901, rpt. 1968)

Gibson, Arrell M. *The Chickasaws* (1981)

Gillis, Norman E. *Early Inhabitants of the Natchez District* (1963)

Gonzales, John E. *A Mississippi Reader: Selected Articles from the Journal of Mississippi History* (1980)

Green, A. Wigfall *The Man Bilbo* (1963)

Hall, James *A Brief History of the Mississippi Territory* (1801, rpt. 1986)

Harris, William C. *Presidential Reconstuction in Mississippi* (1967)
———. *The Day of the Carpetbagger; Republican Reconstruction in Mississippi* (1979)

Harrison, Robert W. *Levee Districts and Levee Building in Mississippi: A Study of State and Local Efforts to Control Mississippi River Floods* (1951)

Haynes, Robert *The Natchez District and the American Revolution* (1976)

Hickman, Nollie *Mississippi Harvest: Lumbering in the Longleaf Pine Belt, 1840–1915* (1962)

Highsaw, Robert B. and Charles N. Fortenberry *The Government and Administration of Mississippi* (1954)

Hobbs, Gambrell A. *Bilbo, Brewer, and Bribery in Mississippi Politics* (1917)

Hoehling, Adolph A. *Vicksburg: 47 Days of Siege* (1969)

Hogan, William R. and Edwin A. Davis (eds.) *William Johnson's Natchez: The Ante-Bellum Diary of a Free Negro* (1951)

Holmes, Jack D. L. *Gayoso: The Life of a Spanish Governor in the Mississippi Valley, 1789–1799* (1965)

Holmes, W. F. *The White Chief: James Kimble Vardaman* (1970)

Hooker, Charles E. *Mississippi* (1899)

Howell, H. Grady, Jr. *Going to Meet the Yankees: A History of the "Bloody Sixth" Mississippi Infantry, C.S.A.* (1981)

Huie, William B. *Three Lives for Mississippi* (1968)

James, D. Clayton *Antebellum Natchez* (1968)

Jones, Laurence C. *Piney Woods and Its Story* (1922)

Kane, Harnett T. *Natchez on the Mississippi* (1947)

Kirwan, Albert D. *Revolt of the Rednecks; Mississippi Politics, 1876–1925* (1964)

Knight, Anna *Mississippi: An Autobiography* (1952)

Korn, Jerry and the Editors of Time-Life Books *War on the Mississippi: Grant's Vicksburg Campaign* (1985)

Lana, Meredith *Defender of the Faith: The High Court of Mississippi* (1977)

Leverett, Rudy H. *Legend of the Free State of Jones* (1984)

Loewen, James W. and Charles Sallis (eds.) *Mississippi: Conflict and Change* (1974)

Lord, Walter *The Past That Would Not Die* (1966)

Lowry, Robert and W. H. McCardle *A History of Mississippi* (1891, rpt. 1978)

Lynch, John R. *Reminiscences of an Active Life: The Autobiography of John Roy Lynch* (1970)

May, Robert *John A. Quitman: Old South Crusader* (1985)

McCord, William *Mississippi: The Long, Hot Summer* (1965)

McElroy, Robert *Jefferson Davis: The Unreal and the Real* 2 vols. (1937)

McLemore, Richard A. (ed.) *A History of Mississippi* 2 vols. (1973)

McMillen, Neil R. *The Citizens' Council: Organized Resistance to the Second Reconstruction* (1971)

Meredith, James *Three Years in Mississippi* (1966)

Miles, Edwin A. *Jacksonian Democracy in Mississippi* (1960)

Mitchell, George *Blow My Blues Away* (1971)

Moody, Anne *Coming of Age in Mississippi* (1968)

Moore, John H. *Agriculture in Ante-Bellum Mississippi* (1958)

Morgan, Chester M. *Redneck Liberal; Theodore G. Bilbo and the New Deal* (1985)

Murphy, James B. *L. Q. C. Lamar: Pragmatic Patriot* (1973)

Neitzel, Robert S. *Archeology of the Fatherland Site: Grand Village of the Natchez* (1965)

Oliver, Nola N. *This Too Is Natchez* (1953)

Oliver, Paul *The Story of the Blues* (1969)

Osborn, George C. *John Sharpe Williams, Planter-Statesman of the Deep South* (1943)
———. *James Kimble Vardaman: Southern Commoner* (1981)

Pemberton, John C. *Pemberton, Defender of Vicksburg* (1942)

Pereyre, Lillian *James Lusk Alcorn: Persistent Whig* (1966)

Pishel, Robert G. *Natchez: Museum City of the Old South* (1959)

Polk, Noel (ed.) *Mississippi's Piney Woods; a Human Perspective* (1986)

Prenshaw, Peggy W. and Jesse O. McKee (eds.) *Sense of Place: Mississippi* (1980)

Rainwater, Percy L. *Mississippi, Storm Center of Secession, 1856–1861* (1969)

Randall, Ruth Painter *I Varina: A Biography of the Girl Who Married Jefferson Davis and Became the First Lady of the South* (1962)

Reeves, Carolyn K. (ed.) *The Choctaw before Removal* (1985)

Rowland, Dunbar *Military History of Mississippi* (1908, rpt. 1978)
——— (ed.) *Jefferson Davis, Constitutionalist: His Letters, Papers, and Speeches* 10 vols. (1923)
———. *History of Mississippi: The Heart of the South* 2 vols. (1925, rpt. 1964)

Sansing, David C. and Carroll Waller *A History of the Mississippi Governor's Mansion* (1977)

Sewell, George A. and Margaret L. Dwight *Mississippi Black History Makers* (rev. ed. 1984)

Shenton, James P. *Robert John Walker: A Politician from Jackson to Lincoln* (1961)

Silver, James W. (ed.) *Mississippi in the Confederacy: As Seen in Retrospect* (1961)
———. *Mississippi: The Closed Society* (rev. ed. 1966)
———. *Running Scared: Silver in Mississippi* (1984)

Skates, John R. *Mississippi: A Bicentennial History* (States and the Nation series) (1979)

Smead, Howard *Blood Justice: The Lynching of Mack Charles Parker* (1986)

Smith, Frank E. *The Yazoo* (Rivers of America series) (1954)
———. *Congressman from Mississippi* (1964)
——— and Audrey Warren *Mississippians All* (1968)

Sorrels, William W. and Charles Cavaonaro *Ole Miss Rebels: Mississippi Football* (1976)

Sterne, Emma Gelders *They Took Their Stand* (1968)

Strode, Hudson *Jefferson Davis* 3 vols. (1955–1964)

Sugarman, Tracy *Stranger at the Gates: A Summer in Mississippi* (1966)

Sullivan, Charles L. *Mississippi Gulf Coast: Portrait of a People* (1985)

Swain, Martha H. *Pat Harrison: The New Deal Years* (1978)

Swearingen, Mack *The Early Life of George Poindexter: A Story of the Old Southwest* (1934)

Sydnor, Charles S. and Claude Bennett *Mississippi History* (1930)
———. *Slavery in Mississippi* (1933, rpt. 1966)

Tucker, Shirley *Mississippi from Within* (1965)

Turitz, Leo and Evelyn *Jews in Early Mississippi* (1983)

Walker, Peter F. *Vicksburg: A People at War, 1860–1865* (1960)

Wayne, Michael *The Reshaping of Plantation Society: The Natchez District, 1860–1880* (1983)

Weathersby, W. H. *History of Educational Legislation in Mississippi from 1798 to 1860* (1921)

Weaver, Herbert *Mississippi Farmers, 1850–1860* (1945)

Weems, Robert C. *The Early Economic Development of Mississippi, 1699–1840* (1953)

Wells, Dean F. and Hunter Cole (eds.) *Mississippi Heroes* (1980)

Wells, Samuel J. and Roseanna Tubby (eds.) *After Removal: The Choctaw in Mississippi* (1986)

Wharton, Vernon L. *The Negro in Mississippi, 1865–1890* (1947)

Whitaker, Arthur P. *The Mississippi Question, 1795–1803* (1934)

Whitehead, Don *Attack on Terror: The FBI against the Ku Klux Klan in Mississippi* (1970)

Wier, Sadue H. with John F. Marszalek *A Black Businessman in White Mississippi, 1886–1974* (1977)

Wilber, Leon A. *Mississippi State Government: The Constitution, Legislature, and Administration* (1969)

Wirt, Frederick M. *The Politics of Southern Equality: Law and Change in a Mississippi County* (1970)

MISSOURI

Missouri is a west north central state. It is bordered on the north by Iowa; on the east by the Mississippi River, Illinois, Kentucky, and Tennessee; on the south by Arkansas; and on the west by Oklahoma, Kansas, Nebraska, and the Missouri River.

FULL NAME State of Missouri
POSTAL ABBREVIATION MO
INHABITANT Missourian
ADMITTED TO THE UNION Aug. 10, 1821.
24th state
POPULATION (est. 1987) 5,103,000.
Percent of US total: 2.10%. Rank: 15th

CAPITAL CITY Jefferson City, located on the Missouri River in central Missouri; population 33,619 (1980). Built on a site selected for the future capital in 1821, it was incorporated as a town in 1825 and as a city in 1839, and has served as the capital since 1826.

STATE NAME AND NICKNAMES From the Missouri Indian word for "canoe possessor," in reference to the tribe that gave its name to the Missouri River. Also known as the Show Me State, the Bullion State, the Cave State, the Lead State, and the Ozark State.

STATE SEAL In the center is a circular emblem supported on both sides by grizzly bears. In the right half of the emblem is the eagle of the Federal coat of arms; in the left is a grizzly bear in a red field and above it a new moon in a blue field; the emblem is encircled by the legend "United We Stand, Divided We Fall." Above it is a visored helmet and 24 stars; below it is a streamer bearing the state motto, along with the date "MDCCCXX." Around this coat of arms is the legend "The Great Seal of the State of Missouri."

MOTTO Salus Populi Supreme Lex Esto (The welfare of the people shall be the supreme law)

SONG "Missouri Waltz," lyrics by J.R. Shannon, music by John Valentine Eppel, arrangement by Frederick Knight Logan.

SYMBOLS
Flower red haw blossom
Tree flowering dogwood
Bird bluebird
Mineral galena
Rock mozarkite

LICENSE PLATE White on red, with white border and legend "Show-Me State."

FLAG Three horizontal stripes of red, white, and blue, with the state coat of arms in the center surrounded by a blue border containing 24 stars.

GEOGRAPHY AND CLIMATE

North of the Missouri River, which divides the state neatly in two, Missouri is mainly heartland plain and prairie; south of the river is the Ozark Plateau, higher and rougher terrain with many large caves and natural springs. The extreme southeastern corner of Missouri, called the "Bootheel," is part of the alluvial plain of the Mississippi River, which forms the state's eastern border. The state climate is moderate and continental, with 25 to 30 tornadoes per year.

AREA 69,697 square miles. Rank: 19th
INLAND WATER 752 square miles
GEOGRAPHIC CENTER Miller, 20 miles SW of Jefferson City
ELEVATIONS *Highest point:* Taum Sauk Mountain, Iron County, 1,772 feet. *Lowest point:* St. Francis River, Dunkin County, 230 feet. *Mean elevation:* 800 feet

MAJOR RIVERS Missouri, Mississippi, Osage, Grand

MAJOR LAKES AND RESERVOIRS Lake of the Ozarks, Stockton, Taneycomo, Table Rock, Bull Shoals, Truman, Cannon

LAND USE

	Thousands of acres
Urban (1982)	1,117
Rural (1982)	39,543
Cropland (1982)	14,998
Pastureland (1982)	12,573
Rangeland (1982)	168
Forestland (1982)	10,986
State parks and recreation areas (1983)	98
National park system (1984)	63
National forest system (1984)	3,082
Tribal lands (1984)	0

TEMPERATURES The highest recorded temperature was 118°F on July 14, 1954, at Warsaw and Union. The lowest was -40°F on February 13, 1905, at Warsaw.

NATIONAL SITES

NATIONAL BATTLEFIELD Wilson's Creek
NATIONAL HISTORIC SITES Jefferson National Expansion Memorial, Harry S. Truman
NATIONAL HISTORIC TRAILS Lewis & Clark, Oregon
NATIONAL MONUMENT George Washington Carver
NATIONAL PARK Glacier
NATIONAL SCENIC RIVER AND RIVERWAY Ozark
NATIONAL WILDLIFE REFUGES Clarence Cannon, Mingo, Squaw Creek, Swan Lake

HISTORY

1682	Region now known as Missouri is claimed for France.
1735	Settlers from Illinois establish first permanent settlement at Sainte Genevieve on Mississippi River.
1752	First Catholic Church in Missouri is founded at Ste. Genevieve.
1762	France cedes Missouri territory to Spain.
1764	St. Louis is founded as a lead mining and fur-trading post by Pierre Liguest Laclède.
1774	Lead mines discovered in southeastern Missouri. Missouri becomes world's leading producer of lead.
1784	Shawnee and Delaware Indians migrate to southeastern Missouri.
1785	Great flood on Mississippi River and Missouri River tributary.
1794	Ste. Genevieve relocated on higher ground.
	Auguste and Pierre Chouteau obtain monopoly of Osage Indian trade.
1799	Daniel Boone leaves Kentucky and settles in Missouri.
1800	Missouri territory returned to France by Spain.
1803	Missouri, as part of the Louisiana Purchase, is acquired by the United States.
1804	Sauk and Fox Indians cede northeast Missouri lands to United States. Later the Indians say treaty was unauthorized.
1806	Salt manufacturing started at Boon's Lick.
1808	First newspaper in Missouri published at St. Louis is the *Missouri Gazette*.
	St. Louis incorporated.
1809	Hostility of Indians on frontier increases.
1812	Earthquake causes considerable damage in New Madrid area.

1818	Missouri Fur Company established.
	Pine lumbering begins.
1821	*August 10.* Missouri admitted into Union as 24th state.
1825	*November 7.* Shawnee Indians cede title to remaining land in state. General removal of Indians follows.
1827	Joseph Robidoux establishes fur–trading post on present site of St. Joseph.
1830	*March 3.* Missouri Compromise passes thereby prohibiting slavery in the Louisiana Territory north of latitude 36°30' but not restricting Missouri.
1831	Joseph Smith, leader of the Latter–Day Saints, announces a Jackson County site as the New Jerusalem. Mormon settlement begins there.
1836	Platte Purchase, comprising six northwestern Missouri counties, is added to the state.
1838	*September.* Open war between the Mormons and the gentiles.
	Cherokee Indians, headed for new reservation, pass through southern Missouri over Trail of Tears.
1839	Mormons emigrate from Missouri to Illinois.
	Independence, where both the Oregon and the Santa Fe trails begin, is known as Gateway to the West.
1856	Guerrilla warfare over slavery question breaks out.
1857	United States Supreme Court prevents Missouri slave, Dred Scott, from gaining freedom. Case becomes one of the major events leading to the Civil War.
1860	*April 3.* Pony Express Service inaugurated, linking St. Joseph to Sacramento, California.
1861	*March 6.* Convention meets to determine state allegiance resulting in a defeat of pro-southern secession.
	April 20. Pro-southern forces capture Liberty arsenal.
	May 10. Camp Jackson captured by federal captain Nathaniel Lyon.
	August 10. Battle of Wilson Creek.
	November 7. General Ulysses S. Grant defeated in Battle of Belmont.
1862	*October 18.* Palmyra executions.
1864	*September 27.* Centralia massacre.
	October 21-23. Confederates defeated at Westport.
1865	*January 11.* Slavery abolished in Missouri.
1870	First stockyards built in Kansas City.
1880	First black newspaper begins publication in St. Louis.
1882	*April.* Jesse James killed at St. Joseph.
1891	First automobile brought into Missouri.
1901	First Missouri State Fair held at Sedalia.
1904	Everyone is singing "Meet Me in St. Louis, Louie" as Louisiana Purchase Exposition (World Fair) opens there.
1908	School of Journalism, first in the world, established at University of Missouri.
1911	*February 5.* State capitol burns.
	October 4. First air mail ever carried is flown from Kinloch Park to Fairgrounds Park, St. Louis, a distance of 10 miles.
1917	*August 5.* Missouri National Guard conscripted for Federal Service.
1918	Missouri mules are lauded for battlefront service in World War I.
1921	WEW, first radio station in state, starts broadcasting from St. Louis University.
1923	President Warren Harding makes first presidential broadcast at St. Louis.
1926	President Calvin Coolidge dedicates Kansas City's Liberty Memorial.
1931	Bagnell Dam completed on Osage River to form 100-square-mile Lake of the Ozarks.
1935	Thomas Hart Benton, controversial Missouri painter, is commissioned to paint murals for state capitol.
1936	Leeds Chevrolet Plant in Kansas City is scene of nation's first sit-down strike.
1944	Harry S. Truman, born in Lamar, is elected vice president on ticket with Franklin Roosevelt.
1945	*April.* Harry Truman becomes president of the United States upon the death of Roosevelt.
1947	KSD-TV, St. Louis, begins broadcasting as first television station of the state.

1952	*September.* President Truman declares Missouri a disaster area due to severe drought.
1953	*July 14.* National monument erected for botanist, George Washington Carver, near Diamond.
1955	Kansas City schools end segregation without incident.
1957	Truman Library opens in Independence, Missouri.
1965	The steel Gateway Arch of St. Louis is completed.
1975	State legislature defeats Equal Rights Amendment. State spends $2.5 million on environmental health.
1977	School busing is initiated as part of desegregation program in Kansas City.
1980	*November.* Controversial "Hancock Amendment," Constitutional Amendment #5, which sets a tax and expenditure limit, is adopted.
1981	*February 18.* Wayne Cryts leads a caravan of 78 trucks to a bankrupt, padlocked grain elevator which holds soybeans he has stored there since 1979. Cryts spends years in court battles fighting, on behalf of the American farmers, against inequities in the judicial system.
	July 10. Ken Rex McElroy, "town bully," is shot to death in a vigilante-style execution in Skidmore.
	October 20. St. Louis Cardinals baseball team wins the World Series.
1983	*January.* The discovery of dioxin contamination at Times Beach and other sites draws national attention and leads to the search for other pollution sites across Missouri and the United States.
	Environmental Protection Agency announces $33 million plan to buy out property owners in Times Beach.
1984	*December.* The Callaway Nuclear Power Plant is completed after years of controversy and protests.
1985	*October.* The St. Louis Cardinals baseball team plays the Kansas City Royals in the "I-70 Series." The Royals win the World Series.
1988	*January.* The St. Louis Cardinals football team moves to Phoenix, Arizona.
	March. Missouri holds its first presidential primary.
	June. Missouri's worst drought since 1934. Mississippi and Missouri rivers experience record lows that create serious problems in river transportation.

DEMOGRAPHY

Population (est. 1987) . . . 5,103,000
Population (1980) 4,916,759
Population density in persons
per square mile (1980) 70.5

POPULATION BY RACE (1980)
American Indian/Aleut/
Eskimo 12,319
Asian/Pacific Islander 23,108
Black 514,274
Hispanic 51,667
White 4,346,267
Other 21,476

POPULATION CHARACTERISTICS (1980)
Percent of state population
Urban 68.1
Rural 31.9
Under 18 . . . . 27.7
65 or older 13.2
College-educated 14.0

Families below poverty line 9.1
Public-assistance recipients 5.9

Per capita personal income
(1986) $13,657
Millionaires per 100,000
residents (1982) 155.8
Average life expectancy in
years (1980) 73.8
Marriage rate per 1,000
residents (1986) 10.0
Divorce rate per 1,000
residents (1986) 5.1
Birth rate per 1,000
residents (1985) 15.4
Infant mortality rate per 1,000
births (1985) 10.5
Abortion rate per 1,000
live births (1985) 261
Crime rate per 100,000
residents (1985)
Violent 578.6
Property 4,075.5

Federal and state prisoners
per 100,000 residents (1984) . . 169
Alcohol consumption in gallons
per capita (1985) 38.7
Deaths from motor vehicle accidents
per 100,000 residents (1985) . . 18.4

MAJOR CITIES

	1984 population (est.)
Columbia	63,294
East St. Louis	51,332
Kansas City	443,075
St. Joseph	74,860
St. Louis	429,296
Springfield	136,939

GOVERNMENT AND POLITICS

Number of US Representatives   8
Electoral votes   10

POLITICAL PARTY NOMINEES FROM STATE
  * winner

Francis Preston Blair Jr. (D)	1868	VP
Benjamin Gratz Brown (D/ Liberal Republican/Liberal Republican Convention of Colored Men)	1872	VP
John Anderson Brooks (Prohibition)	1888	VP
A. King (Continental)	1901	VP
William Wesley Cox (Socialist Labor)	1920	P
Herman Preston Faris (Prohibition)	1924	P
Harry S. Truman* (D)	1944	VP
Harry S. Truman* (D)	1948	P
Gerald Lyman Kenneth Smith (Christian Nationalist)	1948	VP
Rutherford Losey Decker (Prohibition)	1960	P
William R. Rogers (Theological)	1964	VP
William R. Rogers (Theological)	1968	P
Thomas Francis Eagleton (D/ resigned)	1972	VP

PRESIDENTIAL PRIMARY ELECTION In 1988, Missouri sent 83 Democratic delegates and 25 Republican delegates to the national conventions.

CONSTITUTION Missouri has had four constitutions: 1820, 1865, 1875, and the present one, adopted in 1945.

LEGISLATURE The General Assembly is divided into the Senate (34 members, 4-year term, minimum age 30) and the House of Representatives (163 members, 2-year term, minimum age 24). In 1987, the annual salary was $20,852.

JUDICIARY The highest court is the Supreme Court, with 7 judges serving 2-year terms. In 1987, the annual salary was $80,649.

EXECUTIVE The governor serves a 4-year term; the minimum age for holding office is 30. In 1987, the annual salary was $81,000. There are 5 other elected officials.

PRESIDENTIAL VOTE 1948-1988 *(in percents)*

Year	*State Winner*	*Democratic*	*Republican*
1948	Truman (D)	58.1	41.5
1952	Eisenhower (R)	49.1	50.7
1956	Stevenson (D)	50.1	49.9
1960	Kennedy (D)	50.3	49.7
1964	Johnson (D)	64.1	36.0
1968	Nixon (R)	43.7	44.9
1972	Nixon (R)	37.7	62.3
1976	Carter (D)	51.1	47.5
1980	Reagan (R)	44.5	31.2
1984	Reagan (R)	50.0	60.0
1988	Bush (R)	48.0	52.0

GOVERNORS

Territorial Governors

William C.C. Claiborne (acting governor general and intendant of Louisiana)	1803-1804
Amos Stoddard (civil commandant)	1804
William Henry Harrison (governor of District of Lousiana)	1804-1805
James Wilkinson (governor of Louisiana Territory)	1805-1807
Joseph Browne (acting)	1807
Frederick Bates (acting)	1807
Meriwether Lewis	1807-1809

Frederick Bates (acting)	1809-1810
Benjamin Howard	1810-1812
Frederick Bates (acting governor of Missouri Territory)	1812-1813
William Clark	1813-1820

State Governors

Alexander McNair (D)	1820-1824
Frederick Bates (D)	1824-1825
Abraham J. Williams (D/acting)	1825
John Miller (D)	1825-1832
Daniel Dunklin (D)	1832-1836
Lillburn W. Boggs (D)	1836-1840
Thomas Reynolds (D)	1840-1844
M.M. Marmaduke (acting)	1844
John C. Edwards (D)	1844-1848
Austin A. King (D)	1848-1852
Sterling Price (D)	1852-1856
Trusten Polk (D)	1856-1857
Hancock Jackson (D/acting)	1857
Robert M. Stewart (D)	1857-1861
Claiborne F. Jackson (D)	1861
Hamilton R. Gamble (Unionist)	1861-1864
Willard P. Hall (Unionist/acting)	1864-1865
Thomas C. Fletcher (R)	1865-1869
Joseph W. McClurg (R)	1869-1871
B. Gratz Brown (Liberal)	1871-1873
Silas Woodson (D)	1873-1875
Charles H. Hardin (D)	1875-1877
John S. Phelps (D)	1877-1881
Thomas T. Crittenden (D)	1881-1885
John S. Marmaduke (D)	1885-1887
Albert P. Morehouse (D/acting)	1887-1889
David R. Francis (D)	1889-1893
William Joel Stone (D)	1893-1897
Lon V. Stephens (D)	1897-1901
Alexander M. Dockery (D)	1901-1905
Joseph W. Folk (D)	1905-1909
Herbert S. Hadley (R)	1909-1913
Elliot W. Major (D)	1913-1917
Frederick D. Gardner (D)	1917-1921
Arthur M. Hyde (R)	1921-1925
Sam A. Baker (R)	1925-1929
Henry S. Caulfield (R)	1929-1933
Guy B. Park (D)	1933-1937
Lloyd C. Stark (D)	1937-1941
Forrest C. Donnell (R)	1941-1945
Phil M. Donnelly (D)	1945-1949
Forrest Smith (D)	1949-1953
Phil M. Donnelly (D)	1953-1957
James T. Blair Jr. (D)	1957-1961
John M. Dalton (D)	1961-1965
Warren E. Hearnes (D)	1965-1973
Christopher S. Bond (R)	1973-1977
Joseph P. Teasdale (D)	1977-1981
Christopher S. Bond (R)	1981-1985
John Ashcroft (R)	1985-

MINIMUM AGES

Majority	18
Marriage with parental consent	15
Marriage without parental consent	18
Making a will	18
Buying alcohol	21
Jury duty	21
Leaving school	16
Driver's license	16

CAPITAL PUNISHMENT
Number executed 1976-88: 0
On death row Aug. 1, 1988: 61

MILITARY INSTALLATIONS
Total number: 12
Major bases:
  Army: 1

FINANCES

Thousands of dollars

GENERAL REVENUE (1985)

Total general revenue	5,785,785
Total tax revenue	3,352,482
Sales and gross receipts	1,831,397
Individual income taxes	1,053,598
Corporate net income taxes	160,564

GENERAL EXPENDITURE (1985)

Total general expenditure	5,441,768
Education	2,200,860
Public welfare	937,252
Health	179,119
Hospitals	294,105
Natural resources	123,211
Highways	697,890
Police	62,706
Corrections	103,927

FEDERAL AID (1985) 1,935,316

ECONOMY

In agriculture, soybeans, cotton, wheat, corn, and walnuts are the principal cash crops. Livestock and stock products, including hogs, turkeys, and cattle, earn more than half the farm cash receipts, which were $4 billion in 1983. The state produces most of the US supply of lead; limestone, sand and gravel, barite, iron, zinc, coal, and granite are other mining products. Timber concerns in the Ozarks produce varied hardwood products, primarily charcoal, walnut wood, and red cedar. Heavy machinery, transportation equipment, and defense aircraft are Missouri's main manufactures, followed by processed foods, electrical machinery, clothing, shoes, and chemicals. Beer and ale are also important products, with the brewing industry centered around St. Louis. Value added by manufacture was $18 billion in 1982.

EMPLOYMENT (1984)

Thousands of persons

Total number of employed workers	2,207
Construction	82.2
Finance, insurance, and real estate	113.8
Government	332.8
Manufacturing	430.9
Mining	6.0
Services	434.8
Transportation, communications, and utilities	133.9
Wholesale and retail trade	480.4

Percent of civilian labor force unemployed (1984)	7.2

DEPARTMENT OF DEFENSE (1985)

Civilian workers employed	20,991
Military personnel	16,072
Contract awards	$7.613 billion

ENERGY SOURCES FOR ELECTRIC UTILITIES (1983)

	Percent
Coal	96.0
Gas	0.4
Hydroelectric	3.3
Nuclear	0.0
Petroleum	0.3

TRANSPORTATION

Motor vehicles registered in state (1986)	3,683,394
Miles of roads, streets, and highways (1986)	119,398
Miles of Class I railway operated (1986)	5,823
Airports (1983)	419
Major aviation hubs (1983)	2
Largest hub: St. Louis	
Major ports, with gross tonnage in thousands (1985):	
St. Louis	26,620

CULTURE AND EDUCATION

Native American tribes
Missouri was formerly the home of the Delaware, Fox, Illinois, Iowa, Kickapoo, Missouri, Omaha, Osage, Oto, Peoria, Potawatomi, Sauk, Shawnee, Sioux, and Wea tribes. There are no Indian settlements remaining.

Religions, ethnicities, and languages
Missouri has been the recipient of migration from both midwestern and southern states. Much of its population is descended from immigrants from Germany and Ireland who arrived in the early 19th century. There are surviving communities of Germans, Italians, Belgians, and Irish. One-third of the state's people are Roman Catholic, mostly concentrated in the cities, along with Jewish communities; the rest of the state is predominantly Baptist, and there is a strong Mormon presence. In 1980, 3.1 percent of Missouri's population spoke a language other than English at home.

Major museums and libraries
Linda Hall Library, Kansas City
Museum of Science and Natural History, St. Louis
Museum of Westward Expansion, St. Louis
National Museum of Transportation, St. Louis
Nelson Gallery and Atkins Museum of Fine Arts, Kansas City
St. Louis Art Museum
Harry S. Truman Library and Museum, Independence

Major arts organizations
Kansas City Symphony
Lyric Opera of Kansas City
Missouri Repertory Theatre, Kansas City
Opera Theatre of St. Louis
Repertory Theatre of St. Louis
St. Louis Symphony Orchestra
State Ballet of Missouri

Colleges and universities
Number public (1986-87) 28
Number private (1986-87) 64
Total enrollment, in full-time equivalent students (1985) 178,100

Public elementary and secondary schools
Expenditure per pupil in average daily attendance (1986-87) $3,345

Pupil-teacher ratio (1987) 16.4
Average teacher salary (1986-87) $24,383

Major league sports teams
Baseball: Kansas City Royals, St. Louis
Cardinals

Football: Kansas City Chiefs
Hockey: St. Louis Blues

Holidays
Harry S. Truman's Birthday. May 8
State Fair, Sedalia. 3d week in August

MISSOURI IN LITERATURE

John C. Anderson (ed. Glen Barrett) *MacKinaws down the Missouri* (1987)
Journal of a late-nineteenth-century trip by the overland mail route from St. Louis to Montana, and the return on the Missouri by boat.

Herbert Asbury *Up from Methodism* (1930)
Description of life in Farmington, containing an account of Ozark folklore and local traditions.

Conger Beasley Jr. (ed.) *Missouri Short Fiction* (1984)

Henry M. Belden (ed.) *Ballads and Songs Collected by the Missouri Folklore Society* (2d ed. 1955)

Sally Benson *Meet Me in St. Louis* (1941)
Anecdotes of domestic life 1903–1904.

Thomas Hart Benton *An Artist in America* (1937, 3d ed. 1968)
Autobiography of the famous painter, containing Ozark reminiscences and folklore.

Hal G. Borland *The Amulet* (1957)
Novel of Civil War Missouri.

Louis Bromfield *Wild Country* (1948)
Biographical novel of forty years on a Missouri farm.

Joseph M. Carrière *Tales from the French Folklore of Missouri* (1937)
Creole folklore collected near Potasi, in eastern Missouri.

Earl A. Collins *Folk Tales of Missouri* (1935)
———. *Legends and Lore of Missouri* (1951)

Jack Conroy *The Disinherited* (1933, rpt. 1982)
Classic novel of a coalminer's son's attempt to improve his lot.
———. *The Weed King and Other Stories* (1985)

Homer Croy *West of the Water Tower* (1923)
Novel of small town life.
———. *County Cured* (1943)
Autobiographical account of growing up on a small farm in the 1880s.
———. *Jesse James Was My Neighbor* (1949)
History and legends of the famous outlaw.

Dagmar Doneghy *The Border: A Missouri Saga* (1931)
Historical novel of the Kansas-Missouri border war.

Loula G. Erdman *Years of the Locust* (1947)
Novel of farming life.
———. *Life Was Simpler Then* (1963)
Reminiscences of rural life in the years after World War I.

Minnie Jane Forster *Lost Creek, an Ozark Novel of the Civil War* (1952)
Southwest region during the 1860s.

Robert K. Gilmore *Ozark Baptizings, Hangings, and Other Diversions: Theatrical Folkways of Rural Missouri, 1885–1910* (1984)

Leonard Hall *A Journal of the Seasons on an Ozark Farm* (1981); *Stars Upstream: Life along an Ozark River* (1983)
Journalist's essays on Ozark life and landscape.

James P. Jackson *Passages of a Stream: A Chronicle of the Meramec* (1984)

Elijah L. Jacobs and **Forrest E. Wolverton** *Missouri Writers: A Literary History of Missouri, 1780–1955* (1955)

Mitchell F. Jayne *Old Fish Hawk* (1970)
Novel about the friendship between an Osage Indian and a frontier farm boy.

Richard H. Jesse and **Edward A. Allen** (eds.) *Missouri Writers: A Literary History of Missouri, 1780–1955* (1955)

Josephine Johnson *Now in November* (1934)
Pulitzer prize–winning novel of Missouri farmers during the Depression.

MacKinlay Kantor *Romance of Rosy Ridge* (1937)
Romantic folktale of backwoods life just after the Civil War. Kantor also wrote a book of autobiographical and historical essays, *Missouri Bittersweet* (1969).

Rose Wilder Lane *Hill-Billy* (1926); *Cindy, a Romance of the Ozarks* (1928)
Classic early descriptions of the customs and speech of the Ozarks.

Marguerite Lyon *Take to the Hills: A Chronicle of the Ozarks* (1941)
An account of social life and customs.

Florence McCullough (comp.) *Living Authors of the Ozarks and Their Literature* (2d ed. 1945)

John Madson *Up on the River* (1985)
Description of life on the Mississippi between St. Paul and St. Louis.

Tom Moore *Mysterious Tales and Legends of the Ozarks* (1938)

Lucile Morris *Bald Knobbers* (1939)
An account of the outlaw "night riders" of the 1880s.

Ron Powers *White Town Drowsing* (1986)
A journalist rediscovers his roots in Hannibal.

Robert Price *Johnny Appleseed, Man and Myth* (1954)

Vance Randolph *Pissing in the Snow and Other Ozark Folktales* (1976)
Short stories by the celebrated collector of Ozark folklore from Missouri and Arkansas. Randolph's publications include *The Ozarks* (1931), *Ozark Mountain Folks* (1932), *From an Ozark Holler* (1933), *Ozark Folksongs* 4 vols. (1946–1950, rpt. 1980), *Who Blowed Up the Church House? and Other Ozark Folk Tales* (1952) and *Down in the Holler: A Gallery of Ozark Folkspeech* (1953, rpt. 1979).

Eleanor Risley *An Abandoned Orchard* (1932)
Novel about a woman who manages an Ozark orchard, based on actual events.

James Willard Schultz (ed. E. L. Silliman) *Floating on the Missouri* (1988)
Narrative of a pioneer describing the region in the late nineteenth century.

Carle B. Spotts *The Development of Fiction on the Missouri Frontier, 1830–1860* (1935)

Rosemary H. Thomas *It's Good to Tell You: French Folktales from Missouri* (1981)

Mark Twain (pseud. of Samuel L. Clemens) *Tom Sawyer* (1876)
Twain, who dominates Missouri literature, based many incidents in his fiction on his upbringing in Hannibal, and on his riverboat days before the Civil War. The plot of Tom Sawyer is believed to be derived from incidents involving Twain and his childhood friends in Hannibal, which is named "St. Petersburg" in the novel.

Raymond L. Weeks *The Hound-Tuner of Callaway* (1927)
Twenty-eight tales of pioneering.

Miller Williams (ed.) *Ozark, Ozark: A Hillside Reader* (1981)

GUIDES TO RESOURCES

Caldwell, Dorothy J. (ed.) *Missouri Historic Sites Catalog* (1963)

Collier, James E. *Agricultural Atlas of Missouri* (1955)
——. *Geographic Areas of Missouri* (1959)

Cottier, Randy L. *Selected Bibliography of Missouri Archaeology* (1973)

Federal Writers' Project *Missouri: A Guide to the "Show Me" State* (1941)
——. *The WPA Guide to 1930s Missouri* (1986)

Fitzgerald, Alice I. *Missouri's Literary Heritage for Children and Youth: An Annotated Bibliography of Books about Missouri* (1981)

Kinney-Hanson, Sharon (ed.) *Art Museums and Galleries in Missouri: A Directory* (1983)

Rafferty, Milton *Historical Atlas of Missouri* (1982)
——. *Missouri: A Geography* (1983)

Randolph, Vance *Ozark Folklore: An Annotated Bibliography* vol. I (1987)
—— and **Gordon McCann** *Ozark Folklore: An Annotated Bibliography* vol. II (1987)

Schraeder, Walter A. *Bibliography of Missouri Geography: A Guide to Written Material on Places and Regions of Missouri* (1977)

Southern History Publishing Co., St. Louis *Encyclopedia of the History of Missouri* (1901)

Wilson, D. R. *Missouri Historical Tour Guide* (1987)

SELECTED NONFICTION SOURCES

Appler, A. C. *The Younger Brothers* (1892, rpt. 1955)

Atherton, Lewis *The Frontier Merchant in Mid-America* (rev. ed. 1971)

Barrett, Paul W. and **Mary H.** *Young Brothers Massacre* (1988)

Beckwith, Paul E. *Creoles of St. Louis* (1893)

Berthold, Eugenie *Glimpses of Creole Life in Old St. Louis* (1933)

Breihan, Carl W. *The Complete and Authentic Life of Jesse James* (1953)
——. *Quantrill and His Civil War Guerrillas* (1959)

Britton, Rollin J. *Early Days on Grand River and the Mormon War* (1920)

Britton, Wiley *Pioneer Life in Southwest Missouri* (1929)

Brown, A. Theodore *Frontier Community: A History of Kansas City to 1870* (1963)
—— and **Lyle W. Dorsett** *K.C.: A History of Kansas City, Missouri* (1978)

Brownlee, Richard S. *Gray Ghosts of the Confederacy, Guerrilla Warfare in the West, 1861–1865* (1958)

Brugioni, Dino *The Civil War in Missouri as Seen from the Capital City* (1986)

Bryan, John A. (ed.) *Missouri's Contribution to American Architecture* (1928)

Bryan, William S. and **Robert Rose** *A History of Pioneer Families of Missouri* (1935, rpt. 1984)

Castel, Albert *William Clarke Quantrill: His Life and Times* (1962)

Chambers, William N. *Old Bullion Benton, Senator from the New West* (1956)

Chapman, Carl H. *The Archaeology of Missouri* 2 vols. (1980)
—— and **Eleanor F. Chapman** *Indians and Archaeology of Missouri* (1964)

Chittendon, H. M. *History of Early Steamboat Navigation on the Missouri River* 2 vols. (rpt. 1962)

Christ-Janer, Albert *George Caleb Bingham of Missouri: The Story of an Artist* (1940)

Collier, James E. *The Geography of the Northern Ozark Border Region in Missouri* (1953)

Connelley, William E. *Quantrill and the Border Wars* (1956)

Coyle, Elinor M. *Saint Louis; Portrait of a River City* (1966)

Culmer, Frederic A. *A New History of Missouri* (1938)

Cunningham, Mary B. and **Jeanne C. Blythe** *The Founding Family of St. Louis* (1977)

Daniels, Jonathan *The Man of Independence* (1950)

Derr, Ray *Missouri Farmers in Action* (1953)

De Voto, Bernard *Mark Twain's America* (1932)

Dixon, Susan *History of Missouri Compromise and Slavery in American Politics* (1970)

Dorsett, Lyle W. *The Pendergast Machine* (1968)

Dorsey, Florence *Road to the Sea: The Story of James B. Eads and the Mississippi River* (1947)

Ellis, James F. *The Influence of Environment on the Settlement of Missouri* (1929)

Foley, William E. *A History of Missouri: 1673 to 1820* (1971)
—— and **David Rice** *The First Chouteaus: River Barons of Early St. Louis* (1983)

Fuller, Myron L. *The New Madrid Earthquake* (1912, rpt. 1966)

Garwood, Darrell *Crossroads of America, the Story of Kansas City* (1948)

Gerlach, Russel L. *Immigrants in the Ozarks: A Study of Ethnic Geography* (1976)

Giffen, Jerome E. *First Ladies of Missouri: Their Homes and Their Families* (1970)

Gist, Noel P. (ed.) *Missouri: Its Resources, People, and Institutions* (1950)

Gray, Kenneth E. *A Report on Politics in Saint Louis* (1961)

Green, Lorenzo J., Gary Kremer, and **Anthony Holland** *Missouri's Black Heritage* (1980)

Hardy, Richard J. and **Richard R. Dohm** (eds.) *Missouri Government and Politics* (1985)

Haskell, Henry, Jr. and **Richard Fowler** *City of the Future* (1950)

Hawksley, Oscar *Missouri Ozark Waterways* (1965)

Hopkins, Vincent C. *Dred Scott's Case* (1967)

Houck, Louis *History of Missouri from the Earliest Explorations and Settlements until the Admission of the State into the Union* (1908, rpt. 1971)
—— (ed.) *The Spanish Regime in Missouri* 2 vols. (1909)

Hunter, Julius K. *Westmoreland and Portland Places: The History and Architecture of America's Premier Private Streets, 1888–1988* (1988)

Jennings, Marietta *A Pioneer Merchant of St. Louis 1810–1820: The Business Career of Christian Wilt* (1939)

Jones, Charles T., Jr. *George Champlin Sibley: The Prairie Puritan* (1782–1863) (1970)

Kirkendall, Richard S. *A History of Missouri, 1919–1953* vol. V (1986)

Kirschten, Ernest *Catfish and Crystal* (1960)

Knox, Thomas W. *Camp-fire and Cotton-field* (1969)

Lake, Stuart N. *Wyatt Earp, Frontier Marshall* (1955)

Landmarks Commission of Kansas City *Kansas City: A Place in Time* (1977)

Larkin, Lew *Vanguard of Empire: Missouri's Century of Expansion* (1961)

LeSueur, Stephen C. *The 1838 Mormon War in Missouri* (1987)

Love, Robertus *Rise and Fall of Jesse James* (1926)

Lyle, Wes and John Hall *Missouri: Faces and Places* (1977)

Lyon, William H. *The Pioneer Editor in Missouri, 1808–1860* (1965)

March, David D. *The History of Missouri* 4 vols. (1967)

Marshall, Howard W. *Folk Architecture in Little Dixie: A Regional Culture in Missouri* (1981)

McCandless, Perry *A History of Missouri: 1820–1860* vol. II (1972)

McCorkle, John *Three Years with Quantrell* (1966)

McCurdy, Frances Lea *Stump, Bar, and Pulpit: Speechmaking on the Missouri Frontier* (1969)

McDermott, John F. *George Caleb Bingham: River Portraits* (1959)

McReynolds, Edwin C. *Missouri: A History of the Crossroads State* (1962)

Mering, John V. *The Whig Party in Missouri* (1967)

Meyer, Duane *The Heritage of Missouri: A History* (1973)

Milligan, Maurice *Missouri Waltz: Inside Story of the Pendergast Machine* (1948)

Mitchell, Franklin D. *Embattled Democracy: Missouri Democratic Politics, 1919–1932* (1968)

Moore, Glover *The Missouri Compromise, 1819–1821* (1953)

Mott, Frank L. (ed.) *Missouri Reader* (1964)

Musick, James B. *St. Louis as a Fortified Town* (1941)

Nagel, Paul C. *Missouri: A Bicentennial History* (States and the Nation series) (1977)

Oglesby, Richard E. *Manuel Lisa and the Opening of the Missouri Fur Trade* (1963)

Ohman, Marian M. *The History of Missouri Capitols* (1982)
——. *A History of Missouri's Counties, County Seats and Courthouse Squares* (1983)

Parrish, William E. *David Rice Atchison of Missouri: Border Politician* (1961)
——. *Turbulent Partnership: Missouri and the Union, 1861–1865* 2 vols. (1963)
——. *Missouri under Radical Rule, 1865–1870* (1965)
——. *A History of Missouri: 1860 to 1875* vol. III (1973)

Pearson, Nathan W., Jr. *Goin' to Kansas City* (1988)

Penick, James, Jr. *The New Madrid Earthquakes of 1811–1812* (1976)

Peterson, Norma *Freedom and Franchise: The Political Career of B. Gratz Brown* (1965)

Pilcher, Mary T. *Growing Up on a Farm in Missouri* (1985)

Primm, James Neal *Economic Policy in the Development of a Western State, Missouri, 1820–1860* (1954)
——. *Lion of the Valley: St. Louis, Missouri* (1981)

Proetz, Arthur W. *I Remember You, St. Louis* (1963)

Rafferty, Milton D. *The Ozarks: Land and Life* (1980)

Ramsay, Robert L. *Introduction to a Survey of Missouri Place-Names* (1934)
——. *Our Storehouse of Missouri Place Names* (1973)

Reddig, William *Tom's Town: Kansas City and the Pendergast Legend* (1947)

Reid, Loren *Hurry Home Wednesday: Growing Up in a Small Missouri Town, 1905–1921* (1978)

Rhodes, Richard and the editors of Time-Life Books *The Ozarks* (1974)

Rogers, Ann *Lewis and Clark in Missouri* (1981)

Ryle, Walter H. *Missouri: Union or Secession* (1931)

Sanderlin, George *Mark Twain: As Others Saw Him* (1978)

Savage, Charles C. *Architecture of the Private Streets of St. Louis: The Architects and the Houses They Designed* (1987)

Scarf, J. Thomas *History of St. Louis City and County, from Its Earliest Periods to the Present Day* 2 vols. (1883)

Schoolcraft, Henry Rowe (ed. High Parks) *Schoolcraft in the Ozarks* (1955)

Schultz, Gerald *Early History of the North Ozarks* (1937)

Settle, William A., Jr. *Jesse James Was His Name, or, Fact and Fiction Concerning the Careers of the Notorious James Brothers of Missouri* (1966, rpt. 1987)

Shalhope, Robert E. *Sterling Price: Portrait of a Southerner* (1971)

Shaner, Dolph *The Story of Joplin* (1948)

Shoemaker, Floyd C. *Missouri's Struggle for Statehood, 1804–1821* (1916)
——. *Missouri and Missourians: Land of Contrasts and People of Achievement* 5 vols. (1943)

Smith, Elbert B. *Magnificent Missourian: The Life of Thomas Hart Benton* (1958)

Snider, Felix E. and Earl A. Collins *Cape Girardeau, Biography of a City* (1956)

Stocking, Hobart E. *The Road to Santa Fe* (1971)

Switzler, William F. *Switzler's Illustrated History of Missouri, 1541–1877* (1879, rpt. 1975)

Thomas, Tracy and Walt Bodine *Right Here in River City: A Portrait of Kansas City* (1976)

Thompson, Henry C. *Our Lead Belt Heritage* (1955)

Tixier, Victor *Tixier's Travels on the Osage Prairies* (1940)

Trexler, Harrison A. *Slavery in Missouri, 1804–1865* (1914)

Troen, Selwyn K. and Glen E. Holt (eds.) *St. Louis* (1977)

Vestal, Stanley *The Missouri* (Rivers of America series) (1945, rpt. 1964)

Violette, Eugene Morrow *A History of Missouri* (1918, rpt. 1957)

Wecter, Dixon *Sam Clemens of Hannibal* (1952)

Williams, Walter and Floyd C. Shoemaker *Missouri: Mother of the West* 5 vols. (1930)

MONTANA

Montana is a Mountain state, bordered on the north by the Canadian provinces of British Columbia, Alberta, and Saskatchewan; on the east by North Dakota and South Dakota; on the south by Wyoming and Idaho; and on the west by Idaho.

FULL NAME State of Montana
POSTAL ABBREVIATION MT
INHABITANT Montanan
ADMITTED TO THE UNION Nov. 8, 1889. 41st state
POPULATION (est. 1987) 809,000. Percent of US total: 0.33%. Rank: 44th

CAPITAL CITY Helena, located in west central Montana; population 25,000 (1980). Helena was founded as Last Chance Gulch in 1864, three months after gold was discovered at the site, and was incorporated as a town in 1870 and as a city in 1881. From 1875 to 1889 it was the territorial capital, thereafter the state capital.

STATE NAME AND NICKNAMES From the Spanish word *montana*, "mountainous." Also known as the Big Sky Country, the Mountain State, the Stub Toe State, the Bonanza State, and the Treasure State.

STATE SEAL A landscape showing, in the foreground, miners' tools and a plow, and in the background, mountains, trees, and the Great Falls of the Missouri River; along the bottom is a streamer with the state motto. The border bears the inscription

"The Great Seal of the State of Montana."

MOTTO Oro y Plata (gold and silver)

SONGS "Montana," lyrics by Charles C. Cohan, music by Joseph E. Howard. Official state ballad is "Montana Melody" by Carleen and LeGrande Harvey.

SYMBOLS
Flower bitterroot
Tree flowering dogwood
Bird western meadowlark
Gem sapphire and Montana agate
Animal grizzly bear
Fish blackspotted cutthroat trout
Grass bluebunch grass

LICENSE PLATES (1) Dark blue on a white outline of the state against a beige background, with red mountains and the legend "100 Years." (2) Dark blue on beige, with a red outline of the state, a red-white-and-blue logo reading "76 Bicentennial," blue animal skull, and legend "Big Sky."

FLAG On a dark blue field, the emblem, without the border, of the state seal, with the legend "Montana" in yellow above it.

GEOGRAPHY AND CLIMATE

Eastern Montana is flat, treeless grassland, excellent for grazing. The Rocky Mountains, including the Great Divide, rise from the western third of the state. On the west side of the Divide, drainage is toward the Pacific Ocean; from the eastern slopes, water flows into the Missouri and Mississippi rivers; to the north, rivers drain into Hudson Bay. Although it is one of the coldest states, Montana is also semi-arid, making record lows more bearable.

AREA 147,046 square miles. Rank: 4th
INLAND WATER 1,658 square miles
GEOGRAPHIC CENTER Fergus, 12 miles W of Lewistown
ELEVATIONS *Highest point:* Granite Peak, Park County, 12,799 feet. *Lowest point:* Kootenai River, Lincoln County, 1,800 feet. *Mean elevation:* 3,400 feet

MAJOR RIVERS Missouri, Yellowstone, Kootenai

MAJOR LAKES AND RESERVOIRS Flathead, Canyon Ferry, Elwell, Fort Peck, Hungry Horse

LAND USE

	Thousands of acres
Urban (1982)	197
Rural (1982)	64,665
Cropland (1982)	17,197
Pastureland (1982)	3,036
Rangeland (1982)	37,837
Forestland (1982)	5,228
State parks and recreation areas (1983)	49
National park system (1984)	1,221
National forest system (1984)	19,089
Tribal lands (1984)	2,273

TEMPERATURES The highest recorded temperature was 117°F on July 5, 1937, at Medicine Lake. The lowest was -70°F on January 20, 1954, at Rogers Pass.

NATIONAL SITES

NATIONAL BATTLEFIELD Big Hole
NATIONAL HISTORIC SITES Fort Union Trading Post, Grant-Kohrs Ranch
NATIONAL HISTORIC TRAIL Lewis & Clark
NATIONAL MONUMENT Custer Battlefield
NATIONAL PARK Yellowstone
NATIONAL RECREATION AREA Bighorn Canyon
NATIONAL WILDLIFE REFUGES Benton Lake, Bowdoin–Black Coulee/Creedman

Coulee/Hewitt Lake/Lake Thibadeau, Charles M. Russell–Hailstone/Halfbreed Lake/Lake Mason/Nichols, Coulee/UL Bend/War Horse, Medicine Lake–Lamesteer, Lee Metcalf, National Bison Range–Nine-Pipe/Pablo/Swan River, Northwest Montana Wetland Management District, Red Rock Lakes

HISTORY

1743   *January*. Two sons of Pierre Gaultier de Varennes, Sieur de La Vérendrye, glimpse the "Shining Mountains," believed to be the Big Horn Range of present-day Wyoming and Montana.

1805   *Summer*. Meriwether Lewis and William Clark, leading an expedition through the recently purchased Louisiana Territory, pass through Montana.

1807   *November*. Manuel Lisa builds a trading post at the confluence of the Yellowstone and Big Horn rivers.

1809   *November*. While exploring the western slope of the Rocky Mountains for the North West Company, David Thompson builds a post near the present-day town of Thompson Falls.

1818   An Anglo-American agreement extends the US–Canadian border on the 49th parallel to the Rockies, thereby establishing most of Montana's northern border.

1828   Fort Floyd—soon renamed Fort Union—is constructed at the mouth of the Yellowstone River by the American Fur Company.

1832   The *Yellowstone*, first steamboat on the upper Missouri River, reaches Fort Union. Among its passengers is the artist George Catlin.

1837   A smallpox epidemic ravages the Blackfeet Indians and breaks their military supremacy in the region.

1841   Three Catholic priests and three lay brothers establish a mission to the Flathead Indians in the Bitterroot Valley.

1846	The international border is extended to the Pacific on the 49th parallel of latitude. Fort Lewis—soon renamed Fort Benton—is established by the American Fur Company near the headwaters of the Missouri.
1855	The Blackfeet, in return for annuities, accept a reservation in northern Montana.
1860	The steamboat *Chippewa* is the first to travel as far upstream on the Missouri as Fort Benton.
1862–1864	Gold strikes draw thousands of prospectors to Montana and establish Bannack, Virginia City, and Helena.
1864	Vigilantes destroy the notorious Plummer Gang by tracking down and hanging 24 men.
	May 26. Montana Territory is established within its present borders.
1865	Virginia City becomes the capital.
1870	*January 23.* Army troops massacre 173 Blackfeet, largely breaking resistance to white invasion of their lands and pushing them and other tribes completely to the north of the Missouri.
1876	*June 25.* Over 200 men of the Seventh Cavalry Regiment, commanded by George A. Custer, are killed in a Sioux attack at the Battle of Little Big Horn in southeastern Montana.
1877	*October 5.* Virtual end of Indian fighting in Montana as Chief Joseph of the Nez Percé surrenders.
1881–1882	Slaughter of buffalo reaches its peak.
1882	The Anaconda Mine at Butte is found to contain what proves to be the richest body of copper sulphite in the world.
1883	*September 8.* The Northern Pacific line is completed from Lake Superior to the Pacific with the last spike driven at Gold Creek.
	Fewer than 200 buffalo remain in the entire west.
1886	Peak of open-range grazing in Montana, with 664,000 cattle and 986,000 sheep. The hard winter of 1886–1887 kills perhaps half of the cattle.
1887–1888	Indians cede 17.5 million acres north of the Missouri; about 11 million acres remain available to them.
1889	*November 8.* Montana is admitted to the Union as the 41st state.
	Montana is second among states in silver production and first in copper.
1894	Voters choose Helena as the capital of Montana.
1900	Montana, with about six million sheep, is first among states in wool growing.
1910	Farming has supplanted mining as the chief source of income. Almost 5 million acres in homestead claims are filed in this year.
	Glacier National Park is established with 1,013,599 acres.
1914	Labor violence in Butte culminates in the removal of the city's Socialist mayor and the end of recognition for the miners' union.
	Voters approve the vote for women.
	An exhibition in London advances the reputation of Charles Russell of Great Falls, a renowned Western artist.
1916	Jeanette Rankin of Missoula becomes the first woman elected to Congress. She votes against US entry to both world wars—the only legislator to vote against the latter declaration.
1917	*June 8* The death of 164 miners in a North Butte fire sparks a strike by 15,000 workers that is broken by the intervention of federal troops.
1917–1918	A total of 41,133 Montanans see World War I service—more than 10 percent of the population and the highest ratio of any state.
1919–1926	Due to drought and low farm prices, about 20 percent of the state's farms and two million acres pass out of production. Half of all farm mortgages are foreclosed and over half the state's commercial banks fail.
1923	An old-age pension law makes Montana, along with Nevada, the first state to provide such support.
1929	Anaconda's grip on Montana is reflected in its ownership of eight daily newspapers and a million acres of timberland as well as its large mining, smelting, and refining operations.
1930	The number of farms has fallen from 57,677 to 47,495.

1933	In the depths of the Great Depression, more than half of all manufacturing-industry workers are unemployed.
1934	*September 17.* After a four-month strike, Butte miners regain the closed shop they lost in 1914. They also win a 40-hour week and a wage increase.
1936	Over 10,500 workers are employed in the construction of Fort Peck Dam on the Missouri, for many years the largest earth-fill dam in the world.
1942	An Army Air Corps base, later the ICBM-equipped Malmstrom Air Force Base, is constructed at Great Falls.
1951	A large oil strike is made in Willston Basin, in eastern Montana.
1953	Montana is first among states in the production of zinc and manganese, third in copper and silver.
1968	*March 29.* A 250-day strike by 7,200 copper workers ends with $34 million lost in wages; unemployment in Butte has reached half the labor force.
1972	Voters approve a new state constitution.
1974	The average agricultural unit has increased to 2,510 acres from 608 in 1920.
1975	*August 24.* Dedication of Libby Dam.
	Montana adopts a coal severance tax of up to 30 percent, the highest rate in the country.
1976	Senator Mike Mansfield announces his retirement after 33 consecutive years in Congress and 15 as Senate majority leader.
1980	Anaconda closes its copper smelter in Anaconda and its refinery in Great Falls.
1982	Montana is fourth among states in wheat production, second in barley, and seventh in sheep.
1983	*June 30.* After over a hundred years, Anaconda ceases mining operations in Butte, which has yielded almost $4 billion in minerals.
	Dedication of the third and fourth generating plants in Colstrip, all fueled by Montana coal.

DEMOGRAPHY

Population (est. 1987) 809,000
Population (1980) 786,690
Population density in persons
  per square mile (1980) 5.3

POPULATION BY RACE (1980)
American Indian/Aleut/
  Eskimo 37,270
Asian/Pacific Islander 2,503
Black 1,786
Hispanic 9,974
White 740,148
Other 4,983

POPULATION CHARACTERISTICS (1980)
Percent of state population
Urban 52.9
Rural 47.1
Under 18 . . . . 29.5
65 or older 10.7
College-educated 17.3
Families below poverty line 9.2
Public-assistance recipients 3.4

Per capita personal
  income (1986) $11,904
Millionaires per 100,000
  residents (1982) 111.8
Average life expectancy in
  years (1980) 73.9

Marriage rate per 1,000
  residents (1986) 8.3
Divorce rate per 1,000
  residents (1986) 5.3
Birth rate per 1,000
  residents (1985) 16.0
Infant mortality rate per 1,000
  births (1985) 8.3
Abortion rate per 1,000
  live births (1985) 288
Crime rate per 100,000
  residents (1985)
  Violent 157.4
  Property 4,321.5
Federal and state prisoners
  per 100,000 residents (1984) . . 116
Alcohol consumption in gallons
  per capita (1985) 46.8
Deaths from motor vehicle accidents
  per 100,000 residents (1985) . . 27.5

MAJOR CITIES

	Population
Billings (est. 1984)	69,836
Butte-Silver Bow (1980)	37,205
Great Falls (est. 1984)	58,769
Missoula (1980)	33,351

GOVERNMENT AND POLITICS

Number of US Representatives 5
Electoral votes 7

POLITICAL PARTY NOMINEES FROM STATE

Burton Kendall Wheeler (Pro-
gressive/Socialist) 1924 VP
Burton Kendall Wheeler (Socialist) 1928 VP

PRESIDENTIAL PRIMARY ELECTION In 1988,
Montana sent 25 Democratic delegates and
20 Republican delegates to the national
conventions.

CONSTITUTION Montana has had two constitutions: 1889 and the present one, adopted
in 1972.

LEGISLATURE The Legislature is divided
into the Senate (50 members serving staggered terms of four and two years, minimum age 18) and the House of
Representatives (100 members, 2-year
term, minimum age 18). In 1987, the salary
was $52.13 per day for a maximum of 90
days.

JUDICIARY The highest court is the Supreme
Court, with 7 judges serving 8-year terms.
In 1987, the annual salary was $50,452.

EXECUTIVE The governor serves a 4-year
term; the minimum age for holding office
is 25. In 1987, the annual salary was
$50,452. There are 10 other elected offi-
cials.

PRESIDENTIAL VOTE 1948-1988 *(in percents)*

Year	State Winner	Democratic	Republican
1948	Truman (D)	53.1	43.2
1952	Eisenhower (R)	40.1	59.4
1956	Eisenhower (R)	42.9	57.1
1960	Nixon (R)	48.6	51.1
1964	Johnson (D)	59.0	40.6
1968	Nixon (R)	41.6	50.6
1972	Nixon (R)	37.9	57.9
1976	Ford (R)	45.4	52.8
1980	Reagan (R)	32.4	56.8
1984	Reagan (R)	38.2	60.5
1988	Bush (R)	47.0	53.0

GOVERNORS

Territorial Governors
Sidney Edgerton 1864-1866
Green Clay Smith 1866-1869
James M. Ashley 1869-1870
Benjamin F. Potts 1870-1883
J. Schuyler Crosby 1883-1884
B. Platt Carpenter 1884-1885
Samuel T. Hauser 1885-1887
Preston H. Leslie 1887-1889
Benjamin F. White 1889

State Governors
Joseph K. Toole (D) 1889-1893
John E. Rickards (R) 1893-1897
Robert B. Smith (D) 1897-1901
Joseph K. Toole (D) 1901-1908
Edwin L. Norris (D) 1908-1913
Sam V. Stewart (D) 1913-1921
Joseph M. Dixon (R) 1921-1925
John E. Erickson (D) 1925-1933
Frank H. Cooney (D) 1933-1935
W. Elmer Holt (D) 1935-1937

Roy E. Ayres (D) 1937-1941
Sam C. Ford (R) 1941-1949
John W. Bonner (D) 1949-1953
J. Hugo Aronson (R) 1953-1961
Donald Nutter (R) 1961-1962
Tim M. Babcock (R) 1962-1969
Forrest H. Anderson (D) 1969-1973
Thomas L. Hudge (D) 1973-1981
Ted Schwinden (D) 1981-1989
Stanley Stephens (R) 1989-

MINIMUM AGES
Majority 18
Marriage with parental consent . . . 18
Marriage without parental consent . 18
Making a will 18
Buying alcohol 21
Jury duty 18
Leaving school . . . . 16 or 8th grade
Driver's license 15

CAPITAL PUNISHMENT
Number executed 1976-88: 0
On death row Aug. 1, 1988: 6

MILITARY INSTALLATIONS
Total number: 5

Thousands of dollars

GENERAL REVENUE (1985)
Total general revenue . . .	1,388,045
Total tax revenue	640,750
Sales and gross receipts	139,683
Individual income taxes	181,057
Corporate net income taxes . .	62,671

GENERAL EXPENDITURE (1985)
Total general expenditure .	1,317,682
Expenditure	435,947
Public welfare	183,879
Health	48,020
Hospitals	31,192
Natural resources	83,789
Highways	238,970
Police	16,629
Corrections	29,043

FEDERAL AID (1985) 583,689

ECONOMY

Montana's economy is based on cattle and wheat. Sheep, hogs, and horses are other favored livestock; cash crops include barley (for feed), hay, potatoes, sugar beets, oats, and flaxseed. In 1982, cash farm receipts totaled $1.5 billion. Gold, silver, and copper are still mined in the state, along with zinc, lead, manganese, chromite, vermiculite, oil, natural gas, and coal. Most manufacturing in Montana is centered on food, timber, and metals processing. Millions of tourists visit Montana's national parks, ranches, and ski resorts, making the tourist industry one of the state's largest.

EMPLOYMENT (1984)

Thousands of persons
Total number of employed workers	376
Construction	12.6
Finance, insurance, and real estate	13.4
Government	68.3
Manufacturing	22.3
Mining	7.5
Services	59.8
Transportation, communications, and utilities	20.5
Wholesale and retal trade	76.4

Percent of civilian labor force unemployed (1984)	7.4

DEPARTMENT OF DEFENSE (1985)
Civilian workers employed . . .	1,236
Military personnel	3,728
Contract awards	$102 million

ENERGY SOURCES FOR ELECTRIC UTILITIES (1983)

Percent
Coal	22.9
Gas	0.2
Hydroelectric	76.6
Nuclear	0.0
Petroleum	0.1

TRANSPORTATION
Motor vehicles registered in state (1986)	672,547
Miles of roads, streets, and highways (1986)	71,706
Miles of Class I railway operated (1986)	3,274
Airports (1983)	197
Major aviation hubs (1983)	1
Largest hub: Billings	

CULTURE AND EDUCATION

Native American tribes
Montana was formerly the home of the Arikara, Bannock, Blood, Hidatsa, Kalispel, Ojibway, Sematuse, Northern Shoshoni, and Sioux. Groups that continue to live in the state include the Arapaho, Assiniboine, Blackfoot, Cheyenne, Crow, Flathead, Gros Ventre, and Kootenay. Groups that have been relocated to Montana include the Cree and Metis. There are seven federal reservations in Montana.

Religions, ethnicities, and languages
In addition to settlers from the midwestern states, Montana during the late 19th and early 20th centuries attracted miners from Ireland, Wales, Cornwall, Scotland, and Italy, and homesteaders from Germany, Scandinavia, Holland, and Finland. Chinese and American blacks who came in the 1880s were discouraged from remaining. American Indians today represent about 5 percent of the population. In 1980, 5.2

percent of Montana's population spoke a language other than English at home. More than half of Montanans are Roman Catholic; Mormonism is also strong, and there are some 20 Hutterite (German Anabaptist) communes.

Major museums and libraries
Montana Historical Society Museum, Helena
Museum of the Plains Indians, Browning
Museum of the Rockies, Bozeman
C.M. Russell Gallery, Great Falls
Yellowstone Art Center, Billings

Major arts organizations
Billings Symphony Orchestra
Great Falls Symphony Orchestra
Montana Institute of Arts
Montana Repertory Theater, Missoula

Colleges and universities
Number public (1986-87) 10
Number private (1986-87) 7
Total enrollment, in full-time equivalent students (1985) 30,000

Public elementary and secondary schools
Expenditure per pupil in average daily attendance (1986-87) $4,070
Pupil-teacher ratio (1987) 15.6
Average teacher salary (1986-87) $24,370

Holidays
Heritage Day. Late November
State Fair, Great Falls. Late July to early August

MONTANA IN LITERATURE

Nannie T. Alderson (ed. Helena H. Smith) *A Bride Goes West* (1942)
Life on the frontier in the 1880s and '90s by a Virginia-born settler.

John R. Barrows *Ubet* (1934)
Classic tales of stockraising by a pioneer of the 1880s and '90s.

Myron Brinig *Singermann* (1919); *Wide Open Town* (1921); *Sun Sets in the West* (1935)
Novels by a Jewish immigrant to Montana describing life in Butte during the boom years.

Percy Bullchild *The Sun Came Down: The History of the World As My Blackfoot Elders Told It* (1985)
Collection of Blackfoot stories.

Hughie Call *Golden Fleece* (1942)
Reminiscences of a western Montana rancher's wife.

James Crumley *The Wrong Case* (1975)
Violent detective novel set in a small Montana town.

Dan Cushman *Stay Away Joe* (1953)
Novel about life on an Indian reservation. Cushman, a miner, prospector, and journalist since the 1920s, published his memoirs in *Plenty of Room and Air* (1975).

George A. Custer (ed. Milo M. Quaife) *My Life on the Plains* (1966)
Autobiography of military service, 1867–1874.

Thomas J. Dimsdale *The Vigilantes of Montana* (1866, rpt. 1953, 1985)
The author was a schoolmaster and journalist in Virginia City during the infamous vigilante days. This book, a collection of his newspaper articles, was the first published in Montana.

Ivan Doig *This House of Sky: Landscapes of a Western Mind* (1978)
Autobiographical account of growing up in the Rocky Mountain region. Doig has also published two volumes of a proposed trilogy about a Montana family.

Michael Dorris *A Yellow Raft in Blue Water* (1987)
Three generations of Indian women trace the decline of their culture on reservations.

Kate Dunlap (ed. J. Lyman Tyler) *The Montana Gold Rush Diary of Kate Dunlap* (1969)

Federal Writers' Project *Copper Camp: Stories of the World's Greatest Mining Town, Butte, Montana* (1943)

Leslie Fiedler "The Montana Face," "Montana P.S.," "Montana P.P.S." in *The Collected Essays of Leslie Fiedler* (1971)
Essays on Montana myth and reality by a critic who taught at the University of Montana.

Andrew Garcia (ed. Bennett H. Stein) *Tough Trip through Paradise* (1976)
Garcia lived among the Nez Percé and Flathead Indians before their enforced settlement in reservations. His memoirs were discovered in 1943.

Hamlin Garland *General Custer's Last Fight As Seen by Two Moon* (1898). Reprinted in W. Maquin and C. Van Doren (eds.) *Great Documents in American Indian History* (1973)
Narrative of a chief who was present at Little Big Horn, June 25, 1876.

George Bird Grinnell *Blackfoot Lodge Tales* (1962)
Grinnell (1849–1938) was an anthropologist and historian who first visited Montana in 1870, and accompanied Custer's expedition to the Black Hills.

Alfred B. Guthrie *The Big Sky* (1947)
Classic Montana novel about a boy who runs away from home to join the Blackfoot in the Teton Mountains in the 1820s. Guthrie, who grew up in Choteau, published an autobiography, *The Blue Hen's Chick* (1965), and four other novels about Western life.

W. W. Haines *The Winter War* (1961)
Historical novel depicting the pursuit of the Sioux and Cheyenne after the Battle of Little Bighorn.

Dashiel Hammett *Red Harvest* (1929)
Hammett's first detective novel is based on his experiences as a Pinkerton detective in Butte, 1920–1921. The town is thinly disguised as "Poisonville."

Joseph K. Howard *Montana Margins: A State Anthology* (1946)
Anthology of writing about the state. Howard also collected non-fiction essays about the state in *Montana: High, Wide, and Handsome*.

Laton A. Huffman "Last Busting at Bow-Gun," in Michael Kennedy (ed.) *Cowboys and Cattlemen* (1964)
Tale of stockraising by one of the state's first photographers.

Chet Huntley *The Generous Years: Remembrances of a Frontier Boyhood* (1968)
Memoir of frontier life in the early years of the twentieth century.

Dorothy M. Johnson *When You and I Were Young, Whitefish* (1982)
Humorous autobiography of growing up in a small town in the 1920s.

Michael Kennedy (ed.) *The Assiniboines* (1961)
Collection of Native American stories and myths including material collected by James L. Long during the 1940s.

William Kittredge and Annick Smith (eds.) *The Last Best Place: A Montana Anthology* (1989)
Anthology of state literature comprising Native American myths, explorers' journals, accounts by pioneers, early settlers, and miners, and a selection of contemporary fiction and poetry.

Frank B. Linderman *Plenty-Coups, Chief of the Crows* (1930, rpt. 1962)
Transcriptions of the reminiscences of the great warrior chief (1848–1932). Linderman also wrote a memoir of his eventful life, *Montana Adventure: The Recollections of Frank B. Linderman* (1968).

Philip S. Long *Dreams, Dust and Depression* (1972)
Narrative of ranch life during the Depression.

Robert H. Lowie and Luella C. Lowie (trans. and ed.) *Crow Texts* (1960)
Legends and tales of the Crow tribe collected by a pioneer anthropologist and his wife.

Norman Maclean *A River Runs through It and Other Stories* (1976)
Autobiographical narrative of growing up in rural Montana that centers on troutfishing in the Blackfoot River.

Alice Marriott and Carol K. Rachlin *Plains Indian Mythology* (1975)
Collection containing myths and stories of the Montana Cheyenne.

Thomas McGuane *Nobody's Angel* (1982)
Novel about a veteran and drifter who returns to care for his family's ranch.

D'Arcy McNickle *The Surrounded* (1936); *Wind from an Enemy Sky* (1978)
Novels about reservation life in western Montana.

James Miller (ed. Andrew Rolle) *The Road to Virginia City: The Diary of James Knox Polk Miller* (1989)
The adventures of a nineteen-year-old orphan who went west to seek his fortune in 1864.

Clyde Murphy *Glittering Hill* (1944)
Novel set in the Irish mining community of Butte during the prospecting boom.

Elliot Paul *A Ghost Town on the Yellowstone* (1948)
Autobiography describing surveying work in the town of Trembles, 1907–1908.

Mary Ronan (ed. Margaret Ronan) *Frontier Woman: The Story of Mary Ronan* (1973)

Reminiscences of a woman who grew up in Virginia City in the 1860s, married an Indian agent and lived on the Flathead Reservation.

Charles M. Russell *Trails Plowed Under* (1937)
Tales of a cowboy and artist who used the persona of Rawhide Rawlins. More tales by Russell were edited by H. G. Merriam as *Recollections of Charley Russell* (1963).

Osborne Russell *Journal of a Trapper* (1921)
Memoirs of a mountain man who trapped in the Yellowstone region in the 1830s.

James Willard Schultz *Blackfeet and Buffalo: Memories of Life among the Indians* (1962, rpt. 1973)
The author came to Montana in 1877, married a Blackfoot woman and became a member of the tribe. Eugene L. Silliman edited a collection of Schultz's stories, *Many Strange Characters: Montana Frontier Tales* (1982), and Warren L. Hanna gathered his fiction of the years 1880–1894 in *Recently Discovered Tales of Life among the Indians* (1988).

Milton Shawtraw *Thrashin' Time: Memories of a Montana Boyhood* (1970)
Memoir of ranch life in the early twentieth century.

Eugene L. Silliman (ed.) *We Seized Our Rifles: Recollections of the Montana Frontier* (1982)

Wallace Stegner *Wolf Willow: A History, a Story, and a Memory of the Last Plains Frontier* (1962)
Memoir of the author's youth on the Montana/Saskatchewan boundary.

Robert Lewis Taylor *A Roaring in the Wind* (1978)
Historical novel about an easterner's adventures in mid-nineteenth-century Montana.

John Charles Van Dyke *The Mountain* (1916)
Naturalist's account of a journey on horseback across the plains of Montana.

James Welch *Winter in the Blood* (1974); *The Death of Jim Loney* (1979); *Fools Crow* (1986)
Novels about Blackfoot reservation life by a Native American writer.

Clarence Woodcock (ed.) *Stories from Our Elders* (1979)
Legends of Montana Native Americans.

Paul E. Young (ed. Nellie Snyder) *Back Trail of an Old Cowboy* (1983)
Memories of an eastern Montana cowboy, transcribed when he was 91 years old.

GUIDES TO RESOURCES

Brown, Margery and Virginia Griffing *Montana: A Student's Guide to Localized History* (1971)

Federal Writers' Project *Montana: Land of Nakoda* (1942)

Hatcher, Karen A. and Katherine Schaefer *Montana Authors: A Bio-Bibliography* (1985)

MacDonald, Marie P. (Montana State Library Association) *Montana in Print* (1972)

Montana Department of Planning and Economic Development *Montana Data Book* (1970)

Montana Historical Society *Not in Precious Metals Alone: A Manuscript History of Montana* (1976)

Montana Oral History Associations *Directory of Montana Oral History Resources* (1985)

Parpart, Paulette K. and Donald E. Spritzer (Montana Library Association) *The Montana Historical and Genealogical Data Index* (1986)

Taylor, Robert L., Milton J. Edie, and Charles F. Gritzner *Montana in Maps: 1974* (1974)

Wolle, Muriel S. *Montana Pay Dirt: A Guide to the Mining Camps of the Treasure State* (1963)

SELECTED NONFICTION SOURCES

Adams, Ramon F. *From the Pecos to the Powder: A Cowboy's Autobiography* (1965)

Alwin, John A. *Western Montana: A Portrait of the Land and Its People* (1983)

Ambrose, Stephen E. *Crazy Horse and Custer* (1975)

Bakeless, John *Lewis and Clark: Partners in Discovery* (1947)

Baker, Paul E. *The Forgotten Kutenai* (1955)

Barsness, Larry *Gold Camp: Alder Gulch and Virginia City, Montana* (1962)

Beaumont, Greg *Many-Storied Mountains: The Life of Glacier National Park* (1978)

Brown, Dee *Fort Phil Kearny: An American Saga* (1962)
———. *Bury My Heart at Wounded Knee: An Indian History of the American West* (1970)

Bryan, William L. *Montana's Indians: Yesterday and Today* (1985)

Burlingame, Merrill G. *The Montana Frontiers* (1942)
———. *John M. Bozeman: Montana Trailmaker* (1971)
———. and K. R. Toole (eds.) *A History of Montana* 3 vols. (1957)

Calvert, Jerry W. *The Gibraltar: Socialism and Labor in Butte, Montana, 1895–1920* (1988)

Cheney, Roberta C. *Names on the Face of Montana: The Story of Montana's Place Names* (1983)

Clinch, Thomas A. *Urban Populism and Free Silver in Montana* (1970)

Coburn, Walt *Pioneer Cattlemen in Montana: The Story of the Circle C Ranch* (1973)

Connolly, C. P. *The Devil Learns to Vote, the Story of Montana* (1938)

Cushman, Dan *Montana: The Gold Frontier* (1973)
———. *Plenty of Room and Air* (1975)

Dillon, Richard *Meriwether Lewis: A Biography* (1965)

Eunson, Dale *Up on the Rim* (1970)

Ewers, John C. *The Blackfeet: Raiders on the Northwestern Plains* (1958)

Farr, William E. *The Reservation Blackfeet, 1822–1945; a Photographic History of Cultural Survival* (1984)
———. and **Ross Toole** *Montana: Images of the Past* (1978)

Fougera, Katherine G. *With Custer's Cavalry* (1988)

France, Johnny and Malcolm McConnell *Incident at Big Sky: The True Story of Sheriff Johnny France and the Capture of the Mountain Men* (1986)

Fritz, Harry W. *Montana: Land of Contrast* (1984)

Gilluly, Sam *The Press Gang: A Century of Montana Newspapers* (1985)

Glasscock, C. B. *The War of the Copper Kings: Builders of Butte and Wolves of Wall Street* (1935)

Graham, W. A. *The Story of Little Bighorn: Custer's Last Fight* (1926, rpt. 1988)
———. *The Custer Myth: A Source Book of Custeriana* (1986)

Gutfeld, Arnon *Montana's Agony: Years of War and Hysteria, 1917–1921* (1979)

Hamilton, James M. *History of Montana: From Wilderness to Statehood* (1957)

Hanna, Warren *The Grizzlies of Glacier* (1978)

Hebard, Grace R. and E. A. Brininstool *The Bozeman Trail* 2 vols. (1971)

Henry, Will *Custer's Last Stand: Story of the Little Big Horn* (1966)

Heuman, William *Custer: Man and Legend* (1968)

Howard, Joseph K. *Montana: High, Wide, and Handsome* (1959, rpt. 1981)

Jackson, W. Turrentine *Wells Fargo Stagecoaching in Montana Territory* (1979)

James, Don *Butte's Memory Book* (1976)

Johnson, Dorothy M. *The Bloody Bozeman: The Perilous Trail to Montana's Gold* (1971)

Josephson, Hanna *Jeannette Rankin: First Lady in Congress* (1974)

King, Bucky *The Dude Connection* (1983)

Kraenzel, Carl F. *The Great Plains in Transition* (1955)

Lee, Rose H. *The Growth and Decline of Chinese Communities in the Rocky Mountain Area* (1978)

Lopach, James et al. *We the People of Montana* (1983)

Malone, Michael P. *Montana: A History of Two Centuries* (1976)
——— and **Richard E. Roeder** (eds.) *The Montana Past: An Anthology* (1969)

Mangam, William D. *The Clarks of Montana* (1939)
———. *The Clarks: An American Phenomenon* (1941)

Marquis, Thomas B. *The Cheyennes of Montana* (1935)

Mather, R. E. and F. E. Boswell *Hanging the Sheriff: A Biography of Henry Plummer* (1987)

McNelis, Sarah *Copper King at War: The Biography of F. Augustus Heinze* (1968)

Murphy, James E. *Half Interest in a Silver Dollar: The Saga of Charles E. Conrad* (1983)

Myers, Rex C. and Harry W. Fritz (eds.) *Montana and the West: Essays in Honor of K. Ross Toole* (1984)

O'Malley, Richard K. *Mile High, Mile Deep* (1971)

Parfit, Michael *Last Stand at Rosebud Creek: Coal, Power, and People* (1980)

Phillips, Paul C. (ed.) *Forty Years on the Frontier As Seen in the Journals and Reminiscences of Granville Stuart* 2 vols. (1925, rpt. 1957)

Raymer, Robert G. *Montana: The Land and the People* 3 vols. (1930)

Rolle, Andrew F. (ed.) *The Road to Virginia City: The Diary of James Knox Polk Miller* (1960)

Sandoz, Mari *Battle of the Little Bighorn* (1966)

Schoenberg, Wilfred, S. J. *Jesuits in Montana: 1840–1960* (1960)

Sharp, Paul F. *Whoop-Up Country: The Canadian-American West, 1865–1885* (1960)

Smith, Steve *Fly the Biggest Piece Back* (1979)

Smurr, John W. and K. Ross Toole (eds.) *Historical Essays on Montana and the Northwest* (1957)

Spence, Clark C. *Territorial Politics and Government in Montana: 1864–1889* (1975)
———. *Montana: A Bicentennial History* (States and the Nation series) (1978)

Stewart, Edgar I. *Custer's Luck* (1955)

Stout, Tom *Montana: Its Story and Biography* 3 vols. (1921)

Stuart, Granville (ed. Paul C. Phillips) *Pioneering in Montana: The Making of a State, 1864–1887* (1925, 1977)

Swartout, Robert R. (ed.) *Montana Vistas: Selected Historical Essays* (1982)

Thwaites, Reuben G. (ed.) *Original Journals of the Lewis and Clark Expedition, 1804–1806* 8 vols. (1905)

Toole, Kenneth R. *Montana: An Uncommon Land* (1959, rpt. 1977)
———. *Twentieth-Century Montana: A State of Extremes* (1972)
———. *The Rape of the Great Plains* (1976)

Turney-High, H. H. *The Flathead Indians of Montana* (1937)

Van West, Carroll *A Traveler's Companion to Montana History* (1986)

Voynick, Stephen M. *The Great American Sapphire* (rev. ed. 1987)

Wheeler, Burton K. (with Paul Healy) *Yankee from the West: The Candid Turbulent Life Story of the Yankee-born U.S. Senator from Montana* (1962)

White, M. Catherine (ed.) *David Thompson's Journals Relating to Montana, 1802–1812* (1950)

Wolle, Muriel S. *Montana Pay Dirt: A Guide to the Mining Camps of the Treasure State* (1963)

Wright, Robert C. and Kathryn *Montana: Territory of Treasures* (1964)

Yuill, Clifford D., Sr. and Ellan R. *Montana's Historic Homes* (1986)

NEBRASKA

Nebraska is a west north central state, bordered on the north by South Dakota and the Missouri River; on the east by the Missouri River, Iowa, and Missouri; on the south by Kansas and Colorado; and on the west by Wyoming.

FULL NAME State of Nebraska
POSTAL ABBREVIATION NE
INHABITANT Nebraskan
ADMITTED TO THE UNION Mar. 1, 1867.
37th state
POPULATION (est. 1987) 1,594,000.
Percent of US total: 0.66%. Rank: 36th

CAPITAL CITY Lincoln, located in southeast Nebraska; population 180,378 (est. 1984). Originally called Lancaster, it was laid out in 1859. In 1867 it was chosen the state capital and renamed; it was incorporated two years later.

STATE NAME AND NICKNAMES From *niboathka*, "broad river," the Omaha Indian name for the Platte River. Official nickname: the Cornhusker State. Also known as the Tree Planters' State, the Antelope State, and the Bug-eating State.

STATE SEAL A landscape, with a blacksmith at work in the foreground; behind him are a settler's cabin, sheaves of wheat, a steamboat on the Missouri River, and in the distance a train and the Rocky Mountains.

The border carries the legend "Great Seal of the State of Nebraska, March 1st, 1867."

MOTTO Equality Before the Law

SONG "Beautiful Nebraska," lyrics and music by Jim Fras.

SYMBOLS
Flower late goldenrod
Tree cottonwood
Bird western meadowlark
Gem blue agate
Rock prairie agate
Mammal white-tailed deer
Insect honeybee
Fossil mammoth
Grass little blue stem grass

LICENSE PLATE Orange on white, with an orange-and-yellow horizon and setting sun behind the state name in black.

FLAG The state seal in gold and silver on a blue field.

GEOGRAPHY AND CLIMATE

Geographically, Nebraska's eastern third is part of the fertile Central Lowlands, while the remainder belongs to the Great Plains. A steady rise in elevation marks the transition, with the highest points near Nebraska's western border with Wyoming and Colorado. To the north and northwest lie the Sand Hills, some of the country's best rangeland. While Nebraska's climate is semi-arid, the state's many rivers — including the North Platte and Platte, which bisect the state — offer good sources of irrigation.

AREA 77,355 square miles. Rank: 15th
INLAND WATER 711 square miles
GEOGRAPHIC CENTER Custer, 10 miles NW of Broken Bow
ELEVATIONS *Highest point:* Johnson Township, Kimball County, 5,426 feet. *Lowest point:* SE corner of the state, Richardson County, 840 feet. *Mean elevation:* 2,600 feet

MAJOR RIVERS Missouri, North Platte, South Platte

MAJOR LAKES AND RESERVOIRS Lewis and Clark, McConaughy

LAND USE

	Thousands of acres
Urban (1982)	415
Rural (1982)	46,990
Cropland (1982)	20,277
Pastureland (1982)	2,125
Rangeland (1982)	23,096
Forestland (1982)	732
State parks and recreation areas (1983)	137
National park system (1984)	6
National forest system (1984)	442
Tribal lands (1984)	23

TEMPERATURES The highest recorded temperature was 118°F on July 24, 1936, at Minden. The lowest was -47°F on February 12, 1899, at Camp Clarke.

NATIONAL SITES

NATIONAL HISTORIC SITE Chimney Rock
NATIONAL HISTORIC TRAILS Lewis & Clark, Mormon Pioneer, Oregon
NATIONAL MONUMENTS Agate Fossil Beds, Homestead, Scotts Bluff
NATIONAL SCENIC RIVER AND RIVERWAY Missouri National Recreational River
NATIONAL WILDLIFE REFUGES Crescent Lake–North Platte, De Soto, Fort Niobrara–Valentine, Hastings Wetland Management District

HISTORY

1720	*August 13.* A Spanish expedition sent from New Mexico to check French influence in the Great Plains is attacked and defeated in Nebraska by Pawnee Indians.
1739	Pierre and Paul Mallet, French traders, cross Nebraska east to west on their way to Santa Fe, New Mexico.
1803	*April 30.* United States acquires Nebraska territory through the Louisiana Purchase.
1804	Meriwether Lewis and William Clark, leading an expedition through the recently acquired Louisiana Territory, pass through Nebraska along the Missouri shore. They return in 1806 on their way back to St. Louis.
1812	Manuel Lisa of the Missouri Fur Company builds a fort on the Missouri River, about 10 miles north of what is now Omaha.
1819	A scientific party led by Major Stephen H. Long ascends the Missouri to what is now Fort Calhoun aboard the *Western Engineer,* the first steamboat so far north on the river.
1820	Long's party crosses Nebraska east to west, and he proclaims it "almost wholly unfit for cultivation, and of course uninhabitable."
1823	Andrew Drips of the Missouri Fur Company is operating a trading post just north of what is now Bellevue, the oldest existing town in Nebraska.
1833	*November 15.* Baptist missionary Moses Merrill opens, with his wife, a school for Otoe Indians at Bellevue.
1842	John C. Frémont establishes the Platte river valley route as the most popular way to Oregon.
1847	*Spring.* The Mormon Trail is established when pilgrims begin crossing the Platte route westward to their "Promised Land."

1848	Fort Kearny is reestablished as a relief station at the junction of the Oregon Trail, Mormon Trail, and California Trail.
1849	Following the discovery of gold in California, about 40,000 people take the Platte river valley trail west.
	Half the Pawnee population of 10,000 to 12,000 falls victim to a cholera epidemic.
1851–1855	*Nebraska Palladium and Platte Valley Advocate*, published at Bellevue, is the state's first newspaper.
1854	*March 15–16.* In exchange for two reservations, the Oto, Missouri, and Omaha cede all other lands west of the Missouri, thereby opening most of eastern Nebraska to white settlement.
	May 30. Nebraska Territory is created, comprising all the land north of Kansas between the Missouri River and the Continental Divide. To satisfy the South's demand for slave states, the Kansas-Nebraska Act repeals the Missouri Compromise.
	Bellevue and Omaha are founded.
1855	*January 16.* The first territorial legislature meets at Omaha, which is named the capital.
1857	*September 24.* In return for a reservation, the Pawnee cede most of their remaining lands in central Nebraska.
1867	*March 1.* Nebraska is admitted to the Union, essentially within its present borders, as the 37th state. The state capital is established at Lancaster, renamed Lincoln.
	November 13. The Union Pacific Railroad line reaches Cheyenne, Wyoming, from Omaha.
1869	The University of Nebraska, at Lincoln, is chartered. It opens its doors in 1871.
1871	David Butler, the first state governor, is impeached and removed from office for misappropriating state funds.
1872	Completion of a railroad bridge across the Missouri links Omaha to Iowa.
1873	Ogallala becomes Nebraska's cowboy capital, serving for over a decade as an important depot for cattle driven north from Texas.
1874–1877	Grasshoppers plague the state, ruining crops.
1875	A new constitution is adopted to replace the original state charter.
1875–1876	The last significant Indian cessions in the state open up northwestern Nebraska to white settlement.
1877	*September 7.* Sioux leader Crazy Horse is killed at Fort Robinson in northwestern Nebraska.
1879	*January 9.* Indian resistance ends as most of a small band of Northern Cheyenne is killed at Fort Robinson. They are trying to escape after being captured and confined for leaving Indian Territory (Oklahoma).
1883	Union Stockyards Company is organized in Omaha.
1885	Peak of homestead filings in Nebraska—2,142,080 acres.
1889	Nebraska is fourth among states in corn production, with 10 percent of the nation's crop.
1890	The population of 1,058,910 is more than double the 452,402 of 1880.
	Meat products comprise more than one-fourth of the state's manufactured products.
	Populists, exploiting farm distress, win control of both houses of the legislature.
1894	A fusion Democratic-Populist candidate, Silas A. Holcomb, is elected governor, but the Republicans recapture the legislature.
1896	William Jennings Bryan of Lincoln wages the first of his three unsuccessful presidential campaigns as the Democratic party nominee.
	The Democratic-Populist coalition reelects Holcomb and regains the legislature.
1897	Nebraska is the first state to adopt the initiative and referendum.
1901	Nebraska is second to Kansas in the production of winter wheat.
1904	*April 28.* Signing of the Kinkaid Act establishes 640-acre homesteads in northwestern Nebraska and thus ends the reign of cattle barons in the area.
1917	Father E. J. Flanagan establishes Boys Town, near Omaha, for homeless boys.
1919	Legislature forbids the teaching of any subject in any foreign language; the US Supreme Court declares the law unconstitutional in 1923.

1928	Creation of Omaha Community Playhouse, which gives such actors as Henry Fonda and Marlon Brando their start.
1932	Completion of a new state capitol building, with a 437-foot-high tower. Farm prices are the lowest in state history and more than 600,000 acres of farmland are abandoned.
1933	*March 2.* A moratorium is imposed on the foreclosure of farm mortgages.
1934	Rainfall of 14.31 inches is the lowest since 1864; corn production of 21,363,000 bushels is less than 10 percent of the 1928–1932 average. By initiative, a unicameral (single chamber) state legislature is established, the only one in the United States.
1935	The worst year of dust storms in a decade of drought, dust, and heat that turned the state into the "Great American Desert."
1936	George W. Norris, Nebraska's most prominent political figure, is elected to his fifth US Senate term.
1945	With the creation of the Omaha Public Power District, Nebraska becomes the first state in which all electricity comes from public power plants.
1946	A constitutional amendment outlaws the closed shop. The Strategic Air Command, the US Air Force's long-range bombing and missile striking force, is established at Offutt Field, outside Omaha.
1949	Oil is discovered in Cheyenne County.
1955	Omaha, with over six million livestock received, supplants Chicago as the nation's chief livestock center.
1967	A combination sales, income, and franchise tax replaces the state property tax.
1968–1969	The closing of the Swift and Armour meatpacking plants in Omaha is testimony to the relocation of the industry to smaller regional centers.
1970	Interstate Highway 80 is completed through Nebraska.
1974	Cooper Nuclear Station, the largest nuclear power plant between the Mississippi and the West Coast, begins producing electricity at Brownsville.
1977	The legislature adopts the first major revision of the criminal code in more than a century.
1978	Wells are providing 83 percent of the water for Nebraska's 6.7 million acres of irrigated farmland, leading to concerns that the water table may be falling.
1981	Nebraska ranks second among states in sorghum for silage, third in corn for grain and sorghum for grain, fifth in rye, hay, and corn for silage, eighth in soybeans, and tenth in wheat. It is also third in the number of cattle and calves and fifth in hogs.
1982	A law regulates groundwater irrigation pumping; user fees are imposed the following year. Voters adopt a constitutional amendment banning further corporate farming, except by family members.
1985	Because of defaulted farm loans, 13 banks fail, the largest number since the Great Depression.
1986	Kay Orr, a Republican, is the first woman to be elected governor of Nebraska.

DEMOGRAPHY

Population (est. 1987) . . . 1,594,000
Population (1980) 1,569,825
Population density in persons per
    square mile (1980) 20.3

POPULATION BY RACE (1980)
American Indian/Aleut/
    Eskimo 9,197
Asian/Pacific Islander 6,996
Black 48,389
Hispanic 28,020
White 1,490,569
Other 14,855

POPULATION CHARACTERISTICS (1980)
Percent of state population
Urban 66.7
Rural 33.3
Under 18 . . . . 27.5
65 or older 13.0
College-educated 16.1
Families below poverty line 8.0
Public-assistance recipients 3.2

Per capita personal income
    (1986) $13,777
Millionaires per 100,000
    residents (1982) 207.7

Average life expectancy in
years (1980) 75.5
Marriage rate per 1,000
residents (1986) 7.5
Divorce rate per 1,000
residents (1986) 3.9
Birth rate per 1,000
residents (1985) 15.9
Infant mortality rate per 1,000
births (1985) 10.6
Abortion rate per 1,000
live births (1985) 268
Crime rate per 100,000
residents (1985)
Violent 262.6
Property 3,593.1

Federal and state prisoners per 100,000
residents (1984) 107
Alcohol consumption in gallons
per capita (1985) 40.4
Deaths from motor vehicle accidents
per 100,000 residents (1985) . . 14.8

MAJOR CITIES

	Population
Grand Island (1980)	33,180
Lincoln (est. 1984)	180,378
North Platte (1980)	24,509
Omaha (est. 1984)	334,016

GOVERNMENT AND POLITICS

Number of US Representatives   3
Electoral votes   5

POLITICAL PARTY NOMINEES FROM STATE

William Jennings Bryan (D/ Populist/National Silver)	1896	P
Charles Eugene Bently (National)	1896	P
William Jennings Bryan (D/ People's/Silver Republicans)	1900	P
Thomas Henry Tibbles (People's)	1904	VP
William Jennings Bryan (D)	1908	P
Charles Wayland Bryan (D)	1924	VP
Roy M. Harrop (Greenback)	1924	VP
George William Norris (Farmer Labor/declined)	1928	P

PRESIDENTIAL PRIMARY ELECTION In 1988, Nebraska sent 29 Democratic delegates and 25 Republican delegates to the national conventions.

CONSTITUTION Nebraska has had two constitutions: 1866 and the present one, adopted in 1875.

LEGISLATURE The Legislature is unicameral and nonpartisan. There are 49 members serving 4-year terms; the minimum age is 21. In 1987, the annual salary was $4,800.

JUDICIARY The highest court is the Supreme Court, with 7 judges serving 6-year terms. In 1987, the annual salary was $63,512.

EXECUTIVE The governor serves a 4-year term; the minimum age for holding office is 30. In 1987, the annual salary was $58,000. There are 26 other elected officials.

PRESIDENTIAL VOTE 1948-1988 *(in percents)*

Year	State Winner	Democratic	Republican
1948	Dewey (R)	45.9	54.2
1952	Eisenhower (R)	30.9	69.2
1956	Eisenhower (R)	34.5	65.5
1960	Nixon (R)	37.9	32.1
1964	Johnson (D)	52.6	47.4
1968	Nixon (R)	31.8	59.8
1972	Nixon (R)	29.5	70.5
1976	Ford (R)	38.5	59.2
1980	Reagan (R)	26.0	65.9
1984	Reagan (R)	28.8	70.6
1988	Bush (R)	40.0	60.0

GOVERNORS

Territorial Governors

Francis Burt	1854
Thomas B. Cuming (acting)	1854-1855
Mark W. Izard	1855-1857
Thomas B. Cuming (acting)	1857-1858
William Alexander Richardson	1858
Julius Sterling Morton (acting)	1858-1859
Samuel W. Black	1859-1861

Algernon Sidney Paddock
  (acting)   1861
Alvin Saunders   1861-1867

State Governors

David Butler (R)	1867-1871
William Hartford James (R)	1871-1873
Robert Wilkinson Furnas (R)	1873-1875
Silas Garber (R)	1875-1879
Albinus Nance (R)	1879-1883
James W. Dawes (R)	1883-1887
John Milton Thayer (R/acting)	1887-1891
James E. Boyd (D)	1891
John Milton Thayer (R/acting)	1891-1892
James E. Boyd (D)	1892-1893
Lorenzo Crounse (R)	1893-1895
Silas Alexander Holcomb (Populist)	1895-1899
William A. Poynter (Populist)	1899-1901
Charles Henry Dietrich (R)	1901
Ezra Perin Savage (R)	1901-1903
John Hopwood Mickey (R)	1903-1907
George Lawson Sheldon (R)	1907-1909
Ashton C. Shallenberger (D)	1909-1911
Chester Hardy Aldrich (R)	1911-1913
John Henry Morehead (D)	1913-1917
Keith Neville (D)	1917-1919
Samuel Roy McKelvie (R)	1919-1923
Charles Wayland Bryan (D)	1923-1925
Adam McMullen (R)	1925-1929
Arthur J. Weaver (R)	1929-1931
Charles Wayland Bryan (D)	1931-1935
Robert LeRoy Cochran (D)	1935-1941
Dwight Palmer Griswold (R)	1941-1947
Val Peterson (R)	1947-1953
Robert Crosby (R)	1953-1955
Victor Emanuel Anderson (R)	1955-1959
Ralph Brooks (D)	1959-1960
Dwight W. Burney (R)	1960-1961
Frank B. Morrison (D)	1961-1967
Norbert T. Tiemann (R)	1967-1971
James Exon (D)	1971-1979
Charles Thone (R)	1979-1983
Robert Kerrey (R)	1983-1987
Kay A. Orr (D)	1987-

MINIMUM AGES

Majority	19
Marriage with parental consent	17
Marriage without parental consent	18
Making a will	18
Buying alcohol	21
Jury duty	19
Leaving school	16
Driver's license	16

CAPITAL PUNISHMENT
Number executed 1976-88: 0
On death row Aug. 1, 1988: 12

MILITARY INSTALLATIONS
Total number: 7
Major bases: Air Force: 1

FINANCES

Thousands of dollars

GENERAL REVENUE (1985)

Total general revenue	2,003,297
Total tax revenue	1,040,064
Sales and gross receipts	566,078
Individual income taxes	318,848
Corporate net income taxes	48,959

GENERAL EXPENDITURE (1985)

Total general expenditure	2,066,871
Education	692,501
Public welfare	328,762
Health	62,375
Hospitals	114,349
Natural resources	78,543
Highways	369,291
Police	20,207
Corrections	45,828

FEDERAL AID 675,346

ECONOMY

While industrialization is on the increase in Nebraska, the state economy is still based primarily on agriculture. Corn and wheat are the main crops, followed by oats, rye, barley, sugar beets, potatoes, beans, alfalfa, and sorghum. Cattle, dairy products, and poultry are the dominant farm cash producers. The state's more than 60,000 farms generated cash receipts of $6 billion in 1983. Meat and dairy processing are the main state industries, with agricultural machinery, transportation equipment, electrical machinery, rubber and chemicals, and printed materials other important products. Omaha is the center of Nebraska's insurance and financial industries.

EMPLOYMENT (1984)

Thousands of persons

Total number of employed workers	763
Construction	24.0

Finance, insurance, and
real estate 43.2
Government 131.7
Manufacturing 89.0
Mining 1.7
Services 135.4
Transportation, communications,
and utilities 42.8
Wholesale and retail trade 160.8

Percent of civilian labor force
unemployed (1984) 4.4

DEPARTMENT OF DEFENSE (1985)
Civilian workers employed . . . 3,827
Military personnel 12,794
Contract awards . . . . . $193 million

ENERGY SOURCES FOR ELECTRIC UTILITIES (1983)
Percent
Coal 55.5
Gas 0.7
Hydroelectric 7.9
Nuclear 35.7
Petroleum 0.2

TRANSPORTATION
Motor vehicles registered
in state (1986) 1,280,646
Miles of roads, streets,
and highways (1986) 92,199
Miles of Class I railway
operated (1986) 4,426
Airports (1983) 346
Major aviation hubs (1983) 1
Largest hub: Omaha

CULTURE AND EDUCATION

Native American tribes
Nebraska was formerly the home of the Arapaho, Arikara, Cheyenne, Comanche, Fox, Iowa, Kansa, Missouri, Oto, and Pawnee. Groups that continue to live in the state include the Omaha, Ponca, and Sioux. Groups that have been relocated there include the Winnebago. There are three federal reservations in Nebraska.

Religions, ethnicities, and languages
In addition to the settlers, white and black, who arrived in Nebraska after it was opened for settlement, the railroad companies and the state government recruited emigrants from northern Europe. The largest groups were from Germany, Sweden and the other Scandinavian nations, and Bohemia; consequently, the dominant religious groups are the Roman Catholics and Lutherans. In 1980, 4.8 percent of Nebraska's population spoke a language other than English at home.

Major museums and libraries
Joslyn Art Museum, Omaha
Nebraska State Historical Society Museum, Lincoln
Sheldon Memorial Art Gallery, Lincoln

University of Nebraska State Museum, Lincoln

Major arts organizations
Emmy Gifford Children's Theater, Omaha
Nebraska Repertory Theatre, Lincoln
Omaha Ballet
Omaha Symphony Chamber Orchestra
Omaha Symphony Orchestra
Opera/Omaha

Colleges and universities
Number public (1986-87) 18
Number private (1986-87) 15
Total enrollment, in full-time equivalent students (1985) 70,800

Public elementary and secondary schools
Expenditure per pupil in average daily attendance (1986-87) $3,437
Pupil-teacher ratio (1987) 15.1
Average teacher salary (1986-87) $24,138

Holidays
Arbor Day. April 22
State Fair, Lincoln. Early to mid-September

NEBRASKA IN LITERATURE

Bess Streeter Adrich *A Lantern in Her Hand* (1928); *A White Bird Flying* (1931, rpt. 1988)
Popular stories of pioneer life.

Bernice Anderson *Indian Sleep-Man Tales: Authentic Legends of the Otoe Tribe* (1940, rpt. 1984)

Frederic Babcock *Hang Up the Fiddle* (1954)
Novel about a Nebraska boyhood c.1920.

Mildred R. Bennett *The World of Willa Cather* (1988)
Description of the author's Nebraska upbringing.

Margaret Cannell and **Emma L. Snapp** *Signs, Omens, and Portents in Nebraska Folklore* (1933)

Willa S. Cather *O Pioneers!* (1913, rpt. 1989); *My Antonia* (1918, rpt. 1988); *A Lost Lady* (1923, rpt. 1972)
Classic novels of pioneer life.

Richard Crabb *Empire on the Platte* (1967)
Historical novel about rivalry between cattlemen and farmers in the 1870s.

Clyde Davis *Nebraska Coast* (1939)
Pioneers from New York settle in Nebraska in the 1860s.

Virginia Faulkner (ed.) *Roundup: A Nebraska Reader* (1957) Anthology of articles, short stories, and biographical sketches.

George B. Grinnell *Pawnee Hero Stories and Folk-Tales* (1904)

Alice G. Harvey *Nebraska Writers* (rev. ed. 1964)

Paul L. Hedren *First Scalp for Custer: The Skirmish at Warbonnet Creek* (1986)

Charles Tenney Jackson *The Buffalo Wallow* (1953) An account of a boyhood spent in a prairie sodhouse in the 1890s.

John Janovy *Keith County Journal* (1980); *Back in Keith County* (1983) Essays on Nebraska prairie and sandhills.

Alvin S. Johnson *The Battle of the Wild Turkey, and Other Tales* (1961) Tales of the author's Nebraska boyhood.

Bernice Kauffman (comp.) *Nebraska Centennial Literary Map and Guide to Nebraska Authors* (1967)

Wright Morris *The Home Place* (1948); *God's Country and My People* (1968) Evocations of small-town and rural life, including photographs by the author, that constitute a documentary portrait. Morris has described his Nebraska youth in *Will's Boy: A Memoir* (1981).

Charley O'Kieffe *Western Story: The Recollections of Charley O'Kieffe, 1884–1898* (1960) Records of a pioneer's life in the 1880s and '90s.

Louise Pound *The Folksong of Nebraska and the Central West* (1915)

Mari Sandoz *Old Jules* (1935, rpt. 1985) A biography of the author's Swiss immigrant father and a portrait of the northwestern Nebraska community in which she grew up. All of Sandoz's novels, biographies, and nonfictional studies concern the Great Plains and westward expansion, but the novels *Slogum House* (1937, rpt. 1981), *Miss Morissa: Doctor of the Gold Trail* (1955, rpt. 1980), and *Son of the Gamblin' Man* (1960, rpt. 1976) are of particular relevance to Nebraska.

Emma L. Snapp *Proverbial Lore in Nebraska* (1933)

Helen W. Stauffer *Mari Sandoz: Story Catcher of the Plains* (1982)

Dorothy Swain Thomas *Ma Jeeter's Girls* (1932); *The Home Place* (1936) Stories of farm life during the Depression.

Roger L. Welsch (ed.) *A Treasury of Nebraska Pioneer Folklore* (1966, rpt. 1984)
—— *Shingling the Fog and Other Plains Lies* (1980)
—— *Omaha Indian Myths and Trickster Tales* (1981)
—— and **Linda K. Welsch** *Cather's Kitchens: Foodways in Literature and Life* (1987)
—— and **Linda K. Welsch** *Catfish at the Pump: Humor and the Frontier* (1988)

Sophus Keith Winther *Take All to Nebraska* (1936, rpt. 1988); *Mortgage Your Heart* (1937); *This Passion Never Dies* (1938) Trilogy of novels about a Danish immigrant farming family.

GUIDES TO RESOURCES

Brevet's Nebraska Historical Markers and Sites (1974)

Federal Writers' Project *Nebraska; a Guide to the Cornhusker State* (1939, rpt. 1979)

Hunt, N. Jane (ed.) *Nebraska Historical Markers and Sites* (1974)

Johnson, John R. *Representative Nebraskans* (1954)

Junior League of Lincoln, Nebraska (comp.) *An Architectural Album* (1979)

Lonsdale, Richard E. *Economic Atlas of Nebraska* (1977)

Magie, John Q. *A History and Historic Sites Survey of Johnson, Nemaha, Pawnee, and Richardson Counties in Southeastern Nebraska* (1969)

Miewald, Robert D. and **Robert Sittig** *Nebraska Government: Sources and Literature* (1983)

Nebraska Department of Economic Development *Nebraska Statistical Handbook* (1972)

Reed, E. C. *Groundwater Atlas of Nebraska* (1966)

Rife, Janet W. *Germans and German-Russians in Nebraska: A Research Guide to Nebraska Ethnic Studies* (1980)

White, John B. *Nebraska State Historical Society: Published Sources on Territorial Nebraska, an Essay and Bibliography* (1956)

Williams, James H. and **Doug Murfield** (eds.) *Agricultural Atlas of Nebraska* (1977)

SELECTED NONFICTION SOURCES

Allen, William *Starkweather: The Story of a Mass Murderer* (1976)

Andreas, A. T. *History of Nebraska* (1882, rpt. 1976)

Aucoin, James *Water in Nebraska: Use, Politics, Policies* (1984)

Baltensperger, Bradley H. *Nebraska, a Geography* (1985)

Barns, Cass G. *The Sod House* (1930, rpt. 1970)

Blouet, Brian W. and **Frederick C. Luebke** (eds.) *The Great Plains: Environment and Culture* (1979)

Bratt, John *Trails of Yesterday* (1921)

Bremer, Richard G. *Agricultural Change in an Urban Age: The Loup Country of Nebraska, 1910–1970* (1976)

Bryson, Conrey *Winter Quarters* (1986)

Bucklin, Clarissa (ed.) *Nebraska Art and Artists* (1932)

Butcher, Solomon D. *History of Custer County* (1902, rpt. 1965)

Cherny, Robert W. *Populism, Progressivism and the Transformation of Nebraska Politics, 1885–1915* (1981)

Condra, George E. *The Nebraska Story* (1951)

Creigh, Dorothy W. *Adams County: A Story of the Great Plains* (1972)

——. *Nebraska: A Bicentennial History* (States and the Nation series) (1977)

Dick, Everett *Vanguards of the Frontier: A Social History of the Northern Plains and Rocky Mountains from the Fur Traders to the Sod Busters* (1965)
——. *Conquering the Great American Desert: Nebraska* (1975)
——. *The Sod-House Frontier, 1854–1890: A Social History of the Northern Plains from the Creation of Kansas and Nebraska to the Admission of the Dakotas* (1979)

Federal Writers' Project *Origin of Nebraska Place Names* (1938)

Fite, Gilbert C. *The Farmers' Frontier, 1865–1900* (1966)

Fitzpatrick, Lilian L. *Nebraska Place-Names* (1960)

Fletcher, Alice *The Omaha Tribe* (1911)

Glad, Paul W. *The Trumpet Soundeth* (1960)

Hanna, Robert *Sketches of Nebraska* (1984)

Holmes, Louis A. *Fort McPherson, Nebraska, Fort Cottonwood, N.T., Guardian of the Tracks and Trails* (1963)

Hyde, George E. *The Pawnee Indians* (1951)

Johnsgard, Paul A. *The Platte: Channels in Time* (1984)

Kaplan, Beverly S. *Daniel and Agnes Freeman, Homesteaders* (1971)

Keech, C. F. and Ray Bentall *Dunes on the Plains: The Sand Hills Region of Nebraska* (1978)

Kellogg, Orleatha G. *Bloom on the Land: A Prairie Pioneer Experience* (1982)

Killian, Margaret P. (ed. Sharon M. Wiesner) *Born Rich: A Historical Book of Omaha* (2d ed. 1978)

Koenig, Louis W. *Bryan; a Political Biography of William Jennings Bryan* (1971)

Larsen, Lawrence H. and Barbara J. Cottrell *The Gale City: A History of Omaha* (1982)

Lawson, Merlin P. *Climatic Atlas of Nebraska* (1977)
—— and Maurice E. Baker (eds.) *The Great Plains: Perspectives and Prospects* (1981)

Lee, Wayne C. *Wild Towns of Nebraska* (1988)

Luebke, Frederick C. *Immigrants and Politics: The Germans of Nebraska, 1880–1900* (1969)

Manley, Robert N. *Nebraska: Our Pioneer Heritage* (1981)

Mattes, Merrill J. *The Great Platte River Road: The Covered Wagon Mainline via Fort Kearny to Fort Laramie* (1969)

McKee, James L. and Arthur Duerschner *Lincoln, a Photographic History* (1976)

Miewald, Robert D. (ed.) *Nebraska Government and Politics* (1984)

Milner, Clyde A., II *With Good Intentions: Quaker Work among the Pawnees, Otos, and Omahas in the 1870s* (1982)

Morton, J. Sterling and Albert Watkins (eds.) *Illustrated History of Nebraska* 3 vols. (1905–13)

Nicoll, Bruce H. *Know Nebraska* (2d ed. 1961)

Olson, James C. *History of Nebraska* (rev. ed. 1966)

Perkey, Elton *Perkey's Nebraska Place-Names* (1982)

Richards, Bartlett, Jr., with Ruth Van Ackeren *Bartlett Richards: Nebraska Sandhills Cattleman* (1980)

Sandoz, Mari *Love Song to the Plains* (1961, rpt. 1966)

Sheldon, Addison E. *Nebraska: The Land and the People* . . . 3 vols. (1931)

Sherwood, James E. *Nebraska Football: The Coaches, the Players, the Experience* (1987)

Sorenson, Alfred R. *Hands Up: The History of a Crime* (1877, rpt. 1982)

Stilgebouer, Forster G. *Nebraska Pioneers; the Story of Sixty-Five Years of Pioneering in Southwest Nebraska, 1875–1940* (1944)

Weaver, John *The North American Prairie* (1954)

Webb, Walter P. *The Great Plains* (1931, rpt. 1972)

Wedel, Waldo R. *Prehistoric Man on the Great Plains* (1961)

Wilson, Dorothy C. *Bright Eyes: The Story of Susette La Flesche, an Omaha Indian* (1974)

NEVADA

The Mountain state of Nevada is bordered on the north by Oregon and Idaho; on the east by Utah and Arizona; and on the southwest and west by California.

FULL NAME State of Nevada
POSTAL ABBREVIATION NV
INHABITANT Nevadan
ADMITTED TO THE UNION Oct. 31, 1864. 36th state
POPULATION (est. 1987) 1,007,000. Percent of US total: 0.41%. Rank: 41st

CAPITAL CITY Carson City, located near Lake Tahoe in the southwestern corner of the state; population 36,000 (est. 1984). Carson City, named after Kit Carson, was originally the site of a frontier station. Founded in 1858, it became the territorial capital in 1861 and the state capital three years later; it was incorporated as a city in 1969.

STATE NAME AND NICKNAMES From the Spanish word meaning "snowy," condensed from Sierra Nevada, "snowy range," the name given to the California mountain ranges by Spanish sailors traveling near the Pacific Coast. Also known as the Sage State, the Sagebrush State, the Silver State, the Mining State, and the Battle Born State.

STATE SEAL A landscape with agricultural tools in the foreground, on a green field; behind them a miner taking ore from a tunnel in a mountain, and a wagon team bringing ore to a quartz mill; in the distance a railroad and telegraph line, and the sun rising behind snow-capped purple mountains. The inner border consists of 36 stars and the state motto; the outer yellow border reads "The Great Seal of the State of Nevada."

MOTTO All for Our Country

SONG "Home Means Nevada" by Bertha Raffeto

SYMBOLS
Flower sagebrush
Tree single-leaf pinyon
Bird mountain bluebird
Animal desert bighorn sheep
Fish lohonton cutthroat trout
Fossil ichthyosaur
Grass Indian rice grass
Metal silver
Colors silver and blue

LICENSE PLATES (1) Dark blue on white, with a gray mountain scene in the background, and the legend "The Silver State." (2) White on dark blue with a white border, some with the city name.

FLAG On a field of cobalt blue, in the upper left quarter, a five-pointed silver star resting on two sprays of sagebrush, with the letters of the name "Nevada" arrayed around the star and the legend "Battle Born" on a golden scroll above it.

GEOGRAPHY AND CLIMATE

The varied terrain of Nevada includes rugged mountains (the Sierra Nevadas and some 30 other mountain chains in the western region); sandy deserts (the Mojave, at the southern tip of the state, and the alkali deserts surrounding the Great Salt Lake on the northeastern border); and semi-arid grasslands (in central Nevada). With little annual precipitation, Nevada depends on increasingly scarce underground water sources and on manmade lakes such as Lake Mead.

AREA 110,561 square miles. Rank: 7th
INLAND WATER 667 square miles
GEOGRAPHIC CENTER Lander, 26 miles SE of Austin
ELEVATIONS *Highest point:* Boundary Peak, Esmeralda County, 13,143 feet. *Lowest point:* Colorado River, Clark County, 470 feet. *Mean elevation:* 5,500 feet

MAJOR RIVERS Humboldt, Colorado, Truckee

MAJOR LAKES AND RESERVOIRS Pyramid, Walker, Tahoe, Mead

LAND USE

	Thousands of acres
Urban (1982)	199
Rural (1982)	9,788
Cropland (1982)	860
Pastureland (1982)	304
Rangeland (1982)	7,908
Forestland (1982)	357
State parks and recreation areas (1983)	153
National park system (1984)	700
National forest system (1984)	5,424
Tribal lands (1984)	1,145

TEMPERATURES The highest recorded temperature was 122°F on June 23, 1954, at Overton. The lowest was -50°F on January 8, 1937, at San Jacinto.

NATIONAL SITES

NATIONAL MONUMENT Death Valley
NATIONAL PARK Great Basin
NATIONAL RECREATION AREA Lake Mead
NATIONAL WILDLIFE REFUGES Desert National Wildlife Range–Pahranagat, Ruby Lake, Sheldon, Stillwater–Anaho Island/Fallon

HISTORY

1775	Spanish missionary Francisco Garcès crosses southern Nevada on his way to California.
1826	Jedediah Smith leads an expedition through present-day Nevada, traveling east to west, for the Rocky Mountain Fur Company. He returns through central Nevada in 1827.
1828–1830	Peter S. Ogden of the Hudson's Bay Company explores what is now northern Nevada, discovering the Humboldt River and following its course.
1833–1834	Joseph Walker reaches California by passing through northern Nevada from Great Salt Lake on what becomes known as the Humboldt Trail.
1843–1845	John C. Frémont leads two expeditions through Nevada.
1846	Forty of the 87-member Donner wagon-train party perish when heavy snows close the Sierra Nevada passes.
1848	Nevada passes from Mexican to United States sovereignty as a result of the Treaty of Guadalupe Hildago, which ends the Mexican War.
1851	The first permanent settlement in Nevada is Mormon Station (later renamed Genoa), a trading post for California-bound gold-rush migrants.
1854	Norwegian-born John A. Thompson introduces skiing to Nevada when he incorporates the practice into his speedy mail delivery service.
1855–1857	Mormons settle in Carson Valley and what is now Las Vegas but return to Utah to help defend the community there in case of war with federal troops.
1858	Nevada's first newspaper, the *Territorial Enterprise,* is published at Genoa.
1859	The Comstock Lode, the richest mineral area in the United States, is discovered 30 miles north of Genoa. Through 1882 it produces $293 million worth of silver and gold.
1860	About 10,000 prospectors rush from California to the Comstock settlements of Silver City, Gold Hill, and Virginia City.

	An Indian ambush on May 12 kills 76 of 105 whites during the Pyramid Lake War. The Indians are routed on May 31.
1861	Nevada Territory is created. Carson City is made the capital.
1864	Silver strike at Eureka; it yields about $60 million in production through 1881. *October 31.* Despite Nevada's small population, it is admitted to the Union as the 36th state because President Abraham Lincoln needs more Senate votes for passage of the 13th Amendment, abolishing slavery.
1867	The Gold Hill and Virginia City miners' union forces the establishment of a closed shop and a $4-a-day wage for underground workers.
1868–1869	The Central Pacific Railroad crosses Nevada from west to east on its way to its transcontinental rendezvous with the Union Pacific in Utah. Reno and Elko are among the settlements first established as railroad stations.
1869	Gambling is legalized and remains legal until 1910.
1874	The Pyramid Lake and Walker Lake reservations are established for the Northern Paiute Indians.
1875	The University of Nevada opens at Elko, later moving to Reno.
1877	Mineral production of $47 million is a record that, excluding World War I and II years, is not topped until 1951.
1879	Several acts and resolutions are passed by the legislature that seek to prohibit Chinese immigration and labor.
1894	Annual mineral production has dropped to less than $2 million as the Comstock and other mines peter out.
1894–1902	Heyday of the Silver party, which seeks the remonetization of silver. Alone or in union with the Democrats, the party dominates elections to state offices in this period.
1897	*March 17.* Bob Fitzsimmons wins the world heavyweight championship from Jim Corbett in Carson City, establishing a tradition of championship fights held in Nevada.
1900	The population has dropped to 42,335 from 62,266 in 1880 as a result of the fall in output of precious metals. But a second great silver-gold boom opens with the Tonopah strike in southwestern Nevada. Butch Cassidy's gang robs the First National Bank in Winnemucca of $32,640.
1905	Las Vegas is founded as a stop on the San Pedro, Los Angeles, and Salt Lake Railroad.
1907	Dispatch of federal troops helps break a strike at Goldfield by the Western Federation of Miners.
1908	Copper production begins near Ely; the area becomes Nevada's richest mining district.
1910	Mainly as a result of renewed mining, the state population has almost doubled since 1900. There are 220 men to every 100 women.
1922	Only a little more than three percent of Nevada's land is privately owned, and less than one percent is irrigated.
1931	Wide-open gambling is again legalized after a 16-year period in which it is restricted to certain card games. Residency required for divorce, lowered to three months in 1927, is lowered again to six weeks.
1932	The 12-bank Wingfield group fails in the Great Depression, falling into receivership the following year.
1936	Completion of the giant Boulder (later Hoover) Dam, impounding the waters of the Colorado River in Lake Mead and providing power to Nevada.
1942–1944	A $150-million magnesium plant at Henderson provides employment for thousands of Nevadans in World War II.
1945	A tax is imposed on gross gambling receipts, which in fiscal 1987 total $3.7 billion.
1946	"Bugsy" Siegel opens the Flamingo Hotel on a five-mile section of US Highway 91 in Las Vegas—the "Strip." By far the most lavish resort in Nevada, it also ushers in an era of Mob influence in the gaming industry.
1951	Ten years of mostly above-ground nuclear-weapons tests begin in southern Nevada, employing thousands. After 1962 all tests are held underground. A southern branch of the University of Nevada is established at Las Vegas.

1952	A right-to-work law outlaws the closed and union shops.
1955	A state sales tax is enacted.
1966–1969	Howard Hughes buys five Las Vegas Strip casino-hotels, Air West, a television station, airport, charter air service, and some 500 mining claims.
1969	A *Time* magazine article reports that 30 or 40 brothels are operating in 15 of the 17 counties where prostitution is allowed by local option.
1970	Nevada has been the fastest-growing state in the 1960s, its population growing by 71.3 percent to 488,738.
1971	The Atomic Energy Commission reports that, as a result of nuclear tests, 250 square miles of Nevada desert are contaminated by plutonium-237. A state fair-housing law is passed.
1978	A Gold Hill open-pit gold mine is opened but the state's three largest copper mines close.
1979	Nevada declares state sovereignty over 49 million acres of Nevada owned by the federal government, but the action has no legal standing.
1980	Nevada has been the fastest-growing state in the 1970s, its population increasing fivefold since 1950. Almost a third of the state's adults have lived in Nevada five years or less. *November 21.* A fire sweeps through the MGM Grand Hotel in Las Vegas, killing 84 persons.
1981	The service sector, which includes gambling, accounts for 41 percent of state employment, and gambling taxes account for 46 percent of state revenue.
1985	A total of 14.2 million visitors come to Las Vegas, spending $7 billion.
1986	Nevada is first among states in gold, accounting for 56 percent of US production; the Carlin Mine complex in Eureka County is the nation's biggest gold producer. Nevada is also second in silver production and accounts for all mercury and magnesite production and 64 percent of barite production.
1987	Creation of 77,000-acre Great Basin National Park. Construction begins on the Las Vegas Strip of a 3,303-room hotel, the biggest in the world.

DEMOGRAPHY

Population (est. 1987) . . . 1,007,000
Population (1980) 800,493
Population density in persons
   per square mile (1980) 7.2

POPULATION BY RACE (1980)
American Indian/Aleut/
  Eskimo 13,304
Asian/Pacific Islander 14,109
Black 50,791
Hispanic 53,786
White 699,377
Other 21,603

POPULATION CHARACTERISTICS (1980)
    Percent of state population
Urban 85.3
Rural 14.7
Under 18 . . . . 26.9
65 or older 8.2
College-educated 15.1

Families below poverty line 6.3
Public-assistance recipients 2.3

Per capita personal income
  (1986) $15,074
Millionaires per 100,000
  residents (1982) 170.8
Average life expectancy in
  years (1980) 72.6
Marriage rate per 1,000
  residents (1986) 114.2
Divorce rate per 1,000
  residents (1986) 14.0
Birth rate per 1,000
  residents (1985) 16.4
Infant mortality rate per 1,000
  births (1985) 8.6
Abortion rate per 1,000
  live births (1985) 641
Crime rate per 100,000
  residents (1985)
  Violent 718.9
  Property 5,570.8

Federal and state prisoners per
100,000 residents (1984) 376
Alcohol consumption in gallons
per capita (1985) 63.1
Deaths from motor vehicle accidents
per 100,000 residents (1985) . . 28.7

MAJOR CITIES

	Population
Carson City (est. 1984)	36,000
Las Vegas (est. 1984)	183,227
Paradise (1980)	84,818
Reno (est. 1984)	105,615

GOVERNMENT AND POLITICS

Number of US Representatives 2
Electoral votes 4

POLITICAL PARTY NOMINEES FROM STATE

Martin R. Preston (Socialist
Labor) 1908 VP

PRESIDENTIAL PRIMARY ELECTION In 1988, Nevada sent 21 Democratic delegates and 20 Republican delegates to the national conventions.
CONSTITUTION Nevada is using its original constitution, adopted in 1864.

LEGISLATURE The Legislature is divided into the Senate (21 members, 4-year term, minimum age 21) and the Assembly (42 members, 2-year term, minimum age 21). In 1987, the salary for legislators was $130 per day for a maximum of 60 days.
JUDICIARY The highest court is the Supreme Court, with 5 judges serving 6-year terms. In 1987, the annual salary was $73,500.
EXECUTIVE The governor serves a 4-year term; the minimum age for holding office is 25. In 1987, the annual salary was $77,500. There are 23 other elected officials.

PRESIDENTIAL VOTE 1948-1988 *(in percents)*

Year	State Winner	Democratic	Republican
1948	Truman (D)	50.4	47.3
1952	Eisenhower (R)	38.6	6.5
1956	Eisenhower (R)	42.0	58.0
1960	Kennedy (D)	51.2	48.8
1964	Johnson (D)	58.6	41.4
1968	Nixon (R)	39.3	47.5
1972	Nixon (R)	36.3	63.7
1976	Ford (R)	45.8	50.2
1980	Reagan (R)	26.6	92.5
1984	Reagan (R)	32.0	65.8
1988	Bush (R)	38.0	60.0

GOVERNORS

Territorial Governor
James W. Nye 1861-1864

State Governors
Henry G. Blasdel (R)	1864-1871
L.R. Bradley (D)	1871-1879
John H. Kinkead (R)	1879-1883
Jewett W. Adams (D)	1883-1887
Christopher C. Stephenson (R)	1887-1890
Frank Bell (acting)	1890-1891
Roswell K. Colcord (R)	1891-1895
John E. Jones (Silver Party)	1895-1896
Reinhold Sadler (Silver Party/acting)	1896-1899
Reinhold Sadler (Silver Party)	1899-1903
John Sparks (Silver Democrat)	1903-1908
Denver S. Dickerson (Silver Democrat)	1908-1911
Tasker L. Oddie (R)	1911-1915
Emmet D. Boyle (D)	1915-1923
James G. Scrugham (D)	1923-1927
Fredrick B. Balzar (R)	1927-1934
Morley Griswold (R/acting)	1934-1935
Richard Kirman Sr. (D)	1935-1939
Edward P. Carville (D)	1939-1945
Vail Pittman (D/acting)	1945-1947
Vail Pittman (D)	1947-1951
Charles H. Russell (R)	1951-1959
Grant Sawyer (D)	1959-1967
Paul Laxalt (R)	1967-1971

D.N. O'Callaghan (D)   1971-1979
Robert List (R)   1979-1983
Richard H. Bryan (D)   1983-

MINIMUM AGES

Majority	18
Marriage with parental consent	16
Marriage without parental consent	18
Making a will	18
Buying alcohol	21
Jury duty	18
Leaving school	17
Driver's license	16

CAPITAL PUNISHMENT

Number executed 1976-88: 2
On death row Aug. 1, 1988: 44

MILITARY INSTALLATIONS

Total number: 12
Major bases:
  Army: 1
  Navy: 1
  Air Force: 2

FINANCES

Thousands of dollars

GENERAL REVENUE (1985)

Total general revenue	1,397,858
Total tax revenue	940,622
Sales and gross receipts	803,902
Individual income taxes	0
Corporate net income taxes	9

GENERAL EXPENDITURE (1985)

Total general expenditure	1,317,938
Education	464,617
Public welfare	117,390
Health	29,842
Hospitals	25,445
Natural resources	22,302
Highways	198,783
Police	10,351
Corrections	44,887

FEDERAL AID (1985) 387,267

ECONOMY

The state's main farm activity, and by far the biggest cash producer, is cattle and sheep ranching, along with sales of meat, dairy products, and wool. The amount of arable land in the state is relatively small; alfalfa hay for feed is the principal crop, with smaller amounts of wheat, barley, oats, potatoes, onions, and truck vegetables also grown. Farm cash receipts in 1983 were $224 million. Mining is a major income producer; the state's important minerals include copper, gold, mercury, magnesite, diatomite, lithium salts, sand, and gravel. Manufacturing serves both agriculture and mining, with processed metals and foods the leading products. Many goods made out of state are warehoused in Nevada for shipment to California and the Pacific markets. By far the biggest segment of the economy, however, is entertainment and tourism. Gambling, resort hotels, and the quick marriage and divorce industries attract nearly 30 million visitors to the state each year.

EMPLOYMENT (1984)

Thousands of persons

Total number of employed workers	457
Construction	22.3
Finance, insurance, and real estate	20.1
Government	59.0
Mining	6.6
Manufacturing	21.0
Services	187.3
Transportation, communications, and utilities	24.8
Wholesale and retail trade	86.0
Percent of civilian labor force unemployed (1984)	7.8

DEPARTMENT OF DEFENSE (1985)

Civilian workers employed	2,077
Military personnel	9,744
Contract awards	$128 million

ENERGY SOURCES FOR ELECTRIC UTILITIES (1983)

Percent

Coal	71.4
Gas	4.9
Hydroelectric	23.6
Nuclear	0.0
Petroleum	0.1

TRANSPORTATION

Motor vehicles registered in state (1986)	769,076
Miles of roads, streets, and highways (1986)	44,438
Miles of Class I railway operated (1986)	1,451
Airports (1983)	126
Major aviation hubs (1983)	2

  Largest hub: Las Vegas

CULTURE AND EDUCATION

Native American tribes
Nevada was formerly the home of the Mono, Panamint, Ute, and Western Shoshoni tribes. Groups that continue to live in the state include the Northern and Southern Paiute and the Washo. There are 23 federal reservations in Nevada.

Religions, ethnicities, and languages
Although some 95 percent of Nevadans were born in the United States, less than one-quarter were born in Nevada; many are from the western states. There are distinct communities of Basques, Italians, Mexicans, and American Indians. In 1980, 9.7 percent of Nevada's population spoke a language other than English at home. Mormons and Roman Catholics are the predominant religious groups.

Major museums and libraries
Nevada Historical Society Museum, Reno
Nevada Art Gallery, Reno
Nevada State Library, Carson City
Nevada State Museum, Carson City

Major arts organizations
Las Vegas Symphony Orchestra
Nevada Opera Association, Reno
Nevada Dance Theatre, Las Vegas
Reno Symphony Orchestra

Colleges and universities
Number public (1986-87) 6
Number private (1986-87) 3
Total enrollment, in full-time equivalent students (1985) 23,100

Public elementary and secondary schools
Expenditure per pupil in average daily attendance (1986-87) $3,548
Pupil-teacher ratio (1987) 20.4
Average teacher salary (1986-87) $27,340

Holidays
Nevada Day. October 31
State Fair, Reno. Early September

NEVADA IN LITERATURE

Herman W. Albert *Odyssey of a Desert Prospector* (1967)
Memoir of a Tonopah prospector who became a banker.

Emmett L. Arnold *Gold Camp Drifter: 1906–1910* (1973)
Memoirs of a miner and prospector.

Frank Bergon *Shoshone Mike* (1987)
Novel describing events arising from the last Indian massacre in the US, which took place on February 16, 1911.

(Mrs.) Hugh Brown *Lady in Boomtown* (1968)
The author accompanied her husband to Tonopah in 1904, and gives a detailed description of life in a mining boom town.

J. Ross Browne *A Peep at Washoe and Washoe Revisited* (1959)
Descriptions of the Comstock by an eastern journalist who visited during the 1850s and in 1863.

James M. Cain *Past All Dishonor* (1946)
Historical novel set in Virginia City.

Walter Van Tilburg Clark *The Ox-Bow Incident* (1940)
Classic Western tale of a murder and a lynching set in a small Nevada town in 1885. Clark also wrote a semi-autobiographical novel set in Reno, *The City of Trembling Leaves* (1945).

Octavus R. Cohen *Borrasca* (1953)
Prospecting on the Comstock Lode in the 1870s.

Dan De Quille (pseud. of William Wright) *History of the Big Bonanza* (1876, rpt. 1983)
History and legends of the Comstock Lode by a newspaper editor and friend of Mark Twain who lived in Virginia City.

Alfred Doten (ed. Walter Van Tilburg Clark) *The Journals of Alfred Doten, 1849–1903* (1974)
Selection from journals kept during fifty-four years by a Comstock miner who became a journalist.

Wells Drury *An Editor on the Comstock Lode* (1936, rpt. 1984)
A newspaper editor's autobiography of the mining boom.

John Gregory Dunne *Vegas: A Memoir of a Dark Season* (1974)
Personal account of Las Vegas.

Duncan Emrich (ed.) *Comstock Bonanza: Western Americana of J. Ross Browne, Mark Twain, Sam Davis . . .* (1950)
Anthology of writing about the mining boom.

Vardis Fisher *City of Illusion* (1941)
Historical novel of Virginia City and the Comstock Lode.

Harry M. Gorham *My Memories of the Comstock* (1939)
Life in Virginia City, 1877–1903.

Fred H. Hart *The Sazerac Laughing Club* (1878)
Collection of character sketches and local narratives.

Mary M. Mathews *Ten Years in Nevada, or, Life on the Pacific Coast* (1880, rpt. 1985)
Detailed description of mining-boom times by a woman who spent ten years living on the Comstock.

John McPhee *Basin and Range* (1981)
An introduction to the history of the earth, with illustrations drawn from the landscape alongside Route I–80 as it passes through Nevada and the Great Basin.

Beltran Paris (ed. William O. Douglas) *Beltran: Basque Sheepman of the American West* (1979)
A shepherd's account of his working life, origins, and customs.

Zola Helen Ross *Bonanza Queen* (1949); *Tonopah Lady* (1950); *Reno Crescent* (1951)
Romantic adventure novels set in Virginia City and Reno, 1875–1900.

Lalla Scott *Karnee: A Paiute Narrative* (1966)
Biography of a Paiute woman, including descriptions of history and folkways.

John Franklin Swift *Robert Greathouse* (1878)
A novel set during the Gold Rush.

Hunter Thompson *Fear and Loathing in Las Vegas: A Savage Journey to the Heart of the American Dream* (1972)
A view of American culture, exemplified by a district attorneys' conference, from the perspective of a drugged,

itinerant journalist. A classic of the 1960s countercultural movement.

Mark Twain (pseud. of Samuel L. Clemens) *Roughing It* (1872)
Autobiographical account of the twenty-five-year-old writer's journey west, which included a stay in Virginia City working as a journalist.

————. *Mark Twain of the Enterprise* (1957)
Collection of humorous pieces that appeared in the *Virginia City Enterprise.*

Sessions S. Wheeler *Paiute* (1965, rpt. 1986)
Historical novel of mining and Indian fighting set in the years 1859–1860.

GUIDES TO RESOURCES

Armstrong, Robert D. *Nevada Printing History: A Bibliography of Imprints and Publications, 1858–1880* (1982)

Basso, David (ed.) *Nevada Historical Marker Guidebook* (1982)

Cullen, David J. *Historical Northern Nevada* (1986)
————. *Historical Southern Nevada* (1987)

Federal Writers' Project *Nevada: A Guide to the Silver State* (1940, rpt. 1973)

Glass, Mary Ellen and **Al** *Touring Nevada: A Historic and Scenic Guide* (1983)

Higgins, L. James, Jr. *A Guide to the Manuscript Collections at the Nevada Historical Society* (1975)

Lingenfelter, Richard E. and **Karen Rix Gash** *The Newspapers of Nevada: A History and Bibliography, 1854–1979* (1983)

Moody, Eric N. (comp.) *An Index to the Publications of the Nevada Historical Society, 1907–1971* (1977)

Nevada Secretary of State *Political History of Nevada* (issued periodically)

Nevada Statistical Abstract (1977–   )

Paher, Stanley W. (ed.) *Nevada Official Bicentennial Book* (1976)
————. *Nevada, an Annotated Bibliography: Books and Pamphlets Relating to the History and Development of the Silver State* (1980)

Parker, J. Carlyle and **Janet G.** (comps.) *Nevada Biographical and Genealogical Sketch Index* (1986)

Poulton, Helen *Index to the History of Nevada* (1981)

SELECTED NONFICTION SOURCES

Abbe, Donald R. *Austin and the Reese River Mining District: Nevada's Forgotten Frontier* (1985)

Amaral, Anthony *Mustang; Life and Legends of Nevada's Wild Horses* (1977)

Angel, Myron (ed.) *History of Nevada, with Illustrations and Biographical Sketches of Its Prominent Men and Pioneers* (1881, rpt. 1958)

Arnold, Emmett L. *Gold-Camp Drifter: 1906–1910* (1973)

Ashbaugh, Don *Nevada's Turbulent Yesterdays . . . A Study in Ghost Towns* (1963)

Beatty, David and **Robert O.** *Nevada: Land of Discovery* (1976)

Beebe, Lucius M. *Comstock Commotion: The Story of the Territorial Enterprise and Virginia City News* (1954)

Benson, Ivan *Mark Twain's Western Years* (1938, rpt. 1966)

Best, Katharine and **Katharine Hillyer** *Las Vegas, Playtown U.S.A.* (1955)

Browne, J. Ross *A Peep at Washoe and Washoe Revisited* (1959)

Bushnell, Eleanor (ed.) *Sagebrush and Neon* (1973)
————. *The Nevada Constitution: Origin and Growth* (4th rev. ed. 1977)

Carlson, Helen S. *Nevada Place Names: A Geographical Dictionary* (1974, rpt. 1985)

Carpenter, Jay A., Russell R. Elliott, and **Byrd F. W. Sawyer** *The History of Fifty Years of Mining at Tonopah, 1900–1950* (1953)

Cline, Gloria G. *Exploring the Great Basin* (1963, rpt. 1988)
————. *Peter Skene Ogden and the Hudson's Bay Company* (1974)

Crane, Basil K. *Dust from an Alkali Flat: A Forest Ranger Remembers Central Nevada* (1984)

Dangberg, Grace M. *Carson Valley: Historical Sketches of Nevada's First Settlement* (1972)
————. *Conflict on the Carson* (1975)

Douglass, William A. and **Jon Bilbao** *Amerikanuak: Basques in the New World* (1975)

Drury, Wells *An Editor on the Comstock Lode* (1936, rpt. 1984)

Earl, Phillip I. *This Was Nevada* (1986)

Edwards, Jerome E. *Pat McCarran: Political Boss of Nevada* (1982)

Egan, Ferol *Sand in a Whirlwind: The Paiute Indian War of 1860* (1972, rpt. 1985)
————. *Frémont: Explorer for a Restless Nation* (1977, rpt. 1985)

Elliott, Russell R. *Radical Labor in the Nevada Mining Booms, 1900–1920* (1961)
————. *Nevada's Twentieth-Century Mining Boom: Tonopah, Goldfield, Ely* (1966, rpt. 1988)
————. *History of Nevada* (1973)
————. *Servant of Power: A Political Biography of Senator William M. Stewart* (1983)

Fatout, Paul *Mark Twain in Virginia City* (1964)

Findlay, John M. *People of Chance: Gambling in American Society from Jamestown to Las Vegas* (1986)

Fletcher, Fred N. *Early Nevada, the Period of Exploration, 1776–1848* (1929)

Forbes, Jack D. *The Nevada Indian Speaks* (1967)

Fradkin, Philip L. *Fallout: An American Nuclear Tragedy* (1988)

Frady, Steven R. *Red Shirts and Leather Helmets: Volunteer Fire Fighting on the Comstock Lode* (1984)

Freeman, Marie E. *Alpine to Alkali* (1983)

Galbraith, J. K. *Money: Whence It Came, Where It Went* (1975)

Georgetta, Clel *Golden Fleece in Nevada* (1972)

Gillman, M. Ostrander *Nevada: The Great Rotten Borough, 1859–1964* (1966)

Glass, Mary E. *Water for Nevada: The Reclamation Controversy, 1885–1902* (1964, rpt. 1970)
————. *Silver and Politics in Nevada: 1892–1902* (1969)
————. *Nevada's Turbulent '50s: Decade of Political and Economic Change* (1981)

Glasscock, Carl B. *The Big Bonanza: The Story of the Comstock Lode* (1931)
————. *Gold in Them Hills: The Story of the West's Last Wild Mining Days* (1932)

Goldman, Marion S. *Gold Diggers and Silver Miners: Prostitution and Social Life on the Comstock Lode* (1981)

Gortner, Willis A. and **Albert B. Elsasser** *The Martis Indians, Ancient Tribe of the Sierra Nevada* (1986)

Haglund, E. *The Washoe, Paiute and Shoshone Indians of Nevada* (1961)

Hopkins, Sarah W. *Life among the Paiutes; Their Wrongs and Claims* (1883)

Houghton, John G., Clarence M. Sakamoto, and Richard O. Gifford *Nevada's Weather and Climate* (1975)

Houghton, Ruth M. and Leontine B. Nappe (eds.) *Nevada Lifestyles and Lands* (1977)

Houghton, Samuel *A Trace of Desert Waters, the Great Basin Story* (1976)

Hulse, James W. *Lincoln County, Nevada, 1864–1909: History of a Mining Region* (1971)
———. *The Nevada Adventure: A History* (5th rev. ed. 1981)
———. *Forty Years in the Wilderness: Impressions of Nevada, 1940–1980* (1986)

Israel, Fred L. *Nevada's Key Pittman* (1963)

Jackson, Donald D. and the Editors of Time-Life Books *Sagebrush Country, the American Wilderness* (1975)

Jackson, W. Turrentine and Donald J. Pisani *Treasure Hill, Portrait of a Silver Mining Camp* (1963)

James, George W. *The Lake of the Sky: Lake Tahoe in the High Sierras of California and Nevada* (1915)

Jennings, Dean S. *We Only Kill Each Other: The Life and Bad Times of Bugsy Siegel* (1967)

Johnson, Edward *Walker River Paiutes: A Tribal History* (1975)

Johnston, Hank *The Whistles Blow No More: Railroad Logging in the Sierra Nevada, 1874–1942* (1984)

Jones, Florence L. and John F. Cahlan *Water: A History of Las Vegas* 2 vols. (1975)

Knudtsen, Molly F. *Here Is Our Valley* (1975)

Lambert, Florin *Nevada Ghost Towns* (1986)

Laxalt, Robert *Sweet Promised Land* (1957, rpt. 1988)
———. *Nevada: A Bicentennial History* (States and the Nation series) (1977)

Lewis, Oscar *Silver Kings: The Lives and Times of Mackay, Fair, Flood and O'Brien, Lords of the Nevada Comstock Lode* (1947, rpt. 1986)
———. *Sagebrush Casinos: The Story of Legal Gambling in Nevada* (1953)
———. *High Sierra Country* (1955, rpt. 1988)
———. *The Town That Died Laughing: The Story of Austin, Nevada, Rambunctious Early-day Mining Camp, and of Its Renowned Newspaper, The Reveille* (1955, rpt. 1986)

Lillard, Richard G. *Desert Challenge: An Interpretation of Nevada* (1942, 1979)

Lincoln, Francis C. *Mining Districts and Mineral Resources of Nevada* (1923, rpt. 1970)
———. *The Lincoln Highway: The Story of a Crusade That Made Transportation History* (1935)

Linn, Edward *Big Julie of Vegas* (1971)

Lord, Eliot *Comstock Mining and Miners* (1883, rpt. 1959)

Lyman, George D. *The Saga of the Comstock Lode: Boom Days in Virginia City* (1934)
———. *Ralston's Ring: California Plunders the Comstock Lode* (1937)

Mack, Effie M. *Nevada: A History of the State from the Earliest Times through the Civil War* (1936)
———. *Mark Twain in Nevada* (1947)

Manter, Ethel *Rocket of the Comstock: The Story of John William Mackay* (1950)

Mason, Dorothy *The Pony Express in Nevada* (1976)

Meadows, Lorena E. *A Sagebrush Heritage* (1972)

Melton, Rollan *Nevadans* (1988)

Miller, Max *Reno* (1941)

Mills, Lester W. *A Sagebrush Saga* (1956)

Miluck, Nancy C. (ed.) *The Genoa–Carson Valley Book: Where Nevada Began* (1975)
——— (ed.) *Nevada—This Is Our Land: A Survey from Prehistory to the Present* (1978)

Molinelli, Lambert *Eureka and Its Resources: A Complete History of Eureka County, Nevada* (1879, rpt. 1982)

Moody, Eric N. *Southern Gentleman of Nevada Politics: Vail Pittman* (1974)
———. *Western Carpetbagger: The Extraordinary Memoirs of "Senator" Thomas Fitch* (1978)

Morgan, Dale L. *The Humboldt, Highroad of the West* (Rivers of America series) (1943, rpt. 1985)

Murbarger, Nell *Ghosts of the Glory Trail* (1956)

Myles, Myrtle T. *Nevada's Governors from Territorial Days to the Present, 1861–1971* (1972)

Myrick, David F. *Railroads of Nevada and Eastern California* 2 vols. (1962)

Paher, Stanley W. *Nevada Ghost Towns and Mining Camps* (1970)
———. *Las Vegas, as It Began, as It Grew* (1971)
——— (ed.) *Nevada Towns and Tales* (1982)

Paine, Swift *Eilley Orrum, Queen of the Comstock* (1929)

Patterson, Edna B., Louise A. Ulph, and Victor Goodwin *Nevada's Northeast Frontier* (1969)

Puzo, Mario *Inside Las Vegas* (1976)

* Reid, Ed *Las Vegas, City without Clocks* (1961)

Rusco, Elmer *Voting Behavior in Nevada* (1968)
———. *"Good Times Coming?" Black Nevadans in the Nineteenth Century* (1975)

Scrugham, James G. (ed.) *Nevada; a Narrative of the Conquest of a Frontier Land* 3 vols. (1935)

Shepperson, Wilbur S. *Retreat to Nevada: A Socialist Colony of World War I* (1966)
———. *Restless Strangers: Nevada's Immigrants and Their Interpreters* (1970)

Smith, Grant *The History of the Comstock Lode, 1850–1920* (1943)

Stewart, William M. *Reminiscences of Senator William M. Stewart of Nevada* (1908)

Stoutenburg, Adrien and Laura N. Baker *Snowshoe Thompson* (1957)

Strobridge, Idah M. *In Miners' Mirage Land* (1982)

Vogliotti, Gabriel R. *The Girls of Nevada* (1975)

Watson, Margaret *Silver Theater Amusements of the Mining Frontier in Early Nevada, 1850–1864* (1964)

Wheat, Margaret *Survival Arts of the Primitive Paiutes* (1968)

Wheeler, Sessions *The Desert Lake, the Story of Nevada's Pyramid Lake* (1968)
———. *The Nevada Desert* (1971)

Wilhelm, Walt *The Last Rig to Battle Mountain* (1970)

Williams, George, III *Mark Twain: His Life in Virginia City, Nevada* (1986)

Wilson, Thomas C., Advertising Agency, Reno, Nevada *Pioneer Nevada* 2 vols. (1951, 1956)

Zanjani, Sally and Guy L. Rocha *The Ignoble Conspiracy: Radicalism on Trial in Nevada* (1986)

NEW HAMPSHIRE

New Hampshire is a northern New England state, bordered on the north by Quebec, Canada; on the east by Maine and the Atlantic Ocean; on the south by Massachusetts; and on the west by the Connecticut River and Vermont.

FULL NAME State of New Hampshire
POSTAL ABBREVIATION NH
INHABITANT New Hampshirite
ADMITTED TO THE UNION June 21, 1788. 9th state
POPULATION (est. 1987) 1,057,000. Percent of US total: 0.43%. Rank: 40th

CAPITAL CITY Concord, on the Merrimack River in south central New Hampshire; population 31,000 (est. 1984). Originally known as Penacook Plantation, it was settled in 1727 and incorporated as Rumford, Massachusetts, in 1733. After years of litigation by New Hampshire, it was reincorporated there as Concord in 1765. It became a town in 1784, a city in 1853, and has been the state capital since 1808.

STATE NAME AND NICKNAMES Named by Captain John Mason for the county of Hampshire in his native England. Also known as the Granite State, the White Mountain State, the Switzerland of America, and the Mother of Rivers.

STATE SEAL The frigate *Raleigh* resting on the stocks, flying the United States flag of 1777, with a river and a granite boulder in the foreground and in the background the sun rising over the horizon of the sea. The scene is encircled by a laurel wreath. The border reads "Seal of the State of New Hampshire, 1776."

MOTTO Live Free or Die

SONGS "Old New Hampshire," lyrics by John F. Holmes, music by Maurice Hoffmann; "New Hampshire, My New Hampshire," lyrics by Julius Richelson, music by Walter P. Smith.

SYMBOLS
Flower purple lilac
Tree white birch
Bird purple finch
Animal white-tailed deer
Insect ladybug

LICENSE PLATE Dark green on white, with the legend "Live Free or Die."

FLAG On a blue field, the state seal surrounded by a border of laurel leaves and stars.

GEOGRAPHY AND CLIMATE

Narrow New Hampshire is one of the New England states, with the glacier-formed terrain typical of that section of the country. Heavily wooded mountains and hills, covering most of the state, exhibit notches carved by glaciers during the Ice Age. New Hampshire's glacial soils, overlaying granite beds, can be hundreds of feet deep, but are too stony for widespread agriculture, except in narrow bands along the Connecticut and Merrimack river valleys. Overall, New Hampshire's climate is cool, like that of its New England neighbors; the northern mountains register the state's lowest temperatures and highest snowfall.

AREA 9,279 square miles. Rank: 44th
INLAND WATER 286 square miles
GEOGRAPHIC CENTER Belknap, 3 miles E of Ashland
ELEVATIONS *Highest point:* Mount Washington, Coos County, 6,288 feet. *Lowest point:* Atlantic Ocean, sea level. *Mean elevation:* 1,000 feet

MAJOR RIVERS Connecticut, Merrimack, Androscoggin

MAJOR LAKES AND RESERVOIRS Winnipesaukee, Umbagog, Squam, Newfound, Little Sunapee

TIDAL SHORELINE 131 miles, Atlantic coast

LAND USE

	Thousands of acres
Urban (1982)	236
Rural (1982)	4,629
Cropland (1982)	158
Pastureland (1982)	125
Rangeland (1982)	0
Forestland (1982)	4,085
State parks and recreation areas (1983)	71
National park system (1984)	9
National forest system (1984)	819
Tribal lands (1984)	0

TEMPERATURES The highest recorded temperature was 106°F on July 4, 1911, at Nashua. The lowest was -46°F on January 28, 1925, at Pittsburg.

NATIONAL SITES

NATIONAL HISTORIC SITE Saint-Gaudens
NATIONAL SCENIC TRAIL Appalachian
NATIONAL WILDLIFE REFUGE Wapack

HISTORY

1603	Martin Pring is hired by English merchants to explore mouth of the Piscataqua River near present site of Portsmouth.
1605	*July 15.* French explorer, Samuel de Champlain, enters Piscataqua Bay.
1614	Captain John Smith sails along the New Hampshire coast and discovers the Isle of Shoals.
1623	First settlements are founded at Dover and at Little Harbor (now called Rye), territory originally occupied by the Indians, mainly of the Algonkian and Pennacock tribes.
1629	*November 8.* Captain John Mason receives a grant of land in the area and names it New Hampshire after the English county of Hampshire.
1634	Dover becomes site of the first church built in New Hampshire.
1640s	Religious disputes between Anglicans, Puritans, and Quakers leave communities unable to compromise on a single system of government.
1641	New Hampshire submits to jurisdiction of Massachusetts.
1647	An education act that requires towns to provide public education is passed.
1669	Portsmouth passes act which gives £60 yearly for next seven years to Harvard.
1670s	Principal means of livelihood are lumbering, trapping for furs, fishing, and shipbuilding. Social center in every town is the church. Religious toleration prevails.
1676	Major Richard Waldron betrays Indians in a peace treaty agreement to end King Philip's War. Thirteen years later, they take revenge and kill him and other Dover garrisons.
1679	New Hampshire becomes a royal province, separate from Massachusetts.

1685	Uniting with other colonies, New Hampshire becomes part of the Province of New England.
1689–1697	With stockage garrisons, communities seek safety from Indian attacks during King Williams War.
1693	New school law requires each town to provide a schoolmaster.
1734	Religious revival sweeps New Hampshire, mostly due to Congregationalist pastor Jonathan Edwards, whose sermons include "Sinners in the Hands of an Angry God."
1754–1763	French and Indian War. Indians, aided by French, are driven back to Quebec by Rogers's Rangers, famous raiders attached to the British Army.
1756	The New Hampshire *Gazette*, first newspaper in New Hampshire, is published at Portsmouth.
1768	Dartmouth College is opened at Hanover. Originally called Moor's Indian Charity School, it was first located in Connecticut about 1750.
1774	*December 11–12*. Patriots raid British Fort William and Mary in Portsmouth, taking amunition and gunpowder.
1775–1783	Revolutionary War. About 100 New Hampshire privateers help defeat the British. Three American warships are built in Portsmouth Navy Yard.
1776	Of the 13 colonies, New Hampshire is first to declare independence of Great Britain, six months before the signing of the Declaration of Independence.
1784	The state constitution is adopted.
1785	Two-party political system begins in the state.
1788	*June 21*. New Hampshire becomes the ninth state to ratify the US Constitution.
1804	New Ipswich is the site of the state's first cotton factory.
1838	First railroad is built in the state.
1847	First 10-hour day law for factory workers is enacted by New Hampshire legislature.
1853	*March 4*. Franklin Pierce (1804–1869) is inaugurated as 14th president of the United States.
1861–1865	Civil War. Approximately 39,000 men from New Hampshire join the Union forces. Fifth New Hampshire Regiment completes war services with more casualties suffered than any other regiment in the Union Army.
1870	First teachers' college is opened at Plymouth.
1871	School attendance is made compulsory.
1877	Amendment to state's constitution abolishes rule that governor, senators, and representatives be of Protestant faith.
1891	New Hampshire's Library Commission provides free public libraries with state aid.
1900	New Hampshire is now considered an industrial state. Abundant water power draws many factories.
1903	*May 1*. Ending 48 years of prohibition the state legislature agrees to provide licenses for sales of liquor.
1909	New Hampshire adopts the direct primary law.
1917–1919	*World War I*. New Hampshire supplies 20,000 men to serve in the armed forces. The state contributes $80 million to the war effort. Portsmouth busy with shipbuilding.
1919	*January 15*. The state ratifies the 18th Amendment and prohibition becomes law.
1922	WLNH, the state's first radio station, begins broadcasting from Laconia.
1930	Depression begins to be felt as some factories close and wages decrease but New Hampshire continues to advance as a recreational state.
1933	The state ratifies the 21st Amendment (repeal of prohibition).
1936	Spring floods destroy over $7 million worth of property. Works Progress Administration (WPA) and Civilian Conservation Corps (CCC) provide extensive aid to the state.
1941–1945	Under Governor Robert Blood, New Hampshire contributes men, women, and money to the war effort. Shipbuilding in Portsmouth thrives again.
1944	The United Nations International Monetary conference is held at Bretton Woods.

1954	WMUR-TV, New Hampshire's first television station, begins telecasting from Manchester.
1956	Pease Air Force Base, a link in US continental defense, is opened.
1961	The first American to travel in space is Alan B. Shepard, Jr. from East Denny in southeastern New Hampshire.
1962	*December 2.* Thorium deposits, vital to nuclear fuel, discovered in White Mountains constitute a reserve equal to nation's uranium deposits.
1966	Home rule is granted to New Hampshire cities.
1972	*May 31.* Environmental Protection Agency approves the state's clean air plans. New Hampshire ratifies the Equal Rights Amendment.
1973	*July 26.* Ruling that proper safety precautions have been taken, the Atomic Safety and Licensing Board of the Nuclear Regulatory Commission approves construction of an atomic energy plant at Seabrook.
1977	*April 30.* Two thousand demonstrators march on construction site of nuclear plant at Seabrook. State police are called in to arrest those who refuse to leave.
1978	February blizzard causes extensive damage throughout much of the state.
1981	*June 23.* Over 80% of New Hampshire's state workers call in sick adding pressure to their demands for higher salaries.
	Gypsy moths cause severe defoliation.
	August. The state gains its own public radio station.
1986	*January 28.* Sharon Christie McAuliffe, a Concord teacher, is one of seven crew members killed when the space shuttle *Challenger* explodes.
1987	The $5.2 billion Seabrook Nuclear Power plant, completed in 1986 but never put into operation because of controversy, nears testing of evacuation plans.
1988	Public Service Company of New Hampshire, a heavy investor in the Seabrook plant, files bankruptcy plea.

DEMOGRAPHY

Population (est. 1987) . . . 1,057,000
Population (1980) 920,610
Population density in persons per
  square mile (1980) 99.2

POPULATION BY RACE (1980)
American Indian/Aleut/
  Eskimo 1,352
Asian/Pacific Islander 2,929
Black 3,990
Hispanic 5,587
White 910,099
Other 2,240

POPULATION CHARACTERISTICS (1980)
Percent of state population
Urban 52.2
Rural 47.8
Under 18 . . . . 25.8
65 or older 11.7
College-educated 18.4
Families below poverty line 6.1
Public-assistance recipients 3.0

Per capita personal income
  (1986) $15,922
Millionaires per 100,000
  residents (1982) 221.5

Average life expectancy
  in years (1980) 75.0
Marriage rate per 1,000
  residents (1986) 11.4
Divorce rate per 1,000
  residents (1986) 4.6
Birth rate per 1,000
  residents (1985) 15.8
Infant mortality rate per
  1,000 births (1985) 6.8
Abortion rate per 1,000
  live births (1985) 419
Crime rate per 100,000
  residents (1985)
  Violent 139.5
  Property 3,190.5
Federal and state prisoners per
  100,000 residents (1984) 54
Alcohol consumption in gallons
  per capita (1985) 62.3
Deaths from motor vehicle accidents
  per 100,000 residents (1985) . . 18.8

MAJOR CITIES

	1984 population (est.)
Concord	31,000
Manchester	94,937
Nashua	72,458
Portsmouth	27,789

GOVERNMENT AND POLITICS

Number of US Representatives   2
Electoral votes   4

POLITICAL PARTY NOMINEES FROM STATE
  * winner

John Langdon (Democratic-Republican)	1808	VP
John Parker Hale (Free Soil)	1848	P
Franklin Pierce* (D)	1852	P
John Parker Hale (Free Soil)	1852	P
Lyndon Hermyle LaRouche Jr. (US Labor)	1976	P

PRESIDENTIAL PRIMARY ELECTION In 1988, New Hampshire sent 22 Democratic delegates and 23 Republican delegates to the national conventions.

CONSTITUTION New Hampshire has had two constitutions: 1776 and the present one, adopted in 1784.

LEGISLATURE The General Court is divided into the Senate (24 members, 2-year term, minimum age 30) and the House of Representatives (400 members, 2-year term, minimum age 18). In 1987, the salary for legislators was $200 biannually.

JUDICIARY The highest court is the Supreme Court, with 5 judges serving until they reach the age of 70. In 1987, the annual salary was $66,078.

EXECUTIVE The governor serves a 2-year term; the minimum age for holding office is 30. In 1987, the annual salary was $68,005. There are 5 other elected officials.

PRESIDENTIAL VOTE 1948-1988 *(in percents)*

Year	State Winner	Democratic	Republican
1848	Dewey (R)	46.7	52.4
1952	Eisenhower (R)	39.1	60.9
1956	Eisenhower (R)	33.8	66.1
1960	Nixon (R)	46.6	53.4
1964	Johnson (D)	63.6	36.4
1968	Nixon (R)	43.9	52.1
1972	Nixon (R)	34.9	64.0
1976	Ford (R)	43.5	54.7
1980	Reagan (R)	28.4	57.7
1984	Reagan (R)	30.9	68.6
1988	Bush (R)	37.0	63.0

GOVERNORS

Provincial Governors

John Cutt (president)	1680-1681
Richard Waldron (deputy president)	1681-1682
Edward Cranfield (lieutenant governor)	1682-1685
Walter Barefoote (deputy governor)	1685-1686
Joseph Dudley (council president)	1686-1687
Edmund Andros	1687-1689
Simon Bradstreet	1689-1692
John Usher (lieutenant governor)	1692-1697
William Partridge (lieutenant governor)	1697-1698
Samuel Allen	1698-1699
Richard Coote, 1st Earl of Bellamont	1699-1701
William Partridge (lieutenant governor)	1701-1702
Joseph Dudley	1702-1716
Samuel Shute	1716-1723
John Wentworth (lieutenant governor)	1723-1730
Jonathan Belcher	1730-1741
Benning Wentworth	1741-1767
John Wentworth	1767-1775

State Presidents

Matthew Thornton (council president)	1775-1776
Meshech Weare	1776-1785
John Langdon	1785-1786
John Sullivan	1786-1788
John Langdon	1788-1789
John Pickering (acting)	1789
John Sullivan	1789-1790
Josiah Bartlett	1790-1792

State Governors

Josiah Bartlett	1792-1794
John T. Gilman (Federalist)	1794-1805

John Langdon (Democratic-Republican)	1805-1809
Jeremiah Smith (Federalist)	1809-1810
John Langdon (D-R)	1810-1812
William Plumer (D-R)	1812-1813
John T. Gilman (Federalist)	1813-1816
William Plumer (D-R)	1816-1819
Samuel Bell (D-R)	1819-1823
Levi Woodbury (D-R)	1823-1824
David L. Morrill (D-R)	1824-1827
Benjamin Pierce (D-R)	1827-1828
John Bell (D-R)	1828-1829
Benjamin Pierce (D)	1829-1830
Matthew Harvey (D)	1830-1831
Joseph M. Harper (D/acting)	1831
Samuel Dinsmoor (D)	1831-1834
William Badger (D)	1834-1836
Isaac Hill (D)	1836-1839
John Page (D)	1839-1842
Henry Hubbard (D)	1842-1844
John H. Steele (D)	1844-1846
Anthony Colby (Whig)	1846-1847
Jared W. Williams (D)	1847-1849
Samuel Dinsmoor (D)	1849-1852
Noah Martin (D)	1852-1854
Nathaniel B. Baker (D)	1854-1855
Ralph Metcalf (Know-Nothing)	1855-1857
William Haile (R)	1857-1859
Ichabod Goodwin (R)	1859-1861
Nathaniel S. Berry (R)	1861-1863
Joseph A. Gilmore (R)	1863-1865
Frederick Smyth (R)	1865-1867
Walter Harriman (R)	1867-1869
Onslow Stearns (R)	1869-1871
Ezekiel A. Straw (R)	1872-1874
James A. Weston (D)	1874-1875
Person C. Cheney (R)	1875-1877
Benjamin F. Prescott (R)	1877-1879
Natt Head (R)	1879-1881
Charles H. Bell (R)	1881-1883
Samuel W. Hale (R)	1883-1885
Moody Currier (R)	1885-1887
Charles H. Sawyer (R)	1887-1889
David H. Goodell (R)	1889-1891
Hiram A. Tuttle (R)	1891-1893
John B. Smith (R)	1893-1895
Charles A. Busiel (R)	1895-1897
George A. Ramsdell (R)	1897-1899
Frank W. Rollins (R)	1899-1901
Chester B. Jordan (R)	1901-1903
Nahum J. Bachelder (R)	1903-1905
John McLane (R)	1905-1907
Charles M. Floyd (R)	1907-1909
Henry B. Quimby (R)	1909-1911
Robert P. Bass (R)	1911-1913
Samuel D. Felker (D)	1913-1915
Rolland H. Spaulding (R)	1915-1917
Henry W. Keyes (R)	1917-1919
John H. Bartlett (R)	1919-1921
Albert O. Brown (R)	1921-1923
Fred H. Brown (D)	1923-1925
John G. Winant (R)	1925-1927
Huntley N. Spaulding (R)	1927-1929
Charles W. Tobey (R)	1929-1931
John G. Winant (R)	1931-1935
Styles Bridges (R)	1935-1937
Francis P. Murphy (R)	1937-1941
Robert O. Blood (R)	1941-1945
Charles M. Dale (R)	1945-1949
Sherman Adams (R)	1949-1953
Hugh Gregg (R)	1953-1955
Lane Dwinell (R0	1955-1959
Wesley Powell (R0	1959-1963
John W. King (D)	1963-1969
Walter R. Peterson (R)	1969-1973
Meldrim Thomson (R)	1973-1979
Hugh Gallen (D)	1979-1983
John H. Sununu (R)	1983-1989
Judd Gregg (R)	1989-

MINIMUM AGES

Majority	18
Marriage with parental consent	
female	13
male (with judicial consent)	14
Marriage without parental consent	18
Making a will	18
Buying alcohol	21
Jury duty	18
Leaving school	16
Driver's license	16

CAPITAL PUNISHMENT
Number executed 1976-88: 0
On death row Aug. 1, 1988: 0

MILITARY INSTALLATIONS
Total number: 4
Major bases:
  Navy: 1
  Air Force: 1

FINANCES

Thousands of dollars

GENERAL REVENUE (1985)

Total general revenue	1,067,753
Total tax revenue	433,873
Sales and gross receipts	200,416
Individual income taxes	24,480
Corporate net income taxes	95,421

GENERAL EXPENDITURE (1985)

Total general expenditure	1,011,885
Education	200,806
Public welfare	185,046

Health	55,604
Hospitals	43,864
Natural resources	14,888
Highways	162,906
Police	12,161
Corrections	29,584

FEDERAL AID (1985) 419,964

ECONOMY

Because of the state's relatively small amount of arable land, New Hampshire farms produce more dairy and poultry products, especially eggs, than crops. Orchard fruits, hay, and truck vegetables are the main crops. Farm cash receipts were $114 million in 1983, third smallest in the nation that year. Granite ranks first among mining products, followed by sand and gravel, mica and feldspar, garnet and beryl. In 1982 the thriving lumber industry contributed $212 million to New Hampshire's economy, with sawn timber, paper, and pulp the main products. The fishing industry has long been in decline from its height in the 19th century, but lobsters and clams are still caught, yielding $4 million in income in 1983. Manufacturing is the main segment of the state's economy; principal manufactures include electrical and electronic equipment, paper products, leather goods, textiles and apparel, processed foods, chemicals and rubber, and furniture. A tiny shipbuilding industry survives around Portsmouth. Tourism is also an important industry, catering to hikers, skiers, and mountain climbers.

EMPLOYMENT (1984)

Thousands of persons

Total number of employed workers	498
Construction	25.5
Finance, insurance, and real estate	23.5
Government	57.5
Manufacturing	123.3
Mining	0.4
Services	90.4
Transportation, communications, and utilities	15.1
Wholesale and retail trade	104.5
Percent of civilian labor force unemployed (1984)	6.1

DEPARTMENT OF DEFENSE (1985)

Civilian workers employed	1,802
Military personnel	4,122
Contract awards	$678 million

ENERGY SOURCES FOR ELECTRIC UTILITIES (1983)

Percent

Coal	50.2
Gas	0.0
Hydroelectric	22.7
Nuclear	0.0
Petroleum	27.1

TRANSPORTATION

Motor vehicles registered in state (1986)	1,071,247
Miles of roads, streets, and highways (1986)	14,491
Miles of Class I railway operated (1986)	355
Airports (1983)	54
Major aviation hubs (1983)	0

CULTURE AND EDUCATION

Native American tribes
Before 1800, New Hampshire was home to the Ossipee, Nashua, Pennacook, Piscataqua, Squamscot, and Winnipesaukee tribes.

Religions, ethnicities, and languages
New Hampshire's first settlers were mainly of English and Scotch-Irish descent. Until 1819, each town chose an official religion from among the Congregationist, Baptist, Presbyterian, Quaker, and Anglican churches. Since then, immigration has brought an influx of Roman Catholics: one-quarter of the population today is of French Canadian descent, with other groups arriving from central and eastern Europe. There are Greek and Russian Orthodox, Jewish, and Shaker communities. In 1980, 10.4 percent of New Hampshire's population spoke a language other than English at home.

Major museums and libraries
Currier Gallery of Art, Manchester
Hopkins Center Art Gallery, Dartmouth College, Hanover

Major arts organizations
American Stage Festival
New Hampshire Symphony Orchestra, Manchester

Colleges and universities
Number public (1986-87) 12
Number private (1986-87) 16

Total enrollment, in full-time equivalent students (1985) 41,700

Public elementary and secondary schools
Expenditure per pupil in average daily attendance (1986-87) $3,682

Pupil-teacher ratio (1987) 15.9
Average teacher salary (1986-87) $22,625

Holidays
Fast Day. 4th Monday in April

NEW HAMPSHIRE IN LITERATURE

Thomas Bailey Aldrich *The Story of a Bad Boy* (1870)
Part-fictional autobiography of the poet's boyhood in Portsmouth, about which he also wrote a nonfictional study, *An Old Town by the Sea* (1893).

Brooks Atkinson and **W. Kent Olson** *New England's White Mountains: At Home in the Wild* (1978)
Writing and photography celebrating the beauty of wilderness landscape.

Ernest E. Bisbee *The White Mountain Scrapbook of Stories and Legends of the Crystal Hills or White Mountains of New Hampshire* (1939)

Alice Brown *Tiverton Tales* (1899)
Local-color stories of bucolic characters set in a fictional farming community modeled on Hampton Falls.

Stephen Burroughs *Memoirs of the Notorious Stephen Burroughs of New Hampshire* (1798, rpt. 1924)
Narrative of an eighteenth-century reprobate, containing details of contemporary manners and society.

Le Grand Cannon *Look to the Mountain* (1942)
Novel of pioneering in the White Mountains 1769–1777.

Winston Churchill *Coniston* (1906)
Historical novel about a corrupt politician set in the 1860s and '70s.

Anne Downes *The Pilgrim Soul* (1952)
Historical novel of farming in the White Mountains, 1820–1870.

Charles J. Fox *The New Hampshire Book: Being Specimens of the Literature of the Granite State* (1842)

Robert C. Gilmore (ed.) *New Hampshire Literature: A Sampler* (1981)

Donald Hall *String Too Short to Be Saved* (1961, rpt. 1988); *Seasons at Eagle Pond* (1987)
Poet's recollections of summers in boyhood, and vacations as an adult, on a New Hampshire farm.

Ernest Hebert *The Dogs of March* (1979)
Novel about the hardships of an uneducated countryman.

John Jennings *Next to Valour* (1939)
Historical romance set in 1745 during the French and Indian War.

Thomas Starr King *The White Hills: Their Legends, Landscape, and Poetry* (1860)
Essays on the beauty of the natural scene.

Oscar Laighton *Ninety Years at the Isles of Shoals* (1930)
Reminiscences by the brother of the poet Celia Thaxter.

Lorus J. Milne and **Margery Milne** *The Valley: Meadow, Grove and Stream* (1963)
Naturalists' essays on the Oyster River Valley and the tidewater estuary at Durham.

Philbrook Paine *Squarely behind the Beavers* (1963)
Essays on regional traditions and history.

Haydn S. Pearson *New England Flavor: Memories of a Country Boyhood* (1961)
Memoir of farm life at the turn of the century.

Ernest Poole *Nancy Flyer: A Stagecoach Epic* (1949)
Historical novel about the replacement of horse by rail travel. Poole also wrote two novels set in 1930s New Hampshire: *Great Winds* (1933), and *One of Us* (1934).

Thomas Raddall *The Governor's Lady* (1959)
Historical novel about John Wentworth, last royal governor of the state.

Mary Cochrane Rogers *Glimpses of an Old Social Capital* (1924)
Social life of Portsmouth during the eighteenth century seen in a selection from contemporary documents.

Lyman Rutledge *The Isles of Shoals in Lore and Legend* (1965)

Wallace Stegner *Second Growth* (1947)
Novel about summer residents of a small town.

Roger B. Swain *Earthly Pleasures: Tales from a Biologist's Garden* (1981, rpt. 1985)
Essays on a southern New Hampshire farm.

Celia Thaxter *Among the Isles of Shoals* (1873)
Prose sketches of the islands by a nineteenth-century poet.

Newton F. Tolman *North of Monadnock* (1961); *Our Loons Are Always Laughing* (1963)
Essays on regional topics.

Cornelius Weygandt *The White Hills: Mountain New Hampshire, Winnepesaukee to Washington* (1934); *New Hampshire Neighbors: Country Folks and Things in the White Hills* (1937); *November Rowen: A Late Harvest from the Hills of New Hampshire* (1941); *The Heart of New Hampshire: Things Held Dear by Folks of the Old Stocks* (1944)
Essays on regional topics.

Thomas Williams *Whipple's Castle* (1969)
Family chronicle set in a small town, 1930–1960.

GUIDES TO RESOURCES

DeLorme, David *The New Hampshire Atlas and Gazetteer* (1979)

Federal Writers' Project *New Hampshire: A Guide to the Granite State* (1938, rpt. 1975)

Hammond, Otis G. (ed. E. J. Hanrahan) *Check List of New Hampshire Local History* (1971)

Haskell, John D. and **T. D. Seymour Bassett** (eds.) *New Hampshire: A Bibliography of Its History* (1979, rpt. 1983)

Hill, Evan *The Primary State: An Historical Guide to New Hampshire* (1976)

New Hampshire Historical Society *Collections of the New Hampshire Historical Society* (1834–1939)

New Hampshire State Historical Commission *New Hampshire Historical Markers* . . . (5th ed. 1977)

New Hampshire State Library *Genealogical Sources in New Hampshire* (1987)

New Hampshire Vital Statistics (annual)

Noyes, Sybil et al. *Genealogical Dictionary of Maine and New Hampshire* (1939, rpt. 1983)

Tolles, Bryant and **Carolyn K.** *New Hampshire Architecture: An Illustrated Guide* (1979)

SELECTED NONFICTION SOURCES

Adams, Nathaniel *Annals of Portsmouth* . . . (1825, rpt. 1971)

Antevs, Ernest W. *Alpine Zone of Mt. Washington Range* (1932)

Armstrong, John B. *Factory Under the Elms, a History of Harrisville, New Hampshire* (1969)

Bartlett, Josiah (ed. Frank C. Meyers) *The Papers of Josiah Bartlett* (1979)

Belknap, Jeremy *The History of New Hampshire* 3 vols. (1813, rpt. 1973)

Blaisdell, Paul H. *Three Centuries on Winnipesaukee* (2d ed. 1936, rpt. 1975)

Blood, Grace E. *Manchester on the Merrimack* (1948)

Bowles, Ella S. *Let Me Show You New Hampshire* (1938)

Brighton, Ray *Clippers of the Port of Portsmouth and the Men Who Built Them* (1985)
———. *Port of Portsmouth and the Cotton Trade, 1783–1829* (1986)

Brown, Francis *Raymond of the Times* (1951)

Brown, William R. *Our Forest Heritage: A History of Forestry and Recreation in New Hampshire* (1956)

Burt, F. Allen *The Story of Mount Washington* (1960)

Campbell, Catherine H. *New Hampshire Scenery: A Dictionary of Nineteenth-Century Artists of New Hampshire Mountain Landscapes* (1985)

Candee, Richard M. *Atlantic Heights, a World War I Shipbuilders' Community* (1985)

Churgin, Jonah R. *From Truman to Johnson: New Hampshire's Impact on American Politics* (1972)

Cleveland, Mather *New Hampshire Fights the Civil War* (1969)

Cole, Donald B. *Jacksonian Democracy in New Hampshire, 1800–1851* (1970)

Daniell, Jere R. *Colonial New Hampshire—A History* (1981)

Federal Writers' Project *Hands That Built New Hampshire: The Story of Granite State Craftsmen Past and Present* (1940)

Folsom, Elizabeth K. *Colonial Garrisons of New Hampshire* (1937)

Fry, William *New Hampshire as a Royal Province* (1908)

Fuess, Claude M. *Daniel Webster* 2 vols. (1930)

Guyol, Phillip N. *Democracy Fights, a History of New Hampshire in World War II* (1951)

Hadley, Alice M. *Where the Winds Blow Free: Dunbarton, New Hampshire* (1976)

Hammond, Otis G. *Some Things about New Hampshire* (1930)

Hareven, Tamara K. and Randolph *Langenbach* (1978)
——— and Randolph *Amoskeag: Life and Work in an American Factory City* (1978)

Hawthorne, Nathaniel *Life of Franklin Pierce* (1852)

Hayes, John L. *A Reminiscence of the Free-Soil Movement in New Hampshire* (1885)

Hayes, Lyman S. *The Connecticut River Valley in Southern Vermont and New Hampshire* (1929)

Hill, Ralph N. *Yankee Kingdom: Vermont and New Hampshire* (1960)

Holden, Raymond P. *The Merrimack* (Rivers of America series) (1958)

Howells, John M. *The Architectural Heritage of the Piscataqua* (1937)

———. *The Architectural Heritage of the Merrimack* (1941)

Hunt, Elmer M. *New Hampshire Town Names and Whence They Came* (1971)

Jager, Ronald and Grace *New Hampshire: An Illustrated History of the Granite State* (1983)

Kalijarvi, Thorsten V. *The Government of New Hampshire* (1939)

Kilbourne, Frederick W. *Chronicles of the White Mountains* (1916)

King, Thomas S. *The White Hills: Their Legends, Landscape and Poetry* (1866)

Kingsbury, John M. *Oil and Water, the New Hampshire Story* (1975)

Kinney, Charles B. *Church and State: The Struggle for Separation in New Hampshire, 1630–1800* (1955)

Laighton, Oscar *Ninety Years at the Isles of Shoals* (1930)

Leavitt, Richard F. *Yesterday's New Hampshire* (1974)

MacDowell, Marian *The First Twenty Years of the MacDowell Colony* (1951)

Marshall, Gertrude W. *Indian Stream Republic and the Indian Stream War* (1935)

May, Ralph *Early Portsmouth History* (1926)

Mayo, Lawrence S. *John Wentworth, Governor of New Hampshire, 1767–1775* (1921)
———. *John Langdon of New Hampshire* (1937)

Monahan, Robert S. *Mount Washington Reoccupied* (1933)

Morison, Elizabeth F. and Elting E. *New Hampshire: A Bicentennial History* (States and the Nation series) (1976)

Morse, Stearns (ed.) *Lucy Crawford's History of the White Mountains* (1846, rpt. 1978)

Nichols, Roy F. *Franklin Pierce: Young Hickory of the Granite State* (2d ed. 1958)

Penrose, Charles, Jr. *They Live on a Rock in the Sea! The Isles of Shoals in Colonial Days* (1957)

Pichierri, Louis *Music in New Hampshire, 1623–1800* (1960)

Poole, Ernest *The Great White Hills of New Hampshire* (1946)

Randall, Peter E. (ed.) *New Hampshire Years of Revolution, 1774–1783* (1976)
———. *Portsmouth and the Piscataqua* (1982)
———. *Mount Washington: A Guide and Short History* (1983)

Saltonstall, William G. *Ports of Piscataqua* . . . (1941)
———. *Lewis Perry of Exeter: A Gentle Memoir* (1980)

Squires, J. Duane *The Granite State of the United States: A History of New Hampshire from 1623 to the Present* 4 vols. (1956)
———. *The Story of New Hampshire* (1964)

Stackpole, Everett S. *History of New Hampshire* (1916)

Stever, Donald W., Jr. *Seabrook and the Nuclear Regulatory Commission: The Licensing of a Nuclear Power Plant* (1980)

Thompson, Lawrance *Robert Frost: The Early Years, 1874–1915* (1966)
———. *Robert Frost: The Years of Triumph, 1915–1938* (1970)

Turner, Lynn W. *William Plumer of New Hampshire, 1759–1850* (1962)
———. *The Ninth State: New Hampshire's Formative Years* (1983)

Upton, Richard F. *Revolutionary New Hampshire* . . . (1936, rpt. 1971)

Van Deventer, David E. *The Emergence of Provincial New Hampshire, 1623–1741* (1976)

Van Diver, Bradford B. *Roadside Geology of Vermont and New Hampshire* (1987)

Vose, Arthur W. *The White Mountains: Heroes and Hamlets* (1968)

Wight, D. B. *The Androscoggin River Valley: Gateway to the White Mountains* (1968)

Wilson, Harold F. *The Hill Country of Northern New England* (1936)

Winslow, Ola E. *Portsmouth: The Life of a Town* (1966)

Winslow, Richard E., III *Portsmouth-built: Submarines of the Portsmouth Naval Shipyard* (1985)

Wright, James *The Progressive Yankees: Republican Reformers in New Hampshire, 1906–1916* (1987)

NEW JERSEY

New Jersey is a Middle Atlantic state bounded on the north by New York; on the east by the Hudson River, New York, and the Atlantic Ocean; on the south by the Atlantic Ocean and Delaware Bay; and on the west by the Delaware River and Pennsylvania.

FULL NAME State of New Jersey
POSTAL ABBREVIATION NJ
INHABITANT New Jerseyite; New Jerseyan
ADMITTED TO THE UNION Dec. 18, 1787. 3d state
POPULATION (est. 1987) 7,672,000. Percent of US total: 3.15%. Rank: 9th

CAPITAL CITY Trenton, located on the Delaware River in west central New Jersey; population 92,052 (est. 1984). A settlement known as The Falls was founded there by an English Quaker family in 1679; the town was laid out in 1714, renamed in 1721, and incorporated in 1745. It became the state capital in 1790.

STATE NAME AND NICKNAMES Named by Sir John Berkeley and Sir George Carteret after Carteret's native island of Jersey, in the English Channel. Also known as the Garden State, the Clam State, the Camden and Amboy State, the Jersey Blue State, and the Pathway of the Revolution.

STATE SEAL A heraldic shield containing three plows, supported by the Goddess of Liberty, holding the Phyrgian cap, and the Goddess Ceres, holding a cornucopia; above the shield is a visored helmet and a horse's head, below it a streamer with the state motto and the date 1776. Encircling the coat of arms is the legend "The Great Seal of the State of New Jersey."

MOTTO Liberty and Prosperity

SONG None.

SYMBOLS
Flower common meadow violet
Tree northern red oak
Bird eastern goldfinch
Animal horse
Insect honeybee

LICENSE PLATES (1) Yellow on green-blue, with an outline of the state and the legend "Garden State." (2) Blue on yellow, with the legend "Garden State."

FLAG The state coat of arms on a field of buff.

GEOGRAPHY AND CLIMATE

One of the most densely urbanized states, New Jersey also contains areas of wilderness. North of the "waistline" that divides New Jersey into northern and southern portions, meadowlands and marshes mix with forested hills. New Jersey's coast is well known for its long, sandy beaches. The foothills of the Appalachians cut across the northwestern part of New Jersey. In South Jersey, a more thinly settled agricultural area, are the Pine Barrens, a wilderness area that has so far escaped the development rapidly changing the rest of the state.

AREA 7,787 square miles. Rank: 46th
INLAND WATER 319 square miles
GEOGRAPHIC CENTER Mercer, 5 miles SE of Trenton
ELEVATIONS *Highest point:* High Point, Sussex County, 1,803 feet. *Lowest point:* Atlantic Ocean, sea level. *Mean elevation:* 250 feet

MAJOR RIVERS Raritan, Delaware, Hudson, Passaic

MAJOR LAKES AND RESERVOIRS Hopatcong, Budd, Culvers, Wanaque

TIDAL SHORELINE 1,792 miles, Atlantic coast

LAND USE

	Thousands of acres
Urban (1982)	1,163
Rural (1982)	3,342
Cropland (1982)	809
Pastureland (1982)	240
Rangeland (1982)	0
Forestland (1982)	1,848
State parks and recreation areas (1983)	290
National park system (1984)	35
National forest system (1984)	0
Tribal lands (1984)	0

TEMPERATURES The highest recorded temperature was 110°F on July 10, 1936, at Runyon. The lowest was -34°F on January 5, 1904, at River Vale.

NATIONAL SITES

NATIONAL HISTORIC SITES Edison, Pinelands National Reserve
NATIONAL HISTORICAL PARK Morristown
NATIONAL RECREATION AREA Delaware Water Gap Gateway
NATIONAL SCENIC RIVERS AND RIVERWAYS Delaware, Upper Delaware

NATIONAL SCENIC TRAIL Appalachian
NATIONAL WILDLIFE REFUGES Brigantine–Barnegat/Supawna Meadows, Cape May (proposed), Great Swamp

HISTORY

1524	Giovanni de Verrazano sails along the shore of New Jersey.
1609	Henry Hudson lands at Sandy Hook on the northern coast of New Jersey and explores the Hudson River.
1614	Dutch explorer, Cornelius Mey, explores Delaware River. Cape May is named for him.
1618	A Dutch trading post is established at Bergen (now Jersey City).
1623	The Dutch build Fort Nassau on the Delaware River near what is now Gloucester.
1629	Michael Pauw, burgomaster of Amsterdam, is granted site of present-day Jersey City. This is the first recorded land transfer.
1640	Swedish settlers purchase lands from Cape May to Raccoon Creek from the Lenni-Lenape Indians.
1642	First brewery is built at Hoboken.
1655	Under Dutch leader, Peter Stuyvesant, forces overthrow Swedish rule on the Delaware River.
1662	The first church and school are opened at Bergen.
1664	England takes New Jersey and other Dutch possessions in North America after a war between the two nations.
1672	The first Quaker meeting house is built at Shrewsbury.
1676	Earliest recorded iron foundry is established at Shrewsbury.
1682	William Penn and associates buy East Jersey.

1702	East and West Jersey are merged as a royal English colony.
1739	Weekly mail route is established and operated by post boys.
1740	Caspar Wistor builds the first glass factory in New Jersey near Salem.
1753	*September 25.* The first steam engine is imported by England to a copper mine near present-day Arlington.
1758	*October 18.* In a conference between governors and Indian chiefs, Indians, for £1,000, release all titles to New Jersey lands. The first Indian reservation in America is established. It consists of 3,000 acres in Burlington County.
1763	Sandy Hook lighthouse (now the oldest in America) is erected.
1774	*November 22.* Cargo of tea is burned at Greenwich in a protest against the British tax.
1776	*August 2.* New Jersey delegates to the Continental Congress sign the national Declaration of Independence. *November.* General George Washington retreats across New Jersey from Fort Lee. *December 26.* Washington crosses the Delaware River and leads a suprise attack on British soldiers in the Battle of Trenton.
1777	*January 4.* Washington again defeats British in the strategically successful Battle of Princeton.
1779	American forces surprise British at Paulus Hook.
1781	Washington's swift march across New Jersey leads to defeat of British at Yorktown, Virginia. The Americans and British fought nearly 100 engagements in New Jersey.
1783	*June 30.* Princeton becomes national capital until November 20. Washington writes farewell address to army at Rocky Hill.
1787	*December 18.* New Jersey is the third state to ratify the US Constitution.
1804	*July 11.* Aaron Burr kills Alexander Hamilton in a duel at Weehawken.
1811	First steam ferry operates between Hoboken and New York.
1824	On a circular track at Hoboken, John Stevens runs the first steam locomotive in the US.
1838	Samuel F. B. Morse, with the help of Alfred Vail, demonstrates his magnetic telegraph at Morristown.
1844	Reformer Dorothea Dix lobbies state legislature to build asylums and to reform the prison system.
1858	The first transatlantic cable message from Queen Victoria to President James Buchanan is received by John Wright at Trenton. The first dinosaur skeleton found in North America is unearthed at Haddonfield.
1861–1865	Civil War. State legislature appropriates $2 million for war purposes. State records show that New Jersey supplied over 88,000 men to armed forces.
1870	First boardwalk is completed in Atlantic City.
1871	Free public school system is established throughout state.
1874	Compulsory school attendance act is passed.
1876	The Standard Oil Company builds refinery at Bayonne.
1879	Thomas Alva Edison invents the incandescent electric lamp at Menlo Park.
1884	Grover Cleveland is elected president.
1898	Spanish American War. New Jersey supplies three regiments of infantry to the US Army.
1910	Woodrow Wilson is elected governor.
1912	*November 5.* Woodrow Wilson is elected President of the United States.
1917–1918	World War I. Hoboken becomes embarkation port; Camps Dix and Merritt are established as training centers.
1921	WJZ, world's second radio station, begins broadcasting in Newark.
1924	The first dirigible flight across the continent is made by the *Shenandoah* from Lakehurst to San Diego, California in four days.
1927	Holland Tunnel from Jersey City to New York is opened.
1929	The dirigible, *Graf Zeppelin*, starts and completes a 21-day around-the-world trip at Lakehurst.
1931	George Washington Bridge between Fort Lee and Manhattan is opened.
1932	Charles A. Lindbergh, Jr. is kidnapped at Hopewell.

	Amelia Earhart makes first transcontinental non-stop flight by a woman from Los Angeles to Newark.
1934	The steamship, *Morro Castle,* burns off Asbury Park; 134 die.
1936	Bruno Richard Hauptmann is executed at Trenton for murder of Lindbergh baby. Unemployed marchers occupy state capitol for nine days.
1937	German dirigible, *Hindenberg,* is destroyed by fire at Lakehurst; 36 die.
1941–1945	World War II. The state contributes important war supplies and serves as a training and embarkation center.
1947	New Jersey voters ratify a new state constitution which increases the governor's term to four years.
1952	The 118-mile New Jersey Turnpike linking Wilmington, Delaware, and New York City is opened.
1957	*May.* The Walt Whitman Bridge, spanning the Delaware River between Gloucester City and Philadelphia, Pa., is opened. It stimulates industrial growth on the New Jersey side of the river.
1963	*October 21.* All woodlands are closed and hunting season is postponed due to severe drought.
1967	*July.* Property damage of $10 million and 23 deaths result from four days of rioting in Newark.
1970	*July 22.* Ex-mayor of Newark, Hugh Addonizio, is found guilty of 64 counts of conspiracy to commit extortion.
1972	In gubernatorial election, Brendan Byrne, Democratic candidate, receives 68 percent of the votes—the greatest landslide in the state's history.
1978	*May.* Casino gambling begins in Atlantic City on Memorial Day weekend. Monthly gross for June is over $16 million.

DEMOGRAPHY

Population (est. 1987) . . . 7,672,000
Population (1980) 7,365,011
Population density in persons
   per square mile (1980) 945.8

POPULATION BY RACE (1980)
American Indian/Aleut/
   Eskimo 8,394
Asian/Pacific Islander 103,842
Black 924,786
Hispanic 491,867
White 6,127,090
Other 200,046

POPULATION CHARACTERISTICS (1980)
Percent of state population
Urban 69.3
Rural 30.7
Under 18 . . . . 27.0
65 or older 11.7
College-educated 18.6
Families below poverty line 7.6
Public-assistance recipients 7.4

Per capita personal income
   (1986) $18,284
Millionaires per 100,000
   residents (1982) 111.7
Average life expectancy
   in years (1980) 74.0

Marriage rate per 1,000
   residents (1986) 8.0
Divorce rate per 1,000
   residents (1986) 3.7
Birth rate per 1,000
   residents (1985) 13.7
Infant mortality rate per
   1,000 births (1985) 10.8
Abortion rate per 1,000
   live births (1985) 672
Crime rate per 100,000
   residents (1985)
     Violent 572.5
     Property 4,668.8
Federal and state prisoners per
   100,000 residents (1984) 135
Alcohol consumption in gallons
   per capita (1985) 38.3
Deaths from motor vehicle accidents
   per 100,000 residents (1985) . . 12.7

MAJOR CITIES

	1984 population (est.)
Camden	82,537
Elizabeth	107,455
Jersey City	223,004
Newark	314,387
Paterson	138,818
Trenton	92,052
Vineland	53,151

GOVERNMENT AND POLITICS

Number of US Representatives 14
Electoral votes 16

POLITICAL PARTY NOMINEES FROM STATE
  * winner

Richard Stockton (Whig faction)	1820	VP
Theodore Frelinghuysen (Whig)	1844	VP
Winfield Scott (Whig)	1852	P
William Lewis Dayton (R)	1856	VP
Clinton Bowen Fisk (Prohibition)	1888	P
Garret Augustus Hobart* (R)	1896	VP
Matthew Maguire (Socialist Labor)	1896	VP
Woodrow Wilson* (D)	1912	P
Woodrow Wilson* (D)	1916	P
George Ross Kirkpatrick (Socialist)	1916	VP
William J. Wallace (Commonwealth Land)	1924	P
Henry B. Krajewski (Poor Man's)	1952	P
Frank Jenkins (Poor Man's)	1952	VP
Henry B. Krajewski (American Third)	1956	P
Ann Marie Yezo (American Third)	1956	VP
Paul Benjamin Boutelle (Socialist Workers)	1968	VP
Christian Larson (American Independent-NJ)	1976	P
Edmund Otto Matzal (American Independent-NJ)	1976	VP
Jules Levin (Socialist Labor)	1976	P
Carroll Driscoll (independent)	1980	VP
Deirdre Griswold (Workers World)	1980	P
Larry Holmes (Workers World)	1980	VP
Andrea Gonzalez (Socialist Workers)	1984	VP
Dennis L. Serrette (Independent Alliance)	1984	P

PRESIDENTIAL PRIMARY ELECTION In 1988, New Jersey sent 118 Democratic delegates and 64 Republican delegates to the national conventions.

CONSTITUTION New Jersey has had three constitutions: 1776, 1844, and the present one, adopted in 1947.

LEGISLATURE The Legislature is divided into the Senate (40 members serving staggered terms of four and two years, minimum age 30) and the General Assembly (80 members, 2-year term, minimum age 21). In 1987, the annual salary was $25,000.

JUDICIARY The highest court is the Supreme Court, with 7 judges serving initial 7-year terms (if reappointed, they serve until they reach the age of 70). In 1987, the annual salary was $93,000.

EXECUTIVE The governor serves a 4-year term; the minimum age for holding office is 30. In 1987, the annual salary was $85,000. There are no other statewide elected officials.

PRESIDENTIAL VOTE 1948-1988 *(in percents)*

Year	State Winner	Democratic	Republican
1948	Dewey (R)	45.9	50.3
1952	Eisenhower (R)	42.0	56.8
1956	Eisenhower (R)	34.2	64.7
1960	Kennedy (D)	50.0	49.2
1964	Johnson (D)	65.6	33.9
1968	Nixon (R)	44.0	46.1
1972	Nixon (R)	36.8	61.6
1976	Ford (R)	47.9	50.1
1980	Reagan (R)	38.6	52.0
1984	Reagan (R)	39.2	60.1
1988	Bush (R)	43.0	57.0

GOVERNORS

(For the governors of New Netherland, 1624–1664, see the directors of the West India Company under New York. For the governors of New Sweden, 1640–1655, see Pennsylvania.)

Proprietary Governors of East New Jersey

Philip Carteret	1665-1673
temporary Dutch rule	1673-1674
Philip Carteret	1674-1682
Robert Barclay	1682-1688

Proprietary Governors of West New Jersey

Edward Byllinge	1680-1685
John Skene (deputy)	1685-1687
Daniel Coxe	1687-1688

Dominion of New England

Sir Edmund Andros (governor-general)	1688-1692

Proprietary Governors

Andrew Hamilton	1692-1698
Jeremiah Basse	1698-1699
Andrew Hamilton	1699-1703

Royal Government

Edward Hyde, Viscount Cornbury	1703-1708
John Lovelace, 4th Baron Lovelace	1708-1709
Richard Ingoldsby (lieutenant governor)	1709-1710
William Pinhorne (council president)	1710
Robert Hunter	1710-1719
Lewis Morris (council president)	1719-1720
William Burnet	1720-1728
John Montgomerie	1728-1730
Lewis Morris (council president)	1730-1732
William Cosby	1732-1736
John Anderson (council president)	1736
John Hamilton (council president)	1736-1738
Lewis Morris	1738-1746
John Hamilton (council president)	1746-1747
John Reading (council president)	1747
Jonathan Belcher	1747-1757
John Reading (council president)	1757
Thomas Pownall (lieutenant governor)	1757
John Reading (acting governor)	1757-1758
Francis Bernard	1758-1760
Thomas Boone	1760-1761
Josiah Hardy	1761-1763
William Franklin	1763-1776

State Governors

William Livingston (Federalist)	1776-1790
William Paterson (Federalist)	1790-1792
Richard Howell (Federalist)	1792-1801

Joseph Bloomfield (Democratic-Republican)	1801-1802
John Lambert (D-R/acting)	1802-1803
John Bloomfield (D-R)	1803-1812
Aaron Ogden (Federalist)	1812-1813
William S. Pennington (D-R)	1813-1815
Mahlon Dickerson (D-R)	1815-1817
Isaac H. Williamson (Federalist)	1817-1829
Garret D. Wall (D)	1829
Peter D. Vroom (D)	1829-1832
Samuel L. Southard (Whig)	1832-1833
Elias P. Seeley (Whig)	1833
Peter D. Vroom (D)	1833-1836
Philemon Dickerson (D)	1836-1837
William Pennington (Whig)	1837-1843
Daniel Haines (D)	1843-1844
Charles C. Stratton (Whig)	1845-1848
Danile Haines (D)	1848-1851
George F. Fort (D)	1851-1854
Rodman M. Price (D)	1854-1857
William A. Newell (R)	1857-1860
Charles S. Olden (R)	1860-1863
Joel Parker (D)	1863-1866
Marcus L. Ward (R)	1866-1869
Theodore F. Randolph (D)	1869-1872
Joel Parker (D)	1872-1875
Joseph D. Bedle (D)	1875-1878
George B. McClellan (D)	1878-1881
George C. Ludlow (D)	1881-1884
Leon Abbett (D)	1884-1887
Robert S. Green (D)	1887-1890
Leon Abbett (D)	1890-1893
George T. Werts (D)	1893-1896
John W. Griggs (R)	1896-1898
Foster M. Voorhees (R/acting)	1898
David O. Watkins (R/acting)	1898-1899
Foster M. Voorhees (R)	1899-1902
Franklin Murphy (R)	1902-1905
Edward C. Stokes (R)	1905-1908
John Franklin Fort (R)	1908-1911
Woodrow Wilson (D)	1911-1913
James F. Fielder (D/acting)	1913
Leon R. Taylor (D/acting)	1913-1914
James F. Fielder (D)	1914-1917
Walter E. Edge (R)	1917-1919
William N. Runyon (R/acting)	1919-1920
Clarence E. Case (R/acting)	1920
Edward I. Edwards (D)	1920-1923
George S. Silzer (D)	1923-1926
A. Harry Moore (D)	1926-1929
Morgan F. Larson (R)	1929-1932
A. Harry Moore (D)	1932-1935
Clifford R. Powell (R/acting)	1935

Horace G. Prall (R/acting)	1935
Harold G. Hoffman (R)	1935-1938
A. Harry Moore (D)	1938-1941
Charles Edison (D)	1941-1944
Walter E. Edge (R)	1944-1947
Alfred E. Driscoll (R)	1947-1954
Robert B. Meyner (D)	1954-1962
Richard J. Hughes (D)	1962-1970
William T. Cahill (R)	1970-1974
Brendan T. Byrne (D)	1974-1982
Thomas H. Kean (R)	1982-

MINIMUM AGES

Majority	18
Marriage with parental consent	16
(younger with judicial consent)	
Marriage without parental consent	18
Making a will	18
Buying alcohol	21
Jury duty	18
Leaving school	16
Driver's license	17

CAPITAL PUNISHMENT
Number executed 1976-88: 0
On death row Aug. 1, 1988: 28

MILITARY INSTALLATIONS
Total number: 15
Major bases:
Army: 3
Air Force: 1

FINANCES

Thousands of dollars

GENERAL REVENUE (1985)

Total general revenue	13,244,732
Total tax revenue	7,718,790
Sales and gross receipts	4,056,410
Individual income taxes	1,937,007
Corporate net income taxes	923,166

GENERAL EXPENDITURE (1985)

Total general expenditure	11,858,056
Education	3,472,447
Public welfare	2,127,951
Health	267,762
Hospitals	517,713
Natural resources	107,716
Highways	952,203
Police	156,954
Corrections	265,095

FEDERAL AID (1985) | 2,945,210

ECONOMY

Service industries, including finance, insurance, construction, real estate, retailing, utilities, and government, are more important to New Jersey's economy than manufacturing or agriculture, employing nearly half the labor force and growing rapidly in size as the state population increases. In agriculture, Garden State crops include truck vegetables (especially tomatoes and lettuce), orchard fruits, berries, potatoes, ornamentals, hay, and nearly every other edible plant. Dairy products are also important to the state economy. Farm cash receipts were $543 million in 1983, but the number and size of farms is rapidly declining because of development. Mining products include basalt, granite, limestone, iron, zinc, greensand marl, sand, gravel, and clay. Manufactured products are petrochemicals and plastics, computers, electronic and high-tech equipment, bioengineered products, pharmaceuticals, large and small machinery, paper products, printing and publishing, and ceramics, among many others.

EMPLOYMENT (1984)

Thousands of persons

Total number of employed workers	3,592
Construction	132.6
Finance, insurance, and real estate	182.8
Government	525.3
Mining	2.2
Manufacturing	729.4
Services	754.7
Transportation, communications, and utilities	215.9
Wholesale and retail trade	795.9
Percent of civilian labor force unemployed (1984)	6.2

DEPARTMENT OF DEFENSE (1985)

Civilian workers employed	28,961
Military personnel	18,974
Contract awards	$3.862 billion

ENERGY SOURCES FOR ELECTRIC UTILITIES (1983)

Percent

Coal	28.7
Gas	31.7
Hydroelectric*	-0.8
Nuclear	23.2
Petroleum	17.3

* Energy expended for storage exceeded energy produced.

TRANSPORTATION
Motor vehicles registered
in state (1986) 5,267,489
Miles of roads, streets,
and highways (1986) 34,040
Miles of Class I railway
operated (1986) 1,194

Airports (1983) 291
Major aviation hubs (1983) 2
Largest hub: Newark
Major ports, with gross tonnage in
thousands (1985):
Paulsboro 16,101

CULTURE AND EDUCATION

Native American tribes
New Jersey was formerly the home of the
Brotherton and Delaware tribes.

Religions, ethnicities, and languages
New Jersey's first settlers were Dutch and
Swedish farmers and religious refugees
(including Quakers, Baptists, and Puritans) from the New England states. Since
then the state has taken in successive
waves of immigrants, first from northern
Europe and the British Isles, then from
central, eastern, and southern Europe,
Puerto Rico, the black communities of the
American South, Latin America, and most
recently from Southeast Asia. Italians are
presently the largest ethnic group. In 1980,
15.9 percent of New Jersey's population
spoke a language other than English at
home. The state is religiously heterogeneous as well, with most Christian denominations represented, and many Jewish
congregations in the urban and suburban
areas.

Major museums and libraries
Montclair Art Museum
Museum of Art, Princeton University,
Princeton
New Jersey State Museum, Princeton

Major arts organizations
McCarter Theatre Company, Princeton
New Jersey Ballet Company, West
Orange
New Jersey State Opera, Newark
New Jersey Symphony Orchestra,
Newark
Paper Mill Playhouse, Millburn

Colleges and universities
Number public (1986-87) 31
Number private (1986-87) 30
Total enrollment, in full-time equivalent
students (1985) 201,300

Public elementary and secondary schools
Expenditure per pupil in average daily
attendance (1986-87) $6,177
Pupil-teacher ratio (1987) 14.7
Average teacher salary (1986-87) $30,770

Major league sports teams
Basketball: New Jersey Nets
Football: New Jersey Giants
Hockey: New Jersey Devils

Holidays
State Fair. September

NEW JERSEY IN LITERATURE

Henry Charlton Beck *A New Jersey Reader* (1961)
An anthology of stories, both fictional and historical,
relating to the history and folklore of the state. Beck, a
journalist, has also published *Fare to Midlands: Forgotten
Towns of Central New Jersey* (1939), *The Roads of Home: Lanes
and Legends of New Jersey* (1956), and *The Jersey Midlands*
(1962, rpt. 1984).

David S. Cohen *The Folklore and Folklife of New Jersey* (1983)

Jessie Redmon Fauset *Chinaberry Tree* (1931)
Novel about black community life in a small village.

Federal Writers' Project *Stories of New Jersey* (1938, rpt.
1972)

Thomas Fleming *Liberty Tavern* (1976)
Historical novel of the Revolution centering on a New
Jersey tavern.

Amelia M. Gummere (ed.) *The Journal and Essays of John
Woolman* (1922)
The collected writings of Woolman (1720–1772), a Mount
Holly tailor who became a Quaker and abolitionist preacher
in 1743, constitute a detailed record of the social conditions
of his time.

Herbert Halpert *Folktales and Legends from the New Jersey
Pines* 2 vols. (Ph.D. diss., Indiana Univ. 1947)

Bret Harte *Thankful Blossom* (1877)
Romantic tale of a Morristown woman and her suitor.

Nathan C. Heard *Howard Street* (1968)
Life in the Newark ghetto.

Albert Edward Idell *Rogers' Folly* (1957)
Historical novel set in 1844 concerning the adventures of an
exiled family of European aristocrats.

Bruce Lancaster *Trumpet to Arms* (1944)
Novel of the Revolution, with accounts of the battles of
Trenton and Princeton.

Josephine Lawrence *If I Have Four Apples* (1935)
Realistic novel of lower-middle-class life in Newark, the
author's birthplace.

Mark E. Lender and **James K. Martin** (eds.) *Citizen Soldier:
The Revolutionary War Journal of Joseph Bloomfield* (New
Jersey Historical Society) (1982)

James F. McCloy and Ray Miller, Jr. *The Jersey Devil* (1976)
An account of a legend of the Pine Barrens from the 1730s to its last reported sighting in 1966.

John A. McPhee *The Pine Barrens* (1968)
An account of the land, people, and folklore of the region.

Andrew D. Mellick *The Story of an Old Farm* (1889, rpt. 1948 as *Lesser Crossroads*)
Historical account of the Raritan area.

Rita Zorn Moonsammy, David Steven Cohen, and Lorraine E. Williams (eds.) *Pinelands Folklife* (1987)

Prentice Mulford *The Swamp Angel* (1888)
A California journalist's Thoreau-like retirement to a woodland region in the 1880s.

Lawrence Perry *Old First* (1931)
Romantic novel set in Brookfield in the 1870s.

Charles D. Platt *Ballads of New Jersey in the Revolution* (1972)
The state's participation in the Revolution traced through ballads.

Philip Roth *Goodbye, Columbus, and Five Short Stories* (1959)
The title novella concerns an illicit liaison between a Newark boy, closely modelled on Roth himself, and a Radcliffe student.

Francis Hopkinson Smith *The Tides of Barnegat* (1906)
Story of a fishing community.

Samuel Smith *The History of the Colony of Nova-Caesaria, or New Jersey . . . to the Year 1721* (1765)
History of the state by a public official, particularly valuable for its account of the seventeenth century.

Frank R. Stockton *Stories of New Jersey* (1987)

A. M. Sullivan *Songs of the Musconetcong and Other Poems of New Jersey* (1968)
A collection of ballads and poems of historical interest, mostly written along the Musconetcong River.

Horace Traubel *With Walt Whitman in Camden* 3 vols. (1906–1914)
Conversations with the poet 1888–1889.

Cornelius Weygandt *Down Jersey* (1940)
Essays on the folklore and traditions of southern Jersey.

William Carlos Williams *Life along the Passaic River* (1938)
Sketches of life in Paterson, where the poet spent much of his life practicing medicine in a working-class immigrant community.
———. *The Build Up* (1952)
The third volume in a trilogy also comprising *White Mule* (1937) and *In the Money* (1940) that relates the life of a German immigrant printer 1900–1914.

GUIDES TO RESOURCES

Barker, Bette (comp.) *Guide to Family History Sources in the New Jersey State Archives* (1988)

Bassett, William B. *Historic American Buildings Survey of New Jersey* (1977)

Bergman, Edward F. and Thomas Pohl *A Geography of the New York Metropolitan Region* (1975)

Brush, John E. *The Population of New Jersey* (2d ed. 1958)

Burr, Nelson R. *A Narrative and Descriptive Bibliography of New Jersey* (1964)

Center for the Analysis of Public Issues *New Jersey Political Almanac* (annual, 1980–   )

Cohen, David *Folklife in New Jersey: An Annotated Bibliography* (1982)
———. *New Jersey Ethnic History: A Bibliography* (1986)

Federal Writers' Project *New Jersey: A Guide to Its Present and Past* (1939, rpt. 1977)

Garwood, Alfred N. *New Jersey Economic Almanac* (1983)

Grele, Ronald (comp.) *Oral History in New Jersey: A Directory* (New Jersey Historical Commission) (1979)

Kehoe, Helen A. *New Jersey and the Writing of the U. S. Constitution: The Signers. A Bibliography* (1987)

Murrin, Mary R. (comp.) *New Jersey Historical Manuscripts: A Guide to Collections in the State* (1987)

New Jersey Department of Transportation *New Jersey Local Names: Municipalities and Counties* (rev. ed. 1982)

Skemer, Don C. and Robert C. Morris *Guide to the Manuscript Collections of the New Jersey Historical Society* (1979)

Starr, Dennis J. *The Italians of New Jersey: A Historical Introduction and Bibliography* (1985)

Statistical Almanac—New Jersey: A Compilation of Key New Jersey Facts and Figures (1981)

Waldron, Richard (comp.) *Historical Organizations in New Jersey: A Directory* (1977)

SELECTED NONFICTION SOURCES

Archdeacon, Thomas J. *New Jersey Society in the Revolutionary Era* (New Jersey Historical Commission) (1975)

Ashby, William M. *Tales without Hate* (1980)

Bebout, John E. and Ronald G. Grele *Where Cities Meet: The Urbanization of New Jersey* (1964)

Beck, Henry C. *Jersey Genesis: The Story of the Mullica River* (1963)

Blum, John M. *Joe Tumulty and the Wilson Era* (1951)

Carey, George W. *New York–New Jersey: A Vignette of the Metropolitan Region* (1975)

Conners, Richard J. *The Constitution of 1776* (New Jersey Historical Commission) (1975)

Cooley, Henry S. *A Study of Slavery in New Jersey* (1896)

Cranmer, H. Jerome *New Jersey in the Automobile Age: A History of Transportation* (1964)

Craven, Wesley F. *New Jersey and the English Colonization of North America* (New Jersey Historical series) (1964)

Cudahy, Brian J. *Rails under the Mighty Hudson: The Story of the Hudson Tubes, the Pennsy Tunnels and Manhattan Transfer* (1975)

Cunningham, Barbara (ed.) *The New Jersey Ethnic Experience* (1977)

Cunningham, John T. *Made in New Jersey: The Industrial Story of a State* (1954)
———. *Garden State: The Story of Agriculture in New Jersey* (1955)
———. *The New Jersey Shore* (1958)
———. *New Jersey: America's Main Road* (1976)
———. *Newark* (1966)
———. *New Jersey's Five Who Signed* (New Jersey Historical Commission) (1975)
———. *This Is New Jersey, from High Point to Cape May* (3 ed. 1978)

Duke, Harry *Neutral Territory* (1977)

Dwyer, William M. *The Day Is Ours: November 1776–January 1777: An Inside View of the Battles of Trenton and Princeton* (1983)

Edge, Walter E. *A Jerseyman's Journal; Fifty Years of American Business and Politics* (1948, rpt. 1972)

Federal Writers' Project *Entertaining a Nation: The Career of Long Branch* (1940)

Fee, Walter R. *The Transition from Aristocracy to Democracy in New Jersey, 1789–1829* (1933)

Fisher, Edgar J. *New Jersey as a Royal Province, 1738–1776* (History, Economics, and Public Law series) (1911)

Fleming, Thomas *The Forgotten Victory: The Battle of Spring-field, New Jersey—1780* (1973)
———. *New Jersey: A Bicentennial History* (States and the Nation series) (1977)

Funnel, Charles *By the Beautiful Sea: The Rise and High Times of That Great American Resort, Atlantic City* (1975)

Gerlach, Larry R. *The Road to Revolution* (New Jersey Historical Commission) (1975)
———. *Prologue to Independence: New Jersey in the Coming of the American Revolution* (1976)

Gilman, Malcolm C. *Blazing Star: A Documentary Account of a Small Privateer during the American Revolution* (1974)

Hammond, Cleon E. *John Hart: The Biography of a Signer of the Declaration of Independence* (1977)

Harper, Robert W. *John Fenwick and Salem County in the Province of West Jersey, 1609–1750* (1978)

Hayden, Thomas *Rebellion in Newark; Official Violence and Ghetto Response* (1967)

Heston, Alfred M. *South Jersey: A History, 1664–1924* 4 vols. (1924)

Hixson, Richard F. *The Press in Revolutionary New Jersey* (New Jersey Historical Commission) (1975)

Johnson, Virgil S. *Millville Glass: The Early Days* (1971)

Jones, E. Alfred *The Loyalists of New Jersey* (New Jersey Historical Society Collections, Vol. 10) (1927)

Kalata, Barbara N. *A Hundred Years, a Hundred Miles: New Jersey's Morris Canal* (1983)

Kemmerer, Donald L. *Path to Freedom: The Struggle for Self-Government in Colonial New Jersey* (Princeton History of New Jersey series) (1940)

Knapp, C. M. *New Jersey Politics during the Period of the Civil War and Reconstruction* (1924)

Koedel, R. Craig *South Jersey Heritage: A Social, Economic, and Cultural History* (1977)

Kraft, Bayard R. *Under Barnegat's Beam: Light on Happenings along the Jersey Shore* (1960)

Kull, Irving S. (ed.) *New Jersey: A History* 6 vols. (1930–1932)

Kunstler, William M. *The Minister and the Choir Singer: The Hall-Mills Murder Case* (1964)

Landsman, Ned C. *Scotland and Its First American Colony, 1683–1765* (1985)

Lane, Wheaton J. *From Indian Trail to Iron Horse: Travel and Transportation in New Jersey, 1620–1860* (1939)

Lee, Francis B. (ed.) *New Jersey as a Colony and as a State . . .* 4 vols. (1902)

Lee, James *The Morris Canal: A Photographic History* (1974)
———. *Tales the Boatmen Told* (1977)

Leiby, Adrian C. *The Revolutionary War in the Hackensack Valley* (1962)
———. *The Early Dutch and Swedish Settlers of New Jersey* (1964)

Lender, Mark E. *The New Jersey Soldier* (New Jersey Historical Commission) (1975)

Levitt, James H. *New Jersey's Revolutionary Economy* (New Jersey Historical Commission) (1975)
———. *For Want of Trade: Shipping and the New Jersey Ports, 1680–1783* (Collections of the New Jersey Historical Society, vol. 17) (1981)

Link, Arthur F. *Wilson: The Road to the White House* (1947)

Lundin, Leonard *Cockpit of the Revolution: The War for Independence in New Jersey* (1940)

Mahon, Gigi *The Company That Bought the Boardwalk: A Reporter's Story of How Resorts International Came to Atlantic City* (1980)

McCormick, Richard P. *Experiment in Independence: New Jersey in the Critical Period, 1781–1789* (1950)
———. *The History of Voting in New Jersey* (1953)
———. *New Jersey from Colony to State, 1609–1789* (New Jersey Historical series) (1964)

McMahon, William *South Jersey Towns: History and Legend* (1973)

Munn, David C. *Battles and Skirmishes of the American Revolution in New Jersey* (1976)

Murphy, Paul L. (ed.) *The Passaic Textile Strike of 1926* (1974)

Murrin, Mary R. *To Save This State from Ruin: New Jersey and the Creation of the United States Constitution, 1776–1789* (1987)

Myers, William S. (ed.) *The Story of New Jersey* (1945)

Nelson, William (ed.) *New Jersey Coast in Three Centuries* 3 vols. (1902)

New Jersey Department of Transportation *The Development of Transportation in New Jersey: A Brief History* (1975)

Noble, Ranson E. *New Jersey Progressivism before Wilson* (1946)

Norwood, Christopher *About Paterson; the Making and Unmaking of an American City* (1974)

Owen, Lewis F. *The Revolutionary Struggle in New Jersey, 1776–1783* (New Jersey Historical Commission) (1975)

Pierce, Arthur D. *Iron in the Pines: The Story of New Jersey's Ghost Towns and Bog Iron* (1957)
———. *Smugglers' Woods: Jaunts and Journeys in Colonial and Revolutionary New Jersey* (1960)

Pierce, John R. and Arthur G. Tressler *The Research State: A History of Science in New Jersey* (New Jersey Historical series) (1964)

Pingeon, Frances D. *Blacks in the Revolutionary Era* (New Jersey Historical Commission) (1975)

Pomfret, John E. *The Province of West New Jersey: 1609–1702* (1956)
———. *The Province of East New Jersey: 1609–1702* (1962)
———. *The New Jersey Proprietors and Their Lands: 1664–1776* (1964)
———. *Colonial New Jersey: A History* (1973)

Porambo, Ron *No Cause for Indictment; an Autopsy of Newark* (1971)

Prince, Carl E. *New Jersey's Jeffersonian Republicans: The Genesis of an Early Party Machine, 1789–1817* (1967)
———. *William Livingston, New Jersey's First Governor* (1975)

Purvis, Thomas L. *Proprietors, Patronage, and Paper Money: Legislative Politics in New Jersey, 1703–1776* (1986)

Radko, Thomas (ed.) *Discovering New Jersey* (1982)

Regis, Edward *Who Got Einstein's Office?: Eccentricity and Genius at the Institute for Advanced Study* (1987)

Resnick, Abraham *New Jersey: Its People and Culture* (1974)

Rosskam, Edwin *Roosevelt, New Jersey: Big Dreams in a Small Town and What Time Did to Them* (1972)

Ryan, Dennis P. *New Jersey in the American Revolution, 1763–1783: A Chronology* (1974)

Schmidt, George P. *Princeton and Rutgers: The Two Colonial Colleges of New Jersey* (1964)

Schmidt, Hubert G. *Agriculture in New Jersey: A Three-Hundred-Year History* (1973)

Schonbach, Morris *Radicals and Visionaries: A History of Dissent in New Jersey* (New Jersey Historical series) (1964)

Schwartz, Helen *The New Jersey House* (1983)

Scranton, Philip B. (ed.) *Silk City: Studies on the Paterson Silk Industry, 1860–1940* (Collections of the New Jersey Historical Society, vol. 19) (1985)

Singh, Harbans *Paterson and Its Neighboring Communities* (1975)

Sinton, John W. (ed.) *Natural and Cultural Resources of the New Jersey Pine Barrens* (1979)

Spehr, Paul C. *The Movies Begin: Making Movies in New Jersey, 1887–1920* (1977)

Stellhorn, Paul A. (ed.) *The Governors of New Jersey, 1664–1974: Biographical Essays* (1982)

Sternlieb, George and James W. Hughes *The Atlantic City Gamble* (1983)

Stryker, William S. *The Battle of Monmouth* (1927)

Tanner, Edwin P. *The Province of New Jersey, 1664–1738* (1908)

Thomas, George E. and Carl Doebley *Cape May, Queen of the Seaside Resorts: Its History and Architecture* (1976)

Thorpe, Willard (ed.) *The Lives of Eighteen from Princeton* (1946)

Trenton Historical Society *A History of Trenton, 1679–1929* 2 vols. (1929)

Troy, Leo *Organized Labor in New Jersey* (1965)

Turp, Ralph K. *West Jersey under Four Flags* (1975)

Urquhart, F. J. *History of the City of Newark, New Jersey, 1666–1913* 3 vols. (1913)

Van Hoesen, Walter Hamilton *Crafts and Craftsmen of New Jersey* (1973)

Vecoli, Rudolph *The People of New Jersey* (1965)

Veit, Richard *The Old Canals of New Jersey: A Historical Geography* (1963)

Wacker, Peter O. *The Musconetcong Valley of New Jersey* (1968)
———. *Land and People: A Cultural Geography of Preindustrial New Jersey. Origins and Settlement Patterns* (1975)

Widmer, Kemble *The Geology and Geography of New Jersey* (1964)

Wills, Weymer J. *Historic Houses of New Jersey* (1902)

Wilson, Harold F. *The Story of the New Jersey Shore* (1964)

Wood, Gertrude S. *William Paterson of New Jersey* (1933)

Wright, William C. (ed.) *Urban New Jersey since 1870* (1975)

NEW MEXICO

New Mexico is a southwestern Mountain state. It is bordered on the north by Colorado; on the east by Oklahoma and Texas; on the south by Texas and the Mexican states of Chihuahua and Sonora; and on the west by Arizona.

FULL NAME State of New Mexico
POSTAL ABBREVIATION NM
INHABITANT New Mexican
ADMITTED TO THE UNION Jan. 6, 1912.
47th state
POPULATION (est. 1987) 1,500,000.
Percent of US total: 0.62%. Rank: 37th

CAPITAL CITY Santa Fe, located on the Santa Fe River in north central New Mexico; population 52,274 (est. 1984). The oldest capital in the United States, Santa Fe was founded in 1610 under the name Villa Real de la Santa Fe de San Francisco de Asis (Royal City of the Holy Faith of St. Francis of Assisi). In the 1820s it was the western terminus of the Santa Fe Trail. It became the territorial capital in 1851.

STATE NAME AND NICKNAMES From the Aztec word *mexico*, "place of [the god] Mexitli"; the area was named Nuevo Mexico in the 16th century. Also known as the Cactus State, the Spanish State, the Sunshine State, and the Land of Enchantment.

STATE SEAL The coat of arms consists of an American eagle, with arrows in its talons, shielding with its wing a Mexican eagle standing on a cactus and eating a snake (a Mexican national symbol derived from Aztec mythology); below them is a streamer with the state motto. Around the border is the legend "Great Seal of the State of New Mexico, 1912."

MOTTO Crescit Eundo (It grows as it goes)

SONGS "O, Fair New Mexico," lyrics and music by Elizabeth Garrett; "Asi Es Nuevo Mejico," by Amadeo Lucero.

SYMBOLS
Flower yucca flower
Tree nut pine (pinon)
Bird chaparral bird (roadrunner)
Gem turquoise
Animal New Mexico black bear
Fish New Mexico cutthroat trout
Fossil coelophysis
Vegetable pinto bean and the chili
Grass blue grama grass

LICENSE PLATES (1) Red on orange, with the state sun symbol and the legend "Land of Enchantment," some bearing city name. (2) Red on white, with the sun symbol, the legend "Land of Enchantment," and the city name. (3) Red on white with red border, with the sun symbol and the legend "Land of Enchantment."

FLAG The ancient Zia sun symbol, a red circle with four rays pointing in each of the four directions, on a yellow field.

GEOGRAPHY AND CLIMATE

The Great Plains, the Rocky Mountains, and high-plateau grasslands define the eastern, central, and western thirds of New Mexico. The state contains extremes of terrain, including several peaks over 12,000 feet, deep river canyons, such as those carved by the Canadian River in the northeastern corner, and impressive caverns (notably Carlsbad Caverns National Park, in the southwest). Climate and rainfall vary greatly with altitude; the mountain regions receive the most precipitation, while the western plateaus may have only a few inches of rain per year.

AREA 121,593 square miles. Rank: 5th
INLAND WATER 258 square miles
GEOGRAPHIC CENTER Torrance, 12 miles SSW of Willard
ELEVATIONS *Highest point:* Wheeler Peak, Taos County, 13,161 feet. *Lowest point:* Red Bluff Reservation, Eddy County, 2,817 feet. *Mean elevation:* 5,700 feet

MAJOR RIVERS Rio Grande, San Juan, Pecos, Canadian

MAJOR LAKES AND RESERVOIRS Santa Rosa, Conchas, Navajo, Elephant Butte

LAND USE

	Thousands of acres
Urban (1982)	267
Rural (1982)	50,535
Cropland (1982)	2,413
Pastureland (1982)	163
Rangeland (1982)	40,982
Forestland (1982)	4,734
State parks and recreation areas (1983)	109
National park system (1984)	250
National forest system (1984)	10,384
Tribal lands (1984)	6,992

TEMPERATURES The highest recorded temperature was 116°F on July 14, 1936, at Orogrande. The lowest was -50°F on February 1, 1951, at Gavilan.

NATIONAL SITES

NATIONAL HISTORICAL PARK Chaco Culture
NATIONAL MONUMENTS Aztec Ruins, Bandelier, Capulin Mountain, El Morro, Fort Union, Gila Cliff Dwellings, Pecos, Salinas, White Sands
NATIONAL PARK Carlsbad Caverns
NATIONAL WILDLIFE REFUGES Bitter Lake, Bosque del Apache, Grulla, Las Vegas, Maxwell, Sevilleta

HISTORY

1534	Shipwrecked Spanish castaways, including Cabeza de Vaca, enter what is now southeastern New Mexico. Ultimately reaching Spanish settlements in Mexico, they report evidence of considerable wealth, including precious metals.
1540	Seeking the mythical Seven Cities of Cibola, Francisco Vásquez de Coronado crosses New Mexico from west to east but finds only the hovels of Zuñi Indian pueblos.
1598–1599	Led by Juan de Oñate, an expedition of Spanish soldiers and prospective settlers follows the Rio Grande northward, establishing the second-oldest US settlement near present-day Española.
1609	The first royal governor arrives in New Mexico.
1610	Founding of Santa Fe, the oldest state capital in the US.
1680	New Mexico has an estimated 2,800 whites and 16,000 Christianized Indians. *August.* Pueblo Indians revolt, killing about 400 Spanish and forcing the rest to flee from Santa Fe to San Lorenzo.
1692	A Spanish party reoccupies Santa Fe and 23 Indian pueblos.
1706	Founding of Albuquerque, now New Mexico's largest city.
1776	Twenty Franciscan priests are ministering to 18,261 Indians.
1804	Mining of copper deposits begins at Santa Rita; about 2,000 tons of ore are taken out annually before Apache hostility dooms the enterprise.
1821	New Mexico passes from Spanish to Mexican rule. *September.* William Becknell blazes a new trail for traders, leading from Independence, Missouri, to Santa Fe. Nearly 17 million pounds of freight pass over the Santa Fe Trail by 1860.
1821–1830	Anglo-American mountain men hunt for beaver in New Mexico's highland streams, taking as much as $100,000 worth a year in pelts.

1841	A Texas trading expedition of 400 men surrenders to Mexican troops in New Mexico. Many of the prisoners are killed.
1846	*August 18.* US forces under Colonel Stephen Watts Kearny capture Santa Fe without resistance.
1847	Governor Charles Bent is murdered in Taos by an Indian and Mexican uprising. The revolt is crushed within a month.
	The *Sante Fe Republican* is the territory's first English-language newspaper.
1848	The Treaty of Guadalupe Hidalgo, ending the Mexican War, formally cedes the American Southwest to the United States. Spanish and Mexican land grants are to be honored by the terms of the treaty.
1850	*May 25.* New Mexico becomes a territory, including, until 1863, what is now Arizona. The population is 61,547.
1853	*December 30.* The Gadsden Purchase from Mexico adds territory in the south to New Mexico.
1862	A Civil War Confederate force of 3,500 briefly occupies Santa Fe and Albuquerque but retreats after the Battle of Glorieta Pass.
1863	Silver mining begins, at Magdalena and Socorro.
1866	Charles Goodnight opens a cattle trail by taking a herd from Texas through New Mexico to Denver.
1868	A treaty establishes a Navajo reservation on their ancestral lands in northwestern New Mexico and northeastern Arizona.
	A gold rush occurs near Taos.
1869	The largest tract of land held by a single owner in US history—1.7 million acres—is sold to an English syndicate by Lucien Maxwell for $650,000.
1874	Troops under General Philip Sheridan effectively end the depredations of Comanche Indians in eastern New Mexico.
1876–1878	The Lincoln County War pits cattle barons against one another in an area comprising one-fifth of New Mexico. Among the participants is the gunfighter Billy the Kid.
1879	The Atchison, Topeka, and Santa Fe Railroad enters New Mexico through the Raton Pass, soon reaching Albuquerque.
1880	Some families have flocks as large as 250,000 sheep; the wool clip has grown to four million pounds annually.
1881	*July 14.* Sheriff Pat Garrett kills Billy the Kid at a ranch near Fort Sumner.
1885	*May.* Resentful of his people's eviction to an Arizona reservation, Apache Chief Geronimo leads an uprising against white settlers.
1890	Peak of the open-range ranching system in New Mexico, which has 1,340,000 head of cattle. New Mexico's human population of 160,282 is 94 percent rural.
1898	Burt Phillips and Ernest L. Blumenschein settle in Taos, publicizing it as an artists' colony. It later attracts visitors such as D. H. Lawrence.
1900	Over five million acres are in agricultural cultivation.
1909–1912	Drought drives about three-quarters of all homesteaders from New Mexico.
1912	*January 6.* New Mexico is admitted to the Union as the 47th state.
1916	Completion of Elephant Butte Dam and Reservoir, near what is now Truth or Consequences, provides 2.6 million acre-feet of Rio Grande water annually for irrigation.
	March 9. Mexican insurgent Pancho Villa raids the border town of Columbus, destroying part of the town and killing several persons.
1924	First oil production in New Mexico, from Navajo reservation lands in San Juan County.
1930	Creation of Carlsbad Caverns National Park.
1935	About one-third of the population is on relief as a result of the Great Depression.
1937	Mining exceeds agriculture in annual value for the first time.
1943	The World War II atomic-bomb project is located at Los Alamos. The national center was once a ranch school for boys.
1945	*July 16.* The first atomic bomb is successfully tested in the desert near Alamogordo, at the White Sands Proving Grounds.
1948	A constitutional provision denying the vote to Indians is ruled invalid.
1953	Opening of the Santa Fe Opera Company.

1957	Grants is the US uranium-mining center. New Mexico is also first in potash, second in pumice, third in beryl, fourth in natural gas and manganese, and fifth in copper.
1962	Dedication of the $42-million Navajo Dam on the San Juan River.
1966	Dedication of the new state capitol, built in the round and designed to harmonize with indigenous adobe structures.
1967	*June 5.* Hispanics led by Reies Lopez Tijerina raid the Rio Arriba County courthouse in an effort to obtain title to some 2,500 square miles under Old Spanish and Mexican land grants.
1969	Peak oil production of 129 million barrels places New Mexico sixth among states.
1972	The F.B.I. reports that Albuquerque has the highest crime rate among US cities, with 5,926 serious crimes annually per 100,000 population. *July 17.* The Navajo Indian tribe is offered full control of all Bureau of Indian Affairs operations in its area.
1975	New Mexico State University at Las Cruces dedicates the largest solar-heated and -cooled building in the world.
1977	*June 16–22.* Nearly 12,000 acres of timberland are destroyed by a forest fire.
1980	The population of 1,303,143 includes 37 percent with Spanish surnames, compared to 45 percent in 1940. Indians number 104,634. *February 2–3.* Inmates of the state penitentiary, near Santa Fe, kill 33 fellow prisoners in a rampage. Dedication of the 27-antenna Very Large Array, the world's largest radio telescope, strung out along 38 miles of railroad track near Socorro.
1985	Grant County has become the largest copper-producing area in North America.
1986	Governor Toney Anaya declares New Mexico a sanctuary for Central American refugees.

DEMOGRAPHY

Population (est. 1987) . . . 1,500,000
Population (1980) 1,479,445
Population density in persons
    per square mile (1980) 10.7

POPULATION BY RACE (1980)
American Indian/Aleut/
    Eskimo 104,777
Asian/Pacific Islander 6,816
Black 24,042
Hispanic 476,089
White 976,465
Other 187,868

POPULATION CHARACTERISTICS (1980)
Percent of state population
Urban 72.1
Rural 27.9
Under 18 . . . . 32.1
65 or older 8.9
College-educated 17.3
Families below poverty line . . . 14.0
Public-assistance recipients 6.1

Per capita personal income
    (1986) $11,037
Millionaires per 100,000
    residents (1982) 80.5
Average life expectancy
    in years (1980) 74.0

Marriage rate per 1,000
    residents (1986) 9.6
Divorce rate per 1,000
    residents (1986) 6.0
Birth rate per 1,000
    residents (1985) 19.9
Infant mortality rate per
    1,000 births (1985) 9.7
Abortion rate per 1,000
    live births (1985) 219
Crime rate per 100,000
    residents (1985)
    Violent 725.6
    Property 5,900.3
Federal and state prisoners per
    100,000 residents (1984) 137
Alcohol consumption in gallons
    per capita (1985) 50.4
Deaths from motor vehicle accidents
    per 100,000 residents (1985) . . 36.9

MAJOR CITIES
	Population
Albuquerque (est. 1984)	350,575
Las Cruces (est. 1984)	50,275
Roswell (1980)	39,676
Santa Fe (est. 1984)	52,274

GOVERNMENT AND POLITICS

Number of US Representatives   3
Electoral votes   5

POLITICAL PARTY NOMINEES FROM STATE

LaDonna Harris (Citizens)   1980 VP

PRESIDENTIAL PRIMARY ELECTION In 1988, New Mexico sent 28 Democratic delegates and 26 Republican delegates to the national conventions.

CONSTITUTION New Mexico is using its original constitution, adopted in 1911.

LEGISLATURE The Legislature is divided into the Senate (42 members, 4-year term, minimum age 25) and the House of Representatives (70 members, 2-year term, minimum age 21). In 1987, the salary for legislators was $75 per day to a maximum of 60 days in odd-numbered years and 30 days in even-numbered years.

JUDICIARY The highest court is the Supreme Court, with 5 judges serving 8-year terms. In 1987, the annual salary was $60,375.

EXECUTIVE The governor serves a 4-year term; the minimum age for holding office is 30. In 1987, the annual salary was $63,000. There are 8 other elected officials.

PRESIDENTIAL VOTE 1948-1988 *(in percents)*

Year	State Winner	Democratic	Republican
1948	Truman (D)	56.3	43.0
1952	Eisenhower (R)	44.2	55.5
1956	Eisenhower (R)	41.8	57.8
1960	Kennedy (D)	50.2	49.4
1964	Johnson (D)	59.0	40.4
1968	Nixon (R)	39.8	51.9
1972	Nixon (R)	36.6	61.1
1976	Ford (R)	48.1	50.5
1980	Reagan (R)	36.7	54.9
1984	Reagan (R)	39.2	59.7
1988	Bush (R)	48.0	52.0

GOVERNORS

Territorial Governors

James S. Calhoun	1851-1852
John Greiner (acting)	1852
William Carr Lane	1852-1853
W.S. Messervy (acting)	1853
David Meriwether	1853-1856
W.W.H. Davis (acting)	1856-1857
Abraham Rencher	1857-1861
Henry Connelley	1861-1866
W.F.M. Arny (acting)	1866
Robert B. Mitchell	1866-1869
William A. Pile	1869-1871
Marsh Giddings	1871-1875
William G. Ritch (acting)	1875
Samuel B. Axtell	1875-1878
Lewis (Lew) Wallace	1878-1881
Lionel A. Sheldon	1881-1885
Edmund G. Ross	1885-1889
L. Bradford Prince	1889-1893
William T. Thornton	1893-1897
Miguel A. Otero	1897-1906
Herbert J. Hagerman	1906-1907
J.W. Raynolds (acting)	1907
George Curry	1907-1910
William J. Mills	1910-1912

State Governors

William C. McDonald (D)	1912-1917
Ezequiel Cabeza da Baca (D)	1917
Washington E. Lindsey (R)	1917-1919
Octaviano A. Larrazolo (R)	1919-1921
Merritt C. Mechem (R)	1921-1923
James F. Hinkle (D)	1923-1925
Arthur T. Hannett (D)	1925-1927
Richard C. Dillon (R)	1927-1931
Arthur Seligman (D)	1931-1933
A.W. Hockenhull (D)	1933-1935
Clyde Tingley (D)	1935-1939
John E. Miles (D)	1939-1943
John L. Dempsey (D)	1943-1947
Thomas L. Mabry (D)	1947-1951
Edwin L. Mechem (R)	1951-1955
Edwin F. Simms Jr. (D)	1955-1957
Edwin L. Mechem (R)	1957-1959
John Burroughs (D)	1959-1961
Edwin L. Mechem (R)	1961-1962
Tom Bolack (R/acting)	1962-1963
Jack M. Campbell (D)	1963-1967
David F. Cargo (R)	1967-1971
Bruce King (D)	1971-1975
Jerry Apodaca (D)	1975-1979
Bruce King (D)	1979-1983

Toney Anaya (D)   1983-1987
Garrey E. Carruthers (R) 1987-

MINIMUM AGES
Majority 18
Marriage with parental consent . . . 16
Marriage without parental consent . 18
Making a will 18
Buying alcohol 21
Jury duty 18
Leaving school . . . 18 or 10th grade,
            with school/parental consent
Driver's license 15

CAPITAL PUNISHMENT
Number executed 1976-88: 0
On death row Aug. 1, 1988: 2

MILITARY INSTALLATIONS
Total number: 9
Major bases:
  Army: 2
  Air Force: 2

FINANCES

Thousands of dollars
GENERAL REVENUE (1985
Total general revenue   . . . 3,123,960
Total tax revenue 1,439,312
Sales and gross receipts 819,410
Individual income taxes . . . 84,980
Corporate net income taxes . . 64,056

GENERAL EXPENDITURE (1985)
Total general expenditure . 2,861,087
Education 1,263,590
Public welfare 252,481
Health 96,574
Hospitals 131,845
Natural resources 58,537
Highways 312,923
Police 29,483
Corrections 82,430

FEDERAL AID (1985) 891,071

ECONOMY

New Mexico's farm income derives mainly from cattle, dairy products, and sheep; crops include hay, cotton, wheat, sorghum, legumes and hot peppers, fruit, and nuts. Farm receipts were $962 million in 1983. New Mexico is the nation's major producer of uranium, perlite, and potash ore, and also mines significant quantities of copper, helium gas, natural gas, lead, zinc, and coal. Processed foods, ceramic and glass products, wood products, and small electricals are the main manufactures. Value added by manufacture was $1.4 billion in 1982. Federal and defense projects are also an important source of income for the state, as is tourism.

EMPLOYMENT (1984)
Thousands of persons
Total number of employed
  workers 582
Construction 36.3
Finance, insurance, and
  real estate 24.5
Government 129.6
Manufacturing 36.6
Mining 21.4
Services 107.1
Transportation, communications,
  and utilities 29.9
Wholesale and retail trade 117.8

Percent of civilian labor force
  unemployed (1984) 7.5

DEPARTMENT OF DEFENSE (1985)
Civilian workers employed . . . 9,830
Military personnel 16,421
Contract awards . . . . . $492 million

ENERGY SOURCES FOR ELECTRIC UTILITIES (1983)
Percent
Coal 88.8
Gas 10.5
Hydroelectric 0.3
Nuclear 0.0
Petroleum 0.4

TRANSPORTATION
Motor vehicles registered
  in state (1986) 1,320,121
Miles of roads, streets,
  and highways (1986) 53,596
Miles of Class I railway
  operated (1986) 2,062
Airports (1983) 160
Major aviation hubs (1983) 1
  Largest hub: Albuquerque

CULTURE AND EDUCATION

Native American tribes
New Mexico was formerly home to the Comanche, Kiowa, Manso, Pecos, Piro, Ute, and Zuni tribes. Groups that continue to live in the state include the Apache, Jemez, Keres, Lipan, Navajo, Tewa, and

Tiwa. Groups that have been relocated to New Mexico include the Hopi. There are 24 federal reservations.

Religions, ethnicities, and languages

Most of New Mexico's inhabitants belong to one of its three main groups: the Indians, who have lived there for more than 10,000 years; the Hispanos, or Spanish-Americans, descended from the Spanish colonists who began arriving in the 16th century; and the "Anglos," a term that applies to everyone not in the first two categories. Many Anglos are white settlers from Texas. In 1980, 37.8 percent of New Mexico's population spoke a language other than English at home, usually Spanish.

Major museums and libraries

Maxwell Museum of Anthropology, Albuquerque
Museum of New Mexico, Santa Fe
Museum of Navajo Ceremonial Art, Santa Fe

Major arts organizations

New Mexico Repertory Theatre, Albuquerque
New Mexico Symphony Orchestra, Albuquerque
Santa Fe Opera

Colleges and universities

Number public (1986-87) 18
Number private (1986-87) 3
Total enrollment, in full-time equivalent students (1985) 47,200

Public elementary and secondary schools

Expenditure per pupil in average daily attendance (1986-87) $3,537
Pupil-teacher ratio (1987) 19.0
Average teacher salary (1986-87) $26,892

Holidays

Onate Day. Date in July designated annually
Ernie Pyle Day. August 3
State Fair, Albuquerque. Mid-September

NEW MEXICO IN LITERATURE

Edward Abbey *The Brave Cowboy* (1956)
Novel about a rugged individual at odds with authority.
——. *Fire on the Mountain* (1962, rpt. 1978)
An old man's struggle, seen through the eyes of his grandson, to preserve the wilderness from the encroachment of a missile range.

Rudolfo A. Anaya *Bless Me, Ultima* (1972, rpt. 1975)
An account of growing up in a Hispanic community, set against the landscape and folklore of northern New Mexico.

Frank G. Applegate *Indian Stories from the Pueblos* (1929, rpt. 1988); *Native Tales of New Mexico* (1932)
Collections of Indian and Hispanic folklore.

Elliott Arnold *Blood Brothers* (1947)
Romantic historical novel about an Apache and an Indian agent.
——. *The Time of the Gringo* (1953)
Novel about the conquest of New Mexico by Anglo-Americans.

Mary Austin *The Land of Journeys' Endings* (1924)
Lyrical study of the landscape and people of New Mexico and Arizona.
——. *Starry Adventure* (1931)
Novel about a young man's growing up in the Sangre de Cristo Mountains.

Kenneth C. Balcomb *A Boy's Albuquerque, 1898–1912* (1980)
The author recounts his upbringing in New Mexico territory.

Eve Ball *Indeh: An Apache Odyssey* (1980, rpt. 1988)
Oral history of the Apaches.

Adolph F. Bandelier *The Delight Makers* (1890)
Historical novel depicting the daily lives of the inhabitants of Frijoles Canyon. Bandelier was an ethnologist who studied the Pueblo Indians.

Ruth Benedict *Tales of the Cochiti Indians* (1931, rpt. 1981)
Collection of pueblo tales.

Irwin Robert Blacker *Taos* (1959)
Fictional reconstruction of the rebellion of the Pueblo Indians in the province of Nueva Mexico in 1680.

Robert Bright *The Life and Death of Little Jo* (1944, rpt. 1978)
Novel about rural Hispanic communities.

Alice Bullock *Living Legends of the Santa Fe Country* (1972)
——. *The Squaw Tree: Ghosts, Mysteries and Miracles of New Mexico* (1978)

Arthur L. Campa *Spanish Folk-Poetry in New Mexico* (1946)

James H. Carleton *Diary of an Excursion to the Ruins of Abo, Quarai, and Gran Quivira in New Mexico in 1853* (rpt. 1965)
Account of an early archaeological expedition.

Kit Carson *Kit Carson's Own Story of His Life* (1926)
Autobiography narrated about 1856.

Willa Cather *Death Comes to the Archbishop* (1927, rpt. 1971)
A fictional account of the life of Bishop L'Amy (1814–1888) of Santa Fe, who attempted to reform his church's mission to the Pueblo Indians.

Peggy P. Church *The House at Otowi Bridge: The Story of Edith Warner and Los Alamos* (1959, rpt. 1973)
The story of a woman who lived near Los Alamos at the time of the creation of the atomic bomb, and a description of the nuclear project's effect on the region.

Ann N. Clark *Journey to the People* (1969)
Reminiscences of New Mexico by a teacher and writer who won the 1953 Newbery Award.

Agnes M. Cleaveland *No Life for a Lady* (1941, rpt. 1977)
Reminiscences of pioneer life on the San Augustin plains in the 1880s.

Wilbur Coe *Ranch on the Ruidoso: The Story of a Pioneer Family in New Mexico, 1871–1968* (1968)
Narrative of a family of pioneers who came by the Santa Fe trail.

Will Levington Comfort *Apache* (1931)
Fictional biography of Apache chief Dasoda-Lae, known to whites as Mangas Coloradas. The novel depicts his education as a warrior, his assumption of the leadership of his tribe, and his role in fighting for Indian survival.

Harold Courlander *The Fourth World of the Hopis* (1971)
Collection of historical anecdotes and legends.

Stanley Crawford *Mayordomo: Chronicle of an Acequia in Northern New Mexico* (1988)
Autobiographical account of rural labor.

Kyle Crichton *The Proud People* (1944)
Novel about the tribulations of a poor Spanish family, c.1941.

Frank H. Cushing (comp. and trans.) *Zuni Folk Tales* (1931, rpt. 1986)

W. W. H. Davis *El Gringo: New Mexico and Her People* (1857, rpt. 1983)
Davis, a veteran of the Mexican War, returned to New Mexico in 1853 to become U.S. Attorney.

William Eastlake *Go in Beauty* (1956); *Bronc People* (1958); *Portrait of an Artist with Twenty-Six Horses* (1963); *Dancers in the Scalp House* (1976)
Novels and stories about contemporary life in New Mexico.

Aurelio M. Espinosa (ed. J. M. Espinosa) *The Folklore of Spain in the American Southwest: Traditional Spanish Folk Literature in Northern New Mexico and Southern Colorado* (1985)

J. Manuel Espinosa *Spanish Folktales From New Mexico* (1937, rpt. 1977)

Harvey Fergusson *Blood of the Conquerors* (1921)
The first realistic novel about contemporary New Mexico life. Among Fergusson's ten novels about the state, *Wolf Song* (1927, rpt. 1988), about life in Taos in the days of Kit Carson, is regarded as a classic. The trilogy of novels *Followers of the Sun* (1937) traces the development of the state. *Home in the West* (1945) is Fergusson's account of his upbringing.

Lewis Hector Garrard (ed. A. B. Guthrie) *Wah-To-Yah and the Taos Trail, or Prairie Travel and Scalp Dances, with a Look at Las Rancheros* (1850, rpt. 1955)
Classic pioneer memoir.

Byrd Gibbens (ed.) *This Is a Strange Country: Letters of a Westering Family, 1880–1906* (1988)

Janice Giles *Voyage to Santa Fe* (1962)
Saga of the overland journey from Oklahoma in the 1880s.

José Griego y Maestas and **Rudolfo A. Anaya** *Cuentos: Tales from the Hispanic Southwest* (1980)
A bilingual edition of tales collected from Spanish-speaking families in northern New Mexico and southern Colorado.

Tony Hillerman *The Blessing Way* (1970)
First of a series of detective novels centering on a Navaho policeman and highly regarded for their accurate portrayal of Navaho ways.

Paul Horgan *Far from Cibola* (1938)
Novel set in the Depression. Horgan has written several novels with regional New Mexico settings, and three historical studies of the state.

John T. Hughes *Doniphan's Expedition: Containing an Account of the Conquest of New Mexico* (1847, rpt. 1973)

Oliver La Farge *Laughing Boy* (1929)
Pulitzer Prize–winning novel of life among the Navaho.
———. *Behind the Mountains* (1956)
La Farge's second wife recounts her childhood in the Sangre de Cristos Mountains.
———. (ed. David L. Caffey) *Yellow Sun, Bright Sky: The Indian Country Stories of Oliver La Farge* (1988)

Charles H. Lange, Carroll L. Riley, and **Elizabeth M. Lange** (eds.) *The Southwestern Journals of Adolph F. Bandelier, 1885–1888* (1975)
Observations of an ethnographer and early student of Indian life.

Ruth Laughlin *The Wind Leaves No Shadow* (1948, enl. ed. 1951)
Novel about early nineteenth-century settlers in Santa Fe, 1821–1852, centering on the life of La Tules, one of the most important New Mexico women.

D. H. Lawrence *Mornings in New Mexico* (1950)
Essays on landscape and culture written in Taos in the early 1920s.

Aurora L.-W. Lea *Literary Folklore of the Hispanic Southwest* (1953)

Mabel Dodge Luhan *Lorenzo in Taos* (1932)
Autobiographical account of the writer's turbulent friendship with Lawrence. Luhan also wrote two books about the region: *Winter in Taos* (1935) and *Edge of Taos Desert* (1937).

Charles F. Lummis *A New Mexico David, and Other Stories and Sketches about the Southwest* (1891); *The Land of Poco Tiempo* (1893); *Pueblo Indian Folk-Stories* (1910); *Flowers of Our Last Romance* (1929)
Fiction based on regional folktales, and historical studies, by a southern California writer who lived among the Pueblo Indians from 1888–1891. He described the region in a nonfiction study *Mesa, Cañon and Pueblo* (1925).

Mabel Major, Rebecca Smith, and **T. M. Pearce** *Southwest Heritage: A Literary History with Bibliography* (1935, rpt. 1948, 1972)

N. Scott Momaday *House Made of Dawn* (1968)
Novel about a contemporary Indian who attempts to recover the mystical culture of his ancestors.

Dwight and **Carol Myers** (eds.) *In Celebration of the Book: Literary New Mexico* (1982)

John Nichols *The Milagro Beanfield War* (1974)
Novel about conflict between developers and a poor farming community in northern New Mexico.

James Ohio Pattie (ed. M. M. Quaife) *Personal Narrative* (1831, rpt. 1930)
Pattie was a Kentucky-born explorer and trapper who took several lengthy journeys to Santa Fe in the 1820s.

Evelyn Dahl Reed *Coyote Tales from the Indian Pueblos* (1988)

Conrad Richter *The Lady* (1957)
Historical romance set in northern New Mexico in the 1880s.

John D. Robb *Hispanic Folk Songs of New Mexico* (1979)
———. *Hispanic Folk Music of New Mexico and the Southwest* (1980)

Martha A. Sandweiss (ed.) *Denizens of the Desert: A Tale in Word and Picture of Life among the Navaho Indians. The Letters of Elizabeth W. Forster* (1988)

Marc Simmons (ed.) *On the Santa Fe Trail* (1986)
Anthology of narratives by travellers on the trail c.1840– c.1860.

John L. Sinclair *In Time of Harvest* (1943)
Novel about a dirt farmer in the Estancia Valley.

Sabine R. Ulibarri *Tierra Amarilla: Stories of New Mexico* (1971)
Stories of rural New Mexico in a bilingual edition.

Mary R. Van Stone *Spanish Folksongs of New Mexico* (1938)

Frank Waters *People of the Valley* (1941)
Novel about life among the Hispanic residents of a small town in the Sangre de Cristos Mountains.
———. *The Man Who Killed the Deer* (1942)
Novel about the conflict between Indian and white ways of life. Waters also wrote *Book of the Hopi* (1963) and *Pumpkin Seed Point* (1969), accounts of Indian life.

Marta Weigle and **Peter White** *The Lore of New Mexico* (1988)

GUIDES TO RESOURCES

Beck, Warren A. and Ynez D. Haase *Historical Atlas of New Mexico* (1969)

Campa, Arthur L. *A Bibliography of Spanish Folk-Lore in New Mexico (University of New Mexico Bulletin,* Modern Language Series 2) (1930)

Caperton, Thomas J. and LoRheda Fry *Links to the Past: New Mexico's State Monuments* (1977)

Chilton, Lance et al. *New Mexico: A Guide to the Colorful State* (1984)

Davis, Ellis Arthur *The Historical Encyclopedia of New Mexico* 2 vols. (1945)

Ellis, Richard N. (ed.) *New Mexico Historic Documents* (1975)

Federal Writers' Project (ed. Joseph Miller) *New Mexico: A Guide to the Colorful State* (rev. ed. 1962, rpt. 1974)

Garcia, F. Chris and Paul L. Hain *New Mexico Government* (rev. ed. 1981)

Irion, Frederick C. *Selected and Annotated Bibliography on Politics in New Mexico* (1959)

Major, Mabel and T. M. Pearce *Southwest Heritage. A Literary History with Bibliographies* (1972)

Myers, Christine Buder *New Mexico Local and County Histories* (1983)

New Mexico Statistical Abstract (1970–)

Official New Mexico Blue Book (1980–)

Pearce, T. M. (ed.) *New Mexico Place Names: A Geographical Dictionary* (1980)

Saunders, Lyle *A Guide to the Literature of the Southwest* (1942)

Stoddard, Ellwyn R., Richard L. Nostrand, and Jonathan P. West *Borderlands Sourcebook: A Guide to the Literature on Northern New Spain and the American Southwest* (1983)

Swadesh, Frances L. *Twenty Thousand Years of History: A New Mexico Bibliography* (1973)

Trimble, Stephen *From Out of the Rocks: Discovering Ancient Life in New Mexico* (1980)

Tully, Marjorie F. and Juan B. Rael *An Annotated Bibliography of Spanish Folklore in New Mexico and Southern Colorado* (1950)

Twitchell, Ralph E. *Leading Facts of New Mexican History* 5 vols. (1911–1917)
———. *The Spanish Archives of New Mexico* 2 vols. (1914)

Weigle, Marta *A Penitente Bibliography* (1976)

Williams, Jerry L. (ed.) *New Mexico in Maps* (2d ed. 1986)

SELECTED NONFICTION SOURCES

Bailey, Jessie B. *Diego de Vargas and the Reconquest of New Mexico* (1940)

Ball, Larry D. *The United States Marshals of New Mexico and Arizona Territories, 1846–1912* (1978)

Bancroft, Hubert H. *History of Arizona and New Mexico, 1530–1888* (1889)

Bannon, John F. *The Spanish Borderlands Frontier, 1513–1821* (1970)

Baxter, John O. *Las Carneradas: Sheep Trade in New Mexico, 1700–1860* (1987)

Beck, Warren A. *New Mexico; a History of Four Centuries* (1962)

Bolton, Herbert E. *The Spanish Borderlands* (1921)
———. *Coronado, Knight of Pueblos and Plains* (1949)

Boyd, E. *Popular Arts of Spanish New Mexico* (1974)

Brown, Lorin W., Charles L. Briggs, and Marta Weigle *Hispano Folklife of New Mexico* (1978)

Bunting, Bainbridge *Of Earth and Timbers Made: New Mexico Architecture* (1974)
———. *Early Architecture in New Mexico* (1976)

Caiar, Ruth *One Man's Dream: The Story of Jim White— Discoverer and Explorer of Carlsbad Caverns* (1957)

Calvin, Ross *Sky Determines: An Interpretation of the Southwest* (1965)

Campa, Arthur L. *Hispanic Culture in the Southwest* (1979)

Carroll, H. Bailey and J. Villasana Haggard *Three New Mexico Chronicles* (1942)

Chavez, Fray Angelico (comp.) *Origins of New Mexico Families, 1598–1693 and 1693–1821* (1954)

Clark, Ira G. *Water in New Mexico: A History of Its Management and Use* (1987)

Cleland, Robert G. *This Reckless Breed of Men: The Trappers and Fur Traders of the Southwest* (1950, rpt. 1976)

Coan, Charles F. *A History of New Mexico* 3 vols. (1925)

Coe, Wilbur *Ranch on the Ruidoso: The Story of a Pioneer Family in New Mexico, 1871–1968* (1968)

Coke, Van Deren *Photography in New Mexico: From the Daguerreotype to the Present* (1979)

Coles, Robert *The Old Ones of New Mexico* (1973)

Cooke, Philip S. *The Conquest of New Mexico and California* (1878, rpt. 1952)

Coolidge, Dane and Mary *The Navajo Indians* (1930)
——— and Mary Roberts *The Rain-makers: Indians of Arizona and New Mexico* (1929)

Corle, Edwin *The Gila: River of the Southwest* (1951)

Cortés, Carlos E. (ed.) *The Penitentes of New Mexico* (1974)

Crane, Leo *Desert Drums: The Pueblo Indians of New Mexico, 1540–1928* (1928, rpt. 1972)

Davis, W. W. *El Gringo: New Mexico and Her People* (1938, rpt. 1982)

DeBuys, William *Enchantment and Exploitation: The Life and Hard Times of a New Mexico Mountain Range* (1985)

Dewitt, Susan *Historic Albuquerque Today* (1978)

Dickey, Roland F. *New Mexico Village Arts* (1949)

Dozier, Edward P. *The Pueblo Indians of North America* (1970)

Duffus, R. L. *The Santa Fe Trail* (1930)

Ellis, Richard N. (ed.) *New Mexico, Past and Present: A Historical Reader* (1971)

Espinosa, J. Manuel *First Expedition of Vargas into New Mexico, 1692* (1940)
———. *Crusaders of the Rio Grande: The Story of Don Diego de Vargas and the Reconquest and Refounding of New Mexico* (1942)
———. *The Pueblo Indian Revolt of 1696* (1988)

Fergusson, Erna *Murder and Mystery in New Mexico* (1948)
———. *New Mexico: A Pageant of Three Peoples* (1964, rpt. 1973)

Fergusson, Harvey *Rio Grande* (1933, rpt. 1967)

Fincher, E. B. *Spanish-Americans as a Political Factor in New Mexico, 1912–1950* (1974)

Frazer, Robert W. (ed.) *New Mexico in 1850: A Military View* (1968)

Frazier, Kendrick *People of Chaco: A Canyon and Its Culture* (1986)

Garrett, Pat (ed. M. G. Fulton) *The Authentic Life of Billy the Kid* (1927, rpt. 1967)

Gibson, Arrell M. *The Santa Fe and Taos Colonies: Age of the Muses, 1900–1942* (1983)

Granjon, Monseignor Henry *Along the Rio Grande: A Pastoral Visit to Southern New Mexico in 1902* (1986)

Grant, Blanche C. *When Old Trails Were New, the Story of Taos* (1934)

Gregg, Andrew K. *New Mexico in the Nineteenth Century: A Pictorial History* (1968)

Groueff, Stephanie *Manhattan Project: The Untold Story of the Making of the Atomic Bomb* (1968)

Hammond, George P. *Don Juan de Oñate and the Founding of New Mexico* (1927, rpt. 1953)
——— and Agapito Rey *Don Juan de Oñate, Colonizer of New Mexico, 1595–1628* 2 vols. (1953)

Harwood, Thomas *History of New Mexico Missions* 2 vols. (1908)

Hillerman, Tony (ed.) *The Spell of New Mexico* (1976)
———. *The Great Taos Bank Robbery and Other Indian Country Affairs* (1978)

Historic Santa Fe Foundation *Old Santa Fe Today* (3d ed. 1982)

Horgan, Paul *The Centuries of Santa Fe* (1956, rpt. 1976)
———. *Great River: The Rio Grande in North American History* (1960)
———. *Lamy of Santa Fe: His Life and Times* (1975)

Iowa, Jerome *Ageless Adobe: History and Preservation in Southwestern Architecture* (1985)

Irion, Frederick C. (ed.) *New Mexico and Its Natural Resources, 1900–2000* (1959)

James, George W. *New Mexico: The Land of the Delight Makers* (1920)

Johnson, Byron A. and Robert K. Dauner *Early Albuquerque* (1981)

Jordan, Louann and St. George Coe *El Rancho de Las Golondrinas: Spanish Colonial Life in New Mexico* (1977)

Kalloch, Eunice *The First Ladies of New Mexico* (1982)

Keleher, William A. *Turmoil in New Mexico, 1846–1868* (1951, rpt. 1982)
———. *Violence in Lincoln County, 1869–1881: A New Mexico Item* (1957, rpt. 1982)
———. *The Fabulous Frontier: Twelve New Mexico Items* (1962, rpt. 1982)
———. *New Mexicans I Knew: Memoirs, 1892–1969* (1969, rpt. 1983)
———. *The Maxwell Land Grant: A New Mexico Item* (4th ed. 1983)

Kenner, Charles L. *A History of New Mexican–Plains Indian Relations* (1969)

Kern, Robert W. (ed.) *Labor in New Mexico: Unions, Strikes, and Social History since 1881* (1983)

Kessell, John L. *Kiva, Cross, and Crown: The Pecos Indians and New Mexico, 1540–1840* (1966)
———. *The Missions of New Mexico since 1776* (1980)

Kubler, George *The Religious Architecture of New Mexico in the Colonial Period and since the American Occupation* (1940, rpt. 1972)

Kunetka, James W. *City of Fire: Los Alamos and the Atomic Age, 1943–1945* (rev. ed. 1979)

La Farge, Oliver and Arthur N. Morgan *Santa Fe: The Autobiography of a Southwestern Town* (1959)

Larson, Robert W. *New Mexico's Quest for Statehood, 1846–1912* (1968)

Laughlin, Ruth *Caballeros* (1945)

Lavash, Donald R. *Sheriff William Brady, Tragic Hero of the Lincoln County War* (1986)

Lekson, Stephen H. *Great Pueblo Architecture of Chaco Canyon, New Mexico* (1984)

Lister, Robert H. and Florence C. *Those Who Came Before: Southwestern Archaeology in the National Park System* (1983) Last Days (1986)

Looney, Ralph *Haunted Highways: The Ghost Towns of New Mexico* (1968)

Marriott, Alice *Maria: The Potter of San Ildefonso* (1948)

McDonald, Corry *Wilderness: A New Mexico Legacy* (1985)

Moorhead, Max L. *New Mexico's Royal Road: Trade and Travel on the Chihuahua Trail* (1958)

Motto, Sytha *Madrid and Christmas in New Mexico* (1973, rpt. 1981)

Murphy, Dan *New Mexico, the Distant Land; an Illustrated History* (1985)

Myrick, David F. *New Mexico's Railroads: An Historical Survey* (1970)

Nabokov, Peter *Tijerina and the Courthouse Raid* (1969)

Ortiz, Alfonso *New Perspectives on the Pueblos* (1972)

Otero, Miguel A. *My Nine Years as Governor of the Territory of New Mexico, 1897–1906* (1940)

Pearson, Jim B. *The Red River—Twining Area: A New Mexico Mining Story* (1986)

Perrigo, Lynn I. *Hispanos: Historic Leaders in New Mexico* (1984)

Ream, Glen O. *Out of New Mexico's Past* (1980)

Reeve, Agnesa L. *From Hacienda to Bungalow; Northern New Mexico Houses, 1850–1912* (1988)

Rickards, Colin *Sheriff Pat Garrett's Last Days* (1986)

Robb, John D. *Hispanic Folk Music of New Mexico and the Southwest: A Self-Portrait of a People* (1980)

Roberts, Calvin A. and Susan A. *New Mexico* (1988)

Salpointe, Jean B. *Soldiers of the Cross* (1898, rpt. 1967)

Sherman, James E. and Barbara H. *Ghost Towns and Mining Camps of New Mexico* (1975)

Sherman, John (comp.) *Santa Fe, a Pictorial History* (1983)

Simmons, Marc *New Mexico: A Bicentennial History* (States and the Nation series) (1977)
———. *Albuquerque: A Narrative History* (1982)

Smith, Anne M. *New Mexico Indians: Economic, Educational and Social Problems* (1969)

Sonnichsen, C. L. *The Mescalero Apaches* (1958, rpt. 1980)
———. *Tularosa: Last of the Frontier West* (1960, rpt. 1980)

Spears, Beverly *American Adobes: Rural Houses of Northern New Mexico* (1986)

Stanley, F. *Desperadoes of New Mexico* (1928)
———. *Socorro: The Oasis* (1950)
———. *Fort Union* (1953)

Szasz, Ferenc M. *The Day the Sun Rose Twice: The Story of the Trinity Site Nuclear Explosion, July 16, 1945* (1984)

Thomas, Alfred B. *The Plains Indians and New Mexico, 1751–1778* (1940)

Tuan, Yi-Fu, Cyril E. Everard, and Jerrold G. Widdison *The Climate of New Mexico* (1969)

Udall, Sharyn R. *Santa Fe Art Colony, 1900–1942* (1988)

Ungnade, Herbert E. *Guide to the New Mexico Mountains* (2d ed. 1972)

Utley, Robert M. *Four Fighters of Lincoln County* (1986)
———. *High Noon: Violence on the Western Frontier* (1987)

Van Dyke, John C. *The Desert* (1930, rpt. 1978)

Weber, David J. *The Taos Trappers: The Fur Trade in the Far Southwest* (1970)

Weigle, Marta *Brothers of Light, Brothers of Blood: The Penitentes of the Southwest* (1976)
——— (ed.) *Hispanic Villages of Northern New Mexico* (1975)
——— and Peter White *The Lore of New Mexico* (1988)

Young, John V. *The State Parks of New Mexico* (1984)

NEW YORK

New York is a Middle Atlantic state. It is bordered on the north by Lake Ontario, the St. Lawrence River, and the Canadian provinces of Ontario and Quebec; on the east by Lake Champlain, Vermont, Massachusetts, and Connecticut; on the south by the Atlantic Ocean, New Jersey, Pennsylvania, and the Delaware River; and on the west by Pennsylvania, Lake Erie, the Niagara River, and the Canadian province of Ontario.

FULL NAME State of New York
POSTAL ABBREVIATION NY
INHABITANT New Yorker
ADMITTED TO THE UNION July 26, 1788. 11th state
POPULATION (est. 1987) 17,825,000. Percent of US total: 7.33%. Rank: 2d

CAPITAL CITY Albany, located on the Hudson River in east central New York; population 99,451 (est. 1984). Albany is one of the oldest permanent settlements in the United States. It began in 1540 as a French fort. The Dutch built Fort Nassau there in 1614, and Fort Orange in 1624. By 1652 the village of Beverwyck was established; it was renamed Albany by the British when they took it over in 1664. Albany was chartered as a city in 1686 and became the state capital in 1797.

STATE NAME AND NICKNAMES Called New Netherlands by the Dutch, the colony was renamed by the British in honor of the Duke of York and Albany (the future King James II) when they captured it in 1664. Official nickname: Empire State. Also known as the Excelsior State.

STATE SEAL The coat of arms is a shield showing the Hudson River with ships traveling on it, and a smiling sun rising over a mountain. To the left of the shield is the Goddess of Liberty holding the Phrygian cap and treading on a fallen crown; to the right is the blindfolded Goddess of Justice with sword and scales; above it is an eagle perched on a globe, below it on a scroll the state motto. The border reads "The Great Seal of the State of New York."

MOTTO Excelsior (Higher)

SONG None.

SYMBOLS
Flower rose
Tree sugar maple
Bird bluebird
Gem garnet
Animal American beaver
Fish brook or speckled trout
Fossil Eurypterus remipes
Fruit apple
Beverage milk

LICENSE PLATE Dark blue on white, with red stripes and red Statue of Liberty.

FLAG The state coat of arms on a field of blue.

GEOGRAPHY AND CLIMATE

New York's varied geographic regions include the rugged Adirondack Mountains to the northeast; the wide valleys of the Hudson and Mohawk rivers in the central and western part of the state; Appalachian highlands covering nearly all of the western half of New York; and marine plains along the Atlantic Ocean, the St. Lawrence River, and the shores of Lake Erie and Lake Ontario, where there is heavy annual snowfall. There are more than 2,000 lakes in the state. Long Island, 1,723 square miles in area, projects into the Atlantic from New York's southeastern end.

AREA 49,108 square miles. Rank: 30th

INLAND WATER 1,731 square miles

GEOGRAPHIC CENTER Madison, 12 miles S of Oneida, 26 miles SW of Utica

ELEVATIONS *Highest point:* Mount Marcy, Essex County, 5,344 feet. *Lowest point:* Atlantic Ocean, sea level. *Mean elevation:* 1,000 feet

MAJOR RIVERS St. Lawrence, Hudson, Mohawk, Delaware, Niagara

MAJOR LAKES AND RESERVOIRS Erie, Finger Lakes, Champlain, George, Oneida

TIDAL SHORELINE 1,850 miles, Atlantic coast

LAND USE

	Thousands of acres
Urban (1982)	1,811
Rural (1982)	27,386
Cropland (1982)	5,912
Pastureland (1982)	3,872
Rangeland (1982)	0
Forestland (1982)	16,517
State parks and recreation areas (1983)	256
National park system (1984)	35
National forest system (1984)	13
Tribal lands (1984)	0

TEMPERATURES The highest recorded temperature was 108°F on July 22, 1926, at Troy. The lowest was -52°F on February 18, 1979, at Old Forge.

NATIONAL SITES

NATIONAL HISTORIC SITES Eleanor Roosevelt, Home of Franklin Delano Roosevelt, Theodore Roosevelt Birthplace, Theodore Roosevelt Inaugural, Sagamore Hill, St. Paul's Church, Martin Van Buren, Vanderbilt Mansion

NATIONAL HISTORICAL PARKS Saratoga, Women's Rights

NATIONAL MEMORIALS Federal Hall, General Grant, Hamilton Grange

NATIONAL MONUMENTS Castle Clinton, Fort Stanwix, Statue of Liberty

NATIONAL RECREATION AREA Gateway

NATIONAL SCENIC RIVERS AND RIVERWAYS Delaware, Upper Delaware

NATIONAL SCENIC TRAILS Appalachian, North Country

NATIONAL SEASHORE Fire Island

NATIONAL WILDLIFE REFUGES Iroquois, Montezuma, Target Rock–Amagansett/Conscience Point/Morton/Oyster Bay/Seatuck/Wertheim

HISTORY

1524	*April 17.* Giovanni da Verrazano enters New York Bay.
1570	The five tribes of the Iroquois—Mohawk, Oneida, Onondaga, Cayuga, and Seneca—found the League of Five Nations.
1609	Samuel de Champlain discovers the lake that bears his name. *September 3.* Henry Hudson, searching for a passage to China, sails the *Half Moon* into New York Bay.
1612	Crews of Dutch ships *Tiger* and *Fortune* trade with Hudson River Indians and build huts on Manhattan island.
1614	Hendrik Christiaensen builds Fort Nassau, a Dutch trading post near Albany.
1624	Dutch and French Protestant refugees led by Cornelius May establish first permanent European settlement, Fort Orange, Albany.
1625	Dutch settlers led by Willem Verhulst found the colony of New Netherland on Manhattan, which is renamed New Amsterdam.
1626	Peter Minuit, third governor of New Netherland, buys Manhattan from the Indians for 60 guilders.

1629	*July 27.* Dutch West India Company grants Hudson river valley land to the patroons.
1630	Kiliaen van Rensselaer, Amsterdam merchant, founds Rensselaerswyck, which is now Albany, Rensselaer and Columbia counties.
1633	First recorded school in America set up in New Amsterdam.
1636	Jacob van Curler buys land on Long Island and extends Dutch territory.
1654	*July 8.* Jacob Barsimon, first Jewish settler, arrives on Manhattan.
1659	Founding of the Dutch reformed church of Esopus (Kingston).
1664	*September 9.* Governor Peter Stuyvesant surrenders the city of New Amsterdam to Colonel Richard Nicolls, commander of a British squadron, who renames the city New York.
1668	Francis Lovelace, second British governor, purchases Staten Island from the Indians.
1679	Robert Cavelier, Sieur de la Salle, builds Fort Niagara.
1684	The League of Five Nations forms an alliance with the British.
1686	*April 27.* Governor Thomas Donagan grants a municipal charter to New York City.
1688	Huguenot settlers establish New Rochelle.
1690	A French and Indian force sacks Schenectady, but is then defeated at the battle of La Prairie by Peter Schuyler, mayor of Albany, leading English and Dutch frontiersmen. The French continue to raid frontier outposts.
1725	*October 16.* William Bradford publishes the *New York Gazette,* the first New York newspaper.
1731	The French build a fort at Crown Point in an attempt to establish a border between lakes Champlain and Erie.
1735	*August 4.* John Peter Zenger, publisher of the *Weekly Journal,* is acquitted of libel by a jury defying the judge's instructions.
1754	*June 19.* Albany Congress convenes to deal with Indian grievances that are leading to cooperation between the Iroquois and the French. King's College (later Columbia University) founded.
1762	*March 17.* Probable date of the first Saint Patrick's Day parade.
1764	*October.* The state legislative assembly protests taxation on molasses without representation.
1765	*October 7.* State representatives protest the Stamp Act, a tax on paper and documents.
1770	*January 18.* Colonial agitators clash with British troops at the "Battle of Golden Hill" in New York City.
1774	*April.* Eighteen boxes of tea dumped in the harbor at "New York Tea Party." *August 6.* Ann Lee and the Shaker Mission arrive in New York from England.
1775	*May 10.* Ethan Allan and the Green Mountain Boys capture Fort Ticonderoga.
1776	*July 9.* Provincial congress ratifies the Declaration of Independence at White Plains. The declaration is read to Washington and his troops in Manhattan. *August 27.* Washington defeated at the Battle of Long Island. *September 19.* Lord William Howe's troops occupy Manhattan. *Septmeber 22.* Nathan Hale is executed on Long Island by British for espionage. *October 28.* Washington defeated at the Battle of White Plains.
1777	*April 20.* First state constitution adopted at Kingston. *July 9.* George Clinton, 1st governor, inaugurated. *October 17.* Major General John Burgoyne surrenders at Saratoga.
1779	*July 16.* Anthony Wayne's colonial troops capture Stony Point, establishing American control over the lower Hudson Valley.
1781	*October 25.* Colonel Marinus Willett defeats a British and Indian force at Johnstown in the last Revolutionary battle to take place in the state.
1783	*April 3.* Washington Irving born in New York City. *November 3.* Washington bids farewell to his officers in New York City. *November 25.* British evacuate Manhattan.
1784	*May 1.* Governor Clinton founds the State University.
1787	*October 27.* Alexander Hamilton publishes the first issue of *The Federalist.*
1788	*July 26.* New York ratifies the Constitution at Poughkeepsie becoming the 11th state.

1789	*April 30*. George Washington inaugurated as president on the steps of Federal Hall, Manhattan.
1790	*February 1*. First session of the United States Supreme Court, Royal Exchange Building, New York City.
1797	*March 10*. Albany becomes the capital of the state.
1802	*March 16*. United States Military Academy founded at West Point.
1807	*August 17*. Robert Fulton's steamboat *Clermont* sails from New York to Albany in 32 hours.
1813	British troops raid Ogdensburg.
1814	*September 11*. Americans defeat British in the Battle of Lake Champlain.
1817	Construction of the Erie Canal begins at Rome.
1821	Emma Willard founds Troy Female Seminary, first women's college in the United States.
1823	Joseph Smith reports a vision of the golden book of Mormon near Palmyra.
1825	Erie Canal opens.
	Painter Thomas Cole unknowingly founds the Hudson River School, America's first major school of painting.
1827	*July 4*. Freedom for 10,000 when the state abolishes slavery.
1839	According to a dubious legend, the first baseball game played in Cooperstown.
1847	John H. Noyes founds the Oneida Community.
1848	*July 19*. First Women's Rights Convention is held at Seneca Falls.
1857	Frederick Law Olmstead and Calvert Vaux begin designs for Central Park.
1862	The state sends 120 regiments to the Civil War.
1863	*July 13–16*. New York antidraft riots result in 1,000 casualties.
1871	The Tweed Ring, a circle of corrupt city officials, is broken.
1873	*September 20*. Panic closes New York Stock Exchange.
1886	*October 28*. Statue of Liberty dedicated.
1888	*March 11*. The Great Blizzard paralyzes New York City.
1901	Theodore Roosevelt becomes President on the assassination of William McKinley at Buffalo.
1904	*October 27*. First subway in the world begins operating in New York City.
1917	Women granted suffrage in state elections.
1919	Mary M. Lilly and Ida B. Sammis become first women elected to the state legislature.
1924	Fires destroy large portions of the Catskill and Adirondack forests.
1927	*May 20*. Charles A. Lindbergh flies nonstop to Paris, France from Roosevelt Field.
1929	*October 29*. Panic on New York Stock Exchange presages the Great Depression.
1932	Franklin Delano Roosevelt becomes President.
1939	World's Fair opens in Queens.
1950	*March 21*. Construction of the New York State Thruway authorized.
1955	Hurricane Diane causes extensive damage.
1961	World census finds New York world's second-largest city.
1964	Second New York World's Fair.
1965	Nationalist leader Malcolm X is assassinated in New York City.
1966	*November 8*. State lotteries legalized.
1987	*October 19*. The Dow Jones Industrial Average records a record loss of 500 points.

DEMOGRAPHY

Population (est. 1987) . . . 17,825,000
Population (1980) 17,558,072
Population density in persons per
  square mile (1980) 357.5

Black 2,401,842
Hispanic 1,659,245
White 13,961,106
Other 845,077

POPULATION BY RACE (1980)
American Indian/Aleut/
  Eskimo 38,732
Asian/Pacific Islander 310,531

POPULATION CHARACTERISTICS (1980)
Percent of state population
Urban 84.6
Rural 15.4
Under 18 . . . . 26.7

65 or older	12.3
College-educated	18.7
Families below poverty line	10.8
Public-assistance recipients	8.4

Per capita personal income (1986)	$17,118
Millionaires per 100,000 residents (1982)	175.9
Average life expectancy in years (1980)	73.7
Marriage rate per 1,000 residents (1986)	9.9
Divorce rate per 1,000 residents (1986)	3.3
Birth rate per 1,000 residents (1985)	14.4
Infant mortality rate per 1,000 births (1985)	11.0
Abortion rate per 1,000 live births (1985)	746
Crime rate per 100,000 residents (1985)	
Violent	985.9
Property	4,781.8
Federal and state prisoners per 100,000 residents (1984)	182
Alcohol consumption in gallons per capita (1985)	36.6
Deaths from motor vehicle accidents per 100,000 residents (1985)	11.3

MAJOR CITIES

	1984 population (est.)
Albany	99,451
Buffalo	338,982
New York	7,164,742
Bronx	1,172,952
Kings (Brooklyn)	2,253,858
New York (Manhattan)	1,456,012
Queens	1,911,235
Richmond (Staten Island)	370,595
Rochester	242,562
Schenectady	67,981
Syracuse	164,219
Utica	72,935

GOVERNMENT AND POLITICS

Number of US Representatives	34
Electoral votes	36

POLITICAL PARTY NOMINEES FROM STATE
*winner

John Jay	1789	P
George Clinton	1789	P
Aaron Burr	1792	P
Aaron Burr	1796	P
George Clinton	1796	P
John Jay	1796	P
Aaron Burr* (Democratic-Republican)	1800	VP
George Clinton (D-R)	1800	P
John Jay (Federalist)	1800	P
George Clinton* (D-R)	1804	VP
Rufus King (Federalist)	1804	VP
George Clinton* (D-R)	1808	VP
Rufus King (Federalist)	1808	VP
De Witt Clinton (Federalist)	1812	P
Rufus King (Federalist)	1816	P
Daniel D. Tompkins* (D-R)	1816	VP
Daniel D. Tompkins* (D-R)	1820	VP
Martin Van Buren (Whig faction)	1824	VP
Nathan Sanford (Whig faction)	1824	VP
Martin Van Buren* (D-R)	1832	VP
Martin Van Buren* (D-R)	1836	P
Francis Granger (Whig faction)	1836	VP
Martin Van Buren (D-R)	1840	P
James Gillespie Birney (Liberal)	1840	P
James Gillespie Birney (Liberal)	1844	P
Millard Fillmore* (Whig)	1848	VP
Martin Van Buren (Free Soil Democratic)	1848	P
Gerrit Smith (National Liberal)	1848	P
Millard Fillmore (American/Whig)	1856	P
George Brinton McClellan (D)	1864	P
John Cochrane (Independent Republican)	1864	VP
Horatio Seymour (D)	1868	P
Horace Greeley (D/Liberal Republican/Liberal Republican Convention of Colored Men)	1872	P
Charles O'Conor (Straight-out Democratic)	1872	P
Victoria Claflin Woodhull (People's)	1872	P
Frederick Law Olmsted (Independent Liberal Republican)	1872	VP
Samuel Jones Tilden (D)	1876	P
William Almon Wheeler* (R)	1876	VP
Peter Cooper (Greenback)	1876	P
Donald Kirkpatrick (American National)	1876	VP
Chester Alan Arthur* (R)	1880	VP
Grover Cleveland* (D)	1884	P
Grover Cleveland (D)	1888	P
Levi Parsons Morton* (R)	1888	VP
James Langdon Curtis (American)	1888	P

Grover Cleveland* (D)	1892	P
Whitelaw Reid (R)	1892	VP
Charles Horatio Matchett (Socialist Labor)	1892	VP
Charles Horatio Matchett (Socialist Labor)	1896	P
Theodore Roosevelt* (R)	1900	VP
Theodore Roosevelt* (R)	1904	P
Alton Brooks Parker (D)	1904	P
Benjamin Hanford (Socialist)	1904	VP
Charles Hunter Corregan (Socialist Labor)	1904	P
James Schoolcraft Sherman* (R)	1908	VP
Benjamin Hanford (Socialist)	1908	VP
August Gillhaus (Socialist Labor)	1908	P
Theodore Roosevelt (Progressive)	1912	P
August Gillhaus (Socialist Labor)	1912	VP
James Schoolcraft Sherman (R)	1912	VP
Charles Evans Hughes (R)	1916	P
Allan Louis Benson (Socialist)	1916	P
Theodore Roosevelt (Progressive/declined)	1916	P
Franklin Delano Roosevelt (D)	1920	VP
David Leigh Colvin (Prohibition)	1920	VP
August Gillhaus (Socialist Labor)	1920	VP
Verne L. Reynolds (Socialist Labor)	1924	VP
Benjamin Gitlow (Workers)	1924	VP
Alfred Emanuel Smith (D)	1928	P
Benjamin Gitlow (Workers)	1928	VP
Norman Mattoon Thomas (Socialist)	1928	P
Jeremiah D. Crowley (Socialist Labor)	1928	VP
William Frederick Varney (Prohibition)	1928	P
Franklin Delano Roosevelt* (D)	1932	P
Norman Mattoon Thomas (Socialist)	1932	P
James William Ford (Communist)	1932	VP
Eric Hass (Socialist Labor/declined)	1932	P
Franklin Delano Roosevelt* (D)	1936	P
Norman Mattoon Thomas (Socialist)	1936	P
James William Ford (Communist)	1936	VP
David Leigh Colvin (Prohibition)	1936	P
Emil F. Teichert (Socialist Labor)	1936	VP
Franklin Delano Roosevelt* (D)	1940	P
Wendell Lewis Willkie (R)	1940	P
Norman Mattoon Thomas (Socialist)	1940	P
James William Ford (Communist)	1940	VP
Aaron M. Orange (Socialist Labor)	1940	VP
Franklin Delano Roosevelt* (D)	1944	P
Thomas Edmund Dewey (R)	1944	P
Norman Mattoon Thomas (Socialist)	1944	P
Thomas Edmund Dewey (R)	1948	P
Norman Mattoon Thomas (Socialist)	1948	P
Stephen Emery (Socialist Labor)	1948	VP
Farrell Dobbs (Socialist Workers)	1948	P
John G. Scott (Greenback)	1948	P
Symon Gould (Vegetarian)	1948	P
Dwight David Eisenhower* (R)	1952	P
Farrell Dobbs (Socialist Workers)	1952	P
Homer Aubrey Tomlinson (Church of God)	1952	P
Eric Hass (Socialist Labor)	1952	P
Stephen Emery (Socialist Labor)	1952	VP
Charlotta Bass (Progressive/American Labor)	1952	VP
Symon Gould (Vegetarian)	1952	VP
Samuel Herman Friedman (Socialist)	1952	VP
Myra Tanner Weiss (Socialist Workers)	1952	VP
Dwight David Eisenhower* (R)	1956	P
Eric Hass (Socialist Labor)	1956	P
Farrell Dobbs (Socialist Workers)	1956	P
Myra Tanner Weiss (Socialist Workers)	1956	VP
Symon Gould (American Vegetarian)	1956	VP
Samuel Herman Friedman (Socialist)	1956	VP
Symon Gould (American Vegetarian)	1960	P
Eric Hass (Socialist Labor)	1960	P
Homer Aubrey Tomlinson (Theocratic)	1960	P
Farrell Dobbs (Socialist Workers)	1960	P
Myra Tanner Weiss (Socialist Workers)	1960	VP

William Edward Miller (R)   1964 VP
Eric Hass (Socialist Labor)   1964   P
Homer Aubrey Tomlinson
(Theocratic)   1964   P
Clifton De Berry (Socialist
Workers)   1964   P
Edward Shaw (Socialist Workers)   1964 VP
Fred Wolf Halstead (Socialist
Workers)   1968   P
Judith Mage (Peace and Freedom)   1968 VP
Michael Zagarell (Communist)   1968 VP
Gus Hall (Communist)   1972   P
Jarvis Tyner (Communist)   1972 VP
Peter Camejo (Socialist Workers)   1976   P
Gus Hall (Communist)   1976   P
Jarvis Tyner (Communist)   1976 VP
Barry Commoner (Citizens)   1980   P
Ellen McCormack (Independent/Right to Life/Respect
for Life)   1980   P
Percy L. Greaves Jr. (American)   1980   P
David McReynolds (Socialist)   1980   P
Gus Hall (Communist)   1980   P
Clifton De Berry (Socialist
Workers)   1980   P
Matilde Zimmerman (Socialist
Workers)   1980 VP

David Koch (Libertarian)   1980 VP
Geraldine Anne Ferraro (D)   1984 VP
Gus Hall (Communist)   1984   P
Larry Holmes (Workers
World)   1984   P
Nancy Ross (Independent Alliance)   1984 VP

PRESIDENTIAL PRIMARY ELECTION In 1988, New York sent 275 Democratic delegates and 136 Republican delegates to the national conventions.

CONSTITUTION New York has had four constitutions: 1777, 1822, 1846, and the present one, adopted in 1894.

LEGISLATURE The Legislature is divided into the Senate (61 members, 2-year term, minimum age 18) and the Assembly (150 members, 2-year term, minimum age 18). In 1987, the annual salary was $43,000.

JUDICIARY The highest court is the Court of Appeals, with 7 judges serving initial 14-year terms (if reappointed, they serve until they reach the age of 70). In 1987, the annual salary was $115,000.

EXECUTIVE The governor serves a 4-year term; the minimum age for holding office is 30. In 1987, the annual salary was $130,000. There are 3 other elected officials.

PRESIDENTIAL VOTE 1948-1988 *(in percents)*

Year	State Winner	Democratic	Republican
1948	Dewey (R)	45.0	46.0
1952	Eisenhower (R)	43.6	55.5
1956	Eisenhower (R)	38.8	61.2
1960	Kennedy (D)	52.5	47.3
1964	Johnson (D)	68.6	31.3
1968	Humphrey (D)	49.8	44.3
1972	Nixon (R)	40.3	57.3
1976	Carter (D)	51.9	47.5
1980	Reagan (R)	44.0	46.7
1984	Reagan (R)	45.8	53.8
1988	Dukakis (D)	52.0	48.0

GOVERNORS

Directors of the West India Company
Adriaen Jorissen Tienpoint   1623-1624
Cornelis Jacobsen Mey   1624-1625
Willem Verhulst   1625-1626
Peter Minuit   1626-1632
Bastiaen Jansen Krol   1632-1633
Wouter Van Twiller   1633-1638
Willem Kieft   1638-1647
Peter Stuyvesant   1647-1664

English Governors
Richard Nicolls   1664-1668
Francis Lovelace   1668-1673

Dutch Governors
Cornelis Evertsen and war
council   1673
Anthony Colve (governor
general)   1673-1674

English Governors
Edmund Andros   1674-1677

Anthony Brockholls (lieutenant governor)	1677-1678
Sir Edmund Andros	1678-1681
Anthony Brockholls	1681-1683
Thomas Dongan	1683-1688
Sir Edmund Andros	1688
Francis Nicholson (lieutenant governor)	1688-1689
Jacob Leisler (lieutenant governor)	1689-1691
Henry Stoughter	1691
Richard Ingoldsby (commander in chief)	1691-1692
Benjamin Flecher	1692-1698
Richard Coote, 1st Earl of Bellamont	1698-1699
John Nanfan (lieutenant governor)	1699-1700
1st Earl of Bellamont	1700-1701
John Nanfan (lieutenant governor)	1701-1702
Edward Hyde, Viscount Cornbury	1702-1708
John Lovelace, 4th Baron Lovelace	1708-1709
Peter Schuyler (council president)	1709
Richard Ingoldsby (lieutenant governor)	1709-1710
Gerardus Beekman (council president)	1710
Robert Hunter	1710-1719
Peter Schuyler (council president)	1719-1720
William Burnet	1720-1728
John Montgomerie	1728-1731
Rip Van Dam (council president)	1731-1732
William Cosby	1732-1736
George Clarke (council president and lieutenant governor)	1736-1743
George Clinton	1743-1753
Sir Danvers Osborne	1753
James De Lancey (lieutenant governor)	1753-1755
Sir Charles Hardy	1755-1757
James De Lancey (lieutenant governor)	1757-1760
Cadwallader Colden (council president and lieutenant governor)	1760-1761
Robert Monckton	1761
Cadwallader Colden (lieutenant governor)	1761-1762
Robert Monckton	1762-1763
Cadwallader Colden (lieutenant governor)	1763-1765
Sir Henry Moor	1765-1769

Cadwallader Colden (lieutenant governor)	1769-1770
John Murray, 4th Earl of Dunmore	1770-1771
William Tryon	1771-1774
Cadwallader Colden	1774-1775
William Tryon	1775-1778
James Robertson	1779-1781
James Robertson (lieutenant-general)	1782-1783

State Governors

provincial congress	1776-1777
George Clinton	1777-1795
John Jay	1795-1801
George Clinton (Democratic-Republican)	1801-1804
Morgan Lewis (D-R)	1804-1807
Daniel D. Tompkins (D-R)	1807-1817
John Tayler (D-R/acting)	1817
DeWitt Clinton (D-R)	1817-1822
Joseph C. Yates (D-R)	1823-1824
DeWitt Clinton (D-R)	1825-1828
Nathaniel Pitcher (D-R/acting)	1828
Martin Van Buren (D)	1829
Enos T. Throop (D/acting)	1829-1830
Enos T. Throop (D)	1831-1832
William L. Marcy (D)	1833-1838
William H. Seward (Whig)	1839-1842
William C. Bouck (D)	1843-1844
Silas Wright (D)	1845-1846
John Young (Whig)	1847-1848
Hamilton Fish (Whig)	1849-1850
Washington Hunt (Whig)	1851-1852
Horatio Seymour (D)	1853-1854
Myron H. Clark (Whig)	1855-1856
John A. King (R)	1857-1858
Edwin D. Morgan (R)	1859-1862
Horatio Seymour (D)	1863-1864
Reuben E. Fenton (R)	1865-1868
John T. Hoffman (D)	1869-1872
John Adams Dix (R)	1873-1874
Samuel J. Tilden (D)	1875-1876
Lucius Robinson (D)	1877-1879
Alonzo B. Cornell (R)	1880-1882
Grover Cleveland (D)	1883-1885
David B. Hill (D/acting)	1885
David B. Hill (D)	1886-1891
Roswell P. Flower (D)	1892-1894
Levi P. Morton (R)	1895-1896
Frank S. Black (R)	1897-1898
Theodore Roosevelt (R)	1899-1900
Benjamin B. Odell Jr. (R)	1901-1904
Frank W. Higgins (R)	1905-1906
Charles Evans Hughes (R)	1907-1910
Horace White (R/acting)	1910
John Alden Dix (D)	1911-1912
William Sulzer (D)	1913

Martin Glynn (D/acting)	1913-1914
Charles S. Whitman (R)	1915-1918
Alfred E. Smith (D)	1919-1920
Nathan L. Miller (R)	1921-1922
Alfred E. Smith (D)	1923-1928
Franklin D. Roosevelt (D)	1929-1932
Herbert H. Lehman (D)	1933-1942
Charles Poletti (D/acting)	1942
Thomas E. Dewey (R)	1943-1954
Averill Harriman	1955-1958
Nelson Rockefeller (R)	1959-1973
Malcolm Wilson (R/acting)	1973-1974
Hugh J. Carey (D)	1975-1982
Mario M. Cuomo (D)	1983-

MINIMUM AGES

Majority	18
Marriage with parental consent	
female (with judicial consent)	14
male	16
Marriage without parental consent	18
Making a will	18
Buying alcohol	21
Jury duty	18
Leaving school	17
Driver's license	17

CAPITAL PUNISHMENT None

MILITARY INSTALLATIONS
Total number: 36
Major bases:
Army: 2
Air Force: 2

FINANCES

Thousands of dollars

GENERAL REVENUE (1985)

Total general revenue	37,342,447
Total tax revenue	20,702,069
Sales and gross receipts	6,910,616
Individual income taxes	10,394,165
Corporate net income taxes	1,859,979

GENERAL EXPENDITURE (1985)

Total general expenditure	33,358,620
Education	9,448,898
Public welfare	9,621,260
Health	1,046,360
Hospitals	2,210,010
Natural resources	182,482
Police	261,262
Corrections	1,139,288

FEDERAL AID (1985) 11,092,526

ECONOMY

Dairy products—cheese, butter, and milk—yield the greatest share of New York's farm income, followed by cattle and crops such as truck vegetables, grapes, and orchard fruits. Farm cash receipts were $2.7 billion in 1983. The state's mineral wealth is in building stone, gravel, and sand, with smaller quantities of iron, titanium, and grit stones. The principal products of New York's diverse manufacturing base include machinery, electrical products, printed materials, electronic instruments, cameras and photographic supplies, clothing, processed foods, metal products, chemicals, aircraft, and high-tech components. Value added by manufacture was $63 billion in 1982, second only to California. New York City is the world capital of international finance; banks, brokerages, and other financial firms located in New York have close to $1,000 billion in assets. Manhattan is also the center of the publishing, advertising, art, theater, and television industries. Tourism and conventions bring hundreds of million of dollars to the state each year. As a hub of trade to the inner parts of the nation, New York derives considerable revenue from shipping and transportation.

EMPLOYMENT (1984)

Thousands of persons

Total number of employed workers	7,505
Construction	251.8
Finance, insurance, and real estate	703.5
Government	1,317.3
Manufacturing	1,330.2
Mining	6.8
Services	1,962.0
Transportation, communications, and utilities	417.6
Wholesale and retail trade	1,567.9

Percent of civilian labor force unemployed (1984)	7.2

DEPARTMENT OF DEFENSE (1985)

Civilian workers employed	18,804
Military personnel	21,982
Contract awards	$10.033 billion

ENERGY SOURCES FOR ELECTRIC UTILITIES (1983)

Percent

Coal	14.9
Gas	11.8

Hydroelectric	. . . .	24.9		
Nuclear	. . . .	15.6		
Petroleum	. . . .	32.8		

TRANSPORTATION

Motor vehicles registered
in state (1986)   9,515,375
Miles of roads, streets,
and highways (1986) 110,136

Miles of Class I railway
operated (1986) 3,453
Airports (1983)   476
Major aviation hubs (1983) 6
Largest hub: New York
Major ports, with gross tonnage in
thousands (1985):
New York 152,054

CULTURE AND EDUCATION

Native American tribes
New York was formerly home to the Brotherton, Conoy, Delaware, Erie, Mahican, Neutral, Poospatuck, Susquehannock, Tutelo, Wappinger, and Wenro tribes. Groups that continue to live in the state include the Cayuga, Mohawk, Montauk, Oneida, Onondaga, Seneca, Shinnecock, and Tuscarora. There are six federal reservations in New York.

Religions, ethnicities, and languages
New York leads the nation in absorption of immigrants. It has always been exceptionally heterogeneous; by the mid-17th century, when it passed from Dutch to English control, at least 18 languages were already spoken there. During the 19th century New York, and especially New York City, took in millions of Irish, Germans, Italians, Russians, Poles, Greeks, and other Europeans; in the 20th century, its newcomers tended to be Puerto Rican, American black, South and Central American, Asian, and Middle Eastern. Almost every culture, nationality, and religion in the world has representatives here. In the 1970s, immigrants and the children of immigrants constituted one-third of the population. In 1980, 20.1 percent of New York's population spoke a language other than English at home. Approximately 40 percent of the population is Roman Catholic, another 40 percent Protestant, and 15 percent Jewish (the largest Jewish community in the world); there are also substantial Greek Orthodox, Buddhist, and Islamic communities.

Major museums and libraries
New York City
American Museum of Natural History
Brooklyn Museum
Frick Collection
Guggenheim Museum
Jewish Musem
Metropolitan Museum of Art
Museum of Modern Art

Museum of the American Indian
New York Public Library
Pierpont Morgan Library
Whitney Museum of American Art

Upstate
Albright-Knox Art Gallery, Buffalo
Buffalo Museum of Science
George Eastman House of Photography, Rochester
Memorial Art Gallery, University of Rochester
Rochester Museum and Science Center

Major arts organizations
New York City
Alvin Ailey American Dance Theater
American Ballet Theatre
American Place Theatre
Circle in the Square Theater
Dance Theatre of Harlem
Joffrey Ballet
Lincoln Center Theater
Metropolitan Opera Association
New York City Opera
New York Philharmonic
New York Shakespeare Festival

Upstate
Buffalo Philharmonic Orchestra
Empire State Institute for the Performing Arts, Albany
Rochester Philharmonic Orchestra
Studio Arena Theatre, Buffalo
Syracuse Stage

Colleges and universities
Number public (1986-87) 86
Number private (1986-87) 222
Total enrollment, in full-time equivalent students (1985) 763,600

Public elementary and secondary schools
Expenditure per pupil in average daily attendance (1986-87) $6,224
Pupil-teacher ratio (1987) 15.4
Average teacher salary (1986-87) $33,500

Major league sports teams

Baseball: New York Mets, New York Yankees
Basketball: New York Knicks
Football: Buffalo Bills, New York Jets
Hockey: Buffalo Sabres, New York Islanders, New York Rangers

Holidays

Pulaski Day. March 4
Verrazano Day. April 7
State Fair, Syracuse. Late August to early September

NEW YORK STATE IN LITERATURE

Samuel H. Adams *Canal Town* (1944)
Life of a doctor in Palmyra during the building of the Erie Canal.
———. *Banner by the Wayside* (1947)
A touring theatrical company in the Erie Canal region in the mid-nineteenth century.
———. *Grandfather Stories* (1955, rpt. 1988)
Tales of regional customs and history.

Anthony Bailey *Major André* (1987)
Novel based on the last days of John André, British army officer executed for spying on October 2, 1780.

T. Coraghessan Boyle *World's End* (1987)
Novel chronicling the lives of several generations of a Hudson Valley family, from the 17th century to the present day.

John H. Braunlein *Colonial Long Island Folklife* (1976)

John Brick *The Rifleman* (1953)
Novel based on the life of Timothy Murphy, upstate hero of the Revolution, one of a series of historical novels by this author set in the Hudson Valley.

John Burroughs *In the Catskills* (1910) *The Heart of Burroughs, Journals* (1928)
Catskill landscape, flora, and fauna, described by a pioneer naturalist.

Carl L. Carmer *Listen for a Lonesome Drum* (1936)
History of religious sectarianism in the state.
———. *Genesee Fever* (1941)
The Genesee Valley in the 1790s.
———. *The Tavern Lamps Are Burning: Literary Journeys Through Six Regions and Four Centuries of New York State* (1964)
Anthology of writing about upstate New York.
———. *My Kind of Country: Favorite Writings about New York* (1966)

Charles Champlin *Back There Where the Past Was* (1988)
Memoir of growing up in the Finger Lakes area in the 1930s and 1940s.

John Cheever *Bullet Park* (1969)
Satirical novel about an affluent Westchester family.

Henry Conklin *Through Poverty's Vale: A Hardscrabble Boyhood in Upstate New York, 1832–1862* (1974)
Memoir of a rural upbringing.

James Fenimore Cooper *The Spy* (1821)
An itinerant peddler spies for Washington during the Revolution. Often regarded as the first American historical novel.
———. *The Pioneers* (1823)
Novel centering on the settlement of Cooperstown in the 1780s.
———. *The Last of the Mohicans: a Narrative of 1757* (1826)
Romantic frontier adventure and the defense of Fort William Henry during the French and Indian War.
———. *Satanstoe* (1845)
An upstate landowner's journeys to Albany and New York City during the French and Indian Wars.

Susan Fenimore Cooper *Rural Hours* (1850, rpt. 1968)
Seasonal journal containing a detailed account of farm life near Otsego Lake in the 1840s.

Hector St. John de Crevecoeur (ed. A. E. Stone) *Letters from an American Farmer* (1782, rpt. 1951, 1963)
French aristocrat's account of life on a pioneer farm in Orange County before the Revolution.

Philander Deming *Adirondack Stories* (1880) *Tompkins and Other Folks* (1885)
Humorous Adirondack tales.

George Donaldson *Niagara* (1979)
The region's history and folklore.

Walter D. Edmonds *Rome Haul* (1929)
Novel of life on the Erie Canal in the mid-nineteenth century.
———. *Erie Water* (1933)
Novel of the building of the Erie Canal.
———. *Drums Along the Mohawk* (1936)
Mohawk Valley during the Revolution.
———. *Chad Hanna* (1940)
Mohawk Valley boy runs away to join the circus in the 1830s.
———. *In the Hands of the Senecas* (1947)
Upstate pioneers in the 1770s.

Edna Ferber *Saratoga Trunk* (1941)
Romantic novel set in Saratoga Springs during the spa's 1880s heyday.

Hugh Fosburgh *A Clearing in the Wilderness* (1969)
Observations of the ecology of a clearing in the Adirondack forest.

Harold Frederic *Seth's Brother's Wife* (1877)
Upstate rural life.
———. *In the Valley* (1890)
Mohawk Valley during the Revolution.
———. *The Copperhead* (1893)
A farmer's opposition to abolition of slavery is ended by his son's marriage to a reformer's daughter.
———. *The Damnation of Theron Ware* (1896)
Mohawk Valley evangelism.
———. (ed. T. F. O'Donnell) *Stories of New York State* (1966)
Tales of the Mohawk Valley during the Civil War.

John Gardner *Nickel Mountain* (1973)
Novel of working-class life in the Catskills during the 1960s.

Noel Gerson *Savage Gentleman* (1950)
Historical novel set in Schenectady during Queen Anne's War, 1702–1713.

Robert Gessner *Treason* (1944)
Novel about the career of Benedict Arnold.

Anne Grant *Memoirs of an American Lady; with Sketches of Manners and Scenery . . . Previous to the Revolution* (1876)
Loyalist's upstate journal.

Robert Graves *Sergeant Lamb's America* (1940, rpt. 1987)
An Irish soldier serves in the British army under Burgoyne during the Saratoga campaign.

Charles Fenno Hoffman *Greyslaer* (1840)
Romantic historical novel centered on the Revolutionary battle of Oriskany.

James Horan *King's Rebel* (1953)
Historical novel of Indian warfare and the Cherry Valley massacre during the Revolution.
———. *The Neutral Ground* (1941)
Westchester County during the Revolution.

George F. Hummel *Subsoil* (1924); *Heritage* (1935)
Long Island farming during pioneer times.

Washington Irving *A History of New York . . . by Diedrich Knickerbocker* (1809, rpt. 1981)
A burlesque portait of Dutch colonial times that inaugurated the tradition of Knickerbocker fiction.

————. *The Sketch Book* (1819)
Volume of essays, chiefly on English topics, containing "Rip Van Winkle," and "The Legend of Sleepy Hollow," American versions of German folktales, in which Irving used the Catskills and lower Hudson Valley as regional settings.

J. F. Jameson (ed.) *Narratives of New Netherland, 1609–1664* (1909)
Accounts drawn from the diaries of early settlers.

Louis C. Jones (ed.) *Growing up in the Cooper Country: Boyhood Recollections of the New York Frontier* (1965)
————. *Three Eyes on the Past: Exploring New York State Folk Life* (1982)

William Kennedy *Legs* (1983)
Bootlegging in the Catskills and Albany during Prohibition.
————. *Ironweed* (1983)
Third novel in a trilogy depicting social and political life in Albany prior to World War II.
————. *Quinn's Book* (1989)
Novel about an Albany journalist, 1849–1864.

Anne LaBastille *Woodswoman* (1976); *Beyond Black Bear Lake* (1987)
Account of a Thoreau-like attempt to live in and know the Adirondack wilderness.

Bruce Lancaster *Guns of Burgoyne* (1939)
The battle of Saratoga seen through the eyes of a Hessian soldier.
————. *Secret Road* (1952)
Revolutionary espionage on Long Island in 1780.

Jerre G. Mangione *Mount Allegro* (1943)
An Italian American's childhood in Rochester.

Peter Matthiessen *Men's Lives: The Surfmen and Baymen of South Fork* (1988)
Non-fiction account of the vanishing way of life of the fishermen of South Fork, Long Island.

Frances Nutt *Three Fields to Cross* (1947)
Family life on Staten Island during the Revolution.

James K. Paulding *The Dutchman's Fireside* (1831)
Genre account of Dutch farming life in the Hudson Valley before the French and Indian Wars.
————. *The Old Continental* (1841)
Adventures of a common soldier during the Revolution.

Alexandra Phillips *Forever Possess* (1946)
Historical novel set on a Hudson Valley estate at the time of Leisler's rebellion.

Kenneth Roberts *Rabble in Arms* (1933)
Novel of the Saratoga campaign and the defeat of Burgoyne.

Constance Robertson *The Unterrified* (1946)
Novel set in Troy during the Civil War.

Richard Russo *Mohawk* (1986); *The Risk Pool* (1988)
Novels of coming of age in a small upstate town.

Paul Schaefer *Defending the Wilderness: The Adirondack Writings of Paul Schaefer* (1988)
Naturalist's essays and plea for conservation.

Anne G. Sneller *A Vanished World* (1964)
Memoir of eighty years of upstate life, including reminiscences of the Civil War.

Bart Spicer *Brother to the Enemy* (1958)
Historical novel about Benedict Arnold.

Harold W. Thompson *Body, Boots, and Britches: Folktales, Ballads and Speech From Country New York* (1939; rpt. 1962, 1979)

Roland Van Zandt (ed.) *Chronicles of the Hudson: Three Centuries of Travelers' Accounts* (1971)

Edward Westcott *David Harum: a Story of an American Life* (1898)
The life of a Syracuse banker during the Civil War.

Edith Wharton *Hudson River Bracketed* (1929)
A young midwesterner's stay at a Hudson Valley house built in the 1840s, and his discovery of the cultural tradition symbolized by its architecture.

Walt Whitman (ed. H. M. Christman) *Walt Whitman's New York: From Manhattan to Montauk* (1963)
A collection of articles on contemporary issues and historical events written by Whitman for the Brooklyn *Standard*.

Edmund Wilson *Upstate: Records and Recollections of Northern New York* (1971)
Journal of Wilson's life in Talcottville, with observations on local history and folklore.
———— and **Joseph Mitchell** *Apologies to the Iroquois: with a Study of the Mohawks in High Steel* (1959)
The history of upstate New York's original inhabitants.

Rufus R. and Otilie E. Wilson *New York in Literature* (1947)

Lionel D. Wyld *Low Bridge!: Folklore and the Erie Canal* (1962)

NEW YORK CITY IN LITERATURE

Renata Adler *Sketches of Urban Life* (1976)
Episodes in the life of a cultural journalist and novelist.

Sholom Aleichem *The Adventures of Mottel, the Cantor's Son* (1953)
Novel about a Jewish immigrant family.

Sholem Asch (tr. Isaac Goldberg) *Uncle Moses* (1920)
Jewish immigrant life in the sweatshops of the Lower East Side.
————. *East River* (1946)
The fortunes of a Jewish family in the early 1900s.

Louis Auchincloss *Portrait in Brownstone* (1962)
An upper-class Manhattan family 1900–1950.
————. *Tales of Manhattan* (1967); *Skinny Island* (1987)
Stories of high society.
————. *The Country Cousin* (1978)
An ingenue's loss of innocence in '30s Manhattan.

James Baldwin *Go Tell It on the Mountain* (1963)
Novel centering on the religious conversion of a Harlem boy.
————. *Tell Me How Long the Train's Been Gone* (1968)
Harlem life in the 1930s and 1940s.

William Beebe *Unseen Life of New York: As a Naturalist Sees It* (1953)
Account of the city as a bio-region.

Meyer Berger *Meyer Berger's New York* (1960)
Essays by a journalist born on the Lower East Side in 1898.

Arna Bontemps (ed.) *The Harlem Renaissance Remembered* (1972)
Recollections of people and events of the 1920s.

Benjamin A. Botkin (ed.) *New York City Folklore* (1956)

Jimmy Breslin *The Gang That Couldn't Shoot Straight* (1969)
Brooklyn gangsters and politicians.

Henry Cuyler Bunner *Short Sixes* (1917)
Sketches of Manhattan street life.

Abraham Cahan *The Rise of David Levinsky* (1917)
A Russian-Jewish immigrant struggles to rise from the Lower East Side ghetto.

Susan Cahill *Earth Angels* (1976)
Novel about a Catholic girl's upbringing in Queens.

Hortense Calisher *The New Yorkers* (1969)
A wealthy Manhattan Jewish family 1943–1955.

Truman Capote *Breakfast at Tiffany's* (1958)
Novella about the adventures of an amoral girl in the 1950s.

Barbara Cohen et al. (eds.) *New York Observed: Artists and Writers Look at the City, 1650 to the Present* (1987)

Stephen Crane *Maggie: A Girl of the Streets* (1893)
A young Irish working woman's fall into crime and despair.

Countee Cullen *One Way to Heaven* (1932)
A romantic comedy about poor blacks.

Valentine Davies *Miracle on 34th Street* (1947)
The Macy's Santa Claus succeeds in proving his identity in the city courts.

Dorothy S. Davis *Men of No Property* (1955)
Irish immigrant life 1848–1870.

Clarence Day *Life With Father* (1961)
Humorous accounts of Manhattan family life.

E. L. Doctorow *Ragtime* (1975)
Novel of 1920s society.

John Dos Passos *Manhattan Transfer* (1925)
A panorama of metropolitan scenes and characters.

Theodore Dreiser *Sister Carrie* (1900)
Novel of the life of a lower-middle-class showgirl.
————. *The Color of a Great City* (1923)
Sketches of the city 1900–1915.

Susan Edmiston and **Linda D. Cirino** *Literary New York: A History and Guide* (1976)

Jack Finney *Time and Again* (1970)
A detailed evocation of the city in the 1880s.

F. Scott Fitzgerald *The Beautiful and Damned* (1922)
Novel portraying the wealthy decadence of the 1920s.

Paul L. Ford *The Honorable Peter Stirling* (1894)
Novel of 1870s politics partly based on the life of Grover Cleveland.

Rosa Guy *A Measure of Time* (1983)
A black woman's coming of age in Harlem in the 1920s.

Ben Hecht *1001 Afternoons in New York* (1941)
A collection of journalistic sketches and reports.

William D. Howells *A Hazard of New Fortunes* (1890)
A Yankee editor and his wife set up home in Manhattan.

Langston Hughes *Simple Speaks His Mind* (1950)
A Harlem black's opinion on matters of local and national importance.

Albert Idell *Bridge to Brooklyn* (1944)
Family life in Brooklyn c.1883.
————. *Great Blizzard* (1948)
Family story set in Brooklyn and Manhattan between 1884 and the blizzard of 1888.

César Andreu Iglesias (ed.) *Memoirs of Bernardo Vega: A Contribution to the History of the Puerto Rican Community in New York* (trans. of *Memorias de Bernardo Vega*, 1977) (1984)
A personal account of the experiences of Puerto Rican migrants in the early 20th century.

Henry James *Washington Square* (1881)
Short novel of manners portraying late-nineteenth-century society.
————. *The American Scene* (1907)
Observations on New York scenes and people.

Roger Kahn *The Boys of Summer* (1972)
The childhood of a Dodgers fan, and his career as a reporter following the team until its move to Los Angeles.

Myra Kelly *Little Citizens* (1904)
A schoolteacher's stories of her East Side Jewish pupils.

John Kieran *Footnotes on Nature* (1947); *A Natural History of New York City* (1959)
Descriptions of searches for natural life in Manhattan.

Eugene Kinkead *A Concrete Look at Nature: Central Park (and Other) Glimpses* (1974)
Accounts of a naturalist's rambles in the city.

Alexander Klein (ed.) *The Empire City: All the Best Ever Written About New York* (1955)
An anthology of essays and articles by notable writers.

Oscar Lewis *La Vida: A Puerto Rican Family in the Culture of Poverty* (1966)
An anthropologist's study of a Harlem family.

Hamilton W. Mabie *The Writers of Knickerbocker, New York* (1912)

Bernard Malamud *The Assistant* (1971)
Novel about the family of a Brooklyn Jewish grocer.

Mike Marquesee and **Bill Harris** *New York, an Anthology* (1985)
Poetry and prose describing the city by a wide range of writers including Whitman, Bierce, Hansberry, and Capote.

Brander Matthews *Vignettes of Manhattan* (1894)
Sketches of city people and neighborhoods in the late nineteenth century.

Ed McBain *Long Time No See* (1977)
One of a classic detective mystery writer's many novels with a New York setting.

Bucklin Moon *Darker Brother* (1943)
A Southern-born black teenager comes of age in Harlem.

Christopher Morley *Christopher Morley's New York* (1988)
Essays on Manhattan literary and social life in the 1920s.

0. Henry (pseud. of William Sydney Porter) *Voice of the City: Further Stories of the Four Million* (1908); *Trimmed Lamp, and Other Stories of the Four Million* (1908)
New York characters and types.

John O'Hara *Butterfield 8* (1935)
Manhattan nightlife during Prohibition.

Dorothy Parker "The Big Blonde," in *Collected Stories of Dorothy Parker* (1942)
Classic tale of New York society.

David Graham Phillips *Light-Fingered Gentry* (1907)
Financial and political scandals of the 1890s.

Ernest Poole *The Harbor* (1915)
Novel about a man's crusade for improved working conditions set on the Manhattan and Brooklyn waterfront.
————. *His Family* (1917)
Manhattan seen through the eyes of three young working women.

Richard Price *The Wanderers* (1974)
Realistic account of growing up in the Bronx.

V. S. Pritchett *New York Proclaimed* (1965)
Impressionistic essays by a British man of letters.

Frederic Prokosch *Idols of the Cave* (1946)
Cosmopolitan society in the 1930s.

Elmer Rice *Imperial City* (1937)
The financial community in the 1920s and 1930s.

Edward Rivera *Family Installments: Memories of Growing Up Hispanic* (1982)
A part-autobiographical fiction about growing up in Puerto Rico and Manhattan during the 1960s and '70s.

Leo Rosten *The Education of Hyman Kaplan* (1937)
Jewish immigrant life in the 1920s.

Henry Roth *Call It Sleep* (1934)
A Jewish childhood in the ghettos of Brownsville and the Lower East Side.

Damon Runyon *Guys and Dolls* (1950)
Manhattan life in the 1930s and 1940s.

Gene Schermerhorn *Letters to Phil: Memories of a New York Boyhood, 1848–1856* (1982)

Kate Simon *Bronx Primitive* (1983); *A Wider World: Portraits in an Adolescence* (1986)
Memoirs of growing up in the Bronx during World War II.

Isaac Bashevis Singer *Enemies, A Love Story* (1972)
Moral dilemmas of a Polish Jew living in Brooklyn.
————. *The Family Carnovsky* (1972)
Post–World War II Jewish life in Manhattan.

Betty Smith *A Tree Grows in Brooklyn* (1943)
Life of a tenement family before and during World War I.

Ramona Stewart *Casey* (1968)
An Irish-American politician's rise to power c.1850.

Bayrd Still (ed.) *Mirror for Gotham: New York as Seen by Contemporaries from Dutch Days to the Present* (1956)
Collection of eyewitness accounts of Manhattan.

John Tebbel *Voice in the Streets* (1954)
Novel of city politics c.1850.

Jean Toomer *Cane* (1923)
Collection of prose and poetry evoking the artistic development of a Harlem black.

Adriaen Van der Donck *A Description of the New Netherlands* (1968)
The earliest account of the Dutch colony, written in Holland in 1641.

Carl Van Vechten *Nigger Heaven* (1926)
The culture of Harlem during the 1920s.

Jerome Weidman *I Can Get It for You Wholesale* (1937)
An unscrupulous young Jew makes his fortune in the garment industry.

Edith Wharton *The House of Mirth* (1905)
The downfall of a penurious society woman who fails to find a husband.

———. *The Age of Innocence* (1920)
Manners of wealthy society in the 1870s.
———. *Old New York* (1924)
Portraits of Manhattan people.

Tom Wolfe *The Bonfire of the Vanities* (1987)
A satiric novel of fashion and high society set in the 1980s concerning the fall of a wealthy bond trader.

Herman Wouk *Cityboy* (1969)
A Jewish boy's adventures at home, school, and summer camp.

Helen Yglesias *Family Feeling* (1976)
A child of Jewish immigrant parents rises from poverty in Bronx and Brooklyn ghettos to prominence in left-wing intellectual circles.

Louis Zara *Blessed Is the Land* (1954)
Novel about the first Jewish immigrants to New Amsterdam in 1654.

GUIDES TO RESOURCES

Burke, Kate *Searching in New York: A Reference Guide to Public and Private Records* (1987)

Burnham, Alan (ed. Arnold Markowitz) *New York City: An Annotated Bibliography Covering its Growth and Development* (1986)

Federal Writers' Project *New York City Guide* (1939, rpt. 1982)
———. *New York: A Guide to the Empire State* (1940, rpt. 1962)
———. *New York Panorama: A Comprehensive View of the Metropolis Presented in a Series of Articles* (1941, rpt. 1981)

Federation of Historical Services *Handbook to Historic Resources in the Upper Hudson, Mohawk, and Champlain Valleys* (2d ed. 1987)

Flagg, C. A. and J. T. Jennings "Bibliography of New York Colonial History" *Bulletin of the New York State Library*, No. 56 (1901)

Greenberg, Charles (ed.) *New York State Local History: A Checklist of Selected Resources* (1984)

Hepfer, Cindy and William "The Periodicals of New York State" *Serials Review* 11 (Spring 1985)

Harnik, Tema G. *Wherewithal: A Guide to Resources for Museums and Historical Societies in New York State* (1981)

Lopez, Manuel D. *New York: A Guide to Information and Reference Sources* (1980)

Lower Hudson Conference *Directory of Historical Agencies, Museums and Local Historians in Dutchess, Putnam, Rockland and Westchester Counties* (1984)

Mason, Elizabeth and Louis M. Starr *The Oral History Collection of Columbia University* (1979)

Mitchell, George A. (ed.) *The New York Red Book* (annual)

Munger, W. P. *Historical Atlas of New York* (1941)

Nelson A. Rockefeller Institute of Government, State University of New York *New York State Statistical Yearbook* (annual)

Nestler, Harold *Bibliography of New York State Communities: Counties, Towns, and Villages* (1968)

New York State Library *Dictionary Catalog of Official Publications of the State of New York, 1973–1983* (1984)

Office of State History, Albany *Research and Publications in New York State History: A Bibliography* (annual 1968–)

Palmer, Joseph W. (ed.) *Directory of Oral History and Audio-Visual Local History Resources in Public Libraries in New York State* Buffalo: School of Information and Library Studies, State University of New York (1985)

Patterson, Jerry E. *The City of New York: A History Illustrated from the Collections of the Museum of the City of New York* (1978)

Perry, Margaret *The Harlem Renaissance: An Annotated Bibliography* (1982)

Plum, Dorothy A. *Adirondack Bibliography* (1958)

Rayback, Robert J. (ed.) *Richard Atlas of New York State* (1965)

Sealock, Richard and Pauline A. Seely *Long Island Bibliography* (1940)

White, Norval and Elliot Willensky *AIA Guide to New York City* (3d. ed. 1988)
——— and Elliot Willensky *New York: A Physical History* (1988)

SELECTED NONFICTION SOURCES FOR NEW YORK STATE

Abbott, Wilbur C. *New York in Revolution* (1929)

Albion, Robert G. *The Rise of New York Port, 1815–1860* (1970)

Alexander, D. S. *Political History of the State of New York*, 4 vols (1906–1923)

Andrews, Edward D. *The Community Industries of the Shakers* (1933)

Avery, Giles B. *Sketches of Shakers and Shakerism* (1884)

Bailey, Rosalie F. *Pre-Revolutionary Dutch Houses and Families in Northern New Jersey and Southern New York* (1936)

Beauchamp, William M. *History of the New York Iroquois* (1905)
———. "Aboriginal Place Names of New York" *Bulletin of the New York State Museum*, no. 108 (1907, rpt. 1972)

Bishop, Morris *Champlain* (1948)

Bliven, Bruce, Jr. *Battle for Manhattan* (1956)

———. *Under the Guns: New York, 1775–76* (1972)
———. *New York* (1981)

Bonomi, Patricia V. *A Factious People: Politics and Society in Colonial New York* (1971)

Boyle, Robert H. *The Hudson River: A Natural and Unnatural History* (1969)

Boynton, Henry W. *James Fenimore Cooper* (1931)

Bronner, Simon J. *Old-Time Music Makers of New York State* (1987)

Brummer, Sidney D. *A Political History of New York State During the Civil War* (1911)

Buranelli, Vincent (ed.) *The Trial of Peter Zenger* (1957)

Burgess, Anthony *New York* (1977)

Carmer, Carl L. *The Hudson* (Rivers of America series) (rev. ed. 1968, rpt. 1988)

Caro, Robert A. *The Power Broker: Robert Moses and the Fall of New York* (1974)

Clune, Henry W. *The Genesee* (Rivers of America series) (1963)

Cross, Whitney *The Burned-Over District: The Social and Intellectual History of Enthusiastic Religion in Western New York, 1800–50* (1950)

De Sormo, Maitland C. *The Heydays of the Adirondacks* (1974)

Eberlein, H. D. *Manor Houses and Historic Homes of the Hudson Valley* (1924)

Ellis, David M. et al. *A Short History of New York State* (rev. ed.) (1967)

Everest, Allan S. *Run Across the Border: the Prohibition Era in Northern New York* (1978)

Evers, A. *The Catskills, from Wilderness to Woodstock* (1972)

Flick, Alexander C. (ed.) *A History of the State of New York*, 10 vols (1933–1937)

Fox, Dixon R. *Decline of the Aristocracy in the Politics of New York* (1918)

Gerlach, Don R. *Philip Schuyler and the American Revolution in New York, 1733–1777* (1964)

Goodwin, Maud W. *The Dutch and English on the Hudson* (1919)

Halsey, Francis W. *The Old New York Frontier: Its Wars with Indians and Tories, Its Missionary Schools, Peasants and Land Titles 1614–1800* (1901; rpt. 1963)

Hislop, Codman *The Mohawk* (Rivers of America series) (1948)

Hopkins, A. S. *Lake George* (1939)

Howat, John K. *The Hudson River and Its Painters* (1972)
———. (ed.) *American Paradise: The World of the Hudson River School* (1987)

Jackson, Harry F. *Scholar in the Wilderness: Francis Adrian Van der Kemp* (1963)

Jamieson, Paul F. *The Adirondack Reader* (1964)

Kammen, Michael *Colonial New York: A History* (1975)

Keller, Jane E. *Adirondack Park* (1978)

Kennedy, William *O Albany: Improbable City of Political Wizards, Fearless Ethnics, Spectacular Aristocrats, Splendid Nobodies and Underrated Scoundrels* (1985)

Kenney, Alice P. *Stubborn for Liberty: The Dutch in New York* (1975)

Launitz-Schurer, Leopold *Loyal Whigs and Revolutionaries: The Making of the Revolution in New York, 1765–1766* (1980)

Lederer, Richard M. *The Place Names of Westchester County* (1978)

Mark, Irving *Agrarian Conflicts in Colonial New York, 1711–1775* (1940)

Mason, Bernard *Road to Independence: the Revolutionary Movement in New York, 1773–1777* (1966)

McKee, Samuel *Labor in Colonial New York* (1964)

Morison, Samuel E. *Samuel de Champlain* (1972)

Myers, Kenneth *The Catskills: Painters, Writers, and Tourists in the Mountains, 1820–1895* (1988)

Nevins, Allan *Herbert H. Lehman and His Era* (1963)

Niemczycki, M.A.P. *The Origin and Development of the Seneca and Cayuga Tribes of New York State* (1984)

O'Brien, Raymond J. *American Sublime: Landscape and Scenery of The Lower Hudson Valley* (1981)

Oppenheim, Samuel *The Early History of the Jews in New York* (1909)

Parker, Robert A. *A Yankee Saint; John N. Noyes and the Oneida Community* (1935)

Powys, Llewelyn *Henry Hudson* (1928)

Raesly, E. L. *Portrait of New Netherland* (1945)

Ranlet, Philip *The New York Loyalists* (1986)

Rattray, Everett T. *The South Fork: The Land and People of Eastern Long Island* (1979)

Reed, John *The Hudson River Valley* (1960)

Richter, Daniel K. and James H. Merrell (eds.) *Beyond the Covenant Chain: The Iroquois and Their Neighbors, 1600–1800* (1987)

Ritchie, William A. *The Archaeology of New York State* (1969, rpt. 1980)

Rowe, David L. *Thunder and Trumpets: Millerites and Dissenting Religion in Upstate New York, 1800–1850* (1985)

Shaw, Ronald E. *Erie Water West* (1966)

Smith, William Jr. (ed. M. Kammen) *The History of the Province of New York* 2 vols. (1972)

Spiller, Robert E. *Fenimore Cooper: Critic of His Times* (1931)

Thompson, John H. *The Geography of New York State* (1966)

Van der Zee, Henri and Barbara *A Sweet and Alien Land: The Story of Dutch New York* (1978)

Van Zandt, Roland *The Catskill Mountain House* (1966)

Waller, George *Saratoga: Saga of an Impious Era* (1966)

White, William C. *Adirondack Country* (1954)

SELECTED NONFICTION SOURCES FOR NEW YORK CITY

Auletta, Ken *The Streets Were Paved with Gold: The Decline of New York--An American Tragedy* (1980)

Barlow, Elizabeth *The Forests and Wetlands of New York City* (1971)
———. *Frederick Law Olmsted's New York* (1972)

Bayor, Ronald H. *Neighbors in Conflict: The Irish, Germans, Jews and Italians of New York City* (1978)

Bellush, Jewel, and Stephen M. David *Race and Politics in New York City* (1971)

Benton, Barbara *Ellis Island: A Pictorial History* (1985)

Birmingham, Stephen *"Our Crowd": The Great Jewish Families of New York* (1967)

Blanchet, Christian and Bertrand Dard *Statue of Liberty: The First Hundred Years* (1985)

Bloom, Alexander *Prodigal Sons: The New York Intellectuals and Their World* (1986)

Bordman, Gerald *American Musical Theatre: A Chronicle* (1978)

Chapin, Anna A. *Greenwich Village* (1917)

Charyn, Jerome *Metropolis: New York as Myth, Marketplace, and Magical Land* (1986)

Dunshee, Kenneth H. *As You Pass By* (1952)

Ernst, Robert *Immigrant Life in New York City, 1825–1863* (1949)

Fischler, Stan *Uptown, Downtown* (1976)

Friedman, Josh A. *Tales of Times Square* (1986)

Glazer, Nathan and Daniel P. Moynihan *Beyond the Melting Pot: The Negroes, Puerto Ricans, Jews, Italians, and Irish of New York City* (1963)

Goldberger, Paul *The City Observed* (1979)

Hammack, David C. *Power and Society: Greater New York at the Turn of the Century* (1982)

Harrington, Virginia D. *The New York Merchant on the Eve of the Revolution* (1964)

Hayden, Richard S. and Thierry Despont *Restoring the Statue of Liberty* (1986)

Heckscher, August, and Phyllis Robinson *When La Guardia Was Mayor* (1978)

Honig, Donald *The New York Yankees: An Illustrated History* (1981)

Howe, Irving *World of Our Fathers* (1976)

Jastrow, Marie *A Time to Remember: Growing Up in New York Before the Great War* (1979)

Jennison, C. *Wait 'til Next Year: The Yankees, Dodgers, and Giants 1947–1957* (1974)

Johnson, James W. *Black Manhattan* (1930)

Kellner, Bruce (ed.) *The Harlem Renaissance, an Historical Dictionary for the Era* (1984)

Klein, Alexander (ed.) *Empire City: A Treasury of New York* (1955)

Klein, Carole *Gramercy Park: An American Bloomsbury* (1987)

Kolodin, Irving *The Metropolitan Opera: 1883–1939*, New York, 1939.

Kouwenhoven, John A. *Columbia Historical Portrait of New York* (1953; rpt. 1972)

Lancaster, Clay *Old Brooklyn Heights* (1961; rpt. 1979)

Lewis, David L. *When Harlem was in Vogue* (1981)

Lockwood, Charles *Bricks and Brownstone: The New York Row House 1783–1929* (1972)

Loth, David *The City Within a City: The Romance of Rockefeller Center* (1966)

Mandelbaum, Seymour J. *Boss Tweed's New York* (1965; rpt. 1981)

Mann, Arthur *La Guardia Comes to Power* (1933, rpt. 1981)

Mayer, Grace M. *Once Upon a City: New York from 1890 to 1910 As Photographed by Byron* (1958; rpt. 1971)

McCullough, David *The Great Bridge* (1972)

McKay, Claude *Negro Metropolis* (1940)

Monaghan, Frank and Marvin Lowenthal *This Was New York: the Nation's Capital in 1789* (1943)

Moorhouse, Geoffrey *Imperial City: The Rise and Rise of New York* (1988)

Morris, James *The Great Port: A Passage to New York* (1969)

Morris, Jan *Manhattan '45* (1987)

Orsi, Robert A. *The Madonna of 115th Street: Faith and Community in Italian Harlem, 1880–1950* (1985)

Reed, Henry H. *Central Park: A History and Guide* (1967)

Reynolds, Donald M. *The Architecture of New York City* (1988)

Rink, Oliver *Holland on the Hudson* (1988)

Riis, Jacob A. *How the Other Half Lives: Studies Among the Tenements of New York* (1890; rpt. 1971)

Rischin, Moses *The Promised City: New York's Jews, 1870–1914* (1962)

Roskolenko, Harry *The Time That Was Then: The Lower East Side, 1900–1913* (1971)

Schuberth, Christopher J. *The Geology of New York City and Environs* (1968)

Simon, Kate *Fifth Avenue: A Very Social History* (1978)
———. *New York Places and Pleasures: An Uncommon Guide Book* (1971; rpt. 1980)

Sobel, Robert *The Big Board: A History of the New York Stock Market* (1965)

Sutton, Horace *Confessions of a Grand Hotel: The Waldorf Astoria* (1953)

Talese, Gay *The Kingdom and the Power* (1969)

Trachtenberg, Marvin *The Statue of Liberty* (1976)

Werner, M. R. *Tammany Hall* (1968)

Willensky, Elliot *When Brooklyn Was the World* (1986)

NORTH CAROLINA

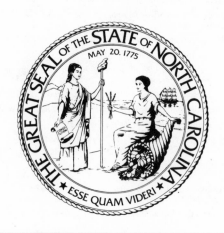

North Carolina, a South Atlantic state, is bordered on the north by Virginia; on the east and southeast by the Atlantic Ocean; on the south by South Carolina and Georgia; and on the west and northwest by Tennessee.

FULL NAME State of North Carolina
POSTAL ABBREVIATION NC
INHABITANT North Carolinian
ADMITTED TO THE UNION Nov. 21, 1789.
  12th state
POPULATION (est. 1987) 6,413,000.
  Percent of US total: 2.64%. Rank: 10th

CAPITAL CITY Raleigh, located in east central North Carolina; population 169,331 (est. 1984). The site, named after Sir Walter Raleigh, was chosen for settlement in 1788, founded and made the state capital in 1792, and incorporated in 1793.

STATE NAME AND NICKNAMES Named in honor of King Charles IX of France and then of King Charles I and King Charles II of England. Also known as the Tarheel State, the Old North State, and the Turpentine State.

STATE SEAL In a landscape of grassy hills, the Goddess of Liberty, holding a Phrygian cap and the Constitution, and the Goddess Ceres, sitting beside a cornucopia and holding three heads of ripe wheat; in the distance is a three-masted ship under sail. Above them is the inscription "May 20, 1775." Around the border are the legends "The Great Seal of the State of North Carolina" and the state motto.

MOTTO Esse Quam Videri (To be rather than to seem)

SONG "The Old North State"

SYMBOLS
Flower dogwood
Tree pine
Bird cardinal
Stone emerald
Rock granite
Mammal gray squirrel
Reptile turtle
Saltwater fish channel bass or red drum
Insect honeybee
Shell Scotch bonnet
Color red and blue
Toast song "A Toast"

LICENSE PLATES (1) Dark blue on white, with red legend "First in Flight," state name in red, and image of Wright Brothers' airplane in flight. (2) Orange-red on white, with orange-red border.

FLAG The flag is divided into a blue segment, occupying one-third of the length, and horizontal red and white segments, occupying the remaining two-thirds. On the blue segment is a white star flanked by the letters N and C in gold; a gold scroll above them reads "May 20th, 1775," another below them reads "April 12th, 1776."

GEOGRAPHY AND CLIMATE

The three main geographical areas of North Carolina are the Coastal Plain and tidal regions, including the Outer Banks, a long series of sandy islands paralleling the coast, and the treacherous waters of Cape Hatteras, Cape Lookout, and Cape Fear; the central Piedmont Plateau, an industrial region of rolling, forested hills; and, to the west, the Appalachian Mountains, containing the Blue Ridge, Unaka, and Smoky ranges.

AREA 52,669 square miles. Rank: 28th
INLAND WATER 3,826 square miles
GEOGRAPHIC CENTER Chatham, 10 miles NW of Sanford
ELEVATIONS *Highest point:* Mount Mitchell, Yancey County, 6,684 feet. *Lowest point:* Atlantic Ocean, sea level. *Mean elevation:* 700 feet

MAJOR RIVERS Yadkin, Pee Dee, Cape Fear, Neuse, Roanoke

MAJOR LAKES AND RESERVOIRS Norman, Fontana, Mattamuskeet, Jordan, Gaston, Kerr, Lake of the Neuse

TIDAL SHORELINE 3,375 miles, Atlantic coast

LAND USE

	Thousands of acres
Urban (1982)	1,622
Rural (1982)	26,481
Cropland (1982)	6,695
Pastureland (1982)	1,980
Rangeland (1982)	0
Forestland (1982)	16,729
State parks and recreation areas (1983)	120
National park system (1984)	378
National forest system (1984)	3,165
Tribal lands (1984)	56

TEMPERATURES The highest recorded temperature was 110°F on August 21, 1983, at Fayettville. The lowest was -34°F on January 21, 1985, at Mitchell.

NATIONAL SITES

NATIONAL HISTORIC SITES Carl Sandburg Home, Fort Raleigh
NATIONAL MEMORIAL Wright Brothers
NATIONAL MILITARY PARK Guilford Courthouse
NATIONAL PARK Great Smoky Mountains
NATIONAL PARKWAY Blue Ridge

NATIONAL SCENIC TRAIL Appalachian
NATIONAL SEASHORES Cape Hatteras, Cape Lookout
NATIONAL WILDLIFE REFUGES Great Dismal Swamp, Mackay Island, Mattamuskeet–Cedar Island/Swanquarter, Pea Island, Pee Dee, Pungo

HISTORY

1524	Italian navigator, Giovanni de Verrazzano, explores the coast of North Carolina for France.
1584	*March 25.* Walter Raleigh is granted patent of discovery.
	July. Sent by Raleigh, Philip Amandas and Arthur Barlowe land on Roanoke Island.
	September. Amandas and Barlowe return to England with high praises for Roanoke and Raleigh is knighted by Queen Elizabeth. The new land is named Virginia.
1585	*August.* Ralph Lane and a group of settlers arrive at Roanoke and begin to build Fort Raleigh.
1586	Sir Francis Drake brings most of the colonists back to England as their supplies had dwindled and replacements were delayed.
1587	A second party of Raleigh-backed colonists, led by John White, lands at Roanoke. *August 18.* Birth of Virginia Dare: the first child born of English parents in America.
1590	White returns to Roanoke but finds the area deserted with no trace of the colonists except the word "CROATOAN" carved in a tree. This expedition becomes known as the Lost Colony.
1629	Sir Robert Heath is granted a charter from Charles I for territory south of Virginia and the region is named *Carolana*—the "Land of Charles."
1653	Robert Green founds a settlement on Albemarle Sound. Virginia settlers begin migration to the territory of Chowan County.
1663	Charles II grants the territory to eight lord proprietors.

1667	*March 11*. The proprietors issue the Fundamental Constitutions, drawn up by philosopher John Locke.
1675	Chowan Indians war with Virginia whites.
1677	*December 3*. John Culpepper leads a rebellion against proprietary rule and tobacco export duties.
1691	Albemarle is renamed North Carolina, with its governor to be deputy, responsible to the Crown.
1700	Arguments erupt between Quakers and Anglicans over the latter's establishment of a Church of England in the Carolinas.
1711	*September*. War begins with the Tuscarora Indians who are eventually defeated and expelled from the province.
1712	*May 9*. An independent governor is appointed for North Carolina.
1718	*November 22*. Pirate Blackbeard (Edward Teach) is killed near Ocracoke Island.
1729	The proprietors of North Carolina are bought out by King George II and the territory is made a royal colony.
1730	An attempt to define North and South Carolina boundaries is made but not completed until 1815.
1747	The first German settlers arrive.
1751	John David publishes the *North Carolina Gazette*.
1753	The first Moravians arrive at Wachovia.
1765	*October 19*. Sons of Liberty burn Lord Bute in effigy at Wilmington and force the stamp master, Dr. William Houston, to resign.
1766	Vessels carrying stamps and stamped paper to Wilmington are prevented from landing.
1768	Backcountry farmers organize as "Regulators" and threaten rebellion against excessive taxes.
1771	*May 17*. The Regulators are defeated at the Battle of Alamance Creek by Governor William Tryon.
1774	*August 25*. The colonies' first provincial congress meets at New Bern, independent of the governor.
	October 25. Fifty-one patriotic Edenton women burn their tea in support of the colonies' cause.
1775	*May 20*. Mecklenburg patriots draw up a list of resolutions declaring themselves a free and independent people.
1776	*February 27*. Patriots defeat Tory Highlanders in three minutes at the Battle of Moore's Creek.
	April 12. North Carolina is the first colony to instruct its delegates to the Continental Congress to vote for independence.
	December 18. The first state constitution is approved by the Provincial Congress.
1780	*October 7*. Patriots defeat 1,100 Loyalist troops at the Battle of King's Mountain.
1781	*March 15*. General Greene and his American troops are defeated by General Cornwallis at the Battle of Guilford Courthouse.
1789	*November 21*. North Carolina is the 12th state to ratify the US Constitution.
1790	Western North Carolina is ceded to the US government, later to become Tennessee.
1792	Raleigh becomes the capital.
1801	Gold is discovered in Cabarrus County.
1812	North Carolina troops serving in the War of 1812 include Cherokee and Lumbee Indians.
1813	Michael Schenck builds the state's first cotton mill in Lincoln County.
1835	The revised state constitution disenfranchises free blacks.
1853	The Holt Mill is the first southern factory to produce colored cotton cloth.
1854	Construction of the Atlantic and North Carolina Railroad is begun.
1861	*May 20*. North Carolina is the last Confederate state to secede from the Union.
1862	*April 26*. Northern troops capture Fort Macon.
1865	*January 15*. Fort Fisher is captured by Confederates.
	March 19-21. Battle of Bentonville results in a narrow and bloody victory for General William T. Sherman.
1868	*June 25*. North Carolina is readmitted to the Union.

1870	Republican Governor William Woods Holden is impeached for corruption.
1876	Reconstruction in North Carolina is officially ended.
1890	Cigarette manufacturing is a leading industry in the state.
1903	*December 17.* Orville and Wilbur Wright make the first successful airplane flight at Kitty Hawk.
1904	James Buchanan Duke's American Tobacco Company controls three-fourths of the nation's tobacco industry.
1909	Statewide prohibition is in effect under the Turlington Act.
1915	Legislature organizes a highway commission.
1917	State public welfare system is formed.
1918	Fort Bragg is established to train troops in psychological and guerrilla warfare.
1920	Tobacco surpasses cotton as the state's major crop.
	January 16. The state ratifies the 18th Amendment.
1926	The Great Smoky Mountains National Park is established in conjunction with Tennessee.
1933	The state government takes over total support of the public school system.
1934	Burlington Industries is the nation's largest weaver of rayon yarns.
1942	Camp LeJeune and Cherry Point marine bases are opened.
1945	Fontana Dam is completed.
1958	The Research Triangle is established due to the unusual proximity of Duke University, University of North Carolina at Chapel Hill and North Carolina State.
1960	*February 1.* The first sit-in is staged by four black freshmen at a Woolworth's lunch counter in Greensboro.
1970	*November 5.* Shooting and fires break out in Henderson due to protests of school segregation.
1975	North Carolina has 595 furniture factories, one of the state's leading industries.
1977	*November 6.* Flash flooding kills five people.
1981	*July.* The University of North Carolina and the federal government reach an agreement on desegregation guidelines for the state school system.

DEMOGRAPHY

Population (est. 1987) . . . 6,413,000
Population (1980) 5,881,385
Population density in persons
  per square mile (1980) 111.7

POPULATION BY RACE (1980)
American Indian/Aleut/
  Eskimo 64,635
Asian/Pacific Islander 21,168
Black 1,316,050
Hispanic 56,607
White 4,453,010
Other 19,566

POPULATION CHARACTERISTICS (1980)
Percent of state population
Urban 48.0
Rural 52.0
Under 18 . . . . 28.1
65 or older 10.3
College-educated 13.4
Families below poverty line . . . 11.6
Public-assistance recipients 5.8

Per capita personal income
  (1986) $12,245
Millionaires per 100,000
  residents (1982) 59.9

Average life expectancy
  in years (1980) 73.0
Marriage rate per 1,000
  residents (1986) 7.9
Divorce rate per 1,000
  residents (1986) 5.0
Birth rate per 1,000
  residents (1985) 14.4
Infant mortality rate per
  1,000 births (1985) 12.1
Abortion rate per 1,000
  live births (1985) 379
Crime rate per 100,000
  residents (1985)
    Violent 475.9
    Property 3,856.0
Federal and state prisoners per
  100,000 residents (1984) 267
Alcohol consumption in gallons
  per capita (1985) 33.0
Deaths from motor vehicle accidents
  per 100,000 residents (1985) . . 23.7

MAJOR CITIES
1984 population (est.)

Asheville	58,567
Charlotte	330,838

Durham	101,997	High Point	66,755
Fayetteville	66,131	Raleigh	169,331
Greensboro	159,314	Winston-Salem	143,366

GOVERNMENT AND POLITICS

Number of US Representatives 11
Electoral votes 13

POLITICAL PARTY NOMINEES FROM STATE

James Iredell	1796	P
Samuel Johnston	1796	P
Nathaniel Macon (Whig faction)	1824	VP
Willie Person Mangum (Whig faction)	1836	P
William Alex Graham (Whig)	1852	VP
James Haywood Southgate (National)	1896	VP
Willie Isaac Bass (Church of God)	1952	VP

PRESIDENTIAL PRIMARY ELECTION In 1988, North Carolina sent 89 Democratic dele-gates and 54 Republican delegates to the national conventions.

CONSTITUTION North Carolina has had three constitutions: 1776, 1868, and the present one, adopted in 1970.

LEGISLATURE The General Assembly is divided into the Senate (50 members, 2-year term, minimum age 25) and the House of Representatives (120 members, 2-year term, minimum age 21). In 1987, the annual salary was $10,140.

JUDICIARY The highest court is the Supreme Court, with 7 judges serving 8-year terms. In 1987, the annual salary was $76,236.

EXECUTIVE The governor serves a 4-year term; the minimum age for holding office is 30. In 1987, the annual salary was $105,000. There are 9 other elected officials.

PRESIDENTIAL VOTE 1948-1988 *(in percents)*

Year	State Winner	Democratic	Republican
1948	Truman (D)	58.0	32.7
1952	Stevenson (D)	53.9	46.1
1956	Stevenson (D)	50.7	49.3
1960	Kennedy (D)	52.1	47.9
1964	Johnson (D)	56.2	43.9
1968	Nixon (R)	29.2	39.5
1972	Nixon (R)	28.9	69.5
1976	Carter (D)	55.2	44.2
1980	Reagan (R)	47.2	49.3
1984	Reagan (R)	37.9	61.9
1988	Bush (R)	42.0	58.0

GOVERNORS

Colonial Governors

William Drummond	1664-1667
Samuel Stephens	1667-1669
Peter Carteret	1670-1673
John Jenkins (council president)	1673-1676
Thomas Eastchurch	1676-1677
Thomas Miller (deputy)	1677
John Culpeper (elected by rebels)	1677-1678
Seth Sothel	1678
John Harvey (deputy)	1679
John Jenkins (council president)	1679-1681
Henry Wilkinson	1681-1683
Seth Sothel	1683-1689
Philip Ludwell	1689-1691
Thomas Jarvis (deputy)	1691-1694
Thomas Harvey (deputy)	1694-1699
Henderson Walker (council president)	1699-1704
Robert Daniel (deputy)	1704-1705
Thomas Cary (deputy)	1705-1706
William Glover (council president)	1706-1708
Thomas Cary (council president)	1708-1711
Edward Hyde (deputy)	1711-1712
Thomas Pollock (council president)	1712-1714
Charles Eden	1714-1722
Thomas Pollock (council president)	1722
William Reed (council president)	1722-1724
George Burrington	1724-1725

Sir Richard Everard	1725-1731
George Burrington	1731-1734
Gabriel Johnston	1734-1752
Nathaniel Rice (council president)	1752-1753
Matthew Rowan (council president)	1753-1754
Arthur Dobbs	1754-1765
William Tryon	1765-1771
James Hasell (council president)	1771
Josiah Martin	1771-1775

State Governors

Richard Caswell	1776-1780
Abner Nash	1780-1781
Thomas Burke	1781-1782
Alexander Martin	1782-1785
Richard Caswell	1786-1787
Samuel Johnston	1787-1789
Alexander Martin (Federalist)	1789-1792
Richard Dobbs Spaight, Sr. (Democratic-Republican)	1792-1795
Samuel Ashe (D-R)	1795-1798
William R. Davie (Federalist)	1798-1799
Benjamin Williams (D-R)	1799-1802
James Turner (D-R)	1802-1805
Nathaniel Alexander (D-R)	1805-1807
Benjamin Williams (D-R)	1807-1808
David Stone (D-R)	1808-1810
Benjamin Smith (D-R)	1810-1811
William Hawkins (D-R)	1811-1814
William Miller (D-R)	1814-1817
John Branch (D-R)	1817-1820
Jesse Franklin (D-R)	1820-1821
Gabriel Holmes (D-R)	1821-1824
Hutchins G. Burton (D-R)	1824-1827
James Iredell (D-R)	1827-1828
John Owen (D)	1828-1830
Montfort Stokes (D)	1830-1832
David L. Swain (D)	1832-1835
Richard Dobbs Spaight, Jr. (D)	1835-1837
Edward B. Dudley (Whig)	1837-1841
John M. Morehead (Whig)	1841-1845
William A. Graham (Whig)	1845-1849
Charles Manly (Whig)	1849-1851
David S. Reid (D)	1851-1854
Warren Winslow (D)	1854-1855
Thomas Bragg (D)	1855-1859
John W. Ellis (D)	1859-1861
Henry T. Clark (D)	1861-1862
Zebulon B. Vance (Conservative)	1862-1865
William W. Holden (Provisional)	1865

Jonathan Worth (Conservative)	1865-1868
William W. Holden (R)	1868-1871
Tod R. Caldwell (R)	1871-1874
Curtis H. Brogden (R)	1874-1877
Zebulon B. Vance (D)	1877-1879
Thomas J. Jarvis (D)	1879-1885
Alfred M. Scales (D)	1885-1889
Daniel G. Fowle (D)	1889-1891
Thomas M. Holt (D)	1891-1893
Elias Carr (D)	1893-1897
Daniel L. Russell (R)	1897-1901
Charles B. Aycock (D)	1901-1905
Robert B. Glenn (D)	1905-1909
William W. Kitchin (D)	1909-1913
Locke Craig (D)	1913-1917
Thomas W. Bickett (D)	1917-1921
Cameron Morrison (D)	1921-1925
Angus W. McLean (D)	1925-1929
O. Max Gardner (D)	1929-1933
J.C.B. Ehringhaus (D)	1933-1937
Clyde R. Hoey (D)	1937-1941
Joseph M. Broughton (D)	1941-1945
R. Gregg Cherry (D)	1945-1949
W. Kerr Scott (D)	1949-1953
William B. Umstead (D)	1953-1954
Luther H. Hodges (D/acting)	1954-1957
Luther H. Hodges (D)	1957-1961
Terry Sanford (D)	1961-1965
Dan K. Moore (D)	1965-1969
Robert W. Scott (D)	1969-1973
James E. Holshouser, Jr. (R)	1973-1977
James B. Hunt, Jr. (D)	1977-1985
James G. Martin (R)	1985-

MINIMUM AGES

Majority	18
Marriage with parental consent	16
Marriage without parental consent	18
Making a will	18
Buying alcohol	21
Jury duty	18
Leaving school	16
Driver's license	16

CAPITAL PUNISHMENT
Number executed 1976-88: 3
On death row Aug. 1, 1988: 79

MILITARY INSTALLATIONS
Total number: 18
Major bases:
  Army: 1
  Air Force: 2
  Marine Corps: 2

FINANCES

Thousands of dollars

GENERAL REVENUE (1985)

Total general revenue . . .	8,288,109
Total tax revenue	5,198,024
Sales and gross receipts . . .	2,161,583
Individual income taxes . .	2,023,463
Corporate net income taxes . .	490,296

GENERAL EXPENDITURE (1985)

Total general expenditure .	7,828,407
Education	3,826,940
Public welfare	945,221
Health	264,267
Hospitals	411,962
Natural resources	183,763
Highways	804,942
Police	101,019
Corrections	258,502

FEDERAL AID (1985) 2,133,677

ECONOMY

North Carolina is the nation's chief tobacco producer; other farm products include cotton, sweet potatoes, soybeans, corn, peanuts, truck vegetables, and fruits. Broilers, hogs, and dairy products are also important contributors to farm cash receipts, which totaled $3.8 billion in 1983. The catch from the state's fishing industry includes menhaden, bluefish, flounder, and mackerel; 1981 had the top yield, 432 million pounds. Leading among manufactures are tobacco products, followed by textiles, processed foods, wood products (including paper and pulp), electrical machinery and fabricated goods, high-tech electronics, and chemicals. Value added by manufacture was $28.5 billion in 1982.

EMPLOYMENT (1984)

Thousands of persons

Total number of employed workers	2,828
Construction	133.0
Finance, insurance, and real estate	104.9
Government	413.7
Manufacturing	830.6
Mining	4.6
Services	398.2
Transportation, communications, and utilities	127.5
Wholesale and retail trade	549.3

Percent of civilian labor force unemployed (1984)	6.7

DEPARTMENT OF DEFENSE (1985)

Civilian workers employed . . .	16,312
Military personnel	98,702
Contract awards	$1.029 billion

ENERGY SOURCES FOR ELECTRIC UTILITIES (1983)

Percent

Coal	74.9
Gas	0.0
Hydroelectric	8.2
Nuclear	16.6
Petroleum	0.3

TRANSPORTATION

Motor vehicles registered in state (1986)	4,738,956
Miles of roads, streets, and highways (1986)	93,630
Miles of Class I railway operated (1986)	3,217
Airports (1983)	284
Major aviation hubs (1983)	3
Largest hub: Charlotte	

CULTURE AND EDUCATION

Native American tribes

North Carolina was formerly home to the Cape Fear, Catawba, Chenaw, Chowanoc, Corree, Eno, Hatteras, Keyauwee, Machapunga, Meherrin, Moratok, Natchez, Neusiok, Ocaneechi, Pamlico, Secotan, Shakori, Sissipahaw, Sugeree, Tuscarora, Tutelo, Waccamaw, Wateree, Waxhaw, Weapemeoc, Woccon, and Yadkin tribes. Groups that continue to live there include the Cherokee (most of whom were forcibly relocated west of the Mississippi in 1838-1839) and Lumbee. There is one federal reservation in North Carolina.

Religions, ethnicities, and languages

Many North Carolinans trace their ancestry to the English and Scottish Highlander settlers of the 1650s, some of whom came from Virginia and other states. Many others are the descendants of African slaves. The Piedmont area was settled mainly by Scotch-Irish, German, and Welsh groups from other states, as well as Huguenots and Swiss. In 1980, 2.4 percent of North Carolina's population spoke a language other than English at home. The Church of England was the established faith until the 18th century; other religions now represented in North Carolina include the Presbyterian, Quaker, Moravian, Lutheran, Reformed, Baptist, and Methodist churches, and Judaism.

Major museums and libraries
Ackland Art Museum, University of
North Carolina, Chapel Hill
North Carolina Museum of Art
North Carolina Museum of History
North Carolina State Museum
Science Museum of Charlotte

Major arts organizations
Charlotte Symphony Orchestra
North Carolina Dance Theater, Winston
Salem
North Carolina Symphony Orchestra,
Raleigh
Opera Carolina

Playmakers Repertory Company, Chapel Hill

Colleges and universities
Number public (1986-87) 74
Number private (1986-87) 51
Total enrollment, in full-time equivalent
students (1985) 249,900

Public elementary and secondary schools
Expenditure per pupil in average daily
attendance (1986-87) $3,473
Pupil-teacher ratio (1987) 18.7
Average teacher salary (1986-87) $24,395

Holidays
Easter Monday. March or April
Halifax Day. April 12
Confederate Memorial Day. May 10
Mecklenburg Day. May 20
State Fair, Raleigh. Mid-October

NORTH CAROLINA IN LITERATURE

Doris Betts *The Scarlet Thread* (1964)
Historical novel set in the late nineteenth century tracing the fortunes of a family in a cotton-producing town in the Piedmont.

James Boyd *Drums* (1925); *Marching On* (1927); *Long Hunt* (1930); *Roll River* (1935); *Bitter Creek* (1939)
Historical novels set during the early nineteenth century and the Civil War. Boyd also wrote a collection of short stories set in a poor rural community, *Old Pines and Other Stories* (1952).

J. Mason Brewer *Worser Days and Better Times: The Folklore of the North Carolina Negro* (1965)

Henry E. Cowan Bryant *Tar Heel Tales* (1972)

Fielding Burke (pseud. of Olive Tilford Dargan) *Call Home the Heart* (1932); *A Stone Came Rolling* (1935)
Novels about the plight of textile workers.

W. J. Cash *The Mind of the South* (1941)
North Carolinian's attempt to define a "Southern" personality.

Richard Chase (ed.) *The Jack Tales, Told by R.M. Ward and His Kindred in the Beech Mountain Section of Western North Carolina* (1943)
——. *Grandfather Tales: American-English Folktales* (1948)
Collection from North Carolina, Virginia, and Kentucky.

Charles W. Chestnutt *The Conjure Woman* (1899); *The Wife of His Youth and Other Stories of the Color Line* (1899)
Folktales and short stories by a black writer who grew up in Fayetteville. Chestnutt's work, which includes three novels, deals chiefly with racial prejudice during Reconstruction.

Burke Davis *The Ragged Ones* (1951); *Yorktown* (1952)
Historical novels of the Revolution noted for their realistic accuracy. Davis also wrote a fictional portrait of life on a tobacco farm, *The Summer Land* (1965).

John Ehle *The Land Breakers* (1964); *The Road* (1967)
Novels of pioneer life beyond the Blue Ridge in the late eighteenth and early nineteenth centuries. Ehle's other regional works include *Move Over, Mountain* (1957), *Kingstree Island* (1959), and *Lion on the Hearth* (1961).

Anderson Ferrell *Where She Was* (1985)
Psychological portrait of a young mother and farmer's wife set against a background of farmland, swamp, and forest.

Inglis Fletcher *Bennett's Welcome* (1950)
Second novel in the twelve-volume "Carolina Series" that

traces the history of settlement from the Roanoke colony through the Revolution.

Adelaide L. Fries *The Road to Salem* (1944, rpt. 1988)
Novel based on the autobiography of a German woman who immigrated to the Wachovia Settlement of Moravian Christians in 1759.

Noel Gerson *The Swamp Fox* (1967)
Fictional biography of General Francis Marion.

Patsy M. Ginns *Rough Weather Makes Good Timber: Carolinians Recall* (1977); *Snowbird Gravy and Dishpan Pie: Mountain People Recall* (1982)

Paul E. Green *Salvation on a String and Other Tales of the South* (1946)
Stories of the farmers of the Cape Fear valley by a dramatist well-known in the 1920s for plays with North Carolina settings.

John Harden *The Devil's Tramping Ground and Other North Carolina Mystery Stories* (1949, rpt. 1972); *Tar Heel Ghosts* (1954)

Bernice K. Harris *Purslane* (1939); *Portulaca* (1941); *Sweet Beulah Land* (1943)
Three novels with idyllic rural settings by a popular regional writer of the '30s and '40s.

W. C. Hendricks (ed.) *Bundle of Troubles and Other Tarheel Tales* (1943)

Richard J. Hooker (ed.) *The Carolina Backcountry on the Eve of the Revolution: The Journal and Other Writings of Charles Woodmason, Anglican Itinerant* (1953)

Belinda Hurmence (ed.) *My Folks Don't Want Me to Talk about Slavery: Twenty-one Oral Histories of Former North Carolina Slaves* (1984)

Frank R. Johnson *Supernaturals among Carolina Folk and Their Neighbors* (1974)
Folk tales of North Carolina and bordering states.

Bruce Lancaster *Phantom Fortress* (1950)
Novel of the Revolution centering on General Marion.

John Lawson (ed. Hugh Talmage Lefler) *A New Voyage to Carolina* (1709, rpt. 1984)
The author was a Scottish surveyor and pioneer who explored the Piedmont and describes Indian life. He was killed by the Tuscarora in 1711.

Grace Lumpkin *To Make My Bread* (1932)
Novel about the textile mill workers' strike in Gastonia in

1929. *See* Mary H. Vorse, *Strike* (1930), for another fictional treatment of this incident.

Mary E. Mebane *Mary* (1981)
An account of life in a black community near Durham.

Heather R. Miller *Gone a Hundred Miles* (1968)
The frontier during the early nineteenth century.

Joseph Mitchell *McSorley's Wonderful Saloon* (1943)
Humorous low-country tales.

Fred T. Morgan *Ghost Tales of the Uwharries* (1968)
Tales from the mountains of central North Carolina.

Robert Morgan *The Blue Valleys* (1989)
Short stories of contemporary life in the Blue Ridge Mountains.

Pauli Murray *Proud Shoes* (1956)
Biography of the author's grandfather, a black Union veteran who ran a school for freed slaves in Durham during Reconstruction.

Ovid W. Pierce *The Plantation* (1953); *On a Lonesome Porch* (1960)
Historical novels set during the Civil War and Reconstruction.

Reynolds Price *A Long and Happy Life* (1961)
Novel about the rural folk of Warren County.

Christian Reid (pseud. of Frances Christine Fisher) *The Land of the Sky* (1876)
Romance set in the western mountains, the best-known of the author's many regional novels and stories describing genteel social manners of the late nineteenth century.

Janet Schaw (ed. Evangeline W. and Charles M. Andrews) *Journal of a Lady of Quality . . . 1774–1776* (1921)
Journal of a Scotswoman, loyal to the British, who traveled in the state just before the Revolution.

Ernest Seeman *American Gold* (1978)
Chronicle of a tobacco town, 1880–1960.

Frank G. Slaughter *In a Dark Garden* (1946); *The Stubborn Heart* (1950)
Period novels by a prolific writer of popular romance, describing the adventures of a Confederate doctor.

Edith H. Smith *Drought and Other North Carolina Yarns* (1955)
Tales of the Piedmont region.

Harden E. Taliaferro *Fisher's River (North Carolina) Scenes and Characters, by "Skitt," "Who Was Raised Thar"* (1959)

Folk humor and tall tales from the backwoods by a writer who, like Augustine B. Longstreet, George W. Harris, and Mark Twain, belongs to the nineteenth-century rustic storytelling tradition.

John K. Terres *From Laurel Hill to Silber's Bog; the Walking Adventures of a Naturalist* (1969)
Observations of a tract of wild land near Chapel Hill.

Albion W. Tourgée *A Fool's Errand* (1879)
Semi-autobiographical novel about a Union colonel who buys a plantation near Greensboro. Tourgée, a well-known carpetbagger, was frustrated by his experience of Reconstruction and wrote several embittered novels based on his experience. *Bricks Without Straw* (1880) is an account of attempts to educate freed slaves.

Don Tracy *Carolina Corsair* (1955)
Romantic historical novel about Blackbeard, the legendary pirate.

Richard Walser *Literary North Carolina: A Brief Historical Survey* (1970)
———. *Tar Heel Laughter* (1983)
Anthology of regional humor.

Manly W. Wellman *The Kingdom of Madison, a Southern Mountain Fastness and Its People* (1973)
Study of a region.

Charles H. Whedbee *Outer Banks Mysteries And Seaside Stories (1978); Outer Banks Tales to Remember* (1985); *Blackbeard's Cup and Stories of the Outer Banks* (1989)

Newman I. White et al. *The Frank C. Brown Collection of North Carolina Folklore* 7 vols. (1952-1964)

Sylvia Wilkinson *Moss on the North Side* (1966)
Novel of a young woman's growing up in a contemporary rural setting.

Reed Wolcott *Rose Hill* (1976)
Oral history of a small North Carolina town.

Thomas Wolfe *Look Homeward, Angel* (1929); *The Web and the Rock* (1939); *You Can't Go Home Again* (1940)
An autobiographical sequence of novels describing the writer's upbringing in, and eventual return to, Asheville.

Constance Fenimore Woolson *For the Mayor* (1883); *Horace Chase* (1894)
Novels set in the North Carolina mountains by a pioneer of regional fiction. Woolson was a regular visitor to Asheville from the 1870s, and portrayed the town in a story "Up in the Blue Ridge," published in *Rodman the Keeper* (1880).

GUIDES TO RESOURCES

Cashion, Jerry *Guide to North Carolina Historical Highway Markers* (7th ed. 1979)

Clay, James W., Douglas M. Orr, Jr., and **Alfred W. Stuart** (eds.) *North Carolina Atlas: Portrait of a Changing Southern State* (1975)

Crabtree, Beth C. and **Ruth C. Langston** (eds.) *The North Carolina Historical Review: Fifty-year Index, 1924–1973* (1984)

Crittenden, Charles C. and **Dan Lacy** *The Historical Records of North Carolina* 3 vols. (1938)

Crutchfield, James A. *The North Carolina Almanac and Book of Facts* (1988)

Federal Writers' Project (ed. Blackwell P. Robinson) *The North Carolina Guide* (1939, rpt. 1955)

Leary, Helen F. and **Maurice R. Stirewalt** (eds.) *North Carolina Research: Genealogy and Local History* (1980)

Lefler, Hugh T. *A Guide to the Study and Reading of North Carolina History* (3rd ed. 1969)

Lonsdale, Richard E. *Atlas of North Carolina* (1967)

McMillan, Laura (comp.) *The North Carolina Portrait Index, 1700–1860* (1963)

North Carolina Department of Cultural Resources, Division of Archives and History *The North Carolina Historical Review* (1924–)
———, Division of Archives and History *Guide to Research Materials in the N.C. State Archives, Section B: County Records* (8th ed. rev. 1982)

North Carolina Department of Secretary of State *North Carolina Manual* (biennial)

North Carolina English Teachers Association and the **North Carolina Library Association** *North Carolina Authors: A Selective Handbook* (1952)

North Carolina Folklore Journal Chapel Hill. (Jan. 1948–)

North Carolina Office of the Governor. Office of State Budget and Management: Research and Planning Services *Profile: North Carolina Counties* (1968–)
———. Office of State Budget and Management: Research and Planning Services *North Carolina Statistical Guide* (6th ed. 1980)

Powell, William S. *North Carolina County Histories: A Bibliography* (1958)
——— (ed.) *North Carolina Lives; the Tar Heel Who's Who* (1962)
———. *North Carolina: A Student's Guide to Localized History* (1965)
———. *The North Carolina Gazetteer* (1976)

———. (ed.) *Dictionary of North Carolina Biography* Vol. 1 (1979); Vol. 2 (1986); Vol. 3 (1988)

Stevenson, George *North Carolina Local History, A Select Bibliography* (1975, rev. ed. 1984)

Thornton, Mary L. *A Bibliography of North Carolina, 1589–1956* (1958)

Walser, Richard and Mary R. Peacock *Young Readers' Picturebook of Tar Heel Authors* (5th ed. 1981)

SELECTED NONFICTION SOURCES

Allcott, John V. *Colonial Homes in North Carolina* (1963)

Anderson, Eric *Race and Politics in North Carolina, 1872–1901* (1981)

Arnett, Alex M. *The Story of North Carolina* (1933)

Arthur, John P. *Western North Carolina; a History* (1914)

Ashe, Samuel A. (ed.) *Biographical History of North Carolina From Colonial Times to the Present* 8 vols. (1905–1917)
———. *History of North Carolina* 2 vols. (1908, rpt. 1925)

Badger, Anthony J. *Prosperity Road: The New Deal, Tobacco, and North Carolina* (1980)

Barrett, John G. *The Civil War in North Carolina* (1963)

Blackmun, Ora *Western North Carolina: Its Mountains and Its People to 1800* (1977)

Bledsoe, Jerry *Just Folks: Visitin' with Carolina People* (1980)

Boykin, James H. *North Carolina in 1861* (1961)

Brooks, Maurice *The Appalachians* (1965)

Burney, Eugenia *Colonial North Carolina* (1975)

Butler, Lindley S. *North Carolina and the Coming of the Revolution* (1976)
——— and Alan D. Watson (eds.) *The North Carolina Experience; an Interpretive and Documentary History* (1984)

Cheney, John L., Jr. (ed.) *North Carolina Government, 1585–1979: A Narrative and Statistical History* (1981)

Clayton, Thomas H. *Close to the Land: The Way We Lived in North Carolina, 1820–1870* (1983)

Connor, R. D. W. *Revolutionary Leaders of North Carolina* (1916, rpt. 1971)
———, William K. Boyd, and J. G. de Roulhac Hamilton *History of North Carolina* 3 vols. (1919)
———. *North Carolina, Rebuilding an Ancient Commonwealth, 1584–1925* 4 vols. (1929)

Conway, Martin *The Outer Banks: An Historical Adventure from Kitty Hawk to Ocracoke* Conway (1984)

Crabtree, Beth G. *North Carolina Governors, 1585–1974: Brief Sketches* (rev. ed. 1974)

Craig, James H. *The Arts and Crafts in North Carolina, 1699–1840* (1965)

Crittenden, Charles C. *Commerce of North Carolina, 1763–1789* (1937)
——— et al. (eds.) *100 Years, 100 Men, 1871–1971* (1971)

Crow, Jeffrey J. *The Black Experience in Revolutionary North Carolina* (1977)

Crow, Vernon H. *North Carolina Government, 1585–1979* (1981)
———. *Storm in the Mountains: Thomas' Confederate Legion of Cherokee Indians and Mountaineers* (1982)

Davis, Burke *The Cowpens-Guilford Courthouse Campaign* (1962)

DeMond, Robert O. *The Loyalists in North Carolina during the Revolution* (1964)

Dill, Alonzo T. *Governor Tryon and His Palace* (1955)

Dunbar, Gary S. *Geographical History of the Outer Banks* (1956)

Durant, David N. *Raleigh's Lost Colony* (1981)

Dykeman, Wilma *The French Broad* (Rivers of America series) (1955)

Edmonds, Helen G. *The Negro and Fusion Politics in North Carolina* (1951)

Ekirch, A. Roger *"Poor Carolina": Politics and Society in Colonial North Carolina 1729–1776* (1981)

Escott, Paul D. *Many Excellent People: Power and Privilege in North Carolina, 1850–1900* (1985)

Evans, W. McKee *To Die Game; the Story of the Lowry Band, Indian Guerrillas of Reconstruction* (1971)
———. *Ballots and Fence Rails; Reconstruction on the Lower Cape Fear* (1987)

Fagg, Daniel W. *Carolina, 1663–1683: The Founding of a Proprietary* (1970)

Fenn, Elizabeth and Peter H. Wood *Natives & Newcomers: The Way We Lived in North Carolina Before 1770* (1983)

Fleer, Jack D. *North Carolina Politics* (1968)

Franklin, John Hope *The Free Negro in North Carolina, 1790–1860* (1943, rpt. 1971)

Hall, Lewis P. *Land of the Golden River; Historical Events and Stories of Southeastern North Carolina and the Lower Cape Fear* (1975)

Hammer, Carl, Jr. *Rhinelanders on the Yadkin* (1965)

Henderson, Archibald *North Carolina: the Old North State and the New* 2 vols. (1941)

Hodges, Luther H. *Businessman in the State House* (1962)

Hughson, Shirley C. *The Carolina Pirates and Colonial Commerce, 1670–1740* (1973)

Hunter, C. L. *Sketches of Western North Carolina* (1877)

James, Hunter *The Quiet People of the Land: A Story of the North Carolina Moravians in Revolutionary Times* (1976)

Johnson, Guion G. *Ante-Bellum North Carolina; a Social History* (1937)

Jones, H. G. *For History's Sake, the Preservation and Publication of North Carolina History, 1663–1903* (1966)
———. *North Carolina Illustrated, 1524–1984* (1983)

Kruman, Marc W. *Parties and Politics in North Carolina, 1836–1865* (1983)

Lane, Mills (ed. Marshall Bullock) *North Carolina* (1985)

Lauterer, Jack *Runnin' on Rims: Appalachian Profiles* (1986)

Lee, E. Lawrence *Indian Wars in North Carolina, 1663–1763* (1963)
———. *The Lower Cape Fear in Colonial Days* (1965)

Lefler, Hugh T. (ed.) *North Carolina History Told by Contemporaries* (4th ed. 1965)
———. *North Carolina: The History of a Southern State* (3rd ed. 1973)
——— and Albert Ray Newsome *North Carolina: The History of a Southern State* (3rd ed. 1973)
——— and William S. Powell *Colonial North Carolina: A History* (1973)

Lemmon, Sarah M. *Frustrated Patriots; North Carolina and the War of 1812* (1973)

Logan, Frenise A. *The Negro in North Carolina, 1878–1894* (1964)

Merrens, Harry R. *Colonial North Carolina in the Eighteenth Century: A Study in Historical Geography* (1964)

Meyer, Duane *The Highland Scots of North Carolina, 1732–1776* (1987)

Moore, Jeanelle C. and Grace R. Hamrick *The First Ladies of North Carolina* (1981)

Morrison, Joseph L. *Josephus Daniels: The Small-d Democrat* (1966)

———. *W. J. Cash: Southern Prophet* (1967)
———. *Governor O. Max Gardner; a Power in North Carolina and New Deal Washington* (1971)

Moss, Bobby, G. *The Patriots at the Cowpens* (1985)

Nathans, Sidney (ed.) *The Way We Lived In North Carolina* 5 vols. (1983)

North Carolina Civil War Documentary (ed. W. Buck Yearns and John G. Barrett) (1980)

O'Donnell, James H. *The Cherokees of North Carolina in the American Revolution* (1976)

Parker, Mattie E. E. (ed.) *North Carolina Charters and Constitutions, 1578–1698* (1963)

Parramore, Thomas C. *Express Lanes & Country Roads: The Way We Lived in North Carolina, 1920–1970* (1983)

Pomeroy, Kenneth B. and James G. Yoho *North Carolina Lands* (1964)

Powell, William S. *The Proprietors of Carolina* (1963)
———. *Paradise Preserved* (1965)
———. *North Carolina: A Bicentennial History* (1977)
———. *The First State University: A Pictorial History of the University of North Carolina* (1979)
———. *North Carolina through Four Centuries* (1988)

Quinn, David B. *Raleigh and the British Empire* (1949)
———. (ed.) *The Roanoke Voyages* 2 vols. (1955)

Ramsey, Robert W. *Carolina Cradle: Settlement of the Northwest Carolina Frontier, 1747–1762* (1987)

Rankin, Hugh F. *The Pirates of North Carolina* (1960)
———. *Upheaval in Albemarle, the Story of Culpepper's Rebellion, 1675–1689* (1962)
———. *North Carolina in the American Revolution* (1965)
———. *The North Carolina Continentals* (1971)

Raper, C. L. *North Carolina: A Study in English Colonial Government* (1904)

Rappoport, Ken *Tar Heel: North Carolina Football* (1976)

Reines, Philip *A Cultural History of the City of Winston-Salem, North Carolina* (1970)

Rights, Douglas L. *The American Indian in North Carolina* (1957)

Roberson, Ruth H. et al. *North Carolina Quilts* (1988)

Roberts, Bruce *The Carolina Gold Rush* (1971)
———. *Old Salem in Pictures* (rev. ed. 1972)

Robinson, Blackwell P. *Battles and Engagements of the American Revolution in North Carolina* (1961)
———. *The Five Royal Governors of North Carolina, 1729–1775* (1963)

Ross, Malcolm *The Cape Fear* (Rivers of America series) (1965)

Russell, Anne *North Carolina Portraits of Faith: A Pictorial History of Religions* (1986)

Russell, Phillips *North Carolina in the Revolutionary War* (1965)

———. *These Old Stone Walls* (1972)

Salley, Alexander S., Jr. *Narratives of Early Carolina, 1650–1708* (1911, rpt. 1959)

Savage, Henry *River of the Carolinas: the Santee* (1956, rpt. 1968)

Schwarzkopf, S. Kent *A History of Mt. Mitchell and the Black Mountains: Exploration, Development, and Preservation* (1985)

Sharpe, Bill *A New Geography of North Carolina* 4 vols. (1954–1965)

Sikes, E. W. *The Transition of North Carolina from Colony to Commonwealth* (1898)

Spitsbergen, Judith M. *Seacoast Life: An Ecological Guide to Natural Seashore Communities in North Carolina* (1983)

Sprunt, James *Chronicles of the Cape Fear River, 1660–1916* (1916)

Stick, David *Graveguard of the Atlantic; Shipwrecks of the North Carolina Coast* (1952)
———. *The Outer Banks of North Carolina, 1584–1958* (1958)
———. *The Cape Hatteras Seashore* (1974)
———. *Roanoke Island: The Beginnings of English America* (1983)

Treacy, M. F. *Prelude to Yorktown, the Southern Campaign of Nathanael Greene, 1780–1781* (1963)

Trenholme, Louise *The Ratification of the Federal Constitution in North Carolina* (1967)

Troxler, Carole W. *The Loyalist Experience in North Carolina* (1976)

Vining, Elizabeth G. *Flora, a Biography* (1966)

Walsh, John E. *One Day at Kitty Hawk: The Untold Story of the Wright Brothers and the Airplane* (1975)

Watson, Harry L. *An Independent People: The Way We Lived in North Carolina, 1770–1820* (1983)

Waugh, Elizabeth C. *North Carolina's Capital, Raleigh* (1967)

Weare, Walter B. *Black Business in the New South; a Social History of the North Carolina Mutual Life Insurance Company* (1973)

Wetmore, Ruth Y. *The North Carolina Indians* (1975)

Wheeler, John H. *Historical Sketches of North Carolina, from 1684 to 1851* (1964)
———. *Reminiscences and Memoirs of North Carolina and Eminent North Carolinians* (1966)

Wood, Phillip J. *Southern Capitalism; the Political Economy of North Carolina, 1880–1980* (1986)

Wrenn, Tony P. *Wilmington, North Carolina: An Architectural and Historical Portrait* (1984)

Zuber, Richard L. *North Carolina during Reconstruction* (1969)

Zug, Charles G. *Turners and Burners: The Folk Potters of North Carolina* (1986)

NORTH DAKOTA

North Dakota is a west north central state. It borders the Canadian provinces of Saskatchewan and Manitoba on the north; the Red River of the North and Minnesota on the east; South Dakota on the south; and Montana on the west.

FULL NAME State of North Dakota
POSTAL ABBREVIATION ND
INHABITANT North Dakotan
ADMITTED TO THE UNION Nov. 2, 1889. 39th state
POPULATION (est. 1987) 672,000. Percent of US total: 0.28%. Rank: 46th

CAPITAL CITY Bismarck, located on the Missouri River in south central North Dakota; population 47,552 (est. 1984). It was founded in 1872 as a military post called Fort Hancock and renamed the following year. The capital of the Dakota Territory was transferred from Yankton to Bismarck in 1883.

STATE NAME AND NICKNAMES From the Dakota Indian word meaning "friends, allies." Official nicknames: the Sioux State, the Flickertail State. Also known as the Land of the Dakotas and the Peace Garden State.

STATE SEAL A landscape showing a leafy tree in a field, its trunk encircled by three sheaves of wheat; to the right, a plow and blacksmith's tools; to the left, a bow and three arrows; in the distance, a mounted Indian chasing a buffalo toward the sunset. The state motto is inscribed in a semicircle across the top, together with 42 stars. The border reads "Great Seal, State of North Dakota, October 1st, 1889."

MOTTO Liberty and Union Now and Forever, One and Inseparable.

SONGS "North Dakota Hymn," lyrics by James W. Foley, music by C.S. Putnam. State march: "Spirit of the Land" by James D. Ployhar.

SYMBOLS
Flower wild prairie rose
Tree American elm
Bird meadowlark
Fossil teredo petrified wood
Grass western wheat grass
Beverage milk
Art gallery Univ. of North Dakota Art Gallery, Grand Forks

LICENSE PLATE Dark blue on a background of orange shading to blue, with the legends "Peace Garden State" and "Centennial" and a blue stripe bearing the dates 1889 and 1989.

FLAG On a blue field, an eagle with outstretched wings, holding an olive branch and arrows in its talons and bearing the shield of the Stars and Stripes on its breast. In its beak it holds a scroll with the legend "E Pluribus Unum" (From Many, One); over its head is a double arch of 13 stars surmounted by a sunburst; below it is a scroll bearing the state name.

GEOGRAPHY AND CLIMATE

North Dakota rises in steps from the eastern Central Lowland region, including the Red River valley and the Drift Prairie, to the Missouri Plateau, part of the Great Plains, in the western half of the state. Deep black soils cover the eastern state, where wheat is the main crop. West of the Missouri River along the Little Missouri are the North Dakota Badlands, a rugged landscape of cliffs, valleys, and buttes.

AREA 70,703 square miles. Rank: 17th
INLAND WATER 1,403 square miles
GEOGRAPHIC CENTER Sheridan, 5 miles SW of McClusky
ELEVATIONS *Highest point:* White Butte, Slope County, 3,506 feet. *Lowest point:* Red River, Pembina County, 750 feet. *Mean elevation:* 1,900 feet

MAJOR RIVERS Red River of the North, Missouri, Sheyenne

MAJOR LAKES AND RESERVOIRS Sakakwea, Oahe, Long, Garrison, Jamestown

LAND USE

	Thousands of acres
Urban (1982)	198
Rural (1982)	41,021
Cropland (1982)	27,039
Pastureland (1982)	1,272
Rangeland (1982)	10,948
Forestland (1982)	438
State parks and recreation areas (1983)	15
National park system (1984)	71
National forest system (1984)	1,106
Tribal lands (1984)	214

TEMPERATURES The highest recorded temperature was 121°F on July 6, 1936, at Steele. The lowest was -60°F on February 15, 1936, at Parshall.

NATIONAL SITES

NATIONAL HISTORIC SITES Fort Union Trading Post, International Peace Garden, Knife River Indian Villages
NATIONAL HISTORIC TRAIL Lewis & Clark
NATIONAL PARK Theodore Roosevelt
NATIONAL SCENIC TRAIL North Country
NATIONAL WILDLIFE REFUGES Arrowwood–Chase Lake/Slade, Audubon, Crosby Wetland Management District, Des Lacs–Lake Zahl, Devils Lake Wetland Management District–Lake Alice/Sullys Hill National Game Preserve, Lake Ilo, Kulm Wetland Management District, Long Lake, Lostwood, J. Clark Salyer, Tewaukon, Upper Souris, Valley City Wetland Management District

HISTORY

1738	*December 3*. French explorer Pierre Gaultier de Varennes, Sieur de La Vérendrye, becomes the first white in North Dakota when he visits Mandan Indians at what is now Menoken.
1797–1798	English explorer David Thompson visits Mandan and Hidatsa Indians in central North Dakota.
1801	Alexander Henry of the North West Company establishes a fur-trading post at Pembina. The X.Y. and Hudson's Bay companies also establish trading posts there.
1803	*December 20*. The US receives most of North Dakota in the Louisiana Purchase.
1804	*October 13*. Meriwether Lewis and William Clark, on their way west to the Pacific, arrive in North Dakota. They create winter quarters on the Missouri River near present-day Washburn and engage the services of Toussaint Charbonneau and his Shoshone Indian wife, Sacajawea, for the trip west. The party returns in 1806.
1812	A group of dispossessed Scottish and Irish peasants sponsored by Thomas Douglas, Earl of Selkirk, establish a farming settlement at Pembina. North Dakota becomes part of Missouri Territory.
1818	An Anglo-American treaty establishes the northern border of what is now North Dakota, and most of the Pembina colonists return north into Canada.
1832	The steamboat *Yellowstone* ascends the Missouri from St. Louis to Fort Union, just beyond the present North Dakota–Montana border.
1851	Settlers arrive at Pembina from Minnesota to form the first permanent white agricultural community in North Dakota.

1857	Fort Abercrombie, first military post in North Dakota, is established on the Red River of the North near Wahpeton.
1859	First steamboat on the Red River arrives at Fort Garry (Winnipeg).
1861	Dakota Territory is organized, including what is now North Dakota and South Dakota.
1863	*January 1*. Free land becomes available under the Homestead Act, which provides 160 acres to a settler cultivating a portion of it for five years.
	The Chippewa (Ojibway) sell 10 million acres in northwestern Minnesota and northeastern North Dakota for $500,000.
1863–1864	In retaliation for the uprising of the Santee Sioux (Dakota) in Minnesota in 1862, federal troops conduct punitive expeditions on the upper Missouri against Sioux tribes, most of whom had taken no part in the fighting.
1867	Fort Totten Indian Reservation, south of Devils Lake, is created for the Sisseton, Wahpeton, and Cut-Head Sioux.
1868	A treaty defines reservation boundaries for other Sioux tribes, including the part of Standing Rock Reservation in what is now North Dakota.
1870	The Fort Berthold Reservation in northwest North Dakota is set aside for the Mandan, Arikara, and Hidatsa Indians.
1871	The Northern Pacific Railroad seeks European immigrants to settle on its land grants, comprising almost a quarter of what is now North Dakota.
1873	The Northern Pacific Railroad reaches Bismarck.
	July 11. The first issue appears of the Bismarck *Tribune*, the state's oldest newspaper.
1876	The first of the bonanza farms—giant wheat farms—is established near Casselton. In all, 91 farms of over 3,000 acres are established, almost all by 1885, after which they are broken up.
	May 11. Federal troops under George A. Custer leave Fort Abraham Lincoln, near Mandan, for their campaign against the Sioux that leads to the disastrous defeat at Little Big Horn.
1881	Sitting Bull's forces, who fled to Canada after defeating Custer, surrender and return to their reservations.
	The Northern Pacific reaches the Montana border.
1882	Nine million acres of north central North Dakota are opened to the public despite protests from the Turtle Mountain Chippewa, who do not cede the land until 1892.
1883	Bismarck becomes the capital of Dakota Territory by offering the best bid—$100,000 and 160 acres of land.
	The University of North Dakota opens at Grand Forks.
	Theodore Roosevelt comes to North Dakota for his health and begins ranching near Medora.
1884	First commercial mining of North Dakota's abundant lignite deposits.
1885	Peak of the first land boom; population has grown to 152,000 from 37,000 in 1880.
1889	*November 2*. North Dakota and South Dakota are admitted to the Union simultaneously as the 39th and 40th states.
1890	North Dakota ranks second to Minnesota in wheat production.
	Of North Dakota's population of 190,183, 43 percent are foreign born, including 25,773 from Norway and 23,045 from Canada.
1906	Second wave of land fever reaches peak with homestead filing of 2.7 million acres, mostly in arid western North Dakota.
1915	Nonpartisan League is formed to further farmers' interests and to fight out-of-state grain milling and elevator companies. The league enters candidates in Republican party primaries.
1916	Lynn J. Frazier, the Nonpartisan League's candidate, is elected governor.
1919	The Bank of North Dakota is created, the only state-owned bank in the United States.
	A graduated income tax and an inheritance tax are adopted.
1922	Opening of a state-owned grain mill and elevator in Grand Forks.
1929–1936	A persistent drought in the Great Plains states severely curtails farm production. Vast amounts of topsoil are blown away by high winds.

1932   Erection of the 19-story state capitol, North Dakota's tallest building other than grain elevators.
        The prohibition clause in the state constitution is repealed. The sale of liquor is legalized in 1936.
1933   Per capita income is only $145, compared to $375 for the United States.
        A moratorium on foreclosure of farm mortgages continues in some form until 1943.
1935   A retail sales tax is adopted.
1936   The wheat crop in this year of severe drought is only 19 million tons.
1941   The International Peace Garden is established on the border with Canada.
1947   After nearly a decade of farm prosperity, per capita income of $1,446 exceeds the national average of $1,316. Construction begins on the Missouri of the giant Garrison Dam.
1949   *June 4*. The Theodore Roosevelt National Memorial Park is dedicated at Medora in recognition of his concern for the conservation of natural resources and wildlife.
1951   *April 4*. Oil is struck in the Williston Basin, near Tioga.
1954   Standard Oil of Indiana opens a 30,000-barrel-a-day oil refinery at Mandan.
1956   The Nonpartisan League joins the Democratic party.
1960   Virtual completion of the Garrison Dam. Impoundment of the Missouri's waters creates 200-mile-long Lake Sakakawea, inundating 550,000 acres.
1961   North Dakota ranks 10th in national oil production.
1963   The state's first large, modern lignite-burning electrical generating station is put into operation.
1966   William A. Guy, a Democrat, wins a record fourth term as governor. He serves a total of 12 years.
1969   Construction begins of a $5.7-billion antiballistic missile complex to defend the Minuteman II missiles at Grand Forks. The ABM complex is decommissioned in 1975 as a result of an agreement with the Soviet Union.
1971   North Dakota ranks second in wheat production, first in barley, and third in hay and oats.
1980   Construction begins at Beulah of the nation's first commercial-scale synthetic-fuels plant, converting lignite into natural gas. In 1985, with the default of $1.5 billion in federally guaranteed loans, the plant passes into the hands of the US Department of Energy, which vainly seeks a buyer.
1981   North Dakota outstrips Kansas in wheat production with a record 328 million bushels.
1988   *June 14*. A North Dakota State University study reports that the spring drought has wiped out at least 40 percent of the wheat crop.

DEMOGRAPHY

Population (est. 1987) 672,000
Population (1980) 652,717
Population density in persons
    per square mile (1980) 9.2

POPULATION BY RACE (1980)
American Indian/Aleut/
    Eskimo 20,157
Asian/Pacific Islander 1,979
Black 2,568
Hispanic 3,903
White 625,536
Other 2,455

POPULATION CHARACTERISTICS (1980)
                Percent of state population
Urban 48.8
Rural 51.2
Under 18 . . . . 29.3
65 or older 12.3

College-educated 15.2
Families below poverty line 9.8
Public-assistance recipients 3.0

Per capita personal income
    (1986) $12,284
Millionaires per 100,000
    residents (1982) 565.5
Average life expectancy
    in years (1980) 75.7
Marriage rate per 1,000
    residents (1986) 7.6
Divorce rate per 1,000
    residents (1986) 13.3
Birth rate per 1,000
    residents (1985) 18.6
Infant mortality rate per
    1,000 births (1985) 9.9
Abortion rate per 1,000
    live births (1985) 230

Crime rate per 100,000
  residents (1985)
  Violent 51.3
  Property 2,554.2
Federal and state prisoners
  per 100,000 residents (1984) . . . 64
Alcohol consumption in gallons
  per capita (1985) 39.4
Deaths from motor vehicle accidents
  per 100,000 residents (1985) . . 13.1

MAJOR CITIES

	Population
Bismarck (est. 1984)	47,552
Fargo (est. 1984)	65,721
Grand Forks (est. 1984)	44,233
Minot (1980)	32,843

GOVERNMENT AND POLITICS

Number of US Representatives   1
Electoral votes   3

POLITICAL PARTY NOMINEES FROM STATE

William Lemke (Union)	1936	P
William Langer (Pioneer)	1956	P
Warren C. Martin (National Statesman)	1984	P

PRESIDENTIAL PRIMARY ELECTION In 1988, North Dakota sent 90 Democratic delegates and 16 Republican delegates to the national conventions.

CONSTITUTION North Dakota is using its original constitution, adopted in 1889.
LEGISLATURE The Legislature is divided into the Senate (53 members, 4-year term, minimum age 18) and the House of Representatives (106 members, 2-year term, minimum age 18). In 1987, the salary for legislators was $180 per month.
JUDICIARY The highest court is the Supreme Court, with 5 judges serving 10-year terms. In 1987, the annual salary was $59,140.
EXECUTIVE The governor serves a 4-year term; the minimum age for holding office is 30. In 1987, the annual salary was $60,856. There are 13 other elected officials.

PRESIDENTIAL VOTE 1948-1988 *(in percents)*

Year	State Winner	Democratic	Republican
1948	Dewey (R)	43.4	52.2
1952	Eisenhower (R)	28.4	71.0
1956	Eisenhower (R)	38.1	61.7
1960	Nixon (R)	44.5	55.4
1964	Johnson (D)	58.0	41.9
1968	Nixon (R)	38.2	55.9
1972	Nixon (R)	35.8	62.1
1976	Ford (R)	45.8	51.6
1980	Reagan (R)	26.3	64.2
1984	Reagan (R)	33.8	64.8
1988	Bush (R)	43.0	57.0

GOVERNORS

Territorial Governors

William Jayne	1861-1863
Newton Edmunds	1863-1866
Andrew J. Faulk	1866-1869
John A. Burbank	1869-1874
John L. Pennington	1874-1878
William A. Howard	1878-1880
Nehemiah G. Ordway	1880-1884
Gilbert A. Pierce	1884-1887
Louis K. Church	1887-1889
Arthur C. Melette	1889

State Governors

John Miller (R)	1889-1891
Andrew H. Burke (R)	1891-1893
Eli C.D. Shortridge (Democrat-Independent)	1893-1895
Roger Allin (R)	1895-1897
Frank A. Briggs (R)	1897-1898
Joseph M. Devine (R/acting)	1898-1899
Frederick B. Fancher (R)	1899-1901
Frank White (R)	1901-1905
Elmore Y. Sarles (R)	1905-1907
John Burke (D)	1907-1913
Louis B. Hanna (R)	1913-1917
Lynn J. Frazier (Nonpartisan League)	1917-1921
Ragnvald A. Nestos (R)	1921-1925

Arthur G. Sorlie (R)	1925-1928
Walter Maddock (Nonpartisan League/acting)	1928-1929
George F. Shafer (R)	1929-1933
William Langer (Nonpartisan League)	1933-1934
Ole H. Olson (R/acting)	1934-1935
Thomas H. Moodie (D)	1935
Walter Welford (R/acting)	1935-1937
William Langer (Independent)	1937-1939
John Moses (D)	1939-1945
Fred G. Aandahl (R)	1945-1951
Norman Brunsdale (R)	1951-1957
John E. Davis (R)	1957-1961
William L. Guy (D)	1961-1973
Arthur A. Link (D)	1973-1981
Allen I. Olson (R)	1981-1985
George Sinner (D)	1985-

MINIMUM AGES

Majority	18
Marriage with parental consent	16
Marriage without parental consent	18
Making a will	18
Buying alcohol	21
Jury duty	18
Leaving school	16
Driver's license	16

CAPITAL PUNISHMENT None

MILITARY INSTALLATIONS
Total number: 8
Major bases:
Air Force: 2

FINANCES

Thousands of dollars

GENERAL REVENUE (1985)

Total general revenue	1,471,930
Total tax revenue	692,213
Sales and gross receipts	293,574
Individual income taxes	76,182
Corporate net income taxes	84,445

GENERAL EXPENDITURE (1985)

Total general expenditure	1,440,294
Education	540,545
Public welfare	177,129
Health	32,594
Hospitals	60,992
Natural resources	49,699
Highways	212,092
Police	6,919
Corrections	10,159

FEDERAL AID (1985) 452,291

ECONOMY

Agricultural goods are North Dakota's chief export. The state's approximately 40,000 farms grow wheat as the main cash crop; significant quantities of potatoes, sugar beets, flax, barley, sunflowers, and soybeans are also grown. Beef and dairy cattle, hogs, sheep, and poultry accounted for about one-third of the state's $2.7 billion in farm cash receipts in 1983. Important mining products are oil, lignite coal, uranium, molybdenum, bentonite, salt, sand, gravel, and clays. Manufactured goods, never a major contributor to the state's economy, include processed foods, farm implements and machinery, and printed materials. Value added by manufacture was $652 million in 1982, second lowest in the nation.

EMPLOYMENT (1984)

Thousands of persons

Total number of employed workers	311
Construction	14.1
Finance, insurance, and real estate	12.2
Government	61.9
Manufacturing	15.5
Mining	7.4
Services	57.5
Transportation, communications, and utilities	16.4
Wholesale and retail trade	67.7
Percent of civilian labor force unemployed (1984)	5.2

DEPARTMENT OF DEFENSE (1985)

Civilian workers employed	1,805
Military personnel	11,274
Contract awards	$207 million

ENERGY SOURCES FOR ELECTRIC UTILITIES (1983)

Percent

Coal	87.7
Gas	0.0
Hydroelectric	12.1
Nuclear	0.0
Petroleum	0.2

TRANSPORTATION

Motor vehicles registered in state (1986)	647,663
Miles of roads, streets, and highways (1986)	86,173
Miles of Class I railway (1986)	4,472
Airports (1983)	451
Major aviation hubs (1983)	0

CULTURE AND EDUCATION

Native American tribes
North Dakota was formerly the home of the Arapaho, Assiniboine, and Cheyenne tribes. Groups that continue to live in the state include the Arikara, Hidatsa, Mandan, Ojibway, and Sioux. There are five federal reservations.

Religions, ethnicities, and languages
Since 1871, North Dakota has attracted immigrants from northern Europe, Canada, and other states. Some cultural traditions are still retained by the state's Norwegian, Icelandic, Czech, and German communities. In 1980, 11.3 percent of North Dakota's population spoke a language other than English at home. About half the state's population is Lutheran, another third Roman Catholic.

Major museums and libraries
North Dakota Historical Society Library, Bismarck
University Museum, Grand Forks

Major arts organizations
Fargo-Moorehead Civic Opera Company, West Fargo
Fargo-Moorhead Symphony Orchestra
North Dakota Ballet, Grand Forks

Colleges and universities
Number public (1986-87) 14
Number private (1986-87) 5
Total enrollment, in full-time equivalent students (1985) 32,500

Public elementary and secondary schools
Expenditure per pupil in average daily attendance (1986-87) $3,174
Pupil-teacher ratio (1987) 15.3
Average teacher salary (1986-87) $22,533

Holidays
State Fair, Minot. 3d week in July

NORTH DAKOTA IN LITERATURE

Johann Bojer *The Emigrants* (1925)
Novel of pioneer life in the Red River Valley translated from the Norwegian.

Hubert E. Collins *Warpath and Cattle Trail* (1928)
Account of a frontier trading post on the Chisholm Trail.

Lewis F. Crawford *Badlands and Bronco Trails* (1926)
Account of the adventures of Ben Arnold Conner, a post–Civil War pioneer.

Elizabeth Custer *Boots and Saddles: or, Life in Dakota with General Custer* (1895, rpt. 1961)
Custer's widow, in an apologia for her husband, describes life at Fort Abraham Lincoln.

Hiram M. Drache *The Challenge of the Prairie: Life and Times of Red River Pioneers* (1970)

Louise Erdrich *Love Medicine* (1984); *The Beet Queen* (1986); *Tracks* (1988)
Three novels of a projected tetralogy describing three generations of several Chippewa Indian families, 1912–1984.

Carolyn Gilman and **Mary J. Schneider** (eds.) *The Way to Independence: Memories of a Hidatsa Indian Family, 1840–1920* (1988)
Reminiscences of three residents of the Fort Berthold Reservation collected by the anthropologist Gilbert L. Wilson in 1906.

Hermann Hagedorn *Roosevelt in the Badlands* (1921)
Description of Roosevelt's life in the 1880s.

Lois Phillips Hudson *The Bones of Plenty* (1962, rpt. 1984); *Reapers of the Dust: A Prairie Chronicle* (1964)
Novel, and short stories, portraying farm life during the Depression.

Lucile M. Kane (trans. and ed.) *Military Life in Dakota: The Journal of Philippe Régis de Trobriand* (1951)
Dakota Territory described by a Frenchman who served with the U.S. cavalry.

Ann Marie Low *Dust Bowl Diary* (1984)
Memoir of life on a stock farm in southeastern North Dakota from 1927.

Aagot Raaen *Grass of the Earth: Immigrant Life in North Dakota* (1950); *Measure of My Days* (1953)
Pioneer memoirs.

Erling N. Rolfsrud *Lanterns over the Prairie* 2 vols (1949, 1950)
Portraits of pioneer settlers.

Theodore Roosevelt *Hunting Trips of a Ranchman* (1885); *Hunting Adventures in the West* (1927)
Descriptions of hunting adventures and ranch life in the Badlands.

Eric Sevareid *Not So Wild a Dream* (1946)
Memoir containing a description of the author's boyhood in North Dakota.

Lucy J. Sypher *The Edge of Nowhere* (1972); *Cousins and Circuses* (1974); *The Spell of the Northern Lights* (1975); *The Turnabout Year* (1976)
Portrait of life in a small town during the early twentieth century.

Eta Bell Thompson *American Daughter* (1986)
Autobiography of a black woman who moved with her farming family to the small town of Driscoll in 1914.

Sophie Trupin *Dakota Diaspora: Memoirs of a Jewish Homesteader* (1988)
Account of life in a small Jewish immigrant community.

Douglas Unger *Leaving the Land* (1984)
Depiction of a small rural community in the western Dakotas and its destruction by agribusiness.

Mary Dodge Woodward *The Checkered Years* (1937)
Diary of woman living on a bonanza farm near Fargo in the 1880s.

GUIDES TO RESOURCES

Berg, Francis M. *Ethnic Heritage in North Dakota* (1983)

Budge, Chrissie E. (ed.) *Bibliography of the Geology and Natural Resources of North Dakota, 1814–1944. With Supplements One and Two* (1946, rpt. 1959)

Bye, John E. *North Dakota Institute for Regional Studies: Guide to Manuscripts and Archives* (1985)

Federal Writers' Project *North Dakota: A Guide to the Northern Prairie State* (1938; 2d ed. 1950, rpt. 1980)

Fridley, Russell *Historic Sites of North Dakota* (1967)
———. *Supplement to Report on Historic Sites of North Dakota* (1967)

Goodman, Lowell R. and R. J. Eidem *The Atlas of North Dakota* (1976)

Liddle, Janice *Index to Mary Ann Barnes Williams' Origins of North Dakota Place Names* (1977)

North Dakota State Library Commission *Who's Who for North Dakota: A Triennial* (1955)

———. *North Dakota in Print* (1972)

———. *Legislative History of North Dakota State Agencies: A Compendium of North Dakota State Agencies, Their Organization, Function and Legislative History* (1978)

Reid, Russell and Clell G. Gannon *Historical and Pictorial Map of North Dakota* (1930)

Roehrick, Kaye L. (ed.) *Brevet's North Dakota Historical Markers and Sites* (1975)

Rylance, Daniel F. (ed.) *North Dakota Government and Politics: A Selected Annotated Bibliography* (1975)
———. *Reference Guide to North Dakota History* (1979)

Sherman, William C. *Prairie Mosaic: An Ethnic Atlas of Rural North Dakota* (1983)

University of North Dakota, Bureau of Business and Economic Research *Statistical Abstract of North Dakota* (1979–)

SELECTED NONFICTION SOURCES

Arnold, Henry V. *History of Grand Forks County* (1900)
———. *History of Old Pembina* (1917)
———. *Early History of Grand Forks* (1918)
———. *Forty Years in North Dakota* (1921)

Bavendick, Frank J. *Climate and Weather in North Dakota* (2d ed. 1952)

Blackorby, Edward C. *Prairie Rebel: The Public Life of William Lemke* (1963)

Brand, Wayne L. and James G. Hector (eds.) *North Dakota Decision Makers* (1972)

Buttree, J. Edmond *The Despoilers; Stories of the North Dakota Grain Fields* (1920)

Crawford, Lewis F. (ed.) *History of North Dakota* 3 vols. (1931)
———. *Ranching Days in Dakota, and Custer's Black Hills Expedition* (1950)

Diede, Pauline Neher (ed. Elizabeth Hampsten) *Homesteading on the Knife River Prairies* (1983)

Drache, Hiram M. *The Day of the Bonanza: A History of Bonanza Farming in the Red River Valley of the North* (1964)

Fossum, Paul R. *The Agrarian Movement in North Dakota* (1925)

Gaston, Herbert E. *The Nonpartisan League* (1920, rpt. 1975)

Gillette, John M. *North Dakota Weather and the Rural Economy* (1945)

Hager, Dorothy *First Ladies of North Dakota* (1967)

Hanson, Nancy E. *Bread Basket of the World* (1985)

Hargreaves, Mary W. M. *Dry Farming in the Northern Great Plains, 1900–1925* (1957)

Holley, Frances C. *Once Their Home; or, Our Legacy from the Dahkotahs; Historical, Biographical, and Incidental, from Far-off Days, Down to the Present* (1890)

Howard, Thomas W. (ed.) *The North Dakota Political Tradition* (1981)

Hudson, John C. *Plains Country Towns* (1985)

Jensen, Ray E. *Climate of North Dakota* (1972)

Kazeck, Melvin E. *North Dakota: Human and Economic Geography* (1956)

Kelsey, Vera *Red River Runs North* (1951)

Knight, Harold V. *Grass Roots: The Story of the North Dakota Farmers' Union* (1947)

Lamar, Howard R. *Dakota Territory, 1861–1889: A Study of Frontier Politics* (1956)

Lawson, Michael L. *Dammed Indians: The Pick-Sloan Plan and the Missouri River Sioux, 1944–1980* (1982)

Lincoln, Kenneth *The Good Red Road: Passages into Native America with Al Logan Slagle* (1987)

Lounsberry, C. A. *North Dakota History and People* 3 vols. (1916)
———. *Early History of North Dakota* (1919)

McDonald, Marie P. *After Barbed Wire: A Pictorial History of the Homestead Rush into the Northern Great Plains, 1900–1919* (1963)

Morlan, Robert L. *Political Prairie Fire: The Nonpartisan League, 1915–1922* (1955)

Nelson, Bruce *Land of the Dacotahs* (1946)

Oihus, Colleen A. *Compendium of History and Biography of North Dakota Containing a History of North Dakota* (1980)
———. *A History of Coal Mining in North Dakota, 1873–1982* (1983)

Omdahl, Lloyd *Organization and Administration of the State Government of North Dakota* 2 vols. (1942)
———. *Insurgents: History of North Dakota Politics 1947–1960* (1961)

Piper, Marion J. *Dakota Portraits: A Sentimental Journal of Pictorial History* (1964)

Rath, George *The Black Sea Germans in the Dakotas* (1977)

Roberts, Norene A. *Fargo's Heritage* (1983)

Robinson, Elwyn B. *Heroes of North Dakota* 2 vols. (1947–1948)
———. *History of North Dakota* (1966)

Russell, Charles E. *The Story of the Nonpartisan League: A Chapter in American Evolution* (1920)

Schneider, Mary J. *North Dakota Indians: An Introduction* (1986)

Schulenberg, Raymond F. *Indians of North Dakota* (1956)

Thompson, Era B. *American Daughter* (1946, rpt. 1986)

Trinka, Zena I. *North Dakota of Today* (1920)
———. *Out Where the West Begins* (1920)

Tweton, Jerome D. and Daniel F. Rylance *The Years of Despair: North Dakota in the Depression* (1973)
——— and Theodore Jelliff *North Dakota: The Heritage of a People* (1976)

Wilkins, Robert P. and Wynona H. *God Giveth the Increase: The History of the Episcopal Church in North Dakota* (1958)
——— and Wynona H. *North Dakota: A Bicentennial History* (States and the Nation series) (1977)

Willard, Daniel E. *The Story of the Prairies; or, The Landscape Geology of North Dakota* (9th ed. 1921)

Williams, Mary A. Barnes *Origins of North Dakota Place Names* (1966)

Wilson, Gilbert (ed.) *Buffalo Bird Woman's Garden: Agriculture of the Hidatsa Indians* (1988)

OHIO

Ohio is an east north central state. It is bordered on the north by Michigan and Lake Erie; on the east by Pennsylvania, West Virginia, and the Ohio River; on the south by the Ohio River, West Virginia and Kentucky; and on the west by Indiana.

FULL NAME State of Ohio
POSTAL ABBREVIATION OH
INHABITANT Ohioan
ADMITTED TO THE UNION Mar. 1, 1803.
  17th state
POPULATION (est. 1987) 10,784,000.
  Percent of US total: 4.43%. Rank: 7th

CAPITAL CITY Columbus, located at the junction of the Scioto and Olentangy rivers in central Ohio; population 566,114 (est. 1984). The site was selected to be the capital in 1812; the capital was moved there from Chillicothe in 1816. Columbus became a city in 1834.

STATE NAME AND NICKNAMES From the Iroquois word *ohio*, "beautiful river" or "large river." Also known as the Buckeye State and the Mother of Modern Presidents.

STATE SEAL The coat of arms shows a 17-rayed sun rising over Mount Logan, behind the Scioto River, with a sheaf of wheat and a bundle of 17 arrows standing in a field in the foreground. Around the border is the inscription "The Great Seal of the State of Ohio."

MOTTO With God, All Things Are Possible.

SONG "Beautiful Ohio," lyrics by Ballad MacDonald, music by Mary Earl.

SYMBOLS
Flower scarlet carnation
Tree buckeye
Bird cardinal
Gem Ohio flint
Beverage tomato juice

LICENSE PLATE Green on white, with county name.

FLAG A double-pointed pennant consisting of five horizontal stripes, three red and two white; at the staff end is a blue triangle bearing a red circle with a white border, around which are arrayed 17 stars.

GEOGRAPHY AND CLIMATE

Ohio's terrain is dominated by the plains along Lake Erie and extending to the south, and the Central Plains, occupying the west and southwest. Along Ohio's eastern border is the western end of the Allegheny Plateau, a more rugged area of winding rivers and bluffs. The Ohio River, which forms Ohio's southern border, provides drainage for most of the state, with Lake Erie draining the northern third.

AREA 41,330 square miles. Rank: 35th
INLAND WATER 326 square miles
GEOGRAPHIC CENTER Delaware, 25 miles NNE of Columbus
ELEVATIONS *Highest point:* Campbell Hill, Logan County, 1,550 feet. *Lowest point:* Ohio River, Hamilton County, 433 feet. *Mean elevation:* 850 feet

MAJOR RIVERS Ohio, Miami, Muskingum, Scioto

MAJOR LAKES AND RESERVOIRS Erie, Grand, Mosquito Creek, Milton

LAND USE

	Thousands of acres
Urban (1982)	2,187
Rural (1982)	22,859
Cropland (1982)	12,447
Pastureland (1982)	2,714
Rangeland (1982)	0
Forestland (1982)	6,380
State parks and recreation areas (1983)	112
National park system (1984)	15
National forest system (1984)	833
Tribal lands (1984)	0

TEMPERATURES The highest recorded temperature was 113°F on July 21, 1934, near Gallipolis. The lowest was -39°F on February 10, 1899, at Milligan.

NATIONAL SITES

NATIONAL HISTORIC SITES Afro-American History and Culture, James A. Garfield, William Howard Taft
NATIONAL MEMORIAL David Berger
NATIONAL MONUMENT Mound City Group
NATIONAL SCENIC TRAIL North Country
OTHER PARKS Perry's Victory and International Peace Memorial
NATIONAL WILDLIFE REFUGES Ottawa–Cedar Point/West Sister Island

HISTORY

1655	Invading Iroquois nearly annihilate the Erie in northern Ohio, laying claim to their Ohio lands.
1669–1670	French explorer Robert Cavelier, Sieur de La Salle, is believed to have crossed Ohio traveling from Lake Erie to the Ohio River.
c.1740	Four Indian tribes—the Miami, Shawnee, Wyandot, and Delaware—have a population of perhaps 15,000 in Ohio.
1748	A group of Virginians organize the Ohio Land Company and plan to colonize a half-million acres.
1749	Celeron de Bienville (or Blainville), a French trader, buries land markers to underline French claims to the Ohio country but does not dissuade English rivals.
1750–1751	Christopher Gist, an agent for the Ohio Land Company, explores the Ohio country.
1761	Christian Frederick Post, a Moravian missionary, builds the first permanent dwelling in Ohio, a log cabin near Bolivar.
1763	By the Treaty of Paris, France cedes to Great Britain all its North American continental possessions east of the Mississippi except for New Orleans.
1772	*August 24.* A Moravian community is established near present-day New Philadelphia; here, the following year, the first school west of the Alleghenies is opened.
1779	American colonists taking part in the Revolutionary War build Fort Laurens, the first American fort in Ohio, at Bolivar, but it is abandoned after six months.
1780–1781	George Rogers Clark and other frontiersmen conduct punitive raids in retaliation for Indian raids on Kentucky settlers.
1782	*March 8.* Frontiersmen massacre 96 Christian Delaware Indians at Gnadenhutten. *August 19.* Sixty-six American soldiers are killed by Indians at Blue Licks.

1788	*April 7.* Marietta, the first permanent white settlement in Ohio, is founded with 48 settlers.
1789	The US Army begins construction of Fort Washington at the site of present-day Cincinnati.
1794	*August 20.* Soldiers under General "Mad Anthony" Wayne break the power of the Indians at the Battle of Fallen Timbers near present-day Toledo.
1795	*August 3.* The Treaty of Greenville leaves to the Indians only about one-fourth of what is now the state of Ohio.
1796	Moses Cleaveland of the Connecticut Land Company plans a town site at present-day Cleveland.
	Zane's Trail is Ohio's first formal road, leading from Jefferson City in the east to Adams County on the Ohio River.
1800	Chillicothe is the territorial capital.
	May 7. Indiana Territory is detached from Ohio.
	Connecticut cedes its claim to the Western Reserve, a strip of land along Lake Erie.
1801	First federal land sale in Ohio, at Cincinnati.
1803	*March 1.* Ohio admitted to the Union as the 17th state.
1804	The future Ohio University is chartered as an academy and thus becomes the first institution of higher learning in the United States north and west of the Ohio River.
	Legislature enacts the first of the "Black Laws" which restrict the rights and movements of blacks.
1811	The steamboat is introduced on the Ohio River.
1812	*February 14.* The legislature votes to establish the state capital on a site named Columbus.
1813	*September 10.* In a major War of 1812 naval battle, Oliver Hazard Perry defeats a British flotilla on Lake Erie.
1817	First abolitionist newspaper in the United States is issued at Mount Pleasant.
1818	First steamboat on Lake Erie.
1820	Cincinnati, with about 25,000, is the largest city in the West except New Orleans.
1827	*June 25.* First issue of the Cincinnati *Daily Gazette*, the first daily newspaper west of Philadelphia.
1832	*December 1.* Completion of the Ohio and Erie Canal, linking Cleveland with Portsmouth on the Ohio River.
1833	National Pike road from Cumberland, Maryland, reaches Columbus.
1837	Oberlin College becomes the first coeducational college in the United States.
1840	Ohio resident William Henry Harrison is elected president.
	Ohio leads all states in wheat production with 16 million bushels.
1842	Wyandots sell their lands in northwest Ohio and go west, leaving no Indian tribes in the state.
1846	Cleveland, Columbus, and Cincinnati are connected by 263 miles of railroad.
1850	Ohio is first among states in corn, horses, sheep, and wool, second in wheat and cattle.
	Cincinnati is third among cities in manufacturing, leading in carriages and wagons.
1856	Rudolph Wurlitzer founds his music house in Cincinnati.
1861–1865	Ohio contributes 346,326 men to the Union cause in the Civil War, more than half the able-bodied men in the state; 24,591 die in battle, of wounds, or disease.
1863	*July.* Confederate cavalry under General John Morgan raid the state, and are captured July 26 near Salineville.
	Exiled Peace Democrat Clement Vallandigham runs for governor, receiving about 40 percent of the vote and carrying 18 counties.
1870	John D. Rockfeller organizes the Standard Oil Company in Cleveland.
1884	First US electric street railway is placed in operation in Cleveland.
1886	*February 23.* Charles Martin Hall discovers the electrolytic process of making aluminum in Oberlin.
	December 10. The American Federation of Trades and Labor is founded in Columbus, with Samuel Gompers as its president.

1892	State legislature makes it unlawful to dismiss a workingman for membership in a labor union.
1896	B. F. Goodrich Company makes the first rubber automobile tire at Akron.
1912	Adoption of Ohio's fourth constitution.
1913	Devastating spring floods take at least 428 lives and cause property damage estimated at $250 million.
1915	Founding of the Cleveland Play House, the oldest continuing regional theater in the United States.
1920	Warren Harding becomes the seventh Ohio native to be elected president of the United States.
1929	Ohio's leading industry is iron and steel, with more than 80 steel plants and rolling mills.
1933	The number of wage earners in Ohio has dropped to 472,000, from a high of 740,000 in 1929, as a result of the Depression.
1934	A state sales tax of three percent is adopted.
1936	*February 14.* A series of sit-down strikes begin in the Akron rubber plants, leading to a share-the-work clause to avoid layoffs.
1937	*January 28.* Ohio River crests at a record 80 feet at Cincinnati; about 750,000 Ohioans are homeless.
	June 19. Two strikers killed, 27 wounded, and hundreds teargassed at the Republic Steel plant in Youngstown.
1955	*September 30.* Opening of the 241-mile, $326-million east-west Ohio Turnpike.
1959	The St. Lawrence Seaway opens Lake Erie ports to international trade.
1967	Carl Stokes of Cleveland is the first popularly elected black mayor of a major US city.
1970	*May 4.* During an anti-Vietnam War protest, four Kent State University students are killed and nine injured by National Guardsmen.
1971	A state income tax is adopted.
1973	Voters approve a constitutional amendment allowing a state lottery.
1978	*November.* Republican James Rhodes is elected to a recordbreaking fourth term as governor.
	December. Cleveland defaults on a $14-million debt owed to six banks.
1980	Ohio is reported to have moved to second place, behind Michigan, in automobile production; Honda Motor Company announces it will open an auto plant in Marysville.
1982	The unemployment rate reaches 14.2 percent of the labor force in November, highest since the Great Depression.

DEMOGRAPHY

Population (est. 1987) . . . 10,784,000
Population (1980) 10,797,624
Population density in persons
  per square mile (1980) . . . 261.3

65 or older 10.8
College-educated 14.8
Families below poverty line 8.0
Public-assistance recipients 6.0

POPULATION BY RACE (1980)
American Indian/Aleut/
  Eskimo 12,240
Asian/Pacific Islander 47,813
Black 1,076,734
Hispanic 119,880
White 9,597,266
Other 63,366

Per capita personal income
  (1986) $13,743
Millionaires per 100,000
  residents (1982) 117.0
Average life expectancy in
  years (1980) 73.5
Marriage rate (1986) 9.0
Divorce rate (1986) 5.0
Birth rate per 1,000
  residents (1985) 15.0
Infant mortality rate per
  1,000 births (1985) 10.3
Abortion rate per 1,000
  live births (1985) 357

POPULATION CHARACTERISTICS (1980)
Percent of state population
Urban 73.3
Rural 26.7
Under 18 . . . . 28.7

Crime rate per 100,000
  residents (1985)
    Violent 420.9
    Property 3,937.8
Federal and state prisoners
  per 100,000 residents (1984) . . 175
Alcohol consumption in gallons
  per capita (1985) 39.3
Deaths from motor vehicle
  accidents per 100,000 residents
  (1985) 15.3

MAJOR CITIES

	1984 population (est.)
Akron	226,877
Canton	89,098
Cincinnati	370,481
Cleveland	546,543
Columbus	566,114
Dayton	181,159
Lorain	72,789
Springfield	70,079
Toledo	343,939
Youngstown	108,042

GOVERNMENT AND POLITICS

Number of US Representatives	21	
Electoral votes	23	

POLITICAL PARTY NOMINEES FROM STATE
  *winner

William Henry Harrison (Whig faction)	1836	P
William Henry Harrison* (Whig)	1840	P
Thomas Morris (Liberal)	1844	VP
Leicester King (Free Soil/Liberal)	1848	VP
George Hunt Pendleton (D)	1864	VP
William Slocum Grosebeck (Independent Liberal Republican)	1872	P
Rutherford Birchard Hayes* (R)	1876	P
Samuel Fenton Cary (Greenback)	1876	VP
Gideon Tabor Stewart (Prohibition)	1876	VP
James Abram Garfield* (R)	1880	P
Henry Adams Thompson (Prohibition)	1884	VP
Allen Granberry Thurman (D)	1888	VP
William McKinley* (R)	1896	P
William McKinley* (R)	1900	P
Seth Hockett Ellis (Union Reform)	1900	P
William Howard Taft* (R)	1908	P
Aaron Sherman Watkins (Prohibition)	1908	VP
William Howard Taft (R)	1912	P
Aaron Sherman Watkins (Prohibition)	1912	VP
Warren Gamaliel Harding* (R)	1920	P
James Middleton Cox (D)	1920	P
Maximilian Sebastian Hayes (Farmer Labor)	1920	VP
Aaron Sherman Watkins (Prohibition)	1920	P
R.G. Barnum (Single Tax)	1920	VP
John Cromwell Lincoln (Commonwealth Land)	1924	VP
Wesley Henry Bennington (Greenback)	1928	VP
Jacob Sechler Coxey (Farmer Labor)	1932	P
John William Bricker (R)	1944	VP
Arla A. Albaugh (Socialist Labor)	1944	VP
Henry A. Romer (America First)	1944	VP
Henry A. Romer (Christian Nationalist)	1948	VP
Curtis Emerson LeMay (American Independent/Courage)	1968	VP
Richard Congress (Socialist Workers)	1980	P

PRESIDENTIAL PRIMARY ELECTION In 1988, Ohio sent 174 Democratic delegates and 88 Republican delegates to the national conventions.

CONSTITUTION Ohio has had two constitutions: 1802 and the present one, adopted in 1851.

LEGISLATURE The General Assembly is divided into the Senate (33 members, 4-year term, minimum age 18) and the House of Representatives (99 members, 2-year term, minimum age 18). In 1987, the annual salary was $34,905.

JUDICIARY The highest court is the Supreme Court, with 7 judges serving 6-year terms. In 1987, the annual salary was $83,250.

EXECUTIVE The governor serves a 4-year term; there is no minimum age for holding office. In 1987, the annual salary was $65,000. There are 28 other elected officials.

PRESIDENTIAL VOTE 1948-1988 *(in percents)*

Year	State Winner	Democratic	Republican
1948	Truman (D)	49.5	49.2
1952	Eisenhower (R)	43.2	56.8
1956	Eisenhower (R)	38.9	61.1
1960	Nixon (R)	46.7	53.3
1964	Johnson (D)	62.9	37.1
1968	Nixon (R)	43.0	45.2
1972	Nixon (R)	38.1	59.6
1976	Carter (D)	38.9	38.7
1980	Reagan (R)	40.9	51.5
1984	Reagan (R)	40.1	58.9
1988	Bush (R)	45.0	55.0

GOVERNORS

State Governors

Edward Tiffin (Democratic-Republican)	1803-1807
Thomas Kirker (D-R)	1807-1808
Samuel Huntington (D-R)	1808-1810
Return Jonathan Meigs (D-R)	1810-1814
Othniel Looker (D-R)	1814
Thomas Worthington (D-R)	1814-1818
Ethan Allen Brown (D-R)	1818-1822
Allen Trimble (D-R)	1822
Jeremiah Morrow (D-R)	1822-1826
Allen Trimble (National Republican)	1826-1830
Duncan McArthur (National Republican)	1830-1832
Robert Lucas (D)	1832-1836
Joseph Vance (Whig)	1836-1838
Wilson Shannon (D)	1838-1840
Thomas Corwin (Whig)	1840-1842
Wilson Shannon (D)	1842-1844
Thomas Bartley (D)	1844
Mordecai Bartley (Whig)	1844-1846
William Bebb (Whig)	1846-1849
Seabury Ford (Whig)	1849-1850
Reuben Wood (D)	1850-1853
William Medill (D)	1853-1856
Salmon P. Chase (R)	1856-1860
William Dennison (R)	1860-1862
David Tod (Union)	1862-1864
John Brough (Union)	1864-1865
Charles Anderson (Union)	1865-1866
Jacob D. Cox (Union)	1866-1868
Rutherford B. Hayes (R)	1868-1872
Edward F. Noyes (R)	1872-1874
William Allen (D)	1874-1876
Rutherford B. Hayes (R)	1876-1877
Thomas L. Young (R)	1877-1878
Richard M. Bishop (D)	1878-1880
Charles Foster (R)	1880-1884
George Hoadly (D)	1884-1886

Joseph B. Foraker (R)	1886-1890
James E. Campbell (D)	1890-1892
William McKinley (R)	1892-1896
Asa S. Bushnell (R)	1896-1900
George K. Nash (R)	1900-1904
Myron T. Herrick (R)	1904-1906
John M. Pattison (D)	1906
Andrew L. Harris (R)	1906-1909
Judson Harmon (D)	1909-1913
James M. Cox (D)	1913-1915
Frank B. Willis (R)	1915-1917
James M. Cox (D)	1917-1921
Harry L. Davis (R)	1921-1923
A.V. Donahey (D)	1923-1929
Myers Y. Cooper (R)	1929-1931
George White (D)	1931-1935
Martin L. Davey (D)	1935-1939
John W. Bricker (R)	1939-1945
Frank J. Lausche (D)	1945-1947
Thomas J. Herbert (R)	1947-1949
Frank J. Lausche (D)	1949-1957
John W. Brown (R)	1957
C. William O'Neill (R)	1957-1959
Michael V. DiSalle (D)	1959-1963
James A. Rhodes (R)	1963-1971
John J. Gilligan (D)	1971-1975
James A. Rhodes (R)	1975-1983
Richard F. Celeste (D)	1983-

MINIMUM AGES

Majority	18
Marriage with parental consent	
female	16
male	18
Marriage without parental consent	18
Making a will	18
Buying alcohol	21
Jury duty	18
Leaving school	18
Driver's license	16

CAPITAL PUNISHMENT

Number executed 1976-88: 0
On death row Aug. 1, 1988: 86

MILITARY INSTALLATIONS
Total number: 19
Major bases:
  Air Force: 1

machinery, machine tools, ceramics, plastics, and chemicals.

FINANCES

Thousands of dollars

GENERAL REVENUE (1985)
Total general revenue . . .	14,775,850
Total tax revenue	8,651,690
Sales and gross receipts	4,625,294
Individual income taxes . . .	2,781,658
Corporate net income taxes . . .	437,129

GENERAL EXPENDITURE (1985)
Total general expenditure . .	14,071,365
Education	5,431,414
Public welfare	3,134,228
Health	389,796
Hospitals	737,236
Natural resources	180,589
Highways	1,424,765
Police	85,359
Corrections	329,694

FEDERAL AID (1985) 4,158,358

ECONOMY

Among the main cash crops are corn and soybeans, wheat, fruits, and vegetables. Dairy cattle, hogs, and poultry contributed about a third of the state's $3.7 billion in farm cash receipts in 1983. As manufacturing and services continue to increase in importance to Ohio's economy, farming decreases, and farmland is undergoing rapid development. Coal is Ohio's leading mining product, followed by oil and natural gas, gypsum and clays, sand and gravel, and building stones such as sandstone. Ohio's principal manufactures include transportation machinery, rubber tires and rubber products, metal parts, electrical

EMPLOYMENT (1984)
Thousands of persons
Total number of employed workers	4,618
Construction	142.9
Finance, insurance, and real estate	211.5
Government	654.5
Manufacturing	125.1
Mining	27.6
Services	903.8
Transportation, communications, and utilities	205.7
Wholesale and retail trade	976.8

Percent of civilian labor force
  unemployed (1984) 9.4

DEPARTMENT OF DEFENSE (1985)
Civilian workers employed . . .	34,318
Military personnel	13,815
Contract awards	$4.648 billion

ENERGY SOURCES FOR ELECTRIC UTILITIES (1983)
Percent
Coal	94.9
Gas	0.1
Hydroelectric	0.1
Nuclear	4.6
Petroleum	0.3

TRANSPORTATION
Motor vehicles registered in state (1986)	8,159,171
Miles of roads, streets, and highways (1986)	113,288
Miles of Class I railway operated (1986)	6,102
Airports (1983)	678
Major aviation hubs (1983)	6

Largest hub: Cleveland
Major ports, with gross tonnage in
  thousands (1985):
Toledo Harbor	18,400
Cincinnati	16,215
Cleveland	13,767
Lorain Harbor	9,426
Conneaut Harbor	9,148

CULTURE AND EDUCATION

Native American tribes
Native American tribes lived in Ohio for some 7,000 years. Ohio was formerly home to the Delaware, Erie, Honniasont, Illinois, Kickapoo, Miami, Neutral, Ojibway, Ottawa, Peoria, Potawatomi, Seneca, Shawnee, and Wyandot tribes.

Religions, ethnicities, and languages
Ohio's mixture of industry and farming has attracted successive waves of immigrants. The early settlers came from other states—chiefly Connecticut, Virginia, and Pennsylvania. During the mid-19th century, immigrants came from Germany, Ireland,

the British Isles, and France. By the turn of the century, they were coming from central, eastern, and southern Europe, as well as from Asia, Turkey, and Mexico; most settled in the industrialized northeast part of the state, which also took in American blacks from the southern states. In 1980, 5.2 percent of Ohio's population spoke a language other than English at home. In addition to the mainstream Protestant denominations, there are large Jewish, Roman Catholic, and Eastern Orthodox congregations in Ohio's cities, and its farm areas have many Amish and Mennonite communities.

Major museums and libraries
Akron Art Museum
Canton Art Institute
Cincinnati Art Museum
Cincinnati Museum of Natural History
Columbus Museum of Art
Dayton Museum of Natural History
Massillon Museum
Ohio Historical Center, Columbus
Taft Museum, Cincinnati
Toledo Museum of Art

Major arts organizations
Cincinnati/New Orleans City Ballet,
   Cincinnati Opera Association
Cincinnati Playhouse-in-the-Park

Cincinnati Symphony Orchestra
Cleveland Opera
Cleveland Orchestra
Cleveland Play House
Cleveland San Jose Ballet
Columbus Symphony Orchestra
Great Lakes Theater Festival, Cleveland
Karamu Theatre, Cleveland
Ohio Ballet
Opera/Columbus

Colleges and universities
Number public (1986-87) 60
Number private (1986-87) 82
Total enrollment, in full-time equivalent students (1985) 383,900

Public elementary and secondary schools
Expenditure per pupil in average daily attendance (1986-87) $3,764
Pupil-teacher ratio (1987) 18.1
Average teacher salary (1986-87) $27,379

Major league sports teams
Baseball: Cincinnati Reds, Cleveland Indians
Basketball: Cleveland Cavaliers
Football: Cincinnati Bengals, Cleveland Browns

Holidays
State Fair, Columbus. Mid-August

OHIO IN LITERATURE

Marguerite Allis *Brave Pursuit* (1954)
Pioneer life during the early 1800s.
———. *Rising Storm* (1955)
Novel about the abolition movement and the underground railroad.

Sherwood Anderson *Winesburg, Ohio* (1919)
Anderson's best-known collection of tales is based on his experience of growing up in Clyde and other towns, and of managing a factory in Elyria. The novels *Windy McPherson's Son* (1916) and *Poor White* (1920) are also set in small towns and depict the oddities of mid-western characters. *A Story-Teller's Story* (1924) is an autobiography describing Anderson's opposition to materialism and standardization.

John Baskin *New Burlington: The Life and Death of an American Village* (1976)
Memoir of a community, composed of autobiographies, that commemorates the rural American culture of the years 1870–1930.

Louis Bromfield *Pleasant Valley* (1945)
In the first of a series of books about his agrarian experiments, Bromfield describes abandoning his work as a novelist, returning to Ohio where he had grown up, and purchasing three adjacent farms. He continued the account in *Malabar Farm* (1948, rpt. 1970, 1978) and *From My Experience: The Pleasures and Miseries of Life on a Farm* (1955). *The Farm* (1933) is a novel about four generations of a rural family, 1815–1915. Bromfield's novels *Green Bay Tree* (1924), *Possession* (1925), and *Early Autumn* (1926) are based on his observations of the Ohio steel industry.

Joan Chase *During the Reign of The Queen of Persia* (1983)
Novel about three generations of women on a northern Ohio farm.

Charles W. Chesnutt *The Wife of His Youth and Other Stories of the Color Line* (1899)
Realistic tales of black society in Cleveland at the turn of the century.

James M. Cox *Journey Through My Years* (1946)
Memoirs of an Ohio governor.

William Coyle (ed.) *Ohio Authors and Their Books . . . 1796–1950* (1962)

Peter Davis *Hometown* (1982)
Study of the culture of a small town.

Margaret V. Dwight (ed. Max Farrand) *A Journey to Ohio in Eighteen-Ten as Recorded in the Journal of Margaret Van Horn Dwight* (1912)
Twenty-year-old's journal of the wagon trip from Connecticut.

Allan W. Eckert *The Frontiersmen* (1967); *Wilderness Empire* (1969)
Historical saga depicting pioneering in eighteenth-century Ohio.

Mary O. Eddy (comp.) *Ballads and Songs from Ohio* (1939)
Versions of 25 English and Scottish popular ballads and almost 300 European and native American folksongs.

Edward Eggleston *The End of the World* (1872); *The Circuit Rider* (1874)
Realistic, historically accurate, novels depicting the Millerite religious movement, and the life of a Methodist preacher, in Ohio in the 1840s.

William D. Ellis *The Bounty Lands* (1952); *Jonathan Blair* (1954); *The Brooks Legend* (1958)
Historical novels about frontier life in Ohio Territory.

Federal Writers' Project *Tales of Old Cincinnati* (1940)

Dorothy Canfield Fisher *The Bent Twig* (1915)
Novel about the family of a college professor based on the author's experience of Columbus in the late nineteenth century.

Herbert Gold *Therefore Be Bold* (1960)
Comic novel about adolescence in a Cleveland suburb during the Depression.

Karen M. Green *Pioneer Ohio Newspapers* (1986)

William C. Howells *Recollections of Life in Ohio from 1813 to 1840* (1895, rpt. 1977)
Memoirs of pioneer life by the novelist's father.

William Dean Howells *A Boy's Town* (1890)
Howells lived in New York and Boston from the age of 35 but retained ties with Hamilton, where his family had moved when he was three. *A Boy's Town* recalls the struggles of his family; *My Year in a Log Cabin* (1893) relates his father's attempts to survive as a paper manufacturer on the Little Miami River; *New Leaf Mills* (1913) is a novel based on this experience; *Years of My Youth* (1916) is an autobiography of his Ohio years; and *The Leatherwood God* (1916) is a novel about a religious lunatic in a small Ohio community in the 1820s.

W. Ralph Janeway *A Selected List of Ohio Authors and Their Books* (1933)

Josephine Johnson *The Inland Island* (1969)
Journal of a year on a farm in southern Ohio.

Jack Matthews *Tales of the Ohio Land* (1978)

Toni Morrison *Sula* (1973)
Novel about a friendship between two young women set in the black community of a small Ohio town.
———. *Beloved* (1987)
Novel about the loss and rediscovery of a black child set in Ohio during Reconstruction.

Conrad Richter *The Trees* (1940); *The Fields* (1946); *The Town* (1950)
Trilogy of historical novels, republished in one volume as *The Awakening Land* (1966), depicting the settlement of Ohio through a chronicle of a family, 1790–1860.

Constance Robertson *Golden Circle* (1953)
Civil war novel describing the "copperheads" and anti-government activities.

Don Robertson *The Greatest Thing since Sliced Bread* (1965); *The Sum and Total of Now* (1966); *The Greatest Things that Almost Happened* (1971)
Trilogy of novels featuring Morris Bird, a youth growing up in the Cleveland area. Robertson's *Paradise Falls Saga* (1978) is a panoramic portrait of a southern Ohio town in the nineteenth century.

Helen H. Santmyer *Ohio Town* (1962)
Memoir of Xenia, 1900–1960. Detailed account of small-town life.
———. *And Ladies of the Club* (1982, rpt. 1984)
A group of women found a literary club in a small southwestern Ohio town in 1868. The novel traces social change through the next 64 years, using the club's meetings as the only constant, unchanging factor in the lives of its members.

Ruth Seid *The Changelings* (1955)
Novel about racial and cultural integration in an Ohio city.

Charles Smart *R.F.D* (1938)
Account of farming during the Depression by an Ohio writer who gave up ambitions to become a novelist to return to the family farm.

Barr Spicer *The Wild Ohio* (1953)
Historical novel of French settlers in the Ohio Valley c.1730.

Jesse Stuart *Land Beyond the River* (1974)
Humorous novel about an Appalachian family.

William Thomas *The Country in the Boy* (1976)
Lyrical evocation of growing up in Ohio in the early twentieth century.

James Thurber *My Life and Hard Times* (1933); *The Thurber Album* (1952)
Comically exaggerated accounts of the author's Columbus upbringing and ancestors.

Frances Trollope *Domestic Manners of the Americans* (1832, rpt. 1949)
Censorious and amusing portrait of American society written by the mother of the novelist Anthony Trollope shortly after returning in 1830 from a two-year stay in Cincinnati.

Dale Van Every *The Voyagers* (1957)
Picaresque adventures on the Ohio River in the 1780s.

William H. Venable *A Buckeye Boyhood* (1911)
Romantic idyll of mid-nineteenth-century boyhood in the Ohio Valley.

David Rains Wallace *Idle Weeds: The Life of a Sandstone Ridge* (1980)
Natural history of a year on a wooded ridge that has been spared from development.

Jessamyn West *Leafy Rivers* (1967)
Novel set in Ohio Territory c.1800.

Brand Whitlock *Forty Years of It* (1914)
Autobiography of a novelist and diplomat born in Urbana describing social change in the years 1880–1940 from an Ohio perspective. Whitlock's novel *J. Hardin and Son* (1923) depicts life on the main street of a small Ohio town.

GUIDES TO RESOURCES

Adams, Marilyn *Ohio Local and Family History Sources in Print* (1984)

Browarek, Matthew F. *A Heritage of Books: A Selected Bibliography of Books and Related Materials on Cleveland* . . . (1984)

Federal Writers' Project *The Ohio Guide* (1940)
———. *The WPA guide to Cincinnati* (1943, rpt. 1987)

Fitak, Madge R. *Place Names Directory: Southeast Ohio* (1980)

Fuller, Sara *The Ohio Black History Guide* (1975)

Gutgesell, Steve *Guide to Ohio Newspapers, 1793–1973* (1976)

Historical Records Survey *Check List of Ohio Imprints, 1796–1820* (1941)

Hochstetter, Nancy (ed.) *Travel Historic Ohio: A Guide to Historic Sites and Markers* (1986)

Howe, Henry *Historical Collections of Ohio* 2 vols. (rev. and enl. ed. 1889–1891)

Lentz, A. *A Guide to the Manuscripts at the Ohio Historical Society* (1972)

Ohio Historical Society *Union Bibliography of Ohio Printed State Documents, 1803–1970* (1973)

Powell, Esther W. (ed.) *Ohio Records and Pioneer Families* vols. 11–19 (1970–1978)

Thompson, Peter G. *Bibliography of the State of Ohio* 2 vols (1890, rpt. 1986)

Yon, Paul D. *Guide to Ohio County and Municipal Government Records for Urban Research* (1973)

SELECTED NONFICTION SOURCES

Alburn, Wilfred H. *This Cleveland of Ours* (1933)

Allen, Lee *The Cincinnati Reds* (1948)

Banta, Richard E. *The Ohio* (Rivers of America series) (1949)

Barnhart, John D. *Valley of Democracy; the Frontier versus the Plantation in the Ohio Valley, 1775–1818* (1953)

Barnholth, William I. *The Cuyahoga-Tuscarawas Portage* (1954)

Beer, Thomas *Hanna* (1929)

Bond, Beverly W., Jr. *The Foundations of Ohio* (*Sesquicentennial History of the State of Ohio*, Vol. 1) (1941)

Boryczka, Raymond and Lorin L. Cary *No Strength without Union: An Illustrated History of Ohio Workers, 1803–1980* (1982)

Brawley, Benjamin *Paul Laurence Dunbar: Poet of His People* (1936)

Campbell, Thomas F. and Edward M. Miggins (eds.) *The Birth of Modern Cleveland, 1865–1930* (1988)

Campen, Richard N. *The Architecture of the Western Reserve, 1800–1900* (1971)
——. *Ohio—An Architectural Portrait* (1973)

Carr, Carolyn K. (ed.) *Ohio, A Photographic Portrait, 1935–1941: Farm Security Administration Photographs* (1980)

Cauffield, Joyce V. and Carolyn E. Banfield (eds.) *The River Book: Cincinnati and the Ohio* (2d ed. 1981)

Chambrun, Clara L. *Cincinnati; Story of the Queen City* (1939)

Clark, Edna M. *Ohio Art and Artists* (1932)

Condit, Carl W. *The Railroad and the City: A Technological and Urbanistic History of Cincinnati* (1977)

Condon, George E. *Cleveland, the Best Kept Secret* (1967)
——. *Yesterday's Cleveland* (1976)
——. *Yesterday's Columbus: A Pictorial History of Ohio's Capital* (1977)

Conlin, Mary L. *Simon Perkins of the Western Reserve* (1968)

Cramer, C. H. *Case Western Reserve* (1976)

Crouch, Tom D. *The Giant Leap: A Chronology of Ohio Aerospace Events and Personalities, 1815–1969* (1971)

Crouse, David E. *The Ohio Gateway* (1938)

Cunningham, Virginia *Paul Laurence Dunbar and His Song* (1947)

DeChambrun, Clara L. *The Story of the Queen City* (1939)

Downard, William L. *The Cincinnati Brewing Industry: A Social and Economic History* (1973)

Downes, Randolph C. *Frontier Ohio; 1788–1803* (1935)
——. *History of Lake Shore Ohio* 3 vols. (1952)

Ellis, William D. *The Cuyahoga* (Rivers of America series) (1966)
——. *Early Settlers of Cleveland* (1976)

Feck, Luke *Yesterday's Cincinnati* (1976)

Federal Writers' Project *Annals of Cleveland, 1815–1935* (1937)

Frary, I. T. *Early Homes of Ohio* (1936)
——. *Ohio in Homespun and Calico* (1942)

Fuller, Sara *The Ohio Black History Guide* (1975)

Galloway, William A. *Old Chillicothe: Shawnee and Pioneer History* (1934)

Gieck, Jack *A Photo Album of Ohio's Canal Era, 1825–1913* (1988)

Harlow, Alvin Fay *The Serene Cincinnatians* (1950)

Hatcher, Harlan *The Buckeye Country: A Pageant of Ohio* (1940)

——. *The Western Reserve: Story of New Connecticut in Ohio* (1949, rpt. 1966)

Havighurst, Walter *River to the West: Three Centuries of the Ohio* (1970)
——. *Ohio: A Bicentennial History* (States and the Nation series) (1976)

Hopkins, Charles E. *Ohio the Beautiful and Historic* (1931)

Howe, Henry *Historical Collections of Ohio* 2 vols. (1888)

Jones, Robert Leslie *History of Agriculture in Ohio to 1880* (1983)

Jordan, Philip D. *Ohio Comes of Age, 1873–1900* (*Sesquicentennial History of the State of Ohio*, Vol. 5) (1943)
——. *The National Road* (1948)

Joyce, Rosemary O. *A Woman's Place: The Life History of a Rural Ohio Grandmother* (1983)

Junior League of Dayton (comp. and ed.) *Dayton: A History in Photographs* (1976)

Knopf, Richard *Indians of the Ohio Country* (1959)

Kusmer, Kenneth L. *A Ghetto Takes Shape: Black Cleveland, 1870–1930* (1976)

Laffoon, Polk, IV *Tornado* (1975)

Leech, Margaret *In the Days of McKinley* (1959)
—— and Harry J. Brown *The Garfield Orbit* (1978)

Lindley, Harlow (comp.) *Ohio in the Twentieth Century* (*Sesquicentennial History of the State of Ohio*, Vol. 6) (1942)

Lund, Staughton *The Fight against Shutdowns: Youngstown's Steel Mill Closings* (1982)

Lupold, Harry F. *The Forgotten People: The Woodland Erie* (1975)
—— and Gladys Haddad (eds.) *Ohio's Western Reserve: A Regional Reader* (1988)

Meade, David *Yankee Eloquence in the Middle West: The Ohio Lyceum, 1850–1870* (1951)

Metzman, Gustav *Cincinnati and Ohio, Their Early Railroads* (1948)

Michener, James A. *Kent State: What Happened and Why* (1971)

Miller, James M. *The Genesis of Culture in the Ohio Valley, 1800–1825* (1938)
——. *The Genesis of Western Culture: The Upper Ohio Valley, 1800–1825* (1938)

Miller, Zane L. *Boss Cox's Cincinnati: Urban Politics in the Progressive Era* (1968)

Nichols, Kenneth *Yesterday's Akron: The First 150 Years* (1975)

Patterson, James T. *Mr. Republican, a Biography of Robert A. Taft* (1972)

Pearson, Ralph (ed.) *Ohio in Century Three: Quality of Life* (1977)

Perry, Dick *Vas You Ever in Zinzinnati?* (1966)

Peskin, Allan *Garfield* (1978)

Pieper, Thomas and James B. Gidney *Fort Laurens, 1778–1779: The Revolutionary War in Ohio* (1976)

Porter, Philip W. *Cleveland: Confused City on a Seesaw* (1976)

Potter, Martha A. *Ohio's Prehistoric Peoples* (1968)

Reid, Whitelaw *Ohio in the War* 2 vols. (1868)

Ronald, Bruce W. and Virginia *Dayton, the Gem City* (1981)

Rose, William G. *Cleveland: The Making of a City* (1950)

Roseboom, Eugene H. *The Civil War Era, 1850–1873* (*Sesquicentennial History of the State of Ohio*, Vol. 4) (1944)

————— and Francis P. Weisenburger *A History of Ohio* (2d ed. 1967, rpt. 1977)

Ross, Steven J. *Workers on the Edge: Work, Leisure, and Politics in Industrializing Cincinnati, 1788–1890* (1985)

Ryan, Daniel J. *Lincoln and Ohio* (1923)

Scheiber, Harry N. *Ohio Canal Era: A Case Study of Government and the Economy* (1970)

Schneider, Norris F. *The Muskingum River: A History and Guide* (1968)

Shetrone, Henry C. *The Indians of Ohio* (1918)

Siebert, Wilbur H. *The Mysteries of Ohio's Underground Railroad* (1951)

Tarbell, Ida *The History of the Standard Oil Company* 2 vols. (1904)

Utter, William T. *The Frontier State, 1803–1825* (*Sesquicentennial History of Ohio*, Vol. 2) (1942)

Walters, Raymond W. *Stephen Foster: Youth's Golden Dream; a Sketch of His Life and Background in Cincinnati, 1846–1850* (1936)

Warner Hoyt L. *Progressivism in Ohio* (1964)

Weisenburger, Francis P. *The Passing of The Frontier, 1825–1850* (*Sesquicentennial History of the State of Ohio*, Vol. 3) (1941)

Wheeler, Kenneth W. (ed.) *For the Union; Ohio Leaders in the Civil War* (1967)

Wheeler, Robert A. *Pleasantly Situated on the West Side* (1980)

Wilcox, Frank N. *Ohio Indian Trails* (1933)

Williams, Charles R. *The Life of Rutherford Birchard Hayes* 2 vols. (1914)

Wittke, Carl (ed.) *History of the State of Ohio* 6 vols. (1941–1944)

OKLAHOMA

The west south central state of Oklahoma is bordered by Colorado and Kansas on the north; Missouri and Arkansas on the east; the Red River and Texas on the south; and Texas and New Mexico on the west.

FULL NAME State of Oklahoma
POSTAL ABBREVIATION OK
INHABITANT Oklahoman
ADMITTED TO THE UNION Nov. 16, 1907. 46th state
POPULATION (est. 1987) 3,272,000. Percent of US total: 1.34%. Rank: 27th

CAPITAL CITY Oklahoma City, the largest city in the state, located on the North Canadian River in central Oklahoma; population 443,172 (est. 1984). It was founded by homesteaders in 1889, on the first day of legal settlement, was incorporated the following year, and became the state capital in 1910.

STATE NAME AND NICKNAMES From the Choctaw Indian words *ukla*, "person," and *huma*, "red." Also known as the Sooner State and the Boomer's Paradise.

STATE SEAL A five-pointed star, bearing in each of its points a symbol of an Indian Nation (one of the "Five Civilized Tribes" relocated to Oklahoma in the 19th century): clockwise from the top, the Chickasaw (an armed warrior), Choctaw (bow, arrows, and tomahawk), Seminole (a man in a canoe near a lakeside settlement), Creek (a plow and a sheaf of wheat), and Cherokee (a seven-pointed star surrounded by oak leaves). In the center, under the state motto, is Justice holding her scales above a white settler and an Indian warrior

shaking hands, a cornucopia at their feet. Forty-five stars are grouped around the central star. The border reads "Great Seal of the State of Oklahoma, 1907."

MOTTO Labor Omnia Vincit (Labor conquers all things)

SONG "Oklahoma," lyrics by Richard Rodgers, music by Oscar Hammerstein.

SYMBOLS
Flower mistletoe
Tree redbud
Bird scissor-tailed flycatcher
Rock barite rose
Animal American buffalo
Reptile collared lizard
Fish white bass
Grass Indian grass
Colors green and white
Poem "Howdy Folks" by David Randolph Milsten

LICENSE PLATES (1) Black on white, with an outline of the state, and the legend "Oklahoma is OK!" over a background of an orange sunset. (2) Blue on white, with an outline of the state and the legend "Oklahoma is OK."

FLAG On a field of sky blue, an Indian warrior's rawhide shield, bearing six painted red crosses and dangling seven eagle feathers, and superimposed on it a peace pipe crossed with an olive branch; below it, in white, the legend "Oklahoma."

GEOGRAPHY AND CLIMATE

Geologically, Oklahoma is a transitional state, occupying an area where the Coastal Plain, Interior Highlands, and Central Lowland come together. Coal, gas, and oil deposits are plentiful; cotton and corn are grown in the wetter and warmer southeastern regions, while wheat is the most important crop in the drier, cooler northwest. Along the Oklahoma Panhandle, a dry, elevated strip extending west along the top of Texas, the High Plains terrain is suited mainly to grazing.

AREA 69,956 square miles. Rank: 18th
INLAND WATER 1,301 square miles
GEOGRAPHIC CENTER Oklahoma, 8 miles N of Oklahoma City
ELEVATIONS *Highest point:* Black Mesa, Cimarron County, 4,973 feet. *Lowest point:* Little River, McCurtain County, 287 feet. *Mean elevation:* 1,300 feet

MAJOR RIVERS Red, Arkansas, Cimarron, Canadian

MAJOR LAKES AND RESERVOIRS Texoma, Eufaula, Oologah, Keystone, Grand Lake o' the Cherokees, Hudson

LAND USE
Thousands of acres
Urban (1982) 851
Rural (1982) 40,795
Cropland (1982) 11,568
Pastureland (1982) 7,138
Rangeland (1982) 15,060
Forestland (1982) 6,539
State parks and recreation
  areas (1983) 100
National park system (1984) 10
National forest system (1984) . . . 461
Tribal lands (1984) 89

TEMPERATURES The highest recorded temperature was 120°F on July 26, 1943, at Tishomingo. The lowest was -27°F on January 18, 1930, at Watts.

NATIONAL SITES

NATIONAL HISTORIC SITE Fort Smith
NATIONAL RECREATION AREA Chickasaw
NATIONAL WILDLIFE REFUGES Optima, Salt Plains, Sequoyah, Tishomingo, Washita, Wichita Mountains Wildlife Refuge

HISTORY

1541	First white men to enter present-day Oklahoma are on an expedition led by Captain-General Francisco Vásquez de Coronado. He claims the land for Spain.
1541–1600	First explorers find scattered bands of Caddo, Wichita, Pawnee, Osage, Comanche, Kiowa, Cheyenne, and Arapaho Indians. Most of them are wandering tribes who set up camps and hunt buffalo.
1650	Don Diego del Castillo spends six months in Wichita Mountains prospecting for silver and gold.
1682	Robert Cavelier, Sieur de La Salle, claims Oklahoma as part of French Louisiana. He is followed by French explorers and traders who enter the Oklahoma region by way of the Red and Arkansas rivers.
1719	Bernard de la Harpe crosses southeastern Oklahoma near present site of Muskogee.
1762	French Louisiana (including Oklahoma) is ceded to Spain.
1800	Spain retrocedes Louisiana to France in the Treaty of Fontainebleau.
1802	Major Jean Pierre Chouteau induces some Osage Indian tribes to leave Missouri and settle in northeastern Oklahoma. He opens a profitable fur trade with them.
1803	The United States purchases Louisiana, including most of Oklahoma, from France.
1804	All of Louisiana north of 33d parallel, which includes present-day Oklahoma, is placed under the Administration of Indian Affairs by Congress. William Henry Harrison becomes first American governor of Oklahoma.
1808–1820	Indian tribes continue migrating to Oklahoma territory. Some tribes, including Choctaws, purchase land.
1821	First Protestant mission is founded on Grand River among the Osage.
1824	Oklahoma's first post office is opened at Miller Courthouse.
1828	First immigrant Creek Indians arrive in Oklahoma and lay out farms.
1829	Cherokees begin their removal to Oklahoma. Sequoyah, inventor of the Indian alphabet, is one of the immigrants.

1832	*July 14*. President Andrew Jackson names a special commission to report on conditions of the Indians in Oklahoma territory.
1833	Seminoles are tricked into signing a removal treaty to Oklahoma. The result is the Seminole War and the final colonization of the tribe in Oklahoma.
1844	*The Cherokee Messenger* is the first newspaper published in Oklahoma. This is followed a month later by *The Cherokee Advocate* published both in English and the Cherokee language.
1858	Butterfield stage and mail route is laid out, crossing Oklahoma.
1861	Civil War. United States abandons its forts in Oklahoma. Majority of Indian tribes align with the Confederates. Thousands of Union Indians flee to Kansas.
1863	Union forces defeat the Confederates at Honey Springs, the most important Civil War battle fought in Oklahoma.
1865	Two months after Robert E. Lee's surrender at Appomatox, Confederate Indians surrender to Union forces.
1866	Indian tribes sign treaties with the US, freeing their slaves and agreeing to an intertribal organization.
1889	*March 2*. A law is passed, authorizing the opening of Oklahoma lands.
	April 22. US opens part of Oklahoma to settlement. Approximately 50,000 settlers rush in on the first day.
1890	*May 2*. Congress creates a Territorial government for the settlers in the "Oklahoma Lands." It is the last territory in the Continental United States. Panhandle is joined to the territory of Oklahoma.
1891	*September 22*. President Benjamin Harrison proclaims 900,000 acres of Indian land in Oklahoma is open for general settlement. A second land rush for homesteads occurs.
1893	The Dawes Commission is created to liquidate the affairs of the Five Civilized Tribes.
1898	Spanish American War. Many Oklahoma and Indian frontiersmen serve with Roosevelt's Rough Riders.
1901	Red Fork–Tulsa Oilfield opens. Tulsa becomes an oil center.
1907	*November 16*. Oklahoma is admitted to the Union as the 46th state.
1910	The state capital is moved from Guthrie to Oklahoma City.
1917	Farmers and Indians protest the draft in the Green Corn Rebellion.
	World War I. Oklahoma furnishes 88,496 men in uniform and purchases over $116,000,000 worth of Liberty Bonds.
1918	Osage County oil fields begin production.
1926	The great Seminole Oil Field is developed, adding to overproduction in the oil industry.
1931	Governor William H. Murray closes the Oklahoma oil wells in an effort to stabilize prices.
1934–35	A severe drought ruins wheat and cotton crops. Farmers abandon their farms and begin migration to California.
1937	Construction begins on the Grand River Dam.
1941–1945	World War II. Oklahoma supplies thousands of its citizens to the armed forces. Large amounts of petroleum and agricultural products go to the Allied armies.
1947	Governor Roy Turner initiates reforms to remove educational institutions from politics. He also promotes a road building program.
1948	*January 12*. The United States Supreme Court rules that legal education opportunities for blacks in Oklahoma must be equal to those for whites.
1949	First television stations begin telecasting: WKY-TV in Oklahoma City and KOTV in Tulsa.
1952	*October 13*. President Harry S. Truman declares Oklahoma a disaster area due to a prolonged and severe drought.
1955	*April 2–3*. Severe tornadoes occur in the state.
1959	*April 7*. After 51 years of prohibition, Oklahoma voters legalize the sale of beer but reject local option and mixed drinks.
1962	*December 3*. Voters approve a 7-million dollar bond issue for University of Oklahoma Medical Center to construct a 600-bed hospital.

1964	*June 26*. National Cowboy Hall of Fame is dedicated as a memorial to the brave men and women who built the West.
	August 14. Wildcat oil well blows out near Canton in northeastern Oklahoma. Gas from well ignites and fire is not brought under control until June 11, 1965.
1967	The Will Rogers World Airport Terminal opens at Oklahoma City.
1970	*October*. Oklahoma is sued by American Civil Liberties Union on grounds that files of some 6,000 "potential troublemakers" are used to prevent those persons from obtaining jobs or entering college.
1973	*July 27*. One of nation's costliest prison riots erupts at the state prison, resulting in deaths of several prisoners, injuries to guards, officials, and other prisoners, and over $20 million in property damage.
1976	A long-delayed prison construction bill is passed.
1978	The prolonged summer drought results in 57 of Oklahoma's 77 counties being declared federal disaster areas.
1981	In the midst of an oil boom Oklahoma raises teachers' salaries by an average of $1,600 per year.
1986	*September–October*. Heavy floods result in great property damage.
1987	Oklahoma's 29 bank failures are second only to Texas.

DEMOGRAPHY

Population (est. 1987) . . . 3,272,000
Population (1980) 3,025,495
Population density in persons
   per square mile (1980) 43.2

POPULATION BY RACE (1980)
American Indian/Aleut/
   Eskimo 169,464
Asian/Pacific Islander 17,274
Black 204,658
Hispanic 57,413
White 2,597,783
Other 36,087

POPULATION CHARACTERISTICS (1980)
Percent of state population
Urban 67.3
Rural 32.7
Under 18 . . . . 28.2
65 or older 12.4
College-educated 15.7
Families below poverty line . . . 10.3
Public-assistance recipients 5.2

Per capita personal income
  (1986) $12,368
Millionaires per 100,000
  residents (1982) 139.3

Average life expectancy
  in years (1980) 73.7
Marriage rate per 1,000
  residents (1986) 10.1
Divorce rate per 1,000
  residents (1986) 7.5
Birth rate per 1,000
  residents (1985) 15.7
Infant mortality rate per
  1,000 births (1985) 11.6
Abortion rate per 1,000
  live births (1985) 269
Crime rate per 100,000
  residents (1985)
    Violent 436.4
    Property 5,577.7
Federal and state prisoners per
  100,000 residents (1984) 235
Alcohol consumption in gallons
  per capita (1985) 30.1
Deaths from motor vehicle accidents
  per 100,000 residents (1985) . . 22.4

MAJOR CITIES

	1984 population (est.)
Enid	52,502
Lawton	85,629
Norman	75,350
Oklahoma City	443,172
Tulsa	374,535

GOVERNMENT AND POLITICS

Number of US Representatives   6
Electoral votes   8

POLITICAL PARTY NOMINEES FROM STATE

V.C. Tisdal (Jobless)   1932   VP

PRESIDENTIAL PRIMARY ELECTION In 1988, Oklahoma sent 51 Democratic delegates and 36 Republican delegates to the national conventions.
CONSTITUTION Oklahoma is using its original constitution, adopted in 1907.

LEGISLATURE The Legislature is divided into the Senate (48 members, 4-year term, minimum age 25) and the House of Representatives (101 members, 2-year term, minimum age 21). In 1987, the annual salary was $20,000.

JUDICIARY The highest courts are the Supreme Court, with 9 judges serving 6-year terms, and the Court of Criminal Appeals, with 3 judges serving 6-year terms. In 1987, the annual salary for judges on both courts was $68,006.

EXECUTIVE The governor serves a 4-year term; the minimum age for holding office is 31. In 1987, the annual salary was $70,000. There are 9 other elected officials.

PRESIDENTIAL VOTE 1948-1988 *(in percents)*

Year	State Winner	Democratic	Republican
1948	Truman (D)	62.8	37.3
1952	Eisenhower (R)	45.4	54.6
1956	Eisenhower (R)	44.9	55.1
1960	Nixon (R)	41.0	59.0
1964	Johnson (D)	55.8	44.3
1968	Nixon (R)	32.0	47.7
1972	Nixon (R)	24.0	73.7
1976	Ford (R)	48.7	50.0
1980	Reagan (R)	35.0	60.5
1984	Reagan (R)	30.7	68.6
1988	Bush (R)	42.0	58.0

GOVERNORS

Territorial Governors

George W. Steele	1890-1891
Robert Martin (acting)	1891-1892
Abraham J. Seay	1892-1893
William C. Renfrow	1893-1897
Cassius M. Barnes	1897-1901
William M. Jenkins	1901
William Grimes (acting)	1901
Thompson B. Ferguson	1901-1906
Frank Frantz	1906-1907

State Governors

Charles N. Haskell (D)	1907-1911
Lee Cruce (D)	1911-1915
Robert L. Williams (D)	1915-1919
James B.A. Robertson (D)	1919-1923
John C. Walton (D)	1923
Martin E. Trapp (D)	1923-1927
Henry S. Johnston (D)	1927-1929
William J. Holloway (D)	1929-1931
William H. Murray (D)	1931-1935
Earnest W. Marland (D)	1935-1939
Leon C. Phillips (D)	1939-1943
Robert S. Kerr (D)	1943-1947
Roy J. Turner (D)	1947-1951
Johnston Murray (D)	1951-1955
Raymond Gary (D)	1955-1959
J. Howard Edmonson (D)	1959-1963
George Nigh (D)	1963
Henry Bellmon (R)	1963-1967
Dewey Barlett (R)	1967-1971
David Hall (D)	1971-1975
David L. Boren (D)	1975-1979
George Nigh (D)	1979-1987
Henry Bellmon (R)	1987-

MINIMUM AGES

Majority	18
Marriage with parental consent	16
Marriage without parental consent	18
Making a will	18
Buying alcohol	21
Jury duty	18
Leaving school	16
Driver's license	16

CAPITAL PUNISHMENT

Number executed 1976-88: 0
On death row Aug. 1, 1988: 93

MILITARY INSTALLATIONS

Total number: 13
Major bases:
  Army: 1
  Air Force: 1

FINANCES

Thousands of dollars

GENERAL REVENUE (1985)

Total general revenue	4,933,429
Total tax revenue	2,982,106
Sales and gross receipts	1,123,120
Individual income taxes	727,100
Corporate net income taxes	104,522

GENERAL EXPENDITURE (1985)

Total general expenditure	4,366,858
Education	1,950,213
Public welfare	701,178
Health	112,881
Hospitals	261,923
Natural resources	77,315
Highways	523,122
Police	39,380
Corrections	136,104

FEDERAL AID (1985) 1,166,536

ECONOMY

Beef cattle and calves, dairy cattle, hogs, and poultry are the main cash producers for Oklahoma's approximately 60,000 farms. Wheat, cotton, corn, soybeans, sorghum, peanuts, fruits, vegetables, and nuts are the important crops, but contributed less than half of the state's $2.7 billion in 1983 cash farm receipts. Oklahoma is an important petroleum and natural gas producer; coal is mined in the eastern part of the state. Manufacturing focuses on processed foods, petroleum products, fabricated metals, aircraft and other transportation equipment, chemicals, and wood products. Value added by manufacture was $8.2 billion in 1982.

EMPLOYMENT (1984)

Thousands of persons

Total number of employed workers	1,439
Construction	51.0
Finance, insurance, and real estate	64.6
Government	245.5
Manufacturing	174.1
Mining	75.0
Services	221.6
Transportation, communications, and utilities	64.5
Wholesale and retail trade	288.3

Percent of civilian labor force unemployed (1984) 7.0

DEPARTMENT OF DEFENSE (1985)

Civilian workers employed	26,840
Military personnel	31,115
Contract awards	$602 million

ENERGY SOURCES FOR ELECTRIC UTILITIES (1983)

Percent

Coal	42.8
Gas	51.7
Hydroelectric	5.5
Nuclear	0.0
Petroleum	0.1

TRANSPORTATION

Motor vehicles registered in state (1986)	2,902,391
Miles of roads, streets, and highways (1986)	111,001
Miles of Class I railway operated (1986)	4,024
Airports (1983)	332
Major aviation hubs (1983)	2
Largest hub: Tulsa	

CULTURE AND EDUCATION

Native American tribes

Oklahoma has been inhabited by Native American tribes for some 15,000 years. During the 19th century the federal government relocated many tribes to the part of Oklahoma designated as Indian Territory. Groups no longer extant in the state include the Apalachicola, Biloxi, Hitchiti, Kichai, Lipan, Miccosukee, Natchez, Ofo, Okmulgee, Tawakoni, Tuskegee, and Waco tribes. Groups that were relocated to Oklahoma—some by agreement, some forcibly—include the Alabama, Caddo, Cayuga, Delaware, Ponca, Seminole, Shawnee, and Wyandot. Groups that continue to live in Oklahoma include the Apache, Arapaho, Cherokee, Cheyenne, Chickasaw, Choctaw, Comanche, Creek, Fox, Illinois, Iowa, Kansa, Kickapoo, Kiowa, Koasati, Miami, Missouri, Modoc, Osage, Oto, Ottawa, Pawnee, Peoria, Piankashaw, Potawatomi, Quapaw, Sauk, Seneca, Tonkawa, Wea, and Wichita. There are 27 federal trust areas in Oklahoma.

Religions, ethnicities, and languages

Many of the black inhabitants of Oklahoma trace their descent from slaves brought by Indians relocated from the South. After the territory was opened for settlement in 1889, settlers arrived from other states and from Europe (particularly Germany, the British Isles, France, and Bohemia), China, Japan, Mexico, and Canada. In 1980, 4.0 percent of Oklahoma's population spoke a language other than English at home. The majority of churchgoers belong to Protestant denominations, chiefly Southern Baptist and

Methodist; there are also communities of Roman Catholics, Greek Orthodox, and Mennonites. The Native American Church is formally recognized.

Major museums and libraries
Thomas Gilcrease Institute of American History and Art, Tulsa
Oklahoma Art Center, Oklahoma City
Oklahoma Historical Society Museum, Oklahoma City
Philbrook Art Center, Tulsa
Southern Plains Indian Museum, Anadarko
Stovall Museum of Science and History, University of Oklahoma, Norman
Woolaroc Museum, Bartlesville

Major arts organizations
Mummers Theater, Oklahoma City
Oklahoma Symphony Orchestra, Oklahoma City
Tulsa Ballet Theatre
Tulsa Little Theater
Tulsa Opera
Tulsa Philharmonic Orchestra

Colleges and universities
Number public (1986-87) 29
Number private (1986-87) 18
Total enrollment, in full-time equivalent students (1985) 126,700

Public elementary and secondary schools
Expenditure per pupil in average daily attendance (1986-87) $3,082
Pupil-teacher ratio (1987) 16.9
Average teacher salary (1986-87) $22,770

Holidays
Youth Day. March 20
Thomas Jefferson's Birthday. April 13
Oklahoma Day. April 22
Bird Day. May 1
Senior Citizen's Day. June 9
Indian Day. 1st Saturday after full moon, September
State Fair, Oklahoma City. Last week of September
Oklahoma Historical Day. October
Will Rogers Day. November 4
Oklahoma Heritage Day. Week of November 16

OKLAHOMA IN LITERATURE

Evan G. Barnard *A Rider of the Cherokee Strip* (1936)
Memoir of pioneer ranching and homesteading.

Thomas C. Battey *The Life and Adventures of a Quaker among the Indians* (1968, rpt. 1972)
Narrative of a missionary and teacher, first published in 1875, who worked among the Kiowa Indians in the 1870s.

John L. Callison *Bill Jones of Paradise Valley, Oklahoma. His Life and Adventures* . . . (1914)
Collection of tall tales, folklore, and pioneer memoirs.

Alberta W. Constant *Oklahoma Run* (1955)
Novel of pioneer farming life in the 1890s.

Courtney R. Cooper *Oklahoma* (1926)
Romantic pioneer saga of the land rush.

Alice L. Covert *Return to Dust* (1939); *The Months of Rain* (1941)
Novels about farmers who cling to their land in times of hardship.

William Cunningham *The Green Corn Rebellion* (1935)
Realistic novel about the sharecroppers' rebellion of 1917.

Edward Donahoe *Madness in the Heart* (1937)
Novel about an oil wildcatter who strikes it rich in 1912, but is then destroyed by his wealth.

John R. Erickson *Panhandle Cowboy* (1980)
An account of modern ranch life in Beaver County.

Thomas Fall *The Ordeal of Running Standing* (1977)
Novel about the upbringing of a Kiowa Indian and his difficult relationship to his cultural heritage.

Edna Ferber *Cimarron* (1930, rpt. 1979)
Historical novel about a newspaperman and his wife who migrate during the land rush of 1889. The novel was inspired by the life of Elva Ferguson, wife of Oklahoma's sixth territorial governor.

Grant Foreman *Sequoyah* (1938, rpt. 1976)
A biography of the Cherokee who invented a syllabary for his language, covering the years between his war service in 1812 and his death in 1842.

Janice Holt Giles *The Kinta Years* (1973)
Memoir of childhood in the prairie town of Kinta in the early 1900s.

Woody Guthrie *Bound for Glory* (1943, rpt. 1970)
The songwriter and singer's account of his life, from his upbringing in Okemah through his involvement with social protest in the 1930s and 1940s.

Nola Henderson *This Much Is Mine!* (1934)
Realistic novel of farm life in the 1920s.

S. E. Hinton *The Outsiders* (1967, rpt. 1980)
A novel about tensions and rivalries among teenagers, written while the author was a student in a Tulsa high school.

William Humphrey *A Time and a Place* (1968)
Short stories of rural people set in northeast Texas and the Oklahoma Dust Bowl.

Washington Irving *A Tour on the Prairies* (1834, rpt. 1985)
Record of the New York writer's expedition from Fort Gibson in 1832. One of the earliest accounts of life on the western frontier.

Marquis James *Cherokee Strip: A Tale of an Oklahoma Boyhood* (1945)
Memoir by a Pulitzer prize-winning biographer and journalist.

Mackinlay Kantor *Gentle Annie* (1942)
Romantic mystery novel about the opening of the Cherokee Strip.

Harold Keith *The Obstinate Land* (1977)
Novel about the struggle over land between farmers and ranchers set during the land rush.

Jack F. Kilpatrick and **Anna Gritts** *Friends of Thunder: Folktales of the Oklahoma Cherokees* (1964)

Edwin Lanham *The Stricklands* (1939)
Novel about the struggle to form a tenant farmers' union during the Dustbowl era.

Mary H. Marable and **Elaine Boylan** *A Handbook of Oklahoma Writers* (1939)

John Joseph Mathews *Wah'Kon-Tah: The Osage and the White Man's Road* (1932)
The story of Quaker Indian agent Laban Miles and his efforts to assist the Osage from 1878 until the oil boom.

George Milburn *Oklahoma Town* (1931); *Catalogue* (1936)
Short stories of small-town life by a native of Coweta. Milburn's concentration on unappealing aspects of human nature attracted unfavorable local publicity at time of publication.

N. Scott Momaday *The Way to Rainy Mountain* (1969)
An account of the folklore, history, and present life of the Kiowa Indians in the Wichita Mountains.

Anne Hodges Morgan and Rennard Strickland (eds.) *Oklahoma Memories* (1981)
Collection of memoirs.

Speer Morgan *Belle Starr* (1979)
Fictional biography of the famous outlaw.

John M. Oskison *Black Jack Davy* (1926)
Novel about conflict between Indians and white tenant farmers.

William A. Owens *Walking on Borrowed Land* (1954)
A black teacher's efforts to overcome segregation and racial prejudice as school principal in a small town during the 1930s.

Will Rogers (ed. Paula M. Love) *The Will Rogers Book* (1971)
Reminiscences of the state's popular homespun philosopher, with a selection of his writing.

John Steinbeck *The Grapes of Wrath* (1939, rpt. 1976)
In this classic novel of agricultural hardship, a sharecropper family is forced to migrate by developers, and sets out for California down Highway 66.

Stanley Vestal *Short Grass Country* (1941)
Collection of folklore.

GUIDES TO RESOURCES

Bell, Robert E. *Oklahoma Archaeology: An Annotated Bibliography* (2d ed. 1978)

Federal Writers' Project *The WPA Guide to 1930s Oklahoma* (1941, rpt. 1986)

Hunt, David C. *Guide to Oklahoma Museums* (1981)

Morris, John W., Charles R. Goins, and Edwin C. McReynolds *Historical Atlas of Oklahoma* (3d ed. 1986)

Morris, Mary E. *Bibliography of Theses on Oklahoma* (1956)

Oklahoma State Library *Oklahoma Authors and Books about Oklahoma in the Collection . . . as of October 1, 1957* (1957)

Teal, Kaye M. *Black History in Oklahoma; a Resource Book* (1971)

University of Oklahoma Bureau for Business and Economic Research *Statistical Abstracts of Oklahoma* (biennial)

Wright, Muriel H. *A Guide to the Indian Tribes of Oklahoma* (1951, rpt. 1986)
———, George H. Shirk, and Kenny H. Franks *Mark of Heritage* (2d ed. 1976)

SELECTED NONFICTION SOURCES

Agnew, Brad *Fort Gibson, Terminal on the Trail of Tears* (1980)

Aldrich, Gene *The Okie Jesus Congressman: The Life of Manuel Herrick* (1974)

Alexander, Charles C. *The Ku Klux Klan in the Southwest* (1965)

Allen, Clinton M. *The Sequoyah Movement* (1925)

Alley, John *City Beginnings in Oklahoma Territory* (1939)

Baldwin, Kathlyn *The 89ers: Oklahoma Land Rush of 1889* (1981)

Bell, Robert E. *Prehistory of Oklahoma* (1984)

Benson, Oliver et al. *Oklahoma Votes, 1907–1962* (1964)

Billington, Monroe L. *Thomas P. Gore: The Blind Senator from Oklahoma* (1967)

Bischoff, John P. *Mr. Iba: Basketball's Aggie Iron Duke* (1980)

Blackburn, Bob L. *Heart of the Promised Land: An Illustrated History of Oklahoma County* (1982)
———. *Images of Oklahoma: A Pictorial History* (1984)

Bonnifield, Mathew Paul *Oklahoma Innovator: The Life of Virgil Browne* (1976)

Bryant, Keith L., Jr. *Alfalfa Bill Murray* (1968)

Burbank, Garin *When Farmers Voted Red: The Gospel of Socialism in the Oklahoma Countryside, 1910–1924* (1976)

Collings, Ellsworth and Alma Miller *The 101 Ranch* (1937)

Costello, David F. *The Prairie World* (1969)

Cross, George L. *Blacks in White Colleges: Oklahoma's Landmark Cases* (1975)
———. *Professors, Presidents, and Politicians: Civil Rights and the University of Oklahoma, 1890–1968* (1981)

Dale, Edward E. *The Range Cattle Industry* (1930)
———. *Cow Country* (1942)
——— and Morris L. Wardell *History of Oklahoma* (1948)

Debo, Angie *And Still the Waters Run: The Betrayal of the Five Civilized Tribes* (1940, rpt. 1984)

———. *Tulsa: From Creek Town to Oil Capital* (1943)
———. *Prairie City, the Story of an American Community* (1944)
———. *Oklahoma, Footloose and Fancy-free* (1949)
———. *Geronimo: The Man, His Times, His Place* (1976)

Decazes, Daisy *Western Oklahoma: A Photographic Essay* (1982)

Deering, Ferdie J. (ed.) *Look at Oklahoma: An Album of Photographs of Some of the Interesting and Beautiful Features of Oklahoma, the 46th State* (1975)

Ellsworth, Scott *Death in a Promised Land: The Tulsa Race Riot of 1921* (1981)

Ezell, John S. *Innovations in Energy: The Story of Kerr-McGee* (1979)

Faulk, Odie B. *Oklahoma, Land of the Fair God* (1986)
———, Kenny H. Franks, and Paul F. Lambert (eds.) *Early Military Forts and Posts in Oklahoma* (1978)

Fischer, John *The High Plains: An Informal History* (1978)

Fischer, LeRoy H. (ed.) *Oklahoma's Governors, 1890–1907: The Territorial Years* (1975)
——— (ed.) *Oklahoma's Governors, 1907–1929: Turbulent Politics* (1981)
——— (ed.) *Oklahoma's Governors, 1929–1955: Depression to Prosperity* (1983)
——— (ed.) *Oklahoma's Governors, 1955–1979: Growth and Reform* (1985)

Foreman, Grant *Sequoyah* (1938)
———. *History of Oklahoma* (1942)

Franklin, Jimmie L. *Born Sober: Prohibition in Oklahoma, 1907–1959* (1971)
———. *Journey toward Hope: A History of Blacks in Oklahoma* (1982)

Franks, Kenny A. *Stand Watie and the Agony of the Cherokee Nation* (1979)
———. *The Oklahoma Petroleum Industry* (1980)

Gibson, Arrell M. *The Chickasaws* (1971)
——— (ed.) *America's Exiles: Indian Colonization in Oklahoma* (1976)

————. *The Oklahoma Story* (1978)
———— (ed.) *Will Rogers: A Centennial Tribute* (1979)
————. *Oklahoma: A History of Five Centuries* (2d ed. 1981)
————. *The History of Oklahoma* (rev. ed. 1984)

Gittinger, Roy *The Formation of the State of Oklahoma, 1803–1906* (1917, rpt. 1974)

Goble, Danney *Progressive Oklahoma: The Making of a New Kind of State* (1980)

Goins, Charles R. and John W. Morris *Oklahoma Homes: Past and Present* (1980)

Gould, Charles N. *Oklahoma Place Names* (1933)

Green, Donald E. (ed.) *Rural Oklahoma* (1977)

Halliburton, R., Jr. *The Tulsa Race War of 1921* (1975)

Harlow, Victor E. *Oklahoma History* (1961)

Haywood, C. Robert *Trails South: The Wagon-Road Economy in the Dodge City–Panhandle Region* (1986)

Henderson, Arn, Frank Parman, and Dortha Henderson *Architecture in Oklahoma: Landmark and Vernacular* (1978)

Hendrickson, Kenneth E., Jr. (ed.) *Hard Times in Oklahoma: The Depression Years* (1983)

Hoig, Stan *David L. Payne: The Oklahoma Boomer* (1980)
————. *The Oklahoma Land Rush of 1889* (1984)

Holden, William C. *A Ranching Saga: The Lives of William Electious Halsell and Ewing Halsell* (1976)

Hurst, Irvin *The 46th Star: A History of Oklahoma's Constitutional Convention and Early Statehood* (1957, rpt. 1980)

Jones, Billy M. and Odie B. Faulk *The Cherokees: An Illustrated History* (1984)

Jordan, H. Glenn and Thomas M. Holm (eds.) *Indian Leaders: Oklahoma's First Statesmen* (1979)

Keith, Harold *Oklahoma Kickoff: An Informal History of the First Twenty-Five Years of Football at the University of Oklahoma, and of the Amusing Hardships That Attended Its Pioneering* (1978)

Ketchum, Richard M. *Will Rogers, His Life and Times* (1973)

Kirkpatrick, Samuel A., David R. Morgan, and Thomas G. Kielhorn *The Oklahoma Voter: Politics, Elections and Political Parties in the Sooner State* (1977)
————. *The Legislative Process in Oklahoma: Policy Making, People, and Politics* (1978)

Knight, Thomas *Sunset on Utopian Dreams: An Experiment of Black Separatism on the American Frontier* (1977)

Kohn, Howard *Who Killed Karen Silkwood?* (1981)

Littlefield, Daniel P. *The Chickasaw Freedmen: A People without a Country* (1980)

Litton, Gaston *History of Oklahoma* 4 vols. (1957)

Marriott, Alice and Carol K. Rachlin *Oklahoma, the Forty-sixth Star* (1973)

Masterson, V. V. *The Katy Railroad and the Last Frontier* (1952)

Mathews, Joseph *Life and Death of an Oilman: The Career of E. W. Marland* (1951)

Maynard, Louis *Down the River* (1971)

McKee, Jesse U. and Jon H. Schlenker *The Choctaws* (1980)

McReynolds, Edwin C. *The Seminoles* (1957)
————. *Oklahoma: A History of the Sooner State* (rev. ed. 1964)
————, Alice Marriott, and Estelle Faulconer *Oklahoma: The Story of Its Past and Present* (rev. ed. 1967)

Meredith, Howard L. and Mary E. (eds.) *Of the Earth: Oklahoma's Architectural History* (1980)

Miller, Worth R. *Oklahoma Populism: A History of the People's Party in the Oklahoma Territory* (1987)

Morgan, Anne H. *Robert S. Kerr: The Senate Years* (1977)
———— and H. Wayne Morgan (eds.) *Oklahoma: New Views of the Forty-sixth State* (1982)

———— and Kennard Strickland (eds.) *Oklahoma Memories* (1981)

Morgan, H. Wayne and Anne H. *Oklahoma: A Bicentennial History* (States and the Nation series) (1977)

Morris, John W. (ed.) *Geography of Oklahoma* (1977)
————. *Ghost Towns of Oklahoma* (1978)
———— (ed.) *Cities of Oklahoma* (1979)
———— (ed.) *Boundaries of Oklahoma* (1980)
———— (ed.) *Drill Bits, Picks, and Shovels: History of Mineral Resources in Oklahoma* (1982)

Nye, Captain W. S. *Carbine and Lance; the Story of Old Fort Sill* (1937)

Rainey, George *The Cherokee Strip* (1933)
————. *No Man's Land* (1937)

Ridings, Sam P. *The Chisholm Trail* (1936)

Rister, Carl C. *Southern Plainsmen* (1938)
————. *Land Hunger: David L. Payne and the Oklahoma Boomers* (1942)
————. *No Man's Land* (1948)
————. *Oil! Titan of the Southwest* (1949)

Savage, William W., Jr. *Singing Cowboys and All That Jazz: A Short History of Popular Music in Oklahoma* (1983)

Scales, James R. *Oklahoma Politics: A History* (1982)

Sears, Paul B. *Deserts on the March* (1935)

Shirk, George H. *Oklahoma Place Names* (rev. ed. 1974)

Shirley, Glenn *Red Yesterdays* (1977)
————. *West of Hell's Fringe: Crime, Criminals, and the Federal Peace Officer in Oklahoma Territory, 1889–1907* (1978)
————. *Temple Houston: Lawyer with a Gun* (1980)

Singer, Mark *Funny Money* (1985)

Skaggs, Jimmy M. (ed.) *Ranch and Range in Oklahoma* (1978)

Smallwood, James M. *An Oklahoma Adventure: Of Banks and Bankers* (1979)

Smith, Michael M. *The Mexicans in Oklahoma* (1980)

Smith, Robert (ed.) *Oklahoma's Forgotten Indians* (1979)

Stewart, Dora A. *Government and Development of Oklahoma Territory* (1933)

Stewart, Roy P. *Born Grown: An Oklahoma City History* (1974)

Stout, Joseph H., Jr. *Frontier Adventurers: American Exploration in Oklahoma* (1976)

Strickland, Rennard *Fire and Spirits: Cherokee Law from Clan to Court* (1975)
————. *The Indians in Oklahoma* (1980)

Thompson, John *Closing the Frontier: Radical Response in Oklahoma, 1889–1923* (1986)

Thurman, Melvina (ed.) *Women in Oklahoma* (1982)

Tilghman, Zoe A. *Outlaw Days: A True History of Early-Day Oklahoma Characters* (1926)

Trafzer, Clifford E. *The Judge: The Life of Robert A. Hefner* (1975)

Tucker, Howard H. *History of Governor Walton's War on the Ku Klux Klan, the Invisible Empire* (1923)

Tyson, Carl N., James H. Thomas, and Udie B. Faulk *The McMan: The Lives of Robert M. Farlin and James H. Chapman* (1977)

Vaughn-Roberson, Courtney Ann and Glen *City in the Osage Hills: A History of Tulsa, Oklahoma* (1984)

Waldby, H. O. *The Patronage System in Oklahoma* (1950)

Walker, Jerald C. E. *The State of Sequoquah: An Impressionistic Look at Eastern Oklahoma* (1985)

Wallace, Ernest and E. Adamson Hoebel *The Comanches: Lords of the South Plains* (1952)

Wardell, Morris L. *A Political History of the Cherokee Nation* (1938)

Wheeler, Robert W. *Jim Thorpe: The World's Greatest Athlete* (1979)

Wilson, Steve *Oklahoma Treasures and Treasure Tales* (1988)

Wilson, Terry P. *The Cart That Changed the World: The Career of Sylvan N. Goldman* (1978)

———. *The Underground Reservation: Osage Oil* (1985)

Wright, Muriel H. and J. B. Thoburn *Oklahoma: A History of the State and Its People* 4 vols (1929)

———. *Our Oklahoma* (1949)

———. *The Story of Oklahoma* (1949)

OREGON

Oregon, a Pacific Northwest state, is bordered by the Columbia River and Washington on the north; by Idaho and the Snake River on the east; by Nevada and California on the south; and by the Pacific Ocean on the west.

FULL NAME State of Oregon
POSTAL ABBREVIATION OR
INHABITANT Oregonian
ADMITTED TO THE UNION Feb. 14, 1859. 33d state
POPULATION (est. 1987) 2,724,000. Percent of US total: 1.12%. Rank: 30th

CAPITAL CITY Salem, located on the Willamette River in northwest Oregon; population 90,323 (est. 1984). It was settled by Methodist missionaries in 1840 and became the territorial capital in 1851. In 1864, when Oregon was admitted to statehood, the capital, which had been moved to Corvallis, was returned to Salem.

STATE NAME AND NICKNAMES Possibly from the French Canadian word *ouragan*, "storm, hurricane," in reference to the stormy Columbia River, or from the Spanish word *orejon*, "big ear," in reference to a local tribe, or from the Spanish word *oregano*, "wild sage." Also known as the Beaver State, the Web-foot State, the Sunset State, the Valentine State, and the Hard-case State.

STATE SEAL Within a shield, a landscape showing a covered wagon pulled by oxen near a stand of fir trees; at the top, the sun sinking into the sea behind a departing British man o' war and an arriving American merchant ship, and an elk at the foot of a mountain; at the bottom, the state motto on a scroll, and a plow and pickaxe near a sheaf of wheat. The shield is surrounded by 33 stars and surmounted by the Federal eagle holding arrows and olive branch. This coat of arms, in gold, is encircled by a gold border reading "State of Oregon, 1859."

MOTTO The Union

SONG "Oregon, My Oregon," lyrics by J.A. Buchanan, music by Henry B. Murtagh.

SYMBOLS
Flower Oregon grape
Tree Douglas fir
Bird western meadowlark
Rock thunderegg
Animal beaver
Fish chinook salmon
Insect swallowtail butterfly
Hostess Miss Oregon

LICENSE PLATES (1) Dark blue on orange, with blue border. (2) Orange on dark blue, with orange border.

FLAG A navy blue field; on one side, the state coat of arms in gold, with the legends "State of Oregon" above it and "1859" below it, both in gold; on the other side, a gold beaver.

GEOGRAPHY AND CLIMATE

The widely varied terrain of Oregon encompasses several major forested mountain ranges—the Coast Range along the Pacific coast, the Klamath Range in southwestern Oregon, the Cascade Range in the west-central part of the state, and the Blue-Wallowa Mountains in the northeast. The Coast Range area, with 120 inches or more of annual precipitation, has the climate of a temperate rain forest. Central, southeastern, and eastern Oregon are mainly lava plains, lunar in appearance; rangeland and riverine lowlands cover the rest of the state.

AREA 97,073 square miles. Rank: 10th
INLAND WATER 889 square miles
GEOGRAPHIC CENTER Crook, 25 miles SSE of Prineville
ELEVATIONS *Highest point:* Mount Hood, Clackamas-Hood River County, 11,239 feet. *Lowest point:* Pacific Ocean, sea level. *Mean elevation:* 3,300 feet

MAJOR RIVERS Columbia, Snake, Willamette

MAJOR LAKES AND RESERVOIRS Upper Klamath, Malheur, Crater, Albert, Goose, Owyhee

TIDAL SHORELINE 1,410 miles, Pacific coast

LAND USE

	Thousands of acres
Urban (1982)	526
Rural (1982)	28,291
Cropland (1982)	4,356
Pastureland (1982)	1,966
Rangeland (1982)	9,392
Forestland (1982)	11,889
State parks and recreation areas (1983)	88
National park system (1984)	195
National forest system (1984)	17,434
Tribal lands (1984)	633

TEMPERATURES The highest recorded temperature was 119°F on August 10, 1898, at Pendleton. The lowest was -54°F on February 10, 1933, at Seneca.

NATIONAL SITES

NATIONAL HISTORIC SITE McLoughlin House
NATIONAL HISTORIC TRAILS Lewis & Clark, Oregon
NATIONAL MEMORIAL Fort Clatsop
NATIONAL MONUMENTS John Day Fossil Beds, Oregon Caves
NATIONAL PARK Crater Lake
NATIONAL WILDLIFE REFUGES Ankeny, Baskett Slough, Columbian White-Tailed Deer, Hart Mountain Substation, Klamath Forest and Upper Klamath, Lewis and Clark, Malheur, Modoc, Sheldon, Umatilla–Cold Springs/McKay Creek, Willamette Valley and Oregon Coastal–Refuge Complex, William L. Finley–Cape Meares/Oregon Island/Three Arch Rocks

HISTORY

1792   *May 11.* Robert Gray, a Yankee captain, enters the mouth of the river that he names for his ship, the *Columbia.*
October 30. A British naval lieutenant, William Broughton, takes formal possession of the Columbia River after sailing upstream for nearly a hundred miles. The previous day he sights and names Mount Hood.

1805–1806   The overland US expedition led by Meriwether Lewis and William Clark reaches present-day Oregon on October 18 on its course down the Columbia. It reaches the Pacific on December 3 and winters at Fort Clatsop on the south bank of the Columbia, returning upstream the following spring.

1811   *April 12.* Fort Astoria is established near the Columbia's mouth by agents of John Jacob Astor's Pacific Fur Company.

1813   *October 15.* In the midst of the War of 1812, Astor's partners sell Fort Astoria to a British rival, the Montreal-based North West Company, which renames it Fort George.

1818   Great Britain and the United States agree to keep the Pacific Northwest open to the nationals of both countries without prejudice to their respective claims of sovereignty.

1828   Mountain man Jedediah Smith explores the Oregon coast, traveling northward from California.

1829	The Hudson's Bay Company, which had acquired the North West Company in 1821, builds three log houses on the future site of Oregon City.
1834	Reverend Jason Lee establishes a Methodist mission to the Flathead Indians near the present site of Salem. Two years later, another mission is begun at the Dalles of the Columbia.
1843	*May 2*. Fifty American settlers in the Willamette River Valley adopt a provisional government to be financed by voluntary contributions. The beginnings of migration over the Oregon Trail add some 800 to 900 settlers in that year.
1845	Asa L. Lovejoy and Francis Pettygrove name and plat Portland.
1846	*June 15*. Oregon becomes US territory as a treaty extends the boundary between the United States and Canada to the Pacific Ocean.
1848	*August 14*. Creation of Oregon Territory, including, until 1853, present-day Washington, northern Idaho, and western Montana.
1850	The first steam-driven lumber mill is established, in Portland.
1852	Salem replaces Oregon City as the seat of government.
1853	Gold is discovered in the Rogue River Valley, drawing miners from California. A brief but bloody war is fought with Rogue River Indians.
	Steamboats are plying the Columbia and Willamette rivers as far inland from Astoria as Salem. In 1857 they reach Eugene.
1855	Umatilla Reservation created in northeastern Oregon for Umatilla, Walla Walla, and Cayuse Indians; Warm Springs Reservation established in the northwest for Wascos, Walla Walla, and (after 1868) Paiutes.
1857	Territory voters approve a constitution rejecting slavery and excluding free blacks. Blacks and Chinese are barred from voting.
1859	*February 14*. Oregon is admitted to the Union as the 33d state.
1868	John West establishes the first salmon cannery in Oregon at a place between Astoria and Portland that he names Westport.
1876	Opening of the University of Oregon, at Eugene.
1883	Northern Pacific Railroad is completed, linking Portland to St. Paul, Minnesota.
1887	The Oregon and California Railroad reaches San Francisco from Portland.
	Samuel Gompers, founder of the American Federation of Labor, organizes 15 Portland skilled-craft unions into a citywide trades assembly.
1900	Portland has, next to San Francisco, the largest Chinese community on the West Coast.
1902	Voters adopt constitutional amendments establishing the initiative and referendum.
	Crater Lake National Park is created.
1905	Nearly two million people attend the Lewis and Clark Exposition in Portland, commemorating the centennial of the expedition.
1909	Oregon is fourth among states in lumber output, which has increased to 1.9 billion board-feet, compared to 444 million board-feet in 1889.
1910	The Baldwin Sheep and Land Company controls 281 square miles of central Oregon rangeland.
1912	Women win the right to vote.
1914	The giant Weyerhaeuser Company is holding 400,000 acres of ponderosa pine and Douglas fir in Oregon for future use.
1923	Aliens ineligible for citizenship are prohibited from owning land in Oregon. This law, aimed at Chinese and Japanese, is ruled unconstitutional in 1949.
1930	The population of 3,319,000 sheep is a peak for Oregon.
1933	A forest fire burns 311,000 acres near Tillamook, along the northern coast.
1937	Completion of Bonneville Dam on the Columbia River.
1938	Voters approve a measure banning picketing by strikers where less than half of the employees are involved. Oregon leads all states in lumbering.
1942–1945	In the World War II effort, a total of 1,174 ocean vessels are built in the Portland area. Portland is the chief shipping port for lend-lease goods to the Soviet Union.
1948	*May 30*. Vanport, a suburb of Portland, is destroyed in a flood.
1949	A state fair-employment practices law is adopted.
1952	Peak lumber production of 9 billion board-feet.
1953	A civil rights law bars discrimination in public accommodations.

1954	Dedication of McNary Dam on the Columbia River.
1955	Equal pay guaranteed to women for equal work.
1959	A fair-housing law is adopted. The Dalles Dam, on the Columbia River, is dedicated.
1965	Oregon produces a record 8,037 million square feet of softwood plywood—65 percent of the national total.
1966	Opening of Astoria Ridge, spanning the Columbia River.
1968	Dedication of the John Dav Dam project, which includes the nation's second largest hydroelectric plant.
1971	Oregon is the first state to pass a law prohibiting the use of nonreturnable beverage bottles and cans.
1973	Statewide land-use planning is adopted.
1975	The unemployment rate of 11.2 percent in July is the highest since the Great Depression, due chiefly to high interest rates, which reduce demand for housing and therefore for wood products.
1977	*March 1*. An aerosol law bans the use of fluorocarbon aerosol cans.
1981	Followers of Indian guru Bhagwan Shree Rajneesh buy a 64,000-acre ranch near Antelope in Wasco County and incorporate it as Rajneeshpuram, with a population of 1,200, the following year. The venture collapses in 1985.

DEMOGRAPHY

Population (est. 1987) . . . 2,724,000
Population (1980) 2,633,149
Population density in persons
  per square mile (1980) 27.1

POPULATION BY RACE (1980)
American Indian/Aleut/
  Eskimo 27,309
Asian/Pacific Islander 34,767
Black 37,059
Hispanic 65,833
White 2,490,192
Other 43,336

POPULATION CHARACTERISTICS (1980)
          Percent of state population
Urban 67.9
Rural 32.1
Under 18 . . . . 27.4
65 or older 11.5
College-educated 17.2
Families below poverty line 7.7
Public-assistance recipients 4.9

Per capita personal income
  (1986) $13,217
Millionaires per 100,000
  residents (1982) 78.7

Average life expectancy in
  years (1980) 75.0
Marriage rate per 1,000
  residents (1986) 8.0
Divorce rate per 1,000
  residents (1986) 5.7
Birth rate per 1,000
  residents (1985) 15.1
Infant mortality rate per 1,000
  births (1985) 10.1
Abortion rate per 1,000
  live births (1985) 374
Crime rate per 100,000
  residents (1985)
  Violent 549.7
  Property 6,531.0
Federal and state prisoners per
  100,000 residents (1984) 152
Alcohol consumption in gallons
  per capita (1985) 38.9
Deaths from motor vehicle accidents
  per 100,000 residents (1985) . . 20.8

MAJOR CITIES
	1984 population (est.)
Eugene	101,602
Medford	41,952
Portland	365,861
Salem	90,323

GOVERNMENT AND POLITICS

Number of US Representatives   5
Electoral votes   7

POLITICAL PARTY NOMINEES FROM STATE

Joseph Lane (National Demo-
   cratic/Social Democratic)   1860 VP
Frank T. Johns (Socialist La-
   bor)   1924 P
Frank T. Johns (Socialist La-
   bor/died)   1928 P
Charles Linza McNary (R)   1940 VP
Theodora Nathan (Libertarian) 1972 VP

PRESIDENTIAL PRIMARY ELECTION In 1988, Oregon sent 51 Democratic delegates and 32 Republican delegates to the national conventions.

CONSTITUTION Oregon is using its original constitution, adopted in 1857. '

LEGISLATURE The Legislative Assembly is divided into the Senate (30 members, 4-year term, minimum age 21) and the House of Representatives (60 members, 2-year term, minimum age 21). In 1987, the salary for legislators was $919 per month plus $62 per day.

JUDICIARY The highest court is the Supreme Court, with 7 judges serving 6-year terms. In 1987, the annual salary was $69,552.

EXECUTIVE The governor serves a 4-year term; the minimum age for holding office is 30. In 1987, the annual salary was $73,500. There are 5 other elected officials.

PRESIDENTIAL VOTE 1948-1988 *(in percents)*

Year	State Winner	Democratic	Republican
1948	Dewey (R)	46.4	49.8
1952	Eisenhower (R)	38.9	60.5
1956	Eisenhower (R)	44.8	55.3
1960	Nixon (R)	47.3	52.6
1964	Johnson (D)	63.7	36.0
1968	Nixon (R)	43.8	49.8
1972	Nixon (R)	42.3	52.5
1976	Ford (R)	47.6	47.8
1980	Reagan (R)	38.7	48.3
1984	Reagan (R)	43.7	55.9
1988	Dukakis (D)	53.0	47.0

GOVERNORS

Provisional Governors
Executive committee   1843-1845
George Abernethy   1845-1849

Territorial Governors
Joseph Lane   1849-1850
Kintzing Pritchett (acting)   1850
John P. Gaines   1850-1853
Joseph Lane   1853
George L. Curry (acting)   1854-1859

State Governors
John Whiteaker (D)   1859-1862
Addison C. Gibbs (R)   1862-1866
George L. Woods (R)   1866-1870
La Fayette Grover (D)   1870-1877
Stephen F. Chadwick (D/
   acting)   1877-1878
William W. Thayer (D)   1878-1882
Zenas F. Moody (R)   1882-1887

Sylvester Pennoyer
   (Democrat-Populist)   1887-1895
William P. Lord (R)   1895-1899
T.T. Geer (R)   1899-1903
George E. Chamberlain (D)   1903-1909
Frank W. Benson (R/act-
   ing)   1909-1910
Jay Bowerman (R/acting)   1910-1911
Oswald West (D)   1911-1915
James Withycombe (R)   1915-1919
Ben W. Olcott (R/acting)   1919-1923
Walter M. Pierce (D)   1923-1927
Isaac Lee Patterson (R)   1927-1929
Albin W. Norblad (R/acting)   1929-1931
Julius L. Meier (Indepen-
   dent)   1931-1935
Charles H. Martin (D)   1935-1939
Charles A. Sprague (R)   1939-1943
Earl Snell (R)   1943-1947
John H. Hall (R/acting)   1947-1949
Douglas McKay (R)   1949-1952
Paul L. Patterson (R/acting)   1952-1955
Paul L. Patterson (R)   1955-1956

Elmo E. Smith (R/acting)	1956-1957
Robert D. Holmes (D)	1957-1959
Mark Hatfield (R)	1959-1967
Thomas L. McCall (R)	1967-1975
Robert W. Straub (D)	1975-1979
Victor Atiyeh (R)	1979-1987
Neil Goldschmidt (D)	1987-

MINIMUM AGES

Majority	18
Marriage with parental consent	17
Marriage without parental consent	18
Making a will	18
Buying alcohol	21
Jury duty	18
Leaving school	16
Driver's license	16

CAPITAL PUNISHMENT
Number executed 1976-88: 0
On death row Aug. 1, 1988: 12

MILITARY INSTALLATIONS
Total number: 5
Major bases:
  Navy: 1

FINANCES

Thousands of dollars

GENERAL REVENUE (1985)

Total general revenue	4,079,361
Total tax revenue	1,982,956
Sales and gross receipts	237,419
Individual income taxes	1,310,731
Corporate net income taxes	153,822

GENERAL EXPENDITURE (1985)

Total general expenditure	3,986,054
Education	1,264,086
Public welfare	501,820
Health	101,538
Hospitals	187,511
Natural resources	123,420
Highways	481,001
Police	47,489
Corrections	86,823

FEDERAL AID (1985) 1,449,139

ECONOMY

Oregon's most important agricultural products are beef and dairy cattle, wheat and hay, ornamentals, potatoes, alfalfa, orchard fruits, and truck vegetables. 1983 farm marketings cash receipts were $1.7 billion. The timber industry, which comprises about 35 percent of total manufacturing in the state and earns more than $3 billion each year, is mainly based on softwood—Douglas fir, ponderosa pine, and hemlock are the main species forested. Much timber is shipped to the Far East. In addition to timber and wood products, smaller quantities of processed foods, apparel, electrical machinery, fabricated metals, transportation equipment, computers, and other high-tech components are produced. Value added to manufacture was nearly $8 billion in 1982. Visitors to Oregon's national and state parks bring in more than $1 billion annually.

EMPLOYMENT (1984)

Thousands of persons

Total number of employed workers	1,859
Construction	29.9
Finance, insurance, and real estate	65.7
Government	194.6
Manufacturing	198.7
Mining	1.6
Services	205.0
Transportation, communications, and utilities	56.2
Wholesale and retail trade	252.4

Percent of civilian labor force unemployed (1984) 9.4

DEPARTMENT OF DEFENSE (1985)

Civilian workers employed	3,107
Military personnel	782
Contract awards	$256 million

ENERGY SOURCES FOR ELECTRIC UTILITIES (1983)

Percent

Coal	0.9
Gas	0.0
Hydroelectric	91.6
Nuclear	7.5
Petroleum	0.0

TRANSPORTATION

Motor vehicles registered in state (1986)	2,263,989
Miles of roads, streets, and highways (1986)	94,578
Miles of Class I railway operated (1986)	2,865
Airports (1983)	341
Major aviation hubs (1983)	2
Largest hub: Portland	
Major ports, with gross tonnage in thousands (1985):	
Portland	21,845

CULTURE AND EDUCATION

Native American tribes

Oregon was formerly the home of some 125 tribes, including the Ahantchuyuk, Alsea, Atfalati, Bannock, Catulamet, Chastacosta, Chelamela, Chepenafa, Chetco, Chinook, Clatskanie, Clatsop, Clowwewalla, Coos, Cowlitz, Dakubetede, Hanis, Kalapuyu, Klickitat, Kuitsh, Kwalhioqua, Lakmiut, Latgawa, Miluk, Multnomah, Nez Perce, Santiam, Siletz, Siuslaw, Takelma, Taltushtuntude, Tenino, Tillamook, Tututni, Tyigh, Umpqua, Upper Coquille, Watlala, Wishram, Yahuskin, Yamel, Yaquina, and Yoncalla tribes. Groups that continue to live in the state include the Cayuse, Clackamus, Klamath, Modoc, Molala, Northern Paiute, Tolowa, Umatilla, Walla Walla, and Wasco. There are five federal reservations.

Religions, ethnicities, and languages

Most of Oregon's inhabitants are descendants of people who emigrated there from other states since the mid-19th century. Recent immigrants come mainly from Scandinavia, Finland, Canada, Germany, the British Isles, and the Soviet Union. In 1980, 5.4 percent of Oregon's population spoke a language other than English at home. About three-quarters of all churchgoers are Protestants (chiefly Methodists, Baptists, Presbyterians, Disciples of Christ, and Lutherans); most of the remainder are Roman Catholics, reflecting the state's substantial Hispanic community.

Major museums and libraries

Museum of Art, University of Oregon, Eugene
Museum of Natural History, University of Oregon, Eugene
Oregon Museum of Science and Industry, Portland
Portland Art Museum

Major arts organizations

Oregon Shakespeare Festival, Ashland
Oregon Symphony Orchestra, Portland
New Rose Theatre, Portland
Pacific Ballet Theatre
Portland Opera Association

Colleges and universities

Number public (1986-87) 21
Number private (1986-87) 24
Total enrollment, in full-time equivalent students (1985) 102,000

Public elementary and secondary schools

Expenditure per pupil in average daily attendance (1986-87) $4,383
Pupil-teacher ratio (1987) 18.3
Average teacher salary (1986-87) $28,000

Major league sports teams

Basketball: Portland Trail Blazers

Holidays

State Fair, Salem. Late August to early September

OREGON IN LITERATURE

Barbara Allen *Homesteading the High Desert* (1987)
Oral histories of homesteading.

T. D. Allen *Troubled Border* (1954)
A novel about the Hudson's Bay Company and the settlement of the Northwest, centering on the character of a company agent.

William Ashworth *The Wallowas: Coming of Age in the Wilderness* (1978)
Essay on the natural life of the Eagle Cap wilderness.

Frederick Homer Balch *Bridge of the Gods: A Romance of Indian Oregon* (1890)
Novel retelling the legend of the origin of the great rock bridge over the Columbia River and the Indians whose existence was dependent on it.

Don Berry *Trask* (1960); *Moontrap* (1962); *To Build a Ship* (1963)
Historical adventure novels of pioneer life.

Archie Binns *Land Is Bright* (1939)
Novel about an Illinois family that migrates in the 1850s.

Marje Blood *A Song Heard in a Strange Land* (1985)
Fictional account of the life of Narcissa Whitman.

Richard Brautigan *The Hawkline Monster: A Gothic Western* (1974)
Novel set in eastern Oregon in 1902.

Samuel L. Campbell *Autobiography . . . 1824–1920: Frontiersman and Oregon Pioneer, Together with His Summary of the Whitman Massacre* (1986)

Robert Cartwell *The Land of Plenty* (1934)
Novel about labor unrest in a lumber mill.

Sam Churchill *Big Sam* (1965)
Account of a lumberjack's life at the turn of the century.

Malcolm Clark (ed.) *Pharisee Among Philistines: The Diary of Judge Matthew P. Deady, 1871–1892* 2 vols. (1975)
A portrait of early Oregon society, especially that of Portland.

Lloyd Coffman *Pioneering in the Wallowas: Four Frontier Tales* (1987)

Ross Cox (ed. Edgar I. Stewart) *The Columbia River: or, Scenes and Adventures during a Residence of Six Years* (1831, rpt. 1957)
This memoir by a clerk of Astor's Fur Company is a major source of information on the pioneer era.

Paul Cranston *To Heaven on Horseback* (1952)
Novel based on the diaries of Narcissa Whitman.

Harold L. Davis *Honey in the Horn* (1935); *Beulah Land* (1949); *Winds of Morning* (1952); *Distant Music* (1957)
Popular novels of westward pioneering, based on historical fact.

Eva E. Dye *McLoughlin and Old Oregon* (1936)
Popular historical novel based on the life of the governor of the Hudson's Bay Company.

Timothy Flint *The Shoshonee Valley* (1830)
Melodramatic romance of the early settlers, the first fictional work to be set in the state.

Theodore T. Geer *Fifty Years in Oregon* (1912)
Reminiscences of an ex-Governor, describing pioneer life from the 1840s.

Jane A. Gould *The Oregon and California Trail Diary of Jane Gould in 1862* (1987)

A. B. Guthrie, Jr. *The Way West* (1949)
Novel about an 1840s wagon train on the Oregon Trail.

Ernest Haycox *The Earthbreakers* (1952)
Novel about pioneers in the 1840s.

Kenneth L. Holmes (ed.) *Covered Wagon Women: Diaries and Letters from the Western Trails, 1840–1890* (1986)

John B. Horner *Oregon Literature* 2d ed. (1902)
———. *Oregon History and Early Literature* (1931)

Dayton O. Hyde *Yamsi: A Heartwarming Journal of One Year on a Wilderness Ranch* (1971)
Account of a year on a cattle ranch in the pine forest of Southern Oregon.

Washington Irving *Astoria* (1836, rpt. 1982)
An account, based on oral testimony, of the attempt to settle Oregon, 1811–1813.

John Jennings *River to the West* (1948)
Fictional account of the founding of Astor's fur trading company.

Suzi Jones (ed.) *Webfoots and Bunchgrassers: Folk Art of the Oregon Country* (Oregon Arts Commission) (1980)
———. *Oregon Folklore* (1977)

Ken Kesey *Sometimes a Great Notion* (1964)
Novel about two brothers and their struggle with each other and the union set in logging country.

Theodor Kirchoff *Oregon East, Oregon West: Travels and Memoirs, 1863–1872* (1987)

Arthur Kreisman (ed.) *Oregon Centennial Anthology, 1859–1959* (1959)

Honoré-Timothée Lempfrit (ed. Patricia Meyer) *Oregon Trail Journal and Letters from the Pacific Northwest, 1848–1853* (1985)

Willard Leonard *Horse Sense* (1984)
Cowboy's memoir of eastern Oregon in the early years of the century.

Bernard Malamud *A New Life* (1961)
Novel about the life of a Jewish professor of English literature at an Oregon college.

Martha G. Masterson *One Woman's West: Recollection of the Oregon Trail and Settling the Northwest Country* (1986)

Martha McKeown *Mountains Ahead* (1961)
Saga of a wagon train on the Oregon Trail in 1847.

Honoré W. Morrow *We Must March: A Novel of the Winning of Oregon* (1925)
Romantic historical novel based on the life of Narcissa Whitman.

Herbert B. Nelson *The Literary Impulse in Pioneer Oregon* (1948)

Alfred Powers *History of Oregon Literature* (1935)

Jarold Ramsey (comp.) *Coyote Was Going There: Indian Literature of the Oregon Country* (1977)

Alexander Ross *Adventures of the First Settlers on the Oregon or Columbia River, 1810–1813* (1849, rpt. 1986)
First-hand account of the fur trade and early settlement.

James Stevens *Homer in the Sagebrush* (1928)
Short stories based on Oregon and Washington folklore.

Arthur C. Todd and **David James** (eds.) *Ever Westward the Land: Samuel James and His Cornish Family on the Trail to Oregon and the Pacific Northwest, 1842–1852* (1986)

William J. Watson *Journal of an Overland Journey to Oregon Made in the Year 1849* (1851, rpt. 1985)

Thames Williamson *Stride of Man* (1928)
Novel about an Oregon pioneer and inventor.

Nathaniel Jarvis Wyeth (ed. Frederick G. Young) *The Correspondence and Journals of Captain Nathaniel J. Wyeth, 1831–6* (1899, rpt. 1973)
The author, a Boston merchant, made several overland expeditions to build a fur-trading and salmon-shipping business.

GUIDES TO RESOURCES

Book, Betty *Oregon Historical Quarterly Index, 1961–1983* (1984)

Cockrell, Nick and **Bill** *Roofs over Rivers: A Guide to Oregon's Covered Bridges* (1978)

Corning, Howard McKinley (ed.) *Dictionary of Oregon History: Compiled from the Research Files of the Former Oregon Writers' Project with Much Added Material* (1956)

Douthit, Nathan *A Guide to Oregon South Coast History* (1986)

Dublin, William B. *Trail's End Oregon City: Where the Past Meets the Present* (1982)

Federal Writers' Project *The Oregon Trail; the Missouri River to the Pacific Ocean* (1939, rpt. 1972)
———. *Mount Hood; a Guide* (1940)
———. *Oregon: End of the Trail* (1940, rpt. 1972)

Franzwa, Gregory M. *Maps of the Oregon Trail* (1982)
———. *The Oregon Trail Revisited* (3d ed. 1983)

Friedman, Ralph *Oregon for the Curious* (2d ed. 1966)

Gorospe, Kathy *American Indian Cultural Resources: A Preservation Handbook* (1985)

Haines, Aubrey L. *Historical Sites along the Oregon Trail* (1973)

Hewlett, Leroy (ed.) *Indians of Oregon; a Bibliography of Materials in the Oregon State Library* (1969)

Information Technology Institute *Northwest Information Directory: A Guide to Unusual Sources and Special Collections* (1986)

Johnson, Daniel M. et al. *Atlas of Oregon Lakes* (1985)

Kimerling, Jon et al. *Atlas of the Pacific Northwest* 7th ed. (1985)

Leasher, Evelyn M. *Oregon Women: A Bio-Bibliography* (1980)

Loy, William *Atlas of Oregon* (1976)

Norman, James B. *Oregon's Architectural Heritage: The National Register Properties of the Portland Area* (1986)

Oregon Arts Commission *Oregon Literary Resource Directory* (n.d.)

Oregon Department of Education *Oregon Women: a Report on Their Education, Employment, and Economic Status* (1987)

Oregon Commission on Indian Services (comp. Gladine G. Johnson) *1987–89 Oregon Directory of American Indian Resources* (1987)

Oregon State Archives *Echoes of Oregon, 1837–1859: A Selection of Records from the Oregon State Archives* (1987)

Owens, Kenneth N. (ed.) and Alton S. Donnelly (trans.) *The Wreck of the Sv. Nikolai: Two Narratives of the First Russian Expedition to the Oregon Country, 1808–1810* (1985)

Preston, Ralph N. *Early Oregon Atlas* (2d ed. 1978)

Southern Oregon Library Association *A Guide to the State of Jefferson; a Union List of Historical Materials Relating to Northern California and Southern Oregon* (1972)

Thompson, Erwin *Whitman Mission National Historic Site* (National Park Service Historical Handbook series no. 37) (1952)

Vaughan, Thomas and Terrence O'Donnell *Portland: A Historical Sketch and Guide* (1976)

SELECTED NONFICTION SOURCES

Abbott, Carl *Portland: Planning, Politics, and Growth in a Twentieth-Century City* (1983)

Aiken, C. Melvin *Archaeology of Oregon* (1984)

Allen, Barbara *Homesteading the High Desert* (1987)

Allen, Opal *Narcissa Whitman; an Historical Biography* (1959)

Bailey, Barbara R. *Main Street, Northeastern Oregon: The Founding and Development of Small Towns* (1982)

Bancroft, Hubert H. *History of Oregon* 2 vols. (1886)

Barker, Burt B. *The McLoughlin Empire and Its Rulers* (1959)

Barrows, William *Oregon: The Struggle for Possession* (7th ed. 1892, rpt. 1973)

Barzee, Clark L. *Oregon in the Making; 60's to Gay 90's . . .* (1936)

Beal, Merrill *"I Will Fight No More Forever": Chief Joseph and the Nez Percé War* (1963)

Beckham, Stephen D. *Requiem for a People: The Rogue Indians and the Frontiersmen* (1971)

Bell, James C. *Opening a Highway to the Pacific, 1838–1846 . . .* (1921, rpt. 1968)

Belton, Howard C. *Under Eleven Governors* (1977)

Bentson, William A. *Historical Capitols of Oregon: An Illustrated Chronology* (1987)

Bosker, Gideon and Lena Lencek *Frozen Music: A History of Portland Architecture* (1985)

Bowen, William H. *The Willamette Valley: Migration and Settlement on the Oregon Frontier* (1978)

Brimlow, George F. *Harney County, Oregon, and Its Range Land* (1951)

Brogan, Phil F. (ed. L. K. Phillips) *East of the Cascades* (1964)

Brosnan, Cornelius J. *Jason Lee, Prophet of the New Oregon* (1932)

Burton, Robert E. *Democrats of Oregon: The Pattern of Minority Politics, 1900–1956* (1970)

Canse, John M. *Pilgrim and Pioneer; Dawn in the Northwest* (1930)

Case, Robert O. *The Empire Builders* (rev. ed. 1949)
——— and Victoria *Last Mountains--The Story of the Cascades* (1945)

Chalmers, Harvey *The Last Stand of the Nez Percé: Destruction of a People* (1962)

Clark, Keith *Redmond: Where The Desert Blooms* (1985)

Clark, Malcolm *Eden Seekers: The Settlement of Oregon, 1818–1862* (1981)

Clark, Roland Keith and Lowell Tiller *Terrible Trail: The Meek Cutoff, 1845* (1966)

Cline, Gloria *Peter Skene Ogden and the Hudson's Bay Company* (1974)

Coons, Frederick B. *The Trail to Oregon* (1954)

Cordano, Vira *Levi Scott, Oregon Trailblazer* (1982)

Corning, Howard M. *Willamette Landings, Ghost Towns of the River* (1947)

Culp, Edwin D. *Early Oregon Days* (1987)

Dicken, Samuel N. and Emily F. *Pioneer Trails of the Oregon Coast* (1971)
———. *The Making of Oregon: A Study in Historical Geography* (1979)

Dillon, Richard H. *Siskiyou Trail: The Hudson's Bay Company Route to California* (1975)

Dobbs, Caroline et al. *Men of Champoeg; a Record of the Lives of the Pioneers Who Founded the Oregon Government* (1932)

Dodds, Gordon B. *Oregon: A Bicentennial History* (States and the Nation series) (1977)

Drawson, Maynard C. *Treasures of the Oregon Country* (3d ed. 1975)

Drury, Clifford M. *Marcus and Narcissa Whitman, and the Opening of Old Oregon* 2 vols. (1973)
———. *Elkanah and Mary Walker, Pioneers among the Spokanes* (1940)

Dryden, Cecil P. *Give All to Oregon! Missionary Pioneers of the Far West* (1968)

Due, John F. and Giles French *Rails to the Mid-Columbia Wheatlands: The Columbia Southern and Great Southern Railroads and the Development of Sherman and Wasco Counties, Oregon* (1979)

Dunham, Wayland A. *Blue Enchantment, the Story of Crater Lake* (1942)

Eaton, Jeanette *Narcissa Whitman, Pioneer of Oregon* (1941)

Fogdall, Alberta B. *Royal Family of the Columbia: Dr. John McLoughlin and His Family* (1978)

Franklin, Dorothy *West Coast Disaster, Columbus Day, 1962* (1964)

Frazier, Neta *Five Roads to the Pacific* (1964)

French, Giles *The Golden Land; a History of Sherman County, Oregon* (1958)
———. *Cattle Country of Peter French* (1964)

Friedman, Ralph *A Touch of Oregon* (1970)

Galbraith, John S. *The Hudson's Bay Company as an Imperial Factor, 1821–1869* (1957)

Gibson, James R. *Farming the Frontier: The Agricultural Opening of the Oregon Country, 1786–1846* (1985)

Gilmore, Janet Crofton *The World of the Oregon Fishboat: A Study in Maritime Folklife* (1986)

Goodall, Mary *Oregon's Iron Dream; a Story of Old Oswego and the Proposed Iron Empire of the West* (1958)

Gray, William H. *A History of Oregon, 1792–1849* (c.1870, rpt. 1973)

Greene, Linda W. *Historic Resource Study: Crater Lake National Park, Oregon* (1984)

Hafen, LeRoy R. and Francis Marion Young *Fort Laramie and the Pageant of the West, 1834–1890* (1984)

Hall, Don A. *On Top of Oregon* (1975)

Hedges, James B. *Henry Villard and the Railways of the Northwest* (1930)

Hendrickson, James E. *Joe Lane of Oregon, Machine Politics and the Sectional Crisis, 1849–1861* (1967)

Hill, William E. *The Oregon Trail, Yesterday and Today: A Brief History and Pictorial Journal . . .* (1987)

Hixon, Adrietta A. *On to Oregon* (1987)

Hobson, Howard *Shooting Ducks: A History of University of Oregon Basketball* (1984)

Howard, Helen A. and Dan L. McGrath *War Chief Joseph* (1941)

Howe, Carol B. *Ancient Tribes of the Klamath Country* (1968)

Jackman, E. R. and John Scharff *Steens Mountain in Oregon's High Desert Country* (1968)

Jansen, William H. *Abraham "Oregon" Smith: Pioneer, Folk Hero, and Tale-Teller* (1977)

Johnson, Robert C. *John McLoughlin; Father of Oregon* (1935, rpt. 1958)

Kresek, Ray *Fire Lookouts of Oregon and Washington* (1985)

LaLande, Jeffrey M. *Medford Corporation: A History of an Oregon Logging and Lumber Company* (1979)
————. *First over the Siskiyous: Peter Skene Ogden's 1826–1827 Journey Through the Oregon–California Borderlands* (1987)

Laut, Agnes C. *The Overland Trail; the Epic Path of the Pioneers to Oregon* ... (1929)

Lavender, David S. *Westward Vision; the Story of the Oregon Trail* (1963)

Lockley, Fred *Oregon's Yesterdays* (1928)
————. *Oregon Trail Blazers* (1929)

Loewenberg, Robert J. *Equality on the Oregon Frontier: Jason Lee and the Methodist Mission, 1834–43* (1976)

Lucia, Ellis *Tough Men, Tough Country* (1963)

Mackey, Harold *The Kalapuyans: A Source Book on the Indians of the Willamette Valley* (1974)

MacPhee, Marnie *Western Oregon: Portrait of a Land and Its People* (1987)

Maddux, Percy *City on the Willamette; the Story of Portland* (1952)

Marlitt, Richard *Nineteenth Street* (1978)

Marshall, Don B. *Oregon Shipwrecks* (1984)

McArthur, Lewis A. *Oregon Geographic Names* (5th ed. rev. and enl. 1982)

McCall, Tom (ed. Steve Neal) *Tom McCall, Maverick: An Autobiography* (1977)

McKinney, Sam *Reach of Tide, Ring of History: A Columbia River Voyage* (1987)

Miller, Emma G. *Clatsop County, Oregon* (1958)

Mills, Randall V. *Stern-Wheelers Up Columbia: A Century of Steamboating in the Oregon Country* (1977)

Minter, Harold A. *Umpqua Valley, Oregon, and Its Pioneers* (1967)

Monaghan, Robert R. *Pronunciation Guide of Oregon Place Names* (1961)

Montgomery, Richard C. *The White-Headed Eagle, John McLoughlin, Builder of an Empire* (1934, rpt. 1971)

Moore, Lucia W. et al. *The Story of Eugene* (1949)

Oliver, Herman *Gold and Cattle Country* (1961)

Pamplin, Robert B. (ed.) *A Portrait of Oregon* (1973)

Parrish, Philip H. *Historic Oregon* (rev. ed. 1949)

Place, Howard and Marian *The Story of Crater Lake National Park* (1974)

Pollard, Lancaster *Oregon and the Pacific Northwest* (1946)

Potter, Miles F. *Oregon's Golden Years: Bonanza of the West* (1976)

Putnam, George P. *In the Oregon Country* (1915)

Richards, Kent D. *Isaac I. Stevens: Young Man in a Hurry* (1979)

Robbins, William G. *Hard Times in Paradise: Coos Bay, Oregon, 1850–1986* (1988)

Roberge, Earl *Columbia, Great River of the West* (1985)

Ruby, Robert H. and Joan A. Brown *Ferryboats on the Columbia River, Including the Bridges and Dams* (1974)

Skinner, Constance L. *Adventures of Oregon; a Chronicle of the Fur Trade* (1920)

Snyder, Eugene E. *Early Portland: Stump-town Triumph, Rival Towns on the Willamette, 1831–1854* (1970)

Spencer, Omar C. *The Story of Sauvies Island* (1950)

Stern, Theodore *The Klamath Tribe: A People and Their Reservation* (1965)

Sutton, Jack *The Pictorial History of Southern Oregon and Northern California* (1959)

Thompson, Erwin N. *Shallow Grave at Waiilatpu: The Sagers' West* (rev. ed. 1973)

Throckmorton, Arthur L. *Oregon Argonauts: Merchant Adventurers on the Western Frontier* (1961)

Turnbull, George S. *Governors of Oregon* (1959)

Vaughan, Thomas (ed.) *The Western Shore: Oregon Country Essays Honoring the American Revolution* (1975)
———— and George A. McMath *A Century of Portland Architecture* (1967)

Vestal, Stanley *Joe Meek, the Merry Mountain Man: a Biography* (1952)

Victor, Frances F. *The Early Indian Wars of Oregon* (1894)

Winther, Oscar O. *The Old Oregon Country: A History of Frontier Trade, Transportation and Travel* (1969)

Woodward, W. C. *Rise and Early History of Political Parties in Oregon, 1843–1868* (1913)

Zucker, Jeff, Kay Hummel, and Bob Hogfoss *Oregon Indians: Culture, History and Current Affairs, an Atlas and Introduction* (1983)

PENNSYLVANIA

Pennsylvania is a Middle Atlantic state. It is bordered on the north by Lake Erie and New York; on the east by New York, New Jersey, and the Delaware River; on the south by Delaware, Maryland, and West Virginia; and on the west by West Virginia and Ohio.

FULL NAME Commonwealth of Pennsylvania
POSTAL ABBREVIATION PA
INHABITANT Pennsylvanian
ADMITTED TO THE UNION Dec. 12, 1787.
  2d state
POPULATION (est. 1987) 11,936,000.
  Percent of US total: 4.91%. Rank: 5th

CAPITAL CITY Harrisburg, located on the Susquehanna River in south central Pennsylvania; population 52,056 (est. 1984). It was first the site of Harris' Ferry, a trading post founded about 1718. It was laid out in 1785 as Louisbourg, but was chartered as a borough in 1791 and as a city in 1860 as Harrisburg. In 1812 it became the state capital.

STATE NAME AND NICKNAMES Named by King Charles II for William Penn; *sylvania* is the Latin word for "woods." Also known as the Keystone State and the Quaker State.

STATE SEAL On one side, a shield divided in three parts, showing at top a ship under full sail, in the center a plow, and at bottom three standing sheaves of wheat; above the shield is an eagle, at its sides an ear of maize and an olive branch. Around the border is the legend "Seal of the State of Pennsylvania." On the reverse, Liberty trampling the lion of Tyranny, with the inscription "Both Can't Survive."

MOTTO Virtue, Liberty, and Independence

SONG None

SYMBOLS
Flower mountain laurel
Tree hemlock
Game bird ruffed grouse
Animal whitetail deer
Dog Great Dane
Fish brook trout
Insect firefly
Fossil trilobite
Beverage milk
Beautification and conservation plant penngift crownvetch

LICENSE PLATES (1) Orange on dark blue, with orange border and outline of a keystone, and the legend "You've Got a Friend in Pennsylvania." (2) Dark blue on orange, with blue border and outline of a keystone and the legend "Keystone State."

FLAG On a field of blue, the state coat of arms: a rococo shield showing a ship under sail, a plow, and three sheaves of wheat, with the Federal eagle above it and harnessed horses on either side, and the state motto on a scroll below them.

GEOGRAPHY AND CLIMATE

Rectangular Pennsylvania is split in two along the state's northeast to southwest axis by the Allegheny section of the Appalachian Mountains. Around Philadelphia in the southeast is a small section of the Atlantic Coastal Plain, shading into the prosperous agricultural area of the eastern Piedmont. Pennsylvania has several major rivers, including the Delaware, Susquehanna, Allegheny, and Ohio, and a narrow shoreline on Lake Erie.

AREA 45,308 square miles. Rank: 33d
INLAND WATER 420 square miles
GEOGRAPHIC CENTER Centre, 2.5 miles SW of Bellefonte
ELEVATIONS *Highest point:* Mount Davis, Somerset County, 3,213 feet. *Lowest point:* Delaware River, Delaware County, sea level. *Mean elevation:* 1,100 feet

MAJOR RIVERS Delaware, Ohio, Allegheny, Susquehanna

MAJOR LAKES AND RESERVOIRS Erie, Arthur, Raystown, Wallenpaupack, Conneaut, Pymatung, Allegheny

TIDAL SHORELINE 89 miles, Atlantic coast

LAND USE

	Thousands of acres
Urban (1982)	2,073
Rural (1982)	25,144
Cropland (1982)	5,896
Pastureland (1982)	2,593
Rangeland (1982)	0
Forestland (1982)	15,300
State parks and recreation areas (1983)	279
National park system (1984)	41
National forest system (1984) . . .	743
Tribal lands (1984)	0

TEMPERATURES The highest recorded temperature was 111°F on July 10, 1936, at Phoenixville. The lowest was -42°F on January 5, 1904, at Smethport.

NATIONAL SITES

NATIONAL BATTLEFIELD Fort Necessity
NATIONAL CEMETERY Gettysburg
NATIONAL HISTORIC SITES Allegheny Portage Railroad, Eisenhower, Friendship Hill, Gloria Dei Church, Hopewell Furnace, Edgar Allan Poe, Steamtown National Historic Site
NATIONAL HISTORICAL PARKS Independence, Valley Forge
NATIONAL MEMORIALS Benjamin Franklin,

Johnstown Flood, Thaddeus Kosciuszko
NATIONAL MILITARY PARK Gettysburg
NATIONAL RECREATION AREA Delaware Water Gap
NATIONAL SCENIC RIVER AND RIVERWAY Delaware, Upper Delaware
NATIONAL SCENIC TRAILS Appalachian, North Country, Potomac, Heritage
NATIONAL WILDLIFE REFUGES Erie, Tinicum National Environmental Center

HISTORY

1609	Henry Hudson explores lower Delaware River.
1634	Voyagers from Virginia establish a small fort at the mouth of the Schuylkill River, near what is now Philadelphia.
1643	John Printz leads a group of Swedes to Tinicum Island (now Essington), the first European settlement in present Pennsylvania.
1655	New Netherlands governor, Peter Stuyvesant, leads a Dutch expedition to take possession of the Swedish colony.
1664	Colonel Richard Nicolls establishes English rule in the region.
1674	The Treaty of Westminster secures English claims.
1681	*March 4.* King Charles II grants English proprietor and Quaker, William Penn, almost all of what is now Pennsylvania.
1682	*October.* Penn arrives in Pennsylvania and issues a writ for an election. Treaties are made with Indians through Penn and good relations last 70 years.
1683	*February.* First witchcraft trial occurs. *March 19.* First assembly accepts frame of government.
1688	Mennonite Quakers begin fight against slavery in Germantown.
1701	*November 8.* Penn issues the Charter of Priviledges. Philadelphia, City of Brotherly Love, is chartered.
1710	French Huguenots, Germans, and Scotch-Irish settle in the province.

1716	First iron forge in the province is built near Pottstown.
1723	First paper money is issued in Philadelphia.
1727	Benjamin Franklin founds Junto, an association opposing slavery, in Philadelphia.
1731	Franklin originates the Library Company of Philadelphia.
1732	Coventry Forge in Chester County manufactures the first steel.
1746	First nail factory is built on Chester Creek.
1754	George Washington builds Fort Necessity near Uniontown.
1755	General Braddock is defeated and killed on the Monongahela by the French.
1758	*November 25.* British General John Forbes captures Fort Duquesne from the French and renames it Fort Pitt.
1763	War ends with British victory. Pennsylvania region is now completely under British rule.
1767	Charles Mason and Jeremiah Dixon finish laying the boundary lines for Maryland and Pennsylvania.
1768	Pennsylvania bitterly opposes the Stamp Act and Townshend Acts.
1774	*September 5.* Philadelphia is the meeting place for the First Continental Congress.
1776	*July 4.* Declaration of Independence is signed at Philadelphia by the Second Continental Congress and a provisional government prepares a new constitution.
1777	*September 11.* British General William Howe defeats George Washington at the Battle of the Brandywine.
	September 30. American forces defeated at the Battle of Paoli.
	November 10. British bombard Fort Mifflin for six days and drive out the American troops.
1777–1778	The Liberty Bell is hidden in Allentown during the British occupation of Philadelphia.
	December 19–June 19. George Washington's Continental Army camps at Valley Forge.
1780	Pennsylvania passes the first law abolishing slavery.
1783	*September 3.* The Treaty of Paris ends the Revolutionary War. Nearly 3,000 Pennsylvania troops march on Philadelphia to obtain "prompt settlement of their accounts."
1787	*December 12.* The Constitutional Convention meets in Philadelphia. Pennsylvania is the second state to ratify the Constitution.
1794	*July.* Pennsylvanians burn the home of Inspector General John Neville in rebellion against the new federal tax on whiskey.
1800	The Capital is moved from Philadelphia to Washington, D.C.
1812	The state capital is established in Harrisburg.
	June 18. War is declared against Great Britain and Pennsylvania is asked to provide 4,000 volunteers.
1841	Pennsylvania legislature forbids use of state jails for fugitive slaves.
1855	For the first time, horsecars are operated in Philadelphia.
1859	*August 2.* The nation's first commercial oil well is drilled by Edwin Drake and his crew at Titusville.
1861	Civil War. Under governorship of Andrew G. Curtin, the state takes a definite stand against secession.
1862	Bethlehem Iron Company is founded.
1863	*July 1-3.* Battle of Gettysburg is a victory for Union forces.
	November 19. President Abraham Lincoln delivers his Gettysburg Address.
1867	The first practical production of Bessemer steel in America occurs at Steelton.
1870	Pittsburgh is the nation's center of the steel industry.
1873	Widespread money panic occurs when the Philadelphia banking house of Jay Cooke fails.
1876	Alexander Graham Bell's new telephone is exhibited at the US Centennial Exhibition at Philadelphia.
1889	*May 31.* Devastating flood occurs at Johnstown.
1897	*February 2.* State capitol at Harrisburg is destroyed by fire.
1898	*August 10.* Cornerstone of new capitol is laid.
1901	Charles M. Schwab becomes the president of the United States Steel Corporation.

1917	The state's mills and factories produce steel and other needed materials for World War I.
1920	Pioneer radio station at Pittsburgh established first permanent commercial broadcasting station in the world.
1933	Pennsylvania appropriates $45 million for its needy during the Depression.
1940	The first section of the Pennsylvania Turnpike is completed.
1941–1945	State industries again turn to military production.
1955	Natural-gas fields in northern Pennsylvania are greatly expanded by new wells.
1956	The first commercial nickel refinery begins operations at Crum Lynne.
1957	The nation's first full-scale nuclear power reactor for civilian purposes starts producing electricity at Shippingport.
1958	The first copper refinery built east of the Mississippi River in more than 50 years begins production near Reading.
1964	*March*. Racial demonstrations and violence occur in Chester and North Philadelphia.
1966	An atomic power station begins operations at Peach Bottom.
1967	*Fall*. A lengthy and violent strike by steel haulers disrupts the economy of western Pennsylvania.
1972	*June*. Tropical storm Agnes causes the state's worst flooding.
1975	*September*. Harrisburg suffers severe flooding.
1977	Unemployment in many depressed areas falls to the lowest levels in six to ten years.
1979	*March 28*. Major accident occurs at Three Mile Island nuclear power plant when the closing of a reactor leads to the release of radiation. *April 3*. The Nuclear Regulatory Commission (NRC) announces that the hydrogen bubble trapped in the reactor vessel has been eliminated. *April 13*. Cold shutdown of Three Mile Island is begun. *June*. Polio epidemic among the state's 18,000 Amish.
1980	Fort Indiantown Gap is pressed into service as a processing center for 19,000 Cuban refugees.
1981	Three Mile Island radioactive waste clean-up will cost $1 billion.
1982	Unemployment reaches over 11 percent statewide as a number of steel plants close.
1985	*May 13*. Philadelphia police bomb the fortified home of radical group MOVE. Eleven are killed and 61 neighboring homes are destroyed by the subsequent fire. *October 3*. Over objections from anti-nuclear groups and the state government, the NRC approves the restarting of the undamaged nuclear reactor at Three Mile Island.
1986	*July 1*. As contracts expire, more than 20,000 municipal and private employees strike.

DEMOGRAPHY

Population (est. 1987) . . . 11,936,000
Population (1980) 11,864,751
Population density in persons
  per square mile (1980) 261.9

POPULATION BY RACE (1980)
American Indian/Aleut/
  Eskimo 8,459
Asian/Pacific Islander 64,381
Black 1,047,609
Hispanic 154,004
White 10,654,325
Other 90,954

POPULATION CHARACTERISTICS (1980)
Percent of state population
Urban 69.3
Rural 30.7
Under 18 . . . . 26.3
65 or older 12.9
College-educated 13.8
Families below poverty line 7.8
Public-assistance recipients 6.7

Per capita personal income
  (1986) $13,944
Millionaires per 100,000
  residents (1982) 216.3

Average life expectancy in
years (1980) 73.6
Marriage rate (1986) 7.4
Divorce rate (1986) 3.4
Birth rate per 1,000
residents (1985) 13.7
Infant mortality rate per 1,000
births (1985) 11.2
Abortion rate per 1,000
live births (1985) 348
Crime rate per 100,000
residents (1985)
Violent 358.6
Property 2,743.3
Federal and state prisoners per
100,000 residents (1984) 105

Alcohol consumption in gallons
per capita (1985) 38.7
Deaths from motor vehicle accidents
per 100,000 residents (1985) . . 14.9

MAJOR CITIES

1984 population (est.)

Allentown	103,899
Bethlehem	69,967
Erie	117,461
Harrisburg	52,056
Lancaster	56,261
Philadelphia	1,646,713
Pittsburgh	402,583
Reading	78,364
Scranton	83,695

GOVERNMENT AND POLITICS

Number of US Representatives 23
Electoral votes 25

POLITICAL PARTY NOMINEES FROM STATE
*winner

James Armstrong	1798	P
Jared Ingersoll (Federalist)	1812	VP
James Ross (Federalist)	1816	VP
Richard Rush (Whig faction)	1820	VP
Richard Rush (Federalist/ National Republican)	1828	VP
John Sergeant (National Republican)	1832	VP
Amos Ellmaker (Anti-Masonic)	1832	VP
Thomas Earle (Liberal)	1840	VP
George Mifflin Dallas* (D)	1844	VP
James Black (Prohibition)	1872	P
James Buchanan* (D)	1856	P
William Freame Johnson (North American)	1856	VP
Winfield Scott Hancock (D)	1880	P
Alfred Henry Love (Equal Rights/declined)	1888	VP
Wharton Barker (People's)	1900	P
Valentine Remmel (Socialist Labor)	1900	VP
Samuel T. Nicholson (Union Reform)	1900	VP
David H. Martin (United Christian)	1900	VP
Silas Comfort Swallow (Prohibition)	1904	P
Silas Comfort Swallow (United Christian/declined)	1908	P
Robert Colvin Macauley (Single Tax)	1920	P
James Hudson Maurer (Socialist)	1928	VP
James Renshaw Cox (Jobless)	1932	VP
James Hudson Maurer (Socialist)	1932	VP
Edward A. Teichert (Socialist Labor)	1944	P
Darlington Hoopes (Socialist)	1944	VP
Edward A. Teichert (Socialist Labor)	1948	P
Dale Learn (Prohibition)	1948	VP
Darlington Hoopes (Socialist)	1952	P
Darlington Hoopes (Socialist)	1956	P
George Sam Taylor (Socialist Labor)	1968	VP

PRESIDENTIAL PRIMARY ELECTION In 1988, Pennsylvania sent 193 Democratic delegates and 96 Republican delegates to the national conventions.

CONSTITUTION Pennsylvania has had five constitutions: 1776, 1790, 1838, 1873, and the present one, adopted in 1968.

LEGISLATURE The General Assembly is divided into the Senate (50 members, 4-year term, minimum age 25) and the House of Representatives (203 members, 2-year term, minimum age 21). In 1987, the annual salary was $35,000.

JUDICIARY The highest court is the Supreme Court, with 7 judges serving 10-year terms. In 1987, the annual salary was $91,500.

EXECUTIVE The governor serves a 4-year term; the minimum age for holding office is 30. In 1987, the annual salary was $85,000. There are 4 other elected officials.

PRESIDENTIAL VOTE 1948-1988 *(in percents)*

Year	State Winner	Democratic	Republican
1948	Dewey (R)	46.9	50.9
1952	Eisenhower (R)	46.9	52.7
1956	Eisenhower (R)	43.3	56.5
1960	Kennedy (D)	51.1	48.7
1964	Johnson (D)	64.9	34.7
1968	Humphrey (D)	47.6	44.0
1972	Nixon (R)	39.1	59.1
1976	Carter (D)	50.4	47.7
1980	Reagan (R)	42.5	49.6
1984	Reagan (R)	46.0	53.3
1988	Bush (R)	49.0	51.0

GOVERNORS

Governors of New Sweden

Peter Minuit	1638
Peter Hollandaer Ridder	1640-1643
Johan Printz	1643-1653
Johan Papegoja	1653-1654
Johan Classon Rising	1654-1655

(Pennsylvania shared governors with New York from 1655 to 1681. In addition to governors, Pennsylvania also had proprietors: William Penn from 1681 to 1718; John Penn, Richard Penn, and Thomas Penn from 1718 to 1746; Richard Penn and Thomas Penn from 1746 to 1771; Thomas Penn and John Penn from 1771 to 1776.)

Provincial Governors

William Markham (deputy governor)	1681-1682
William Penn	1682-1684
Thomas Lloyd (council president)	1684-1688
John Blackwell (deputy governor)	1688-1690
Thomas Lloyd (council president)	1690-1691
Thomas Lloyd (deputy governor)	1691-1692
William Markham (deputy governor of the Lower Counties)	1691-1692

Governors Appointed by the English Crown

Benjamin Fletcher (governor of New York)	1692-1695
William Markham (deputy governor)	1692-1695

Provincial Governors

William Markham (deputy governor)	1695-1699
William Penn	1699-1701
Andrew Hamilton	1701-1703
Edward Shippen	1703-1704
John Evans	1704-1709
Charles Gookin	1709-1717
Sir William Keith	1717-1726
Patrick Gordon	1726-1736
James Logan	1736-1738
George Thomas	1738-1747
Anthony Palmer	1747-1748
James Hamilton	1748-1754
Robert Hunter Morris	1754-1756
William Denny	1756-1759
James Hamilton	1759-1763
John Penn	1763-1771
James Hamilton	1771
Richard Penn (lieutenant governor)	1771-1773
James Hamilton	1773
John Penn	1773-1776
Thomas Wharton Jr. (president of the Council of Safety)	1776-1777

Presidents of the Supreme Executive Council

Thomas Wharton Jr.	1777-1778
George Bryan (acting)	1778
Joseph Reed	1778-1781
William Moore	1781-1782
John Dickinson	1782-1785
Benjamin Franklin	1785-1788
Thomas Mifflin	1788-1790

State Governors

Thomas Mifflin	1790-1799
Thomas McKean (Democratic-Republican)	1799-1808
Simon Snyder (D-R)	1808-1817
William Findlay (D-R)	1817-1820
Joseph Hiester (Independent Democrat)	1820-1823
John Andrew Shulze (D-R)	1823-1829

George Wolf (D)	1829-1835
Joseph Ritner (Anti-Masonic)	1835-1839
David Rittenhouse Porter (D)	1839-1845
Francis Rawn Shunk (D)	1845-1848
William Freame Johnston (Whig)	1848-1852
William Bigler (D)	1852-1855
James Pollock (Whig/Know-Nothing)	1855-1858
William Fisher Packer (D)	1858-1861
Andrew Gregg Curtin (R)	1861-1867
John White Geary (R)	1867-1873
John Frederick Hartranft (R)	1873-1879
Henry Martyn Hoyt (R)	1879-1883
Robert Emory Pattison (D)	1883-1887
James Addams Beaver (R)	1887-1891
Robert Emory Pattison (D)	1891-1895
Daniel H. Hastings (R)	1895-1899
William A. Stone (R)	1899-1903
Samuel W. Pennypacker (R)	1903-1907
Edwin S. Stuart (R)	1907-1911
John K. Tener (R)	1911-1915
Martin G. Brumbaugh (R)	1915-1919
William G. Sproul (R)	1919-1923
Gifford Pinchot (R)	1923-1927
John S. Fisher (R)	1927-1931
Gifford Pinchot	1931-1935
George H. Earle (D)	1935-1939
Arthur H. James (R)	1939-1943
Edward Martin (R)	1943-1947
John C. Bell (R)	1947
James H. Duff (R)	1947-1951
John S. Fine (R)	1951-1955
George M. Leader (D)	1955-1959
David L. Lawrence (D)	1959-1963
William W. Scranton (R	1963-1967
Raymond P. Shafer (R)	1967-1971
Milton J. Shapp (D)	1971-1979
Richard Thornburgh (R)	1979-1987
Robert P. Casey (D)	1987-

MINIMUM AGES

Majority	21
Marriage with parental consent	16
Marriage without parental consent	18
Making a will	18
Buying alcohol	21
Jury duty	18
Leaving school	16
Driver's license	17

CAPITAL PUNISHMENT
Number executed 1976-88: 0
On death row Aug. 1, 1988: 101

MILITARY INSTALLATIONS
Total number: 22
Major bases:
  Army: 1
  Navy: 4

FINANCES

Thousands of dollars

GENERAL REVENUE (1985)

Total general revenue	16,662,092
Total tax revenue	10,162,436
Sales and gross receipts	5,056,989
Individual income taxes	2,588,913
Corporate net income taxes	942,971

GENERAL EXPENDITURE (1985)

Total general expenditure	15,088,135
Education	4,840,697
Public welfare	3,927,081
Health	433,175
Hospitals	790,851
Natural resources	235,495
Highways	1,770,360
Police	182,591
Corrections	244,029

FEDERAL AID (1985) 4,963,560

ECONOMY

Dairy products, eggs, and cattle are Pennsylvania's main farm products, along with buckwheat, corn, tobacco, vegetables, orchard fruits, grapes, and mushrooms. Farm marketing cash receipts in 1983 were nearly $3 billion. Pennsylvania is the nation's leading grower of Christmas trees. In mining, iron ore and anthracite coal (annual yield: 6 million tons) are still the major products, feeding the state's primary metals manufacturing base. Also mined are oil, natural gas, limestone, slate, clay, sand, salt, and small amounts of precious and strategic metals. Manufacturing in Pennsylvania is highly developed: among the major products are steel (mainly from Pittsburgh and Bethlehem), processed stones and minerals (mainly portland cement and lime), petroleum products, transportation equipment, heavy machinery, processed foods (notably chocolate, ice cream, and sausages), paper and pulp, plastics and chemicals, ceramics and glass, textiles and apparel. Value added to manufacture was $45 billion in 1982, among the nation's highest. Financial, legal, data processing, and other services make up an increasing proportions of the state's economy, as does tourism.

EMPLOYMENT (1984)

Thousands of persons

Total number of employed workers	4,988
Construction	175.7
Finance, insurance, and real estate	253.5
Government	670.2
Manufacturing	1,119.8
Mining	38.7
Services	1,108.3
Transportation, communications, and utilities	246.3
Wholesale and retail trade	1,032.8
Percent of civilian labor force unemployed (1984)	9.1

DEPARTMENT OF DEFENSE (1985)

Civilian workers employed	55,743
Military personnel	6,711
Contract awards	$4.149 billion

ENERGY SOURCES FOR ELECTRIC UTILITIES (1983)

Percent

Coal	78.0
Gas	0.1
Hydroelectric	0.9
Nuclear	11.9
Petroleum	9.1

TRANSPORTATION

Motor vehicles registered in state (1986)	7,477,017
Miles of roads, streets, and highways (1986)	115,663
Miles of Class I railway operated (1983)	5,113
Airports (1983)	720
Major aviation hubs (1983)	3
Largest hub: Pittsburgh/Wheeling	

Major ports, with gross tonnage in thousands (1985):

Philadelphia	32,690
Pittsburgh	28,552
Marcus Hook	27,418

CULTURE AND EDUCATION

Native American tribes

Pennsylvania was formerly home to the Conoy, Delaware, Erie, Honniasont, Nanticoke, Seneca, Shawnee, Susquehannock, Tuscarora, Tutelo, and Wenro tribes.

Religions, ethnicities, and languages

Because the Quakers founded Pennsylvania on principles of religious tolerance, the state has sheltered a wide variety of religious groups, including more than 100 present today. Some 40 percent of churchgoers are Roman Catholic, mainly in the cities, where there are also Jewish and Greek Orthodox congregations; in the rural areas are communities of Amish, Mennonites, Brethren, and Moravians. Other large Protestant groups include the Presbyterians, Methodists, Lutherans, and United Church of Christ. During the 18th and early 19th centuries, people of English descent settled in the southeast, Scotch-Irish in the south central area, Germans in the interior, and American blacks in the cities. Southern and eastern Europeans, now the largest population groups, began to arrive in the late 19th century, Hispanics and Southeast Asians in the 20th. In 1980, 6.9 percent of Pennsylvania's population spoke a language other than English at home.

Major museums and libraries

Academy of Natural Sciences Museum, Philadelphia
Art Museum, Pittsburgh
Brandywine River Museum, Chadd's Ford
Carnegie Museum of Natural History, Pittsburgh
Franklin Institute Science Museum, Philadelphia
Frick Art Museum, Pittsburgh
Pennsylvania Academy of the Fine Arts, Philadelphia
Philadelphia Museum of Art
Rodin Musem, Philadelphia
University Museum, University of Pennsylvania, Philadelphia
William Penn Memorial Museum, Harrisburg

Major arts organizations

Civic Light Opera, Pittsburgh
Fulton Opera House, Lancaster
Opera Company of Philadelphia
Pennsylvania and Milwaukee Ballet, Philadelphia
Philadelphia Drama Guild
Philadelphia Orchestra
Pittsburgh Opera Company
Pittsburgh Public Theater
Pittsburgh Symphony Orchestra

Pittsburgh Theatre
Walnut Street Theatre, Pittsburgh

Colleges and universities
Number public (1986-87) 62
Number private (1986-87) 150
Total enrollment, in full-time equivalent
students (1985) 422,300

Public elementary and secondary schools
Expenditure per pupil in average daily
attendance (1986-87) $4,691
Pupil-teacher ratio (1987) 16.3
Average teacher salary (1986-87) $28,042

Major league sports teams
Baseball: Philadelphia Phillies, Pittsburgh
Pirates
Basketball: Philadelphia 76ers
Football: Philadelphia Eagles, Pittsburgh
Steelers
Hockey: Philadelphia Flyers, Pittsburgh
Penguins

Holidays
State Fair, Harrisburg. 2d week in
January

PENNSYLVANIA IN LITERATURE

Hervey Allen *The City in the Dawn* (1950)
Abridged version of a trilogy of historical novels that begins with *The Forest and the Fort* (1943), set in western Pennsylvania at the time of Pontiac's rising.

Ammon M. Aurand *Aurand's Collection of Pennsylvania German Stories and Poems* (1916)
——. *Pennsylvania German Dialect Stories and Poems* (1939)

Irving Bacheller *In the Days of Poor Richard* (1922)
Novel set in Revolutionary times containing a portrait of Franklin.

James Boyd *Roll River* (1935)
Realistic historical novel about four generations of a nineteenth-century Harrisburg family.

David Boyer *The Sidelong Glimpses of a Pigeon Watcher* (1968)
Comic novel about an eccentric Philadelphia cab driver.

David Bradley *The Chaneysville Incident* (1981)
Historical novel centering on the early-nineteenth-century murder of a group of slaves.

Millen Brand and **George A. Tice** *Fields of Peace: A Pennsylvania German Album* (1970)
Evocation, in photographs and verse, of the life of the Amish community.

John J. Burke *The Writer in Philadelphia, 1682–1982* (1983)

K. C. Constantine *The Rocksburg Railroad Murders* (1972)
First of a series of detective novels about the police chief of a small western Pennsylvania town in the 1970s.

Marcia Davenport *Valley of Decision* (1942)
Saga of an iron-working family from 1873 to the 1940s.

Margaret Wade Deland *Old Chester Tales* (1898)
Collection of sketches of small-town life in a fictional community closely based on Manchester near Pittsburgh. Though dated, Deland's fiction gives an accurate portrayal of middle-class life at the turn of the century.

David P. Demarest (ed.) *From These Hills, from These Valleys: Selected Fiction about Western Pennsylvania* (1976)
Anthology of writing, 1760–1970.

Pete Dexter *God's Pocket* (1983)
Novel set in a blue-collar Philadelphia neighborhood.

Federal Writers' Project *Tales of Pioneer Pittsburgh: Sponsored by the Western Pennsylvania Committee on Folklore* (1937)

Charles Flood *Monmouth* (1961)
Historical novel of the Revolution, with an account of Valley Forge.

Benjamin Franklin *Autobiography* (1818, ed. L. W. Labaree, 1964)
Franklin's unfinished narrative of his life until 1757 offers glimpses of Philadelphia society and a detailed portrait of a colonial American businessman.

Earl C. Haag (ed.) *A Pennsylvania German Anthology* (1988)
Collection of dialect writing.

Josephine Herbst *Satan's Sergeants* (1941)
Novel about social tension in a Bucks County community in the 1930s.

Joseph Hergesheimer *The Three Black Pennys* (1917)
Classic novel of the decline of a family that owes its wealth to the iron industry.

Albert Idell *Centennial Summer* (1943)
Story of family life in Philadelphia in 1876. The Rogers family's later life in Brooklyn was described in two sequels.

Joseph Jackson *Literary Landmarks of Philadelphia* (1939)

Mildred Jordan *Echo of the Flute* (1958)
Novel about a Philadelphia family, 1776–1793.

MacKinlay Kantor *Long Remember* (1934)
The Battle of Gettysburg seen through the eyes of a resident of the town.

Stephen Longstreet *Gettysburg* (1961)
Novel describing reactions of ordinary townsfolk to the battle.

Tom McHale *Principato* (1971)
Novel set in the Italian/Irish community of South Philadelphia.

David McKain *Spellbound: Growing Up in God's Country* (1988)
Autobiography of growing up in a small town in the Alleghenies during the 1940s and '50s.

Silas Weir Mitchell *Hugh Wynne, Free Quaker* (1897); *Red City* (1908)
Classic historical novels of Philadelphia life during and after the Revolution.

Christopher Morley *Travels in Philadelphia* (1920)
Essays on city neighborhoods.

Albert C. Myers (ed.) *Sally Wister's Journal: A True Narrative, Being a Quaker Maiden's Account of Her Experiences with Officers of the Continental Army, 1777–1778* (1902)
——. *Narratives of Early Pennsylvania, West New Jersey, and Delaware, 1630–1707* (1989)
Twenty early accounts of Dutch, Swedish, German, and Welsh settlement of the Delaware Bay.

John O'Hara *49 Stories* (1962)
Collection of stories of the eastern Pennsylvania town in which much of O'Hara's realistic fiction about upper-middle-class society takes place.

Jay Parini *The Patch Boys* (1986)
Novel about coming of age in an Italian-Polish coal mining town in 1925.

Cornelia Parker *Fabulous Valley* (1956)
Novel about the 1859 discovery of oil.

David Philipson (ed.) *Letters of Rebecca Gratz* (1929, rpt. 1975)
Correspondence of a prominent early-nineteenth-century Philadelphia philanthropist who was the model of the character of Rebecca in Walter Scott's *Ivanhoe*.

Conrad Richter *The Free Man* (1943)
Historical novel about a German immigrant to pre-Revolutionary Philadelphia.

Earl F. Robacker *Pennsylvania German Literature* (1943)

Don Robertson *The Three Days* (1959)
Fictional account of the Battle of Gettysburg.

Michael Shaara *The Killer Angels* (1974)
Pulitzer prize–winning novel depicting the Battle of Gettysburg from the point of view of officers on both sides.

Elsie Singmaster *Kathy Gaumer* (1915)
First in a series of novels about Pennsylvania Germans that was the first fictional treatment of this culture. The author was also well-known for her biography of Thaddeus Stevens (1947) and *Gettysburg* (1913), a collection of stories about the battle.

Neil Swanson *The Judas Tree* (1933)
Historical novel of the 1763 siege of Fort Pitt.
———. *The First Rebel* (1937)
Historical novel of King George's War, 1744–1748.

Agnes Sligh Turnbull *The Day Must Dawn* (1942)
Novel of pioneer life in western Pennsylvania before the Revolutionary War. The author was known for her numerous novels, both with historical and contemporary settings, about the Scottish people of the western coal regions. *The King's Orchard* (1963) is a fictional biography of James O'Hara, Washington's quartermaster and a prominent early citizen of Pittsburgh.

John Updike *The Olinger Stories* (1964)
Stories that, like parts of the later "Rabbit" sequence, describe a manufacturing town much like the author's native Shillington.

Cornelius Weygandt *Philadelphia: The Place and the People* (1925)
Informal, nostalgic description of the city. The author wrote of the state's culture in a similar style in *The Red Hills* (1929) and *The Blue Hills* (1936).

Richard Wheeler (ed.) *Witness to Gettysburg* (1987)
Collection of first-hand accounts by soldiers on both sides.

John E. Wideman *Hiding Place* (1981); *Sent for You Yesterday* (1983); *Damballah* (1988)
Collections of related stories set in the black community of Homewood in Pittsburgh's east end.

GUIDES TO RESOURCES

Clawser, N. Clair *A Guide to Pennsylvania Towns* (4th ed. 1982)

Clint, Florence *Pennsylvania Area Key: A Guide to the Genealogical Records of the State of Pennsylvania, Including Maps, Histories, Charts and Other Helpful Materials* (2d ed. 1976)

Federal Writers' Project *The WPA Guide to Philadelphia* (1937, rpt. 1988)
———. *Pennsylvania: A Guide to the Keystone State* (1940)

McBride, David *The Afro-American in Pennsylvania: A Critical Guide to Sources in the Pennsylvania State Archives* (1979)

Miller, E. Willard *An Economic Atlas of Pennsylvania* (1964)
——— and **Ruby M.** *Pennsylvania—Architecture and Culture: A Bibliography* (1985)
——— and **Ruby M.** *Pennsylvania—Natural Resources and Economic Development: A Bibliography* (1985)
——— and **Ruby M.** *Pennsylvania—Transportation: A Bibliography* (1985)

——— and **Ruby M.** *Pennsylvania—History and Politics: A Bibliography* (1986)

Pennsylvania Historical and Museum Commission *Guide to the Historical Markers of Pennsylvania, Erected by the Pennsylvania Historical and Museum Commission* (4th ed. 1975)

Pennsylvania State Library Division of Library Services *A Guide to the Genealogy/Local History Section of the State Library of Pennsylvania* (1986)

Stevens, S. K. (rev. Donald H. Kent) *Pennsylvania History in Outline* (4th ed. 1976)

Wilkinson, Norman B. (ed. S. K. Stevens and D. H. Kent) *Bibliography of Pennsylvania History* (1957)

Wurman, Richard and **John A. Gallery** *Man-Made Philadelphia: A Guide to Its Physical and Cultural Environment* (1972)

SELECTED NONFICTION SOURCES

Alderfer, Harold F. *Pennsylvania Local Government, 1681–1974* (1975)

Arbuckle, Robert D. *Pennsylvania Speculator and Patriot: The Entrepreneurial John Nicholson, 1757–1800* (1975)

Aurand, Harold W. *From the Molly Maguires to the United Mine Workers: The Social Ecology of an Industrial Union, 1869–1897* (1971)

Baldwin, Leland D. *Pittsburgh: The Story of a City* (1937)
———. *Whiskey Rebels: The Story of a Frontier Uprising* (1939)

Baltzell, E. Digby *The Philadelphia Gentlemen: The Making of a National Upper Class* (1958, rpt. 1979)

Beard, Charles A. (ed.) *The Journal of William Maclay, United States Senator from Pennsylvania, 1789–1791* (1927)

Beers, Paul B. *Profiles from the Susquehanna Valley; Past and Present Vignettes* . . . (1973)
———. *Profiles in Pennsylvania Sports: Athletic Heroes and Exploits* . . . (1975)

Bell, Whitfield J., Jr. *John Morgan: Continental Doctor* (1965)

Billinger, Robert D. *Pennsylvania's Coal Industry* (1954)

Binder, Frederick M. *Coal Age Empire: Pennsylvania Coal and Its Utilization to 1860* (1974)

Bining, Arthur C. *Pennsylvania Iron Manufacture in the Eighteenth Century* (1973)

Binzen, Peter *White Town USA* (1970)

Bodnar, John *Anthracite People: Families, Unions and Work, 1900–1940* (1983)

Boland, Charles M. *Ring in the Jubilee: The Epic of America's Liberty Bell* (1973)

Book, Janet M. *Northern Rendezvous: Harrisburg during the Civil War* (1951)

Borie, Beauveau, IV *Farming and Folk Society: Threshing among the Pennsylvania Germans* (1986)

Bradley, Edward S. *Henry Charles Lea, 1825–1909: A Biography* (1931)

Brailsford, Mabel *The Making of William Penn* (1939)

Bridenbaugh, Carl and **Jessica** *Rebels and Gentlemen: Philadelphia in the Age of Franklin* (1962)

Brodie, Fawn M. *Thaddeus Stevens: Scourge of the South* (1959)

Brown, Ira V. *Pennsylvania Reformers: From Penn to Pinchot* (1966)

Brunhouse, Robert L. *The Counter-Revolution in Pennsylvania, 1776–1790* (1971)

Buck, Solon J. and **Elizabeth H.** *The Planting of Civilization in Western Pennsylvania* (1939)

Burmeister, Walter *The Susquehanna River and Its Tributaries* (1975)

Burnett, Edmund C. *The Continental Congress* (1941)

Burt, Nathaniel *The Perennial Philadelphians: The Anatomy of an American Aristocracy* (1963)

Canby, Henry S. *The Brandywine* (1941)

Carter, Jane L. *The Paper Makers: Early Pennsylvanians and Their Water Mills* (1982)

Chew, Paul A. (ed.) *250 Years of Art in Pennsylvania* (1959)

Clark, Dennis *The Irish in Philadelphia: Ten Generations of Urban Experience* (1973)
——— (ed.) *Philadelphia, 1776–2076: A Three Hundred Year View* (1975)

Clarkson, Thomas *Memories of the Private and Public Life of William Penn* (1849)

Cochran, Thomas C. *Pennsylvania: A Bicentennial History* (States and the Nation series) (1978)

Coddington, Edwin B. *The Gettysburg Campaign: A Study in Command* (1968)

Cohen, Bernard I. (ed.) *Benjamin Franklin's Experiments* (1942)

Coleman, John M. *Thomas McKean: Forgotten Leader of the Revolution* (1975)

Cornell, William A. *Our Pennsylvania Heritage* (rev. ed. 1973)

Crippen, Lee F. *Simon Cameron, the Antebellum Years* (1942)

Cummings, Hubertis M. *The Mason and Dixon Line: Story for a Bicentenary, 1763–1963* (1962)

Current, Richard N. *Old Thad Stevens: A Story of Ambition* (1943)

Davies, Edward J. *The Anthracite Aristocracy: Leadership and Social Change in the Hard Coal Regions of Northeastern Pennsylvania, 1800–1930* (1985)

Davis, Allen F. and **Mark H. Haller** (eds.) *The Peoples of Philadelphia: A History of Ethnic Groups and Lower-Class Life, 1790–1940* (1973)

DeArmond, A. J. *Andrew Bradford, Colonial Journalist* (1949)

Del Tredici, Robert *The People of Three Mile Island* (1980)

Dickson, Harold E. *One Hundred Pennsylvania Buildings* (1954)
———. *Pennsylvania Painters* (1955)

Doerflinger, Thomas M. *A Vigorous Spirit of Enterprise: Merchants and Economic Development in Revolutionary Philadelphia* (1986)

Dolson, Hildegarde *The Great Oildorado: The Gaudy and Turbulent Years of the First Oil Rush* (1959)

Dunaway, Wayland F. *A History of Pennsylvania* (2d ed. 1961)

Eastman, Frank M. *Courts and Lawyers of Pennsylvania: A History, 1623–1923* 3 vols. (1922)

Egle, William H. *Pennsylvania Women in the American Revolution* (1898, rpt. 1972)

Endy, Melvin B. *William Penn and Early Quakerism* (1973)

Ershkowitz, Miriam and **Joseph Zikmund** (eds.) *Black Politics in Philadelphia* (1973)

Evans, Frank B. *Pennsylvania Politics, 1872–1877: A Study in Political Leadership* (1966)

Faris, John T. *Old Trails and Roads in Penn's Land* (1927)

Fletcher, Stevenson W. *Pennsylvania Agriculture and Country Life* 2 vols. (1950, 1955)

Ford, Daniel F. *Three Mile Island: Thirty Minutes to Meltdown* (1982)

Ford, Edward *David Rittenhouse, Astronomer-Patriot, 1732–1796* (1946)

Gibson, James E. *Dr. Bodo Otto and the Medical Background of the American Revolution* (1937)

Gilchrist, Agnes A. *William Strickland: Architect and Engineer* (1950)

Glass, Joseph W. *The Pennsylvania Culture Region: A View from the Barn* (1986)

Govan, Thomas P. *Nicholas Biddle, Nationalist and Public Banker, 1786–1844* (1959)

Gray, Mike and **Ira Rosen** *The Warning: Accident at Three Mile Island* (1982)

Hamilton, Fred J. *Rizzo* (1973)

Hanna, William S. *Benjamin Franklin and Pennsylvania Politics* (1964)

Hassler, Warren W., Jr. *Crisis at the Crossroads: The First Day at Gettysburg* (1970)

Hawke, David *In the Midst of a Revolution* (1961)

Heiges, George L. *Henry William Stiegel and His Associates: A Story of Early American Industry* (1948)

Higginbotham, Sanford W. *The Keystone in the Democratic Arch: Pennsylvania Politics 1800–1816* (1952)

Hull, William I. *William Penn, a Topical Biography* (1937, rpt. 1971)

Illick, Joseph E. *Colonial Pennsylvania: A History* (1976)

James, Reese D. *Old Drury of Philadelphia: A History of the Philadelphia Stage from 1800–1835* (1932)

Jensen, Arthur L. *The Maritime Commerce of Colonial Philadelphia* (1963)

Kelley, Joseph J. *Life and Times in Colonial Philadelphia* (1973)
———. *Pennsylvania, the Colonial Years, 1681–1776* (1980)

Kent, Barry C. *Susquehanna's Indians* (1984)

Kent, Donald H. *The French Invasion of Western Pennsylvania* (1981)

Klein, Philip S. *Pennsylvania Politics, 1817–1832; a Game without Rules* (1940, rpt. 1974)
——— and **Ari Hoogenboom** *A History of Pennsylvania* (1973)

Lemay, J. A. Leo *Ebenezer Kinnersley, Franklin's Friend* (1964)

Lemon, James T. *The Best Poor Man's Country: A Geographical Study of Early Southern Pennsylvania* (1972)

Lichten, Frances *Folk Art of Rural Pennsylvania* (1946)
———. *Folk Art Motifs of Pennsylvania* (1954)

Livingood, James W. *The Philadelphia-Baltimore Trade Rivalry, 1780–1860* (1947)

Lubove, Roy (ed.) *Pittsburgh* (1976)

Lukacs, John *Philadelphia: Patricians and Philistines, 1900–1950* (1981)

Magda, Matthew S. *Monessen: Industrial Boomtown and Steel Community, 1898–1980* (1985)

McClure, Alexander K. *Old Time Notes of Pennsylvania* 2 vols. (1905)

McCullough, David G. *The Johnstown Flood* (1968)

Meyer, Carolyn *Amish People: Plain Living in a Complex World* (1976)

Miller, Richard G. *Philadelphia—the Federalist City: A Study of Urban Politics, 1789–1801* (1976)

Moses, M. J. *Fabulous Forrest: The Record of an American Actor* (1929)

Mueller, Henry R. *The Whig Party in Pennsylvania* (1922)

Newcomb, Benjamin H. *Franklin and Galloway: A Political Partnership* (1972)

Oblinger, Carl *Cornwall: The People and Culture of an Industrial Camelot, 1890–1980* (1984)

Panaccio, Tim *Beast of the East: Penn State vs Pitt: A Game-by-Game History of America's Greatest Football Rivalry* (1982)

Pennsylvania Historical Association *Pennsylvania Religious Leaders* (1985)

Platt, John D. R. *The City Tavern: Independence National Historical Park, Philadelphia, Pennsylvania* (1973)

Pound, Arthur *The Penns of Pennsylvania and England* (1932)

Powell, H. Benjamin *Philadelphia's First Fuel Crisis: Jacob Cist and the Development Market for Pennsylvania Anthracite* (1978)

Powell, John H. *Bring Out Your Dead: The Great Plague of Yellow Fever in Philadelphia in 1793* (1949)

Quimby, Ian M. G. *Apprenticeship in Colonial Philadelphia* (1985)

Raymond, Eleanor *Early Domestic Architecture of Pennsylvania* (1931)

Reiser, Catherine E. *Pittsburgh's Commercial Development, 1800–1850* (1951)

Richman, Irwin *The Brightest Ornament: A Biography of Nathaniel Chapman, M.D.* (1967)
———. *Pennsylvania Architecture* (1969)

Ricker, Ralph R. *The Greenback-Labor Movement in Pennsylvania* (1966)

Riedman, Sarah R. and Clarence C. Green *Benjamin Rush: Physician, Patriot, Founding Father* (1964)

Roberts, Ellis W. *The Breaker Whistle Blows: Mining Disasters and Labor Leaders in the Anthracite Region* (1984)

Rohrer, Gertrude M. (comp.) *Music and Musicians of Pennsylvania* (1940)

Rosenberg, Max *The Building of Perry's Fleet on Lake Erie, 1812–1813* (1974)

Rowell, John W. *Yankee Cavalrymen: Through the Civil War with the Ninth Pennsylvania Cavalry* (1971)

Ruck, Rob *Sandlot Seasons: Sport in Black Pittsburgh* (1987)

Russ, William A. *How Pennsylvania Acquired Its Present Boundaries* (1966)

Sack, Saul *History of Higher Education in Pennsylvania* 2 vols. (1963)

Salay, David L. (ed.) *Hard Coal, Hard Times: Ethnicity and Labor in the Anthracite Region* (1984)

Sapio, Victor A. *Pennsylvania and the War of 1812* (1970)

Sass, Steven A. *The Pragmatic Imagination: A History of the Wharton School, 1881–1981* (1982)

Saylor, Roger B. *The Railroads of Pennsylvania* (1964)

Schwartz, Laurens R. *Jews and the American Revolution: Haym Salomon and Others* (1987)

Schwartz, Sally *A Mixed Multitude: The Struggle for Toleration in Colonial Pennsylvania* (1989)

Schweitzer, Mary M. *Custom and Contract: Household, Government, and the Economy in Colonial Pennsylvania* (1987)

Scranton, Philip *Proprietary Capitalism: The Textile Manufacture at Philadelphia, 1800–1885* (1983)
——— and Walter Licht *Work Sights: Industrial Philadelphia, 1890–1950* (1986)

Secor, Robert (ed.) *Pennsylvania 1776* (1976)

Shank, William H., 2d *Great Floods of Pennsylvania* (1974)
———. *Historic Bridges of Pennsylvania* (2d ed. 1974)

Sharpless, Isaac *Political Leaders of Provincial Pennsylvania* (1919)

Singmaster, Elsie *I Speak for Thaddeus Stevens* (1947)

Smeltzer, Gerald *Canals along the Lower Susquehanna* (1963)

Snyder, Charles M. *The Jacksonian Heritage: Pennsylvania Politics, 1833–1848* (1958)

Soderlund, Jean R. et al. (eds.) *William Penn and the Founding of Pennsylvania, 1680–1684: A Documentary History* (1983)

Stevens, Sylvester K. *Pennsylvania: Keystone State* 2 vols. (1956)
———. *Pennsylvania, Birthplace of a Nation* (1964)

Stille, Charles J. *Major-General Anthony Wayne and the Pennsylvania Line in the Continental Army* (1968)

Stradley, Leighton P. *Early Financial and Economic History of Pennsylvania* (1942)

Strohmeyer, John *Crisis in Bethlehem: Big Steel's Struggle to Survive* (1986)

Swetnam, George *Pennsylvania Transportation* (1964)

Tatum, George *Penn's Great Town; 250 Years of Philadelphia Architecture Illustrated in Prints and Drawings* (1961)

Thompson, Ray *The Walking Purchase Hoax of 1737* (1973)

Tinkcom, Harry M. *The Republicans and Federalists in Pennsylvania, 1790–1801: A Study in National Stimulus and Local Response* (1950)

Tolles, Frederick B. *Meeting House and Courting House: The Quaker Merchants of Colonial Philadelphia, 1682–1763* (1948)

Tonkin, Dudley *My Partner, the River: The White Pine Story on the Susquehanna* (1958)

Trussell, John B. B., Jr. *Pennsylvania Military History* (1975)
———. *Birthplace of an Army: A Study of the Valley Forge Encampment* (1983)
———. *William Penn, Architect of a Nation* (1983)

Van Trump, James D. *Life and Architecture in Pittsburgh* (1983)

Ver Steeg, Clarence *Robert Morris: Revolutionary Financier* (1954)

Wainwright, Nicholas B. (ed.) *A Philadelphia Perspective: The Diary of Sidney George Fisher Covering the Years 1834–1871* (1967)

Wakefield, Manville B. *Canal Boats to Tidewater: The Story of the Delaware and Hudson Canal* (1965)

Wall, Joseph F. *Andrew Carnegie* (1970)

Wallace, Anthony F. C. *St. Clair: A Nineteenth-Century Coal Town's Experience with a Disaster-Prone Industry* (1987)

Wallace, Paul A. W. *The Muhlenbergs of Pennsylvania* (1950)
———. *Indian Paths of Pennsylvania* (1971)
———. *Indians in Pennsylvania* (rev. ed. 1981)

Warner, Sam B. *The Private City: Philadelphia in Three Periods of Its Growth* (1968)

Watson, John F. *Annals of Philadelphia and Pennsylvania in Olden Time* . . . 3 vols. (1905)

Weigley, Russell F. (ed.) *Philadelphia: A 300 Year History* (1982)

White, Theo B. *Fairmount, Philadelphia's Park: A History* (1975)

Wildes, Harry E. *The Delaware* (Rivers of America series) (1940)
———. *Lonely Midas: The Story of Stephen Girard* (1943)
———. *William Penn* (1974)

Williams, Richard E. (ed. Cheryl Dorschner) *Called and Chosen: The Story of Mother Rebecca Jackson and the Philadelphia Shakers* (1981)

Williams, William H. *America's First Hospital: The Pennsylvania Hospital, 1751–1841* (1976)

Wilson, George *Yesterday's Philadelphia* (1975)

Wilson, Robert H. *Philadelphia, U.S.A.* (1975)

Wolf, Edwin *Philadelphia, Portrait of an American City: A Bicentennial History* (1975)

Wolf, Stephanie G. *An Urban Village: Population, Community and Family Structure in Germantown, Pennsylvania* (1976)

Wood, Jerome H., Jr. *Conestoga Crossroads: Lancaster, Pennsylvania, 1730–1790* (1979)

Wood, Ralph *The Pennsylvania Germans* (1942)

Wright, Esmond *Franklin of Philadelphia* (1986)

RHODE ISLAND

The New England state of Rhode Island is bordered on the north and east by Massachusetts; on the south by Block Island Sound and Rhode Island Sound; and on the west by Connecticut.

FULL NAME State of Rhode Island and Providence Plantation

POSTAL ABBREVIATION RI

INHABITANT Rhode Islander

ADMITTED TO THE UNION May 29, 1790. 13th state

POPULATION (est. 1987) 986,000. Percent of US total: 0.41%. Rank: 43d

CAPITAL CITY Providence, located on the Providence River and Narragansett Bay in eastern Rhode Island; population 154,148 (est. 1984). The Baptist dissenter Roger Williams founded Providence in 1636 after his exile from Plymouth Colony. Until 1900 it shared capital status with Newport.

STATE NAME AND NICKNAMES Probably from the Dutch *roodt eylandt*, "red island," in reference to its red clay shores. Possibly from the explorer Giovanni da Verrazano's comparison of Block Island to the Mediterranean island of Rhodes in 1524. Also known as Little Rhody, the Smallest State, the Land of Roger Williams, the Plantation State, and the Ocean State.

STATE SEAL An anchor, and above it, on a scroll, the state motto; around the border, in gold on blue, the legend "Seal of the State of Rhode Island and Providence Plantations, 1636."

MOTTO Hope

SONG "Rhode Island," lyrics and music by T. Clarke Brown

SYMBOLS
Flower violet
Tree red maple
Bird Rhode Island Red chicken
Mineral bowenite
Rock cumberlandite
American folk art symbol Charles I.D. Looff Carousel

LICENSE PLATE Blue on white, with blue border, anchor, and legend "Ocean State."

FLAG On a white field, the state coat of arms: a gold anchor and below it a blue ribbon with the state motto in gold, encircled by thirteen gold stars.

GEOGRAPHY AND CLIMATE

Narragansett Bay is the central feature of Rhode Island, the smallest state. The bay, containing the Newport islands, cuts up from Rhode Island Sound into the eastern part of the state as far north as Providence. The central and western part of Rhode Island is mainly flat, with glacial till soil that is best suited for pasturage. Rocky coastline alternates with sandbars and salt marsh.

AREA 1,212 square miles. Rank: 50th

INLAND WATER 157 square miles

GEOGRAPHIC CENTER Kent, 1 mile SSW of Crompton

ELEVATIONS *Highest point:* Jerimoth Hill, Providence, 812 feet. *Lowest point:* Atlantic Ocean, sea level. *Mean elevation:* 200 feet

MAJOR RIVERS Pawtuxet, Sakonnet, Blackstone/Seekonk, Woonasquatucket, Pawcatuck, Moshassuck

MAJOR RESERVOIR Scituate

TIDAL SHORELINE 384 miles, Atlantic coast

LAND USE

	Thousands of acres
Urban (1982)	140
Rural (1982)	508
Cropland (1982)	27
Pastureland (1982)	36
Rangeland (1982)	0
Forestland (1982)	406
State parks and recreation areas (1983)	11
National park system (1984)	0
National forest system (1984)	0
Tribal lands (1984)	0

TEMPERATURES The highest recorded temperature was 104°F on August 2, 1975, at Providence. The lowest was -23°F on January 11, 1942, at Kingston.

NATIONAL SITES

NATIONAL HISTORIC SITE Touro Synagogue
NATIONAL MEMORIAL Roger Williams
NATIONAL WILDLIFE REFUGES Ninigret–Block Island/Nantucket/Sachuest Point/Salt Meadow/Trustom Pond

HISTORY

1511	Miguel Corte Real, a Portuguese navigator, sails along the Rhode Island coast. Probably, he is the first white man to see the land.
1524	Giovanni da Verrazano, sailing for France, explores Narragansett Bay.
1614	Adriaen Block may have named the region. He was a Dutch navigator who referred to a Narragansett Bay island as "Roodt Eyland" (Red Island).
1635	The first white explorers find five peaceful Indian tribes living along the coast. They all belong to the Algonkian family.
1636	Roger Williams is called "Father of Rhode Island." Seeking religious freedom he leaves Massachusetts and starts first permanent settlement at Providence, Rhode Island.
1638	Anne Hutchinson and others, also seeking religious freedom, move to Aquidneck Island in Narragansett Bay.
1639	First Baptist church in America organized at Providence.
1641	Benedict Arnold, great grandfather of Benedict Arnold, Revolutionary War traitor, purchases land at Pawtucket, north of Providence.
1644	Name of Aquidneck is officially changed to Rhode Island. Earl of Warwick grants Rhode Island its first charter.
1647	*May 29–31.* General Assembly draws up a constitution that calls for separation of church and state.
1654	Rhode Island Colony grants first naval commission to a Newport vessel.
1657	Benedict Arnold becomes president of colony. He serves as governor three more times. First Quakers settle in Rhode Island.
1658	Fifteen Jewish families from Holland arrive in Newport.
1663	Providence sets aside lands for maintenance of a school. *July 8.* Charles II grants Rhode Island a charter guaranteeing religious freedom.
1664	Block Island becomes part of the colony of Rhode Island.
1671	Forge, sawmill, and carpenter shops are set up at Pawtucket Falls.

1675	*December 19*. The Great Swamp Fight breaks the power of the Narragansetts under Chief Canonchet.
1676	*August 12*. King Philip is killed and the war ends between Indians and white settlers.
1680	First warehouse and wharf are built in Providence.
1693	First postal route between Boston and Rhode Island is established.
1704	First Trinity Church building erected in Newport.
1711	Quarantine act against smallpox legislated for first time.
1723	Execution of 26 pirates at Newport.
1727	First Rhode Island printing press established.
1732	Colony's first newspaper, *Rhode Island Gazette,* issued at Newport.
1754	Providence Library Assocation is chartered.
1763	Rhode Island College incorporated. It becomes Brown University in 1804.
1765	Governor Samuel Ward refuses oath to enforce the Stamp Act.
1772	*June 9*. Colonists burn the British revenue cutter *Gaspée* in rebellion of trade regulations.
1774	Rhode Island prohibits the importation of slaves.
1776	*May 4*. Rhode Island becomes the first colony to declare its independence from England. The colony sends General Nathanael Greene to fight for independence.
1778	*August 29*. British seize Newport and evacuate American troops.
1781	Public reception given to General George Washington in Newport.
1784	The Rhode Island assembly abolishes slavery.
1790	*May 29*. Rhode Island is last of 13 original colonies to ratify the US Constitution. Delegates refuse to sign until amendments recognize rights of smaller states.
1793	Samuel Slater and Moses Brown establish the first cotton textile mill in Pawtucket.
1813	British occupy Block Island during the second war with Great Britain. Commodore Oliver Hazard Perry of Rhode Island defeats British in Lake Erie naval battle.
1824	First recorded strike involving female employees occurs in Pawtucket.
1835	First train runs between Boston and Providence.
1842	Dorr's Rebellion results in the adoption of a more liberal state constitution.
1852	State legislature abolishes capital punishment.
1861	First Rhode Island troops join Union Forces in Civil War. More than 24,000 Rhode Islanders serve in the Union Army.
1870	State legislature abolishes imprisonment for debts.
1885	Prohibition amendment added to State Constitution but it is repealed in 1889.
1895	"Rhode Island Red" hen officially recognized as a new breed.
1903	Wireless telegraph installed in Rhode Island.
1917–1918	Nearly 28,000 Rhode Islanders serve in armed forces during World War I.
1920	National prohibition amendment is not ratified by Rhode Island. State legislature ratifies the 19th Amendment (nationwide suffrage for women).
1922	Radio broadcasting begins over stations WEAN and WJAR.
1925	Department of State Police created.
1931	General Nathanael Greene statue at State House is dedicated.
1933	Rhode Islanders approve the 21st Amendment which repeals prohibition.
1938	Disastrous hurricane and tidal wave kill over 300 persons and cause over $100 million in property damage.
1941–1945	World War II. Providence shipyards build 64 combat and cargo ships.
1946	Law requiring employers to pay women equal wages to men is passed.
1954	Two severe hurricanes cause great damage.
1955	Rhode Island is declared a major disaster area because of flooding.
1956	Rhode Islanders approve bond issue for Korean War veterans' bonus.
1969	Newport Bridge, a 1,600-foot suspension span, is completed across Narragansett Bay.
1971	Democrat governor, Frank Licht, signs first income tax into operation.

1972	Brown University announces expansion of medical program resulting in the first full medical school in the state.
1973	State prison riot causes much damage. Reform-minded warden resigns.
1976	Rhode Island's US Bicentennial celebration, "Operation Sail," results in an armada of square riggers to Newport and then on to New York City.
1979	Energy is critical issue with an unprecedented midyear gasoline shortage. Faculty strike occurs at University of Rhode Island.
1983	State's economic condition improves steadily after general depression.
1988	*August 8*. Rhode Island celebrates V.J. Day, the second Monday in August. It is the only state that still celebrates the victory over Japan in World War II.

DEMOGRAPHY

Population (est. 1987) 986,000
Population (1980) 947,154
Population density in persons
  per square mile (1980) . . . 781.5

POPULATION BY RACE (1980)
American Indian/Aleut/
  Eskimo 2,898
Asian/Pacific Islander 5,303
Black 27,584
Hispanic 19,707
White 896,692
Other 14,677

POPULATION CHARACTERISTICS (1980)
    Percent of state population
Urban 87.0
Rural 13.0
Under 18 . . . . 25.7
65 or older 13.4
College-educated 15.3
Families below poverty line 7.7
Public-assistance recipients 7.2

Per capita personal income
  (1986) $14,670
Millionaires per 100,000
  residents (1982) 83.9

Average life expectancy in
  years (1980) 74.8
Marriage rate (1986) 8.2
Divorce rate (1986) 3.7
Birth rate per 1,000
  residents (1985) 14.0
Infant mortality rate per 1,000
  births (1985) 9.5
Abortion rate per 1,000
  live births (1985) 572
Crime rate per 100,000
  residents (1985)
  Violent 335.5
  Property 4,567.0
Federal and state prisoners per
  100,000 residents (1984) 128
Alcohol consumption in gallons
  per capita (1985) 43.3
Deaths from motor vehicle accidents
  per 100,000 residents (1985) . . 11.3

MAJOR CITIES
	Population
Pawtucket (est. 1984)	72,803
Providence (est. 1984)	154,148
Warwick (1980)	87,123
Woonsocket (est. 1984)	45,162

GOVERNMENT AND POLITICS

Number of US Representatives   2
Electoral votes   4

POLITICAL PARTY NOMINEES FROM STATE

Henry Brewer Metcalf (Prohi-
  bition)   1900 VP
Florence Garvin (National
  Greenback)   1936 VP
Richard Walton (Citizens)   1984 VP

PRESIDENTIAL PRIMARY ELECTION In 1988, Rhode Island sent 26 Democratic delegates and 21 Republican delegates to the national conventions.

CONSTITUTION Rhode Island is using its original constitution, adopted in 1842.
LEGISLATURE The General Assembly is divided into the Senate (50 members, 2-year term, minimum age 18) and the House of Representatives (100 members, 2-year term, minimum age 18). In 1987, the salary for legislators was $5 per day for a maximum of 60 days.
JUDICIARY The highest court is the Supreme Court, with 5 judges serving for life. In 1987, the annual salary was $78,642.
EXECUTIVE The governor serves a 2-year term; there is no minimum age for holding office. In 1987, the annual salary was $69,900. There are 4 other elected officials.

PRESIDENTIAL VOTE 1948-1988 *(in percents)*

Year	State Winner	Democratic	Republican
1948	Truman (D)	57.6	41.4
1952	Eisenhower (R)	49.1	50.9
1956	Eisenhower (R)	41.7	58.3
1960	Kennedy (D)	63.6	36.4
1964	Johnson (D)	80.9	19.1
1968	Humphrey (D)	64.0	31.8
1972	Nixon (R)	46.8	53.0
1976	Carter (D)	55.4	44.1
1980	Carter (D)	47.7	37.2
1984	Reagan (R)	47.9	51.8
1988	Dukakis (D)	56.0	44.0

GOVERNORS

Colonial Governors

Benedict Arnold	1663-1666
William Brenton	1666-1669
Benedict Arnold	1669-1672
Nicholas Easton	1672-1675
William Coddington	1674-1676
Walter Clarke	1676-1677
Benedict Arnold	1677-1678
William Coddington	1678
John Cranston	1678-1680
Peleg Sanford	1680-1683
William Coddington, Jr.	1683-1685
Henry Bull	1685-1686
Walter Clarke	1686
John Coggeshall (acting)	1689-1690
Henry Bull	1690
John Easton	1690-1695
Caleb Carr	1695
Walter Clarke	1696-1698
Samuel Cranston	1698-1727
Joseph Jenckes	1727-1732
William Wanton	1732-1733
John Wanton	1734-1740
Richard Ward	1740-1743
William Greene	1743-1745
Gideon Wanton	1745-1746
William Greene	1746-1747
Gideon Wanton	1747-1748
William Greene	1748-1755
Stephen Hopkins	1755-1757
William Greene	1757-1758
Stephen Hopkins	1758-1762
Samuel Ward	1762-1763
Stephen Hopkins	1763-1765
Samuel Ward	1765-1767
Stephen Hopkins	1767-1768
Josias Lyndon	1768-1769
Joseph Wanton	1769-1775
Nicholas Cooke	1775-1778
William Greene	1778-1786

State Governors

John Collins (Country)	1786-1790
Arthur Fenner (Anti-Federalist/Democratic-Republican)	1790-1805
Paul Mumford (D-R/acting)	1805
Henry Smith (D-R/acting)	1805-1806
Isaac Wilbour (D-R/acting)	1806-1807
James Fenner (D-R)	1807-1811
William Jones (Federalist)	1811-1817
Nehemiah R. Knight (D-R)	1817-1821
William C. Gibbs (D-R)	1821-1824
James Fenner (D-R)	1824-1831
Lemuel H. Arnold (National Republican/Whig)	1831-1833
John Brown Francis (National Republican/Whig)	1833-1838
William Sprague (Whig/Antimason)	1838-1839
Samuel Ward King (Whig/Antimason)	1839-1843
James Fenner (Law and Order)	1843-1845
Charles Jackson (Liberation)	1845-1846
Byron Diman (Whig/Law and Order)	1846-1847
Elisha Harris (Whig/Law and Order)	1847-1849
Henry B. Anthony (Whig/Law and Order)	1849-1851
Philip Allen (D)	1851-1853
Francis M. Dimond (D/acting)	1853-1854
William W. Hoppin (Whig/Know-Nothing/Republican)	1854-1857
Elisha Dyer (R)	1857-1859
Thomas G. Turner (R)	1859-1860
William Sprague (Union Democrat)	1860-1863
William C. Cozzens (Union Democrat/acting)	1863
James Y. Smith (R)	1863-1866

Ambrose E. Burnside (R)	1866-1869
Seth Padelford (R)	1869-1873
Henry Howard (R)	1873-1875
Henry Lippitt (R)	1875-1877
Charles C. Van Zandt (R)	1877-1880
Alfred H. Littlefield (R)	1880-1883
Augustus O. Bourn (R)	1883-1885
George P. Wetmore (R)	1885-1887
John W. Davis (D)	1887-1888
Royal C. Taft (R)	1888-1889
Herbert W. Ladd (R)	1889-1890
John W. Davis (D)	1890-1891
Herbert W. Ladd (R)	1891-1892
D. Russell Brown (R)	1892-1895
Charles W. Lippitt (R)	1895-1897
Elisha Dyer (R)	1897-1900
William Gregory (R)	1900-1901
Charles D. Kimball (R)	1901-1903
Lucius F.C. Garvin (D)	1903-1905
George H. Utter (R)	1905-1907
James H. Higgins (D)	1907-1909
Aram J. Pothier (R)	1909-1915
R. Livingston Beeckman (R)	1915-1921
Emery J. San Souci (R)	1921-1923
William S. Flynn (D)	1923-1925
Aram J. Pothier (R)	1925-1928
Norman S. Case (R)	1928-1933
Theodore F. Green (D)	1933-1937
Robert E. Quinn (D)	1937-1939
William H. Vanderbilt (R)	1939-1941
J. Howard McGrath (D)	1941-1945
John O. Pastore (D)	1945-1951
Dennis J. Roberts (D)	1951-1959
Christopher Del Sesto (R)	1959-1961
John A. Notte, Jr. (D)	1961-1963
John H. Chafee (R)	1963-1969
Frank Licht (D)	1969-1973
Philip W. Noel (D)	1973-1977
J. Joseph Garrahy (D)	1977-1985
Edward D. Di Prete (R)	1985-

MINIMUM AGES

Majority	18
Marriage with parental consent	
female	16
male	18
Marriage without parental consent	18
Making a will	18
Buying alcohol	21
Jury duty	18
Leaving school	16
Driver's license	16

CAPITAL PUNISHMENT
None

MILITARY INSTALLATIONS
Total number: 8
Major bases:
  Navy: 1

FINANCES

Thousands of dollars

GENERAL REVENUE (1985)

Total general revenue	1,859,583
Total tax revenue	862,070
Sales and gross receipts	454,392
Individual income taxes	281,742
Corporate net income taxes	70,504

GENERAL EXPENDITURE (1985)

Total general expenditure	1,786,915
Education	489,448
Public welfare	431,764
Health	71,673
Hospitals	107,900
Natural resources	12,241
Highways	117,231
Police	17,625
Corrections	37,711

FEDERAL AID (1985) 573,163

ECONOMY

Rhode Island's chief farm products are dairy products, chickens and eggs, potatoes, feed corn, apples and other orchard fruits, hay, and vegetables. Agriculture is a small part of the state economy, with farm marketing cash receipts $31 million in 1983, second lowest in the nation (after Alaska). The state's commercial fishing industry brings in about twice as much income as does agriculture, $66 million in 1983; the catch is mainly lobster, cod, scrod, flounder, hake, scup, whiting, mackerel, and herring. Machinery and primary metals refining and fabrication are the biggest manufactured products, followed by defense equipment (ships and submarines), electrical machinery, jewelry and metalware, textiles, plastics and chemicals, and high-tech instruments. Value added by manufacture was $3.8 billion in 1982, higher than that of many larger states.

EMPLOYMENT (1984)

Thousands of persons

Total number of employed workers	464
Construction	12.6
Finance, insurance, and real estate	22.6
Government	57.4
Manufacturing	120.6
Mining	0.1
Services	97.2

Transportation, communications,
utilities 13.7
Wholesale and retail trade 88.0

Percent of civilian labor force
unemployed (1984) 5.3

DEPARTMENT OF DEFENSE (1985)
Civilian workers employed . . . 4,715
Military personnel 4,037
Contract awards . . . . . $431 million

ENERGY SOURCES FOR ELECTRIC UTILITIES (1983)
Percent
Coal 0.0
Gas 42.5

Hydroelectric 0.5
Nuclear 0.0
Petroleum 57.2

TRANSPORTATION
Motor vehicles registered
in state (1986) 631,818
Miles of roads, streets,
and highways (1986) 5,997
Miles of Class I railway
operated (1986) . . . . N/A
Airports (1983) 18
Major aviation hubs (1983) 1
Largest hub: Providence

CULTURE AND EDUCATION

Native American tribes
Rhode Island was formerly home to the Niantic, Nipmuc, Pequawket, Pequot, and Sakonnet tribes. Groups that continue to live in the state include the Narragansett and Wampanoag.

Religions, ethnicities, and languages
Founded as a refuge for religious dissenters, Rhode Island in its colonial days took in many English Protestants, Quakers, French Huguenots, and Sephardic Jews from Portugal. Irish Catholics, who now make up the state's largest group, began to arrive in the 1820s. Together with the French Canadians, Portuguese, Cape Verdeans, Italians, Poles, Ukrainians, and Lithuanians who came in the late 19th and early 20th centuries, they have made Rhode Island the state with the highest concentration of Roman Catholics (almost 65 percent of the state's churchgoers). Immigrants also came from Germany, Greece, Armenia, Syria, and more recently from the American South, the Portuguese islands, Latin America, and Southeast Asia. In 1980, 16.5 percent of Rhode Island's population spoke a language other than English at home.

Major museums and libraries
Haffenreffer Museum, Bristol
Museum of Art, Rhode Island School of Design, Providence
Newport Historical Society Museum
Providence Athenaeum
Redwood Library, Newport

Major arts organizations
Rhode Island Philharmonic Orchestra, Providence
State Ballet of Rhode Island
Trinity Repertory Company, Providence

Colleges and universities
Number public (1986-87) 3
Number private (1986-87) 10
Total enrollment, in full-time equivalent students (1985) 53,000

Public elementary and secondary schools
Expenditure per pupil in average daily attendance (1986-87) $4,574
Pupil-teacher ratio (1987) 15.0
Average teacher salary (1986-87) $32,026

Holidays
Rhode Island Independence Day. May 4
Victory Day. 2d Monday in August

RHODE ISLAND IN LITERATURE

Israel Angell *Diary of Colonel Israel Angell* (1899, rpt. 1971)
Eyewitness account of the Revolution.

Louis Auchincloss *The House of Five Talents* (1960)
Chronicle novel of a wealthy family, 1880–1940, depicting Newport society in its heyday.

Robert Bray and **Paul Bushnell** (eds.) *Diary of a Common Soldier in the American Revolution, 1775–1783: An Annotated Edition of the Military Journal of Jeremiah Greenman* (1978)
Greenman's journal, one of the very few eyewitness accounts of the entire war, was discovered in Illinois in the early 1980s.

David C. De Jong *Benefit Street* (1942)
Novel set in a seedy Providence boardinghouse in 1938.

Maud Howe Elliott *This Was My Newport* (1944)
Memoir of Newport upper-class society.

Adelos Gorton *The Life and Times of Samuel Gorton* (1907)
Biography of the rebel against Puritan dogma and founder of a sect, the Gortonites, who established a community at Warwick.

Caroline Hazard *Narragansett Ballads* (1984)

Thomas Robinson Hazard *Recollections of Olden Times* (1879); *Jonny Cake Letters* (1882)
Hazard (1797–1886), better-known as "Shepherd Tom," was a sheepfarmer, textile manufacturer, and eccentric collector of tall tales who campaigned against Puritan values

and espoused a number of humane causes. His books preserve both authentic and bogus Rhode Island folklore. *The Jonny Cake Letters of "Shepherd Tom"* appeared in 1915.

Thomas Wentworth Higginson *Oldport Days* (1873)
An evocation of Newport during the years of its decline as a port and growing popularity as a resort.

Henry James *The Ivory Tower* (1917)
Unfinished novel set in late-nineteenth-century Newport.

Hortense Lion *Mill Stream* (1941)
Historical novel of Providence, 1790–1812.

Benjamin Lippincott *Indians, Privateers, and High Society: A Rhode Island Sampler* (1961)
Collection of historical essays.

Edward McSorley *Our Own Kind* (1946)
Novel of an Irish immigrant family in South Providence in the early twentieth century.

David Plante *The Family* (1978)
Novel of a French-Canadian childhood in Providence.

Gilbert Rees *I Seek a City* (1950)
Fictional autobiography of Roger Williams, founder of the state.

Jeanne L. Richardson (comp.) *A Bibliography of Selected Contemporary Rhode Island Authors* (1984)

Samuel Rogers *Dusk at the Grove* (1934)
Novel of domestic life set at a summer house, 1909–1931.

William Schofield *Ashes in the Wilderness* (1942)
Novel about King Phillip's War.

William S. Simmons *Old Light on Separate Ways: The Narragansett Diary of Joseph Fish* (1982)

Harriet Beecher Stowe *The Minister's Wooing* (1859, rpt. 1982)
Romance set in Newport, partly based on the life of the author's sister, and reflecting Stowe's questioning of the Calvinist basis of New England Christianity.

Thornton Wilder *Theophilus North* (1973)
Comic, episodic novel portraying incidents in the life of a tutor to children of the Newport wealthy in 1929.

Chilton Williamson, Jr. *Saltbound: A Block Island Winter* (1980)

John T. Winterich *Another Day, Another Dollar* (1947)
Memoir of growing up in Providence at the turn of the century.

GUIDES TO RESOURCES

Austin, John O. *Genealogical Dictionary of Rhode Island* (1887, rpt. 1982)

Coyle, Wallace *Roger Williams: A Reference Guide* (1977)

Davis, Hadassah and **Natalie Robinson** *History You Can See: Scenes of Change in Rhode Island, 1790–1910*

Federal Writers' Project *Rhode Island: A Guide to the Smallest State* (1937, rpt. 1973)

Lamar, Christine *A Guide to Genealogical Materials at the Rhode Island Historical Society Library* (rev. ed. 1985)

Olsen, Stephen, Donald D. Robadue, Jr., and **Virginia Lee** *An Interpretive Atlas of Narragansett Bay* (1980)

Parks, Roger (ed.) *Rhode Island: A Bibliography of Its History* (Bibliographies of New England History, vol. 5) (1983)

Rhode Island Department of Economic Development *Rhode Island Basic Economic Statistics* (1965–)

Sanderson, Edward F. and **W. M. Woodward** *Providence: A Citywide Survey of Historical and Architectural Resources* (1986)

Sea Grant Program *Rhode Island Marine Bibliography* (1973)

Sperry, Kip *Rhode Island Sources for Family Historians and Genealogists* (1986)

Wright, Marion I. and **Robert J. Sullivan** *The Rhode Island Atlas* (1982)

SELECTED NONFICTION SOURCES

Alderman, Clifford L. *The Rhode Island Colony* (1969)

Aldrich, Nelson *Old Money* (1988)

Arnold, Samuel G. *History of the State of Rhode Island and Providence Plantations (1859–60)* 2 vols. (4th ed. 1894, rpt. 1970)

Bates, Frank G. *Rhode Island and the Formation of the Union* (Studies in History, Economics and Public Law, vol. 10, no. 2) (1898, rpt. 1967)

Bavier, Robert N. *America's Cup Fever: An Inside View of Fifty Years of America's Cup Competition* (rev. ed. 1981)

Beals, Carleton *Colonial Rhode Island* (1970)

Boss, Judith A. *Newport: A Pictorial History* (1981)

Bridenbaugh, Carl *Fat Mutton and Liberty of Conscience: Society in Rhode Island, 1636–1690* (1974)
———. *Silas Downer: Forgotten Patriot; His Life and Writings* (1974)

Brigham, Herbert O. *The Old Stone Mill* (1948)

Brockunier, S. H. *The Irrepressible Democrat: Roger Williams* (1940)

Buhle, Paul et al. (eds.) *A History of Rhode Island Working People* (1983)

Carpenter, Ralph E. *The Arts and Crafts of Newport, Rhode Island, 1640–1820* (1954)

Carroll, Charles C. *Rhode Island, Three Centuries of a Democracy* 4 vols. (1932)

Chapin, Anna A. and **Charles V.** *A History of the Rhode Island Ferries, 1640–1923* (1925)

Chapin, Howard M. *Rhode Island Privateers in King George's War, 1739–1748* (1926)

Chyet, Stanley F. *Lopez of Newport: Colonial American Merchant Prince* (1970)

Coleman, Peter J. *The Transformation of Rhode Island, 1790–1861* (1969)

Conley, Patrick T. *Democracy in Decline: Rhode Island's Constitutional Development, 1776–1841* (1977)
———. *Rhode Island Profile* (1983)
——— and **Paul R. Campbell** *Rhode Island Historical Development: An Interpretative Essay* (1985)
———. *An Album of Rhode Island History, 1636–1986* (1986)
———, **Robert O. Jones**, and **W. M. Woodward** *The State Houses of Rhode Island: An Architectural and Historical Legacy* (1986)

Corbett, Scott *Rhode Island* (1969)

Coughtry, Jay *The Notorious Triangle: Rhode Island and the African Slave Trade, 1700–1807* (1981)

Crane, Elaine F. *A Dependent People: Newport, Rhode Island in the Revolutionary Era* (1985)

Crolius, Peter C. *A Wickford Anthology* (1985)
——— (ed.) *The Rhode Island Scene* (1986)

Cunha, M. Rachel (ed. Patrick T. Conley) *The Portuguese in Rhode Island: A History* (1985)

Daniels, Bruce C. *Dissent and Conformity on Narragansett Bay: The Colonial Rhode Island Town* (1984)

Davis, Arthur W. *Yachting in Narragansett Bay, 1921–1945* (1946)

Dearden, Paul F. *The Rhode Island Campaign of 1778: Inauspicious Dawn of Alliance* (1980)

Denis, Michael J. *Rhode Island Towns and Counties* (1983)

Dennison, George M. *The Dorr War: Republicanism on Trial, 1831–1861* (1976)

Dershowitz, Alan M. *Reversal of Fortune: Inside the von Bulow Case* (1986)

Downing, Antoinette F. *Early Homes of Rhode Island* (1937)
——— and V. J. Scully, Jr. *The Architectural Heritage of Newport, Rhode Island, 1640–1915* (2d ed. 1967)

Dunlap, G. D. *America's Cup Defenders* (1970)

Ernst, James *Roger Williams, New England Firebrand* (1932, rpt. 1969)

Field, Edward *Esek Hopkins, Commander-in-Chief of the Continental Navy, 1775–1778* (1898)
———. *The State of Rhode Island* 3 vols. (1902)

Fleming, Donald *Science and Technology in Providence, 1760–1914* (1952)

Foster, Geraldine S. (ed. Patrick T. Conley) *The Jews in Rhode Island: A Brief History* (1985)

Gettleman, Marvin E. *The Dorr Rebellion* (1973)

Gilkeson, John S., Jr. *Middle-Class Providence, 1820–1940* (1986)

Gleeson, Paul F. *Rhode Island, the Development of a Democracy* (1957)

Goldblatt, Burt *Newport Jazz Festival: The Illustrated History* (1977)

Goodman, Jay S. *The Democrats and Labor in Rhode Island, 1952–1962* (1967)

Gorton, Adelos *The Life and Times of Samuel Gorton* (1907)

Guinness, Desmond and Julius T. Sadler, Jr. *Newport Preserv'd: Architecture of the 18th Century* (1982)

Hazard, Caroline *The Narragansett Friends Meeting in the Eighteenth Century* (1899)

Hazleton, Robert M. *Let Freedom Ring: A Biography of Moses Brown* (1957)

Hedges, James B. *The Browns of Providence Plantations: Colonial Years* (1952)
———. *The Browns of Providence Plantations: The Nineteenth Century* (1968)

Hitchcock, Henry R. *Rhode Island Architecture* (1939, rpt. 1968)

James, Sydney V. *Colonial Rhode Island: A History* (1975)

Kimball, Gertrude S. (ed.) *Pictures of Rhode Island in the Past, 1642–1833, by Travellers and Observers* (1900)
——— (ed.) *The Correspondence of the Colonial Governors of Rhode Island, 1723–1775* 2 vols. (1902–1903)

Lippincott, Bertram *Indians, Privateers, and High Society; a Rhode Island Sampler* (1961)

Lovejoy, David S. *Rhode Island Politics and the American Revolution, 1760–1776* (1958)

Macaulay, David *Mill* (1983)

Mayer, Kurt B. *Economic Development and Population Growth in Rhode Island* (1953)
——— and Sidney Goldstein *Migration and Economic Development in Rhode Island* (1958)

McLoughlin, William G. *Rhode Island: A Bicentennial History* (States and the Nation series) (1978)

Mohr, Ralph S. *Governors for Three Hundred Years, 1638–1959; Rhode Island and Providence Plantations* (1959)
———. *Rhode Island Footprints on the Sands of Time: A Bicentennial Remembrance* (1975)

Morgan, E. S. *Roger Williams, the Church and the State* (1967)

Mowry, Arthur M. *The Dorr War: or the Constitutional Struggle in Rhode Island* (1901)

Mullins, Lisa C. (ed.) *Early Architecture of Rhode Island* (1988)

Patten, David *Rhode Island Story* (1954)

Polishook, Irwin H. *Rhode Island and the Union, 1774–1795* (1969)

Preston, Howard Willis *Rhode Island and the Sea* (1932)

Richman, Irving B. *Rhode Island, a Study in Separatism* (1905)
———. *Rhode Island, Its Making and Its Meaning* (1908)

Rogers, Horatio *Mary Dyer of Rhode Island: The Quaker Martyr* (1896)

Rugg, W. K. *Unafraid: A Life of Anne Hutchinson* (1930)

Simister, Florence P. *The Fire's Center: Rhode Island in the Revolutionary Era* (1979)

Smith, Judith E. *Family Connections: A History of Italian and Jewish Lives in Providence, Rhode Island, 1900–1940* (1985)

Staples, William R. (ed. Reuben A. Guild) *Rhode Island in the Continental Congress, 1765–1790 . . .* (1870, rpt. 1971)
———. (ed. Richard M. Deasy) *The Documentary History of the Destruction of the Gaspee* (1986)

Stone, Herbert L. (rev. by William H. Taylor) *The America's Cup Races* (1958)

Straus, Oscar S. *Roger Williams, the Pioneer of Religious Liberty* (1936)

Sutton, Robert W., Jr. (ed.) *Rhode Island Local Government: Past, Present, Future* (1974)

Thompson, Mack E. *Moses Brown* (1962)

Van Rensselaer, May *Newport: Our Social Capital* (1905)

Walker, Anthony *So Few the Brave: Rhode Island Continentals, 1775–1783* (1981)

Weeden, William B. *Early Rhode Island: A Social History of the People 1763–1790* (1910)

Whipple, Chandler *The Indian and the White Man in Massachusetts and Rhode Island* (1974)

Wilson, Arthur E. *Weybosset Bridge* (1947)

Winslow, Ola E. *Master Roger Williams* (1957, rpt. 1973)

Withey, Lynne *Urban Growth in Colonial Rhode Island: Newport and Providence in the Eighteenth Century* (1984)

Woodward, Carl R. *Plantation in Yankeeland; the Story of Cocumscussoc, Mirror of Colonial Rhode Island* (1971)

Wright, William *The Von Bulow Affair* (1983)

SOUTH CAROLINA

South Carolina is a South Atlantic state. Roughly triangular in shape, it is bordered on the north by North Carolina; on the southeast by the Atlantic Ocean; and on the southwest by Georgia and the Savannah River.

FULL NAME State of South Carolina
POSTAL ABBREVIATION SC
INHABITANT South Carolinian
ADMITTED TO THE UNION May 23, 1788.
 8th state
POPULATION (est. 1987) 3,425,000.
 Percent of US total: 1.41%. Rank: 24th

CAPITAL CITY Columbia, located on the Congaree River in central South Carolina; population 98,634 (est. 1984). The site was settled about 1700 and was chosen in 1786 as a compromise site for the state capital. It was incorporated as a village in 1805 and a city in 1854.

STATE NAME AND NICKNAMES Named in honor of King Charles IX of France and then of King Charles I and King Charles II of England. Also known as the Rice State, the Swamp State, the Keystone of the South Atlantic Seaboard, the Iodine State, and the Palmetto State.

STATE SEAL Within a circle, two ellipses, showing the obverse and reverse of the seal. On the left, the arms, showing a palmetto tree with 12 spears bound to its trunk and the legend "Quis Separabit" (Who Shall Separate?) on a ribbon; hanging from its branches two shields, inscribed "March 26" and "July 4"; below it an uprooted oak, and the legend "Meliorem Lapsa Locavit, 1776" (Having Fallen, It Has Set Up a Better One); around the border, the legend "South Carolina," and one of the state mottoes. On the right, the figure of Hope ("Spes") walking toward the rising sun on a seashore strewn with weapons, a laurel sprig in her hand, and around the border the second state motto.

MOTTOES Animus Opibusque Parati (Prepared in mind and resources); Dum Spiro Spero (While I breathe I hope)

SONGS "Carolina," lyrics by Henry Timrod, music by Anne Custis Burgess; "South Carolina On My Mind."

SYMBOLS
Flower yellow jessamine
Tree palmetto tree
Bird Carolina wren
Gem amethyst
Stone blue granite
Animal white-tailed deer
Fish striped bass or rockfish
Fruit peach
Shell lettered olive
Beverage milk
Dance the shag

LICENSE PLATE Dark blue on white, with state name in red and state tree in light blue.

FLAG On a blue field, a palmetto tree, and in the upper right corner a crescent moon.

GEOGRAPHY AND CLIMATE

South Carolina contains three geographic zones: the Coastal Plain, a low-lying, marshy region stretching in from the Atlantic coast about 100-150 miles; the Piedmont, hilly land rising gradually in elevation; and in the extreme western corner of the state the Blue Ridge range of the Appalachians. Below the long crescent beach that comprises South Carolina's northern shoreline is a series of semitropical coastal islands, the Sea Islands. The state has a humid subtropical climate.

AREA 31,113 square miles. Rank: 40th
INLAND WATER 910 square miles
GEOGRAPHIC CENTER Richland, 13 miles SE of Columbia
ELEVATIONS *Highest point:* Sassafras Mountain, Pickens County, 3,560 feet. *Lowest point:* Atlantic Ocean, sea level. *Mean elevation:* 350 feet

MAJOR RIVERS Pee Dee, Santee, Edisto, Savannah

MAJOR LAKES AND RESERVOIRS Marion, Moultrie, Murray, Hartwell, Keowee, Catawba, Clark Hill

TIDAL SHORELINE 2,876 miles, Atlantic coast

LAND USE

	Thousands of acres
Urban (1982)	839
Rural (1982)	16,681
Cropland (1982)	3,579
Pastureland (1982)	1,208
Rangeland (1982)	0
Forestland (1982)	11,026
State parks and recreation areas (1983)	81
National park system (1984)	21
National forest system (1984)	1,382
Tribal lands (1984)	0

TEMPERATURES The highest recorded temperature was 111°F on June 28, 1954, at Camden. The lowest was -19°F on January 21, 1985, at Caesars Head.

NATIONAL SITES

NATIONAL BATTLEFIELD Cowpens
NATIONAL HISTORIC SITES Historic Camden, Ninety Six
NATIONAL MILITARY PARK Kings Mountain
NATIONAL MONUMENTS Congaree Swamp, Fort Sumter
NATIONAL WILDLIFE REFUGES Cape Romain, Carolina Sandhills, Pinckney Island, Santee, Savannah

HISTORY

1521	Francisco Gordillo, sailing from San Domingo, cruises the Carolina coast, capturing and enslaving Indians.
1525	Hilton Head island is discovered by Pedro de Quexos.
1526	Spanish explorer, Lucas Vazquez de Ayllón, erects the first settlement, but it is soon abandoned.
1566	A Spanish settlement is established at Santa Elena (Hilton Head).
1663	Charles II grants the region to eight lord proprietors.
1670	*March.* Charles Town is established at Albermarle Point.
1680	Charles Town is moved to Oyster Point.
	45 French Protestants arrive from England.
1686	Spanish from St. Augustine raid Edisto Island and Port Royal.
1693	The populace is granted power to initiate legislation.
1695	Approximately 500 French Huguenots live in and around Charles Town.
1698	The first library is established in Charles Town by Thomas Bray.
1703	*May 8.* The province issues its first paper money.
1706	*November 30.* The province is divided into 12 parishes as the Church of England becomes the state church.
1712	The Carolinas are made into two separate provinces, each with its own governor.
1715	The Yamasee War breaks out with the massacre of 90 at Pocataligo and 100 at Port Royal.
	Under a reactionary policy, proprietors could not give aid during the Indian war.
1719	Colonists overthrow the British proprietors and elect James Moore as governor.
1725	Pelt trading and rice plantations supply an economic basis for the society.
1729	The English Crown purchases the province from the lord proprietors.

1730	Nine townships are laid out to extend the settlement and provide for a better defense.
	Boundary lines, defining the two Carolinas, are begun but not completed until 1815.
1736	The Dock Street Theatre is built in Charles Town.
1739	Twenty-one whites are killed in the Stono slave insurrection.
1740	Shipbuilding begins at Charles Town and Beaufort.
	Nearly half of Charles Town is destroyed by fire.
1744	Commerical production of indigo is made possible by Eliza Lucas.
1755	*November 30.* Joseph Salvador purchases land near Fort Ninety Six for Jewish settlement.
1769	"Regulators" attempt to suppress horse-stealing and arson in the inland settlements.
1773	America's first public museum is organized at Charles Town.
1775	*June 4.* A council of safety is appointed to manage the affairs of the colony.
	September 15. Royal administration ends when Governor William Campbell dissolves the assembly and flees.
1776	*March 26.* The patriots draw up a state constitution.
	June 28. Colonel William Moultrie successfully defends Fort Sullivan against British fleet.
1777	*May 20.* Cherokee cede to South Carolina all their land except a small area in the Northwest.
1778	*March 19.* A revised state constitution disestablishes the Anglican Church.
1780	*May 12.* Charles Town surrenders to the British after a two-month siege.
	August 16. Earl Charles Cornwallis defeats General Horatio Gates's American troops at Camden.
	October 7. British Major Patrick Ferguson and Loyalists are defeated at Kings Mountain.
1781	*January 17.* American General Dan Morgan defeats Cornwallis at Cowpens.
	September 8. American troops, led by General Nathanael Greene, lose the battle at Eutaw Springs, but severely weaken British forces.
1782	*December 12.* The British evacuate Charles Town.
1783	Charles Town is renamed Charleston.
1788	*May 23.* South Carolina is the eighth state to ratify the US Constitution.
1790	The capital is moved from Charleston to Columbia to ease the struggle between the aristocratic Low country and the poorer, industrial Up country.
1793	Eli Whitney invents the cotton gin in Georgia and the industry in South Carolina comes to rule the land. Demand for black slave labor increases greatly.
1800	The Santee Canal is completed.
1803	South Carolina legislature re-opens slave trade with Latin America and the West Indies.
1810	Suffrage is extended to all white males.
1822	A slave conspiracy, led by Denmark Vessey, is suppressed.
1828	The *Southern Review* is founded, maintaining Charleston's status as cultural center of the South.
1830	*January.* Robert Y. Hayne of South Carolina and Daniel Webster of Massachusetts debate philosophies of American government.
	September 20. A public meeting on states' rights is held in Columbia.
1832	A special state convention nullifies the Tariff Act.
	December 28. John C. Calhoun, South Carolina's spokesman for nullification, resigns as vice president.
1833	The South Carolina Railroad, running between Charleston and Hamburg, is completed.
1860	*December 20.* South Carolina is the first state to secede from the Union.
1861	*April 12.* Confederate troops fire on Fort Sumter, leading the nation into the Civil War.
1865	*February 17.* General William T. Sherman burns Columbia.
1868–1874	During the "Rule of the Robbers" public debt rises from $5 million to $20 million while patients in state hospitals go without food.

1868	*June 25.* The state is readmitted to the Union.
1876	White militants called Red Shirts support the gubernatorial candidate Wade Hampton, a former Confederate general, and intimidate black voters.
1877	*April.* Federal troops are removed, Congressional reconstruction is ended, and Hampton takes office.
1886	*August 31.* An earthquake centered in Charleston kills 92 and causes $8 million in damage.
1890	Benjamin R. Tillman, leader of the Farmers Alliance and industrial workers, is elected governor.
1893	*August 24.* A hurricane kills 1,000 along the coast.
1895	Blacks are disenfranchised by revisions in the constitution.
1896	South Carolina holds its first direct primary election.
1910	Rice production has mostly ended and cotton is the leading crop until 1950.
1915	State-wide prohibition is enacted.
1917	Camp Wadsworth in Spartanburg is a training center for troops for World War I.
1921	The boll weevil destroys much of the cotton crop. Many farmers turn to cattle raising.
1930	The tenant system is characteristic of 65% of the state farms. Breher Shoals dam and power house on the Saluda River is completed.
1940	The textile industry employs 75% of the state's industrial workforce. *June.* Fort Jackson is made a permanent military post. *August.* Hurricane kills 40.
1951	The Savanah River Plant of the United States Atomic Energy Commission is erected. Its main purpose is to manufacture plutonium for nuclear weapons.
1952	*January 28.* The Supreme Court upholds segregation in South Carolina and this decision is reaffirmed by a three-judge federal court in March.
1963	Black student Harvey B. Gantt enrolls in Clemson College, challenging segregation in the last state to adopt integration.
1964	Schools desegregate without incident.
1968	*February 7.* Classes at South Carolina State College are suspended following violence and student rioting against segregation in a local bowling alley in Orangeburg. *February 8.* Three blacks are killed by police during rioting in Orangeburg. National Guardsmen seal off the deserted college campuses.
1970	Sixty-two percent of the state's land is woodland. *January 15.* State police close one of the nation's first anti-war GI coffeehouses near Fort Jackson.
1971	*February 16.* Twenty-two whites are indicted on riot charges for overturning two school buses carrying black students in March, 1970.
1973	*March 31–April 1.* A tornado devastates the state.

DEMOGRAPHY

Population (est. 1987) . . . 3,425,000
Population (1980) 3,122,874
Population density in persons
  per square mile (1980) 100.4

POPULATION BY RACE (1980)
American Indian/Aleut/
  Eskimo 5,758
Asian/Pacific Islander 11,807
Black 948,146
Hispanic 33,414
White 2,145,122
Other 8,375

POPULATION CHARACTERISTICS (1980)
           Percent of state population
Urban 54.1
Rural 45.9
Under 18 . . . . 30.1
65 or older 9.2
College-educated 14.2
Families below poverty line . . . 13.1
Public-assistance recipients 7.6

Per capita personal income
  (1986) $11,096
Millionaires per 100,000
  residents (1982) 68.2

Average life expectancy
in years (1980) 71.9
Marriage rate per 1,000
residents (1986) 16.0
Divorce rate per 1,000
residents (1986) 4.0
Birth rate per 1,000
residents (1985) 14.7
Infant mortality rate per 1,000
births (1985) 14.0
Abortion rate per 1,000
live births (1985) 228
Crime rate per 100,000
residents (1985)
Violent 674.6
Property 4,462.8

Federal and state prisoners per
100,000 residents (1984) 297
Alcohol consumption in gallons
per capita (1985) 38.0
Deaths from motor vehicle accidents
per 100,000 residents (1985) . . 28.4

MAJOR CITIES

	1984 population (est.)
Charleston	67,108
Columbia	98,634
Greenville	57,351
Spartanburg	43,880

GOVERNMENT AND POLITICS

Number of US Representatives   6
Electoral votes   8

POLITICAL PARTY NOMINEES FROM STATE
*winner

John Rutledge	1789	P
Thomas Pinckney	1796	P
Charles Cotesworth Pinckney	1796	P
Charles Cotesworth Pinckney (Federalist)	1800	VP
Charles Cotesworth Pinckney (Federalist)	1804	P
Charles Cotesworth Pinckney (Federalist)	1808	P
John Caldwell Calhoun* (Democratic-Republican)	1824	VP
John Caldwell Calhoun* (D-R)	1828	VP
James Strom Thurmond (States' Rights Democrat)	1948	P

PRESIDENTIAL PRIMARY ELECTION In 1988, South Carolina sent 48 Democratic delegates and 37 Republican delegates to the national conventions.

CONSTITUTION South Carolina has had seven constitutions: 1776, 1778, 1790, 1861, 1865, 1868, and the present one, adopted in 1895.

LEGISLATURE The General Assembly is divided into the Senate (46 members, 4-year term, minimum age 25) and the House of Representatives (124 members, 2-year term, minimum age 21). In 1987, the annual salary was $10,000.

JUDICIARY The highest court is the Supreme Court, with 5 judges serving 10-year terms. In 1987, the annual salary was $80,657.

EXECUTIVE The governor serves a 4-year term; the minimum age for holding office is 30. In 1987, the annual salary was $81,600. There are 8 other elected officials.

PRESIDENTIAL VOTE 1948-1988 *(in percents)*

Year	State Winner	Democratic	Republican
1948	J. Strom Thurmond (States' Rights Democrat), 72.0	24.1	3.0
1952	Stevenson (D)	50.7	49.3
1956	Stevenson (D)	45.4	25.2
1960	Kennedy (D)	51.2	48.8
1964	Goldwater (R)	41.1	58.9
1968	Nixon (R)	29.6	38.1
1972	Nixon (R)	27.7	70.8
1976	Carter (D)	56.2	43.1
1980	Reagan (R)	48.1	49.4
1984	Reagan (R)	35.6	63.6
1988	Bush (R)	38.0	62.0

GOVERNORS

Proprietary Governors

William Sayle	1669-1671
Joseph West	1671-1672
Sir John Yeamans	1672-1674
Joseph West	1674-1682
Joseph Morton	1682-1684
Sir Richard Kyrle	1684
Joseph West	1684-1685
Robert Quary	1685
Joseph Morton	1685-1686
James Colleton	1686-1690
Seth Sothell	1690-1692
Phillip Ludwell	1692-1693
Thomas Smith	1693-1694
Joseph Blake (acting)	1694-1695
John Archdale	1695-1696
Joseph Blake	1696-1700
James Moore	1700-1703
Sir Nathaniel Johnson	1703-1709
Edward Tynte	1709-1710
Robert Gibbes	1710-1712
Charles Craven	1712-1716
Robert Daniel (deputy governor)	1716-1717
Robert Johnson	1717-1719

Royal Governors

James Moore	1719-1721
Sir Francis Nicholson	1721-1725
Arthur Middleton	1725-1730
Robert Johnson	1730-1735
Thomas Broughton (lieutenant governor)	1735-1737
William Bull (lieutenant governor)	1737-1743
James Glen	1743-1756
William H. Lyttelton	1756-1760
William Bull, 2d (lieutenant governor)	1760-1761
Thomas Boone	1761-1764
William Bull, 2d (lieutenant governor)	1764-1766
Lord Charles Greville Montagu	1766-1768
William Bull, 2d (lieutenant governor)	1768
Lord Charles Greville Montagu	1768-1769
William Bull, 2d (lieutenant governor)	1769-1771
Lord Charles Greville Montagu	1771-1773
William Bull, 2d (lieutenant governor)	1773-1775
Lord William Campbell	1775

State Governors

John Rutledge (president)	1776-1778
Rawlins Lowndes (president)	1778-1779
John Rutledge	1779-1782
John Mathewes	1782-1783
Benjamin Guerard	1783-1785
William Moultrie	1785-1787
Thomas Pinckney	1787-1789
Charles Pinckney	1789-1792
William Moultrie (Federalist)	1792-1794
Arnoldus Vanderhorst (Federalist)	1794-1796
Charles Pinckney (Democratic-Republican)	1796-1798
Edward Rutledge (Federalist)	1798-1800
John Drayton (D-R)	1800-1802
James B. Richardson (D-R)	1802-1804
Paul Hamilton (D-R)	1804-1806
Charles Pinckney (D-R)	1806-1808
John Drayton (D-R)	1808-1810
Henry Middleton (D-R)	1810-1812
Joseph Alston (D-R)	1812-1814
David R. Williams (D-R)	1814-1816
Andrew Pickens (D-R)	1816-1818
John Geddes (D-R)	1818-1820
Thomas Bennett (D-R)	1820-1822
John L. Wilson (D-R)	1822-1824
Richard I. Manning (D-R)	1824-1826
John Taylor (D-R)	1826-1828
Stephen D. Miller (D-R)	1828-1830
James Hamilton, Jr. (D)	1830-1832
Robert Y. Hayne (D)	1832-1834
George McDuffie (D)	1834-1836
Pierce M. Butler (D)	1836-1838
Patrick Noble (D)	1838-1840
B.K. Henegan (D/acting)	1840
John P. Richardson (D)	1840-1842
James H. Hammond (D)	1842-1844
William Aiken (D)	1844-1846
David Johnson (D)	1846-1848
Whitemarsh B. Seabrook (D)	1848-1850
John H. Means (D)	1850-1852
John L. Manning (D)	1852-1854
James H. Adams (D)	1854-1856
Robert F.W. Allston (D)	1856-1858
William H. Gist (D)	1858-1860
Francis W. Pickens (D)	1860-1862
Milledge L. Bonham (D)	1862-1864
Andrew G. Magrath (D)	1864-1865
Benjamin F. Perry (D/provisional)	1865
James L. Orr (Provisional)	1865-1868
Robert K. Scott (Conservative)	1868-1872
Franklin J. Moses, Jr. (R)	1872-1874
Daniel H. Chamberlain (R)	1874-1876
Wade Hampton (R)	1876-1879

William D. Simpson (D/acting)	1879-1880
Thomas B. Jeter (D)	1880
Johnson Hagood (D)	1880-1882
Hugh S. Thompson (D)	1882-1886
John C. Sheppard (D/acting)	1886
John P. Richardson (D)	1886-1890
Benjamin R. Tillman (D)	1890-1894
John G. Evans (D)	1894-1897
William H. Ellerbe (D)	1897-1899
Miles B. McSweeney (D)	1899-1903
Duncan C. Heyward (D)	1903-1907
Martin F. Ansel (D)	1907-1911
Coleman L. Blease (D)	1911-1915
Charles A. Smith (D/acting)	1915
Richard I. Manning (D)	1915-1919
Robert A. Cooper (D)	1919-1922
Wilson G. Harvey (D)	1922-1923
Thomas G. McLeod (D)	1923-1927
John G. Richards (D)	1927-1931
Ibra C. Blackwood (D)	1931-1935
Olin D. Johnston (D)	1935-1939
Burnet R. Maybank (D)	1939-1941
J.E. Harley (D)	1941-1942
R.M. Jeffries (D)	1942-1943
Olin D. Johnston (D)	1943-1945
R.J. Williams (D)	1945-1947
J. Strom Thurmond (D)	1947-1951
James F. Byrnes (D)	1951-1955
George B. Timmerman, Jr. (D)	1955-1959
Ernest F. Hollings (D)	1959-1963
Donald S. Russell (D)	1963-1965
Robert E. McNair (D)	1965-1971
John C. West (D)	1971-1975
James B. Edwards (R)	1975-1979
Richard W. Riley (D)	1979-1987
Carroll A. Campbell, Jr. (R)	1987-

MINIMUM AGES

Majority	18
Marriage with parental consent female	14
male	18
Marriage without parental consent	18
Making a will	18
Buying alcohol	21
Jury duty	18
Leaving school	16
Driver's license	16

CAPITAL PUNISHMENT
Number executed 1976-88: 2
On death row Aug. 1, 1988: 41

MILITARY INSTALLATIONS
Total number: 19
Major bases:
  Army: 1
  Navy: 2
  Air Force: 2

FINANCES

Thousands of dollars

GENERAL REVENUE (1985)

Total general revenue	4,544,945
Total tax revenue	2,732,346
Sales and gross receipts	1,497,892
Individual income taxes	850,814
Corporate net income taxes	199,771

GENERAL EXPENDITURE (1985)

Total general expenditure	4,399,862
Education	2,076,648
Public welfare	505,108
Health	216,642
Hospitals	270,446
Natural resources	101,392
Highways	381,574
Police	44,773
Corrections	149,397

FEDERAL AID (1985) 1,323,560

ECONOMY

South Carolina's main cash crops are tobacco, soybeans, cotton, corn, vegetables, peaches, other fruits, and nuts. Farm marketings cash receipts in 1983 were slightly more than $1 billion, of which about one-third was generated by sales of poultry, cattle, hogs, and dairy products. Both timber and fishing industries contribute to the state's economy; timber-based industries constitute about 8 percent of the total manufacturing base, while the catch of crab, oysters, shrimp, and other fish and shellfish yielded $20 million in 1983. South Carolina's principal mined products are clays, limestone, cyanite, barite, vermiculite, cement, sand, and gravel. Manufacturing is centered primarily around textile production and food processing; other manufactures include paper and wood products, chemicals, electrical machinery, transportation equipment, and ceramics.

EMPLOYMENT (1984)

Thousands of persons

Total number of employed workers	1,374
Construction	81.6
Finance, insurance, and real estate	54.4
Government	240.1
Manufacturing	378.2

Mining 1.8
Services 196.6
Transportation, communications,
   and utilities 55.5
Wholesale and retail trade 262.0

Percent of civilian labor force
   unemployed (1984) 7.1

DEPARTMENT OF DEFENSE (1985)
Civilian workers employed . . . 20,545
Military personnel 44,373
Contract awards . . . . . $490 million

ENERGY SOURCES FOR ELECTRIC UTILITIES (1983)
Percent
Coal 37.4
Gas 0.1

Hydroelectric 6.6
Nuclear 55.7
Petroleum 0.2

TRANSPORTATION
Motor vehicles registered
   in state (1986) 2,304,208
Miles of roads, streets,
   and highways (1986) 63,296
Miles of Class I railway
   operated (1986) 2,533
Airports (1983) 137
Major aviation hubs (1983) 3
   Largest hub: Charleston
Major ports, with gross tonnage in
   thousands (1985):
   Charleston 8,882

CULTURE AND EDUCATION

Native American tribes
South Carolina was formerly home to the Chenaw, Cherokee, Chiaha, Chickasaw, Congaree, Cusabo, Eno, Keyauwee, Natchez, Pedee, Saluda, Santee, Sewee, Shakori, Shawnee, Sissipahaw, Wateree, Waxhaw, and Yamasee. Groups that continue to live in the state include the Catawba, Lumbee, and Waccamaw.

Religions, ethnicities, and languages
Blacks and whites arrived together in 1670 to establish the South Carolina's first permanent settlement, and for most of the state's history blacks were in the majority. Most white South Carolinians trace their ancestry to the early English, Scotch, and Irish settlers; other early immigrants were Huguenot, German, Swiss, Welsh, and Dutch. In 1980, 2.5 percent of South Carolina's population spoke a language other than English at home. The leading Protestant denominations are Baptists and Methodists, followed by Presbyterians, Lutherans, and Episcopalians; there are also Roman Catholic and Jewish congregations.

Major museums and libraries
Charleston Museum
Columbia Museum of Art and Science
Gibbes Art Gallery, Charleston

Major arts organizations
Charleston Ballet Theatre
Charleston Opera Company
Dock Street Theatre, Charleston
Symphony orchestras of Charleston,
   Greenville, Columbia

Colleges and universities
Number public (1986-87) 33
Number private (1986-87) 29
Total enrollment, in full-time equivalent students (1985) 109,300

Public elementary and secondary schools
Expenditure per pupil in average daily
   attendance (1986-87) $3,096
Pupil-teacher ratio (1987) 17.3
Average teacher salary (1986-87) $24,043

Holidays
Robert E. Lee's Birthday. January 19
Confederate Memorial Day. May 10
Jefferson Davis's Birthday. June 3
State Fair, Columbia. Mid-October

SOUTH CAROLINA IN LITERATURE

Jane Barry *Long March* (1955)
   A historical novel of the Revolution centering on General Morgan and the Battle of Cowpens.

Hamilton Basso *Courthouse Square* (1936); *Wine of the Country* (1940); *The View from Pompey's Head* (1954)
   Basso was a New Orleans-born New York journalist who, in much of his fiction, portrayed the moral values and cultural distinctiveness of Southern society in Louisiana and South Carolina. *The View from Pompey's Head*, set in a fictional South Carolina port, was made into a successful film.

John Bennett *Madame Margot* (1921)
   Romantic novel about a creole woman based on a Charleston legend.

Bert W. Bierer *South Carolina Indian Lore* (1972)

Gwen Bristow *Celia Garth* (1959)
   Novel of Charleston in the last years of the Revolution.

Guy and **Candie Carawan** *Ain't You Got a Right to the Tree of Life: The People of John's Island, South Carolina* (1966) . . . Collection of folklore and oral history.
———. *Ain't You Got a Right to the Tree of Life* (1989)
   Folklore and music of Johns Island.

Mary B. Chestnut *A Diary from Dixie* (1905, rpt. 1929, 1961); (ed. Ben A. Williams, 1949, rpt. 1980); *Mary Chesnut's Civil War* (ed. C. Vann Woodward) (1981)
   The most celebrated of all American diaries, written

1861–1865, and then re-composed by its author in 1880. Mary Chesnut, who traveled widely, was a keen observer of war, politics, and the gradual collapse of Southern society.

Alice Childress *A Short Walk* (1979)
Fictional biography of a black woman, born in Charleston, who flees her marriage to join Marcus Garvey's campaign for racial equality.

Hennig Cohen (ed.) *Articles in Periodicals and Serials on South Carolina Literature and Related Subjects, 1950–1955* (1956)

Sarah Morgan Dawson (ed. James I. Robertson) *A Confederate Girl's Diary* (1960, rpt. 1972)

John William De Forest *Kate Beaumont* (1872)
Realistic novel of Charleston plantation society and life among poor white tenant farmers. De Forest was head of the South Carolina Freedmen's Bureau during Reconstruction.

Thomas Dixon, Jr. *The Clansman* (1905)
One of three novels by Dixon displaying hostility for the aims of Reconstruction and sympathy for the Ku Klux Klan. The novel was the basis of D.W. Griffith's classic film *Birth of a Nation* (1915).

Margaret W. Ehrhardt (ed.) *South Carolina Authors and Materials for Elementary and Secondary Media Centers* (1986)

Howard Fast *Freedom Road* (1944)
Novel about the efforts of a young black Union army veteran to change the social order on his native plantation.

Federal Writers' Project *South Carolina Folktales: Stories of Animals and Supernatural Beings* (1941, rpt. 1975)
———. (ed. Belinda Hurmence) *Before Freedom, When I Just Can Remember* (1989)
Twenty-seven narratives of slavery and freedom collected during the Depression.

Mamie Garvin Fields (with Karen Fields) *Lemon Swamp and Other Places: A Carolina Memoir* (1983)

William Price Fox *Moonshine Light, Moonshine Bright* (1967)
Humorous novel of two boys' adventures with a bootlegger in Columbia in the 1940s.

Noel Gerson *Imposter*
A swashbuckling adventure set in Port Royal at the time of the 1692 earthquake.

Nell S. Graydon *South Carolina Ghost Tales* (1969)

Francis Griswold *A Sea Island Lady* (1939); *The Tides of Malverne* (1941)
Chronicle novel of a Beaufort family, 1860-1920, and a novel about life on a Charleston plantation.

DuBose Heyward *Porgy* (1925)
Heyward's first and most famous novel, a depiction of black life on Charleston's "Catfish Row," was a landmark in the literature of Southern black life, and formed the basis of George Gershwin's opera *Porgy and Bess* (1935), for which Heyward wrote the lyrics. He again described Charleston black society in *Mamba's Daughters* (1929), but in the novel *Peter Ashley* (1932), he describes the predicament of a Charleston aristocrat who is forced to weigh abolitionist beliefs against love of his country.

Josephine Humphreys *Dreams of Sleep* (1984)
Novel about domestic events in Charleston.
———. *Rich In Love* (1987)
Novel about a seventeen-year-old girl set in Mount Pleasant.

Alvah F. Hunter *A Year on a Monitor and the Destruction of Fort Sumter* (1987)
Memoir of wartime service by a young enlisted man.

Guy B. Johnson *Folk Culture on St. Helena Island, South Carolina* (1930)

Charles W. Joyner *Folk Song in South Carolina* (1971)

John Pendleton Kennedy *Horseshoe Robinson* (1835)
Historical romance of the Revolution centering on the Battle of Kings Mountain, and depicting guerilla warfare.

James Kilgo *Deep Enough for Ivorybills* (1988)
A study of the natural history and folklife of the swampy region of the Great PeeDee River.

Emma LeConte (ed. Earl S. Miers) *When the World Ended: The Diary of Emma LeConte* (1957, rpt. 1987)
Sherman's siege of Columbia recorded in a seventeen-year-old's journal.

Stephen Longstreet *A Few Painted Feathers* (1963)
Historical novel of the Revolution.

Edward Manigault (ed. Warren Ripley) *Siege Train: The Journal of a Confederate Artilleryman in the Defense of Charleston* (1986)

Floride M. Martin *A Chronological Survey of South Carolina Literature* (1983)

Isaac Jenkins Mikell *Rumbling of the Chariot Wheels* (1923)
Reminiscences of plantation life on Edisto Island and in the Low Country, including anecdotes of General Sherman.

Robert Molly *Charleston: A Gracious Heritage* (1947)
Essay on history and social customs.

Elsie Clews Parsons *Folklore of the Sea Islands, South Carolina* (1923)

William Peden and **George Garrett** (eds.) *New Writings in South Carolina* (1971)

Julia Peterkin *Green Thursday* (1924); *Black April* (1927); *Scarlet Sister Mary* (1928); *Bright Skin* (1932); *Roll, Jordan, Roll* (1933); *The Collected Stories of Julia Peterkin* (ed. Frank Durham) (1970)
The stories and novels of Peterkin, owner and manager of a plantation near Fort Motte, are exclusively devoted to the lives and folklore of the Gullah blacks. *Scarlet Sister Mary* won the Pulitzer prize.

Josephine Pinckney *Hilton Head* (1941); *Three O'Clock Dinner* (1945); *Great Mischief* (1948)
Historical novels set in Charleston and on a resort island.

Elizabeth Warris Pringle *Woman Rice Planter* (1913); *Chronicles of Chicora Wood* (1922)
Autobiographical accounts of plantation life.

Warren Ripley (ed.) *Siege Train: The Journal of a Confederate Artilleryman in Defense of Charleston* (1986)
Life on the front line 1863–1864 as seen by Major Edward Manigault.

Nancy Roberts *South Carolina Ghosts, from the Coast to the Mountains* (1983)

Ben Robertson *Red Hills and Cotton: An Upcountry Memory* (1942)
Autobiographical account of the Piedmont.

Theodore Rosengarten *Tombee: Portrait of a Cotton Planter, with the Journal of Thomas B. Chaplin (1822–1890)* (1987)
Biography of a cotton planter who owned a plantation on St. Helena Island and kept a journal between 1845 and 1858.

Louis B. Rubin, Jr. *The Golden Weather* (1961)
Account of a thirteen-year-old Jewish boy's summer in Charleston in 1936.

Archibald Rutledge *Old Plantation Days* (1911); *Home By the River* (1941); *Santee Paradise* (1956); *The World Around Hampton* (1960)
Fictional and non-fictional evocations of the South Carolina coast, low country, and plantation life by a celebrated poet whose ancestral home was the Hampton Plantation.

Herbert Ravenel Sass *War Drums* (1928); *Look Back to Glory* (1938)
Romantic historical novels set in tidewater South Carolina before the Civil War. Sass also wrote *A Carolina Rice Plantation of the Fifties* (1936), a historical study of antebellum life.

William Gilmore Simms *The Yemassee* (1835); *The Partisan* (1935)
Charleston-born Simms, a planter, politician, and leading secessionist, wrote more than eighty books, most of which preserve some aspect of South Carolina history and manners. *The Yemassee*, the first American work of fiction to deal with the Indians, depicts the Yemassee rebellion of 1715–1718. *The Partisan* is the first volume of a trilogy of novels dealing with the events of the Revolution that concludes with *Katherine Walton* (1851), an account of the British

occupation of Charleston. In *The Wigwam and the Cabin* (1845), a collection of tales, Simms described life in the backwoods.

University of South Carolina. The Library *Historic South Carolina: A Literary Tour of the State* (1974)

Louisa Susannah Wells *The Journal of a Voyage from Charleston, South Carolina to London Undertaken during the American Revolution* (1906, rpt. 1968)

Eliza Yonge Wilkinson (ed. Caroline Gilman) *Letters . . . during the Invasion and Possession of Charleston, S.C. by the British in the Revolutionary War* (1839, rpt. 1969)

Owen Wister *Lady Baltimore* (1906)
Romantic novel of life in Charleston.

Thomas J. Woofter *Black Yeomanry: Life on St. Helena Island* (1930)
Study of customs and folklore in a black community.

Louis B. Wright *Barefoot in Arcadia: Memories of a More Innocent Era* (1974)
Literary scholar's memories of growing up in Greenwood, 1900–1920.

GUIDES TO RESOURCES

Bailey, N. Louise, Mary L. Morgan, and **Carolyn R. Taylor** *Biographical Directory of the South Carolina Senate, 1776–1985* (1986)

Bass, Carolyn M. *A Bibliography of Articles, Pamphlets and Brochures on South Carolina History* (1985)

Carroll, Bartholomew R. *Historical Collections of South Carolina* 2 vols. (1836)

Clay, James W. and **Douglas M. Orr, Jr.** (eds.) *Metrolina Atlas* (1972)

Cote, Richard N. *Local and Family History in South Carolina: A Bibliography* (1981)
—— and **Patricia H. Williams** (eds.) *The Dictionary of South Carolina Biography* vol. 1 (1985)

Easterby, J. H. and **Noel Polk** *Guide to the Study and Reading of South Carolina History* (1950, rpt. 1975)

Edgar, Walter B. (ed.) *Biographical Directory of the South Carolina House of Representatives* (1974–)

Federal Writers' Project *South Carolina: A Guide to the Palmetto State* (1941, rpt. 1988)

Hicks, Theresa M. *South Carolina, a Guide for Genealogists* (1985)

Johnson, Elmer D. (comp.) *South Carolina: A Documentary Profile of the Palmetto State* (1971)

Jones, Lewis P. *Books and Articles on South Carolina History: A List for Laymen* (1970)

Mills, Robert *Atlas of the State of South Carolina* (1825, rpt. 1979)
——. *Statistics of South Carolina* (1826)

Moore, Caroline T. *Records of the Secretary of the Province of South Carolina, 1692–1721* (1978)

Moore, J. H. *Research Materials in South Carolina* (1967)

Neuffer, Claude H. *Names in South Carolina* 30 vols. (1954–1983, rpt. 1984)

Petty, Julian *The Growth and Distribution of Population in South Carolina* (1943, rpt. 1975)

Rogers, George C. *A South Carolina Chronology, 1497–1970* (1973)

South Carolina Department of History and Archives *Official South Carolina Historical Markers: A Directory* (1978)
——. *A Checklist of South Carolina State Publications* (1982– quarterly)
——. *A Guide to Local Government Records in South Carolina Archives* (1988)

South Carolina Research and Statistical Services Division *South Carolina Statistical Abstract* (1985)

Turnbull, R. J. *Bibliography of South Carolina, 1563–1950* 6 vols. (1956)

University of South Carolina. Bureau of Business and Economic Research *The Carolina Economy: Resource Chartbook to the Future* (1975)

Wauchope, George A. *Writers of South Carolina* (1910)

SELECTED NONFICTION SOURCES

Baldwin, Agnes L. *First Settlers of South Carolina 1670–1700* (1985)

Ball, William W. *The State that Forgot: South Carolina's Surrender to Democracy* (1932)

Ballard, Allen B. *One More Day's Journey; the Story of a Family and a People* (1984)

Bancroft, Frederic *Calhoun and the South Carolina Nullification Movement* (1928, rpt. 1966)

Barnwell, John *Love of Order: South Carolina's First Secession Crisis* (1982)

Barrett, John G. *Sherman's March through the Carolinas* (1976)

Bass, Robert D. *Swamp Fox: The Life and Campaigns of General Francis Marion* (1976)
——. *Ninety Six, the Struggle for the South Carolina Back Country* (1978)

Bennett, John *Madame Margot: A Legend of Charleston* (1951)

Bleser, Carol *The Hammonds of Redcliffe* (1981)

Boddie, William W. *History of Williamsburg* (1923)

Boucher, Chauncey S. *The Nullification Controversy in South Carolina* (1968)

Bowes, Frederick P. *The Culture of Early Charleston* (1942)

Brinsfield, John W. *Religion and Politics in Colonial South Carolina* (1983)

Burton, E. Milby *The Siege of Charleston, 1861–1865* (1982)

Burton, Orville V. *In My Father's House Are Many Mansions; Family and Community in Edgefield, South Carolina* (1985)

Bussman, Marlo P. *Born Charlestonian: The Story of Elizabeth O'Neill Verner* (1969)

Carlton, David L. *Mill and Town in South Carolina, 1880–1920* (1982)

Carter, Luther F. and **David S. Mann** (eds.) *Government in the Palmetto State* (1983)

Cauthen, Charles E. *South Carolina Goes to War, 1860–1865* (1950)

Channing, Steven A. *Crisis of Fear: Secession in South Carolina, 1859–1860* (1968)

Chesnutt, David R. *South Carolina's Expansion into Colonial Georgia, 1720–1765* (1973)

Clark, E. Culpepper *Francis Warrington Dawson and the Politics of Reconstruction: South Carolina, 1874–1889* (1980)

Clarke, Erskine *Wrestlin' Jacob: A Portrait of Religion in the Old South* (1979)

Clowse, Converse *Economic Beginnings in Colonial South Carolina, 1670–1730* (1971)

Coit, Margaret L. *John C. Calhoun: American Portrait* (1950)

Creel, Margaret W. *A Peculiar People: Slave Religion and Community Culture among the Gullahs* (1989)

Davidson, Chalmers G. *The Last Foray: The South Carolina Planters of 1860* (1971, rpt. 1987)

Davis, Evangeline *Charleston: House and Gardens* (3d ed. 1975)

De Vorsey, Louis *The Georgia–South Carolina Boundary* (1982)

Draper, Lyman C. *King's Mountain and Its Heroes* (1881, rpt. 1967)

Drayton, John *Memoirs of the American Revolution as Relating to the State of South Carolina* (1821, rpt. 1969)

Edmunds, John B. *Francis W. Pickens and the Politics of Destruction* (1986)

Elliott, William *Carolina Sports by Land and Water* (1846)

Elzas, Barnett *The Jews of South Carolina from the Earliest Times to the Present Day* (1905, rpt. 1983)

Ervin, Sara S. *South Carolinians in the Revolution* (1949, rpt. 1981)

Fetters, Thomas T. *Palmetto Traction: Electric Railways of South Carolina* (1978)

Frakes, George E. *Laboratory for Liberty: The South Carolina Legislative Committee System 1719–1776* (1970)

Green, Edwin L. *Indians of South Carolina* (1920)

Greene, Jack P. (ed.) *Come to Carolina: Two Colonial South Carolina Promotional Pamphlets* . . . (1987)

Guess, William F. *South Carolina* (1960)

Hamer, Philip M. and George Rogers (eds.) *The Papers of Henry Laurens* 10 vols. (1968, rpt. 1986)

Heitzler, Michael J. *Historic Goose Creek, South Carolina, 1670–1980* (1983)

Hemphill, W. Edwin (ed.) *The Papers of John C. Calhoun* vols. 4–16 (1986)

Hennig, Helen K. (ed.) *Columbia, Capital City of South Carolina, 1786–1936* (1936)
———. *Great South Carolinians* vol. 1– (1970–)

Herd, E. Don *The South Carolina Upcountry: Historical and Biographical Sketches* (1981–1982)

Heyward, Duncan C. *Seed from Madagascar* (1937)

Higginson, Thomas W. *Army Life in a Black Regiment* (1962, rpt. 1984)

Hilborn, Nat and Sam *Battleground of Freedom: South Carolina in the Revolution* (1970)

Hirsch, Arthur H. *The Huguenots of Colonial South Carolina* (1928, rpt. 1962)

Holst, Hermann E. von *John C. Calhoun* (1980)

Hough, Franklin B. (ed.) *The Siege of Charleston by the British Fleet and Army under the Command of Admiral Arbuthnot and Sir Henry Clinton* (1867, rpt. 1975)

Houston, David F. *A Critical Study of Nullification in South Carolina* (1896, rpt. 1967)

Irving, John B. *The South Carolina Jockey Club* (1857, rpt. 1975)

Iseley, N. Jane *Plantations of the Low Country, South Carolina 1697–1865* (1985)

Jarrell, Hampton M. *Wade Hampton and the Negro: The Road Not Taken* (1949)

Jervey, Theodore Dehon *Robert Y. Hayne and His Times* (1909)

Johnson, Michael P. and James L. Roark *Black Masters: A Free Family of Color in the Old South* (1984)
——— and James L. Roark (eds.) *No Chariot Let Down: Charleston's Free People of Color on the Eve of the Civil War* (1984)

Jones, Lewis P. *South Carolina: A Synoptic History for Laymen* (1971)

Kennedy, Robert M. and Thomas J. Kirkland *Historic Camden* 2 vols. (1905)

Kiser, Clyde V. *Sea Island to City: A Study of St. Helena Islanders in Harlem and Other Urban Centers* (1932, rpt. 1969)

Koger, Larry *Black Slaveowners; Free Black Slave Masters in South Carolina, 1790–1860* (1985)

Lachicotte, Alberta *Rebel Senator: Strom Thurmond* (1966)

Lambert, Robert S. *South Carolina Loyalists in the American Revolution* (1987)

Lamson, Peggy *The Glorious Failure: Black Congressman Robert Brown Elliott and the Reconstruction in South Carolina* (1973)

Land, Aubrey C. *Bases of Plantation Society* (1969, rpt. 1986)

Lander, Ernest M. *A History of South Carolina, 1865–1960* (1970)
——— (comp.) *Perspectives in South Carolina History* (1973)
———. *Reluctant Imperialists: Calhoun, the South Carolinians, and the Mexican War* (1980)

Lane, Mills *South Carolina* (1984)
———. *Architecture of the Old South: South Carolina* (1988)

Laurens, Henry *A South Carolina Protest against Slavery* (1861)

Lawson, Dennis T. *A Guide to Historic Georgetown County, South Carolina* (1974)

Leiding, Harriette K. *Historic Houses of South Carolina* (1921)

Leland, John A. *A Voice from South Carolina* (1971)

Lesesne, J. Mauldin *The Bank of the State of South Carolina* (1970, rpt. 1986)

Lofton, John *Denmark Vesey's Revolt; the Slave Plot That Lit a Fuse to Fort Sumter* (1983)

Logan, John H. *History of the Upper Country of South Carolina* (1859)

Madden, Richard C. *Catholics in South Carolina: A Record* (1985)

Marion, John F. *The Charleston Story: Scenes from a City's History* (1978)

Mazyck, Arthur *Charleston in 1883* (1983)

McClure, Harlan and Vernon Hodges *South Carolina Architecture, 1670–1970* (1970)

McCrady, Edward *The History of South Carolina* 4 vols. (1897–1902, rpt. 1969)

Messmer, Catherine C. *South Carolina's Low Country: A Past Preserved* (1988)

Milling, Chapman J. *Red Carolinians* (1940)

Mitchell, Broadus *William Gregg, Factory Master of the Old South* (1928)

Montgomery, Mabel *Worthwhile South Carolinians* (1934)

Neal, William J. *Living with the South Carolina Shore* (1984)

Neuffer, Claude H. and Irene *The Name Game; from Oyster Point to Keewee* (1972)

O'Brien, Michael and David Moltke-Hansen (eds.) *Intellectual Life in Antebellum Charleston* (1986)

Pancake, John S. *"This Destructive War." The British Campaign in the Carolinas, 1780–1782* (1985)

Peare, Catherine *Mary McLeod Bethune* (1951)

Pearson, Elizabeth W. (ed.) *Letters from Port Royal, 1862–1868* (1906, rpt. 1969)

Pike, James Shepherd *The Prostrate State* (1968)

Quattlebaum, Paul *The Land Called Chicora: The Carolinas under Spanish Rule with French Intrusions, 1520–1670* (1956, rpt. 1975)

Ravenel, Harriett H. *Eliza Pinckney* (1986)

Reynolds, John S. *Reconstruction in South Carolina* (1969)

Rhett, James M., III *Charleston Then and Now* (1975)

Rippy, James Fred *Joel R. Poinsett, Versatile American* (1935)

Rivers, William J. *A Sketch of the History of South Carolina to the Close of the Proprietary Government by the Revolution of 1719* (1956, rpt. 1972)

Roberts, Nancy *The Faces of South Carolina* (1976)

Robertson, Ben *Red Hills and Cotton* (1942)

Rogers, George C., Jr. *Charleston in the Age of the Pickneys* (1969)

Rose, Willie Lee *Rehearsal for Reconstruction: The Port Royal Experiment* (1964)

Rutledge, Archibald H. *Plantation Game Trails* (1921)

Sally, Alexander S., Jr. *Art in the Province of South Carolina* (1935)
————. *The State Houses of South Carolina, 1751–1936* (1936)

Savage, Henry *River of the Carolinas: The Santee* (1956, rpt. 1968)

Sherman, Richard P. *Robert Johnson, Proprietary and Royal Governor of South Carolina* (1966)

Simkins, Francis B. *The Tillman Movement in South Carolina* (1926)
———— and Robert H. Woody *South Carolina during Reconstruction* (1932, rpt. 1966)

Simons, Albert and Samuel Lapham, Jr. (eds.) *The Early Architecture of Charleston* (2d ed. 1970)

Simons, Elizabeth P. *Music in Charleston from 1732 to 1919* (1927)

Sirmans, M. Eugene *Colonial South Carolina: A Political History, 1663–1763* (1966)

Sloan, Eugene R. *Scenic South Carolina* (rev. ed. 1971)
————. *South Carolina: A Journalist and His State* (1971)

Smythe, Augustine T. et al. *The Carolina Low Country* (1931)

Stoney, Samuel Gaillard *Plantations of the Carolina Low Country* (1938)
————. *This Is Charleston* (rev. ed. 1970)

Swanberg, William A. *First Blood: The Story of Fort Sumter* (1957)

Taylor, Rosser H. *Ante-Bellum South Carolina: A Social and Cultural History* (1942, rpt. 1970)

Thompson, Henry T. *The Foundation of the Public School System of South Carolina* (1927)

Tindall, George B. *South Carolina Negroes, 1877–1900* (1952, rpt. 1970)

Townsend, Leah *South Carolina Baptists, 1670–1805* (1935)

Uhlendorf, Bernard A. (ed. and tr.) *The Siege of Charleston* (1938, rpt. 1968)

Van Deusen, John G. *Economic Bases of Disunion in South Carolina* (1928, rpt. 1970)

Waddell, Gene *Indians of the South Carolina Low-country, 1562–1751* (1980)

Wallace, David D. *South Carolina: A Short History, 1520–1948* (1951, rpt. 1966)

Walsh, Richard *Charleston's Sons of Liberty: A Story of the Artisans 1763–1789* (1968)

Weir, Robert M. *Colonial South Carolina: A History* (1983)

Whitney, Edison L. *Government of the Colony of South Carolina* (1895, rpt. 1970)

Wikramanayake, Marina *A World in Shadow, the Free Black in Antebellum South Carolina* (1973)

Williams, Alfred B. *Hampton and His Red Skirts* (1935)

Williamson, Joel *After Slavery: The Negro in South Carolina during Reconstruction, 1861–1877* (1965, rpt. 1975)

Wood, Peter H. *Black Majority: Negroes in Colonial South Carolina from 1670 through the Stone Rebellion* (1974)

Woofter, T. J. *Black Yeomanry: Life on St. Helena Island* (1930, rpt. 1978)

Wooten, Bayard and Samuel G. Stoney *Charleston; Azaleas and Old Bricks* (1937)

Wright, Louis B. *South Carolina, a Bicentennial History* (States and the Nation series) (1976)

SOUTH DAKOTA

South Dakota, a west north central state, is bordered on the north by North Dakota; on the east by the Red River of the North, Minnesota, and Iowa; on the south by the Missouri River and Nebraska; and on the west by Wyoming and Montana.

FULL NAME State of South Dakota
POSTAL ABBREVIATION SD
INHABITANT South Dakotan
ADMITTED TO THE UNION Nov. 2, 1889.
 40th state
POPULATION (est. 1987) 709,000.
 Percent of US total: 0.29%. Rank: 45th

CAPITAL CITY Pierre, located on the Missouri River in central South Dakota; population 11,973 (1980). The site was the capital of the Arikara Indian nation prior to 1800, when a settlement was founded as the western terminus of the Chicago and North Western Railway. Pierre became the temporary capital in 1889 and the permanent capital in 1890.

STATE NAME AND NICKNAMES From the Dakota Indian word meaning "friends, allies." Also known as the Sunshine State, the Coyote State, the Blizzard State, and the Artesian State.

STATE SEAL A landscape showing a farmer plowing with a team of horses; in the distance is a steamboat traveling on the river, with a smelting furnace, hoist house, mill, dump, and three ranges of hills on the left bank, and on the right bank a herd of cattle grazing near a field of corn. Across the top is a scroll with the state motto. The

border reads "State of South Dakota, Great Seal, 1889," in gold letters on blue.

MOTTO Under God the People Rule

SONG "Hail! South Dakota," lyrics and music by Deecort Hammitt.

SYMBOLS
Flower American pasque flower
Tree Black Hills spruce
Bird ring-necked pheasant
Gem fairburn agate
Mineral rose quartz
Fish walleye
Insect honeybee
Grass western wheat grass

LICENSE PLATE Red on white, with red legend "1889-1989" and blue image of Mount Rushmore memorial.

FLAG On a field of sky blue, the state seal, either in dark blue on a white background, or in dark blue on a sky-blue background, surrounded by a gold sunburst, with the gold legend "South Dakota" curved along the top edge and the gold legend "The Sunshine State" curved along the bottom. Also in use is an earlier flag, showing the seal on one side and the sun on the other.

GEOGRAPHY AND CLIMATE

The Upper Missouri River Basin splits South Dakota into two roughly equal parts: the east-river region, a fertile area of prairie plain, and the west-river region, a land of mesas and canyons that includes the South Dakota Badlands, a rugged area unusually rich in fossils. The state's climate is typically continental—dry, hot in summer, and cold in winter.

AREA 77,116 square miles. Rank: 16th
INLAND WATER 1,164 square miles
GEOGRAPHIC CENTER Hughes, 8 miles NE of Pierre
ELEVATIONS *Highest point:* Harney Peak, Pennington County, 7,242 feet. *Lowest point:* Big Stone Lake, Roberts County, 962 feet. *Mean elevation:* 2,200 feet

MAJOR RIVERS Missouri, James, Cheyenne

MAJOR LAKES AND RESERVOIRS Oahe, Lewis and Clark, Campbell, Traverse, Francis Case

LAND USE

	Thousands of acres
Urban (1982)	231
Rural (1982)	44,506
Cropland (1982)	16,947
Pastureland (1982)	2,703
Rangeland (1982)	22,784
Forestland (1982)	562
State parks and recreation areas (1983)	90
National park system (1984)	183
National forest system (1984)	2,348
Tribal lands (1984)	2,652

TEMPERATURES The highest recorded temperature was 120°F on July 6, 1936, at Gannvalley. The lowest was -58°F on February 17, 1936, at McIntosh.

NATIONAL SITES

NATIONAL HISTORIC TRAIL Lewis & Clark
NATIONAL MEMORIAL Mount Rushmore
NATIONAL MONUMENT Jewel Cave
NATIONAL PARKS Badlands, Wind Cave
NATIONAL WILDLIFE REFUGES Lacreek, Lake Andes–Karl E. Mundt, Madison Wetland Management District, Sand Lake–Pocasse, Waubay

HISTORY

1743	*March 30.* Two sons of explorer Pierre Gaultier de Varennes, Sieur de La Vérendrye, bury an inscribed lead plate near present-day Pierre. Seeking a water route to the Pacific, they follow the Missouri downstream.
1775	Pierre Dorion of St. Louis, a French Canadian, arrives at a Yankton Sioux (Dakota) village on the lower James River and marries into the tribe, thereby becoming the first white resident of what is to become South Dakota.
1794–1796	Jean Baptiste Truteau builds winter quarters on the Missouri near the subsequent site of Fort Randall.
1804	*August 22.* Traveling upstream from St. Louis on their expedition to the Pacific, Meriwether Lewis and William Clark enter South Dakota, spending 54 days in the future state. They return in 1806.
1815–1850	Heyday of the upper Missouri fur trade. Traders buy beaver, muskrat, and otter pelts, buffalo hides, and deerskins from Indians.
1831	*June 19.* The *Yellowstone*, first steamboat on the Missouri, reaches Fort Tecumseh (present-day Fort Pierre) from St. Louis. Among the passengers is the artist George Catlin.
1851	Indians cede to the United States all lands east of the Big Sioux River in present South Dakota.
1857	A group of Iowa businessmen lay out Sioux Falls.
1858	The Yankton Sioux sell 14 million acres of land between the Big Sioux and Missouri rivers for 12 cents an acre.
1861	*March 2.* Dakota Territory is organized, including what is now North Dakota and South Dakota. There are 2,402 white inhabitants. The first federal land office opens at Vermillion.
1862	Yankton becomes the territorial capital and remains so until 1883.

1868	*April 29.* The Fort Laramie Treaty sets aside what is now South Dakota west of the Missouri as an Indian reservation.
1873	The Dakota Southern Railroad reaches Yankton from Sioux City, Iowa.
1874	*July 30.* Gold is discovered in the Black Hills, in Indian territory. By the spring of 1876 about 10,000 whites are in the area.
1876	As part of a campaign to force Indian bands on reservations, George A. Custer leads federal cavalrymen into Montana, where they are annihilated at the Battle of Little Big Horn on June 25. But later in the year the Sioux agree to cede the Black Hills region. *August 2.* Wild Bill Hickok is shot in the Black Hills mining town of Deadwood while holding aces over eights (the "dead man's hand"). Calamity Jane is later buried next to him.
1877	George Hearst buys the Homestake Mine claim for $70,000. By 1935 the mine has produced $301 million worth of gold bullion—84 percent of the total taken from the Black Hills.
1880	Railroad lines reach the Missouri at Pierre and Chamberlain.
1881	Sitting Bull returns to western South Dakota after five years spent in Canada following the Battle of Little Big Horn.
1882	The University of South Dakota is founded at Vermillion.
1883	Peak of the land boom; filings at public land offices in southern Dakota total 5,410,687 acres, about 23 percent of the national total.
1885	The population of southern Dakota has risen to 248,569 from 81,781 in 1880.
1889	The Great Sioux Reservation is reduced by about nine million acres and broken up into five smaller reservations. *November 2.* North Dakota and South Dakota enter the Union as the 39th and 40th states, respectively. Pierre becomes the capital of South Dakota.
1890	An Indian messianic movement featuring "ghost" dances alarms whites. *December 15.* Sitting Bull is killed. *December 29.* Federal cavalry massacre 146 Indians at Wounded Knee Creek in southwestern South Dakota. Thirty-one soldiers also are killed.
1897	State prohibition of liquor is repealed by popular referendum.
1904–1913	A series of agreements with the Teton Sioux make over four million acres of reservation lands available for purchase by whites. The population of the western half of the state increases from 57,575 in 1905 to 137,687 in 1910.
1909	John Morrell & Company opens a meatpacking plant at Sioux Falls. Meatpacking gradually replaces flour milling as the chief industry.
1917	Legislation permits the state to extend loans to farmers. The program ends in 1928 due to mismanagement and corruption.
1918	Ostracized for failing to support World War I, all but one of 17 Hutterite communities emigrate to Canada. They later return.
1919	The legislature votes to establish state hail insurance and a state-owned coal mine and cement plant. All but the cement plant (at Rapid City) prove uneconomic and are liquidated in the 1930s.
1930	The agricultural depression of the 1920s has dropped the price of farmland in half since 1921.
1932	Farm foreclosures reach a peak of 3,864. For the first time in state history, the Democrats win every state electoral office and overwhelming control of the legislature.
1935	Taxes on net income, retail sales, and gold ore are adopted. The four percent tax on the latter provides one-third of the state budget.
1941	Completion of Mount Rushmore National Memorial, with the giant carved heads of Washington, Jefferson, Lincoln, and Theodore Roosevelt.
1943	The state income tax is repealed.
1947	Following adoption of a right-to-work constitutional amendment the previous year, the closed shop is outlawed.
1953	The state's first commercial oil well is drilled in Harding County.
1955	A law prohibits the formation of new Hutterite communities or the expansion of existing ones.

1956	Fort Randall Dam, the first of four dams on the Missouri River in South Dakota intended for flood control, power, and irrigation, is completed.
1958	With a sale of 1,522,415 head, Sioux Falls Stock Yards moves into 10th place among the nation's livestock markets.
1963	One hundred fifty Minuteman intercontinental ballistic missiles are put in place at Wall.
1964	Completion of the Oahe Dam, the largest of the four Missouri River dams in South Dakota.
1970	Almost 22 percent of the population is working on farms—a higher proportion than in any other state.
1972	*June 9.* At least 236 people are killed when a flash flood inundates Rapid City and other communities on the eastern edge of the Black Hills.
	November 7. Democrats win control of both legislative houses for the first time since 1936, but Senator George McGovern of Mitchell, the Democratic party presidential candidate, fails to carry his home state.
1973	South Dakota is fourth among states in hog production, fifth in sheep, and eighth in cattle.
	American Indian Movement members and supporters seize Wounded Knee and hold it for 70 days to dramatize their demands for reforms in Indian tribal government. Two persons are killed.
1974	South Dakota ranks first among states in the production of rye, second in flaxseed, third in oats and durum wheat. The size of the average farm is 1,046 acres, compared to 439 acres in 1935.
	Richard Kneip, a Democrat, wins an unprecedented third term as governor.
1976	The state's eight Indian tribes report an enrolled population of 46,350, of which 29,750 are on reservations.
1978	South Dakota leads in gold production for the last time; thereafter the state is increasingly outstripped by Nevada.
1979	Sioux tribes win an award of $105 million over 102 years for the forced cession of the Black Hills region.
1982	Reductions in federal funding for housing and job training drive unemployment on Indian reservations to levels of 75 to 90 percent.
	Citicorp, the nation's largest bank holding company, moves its credit-card operations to Sioux Falls.

DEMOGRAPHY

Population (est. 1987)	709,000
Population (1980)	690,768
Population density in persons per square mile (1980)	9.0

POPULATION BY RACE (1980)

American Indian/Aleut/ Eskimo	45,101
Asian/Pacific Islander	1,728
Black	2,144
Hispanic	4,028
White	638,955
Other	2,250

POPULATION CHARACTERISTICS (1980)

Percent of state population

Urban	46.4
Rural	53.6
Under 18	29.8
65 or older	13.2
College-educated	14.2
Families below poverty line . . .	13.1
Public-assistance recipients	4.2

Per capita personal income (1986)	$11,850
Millionaires per 100,000 residents (1982)	172.9
Average life expectancy in years (1980)	75.0
Marriage rate per 1,000 residents (1986)	10.5
Divorce rate per 1,000 residents (1986)	3.6
Birth rate per 1,000 residents (1985)	17.3
Infant mortality rate per 1,000 births (1985)	8.4
Abortion rate per 1,000 live births (1985)	140
Crime rate per 100,000 residents (1985)	
Violent	124.7
Property	2,591.2
Federal and state prisoners per 100,000 residents (1984)	123

418

Alcohol consumption in gallons
per capita (1985) 35.8
Deaths from motor vehicle accidents
per 100,000 residents (1985) . . 18.4

MAJOR CITIES

	Population
Aberdeen (1980)	25,851
Sioux Falls (est. 1984)	87,776
Rapid City (1980)	46,492
Watertown (1980)	15,649

GOVERNMENT AND POLITICS

Number of US Representatives   1
Electoral votes   3

POLITICAL PARTY NOMINEES FROM STATE

George Stanley McGovern (D) 1972   P

PRESIDENTIAL PRIMARY ELECTION In 1988, South Dakota sent 19 Democratic delegates and 18 Republican delegates to the national conventions.
CONSTITUTION South Dakota is using its original constitution, adopted in 1889.
LEGISLATURE The Legislature is divided into the Senate (35 members, 2-year term,

minimum age 25) and the House of Representatives (70 members, 2-year term, minimum age 25). In 1987, the annual salary was $3,200 in odd-numbered years, $2,800 in even-numbered years.
JUDICIARY The highest court is the Supreme Court, with 5 judges serving 8-year terms. In 1987, the annual salary was $56,975.
EXECUTIVE The governor serves a 4-year term; there is no minimum age for holding office. In 1987, the annual salary was $57,324. There are 9 other elected officials.

PRESIDENTIAL VOTE 1948-1988 *(in percents)*

Year	State Winner	Democratic	Republican
1948	Dewey (R)	40.7	51.8
1952	Eisenhower (R)	30.7	69.3
1956	Eisenhower (R)	41.6	58.4
1960	Nixon (R)	41.8	58.2
1964	Johnson (D)	55.6	44.4
1968	Nixon (R)	42.0	53.3
1972	Nixon (R)	45.5	54.2
1976	Ford (R)	48.9	50.4
1980	Reagan (R)	31.7	60.5
1984	Reagan (R)	36.5	63.0
1988	Bush (R)	47.0	53.0

GOVERNORS

Territorial Governors

William Jayne	1861-1863
Newton Edmunds	1863-1866
Andrew J. Faulk	1866-1869
John A. Burbank	1869-1874
John L. Pennington	1874-1878
William A. Howard	1878-1880
Nehemiah G. Ordway	1880-1884
Gilbert A. Pierce	1884-1889
Arthur C. Mellette	1889

State Governors

Arthur C. Mellette (R)	1889-1893
Charles H. Sheldon (R)	1893-1897
Andrew E. Lee (Populist-Democrat)	1897-1901
Charles N. Herreid (R)	1901-1905
Samuel H. Elrod (R)	1905-1907
Coe I. Crawford (R)	1907-1909
Robert S. Vessey (R)	1909-1913
Frank M. Byrne (Republican-Progressive)	1913-1917
Peter Norbeck (R)	1917-1921
William H. McMaster (R)	1921-1925
Carl Gunderson (R)	1925-1927
William J. Bulow (D)	1927-1931
Warren E. Green (R)	1931-1933
Thomas Berry (D)	1933-1937
Leslie Jensen (R)	1937-1939
Harlan J. Bushfield (R)	1939-1943
Merrell Q. Sharpe (R)	1943-1947
George T. Mickelson (R)	1947-1951
Sigurd Anderson (R)	1951-1955
Joe J. Foss (R)	1955-1959
Ralph Herseth (D)	1959-1961
Archie Gubbrud (R)	1961-1965
Nils A. Boe (R)	1965-1969
Frank Farrar (R)	1969-1971

Richard S. Kneip (D)	1971-1978
Harvey Wollman (D)	1978-1979
William J. Janklow (R)	1979-1987
George S. Mickelson (R)	1987-

MINIMUM AGES

Majority	18
Marriage with parental consent	16
Marriage without parental consent . .	18
Making a will	18
Buying alcohol	21
Jury duty	18
Leaving school	16
Driver's license	16

CAPITAL PUNISHMENT
Number executed 1976-88: 0
On death row Aug. 1, 1988: 0

MILITARY INSTALLATIONS
Total number: 2
Major bases:
  Air Force: 2

FINANCES

Thousands of dollars

GENERAL REVENUE (1985)

Total general revenue	929,400
Total tax revenue	355,452
Sales and gross receipts	293,444
Individual income taxes	0
Corporate net income taxes . .	16,938

GENERAL EXPENDITURE (1985)

Total general expenditure . .	964,490
Education	254,490
Public welfare	119,877
Health	27,796
Hospitals	31,554
Natural resources	50,515
Highways	181,058
Police	9,038
Corrections	17,573

FEDERAL AID (1985) 480,179

ECONOMY

South Dakota derives its principal income from the sale of cattle and calves, beef, and dairy products. Farm marketings cash receipts were $2.6 billion in 1983, of which $930 million were from the sale of cash crops—wheat, hay, corn, flax, soybeans, barley, sorghum, and rye. Gold is the most profitable of mined products, but limestone, gypsum, sand, gravel, bentonite, feldspar, coal, and oil are also economically important. The state's manufacturing sector is not highly diversified; it is dominated by food processing—meatpacking and flour milling—with development of other industrial products growing more slowly. Value added by manufacture was $1.1 billion in 1982. Tourism rivals manufacturing as an employer and source of revenue.

EMPLOYMENT (1984)
Thousands of persons

Total number of employed persons	331
Construction	8.9
Finance, insurance, and real estate	13.1
Government	57.0
Manufacturing	28.6
Mining	2.6
Services	58.0
Transportation, communications, and utilities	12.0
Wholesale and retail trade	64.5

Percent of civilian labor force
  unemployed (1984) 4.3

DEPARTMENT OF DEFENSE (1985)

Civilian workers employed . . .	1,404
Military personnel	5,854
Contract awards	$78 million

ENERGY SOURCES FOR ELECTRIC UTILITIES (1983)
Percent

Coal	29.2
Gas	0.0
Hydroelectric	70.6
Nuclear	0.0
Petroleum	0.1

TRANSPORTATION

Motor vehicles registered in state (1986)	664,060
Miles of roads, streets, and highways (1986)	73,468
Miles of Class I railway operated (1986)	1,277
Airports (1983)	165
Major aviation hubs (1983)	1
Largest hub: Sioux Falls	

CULTURE AND EDUCATION

Native American tribes
South Dakota was formerly the home of the Arapaho, Arikara, Cheyenne, Omaha, Ponca, Sutaio, and Winnebago tribes. Groups that continue to live in the state include the Sioux. There are 9 federal reservations in South Dakota.

Religions, ethnicities, and languages
Many of South Dakota's settlers arrived from other states in the upper Mississippi Valley. Most of the immigrants who arrived in the late 19th and early 20th centuries were from Canada and from northern and eastern Europe; the main ethnic groups are Norwegians and other Scandinavians, Germans, Czechs, Dutch, Finns, Welsh, and Russians. In 1980, 7.8 percent of South Dakota's population spoke a language other than English at home. The largest religious groups are Roman Catholics, Lutherans, Methodists, United Church of Christ, Presbyterians, Episcopalians, and Baptists; there are also Hutterite and Mennonite colonies in the state. American Indians, many of whom practice tribal religions, constitute about 6 percent of the population.

Major museums and libraries
Library of the State Historical Society, Pierre
W.H. Over Dakota Museum, University of South Dakota
Sioux Indian Museum, Rapid City
South Dakota Memorial Art Center, Brookings

Major arts organizations
South Dakota Symphony, Sioux Falls

Colleges and universities
Number public (1986-87) 8
Number private (1986-87) 10
Total enrollment, in full-time equivalent students (1985) 27,000

Public elementary and secondary schools
Expenditure per pupil in average daily attendance (1986-87) $3,190
Pupil-teacher ratio (1987) 15.6
Average teacher salary (1986-87) $19,518

Holidays
State Fair, Huron. Late August to early September

SOUTH DAKOTA IN LITERATURE

J. Leonard Bates (ed.) *Tom Walsh in Dakota Territory: Personal Correspondence of Senator Thomas J. Walsh and Elinor C. Clements* (1966)
Accounts of pioneer life in Spink County.

Ike Blasingame *Dakota Cowboy: My Life in the Old Days* (1958)
Recollections of a cowboy who worked for the Matador Cattle Company during the early years of the century.

William H. Briggs *Dakota in the Morning* (1942)
Growth of a pioneer town as seen through the eyes of a small boy.

Dee Brown *Bury My Heart at Wounded Knee: An Indian History of the American West* (1970)
A historical narrative using the Sioux Massacre as a point of departure.

William M. Chapman *Remember the Wind: A Prairie Memoir* (1965)
Portrayal of Sioux life by an an easterner who spent three years on the Standing Rock Reservation.

Oscar W. Coursey *Literature of South Dakota* 4th ed. (1925)

Pete Dexter *Deadwood* (1986)
Historical novel about the murder of Wild Bill Hickok in 1876.

Federal Writers' Project *Sodbusters: Tales of Southeastern South Dakota* 1938

Hamlin Garland *Main-Travelled Roads* (1891)
Garland's sketches of homestead life in the Midwest include material based on his own upbringing in Ordway, Brown County. His novel *Moccasin Ranch* (1909) also depicts Dakota homesteading.

Oakley Hall *The Bad Lands* (1978)
Novel portraying conflict between cattlemen and farmers during the 1880s.

Ethel Hueston *Calamity Jane of Deadwood Gulch* (1937)
Popular history of the folk hero of the Wild West.

William J. Hyde *Dig or Die, Brother Hyde* (1954)
Memoir by a Methodist clergyman who worked at Groton and Faulkton during the mining boom.

Lucile M. Kane (trans. and ed.) *Military Life in Dakota: The Journal of Philippe Régis de Trobriand* (1951)
De Trobriand kept a detailed journal during his command of Fort Stevenson in 1867.

Edith Eudora Kohl *Land of the Burnt Thigh* (1938, rpt. 1986)
The story of Edith and Ida Ammons, homesteading pioneers near the Lower Brule Indian Reservation in 1907.

Rose Wilder Lane *Let the Hurricane Roar* (1933); *Free Land* (1938)
Classic novels of pioneer life in the 1870s and 1880s.

Luther Standing Bear *My People the Sioux* (1928); *Land of the Spotted Eagle* (1933)
Memoirs of a Dakota chief, with detailed accounts of Indian life and customs.

John R. Milton (ed.) *The Literature of South Dakota* (1976)
An anthology of writing about the state from Lewis and Clark to Vine Deloria.

Ole Rölvaag *Giants in the Earth* (1927); *Peder Victorious* (1929)
Classic novels of pioneer life on the Great Plains in the 1880s.

Edwin C. Torrey *Early Days in Dakota* (1925)
Sketches of pioneer life in eastern South Dakota by an Aberdeen journalist.

Stewart Edward White *The Claim Jumpers* (1901)
Novel of the gold-mining boom set in Keystone.

Walker D. Wyman *Nothing but Prairie and Sky: Life on the Dakota Range in the Early Days* (1954)
Description of pioneer life based on original notes of Bruce Siberts, rancher, 1890–1906.

GUIDES TO RESOURCES

Carlson, Loren M. *Bibliography of South Dakota Government* (1951)

Clem, Alan L. and George M. Platt *A Bibliography of South Dakota Government and Politics* (1965)
——. *South Dakota Political Almanac* (1969)
——. *Brevet's South Dakota Historical Markers* (1974)

Federal Writers' Project *South Dakota Historical Collections* 38 vols. (1905–1974)
——. *A Selected List of South Dakota Books* (1943)
——. *South Dakota: A Guide to the State* (rev. ed. 1952)

Hogan, Edward Patrick, Lee A. Opheim, and Scott H. Zieske (eds.) *Atlas of South Dakota* (1970)

Little, John J. and Paul Putz *Historic Sites of South Dakota: A Guidebook* (1980)

Parmelee, Gertrude *A South Dakota Bibliography* (1960)

South Dakota Committee on the Humanities (ed. Herbert T. Hoover) *Planning for the South Dakota Centennial: A Bibliography* (1984)

South Dakota Library Association (ed. Sue Laubersheimer) *South Dakota: Changing, Changeless 1889–1989: A Selected Annotated Bibliography* (1985)

Turchen, Lesta V. and James D. McLaird *County and Community: A Bibliography of South Dakota Local Histories* (1979)

SELECTED NONFICTION SOURCES

Anson, Robert Sam *McGovern: A Biography* (1972)

Atherton, Loren G. and Nora M. *South Dakota Geography* (1936)

Beadle, William H. H. *Dakota: Its Geography, History and Resources* (1899)

Beine, George H. (ed. Shirley Holmes Cochell) *Land of the Coyote* (1972)

Bennett, Estelline *Old Deadwood Days* (1935, rpt. 1982)

Berg, Francie M. *South Dakota: Land of Shining Gold* (1982)

Brown, Jesse and A. M. Willard *The Black Hills Trails; a History of the Struggles of the Pioneers in the Winning of the Black Hills* (1924)

Butler, Mike *92 Days in the Saddle* (1975)

Casey, Robert J. *The Black Hills and Their Incredible Characters* (1949)

Cash, Joseph H. *Working the Homestake* (1973)

Cassells, E. Steve *Prehistoric Hunters of the Black Hills* (1986)

Clem, Alan L. *Prairie State Politics: Popular Democracy in South Dakota* (1967)

Clowser, Don C. *Deadwood, the Historic City* (1969)

Coursey, O. W. *Biography of Senator Alfred Beard Kittredge, His Complete Life Work* (1915)
——. *Beautiful Black Hills; a Comprehensive Treatise on the Black Hills of South Dakota . . .* (1926)

Curley, Edwin A. *Guide to the Black Hills* (2d ed. rev. and enl. 1973)

Dalthorp, Charles (ed.) *South Dakota's Governors* (1953)

Dimmette, Celia P. *Take Me Home: Life on the Family Farm* (1979)

Dollard, Robert *Recollections of the Civil War and Going West to Grow Up with the Country* (1906)

Driscoll, R. E. *Seventy Years of Banking in the Black Hills* (1948)

Durand, George H. *Joseph Ward of Dakota* (1913, rpt. 1935)

Duratschek, Sr. M. Claudia *The Beginnings of Catholicism in South Dakota* (1943)
——. *Under the Shadow of His Wings* (1943)
——. *Crusading Along Sioux Trails: A History of the Catholic Missions of South Dakota* (1947)

Farber, William O., Thomas C. Geary, and William H. Cape *Government of South Dakota* (1968)

Federal Writers' Project *South Dakota Place Names* (1941, rpt. 1973)

Fielder, Mildred *Railroads of the Black Hills* (1964)
——. *Wild Bill and Deadwood* (1965)
——. *The Treasure of Homestake Gold* (1970)
——. *A Guide to Black Hills Ghost Mines* (1972)

Fite, Gilbert C. *Peter Norbeck: Prairie Statesman* (1948)
——. *Mount Rushmore* (1952)

Hagedorn, Hermann *Roosevelt in the Bad Lands* (1921)

Hanson, Joseph M. *South Dakota in the World War, 1917–1919* (1940)

Hassrick, Royal B. *The Sioux: The Life and Customs of a Warrior Society* (1964, rpt. 1988)

Hebert, Frank *History of Southeastern Dakota: Its Settlement and Growth* (1881)
——. *Forty Years Prospecting in the Black Hills of South Dakota* (1921)

Hitchman, Sue *North of Pierre, 1740–1984* (1985)

Holley, Frances *Once Their Home, or Our Legacy from the Dakotahs* (1892)

Hughes, Richard B. (ed. Agnes W. Spring) *Pioneer Years in the Black Hills* (1957)

Humphrey, Seth K. *Following the Prairie Frontier* (1931)

Hunkins, Ralph V. and John C. Lindsey *South Dakota: Its Past, Present and Future* (1932)

Hurt, Wesley R. and William E. Lass *Frontier Photographer: Stanley J. Morrow's Dakota Years* (1956)

Huseboe, Arthur R. (ed.) *Big Sioux Pioneers: Essays about the Settlement of the Dakota Prairie Frontier* (1980)

Jackson, Donald *Custer's Gold—the United States Cavalry Expedition of 1874* (1966)

Jennewein, J. Leonard *Calamity Jane, of the Western Trails* (1952)
—— and Jane Boorman (eds.) *Dakota Panorama* (1961, rpt. 1974)

Johnson, Willis E. *South Dakota, a Republic of Friends* (1923)

Johnston, Sister Mary Antonio *Federal Relations with the Great Sioux Indians of South Dakota, 1887–1933* (1948)

Karolevitz, Robert F. *Yankton: A Pioneer Past* (1970)
——. *Pioneer Church in a Pioneer City* (1971)
——. *Challenge: The South Dakota Story* (1975)

Kaufman, Fred S. *Custer Passed Our Way* (1971)

Krause, Richard A. *The Leavenworth Site: Archaeology of an Historic Arikara Community* (1972)

Lange, Dietrich *The Lure of the Black Hills* (1916)

Lawson, Michael L. *Dammed Indians: The Pick-Sloan Plan and the Missouri River Sioux, 1944–1980* (1982)

Lee, Bob (ed.) *Gold, Gals, Guns, Guts* (1976)
—— and Dick Williams *Last Grass Frontier: The South Dakota Grower Heritage* (1964)

Lewis, Faye C. *Nothing to Make a Shadow* (1972)

Lowe, Barrett *Heroes and Hero Tales of South Dakota* (1931)
——. *Twenty Million Acres; the Story of America's First Conservationist, William Henry Harrison Beadle* (1937)

Mails, Thomas E. *Sundancing at Rosebud and Pine Ridge* (1978)

McGregor, James H. *The Wounded Knee Massacre, from the Viewpoint of the Sioux* (1940)

Milton, John R. *South Dakota: A Bicentennial History* (States and the Nation series) (1977)

Nelson, Paula *After the West Was Won: Homesteaders and Town Builders in Western South Dakota, 1900–1917* (1986)

O'Dell, Thomas E. *Mato, Paha; the Story of Bear Butte, Black Hills Landmark and Indian Shrine, Its Scenic, Historic, and Scientific Uniqueness* (1942)

O'Harra, Cleophas C. *The White River Badlands* (1920)
——— and Joseph P. Connolly *The Geology, Mineralogy and Scenic Features of Custer State Park, South Dakota* (1926)
——— and Joseph P. Connolly *Mineral Wealth of the Black Hills* (1929)

Parker, Watson *Gold in the Black Hills* (1966)
———. *Black Hills Ghost Town* (1974)
———. *Deadwood: The Golden Years* (1981)

Peattie, Roderick (ed.) *The Black Hills* (1952)

Peterson, Purl D. *Through the Black Hills and Bad Lands of South Dakota* (1929)

Pressler, Larry *U.S. Senators from the Prairie* (1982)

Price, S. Goodale *Black Hills, the Land of Legend* (1935)

Putney, Effie F. *In the South Dakota Country* 2 vols. (1922–1927)

Rath, George *The Black Sea Germans in the Dakotas* (1977)

Robinson, Doane *History of South Dakota* 2 vols. (1904)
———. *Doane Robinson's Encyclopedia of South Dakota* (1925)
———. *History of South Dakota, Sui Generis; Stressing the Unique and Dramatic in South Dakota History* (1930)

Rosen, Peter *Pa-ha-sa-pa, or the Black Hills of South Dakota* (1895)

Sampson, York (ed.) *South Dakota, Fifty Years of Progress, 1889–1939* (1939)

Sanford, Rev. John I. (comp.) *The Black Hills Souvenir, a Pictorial and Historic Description of the Black Hills* (1902)

Schell, Herbert A. *History of South Dakota* (1975)

Schuler, Harold H. *The South Dakota Capitol in Pierre* (1985) (1915)

Smith, George M. *South Dakota, Its History and Its People* (1915)

Smith, Rex A. *The Carving of Mount Rushmore* (1985)

Sneve, Virginia D. *Dakota's Heritage: A Compilation of Indian Place Names in South Dakota* (1973)
——— (ed.) *South Dakota Geographic Names* (1973)

South Dakota Legislature. State Legislative Research Council *The Administrative Organization of South Dakota State Government* (1972)

Spindler, Will H. *Tragedy Strikes at Wounded Knee, and Other Essays on Indian Life in South Dakota and Nebraska* (1972)

Spring, Agnes W. *The Cheyenne and Black Hills Stage and Express Routes* (1949)

Stutenroth, Stella M. *Daughters of Dacotah* (1942)

Tallent, Annie D. *The Black Hills, the Last Hunting Ground of the Dakotahs* (1899)

Thomson, Frank *Ninety-Six Years in the Black Hills* (1974)

Torrey, Edwin C. *Early Days in Dakota* (1925)

Van Nuys, Laura B. *The Family Band: From the Missouri to the Black Hills, 1881–1900* (1961)

Williamson, William *An Autobiography* (1964)

Wold, Josephine *Fort Abercrombie Centennial, 1857–1957* (1957)

Zeitner, June C. and Lincoln Borglum *Borglum's Unfinished Dream: Mount Rushmore* (1976)

Zimmerman, Larry J. *Peoples of Prehistoric South Dakota* (1985)

TENNESSEE

The east south central state of Tennessee is bordered on the north by Kentucky and Virginia; on the east by North Carolina; on the south by Georgia, Alabama, and Mississippi; and on the west by the Mississippi River, Arkansas, and Missouri.

FULL NAME State of Tennessee
POSTAL ABBREVIATION TN
INHABITANT Tennessean
ADMITTED TO THE UNION June 1, 1796. 16th state
POPULATION (est. 1987) 4,855,000. Percent of US total: 2.00%. Rank: 34th

CAPITAL CITY Nashville, located on the Cumberland River in north central Tennessee; population 462,450 (est. 1984). It was founded in 1779 as Fort Nashborough, incorporated as a town and renamed in 1784, incorporated as a city in 1806, and made the state capital in 1843.

STATE NAME AND NICKNAMES From the Cherokee word *tanasi*, the name given to two villages on the Little Tennessee River. Also known as the Volunteer State, the Big Bend State, and the Mother of Southwestern Statesmen.

STATE SEAL The top half, under the legend "XVI," shows a plough, sheaf of wheat, and cotton plant, with "Agriculture" inscribed beneath; the bottom half shows a sailboat, over the legend "Commerce." The border reads "The Great Seal of the State of Tennessee, 1796."

MOTTO Agriculture and Commerce (unofficial; from the state seal)

SONGS "My Homeland, Tennessee," by Nell Grayson Taylor and Roy Lamont Smith; "When It's Iris Time in Tennessee" by Willa Mae Waid; "My Tennessee" by Francis Hannah Tranum; "The Tennessee Waltz" by Redd Stewart and Pee Wee King; "Rocky Top," by Boudleaux and Felice Bryant.

SYMBOLS
Flower iris
Wildflower passion flower
Tree tulip poplar
Bird mockingbird
Gem Tennessee pearl
Rock limestone
Wild animal raccoon
Insect firefly and ladybug
Fine art porcelain painting
Folk dance square dance
Poem "Oh Tennessee, My Tennessee" by William Lawrence
Language English
Railroad museum Tennessee Valley Railroad Museum in Hamilton County

LICENSE PLATES (1) Red on white, with the state's three-star symbol and state name in blue. (2) Dark blue on white, with blue state outline bearing legend "Volunteer State."

FLAG A red field, ending in a thin vertical stripe of white and a wider one of blue; in the center, a blue circle enclosed in a border of white, containing three white five-pointed stars with points nearly touching in the center.

GEOGRAPHY AND CLIMATE

Long, narrow Tennessee contains picturesque mountain and valley terrain in the east, notably the Great Smoky Range of the Unaka Mountains and the Great Appalachian Valley. Wide basins and plateaus mark central Tennessee, while western Tennessee, part of the Gulf Coastal Plain, rolls gently to the swampy alluvial plain of the Mississippi River, which forms the state's western border.

AREA 42,144 square miles. Rank: 16th
INLAND WATER 989 square miles
GEOGRAPHIC CENTER Rutherford, 5 miles NE of Murfreesboro
ELEVATIONS *Highest point:* Clingmans Dome, Sevier County, 6,643 feet. *Lowest point:* Mississippi River, Shelby, 182 feet. *Mean elevation:* 900 feet

MAJOR RIVERS Mississippi, Tennessee, Cumberland

MAJOR LAKES AND RESERVOIRS Kentucky, Douglas, Cherokee, Center Hill, Dale Hollow, J. Perry Priest, Watts Bar, Tims Ford

LAND USE

	Thousands of acres
Urban (1982)	1,000
Rural (1982)	23,189
Cropland (1982)	51,592
Pastureland (1982)	5,356
Rangeland (1982)	0
Forestland (1982)	11,026
State parks and recreation areas (1983)	167
National park system (1984)	266
National forest system (1984)	1,212
Tribal lands (1984)	0

TEMPERATURES The highest recorded temperature was 113°F on August 9, 1930, at Perryville. The lowest was -32°F on December 30, 1917, at Mountain City.

NATIONAL SITES

NATIONAL BATTLEFIELDS Fort Donelson, Stones River
NATIONAL CEMETERIES Fort Donelson, Shiloh, Stones River
NATIONAL HISTORIC SITE Andrew Johnson
NATIONAL HISTORICAL PARK Cumberland Gap
NATIONAL MILITARY PARK Chickamauga and Chattanooga, Shiloh
NATIONAL PARK Great Smoky Mountains

NATIONAL PARKWAY Natchez Trace
NATIONAL SCENIC RIVERS AND RIVERWAYS Big South Fork National River and Recreation Area, Obed Wild and Scenic River
NATIONAL SCENIC TRAILS Appalachian, Natchez Trace
NATIONAL WILDLIFE REFUGES Cross Creeks, Hatchie, Reelfoot–Lake Isom, Tennessee

HISTORY

1540	Indian villages in the Tennessee Valley are ransacked by Spanish marauders.
1673	James Needham and Gabriel Arthur explore eastern Tennessee for Virginia.
1682	Robert Cavelier, Sieur de La Salle, claims Tennessee for France and constructs Fort Prud'homme.
1730	Sir Alexander Cuming negotiates the first treaty between the English and the Cherokee.
1738	A smallpox epidemic wipes out half of the Cherokee population.
1750	Dr. Thomas Walker discovers the Cumberland Gap.
1756	Fort Loudon is established and garrisoned by South Carolina.
1760	*August.* War breaks out between settlers and Cherokee. Fort Loudon settlers and garrison are massacred.
1763	France cedes all claims to land east of the Mississippi to Great Britain.
1769	William Bean founds settlement at Boone's Creek.
1772	Watuga Association is founded by residents to create a homespun government.
1775	*March 17.* The Treaty of Sycamore Shoals.
1777	The Watuga settlements are annexed by North Carolina as Washington County.
1779	James Robertson, the "Father of Tennessee," reaches Cumberland Settlement.
1780	*May 1.* The Cumberland Settlement is signed.
	October 7. Tennessee troops help defeat the British at the Battle of King's Mountain in South Carolina.

1784	*December.* The state of Franklin is established out of land ceded by North Carolina to the federal government. North Carolina refuses to recognize the state.
1786	White's Fort is built on the site of Knoxville.
1790	*May 26.* The "Territory of the United States South of the Ohio River" is established.
1795	The Walton Wagon Road is completed between Knoxville and Nashville.
1796	*February 6.* A state constitution is adopted. A petition to outlaw slavery is defeated.
	June 1. Tennessee becomes the 16th state admitted to the Union.
1800	The Great Revival.
1819	The *General Jackson* is the first steamboat to make its way up the Cumberland to Nashville.
	Elihu Embee founds the *Manumission Intelligencer.*
1827	The Cherokee adopt a written constitution.
1828	The *Cherokee Phoenix* is published.
1835	Free blacks are disenfranchised.
1838	The Cherokee are removed to Oklahoma along the Trail of Tears.
1842	The first train in Tennessee makes an exhibition run over the Legrange & Memphis Railroad.
1843	Nashville becomes the state capital.
1847	The New Orleans and Ohio Telegraph Company is chartered.
1850	*June 3–12.* The Southern Convention meets in Nashville.
1860	A special session of the General Assembly votes to submit the secession question to a statewide referendum.
1861	*June 8.* Tennessee is the last of 11 southern states to secede from the Union.
1862	*February.* General Ulysses S. Grant captures Fort Henry and Fort Donelson.
	April 6–7. Confederates are defeated by Grant at the Battle of Shiloh.
	June 6. Memphis falls.
	December 31. Battle of Stone's River or Murfreesboro.
1863	*November 24–25.* The Union victory at Chattanooga opens the way to Atlanta.
1864	*April 12.* Confederate troops capture Fort Pillow.
	December 15–16. The Battle of Nashville.
1865	*January.* A constitutional convention is held in Nashville, dominated by radical Unionists.
	April 6. Governor William G. "Parson" Brownlow is inaugurated, beginning radical reconstruction.
1866	*July 24.* Tennessee is the first to have its statehood restored.
1869	*February 25.* Governor DeWitt C. Senter succeeds Brownlow, ending radical reconstruction.
1871	"The Fisk Jubilee Singers" leave on their first concert tour.
1878	The worst yellow fever epidemic in US history strikes Memphis, killing 5,000 out of 19,000.
1883	The General Assembly approves a funding measure that scales down the state debt, resolving an issue that had dominated postwar politics.
1886	"The War of the Roses." Robert L. Taylor, Democratic candidate for governor defeats his brother, Alfred A. Taylor, Republican candidate.
1890	In the "Agrarian Revolt" the Farmer's alliance seizes control of the Democratic party and the governorship.
1891–1892	The Coal Creek Strike.
1895	*September 18–20.* The Chickamauga & Chattanooga National Military Park is dedicated.
1897	*May–November.* The Tennessee Centennial Exposition is held in Nashville.
1905–1906	The Black Patch Wars.
1907	The local option law is extended to include all cities and towns, making all of rural Tennessee legally dry.
1908	*November 9.* Edward Ward Carmack, in a dispute arising out of a bitter contest for the gubernatorial nomination, is shot dead by Robin Cooper.

1909	Public opinion, inflamed by Carmack's murder, forces mandatory statewide prohibition through the General Assembly over Governor Malcolm R. Patterson's veto.
1920	The state's vote for women's suffrage is decisive in adding the 19th Amendment to the Federal Constitution.
1922	The first commercial radio station in Tennessee begins broadcasting in Nashville.
1923	Governor Austin Peay enacts the Administration Reorganization Bill.
1925	John Scopes is found guilty of teaching evolution in Dayton public schools.
	November 28. George B. Hay inaugurates the WSM "Barn Dance," predecessor of the "Grand Ole Opry."
1926	Great Smoky National Park in North Carolina and Tennessee is created.
1930	Coldwell & Company, the South's largest financial institution, collapses. The Tennessee state government loses over $6.5 million.
1933	*August 31*. The Tennessee Valley Authority (TVA) is created by an act of Congress.
1935	Construction begins on modern airports for Nashville, Chattanooga, and Memphis.
1936	*March 4*. Norris Dam, the first unit of the TVA, is completed.
1943	The Grand Ole Opry chooses the Ryman Auditorium as its permanent quarters.
1945	Holston Ordnance Works at Kingsport becomes one of the world's largest manufacturers of conventional explosives.
	August 6. The existence of the atomic bomb administrative center at Oak Ridge, begun in 1942, is revealed.
	Dr. Dorothy Brown graduates from Meharry Medical College to become the first black woman to practice general surgery in the South.
1956	The National Guard is called out to put down rioting and ensure integration at Clinton.
1960	Downtown lunch counters in Nashville are integrated after a series of "sit-ins."
1964	NAACP lawyer A. W. Willis becomes the first black elected to the General Assembly in the twentieth century.
1968	*April 4*. The Reverend Martin Luther King, Jr. is assassinated in Memphis.
1970	For the first time since Reconstruction, Republicans win control of all three major statewide offices.
1972	Opryland USA opens, attracting 1.4 million visitors in its first year.
1974	*April 3*. Tennessee is declared a disaster area due to tornado damage.
	Tennessee sends its first woman (Marilyn Lloyd [Bouguard]) and its first black (Harold Ford) to Congress.
1975	*March 13–15*. Floods across the state create damages estimated in the millions.
1976	The Adventure II project reenacts the flatboat voyage of pioneers to settle Nashville.
1978	Firemen, policemen, and teachers strike in Memphis.
	The US Supreme Court blocks completion of TVA's Tellico Dam on the basis of the Endangered Species Act.
1980	Former Governor Ray Blanton is convicted of selling liquor licenses.
1982	*May 1*. Knoxville World Fair opens.
1983	United American Bank of Knoxville collapses, the fourth largest bank failure in US history.
1985	Opryland USA launches the *General Jackson*, one of America's largest paddleboats.

DEMOGRAPHY

Population (est. 1987)	4,855,000	Black	725,949
Population (1980)	4,591,120	Hispanic	34,081
Population density in persons		White	3,835,078
per square mile (1980)	108.9	Other	10,657

POPULATION BY RACE (1980)

American Indian/Aleut/ Eskimo	5,103
Asian/Pacific Islander	13,963

POPULATION CHARACTERISTICS (1980)

Percent of state population

Urban	60.4
Rural	39.6

Under 18 . . . . 28.3
65 or older 11.3
College-educated 11.9
Families below poverty line . . . 13.1
Public-assistance recipients 6.4

Per capita personal income
(1986) $11,831
Millionaires per 100,000
residents (1982) 113.8
Average life expectancy in
years (1980) 73.3
Marriage rate (1986) 12.2
Divorce rate (1986) 6.1
Birth rate per 1,000
residents (1985) 14.8
Infant mortality rate per 1,000
births (1985) 12.4
Abortion rate per 1,000
live births (1985) 315

Crime rate per 100,000 residents
(1985)
Violent 539.6
Property 3,994.6
Federal and state prisoners
per 100,000 residents (1984) . . 162
Alcohol consumption in gallons
per capita (1985) 32.0
Deaths from motor vehicle accidents
per 100,000 residents (1985) . . 23.1

MAJOR CITIES

	1984 population (est.)
Chattanooga	164,400
Clarksville	58,532
Knoxville	173,972
Memphis	648,399
Nashville-Davidson	462,450

GOVERNMENT AND POLITICS

Number of US Representatives 9
Electoral votes 11

POLITICAL PARTY NOMINEES FROM STATE
* winner

Andrew Jackson	1824	P
Andrew Jackson	1824	VP
Andrew Jackson* (Democratic-Republican)	1828	P
Andrew Jackson* (D-R)	1832	P
Hugh Lawson White (Whig faction)	1836	P
James Knox Polk (D-R faction)	1840	VP
James Knox Polk* (D)	1844	P
Andrew Jackson Donelson (American/Whig)	1856	VP
John Bell (Constitutional Union)	1860	P
Andrew Johnson* (D, elected on R ticket)	1864	VP
James R. Greer (American/declined)	1888	VP
Ira Landrith (Prohibition)	1916	VP
Alvin York (Prohibition/declined)	1936	VP
Estes Kefauver (D/Liberal)	1956	VP
John Kasper (National States' Rights)	1964	P
Thomas Jefferson Anderson (American)	1972	VP
Thomas Jefferson Anderson (American)	1976	P
Delmar Dennis (American)	1984	P

PRESIDENTIAL PRIMARY ELECTION In 1988, Tennessee sent 77 Democratic delegates and 45 Republican delegates to the national conventions.

CONSTITUTION Tennessee has had three constitutions: 1796, 1835, and the present one, adopted in 1870.

LEGISLATURE The General Assembly is divided into the Senate (33 members, 4-year term, minimum age 30) and the House of Representatives (99 members, 2-year term, minimum age 21). In 1987, the annual salary was $12,500.

JUDICIARY The highest court is the Supreme Court, with 5 judges serving 8-year terms. In 1987, the annual salary was $56,975.

EXECUTIVE The governor serves a 4-year term; the minimum age for holding office is 30. In 1987, the annual salary was $85,000. There are 3 other elected officials.

PRESIDENTIAL VOTE 1948-1988 *(in percents)*

Year	State Winner	Democratic	Republican
1948	Truman (D)	49.1	36.9
1952	Eisenhower (R)	49.7	50.0
1956	Eisenhower (R)	48.6	49.2
1960	Nixon (R)	45.8	52.8
1964	Johnson (D)	55.5	44.5
1968	Nixon (R)	28.1	37.9
1972	Nixon (R)	29.8	67.7
1976	Carter (D)	55.9	42.9
1980	Reagan (R)	48.4	48.7
1984	Reagan (R)	41.6	57.8
1988	Bush (R)	42.0	58.0

GOVERNORS

Territorial Governor
William Blount — 1790-1796

State Governors
John Sevier (Democratic-Republican) — 1796-1801
Archibald Roane (D-R) — 1801-1803
John Sevier (D-R) — 1803-1809
Willie Blount (D-R) — 1809-1815
Joseph McMinn (D-R) — 1815-1821
William Carroll (D-R) — 1821-1827
Sam Houston (D-R) — 1827-1829
William Hall (D-R/acting) — 1829
William Carroll (D) — 1829-1835
Newton Cannon (Whig) — 1835-1839
James K. Polk (D) — 1839-1841
James C. Jones (Whig) — 1841-1845
Aaron V. Brown (D) — 1845-1847
Neill S. Brown (Whig) — 1847-1849
William Trousdale (D) — 1849-1851
William B. Campbell (Whig) — 1851-1853
Andrew Johnson (D) — 1853-1857
Isham G. Harris (D) — 1857-1862
Andrew Johnson (military) — 1862-1865
William G. Brownlow (R) — 1865-1869
DeWitt C. Senter (Conservative Republican) — 1869-1871
John C. Brown (D) — 1871-1875
James D. Porter (D) — 1875-1879
Albert S. Marks (D) — 1879-1881
Alvin Hawkins (R) — 1881-1883
William B. Bate (D) — 1883-1887
Robert L. Taylor (D) — 1887-1891
John P. Buchanan (D) — 1891-1893
Peter Turney (D) — 1893-1897
Robert L. Taylor (D) — 1897-1899
Benton McMillin (D) — 1899-1903
James B. Frazier (D) — 1903-1905
John I. Cox (D) — 1905-1907
Malcolm R. Patterson (D) — 1907-1911
Ben W. Hooper (R) — 1911-1915
Thomas C. Rye (D) — 1915-1919
Albert H. Roberts (D) — 1919-1921
Alfred A. Taylor (R) — 1921-1923
Austin Peay (D) — 1923-1927
Henry H. Horton (D) — 1927-1933
Hill McAlister (D) — 1933-1937
Gordon Browning (D) — 1937-1939
Prentice Cooper (D) — 1939-1945
Jim Nance McCord (D) — 1945-1949
Gordon Browning (D) — 1949-1953
Frank G. Clement (D) — 1953-1959
Buford Ellington (D) — 1959-1963
Frank G. Clement (D) — 1963-1967
Buford Ellington (D) — 1967-1971
Winfield Dunn (R) — 1971-1975
Ray Blanton (D) — 1975-1979
Lamar Alexander (R) — 1979-1987
Ned R. McWherter (D) — 1987-

MINIMUM AGES
Majority — 18
Marriage with parental consent — 16
Marriage without parental consent — 18
Making a will — 18
Buying alcohol — 21
Jury duty — 18
Leaving school — 16
Driver's license — 16

CAPITAL PUNISHMENT
Number executed 1976-88: 0
On death row Aug. 1, 1988: 70

MILITARY INSTALLATIONS
Total number: 13
Major bases:
  Navy: 1

FINANCES

Thousands of dollars
GENERAL REVENUE (1985)
Total general revenue — 5,351,295
Total tax revenue — 2,998,373

Sales and gross receipts . . . 2,292,690
Individual income taxes 61,825
Corporate net income taxes . . 259,198

GENERAL EXPENDITURE (1985)
Total general expenditure . 5,025,340
Education 2,002,990
Public welfare 852,837
Health 191,376
Hospitals 252,606
Natural resources 87,499
Highways 700,620
Police 35,299
Corrections 155,683

FEDERAL AID (1985) 2,049,340

ECONOMY

Tennessee's approximately 80,000 farms produce tobacco, cotton, soybeans, corn, hay, wheat, apples, potatoes, vegetables, and strawberries. Beef and dairy cattle are the principal livestock; hogs, sheep, poultry, horses, and mules are also raised. In 1983, farm marketings cash receipts were $1.9 billion, with income almost evenly split between crops and livestock. Mining products include marble, sandstone and limestone, crushed stone, zinc, phosphate, bituminous coal, clay, and pyrite. Chemicals are the main manufactured product, followed by processed foods, textiles, machinery, ceramics and glass, paper and printed materials, rubber goods, fabricated metals (notably aluminum), and metal products. Value added by manufacture was $17.8 billion, among the highest in the South.

EMPLOYMENT (1984)
Thousands of persons
Total number of employed
  workers 2,033
Construction 76.3
Finance, insurance, and
  real estate 85.8
Government 293.0
Manufacturing 497.6
Mining 7.9
Services 345.2
Transportation, communications,
  and utilities 88.5
Wholesale and retail trade 414.7

Percent of civilian labor force
  unemployed (1984) 8.6

DEPARTMENT OF DEFENSE (1985)
Civilian workers employed . . . 7,300
Military personnel 10,991
Contract awards . . . . . $793 million

ENERGY SOURCES FOR ELECTRIC UTILITIES (1983)
Percent
Coal 65.2
Gas 0.1
Hydroelectric 14.3
Nuclear 20.2
Petroleum 0.2

TRANSPORTATION
Motor vehicles registered
  in state (1986) 3,932,220
Miles of roads, streets,
  and highways (1986) 83,851
Miles of Class I railway
  operated (1986) 2,537
Airports (1983) 169
Major aviation hubs (1983) 4
  Largest hub: Memphis
Major ports, with gross tonnage in
  thousands (1985):
  Memphis 10,375

CULTURE AND EDUCATION

Native American tribes
Tennessee was formerly home to the Catawba, Cherokee, Chiaha, Chickasaw, Creek, Kaskinampo, Natchez, Ofo, Shawnee, and Tuskegee.

Religions, ethnicities, and languages
Tennessee was settled mainly by the English, together with some Scotch, Irish, German, Dutch, and French settlers, and most of Tennessee's white inhabitants are of English descent. More than 99 percent of Tennesseans were born in the United States. In 1980, 1.9 percent of Tennessee's population spoke a language other than English at home. The United Methodist and Southern Baptist denominations are the largest, representing about two thirds of the churchgoing population.

Major museums and libraries
American Museum of Atomic Energy,
  Oak Ridge
Brooks Museum of Art, Memphis
Tennessee State Museum, Memphis

Major arts organizations
Chattanooga Opera
Cumberland County Playhouse, Cross-
ville
Nashville Ballet
Opera Memphis
Symphony orchestras of Chattanooga,
Knoxville, Memphis, Nashville

Colleges and universities
Number public (1986-87) 24
Number private (1986-87) 58

Total enrollment, in full-time equivalent
students (1985) 153,000

Public elementary and secondary schools
Expenditure per pupil in average daily
attendance (1986-87) $2,842
Pupil-teacher ratio (1987) 19.9
Average teacher salary (1986-87) $23,231

Holidays
Andrew Jackson's Birthday. March 15
Nathan Bedford Forrest's Birthday.
July 13
State Fair, Nashville. Mid-September

TENNESSEE IN LITERATURE

James Agee *The Morning Watch* (1950, rpt. 1976)
A study of the thoughts of a young church-school boy at his
first Good Friday service.
———. *A Death in the Family* (1957, rpt. 1971)
Events in the life of an East Tennessee family in 1915
following the death of the father in an automobile accident.

Hervey Allen *Action at Aquila* (1938)
Historical novel of the Civil War in the Shenandoah Valley
in 1864.

Anne Wetzell Armstrong *This Day and Time* (1930, rpt.
1970)
An East Tennessee countrywoman returns to her rural
home, which is portrayed as a source of spiritual strength.

Charles Barley Bell and **Harriet P. Miller** *A Mysterious
Spirit: The Bell Witch of Tennessee* (1972)
Two accounts of a local legend.

Octavia L. Z. Bond *Old Tales Retold; or, Perils and Adventures
of Tennessee Pioneers* (1906, rpt. 1973)
Narratives of de Soto, Robertson, Sevier and others.

Arna Bontemps *Chariot in the Sky: A Story of the Jubilee Singers*
(1951, rpt. 1971)
A narrative told through the life of Caleb Willows, who was
born in slavery but attended Fisk University after the Civil
War.

John M. Bradbury *The Fugitive: A Critical Account* (1958, rpt.
1964)

Campbell H. Brown (ed.) *The Reminiscences of Newton
Cannon, First Sergeant, 11th Tennessee Cavalry, C.S.A.* (1963)

William Gannaway Brownlow *Sketches of the Rise, Progress
and Decline of Succession; with a Narrative of Personal Adventures among the Rebels* (1862, rpt. 1968)

Maristan Chapman *Happy Mountain* (1928)
First in a sequence of lyrical novels of the Cumberland
region written by a Chattanooga man, John Stanton
Higham, and his wife.

Louise Cowan *The Fugitive Group: A Literary History* (1959)

Alfred Leland Crabb *A Mockingbird Sang at Chickamauga*
(1949)
One of the author's eleven historical novels dealing with
the Civil War and pioneer times in Tennessee and Kentucky.

Davy Crockett (ed. Paul A. Hutton) *A Narrative of the Life
of David Crockett of the State of Tennessee* (1834, rpt. 1987)

Louise L. Davis *Frontier Tales of Tennessee* (1976); *More Tales
of Tennessee* (1978)
Thirty stories about people who played an important part
in state history.

Anne Downes *Quality of Mercy* (1959)
Novel about Jackson's campaign against the Creek Indians
in 1813.

Robert Drake *The Single Heart* (1971)
Autobiographical tales of growing up in Ripley.

John Ehle *The Land Breakers* (1963)
Novel about mountain pioneers c.1780.

Sarah Barnwell Elliot *Jerry* (1891)
Classic novel of a mountain boy's upbringing and rise to
prosperity.

Shelby Foote *Shiloh* (1952)
Fictional account of the battle closely based on actual
events.

Jesse Hill Ford *The Liberation of Lord Byron Jones* (1965)
Novel about racial tensions in a small town. Ford has also
written a short story collection set in the same town, *Fishes,
Birds and Sons of Men* (1967) and a historical novel set during
the Civil War in West Tennessee, *The Raider* (1975).

John Rolfe Gardiner *Great Dream from Heaven* (1975)
Novel about the Coal Creek Rebellion of 1889.

Noel B. Gerson *The Cumberland Rifles* (1952, rpt. 1979)
A historical romance set in the time of the free state of
Franklin.
———. *The Slender Reed: A Biographical Novel of James K. Polk*
(1965)

Ely Green *Ely: An Autobiography* (1966)
The illegitimate son of a black woman and a white man
recalls his boyhood in Sewanee, Tennessee, where he was
born in 1893.

Will T. Hale *The Backward Trail* (1899)
Stories of pioneer life by a journalist and poet who was
among the first writers to record Tennessee dialect.

George Washington Harris *Sut Lovingood's Yarns* (1867)
Tales and anecdotes written in the persona of a semi-
literate mountain man. Harris's tales, along with the
popular Crockett almanacs, with their yarns of pioneer
adventure, are regarded as an important part of the tradition
of regional humor that gave rise to Mark Twain.

William C. Hardy (ed. Arna Bontemps) *Father of the Blues;
An Autobiography of W.C. Hardy* (1970)
The autobiography of a prominent black musician and
Beale Street performer.

Mildred Haun *The Hawk's Done Gone, and Other Stories* (1968)
Stories of the east Tennessee mountain people.

Ben W. Hooper (ed. Everett R. Boyce) *The Unwanted Boy:
The Autobiography of Governor Ben W. Hooper* (1963)
The first Republican to be elected governor recounts his
political career and describes the state in the post-
Reconstruction period.

M. V. Ingram *An Authenticated History of the Famous Bell Witch*
(1961, rpt. 1974)
An account of a supernatural incident that took place in
Robertson County during the early nineteenth century.

Madison Jones *A Buried Land* (1963); *Passage through Gehenna*
(1978)
Realistic novels of contemporary rural life.

May Justus *The Complete Peddler's Pack: Games, Songs,
Rhymes, and Riddles from Mountain Folklore* (1967)
Folktales and songs of the Smoky Mountains.

Harry H. Kroll *I Was a Sharecropper* (1937)
Autobiography describing the hardships of primitive rural life by a novelist whose fiction, *Three Brothers and Seven Daddies* (1932) and *The Cabin in the Cotton* (1931) is also set in poor rural areas.

Bruce Lancaster *No Bugles Tonight* (1948)
Civil War romance about a Union agent.

John A. Leland *Othneil Jones* (1956)
Romance about a pioneer who serves with Marion's raiders in 1781.

Perry Lentz *Falling Hills* (1967)
Fictional account of the Fort Pillow Massacre, in which a Union fort was captured.

Michael A. Lofaro (ed.) *The Tall Tales of Davy Crockett: The Second Nashville Series of Crockett Almanacs, 1838–1841* (1987)

Andrew Lytle *The Velvet Horn* (1959)
Novel about five orphaned children living in the Cumberland hills during the late nineteenth century.

Richard Marius *Coming of Rain* (1969)
Novel set in a small town during Reconstruction.

Charles Hodge Mathes *Tall Tales from Old Smoky* (1976)
Sixteen tales of mountain people originally published 1923–1936.

Ben H. McClary *Our Literary Heritage: A Guide for Tennessee in Literature* (1962)

William Lynwood Montell *Don't Go Up Kettle Creek: Verbal Legacy of the Upper Cumberland* (1983)
An oral history of the people of the Cumberland River between Burnside, Kentucky and Carthage, Tennessee, including numerous legends and folktales.

James Mooney *Myths of the Cherokee* American Indian History Series, Bureau of American Ethnology (1800, rpt. 1970)

John Trotwood Moore *Hearts of Hickory* (1926)
Romantic historical novel about the exploits of Andrew Jackson and David Crockett.

Mary Noailles Murfree (pseud. Charles Egbert Craddock) *In the Tennessee Mountains* (1884, rpt. 1970)
Popular local color stories emphasizing picturesque details of regional life. Murfree was among the first American writers to attempt realistic portrayal of local character, and laid the foundation of Appalachian regional writing.

Meredith Nicholson *Cavalier of Tennessee* (1928)
Romantic historical novel about Andrew Jackson.

Orlando M. Poe *Personal Recollections of the Occupation of East Tennessee and the Defense of Knoxville* (1889, rpt. 1963)

Frank J. Ray *Tennessee Writers: A Bibliographical Index* (1929)

Bella Rodman *Lions in the Way* (1966)
A fictional treatment of high school integration in a small town.

Elizabeth Seeman *In the Arms of the Mountain: An Intimate Journal of the Great Smokies* (1961)
A journal of a couple's attempt to flee Chicago and support themselves by farming in the Smoky Mountains.

John L. Stewart *The Burden of Time: The Fugitives and Agrarians* (1965)

Irving Stone *The President's Lady: A Novel about Rachel and Andrew Jackson* (1961, rpt. 1968)
A historical novel closely based on actual events.

Thomas S. Stribling *Teeftallow* (1926)
Realistic novel of farming people set in the hills of west Tennessee.

Peter Taylor *Collected Stories* (1969)
Stories of affluent Tennessee and Kentucky society, chiefly concerning the nuances of Southern tradition and mores. *A Summons to Memphis* (1986) is a novel centering on the narrator's Nashville upbringing.

Robert Love Taylor *Governor Bob Taylor's Tales* (1896)
Classic regional stories and humorous anecdotes.

Robert Penn Warren *Flood* (1964)
Novel about a West Tennessee community disrupted by the construction of a dam. The Kentucky-born author, a prominent member of The Fugitives, has written several prose works with Tennessee settings, including *At Heaven's Gate* (1943), a novel suggested by the career of the politician Luke Lea, and *Meet Me in the Green Glen* (1971), a novel about a farmer.

Ray Wilbanks (ed.) *Literature of Tennessee* (1984)

Richard Wright *Black Boy: A Record of Childhood and Youth* (1947, rpt. 1969)
The novelist describes his upbringing in Jackson and Memphis.

Thomas D. Young *Tennessee Writers* (1981)

GUIDES TO RESOURCES

Alderson, William T. and **Robert H. White** *A Guide to the Study and Reading of Tennessee History* (1959)

Bauer, Harry C. (comp.) *An Indexed Bibliography of the Tennessee Valley Authority* (1933–40, various editions)

Beasley, Gladys M. and **Mary F. Brown** *Tennessee Through the Printed Page: A Classifed List of Material Relating to Tennessee for School Libraries* (1942)

Cram, Kendall J. *Guide to the Use of Genealogical Material in the Tennessee State Library and Archives* (1964)

Crawford, Charles W. (ed.) *Governors of Tennessee* (1979–)

Federal Writers' Project *Tennessee: A Guide to the State* (1939, rpt. 1986)

Fulcher, Richard C. (comp.) *Guide to County Records and Genealogical Resources in Tennessee* (1987)

Goehring, Eleanor *Tennessee Folk Culture: An Annotated Bibliography* (1982)

Hauck, Richard B. *Crockett, a Bio-bibliography* (1982)

Morris, Eastin (ed. Robert M. McBride) *The Tennessee Gazetteer, or Topographical Dictionary* (1834, rpt. 1971)

Rhea, Matthew (ed. Robert M. McBride) *Map of the State of Tennessee, 1832* (1971)

Smith, Sam B. (ed.) *Tennessee History, a Bibliography* (1974)

Stokely, Jim and **Jeff D. Johnson** (eds.) *An Encyclopedia of East Tennessee* (1981)

Tennessee State Library and Archives *Writings on Tennessee Counties* (1967)
———. *A List of Tennessee State Publications* (annual 1971–)

West Tennessee Historical Society *The West Tennessee Historical Guide to Archives and Collections* (1979)

SELECTED NONFICTION SOURCES

Abernethy, Thomas P. *From Frontier to Plantation in Tennessee; a Study in Frontier Democracy* (1932, rpt. 1967)

Acuff, Roy with **William Neely** *Roy Acuff's Nashville: The Life and Good Times of Country Music* (1983)

Alderman, Pat *The Overmountain Men; Early Tennessee History, 1760–1795* (1970, rpt. 1986)

Alderson, William T. (ed.) *Tennessee Lives* (1971)
——— and **Robert M. McBride** (eds.) *Landmarks of Tennessee History* (1965)

Alexander, Thomas B. *Political Reconstruction in Tennessee* (1950, rpt. 1968)
————. *Thomas A. R. Nelson of East Tennessee* (1956)

Allen, Leslie H. (ed.) *Bryan and Darrow at Dayton: The Record and Documents of the "Bible-Evolution Trial"* (1967)

Allison, John *Dropped Stitches in Tennessee History* (1897, rpt. 1971)

Arnow, Harriette L. S. *Flowering of the Cumberland* (1963)

Bailey, Fred A. *Class and Tennessee's Confederate Generation* (1987)

Bakeless, John *Master of the Wilderness: Daniel Boone* (1939)

Barnett, Paul *Industrial Development in Tennessee* (1941)

Barrett, Albert T. *Tennessee* (1904)

Bergeron, Paul H. *Antebellum Politics in Tennessee* (1982)

Blair, Walter *Davy Crockett, Legendary Frontier Hero* (1986)

Blanche, Henry C. *The Tennessee Yeomen, 1840–1860* (1942)

Blumstein, James F. and Benjamin Walter (eds.) *Growing Metropolis: Aspects of Development in Nashville* (1975)

Bowman, Elizabeth S. *Land of High Horizons* (1938)

Brandau, Roberta S. (ed.) *History of Homes and Gardens in Tennessee* (1936)

Brewer, Alberta and Carson *Valley So Wild: A Folk History* (1975)

Brown, John P. *Old Frontiers: The Story of the Cherokee Indians* (1938, rpt. 1971)

Bruce, H. Addington *Daniel Boone and the Wilderness Road* (1910)

Bryant, F. Carlene *We're All Kin: A Cultural Study of a Mountain Neighborhood* (1981)

Burke, James W. *David Crockett: The Man Behind the Myth* (1984)

Caldwell, Mary F. *Tennessee: The Dangerous Example; Watauga to 1849* (1974)

Callahan, North *Smoky Mountain Country* (1952)
————. *TVA: Bridge over Troubled Waters* (1980)

Campbell, Carlos C. *Birth of a National Park in the Great Smoky Mountains* (1960)

Campbell, John C. *The Southern Highlander and His Homeland* (1921)

Cansler, Charles W. *Three Generations: The Story of a Colored Family of Eastern Tennessee* (1961)

Capers, Gerald M. *Biography of a River Town: Memphis, Its Heroic Age* (1939)

Cartwright, Joseph H. *The Triumph of Jim Crow: Tennessee Race Relations in the 1880s* (1976)

Case, Earl C. *The Valley of East Tennessee: The Adjustment of Industry to Natural Environment* (1925)

Chandler, William V. *The Myth of TVA: Conservation and Development in the Tennessee Valley, 1933–1983* (1984)

Cimprich, John *Slavery's End in Tennessee, 1861–1865* (1985)

Clark, Blanche H. *The Tennessee Yeoman, 1840–1860* (1942)

Conkin, Paul K. *Gone with the Ivy: A Biography of Vanderbilt University* (1985)

Connelly, Thomas L. *Army of the Heartland: The Army of Tennessee, 1861–1862* (1967)
————. *Autumn of Glory; the Army of Tennessee, 1862–1865* (1974)
————. *Civil War Tennessee: Battles and Leaders* (1979)

Corlew, Robert E. *Tennessee, a Short History* (2d ed. 1981)

Coulter, E. Merton *William G. Brownlow, Fighting Parson of the Southern Highlands* (1937, rpt. 1971)

Creekmore, Betsey B. *Arrows to Atoms: The Story of East Tennessee* (1959)

Crow, Vernon H. *Storm in the Mountains: Thomas' Confederate Legion of Cherokee Indians and Mountaineers* (1982)

Crutchfield, James A. *Tennesseans at War: Volunteers and Patriots in Defense of Liberty* (1986)

Davenport, F. Garvin *Cultural Life in Nashville on the Eve of the Civil War* (1941)

Davidson, Donald *The Tennessee: The New River, Civil War to TVA* (Rivers of America series) (1948)
————. *The Tennessee: The Old River, Frontier to Secession* (Rivers of America series) (1978)

DeCamp, L. Sprague *The Great Monkey Trial* (1968)

Diekhoff, John S. et al. *A Study of Private Higher Education in Tennessee* (1970)

Dixon, Max *The Watagans* (1976)

Dorson, Richard M. *Davy Crockett, American Comic Legend* (1977)

Downey, Fairfax *Storming the Gateway: Chattanooga, 1863* (1960, 1969)

Doyle, Don H. *Nashville in the New South, 1880–1930* (1985)
————. *Nashville since the 1920s* (1985)

Droze, Wilmon H. *High Dams and Slack Waters: TVA Rebuilds a River* (1965)

Dunn, Durwood *Cades Cove: The Life and Death of a Southern Appalachian Community, 1818–1937* (1988)

Durham, Walter T. *Great Leap Westward: History of Sumner County, from Its Beginning to 1805* (1969)
————. *Daniel Smith: Frontier Statesman* (1976)

Dykeman, Wilma *The French Broad* (Rivers of America series) (1955, rpt. 1974)
————. *Tennessee, a Bicentennial History* (States and the Nation series) (1975)
———— and Jim Stokeley *Highland Homeland: The People of the Great Smokies* (1978)

East Tennessee Historical Society *History of Knoxville* (1945)

Edwards, Olga J. and Izora W. Frizzell *The "Connection" in East Tennessee* (1969)

Egerton, John *Visions of Utopia: Nashoba, Rugby, Ruskin, and the "New Communities" in Tennessee's Past* (1977)

Eller, Ronald D. *Miners, Millhands, and Mountaineers: Industrialization of the Appalachian South, 1880–1930* (1982)

Folmsbee, Stanley J., Robert E. Corlew, and Enoch L. Mitchell *History of Tennessee* 4 vols. (1960)

Freeman, Thomas H., IV *An Economic History of Tennessee* (1965)

Gatewood, Willard B., Jr. (ed.) *Controversy in the Twenties: Fundamentalism, Modernism, and Evolution* (1969)

Gerson, Noel B. *Franklin: America's "Lost State"* (1968)

Gilmore, James R. *The Rear-Guard of the Revolution* (1903, rpt. 1974)

Ginger, Ray *Six Days or Forever? Tennessee v. John Thomas Scopes* (1958, rpt. 1969)

Goodman, William *Inherited Domain: Political Parties in Tennessee* (1954)

Goodspell's General History of Tennessee (1887, rpt. 1973)

Gorman, Joseph B. *Kefauver: A Political Biography* (1971)

Graham, Hugh D. *Crisis in Print: Desegregation in the Press in Tennessee* (1967)

Greene, Lee S. and Robert S. Avery *Government in Tennessee* (1962)
———— and Jack E. Holmes "Tennessee: A Politics of Peaceful Change" in *The Changing Politics of the South* (William C. Havard ed. 1972)
————, David H. Grubbs, and Victor C. Hobday *Government in Tennessee* (3d ed. 1975)

————. *Lead Me On: Frank Good Clement and Tennessee Politics* (1982)

Groves, Leslie R. *Now It Can Be Told: The Story of the Manhattan Project* (1962)

Guild, J. C. *Old Times in Tennessee* (1878, rpt. 1971)

Hall, Joseph S. (ed.) *Sayings from the Old Smoky, Some Traditional Phrases, Expressions, and Sentences Heard in the Great Smoky Mountains and Nearby Areas; an Introduction to a Southern Mountain Dialect* (1972)

Hamer, Philip M. (ed.) *Tennessee: A History, 1673–1932* 4 vols. (1933)

Hamilton, James J. *The Battle of Fort Donelson* (1968)

Harper, Herbert L. (ed.) *Houston and Crockett: Heroes of Tennessee and Texas, an Anthology* (1986)

Hart, Roger L. *Redeemers, Bourbons, and Populists: Tennessee, 1870–1896* (1978)

Hauck, Richard B. *Davy Crockett: A Handbook* (1986)

Hay, George "The Story of the Grand Ole Opry," in Robert Shelton and Burt Goldblatt (eds.) *The Country Music Story* (1966)

Haywood, John *The Civil and Political History of the State of Tennessee* (1823, rpt. 1969)
————. *Natural and Aboriginal History of Tennessee* (1823, rpt. 1959)

Heiskell, S. G. *Andrew Jackson and Early Tennessee History* (1920)

Holly, J. Fred *Protective Labor Legislation and Its Administration in Tennessee* (1956)

Hoobler, James A. *Cities under the Gun: Images of Occupied Nashville and Chattanooga* (1986)

Horn, Stanley F. *The Army of Tennessee: A Military History* (1941, rpt. 1968)
———— (ed.) *Tennessee's War, 1861–1869* (1965)
————. *The Decisive Battle of Nashville* (1956, rpt. 1968)

Hubbard, Preston J. *Origins of the TVA, the Muscle Shoals Controversy, 1920–1932* (1961, rpt. 1968)

Humphrey, Steve *"That D———d Brownlow": Being a Saucy and Malicious Description of William Gannaway Brownlow . . .* (1978)

Isaac, Paul E. *Prohibition and Politics: Turbulent Decades in Tennessee, 1885–1920* (1965)

Johnson, Charles W. and Charles O. Jackson *City Behind a Fence: Oak Ridge, Tennessee, 1942–1946* (1981)

Jones, Billy M. (ed.) *Heroes of Tennessee* (1979)

Jones, Robert B. *Tennessee at the Crossroads: The State Debt Controversy, 1870–1883* (1977)

Jordan, Thomas and J. P. Pryor *The Campaigns of Lieut.-Gen. N. B. Forrest* (1868)

Keever, Rosalie A. (comp.) *Some Pioneer Preachers and Teachers of Tennessee* (1974)

Kelley, Sarah F. *General James Robertson: The Founder of Nashville* (1980)

Kelly, James C. *From Settlement to Statehood: Pictorial History of Tennessee to 1796* (1977)

Kephart, Horace *Our Southern Highlanders* (1913, rpt. 1976)

Key, V. O., Jr. "Tennessee: The Civil War and Mr. Crump" in *Southern Politics in State and Nation* (1949)

Korn, Jerry and the Editors of Time-Life Books *The Fight for Chattanooga: Chickamauga to Missionary Ridge* (1985)

Lamon, Lester C. *Black Tennesseans, 1900–1930* (1977)
————. *Blacks in Tennessee, 1791–1970* (1981)

Lee, David D. *Tennessee in Turmoil: Politics in the Volunteer State, 1920–1932* (1979)

Lewis, Thomas M. and Madeline Kneberg *Tribes That Slumber: Indians of the Tennessee Region* (1958, rpt. 1970)

Lofaro, Michael A. (ed.) *Davy Crockett: The Man, the Legend, the Legacy, 1786–1986* (1985)
———— and Joe Cummings (eds.) *Crockett at Two Hundred, New Perspectives on the Man and the Myth* (1989)

Lomax, John, III *Nashville: Music City USA* (1985)

Luther, Edward T. *Our Restless Earth: The Geologic Regions of Tennessee* (1977)

Lytle, Andrew N. *Bedford Forrest and His Critter Company* (1960)

Majors, William R. *The End of Arcadia: Gordon Browning and Tennessee Politics* (1982)

Maslowski, Peter *Treason Must Be Made Odious: Military Occupation and Wartime Reconstruction in Nashville, Tennessee 1862–1886* (1978)

Masterson, William H. *William Blount* (1954, rpt. 1970)

Mayors, William R. *The End of Arcadia: Gordon Browning and Tennessee Politics* (1982)
————. *Editorial Wild Oats: Edward Ward Carmack and Tennessee Politics* (1984)
————. *Change and Continuity: Tennessee Politics since the Civil War* (1986)

McBride, Robert M. (ed.) *More Landmarks of Tennessee History* (1969)

McCague, James *The Cumberland* (Rivers of America series) (1973)

McCormack, Edward M. *Slavery on the Tennessee Frontier* (1977)

McCraw, Thomas K. *TVA and the Power Fight, 1933–1939* (1971)

McFerrin, John B. *Caldwell and Company: A Southern Financial Empire* (1969)

McIlwaine, Shields *Memphis, Down in Dixie* (1948)

McKee, Margaret and Fred Chisenhall *Beale Black and Blue: Life and Music on Black America's Main Street* (1981)

McKellar, Kenneth D. *Tennessee Senators As Seen by One of Their Successors* (1942, rpt. 1944)

McKinney, Gordon B. *Southern Mountain Republicans, 1865–1900: Politics and the Appalachian Community* (1978)

McMillan, Laurence *The Schoolmaker: Sawney Webb and the Bell Buckle Story* (1971)

Miller, William D. *Memphis During the Progressive Era, 1900–1917* (1957)
————. *Mr. Crump of Memphis* (1964)

Minton, John Dean *The New Deal in Tennessee, 1932–1938* (1979)

Montgomery, James R. *To Foster Knowledge: A History of the University of Tennessee* (1984)

Moore, John T. and A. P. Foster *Tennessee: The Volunteer State, 1769–1923* 4 vols. (1923)

Morgan, Arthur E. *The Making of the TVA* (1974)

Munzer, Martha E. *Valley of Vision; the TVA Years* (1969)

Nall, James D. *The Tobacco Night Riders of Kentucky and Tennessee 1905–1909* (1939)

National Park Service *At Home in the Smokies: A History Handbook for Great Smoky Mountains National Park, North Carolina and Tennessee* (1984)

National Portrait Gallery/Tennessee State Museum *Davy Crockett, Gentleman From the Cane* (1986)

Norton, Herman A. *Religion in Tennessee, 1777–1945* (1981)

Nurick, Aaron J. *Participation in Organizational Change: The TVA Experiment* (1985)

Overholt, James *These Are Our Voices: The Story of Oak Ridge, 1942–1970* (1987)

Parker, Barry *The Tennesseans: A People and Their Land* (1981)

Parks, Joseph H. *John Bell of Tennessee* (1950)

Patterson, Caleb *The Negro in Tennessee, 1790–1865* (1922, rpt. 1968)

Patton, James W. *Unionism and Reconstruction in Tennessee, 1860–1869* (1934, rpt. 1966)

Perry, Jennings *Democracy Begins at Home: The Tennessee Fight on the Poll Tax* (1944)

Phelan, James *History of Tennessee: The Making of a State* (1988)

Phillips, Margaret I. *The Governors of Tennessee* (1978)

Porter, Eliot *Appalachian Wilderness; the Great Smoky Mountains* (1970)

Pride, Richard A. and J. David Woodard *The Burden of Busing: The Politics of Desegregation in Nashville* (1985)

Putnam, Albigence W. *History of Middle Tennessee; or, Life and Times of Gen. James Robertson* (1859, rpt. 1971)

Ramsey, James G. M. *The Annals of Tennessee to the End of the Eighteenth Century* (1853, rpt. 1971)

Robertson, Mary E. *The Attitude of Tennesseans toward the Union, 1847–1861* (1961)

Robinson, Dan *Bob Taylor and the Agrarian Revolt in Tennessee* (1935)

Robinson, George O. *The Oak Ridge Story: The Saga of a People Who Share in History* (1950)

Rourke, Constance *Davy Crockett* (1962)

Scott, Mingo *The Negro in Tennessee Politics and Governmental Affairs, 1865–1965* (1965)

Severn, Bill *Frontier President: James K. Polk* (1965)

Shackford, James A. (ed. John B. Shackford) *David Crockett: The Man and the Legend* (1956, rpt. 1986)

Shapiro, Henry D. *Appalachia on Our Mind: The Southern Mountains and Mountaineers in the American Consciousness, 1870–1920* (1978)

Shellenbarger, John D. *The Battle of Spring Hill* (1913)
———. *The Battle of Franklin, Tennessee* (1916)

Shields, A. Randolph *The Cades Cove Story* (1977)
———. *The Families of Cades Cove, 1821–1936* (1981)

Siler, Thomas T. *Tennessee Towns: From Adams to Yorkville* (1985)

Street, James *The Struggle for Tennessee* (1985)

Stupka, Arthur *Great Smoky Mountains National Park* (1960)

Sulzer, Elmer G. *Ghost Railroads of Tennessee* (1975)

Swados, Harvey *Standing Up for the People: The Life and Work of Estes Kefauver* (1972)

Taylor, A. Elizabeth *The Woman's Suffrage Movement in Tennessee* (1957)

Taylor, Alrutheus A. *The Negro in Tennessee, 1865–1880* (1944)

Taylor, O. W. *Early Tennessee Baptists, 1768–1832* (1957)

Temple, Oliver P. *East Tennessee and the Civil War* (1899, rpt. 1971)

Tennessee Valley Authority *A History of the Tennessee Valley Authority* (1983)

Thomas, James P. *From Tennessee Slave to St. Louis Entrepreneur: The Autobiography of James Thomas* (1984)

Thornborough, Laura *The Great Smoky Mountains* (1937, rev. ed. 1962)

Thorogood, James E. *A Financial History of Tennessee since 1870* (1949)

Watkins, Floyd C. and Charles H. *Yesterday in the Hills* (1963)

Wheeler, William B. and Michael J. McDonald *TVA and the Tellico Dam, 1936–1979: A Bureaucratic Crisis in Post-Industrial America* (1986)

Whitman, Wilson *God's Valley: People and Power along the Tennessee River* (1939)

Williams, Emma I. *Historic Madison, the Story of Jackson and Madison County, Tennessee* (1946)

Williams, Frank B. *Tennessee's Presidents* (1981)

Williams, Samuel Cole *History of the Lost State of Franklin* (1924, rpt. 1970)
———. *Lieutenant Henry Timberlake's Memories, 1756–1765* (1927, rpt. 1948)
——— (ed.) *Early Travels in the Tennessee Country* (1928, rpt. 1970)
———. *Beginnings of West Tennessee in the Land of the Chickasaws, 1541–1841* (1930, rpt. 1971)
———. *Dawn of Tennessee Valley and Tennessee History, 1541–1776* (1937)
———. *The Admission of Tennessee into the Union* (1945)

Wilson, Samuel T. *The Southern Mountaineers* (1914)

Wright, James B. *Great Smoky Mountains National Park* (1929)

Yelling, Carol Lynn (ed.) *Tennessee Women, Past and Present* (1977)

TEXAS

The west south central state of Texas is bordered on the north by Oklahoma and the Red River; on the east by Arkansas, Louisiana, and the Sabine River; on the southeast by the Gulf of Mexico; on the southwest by the Rio Grande and the Mexican states of Tamaulipas, Nuevo Leon, Coahuila, and Chihuahua; and on the west by New Mexico.

FULL NAME State of Texas
POSTAL ABBREVIATION TX
INHABITANT Texan
ADMITTED TO THE UNION Dec. 29, 1845. 28th state
POPULATION (EST. 1987) 16,789,000. Percent of US total: 6.90%. Rank: 3d

CAPITAL CITY Austin, located on the Colorado River in east central Texas; population 397,001 (est. 1984). Founded as Waterloo in 1835, it was renamed in 1839, when it was selected to be the capital of the Republic of Texas. It was incorporated in 1840. The government was temporarily moved to Houston during the war with Mexico, 1842-1845.

STATE NAME AND NICKNAMES From the Caddo Indian word *teysha*, "hello friend," or *tejas*, "friendship," a term applied by the Spanish to friendly tribes from Oklahoma to Louisiana. Also known as the Lone Star State, the Beef State, and the Banner State.

STATE SEAL On an azure field, a white five-pointed star encircled by a branch of live oak and a branch of olive; around the border, the legend "The State of Texas."

MOTTO Friendship

SONGS "Texas, Our Texas," by William J. Marsh and Gladys Yoakum Wright; state flower song: "Bluebonnets," lyrics by Julia D. Booth, music by Lora C. Crockett.

SYMBOLS
Flower bluebonnet
Tree pecan
Bird mockingbird
Plays "The Lone Star," "Texas," "Beyond the Sundown," "Fandangle"

LICENSE PLATES (1) Dark blue on white, with red state name and outline of state; some also with red legends "Sesquicentennial" and "1836-1986." (2) Dark blue on white, with outline of state. (3) Dark blue on white, with star.

FLAG The third nearest the staff is blue, with a white star in the center; the remaining segment is divided in half horizontally, the top half white, the bottom half red; all three segments have the same dimensions.

GEOGRAPHY AND CLIMATE

Texas's immense landscape rises in broad steps from the Gulf of Mexico to the state's western border. The fertile crescent of Texas's Gulf Coastal Plain ends 50 to 200 miles inland at the Balcones Escarpment, where the land abruptly changes to central plain and tableland and the Texas Hill Country in the northwest. West of the central plains and the Hill Country are the High Plains, dry, windswept rangeland, and, to the south, the dry Trans-Pecos region, centered on the Pecos River. A spur of the Rockies reaches down into western Texas near the Big Bend of the Rio Grande River.

AREA 266,807 square miles. Rank: 2d
INLAND WATER 4,790 square miles
GEOGRAPHIC CENTER McCulloch, 15 miles NE of Brady
ELEVATIONS *Highest point:* Guadalupe Peak, Culberson County, 8,749 feet. *Lowest point:* Gulf of Mexico, sea level. *Mean elevation:* 1,700 feet

MAJOR RIVERS Rio Grande, Red, Pecos, Brazos, Colorado, Trinity, Sabine, Neches

MAJOR LAKES AND RESERVOIRS Texoma, Toledo Bend, International Falcon, Meredith, Livingston, Conroe, Choke Canyon, Sam Rayburn, Amistad

TIDAL SHORELINE 3,359 miles, Gulf coast

LAND USE

	Thousands of acres
Urban (1982)	4,388
Rural (1982)	157,431
Cropland (1982)	33,320
Pastureland (1982)	17,043
Rangeland (1982)	95,353
Forestland (1982)	9,324
State parks and recreation areas (1983)	194
National park system (1984) . .	1,099
National forest system (1984) . .	1,994
Tribal lands (1984)	0

TEMPERATURES The highest recorded temperature was 120°F on August 12, 1936, at Seymour. The lowest was -23°F on February 8, 1933, at Seminole.

NATIONAL SITES

HISTORIC SITES Fort Davis, Palo Alto Battlefield
NATIONAL HISTORICAL PARKS Lyndon B. Johnson, San Antonio Missions
NATIONAL MEMORIAL Chamizal
NATIONAL MONUMENT Aliates Flint Quarries
NATIONAL PARK Big Bend Guadalupe Mountains
NATIONAL PRESERVE Big Thicket

NATIONAL RECREATION AREAS Amistad, Lake Meredith
NATIONAL SCENIC RIVER AND RIVERWAY Rio Grande Wild and Scenic River
NATIONAL SEASHORE Padre Island
NATIONAL WILDLIFE REFUGES Anahuac–Sea Rim, Aransas, Attwater, Prairie Chicken, Brazoria, Buffalo Lake, Hagerman, Laguna, Atascosa, Mulesh–Brulla, Santa Ana

HISTORY

1519	The first recorded visitor, a Spaniard, Alonso Alvarez de Piñeda, explores and maps the Texas coast.
1528	*November 6.* Alvar Cabeza de Vaca and three other Spaniards are shipwrecked on the Texas coast. For six years they travel among the Indians and bring back stories of Indian cities of great wealth.
1541	Vásquez de Coronado, searching for the seven "golden" cities of Cibola, travels through West Texas.
1542	Survivors of Hernando de Soto's expedition reach the High Plains of Texas. Spain bases its claims to Texas on these and other explorations.
1659	*December 8.* Mission Nuestra Señora de Guadalupe de El Paso is founded, beginning settlement by the Spanish in the El Paso vicinity.
1680	Refugees from the revolt of the pueblos in New Mexico settle along the Rio Grande River.
1681	Mission Corpus Christi de la Isleta del Sur is founded.
1682	Franciscan missionaries construct two missions in Texas near site of El Paso.

1685	*February 18.* French exploration begins in Texas when Robert Cavelier, Sieur de la Salle, establishes colony, Fort St. Louis.
1687	La Salle is murdered by one of his own men in a quarrel. Disease and Indians kill most of the colonists and the French colony fails.
1691	Texas officially becomes a Spanish province.
1718	*May 1.* Mission San Antonio (later the Alamo) is founded.
1731	By this date Spain has sent more than 90 expeditions into the Texas region and has established missions throughout the area.
1772	San Antonio becomes the seat of Spanish government in Texas. Colonization proceeds slowly.
1799	Anglo-American invasion of Mexico, led by Philip Nolan, is crushed by the Spanish in 1801. Nolan is killed.
1803	Louisiana is purchased by the US, increasing threat of American invasions into the Texas area.
1821	Mexico breaks away from Spain, and Texas becomes part of the Republic of Mexico. By the Treaty of Florida, US gives up its claims to Texas. Stephen F. Austin founds the first Anglo-American settlement, Sal Felipe de Austin, on the Brazos river.
1825	*March 24.* First American immigrants are permitted to establish colonies in Coahvilla, the Mexican state of Texas.
1830	*April 6.* Mexico enacts law checking further immigration of US citizens into Texas. No black slaves are to be imported.
1835	*October 2.* Settlers win Battle of Gonzales, first battle of the Texas Revolution. *October 12.* Stephen Austin's volunteer army marches on San Antonio. *November 3.* Provisional government is created. *December 9.* San Antonio is captured.
1836	*February 23.* General Santa Anna's Mexican Army lays siege to the Alamo. *March 6.* The Alamo is captured. *March 17.* Constitution adopted by state convention meeting at Washington. *April 21.* General Sam Houston defeats Mexican Army and wins Texas Revolution. *September 1.* Houston is elected president of the Republic of Texas.
1845	*December 29.* Texas is admitted as the 28th state.
1846	*May 8.* First battle of the US-Mexican War is won by General Zachary Taylor at Palo Alto.
1848	Mexican War ends and Mexico gives up all claims to Texas.
1851	Construction is started on first railroad in Texas.
1853	King Ranch, largest in the US, is established.
1861	*February 1.* Texas secedes from the Union and joins the Confederate States. *March 16.* Sam Houston is deposed as governor for refusing to take oath of allegiance to the Confederacy.
1865	*May 12–13.* Last battle of Civil War is fought at Palmito Hill near the mouth of the Rio Grande River. (Soldiers in Texas had not heard of the war's end.)
1866	Jesse Chisholm leads the first cattle drive from Texas to Kansas, opening the era of cattle drives.
1870	*March 30.* US Congress grants Texas readmission to the Union.
1876	Present state constitution is adopted.
1890	*October 14.* Dwight D. Eisenhower is born in Denison.
1898	Spanish-American War. Theodore Roosevelt trains the "Rough Riders" at San Antonio.
1900	*September 8.* Storm hits Galveston with enormous tidal wave, taking 6,000 lives.
1901	Oilmen discover the great Spindletop oil field.
1910	The first US Army airplane is flown at Fort Sam Houston.
1915	Compulsory education law is passed.
1920	State's first radio station, WRR, begins broadcasting in Dallas.
1924	Texas becomes second state to elect a woman governor, Mrs. Miriam A. Ferguson.
1928	Construction of Randolph Field, "West Point of the Air," begins. *June 26–29.* The Democratic party holds national convention in Houston, nominating Alfred E. Smith for president and Joseph Robinson for vice president. They lose the November election to Herbert Hoover and Charles Curtis.

1930	East Texas oil field is discovered.
1936	The Texas Centennial Exposition, celebrating 100 years of independence, is held in Dallas.
1941	World War II. About 1,250,000 members of the US armed forces train in Texas. Audie Murphy of Farmersville gains fame as "the nation's most decorated soldier of World War II."
1947	*April 16–18.* A ship explosion at a refinery dock in Texas City kills about 575 people and injures about 4,000. The city is almost totally destroyed by the blast.
1948	First television station in Texas, WBAP-TV, begins broadcasting at Fort Worth.
1953	After a bitter dispute in Congress, President Eisenhower signs a bill that restores the oil-rich tidelands to state ownership.
1957	*June 27–28.* Hurricane Audrey causes great damage along the Texas coast. Over 500 persons killed.
1963	*November 22.* President John F. Kennedy is assassinated in Dallas. Texas Governor John Connally is severely wounded. Vice President Lyndon B. Johnson takes the presidential oath of office at Love Air Force field in Dallas.
	November 24. Millions of people watch on television as Lee Harvey Oswald, accused assassin of President Kennedy, is killed by Jack Ruby.
1964	*March 14.* Jack Ruby is found guilty of Oswald's murder by a Dallas jury.
1970	*January 1.* University of Texas defeats Notre Dame in Cotton Bowl to complete undefeated season.
1973	*January 22.* Lyndon Johnson dies. The Manned Spacecraft Center is renamed the Lyndon B. Johnson Space Center.
1977	President Carter's energy program is greatly opposed by oil and gas industry.
1979	Texas shoreline is dealt devastating blow by a large oil spill.
1982	Unemployment rate in Texas is among the lowest in the nation.
1983	Economic growth in state is stalled for the first time since the 1930s.
1985	Downward spiral in world oil prices severely affects state's economy.
1986	150th anniversary of independence from Mexico.
1987	*September 13.* Pope John Paul II visits San Antonio.
1989	*February.* Dallas Cowboys purchased by Arkansas businessman who fires Tom Landry, coach since the team's founding.

DEMOGRAPHY

Population (est. 1987) . . . 16,789,000
Population (1980) 14,227,574
Population density in persons
   per square mile (1980) 53.3

POPULATION BY RACE (1980)
American Indian/Aleut/
   Eskimo 40,074
Asian/Pacific Islander 120,306
Black 1,710,250
Hispanic 2,985,643
White 11,197,663
Other 1,160,090

POPULATION CHARACTERISTICS (1980)
Percent of state population
Urban 79.6
Rural 20.4
Under 18 . . . . 30.2
65 or older 9.6
College-educated 16.0
Families below poverty line . . . 11.1
Public assistance recipients 4.0

Per capita personal income
   (1986) $13,523
Millionaires per 100,000
   residents (1982) 257.3
Average life expectancy in
   years (1980) 73.6
Marriage rate (1986) 12.2
Divorce rate (1986) 6.0
Birth rate per 1,000
   residents (1985) 19.2
Infant mortality rate per 1,000
   live births (1985) 9.8
Abortion rate per 1,000
   live births (1985) 320
Crime rate per 100,000
   residents (1985)
   Violent 658.9
   Property 6,749.2
Federal and state prisoners per
   100,000 residents (1984) 221
Alcohol consumption in gallons per
   capita (1985) 48.9

Deaths from motor vehicle accidents
per 100,000 residents (1985) . . 22.5

MAJOR CITIES

1984 population (est.)

Amarillo	162,863
Arlington	213,832
Austin	397,001
Beaumont	123,356
Corpus Christi	258,067
Dallas	974,234
El Paso	463,809
Fort Worth	414,562
Houston	1,705,697
Lubbock	178,529
San Antonio	842,779

GOVERNMENT AND POLITICS

Number of US Representatives 27
Electoral votes 29

POLITICAL PARTY NOMINEES FROM STATE
*winner

Benjamin J. Chambers (Green-back Labor)	1880	P
Samuel Evans (Union Labor/declined)	1888	VP
James Britton Cranfill (Prohibition)	1892	VP
George W. Carroll (Prohibition)	1904	VP
James Edward Ferguson (American)	1920	P
John Nance Garner* (D)	1932	VP
John Nance Garner* (D)	1936	VP
Lyndon Baines Johnson* (D)	1960	VP
Lyndon Baines Johnson* (D/Liberal)	1964	P
Richard K. Troxell (Constitution)	1968	P
George Herbert Walker Bush* (R)	1980	VP
George Herbert Walker Bush* (R)	1984	VP
Bob Richards (Populist)	1984	P
George Herbert Walker Bush* (R)	1988	P
Lloyd Bentsen (D)	1988	VP

PRESIDENTIAL PRIMARY ELECTION In 1988, Texas sent 197 Democratic delegates and 111 Republican delegates to the national conventions.

CONSTITUTION Texas has had five constitutions: 1845, 1861, 1866, 1869, and the present one, adopted in 1876.

LEGISLATURE The Legislature is divided into the Senate (31 members, 4-year term, minimum age 26) and the House of Representatives (150 members, 2-year term, minimum age 21). In 1987, the annual salary was $7,200 plus $30 per day for a maximum of 140 days.

JUDICIARY The highest courts are the Supreme Court and the Court of Criminal Appeals. In each, there are 9 judges serving 6-year terms. In 1987, the annual salary was $78,795.

EXECUTIVE The governor serves a 4-year term; the minimum age for holding office is 30. In 1987, the annual salary was $91,600. There are 29 other elected officials.

PRESIDENTIAL VOTE 1948-1988 *(in percents)*

Year	State Winner	Democratic	Republican
1948	Truman (D)	65.4	24.6
1952	Eisenhower (R)	46.7	53.1
1956	Eisenhower (R)	44.0	55.3
1960	Kennedy (D)	50.5	48.5
1964	Johnson (D)	63.3	36.5
1968	Humphrey (D)	41.1	39.9
1972	Nixon (R)	33.3	66.2
1976	Carter (D)	51.1	48.0
1980	Reagan (R)	41.4	55.3
1984	Reagan (R)	36.1	63.6
1988	Bush (R)	44.0	56.0

GOVERNORS

J. Pinckney Henderson (D)	1846-1847
George T. Wood (D)	1847-1849
P. Hansborough Bell (D)	1849-1853
James W. Henderson (D/ acting)	1853
Elisha M. Pease (D)	1853-1856
Hardin R. Runnels (D)	1857-1859
Sam Houston (Independent/ Unionist)	1859-1861
Edward Clark (D/acting)	1861
Francis R. Lubbock (D)	1861-1863
Pendleton Murrah (D)	1863-1865
Andrew J. Hamilton (Con- servative)	1865-1866
James W. Throckmorton (Conservative)	1866-1867
Elisha M. Pease (R)	1867-1869
Edmund J. Davis (R)	1870-1874
Richard Coke (D)	1874-1876
Richard B. Hubbard (D)	1876-1879
Oran M. Roberts (D)	1879-1883
John Ireland (D)	1883-1887
Lawrence S. Ross (D)	1887-1891
James S. Hogg (D)	1891-1895
Charles A. Culberson (D)	1895-1899
Joseph D. Sayers (D)	1899-1903
W.T. Lanham (D)	1903-1907
Thomas M. Campbell (D)	1907-1911
Oscar B. Colquitt (D)	1911-1915
James E. Ferguson (D)	1915-1917
William P. Hobby (D)	1917-1921
Pat M. Neff (D)	1921-1925
Miriam A. Ferguson (D)	1925-1927
Dan Moody (D)	1927-1931
Ross Sterling (D)	1931-1933
Miriam A. Ferguson (D)	1933-1935
James V. Allred (D)	1935-1939
W. Lee O'Daniel (D)	1939-1941
Coke R. Stevenson (D)	1941-1947
Beauford H. Jester (D)	1947-1949
Allan Shivers (D)	1949-1957
Price Daniel (D)	1957-1963
John B. Connally (D)	1963-1969
Preston Smith (D)	1969-1973
Dolph Briscoe (D)	1973-1979
William Clements (R)	1979-1983
Mark White (D)	1983-1987
William Clements (R)	1987-

MINIMUM AGES

Majority	18
Marriage with parental consent (with judicial consent)	14
Marriage without parental consent	18
Making a will	18
Buying alcohol	21
Jury duty	18
Leaving school	17
Driver's license	16

CAPITAL PUNISHMENT
Number executed 1976-88: 27
On death row Aug. 1, 1988: 269

MILITARY INSTALLATIONS
Total number: 45
Major bases:
  Army: 4
  Navy: 2
  Air Force: 7

FINANCES

Thousands of dollars

GENERAL REVENUE (1985)

Total general revenue	18,795,846
Total tax revenue	11,540,836
Sales and gross receipts	7,612,317
Individual income taxes	0
Corporate net income taxes	0

GENERAL EXPENDITURE (1985)

Total general expenditure	17,535,597
Education	9,545,476
Public welfare	2,145,603
Health	371,724
Hospitals	1,014,477
Natural resources	305,670
Highways	1,650,470
Police	148,706
Corrections	464,312

FEDERAL AID (1985) 4,476,730

ECONOMY

Texas ranks first among states in many economic measures: in livestock production, in cotton and sorghum, and in oil production. On Texas farms, wheat, rice, corn, cotton, peanut, barley, and vegetables are important crops, while Texas cattle are widely considered to be among the finest in the nation. Farm marketings cash receipts were $8.97 billion, third-highest in the US for that year, with livestock production accounting for about three-fifths of that. Oil and natural gas are the major mining products, but iron, uranium, magnesium, sulfur, helium, salt, and sand and gravel are also important. Among the principal manufactures are petroleum products and petrochemicals, processed foods, transportation equipment, agricultural and drilling equipment, electronics, fabricated metals, apparel, and stone and ceramic products. Value added by manufacture was $53 billion in 1982, third after New York and California. Federal and defense installations and R & D bring significant income to Texas, as does tourism. The state's deepwater ports and extensive highway and rail system make it an important hub for shipping goods to the interior of the nation.

EMPLOYMENT (1984)

Thousands of persons

Total number of employed workers	7,387
Construction	430.4
Finance, insurance, and real estate	414.9
Government	1,082.0
Manufacturing	996.8
Mining	269.9
Services	1,257.5
Transportation, communications, and utilities	371.1
Wholesale and retail trade	1,614.0
Percent of civilian labor force unemployed (1984)	5.9

DEPARTMENT OF DEFENSE (1985)

Civilian workers employed	66,649
Military personnel	127.176
Contract awards	$10.562 billion

ENERGY SOURCES FOR ELECTRIC UTILITIES (1983)

	Percent
Coal	42.4
Gas	56.0
Hydroelectric	0.5
Nuclear	0.0
Petroleum	1.0

TRANSPORTATION

Motor vehicles registered in state (1986)	12,406,608
Miles of roads, streets, and highways (1986)	285,962
Miles of Class I railway operated (1986)	12,802
Airports (1983)	1,543
Major aviation hubs (1983)	10

Largest hub: Dallas/Fort Worth

Major ports, with gross tonnage in thousands (1985):

Houston	90,669
Corpus Christi	42,682
Texas City	33,441
Beaumont	26,842
Port Arthur	15,755
Freeport	12,918

CULTURE AND EDUCATION

Native American tribes

Texas was formerly home to the Apache, Aranama, Atakapa, Bidai, Biloxi, Caddo, Choctaw, Coahuiltec, Comanche, Creek, Eyeish, Humano, Karan Kawau, Kichai, Kiowa, Koasati, Lipan, Pascagoula, Patiri, Quapaw, Socatino, Tawakoni, Tonkawa, Waco, and Wichita tribes. Groups that continue to live in the state include the Shawnee. Groups that have been relocated to Texas include the Alabama.

Religions, ethnicities, and languages

Texas is a state of great cultural and ethnic diversity. There are three main groups: the Mexican-Americans, who are Roman Catholics and who represent about 20 percent of the population; blacks, a mostly Protestant group, many of whom are the descendants of slaves; and Anglos, a term that encompasses all other cultures. Immigrant groups from Europe in the 19th and 20th centuries included Germans, Swedes, Czechs, Polish, Irish, Italians, Norwegians, Danes, and Greeks. In 1980, 21.8 percent of Texas's population spoke a language other than English at home, usually Spanish.

Baptists and Methodists are the leading Protestant groups; more than a third of the churchgoers are Roman Catholic.

Major museums and libraries

Alamo Museum, San Antonio
Amon Carter Museum of Western Art, Forth Worth
Dallas Museum of Fine Arts
Dallas Museum of Natural History
Fort Worth Art Museum
Institute of Texan Culture, San Antonio
Kimbell Art Museum, Fort Worth
The Museum of Fine Arts, Houston
Panhandle-Plains Historical Museum, Canyon
San Jacinto Museum, Houston
Texas Memorial Museum, Austin

Major arts organizations

Alley Theatre, Houston
Dallas Opera
Dallas Symphony Orchestra
Dallas Theatre Center
Fort Worth Ballet
Houston Ballet

Houston Grand Opera Association
Houston Symphony Orchestra
San Antonio Symphony Orchestra
Texas Opera Theater, Houston

Colleges and universities
Number public (1986-87) 100
Number private (1986-87) 63
Total enrollment, in full-time equivalent
students (1985) 566,700

Public elementary and secondary schools
Expenditure per pupil in average daily
attendance (1986-87) $3,551
Pupil-teacher ratio (1987) 17.3
Average teacher salary (1986-87) $26,255

Major league sports teams
Baseball: Houston Astros, Texas Rangers
Basketball: Dallas Mavericks, Houston
Rockets
Football: Dallas Cowboys, Houston Oilers

Holidays
Confederate Heroes Day. January 19
Texas Independence Day. March 2
San Jacinto Day. April 21
Emancipation Day. June 19
Lyndon B. Johnson's Birthday. August
27
State Fair, Dallas. Mid-October

TEXAS IN LITERATURE

Francis E. Abernethy *Tales From the Big Thicket* (1966)
A collection of folklore.

Andy Adams *The Log of a Cowboy* (1903, rpt. 1964, 1976)
The story of an 1882 cattle drive from the Mexican border
to Montana, narrated by a young man whose family has
settled in San Antonio shortly after the Civil War. This is
one of the earliest works of Texas fiction, and the best-
known of Adams' descriptions of pioneer life, which
include *A Texas Matchmaker* (1904), *Wells Brothers: The Young
Cattle Kings* (1911), and *The Ranch on the Beaver* (1927)

John Houghton Allen *Southwest* (1952)
Essays about ranch life on the south Texas border.

Dillon Anderson *I and Claudie* (1951)
Picaresque novel about two men wandering in the '30s.

Carlos Ashley *That Spotted Cow and Other Texas Hill Country
Ballads* (1975)
Verse collected and composed by the state laureate.

Roy Bedichek *Adventures With a Texas Naturalist* (1947);
Karankaway Country (1950, rpt. 1974)
Classic works on the Texas landscape.

Mody C. Boatright *Folklore of the Oil Industry* (1963)
Tales and songs of the pre-1940 oilfields.

Elroy Bode *To Be Alive* (1979)
Sketches of contemporary Texas life.

William Brammer *The Gay Place* (1961)
A three-part novel about Texas politics of the 1950s,
centered on a fictional governor who resembles LBJ.

Bill Brett *The Stolen Steers: A Tale of the Big Thicket* (1977)
A folktale of frontier life in southwestern Texas.

J. Mason Brewer *Dog Ghosts, and Other Texas Negro Folk Tales*
(1958)

Mamie Sypert Burns *This I Can Leave You: A Woman's Days
on the Pitchfork Ranch* (1986)
A woman's view of life in the male domain of cow-herding.

Benjamin Capps *The Trail to Ogallala* (1964, rpt. 1985)
Novel about a cattle drive from San Antonio to Nebraska.
Generally valued as the finest of Capps' numerous works on
the plains, which also include *A Woman of the People* (1966),
a tale of two white women captured by Comanches in 1854,
and *The White Man's Road* (1969), a novel set on the Fort Sill
reservation c.1900.

Forrest Carter *Gone to Texas* (1975)
A fictional account of the outlaw Josey Wales.

Madison Cooper *Sironia, Texas* 2 vols. (1952)
A satiric account of a Texan town, based on the author's
native Waco. Reputedly the longest American novel.

Jim W. Corder *Lost in West Texas* (1987)
Reminiscences and sketches of daily life in a remote region
of west Texas.

Al Dewlen *The Bone Pickers* (1958)
Novel about a wealthy Amarillo family.
————. *Servants of Corruption* (1971)
A satirical novel about an evangelical church in the Pan-
handle.

Bertha M. Dobie *Growing Up in Texas* (1972)
Reminiscences of pioneer life 1880–1940 collected from
thirteen Texans.

J. Frank Dobie *Coronado's Children: Tales of Lost Mines and
Buried Treasures of the Southwest* (1930)
The first, and one of the best-known works, by a writer
whose efforts to portray Texas lives and gather local
folklore did much to establish a tradition of regional fiction.
Dobie's other Texan writing includes: *Apache Gold and
Yaqui Silver, The Ben Lilly Legend, Cow People, I'll Tell You
a Tale, Life and Literature of the Southwest, The Longhorns, The
Mustangs, Rattlesnakes, Some Part of Myself, Tales of Old-Time
Texas, A Vaquero of the Brush Country.*

William O. Douglas *Farewell to Texas: A Vanishing Wilderness*
(1967)
A survey of natural Texas, and a plea for its preservation.

H. G. Dulaney and **Edward Phillips** (eds.) *Speak Mr.
Speaker* (1978)
A biography of Sam Rayburn, longest-serving US congress-
man, with selections from his writing.

Ella E. B. Dumont (ed. Tommy J. Boley) *Ella Elgar Bird
Dumont: An Autobiography of a West Texas Pioneer* (1988)
Memoirs of a King County pioneer of the late 1800s who
married a Texas Ranger and later became a sculptor.

Loula Grace Erdman *The Edge of Time* (1950)
Novel about a pioneer couple in the Panhandle c.1885.

Winston M. Estes *Another Part of the House* (1970); *Andy
Jessup* (1975)
Novels about coming-of-age during the 1930s.

Edna Ferber *Giant* (1952, rpt. 1979)
Novel about a dynasty of ranchers and oilmen, 1920–1960.

Sue Flanagan *Sam Houston's Texas* (1964)
A biography and selection of Houston's writing.

Baylis J. Fletcher *Up the Trail in '79* (1967)
An eyewitness account of a five-month cattle drive up the
Chisholm Trail.

Horton Foote *The Chase* (1956)
Novel about an escaped convict's return to a small Gulf
Coast town.

John Salmon Ford (ed. S. B. Oates) *Rip Ford's Texas* (1963,
rpt. 1987)
Memoirs of a pioneer who settled in 1836.

Walter Fulcher *The Way I Heard It: Tales of the Big Bend*
(1987)
Folktales of traditional Western subjects.

Wayne Gard *Sam Bass* (1936)
Biography of a famous outlaw from Denton County who was shot by Texas Rangers in 1878.

Peter Gent *North Dallas Forty* (1973)
Novel about a football team, closely based on the Dallas Cowboys.

Fred Gipson *Hound-Dog Man* (1949)
A classic novel about a boy's initiation into adult life on the west Texas frontier at the turn of the century. The best-known of the author's portrayals of the Texas hill country, which include *Old Yeller* (1956) and *Savage Sam* (1962).

William Goyen *The House of Breath* (1949)
Novel about a boy growing up in Trinity, east Texas.

Don Graham (ed.) *South by Southwest: Twenty-four Stories from Modern Texas* (1986)
An anthology of works by contemporary writers, including Paul Horgan and William A. Owens.

Katherine C. Graham *Under the Cottonwood*
A saga of five generations of a 19th-century Texas black family.

John Graves *Goodbye to a River* (1960)
Memoir of rural life on the Brazos River. Graves also described his farm in *Hard Scrabble: Observations on a Patch of Land* (1974), and *From a Limestone Ledge* (1980).

Leon Hale *Bonney's Place* (1972)
Novel set in the Piney Woods region about an elderly man's search for a debtor, containing realistic portrayals of rural life. Hale is also the author of two popular collections of east Texas journalism, *Turn South at the Second Bridge* (1965) and *A Smile From Katie Hattan* . . . . (1982)

Rolando Hinojosa *The Valley* (1983)
The first of a sequence of novels depicting life in Mexican-American communities in the valley of the Rio Grande.

Carol Hoff *Johnny Texas* (1950)
Classic juvenile novel about a boy's life on a ranch.

Ada Morehead Holland *Brush Country Woman* (1986)
The life of Helen Sewell, who moved with her family to south Texas at age eleven in 1908, and later, as wife of a Texas Ranger, ran a ranch near Hebbronville.

Paul Horgan *Whitewater* (1970)
A Pulitzer Prize–winning novel about growing up in a small west Texas town.

William Humphrey *Home From the Hill* (1958); *The Ordways* (1965)
Novels about Texas families set in the 1930s and Reconstruction.
———. *A Time and a Place* (1968)
Stories set in northeastern Texas.
———. *Farther Off From Heaven* (1977)
Memoir of an upbringing in Clarksville.

John Holland Jenkins (ed. J. H. Jenkins, III) *Recollections of Early Texas* (1987)
Memoirs of a pioneer who witnessed conflict with the Indians and Mexicans.

Elmer Kelton *The Day the Cowboys Quit* (1971)
A novel based on a strike that took place in the Panhandle in 1883.
———. *The Time It Never Rained* (1973)
A farmer's struggle to survive a drought in the 1950s.
———. *The Good Old Boys* (1978)
Ranch life in west Texas c.1900.

Laura Krey *And Tell of Time* (1938)
A novel about plantation life in Fort Bend County during Reconstruction, noted for its historical accuracy and conservative attachment to the pre–Civil War way of life.

Aaron Latham *Urban Cowboy* (1980)
Single life in the bars of Houston.

Tom Lea *The Wonderful Country* (1952)
Novel about life on the Mexican border in the 1870s.
———. *The Hands of Cantu* (1964)
A romance set in Spanish Texas and Mexico.

James Ward Lee *Classics of Texas Fiction* (1987)
A collection of syndicated short reviews.

Alan Le May *The Searchers* (1978)
———. *The Unforgiven* (1978)
Classic western novels.

Howard N. Martin *Myths and Folktales of the Alabama-Coushatta Indians of Texas* (1977)

Larry McMurtry *Horseman, Pass By* (1961)
Novel set in Archer County during the 1950s about the differing values of three generations of Texans, personified by an old cattle rancher, an oil speculator, and a boy who admires both.
———. *Leaving Cheyenne* (1962)
Novel about the lives of the three members of a love triangle set in rural north central Texas.
———. *The Last Picture Show* (1966)
A satirical account of adolescence in south Texas.
———. *In a Narrow Grave: Essays on Texas* (1968)
———. *Lonesome Dove* (1985)
Two retired Texas Rangers drive a herd of cattle from the Rio Grande to the Yellowstone in the mid-1870s.

James Michener *Texas* (1985)
A fictional treatment of Texas history, 1535–present.

Elton Miles *Tales of the Big Bend* (1977); *More Tales of the Big Bend* (1987)
Stories and legends of west Texas.

Andrew Forest Muir (ed.) *Texas in 1837* (1988)
An anonymous account of the first year of the Texas republic, apparently written by a settler from Ohio.

Patrick B. Mullen *I Heard the Old Fishermen Say: Folklore of the Texas Gulf Coast* (1978, rpt. 1988)

Hermes Nye *Fortune Is a Woman* (1958)
Comic novel about a young lawyer's struggle to establish himself in Dallas during the Depression.

O. Henry (William Sydney Porter) (ed. Marian McClintock and Michael Simms) *O. Henry's Texas Stories*
Humorous accounts of Texas life c.1900.

Frederick Law Olmsted *A Journey Through Texas; or, A Saddletrip on the Southwestern Frontier* (1857, rpt. 1978)
The celebrated landscape architect's impressions of the frontier before the Civil War.

Waterman L. Ormsby (ed. L. H. Wright and J. M. Bynum) *The Butterfield Overland Mail* (1942, rpt. 1955)
The author, a New York journalist, was the first and only through passenger on the transcontinental mail line from Missouri to San Francisco.

William A. Owens *This Stubborn Soil* (1966, rpt. 1988)
Autobiographical account of growing up in Pin Hook, a small north Texas community, in the early years of the century.

William Peery (ed.) *Twenty-one Texas Short Stories* (1954)
An anthology including works by Katherine Ann Porter, J. Frank Dobie, William Goyen, and George Sessions Perry.

George Sessions Perry *Hold Autumn in Your Hand* (1941)
Novel about a tenant farmer on the Brazos River in the 1930s, often favorably compared with John Steinbeck's *Grapes of Wrath*.

Katherine Anne Porter *Pale Horse, Pale Rider* (1939)
Three short novels.

Lawrence Clark Powell *Southwest Classics* (1982)

Sallie Reynolds Matthews *Interwoven* (1936, rpt. 1958, 1980)
Memoir of domestic life in rural Texas 1860–1940.

Tomas Rivera (trans. Hermione Rios) *. . . y no se lo trago la tierra* (1970)
Sketches of migrant farm workers.

Frank Roderus *Duster: The Story of a Texas Cattle Drive* (1977)
Tale of cowboys during Reconstruction.

Jane Gilmore Rushing *Against the Moon* (1968)
An ironically realistic portrait of family life in rural west Texas, one of the author's five novels set in that area.

Leonard Sanders *The Wooden Horseshoe* (1964)
Small-town intrigues and politics in the 1960s.

Winfred M. Sanford (ed. E. S. Miles) *Windfall and Other Stories* (1980, rpt. 1988)
Stories of oil speculators set in north Texas in the 1920s.

Dorothy Scarborough *The Wind* (1925, rpt. 1988)
A tragic novel depicting the hardships faced by pioneer women in west Texas during the drought of the 1880s. Scarborough also wrote four novels partly set in the cotton-growing region around Waco, and in the Brazos valley.

Edwin Shrake *Blessed McGill* (1968)
Novel about a young man's upbringing in Austin during Reconstruction.

C. W. Smith *The Thin Men of Haddam* (1973)
Novel about a Mexican-American ranch foreman in a west Texas town.

Hart Stilwell *The Uncovered Wagon* (1947, rpt. 1985)
Novel about an intinerant poor family in the early years of the century.

Alexander Edwin Sweet (ed. Virginia Eisenhour) *Alex Sweet's Texas* (1986)
Collected articles by a nineteenth-century humorist whose writing appeared in the *Galveston Daily News* during the 1870s and '80s.

John W. Thomason, Jr. *Lone Star Preacher* (1941)
Short stories about a Methodist minister and army chaplain during the Civil War and Reconstruction.

John O. West (ed.) *Mexican-American Folklore* (1988)

John W. Wilson *High John the Conqueror* (1948)
Novel about black farmers during the Depression.

GUIDES TO RESOURCES

Adams, Ramon *Six-Guns and Saddle Leather: A Bibliography of Books and Pamphlets on Western Outlaws and Gunmen* (1954)

Arbingast, Stanley A., Lorrin C. Kennamer, and **Michael E. Bonnine** *Atlas of Texas* (5th rev. ed. 1976)

Bebout, Lois (ed.) *Texas Reference Sources: A Selective Guide* (Texas Library Assoc.) (3d. ed. 1987)

Best, Hugh *Debrett's Texas Peerage* (1983)

Bratcher, James T. *Analytical Index to the Publications of the Texas Folklore Society* (1973)

Cable, Carole *Texas Architecture of the 80's: A Bibliography* (1986)

Cruz, Gilberto R. and **James Arthur Irby** (eds.) *Texas Bibliography: A Manual on History Research Materials* (1982)

Cummins, L. T. and **A. R. Bailey** *A Guide to the History of Texas* (1988)

De Boe, David Cornelius and **Barbara F. Immroth** *Teaching Texas History; an All-Level Resource Guide* (1985)

Dingus, Anne *Book of Texas Lists* (1982)

Dobie, J. Frank *Guide to the Life and Literature of the Southwest* (1952)

Federal Writers' Project *Texas: A Guide to the Lone Star State* (1940, rev. ed. 1969)
———. *The WPA Guide to Texas* (1986)

Fleischmann, Arnold, et al. *A Bibliography of Texas Government and Politics* (1985)

Graff, Harvey J., Charles Barton, and **Alan R. Baron** *Dallas, Texas; a Bibliographical Guide to the Sources of Its Social History to 1930* (1979)

Greene, A. C. *The 50 Best Books on Texas* (1982)

Harmon, Robert B. *Government and Politics in Texas: An Information Source Survey* (1980)

Immroth, Barbara F. *Texas in Children's Books: An Annotated Bibliography* (1986)

Jenkins, John H. *Basic Texas Books: An Annotated Bibliography of Selected Works for a Research Library* (1987)

Jimenez, Rebecca S. et al. (eds.) *Baylor University Institute for Oral History: A Guide to the Collections, 1970–85* (1985)

King, Valentine O. *Valentine Overton King's Index to Books About Texas Before 1889: A Facsimile of the Original in the Collection of the Texas State Library* (1976)

Livingston, Ronald H. *Livingston's Directory of Texas Historical and Genealogical Organizations* (1984)

Nichols, Margaret I. *Current Texas Reference Sources: A Sesquicentennial Guide* (1985)

Nunnerlyn, Tom *Texas Local History: A Source Book for . . . Town and County Histories . . .* (1983)

Parker, Lois W. *The Big Thicket of Texas: A Comprehensive Bibliography* (1977)

Pevoto, Charlotte W. *Cattle Barons and the Mansions They Built in Texas, 1870–1905: A Bibliography* (1984)
———. *Texas Courthouses, Past and Present: A Bibliography* (1984)

Pluta, Joseph E., Rita J. Wright, and **Mildred C. Anderson** *Texas Fact Book* (1983–)

Pool, William C. *The Historical Atlas of Texas* (1976)

Robinson, Barbara J. and **J. Cordell Robinson** *The Mexican American: A Critical Guide to Research Aids and Index* (1980)

Roseman, Rick and **Bill Sanderson** *Annually in Texas* (1985)

Stephens, A. Ray and **William M. Holmes** *Historical Atlas of Texas* (1988)

Stevens, Michael D. and **Kathleen Beatty** *The Texas Constitution and Its Impact: An Annotated Bibliography* (1973)

Streeter, Thomas W. *Bibliography of Texas, 1795–1845* 5 vols. (1955–1960)

Tate, Michael L. *The Indians of Texas; an Annotated Research Bibliography* (1986)

Texas History Education Advisory Committee *The Texas History Teacher's Guide to Supplementary Materials and Professional Bibliography* (1973)

Texas State Library Archives Division *Guide to Genealogical Resources in the Texas State Archives* (3d ed. 1984)

Texas State Library Bibliographies *Governors of Texas; Legislature Landmarks of Texas; One Hundred Fifty Years of Texas Growth; Texans in the Military; Texas Books and Writers: 150 Years; The Texas Revolution* (1986)
———. **Information Services Division** *Genealogical Resources and the Texas State Library* (1984)

Tyler, Paula E. and **Ron** *Texas Museums: A Guidebook* (1983)

Webb, Walter P. and **H. Bailey Carroll** (ed. Eldon S. Branda) *Handbook of Texas* 2 vols. (1952) and *Supplement* (vol. 3) (1977)

Winegarten, Ruth *Finder's Guide to the Texas Women: A Celebration of History Exhibit Archives* (1984)

Winkler, Ernest W. *Check List of Texas Imprints, 1846–1860* (1949)
——— and **Llerena Friend** *Check List of Texas Imprints, 1861–1876* (1963)

Wright, Rita J. *Texas Sources: A Bibliography* (1976)

SELECTED NONFICTION SOURCES

Adair, Anthony Garland (ed.) *Heroes of the Alamo* (1957)

Adler, Larry *The Texas Rangers* (1979)

Ashford, Gerald *Spanish Texas; Yesterday and Today* (1971)

Aten, Lawrence E. *Indians of the Upper Texas Coast* (1983)

Atwood, E. Bagby *The Regional Vocabulary of Texas* (1962, rpt. 1969)

Austerman, Wayne R. *Sharps Rifles and Spanish Mules; the San Antonio–El Paso Mail, 1851–1881* (1985)

Bainbridge, John *The Super-Americans* (1961, rpt. 1972)

Baker, T. Lindsay *Building the Lone Star; an Illustrated Guide to Historic Sites* (1986)
———. *Ghost Towns of Texas* (1986)

Bancroft, Hubert H. *North Mexican States and Texas, 1883–1889* 2 vols. (1883–1889)

Banks, Clinton Stanley *The Texas Reader* (1960)

Barker, Eugene Campbell *The Life of Stephen F. Austin, Founder of Texas, 1793–1836* (1926, rpt. 1969)
———. *Mexico and Texas, 1821–1835* (1965)

Barr, Alwyn *Black Texans: A History of Negroes in Texas, 1528–1971* (1973)
——— and Robert A. Calvert *Black Leaders: Texans for Their Times* (1981)

Bauman, Richard and Roger D. Abrahams *And Other Neighborly Names: Social Process and Cultural Change in Texas Folklore* (1981)

Binkley, William C. *The Expansionist Movement in Texas, 1836–1850* (1925, rpt. 1974)
———. *The Texas Revolution* (1952)

Blodgett, Jan *Land of Bright Promise: Advertising the Texas Panhandle and South Plains, 1870–1917* (1988)

Bolton, Hubert Eugene *Texas in the Middle Eighteenth Century* (1915, rpt. 1962)

Bomar, George W. *Texas Weather* (1983)

Bones, Jim and John Graves *Texas Heartland: A Hill Country Year* (1975)

Brook, Stephen *Honkytonk Gelato* (1985)

Caerver, Don M. and Linda B. Hall *Texas and the Mexican Revolution* (1988)

Calvert, Robert, Randolph Campbell, and Donald Chipman *The Dallas Cowboys and the NFL* (1970)

Carter, Hodding *Doomed Road of the Empire* (1963)

Casey, Robert J. *The Texas Border and Some Borderlines, a Chronicle and a Guide* (1950)

Castaneda, Carlos *The Mexican Side of the Texas Revolution* (1928)

Chance, Joseph E. *The Second Texas Infantry: From Shiloh to Vicksburg* (1984)

Clark, Joseph L. *A History of Texas: Land of Promise* (1939)

Clark, Sara *The Capitols of Texas: A Visual History* (1976)

Conaway, James *The Texans* (1976)

Conger, Roger N. *Frontier Forts of Texas* (1966)

Connor, Seymour V. (ed.) *The Saga of Texas* 6 vols. (1965)
———. *Texas: A History* (1971)

Crawford, Ann F. and Crystal S. Ragsdale *Women in Texas* (1982)

Cueller, Robert A. *A Social and Political History of the Mexican-American Population of Texas, 1929–1963* (1974)

Dana, Anna M. *Under the Texas Sun: Adventures of a Texas Cowpuncher* (1986)

Daniell, Lewis E. *Texas; the Country and Its Men; Historical, Biographical, Descriptive* (1924)

Davis, John L. *Houston: A Historical Portrait* (1983)

De Leon, Arnoldo *They Called Them Greasers: Anglo Attitudes Toward Mexicans in Texas, 1821–1900* (1983)

Doughty, Robin W. *At Home in Texas: Early Views of the Land* (1987)

Downey, Fairfax D. *Texas and the War with Mexico* (1961)

Driskill, Frank A. and Noel Grisham *Historic Churches of Texas: The Land and the People* (1980)

Duke, Cordia S. and Joe B. Frantz *6000 Miles of Fence: Life on the XIT Ranch of Texas* (1961)

Farrell, Mary and Elizabeth Silverthorne *First Ladies of Texas: The First One Hundred Years* (1976)

Faulk, Odie B. *The Last Years of Spanish Texas, 1778–1821* (1964)

Fehrenbach, T. R. *Lone Star; A History of Texas and the Texans* (1968)
———. *Seven Keys to Texas* (1983)
———. *Texas: A Salute from Above* (1985)

Ferguson, Walter K. *Geology and Politics in Frontier Texas, 1845–1909* (1969)

Fergusson, Harvey *Rio Grande* (1933)

Foote, Henry S. *Texas and Texans or Advance of Anglo-America* 2 vols. (1935)

Foote, Horton *Harrison, Texas* (1956)

Foster, Nancy H. *The Alamo and Other Texas Missions to Remember* (1984)

Frantz, Joe B. and Julian E. Choate, Jr. *The American Cowboy* (1955)
———. *Texas: A Bicentennial History* (1976)
———. *The Forty-Acre Follies* (1983)

Frary, Michael and William A. Owens *Impressions of the Big Thicket* (1973)

Friend, Llerena *Sam Houston: The Great Designer* (1954)

Fuermann, George *The Reluctant Empire* (1957)

Gallaway, B. P. *The Ragged Rebel: A Common Soldier in W. H. Parsons' Texas Cavalry, 1861–1865* (1988)

Gehlbach, Frederick *Mountain Islands and Desert Seas* (1981)

Gillett, James B. *Six Years With the Texas Rangers: 1875 to 1881* (1925)

Goodwyn, Frank *Lone Star Land: 20th Century Texas in Perspective* (1955)

Graham, Don, James W. Lee, and William T. Pilkington (eds.) *The Texas Literary Tradition: Fiction, Folklore, History* (1983)

Gray, William F. *From Virginia to Texas* (1909, rpt. 1965)

Greer, James K. (ed.) *A Texas Ranger and Frontiersman: The Days of Buck Barry in Texas 1845–1906* (1932)

Haley, J. Evetts *Charles Goodnight: Cowman and Plainsman* (1936)
———. *Life on the Texas Range* (photographs by Erwin E. Smith) (1953, rpt. 1973)
———. *XIT Ranch of Texas and the Early Days of the Llano Estacado* (1953, rpt. 1977)

Haley, James L. *Texas, an Album of History* (1985)

Hatcher, Mattie A. *The Opening of Texas to Foreign Settlements, 1801–1821* (1927)

Helgesen, Sally *Wildcatters: A Story of Texans, Oil and Money* (1981)

Hill, Jim Dan *The Texas Navy* (1937, rpt. 1962)

Hinojosa, Gilberto M. *A Borderland Town in Transition: Laredo, Texas, 1755–1870* (1983)

Hogan, William Ransom *The Texas Republic: A Social and Economic History* (1969)

Holley, Mary Austin *Texas* (1985)

Holmes, John *Texas Sport: The Illustrated History* (1984)

Hopewell, Clifford *Sam Houston; Man of Destiny* (1986)

Horgan, Paul *The Great River: The Rio Grande in North American History* (1954)

Hunter, J. Marvin (ed.) *The Trail Drivers of Texas* (1985)

Hurt, Harry III *Texas Rich* (1981)

Jordan, Terry G. *German Seed in Texas Soil: Immigrant Farmers in Nineteenth-Century Texas* (1966)
——. *Texas Log Buildings: A Folk Architecture* (1978)
—— with John L. Bean, Jr., and William M. Holmes *Texas; a Geography* (1984)
——. *Texas Log Buildings* (1987)

Keating, Bern *An Illustrated History of the Texas Rangers* (1980)

Kilgore, Dan *How Did Davy Die?* (1978)

Lanning, Jim and Judy (eds.) *Texas Cowboys; Memories of the Early Days* (1984)

Lich, Colen E. and Dona B. Reeves-Marquardt (eds.) *Texas Country; the Changing Rural Scene* (1986)

Lomax, John A. *Cowboy Songs and Other Frontier Ballads* (1910)
——. *Songs of the Cattle Trails and Cow Camp* (1919, rpt. 1979)
——. *Adventures of a Ballad Hunter* (1947)

Lord, Walter *A Time to Stand* (1961)

Loughmiller, Campbell and Lynn (eds.) *Big Thicket Legacy* (1977)

Lowe, Richard G. and Randolph B. Campbell *Planters and Plain Folk: Farming in Antebellum Texas* (1987)

Lowrie, Samuel H. *Culture Conflict in Texas* (1967)

Lynch, Gerald *Roughnecks, Drillers, and Tool Pushers: Thirty-Three Years in the Oil Fields* (1987)

Madsen, William *Mexican-Americans of South Texas* (1973)

Malone, Ann P. *Women on the Texas Frontier* (1983)

Malone, Bill C. *Country Music U.S.A.* (1968)

Maysel, Lou *Here Come the Longhorns, 1893–1970* 2 vols. (1978)

McCoy, Dorothy Abbott *Texas Ranchmen* (1987)

McDonald, Archie P. (comp.) *The Texas Experience* (1986)

McKay, Seth Shepard *Texas Politics, 1906–1944* (1952)

McMurtry, Larry *In a Narrow Grave, Essays on Texas* (1968)

Meining, D. W. *Imperial Texas, an Interpretive Essay in Cultural Geography* (1969)

Merk, Frederick *Slavery and the Annexation of Texas* (1972)

Montaigne, Sanford H. *Blood Over Texas* (1976)

Montejano, David *Anglos and Mexicans in the Making of Texas, 1836–1986* (1987)

Moore, Richard R. *West Texas After the Discovery of Oil; a Modern Frontier* (1971)

Morfí, Fray Juan Agustín (trans. C. E. Castañeda) *History of Texas, 1673–1779* (1967)

Morton, Robert A. *Living with the Texas Shore* (1983)

Muench, David *Texas* (1980)

Muir, Andrew Forest (ed.) *Texas in 1837* (1988)

Myers, John M. *The Alamo* (1948)

Newcomb, W. W., Jr. *The Indians of Texas: From Prehistoric to Modern Times* (1961)

Nunn, W. C. *Texas under the Carpetbaggers* (1962)

O'Connor, Robert F. (ed.) *Texas Myths* (1986)

Olien, Roger M. *Life in the Oil Fields* (1986)

Owens, William A. *Texas Folksongs* (1950, rpt. 1976)
——. *Tell Me a Story, Sing Me a Song* (1983)

Paredes, Americo *With His Pistol in His Hand: A Border Ballad and Its Hero* (1971)

Pena, Manuel *The Texas-Mexican Conjunto: History of a Working-Class Music* (1985)

Phelan, Richard *Texas Wild* (1976)

Presley, James *Saga of Wealth: The Rise of the Texas Oilmen* (1983)

Pruitt, Richard *Texas Women* (1984)

Ramsay, Jack C. *Thunder Beyond the Brazos; Mirabeau B. Lamar, a Biography* (1984)

Rathjen, Frederick W. *The Texas Panhandle Frontier* (1973, rpt. 1985)

Rector, Ray *Cowboy Life on the Texas Plains* (1982)

Reyna, José R. *Raza Humor: Chicano Joke Tradition in Texas* (1980)

Rice, Lawrence D. *The Negro in Texas, 1874–1900* (1971)

Richardson, Rupert N. *The Comanche Barrier to South Plains Settlement* (1933)
——. *The Frontier of Northwest Texas, 1846 to 1876* (1963)
——, Adrian N. Anderson, and Ernest Wallace *Texas: The Lone Star State* (5th ed. 1988)

Rittenhouse, Jack DeVere *Maverick Tales: True Stories of Early Texas* (1971)

Robinson, Willard B. *The People's Architecture; Texas Court-houses, Jails, and Municipal Buildings* (1983)

Roemer, Ferdinand *Texas* (1935, rpt. 1983)

Roland, Charles P. *Albert Sidney Johnston: Soldier of Three Republics* (1964, rpt. 1987)

Ruff, Ann *Unsung Heroes of Texas: Stories of Courage and Honor from Texas History and Legend* (1985)

Rundell, Walter Jr. *Early Texas Oil: A Photographic History, 1866–1936* (1977)

Santos, Richard G. *Santa Anna's Campaign Against Texas, 1835–1836* (1968)

Schofield, Donald F. *Indians, Cattle, Ships, and Oil* (1985)

Seale, William *Texas in Our Time; a History of Texas in the Twentieth Century* (1972)

Sewell, Gerald and Mary Beth Rogers *The Story of Texas Public Lands; a Unique Heritage* (1973)

Siegel, Stanley *A Political History of the Texas Republic, 1836–45* (1956)

Silverthorne, Elizabeth *Plantation Life in Texas* (1986)

Smallwood, James M. *Time of Hope, Time of Despair* (1980)

Smith, Justin H. *The Annexation of Texas* (1971)

Smithwick, Noah *The Evolution of a State, or, Recollections of Old Texas Days* (1900, rpt. 1983)

Sonnichsen, C. L. *I'll Die Before I'll Run: The Story of the Great Feuds of Texas* (1951)
——. *Pass of the North: Four Centuries on the Rio Grande* 2 vols. (1968, 1980)

Sowell, Andrew J. *Rangers and Pioneers of Texas* (1964)

Speck, Lawrence W. *Landmarks of Texas Architecture* (1987)

Spratt, John S. *The Road to Spindletop: Economic Change in Texas, 1875–1901* (1970)

Stapp, William P. *The Prisoners of Perote* (1977)

Tarpley, Fred *1001 Texas Place Names* (1980)

Texas Monthly *Texas, Our Texas; 150 Moments That Made Us the Way We Are* (1986)

Thompson, Jerry D. *Vaqueros in Blue and Gray* (1976)

Thompson, Thomas *Blood and Money* (1976)

Thrall, Homer S. *A Pictorial History of Texas, from the Earliest Visits of European Adventurers, to A. D. 1879* (4th ed. 1972)

Tinkle, Lon *Thirteen Days to Glory: The Siege of the Alamo* (1958)

Tyler, Ronnie C. and **Lawrence R. Murphy** *The Slave Narratives of Texas* (1974)

Webb, Walter Prescott and **H. Bailey Carroll** (eds.) *The Handbook of Texas* 3 vols. (1952–1976)
———. *The Great Plains* (1931)
———. *The Texas Rangers* (1935, rpt. 1971)
———. *The Great Frontier* (1964)

Weedle, Robert S. *Wilderness Manhunt* (1973)

Weems, John E. with **Jane Weems** *Dream of Empire; a Human History of the Republic of Texas 1836–1846* (1971)

Welch, June R. *People and Places in the Texas Past* (1974)

Wells, Tom H. *Commodore Moore and the Texas Navy* (1988)

Weniger, Del *Explorers' Texas: The Lands and Waters* (1984)

Whisenhunt, Donald W. *The Chronology of Texas History Through 1920* (1982)
———. (ed.) *Texas: A Sesquicentennial Celebration* (1984)

Wiley, Nancy *The Great State Fair of Texas: An Illustrated History* (1985)

Williams, J. W. (ed. K. F. Neighbours) *Old Texas Trails* (1979)

Winfrey, Dorman H. et al. *Indian Tribes of Texas* (1971)

Wooten, Dudley C. (ed.) *A Comprehensive History of Texas, 1685 to 1897* (1986)

Worcester, Donald Emmet *The Texas Longhorn--Relic of the Past, Asset for the Future* (1987)

UTAH

Utah, a Mountain state, is bordered on the north by Idaho and Wyoming; on the east by Colorado; on the south by Arizona; and on the west by Nevada.

FULL NAME State of Utah
POSTAL ABBREVIATION UT
INHABITANT Utahn
ADMITTED TO THE UNION Jan. 4, 1896.
45th state
POPULATION (est. 1987) 1,680,000.
Percent of US total: 0.69%. Rank: 35th

CAPITAL CITY Salt Lake City, the largest city in the state, located on the Great Salt Lake in north central Utah; population 164,844 (est. 1984). It was founded by Mormon pioneers in 1847 and named Great Salt Lake City (the name was changed in 1868). In 1849-1850 it was the capital of the provisional state of Deseret; it served as the territorial capital of Utah in 1850, 1857, and from 1859 to 1896, when it became state capital.

STATE NAME AND NICKNAMES From the White Mountain Apache word *yuttahih*, "one who is higher up," or "mountaintop dwellers," their term for the Navajo. Also known as the Beehive State, the Mormon State, the Land of the Saints, and the Salt Lake State.

STATE SEAL A shield bearing a beehive flanked by the state flower, with the state motto and the date "1847," and six arrows piercing the shield at the top; above it is a crouching eagle, and crossed behind it are two spears from which are draped American flags. The border reads "The Great Seal of the State of Utah, 1896."

MOTTO Industry

SONG "Utah We Love Thee" by Evan Stephens.

SYMBOLS
Flower sego lily
Tree blue spruce
Bird seagull
Gem topaz
Animal elk
Fish rainbow trout
Insect honeybee
Emblem beehive

LICENSE PLATES (1) Blue on white, with image of skier and blue-and-red legend "Ski Utah! Greatest Show on Earth." (2) Dark blue on white, with beehive symbol.

FLAG A blue field bearing a variant of the emblem of the state seal: the pictorial elements are identical, but the state name appears below the beehive, the date "1847" immediately below the shield, and the date "1896" at the bottom.

GEOGRAPHY AND CLIMATE

The arid landscape of Utah is mainly desert, mountain, and plateau. The spectacular red deserts of the Colorado Plateau occupy most of the southeastern part of the state; the Wasatch Range and Uinta Mountains of the Middle Rockies are in the northeast. The west contains the alkali deserts of the Basin and Range region. The Great Salt Lake is in northwestern Utah, an area once covered by a vast inland lake.

AREA 84,899 square miles. Rank: 11th
INLAND WATER 2,826 square miles
GEOGRAPHIC CENTER Sanpete, 3 miles N of Manti
ELEVATIONS *Highest point:* Kings Peak, Duchesne County, 13,528 feet. *Lowest point:* Beaverdam Creek, Washington County, 2,000 feet. *Mean elevation:* 6,100 feet

MAJOR RIVERS Colorado, Green, Sevier, Bear, Virgin

MAJOR LAKES AND RESERVOIRS Great Salt Lake, Utah, Bear, Powell, Flaming Gorge

LAND USE

	Thousands of acres
Urban (1982)	274
Rural (1982)	16,247
Cropland (1982)	2,039
Pastureland (1982)	490
Rangeland (1982)	8,489
Forestland (1982)	3,235
State parks and recreation areas (1983)	96
National park system (1984)	2,023
National forest system (1984)	9,129
Tribal lands (1984)	2,286

TEMPERATURES The highest recorded temperature was 117°F on July 5, 1985, at St. George. The lowest was -69°F on February 1, 1985, at Peter's Sink.

NATIONAL SITES

NATIONAL HISTORIC SITE Golden Spike
NATIONAL HISTORIC TRAIL Mormon Pioneer
NATIONAL MONUMENTS Cedar Breaks, Dinosaur, Hovenweep Natural Bridges, Rainbow Bridge, Timpanogos Cave
NATIONAL PARKS Arches, Bryce Canyon, Canyonlands, Capitol Reef, Zion
NATIONAL RECREATION AREA Glen Canyon
NATIONAL WILDLIFE REFUGES Bear River Migratory Bird Refuge, Fish Springs, Ouray–Browns Park

HISTORY

1776	Friars Francisco Atanasio Domínguez and Silvestre Velez de Escalante enter present-day Utah in seeking an overland route from New Mexico to California.
1824–1825	Jim Bridger discovers Great Salt Lake, which he evidently believes is an arm of the Pacific Ocean.
1825	An expedition led by Peter Skene Ogden of the Hudson's Bay Company clashes with American fur trappers in northwestern Utah.
1826–1827	Mountain man Jedediah Smith leads an expedition from Utah to California and back again to Utah.
1829–1830	Fur trappers hold annual summer rendezvous at Bear Lake in Utah, trading beaver pelts and obtaining supplies for the coming winter.
1843–1845	John C. Frémont leads two expeditions through Utah, surveying Great Salt Lake, Utah Lake, and several rivers.
1844–1845	Miles Goodyear, the first white settler, builds a cabin at what is now Ogden.
1845–1846	As a result of persecution in Illinois, leaders of the Church of Jesus Christ of Latter-day Saints (Mormons) decide on a mass migration to the Great Basin, including what is now western Utah.
1847	*July 24.* Led by Brigham Young, a pioneering band of Mormons arrive in Salt Lake Valley to establish a settlement.
1848	By the Treaty of Guadalupe Hidalgo ending the Mexican War, the entire Southwest, including Utah, passes from Mexico to the United States. Arrival of seagulls helps stem a devastating infestation of crickets and enables the colonists to harvest a partial crop of grain and vegetables.
1849	Provo, in Utah Valley, is founded by 30 families. *March 12.* Mormon leaders declare the state of Deseret, its proposed boundaries

embracing practically all of present Utah, Nevada, and Arizona, and portions of Oregon, Wyoming, Colorado, New Mexico, Idaho, and California.

1850   Congress establishes Utah Territory, which also contains parts of present-day Colorado, Wyoming, and Nevada. The population is 11,380.

1852   Plural marriage is publicly announced and thereafter defended as a Mormon religious tenet.

1856–1860 About 8,000 Mormon immigrants come to the United States bound for Utah. More than 3,000 of these walk from Iowa to Salt Lake City in "handcart companies."

1857   About 2,500 army troops enter Utah Territory to accompany a newly appointed governor replacing Brigham Young; Mormons vow to resist.
September 7–11. At Mountain Meadows, Mormon militia and their Indian allies massacre 120 persons passing through Utah to California.

1858   *June 12.* Mormons accept a presidential amnesty and the establishment of Camp Floyd in Cedar Valley for federal troops.

1862   Congress prohibits plural marriage, disincorporates the Mormon Church, and restricts the church's property to $50,000. For many years the law is not enforced because of Mormon control of the courts in Utah.

1865   Ute Indians agree to move to a reservation in the Uintah Basin. Raids by dissidents kill about 50 Mormons in the following three years.

1867   The installation of an organ in the Salt Lake Tabernacle enhances the performances of the fledgling Mormon Tabernacle Choir.

1868   Utah Territory is reduced to the present state borders.
Creation of Zion's Cooperative Mercantile Institution, a church-sponsored wholesale establishment supplying retail stores in every Mormon town.

1869   *May 10.* The first transcontinental railroad is completed, uniting the Union Pacific and Central Pacific lines at Promontory, Utah. Mormon labor constructs the road within Utah.

1870   *January 10.* The Mormon-owned Utah Central Railroad connects Salt Lake City to the transcontinental line.
February 12. Women receive the right to vote, just two months after Wyoming Territory becomes the first to extend the franchise.
Dissenting Mormons unite with non-Mormons to organize the Liberal party, opposed to church policies. In response, Mormons form the People's party, which easily elects its candidates.

1872   Ontario Ledge silver strike at Park City; from 1877 to 1904 the mine yields almost 38 million ounces of silver. Lead amounts to 23.5 percent of national production.

1882   Utah has a population of 120,283 Mormons, 14,136 gentiles (non-Mormons), and 6,888 ex-Mormons.

1885   As a result of determined federal efforts to enforce the law against polygamy, 23 persons are convicted and sent to jail. Many polygamous Mormons, including church leaders, go underground. Before prosecutions are virtually abandoned in the early 1890s, over 1,000 Utah Mormons are fined and/or imprisoned.

1887   Seeking statehood, the Legislative Assembly, with the support of Mormon leaders, enacts a law prohibiting the practice of polygamy.

1890   *October 6.* A general conference of Mormons unanimously advises church members to refrain from the practice of polygamy.
Peak year for sheep raising, with four million grazing in Utah.

1891   *June 10.* The People's party is dissolved as Mormon leaders seek rapprochement with the national parties. The Liberals dissolve in 1893.

1893   Completion and dedication of the imposing Salt Lake City Temple.

1895   A constitution established for Utah guarantees no union of church and state and declares that polygamous marriage is "forever prohibited."

1896   *January 4.* Utah's seventh application for statehood is successful, with the territory admitted to the Union as the 45th state.

1900   Emery and Carbon counties comprise the coal center of the West, with annual production of about a million tons. Two hundred men die in an explosion at Scofield's Winter Quarters Mine.

1905   Over a million acres of the Uintah Reservation are opened to white settlement.

Copper production surpasses silver in value to become the state's leading mineral product.

1906   Founding of the Utah Copper Company's Bingham Canyon mine, the largest open-pit copper mine in the world.

1911   Completion of the Strawberry Reservoir, the first federal reclamation project in Utah, diverts Colorado River water for irrigation and power.

1915   *November 19.* Industrial Workers of the World member Joe Hill is executed for the murder of a Salt Lake City grocer and his son.

1919   Salt Lake Valley is the greatest smelting district in North America, producing 4.45 million tons of metal per year.
Zion National Park is established.

1920   Total acreage of Utah farms has reached 5 million, or almost 10 percent of the state's land area. Improved land has reached its virtual maximum of 1.7 million acres. Sugar beet is the leading cash crop.

1924   A coal mine explosion in Castle Gate kills 172 men.

1928   Bryce Canyon National Park is established.

1930   Legislature adopts taxes on business profits, uniform rates for all tangible property, and graduated rates on personal and corporate income.

1932   Over 61,000 persons—35.8 percent of Utah's work force—are unemployed in the depths of the Great Depression. Republican US Senator Reed Smoot is unseated after 29 years of service.

1933   In spite of the Mormon stricture against alcoholic beverages, Utahns vote in favor of repealing both state and federal prohibition.

1934   Almost 21 percent of the population is on relief, a proportion exceeded in only four states.

1942–1945   In World War II, Utah is the site of 10 major military bases and an army hospital; the war brings an estimated 49,500 new jobs to the state. A steel plant, later sold to US Steel, is constructed west of Orem. Over 8,000 Pacific Coast Japanese-Americans are interned near Delta.

1955   A right-to-work law is adopted, outlawing the closed shop.

1958   Utah is second among states in the production of copper, gold, silver, molybdenum, and uranium, and third in lead and potash.

1963   Utah has more than 17,000 employees in defense industries, and defense is the state's single largest manufacturing sector.

1964   Completion of the Flaming Gorge Dam on the Green River.

1975   Utah's birth rate of 26 per 1,000 population is almost double the national rate of 14.8. Mormons comprise an estimated 70 percent of the state population of about 1,219,000.
Record oil production of 42 million barrels makes Utah ninth in ranking among states.

1977   *January 17.* Gary Gilmore is executed by firing squad for the murder of a Provo man; it is the first execution in the United States in 10 years.

1985   Great Salt Lake surpasses the high-water mark set in 1873, flooding lakefront property, farmland, highways, and a rail causeway.

DEMOGRAPHY

Population (est. 1987) . . .	1,680,000	White 1,382,550
Population (1980)	1,461,037	Other 34,930
Population density in persons		
per square mile (1980)	17.2	

POPULATION CHARACTERISTICS (1980)

Percent of state population

Urban	84.4
Rural	15.6
Under 18	37.0
65 or older	7.5
College-educated	20.3
Families below poverty line	7.7
Public-assistance recipients	3.2

POPULATION BY RACE (1980)

American Indian/Aleut/	
Eskimo	19,256
Asian/Pacific Islander	15,076
Black	9,225
Hispanic	60,302

Per capita personal income (1986)	$10,743
Millionaires per 100,000 residents (1982)	273.7
Average life expectancy in years (1980)	75.8
Marriage rate (1986)	10.1
Divorce rate (1986)	5.1
Birth rate per 1,000 residents (1985)	23.4
Infant mortality rate per 1,000 births (1985)	10.3
Abortion rate per 1,000 live births (1985)	116

Crime rate per 100,000 residents (1985)	
Violent	266.7
Property	5,211.7
Federal and state prisoners per 100,000 residents (1984)	81
Alcohol consumption in gallons per capita (1985)	26.7
Deaths from motor vehicle accidents per 100,000 residents (1985) . .	18.4

MAJOR CITIES

	1984 population (est.)
Ogden	68,183
Orem	60,884
Provo	74,138
Salt Lake City	164,844

GOVERNMENT AND POLITICS

Number of US Representatives	3
Electoral votes	5

POLITICAL PARTY NOMINEES FROM STATE

Parley Parker Christensen (Farmer Labor)	1920	P
Joseph Bracken Lee (Texas Constitutional)	1956	VP
Joseph Bracken Lee (Conservative Party of NJ)	1960	P

PRESIDENTIAL PRIMARY ELECTION In 1988, Utah sent 27 Democratic delegates and 26 Republican delegates to the national conventions.

CONSTITUTION Utah is using its original constitution, adopted in 1895.

LEGISLATURE The Legislature is divided into the Senate (29 members, 4-year term, minimum age 25) and the House of Representatives (150 members, 2-year term, minimum age 21). In 1987, the salary for legislators was $65 per day for a maximum of 45 days.

JUDICIARY The highest court is the Supreme Court, with 5 judges serving initial 3-year terms and 10-year terms upon retention. In 1987, the annual salary was $58,000.

EXECUTIVE The governor serves a 4-year term; the minimum age for holding office is 30. In 1987, the annual salary was $60,000. There are 4 other elected officials.

PRESIDENTIAL VOTE 1948-1988 *(in percents)*

Year	State Winner	Democratic	Republican
1948	Truman (D)	54.0	45.0
1952	Eisenhower (R)	41.1	58.9
1956	Eisenhower (R)	35.4	64.6
1960	Nixon (R)	45.2	54.8
1964	Johnson (D)	54.7	45.3
1968	Nixon (R)	37.1	56.5
1972	Nixon (R)	26.4	67.6
1976	Ford (R)	33.6	62.4
1980	Reagan (R)	20.6	72.8
1984	Reagan (R)	24.7	74.5
1988	Bush (R)	33.0	67.0

GOVERNORS

Governor, State of Deseret

Brigham Young	1849-1851

Territorial Governors

Brigham Young	1851-1857
Alfred Cumming	1857-1861
Francis H. Wootton (acting)	1861
John W. Dawson	1861
Frank Fuller (acting)	1861-1862
Stephen S. Harding	1862-1863
James Duane Doty	1863-1865
O.H. Irish (acting)	1865
Charles Durkee	1865-1869

Edwin P. Higgins (acting)	1869-1870
Stephen A. Mann (acting)	1870
J. Wilson Shaffer	1870
Vernon H. Vaughan (acting)	1870-1871
George A. Black (acting)	1871
George L. Woods	1871-1874
Samuel B. Axtell	1874-1875
George B. Emery	1875-1880
Eli H. Murray	1880-1886
Caleb W. West	1886-1889
Arthur L. Thomas	1889-1893
Caleb W. West	1893-1896

State Governors

Heber M. Wells (R)	1896-1905
John C. Cutler (R)	1905-1909
William Spry (R)	1909-1917
Simon Bamberger (D)	1917-1921
Charles R. Mabey (R)	1921-1925
George H. Dern (D)	1925-1933
Henry H. Blood (D)	1933-1941
Herbert B. Maw (D)	1941-1949
J. Bracken Lee (R)	1949-1957
George D. Clyde (R)	1957-1965
Calvin L. Rampton (D)	1965-1977
Scott M. Matheson (D)	1977-1985
Norman H. Bangerter (R)	1985-

MINIMUM AGES

Majority	18
Marriage with parental consent	no minimum age
Marriage without parental consent	18
Making a will	18
Buying alcohol	21
Jury duty	18
Leaving school	18
Driver's license	16

CAPITAL PUNISHMENT
Number executed 1976-88: 3
On death row Aug. 1, 1988: 6

MILITARY INSTALLATIONS
Total number: 13
Major bases:
    Army: 1
    Air Force: 3

FINANCES

Thousands of dollars

GENERAL REVENUE (1985)

Total general revenue	2,582,538
Total tax revenue	1,323,699
Sales and gross receipts	728,433
Individual income taxes	430,711
Corporate net income taxes	52,191

GENERAL EXPENDITURE (1985)

Total general expenditure	2,563,524
Education	1,174,019
Public welfare	310,476
Health	90,126
Hospitals	107,987
Natural resources	65,078
Highways	378,052
Police	24,022
Corrections	54,672

FEDERAL AID (1985) 759,414

ECONOMY

The relatively small amount of arable land in Utah produces wheat, sugar beets, hay, barley, corn, potatoes, oats, vegetables, and orchard fruits. Cattle, sheep, and turkeys are the main livestock. Utah's farm marketings cash receipts in 1983 were $579 million. Mining is a major contributor to the state's economy; products include oil, coal, natural gas, and many metals, including uranium, copper, beryllium, magnesium, gold, lead, molybdenum, and silver. The Utah timber industry harvests western softwoods, mainly species of fir, pine and spruce. In manufacturing, metals processing and fabrication ranks with food processing as the top activities. Other manufactures include high-tech electronics, transportation equipment, wood and paper products, and petrochemicals.

EMPLOYMENT (1984)

Thousands of persons

Total number of employed workers	674
Construction	35.0
Finance, insurance, and real estate	29.8
Government	131.1
Manufacturing	94.2
Mining	12.7
Services	121.3
Transportation, communications, and utilities	36.4
Wholesale and retail trade	140.9

Percent of civilian labor force unemployed (1984) 6.5

DEPARTMENT OF DEFENSE (1985)

Civilian workers employed	23,641
Military personnel	6,172
Contract awards	$789 million

ENERGY SOURCES FOR ELECTRIC UTILITIES (1983)

	Percent
Coal	87.9
Gas	0.6
Hydroelectric	11.2
Nuclear	0.0
Petroleum	0.3

TRANSPORTATION

Motor vehicles registered in state (1986)	1,110,633
Miles of roads, streets, and highways (1986)	49,938
Miles of Class I railway operated (1986)	1,483
Airports (1983)	95
Major aviation hubs (1983)	1
Largest hub: Salt Lake City	

CULTURE AND EDUCATION

Native American tribes

Utah was formerly the home of the Bannock, Northern Shoshoni, and Western Shoshoni tribes. Groups that continue to live in the state include the Gosiute, Navajo, Southern Paiute, and Ute. There are 6 federal reservations in Utah.

Religions, ethnicities, and languages

The dominant religious group in Utah is the Church of Jesus Christ of Latter-day Saints (Mormons), which represents 70 percent of the population, and whose world headquarters are in Salt Lake City. Many Utahns are descended from the Mormon pioneers who arrived in 1847. Many others are descended from Mormon converts who emigrated from other countries, chiefly Scandinavia and Britain. Other religious groups include Protestants, Roman Catholics, Jews, Buddhists, and Greek Orthodox. In 1980, 7.4 percent of Utah's population spoke a language other than English at home. Ethnic communities in Utah include American Indians, Chicanos, blacks, Asians, and Greeks.

Major museums and libraries

Departments of Geneology and History, Church of Jesus Christ of Latter-day Saints, Salt Lake City

B.F. Larsen Gallery of Art, Brigham Young University, Provo
Utah Museum of Fine Arts, University of Utah, Salt Lake City
Utah Museum of Natural History, University of Utah, Salt Lake City

Major arts organizations

Pioneer Theatre Company, Salt Lake City
Utah Opera Company, Salt Lake City
Utah Symphony Orchestra, Salt Lake City

Colleges and universities

Number public (1986-87) 9
Number private (1986-87) 5
Total enrollment, in full-time equivalent students (1985) 84,100

Public elementary and secondary schools

Expenditure per pupil in average daily attendance (1986-87) $2,455
Pupil-teacher ratio (1987) 23.4
Average teacher salary (1986-87) $26,908

Major league sports teams

Basketball: Utah Jazz

Holidays

Pioneer Day. July 24
State Fair, Salt Lake City. September

UTAH IN LITERATURE

Edward Abbey *Desert Solitaire* (1968, rpt. 1985)
Autobiographical essays on the author's experiences as a park ranger and forest fire lookout in southeastern Utah. A classic defense of the wilderness.
———. *Slickrock* (1971)
Description of the canyon country of southern Utah.

Amelia Bean *The Fancher Train* (1958)
Novel about the Mountain Meadows Massacre of 1857.

Forrester Blake *Wilderness Passage* (1953)
Novel about conflicts between Mormon settlers and the US Army.

Violet Boyce and **Mabel Harmer** *Upstairs to a Mine* (1988)
Biography of a woman who was brought up near the Bingham mine.

George R. Brooks (ed.) *The Southwest Expedition of Jedediah S. Smith: His Personal Account of the Journey to California, 1826–27* (1977)

Juanita Brooks (ed.) *On the Mormon Frontier: The Diary of Hosea Stout, 1844–1861* (1964, rpt. 1982)
———. *Frontier Tales: True Stories of Real People* (1972)
———. *Quicksand and Cactus: A Memoir of the Southern Mormon Frontier* (1982)

F. S. Buchanan (ed.) *A Good Time Coming: Mormon Letters to Scotland* (1988)
Correspondence of Mormon immigrants who came to Utah between 1853 and 1872.

Richard F. Burton *The City of the Saints* (1862, rpt. 1962)
Portrait of early Mormon society.

Charles L. Camp (ed.) *James Clyman, Frontiersman: The Adventures of a Trapper and Covered-Wagon Emigrant as Told in His Own Reminiscences and Diaries* (1960)

Ray R. Canning and **Beverley Beeton** (eds.) *The Genteel Gentile: Letters of Elizabeth Cumming, 1857-1858* (1977)
The Utah War as seen by the wife of the state's second governor.

Vera Christensen and **Elizabeth Nuhm** *The Big Cache: Fantasy, Fact and Folklore* (1976)

William Clayton *William Clayton's Journal: A Daily Record of the Journey of the Original Company of Mormon Pioneers . . .* (1921, rpt. 1973)

Robert G. Cleland and **Juanita Brooks** (eds.) *A Mormon Chronicle: The Diaries of John D. Lee* 2 vols. (1955, rpt. 1983)
Observations of a prominent Mormon who lived in Southern Utah near the site of the Mountain Meadows Massacre.

Everett L. Cooley *Utah: A Student's Guide to Localized History* (1968)

Levette Jay Davidson *Rocky Mountain Life in Literature* (1936)
―――― and **Prudence Bostwick** *The Literature of the Rocky Mountain West, 1803–1903* (1939)

Clarence E. Dulton *Report on the Geology of the High Plains of Utah* (1880)
Government surveyor's report on the Tushar range that is one of the earliest descriptions of southern Utah landscape.

S. George Ellsworth (ed.) *Dear Ellen: Two Mormon Women and Their Letters* (1974)
Views of polygamous marriage during the early twentieth century.

Austin E. Fife and **Alta Fife** *Saints of Sage and Saddle: Folklore Among the Mormons* (1956, rpt. 1966, 1980)

Vardis Fisher *Children of God: An American Epic* (1939, rpt. 1977)
An epic novel of the founding and establishment of the Mormon Church.

Edward A. Geary *Goodbye to Poplarhaven: Recollections of a Utah Boyhood* (1985)

Linda M. Hasselstrom (ed.) *Journal of a Mountain Man: James Clyman* (1984)

Cassie H. Hock "The Mormons in Fiction," *University of Colorado Studies* 26 (1941)

William Kittson "Journal of Ogden's 1824–25 Snake Country Expedition," *Utah Historical Quarterly* 22 (1954)

Alfred Lambourne *Our Inland Sea: The Story of a Homestead* (1909)
Narrative of a poet and landscape painter who lived alone on Gunnison Island in the Great Salt Lake for fourteen months.

Harold D. Langley (ed.) *To Utah with the Dragoons and Glimpses of Life in Arizona and California 1858-1859* (1974)
The eyewitness reports of an anonymous young soldier who served during the Utah expedition.

A. Karl Larson and **K. M. Larson** *The Diary of Charles Lowell Walker* (1980)
By a Mormon pioneer of southern Utah.

Brigham D. Madsen (ed.) *A Forty-Niner in Utah: With the Stansbury Exploration of Great Salt Lake: Letters and Journal of John Hudson 1849-50* (1981)

Maurice P. Marchant "Mormons in Literature: A Book List to Set the Record Straight," *Library Journal* 88 (1963)

David E. Miller and **David H. Miller** (eds.) *Peter Skene Ogden's Snake Country Journals, 1827–28 and 1828–29*

Dale L. Morgan (ed.) *Overland in 1846: Diaries and Letters of the California-Oregon Trail* (1963)

William Mulder and **A. Russell Mortensen** *Among the Mormons: Historic Accounts by Contemporary Observers* (1958)

William R. Palmer *Why the North Star Stands Still and Other Indian Legends* (1957)
―――――. *Stories of Our Ancestors: A Collection of Northern Ute Indian Tales* (1974)

Parley J. Paskett *Wild Mustangs* (1988)
A firsthand account of wild horse catching in the Utah/Nevada desert in the 1930s.

Parley P. Pratt *The Autobiography of Parley P. Pratt* (1874, rpt. 1961)

Osborne Russell (ed. Aubrey L. Haines) *Journal of a Trapper* (1955)

Gene Allred Sessions *Mormon Thunder* (1982)
The words of Jedediah M. Grant are used to create an autobiography of the great preacher of the Mormon Reformation.

Wallace Stegner *Mormon Country* (1942, rpt. 1981)
The folklore and customs of Mormon society in the 1940s. Stegner has also written *The Gathering of Zion: The Story of the Mormon Trail* (1964) and *The Sound of Mountain Water* (1985), which contains an essay on the flooding of Glen Canyon.

Annie Clark Tanner *A Mormon Mother* (1969)
A memoir of an unhappy polygamous marriage.

Maurine Whipple *The Giant Joshua* (1941)
Novel describing the founding of the Virgin River colony.

William A. Wilson *On Being Human: The Folklore of Mormon Missionaries* (1988)

Ann Zwinger *Wind in the Rock* (1978)
Essay on the natural beauty of five southern Utah canyons.

GUIDES TO RESOURCES

Alter, Cecil J. "Bibliographers' Choice of Books on Utah and the Mormons," *Utah Historical Quarterly* 24 (1956)

Bitton, Davis *Guide to Mormon Diaries and Autobiographies* (1977)

Carr, Stephen L. *The Historical Guide to Utah Ghost Towns* (1972)

Federal Writers' Project *Utah: A Guide to the State* (1941, rpt. 1954)
―――――. *Provo: Pioneer Mormon City* (1942)

Geer, Dean C., Klaus D. Gurgel, Wayne L. Wahlquist, Howard A. Christy, and **Gary B. Peterson** *Atlas of Utah* (1981)

Jackson, Ronald Vern *Utah Historical and Biographical Index* vol. 1 (1984)

Jaussi, Laureen and **Gloria Chaston** *Genealogical Records of Utah* (1974)

Kunz, Phillip R. and **Merlin B. Brinkerhoff** *Utah in Numbers: Comparisons, Trends, and Descriptions* (1969)

Merrill Library *Name Index to the Library of Congress Collection of Mormon Diaries* (1942)

University of Utah, Bureau of Economic and Business Research *Statistical Abstract of Utah* (1987–)

Wahlquist, Wayne L. et al. (eds.) *Atlas of Utah* (1982)

Washington, Mary *An Annotated Bibliography of Western Manuscripts in the Merrill Library . . . Logan, Utah* (1988)

SELECTED NONFICTION SOURCES

Alder, Douglas D. (ed.) *Cache Valley: Essays on Her Past and People* (1976)

Alexander, Thomas G. and **James B. Allen** *Mormons and Gentiles: A History of Salt Lake City* (1984)

Allen, James B. and **Glen M. Leonard** *The Story of the Latter-day Saints* (1976)

Allred, LaNora P. *Spanish Fork: City on the Rio De Aquas Calientes* (1981)

Alter, J. Cecil *James Bridger, Trapper, Frontiersman, Scout and Guide: A Historical Narrative* (1925)
————. *Utah, The Storied Domain* 3 vols. (1932)
————. *Early Utah Journalism* (1938, rpt. 1970)

Anderson, Leroy C. *Joseph Morris and the Saga of the Morrisites* (1988)

Anderson, Nels *Desert Saints: The Mormon Frontier in Utah* (1942)

Andrew, Laurel B. *The Early Temples of the Mormons* (1978)

Arrington, Leonard J. *Great Basin Kingdom* (1958)
————. *The Changing Economic Structure of the Mountain West, 1850–1950* (1963)
————. *Brigham Young: American Moses* (1985)
————. *David Eccles: Pioneer Western Industrialist* (1988)
———— and **Thomas G. Alexander** *A Dependent Commonwealth: Utah's Economy from Statehood to the Great Depression* (1974)
———— and **Davis Bitton** *The Mormon Experience* (1979)
————, **Feramorz Y. Fox,** and **Dean L. May** *Building the City of God: Community and Cooperation Among the Mormons* (1976)
———— and **Gary B. Hansen** *The Richest Hole on Earth: A History of the Bingham Copper Mine* (1988)
———— and **George Jensen** *The Defense Industry of Utah* (1965)
———— and **William Roper** *William Spry: Man of Firmness, Governor of Utah* (1971)

Bailey, Paul *Jacob Hamblin: Buckskin Apostle* (1948)

Bancroft, Hubert H. *History of Utah, 1540–1887* (1890)

Baskin, R. H. *Reminiscences of Early Utah* (1914)

Benally, Clyde et al. *Dinéjí Nákéé Nááhané: A Utah Navajo History* (1982)

Bennett, Richard E. *Mormons at the Missouri, 1846–1852* (1987)

Bergera, Gary J. and **Ronald L. Priddis** *Brigham Young University: A House of Faith* (1985)

Binns, Archie *Peter Skene Ogden: Fur Trader* (1967)

Bolton, Herbert E. *Spanish Borderlands* (1921)
————. *Pageant in the Wilderness* (1951)

Boyce, Violet and **Mabel Harmer** *Upstairs to a Mine* (1976)

Brooks, Juanita *The Mountain Meadows Massacre* (1950; rev. ed. 1962)
————. *The History of the Jews in Utah and Idaho* (1973)
————. *Emma Lee* (1988)

Brough, R. Clayton *Mosida, Utah: Past, Present & Future* (1974)

Call, Craig M. (ed.) *Provo Historic Buildings Tour* (3d. ed, 1979)

Calman, Charles J. *The Mormon Tabernacle Choir* (1979)

Cannon, Anthony S. (ed.) *Popular Beliefs and Superstitions From Utah* (1984)

Cannon, Frank J. and **Harvey J. O'Higgins** *Under the Prophet in Utah: The National Menace of a Political Priestcraft* (1911)

Cannon, Hal (ed.) *Utah Folk Art* (1980)

Carter, Thomas and **Peter Goss** *Utah's Historic Architecture, 1847–1940* (1988)

Chamberlin, Ralph V. *The University of Utah* (1960)

Chavez, Fra Angelico (trans.) and **Ted J. Warner** (ed.) *The Domínguez-Escalante Journal* (1976)

Cline, Gloria Griffen *Exploring the Great Basin* (1963)

Cowan, Ila W. (ed.) *Jensen, Utah: Where Is It? Who Are Its People?* (1979)

Crampton, C. Gregory (ed.) Issue on the Indian tribes of Utah. *Utah Historical Quarterly* (Spring 1971)

Creer, Leland H. *Founding of an Empire: The Exploration and Colonization of Utah, 1776–1856* (1947)

Davies, J. Kenneth *Deseret's Sons of Toil: A History of the Worker Movements of Territorial Utah, 1852–1896* (1977)

Deseret News Publishing Company *Home in the Hills of Bridger Land: The History of Hyrum From 1860 to 1969* (1969)

De Voto, Bernard *Across the Wide Missouri* (1964)

Dixon, Madoline Cloward *Peteetneet Town: A History of Payson, Utah* (1974)

Driggs, Howard R. *Timpanogos Town: Story of Old Battle Creek and Pleasant Grove, Utah* (1948)

Dunham, Dick and **Vivian** *Our Strip of Land: A History of Daggett County, Utah* (1947)
————. *Flaming Gorge Country: The Story of Daggett County, Utah* (1977)

Dunn, Marion *Bingham Canyon* (1973)

Dwyer, Robert J. *The Gentile Comes to Utah* (1941, rpt. 1971)

Fife, Austin and **Alta** *Forms upon the Frontier* (1988)

Gardner, Hamilton *History of Lehi Including a Biographical Section* (1913)

Gerlach, Larry R. *Blazing Crosses in Zion: The Ku Klux Klan in Utah* (1982)

Goldberg, Robert A. *Back to the Soil: The Jewish Farmers of Clarion, Utah, and Their World* (1986)

Hafen, Leroy R. "Etienne Provost, Mountain Man and Utah Pioneer," *Utah Historical Quarterly* 36 (1968)
————. *Broken Hand, the Life of Thomas Fitzpatrick: Mountain Man, Guide, and Indian Agent* (1973)
———— and **Ann** *The Utah Expedition, 1857–58: A Documentary Account* (1958)

Haglund, Carl T. and **Philip F. Notarianni** *The Avenues of Salt Lake City* (1980)

Hansen, Klaus J. *Quest for Empire* (1967)

Haseltine, James L. *One Hundred Years of Utah Painting* (1965)

Heinerman, Joseph "Early Pioneer Cultural Societies," *Utah Historical Quarterly* Winter (1979)

Hintze, Lehi F. *Geological History of Utah* (1973)

Hunter, Milton R. *Brigham Young the Colonizer* (1940)
————. *Utah in Her Western Setting* (1943)
————. *Utah: The Story of Her People, 1540–1947* (1946)

Jackson, Donald and **Mary Lee Spence** *The Expeditions of John Charles Frémont* (1970–1973)

Janecek, George, Kent Miles, and **Arthur Rothstein** *The Other Utahns: A Photographic Portfolio* (1988)

Jefferson, James, Robert W. Delaney, and **Gregory C. Thompson** *The Southern Utes: A Tribal History* (1971)

Kane, Elizabeth Wood (ed. Everett L. Cooley) *Twelve Mormon Homes Visited in Succession on a Journey Through Utah to Arizona* (1974)

Kelly, Charles "Antoine Robidoux," *Utah Historical Quarterly* 6 (1933)

Kenner, S. A. *Utah As It Is: With a Comprehensive Statement of Utah As It Was* (1904)

Kimball, Stanley B. *The Latter-day Saints Immigrant Guide* (1983)

Korns, J. Roderick "West From Fort Bridger," *Utah Historical Quarterly* 19 (1951)

Lange, Dorothea, Russell Lee, and Arthur Rothstein *Life and Land: Farm Security Administration Photographs in Utah, 1936–1941* (1988)

Larson, Gustive O. "The Mormon Reformation," *Utah Historical Quarterly* (January 1958)
––––––. *The "Americanization" of Utah for Statehood* (1971)

Long, E. B. *The Saints and the Union: Utah Territory During the Civil War* (1981)

Lyman, E. Leo *Political Deliverance: The Mormon Quest for Utah Statehood* (1985)

Lythgoe, Dennis L. *Let 'Em Holler: A Political Biography of J. Bracken Lee* (1982)

Madsen, Brigham D. *Corinne: The Gentile Capital of Utah* (1980)
––––––. *Gold Rush Sojourners in Great Salt Lake City 1849 and 1850* (1983)
––––––. *The Shoshoni Frontier and the Bear River Massacre* (1985)

Martin, Thomas K., Tim B. Heaton and Stephen J. Bahr *Utah in Demographic Perspective* (1986)

Matheson, Scott M. *Out of Balance* (1986)

May, Dean L. *Utah: A People's History* (1987)

McPhee, William M. *The Trail of the Leprechaun: Early History of a Utah Mining Camp* (1977)

Merrill, Yvonne Young *Cache Valley: In and Out and Round About* (1970)

Miller, David E. *Hole-in-the-Rock: An Epic in the Colonization of the Great American West* (1959, rpt. 1966)

Miller, Marilyn McMeen and John Clifton Moffitt *Provo: A Story of People in Motion* (1974)

Moffitt, John Clifton *The History of Public Education in Utah* (1946)
––––––. *The Story of Provo, Utah* (1975)

Morgan, Dale L. *The State of Deseret* (1940, rpt. 1988)
––––––. *Jedediah Smith and the Opening of the West* (1953)

Neff, Andrew L. *History of Utah: 1847–1869* (1940)

Nelson, Lowry *Some Social and Economic Features of American Fork, Utah* (1933)
––––––. *The Mormon Village: A Pattern and Technique of Land Settlement* (1952)

Nevins, Allan *Frémont, Pathmarker of the West* (1939; rev. ed. 1955)

Newbold, Noal C. and Bea Kummer *Silver and Snow: The Story of Park City* (1968)

Notarianni, Philip F. *Faith, Hope, and Prosperity: The Tintic Mining District* (1982)

O'Dea, Thomas F. *The Mormons* (1957)

Oswald, Delmont R. *The Life and Adventures of James P. Beckwourth* (1972)

Papanikolas, Helen Z. *The Peoples of Utah* (n.d.)

Peterson, Charles S., John F. Yurtinus, David E. Atkinson, and A. Kent Powell *Mormon Battalion Trail Guide* (1972)
––––––. *Utah: A Bicentennial History* (1977)

Poll, Richard D., Thomas G. Alexander, Eugene E. Campbell, and David E. Miller *Utah's History* (1978)

Powell, Allan Kent *The Next Time We Strike: Labor in Utah's Coal Fields, 1900–1933* (1988)

Pruess, Charles *Exploring with Frémont* (1958)

Ravsten, Ben. J., and Eunice P. Ravsten *History of Clarkston: The Granary of Cache Valley 1864–1964* (1966)

Rice, Claton *Ambassador to the Saints* (1965)

Ricks, Joel E. *Forms and Methods of Early Mormon Settlement in Utah* (1964)
–––––– and Everett L. Cooley *The History of a Valley: Cache Valley, Utah-Idaho* (1956)

Ringholtz, Raye Carleson *Historic Buildings on Capitol Hill, Salt Lake City* (1981)

Rockwell, Wilson *Utes: A Forgotten People* (1956)

Ross, Marvin C. *The West of Alfred Jacob Miller* (1966)

Russell, Carl P. *Firearms, Traps, and Tools of the Mountain Men* (1967)

Shelley, George F. *Early History of American Fork With Some History of a Later Day* (1945)

Shoumatoff, Alex *The Mountain of Names: An Informal History of Kinship* (1985)

Simmonds, A. J. *On the Big Range: A Centennial History of Cornish and Trenton, Cache County, Utah 1870–1970* (1970)
––––––. *The Gentile Comes to Cache Valley: A Study of the Logan Apostasies of 1874 and the Establishment of Non-Mormon Churches in Cache Valley, 1873–1913* (1976)

Snow, Eliza R. *Biography and Family Record of Lorenzo Snow* (1884)

Stott, Clifford L. *Search for Sanctuary: Brigham Young and the White Mountain Expedition* (1984)

Stout, Wayne *History of Utah, 1896–1929* (1968)

Sutton, Wain (ed.) *Utah: A Centennial History*

Thompson, George A. and Fraser Buck *Treasure Mountain Home: A Centennial History of Park City, Utah* (1968)

Thomson, Mildred Hatch *Rich Memories: Some of the Happenings in Rich County From 1863 to 1960* (1962)

Tippetts, Della Ludlow *A Town Is Born: Benjamin, Utah County, Utah* (1969)

Tuttle, Daniel S. *Missionary to the Mountain West: Reminiscences of Episcopal Bishop Daniel S. Tuttle 1866–1886* (1987)

Underhill, Ruth Murray *The Navajo* (1971)

Unruh, John D., Jr. *The Plains Across: the Overland Emigrants and the Trans-Mississippi West, 1840–1860* (1979)

Van Wagoner, Richard S. *Mormon Polygamy: A History* (1986)

Wadsworth, Nelson B. *Through Camera Eyes* (1973)

Warrum, Noble *Utah Since Statehood* 4 vols. (1919–1920)

Watters, Leon L. *The Pioneer Jews of Utah* (1952)

Weeks, Clyde E., Jr. *Sagebrush to Steel; An Orem Centennial History, 1861–1961* (1961)

Wheat, Carl I. (ed.) *Mapping the Trans-Mississippi West, 1540–1861* (1957–1963)

Wild, Jennie Adams *Alpine Yesterdays: A History of Alpine, Utah County, Utah 1850–1980* (1982)

Young, L. E. *The Founding of Utah* (1923)

VERMONT

Vermont is a New England state, bordered on the north by the Canadian province of Quebec; on the east by the Connecticut River and New Hampshire; on the south by Massachusetts; and on the west by New York and Lake Champlain.

FULL NAME State of Vermont
POSTAL ABBREVIATION VT
INHABITANT Vermonter
ADMITTED TO THE UNION Mar. 4, 1791.
 14th state
POPULATION (est. 1987) 548,000.
 Percent of US total: 0.23%. Rank: 48th

CAPITAL CITY Montpelier, located on the Winooski River in north central Vermont; population 8,241 (1980). Montpelier was chartered in 1781 and became the state capital in 1805. It was incorporated as a village in 1828 and a city in 1895.

STATE NAME AND NICKNAME From the French words *verd mont*, "green mountain" (in 17th-century spelling). Also known as the Green Mountain State.

STATE SEAL Across the middle, a forest, out of which rises a stylized pine tree with fourteen branches; to the right a cow, and to the left the head of a spear; at the bottom, the state name and motto. Four sheaves of wheat occupy the corners of the design. The border is made of arrowheads.

MOTTO Freedom and Unity

SONG "Hail, Vermont!" by Josephine Hovey Perry.

SYMBOLS
Flower red clover
Tree sugar maple
Bird hermit thrush
Animal Morgan horse
Insect honeybee
Beverage milk
Soil Tunbridge soil series

LICENSE PLATES (1) White on dark green, with maple tree and legend "Green Mountain State," the license number outlined by a white border. (2) White on dark green, with a white border and legend "Green Mountains."

FLAG A blue field bearing the state coat of arms: a shield showing a landscape, with a pine tree reaching into a yellow sky, three sheaves of wheat on its left, a red cow on its right, and blue mountains in the distance; below the shield, two crossed pine branches, and a red scroll with the state name and motto; above it, a buck's head on a blue and yellow scroll.

GEOGRAPHY AND CLIMATE

The geographical backbone of Vermont is the Green Mountains, a range of the Appalachians, running north-south through the center of the state. Heavily forested hills cover nearly all the rest of Vermont, of which less than 20 percent is level terrain suitable for agriculture. Vermont has some 400 lakes but no large rivers (the Connecticut River, forming the eastern border, is entirely within New Hampshire); the climate is generally cool, with heavy snowfall—up to 110 inches in the mountains.

AREA 9,614 square miles. Rank: 43d
INLAND WATER 341 square miles
GEOGRAPHIC CENTER Washington, 3 miles E of Roxbury
ELEVATIONS *Highest point:* Mount Mansfield, Lamoille County, 4,393 feet. *Lowest point:* Lake Champlain, Franklin County, 95 feet. *Mean elevation:* 1,000 feet

MAJOR RIVERS Connecticut, Winooski, Lamoille, White

MAJOR LAKES AND RESERVOIRS Champlain, Mephremagog, Bomoseen

LAND USE

	Thousands of acres
Urban (1982)	97
Rural (1982)	5,377
Cropland (1982)	648
Pastureland (1982)	501
Rangeland (1982)	0
Forestland (1982)	4,087
State parks and recreation areas (1983)	177
National park system (1984)	4
National forest system (1984)	630
Tribal lands (1984)	0

TEMPERATURES The highest recorded temperature was 105°F on July 4, 1911. The lowest was -50°F on December 30, 1933, at Bloomfield.

NATIONAL SITES

NATIONAL SCENIC TRAIL Appalachian
NATIONAL WILDLIFE REFUGE Missisquoi

HISTORY

1609	Explorers for France led by Samuel de Champlain are the first white men to enter the region. They call the mountains *Verd Mont* (Green Mountains).
1666	French build their first settlement, Forte Sainte Anne, on an island in Lake Champlain.
1690	Trading post is constructed by British, Chimney Point Fort, in southeastern Vermont.
1704	Indians and French soldiers journey through Vermont on way to the French-English battle for Deerfield, Massachusetts.
1724	British establish first permanent settlement, Fort Dummer, in the southeast corner of the region.
1752	First maple sugar and syrup made by whites. (Vermont still makes more maple sugar and syrup than any other state.)
1759	Robert Rogers, scout for British Army, and his group, Rogers' Rangers, destroy Indian village. Many Indian raids follow.
1762	First church organized at Bennington.
1763	Treaty of Paris. French give up claims to Vermont.
1769	Dartmouth College, formerly Moor's Indian Charity School, is incorporated by a charter grant from George III of England.
1770	Ethan Allen forms a military force to protect the area. They are known as the Green Mountain Boys.
1775	Ethan Allen and his Green Mountain Boys capture Fort Ticonderoga, at the head of Lake Champlain, from the British—one of the first important American victories of the Revolutionary War.
1777	*January 15.* Vermonters declare their independence from Great Britain.
	July 2–8. Vermont drafts a constitution and becomes the first state to abolish slavery.
	August 16. American troops defeat British General John Burgoyne at Bennington.
1781	First Vermont newspaper is published at Westminster.
1784–1885	First bridge is built across Connecticut River at Bellows Falls. It is a toll bridge.
1785	First marble quarry in US in operation. Vermont also quarries much granite.

1790	New York sells its claims to Vermont for $30,000.
1791	*March 4*. Vermont admitted to the Union as the 14th state. University of Vermont is chartered.
1793	Bennington manufactures the first of its famous pottery. Copper is discovered near Stratford.
1797	Legislature orders towns to support schools.
1800	Middlebury College is chartered.
1802	First canal in the United States is built at Bellows Falls.
1805	The capital of the state is permanently established at Montpelier.
1809	State prison established at Windsor.
1809	Fort Cassin, west-central Vermont, is defended against the British during the War of 1812.
1814	*September 11*. Vermont soldiers fight in New York's Battle of Plattsburgh which gives Americans final control of Lake Champlain.
1823	Champlain canal opens allowing for easier trade with New York. First normal school for the education of teachers in the US is established at Concord.
1825	General Lafayette tours the state.
1830	Vermonter Thaddeus Fairbanks invents the platform scale.
1838	John Humphrey Noyes establishes his experimental community at Putney but his free love ideals are rejected by neighbors and the group is moved to New York in 1847.
1848	First railroad in the state is opened in central Vermont.
1861	Civil War begins. Vermont is first state to offer troops to Lincoln.
1864	*October*. Confederate raid at St. Albans.
1865	Vermont ratifies the 13th Amendment abolishing slavery.
1896	Rudyard Kipling leaves his Brattleboro, Vermont home for England after writing two *Jungle Books* and *Captains Courageous* there.
1898	Spanish-American War. Vermont-born Admiral George Dewey is victorious at Manila Bay. Admiral Clark, also a Vermonter, defeats the Spanish at Santiago Bay.
1910	First airplane flight at St. Johnsbury in northeastern Vermont.
1923	*August 3*. Calvin Coolidge inaugurated as US President after death of Warren Harding. He is sworn into the presidency by his father in his parents' farmhouse in Plymouth Notch, Vermont.
1924	Calvin Coolidge is nominated and elected president.
1927	Floods kill 60 people and cause millions of dollars in damage.
1930	First radio station in the state, WSYS, begins broadcasting at Rutland.
1931	State income tax is adopted.
1933–1934	The first ski tow in the US is in operation at Woodstock in central Vermont.
1938	Severe hurricane causes death of five people and $12 million in damage.
1941	*September 11*. Vermont legislature defines "armed conflict" and literally declares war on Germany before the US does.
1943	George Lansing Fox from Gelman, Vermont, is one of the "Four Immortal Chaplains" who perish in the torpedoing of *S.S. Dorchester*.
1944	Lyndon State College is established in Lyndonville in northern Vermont.
1954	WCAX-TV, first television station in state, begins broadcasting from Burlington.
1959	Vermont celebrates 350th anniversary of Lake Champlain's discovery.
1964	For the first time in the presidential-election history of the state, Vermont voters favor a Democrat, Lyndon Johnson. Democrats sweep other top state offices.
1972	Vermont's Supreme Court rules unanimously that the state's 125-year-old abortion law is unconstitutional. Stringent laws are enacted to regulate pollution sources such as non-returnable containers.
1973	*June*. Heavy rains cause disastrous flooding.
1976	*January 26*. The Vermont Nuclear Power Corporation closes its generating plant in Vernon as a safety precaution.
1979	Rising costs and declining enrollments cause serious fiscal problems for the state's numerous small private colleges.
1983	State now has a total of 31 commercial radio and television stations.
1987	*September*. State fair at Rutland draws record crowds.

DEMOGRAPHY

Population (est. 1987) 548,000
Population (1980) 511,456
Population density in persons
   per square mile (1980) 53.2

POPULATION BY RACE (1980)
American Indian/Aleut/
   Eskimo 984
Asian/Pacific Islander 1,355
Black 1,135
Hispanic 3,304
White 506,736
Other 1,246

POPULATION CHARACTERISTICS (1980)
        Percent of state population
Urban 33.8
Rural 66.2
Under 18 . . . . 26.2
65 or older 11.9
College-educated 19.5
Families below poverty line 8.9
Public-assistance recipients 6.4

Per capita personal income
   (1986) $12,845
Millionaires per 100,000
   residents (1982) 134.6

Average life expectancy in
   years (1980) 74.5
Marriage rate (1986) 10.4
Divorce rate (1986) 4.4
Birth rate per 1,000
   residents (1985) 14.8
Infant mortality rate per 1,000
   births (1985) 7.3
Abortion rate per 1,000
   live births (1985) 448
Crime rate per 100,000
   residents (1985)
     Violent 149.2
     Property 3,827.7
Federal and state prisoners per
   100,000 residents (1984) 101
Alcohol consumption in gallons
   per capita (1985) 46.7
Deaths from motor vehicle accidents
   per 100,000 residents (1985) . . 21.7

MAJOR CITIES
	Population
Bennington (1980)	15,815
Burlington (est. 1984)	37,817
Essex (1980)	14,392
Rutland (1980)	18,436

GOVERNMENT AND POLITICS

Number of US Representatives   1
Electoral votes   3

POLITICAL PARTY NOMINEES FROM STATE

John Wolcott Phelps (American)   1880   P

PRESIDENTIAL PRIMARY ELECTION In 1988, Vermont sent 19 Democratic delegates and 17 Republican delegates to the national conventions.
CONSTITUTION Vermont has had three constitutions: 1777, 1786, and the present one, adopted in 1793.

LEGISLATURE The General Assembly is divided into the Senate (30 members, 2-year term, minimum age 18) and the House of Representatives (150 members, 2-year term, minimum age 18). In 1987, the salary of legislators was $340 per week.
JUDICIARY The highest court is the Supreme Court, with 5 judges serving 6-year terms. In 1987, the annual salary was $60,300.
EXECUTIVE The governor serves a 2-year term; there is no minimum age for holding office. In 1987, the annual salary was $63,600. There are 5 other elected officials.

PRESIDENTIAL VOTE 1948-1988 *(in percents)*

Year	State Winner	Democratic	Republican
1948	Dewey (R)	36.9	61.5
1952	Eisenhower (R)	28.2	71.5
1956	Eisenhower (R)	27.8	72.2
1960	Nixon (R)	41.4	58.7
1964	Johnson (D)	66.3	33.7
1968	Nixon (R)	43.5	52.8
1972	Nixon (R)	36.6	62.9
1976	Ford (R)	43.1	54.4
1980	Reagan (R)	38.4	44.4
1984	Reagan (R)	40.8	57.9
1988	Bush (R)	49.0	51.0

GOVERNORS

Thomas Chittenden	1778-1789
Moses Robinson	1789-1790
Thomas Chittenden	1790-1797
Paul Brigham (acting)	1797
Isaac Tichenor (Federalist)	1797-1807
Israel Smith (Democratic-Republican)	1807-1808
Isaac Tichenor (Federalist)	1808-1809
Jonas Galusha (D-R)	1809-1813
Martin Chittenden (Federalist)	1813-1815
Jonas Galusha (D-R)	1815-1820
Richard Skinner (D-R)	1820-1823
Cornelius P. Van Ness (D-R)	1823-1826
Ezra Butler (National Republican)	1826-1828
Samuel C. Crafts (National Republican)	1828-1831
William A. Palmer (Anti-Masonic)	1831-1835
Silas H. Jennison (Whig)	1835-1841
Charles Paine (Whig)	1841-1843
John Mattocks (Whig)	1843-1844
William Slade (Whig)	1844-1846
Horace Eaton (Whig)	1846-1848
Carlos Coolidge (Whig)	1848-1850
Charles K. Williams (Whig)	1850-1852
Erastus Fairbanks (Whig)	1852-1853
John S. Robinson (D)	1853-1854
Stephen Royce (R)	1854-1856
Ryland Fletcher (R)	1856-1858
Hiland Hall (R)	1858-1860
Erastus Fairbanks (R)	1860-1861
Frederick Holbrook (R)	1861-1863
John Gregory Smith (R)	1863-1865
Paul Dillingham (R)	1865-1867
John B. Page (R)	1867-1869
Peter T. Washburn (R)	1869-1870
George W. Hendee (R/acting)	1870
John W. Stewart (R)	1870-1872

Julius Converse (R)	1872-1874
Asahel Peck (R)	1874-1876
Horace Fairbanks (R)	1876-1878
Redfield Proctor (R)	1878-1880
Roswell Farnham (R)	1880-1882
John L. Barstow (R)	1882-1884
Samuel E. Pingree (R)	1884-1886
Ebenezer J. Ormsbee (R)	1886-1888
William P. Dillingham (R)	1888-1890
Carroll S. Page (R)	1890-1892
Levi K. Fuller (R)	1892-1894
Urban A. Woodbury (R)	1894-1896
Josiah Grout (R)	1896-1898
Edward C. Smith (R)	1898-1900
William W. Stickney (R)	1900-1902
John G. McCullough (R)	1902-1904
Charles J. Bell (R)	1904-1906
Fletcher D. Proctor (R)	1906-1908
George H. Prouty (R)	1908-1910
John A. Mead (R)	1910-1912
Allen M. Fletcher (R)	1912-1915
Charles W. Gates (R)	1915-1917
Horace F. Graham (R)	1917-1919
Percival W. Clement (R)	1919-1921
James Hartness (R)	1921-1923
Redfield Proctor (R)	1923-1925
Franklin S. Billings (R)	1925-1927
John E. Weeks (R)	1927-1931
Stanley C. Wilson (R)	1931-1935
Charles M. Smith (R)	1935-1937
George D. Aiken (R)	1937-1941
William H. Wills (R)	1941-1945
Mortimer R. Proctor (R)	1945-1947
Ernest W. Gibson (R)	1947-1951
Lee E. Emerson (R)	1951-1955
Joseph B. Johnson (R)	1955-1959
Robert T. Stafford (R)	1959-1961
F. Ray Keyser, Jr. (R)	1961-1963
Philip H. Hoff (D)	1963-1969
Deane C. Davis (R)	1969-1973
Thomas Salmon (D)	1973-1977
Richard A. Snelling (R)	1977-1985
Madeleine Kunin (D)	1985-

Majority 18
Marriage with parental consent 16
Marriage without parental consent . . 18
Making a will 18
Buying alcohol 21
Jury duty 18
Leaving school 18
Driver's license 18

CAPITAL PUNISHMENT
Number executed 1976-88: 0
On death row Aug. 1, 1988: 0

MILITARY INSTALLATIONS
Total number: 3

FINANCES

Thousands of dollars

GENERAL REVENUE (1985)
Total general revenue 984,361
Total tax revenue 458,654
Sales and gross receipts 231,055
Individual income taxes 145,149
Corporate net income taxes . . 34,958

GENERAL EXPENDITURE (1985)
Total general expenditure . . 953,729
Education 314,291
Public welfare 171,530
Health 37,352
Hospitals 20,748
Natural resources 30,047
Highways 119,655
Police 16,182
Corrections 20,557

FEDERAL AID (1985) 336,386

ECONOMY

Vermont's farms produce milk, cheese, and other dairy products, grass and hay, apples and other orchard fruits, and maple sugar and syrup. Farm marketings cash receipts were $114 million in 1983. High-quality granite, marble, and slate are the major quarried products. Machines and machine tools are the main manufactures, along with high-tech electronics, processed foods, and stone products. The tourist industry, oriented toward skiers, hikers, and denizens of summer resorts, is likely to become the state's largest, despite the decline in skiing over the last few years.

EMPLOYMENT (1984)

Thousands of persons
Total number of employed
  workers 255
Construction 12.1
Finance, insurance, and
  real estate 9.4
Government 36.6
Manufacturing 48.7
Mining 0.5
Services 51.6
Transportation, communications,
  and utilities 9.2
Wholesale and retail trade 46.7

Percent of civilian labor force
  unemployed (1984) 4.3

DEPARTMENT OF DEFENSE (1985)
Civilian workers employed 606
Military personnel 74
Contract awards . . . . . $163 million

ENERGY SOURCES FOR ELECTRIC UTILITIES (1983)
Percent
Coal 1.1
Gas 0.3
Hydroelectric 23.9
Nuclear 73.3
Petroleum 0.1

TRANSPORTATION
Motor vehicles registered
  in state (1986) 418,191
Miles of roads, streets,
  and highways (1986) 14,049
Miles of Class I railway
  operated (1986) 102
Airports (1983) 60
Major aviation hubs (1983) 1
  Largest hub: Burlington

CULTURE AND EDUCATION

Native American tribes
Vermont was formerly home to the Mahican, Pennacook, and Pocomtuc tribes.

Religions, ethnicities, and languages
Vermont's inhabitants are mostly Yankees, descended from English Protestant settlers who came from nearby states. Vermont has also taken in groups of Scottish, Irish, French Canadian, Italian, Welsh, Polish, and Spanish immigrants. In 1980, 6.6 percent of Vermont's population spoke a language other than English at home. Most Protestant denominations are represented,

with the United Church of Christ, Presbyterians, Methodists, Baptists, and Episcopalians leading; Roman Catholics represent somewhat less than a third of the population.

Major museums and libraries
Bennington Museum
Fairbanks Museum of Natural Science, St. Johnsbury
Robert Hall Fleming Museum, University of Vermont, Burlington
Shelburne Museum

Major arts organizations
Brattleboro Museum Center Opera Theatre
Vermont Symphony Orchestra, Burlington

Colleges and universities
Number public (1986-87) 6
Number private (1986-87) 16
Total enrollment, in full-time equivalent students (1985) 25,600

Public elementary and secondary schools
Expenditure per pupil in average daily attendance (1986-87) $4,459
Pupil-teacher ratio (est. 1987) 14.1
Average teacher salary (1986-87) $23,293

Holidays
Town Meeting Day. 1st Tuesday in March
Bennington Battle Day. August 16
State Fair, Rutland. Early September

VERMONT IN LITERATURE

Clifford Alderman *Arch of Stars* (1950)
Historical romance about Ethan Allen.

Ethan Allen *Narrative of Colonel Ethan Allen's Captivity* (1779, rpt. 1986)
Revolutionary War hero's account of his capture and imprisonment by the British from late 1775 to mid-1778.

Marguerite Allis *Not without Peril* (1941)
Historical novel based on life of Jemima Sartwell, an early settler.

Consuelo Northrop Bailey *Leaves Before the Wind: The Autobiography of Vermont's Own Daughter, Consuelo Northrop Bailey* (1976)
Memoir by the state's first woman lieutenant-governor.

Arthur W. Biddle and **Paul A. Eschholz** (eds.) *The Literature of Vermont: A Sampler* (1973)
An anthology with biographical notes.

Howard Breslin *Tamarack Tree* (1947)
Historical novel based on the 1840 Whig political rally held near Stratton.

Deane C. Davis *Justice in the Mountains* (1980)
A former governor recounts his days as a country lawyer in the 1920s and '30s.

Robert Luther Duffus *Williamstown Branch* (1958)
Memoir of growing up in a small town at the turn of the century. The author's novel *Victory on West Hill* (1942) is also set in the state.

Dorothea Canfield Fisher *Vermont Tradition: The Biography of an Outlook on Life* (1953)
Nonfiction study of the state drawn from numerous oral and written histories, by an ardent partisan of local character. Vermont society and landscape is a prominent feature of all Fisher's writing, which includes the novels *The Brimming Cup* (1921) and *Seasoned Timber* (1939), and the short story collections *Hillsboro People* (1915), *The Real Motive* (1916), and *Four-Square* (1949). She also wrote a memoir of her locality, *Memories of Arlington* (1955, rpt. 1957).

John Gardner *October Light* (1976)
Novel about an old Bennington hill farmer and his opposition to modern values and customs.

Edward Hoagland *The Courage of Turtles* (1970, rpt. 1985)
Naturalist and traveler's essays on the contrast between life in New York City and in Vermont.

Seth Hubbell *A Narrative of the Suffering of Seth Hubbell in His Beginning a Settlement in the Town of Wolcott . . .* (1824)
Early settler's account of his migration with an ox team from Connecticut.

Lee P. Huntington *Hill Song: A Country Journal* (1985)
Essays on the Vermont seasons.

Keith W. Jennison *Vermont is Where You Find It* (1941); *Green Mountains and Rock Ribs* (1954)
Commentary on Vermont in words and photographs.

Diana Kappel-Smith *Wintering* (1984, rpt. 1986)
Naturalist's reflections on the seasons from a farm in northern Vermont.

Melissa Mather *Rough Road Home* (1958, rpt. 1986, 1988)
A woman's account of personal hardships on an upland farm.

Elliot Merrick *From This Hill Look Down* (1934); *Green Mountain Farm* (1948)
Accounts of rural life by a man who moved his family to a rundown farm during the Depression.

Don Mitchell *Moving Upcountry: A Yankee Way of Knowledge* (1984); *Living Upcountry: A Pilgrim's Progress* (1986)
Autobiographical essays on the Vermont way of life, and the attractions of rural custom.

Howard F. Mosher *Where the Rivers Flow North* (1978)
Short stories set in Jay Peak country near the Canadian border.

Robert N. Peck *A Day No Pigs Would Die* (1973)
Novel about a young man's coming of age in a Shaker settlement near Rutland in the 1920s.

Noel Perrin *First Person Rural: Essays of a Sometime Farmer* (1978); *Second Person Rural: More Essays of a Sometime Farmer (1980); Third Person Rural: Further Essays of a Sometime Farmer* (1983)
Autobiographical essays by a city-born writer living on a Vermont farm who faces practical problems and examines rural mores.

Rowland E. Robinson *Danvis Folks* (1894)
The author, a Quaker-born farmer from the Champlain Valley, explains in the preface to this book that he writes "with less purpose of telling any story than of recording the manners, customs, and speech in vogue fifty or sixty years ago." His best-known book is now the non-fictional *Vermont: A Study of Independence* (1892), but most of his prolific output consists of a partly-fictional but accurate portrayal of rural life and custom. His stories "Out of Bondage" and "The Mole's Path" (1905) record his experience of assisting slaves on the Underground Railroad.

Lee W. Storrs *Stagecoach North: Being an Account of The First Generation in the State of Vermont* (1941)
Study of Vermont life and customs 1791–1841, centering on the town of Middlebury. Storrs also wrote a compendium

of state lore and local history, *The Green Mountains of Vermont* (1955).

Daniel Pierce Thompson *The Green Mountain Boys* (1839) Historical romance of Revolutionary times, incorporating first-hand accounts and local history.

Frederick F. Van de Water *Reluctant Rebel* (1948); *Catch a Falling Star* (1949); *Wings of the Morning* (1956); *Day of Battle* (1958) Tetralogy of historical novels set during the Revolution.

The author also wrote an account of moving from New York to Vermont, *A Home in the Country* (1937).

Mildred Walker *The Quarry* (1947); *Southwest Corner* (1951) Realistic novels about village life, the first concerning the period following the Civil War, the second an account of an old woman's search for a companion.

Susan Warner *Queechy* (1852) Pious and sentimental tale, widely read in its time, about the hardships and social rise of an orphan girl in a small Vermont town.

GUIDES TO RESOURCES

Allen, Ethan and **Ira** *Biographical Sketches and Documents* (1947)

Bassett, Seymour (ed.) *Vermont, a Bibliography of Its History* (1981)

DeLorme, David *The Vermont Atlas and Gazetteer* (1978–1979)

Federal Writers' Project (ed. Ray Bearse) *Vermont: A Guide to the Green Mountain State* (3d ed. rev. 1968)

Hemenway, Abby M. (comp.) *Vermont Historical Gazetteer* 5 vols. (1871)

Meeks, Harold A. *The Geographic Regions of Vermont: A Study in Maps* (1975)

Parks, Roger (ed.) *Vermont: A Bibliography of its History* (1989)

SELECTED NONFICTION SOURCES

Alderman, Clifford L. *Gathering Storm: The Story of the Green Mountain Boys* (1970)

Allen, Ira *The Natural and Political History of the State of Vermont, One of the United States of America* . . . (1798, rpt. 1969)

Allerton, Robert *A Yankee Saint: John Humphrey Noyes and the Oneida Community* (1935)

Beck, Jane C. (ed.) *Always in Season: Folk Art and Traditional Culture in Vermont* (1982)

Benedict, George *Vermont in the Civil War* 2 vols. (1886)

Bogart, Ernest L. *Peacham: The Story of a Vermont Hill Town* (1948)

Bogart, Walter T. *The Vermont Lease Lands* (1950)

Bryan, Frank M. *Yankee Politics in Rural Vermont* (1974)

Cabot, Mary R. *Annals of Brattleboro* 2 vols. (1921)

Congdon, Herbert Wheaton *Old Vermont Houses: The Architecture of a Resourceful People* (rev. ed. 1946, rpt. 1968)

Crane, Charles E. *Let Me Show You Vermont* (1937)

Crittenden, Lucius E. *The Capture of Ticonderoga* (1872)

Crockett, Walter Hill *Vermont: The Green Mountain State* 5 vols. (1921)
———. *The Lakes of Vermont* (1928)
———. *Vermonters; a Book of Biographies* (1932)
———. *A History of Lake Champlain: A Record of More Than Three Centuries, 1609–1936* (1937)

Curtis, Jane, Will Curtis, and **Frank Lieberman** *Return to These Hills; the Vermont Years of Calvin Coolidge* (1985)

Dana, Henry S. *History of Woodstock* (1889)

Dean, Leon W. *The Admission of Vermont into the Union* (1941)

Everest, Allan S. *The War of 1812 in the Champlain Valley* (1981)

Flint, Winston A. *Progressive Movement in Vermont* (1941)

Fuess, Claude M. *Calvin Coolidge, the Man from Vermont* (1940)

Greene, Stephen (ed.) *Treasury of Vermont Life* (1956)

Hagerman, Robert L. *Mansfield: The Story of Vermont's Loftiest Mountain* (1971, rpt. 1975)

Hall, Benjamin H. *History of Eastern Vermont* (1858)

Haviland, William A. and **Marjory W. Power** *The Original Vermonters: Native Inhabitants, Past and Present* (1981)

Hemenway, Abby M. (ed. Brenda C. Morrissey) *Abby Hemenway's Vermont: Unique Portrait of a State* (1972)

Hill, Ellen C. and **Marilyn S. Blackwell** *Across the Onion: A History of East Montpelier, Vermont, 1781–1981* (1982)

Hill, Ralph N. *The Winooski, Heartway of Vermont* (Rivers of America series) (1949)
———. *Contrary Country: A Chronicle of Vermont* (2d ed. 1961)
———. *Yankee Kingdom: Vermont and New Hampshire* (rev. ed. 1973)
——— (ed.) *Vermont Album: A Collection of Early Vermont Photographs* (1974)
———. *Lake Champlain: Key to Liberty* (1976)

Holbrook, Stewart H. *Ethan Allen* (1940, rpt. 1958)

Horton, Guy Bertram, Henry A. Stoddard, and **Harold J. R. Stillwell** (ed. Royal B. Cutts) *The Grange in Vermont* (1926, rpt. 1968)

Hoyt, Edwin P. *The Damndest Yankee: Ethan Allen and His Clan* (1976)

Huden, John C. *Archaeology in Vermont* (1957)
———. *Indian Place Names in Vermont* (1957)

Jellison, Charles A. *Ethan Allen: Frontier Rebel* (1969)

Johnson, Charles W. *The Nature of Vermont: Introduction and Guide to a New England Environment* (1980)

Jones, Matt B. *Vermont in the Making, 1750–1777* (1939, rpt. 1968)

Jones, Robert C., Whitney J. Maxfield, and **William G. Gove** *Vermont's Granite Railroads: The Montpelier and Wells River and the Barre & Chelsea* (1985)

Judd, Richard M. *The New Deal in Vermont, Its Impact and Aftermath* (1979)

Lamb, Wallace E. *The Lake Champlain and Lake George Valleys* (1940)

Lloyd, Susan M. *The Putney School: A Progressive Experiment* (1987)

Lowenthal, David *George Perkins Marsh: Versatile Vermonter* (1958)

Ludlum, David M. *Social Ferment in Vermont, 1791–1850* (1939)

McCoy, Donald R. *Calvin Coolidge: The Quiet President* (1967)

Meeks, Harold A. *Time and Change in Vermont: A Human Geography* (1986)

Melancthon, W. Jacobus *A Canal across Vermont* (1955)

Mellin, Jeanne *The Morgan Horse* (1961)

Merrill, Perry H. *Vermont under Four Flags; a History of the Green Mountain State 1635–1975* (1975)

Meyer, Peter *Death of Innocence: A Case of Murder in Vermont* (1985)

Monahan, Robert S. *Mount Washington Reoccupied* (1933)

Morrissey, Charles T. *Vermont: A Bicentennial History* (States and the Nation series) (1981)

Muller, Charles G. *The Proudest Day, McDonough on Lake Champlain* (1960)

Newton, Earle *The Vermont Story; a History of the People of the Green Mountain State 1749–1949* (1949)

Nuquist, Andrew E. *Town Government in Vermont* (1964)

Palmer, Peter S. *History of Lake Champlain, 1609–1814* (1901)

Pell, John *Ethan Allen* (1929)

Perrin, Noel *Amateur Sugar Maker* (1972)

Pike, Robert E. *Drama on the Connecticut* (1975)

Resch, Tyler *The Shires of Bennington: A Sampler of Green Mountain Heritage* (1975)

Robbins, Daniel *The Vermont Statehouse: A History and Guide* (1980)

Robinson, Rowland Evans *Vermont: A Study of Independence* (1892, rpt. 1973)

Ross, Isabel *Grace Coolidge and Her Era* (1962)

Rozwenc, Edwin C. *Agricultural Policies in Vermont, 1860–1945* (1981)

Shaughnessy, James *The Rutland Road* (1964)

Simpson, Ruth M. Rasey *Hand-hewn in Old Vermont* (1979)

Slade, William, Jr. *Vermont State Papers: Records and Documents Relative to the Early History of the State* (1823)

Stameshkin, David M. *The Town's College; Middlebury College, 1800–1915* (1985)

Stevens, Ethel M. *Footprints down the Centuries; a Vermont Heritage* (1961)

Stilwell, Lewis D. *Migration from Vermont* (1948)

Swift, Esther M. *Vermont Place-Names: Footprints of History* (1977)

Thompson, Charles Miner *Independent Vermont* (1942)

Van de Water, Frederic *The Reluctant Republic 1724–1791* (1941)

Wardner, Henry S. *The Birthplace of Vermont* (1927)

Webb, Kenneth *From Plymouth Notch to President: The Farm Boyhood of Calvin Coolidge* (1978)

White, William A. *A Puritan in Babylon: The Story of Calvin Coolidge* (1938)

Wilbur, James B. *Ira Allen, Founder of Vermont, 1751–1814* 2 vols. (1928)

Wilgus, William J. *The Role of Transportation in the Development of Vermont* (1945)

Williams, Samuel *The Natural and Civil History of Vermont* (1809)

Williamson, Chilton *Vermont in Quandary 1763–1825* (1949)

Wilson, Harold F. *The Hill Country of Northern New England: Its Social and Economic History 1790–1930* (1936, rpt. 1967)

Woodward, Florence M. *The Town Proprietors in Vermont: The New England Proprietorship in Decline* (1936)

VIRGINIA

OBVERSE

Virginia is a South Atlantic state. It is roughly triangular in shape, bordered on the northeast by West Virginia and Maryland; on the east by the Potomac River, Chesapeake Bay, Maryland, and the Atlantic Ocean; to the south by North Carolina and Tennessee; to the west by Kentucky and West Virginia; and to the northwest by West Virginia.

FULL NAME Commonwealth of Virginia
POSTAL ABBREVIATION VA
INHABITANT Virginian
ADMITTED TO THE UNION June 25, 1788.
10th state
POPULATION (est. 1987) 5,904,000.
Percent of US total: 2.43%. Rank: 12th

CAPITAL CITY Richmond, located on the James River in east central Virginia; population 219,056 (est. 1984). In 1637 a trading post was built on the site, followed by Fort Charles in 1644. The town was laid out 1737 and incorporated in 1742; the state capital was moved there from Williamsburg in 1779.

STATE NAME AND NICKNAMES Named in honor of Queen Elizabeth I of England, the "Virgin Queen." Also known as the Old Dominion, the Cavalier State, the Mother of Presidents, the Mother of Statesmen, and the Mother of States.

STATE SEAL On one side, the state coat of arms: the Goddess of Virtue, in Amazon dress, wearing a helmet and sheathed sword and resting on her spear; under her foot, the vanquished body of Tyranny, dressed as a Roman, with a whip and chains in his hands and a crown fallen from his head; at the top is the state name, at the bottom the state motto. On the reverse,

three Goddesses: Eternity, holding a globe and phoenix; Liberty, holding her staff and Phrygian cap; and Ceres, holding an ear of wheat and a cornucopia; above them, the legend "Perseverando" (By persevering). Both sides are bordered by garlands of Virginia creeper.

MOTTO Sic Semper Tyrannis (Thus ever to tyrants)

SONG "Carry Me Back to Old Virginia" by James B. Bland

SYMBOLS
Flower American dogwood
Tree American dogwood
Bird cardinal
Dog American foxhound
Shell oyster shell
Beverage milk

LICENSE PLATES (1) Blue on white, with blue border, state name in red, and gold state seal. (2) Dark blue on white, with blue border. (3) Dark blue on white, with blue border, state name in red, red legend "Independence Bicentennial, 1776-1976," and blue silhouette of George Washington surrounded by red stars.

FLAG On a dark blue field, the state coat of arms in a white border.

GEOGRAPHY AND CLIMATE

Like that of other Atlantic Coast states, Virginia's terrain can be divided into three major regions: the low-lying Coastal Plain (called the Tidewater) along the Atlantic and Chesapeake Bay; the central Piedmont, fertile, rolling hills; and the Appalachian Mountains in the western state. In Virginia, the Appalachians comprise three areas: the Blue Ridge, where the state's highest elevations can be found; the Ridge and Valley Province; and the Appalachian Plateau along the western border. Virginia's mild climate and rich soils make it ideal for agriculture.

AREA 40,767 square miles. Rank: 36th
INLAND WATER 1,063 square miles
GEOGRAPHIC CENTER Buckingham, 5 miles SW of Buckingham
ELEVATIONS *Highest point:* Mount Rogers, Grayson Smyth County, 5,729 feet. *Lowest point:* Atlantic Ocean, sea level. *Mean elevation:* 950 feet

MAJOR RIVERS James, Potomac, Rappahannock, Shenandoah, Roanoke

MAJOR LAKES AND RESERVOIRS Smith Mountain, Anna, Gaston, Philpott, John H. Kerr

TIDAL SHORELINE 3,315 miles, Atlantic coast

LAND USE

	Thousands of acres
Urban (1982)	1,219
Rural (1982)	21,292
Cropland (1982)	3,397
Pastureland (1982)	3,392
Rangeland (1982)	0
Forestland (1982)	13,625
State parks and recreation areas (1983)	50
National park system (1984)	310
National forest system (1984)	3,226
Tribal lands (1984)	0

TEMPERATURES The highest recorded temperature was 110°F on July 15, 1954, at Balcony Falls. The lowest was -30°F on January 22, 1985, at Mountain Lake Biological Station.

NATIONAL SITES

NATIONAL BATTLEFIELD Petersburg
NATIONAL BATTLEFIELD PARKS Manassas, Richmond
NATIONAL CAPITAL PARKS
NATIONAL CEMETERIES Fredericksburg, Poplar Grove, Yorktown
NATIONAL HISTORIC SITES Green Springs Historic District, Jamestown, Maggie L. Walker
NATIONAL HISTORICAL PARKS Appomattox Court House, Colonial, Cumberland Gap
NATIONAL MEMORIALS Arlington House/The Robert E. Lee Memorial, Red Hill, Patrick Henry
NATIONAL MILITARY PARK Fredericksburg and Spotsylvania

NATIONAL MONUMENTS Booker T. Washington, George Washington Birthplace
NATIONAL PARK Shenandoah
NATIONAL PARKWAYS Blue Ridge, George Washington Memorial
NATIONAL SCENIC TRAILS Appalachian, Potomac, Heritage
NATIONAL SEASHORE Assateague Island
OTHER PARKS Prince William Forest, Wolf Trap Farm Park for the Performing Arts
NATIONAL WILDLIFE REFUGES Back Bay–Fisherman Island/Plum Tree Island, Chicoteague–Wallops Island, Great Dismal Swamp, Mackay Island, Mason Neck, Presquile

HISTORY

1585	*August 17.* Settlers led by Sir Walter Raleigh reach Roanoke Island.
1587	*August 18.* Birth of Virginia Dare, first English child born in the New World.
1591	Supply mission from England finds the colony abandoned.
1607	*May 13.* Jamestown, first permanent European settlement in the New World, is established.
	December. John Smith captured by Indians but spared, according to later account, by Pocahontas.
1609	During "the Starving Time," more than 400 colonists die. First marriage in the New World takes place between Anne Burrows and John Laydon.

1610	*May 23.* Sir Thomas Gates, first governor, arrives.
	June 10. Colonists abandon Jamestown, but meet a relief party at the mouth of the James River and return.
1612	John Rolfe begins cultivation of tobacco.
1613	Pocahontas becomes the first Indian convert to Christianity.
1614	*April 5.* John Rolfe marries Pocahontas, initiating eight years of peace between Indians and settlers, and exports 10 tons of tobacco to England.
1619	*June 30.* First meeting of the House of Burgesses, first legislative body in the New World, at Jamestown.
	August 30. Twenty Africans arrive on a Dutch trading ship, and are purchased as indentured servants.
1622	*March 22.* Indians kill 347 colonists.
1624	*June 16.* Virginia becomes a royal colony. Doctrine of no taxation without representation is first proposed.
1629	*October 30.* Province of North Carolina is divided from Virginia.
1632	Province of Maryland divided from Virginia.
1634	*February 12.* Syms Free School (later Hampton Academy), oldest free school in the New World, is endowed.
1635	Colonists assert the right to self-government by defying Sir John Harvey, the royal governor.
1644	*April 18.* About 300 colonists killed by Indians.
1649	*January 30.* Colonists declare allegiance to Charles II after execution of Charles I.
1661	Slavery is legalized.
1670	Suffrage limited to landowners.
1675	Susquehannock Indian War begins.
1676	Nathaniel Bacon's rebellion ends with his death on October 26.
1682	Riots protest falling tobacco prices.
1693	*February 8.* College of William and Mary founded.
1699	Middle Plantation (later Williamsburg) becomes the seat of government.
1716	*August–September.* Governor Spotswood leads an expedition across the Blue Ridge Mountains.
1736	*August 6.* First Virginia newspaper published at Williamsburg.
1754	*May 28.* George Washington leads Virginia militia against French forces in the Ohio Valley, so precipitating the French and Indian War.
1755	*July 9.* General Edward Braddock fatally wounded during an attack on Fort Duquesne. Washington leads a retreat.
1760	*March 25.* Thomas Jefferson becomes a boarding student at the College of William and Mary.
1763	French and Indian War ends.
	December 1. Patrick Henry challenges British rule in the "Parsons' Cause."
1765	*May 29.* Patrick Henry, protesting the Stamp Act, incites the House of Burgesses to treason and presents the "Virginia Resolutions."
1774	*August 1.* First Virginia Convention meets to choose delegates to the Continental Congress.
1775	*March 23.* Patrick Henry, calling for the colony to be put on a war footing, delivers his "give me liberty, or give me death" speech at the second Virginia Convention.
	June 15. Washington chosen commander of the Continental Army.
1776	*May 6.* Fifth Virginia Convention meets at Williamsburg, supports independence, and elects Patrick Henry first governor of the Commonwealth of Virginia.
	July 4. Declaration of Independence, written by Jefferson, adopted by Congress.
1778	*July 9.* Virginia ratifies the Articles of Confederation.
1779	*May 9.* British troops land at Portsmouth and raid surrounding area.
1780	*April 30.* Governor Jefferson moves the seat of government to Richmond.
	December 30. Benedict Arnold, leading a force of 27 British ships, enters the James River.
1781	*January 5.* Arnold occupies Richmond.
	October 19. Cornwallis surrenders at Yorktown.
1784	*February 5.* Virginia's first daily newspaper, the *Alexandria Gazette*, published.

1788	*June 26*. Virginia ratifies the federal Constitution.
1789	*April 30*. Washington inaugurated first president.
	December 3. Virginia cedes land for a seat of federal government to the US.
1799	The *Chesapeake,* first ship constructed by the federal government, built at Gosport.
1801	*March 4*. Thomas Jefferson inaugurated president.
1807	*May 22*. Aaron Burr tried in Richmond.
	June 22. British frigate attacks the *Chesapeake* off the Virginia capes.
1809	*March 4*. James Madison inaugurated president.
1814	*August 24*. President Madison flees Washington for Virginia as British enter the Capital.
1816	*August 19*. Western Virginians meet at Staunton to demand a new state constitution equalizing representation for the western part of the state.
1819	University of Virginia founded.
1831	*August 21*. Nat Turner's slave rebellion leads to stricter laws regulating slavery.
1832	A bill to abolish slavery is narrowly defeated in the House of Delegates.
1851	*October 25*. New state constitution instituting universal white male suffrage is ratified.
1859	*October 16*. John Brown siezes the US arsenal at Harpers Ferry.
	December 2. Brown hanged for treason.
1861	*February 4*. Washington "peace conference" called by the Virginia legislature is attended by 21 states.
	April 17. State Convention votes for secession from the Union rather than provide federal troops.
	April 25. Virginia joins the Confederacy.
	May 21. Richmond becomes the capital of the Confederacy.
	July 21. First Battle of Manassas.
1862	*March 8*. The *Merrimac* sinks two Union frigates at Hampton Roads.
	March 9. The *Merrimac* fights the *Monitor* in the first engagement between armored ships.
	August 9. Confederates win the Battle of Cedar Mountain.
	August 30. Confederates win the second Battle of Manassas.
	December 13. Confederates win the Battle of Fredericksburg.
1863	*May 2*. Battle of Chancellorsville. Stonewall Jackson killed.
	June 20. West Virginia admitted to the Union.
1864	*May 5*. Battle of the Wilderness.
	May 12. Battle of Spotsylvania. Confederate General Edward Johnson and two-thirds of his troops captured.
	June 3. Battle of Cold Harbor.
	June 15. Battle of Petersburg.
	October 19. Battle of Cedar Creek.
1865	*February 3*. President Lincoln meets with Confederate peace commissioners in Hampton Roads.
	April 2. Richmond is evacuated.
	April 9. Lee surrenders at Appomattox.
1867	*March 2*. Virginia designated "Military District 1" under the Reconstruction Act.
	May 13. Jefferson Davis indicted for treason in Richmond.
1869	*October 8*. The legislature ratifies the 14th and 15th Amendments to the Constitution as required by the Reconstruction Act.
1870	*January 26*. Virginia readmitted to the Union.
1879	*February*. General William Mahone founds the Readjuster Party over the issue of state debt.
1889	*April 24*. Simpson Dry Dock, the largest in the world, is opened at Newport News.
1900	*May 12*. Legislature passes the "Jim Crow" laws.
1907	*April 26*. Jamestown Exposition commemorates the 300th anniversary of the landing of English settlers at Cape Henry.
1915	*June 14*. Supreme Court decrees that West Virginia must share the burden of Virginia's pre-war debt.
1918	College of William and Mary admits women.

1920	University of Virginia admits women.
	November 2. Virginia women vote, although the state had voted against the 19th Amendment.
1954	*May 17.* Supreme Court's ruling on racial segregation in schools calls state constitution into question.
	June 25. Governor Stanley proclaims opposition to school racial integration.
1957	Completion of the Hampton Roads Bridge-Tunnel.
1958	Governor Almond closes nine schools rather than accept integration.
1964	Supreme Court orders Prince Edward County schools reopened. They had been closed in 1959 to avoid racial integration.
	Chesapeake Bay Bridge-Tunnel is completed.
	U.S.S. Enterprise, first atomic-powered aircraft carrier, launched at Newport News.

DEMOGRAPHY

Population (est. 1987) . . . 5,904,000
Population (1980) 5,346,797
Population density in persons
    per square mile (1980) 131.2

POPULATION BY RACE (1980)
American Indian/Aleut/
    Eskimo 9,336
Asian/Pacific Islander 66,209
Black 1,008,311
Hispanic 79,873
White 4,229,734
Other 32,689

POPULATION CHARACTERISTICS (1980)
Percent of state population
Urban 66.0
Rural 34.0
Under 18 . . . . 27.5
65 or older 9.5
College-educated 19.2
Families below poverty line 9.2
Public-assistance recipients 4.6

Per capita personal income
    (1986) $15,734
Millionaires per 100,000
    residents (1982) 89.3
Average life expectancy in
    years (1980) 73.4
Marriage rate (1986) 11.5

Divorce rate (1986) 4.3
Birth rate per 1,000
    residents (1985) 14.6
Infant mortality rate per 1,000
    births (1985) 11.1
Abortion rate per 1,000
    live births (1985) 412
Crime rate per 100,000
    residents (1985)
    Violent 306.0
    Property 3,553.8
Federal and state prisoners per
    100,000 residents (1984) 188
Alcohol consumption in gallons per
    capita (1985) 37.1
Deaths from motor vehicle accidents
    per 100,000 residents (1985) . . 17.1

MAJOR CITIES

	1984 population (est.)
Arlington	154,200
Hampton	125,992
Lynchburg	67,296
Newport News	154,560
Norfolk	279,683
Portsmouth	107,961
Richmond	219,056
Roanoke	100,688
Virginia Beach	308,664

GOVERNMENT AND POLITICS

Number of US Representatives   10
Electoral votes   12

POLITICAL PARTY NOMINEES FROM STATE
*winner

George Washington* (Federalist)	1789	P
George Washington* (Federalist)	1792	P

Thomas Jefferson* (Democratic-Republican)	1792	P/VP
George Washington (Federalist)	1796	P
Thomas Jefferson (Democratic-Republican)	1796	P
Thomas Jefferson* (D-R)	1800	P
Thomas Jefferson* (D-R)	1804	P
James Madison* (D-R)	1808	P
James Monroe (D-R)	1808	VP

James Madison* (D-R)	1812	P
James Monroe* (D-R)	1816	P
John Marshall (Federalist)	1816	VP
James Monroe* (D-R)	1820	P
John Floyd (Independent)	1832	P
John Tyler (Whig faction)	1836	VP
John Tyler* (Whig)	1840	VP
John Tyler (National Democratic Tyler)	1844	P
Littleton Walker Tazewell (D-R faction)	1840	VP
James Gaven Field (People's)	1892	VP
Donald L. Munro (Socialist Labor)	1908	VP
James Arthur Edgerton (Prohibition)	1928	VP
Harry Flood Byrd (America First/Constitution)	1952	VP
Harry Flood Byrd (States' Rights Party of KY/South Carolinians for Independent Elections)	1956	P
Thomas Coleman Andrews (States Rights/Constitution)	1956	P
C. Benton Coiner (Constitution Party of VA)	1960	P
Edward M. Silverman (Constitution Party of VA)	1960	VP
Thomas Coleman Andrews (Independent States' Rights)	1964	P
Roger Lea MacBride (Libertarian)	1976	P
Sonia Johnson (Citizens)	1984	P
Lyndon H. LaRouche,Jr. (Independent Democrat)	1984	P

PRESIDENTIAL PRIMARY ELECTION In 1988, Virginia sent 85 Democratic delegates and 50 Republican delegates to the national conventions.

CONSTITUTION Virginia has had six constitutions: 1776, 1830, 1851, 1869, 1902, and the present one, adopted in 1970.

LEGISLATURE The General Assembly is divided into the Senate (40 members, 4-year term, minimum age 21) and the House of Delegates (100 members, 2-year term, minimum age 21). In 1987, the annual salary was $18,000 plus $77 per day.

JUDICIARY The highest court is the Supreme Court, with 7 judges serving 12-year terms. In 1987, the annual salary was $83,304.

EXECUTIVE The governor serves a 4-year term; the minimum age for holding office is 30. In 1987, the annual salary was $85,000. There are 2 other elected officials.

PRESIDENTIAL VOTE 1948-1988 *(in percents)*

Year	State Winner	Democratic	Republican
1948	Truman (D)	47.9	41.0
1952	Eisenhower (R)	43.4	56.3
1956	Eisenhower (R)	38.4	55.4
1960	Nixon (R)	47.0	52.4
1964	Johnson (D)	53.5	46.2
1968	Nixon (R)	32.5	43.4
1972	Nixon (R)	30.1	67.8
1976	Ford (R)	48.0	49.3
1980	Reagan (R)	40.3	53.0
1984	Reagan (R)	37.1	62.3
1988	Bush (R)	40.0	60.0

GOVERNORS

Company Governors

Edward M. Wingfield (council president)	1607
John Ratcliffe (council president)	1607-1608
John Smith (council president)	1608-1609
Lord De La Warr	1609-1618
George Percy (council president)	1609-1610
Sir Thomas Gates (lieutenant governor)	1610
George Percy (deputy governor)	1611
Sir Thomas Dale (deputy governor)	1611
Sir Thomas Gates (lieutenant governor)	1611-1614
Sir Thomas Dale (deputy governor)	1614-1616
George Yeardley (deputy governor)	1616-1617
Samuel Argall (deputy governor)	1617-1619
Sir George Yeardley	1619-1621
Sir Francis Wyatt	1621-1624

Royal Governors

Sir Francis Wyatt	1624-1626
Sir George Yeardley	1626-1627
Francis West	1627-1629
John Pott	1629-1630
Sir John Harvey	1630-1635
John West	1635-1637
Sir John Harvey	1637-1639
Sir Francis Wyatt	1639-1642
Sir William Berkeley	1642-1652

Commonwealth Governors

Richard Bennett	1652-1655
Edward Digges	1655-1656
Samuel Mathews	1656-1660

Royal Governors

Sir William Berkeley	1660-1677
Herbert Jeffreys (lieutenant governor)	1677-1678
Thomas, Lord Culpeper	1678-1683
Sir Henry Chicheley (deputy governor)	1678-1680
Francis, Lord Howard of Effingham	1684-1692
Francis Nicholson (lieutenant governor)	1690-1692
Sir Edmund Andros	1692-1698
Francis Nicholson	1698-1705
Edward Nott	1705-1706
Edmund Jennings (council president)	1706-1710
Alexander Spotswood (lieutenant governor)	1710-1722
Hugh Drysdale (lieutenant governor)	1722-1726
Robert Carter (council president)	1726-1727
William Gooch (lieutenant governor)	1727-1749
Thomas Lee (council president)	1749-1750
Lewis Burwell (council president)	1750-1751
Robert Dinwiddie (lieutenant governor)	1751-1758
John Blair (council president)	1758
Francis Fauquier (lieutenant governor)	1758-1768
John Blair (council president)	1768
Lord Botetourt	1768-1770
William Nelson (council president)	1770-1771
Earl of Dunmore	1771-1776

State Governors

Patrick Henry	1776-1779
Thomas Jefferson	1779-1781
Thomas Nelson, Jr.	1781
Benjamin Harrison	1781-1784
Patrick Henry	1784-1786
Edmund Randolph	1786-1788
Beverley Randolph	1788-1791
Henry Lee	1791-1794
Robert Brooke	1794-1796
James Wood, Jr. (Democratic-Republican)	1796-1799
James Monroe (D-R)	1799-1802
John Page (D-R)	1802-1805
William H. Cabell (D-R)	1805-1808
John Tyler, Sr. (D-R)	1808-1811
James Monroe (D-R)	1811
George William Smith (D-R)	1811
James Barbour (D-R)	1812-1814
Wilson Cary Nicholas (D-R)	1814-1816
James P. Preston (D-R)	1816-1819
Thomas Mann Randolph (D-R)	1819-1822
James Pleasants, Jr. (D-R)	1822-1825
John Tyler (D-R)	1825-1827
William B. Giles (D-R)	1827-1830
John Floyd (D)	1830-1834
Littleton W. Tazewell (D)	1834-1836
Wyndham Robertson (D)	1836-1837
David Campbell (D)	1837-1840
Thomas Walker Gilmer (Whig)	1840-1841
John Rutherford (Whig/acting)	1841-1842
John M. Gregory (Whig/acting)	1842-1843
James McDowell (Whig)	1843-1846
William Smith (D)	1846-1849
John B. Floyd (D)	1849-1852
Joseph Johnson (D)	1852-1856
Henry A. Wise (D)	1856-1860
John Letcher (D)	1860-1864
William Smith (D)	1864-1865
Francis H. Pierpont (R)	1865-1868
Henry H. Wells (R)	1868-1869
Gilbert G. Walker (R)	1869-1874
James L. Kemper (D)	1874-1878
Frederick Holliday (Conservative)	1878-1882
William E. Cameron (Readjuster)	1882-1886
Fitzhugh Lee (D)	1886-1890
Philip W. McKinney (D)	1890-1894
Charles T. O'Ferrall (D)	1894-1898
J. Hoge Tyler (D)	1898-1902
Andrew J. Montague (D)	1902-1906
Claude A. Swanson (D)	1906-1910
William H. Mann (D)	1910-1914
Henry C. Stuart (D)	1914-1918
Westmoreland Davis (D)	1918-1922
E. Lee Trinkle (D)	1922-1926
Harry Flood Byrd, Sr. (D)	1926-1930

John Garland Pollard (D)	1930-1934
George C. Peery (D)	1934-1938
James H. Price (D)	1938-1942
Colgate W. Darden, Jr. (D)	1942-1946
William M. Tuck (D)	1946-1950
John S. Battle (D)	1950-1954
Thomas B. Stanley (D)	1954-1958
J. Lindsay Almond, Jr. (D)	1958-1962
Albertis S. Harrison, Jr. (D)	1962-1966
Mills E. Godwin, Jr. (D)	1966-1970
Linwood Holton (R)	1970-1974
Mills E. Godwin, Jr. (R)	1974-1978
John Dalton (R)	1978-1982
Charles S. Robb (D)	1982-1986
Charles L. Bailles (D)	1986-

MINIMUM AGES

Majority	18
Marriage with parental consent	16
Marriage without parental consent	18
Making a will	18
Buying alcohol	21
Jury duty	18
Leaving school	17
Driver's license	16

CAPITAL PUNISHMENT

Number executed 1976-88: 7
On death row Aug. 1, 1988: 37

MILITARY INSTALLATIONS

Total number: 37
Major bases:
  Army: 6
  Navy: 8
  Air Force: 1
  Marine Corps: 1

FINANCES

Thousands of dollars

GENERAL REVENUE (1985)

Total general revenue	7,687,100
Total tax revenue	4,469,391
Sales and gross receipts	1,845,506
Individual income taxes	1,948,199
Corporate net income taxes	287,747

GENERAL EXPENDITURE (1985)

Total general expenditure	7,233,655
Education	3,026,592
Public welfare	953,185
Health	224,645
Hospitals	520,606
Natural resources	78,013
Highways	997,075
Police	134,165
Corrections	360,906

FEDERAL AID (1985) 1,816,529

ECONOMY

The agricultural segment of Virginia's economy is centered on dairy products, with chickens, turkeys, and hogs also important. Cash crops include tobacco, wheat, orchard fruits, and peanuts. Farm marketing cash receipts in 1983 were $1.4 billion, of which $858 million were derived from livestock and livestock products. Minerals produced include bituminous coal, granite and other building stones, kyanite, titanium, pyrite, clay, sand, and gravel. The Chesapeake Bay feeds Virginia's thriving fishing industry, which pulled in a record catch of 751 million pounds of fish and shellfish in 1983. Shipbuilding is Virginia's main heavy industry; other products include chemicals, clothing, processed foods, light machinery, paper and pulp, wood products, and processed stone. Value added by manufacture was $17 billion in 1982. Federal expenditures for government services (in large part to the area near Washington, D.C.) and defense installations account for an unusually large percentage of the state's economy.

EMPLOYMENT (1984)

Thousands of persons

Total number of employed workers	2,698
Construction	131.8
Finance, insurance, and real estate	117.2
Government	504.4
Manufacturing	420.1
Mining	18.1
Services	492.8
Transportation, communications, and utilities	127.6
Wholesale and retail trade	513.0

Percent of civilian labor force unemployed (1984)	5.0

DEPARTMENT OF DEFENSE (1985)

Civilian workers employed	107,247
Military personnel	96,588
Contract awards	$6.167 billion

ENERGY SOURCES FOR ELECTRIC UTILITIES (1983)

Percent

Coal	42.6
Gas	0.8
Hydroelectric	3.1
Nuclear	49.5
Petroleum	4.0

TRANSPORTATION
Motor vehicles registered
in state (1986) 4,531,780
Miles of roads, streets,
and highways (1986) 65,802
Miles of Class I railway
operated (1986) 3,729
Airports (1983) 270

Major aviation hubs (1983) 3
Largest hub: Norfolk/Virginia Beach/
Portsmouth/Chesapeake
Major ports, with gross tonnage in
thousands (1985):
Norfolk Harbor 47,181
Newport News 19,169

CULTURE AND EDUCATION

Native American tribes
Virginia was formerly home to the Cherokee, Manahoac, Meherrin, Monacan, Nahyssan, Nottaway, Ocaneechi, Powhatan, Mattaponi, Pamunkey, Potomac, Chickahominy, Saponi, Shakori, Shawnee, and Tutelo tribes.

Religions, ethnicities, and languages
Virginia's white inhabitants are mainly descended from Scotch-Irish and English settlers, many of whom came from the states just to the north. Blacks, who now represent about one fifth of the population, represented one half during the revolutionary era. In 1980, 4.4 percent of Virginia's population spoke a language other than English at home. The Church of England, the state religion in colonial days, was disestablished by Jefferson's Statute for Religious Freedom in 1786; the largest groups now are the Methodists, Baptists, and Roman Catholics.

Major museums and libraries
Chrysler Museum, Norfolk
Mariners Museum, Newport News
Museum of the Confederacy, Richmond
Abby Aldrich Rockefeller Folk Art Collection, Williamsburg
Virginia Museum of Fine Arts

Major arts organizations
Barter Theatre, Abingdon
Richmond Ballet
Richmond Symphony
Virginia Opera, Norfolk
Virginia Stage Company, Richmond
Virginia Symphony, Richmond
Wolf Trap Opera Company, Vienna

Colleges and universities
Number public (1986-87) 39
Number private (1986-87) 36
Total enrollment, in full-time equivalent
students (1985) 204,900

Public elementary and secondary schools
Expenditure per pupil in average daily
attendance (1986-87) $3,809
Pupil-teacher ratio (1987) 16.8
Average teacher salary (1986-87) $26,401

Holidays
Lee-Jackson-King Day. 3d Monday in
January
State Fair, Richmond. Late September to
early October

VIRGINIA IN LITERATURE

Sherwood Anderson *Puzzled America* (1935)
  Collection of essays containing writing on the people and customs of southwest Virginia, where Anderson built a house in 1926.

George William Bagby *The Old Virginia Gentleman, and Other Sketches* (1910)
  Collected "local color" sketches of the old South by a popular humorist and journalist.

Arna W. Bontemps *Black Thunder* (1936)
  Novel based on Gabriel Prosser's slave revolt of 1800 in Richmond.

Lucy Breckinridge (ed. Mary D. Robertson) *Lucy Breckinridge of Grove Hill: The Journal of a Virginia Girl, 1862–1864* (1979)

Rita Mae Brown *High Hearts* (1986)
  Novel set during the Civil War focusing on its effect on the lives of women and slaves.

William Wells Brown *Clotel: or, the President's Daughter; a Narrative of Slave Life in the United States* (1853, rpt. 1969)

The first known work of fiction by a black American, telling the story of the illegitimate daughter of Thomas Jefferson and his black mistress.

William Byrd (ed. Louis B. Wright) *The Prose Works of William Byrd of Westover* (1966)
  The witty and sardonic planter and public official from Westover was a keen observer of the manners of his time (1674–1744). Careless of posterity, he apparently wrote primarily to amuse himself: his diaries, letters, and tracts remained unknown until the mid-nineteenth century, when he was recognized as a major writer of the colonial period.

James Branch Cabell *Let Me Lie, Being in the Main an Ethnological Account of the Remarkable Commonwealth of Virginia and the Making of Its History* (1947)
  Eccentric essays on Virginia history and customs.

William Alexander Caruthers *The Cavaliers of Virginia, or the Recluse of Jamestown* (1834)
  Historical novel depicting Nathaniel Bacon's 1676 rebellion against the royal governor. Caruthers, whose romantic style

resembles that of Walter Scott, was, with William G. Simms, John P. Kennedy, and his friend James K. Paulding, one of the founders of American historical fiction. In *The Knights of the Horseshoe* (1845), he portrayed Governor Spotswood's expedition across the Blue Ridge in 1716.

Willa Cather *Sapphira and the Slave Girl* (1940)
Novel set in rural hill country during the 1850s in which a man assists a mulatto slave girl in fleeing to Canada.

Harry M. Caudill *Dark Hills to Westward* (1969)
Novel based on the life of Jennie Wiley, a pioneer captured by Indians in 1789.

Federico F. Cavada *Libby Life: Experiences of a Prisoner of War in Richmond, Virginia; 1863–1864* (1985)

John Esten Cooke *The Virginia Comedians* (1854)
Cooke, a veteran of the Confederate army who served with J.E.B. Stuart, made a popular reputation before the war with his romantic histories of colonial times in the old dominion. His war novels include *Surry of Eagle's Nest* (1866), dealing with Jackson's campaigns, and *Mohun* (1869), which portrays Lee. *The Heir of Gaymount* (1870) depicts Reconstruction. His *Virginia: A History of the People* (1883) is a popular and partisan history of the state.

Stephen Crane *The Red Badge of Courage* (1895)
Classic novel of the Civil War describing the battle of Chancellorsville through the eyes of a young Union recruit.

Scott C. Davies *The World of Patience Gromes: Making and Unmaking a Black Community* (1988)
Nonfiction account of a community in the Fulton district of Richmond.

Arthur K. Davis, Jr. *Traditional Ballads of Virginia . . .* (1929)
————. *Folksongs of Virginia: A Descriptive Index* (1949)
————. *More Traditional Ballads of Virginia . . .* (1960)

John Davis *The First Settlers of Virginia (1805); Captain Smith and Pocahontas* (1805)
These novels by an English traveller are the earliest of many fictional treatments of the Pocahontas legend.

Annie Dillard *Pilgrim at Tinker Creek* (1974)
Personal narrative of experiences and discoveries in the Roanoke Valley. An influential contribution to American writing about man's relation to nature.

Clifford Dowdey *Bugles Blow No More* (1937); *Proud Retreat* (1954)
Historical novels set in Richmond during the Civil War.

David Garnett *Pocahontas* (1933)
Historically accurate biographical novel, partly set in London.

Ellen Glasgow *The Voice of the People* (1900, rpt. 1972)
Glasgow's first novel with a Virginia setting, one of the earliest fictional portraits of a Southerner who is not a member of the social elite, concerns a tenant farmer's son who defeats class prejudice, becomes governor of the state, but is murdered by a lynch mob. With the intention of correcting the romantic preconceptions of the "Southern myth," the Pulitzer prize–winning novelist wrote numerous works that portray social changes arising from Reconstruction. Her most admired work was *The Romantic Comedians* (1926), a satiric social comedy. Her autobiography, *The Woman Within* (1954), was published posthumously.

Henry Glassie *Folk Housing in Middle Virginia* (1975)
Study of regional folkways.

Constance Harrison *Recollections Grave and Gay* (1911)
Memoirs of the Civil War by the wife of Burton Harrison, secretary to Jefferson Davis.

Isaac Jefferson (ed. James A. Bear) *Jefferson at Monticello* (as dictated to Charles Campbell) (1967, rpt. 1988)
Memoirs of one of Thomas Jefferson's slaves. This account, together with that of Hamilton Pierson, is the primary source of information on Jefferson's private life 1781–1820.

Thomas Jefferson *Notes on the State of Virginia* (1784)
Information on the geography, fauna and flora, and social and political life of the state.

Howard Mumford Jones *The Literature of Virginia in the Seventeenth Century* (1968)

Mary Johnston *To Have and To Hold* (1900)
Historical romance, set in 1619, about arranged marriages between settlers. The author's phenomenally successful romantic adaptations of history included *The Long Roll* (1911) and *Cease Firing* (1912), a two-part account of the fortunes of two Virginia families during the Civil War.

John Pendleton Kennedy *Swallow Barn* (1832, rev. ed. 1851)
Sketches of plantation life in the humorous bucolic style of Washington Irving. This book is often credited with initiating the romantic image of the Southern plantation.

Bruce Lancaster *Roll, Shenandoah* (1956)
Novel based on General Sheridan's campaigns.

John Lankford (ed.) *Captain John Smith's America: Selections from His Writings* (1967)

Bernard Mayo *Jefferson Himself: The Personal Narrative of a Many-Sided American* (1970)
Anthology of passages from diaries and letters.

Thomas Nelson Page *In Ole Virginia* (1887)
Nostalgic tales of the Old Dominion.

Hamilton Wilcox Pierson (ed. James A. Bear) *The Private Life of Thomas Jefferson* (1967, rpt. 1988)

Francis Coleman Rosenberger (ed.) *Virginia Reader: A Treasury of Writings* (1948)

Nathan Schachner *King's Passenger* (1942)
Historical novel about Nathaniel Bacon's rebellion against the colonial governor.

Francis Hopkinson Smith *Colonel Carter of Cartersville* (1891)
Smith, a successful engineer, was a talented raconteur who amused his friends with after-dinner stories. The success of his first publication, a tale of an old Virginia gentleman, caused him to abandon his profession and devote his life to the writing of novels and stories containing picturesque anecdotes of Virginia life.

John Smith *A True Relation of Such Occurences and Accidents of Note as Hath Happened in Virginia* (1608, rpt. 1884, 1910, 1986)
The soldier-adventurer Smith was one of the 105 settlers who came ashore at Jamestown on May 13, 1607. His letter of 1608 to the Virginia Company, sponsor of the expedition, was printed in London and so became the first book written in the New World. A plain, unadorned account of hardships, it is generally regarded as more reliable than his later work *A Generall Historie of Virginia* (1624), which includes the romantic, and possibly fabricated, tale of his rescue by Pocahontas.

Harriet Beecher Stowe *Dred: A Tale of the Great Dismal Swamp* (1856)
An abolitionist novel of a rebellious slave who provides refuge for other escapees. Stowe's fiction is closely based on fact; Nat Turner's rebellion was among her sources.

William Styron *The Confessions of Nat Turner* (1967)
Novel based on the slave rebellion of 1831 in Southampton County, giving an account of antebellum Virginia. Styron's first novel, *Lie Down in Darkness* (1951), portrays the decline of a Tidewater family.

Allen Tate *The Fathers* (1938)
Novel about a young man's uneasy relationship to traditional Southern values in the days immediately before the Civil War.

William M. Thackeray *The Virginians* (1859)
The English novelist's visit to Richmond in the early 1850s may have inspired this historical novel of the Revolution, a sequel to *Henry Esmond* (1852).

Amélie Rives Troubetzkoy *The Quick or the Dead?* (1888)
Romantic novel set on a plantation resembling the author's home Castle Hill near Charlottesville. This plantation appears in several of her later novels, most of which depict the social and moral dilemmas of resourceful, intelligent women. Her most popular work was *World's End* (1914).

Nathaniel Beverly Tucker *George Balcombe* (1836)
Novel portraying upper-class society and regional politics.

Tucker was a passionate advocate of Southern traditions, and predicted the Civil War in his novel *The Partisan Leader* (1836).

Claudine Weatherford *The Art of Queena Stovall: Images of Country Life* (1986)

Folk-life study and biography of a black artist from a rural community in the Blue Ridge piedmont.

Jere Wheelwright *Gray Captain* (1954)
Novel about Confederate infantry in northern Virginia in 1864.

GUIDES TO RESOURCES

Anderson, Della *101 Virginia Women Writers: A Select Bibliography* (Virginia Women's Cultural History Project) (1984)

Duncan, Richard R. (comp.) *Theses and Dissertations on Virginia History: A Bibliography* (1986)

Federal Writers' Project *Virginia: A Guide to the Old Dominion* (1940, rpt. 1980)
———. *Jefferson's Albemarle: A Guide to Albemarle County and the City of Charlottesville, Virginia* (1941)

Haynes, Donald (ed.) *Virginiana in the Printed Book Collections of the Virginia State Library* 2 vols. (1975)

Hogg, Anne M. (ed.) *Virginia Cemeteries: A Guide to Resources* (1986)

Kocher, A. Lawrence and **Howard Dearstyne** *Colonial Williamsburg, Its Buildings and Gardens: A Descriptive Tour of the Restored Capital of the British Colony of Virginia* (2d rev. ed. 1976)

Loth, Calder *The Virginia Landmarks Register* (3d ed. 1986)

McCombs, Dorothy F. *The Appalachian Region of Virginia: A Guide to Library Materials* (1981)

Morris, Shirley *The Pelican Guide to Virginia* (1981)

Perdue, Charles L., Thomas E. Barden, and **Robert K. Phillips** (comps. and eds.) *An Annotated Listing of Folklore Collected by Workers of the Virginia Writers' Project, Work Projects Administration: Held in the Manuscripts Department at Alderman Library of the University of Virginia.* (University of Virginia Library. Manuscripts Department) (1979)

Peters, Margaret T. (comp.) *A Guidebook to Virginia's Historical Markers* (1985)

Robertson, James I. *Civil War Sites in Virginia: A Tour Guide* (1982)

Salmon, Emily J. (ed.) *A Hornbook of Virginia History* (3d ed. 1983)

Swem, Earl Gregg (comp.) *Virginia Historical Index* 2 vols. (1934–1936)

Tyler, Lyon Gardiner *Encyclopedia of Virginia Biography* 5 vols. (1915)

Virginia State Library *Virginia Local History: A Bibliography* (1976)

SELECTED NONFICTION SOURCES

Ambler, Charles H. *Sectionalism in Virginia from 1776 to 1861* (1910)
———. *Thomas Ritchie: A Study in Virginia Politics* (1913)

Ammon, Harry *James Monroe: The Quest for National Identity* (1971)

Andrews, Matthew P. *Virginia, the Old Dominion* (1937)

Ashe, Dora J. *Four Hundred Years of Virginia, 1584-1984: An Anthology* (1985)

Bailey, Kenneth P. *The Ohio Company of Virginia and the Westward Movement, 1748–1792* (1939)

Baker-Crothers, Hayes *Virginia and the French and Indian War* (1928)

Ballagh, James C. *White Servitude in the Colony of Virginia* (1895)
———. *A History of Slavery in Virginia* (1902)

Barbour, Philip L. *The Three Worlds of Capt. John Smith* (1964)
———. *Pocahontas and Her World . . .* (1970)
———. (ed.) *The Complete Works of Captain John Smith* 3 vols. (1986)

Beatty, Richard C. *William Byrd of Westover* (1932)

Beeman, Richard R. *The Old Dominion and the New Nation, 1788–1801* (1972)
———. *Patrick Henry: A Biography* (1974)

Berman, Myron *Richmond's Jewry, 1769–1976: Shabbat in Shockoe* (1979)

Beveridge, Albert J. *The Life of John Marshall* 4 vols. (1916–19)

Beverley, Robert (ed. Louis B. Wright) *The History and Present State of Virginia* (1705, rpt. 1947)

Bill, Alfred H. *The Beleaguered City, Richmond, 1861–1865* (1946)

Billings, Warren M. *The Old Dominion in the Seventeenth Century: A Documentary History of Virginia, 1606–1689* (1975)
———, **John E. Selby,** and **Thad W. Tate** *Colonial Virginia: A History* (1986)

Breen, T. H. *Tobacco Culture: The Mentality of the Great Tidewater Planters on the Eve of Revolution* (1985)

Brewer, James H. *The Confederate Negro, Virginia's Craftsmen and Military Laborers, 1861–1865* (1969)

Briceland, Alan V. *Westward from Virginia: The Exploration of the Virginia-Carolina Frontier, 1650–1710* (1987)

Bridenbaugh, Carl *Seat of Empire: The Political Role of Eighteenth-Century Williamsburg* (1963)
———. *Jamestown, 1544–1699* (1980)

Brock, Robert A. *Virginia and Virginians* 2 vols. (1888, rpt. 1973)

Brodie, Fawn M. *Thomas Jefferson: An Intimate Portrait* (1974)

Brown, Alexander *The Cabells and Their Kin* (1939)
———. *English Politics in Early Virginia History* (1901, rpt. 1968)

Brown, Imogene E. *American Aristides: A Biography of George Wythe* (1981)

Bruce, Philip A. *Economic History of Virginia in the Seventeenth Century* 2 vols. (1896, rpt. 1935)
———. *Social Life in Virginia in the Seventeenth Century* (1907)
———. *Institutional History of Virginia in the Seventeenth Century* 2 vols. (1910, rpt. 1964)
———. *The Virginia Plutarch* 2 vols. (1929)

Bruce, William C. *Below the James; a Plantation Sketch* (1918)
———. *John Randolph of Roanoke, 1773–1833; a Biography Based Largely on New Material* 2 vols. (1922)

Brugger, Robert J. *Beverley Tucker: Heart Over Head in the Old South* (1978)

Buckley, Thomas E. *Church and State in Revolutionary Virginia, 1776–1787* (1977)

Buni, Andrew *The Negro in Virginia Politics, 1902–1965* (1967)

Byrd, Robert O. *Decision at Richmond, June 1788; a Documentary Drama of the Constitutional Ratification Convention in Virginia* (1986)

Campbell, Charles *History of the Colony and Ancient Dominion of Virginia* (1860, rpt. 1965)

Campbell, Norine D. *Patrick Henry: Patriot and Statesman* (1969)

Carroll, Nan *Gentlemen of Virginia: Biographical Sketches of Twenty Virginians Who Were Instrumental to the American Revolution* (1975)

Carson, Jane *Colonial Virginians at Play* (1965)

Chesson, Michael B. *Richmond After the War* (1981)

Chinard, Gilbert (ed.) *A Huguenot Exile in Virginia . . .* (1934)
——. *Thomas Jefferson, the Apostle of Americanism* (2d ed. 1943)

Cooke, John Esten *Virginia; a History of the People* (1911)

Couch, Jill and Ernie *Virginia Trivia* (1987)

Coulling, Mary P. *The Lee Girls* (1987)

Craven, Avery O. *White, Red, and Black: The Seventeenth-Century Virginian* (1971)

Cresson, W. P. *James Monroe* (1940)

Culliford, S. G. *William Strachey, 1572–1621* (1965)

Dabney, Virginius *Virginia, the New Dominion: A History from 1607 to the Present* (1971, rpt. 1983)
——. *Across the Years: Memories of a Virginian* (1978)
——. *Mr. Jefferson's University: A History* (1981)
——. *The Jefferson Scandals: A Rebuttal* (1981)
——. *Virginius Dabney's Virginia: Writings about the Old Dominion* (1986)

Daniels, Jonathan *The Randolphs of Virginia* (1972)

Davis, Richard Beale *Francis Walker Gilmer, Life and Learning in Jefferson's Virginia* (1939)
——. *George Sandys: Poet Adventurer* (1955)
——. (ed.) *William Fitzhugh and His Chesapeake World, 1676–1701: The Fitzhugh Letters and Other Documents* (1963)
——. *Intellectual Life in Jefferson's Virginia, 1790–1830* (1964)
——. *Literature and Society in Early Virginia, 1608–1840* (1973)

Dewey, Frank L. *Thomas Jefferson, Lawyer* (1986)

Dill, Alonzo T. *Carter Braxton, Virginia Signer: A Conservative in Revolt* (1983)

Dodson, Leonidas *Alexander Spotswood, Governor of Colonial Virginia, 1710–1722* (1932)

Dowdey, Clifford *Experiment in Rebellion* (1946)
——. *Lee* (1965)
——. *The Virginia Dynasties* (1969)
——. *The Golden Age: A Climate for Greatness, Virginia 1732–1775* (1970)

Dunaway, Wayland F. *History of the James River and Kanawha Co.* (1923, rpt. 1969)

Eckenrode, H. J. *The Revolution in Virginia* (1916, rpt. 1926)
——. *The Political History of Virginia During the Reconstruction* (1966)

Edelhart, Mike *The Virginians* (1982)

Edmunds, Pocahontas W. *Virginians Out Front* (1972)

Ely, James W., Jr. *The Crisis of Conservative Virginia: The Byrd Organization and the Politics of Massive Resistance* (1976)

Emerson, Everett H. *Captain John Smith* (1971)

Engs, Robert Francis *Freedom's First Generation: Black Hampton, Virginia, 1861–1890* (1979)

Fishwick, Marshall *Virginia: A New Look at the Old Dominion* (1959)
——. *Springlore in Virginia* (1978)

Fiske, John *Old Virginia and Her Neighbors* 2 vols. (1897)

Fleet, Betsy and John D. P. Fuller (eds.) *Green Mount: A Virginia Plantation Family during the Civil War* (1977)

Flexner, James Thomas *George Washington: A Biography* 4 vols. (1965–72)
——. *Washington: The Indispensable Man* (1974)

Flippin, Percy S. *The Royal Government in Virginia, 1624–1775* (1919)

Freehling, Alison G. *Drift Toward Dissolution: The Virginia Slavery Debate of 1831–1832* (1982)

Freeman, Douglas S. *George Washington* 7 vols. (1948–1957)
——. *R. E. Lee* 4 vols. (1934–1935)

Friddell, Guy *What Is It About Virginia?* (1966)
——. *We Began at Jamestown* (1968)

Gewehr, Wesley Marsh *The Great Awakening in Virginia, 1740–1790* (1930, rpt. 1965)

Gottmann, Jean *Virginia in Our Century* (1969)

Hagemann, James A. *The Heritage of Virginia: The Story of Place Names in the Old Dominion* (1986)

Hale, Nathaniel C. *Virginia Venturer. A Historical Biography of William Claiborne, 1660–1677* (1951)

Harrell, Isaac S. *Loyalism in Virginia: Chapters in the Economic History of the Revolution* (1926)

Hart, Freeman H. *The Valley of Virginia in the American Revolution* (1942)

Hast, Adele *Loyalism in Revolutionary Virginia: The Norfolk Area and the Eastern Shore* (1982)

Hatch, Alden *The Byrds of Virginia* (1969)

Heineman, Ronald L. *Depression and New Deal in Virginia* (1983)

Hemphill, W. Edwin, Marvin W. Schlegel, and Sadie E. Engelberg *Cavalier Commonwealth* (1957)

Henri, Florette (ed. Carolyn Tragger) *George Mason of Virginia* (1971)

Herndon, Melvin *Tobacco in Colonial Virginia: "The Sovereign Remedy"* (1957)

Hilldrup, Robert L. *The Life and Times of Edmund Pendleton* (1939)

Hughes, Roscoe D. and Henry D. Leidheiser (eds.) *Exploring Virginia's Human Resources* (1965)

Hughes, Rupert *George Washington: The Human Being and the Hero, 1732–1762* (1926)
——. *George Washington: The Rebel and the Patriot, 1762–1777* (1927)

Isaac, Rhys *The Transformation of Virginia, 1740–1790* (1982)

Jester, Annie (ed.) *Adventurers of Purse and Person, Virginia, 1607–1625* (1964)

Johnson, Brooks *Mountaineers to Main Streets: The Old Dominion as Seen through the Farm Security Administration Photographs* (1985)

Jones, Hugh (ed. Richard L. Morton) *The Present State of Virginia* (1724, rpt. 1956)

Jordan, Daniel P. *Political Leadership in Jefferson's Virginia* (1983)

Katcher, Philip R. N. *The Army of Northern Virginia* (1975)

Kegley, F. B. *Kegley's Virginia Frontier; the Beginning of the Southwest; the Roanoke of Colonial Days, 1740–1783* (1938)

Kercheval, Samuel (ed. Oren F. Morton) *A History of the Valley of Virginia* (4th ed. 1925)

Ketcham, Ralph *James Madison: A Biography* (1971)

Kilpatrick, James J. *The Sovereign States: Notes of a Citizen of Virginia* (1957)

Kimball, Marie *Jefferson--War and Peace, 1776–1784* (1947)

Koontz, Louis K. *The Virginia Frontier, 1754–1763* (1925)
——. *Robert Dinwiddie, His Career in American Colonial Government and Westward Expansion* (1941)

Korn, Jerry *Pursuit to Appomattox* (1987)

Lee, Edmund *Lee of Virginia, 1642–1892* (1895)

Lebsock, Suzanne *Virginia Women: A Share of Honour* (1987)

Lehman, Karl *Thomas Jefferson; American Humanist* (1985)

Lewis, Jan *The Pursuit of Happiness: Family and Values in Jefferson's Virginia* (1985)

Lewis, Ronald L. *Coal, Iron, and Slaves: Industrial Slavery in Maryland and Virginia, 1715–1865* (1979)

Lisitsky, Gene *Thomas Jefferson* (1935)

Little, John P. *History of Richmond* (1851, rpt. 1933)

Lockridge, Kenneth A. *The Diary, and Life, of William Byrd II of Virginia, 1674–1744* (1987)

Maddex, Jack P., Jr. *The Virginia Conservatives, 1867–1879: A Study in Reconstruction Politics* (1970)

Malone, Dumas *Jefferson and His Times* 6 vols. (1948–1981)

Mapp, Alf J., Jr. *The Virginia Experiment: The Old Dominion's Role in the Making of America, 1607–1781* (1957)

Marambaud, P. *William Byrd of Westover, 1674–1744* (1971)

Mason, Kate Rowland *The Life of George Mason, 1725–1792* 2 vols. (1892)

Mayo, Bernard *Myths and Men: Patrick Henry, George Washington, Thomas Jefferson* (1959)

McCary, Ben C. *Indians in Seventeenth-Century Virginia* (1957)

McColley, Robert *Slavery and Jeffersonian Virginia* (1964)

McDonald, James J. (ed. J.A.C. Chandler) *Life in Old Virginia* (1907)

Meade, Robert D. *Patrick Henry: Patriot in the Making* (1957)
———. *Patrick Henry: Practical Revolutionary* (1969)

Middleton, Arthur P. *Tobacco Coast; a Maritime History of the Chesapeake Bay in the Colonial Era* (1953)

Miller, Helen H. *George Mason: Gentleman Revolutionary* (1975)

Miller, Marj R. *Place-Names of the Northern Neck of Virginia* (1983)

Mitchell, Mary H. *Hollywood Cemetery: The History of a Southern Shrine* (1985)

Moger, Allen W. *Virginia: Bourbonism to Byrd, 1870–1925* (1968)

Morgan, Edmund S. *Virginians at Home: Family Life in the Eighteenth Century* (1952)
———. *American Slavery, American Freedom: The Ordeal of Colonial Virginia* (1975)

Morgan, George *The True Patrick Henry* (1907)
———. *The Life of James Monroe* (1921)

Morton, Louis *Robert Carter of Nomini Hall: A Virginia Tobacco Planter of the Eighteenth Century* (1945)

Morton, Richard L. *The Negro in Virginia Politics, 1865–1902* (1919)
———. *Colonial Virginia* 2 vols. (1960)

Mossiker, F. *Pocahontas: The Life and Legend* (1976)

Munford, Beverley B. *Virginia's Attitude toward Slavery and Secession* (1969)

Muse, Benjamin *Virginia's Massive Resistance* (1961)

Niles, Blair *The James: From Iron Gate to the Sea* (rev. ed. 1945)

Noël Hume, Ivor *Here Lies Virginia* (1963)

Oates, Stephen B. *The Fires of Jubilee: Nat Turner's Fierce Rebellion* (1975)

O'Neal, William B. *Architecture in Virginia* (1968)

Page, Thomas N. *The Old South: Essays Social and Political* (1892)
———. *Social Life in Old Virginia before the War* (1897, rpt. 1970)

Patrick, Rembert W. *The Fall of Richmond* (1960)

Pendleton, William C. *Political History of Appalachian Virginia, 1776–1927* (1927)

Peterson, Merrill D. *Thomas Jefferson and the New Nation: A Biography* (1970)

Pilcher, George W. *Samuel Davies: Apostle of Dissent in Colonial Virginia* (1971)

Pulley, Raymond H. *Old Virginia Restored: An Interpretation of the Progressive Impulse, 1870–1930* (1968)

Quinn, David B. *The Roanoke Voyages, 1584–1590* (1955)
——— and Alison M. Quinn (eds.) *Virginia Voyages from Hakluyt* (1973)

Rake, William A. *The Blue Ridge* (1977)

Reniers, Perceval *The Springs of Virginia; Life, Love and Death at the Waters, 1775–1900* (1941)

Robert, Joseph C. *The Road from Monticello: A Study of the Virginia Slavery Debate of 1832* (1941)
———. *The Tobacco Kingdom: Plantation, Market, and Factory in Virginia and North Carolina, 1800–1860* (1965)

Robertson, James I. *Virginia, 1861–1865; Iron Gate to the Confederacy* (1961)

Rouse, Parke, Jr. *Virginia and the English Heritage in America* (1966)
———. *Planters and Pioneers, Life in Colonial Virginia* (1968)
———. *Virginia, a Pictorial History* (1975)

Rubin, Louis D., Jr. *Virginia, a Bicentennial History* (States and the Nation series) (1977, rpt. 1984)
———. *No Place on Earth: Ellen Glasgow, James Branch Cabell, and Richmond-in-Virginia* (1959)

Rutland, Robert A. *George Mason: Reluctant Statesman* (1963)

Rutman, Darrett B. (ed.) *The Old Dominion: Essays for Thomas Perkins Abernethy* (1964)

Sams, Conway W. *The Conquest of Virginia: The Forest Primeval* (1916)
———. *The Conquest of Virginia: The First Attempt* (1924)
———. *The Conquest of Virginia: The Second Attempt* (1929)

Sanborn, Margaret *Robert E. Lee* 2 vols. (1966, 1967)

Selby, John E. *The Revolution in Virginia, 1775–1783* (1988)

Shanks, Henry T. *The Secession Movement in Virginia, 1847–1861* (1934)

Shea, William L. *The Virginia Militia in the Seventeenth Century* (1983)

Sheehan, Bernard W. *Savagism and Civility: Indians and Englishmen in Colonial Virginia* (1980)

Shifflett, Crandall A. *Patronage and Poverty in the Tobacco South; Louisa County, Virginia, 1860–1900* (1982)

Siegel, Frederick F. *The Roots of Southern Distinctiveness: Tobacco and Society in Danville, Virginia, 1780–1865* (1987)

Smith, Bradford *Captain John Smith, His Life and Legend* (1953)

Sobel, Mechal *The World They Made Together: Black and White Values in Eighteenth-Century Virginia* (1987)

Soltow, James H. *The Economic Role of Williamsburg* (1965)

Stewart, Peter C. *The Tobacco Kingdom: Plantation, Market, and Factory in Virginia and North Carolina, 1800–1860* (1938)

Stith, William *The History of the First Democracy and Settlement of Virginia* (1747, rpt. 1965)

Sydnor, Charles S. *Gentlemen Freeholders; Political Practices in Washington's Virginia* (1952)

Talpalar, Morris *The Sociology of Colonial Virginia* (1960)

Tate, Allen *Stonewall Jackson* (1928)

Tate, Thad W. and David L. Ammerman (eds.) *The Chesapeake in the Seventeenth Century: Essays on Anglo-American Society and Politics* (1979)

Taylor, Alrutheus A. *The Negro in the Reconstruction of Virginia* (1926)

Thomas, Emory M. *The Confederate State of Richmond; a Biography of the Capital* (1971)

————. *Bold Dragoon: The Life of J. E. B. Stuart* (1986, rpt. 1988)

Tyler, Lyon G. (ed.) *Narratives of Early Virginia, 1606–1625* (1907, rpt. 1959)

Tyler, Moses C. *Patrick Henry* (1980)

Van Schreeven, William J. *The Conventions and Constitutions of Virginia, 1776–1966* (1967)
————, Robert L. Scribner, and Brent Tarter *Revolutionary Virginia, the Road to Independence* 7 vols. (1973–1983)

Vaughan, Alden T. *American Genesis: Captain John Smith and the Founding of Virginia* (1975)

Washburn, Wilcomb E. *The Governor and the Rebel; a History of Bacon's Rebellion in Virginia* (1959)

Waterman, Thomas T. *The Mansions of Virginia, 1706–1776* (1946)

Wertenbaker, Thomas J. *Patrician and Plebian in Virginia or the Origin and Development of the Social Classes of the Old Dominion* (1910)
————. *Virginia Under the Stuarts* (1914)
————. *The Planters of Colonial Virginia* (1922)
————. *The Torchbearer of the Revolution: The Story of Bacon's Rebellion and Its Leader* (1940)
————. *Give Me Liberty: the Struggle for Self-Government in Virginia* (1958)
————. (ed. Marvin Wilson Schlegel) *Norfolk, Historic Southern Port* (2d ed. 1962)

Whiffen, Marcus *The Eighteenth-Century Houses of Williamsburg: A Study of Architecture and Building in the Colonial Capital of Virginia* (rev. ed. 1984)

Wibberley, Leonard *Man of Liberty* (1968)

Wilkinson, J. Harvie, III *Harry Byrd and the Changing Face of Virginia Politics, 1945–1966* (1968)

Willison, George F. *Patrick Henry and His World: A Biography* (1969)

Wilstach, Paul *Tidewater Virginia* (1929)
————. *Mount Vernon, Washington's Home and the Nation's Shrine* (4th ed. 1930)

Woodlief, Ann *In River Time: The Way of the James* (1985)

Wright, Louis B. *The First Gentlemen of Virginia: Intellectual Qualities of the Early Colonial Ruling Class* (1940)

Wust, Klaus *The Virginia Germans* (1969)

Wynes, Charles Eldridge *Race Relations in Virginia, 1870–1902* (1961)
———— (ed.) *Southern Sketches from Virginia, 1881–1901: Orra Langhorne* (1964)

Younger, Edward E. and James T. Moore (eds.) *The Governors of Virginia, 1860–1978* (1982)

WASHINGTON

The Pacific Northwest state of Washington is bordered on the north by the Canadian province of British Columbia; on the east by Idaho; on the south by Oregon and the Columbia River; on the west by the Pacific Ocean; and on the northwest by Puget Sound, Juan de Fuca Strait, and Strait of Georgia.

FULL NAME State of Washington
POSTAL ABBREVIATION WA
INHABITANT Washingtonian
ADMITTED TO THE UNION Nov. 11, 1889.
42d state
POPULATION (est. 1987) 4,538,000.
Percent of US total: 1.87%. Rank: 18th

CAPITAL CITY Olympia, located on Puget Sound in northwestern Washington; population 27,447 (1980). Settled in 1845 and laid out as Smithfield in 1851, it became the territorial capital in 1853 and was chartered as a city six years later.

STATE NAME AND NICKNAMES Named in honor of George Washington. Also known as the Evergreen State and the Chinook State.

STATE SEAL The bust of George Washington, derived from the Gilbert Stuart por-

trait, encircled by the words "The Seal of the State of Washington, 1889."

MOTTO Alki (By and by)

SONG "Washington My Home" by Helen Davis.

SYMBOLS
Flower pink rhododendron
Tree western hemlock
Bird willow goldfinch
Gem petrified wood
Fish steelhead trout
Dance square dance

LICENSE PLATES (1) Dark blue on white, with blue border, red legend "Centennial Celebration," and picture of Mount Rainier. (2) Blue on white, with blue border.

FLAG The state seal on a field of dark green.

GEOGRAPHY AND CLIMATE

Of Washington's seven major geographical regions, the most notable are the Olympic Peninsula, a wild, mountainous, temperate rain forest; the populous lowlands around Puget Sound; the high Cascade Mountains, cutting Washington in two along the north-south axis; the fertile plateau of the Columbia Basin of the Columbia and Snake rivers in the central state; and the mineral-rich highland regions of eastern Washington.

AREA 68,138 square miles. Rank: 20th
INLAND WATER 1,627 square miles
GEOGRAPHIC CENTER Chelan, 10 miles WSW of Wenatchee

ELEVATIONS *Highest point:* Mount Rainier, Pierce County, 14,410 feet. *Lowest point:* Pacific Ocean, sea level. *Mean elevation:* 1,700 feet

MAJOR RIVERS Columbia, Snake, Yakima, Pend Oreille

MAJOR LAKES AND RESERVOIRS Chelan, Franklin D. Roosevelt

TIDAL SHORELINE 3,026 miles, Pacific coast

LAND USE

	Thousands of acres
Urban (1982)	990
Rural (1982)	28,462
Cropland (1982)	7,793
Pastureland (1982)	1,345
Rangeland (1982)	5,637
Forestland (1982)	12,690
State parks and recreation areas (1983)	220
National park system (1984)	1,913
National forest system (1984)	10,041
Tribal lands (1984)	2,077

TEMPERATURES The highest recorded temperature was 118°F on August 5, 1961, at Ice Harbor Dam. The lowest was -48°F on December 30, 1968, at Mazama and Winthrop.

NATIONAL SITES

NATIONAL HISTORIC SITES Ebey's Landing, Fort Vancouver, Whitman Mission
NATIONAL HISTORIC TRAILS Lewis & Clark, Oregon
NATIONAL HISTORICAL PARK San Juan Island
NATIONAL PARKS Mount Rainier, North Cascades, Olympic
NATIONAL RECREATION AREAS Coulee Dam Lake, Chelan Ross Lake

NATIONAL WILDLIFE REFUGES Columbia–Saddle Mountain, Columbian White-Tailed Deer–Dungeness, Lewis and Clark/San Juan Islands, Conboy Lake, Lower Columbia River Complex, McNary, Nisqually Flats, Ridgefield, Toppenish, Turnbull, Umatilla, Willapa–Washington Islands

HISTORY

1775	*July 14.* Bruno Heceta, commanding the flagship *Santiago*, lands at Point Grenville and takes possession of the region for Spain.
1787	Charles Barkley, a British captain and trader, discovers the Juan de Fuca Strait.
1792	*May 11.* Robert Gray, an American captain and trader, discovers the mouth of the river he names for his ship, the *Columbia*. *June 4.* After more than a month exploring the inlets and islands of Puget Sound, Captain George Vancouver of the British navy takes possession of the entire region, naming it New Georgia. *October 30.* Lieutenant William Broughton, commanding one of the ships in the Vancouver expedition, explores the Columbia River inland almost as far as present-day Portland, Oregon, formally claiming British possession.
1805	*October 11.* Traveling overland from St. Louis in leading a US expedition to the Pacific coast, Meriwether Lewis and William Clark reach the Snake River at its confluence with the Clearwater and follow it to the Pacific Ocean. They return along the same route in 1806.
1810	Finan McDonald and Jacques Finlay build a fur-trading depot near present-day Spokane for the Montreal-based North West Company.
1811	David Thompson of the North West Company follows the Columbia from its source in Canada through Washington to the Pacific Ocean.

1818	Donald McKenzie of the North West Company builds Fort Nez Percé (later Fort Walla Walla) as a trade center and supply depot. In that year an Anglo-American agreement leaves the Pacific Northwest open to nationals of either country.
1825	Fort Vancouver is established as the headquarters in the Pacific Northwest for the Hudson's Bay Company, which has merged with the North West Company.
1833	Fort Nisqually, at the southern tip of Puget Sound, is established as a farm and shipping point for the Hudson's Bay Company.
1834–1837	Some 405,000 pelts—mostly beaver—are received at Fort Vancouver.
1836	Marcus and Narcissa Whitman found a mission to the Nez Percé Indians at Waiilatpu, about 25 miles east of Fort Walla Walla.
1846	*June 15.* A treaty establishes the Canadian–US border in the Pacific Northwest, placing what is now Washington on the US side.
1847	*November 29.* Fourteen persons, including the Whitmans, are massacred by Indians at the Waiilatpu mission, which has also been serving as a supply and rest station for pioneers traveling on the Oregon Trail.
1848	*August 14.* Oregon Territory is created, including what is now Washington.
1853	*March 2.* Creation of Washington Territory, including the present state and, until 1863, northern Idaho, and western Montana. Olympia is the capital.
1855	Indian warfare breaks out as prospectors flock to a gold strike in northeastern Washington. Indians in western Washington resisting resettlement in reservations massacre settlers.
1858	Federal troops and militia defeat a confederacy of the Yakima, Spokane, Coeur d'Alene, Nez Percé and Palouse tribes. Eastern Washington is then opened to white settlement and treaties creating reservations are ratified.
1861	*November 4.* Territorial University (later the University of Washington) opens in Seattle with only one college-level student.
1867	Four brothers establish the first salmon cannery on the Columbia River.
1885	Anti-Chinese riots result in federal troops being sent to Seattle.
1887	*June 6.* The first train on the Northern Pacific Railroad's transcontinental line reaches Tacoma.
1889	*November 11.* Washington is admitted to the Union as the 42d state.
1890	The population is 357,232.
1893	Seattle is the Pacific terminus of the transcontinental Great Northern Railroad line.
1895	Peak salmon catch from the Columbia River—634,000 cases.
1897	The discovery of gold in the Yukon's Klondike fosters the growth of Seattle as a supply and transportation center.
1899	Mount Rainier National Park established.
1902	Yacolt Burn destroys 700,000 forested acres south of Puget Sound.
1905	With 3,917 million board-feet cut, Washington has become the leading lumbering state, doubling 1900 production. It holds first rank until 1938.
1909	Alaska-Yukon-Pacific Exposition draws many visitors to Seattle.
1910	Women receive the right to vote.
1912	The initiative, referendum, and recall are enacted into law.
1912	The timber-products industry is employing two-thirds of the state's wage earners.
1913	Peak Puget Sound salmon production of over 2.5 million cases.
1916	Formation by William E. Boeing of the airplane factory that takes his name the following year. *November 5.* Seven die on the Everett docks as participants in a free-speech demonstration organized by the Industrial Workers of the World battle special deputies.
1917	Washington leads all states in apples, accounting for 20 percent of the nation's commercial crop.
1919	An Armistice Day clash in Centralia between American Legionnaires and members of the Industrial Workers of the World leaves seven dead. A mob lynches an IWW organizer and burns down the local union hall.
1921	A law aimed at Chinese and Japanese prohibits aliens ineligible for citizenship to own land in Washington.

1926	Peak lumber production of 7,541 million board-feet.
1933	In the depths of the Great Depression, the number of people working for wages is half that in 1926. A state sales tax is adopted to raise revenue.
1937	Completion of Bonneville Dam, the first major power project on the Columbia River.
	Pierce County produces about one-fifth of all US raspberries and blackberries.
1938	Creation of Olympic National Park.
1941	The Weyerhaeuser Corporation opens the first US tree farm, near Aberdeen.
1942	A total of 14,559 persons of Japanese birth or ancestry are moved from Washington to World War II relocation camps.
1942–1945	Washington receives billions in World War II contracts; Puget Sound yards produce warships, and Boeing's output includes B-17 and B-29 bombers.
1943–1945	The secret Hanford Engineering Works near Richland produces plutonium for the first nuclear weapons.
1949	Washington ranks second among states in pears, apricots, cherries, and green peas. It ranks third in peaches, prunes, strawberries, and asparagus.
1950	Washington is the leading state in the production of aluminum.
1957	Completion of the Chief Joseph Dam on the upper Columbia River.
1962	Seattle is host for the Century 21 Exposition.
1963	Completion of a floating bridge over Lake Washington comes two years after a similar one spanning the Hood Canal.
1967	A state fair-housing law is adopted.
1968	Establishment of North Cascades National Park.
1971	Employment at Boeing plants in Washington, over 95,000 in 1968, has fallen to 37,000 because of a sharp drop in aircraft and aerospace orders.
1972	Daniel Evans, the Republican governor, wins an unprecedented third four-year term. A state equal rights amendment is adopted.
1974	Spokane's Expo '74 draws 5.2 million visitors.
1976	Dedication of Seattle's $60-million domed stadium, the Kingdome.
1979	The US Supreme Court upholds the treaty rights of Washington's Indians to catch half of all salmon returning to traditional, off-reservation waters, a provision that has incensed the state's sports fishermen.
1980	*May 18.* The eruption of Mount St. Helens in southwestern Washington leaves over 60 persons dead and spews volcanic ash over large areas.
1983	Washington, third among states in wheat production, has a record crop of 172.6 million bushels. It also ranks second in potatoes.
1983	The Washington Public Supply System defaults on over $2 billion worth of bonds intended to finance two nuclear power plants.
1985	The US Navy decides to make Everett home quarters for a 15-ship battle group.

DEMOGRAPHY

Population (est. 1987) . . . 4,538,000
Population (1980) 4,132,204
Population density in persons
    per square mile (1980) 60.6

POPULATION BY RACE (1980)
American Indian/Aleut/
    Eskimo 60,771
Asian/Pacific Islander 102,503
Black 105,544
Hispanic 119,986
White 3,777,296
Other 84,049

POPULATION CHARACTERISTICS (1980)
            Percent of state population
Urban 73.5
Rural 26.5

Under 18 . . . . 27.6
65 or older 10.4
College-educated 18.8
Families below poverty line 7.2
Public-assistance recipients 4.9

Per capita personal income
    (1986) $14,498
Millionaires per 100,000
    residents (1982) 243.2
Average life expectancy
    in years (1980) 75.1
Marriage rate per 1,000
    residents (1986) 9.9
Divorce rate per 1,000
    residents (1986) 5.8
Birth rate per 1,000
    residents (1985) 17.3

Infant mortality rate per 1,000
   births (1985) 10.2
Abortion rate per 1,000
   live births (1985) 458
Crime rate per 100,000
   residents (1985)
   Violent 437.0
   Property 6,442.6
Federal and state prisoners per
   100,000 residents (1984) 160
Alcohol consumption in gallons
   per capita (1985) 39.0

Deaths from motor vehicle accidents
   per 100,000 residents (1985) . . 16.8

MAJOR CITIES

	1984 population (est.)
Everett	56,766
Seattle	488,474
Spokane	173,349
Tacoma	159,435

GOVERNMENT AND POLITICS

Number of US Representatives   8
Electoral votes   10

POLITICAL PARTY NOMINEES FROM STATE

William Bouck (Farmer Labor/
   withdrew)   1924 VP
Frank B. Hemenway (Liberty)   1932 VP
Anna Milburn (Greenback/de-
   clined)   1940 P
Frederick C. Proehl (Greenback)   1952 P
Frederick C. Proehl (Greenback)   1956 P

PRESIDENTIAL PRIMARY ELECTION In 1988, Washington sent 71 Democratic delegates

and 41 Republican delegates to the national conventions.

CONSTITUTION Washington is using its original constitution, adopted in 1889.

LEGISLATURE The Legislature is divided into the Senate (49 members, 4-year term, minimum age 18) and the House of Representatives (98 members, 2-year term, minimum age 18). In 1987, the annual salary was $16,500 plus $50 per day.

JUDICIARY The highest court is the Supreme Court, with 9 judges serving 6-year terms. In 1987, the annual salary was $82,700.

EXECUTIVE The governor serves a 4-year term; the minimum age for holding office is 18. In 1987, the annual salary was $83,800. There are 8 other elected officials.

PRESIDENTIAL VOTE 1948–1988 *(in percents)*

Year	State Winner	Democratic	Republican
1948	Truman (D)	52.6	42.7
1952	Eisenhower (R)	44.7	54.3
1956	Eisenhower (R)	45.4	53.9
1960	Nixon (R)	48.3	50.7
1964	Johnson (D)	62.0	37.4
1968	Nixon (R)	45.2	47.3
1972	Nixon (R)	38.6	56.9
1976	Ford (R)	46.1	50.0
1980	Reagan (R)	37.3	49.7
1984	Reagan (R)	42.9	56.2
1988	Dukakis (D)	51.0	49.0

GOVERNORS

Territorial Governors
Isaac Ingals Stevens   1853-1857
Fayette McMullin   1857-1859
Richard D. Gholson   1859-1861
William Pickering   1862-1867
Marshall F. Moore   1867-1869
Alvan Flanders   1869-1870
Edward S. Saloman   1870-1872
Elisha P. Ferry   1872-1880

William A. Newell   1880-1884
Watson C. Squir   1884-1887
Eugene Semple   1887-1889
Miles Conway Moore   1889

State Governors
Elisha P. Ferry (R)   1889-1893
John Harte McGraw (R)   1893-1897
John Rankin Rogers
   (Democrat/Populist)   1897-1901
Henry McBride (R/acting)   1901-1905

Albert Edward Mead (R)	1905-1909
Samuel G. Cosgrove (R)	1909
Marion E. Hay (R/acting)	1909-1913
Ernest Lister (D)	1913-1919
Louis Folwell Hart (R/act- ing)	1919
Louis Folwell Hart (R)	1919-1925
Roland H. Hartley (R)	1925-1933
Clarence D. Martin (D)	1933-1941
Arthur B. Langlie (R)	1941-1945
Monrad C. Wallgren (D)	1945-1949
Arthur B. Langlie (R)	1949-1957
Albert D. Rosellini (D)	1957-1965
Daniel J. Evans (R)	1965-1977
Dixie Lee Ray (D)	1977-1981
John Spellman (R)	1981-1985
Booth Gardner (D)	1985-

MINIMUM AGES

Majority	18
Marriage with parental consent	17
Marriage without parental consent	18
Making a will	17
Buying alcohol	21
Jury duty	18
Leaving school	18
Driver's license	16

CAPITAL PUNISHMENT
Number executed 1976-88: 0
On death row Aug. 1, 1988: 7

MILITARY INSTALLATIONS
Total number: 23
Major bases:
  Army: 2
  Navy: 3
  Air Force: 2

FINANCES

Thousands of dollars

GENERAL REVENUE (1985)

Total general revenue	7,407,484
Total tax revenue	4,585,551
Sales and gross receipts	3,449,085
Individual income taxes	0
Corporate net income taxes	0

GENERAL EXPENDITURE (1985)

Total general expenditure	7,401,755
Education	3,291,974
Public welfare	1,208,519
Health	227,937
Hospitals	261,540
Natural resources	206,091
Highways	863,099

Police	56,320
Corrections	221,626

FEDERAL AID (1985) 1,826,295

ECONOMY

Washington's economy is supported by the state's wealth of natural resources. Wheat and dairy products are the main farm products, with crops yielding about twice the income of livestock. Cash crops include hay, potatoes, vegetables, fruits, hops, flower bulbs, and apples (Washington grows more apples than any other state); cattle, horses, and sheep are the preferred livestock. Farm marketings cash receipts were $3 billion in 1983. The timber and forestry industry, one of Washington's biggest, employed more than half of all manufacturing workers in the state in 1982 to produce a wide variety of lumber, plywood, pulp, paper, and other wood products. Douglas fir is the most important harvested tree. The catch of salmon, halibut, Pacific cod, herring, tuna, oysters, clams, crabs, and other fish and shellfish taken by the state's fisheries was over 150 million pounds in 1983, worth more than $60 million. Coking coal, portland cement, lime, sand, and gravel are among the important mineral products; metals extracted include gold, silver, copper, zinc, lead, manganese, iron, nickel, and tungsten. The manufacturing sector is focused on resources processing, generating large quantities of wood and wood products, processed foods, and processed minerals, along with petrochemical products created from oil and natural gas shipped or piped into the state. The sale of energy generated by hydroelectric plants also contributes substantially to Washington's economy.

EMPLOYMENT (1984)

Thousands of persons

Total number of employed workers	1,859
Construction	76.6
Finance, insurance, and real estate	94.5
Government	339.0
Manufacturing	284.8
Mining	2.6
Services	349.6
Transportation, communications, and utilities	90.1
Wholesale and retail trade	403.1

Percent of civilian labor force
   unemployed (1984) 9.5

DEPARTMENT OF DEFENSE (1985)
Civilian workers employed . . . 29,509
Military personnel 43,669
Contract awards . . . . $3.559 billion

ENERGY SOURCES FOR ELECTRIC UTILITIES (1983)
                                      Percent
Coal 6.4
Gas 0.0
Hydroelectric 89.8
Nuclear 3.7
Petroleum 0.0

TRANSPORTATION
Motor vehicles registered
   in state (1986) 3,752,242
Miles of roads, streets,
   and highways (1986) 80,478
Miles of Class I railway
   operated (1986) 3,562
Airports (1983) 382
Major aviation hubs (1983) 2
   Largest hub: Seattle/Tacoma
Major ports, with gross tonnage in
   thousands (1985):
   Seattle 16,230
   Tacoma Harbor 15,795
   Anacortes 10,208

CULTURE AND EDUCATION

Native American tribes
Washington was formerly the home of the Cathlamet, Cathalpotle, Cayuse, Chehalis, Chelan, Chilluckittequaw, Chimakum, Clackamus, Clatskanie, Coast Salish, Copalis, Duwamish, Hoh, Humptulips, Klickitat, Kootenay, Kwaiailk, Kwalhioqua, Methow, Mical, Nooksack, Ntlakyapamuk, Okanagan, Ozette, Pshwanwapam, Sahehwamish, Samish, Satsop, Semiahmoo, Sinkakaius, Skagit, Skilloot, Skin, Snoqualmie, Stalo, Suquamish, Swallah, Swinomish, Taidnapam, Umatilla, Walla Walla, Wanapam, Wauyukma, and Wynoochie. Groups that continue to live in the state include the Cowliz, Kalispel, Lake, Lumni, Makah, Muckleshoot, Nez Percé, Nisqually, Palouse, Puyallup, Quileute, Quinault, Sanpoil, Skokomish, Snohomish, Spokane, Squaxin, Twana, Wenatchee, Wishram, and Yakima. Groups that have been relocated to Washington include the Tenino. There are 26 federal reservations in the state.

Religions, ethnicities, and languages
Washington's 19th-century settlers came mainly from the Midwest, and from Canada, Scandinavia, and Japan; recent immigrants have also come from Britain and Germany. In 1980, 6.9 percent of Washington's population spoke a language other than English at home. Roman Catholics, Lutherans, and Methodists are the most populous religious groups.

Major museums and libraries
Thomas Burke Memorial, Washington State Museum, University of Washington, Seattle
Museum of History and Industry, Seattle
Pacific Science Center, Seattle
Seattle Art Museum
Tacoma Art Museum

Major arts organizations
A Contemporary Theatre, Seattle
Pacific Northwest Ballet
Seattle Opera
Seattle Repertory Theatre
Seattle Symphony Orchestra
Spokane Symphony Orchestra

Colleges and universities
Number public (1986-87) 32
Number private (1986-87) 20
Total enrollment, in full-time equivalent students (1985) 170,700

Public elementary and secondary schools
Expenditure per pupil in average daily attendance (1986-87) $3,808
Pupil-teacher ratio (1987) 20.5
Average teacher salary (1986-87) $28,746

Major league sports teams
Baseball: Seattle Mariners
Basketball: Golden State Warriors, Seattle Supersonics
Football: Seattle Seahawks

WASHINGTON IN LITERATURE

Jane Adams *Seattle Green* (1987)
Historical novel of pioneers in Seattle.

Archie Binns *Mighty Mountain* (1940)
Historical novel about Puget Sound in the mid-nineteenth century, one of many historical works by the Washington-born author. Binns also wrote several nonfiction works about the region, including the memoir *The Roaring Land* (1942), and *Gateway: The Story of the Port of Seattle* (1941).

Bruce Brown *Mountain in the Clouds: A Search for the Wild Salmon* (1982)
Naturalist's essay on the salmon of the Olympic Peninsula.

Ella E. Clark *Indian Legends of the Pacific Northwest* (1953)

Joseph A. Costello *The Siwash: Their Life, Legends, and Tales, Puget Sound and Pacific Northwest* (1895, rpt. 1986)

Ivan Doig *Winter Brothers: A Season at the Edge of America* (1980)
A journal of the Washington wilderness in which the author combines his own thoughts with passages of James G. Swan's classic account of pioneer life, *The Northwest Coast* (1857).

William O. Douglas *Of Men and Mountains* (1950); *My Wilderness: The Pacific West* (1960)
The Washington-born Supreme Court justice, who was brought up in Yakima, wrote several autobiographical volumes on the value of wilderness land and the dangers of development.

Federal Writers' Project *Tales of Frontier Life as Told by Those Who Remember the Days of the Territory and Early Statehood of Washington* (1938)

Edna Ferber *Great Son* (1945)
Novel about four generations of a Seattle family, 1851–1940.

A. B. Guthrie *The Way West* (1949)
Historical novel of pioneer days.

Vi Hilbert *Haboo: Native American Stories from Puget Sound* (1985)

Stewart H. Holbrook (ed.) *Promised Land: A Collection of Northwest Writing* (1945)

Richard Hoyt *Decoys* (1981)
Detective story set in Seattle.

Rich Ives (ed.) *The Truth About the Territory: Contemporary Nonfiction from the Northwest* (1988)
An anthology of writing concerning the geography, climate, and people of the Northwest.
——— (ed.) *From Timberline to Tidepool; Contemporary Fiction from the Northwest* (1986)
Collection of short stories.

Nard Jones *Scarlet Petticoat* (1941)
Historical novel of fur-trading on the Columbia River. The author also wrote historical fiction concerning wheat farming (*Wheat Women*, 1933), and steamboating (*Swift Flows the River*, 1946).

Phoebe Goodell Judson *A Pioneer's Search for an Ideal Home* (1925, rpt. 1984)
Classic pioneer memoir by a woman who migrated to Puget Sound in 1853 and eventually found her ideal home at the head of the Nooksack River.

W. Storrs Lee (ed.) *Washington State: A Literary Chronicle* (1969)

Ellis Lucia (ed.) *This Land Around Us: A Treasury of Pacific Northwest Writing* (1969)

Norman MacDonald *Song of the Axe* (1957)
Novel about early 1900s lumberjacks.

Allis McKay *They Come to a River* (1941)
Historical novel depicting the development of the apple-growing industry in the early years of the century.

Ezra Meeker *Pioneer Reminiscences of Puget Sound* (1905, rpt. 1980)

Nicholas O'Connell *At The Field's End: Interview with Twenty Pacific Northwest Writers* (1987)

Charlotte Paul *Gold Mountain* (1953)
Portrait of a small logging town in the 1880s.

Lancaster Pollard "A Checklist of Washington Authors," and "Washington Literature" *Pacific Northwest Quarterly* (29, 1938; 31, 1940; 35, 1944)

Robert Michael Pyle *Wintergreen: Listening to the Land's Heart* (1986, rpt. 1988)
Naturalist's account of the Willapa Hills, containing an indictment of the effects of logging.

Lex Runciman and **Steven Sher** (eds.) *Northwest Variety: Personal Essays by 14 Regional Authors* (1987)

Thomas Ripley *Green Timber* (1968)
Memoir of the Tacoma boom of the 1890s.

Lillian Schlissel (ed.) *Women's Diaries of the Westward Journey* (1982)

Paul Schullery (ed.) *Island in the Sky: Pioneering Accounts of Mt. Rainier, 1833–1894* (1987)

Philip Henry Sheridan *Indian Fighting in the Fifties in Oregon and Washington Territories* (1987)
Excerpts from a soldier's memoirs.

Armstrong Sperry *River of the West* (1952)
Fictional account of Captain Gray's discovery of the Columbia River.

James G. Swan *The Northwest Coast: or, Three Years' Residence in Washington Territory* (1857, rpt. 1972)
Classic work of anthropology containing detailed observations of the customs and folklore of northwest Indians. A record of Indian arts and culture can also be found in George P. Castile (ed.) *The Indians of Puget Sound: The Notebooks of Myron Eells* (1986)

GUIDES TO RESOURCES

Abbott, Newton C. and **Fred E. Carver** *The Evolution of Washington Counties* (1978)

Beaver, Lowell J. *Historic Memories from Monuments and Plaques of Western Washington* (1964)

Day, Alan E. *Search for the Northwest Passage: An Annotated Bibliography* (1986)

Federal Writers' Project *Washington, a Guide to the Evergreen State* (1941, rpt. 1972)

Information Technology Institute, Center for Urban Education *Northwest Information Directory: A Guide to Unusual Sources and Special Collections* (1986)

Knight, Margot H. (comp.) *Directory of Oral History in Washington State* Washington State University (1981)

Lenggenhager, Werner *Historical Markers and Monuments of the State of Washington* 2 vols. (1967–1970)

Nicandri, David L. "Washington State: A Bibliography," *Pacific Northwest Quarterly* (July 1983)

State of Washington, Division of Archives and Records Management *Washington: The Road to Statehood, 1853–1889* (1987)

Scott, James W. and **Roland L. De Lorme** *Historical Atlas of Washington* (1988)

Walls, Robert E. *A Bibliography of Washington State Folklore and Folklife* (1988)

SELECTED NONFICTION SOURCES

Alt, David D. *Roadside Geology of Washington* (1984)

Anderson, Bern E. *Surveyor of the Sea: The Life and Voyages of Captain George Vancouver* (1960)

Anderson, D. Victor *Illusions of Power: A History of the Washington Public Power Supply System (WPPSS)* (1985)

Anderson, Helen *How, When and Where, on Hood Canal* (1960)

Andrus, H. Phillip et al. *Seattle* (1976)

Avery, Mary W. *History and Government of the State of Washington* (1961)
———. *Washington: A History of the Evergreen State* (1965)

Bagley, Clarence B. *History of Seattle from the Earliest Settlement to the Present Time* 3 vols. (1916)

Bancroft, Hubert H. *History of Washington, Idaho, and Montana* (1890)
———. *History of the Northwest Coast* 2 vols. (1900)

Bancroft-Hunt, Norman *People of the Totem: The Indians of the Pacific Northwest* (1988)

Barkan, Frances B. (ed.) *The Wilkes Expedition: Puget Sound and the Oregon Country* (1987)

Barto, Harold E. *History of the State of Washington* (2d ed. 1953)

Baylies, Francis *History of The Northwest Coast* (1826, 1851 rpt. 1986)

Beal, Merrill D. *"I Will Fight No More Forever": Chief Joseph and the Nez Percé War* (1966)

Becher, Edmund T. *Spokane Corona: Eras and Empires* (1974)

Becker, Ethel *Here Comes the Polly* (1971)

Beckett, Paul L. *From Wilderness to Enabling Act; the Evolution of a State of Washington* (1968)

Binns, Archie *Northwest Gateway; the Story of the Port of Seattle* (1941)
———. *The Roaring Land* (1942)
———. *Sea in the Forest* (1953)

Blair, Karen J. *Women in the Pacific Northwest: An Anthology* (1988)

Bonney, William P. *History of Pierce County, Washington* 3 vols. (1927)

Bowden, Angie B. *Early Schools in Washington Territory* (1935)

Brier, Howard M. *Sawdust Empire; the Pacific Northwest* (1958)

Brockman, C. Frank *The Story of the Petrified Forest, Ginkgo State Park, Washington* (1952)
———. *The Story of Mount Rainier National Park* (2d ed. 1952)

Brown, J. C. (ed.) *Valley of the Strong: Stories of Yakima and Central Washington History* (1974)

Buerge, David *Seattle in the 1880s* (1986)

Carpenter, Cecilia S. *They Walked Before: The Indians of Washington State* (1977)

Chasen, Daniel J. *The Water Link: A History of Puget Sound as a Resource* (1981)

Clark, Norman H. *Mill Town; a Social History of Everett, Washington* . . . (1971)
———. *Washington: A Bicentennial History* (States and the Nation series) (1976)
———. *The Dry Years: Prohibition and Social Change in Washington* (rev. ed. 1988)

Cochran, John E. *Pioneer Days in Eastern Washington* (1943)

Cox, Thomas *Mills and Markets: A History of the Pacific Coast Lumber Industry to 1900* (1974)

———. *The Park Builders: A History of State Parks in the Pacific Northwest* (1989)

Danner, Wilbert R. *Geology of Olympic National Park* (1955)

Dembo, Jonathan *Union and Politics in Washington State, 1885–1935* (1983)

Denny, Arthur A. *Pioneer Days on Puget Sound* (1888, rpt. 1965)

Dodds, Gordon B. *The American Northwest: A History of Oregon and Washington* (1986)

Downing, John *The Coast of Puget Sound: Its Processes and Development* (1983)

Drucker, Philip *Indians of the Northwest Coast* (1963)

Drury, Clifford M. *Marcus Whitman, M.D.: Pioneer and Martyr* (1937)
———. *Elkanah and Mary Walker: Pioneers among the Spokanes* (1940)
———. *A Teepee in His Front Yard; a Biography of H. T. Cowley, One of the Four Founders of the City of Spokane, Washington* (1949)

Dryden, Cecil *Up the Columbia for Furs* (1950)

Edwards, G. Thomas and **Carlos A. Schwantes** (eds.) *Experiences in a Promised Land: Essays in Pacific Northwest History* (1986)

Evans, Elwood *Puget Sound: Its Past, Present and Future* (1869)
———. *Washington Territory: Her Past, Her Present, and the Elements of Wealth Which Ensure Her Future* (1877)

Fahey, John *The Kalispel Indians* (1986)
———. *The Inland Empire: Unfolding Years, 1879–1929* (1987)

Farber, Jim *An Irreverent Guide to Washington State* (1974)

Fargo, Lucile F. *Spokane Story* (1957)

Ficken, Robert E. *Lumber and Politics: The Career of Mark E. Reed* (1979)
———. *The Forested Land: A History of Lumbering in Western Washington* (1987)
——— and **Charles P. LeWarne** *Washington: A Centennial History* (1988)

Fielder, John *Washington: Magnificent Wilderness* (1986)

Friedheim, Robert L. *The Seattle General Strike* (1964)

Fuller, George W. *History of the Pacific Northwest* (1941)

Gault, Lila *The House Next Door: Seattle's Neighborhood Architecture* (1981)

Gee, Nancie *Reflections in Pike Place Markets* (1968)

Goodhue, Cornelia *Journey into the Fog; the Story of Vitus*

Grater, Russell K. *Guide to Mount Rainier National Park* (1949); *Bering and the Bering Sea* (1944)

Haines, Aubrey L. *Mountain Fever; Historic Conquests of Rainier* (1962)

Hazard, Joseph Taylor *Companion of Adventure: A Biography of Isaac Ingalls Stevens, First Governor of Washington Territory* (1952)

Heckman, Hazel *Island in the Sound* (1967)

Henry, John Frazier *Early Maritime Artists of the Pacific Northwest Coast, 1741–1841* (1984)

Hershman, Marc J., Susan Heikkala, and **Caroline Tobin** *Seattle's Waterfront: A Walker's Guide to the History of Elliott Bay* (1981)

Hidy, Ralph W., Frank Ernest Hill, and **Allen Nevins** *Timber and Men: The Weyerhaeuser Story* (1963)

Hildebrand, Lorraine Barker *Straw Hats, Sandals, and Steel: The Chinese in Washington State* (1977)

Hitchman, Robert *Place Names of Washington* (1985)

Holbrook, Sabra *Taming the Columbia River: The Challenge of United States–Canadian Cooperation* (1967)

Holbrook, Stewart Hall *The Columbia* (Rivers of America series) (1956, rpt. 1965)

Hult, Ruby E. *The Untamed Olympics; the Story of a Peninsula* (1954)

Hunt, Herbert *Tacoma: Its History and Its Builders, A Half Century of Activity* 3 vols. (1916)

Hussey, John A. *The History of Fort Vancouver and Its Physical Structure* (1957)

Hynding, Alan *The Public Life of Eugene Semple: Promoter and Politician of the Pacific Northwest* (1973)

Johannsen, Robert W. *Frontier Politics and the Sectional Conflict* (1955)

Johansen, Dorothy and Charles M. Gates *Empire of the Columbia* (2d ed. 1967)

Johnsen, Kenneth G. *Apple Country Interurban: A History of the Yakima Valley Transportation Company and the Yakima Interurban Trolley Lines* (1979)

Johnston, Norman J. *Washington's Audacious State Capital and Its Builders* (1987)

Jones, Nard *Seattle* (1973)

Josephy, Alvin M., Jr. *The Nez Percé Indians and the Opening of the Northwest* (1965)

Kirk, Ruth *The Oldest Man in America: An Adventure in Archaeology* (1970)
———. *Washington State National Parks, Historic Sites, Recreation Areas, and Natural Landmarks* (1974)
——— and Richard D. Daugherty *Hunters of the Whale: An Adventure in Northwest Coast Archaeology* (1974); *Exploring Washington Archaeology* (1978)

Kline, M. S. and G. A. Bayless *Ferryboats: A Legend on Puget Sound* (1984)

Lavender, David *Land of Giants: The Drive to the Pacific Northwest, 1750–1950* (1958)

Leigland, James and Robert Lamb *WPP$$: Who Is to Blame for the WPPSS Disaster?* (1986)

LeWarne, Charles P. *Utopias on Puget Sound, 1885–1915* (1975)
———. *Washington State* (1986)

MacDonald, Nobert *Distant Neighbors* (1988)

MacKay, Douglas *The Honourable Company: A History of the Hudson's Bay Company* (1936)

Mansfield, Harold *Vision: A Saga of the Sky* (1956)

Marshall, Louise B. *High Trails; Guide to the Pacific Crest Trail in Washington* (4th ed. 1973)

McCurdy, James G. *By Juan de Fuca's Strait: Pioneering along the Northwestern Edge of the Continent* (1937)
———. (ed. Gordon Newell) *Indian Days at Neah Bay* (1961)

McDonald, Lucile *Coast Country; a History of Southwest Washington* (1966)

McFear, Tom (ed.) *Indians of the North Pacific Coast* (1966)

Meany, Edmond S. *Vancouver's Discovery of Puget Sound; Portraits and Biographies of the Men Honored in the Naming of Geographic Features of Northwestern America* (1907, rpt. 1957)
——— (ed.) *Mount Rainier, a Record of Exploration* (1916)
———. *History of the State of Washington* (1941)

Meinig, Donald W. *The Great Columbia Plain: A Historical Geography, 1805–1910* (1968, rpt. 1984)

Miles, John C. *Koma Kulshan: The Story of Mount Baker* (1984)

Miller, Don C. *Ghost Towns of Washington and Oregon* (1977)

Mills, Randall *Stern-Wheelers up Columbia: A Century of Steamboating in the Oregon County* (1947)

Molenaar, Dee *The Challenge of Rainier; a Record of the Explorations and Ascents, Triumphs and Tragedies, on the Northwest's Greatest Mountain* (1971)

Morgan, Lane and Murray *Seattle, a Pictorial History* (1982)

Morgan, Murray *The Dam* (1954)
———. *The Last Wilderness* (1955)
———. *Century 21: The Story of the Seattle World's Fair* (1962)
———. *Puget's Sound; a Narrative of Early Tacoma and the Southern Sound* (1979)
———. *The Mill on the Boot: The Story of the St. Paul & Tacoma Lumber Company* (1982)
———. *Skid Road: An Informal Portrait of Seattle* (rev. ed. 1982)
——— and Rosa *South on the Sound: An Illustrated History of Tacoma and Pierce County* (1984)

Munson, Kenneth G. and Gordon Swanborough *Boeing* (1972)

Nelson, Gerald B. *Seattle: The Life and Times of an American City* (1977)

Nesbit, Robert C. *"He Built Seattle": A Biography of Judge Thomas Burke* (1961)

Newell, Gordon *Rogues, Buffoons and Statesmen* (1975)

O'Connor, Harvey *Revolution in Seattle* (1964)

Parnatt, Smitty *Gods and Goblins: A Field Guide to Place Names of Olympic National Park* (1984)

Phillips, James W. *Washington State Place Names* (1971)

Pollard, Lancaster *A History of the State of Washington* 4 vols. (1937)

Potts, Ralph B. *Seattle Heritage* (1955)

Richards, Kent D. *Isaac I. Stevens: Young Man in a Hurry* (1979)

Richardson, David *Puget Sounds: A Nostalgic Review of Radio and TV in the Great Northwest* (1981)

Ripley, Thomas *Green Timber* (1968)

Robbins, William G., Robert J. Frank, and Richard E. Ross (eds.) *Regionalism and the Pacific Northwest* (1983)

Ruby, Robert H. and John A. Brown *A Guide to the Indian Tribes of the Pacific Northwest* (1986)

Sale, Roger *Seattle, Past to Present* (1976)

Scott, James W., Melly A. Reuling, and Don Bales *Washington Public Shore Guide: Marine Waters* (1986)

Shane, Scott *Discovering Mount St. Helens; a Guide to the National Volcanic Monument* (1985)

Seattle Historical Society *Seattle Country (1842–1952)* (1952)

Sheller, Roscoe *Courage and Water, a Story of Yakima Valley's Sunnyside* . . . (1952)
———. *Blowsand* (1963)

Shorett, Alice and Murray Morgan *The Pike Place Market: People, Politics, and Produce* (1982)

Snowden, Clinton A. *History of Washington: The Rise and Progress of an American State* 6 vols. (1909)

Speidel, William C. *Sons of the Profits: or, There's No Business like Grow Business. The Seattle Story, 1851–1901* (1967)

Splawn, A. J. *Ka-mi-akin, the Last Hero of the Yakimas* (1944)

Steelquist, Robert U. *Washington Mountain Ranges* (1986)
———. *Washington's Coast* (1987)

Steinbrueck, Victor *Seattle Cityscape* (1962)
———. *Seattle Cityscape #2* (1973)

Stevens, Hazard *The Life of Isaac Ingalls Stevens* 2 vols. (1900)

Stewart, Edgar I. *Washington: Northwest Frontier* 4 vols. (1957)

Sugai, Wayne H. *Nuclear Power and Ratepayer Protest: The Washington Public Power Supply System Crisis* (1987)

Sundborg, George *Hail, Columbia: The Thirty-Year Struggle for Grand Coulee Dam* (1954)

Swanson, Thor et al. (eds.) *Political Life in Washington: Governing the Evergreen State* (1985)

Sweetman, Maud *What Price Politics: The Inside Story of Washington State Politics* (1927)

Tabor, Rowland W. *Guide to the Geology of Olympic National Park* (1975)

Thompson, Erwin N. *San Juan Island National Historical Park, Washington* (1972)

Van Syckle, Edwin *The River Pioneers: Early Days on Grays Harbor* (1982)

Walkinshaw, Robert *On Puget Sound* (1929, rpt. 1951)

Warren, James R. *King County and Its Queen City, Seattle: An Illustrated History* (1981)

Washington Secretary of State *Indians in Washington* (1955)

White, Richard *Land Use, Environment, and Social Change: The Shaping of Island County, Washington* (1980)

Williams, Richard L. and the Editors of Time-Life Books *The Cascades* (1974)

Winther, Oscar O. *The Great Northwest: A History* (1952)

Wood, Bryce *San Juan Island: Coastal Place Names and Cartographic Nomenclature* (1980)

Wood, Charles and **Dorothy** *Spokane, Portland and Seattle Ry.; the Northwest's Own Railway* (1974)

Wood, Robert L. *Across the Olympic Mountains: The Press Expedition, 1889–90* (1967, rpt. 1989)

Woodbridge, Sally B. and **Roger Montgomery** *A Guide to Architecture in Washington State: An Environmental Perspective* (1980)

WEST VIRGINIA

West Virginia, a South Atlantic state, has an irregular shape: it is bordered on the north by Pennsylvania, Maryland, and the Potomac River; on the northeast by Maryland; on the southeast and south by Virginia; on the southwest by Kentucky; and on the west and northwest by Ohio.

FULL NAME State of West Virginia
POSTAL ABBREVIATION WV
INHABITANT West Virginian
ADMITTED TO THE UNION June 20, 1863. 35th state
POPULATION (est. 1987) 1,897,000. Percent of US total: 0.78%. Rank: 34th

CAPITAL CITY Charleston, located at the junction of the Elk and Kanawha rivers in western West Virginia; population 59,371 (est. 1984). It was founded as Charles Town in 1788, was incorporated as a town in 1794 and as a city in 1870, and replaced Wheeling as the capital in 1885.

STATE NAME AND NICKNAMES See Virginia, from which West Virginia was separated in 1861. Also known as the Mountain State, the Switzerland of America, and the Panhandle State.

STATE SEAL On one side, the emblem of the state coat of arms: an ivy-covered boulder inscribed with the date "June 20, 1863"; on the left a farmer in hunter's dress, holding an ax and plow handles, with wheat and corn beside him; on the right a miner holding a pickax, with a petroleum barrel, lumps of coal, and an anvil and hammer beside him; at their feet, crossed rifles topped by a Phrygian cap. Around the border is the legend "State of West Virginia" and the state motto. On the reverse, a landscape: in the foreground, cattle and

sheep in a meadow; behind them a river, with petroleum and salt works on one bank, a factory on the other; in the distance, a railroad viaduct on the side of a wooded mountain, and a log farmhouse on the side of a cultivated mountain; above, the sun emerging from clouds, with the motto "Libertas et Fidelitate" (Freedom and Loyalty) in the rays.

MOTTO Montani Semper Liberi (Mountaineers are always free)

SONGS "This Is My West Virginia" by Iris Bell; "West Virginia My Home Sweet Home" by Julian G. Hearne, Jr.; "The West Virginia Hills," lyrics by David King, music by H. E. Engle.

SYMBOLS
Flower big laurel
Tree sugar maple
Bird cardinal
Animal black bear
Fish brook trout
Fruit apple

LICENSE PLATE Black on white, with legend "Wild, Wonderful West Virginia" and an outline of the state in orange.

FLAG On a white field bordered by blue, the emblem of the state coat of arms enclosed in a yellow shield, with the legend "State of West Virginia" on a ribbon above it and a rhododendron wreath surrounding it.

GEOGRAPHY AND CLIMATE

West Virginia, highest in mean elevation of any state east of the Mississippi, is dominated by the narrow peaks and valleys of the Appalachians. Two major mountain regions, the Allegheny Plateau in the western two-thirds of the state and the Appalachian Valley in the eastern third, give the state its rugged character. Panhandles jut out from the east, along Maryland's southern border, and to the north, partly dividing Pennsylvania from Ohio. The state's climate is mainly humid continental.

AREA 24,231 square miles. Rank: 41st
INLAND WATER 112 square miles
GEOGRAPHIC CENTER Braxton, 4 miles E of Sutton
ELEVATIONS *Highest point:* Spruce Knob, Pendleton County, 4,863 feet. *Lowest point:* Potomac River, Jefferson County, 240 feet. *Mean elevation:* 1,500 feet

MAJOR RIVERS Ohio, Shenandoah, Kanawha, Big Sandy, Monongahela

MAJOR LAKES AND RESERVOIRS East Lynn, Mount Storm, Tygart, Bluestone, Sutton, Summersville

LAND USE

	Thousands of acres
Urban (1982)	312
Rural (1982)	13,722
Cropland (1982)	1,093
Pastureland (1982)	1,869
Rangeland (1982)	0
Forestland (1982)	10,423
State parks and recreation areas (1983)	150
National park system (1984)	3
National forest system (1984)	1,861
Tribal lands (1984)	0

TEMPERATURES The highest recorded temperature was 112°F on July 10, 1936, at Martinsburg. The lowest was -37°F on December 30, 1917, at Lewisburg.

NATIONAL SITES

NATIONAL HISTORICAL PARKS Chesapeake and Ohio Canal, Harpers Ferry
NATIONAL SCENIC RIVER AND RIVERWAY New River Gorge
NATIONAL SCENIC TRAIL Appalachian

HISTORY

1669–1670	John Lederer, German physician, reaches the crest of the Blue Ridge Mountains overlooking western Virginia.
1671	An English expedition "for the finding out the ebbing and flowing of the South Sea," reaches the Falls of Great Kanawha River.
1716	Lieutenant-Governor Alexander Spotswood and accompanying party penetrate western Virginia to the peaks of the Alleghenies.
1725	An Indian trader, John Van Nehne, explores the northern part of western Virginia.
1726	According to tradition, Welshman Morgan Morgan makes first permanent settlement at Bunker Hill on Mill Creek (Berkeley County).
1727	Germans from Pennsylvania establish settlement now called Shepherdstown on the Potomac River. Indians often attack the new settlers, who are taking over their hunting grounds.
1742	Coal is discovered along what is now called Coal River.
1744	All territory between the Allegheny Mountains and the Ohio River is ceded to the English by Indians of the Six Nations for 400 pounds.
1748	George Washington surveys land in western Virginia for Lord Fairfax and visits "The famed warm springs at Bath" (Berkeley Springs). France, with aid from Canadian militiamen and Indians, attempts to reinforce claims to Ohio Valley.
1748–1949	The *Harpers Ferry* begins carrying passengers across the Shenandoah River.
1750	First frontier fort, Fort Ohio, is built at Ridgeley in what is now Mineral County.
1755	*July 3.* The settlement of Draper's Meadows in New River section is attacked by Shawnee Indians. Nearly all the settlers are killed or captured.
1763	Treaty of Paris ends the French and Indian War, but Indian attacks continue in the region.
1766	Survey of Mason-Dixon Line reaches western boundary between Maryland and western Virginia.
1768	First recorded flood of Ohio River.

1772	George R. Clark explores Ohio and Kanawha rivers.
1774	*October 10*. General Andrew Lewis leads troops over the mountains and defeats Shawnee Indians at Point Pleasant, where the Kanawha and Ohio rivers meet.
1776	The residents of western Virginia petition the Continental Congress to establish a separate government for their region.
1777	*September*. Indians unsuccessfully besiege Fort Henry.
	November 10. Indian chieftain Cornstalk, his son, and Chief Red Hawk are murdered by whites at Fort Randolph.
1782	*September 10*. Second siege of Fort Henry. This is considered by many the last battle of the Revolution.
1789	Daniel Boone is commissioned lieutenant colonel of the Kanawha Militia.
1790	The *Potomak Guardian and Berkeley Advertiser*, western Virginia's first newspaper, is published in Shepherdstown.
	First US census shows population of West Virginia at 55,873.
1794	*December 19*. Charlestown (Charleston) is established.
	Iron Furnace is erected at King's Creek.
1795	Daniel Boone and family leave Kanawha Valley.
1806	First salt well is drilled in Great Kanawha Valley, increasing production from 150 to 1250 pounds a day by 1808.
1810	Western Virginia protests unequal representation in Virginia legislature.
	Oil is discovered.
1815	First discovery that natural gas can be conserved from wells.
1831	Slavery debates magnify divisions in Virginia's political and social thought.
1859	*October 16*. John Brown, ardent abolitionist, seizes the arsenal at Harpers Ferry but is captured, tried, and hanged in Charleston on December 2.
1861	*May 23*. Virginia's ordinance for secession is ratified, but a large majority of voters in the western counties voice their opposition.
1862	*May 23*. Union troops defeat Confederates at Lewisberg.
1863	*April 20*. President Lincoln issues a proclamation admitting West Virginia to the Union after a 60-day waiting period.
	April 27. Confederate General William Jones attempts to burn the suspension bridge over the Monongahela River.
	April 29. Jones defeats Union troops at Fairmont and burns the library of Francis H. Pierpont.
	June 20. West Virginia admitted to the Union as 35th state.
1865	*April 9*. The Civil War ends.
	First free public school in state opens in Charleston.
1866	*May 24*. Voters ratify constitutional amendment denying citizenship to all who aided the Confederacy.
1867	Land grant agricultural college founded at Morgantown (now West Virginia University).
1869	*February 10*. Charleston is named the seat of government "on and after April 1, 1870." The seat is shifted to Wheeling in 1875 but restored to Charleston permanently in 1885.
1871	*April 27*. All persons stripped of their voting privileges in 1866 have their citizenship restored.
1882	Twenty-year-long Hatfield–McCoy feud erupts in southern Appalachia (Tug Valley).
1898	Spanish American War. West Virginia furnishes two regiments of volunteer infantry.
1902	"Mother" Mary Jones campaigns to unionize 7,000 miners in Kanawha Valley.
1907	Monogah Mine explosion kills 361 men.
1912	Paint Creek Miners strike to gain recognition of the United Mine Workers of America. Martial law imposed until January 1913.
	State prohibition becomes effective.
1917–1918	World War I. West Virginia Selective Service registrants number nearly 325,000. Over 45,000 see active service and 624 are killed in action.
1920	UMWA membership booms in Mingo County following the "Matewan Massacre."

1921	*January 3*. State capitol at Charleston is destroyed by fire.
1924	*April 1*. A strike begins against the coal operators in the north. The bitter struggle goes on for three years.
1930–1934	High death-rate of Hawks Nest Tunnel workers due to silicosis. Governor Holt suppresses mention of tragedy in WPA state guide.
1932	WSAZ, the first radio station in the state, begins broadcasting from Huntington.
1934	State prohibition law is repealed.
1938	The Mingo Oak, largest and oldest white oak tree in the US, is declared dead and felled with ceremony.
1939	West Virginia makes the final payment of its debt to Virginia.
1940	A mine explosion in McDowell County kills 93 miners.
1941–1945	World War II. First and largest synthetic rubber plant in the US opens near Charleston. West Virginia industries furnish many chemical products.
1949	Huntington is the site of the first television station in the state, WSAZ-TV.
1954	State legislature passes a law allowing blacks to attend state colleges and universities.
1956	New aluminum plant opens at Ravenswood.
1959	Operations begin at the National Radio Astronomy Observatory at Green Bank.
1960	JFK defeats Hubert Humphrey in West Virginia presidential primary, virtually assuring Kennedy of Democratic nomination and ending the political issue of his Catholicism.
1962	The state legislature votes approval of funds to supply birth control information and aid to welfare recipients.
1965	*Janaury 18*. Capital punishment is abolished.
1968	Seventy-eight die in Farmington mine explosion.
1969	Former Governor W. W. "Wally" Barron sentenced to a five-year prison term for tampering with a jury.
1972	*February 26*. A coalwaste dam collapses at Buffalo Creek resulting in a flood that kills 118 people.
1973	Arnold Miller, a retired West Virginia coalminer, runs for President of the UMWA as candidate of the reformist Miners for Democracy and defeats incumbent "Tony" Boyle.
1978	The state records its second successive record-breaking winter with heavy snow, rain, and flash floods.
1981	State's economy repeated its unstable pattern, showing major gains in gas and oil industries and a depression in the steel and coal mining industries.
1982	*August*. Unemployment climbs to 13.6 percent, a level close to the nation's highest.
1983	*July*. Governor John D. Rockefeller IV imposes major cutbacks in state spending as the state's recession continues.
1985	West Virginia continues to have the highest unemployment rate in the nation.
1985	*November 7*. Heavy flooding causes loss of life and property.
1987	The unemployment rate drops to a single digit level for the first time in several years, but state government still contends with fiscal crisis.
1988	*November 19*. West Virginia University football team completes first undefeated season in program's 98-year history.

DEMOGRAPHY

Population (est. 1987) . . . 1,897,000
Population (1980) 1,950,258
Population density in persons per
  square mile (1980) 80.5

POPULATION BY RACE (1980)
American Indian/Aleut/
  Eskimo 1,610
Asian/Pacific Islander 5,194
Black 65,061

Hispanic 12,707
White 1,874,751
Other 3,038

POPULATION CHARACTERISTICS (1980)
                Percent of state population
Urban 36.2
Rural 63.8
Under 18 . . . . 28.7
65 or older 12.2
College-educated 10.5

Families below poverty line . . . 11.7
Public-assistance recipients 6.0

Per capita personal
income (1986) $10,530
Millionaires per 100,000
residents (1982) 30.6
Average life expectancy
in years (1980) 72.9
Marriage rate per 1,000
residents (1986) 7.1
Divorce rate per 1,000
residents (1986) 5.1
Birth rate per 1,000
residents (1985) 13.2
Infant mortality rate per 1,000
births (1985) 10.5
Abortion rate per 1,000
live births (1985) 185

Crime rate per 100,000
residents (1985)
Violent 164.5
Property 2,152.2
Federal and state prisoners per
100,000 residents (1984) 81
Alcohol consumption in gallons per
capita (1985) 31.1
Deaths from motor vehicle accidents
per 100,000 residents (1985) . . 21.7

MAJOR CITIES

	1984 population (est.)
Charleston	59,371
Huntington	61,086
Parkersburg	39,379
Wheeling	42,080

GOVERNMENT AND POLITICS

Number of US Representatives 4
Electoral votes 6

POLITICAL PARTY NOMINEES FROM STATE

Henry Gassaway Davis (D)   1904   VP
John William Davis (D)   1924   P
Joseph B. Lightburn (Constitu-
tion)   1964   P

PRESIDENTIAL PRIMARY ELECTION In 1988,
West Virginia sent 44 Democratic delegates and 28 Republican delegates to the
national conventions.
CONSTITUTION West Virginia has had two

constitutions: 1863 and the present one,
adopted in 1872.
LEGISLATURE The Legislature is divided
into the Senate (34 members, 4-year term,
minimum age 25) and the House of Delegates (100 members, 2-year term, minimum age 18). In 1987, the annual salary
was $6,500.
JUDICIARY The highest court is the Supreme
Court, with 5 judges serving 12-year terms.
In 1987, the annual salary was $55,000.
EXECUTIVE The governor serves a 4-year
term; the minimum age for holding office is
30. In 1987, the annual salary was $72,000.
There are 5 other elected officials.

PRESIDENTIAL VOTE 1948-1988 *(in percents)*

Year	State Winner	Democratic	Republican
1948	Truman (D)	57.3	42.2
1952	Stevenson (D)	51.9	48.1
1956	Eisenhower (R)	45.9	54.1
1960	Kennedy (D)	52.7	47.3
1964	Johnson (D)	67.9	32.1
1968	Humphrey (D)	49.6	40.8
1972	Nixon (R)	36.4	63.6
1976	Carter (D)	58.0	41.9
1980	Carter (D)	49.8	45.3
1984	Reagan (R)	44.3	54.7
1988	Dukakis (D)	52.0	48.0

GOVERNORS

Arthur I. Boreman (R)	1863-1869
Daniel D.T. Farnsworth (R/ acting)	1869
William E. Stevenson (R)	1869-1871
John J. Jacob (R)	1871-1877
Henry M. Mathews (R)	1877-1881
Jacob B. Jackson (D)	1881-1885
E. Willis Wilson (D)	1885-1890
A. Brooks Fleming (D)	1890-1893
William A. MacCorkle (D)	1893-1897
George W. Atkinson (R)	1987-1901
Albert B. White (R)	1901-1905

William M. O. Dawson (R)	1905-1909
William E. Glasscock (R)	1909-1913
Henry D. Hatfield (R)	1913-1917
John J. Cornwell (D)	1917-1921
Ephraim F. Morgan (R)	1921-1925
Howard M. Gore (R)	1925-1929
William G. Conley (R)	1929-1933
H. Guy Kump (D)	1933-1937
Homer A. Holt (D)	1937-1941
M. Mansfield Neely (D)	1941-1945
Clarence W. Meadows (D)	1945-1949
Okev L. Patterson (D)	1949-1953
William C. Marland (D)	1953-1957
Cecil H. Underwood (R)	1957-1961
William W. Barron (D)	1961-1965
Hulett C. Smith (D)	1965-1969
Arch A. Moore (R)	1969-1977
John D. Rockefeller 4th (D)	1977-1985
Arch A. Moore (D)	1985-1989
Gaston Caperton (D)	1989-

MINIMUM AGES

Majority	18
Marriage with parental consent . . . minimum (under 16 with judicial approval)	no
Marriage without parental consent .	18
Making a will	18
Buying alcohol	21
Jury duty	18
Leaving school	16
Driver's license	16

CAPITAL PUNISHMENT
None

MILITARY INSTALLATIONS
Total number: 2

FINANCES

Thousands of dollars

GENERAL REVENUE (1985)

Total general revenue . . .	2,964,217
Total tax revenue	1,855,583
Sales and gross receipts . . .	1,136,514
Individual income taxes	503,186
Corporate net income taxes . .	98,766

GENERAL EXPENDITURE (1985)

Total general expenditure .	2,779,542
Education	1,192,378
Public welfare	355,305
Health	87,469
Hospitals	54,743
Natural resources	73,055
Highways	426,094
Police	24,423
Corrections	24,268

FEDERAL AID (1985) 904,024

ECONOMY

Among cash crops, corn, barley, potatoes, and oats are the most important; livestock raising (dairy products, cattle, hogs, and poultry) yields the most income. In 1983, farm marketing cash receipts were $228 million, lowest in the South. Hardwoods such as cherry and oak are the mainstay of the state's timber industry; commercial timber is also produced from softwoods such as white pine and red spruce. Bituminous coal is by far the most valuable mined product; other minerals include natural gas, various salts, clays, sand, and gravel. West Virginia's leading manufactures include chemicals, rubber, primary and fabricated metals, ceramics, fine glass, processed foods, and electrical machinery. Value added by manufacture was $4 billion in 1982.

EMPLOYMENT (1984)

Thousands of persons

Total number of employed workers	653
Construction	22.3
Finance, insurance, and real estate	23.2
Government	131.6
Manufacturing	91.1
Mining	48.4
Services	107.7
Transportation, communications, and utilities	39.5
Wholesale and retail trade	131.2

Percent of civilian labor force unemployed (1984)	15.0

DEPARTMENT OF DEFENSE (1985)

Civilian workers employed . . .	1,599
Military personnel	441
Contract awards	$90 million

ENERGY SOURCES FOR ELECTRIC UTILITIES (1983)

Percent

Coal	99.0
Gas	0.0
Hydroelectric	0.6
Nuclear	0.0
Petroleum	0.4

TRANSPORTATION

Motor vehicles registered in state (1986)	1,170,138
Miles of roads, streets, and highways (1986)	35,143

Miles of Class I
  railway (1986) 3,156
Airports (1983) 94
Major aviation hubs (1983) 1

Largest hub: Charleston/Dunbar
Major ports, with gross tonnage in
thousands (1985):
Huntington 19,644

CULTURE AND EDUCATION

Native American tribes
There were Indian cultures in West Virginia for some 14,000 years. The state was formerly home to the Honniasont, Moneton, and Nahyssa tribes.

Religions, ethnicities, and languages
In 1980, 2.1 percent of West Virginia's population spoke a language other than English at home. Most white residents are descended from the early German and Scotch-Irish settlers; many of the black residents are descended from freed slaves. Immigrant groups of the late 18th and early 20th centuries include Hungarians, Irish, Italians, and Poles. The largest religious groups in West Virginia are the Methodists, Baptists, Presbyterians, Episcopalians, and Roman Catholics; the Disciples of Christ Church was founded there.

Major museums and libraries
Huntington Galleries
Scientific and Cultural Center, Charleston
Sunrise Museums, Charleston

Major arts organizations
Children's Theater, Charleston
Charleston Symphony Orchestra
Wheeling Symphony Orchestra

Colleges and universities
Number public (1986-87) 16
Number private (1986-87) 13
Total enrollment, in full-time equivalent students (1985) 58,400

Public elementary and secondary schools
Expenditure per pupil in average daily attendance (1986-87) $3,619
Pupil-teacher ratio (1987) 15.3
Average teacher salary (1986-87) $22,428

Holidays
West Virginia Day. June 20
State Fair, Lewisburg (Fairlea). Late August

WEST VIRGINIA IN LITERATURE

James Taylor Adams *Death in The Dark: A Collection of Factual Ballads of American Mine Disasters* (1941, rpt. 1975, 1977)
Twenty ballads of the coalfields, with historical annotations.

Mary M. Atkeson *A Study of the Literature of West Virginia, 1822–1922* (1922)

John Peale Bishop *Act of Darkness* (1935)
The West Virginia–born poet's only novel, based on his boyhood in Jefferson County, depicts the physical and moral decline of a small town in 1905.

W. E. Blackhurst *Sawdust in Your Eyes* (1963)
Tales of logging in Pocahontas County.
———. *Of Men and a Mighty Mountain* (1965)
The development of the lumber town of Cass, partly based on the author's own experiences.

Marie Boette (ed.) *Sing a Hipsy Doodle and Other Folk Songs of West Virginia* (1971)

Vito J. Brenni and **Joyce Binder** *West Virginia Authors: A Biobibliography* (1968)

Philip M. Conley *West Virginia Reader: Stories of Early Days* (1970)

Albert Benjamin Cunningham *Manse at Barren Rocks* (1918); *Singing Mountains* (1919)
Chronicles of daily life in a rural settlement.

William Demby *Beetlecreek* (1950)
Novel about race relations in a small town.

Howard Fast *Power* (1962)
Novel about labor unrest in the coal mines during the 1920s and '30s.

Patrick Gainer *Folk Songs from the West Virginia Hills* (1975); *Witches, Ghosts, and Signs: Folklore of the Southern Appalachians* (1975)

Zane Grey *Betty Zane* (1904)
Romantic historical novel about a Revolutionary war heroine of Fort Henry.

Davis Grubb *Night of the Hunter* (1953)
Psychological drama about a killer's pursuit of two children in the Ohio Valley by a West Virginia author who set several of his novels, including *The Watchman* (1961), in small towns of the region.

Ann Hebson *The Lattimer Legend* (1961)
Novel about seven generations of a West Virginia family, centering on the Civil War.

Gay J. James *Appalachian Ghost Stories and Other Tales* (1975)

William A. MacCorkle *The Recollections of Fifty Years of West Virginia* (1928)
Memoirs of a state governor, 1893–1897.

Margaret P. Montague *Sowing of Alderson Cree* (1907); *In Calvert's Valley* (1909)
Novels of mountain people. The author also compiled a collection of tales of Tony Beaver, the legendary lumberjack.

Ruth Ann Musick *The Telltale Lilac Bush and Other West Virginia Ghost Tales* (1965, rpt. 1976)
Tales recounted to the author by mountain people.
———. *Green Hills of Magic: West Virginia Folktales from Europe* (1970)
Folklore of immigrant communities.

Charlton Ogburn *Winespring Mountain* (1973)
Novel about a young idealist's fight to save a region from strip mining.

Breece D'J Pancake *The Stories of Breece D'J Pancake* (1983)
A realistic depiction of the lives of poor hill-country farmers.

Jayne Anne Phillips *Machine Dreams* (1984)
Narrative of the lives of four members of a working-class family in a small West Virginia town. The author's short story collection, *Black Tickets* (1979), has a similar setting.

Jack Preble *Land of Canaan* (1965)
Stories of the inhabitants of Canaan Valley.

Mary Lee Settle *The Beulah Quintet* (1956–1980)
The author's five novels about the founding and development of the state begin with *O Beulah Land* (1956), an account of early settlers between 1754 and 1774, and continue with *Know Nothing* (1960), set in a farming community just before the Civil War. *The Scapegoat* (1980)

depicts a 1912 coalminers' strike and the conflict between traditional and progressive values.

Charles Shetler *West Virginia Civil War Literature: An Annotated Bibliography* (1963)

Hubert D. Skidmore *Hawks' Nest* (1941)
Novel about workers on a tunnel-drilling project in the early 1930s, written to expose the dangers of silicosis. The author also wrote a social comedy set in a small West Virginia town in the 1920s, *O Careless Love* (1949).

William D. Smith *Multitude of Men* (1960)
Novel about labor conflicts in a steel mill in the 1940s.

Booker T. Washington *Up from Slavery: An Autobiography* (1963)
Containing an account of Washington's early life in Malden, where he worked in a saltworks, in a coal mine, and as a domestic servant.

Warren Wood *Representative Authors of West Virginia* (1926)

GUIDES TO RESOURCES

Clagg, Sam *West Virginia Historical Almanac* (1975)

Cohen, Stan *Historic Sites of West Virginia: A Pictorial Guide* (2d ed. 1985)

Davis, Innis and **Emily Johnson** *A Bibliography of West Virginia* (1939)

Federal Writers' Project *West Virginia: A Guide to the Mountain State* (1941, rpt. 1980)

Forbes, Harold M. *West Virginia History: A Bibliography and Guide to Research* (1981)

Gannett, Henry *A Gazetteer of West Virginia* (1904)

Munn, Robert F. *Index to West Virginia* (1960)

Nodyne, Kenneth R. and **Dennis E. Lawther** *The Wheeling Area, an Annotated Bibliography* (1981)

North, E. Lee *The 55 West Virginias: A Guide to the State's Counties* (1985)

Shawkey, Morris P. *West Virginia in History, Life, Literature, and Industry* 5 vols. (1928)

West Virginia University *Appalachian Bibliography* (2d ed. 1972)
———. *Guide to Manuscripts and Archives in West Virginia* (3d ed. 1974)

SELECTED NONFICTION SOURCES

Abernethy, Thomas P. *Three Virginia Frontiers* (1940)

Alvord, Clarence W. and **Lee Bidgood** *The First Explorations of the Trans-Allegheny Region by Virginians, 1650–1674* (1912)

Ambler, Charles H. *A History of Transportation in the Ohio Valley* (1932)
———. *George Washington and the West* (1936)
———. *Francis H. Pierpont, Union War Governor of Virginia and Father of West Virginia* (1937)
———. *West Virginia: Stories and Biographies* (1937)
———. *The Makers of West Virginia and Their Work* (1942)
———. *A History of Education in West Virginia from Early Colonial Times to 1949* (1951)
——— and **F. P. Summers** *West Virginia, the Mountain State* (2d ed. 1958)

Ash, Jerry W. and **Stratton L. Douthat** *West Virginia USA* (1976)

Auvil, Myrtle *Covered Bridges of West Virginia, Past and Present* (2d ed. 1973)

Bailey, Kenneth P. *The Ohio Company of West Virginia and the Westward Movement 1748–1792* (1939)

Barns, William P. *The West Virginia State Grange: The First Century, 1873–1973* (1973)

Bissell, Richard *The Monongahela* (Rivers of America series) (1952)

Boyd, Peter *History of Northern West Virginia Panhandle Embracing Ohio, Marshall, Brooke, and Hancock Counties* 2 vols. (1927)

Brantner, J. H. *Historical Collections of Moundsville, West Virginia* (1947)

Brown, Stephen W. *Voice of the New West: John G. Jackson, His Life and Times* (1985)

Callahan, James M. *Semi-Centennial History of West Virginia* (1913)
———. *History of West Virginia, Old and New* 3 vols. (1923)

———. *History of the Making of Morgantown: A Type Study in Trans-Appalachian Local History* (1926)

Caruso, John A. *The Appalachian Frontier: America's First Surge Westward* (1959)

Cherniack, Martin *The Hawk's Nest Incident: America's Worst Industrial Disaster* (1986)

Clarkson, Roy B. *Tumult on the Mountain: Lumbering in West Virginia, 1770–1920* (1964)

Coffey, William E., **Carolyn M. Karr**, and **Frank S. Riddel** *West Virginia Government* (1984)

Cometti, Elizabeth and **Festus P. Summers** (eds.) *The Thirty-Fifth State: A Documentary History of West Virginia* (1966)

Conley, Phil *The West Virginia Encyclopedia* (1929)
———. *History of West Virginia Coal Industry* (1960)
——— and **Boyd B. Stutler** *West Virginia, Yesterday and Today* (4th ed. 1966)

Cook, Roy *The Family and Early Life of Stonewall Jackson* (5th ed. 1967)

Corbin, David A. *Life, Work and Rebellion in the Coal Fields: Southern West Virginia Coal Mines, 1880–1922* (1981)

Core, Earl L. *The Wondrous Year: West Virginia Through the Seasons* (1975)
———. *Natural History of the Cass Scenic Railroad* (2d ed. 1978)

Curry, Richard O. *A House Divided: A Statehood Politics and the Copperhead Movement in West Virginia* (1964)

Davis, Dorothy *John George Jackson* (1976)

Dayton, Ruth W. *Greenbrier Pioneers and Their Homes* (1942, rpt. 1977)

Dillon, Lacy A. *They Died in the Darkness* (1976)

Diss Debar, Joseph H. *The West Virginia Handbook and Immigrant's Guide* (1870)

Dodge, Jacob R. *West Virginia: Its Farms and Forests, Mines and Oil-Wells* (1865)

Ernst, Harry W. *The Primary That Made a President: West Virginia, 1960* (1962)

Fetherling, Dale *Mother Jones, the Miners' Angel: A Portrait* (1974)
———. *Wheeling: An Illustrated History* (1983)

Greene, Laurence *The Raid, a Biography of Harper's Ferry* (1953)

Hall, Granville D. *The Rending of Virginia, a History* (1902)
———. *Lee's Invasion of Northwest Virginia in 1861* (1911)

Haymond, Henry *History of Harrison County, West Virginia, from the Early Days of Northwestern Virginia to the Present* (1910, rpt. 1973)

Hinton, Richard J. *John Brown and His Men, with Some Account of the Road They Traveled to Reach Harper's Ferry* (1894, rpt. 1968)

Hume, Brit *Death and the Mines; Rebellion and Murder in the United Mine Workers* (1971)

Janssen, Quinith and William Fernbach *West Virginia Place Names* (1984)

Jefferds, Joseph C., Jr. *Captain Matthew Arbuckle: A Documentary Biography* (1981)

Jones, Mary H. *Autobiography of Mother Jones* (1925, rpt. 1969)

Keller, Alan *Thunder at Harper's Ferry* (1958)

Lane, Winthrop *Civil War in West Virginia; a Story of the Industrial Conflict in the Coal Mines* (1921, rpt. 1969)

Lee, Howard B. *Bloodletting in Appalachia* (1969)
———. *My Appalachia; Pipestem State Park Today and Yesterday* (1971)
———. *Lost Tales of Appalachia* (1977)
———. *Looking Backward One Hundred Years in Appalachia* (1981)

Libby, Bill *Clown: A Biography of Hot Rod Hundley* (1970)

Lewis, Virgil A. *Life and Times of Anne Bailey, the Pioneer Heroine of the Great Kanawha Valley* (1891)

Lowry, Terry *September Blood: The Battle of Carnifex Ferry* (1985)

Lowther, Minnie K. *Blennerhassett Island in Romance and Tragedy* (1936, rpt. 1974)

Lunt, Richard D. *Law and Order vs. the Miners, West Virginia, 1907–1933* (1979)

May, Earl C. *Principio to Wheeling 1715–1945: A Pageant of Iron and Steel* (1945)

McAteer, James D. *Coal Mine Health and Safety: The Case of West Virginia* (1973)

McClellan, Major-General George *Report on the Organization and Campaigns of the Army of the Potomac: to Which Is Added an Account of the Campaign in West Virginia* . . . (1864)

McCormick, Kyle *The New-Kanawha River and the Mine War of West Virginia* (1959)

McGregor, James Clyde *The Disruption of Virginia* (1922)

McKeown, Bonni *Peaceful Patriot: The Story of Tom Bennett* (1980)

McWhorter, Lucullus V. *The Border Settlers of Northwestern Virginia from 1768 to 1795* . . . (1915)

Mooney, Fred (ed. J. William Hess) *Struggle in the Coalfields: The Autobiography of Fred Mooney* (1967)

Moore, George E. *A Banner in the Hills; West Virginia's Statehood* (1963)

Morgan, John G. *West Virginia Governors, 1863–1980* (2d ed. 1980)

Munn, Robert F. *The Coal Industry in America* (1965)

Nelson, Truman *The Old Man; John Brown at Harper's Ferry* (1973)

North, E. Lee *Fifty-Five West Virginias* (1985)

Nugent, Tom *Death at Buffalo Creek: The 1972 Flood Disaster* (1973)

Oates, Stephen B. *To Purge This Land with Blood: A Biography of John Brown* (1970)

Parker, Granville *The Formation of the State of West Virginia, and Other Incidents in the Late War* (1875)

Pepper, Charles M. *The Life and Times of Henry Gassaway Davis, 1823–1916* (1920)

Perry, Huey *"They'll Cut Off Your Project"; a Mingo County Chronicle* (1972)

Peterson, Bill *Coaltown Revisited: An Appalachian Notebook* (1972)

Powell, Scott *History of Marshall County* (1925)

Price, Paul H. *A Geologist at Large in Appalachia, 1923–1969* (1978)

Raymond, Richard D. *The Myth of the Appalachian Brain Drain: A Case Study of West Virginia* (1972)

Redpath, James (ed.) *Echoes of Harper's Ferry* (1860, rpt. 1969)

Rice, Otis K. *The Allegheny Frontier: West Virginia Beginnings, 1730–1830* (1970)
———. *West Virginia: A History* (1985)

Ross, William R. *The Electoral Process in West Virginia* (1971)

Safford, William H. *The Life of Harman Blennerhassett, Comprising an Authentic Narrative of the Burr Expedition* (1850, rpt. 1972)

Shetler, Charles *Guide to the Study of West Virginia History* (1960)

Smith, Merritt R. *Harpers Ferry Armory and the New Technology: The Challenge of Change* (1977)

Stutler, Boyd B. *West Virginia in the Civil War* (2d ed. 1966)

Summers, George W. *The Mountain State. A Description of the Natural Resources of West Virginia* . . . (1893)

Tam, W. P., Jr. *The Smokeless Coal Fields of West Virginia; a Brief History* (1963)

Thoenen, Eugene D. *History of the Oil and Gas Industry in West Virginia* (1964)

Trent, W. W. *Mountaineer Education: A Story of Education in West Virginia, 1885–1957* (1960)

Tribe, Ivan M. *Mountaineer Jamboree: Country Music in West Virginia* (1984)

Warren, Robert Penn *John Brown: The Making of a Martyr* (1929)

West, Jerry and Bill Libby *Mr. Clutch: The Jerry West Story* (1969)

Willey, William P. *An Inside View of the Formation of the State of West Virginia* . . . (1901)

Williams, John A. *West Virginia: A Bicentennial History* (States and the Nation series) (1976)
———. *West Virginia and the Captains of Industry* (1976)

Withers, Alexander S. *Chronicles of Border Warfare* (1895, rpt. 1971)

WISCONSIN

The east north central state of Wisconsin is bordered on the north by Lake Superior, Michigan, and the Brule River; on the east by Michigan, the Menominee River, and Lake Michigan; on the south by Illinois; and on the east by the St. Croix and Mississippi rivers, Iowa, and Minnesota.

FULL NAME State of Wisconsin
POSTAL ABBREVIATION WI
INHABITANT Wisconsinite
ADMITTED TO THE UNION May 29, 1848.
30th state
POPULATION (est. 1987) 4,807,000.
Percent of US total: 1.98%. Rank: 17th

CAPITAL CITY Madison, located between Lake Mendota and Lake Monona in south central Wisconsin; population 170,745 (est. 1984). It was founded in 1836 and was named the territorial capital while it was still uninhabited. It was incorporated as a village in 1846 and as a city in 1856.

STATE NAME AND NICKNAMES From a Chippewa word meaning "grassy place," in reference to the area around the Wisconsin River. Also known as the Badger State and the Copper State.

STATE SEAL The state coat of arms: a heraldic shield, quartered, showing clockwise from top left a plow, a pick and shovel, an anchor, and an arm and hammer; in the center a medallion bearing the shield of the Stars and Stripes surrounded by the national motto "E Pluribus Unum" (From Many, One); on the left of the shield a sailor, on the right a miner, below it a cornucopia and a pyramid of lead ingots, above it a badger and the state motto on a ribbon. The border reads "Great Seal of the State of Wisconsin" and contains at bottom a scroll with 13 stars.

MOTTO Forward

SONG "On, Wisconsin" by William T. Purdy.

SYMBOLS
Flower wood violet
Tree sugar maple
Bird robin
Mineral galena
Rock red granite
Animal badger
Domestic animal dairy cow
Wild animal white-tailed deer
Fish muskellunge
Insect honeybee
Soil antigo silt loam
Symbol of peace mourning dove

LICENSE PLATES (1) Red on white, with a blue-and-red image of a seashore and farm and the blue legend "America's Dairyland." (2) Blue on white, with same legend and image as above. (3) Dark blue on gold, with legend "America's Dairyland."

FLAG On a field of royal blue, the state coat of arms, with the state name in white above it and the date "1848" in white below it.

GEOGRAPHY AND CLIMATE

The heartland state of Wisconsin is composed primarily of rolling highlands and plains—granitic uplands in the north, a broad sandstone plain in the central area of the state, a narrow coastal plain along the bank of Lake Superior, and eroded limestone and sandstone uplands in the southwest. The southeast has wide lowlands cut by three north-south ridges. Hundreds of small lakes dot northern Wisconsin; the remnants of glacier activity from the last Ice Age can be found in most of the rest of the state as well.

AREA 56,153 square miles. Rank: 26th
INLAND WATER 1,727 square miles
GEOGRAPHIC CENTER Wood, 9 miles SE of Marshfield
ELEVATIONS *Highest point:* Timms Hill, Price County, 1,951 feet. *Lowest point:* Lake Michigan, 581 feet. *Mean elevation:* 1,050 feet

MAJOR RIVERS Mississippi, Wisconsin, St. Croix, Black, Chippewa, Menominee

MAJOR LAKES AND RESERVOIRS Superior, Winnebago, Poygan, Mendota, Pentenwell, Chippewa, Big Eau Pleine

LAND USE

	Thousands of acres
Urban (1982)	1,125
Rural (1982)	30,890
Cropland (1982)	11,457
Pastureland (1982)	3,394
Rangeland (1982)	0
Forestland (1982)	13,393
State parks and recreation areas (1983)	121
National park system (1984)	66
National forest system (1984)	2,023
Tribal lands (1984)	332

TEMPERATURES The highest recorded temperature was 114°F on July 13, 1936, at Wisconsin Dells. The lowest was -54°F on January 24, 1922, at Danbury.

NATIONAL SITES

NATIONAL LAKESHORE Apostle Islands
NATIONAL SCENIC RIVERS AND RIVERWAYS Lower St. Croix, St. Croix
NATIONAL SCENIC TRAILS Ice Age, North Country
NATIONAL SCIENTIFIC RESERVE Ice Age
NATIONAL WILDLIFE REFUGES Cassville District, Horicon–Fox River/Gravel Island/Green Bay/Wisconsin Wetland Management District, La Crosse District, Necedah, Trempealeau, Upper Mississippi River Wild Life and Fish Refuge

HISTORY

1634	French explorer Jean Nicolet lands on the shores of Green Bay.
1658–1660	Two French fur traders, Pierre Espirit Radisson and Médard Chouart, Sieur des Groseilliers, visit the Wisconsin shore of Lake Superior.
1672	Mission built at DePere by French Jesuit priests.
1673	*June 17.* Louis Jolliet and Father Jacques Marquette arrive at the Mississippi River after ascending the Fox River from Green Bay, paddling to its head, portaging to the Wisconsin River, and following the Wisconsin into the Mississippi.
1684	First French post at Green Bay.
1763	All French possessions east of the Mississippi ceded to Great Britain.
1781	Traditional date of settlement at Prairie du Chien.
1783	Northwest Territory, including present-day Wisconsin, ceded by Britain to the United States.
1791	Fur trader Jacques Vieau establishes posts at Kewaunee, Sheyboygan, Manitowoc, and Milwaukee.
1800–1809	Wisconsin is part of the Indiana Territory.
1809–1818	The Illinois Territory includes Wisconsin.
1814	Fort Shelby, first US military post in Wisconsin, built at Prairie du Chien. Seized by British the same year. Abandoned in 1815, after conclusion of the War of 1812.
1816	Fort Shelby rebuilt as Fort Crawford. Fort Howard erected at Green Bay. A law excludes foreigners from the pelt trade, leaving American traders to prosper.
1817	First school in Wisconsin opened at Green Bay.

1818	*December 3.* Wisconsin region attached to Michigan Territory on elevation of Illinois to statehood.
1824	Earliest lead mining settlement, at Hazel Green. Miners—some from the South, others from Cornwall—are dubbed "Badgers."
1830s	Pennsylvania artist, George Catlin, travels the Mississippi painting portraits of Indians and frontier landscapes of Wisconsin.
1832	*August 2.* Sauk and Fox Indians, led by Black Hawk, routed and massacred at Battle of Bad Axe, near LaCrosse.
1833	*December 11.* First Wisconsin newspaper, the weekly Green Bay *Intelligencer*, is established.
1834	First public land sale, at Mineral Point.
1835	Three men purchase the site of Milwaukee.
1836	Wisconsin becomes a territory; Madison, though still uninhabited by whites, is chosen as capital site.
1847	Special census shows population to be 219,456.
1848	*May 29.* Wisconsin is admitted to the Union as the 30th state.
	In the last of a series of Indian treaty cessions between 1829 and 1848, the Menominee cede their lands east of the Wisconsin and north of the Fox.
1849	*February 5.* University of Wisconsin is founded with its main campus at Madison.
1853	Railroad links Milwaukee and Madison.
1854	First great wave of German immigration reaches crest. (Second was during 1881–1884.)
1861–1865	Wisconsin furnishes 91,379 men to the Union Army in the Civil War; death toll, 10,752.
1871	*October 8–10.* With state still five-sixths covered by virgin forest, over 1,000 people perish in a fire that devastates six counties—600 die at Peshtigo alone.
1872	Last great wheat crop of 26 million bushels.
	Dairy preacher, William Dempster Hoard, forms the Wisconsin Dairy Men's Association.
1880	State population is 1,315,497.
1900	Wisconsin is the leading lumber-producing state.
1905	Civil service adopted for state employees.
1910	Milwaukee sets precedents by electing the first Socialist congressman (Victor Berger) and the first Socialist mayor of a big city (Emil Seidel).
1911	State income tax and seven major labor laws enacted.
1913	First state compulsory workmen's compensation law in the US.
1919	Wisconsin becomes the leading dairying state.
1921	Formation of the Green Bay Packers, one of the earliest professional football teams.
1924	Senator Robert M. La Follette of Madison runs for president as a third-party candidate but carries only Wisconsin.
1925–1926	Wisconsin native Frank Lloyd Wright establishes Taliesin, near Spring Green, as an architectural studio-workshop.
1932	First state unemployment compensation law in the US enacted.
1943	State Civil War debt of $1,183,700 is retired.
1950	Senator Joseph McCarthy of Appleton begins his career as a Red hunter by claiming the State Department is harboring Communists.
1961	Menominee Indian reservation is terminated, becoming Menominee County.
1970	Population is 4,417,821.
1975	Menominee County fails economically and politically and is returned to reservation status.
1977	A no-fault state law substitutes "irretrievable breakdown of marriage" for all existing grounds for divorce.
	More than 80 percent of Wisconsin's agricultural receipts are from livestock and dairy products.
1981	"The beer that made Milwaukee famous" leaves town when the Joseph Schlitz Brewing Company closes its brewery after 133 years of operation.
1982	A $70-million shopping center opens in downtown Milwaukee, preserving many historic structures.

1987	Voters approve constitutional amendments legalizing parimutuel betting and a state lottery.
1988	*January 27.* Only months after acquiring American Motors, the Chrysler Corporation announces it will close the Kenosha plant, idling 5,500 workers.
	Milwaukee Mayor Henry Maier steps down after 28 years in office—a record for big-city mayors.

DEMOGRAPHY

Population (est. 1987) . . . 4,807,000
Population (1980) 4,705,642
Population density in persons
   per square mile (1980) 83.8

POPULATION BY RACE (1980)
American Indian/Aleut/
   Eskimo 29,497
Asian/Pacific Islander 18,165
Black 182,593
Hispanic 62,981
White 4,442,598
Other 32,482

POPULATION CHARACTERISTICS (1980)
Percent of state population
Urban 64.2
Rural 35.8
Under 18 . . . . 28.9
65 or older 12.0
College-educated 14.9
Families below poverty line 6.3
Public-assistance recipients 6.1

Per capita personal income
   (1986) $13,796
Millionaires per 100,000
   residents (1982) 90.6
Average life expectancy in
   years (1980) 75.4
Marriage rate per 1,000
   residents (1986) 8.0

Divorce rate per 1,000
   residents (1986) 3.5
Birth rate per 1,000
   residents (1985) 15.3
Infant mortality rate per 1,000
   births (1985) 8.7
Abortion rate per 1,000
   live births (1985) 246
Crime rate per 100,000
   residents (1985)
   Violent 257.9
   Property 3,838.9
Federal and state prisoners per
   100,000 residents (1984) 102
Alcohol consumption in gallons
   per capita (1985) 53.2
Deaths from motor vehicle accidents
   per 100,000 residents (1985) . . 15.6

MAJOR CITIES
1984 population (est.)

Appleton	62,361
Eau Claire	53,899
Green Bay	90,003
Janesville	51,503
Kenosha	75,657
Madison	170,745
Milwaukee	620,811
Oshkosh	50,150
Racine	83,436
Waukesha	51,578

GOVERNMENT AND POLITICS

Number of US Representatives   9
Electoral votes   11

POLITICAL PARTY NOMINEES FROM STATE

Emil Seidel (Socialist)	1912	VP
Robert Marion La Follette (Progressive/Socialist)	1924	P
George A. Nelson (Socialist)	1936	VP
Douglas MacArthur (America First/Constitution)	1952	P
Georgia Cozzini (Socialist Labor)	1956	VP
Georgia Cozzini (Socialist Labor)	1960	VP
Frank Paul Zeidler (Socialist)	1976	P
William E. Dyke (American Independent)	1976	VP
Diane Drufenbrock (Socialist)	1980	VP
Patrick Joseph Lucey (Independent)	1980	VP

PRESIDENTIAL PRIMARY ELECTION In 1988, Wisconsin sent 88 Democratic delegates and 47 Republican delegates to the national conventions.

CONSTITUTION Wisconsin is using its original constitution, adopted in 1848.

LEGISLATURE The Legislature is divided into the Senate (33 members, 4-year term, minimum age 18) and the Assembly (99 members, 2-year term, minimum age 18). In 1987, the annual salary was $29,997. **JUDICIARY** The highest court is the Supreme Court, with 7 judges serving 10-year terms. In 1987, the annual salary was $76,859.

EXECUTIVE The governor serves a 4-year term; there is no minimum age for holding office. In 1987, the annual salary was $86,149. There are 5 other elected officials.

PRESIDENTIAL VOTE 1948-1988 *(in percents)*

Year	State Winner	Democratic	Republican
1948	Truman (D)	50.7	46.3
1952	Eisenhower (R)	38.7	61.0
1956	Eisenhower (R)	37.8	61.6
1960	Nixon (R)	48.1	51.8
1964	Johnson (D)	62.1	37.7
1968	Nixon (R)	44.3	47.9
1972	Nixon (R)	43.7	53.4
1976	Carter (D)	49.4	47.8
1980	Reagan (R)	43.2	47.9
1984	Reagan (R)	45.1	54.3
1988	Dukakis (D)	52.0	48.0

GOVERNORS

Territorial Governors

Henry Dodge	1836-1841
James Duane Doty	1841-1844
Nathaniel P. Tallmadge	1844-1845
Henry Dodge	1845-1848

State Governors

Nelson Dewey (D)	1848-1852
Leonard J. Farwell (Whig)	1852-1854
William A. Barstow (D)	1854-1856
Arthur MacArthur (acting)	1856
Coles Bashford (R)	1856-1858
Alexander W. Randall (R)	1858-1862
Louis P. Harvey (R)	1862
Edward P. Salomon (R)	1862-1864
James T. Lewis (R)	1864-1866
Lucius Fairchild (R)	1866-1872
Cadwallader C. Washburn (R)	1872-1874
William R. Taylor (Democratic/Greenback)	1874-1876
Harrison Ludington (R)	1876-1878
William E. Smith (R)	1878-1882
Jeremiah M. Rusk (R)	1882-1889
William D. Hoard (R)	1889-1891
George W. Peck (D)	1891-1895
William H. Upham (R)	1895-1897
Edward Scofield (R)	1897-1901
Robert M. La Follette, Sr. (R)	1901-1906
James O. Davidson (R)	1906-1911
Francis E. McGovern (R)	1911-1915
Emanuel L. Philipp (R)	1915-1921
John J. Blaine (R)	1921-1927
Fred R. Zimmerman (R)	1927-1929
Walter J. Kohler, Sr. (R)	1929-1931
Philip F. La Follette (R)	1931-1933
Albert G. Schmedeman (D)	1933-1935
Philip F. La Follette (Progressive)	1935-1939
Julius P. Heil (R)	1939-1943
Walter S. Goodland (R)	1943-1947
Oscar Rennebohm (R)	1947-1951
Walter J. Kohler, Jr. (R)	1951-1957
Vernon Thomson (R)	1957-1959
Gaylord A. Nelson (D)	1959-1963
John W. Reynolds (D)	1963-1965
Warren P. Knowles (R)	1965-1971
Patrick J. Lucey (D)	1971-1977
Martin J. Schrieber (D)	1977-1979
Lee Sherman Dreyfus (R)	1979-1983
Anthony S. Earl (D)	1983-1987
Tommy G. Thompson (R)	1987-

MINIMUM AGES

Majority	18
Marriage with parental consent	16
Marriage without parental consent	18
Making a will	18
Buying alcohol	21
Jury duty	18
Leaving school	16
Driver's license	16

CAPITAL PUNISHMENT
None

MILITARY INSTALLATIONS
Total number: 6
Major bases:
  Army: 1

FINANCES

Thousands of dollars

GENERAL REVENUE (1985)
Total general revenue . . . 8,185,352

Total tax revenue	5,066,390
Sales and gross receipts . . .	2,203,026
Individual income taxes . .	2,009,109
Corporate net income taxes . .	413,645

GENERAL EXPENDITURE (1985)

Total general expenditure .	7,993,884
Education	2,716,007
Public welfare	1,794,896
Health	311,477
Hospitals	233,185
Natural resources	151,684
Police	41,656
Corrections	186,159

FEDERAL AID (1985) 2,111,744

ECONOMY

Dairying is the biggest income-producer on Wisconsin's approximately 90,000 farms. In 1983, dairy products (primarily milk, butter, and cheese) and livestock brought in more than $4 billion of the $5.2 billion in farm marketing cash receipts. Cash crops include feed corn, peas and beans, cabbage, beets, and other vegetables, hay, berries, and apples. Sand, gravel, clays, dolomite, and iron and zinc ores are the principal products of the state's small mining industry. Heavy machinery, transportation equipment (especially cars and trucks), hardware, and metals-processing machines are among Wisconsin's important manufactures, as are processed foods (notably beer and ale), paper, rubber products, chemicals, and leather goods. Value added by manufacture was $22.6 billion in 1982.

EMPLOYMENT (1984)

Thousands of persons

Total number of employed workers	2,218
Construction	58.3
Finance, insurance, and real estate	102.2
Government	313.6
Manufacturing	517.8
Mining	1.8
Services	403.9
Transportation, communications, and utilities	89.7
Wholesale and retail trade	453.8
Percent of civilian labor force unemployed (1984)	7.3

DEPARTMENT OF DEFENSE (1985)

Civilian workers employed . . .	3,152
Military personnel	912
Contract awards	$1.065 billion

ENERGY SOURCES FOR ELECTRIC UTILITIES (1983)

Percent

Coal	69.6
Gas	0.5
Hydroelectric	5.8
Nuclear	23.6
Petroleum	0.3

TRANSPORTATION

Motor vehicles registered in state (1986)	3,120,026
Miles of roads, streets, and highways (1986)	108,667
Miles of Class I railway operated (1986)	3,647
Airports (1983)	416
Major aviation hubs (1983)	3
Largest hub: Milwaukee	

CULTURE AND EDUCATION

Native American tribes
Wisconsin was formerly home to the Noquet, Oto, Ottawa, Peoria, Sauk, Seneca, Sioux, Tobacco, Wea, and Wyandot tribes. Groups that continue to live in the state include the Ojibway, Potawatomi, and Winnebago. Groups that have been relocated to Wisconsin include the Oneida. There are 15 federal reservations in the states.

Religions, ethnicities, and languages
Early settlers came from states to the south and northeast. In the late 19th century, Wisconsin took in settlers from northern Europe, particularly Germany, Norway, Sweden, and Britain; in the early 20th century, immigrants came from eastern Europe, particularly Poland. In 1980, 5.8 percent of Wisconsin's population spoke a language other than English at home. Churchgoers are split fairly evenly between Roman Catholics and Protestants, of which the Lutherans, United Church of Christ, Methodists, and Presbyterians are the largest groups.

Major museums and libraries
Milwaukee Art Center
Milwaukee Public Museum
Museum of the State Historical Society of Wisconsin
Paine Art Center and Arboretum, Oshkosh

Major arts organizations
Florentine Opera Company, Milwaukee
Madison Symphony Orchestra
Milwaukee Repertory Theater
Milwaukee Symphony Orchestra
Pennsylvania and Milwaukee Ballet
Wisconsin Chamber Orchestra, Madison

Colleges and universities
Number public (1986-87) 29
Number private (1986-87) 33
Total enrollment, in full-time equivalent
students (1985) 211,700

Public elementary and secondary schools
Expenditure per pupil in average daily
attendance (1986-87) $4,607
Pupil-teacher ratio (1987) 16.3
Average teacher salary (1986-87) $29,000

Major league sports teams
Baseball: Milwaukee Brewers
Football: Green Bay Packers

Holidays
State Fair, West Allis. Mid-August

WISCONSIN IN LITERATURE

Waldemar Ager (trans. T. M. Ager) *Sons of the Old Country* (1926, rpt. 1984)
Novel of Norwegian immigrants in Wisconsin lumber mills before and during the Civil War.

Jerry Apps *The Land Still Lives* (1970)
Description of moving to a farm north of Madison.

Victor Barnouw (ed.) *Wisconsin Chippewa Myths and Tales and Their Relation to Chippewa Life: Based on Folktales collected by Victor Barnouw, Joseph B. Casagrande, Ernestine Friedl, and Robert E. Ritzenthaler* (1977)

August W. Derleth *Wisconsin Regional Literature* (1942)
———. *Wisconsin Earth: A Sac Prairie Sampler* (1948)
Anthology of passages from the author's numerous romantic historical novels of the Black Hawk country, the first of which was *Wind Over Wisconsin* (1938). The "Sac Prairie Saga," as Derleth's prose and verse was known, traced the history of Sauk City from 1830 to 1930. He also wrote a biography of Zona Gale, *Still Small Voice* (1940).

Charles Dickinson *Crows* (1985)
Novel about life in a small town.

Virginia S. Eifert *Journeys in Green Places: The Shores and Woods of Wisconsin's Door Peninsula* (1963)
Lyrical nature writing.

Edna Ferber *Dawn O'Hara* (1911)
The author's first novel was based on her experiences as a Milwaukee journalist. *Come and Get It* (1936) portrays the lumber industries of northern Wisconsin, and Ferber's autobiography, *A Peculiar Treasure* (1938), tells of her growing up in the state.

Zona Gale *Friendship Village* (1908); *Mothers to Men* (1911); *When I Was a Little Girl* (1913)
Short stories by a popular Wisconsin regionalist who portrayed her home town of Portage. In the novel *Miss Lulu Bett* (1920), the sentimentality of her earlier work is supplanted by an ironic realism.

Robert E. Gard *Wisconsin Is My Doorstep: A Dramatist's Yearbook of Wisconsin Lore* (1948); *Wisconsin Lore* (1962); *The Trail of the Serpent: The Fox River Valley, Lore and Legend* (1962); *This Is Wisconsin* (1969)
Collections of regional folklore and history.

Hamlin Garland *A Son of the Middle Border* (1917)
The first volume of an autobiography. Garland was born on a farm near West Salem, and based his finest work on his experience as a farm worker on the "middle border"—those portions of Wisconsin, Minnesota, Iowa, and Dakota in which he and his family lived. *Boy Life on the Prairies* (1907) also deals with his life in Wisconsin.

Walter Havighurst *The Winds of Spring* (1940)
Historical novel of pioneering, 1840–1870.

Mary E. Hazeltine *One Hundred Years of Wisconsin Authorship, 1836-1937* (1937)

Hjalmar Holland *Old Peninsula Days: Tales and Sketches of the Door County Peninsula* (1925, rpt. 1972)

Margaret Gleason *Wisconsin Folklore and Tall Tales: A Selected List* (1950)

Juliette Kinzie *Wau-Bun: The Early Day in the Northwest* (1856, rpt. 1987)
Memoir by the wife of an Indian agent describing the Winnebago uprising of 1827 and the Black Hawk War of 1832.

Henry E. Legler *Narratives of Early Wisconsin Travellers Prior to 1800* (1906)

Aldo Leopold *A Sand County Almanac* (1949)
Classic work of nature writing, consisting of seasonal observations, with a plea for recognition of the value of wilderness to civilization.

Edward Lueders *The Clam Lake Papers: A Winter in the North Woods* (1977)
Naturalist's account of living in a small cabin near Clam Lake.

John Muir *The Story of My Boyhood and Youth* (1913, rpt. 1965)
Autobiography of the great naturalist covering his years as a student at the University of Wisconsin and boyhood on a Wisconsin farm.

Jessica N. North *Morning in the Land* (1941)
Historical novel describing the founding of Milwaukee, 1840–1861.

Sterling North *Night Outlasts the Whippoorwill* (1936)
Novel set in a small town during World War I.

Harry B. Peters (ed.) *Folk Songs out of Wisconsin* (1977)

William Gray Purcell *St. Croix Trail Country: Recollections of Wisconsin* (1967)
Recollections of a late-nineteenth-century boyhood in northwestern Wisconsin.

Charles R. Rounds *Wisconsin Authors and Their Works* (1918)

Leslie E. Schlytter *The Tall Brothers* (1941)
Novel of a lumber town in the early twentieth century.

Mark Schorer *A House Too Old* (1935)
Chronicle novel of a Wisconsin town, 1835-1935.

William F. Steuber *The Landlooker* (1957)
Historical novel about Chicago and the Wisconsin frontier in 1871.

William A. Titus *Wisconsin Writers: Sketches and Studies* (1930)

Glenway Westcott *The Apple of the Eye* (1924); *The Grandmothers* (1927); *The Babe's Bed* (1930)
Westcott, a disciple of Somerset Maugham, was born on a Wisconsin farm and used rural and small-town life as settings for these novels and the collection of short stories *Goodbye Wisconsin* (1928).

Erna Oleson Xan *Wisconsin My Home: The Story of Thurine Oleson as Told to Her Daughter* (1950, rpt. 1975)
Memoir of a Norwegian immigrant.

GUIDES TO RESOURCES

Berry-Caban, Cristobal S. (comp.) *Hispanics in Wisconsin: A Bibliography of Resource Materials (1981)*

Brevet's Wisconsin Historical Markers and Sites (1974)

Collins, Charles W. *An Atlas of Wisconsin* (2d ed. 1972)

Federal Writers' Project *Wisconsin, a Guide to the Badger State* (1941, rpt. 1973)

Fleckner, John A. and Stanley Mallach (eds.) *Guide to Historical Resources in Milwaukee Area Archives* (1976)

Governor's Commission on Human Rights (comp. Joyce M. Erdman) *Handbook on Wisconsin Indians* (1966)

Hochstetter, Nancy (ed.) *Travel Historic Wisconsin: A Guide to Wisconsin's Historical Markers* (1986)

Lankevich, George J. (comp. and ed.) *Milwaukee: A Chronological and Documentary History, 1673–1977* (1977)

Paul, Justus F. and Barbara D. (eds.) *The Badger State: A Documentary History of Wisconsin* (1979)

Robinson, Arthur H., Jerry B. Cupver, et al. *The Atlas of Wisconsin* (1974)

Schlinkert, Leroy *Subject Bibliography of Wisconsin History* (1946)

Welch, N. Candia and Douglas G. Marshall *Wisconsin Upper Great Lakes Region: A Descriptive Bibliography, 1935–1968* (1968)

Wisconsin State Historical Society *Dictionary of Wisconsin Biography* (1960)

———. *Official Historical Markers of Wisconsin* (1965)

Wisconsin State Bureau of Planning and Budget *Wisconsin Statistical Abstract* (annual)

SELECTED NONFICTION SOURCES

Anderson, Harry H. and Frederick I. Olson *Milwaukee, at the Gathering of the Waters* (1981)

Austin, H. Russell *The Milwaukee Story: The Making of an American City* (rev. ed. 1957)

———. *The Wisconsin Story: The Building of a Vanguard State* (1964)

Barton, Albert O. *La Follette's Winning of Wisconsin (1894–1904)* (1922)

Barton, John R. *Rural Artists in Wisconsin* (1948)

Billington, Ray A. *Frederick Jackson Turner: Historian, Scholar, Teacher* (1973)

Clark, James I. *Chronicles of Wisconsin* (1955–1956)

———. *Wisconsin Meets the Great Depression* (1956)

———. *Henry Dodge: Frontiersman* (1957)

Conzen, Kathleen N. *Immigrant Milwaukee, 1836–1860; Accommodation and Community in a Frontier City* (1976)

Crane, Wilder and H. Clarke Hagensick *Wisconsin Government and Politics* (1976)

Current, Richard N. *The Civil War Era, 1848–1873* (1976)

———. *Wisconsin: A Bicentennial History* (States and the Nation series) (1977)

Doan, Edward N. *The La Follettes and the Wisconsin Idea* (1947)

Donoghue, James R. *Local Government in Wisconsin* (1979)

Douglas, John *The Indians in Wisconsin's History* (1954)

Dunn, James T. *The St. Croix: Midwest Border River* (Rivers of America series) (1965)

Emerson, Charles Leon *Wisconsin; Scenic and Historic Trails* (1933)

Engel, Harold A. *Wisconsin Place Names; a Pronouncing Gazetteer* (1969)

Epstein, Leon D. *Politics in Wisconsin* (1958)

Ettenheim, Sarah C. *How Milwaukee Voted, 1848–1980* (1980)

Gara, Larry *A Short History of Wisconsin* (1962)

Garber, Randy (ed.) *Built in Milwaukee* (1984)

Gard, Robert E. and L. G. Sorden *The Romance of Wisconsin Place Names* (1968)

Gray, James *Pine, Stream and Prairie; Wisconsin and Minnesota in Profile* (1945)

Griffith, Robert W., Jr. *The Politics of Fear: Joseph R. McCarthy and the Senate* (1971)

Hoan, Daniel W. *City Government; the Record of the Milwaukee Experiment* (1936)

Hoeveler, Diane L. (ed.) *Milwaukee Women Today* (1979)

———. *Milwaukee Women Yesterday* (1979)

Holmes, Frederick L. *Badger Saints and Sinners . . .* (1939)

———. *Old World Wisconsin; around Europe in the Badger State* (1944)

———. *Side Roads; Excursions into Wisconsin's Past* (1949)

Howe, Frederic C. *Wisconsin: An Experiment in Democracy* (1912)

Keesing, Felix M. *The Menomini Indians of Wisconsin* (1939, rpt. 1971)

Kellogg, Louise P. *The French Regime in Wisconsin and the Northwest* (1926, rpt. 1968)

———. *The British Regime in Wisconsin and the Northwest* (1935, rpt. 1971)

Kolehmainen, John I. *Haven in the Woods; the Story of the Finns in Wisconsin* (1951)

Lampard, Eric E. *The Rise of the Dairy Industry in Wisconsin* (1962)

Lawson, Marion *Solomon Juneau, Voyageur* (1960)

Le Sueur, Meridel *North Star Country* (1945, rpt. 1984)

Lesy, Michael *Wisconsin Death Trip* (1973)

Maney, Patrick J. *"Young Bob" La Follette: A Biography of Robert M. La Follette, Jr., 1895–1953* (1978)

Margulies, Herbert F. *The Decline of the Progressive Movement in Wisconsin, 1890–1920* (1968)

Martin, Lawrence *The Physical Geography of Wisconsin* (1916)

Mattern, Carolyn J. *Soldiers When They Go: The Story of Camp Randall, 1861–1865* (1981)

Maxwell, Robert S. (ed. Gerald E. Stearn) *La Follette* (1969)

McShane, Clay *Technology and Reform: Street Railways and the Growth of Milwaukee, 1887–1900* (1975)

Mead, Howard, Jill Dean, and Susan Smith (comps.) *Portrait of the Past; a Photographic Journey through Wisconsin* 2 vols. (1971–1973)

Merk, Frederick *Economic History of Wisconsin during the Civil War Decade* (1916)

Miller, John E. *Governor Philip F. La Follette, the Wisconsin Progressives, and the New Deal* (1982)

Nailen, R. L. and James S. Haight *Beertown Blazes: A Century of Milwaukee Firefighting* (2d ed. 1982)

Nesbit, Robert C. *Wisconsin; a History* (1973)

Nolan, Alan T. *The Iron Brigade: A Military History* (1961)

Nute, Grace L. *Lake Superior* (1944)

Ozanne, Robert W. *The Labor Movement in Wisconsin: A History* (1984)

Perrin, Richard W. *Historic Wisconsin Buildings; a Survey of Pioneer Architecture, 1835–1870* (1962)
———. *The Architecture of Wisconsin* (1967)
———. *Milwaukee Landmarks: An Architectural Heritage, 1850–1950* (1968)

Quaife, Milo M. *Wisconsin: Its History and Its People, 1634–1924* 4 vols. (1924)

Quimby, George I. *Indian Life in the Upper Great Lakes, 11,000 B.C. to A.D. 1800* (1960)

Raney, William F. *Wisconsin; a Story of Progress* . . . (1940, rpt. 1963)

Ritzenthaler, Robert E. *Prehistoric Indians of Wisconsin* (1953)

Schaefer, Joseph *A History of Agriculture in Wisconsin* (1922)
———. *The Wisconsin Lead Region* (1932)
———. *The Winnebago-Horicon Basin: A Type Study in Western History* (1937)

Schenker, Eric *The Port of Milwaukee: An Economic Review* (1967)

Schmandt, Henry I., Joan C. Goldbach, and Donald B. Vogel *Milwaukee: A Contemporary Urban Profile* (1971)

Schultz, Gwen *Wisconsin's Foundations: A Review of the State's Geology and Its Influence on Geography and Human Activity* (1986)

Smith, Alice E. *James Duane Doty: Frontier Promoter* (1954)
———. *Millstone and Saw; the Origins of Neenah-Menasha* (1966)
———. *From Exploration to Statehood* (1973)

Soltow, Lee *Patterns of Wealthholding in Wisconsin since 1850* (1971)

Still, Bayrd *Milwaukee: The History of a City* (1948)

Strang, William A. *Wisconsin's Economy in 1990: Our History, Our Present, Our Future* (1982)

Thelen, David P. *The New Citizenship; Origins of Progressivism in Wisconsin, 1885–1900* (1972)
———. *Robert M. La Follette and the Insurgent Spirit* (1976)

Thwaites, Reuben G. *Father Marquette* (1902)
———. *The French Regime in Wisconsin, 1727–48* (1906)
———. *Wisconsin; the Americanization of a French Settlement* (1908, rpt. 1973)

Titus, William A. *History of the Fox River Valley, Lake Winnebago and the Green Bay Region* 3 vols. (1930)

Trotter, Joe W., Jr. *Black Milwaukee: The Making of an Industrial Proletariat, 1915–45* (1985)

Turner, Jennie M. *Wisconsin Pioneers* (1929)

Twining, Charles E. *Downriver: Orrin H. Ingram and the Empire Lumber Company* (1975)

Walsh, Margaret *The Manufacturing Frontier; Pioneer Industry in Antebellum Wisconsin, 1830–1860* (1972)

Wekkin, Gary *Democrat versus Democrat: The National Party's Campaign to Close the Wisconsin Primary* (1984)

Wells, Robert W. *Fire at Peshtigo* (1968)
———. *This Is Milwaukee* (1970)
———. *Yesterday's Milwaukee* (1976)

Whyte, Bertha K. *Wisconsin Heritage* (1954)

Zeitlin, Richard H. *Old Abe the War Eagle: A True Story of the Civil War and Reconstruction* (1986)

WYOMING

The Mountain state of Wyoming is bordered on the north by Montana; on the east by South Dakota and Nebraska; on the south by Colorado and Utah; and on the west by Utah and Idaho.

FULL NAME State of Wyoming
POSTAL ABBREVIATION WY
INHABITANT Wyomingite
ADMITTED TO THE UNION July 10, 1890.
44th state
POPULATION (est. 1987) 490,000.
Percent of US total: 0.20%. Rank: 50th

CAPITAL CITY Cheyenne, the largest city in the state, located on Crow Creek in southeast Wyoming; population 47,283 (1980). Founded by squatters in 1867, it was incorporated and made the state capital in 1869.

STATE NAME AND NICKNAMES From a Delaware Indian term, *mecheweaming*, "at the big flats." Also known as the Equality State, the Big Wyoming State, and the Cowboy State.

STATE SEAL The figure of a woman in Greek dress, holding a banner with the legend "Equal Rights," and standing on a pedestal bearing an eagle and a shield, on which is a star with the number 44; on either side, pillars holding lamps of knowledge and

entwined with banners reading "Livestock," "Grain," "Mines," and "Oil"; on the left a rancher, on the right a miner, at the bottom the legend "1869-1890." The border reads "Great Seal of the State of Wyoming."

MOTTO Equal Rights

SONG "Wyoming," lyrics by Charles E. Winter, music by George E. Knapp.

SYMBOLS
Flower Indian paintbrush
Tree cottonwood
Bird meadowlark
Gem jade

LICENSE PLATE Red on white, with state name in blue and blue legend "Centennial, 1890-1990," a silhouette of white mountains against blue sky, and a red horse with rider.

FLAG A field of blue, with a border of white and an outer border of red; in the center, a white silhouette of a buffalo, bearing the state seal in blue.

GEOGRAPHY AND CLIMATE

The Rockies dominate Wyoming's physiography. More than a dozen north-south ranges rise from the western part of the state, including the Tetons, the Wind River Range, and the Big Horn Mountains. Although primarily a mountain state, Wyoming also contains a vast area of Great Plains in the eastern quarter. Wyoming's spectacular geography includes the US's best-known national parks: Yellowstone and Grand Teton, as well as the Flaming Gorge on the Green River and scores of glaciers in the major mountain ranges.

AREA 97,809 square miles. Rank: 9th
INLAND WATER 820 square miles
GEOGRAPHIC CENTER Fremont, 58 miles ENE of Lander
ELEVATIONS *Highest point:* Gannett Peak, Fremont County, 13,804 feet. *Lowest point:* B. Fouche River, Crook County, 3,100 feet. *Mean elevation:* 6,700 feet

MAJOR RIVERS North Platte, Bighorn, Green, Snake, Yellowstone, Powder

MAJOR LAKES AND RESERVOIRS Yellowstone, Bighorn, Jackson, Flaming Gorge, Pathfinder, Seminoe

LAND USE
Thousands of acres
Urban (1982) 148
Rural (1982) 32,240
Cropland (1982) 2,587
Pastureland (1982) 755
Rangeland (1982) 26,915
Forestland (1982) 987
State parks and recreation
 areas (1983) 123
National park system (1984) . . 2,392
National forest system (1984) . . 9,717
Tribal lands (1984) 1,793

TEMPERATURES The highest recorded temperature was 114°F on January 12, 1900, at Basin. The lowest was -63°F on February 9, 1933, at Moran.

NATIONAL SITES

NATIONAL HISTORIC SITE Fort Laramie
NATIONAL HISTORIC TRAILS Mormon Pioneer, Oregon
NATIONAL MONUMENTS Devils Tower, Fossil Butte
NATIONAL PARKS Grand Teton, Yellowstone
NATIONAL RECREATION AREAS Bighorn Canyon, Flaming Gorge
NATIONAL WILDLIFE REFUGES Bamforth, Hutton Lake, National Elk Refuge, Pathfinder, Seedskadee

HISTORY

1743   *January.* Two sons of Pierre Gaultier de Varennes, Sieur de La Vérendrye, sight what was probably the Big Horn Mountains of present-day Montana and Wyoming.
1807–1808   Fur trapper John Colter travels extensively in the Wyoming region, reaching as far west as the Yellowstone area.
1811   An expedition under Wilson Price Hunt crosses Wyoming on its way to the Pacific Ocean.
1812   Traveling west to east, Robert Stuart discovers South Pass, later part of the Oregon Trail.
1824   William Ashley leads a party of 43 traders and trappers that includes such famous mountain men as Jim Bridger, Thomas Fitzpatrick, and Jedediah Smith.
1834   Traders Robert Campbell and William Sublette build a fur-trading post that later becomes the US Army's Fort Laramie.
1842   Jim Bridger and Louis Vásquez build Fort Bridger in southwestern Wyoming, later leasing it to the government.
1848   The Treaty of Guadalupe Hidalgo, ending the Mexican War, puts all of present-day Wyoming in US possession. Parts of Wyoming had earlier passed into US hands by the Louisiana Purchase (1803), the annexation of Texas (1845), and the Anglo-American agreement of 1846.
1849   Following the discovery of gold in California, 22,000 people pass through Wyoming on the California and Oregon trails.
1851   The first Fort Laramie treaty creates boundaries within Wyoming for the Sioux, Crow, Cheyenne, and Arapaho.

1854	Thirty soldiers are killed by Sioux near Fort Laramie.
1864	Congress awards huge land grants to the Union Pacific Railroad to build part of a transcontinental rail line; 4,582,520 acres of the grant are in Wyoming.
1866	*December 21.* Sioux warriors, led by Red Cloud and Crazy Horse, ambush and massacre 80 soldiers in north-central Wyoming.
1867	Major gold discovery is made in South Pass.
	The Union Pacific Railroad enters Wyoming.
	Cheyenne, the first settlement, has perhaps 6,000 residents by the end of the year.
1868	*July 25.* Wyoming Territory is created by the Wyoming Organic Act, comprising the present state's borders. Cheyenne becomes the capital.
	December. The Union Pacific rail line is completed through Wyoming.
	By the terms of the second Fort Laramie treaty, the Sioux in Wyoming are to be moved east to the Dakotas, but northeastern Wyoming is made an Indian hunting ground off limits to whites. The Shoshone agree to move to a reservation east of Wind River, to which the Arapaho are also moved in 1877.
1869	*October 12.* Wyoming's first legislature convenes in Cheyenne.
	December 10. Women (outnumbered six to one by men) are given the right to vote and hold office. In honor of this event, this date is celebrated annually as Wyoming Day.
1872	Yellowstone National Park is created, the first US national park.
1876	A new treaty opens northeastern Wyoming to white settlement.
1880	The population of Wyoming Territory is 20,789, of which half live in seven towns along the Union Pacific rail line. Three coal mines yield 527,814 tons, mostly for the railroad.
1884	The Union Pacific starts to sell large quantities of its land at an average price of $1 an acre.
1885	*September 2.* Eighty-five Chinese coal miners are killed by a mob in Rock Springs and hundreds more chased out. Federal troops sent to restore order remain until 1898.
1885–1886	At the peak of the cattle boom, Wyoming has about 1.5 million cattle grazing.
1887	The University of Wyoming opens in Laramie with a faculty of seven and a student body of 42.
1890	*July 10.* Wyoming is admitted to the Union as the 44th state.
1892	Big cattlemen hire gunmen to eliminate small ranchers and homesteaders suspected of rustling cattle. The Johnson County War culminates in their unsuccessful attempt to storm Buffalo.
1895	Cody established and named for William F. Cody (Buffalo Bill), who shot bison to feed railroad workers in Wyoming before organizing his Wild West show.
1897	First Frontier Days celebration in Cheyenne, featuring what becomes the world's oldest and biggest rodeo.
1897–1909	Sixteen men and perhaps 10,000 sheep are killed by cattlemen unwilling to share the open range. By the end of this period, however, Wyoming's six million sheep outnumber cattle seven to one, and Wyoming leads all states in wool.
1905	The Shoshone and Arapaho relinquish 1,346,320 acres of their reservation, which become available for white settlement.
1906	Devils Tower becomes the first national monument.
1921	The number of homestead entries reaches a peak of 15,044, covering 5,145,427 acres. Much of this land is later abandoned or sold.
1922	The 9,481-acre federal Teapot Dome oil reserve is leased without competitive bidding, leading to a major scandal.
1923	Forty-four million barrels of oil are produced in Wyoming—the peak production for many years.
1924	Thirty-five of Wyoming's 120 banks close, victims of low, post–World War I farm prices.
1925	Nellie Tayloe Ross takes office as the first woman governor in the United States.
1929	*November 24.* Death of Francis E. Warren, senator from Wyoming for a record 37 years.
	Creation of Grand Teton National Park.

1933	One Wyoming resident in five is receiving some form of relief during the Great Depression. The unemployed number 20,000.
1935	A two percent sales tax is adopted.
1942–1945	A World War II relocation center for persons of Japanese birth or ancestry houses a population of 10,872 in the Heart Mountain area of northwestern Wyoming.
1945	Total cash receipts from farming and ranching have doubled since 1939.
1952	Mining and refining of trona for soda ash begins in Sweetwater County, supplying most of the nation's output.
1960	With 1,357,225 tons, Wyoming is second in the production of uranium ore.
1962	US Steel completes an iron-ore mine and mill complex at South Pass.
1963	A right-to-work law abolishes the closed shop.
1965	Completion of the installation of Minuteman intercontinental ballistic missiles at Warren Air Force Base, near Cheyenne.
1968	Voters approve a constitutional amendment establishing the initiative and referendum.
1969	A mineral severance tax of one percent is adopted.
1970	Peak oil production of 160 million barrels places Wyoming fifth among states.
1980	Population has grown 41 percent in the 1970s, from 332,416 to 469,557, chiefly because of a surge in demand for the state's energy resources.
1981	The unemployment rate of 3.7 percent is the second lowest among states.
1983	Amtrak discontinues passenger trains through Wyoming, leaving the state without passenger rail service.
1986	Wyoming, with six of the nation's 10 biggest coal mines (all strip mines), is second in coal production with 136.8 million tons.
	Installation of the nation's first operational MX intercontinental ballistic missiles, at Warren Air Force Base.

DEMOGRAPHY

Population (est. 1987) 490,000
Population (1980) 469,557
Population density in persons
   per square mile (1980) 4.8

POPULATION BY RACE (1980)
American Indian/Aleut/
   Eskimo 7,125
Asian/Pacific Islander 1,969
Black 3,364
Hispanic 24,499
White 447,716
Other 10,642

POPULATION CHARACTERISTICS (1980)
Percent of state population
Urban 62.7
Rural 37.3
Under 18 . . . . 30.0
65 or older 7.9
College-educated 17.2
Families below poverty line 5.8
Public-assistance recipients 1.9

Per capita personal income
   (1986) $13,230
Millionaires per 100,000
   residents (1982) 254.9

Average life expectancy in
   years (1980) 73.9
Marriage rate per 1,000
   residents (1986) 10.5
Divorce rate per 1,000
   residents (1986) 7.0
Birth rate per 1,000
   residents (1985) 17.4
Infant mortality rate per 1,000
   births (1985) 8.0
Abortion rate per 1,000
   live births (1985) 125
Crime rate per 100,000
   residents (1985)
   Violent 293.0
   Property 4,064.1
Federal and state prisoners per
   100,000 residents (1984) 137
Alcohol consumption in gallons
   per capita (1985) 45.6
Deaths from motor vehicle accidents
   per 100,000 residents (1985) . . 29.9

MAJOR CITIES

	Population
Casper (est. 1984)	49,588
Cheyenne (1980)	47,283
Laramie (1980)	24,410
Rock Springs (1980)	19,458

GOVERNMENT AND POLITICS

Number of US Representatives   1
Electoral votes   3

POLITICAL PARTY NOMINEES FROM STATE

None

PRESIDENTIAL PRIMARY ELECTION In 1988, Wyoming sent 18 Democratic delegates and 18 Republican delegates to the national conventions.
CONSTITUTION Wyoming is using its original constitution, adopted in 1889.
LEGISLATURE The Legislature is divided into the Senate (30 members, 4-year term, minimum age 25) and the House of Representatives (64 members, 2-year term, minimum age 21). In 1987, the salary of legislators was $75 per day.
JUDICIARY The highest court is the Supreme Court, with 5 judges serving 8-year terms. In 1987, the annual salary was $63,500.
EXECUTIVE The governor serves a 4-year term; the minimum age for holding office is 30. In 1987, the annual salary was $70,000. There are 4 other elected officials.

PRESIDENTIAL VOTE 1948-1988 *(in percents)*

Year	State Winner	Democratic	Republican
1948	Truman (D)	51.6	47.3
1952	Eisenhower (R)	37.1	62.7
1956	Eisenhower (R)	39.9	60.1
1960	Nixon (R)	45.0	55.0
1964	Johnson (D)	56.6	43.4
1968	Nixon (R)	35.5	55.8
1972	Nixon (R)	30.5	69.0
1976	Ford (R)	39.8	59.3
1980	Reagan (R)	28.0	62.6
1984	Reagan (R)	27.7	69.1
1988	Bush (R)	39.0	61.0

GOVERNORS

Territorial Governors

John A. Campbell	1869-1875
John M. Thayer	1875-1878
John W. Hoyt	1878-1882
William Hale	1882-1885
Francis E. Warren	1885-1886
George W. Baxter	1886
Thomas Moonlight	1887-1889
Francis E. Warren	1889-1890

State Governors

Francis E. Warren (R)	1890
Amos W. Barber (R/acting)	1890-1891
John E. Osborne (D)	1893-1895
William A. Richards (R)	1895-1899
De Forest Richards (R)	1899-1903
Fenimore Chatterton (R/ acting)	1903-1905
Bryant B. Brooks (R)	1905-1911
Joseph M. Carey (D)	1911-1915
John B. Kendrick (D)	1915-1917
Frank L. Houx (D/acting)	1917-1919
Robert D. Carey (R)	1919-1923
William B. Ross (D)	1923-1924
Frank E. Lucas (R/acting)	1924-1925
Nellie Tayloe Ross (D)	1925-1927
Frank C. Emerson (R)	1927-1931
Alonzo M. Clark (R/acting)	1931-1933
Leslie A. Miller (D)	1933-1939
Nels H. Smith (R)	1939-1943
Lester C. Hunt (D)	1943-1949
Arthur Griswold Crane (R/ acting)	1949-1951
Frank A. Barrett (R)	1951-1953
C. J. Rogers (R/acting)	1953-1955
Milward L. Simpson (R)	1955-1959
J. J. Hickey (D)	1959-1961
Jack R. Gage (D/acting)	1961-1963
Clifford P. Hansen (R)	1963-1967
Stanley K. Hathaway (R)	1967-1975
Ed Herschler (D)	1975-1987
Mike Sullivan (D)	1987-

MINIMUM AGES

Majority	19
Marriage with parental consent . . .	16
Marriage without parental consent .	19
Making a will	19
Buying alcohol	21
Jury duty	19
Leaving school	16
Driver's license	16

CAPITAL PUNISHMENT
Number executed 1976-88: 0
On death row Aug. 1, 1988: 3

MILITARY INSTALLATIONS
Total number: 3

FINANCES

Thousands of dollars

GENERAL REVENUE (1985)
Total general revenue   . . . 1,704,131
Total tax revenue   806,416
Sales and gross receipts 230,151
Individual income taxes 0
Corporate net income taxes 0

GENERAL EXPENDITURE (1985)
Total general expenditure . 1,364,564
Education 418,049
Public welfare 89,584
Health 32,444
Hospitals 27,753
Natural resources 46,823
Highways 295,229
Police 13,019
Corrections 18,870

FEDERAL AID (1985)   503,437

ECONOMY

Wyoming's ranches produced $478 million in livestock marketings receipts in 1983; total farm marketings were $593 million. Cattle are the dominant stock, followed by horses and poultry; cash crops, such as wheat, hay, oats, corn, barley, alfalfa, sugar beets, and potatoes, are used primarily for feed. Mining brings more income to the state than any other industry; oil, coal, natural gas, uranium (Wyoming is the nation's major supplier), iron ore, and sand and gravel are the important mineral products. The value of mineral shipments and receipts was $8.2 billion in 1982. Processed minerals and processed foods are the major contributors to the state's manufacturing sector; electronic instruments are also an important product.

EMPLOYMENT (1984)
Thousands of persons
Total number of employed
  workers 238
Construction 13.0
Finance, insurance, and
  real estate 8.0
Government 49.7
Manufacturing 8.3
Mining 27.2
Services 32.2
Transportation, communications,
  and utilities 15.9
Wholesale and retail trade 44.7

Percent of civilian labor force
  unemployed (1984) 6.3

DEPARTMENT OF DEFENSE (1985)
Civilian workers employed . . . 1,078
Military personnel 3,747
Contract awards . . . . . $125 million

ENERGY SOURCES FOR ELECTRIC UTILITIES (1983)
Percent
Coal 95.4
Gas 0.0
Hydroelectric 4.4
Nuclear 0.0
Petroleum 0.2

TRANSPORTATION
Motor vehicles registered
  in state (1986) 440,155
Miles of roads, streets,
  and highways (1986) 38,931
Miles of Class I railway
  operated (1986) 1,993
Airports (1983) 104
Major aviation hubs (1983) 0

CULTURE AND EDUCATION

Native American tribes
Wyoming was formerly the home of the Bannock, Cheyenne, Comanche, Crow, Sioux, Spokane, and Ute tribes. Groups that continue to live in the state include the Arapaho and Northern Shoshoni. There is one federal reservation in Wyoming.

Religions, ethnicities, and languages
The majority of Wyoming's population is descended from settlers of European stock who came from the Midwest and Texas. There are cultural communities of Scandinavians, Italians, Germans, and Mexicans. Some 18 percent of the state's churchgoers are Roman Catholic; another 6 percent belong to the Church of Jesus Christ of Latter-day Saints (Mormons); and the rest belong mainly to Protestant denominations, of which the Methodist, Episcopalian, Presbyterian, and Lutheran churches are the most populous. In 1980, 6.3 per-

cent of Wyoming's population spoke a language other than English at home.

Major museums and libraries
Buffalo Bill Museum, Cody
Plains Indian Museum, Cody
Winchester Museum, Cody
Wyoming Pioneer Museum, Douglas

Major arts organizations
Casper Civic Symphony
Casper Symphony Association
Cheyenne Choral Society
Cheyenne Symphony Orchestra

Colleges and universities
Number public (1986-87) 8
Number private (1986-87) 3
Total enrollment, in full-time equivalent students (1985) 17,000

Public elementary and secondary schools
Expenditure per pupil in average daily attendance (1986-87) $6,253
Pupil-teacher ratio (1987) 14.0
Average teacher salary (1986-87) $28,230

Holidays
State Fair, Douglas. Late August

WYOMING IN LITERATURE

Floyd C. Bard (ed. Agnes W. Spring) *Horse Wrangler's Sixty Years in the Saddle in Wyoming and Montana* (1960)
Memoir of the life of a Wyoming cattleman and rancher in the late nineteenth and early twentieth centuries.

Maxwell S. Burt *The Diary of a Dude Wrangler* (1924)
Memoir by a popular regional writer of the 1920s and '30s who also wrote the nonfiction study *Powder River: Let'er Buck* (1939, rpt. 1971).

Sally Carrighar *One Day at Teton Marsh* (1947)
Essay on the ecology and wildlife of a pond near Jackson Hole.

Margaret I. S. Carrington *Ab-sa-ra-ka, Land of Massacre: Being the Experience of an Officer's Wife on the Plains* (1975)
Journal written in 1878 giving an account of army life, Indian warfare, and the events leading up to the Fetterman massacre.

James Chisholm (ed. Lola M. Homsher) *South Pass, 1868: James Chisholm's Journal of the Wyoming Gold Rush* (1960)
Detailed account of mining camp life by a Chicago journalist.

Ella E. Clark *Indian Legends from the Northern Rockies* (1966, rpt. 1988)

Peggy S. Curry *Oil Patch* (1959)
Novel set in an oil drilling camp in the late 1930s.

Gretel Ehrlich *The Solace of Open Spaces* (1985)
Account of the landscape and people of the high plains country.

Howard Fast *The Last Frontier* (1941)
Fictional account of the flight to Wyoming of a band of Cherokee Indians in 1878.

John Charles Frémont *Report on the Exploring Expedition to the Rocky Mountains in the Year 1842* . . . (1845)
The earliest descriptions of the Wind River Range.

Zane Grey *U. P. Trail* (1918)
Fictional account of the building of the Union Pacific Railroad across Wyoming in the late 1860s.

Grace R. Hebard *Washakie* (1930)
Historical narrative of Indian resistance to white incursions and the railroad.

Donald Hough *Snow Above Town* (1943); *The Cocktail Hour in Jackson Hole* (1956)
Sketches of life in the Grand Tetons.

Emerson Hough *Story of the Cowboy* (1897)
First of several novels set in Wyoming by a writer who specialized in romantic portrayals of westward migration. His best-known work was *The Covered Wagon* (1922), about the Oregon Trail.

Washington Irving *The Adventures of Captain Bonneville* (1837, rpt. 1961)
Narrative of an expedition to the northwestern states (1832-1835) undertaken by the West Point graduate Louis de Bonneville, and composed by Irving from his papers.

Dean F. Krakel *The Saga of Tom Horn: The Story of a Cattlemen's War* (1988)
Novel set in southern Wyoming in the 1890s.

John McPhee *Rising from the Plains* (1986)
Essay on the geology of the state, with a portrait of David Love, Rocky Mountain geologist.

Asa Shinn Mercer *The Banditti of the Plains, or the Cattleman's Invasion of Wyoming in 1892: The Crowning Infamy of the Ages* (1894, rpt. 1983)
Homesteader's protest against the incursions of ranchers.

Olaus and **Margaret E. Murie** *Wapiti Wilderness* (1966, rpt. 1985)
Account of the naturalist authors' lives in Jackson Hole and the Grand Tetons.

Edgar Wilson Nye (ed. T. A. Larson) *Bill Nye's Western Humor* (1968); *The Best of Bill Nye's Humor* (1973)
Nye, the first Wyoming author to gain a national reputation, began work on a Laramie newspaper in 1876. His humorous journalism, collected in book form in the 1880s, is in the tradition of sagebrush philosophy.

Mary O'Hara *My Friend Flicka* (1941); *Thunderhead* (1943); *The Green Grass of Wyoming* (1946)
Classic works for young adults on the wild horse of the West written on a Wyoming ranch.

Ted Olson *Ranch on the Laramie* (1972)
Memoir of a ranch upbringing before World War I.

Tillie Olsen *Yonnondio: From the Thirties* (1974)
Unfinished novel, set in the 1920s and written in the '30s, that traces a poor family's attempts to make a living mining and farming in Wyoming.

Elizabeth Page *Wild Horses and Gold* (1936)
Story of Sheriff F. B. Wickwire of Big Horn County, who drove a herd of seventy horses from the Big Horn Basin to the Klondike during the gold rush of 1899.

Francis Parkman *The Oregon Trail* (1847)
Journal of the naturalist and explorer's life among the Indians.

John K. Rollinson *Pony Trails in Wyoming: Hoofprints of a Cowboy and US Ranger* (1989)
The author, a runaway from New York, joined a cattle ranch in 1890 and later became a park ranger.

Jack Schaefer *Shane* (1949, rpt. 1984)
Classic western about the struggle between cattlemen and homesteaders in the 1890s. Other westerns with Wyoming settings include Louis L'Amour *Bendigo Shafter* (1979); Ernest Haycox *Deep West* (1937); and James Boyd *Bitter River* (1939).

John Seelye *The Kid* (1982)
Novel set in a cowtown in the 1890s.

Elinore P. Stewart *Letters of a Woman Homesteader* (1914, rpt. 1988)
The author took up homesteading in Burnt Cork, south-

western Wyoming, in 1909. A sequel is entitled *Letters on an Elk Hunt.*

Mae and **Jerry Urbanek** *Know Wyoming, a Guide to Its Literature* (1969)

Owen Wister *The Virginian* (1902)
The Philadelphia-born author based the opening chapter of

his classic western novel, the first of its kind, on his experience of Medicine Bow in 1885.

Ann Zwinger *Run, River, Run* (1975)
Narrative of an expedition on the Green River from its source in the Wind River Range to its confluence with the Colorado in Utah.

GUIDES TO RESOURCES

Bonney, Orrin H. *Guide to Wyoming Mountain and Wilderness Areas* (3d ed. 1977)

Brown, Robert Harold *Wyoming Occupance Atlas* (1970)

Davis, Lynne and **Meade** *Jackson Hole from A to Z: Names, Places, Fact and Myth* (1979)

Day, Alan E. *Search for the Northwest Passage: An Annotated Bibliography* (1986)

Federal Writers' Project *Wyoming: A Guide to Its History, Highways, and People* (1941, rpt. 1981)

Fritz, William *Roadside Geology of the Yellowstone Country* (1985)

The Historical Encyclopedia of Wyoming 2 vols. (1970)

Martner, Brooks E. *Wyoming Climate Atlas* (1986)

Roberts, David L. and **Phil** *Wyoming Almanac* (1988)

Trenholm, Virginia Cole (ed.) *Wyoming Blue Book* (1974)

University of Wyoming. Division of Business and Economic Research *Wyoming Data Book* (annual)

Wilson, D. Ray *Wyoming Historical Tour Guide* (1984)

SELECTED NONFICTION SOURCES

Alter, J. Cecil *James Bridger* (rev. ed. 1962, rpt. 1973)

Athearn, Robert G. *Union Pacific Country* (1971)

Bancroft-Hunt, Norman *People of the Totem: The Indians of The Pacific Northwest* (1988)

Bartlett, Richard A. *Nature's Yellowstone* (1974)

Bauer, Clyde M. *Yellowstone: Its Underwood* (1963)

Beal, Merrill D. *"I Will Fight No More Forever": Chief Joseph and the Nez Percé War* (1966)

Beale, Merrill *The Story of Man in Yellowstone* (1949, 1956, 1960)

Betts, Robert B. *Along the Ramparts of the Tetons; the Saga of Jackson Hole, Wyoming* (1978)

Blair, Karen J. *Women in The Pacific Northwest: An Anthology* (1988)

Bragg, Bill *Wyoming's Wealth: A History of Wyoming* (1976)

Brink, Beverley E. *Wyoming, Land of Echoing Canyons* (1986)

Brown, Dee *The Felterman Massacre* (1971)

Brown, Robert H. *Wyoming: A Geography* (1980)

Buerge, David *Seattle in the 1880s* (1986)

Burns, Robert H., A. S. Gillespie, and **W. G. Richardson** *Wyoming's Pioneer Ranches* (1955)

Burroughs, John R. *Guardian of the Grasslands, the First Hundred Years of the Wyoming Stock Growers Association* (1971)

Burt, Maxwell S. *Powder River: Let 'er Buck* (Rivers of America series) (1939, rpt. 1971)

Burt, Nathaniel *Jackson Hole Journal* (1983)

Calkins, Frank J. *Jackson Hole* (1973)

Combs, Barry B. *Westward to Promontory; Building the Union Pacific across the Plains and Mountains* (1969)

Crandall, Hugh (ed. Gweneth DenDooven) *Grand Teton: The Story behind the Scenery* (1978)

Dodds, Gordon B. *The American Northwest: A History of Oregon and Washington* (1986)

Drucker, Philip *Indians of the Northwest Coast* (1963)

Drury, Clifford M. *Marcus Whitman, M.D.: Pioneer and Martyr* (1937)
———. *Elkanah and Mary Walker: Pioneers among the Spokones* (1940)

Edwards, G. Thomas and **Carlos A. Schwantes** (eds.) *Experiences in a Promised Land: Essays in Pacific Northwest History* (1986)

Fowler, Loretta *Arapahoe Politics, 1851–1978: Symbols in Crises of Authority* (1982)

Friedheim, Robert L. *The Seattle General Strike* (1964)

Gage, Jack R. *Geography of Wyoming* (1940)

Gilmore, John S. and **Mary K. Duff** *Boom Town Growth Management: A Case Study of Rock Springs–Green River, Wyoming* (1975)

Gorzalka, Ann *The Saddlemakers of Sheridan, Wyoming* (1984)

Gould, Lewis L. *Wyoming: A Political History, 1868–1896* (1968)

Gowans, Fred R. and **Eugene E. Campbell** *Fort Bridger: Island in the Wilderness* (1975)

Hafen, LeRoy R. and **F. M. Young** *Fort Laramie and the Pageant of the West, 1834–1890* (1938)

Haines, Aubrey *Yellowstone National Park, Its Exploration and Establishment* (1974)

Harris, Burton *John Colter, His Years in the Rockies* (1952)

Hedren, Paul L. *Fort Laramie in 1876: Chronicle of a Frontier Post at War* (1988)

Hendrickson, Gordon O. *Peopling the High Plains: Wyoming's European Heritage* (1977)

Henry, John Frazier *Early Maritime Artists of the Pacific Northwest Coast, 1741–1841* (1984)

Janetski, Joel C. *The Indians of Yellowstone Park* (1987)

Kirk, Ruth and **Richard D. Daugherty** *Exploring Washington Archaeology* (1978)

Lain, Gayle and **Sheryl** *Wyoming, the Proud Land* (1968)

Langford, Nathaniel P. *The Discovery of Yellowstone Park* (1972)

Larson, T. A. *History of Wyoming* (2d ed. rev. 1978)

Lavender, David *Land of Giants: The Drive to the Pacific Northwest, 1750–1950* (1958)
———. *Fort Laramie and the Changing Frontier* (1984)

League of Women Voters of Wyoming *A Look at Wyoming Government* (4th ed. rev. 1979)

LeWarne, Charles P. *Washington State* (1986)

Linford, Velma *Wyoming, Frontier State* (1947)

MacDonald, Norbert *Distant Neighbors* (1988)

Marler, George D. *The Story of Old Faithful* (1953)

McFeat, Tom (ed.) *Indians of the North Pacific Coast* (1966)

Mead, Jean *Wyoming in Profile* (1982)

Miller, Donald C. *Ghost Towns of Wyoming* (1977, rpt. 1982)

Moore, Vandi *Brands on the Boswell: A Narrative History of One of Wyoming's Earliest Ranches* (1986)

Munkres, Robert L. *Saleratus and Sagebrush: The Oregon Trail through Wyoming* (1974)

Murray, Robert A. *Military Posts in the Powder River Country of Wyoming, 1865–1894* (1968)
———. *Military Posts of Wyoming* (1974)

Nadeau, Remi A. *Fort Laramie and the Sioux Indians* (1967)

Richard, John B. *Government and Politics of Wyoming* (2d ed. 1969)

Richards, Kent D. *Isaac I. Stevens: Young Man in a Hurry* (1979)

Robbins, William G., Robert J. Frank, and Richard E. Ross (eds.) *Regionalism and the Pacific Northwest* (1983)

Rollinson, John K. *Wyoming Cattle Trails, History of the Migration of Oregon-Raised Herds to Mid-Western Markets* (1948)

Sandoval, Judith H. et al. *Historic Ranches of Wyoming* (1986)

Smith, Helena H. *The War on Powder River* (1967)

Thybony, Scott, Robert G. Rosenberg, and Elizabeth M. Rosenberg *The Medicine Bows: Wyoming's Mountain Country* (1985)

Urbanek, Mae *Wyoming Wonderland* (1964)
———. *Wyoming Place Names* (1974, rpt. 1987)

Vannoy-Rhoades, Cynthia *Seasons on a Ranch* (1986)

Vestal, Stanley *Jim Bridger: Mountain Man* (1970)

Vinton, Stallo *John Colter, Discoverer of Yellowstone Park* (1926)

Wall, J. Tom *Crossing Old Trails to New in North Central Wyoming* (1973)

Wasden, David J. *From Beaver to Oil: A Century in the Development of Wyoming's Big Horn Basin* (1972)

Williams, Roger L. *Aven Nelson of Wyoming* (1984)

Wirther, Oscar O. *The Great Northwest: A History* (1952)

Woodbridge, Sally B. and Roger Montgomery *A Guide to Architecture in Washington State: An Environmental Perspective* (1980)

Woods, L. Milton *The Wyoming Country before Statehood; Four Hundred Years under Six Flags* (1971)
———. *Sometimes the Books Froze: Wyoming's Economy and Its Banks* (1985)

Wright, Gary A. *People of the High Country: Jackson Hole before the Settlers*

Wyoming Natural Resources Research Institute *Wyoming Weather Facts* (1966)

Wyoming 75th Anniversary Commission *Wyoming: The 75th Year* (1965)

WASHINGTON, DISTRICT OF COLUMBIA

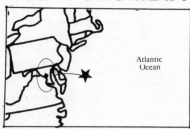

The municipal corporation of Washington, D.C., capital of the United States, is a unique entity, neither state nor city. Located on the western border of Maryland, at the junction of the Potomac and Anacostia rivers, it is bounded on the northwest, northeast, and southeast by Maryland and on the west and southwest by the Potomac River and Virginia.

FULL NAME Washington, District of Columbia

POSTAL ABBREVIATION DC

INHABITANT Washingtonian

FOUNDED 1791, site selected by President Washington; capital transferred from Philadelphia in 1800.

POPULATION (est. 1987) 626,000.

NAME AND NICKNAMES Named in honor of George Washington and Christopher Columbus. Also known as D.C., the District.

SEAL A figure of Justice laying a wreath before a statue of George Washington; in the background are the Capitol Building and an American eagle.

MOTTO Justitia Omnibus (Justice to all)

SYMBOLS
Flower American beauty rose
Tree scarlet oak
Bird wood thrush

LICENSE PLATE Blue on white, with legend "A Capital City," two red horizontal stripes, and in the center two red bars topped by three red stars.

GEOGRAPHY AND CLIMATE

Washington, D.C. is located in a once-swampy depression on the east bank of the Potomac. The District is famous for its unusually hot, humid summers and cold, damp winters.

AREA 68.25 square miles
INLAND WATER 6 square miles
GEOGRAPHIC CENTER 4th and L Streets, NW part of the city
ELEVATIONS *Highest point:* Tenleytown, in the NW, 410 feet. *Lowest point:* Potomac River, 1 foot. *Mean elevation:* 150 feet

MAJOR RIVERS Potomac, Anacostia

MAJOR LAKES AND RESERVOIRS None

LAND USE Washington is completely urban and is the center of a metropolitan area that includes parts of Maryland and Virginia. The federal government and organizations that are tax-exempt own more than half its land.

TEMPERATURES The highest recorded temperature was 106° F on July 20, 1930. The lowest was -15° F on February 11, 1899.

NATIONAL SITES

NATIONAL CEMETERY Battleground
NATIONAL HISTORIC SITES Ford's Theatre, Sewall-Belmont House, M. McLeod Bethune Council House, Old Post Office Tower, Pennsylvania Avenue
NATIONAL HISTORICAL PARK Chesapeake and Ohio Canal
NATIONAL MALL National Mall
NATIONAL MEMORIALS Lincoln Memorial, Lyndon Baines Johnson Memorial Grove

on the Potomac, John F. Kennedy Center for Performing Arts, Theodore Roosevelt Island, Thomas Jefferson Memorial, Washington Monument
NATIONAL SCENIC TRAIL Potomac Heritage
OTHER PARKS Constitution Gardens, Frederick Douglass Home, Rock Creek Park, Vietnam Veterans Memorial
WHITE HOUSE

HISTORY

1608	English captain and colonizer John Smith sails past the future District of Columbia to Little Falls.
1612	Smith publishes a topographical map showing the Indian town of Nacotchtant, the region's first recorded settlement.
1622	British trader Henry Fleet involuntarily becomes D.C.'s first white resident when he is held captive by Indians for several years.
1662	George Thompson gets first D.C. land patent from Maryland.
1700s	Scotch and Irish fur trappers hunt in the region. Farmers, mainly from the British Isles, build homes along the east side of the Potomac River.
1749	George Washington helps lay out Alexandria on the west side of the Potomac River.
1783	The Continental Congress decides to establish a permanent federal city for its meetings, yet the exact location is debated due to slavery issues.
1791	With congressional approval, George Washington selects present D.C. site for the Capital. Major Charles P. L'Enfant commissioned to design the city.
1792	L'Enfant is dismissed. Surveyor Andrew Ellicott and, briefly, mathematician Benjamin Benneker interpret and redesign L'Enfant's original plans.
1793	Construction of the Capitol, designed by William Thornton, begins.
1798	Construction of the White House begins. James Hoban is the original architect.
1800	*June.* The government moves from Philadelphia to Washington. *November 17.* Congress holds first meeting in the White House. *December 1.* The District is officially named the nation's capital.
1802	The public-elected city council receives sole power to select mayor.
1809	Washington-Alexandria bridge is opened.
1812–1814	War of 1812. British capture and burn Washington.
1815	*February 17.* Treaty ending the war is ratified.
1817	President James Monroe occupies the reconstructed White House burned by the British.
1835	The Baltimore and Ohio Railroad reaches Washington.

1836	The Smithsonian Institution is founded.
1842	English novelist Charles Dickens dubs Washington "the City of Magnificent Intentions."
1844	The first telegraph message is sent from Washington to Baltimore.
1848	Seventy-six Washington house-slaves escape with abolitionists on the *Pearl*, but the small vessel is later captured.
1860	Washington's population is 18 percent black.
1861–1865	The Civil War. Lincoln orders Washington militia into Federal Service. The first great expansion of the city occurs to accommodate large Union armies.
1865	*April 14*. President Lincoln is shot at Ford's Theater. He dies on April 15th.
1870	Since 1860 Washington's population has more than doubled.
1878	*June 11*. A Commission form of city government becomes permanent in an attempt to ease growing conflicts between local governments and Congressional overseers.
1879	The first electric lights are installed in the Capitol and the first apartment house is erected.
1883	First long-distance telephone communicaton made with Baltimore.
1885	Washington Monument dedicated.
1895	*February 11*. Georgetown is made part of Washington.
1897	Original Library of Congress building completed.
1898	Spanish-American War. President McKinley delivers war message to Congress. *May*. First D.C. volunteers are off to war.
1902	Municipal park commission partially adopts L'Enfant's original design as guide for reshaping the city.
1907	Carrie Nation raids Washington saloons and is jailed.
1912	Japan gives 3,000 cherry trees to Washington.
1917–1918	World War I. President Wilson's war message to Congress brings the great "War Populations" to the Capital.
1922	Lincoln Memorial dedicated.
1931–1932	Great Depression worsens. Hunger marchers invade Washington and army riots occur when the government fails to pay veterans' bonuses.
1934–1940	Greater centralization of power in the federal government brings in thousands of employees from all parts of the country. Many new offices constructed.
1941–1945	Wartime causes even greater expansion of the city. Office space created in nearby Virginia and Maryland eases some commuter traffic.
1943	The Pentagon completed.
1955	The National Educational Association opens its $5-million headquarters.
1961	Twenty-third Amendment grants citizens voting rights in presidential elections.
1962	*July*. An advisory council is appointed by President John F. Kennedy for the redesigning of Pennsylvania Avenue, the ceremonial boulevard of the Capital.
1963	*May 27*. Kennedy asks Congress to authorize a rapid transit system. *August 28*. Martin Luther King, Jr. delivers his "I Have a Dream" speech to 250,000 at Lincoln Memorial. *November 25*. President Kennedy's funeral draws leaders from all over the world and hundreds of thousands to the city in an outpouring of national grief.
1964	*November 3*. Citizens of the District are eligible to vote in the federal election for the first time. Voters favor Lyndon B. Johnson by 85.6 percent.
1965	Congress approves $75 million for a third building for the Library of Congress to be named for President James Madison. $100,000 is apportioned to the Franklin D. Roosevelt Memorial.
1966	Racial disturbances continue to plague the city.
1967	City commission government is replaced with a modified home rule. Nearly 74 percent of the city's population is black.
1968	*April 4*. The assassination of Martin Luther King, Jr. sets off six days of intense violence. President Nixon calls in troops to quell the looting and burning.
1969	*November 15*. Over 250,000 peace marchers parade down Pennsylvania Avenue in an appeal for a speedy withdrawal of US troops from Vietnam.

1970   Increased efforts are made to solve Washington's chronic problems in transportation, crime, education, social services, and revenue.

1971   *June 17.* Five men arrested for burglarizing the Democratic National Committee's Headquarters at the Watergate complex.
September 8. The $70-million John F. Kennedy Center for the Performing Arts opens.

1972   *September.* Congress approves a 7 percent across-the-board pay raise for teachers and boosts three city taxes to finance it. Public education remains an item of intense controversy.
December. Congressional bill passes allowing citizens to elect their own mayor.

1974   Federal City College, the first urban land-grant college, is granted accreditation in its sixth year of operation.

1975   *January 2.* Justice Thurgood Marshall swears in Walter Washington as the first popularly elected mayor in 100 years.
Washington ranks second to New York City in highest per capita indebtedness.

1978   *June 1.* The new East Building of the National Gallery of Art opens.

1980   *November 4.* City-run lottery and numbers games are approved by the electorate.

1982   *November.* Vietnam Veterans Memorial is dedicated.

1984   The nation's first initiative guaranteeing homeless people overnight shelter is approved.

1987   *June 3.* Statehood movement receives a boost when District of Columbia Committee votes to approve bill to establish the state of New Columbia. Many opponents argue such a move would be unconstitutional.

DEMOGRAPHY

Population (est. 1987) 626,000
Population (1980) 638,432
Population density in persons
    per square mile (1980) . . 9,252.6

POPULATION BY RACE (1980)
American Indian/Aleut/
    Eskimo. 1,031
Asian/Pacific Islander 6,635
Black 488,229
Hispanic 17,652
White 171,796
Other 9,960

POPULATION CHARACTERISTICS (1980)
Percent of state population
Urban 100.0
Rural 0.0
Under 18 . . . . 22.5
65 or older 11.6
College-educated 28.1
Families below poverty line . . . 15.1
Public-assistance recipients . . . 15.5

Per capita personal income
    (1986) $18,980
Millionaires per 100,000 residents
    (1982) . . included under Maryland

Average life expectancy in
    years (1980) 69.2
Marriage rate per 1,000
    residents (1986) 8.1
Divorce rate per 1,000
    residents (1986) 3.8
Birth rate per 1,000
    residents (1985) 32.8
Infant mortality rate per 1,000
    births (1985) 22.1
Abortion rate per 1,000
    live births (1982) 1,186
Crime rate per 100,000
    residents (1985)
    Violent 1,505.2
    Property 6,834.0
Federal and state prisoners per
    100,000 residents (1984) 701
Alcohol consumption in gallons
    per capita (1985) 51.7
Deaths from motor vehicle accidents
    per 100,000 residents (1985) . . 9.6

MAJOR CITY
1984 population (est.)
District of Columbia   622,823

GOVERNMENT AND POLITICS

Number of US Representatives

1 non-voting

Electoral votes   3

POLITICAL PARTY NOMINEES FROM DISTRICT

Belva Ann Bennett Lockwood (Equal Rights/Woman's Rights)	1884	P
Belva Ann Bennett Lockwood (Equal Rights/Woman's Rights	1888	P
Charles Owen Nations (American)	1924	P
Merritt Barton Curtis (Constitutional Party of Washington; Tax Cut/America First/ American)	1960	P
Julius Hobson (People's)	1972	VP

PRESIDENTIAL PRIMARY ELECTION In 1988, the District of Columbia sent 24 Democratic delegates and 14 Republican delegates to the national conventions.

CITY GOVERNMENT Washington, D.C., functions under federal law. Since 1974, when Congress granted the district limited rights of self-government, it has been administered by a mayor and city council. The council is unicameral, with 13 members serving 4-year terms; the minimum age is 18. The mayor also serves a 4-year term; in 1987, the annual salary for the office was $81,380. The mayor and council have the authority to levy taxes, but the city's budget is controlled by Congress, which retains final decision-making authority.

JUDICIARY The highest court is the Court of Appeals, with 9 judges serving 15-year terms. In 1987, the annual salary was $95,000.

PRESIDENTIAL VOTE 1964-1988 *(in percents)*

Year	State Winner	Democratic	Republican
1964	Johnson (D)	85.5	14.5
1968	Johnson (D)	81.8	18.2
1972	McGovern (D)	78.1	21.6
1976	Carter (D)	81.6	16.5
1980	Carter (D)	74.8	13.4
1984	Mondale (D)	85.4	13.7
1988	Dukakis (D)	86.0	14.0

MINIMUM AGES

Majority	18
Marriage with parental consent	16
Marriage without parental consent	18
Making a will	18
Jury duty	18
Leaving school (younger if employed)	16
Driver's license	18

MILITARY INSTALLATIONS

Total number: 9

Major bases:

  Army: 2

  Navy: 2

  Air Force: 1

FINANCES

REVENUES

(est. fiscal 1987)   ... $2,931,793,000

EXPENDITURES

(est. fiscal 1987) $2,931,793,000

ECONOMY

The federal government and the services it requires are the primary industries of Washington, D.C., which has one of the nation's largest communications networks. Tourism is the other important source of income, with tens of millions of tourists visiting the District every year. Hundreds of lobbying groups, professional organizations, businesses, and labor unions have Washington offices; the city is a major convention center.

EMPLOYMENT (1984)

Thousands of persons

Total number of employed workers	291
Construction	10.8
Finance, insurance, and real estate	35.4
Government	258.2
Manufacturing	14.5
Mining	0.1

Services	203.7
Transportation, communications, and utilities	26.0
Wholesale and retail trade	62.9

Percent of civilian labor force
unemployed (1984) 9.0

DEPARTMENT OF DEFENSE (1985)
Civilian workers employed . . 16,861
Military personnel 12,710
Contract awards . . . . $1.104 billion

ENERGY SOURCES FOR ELECTRIC UTILITIES (1983)
Percent
Coal 0.0

Gas 0.0
Hydroelectric 0.0
Nuclear 0.0
Petroleum 100.0

TRANSPORTATION
Motor vehicles registered
in district (1986) 289,360
Miles of roads, streets,
and highways (1986) 1,102
Miles of Class I railway
operated (1986) 47
Airports (1983) 16
Major aviation hubs (1983) 1
Largest hub: D.C.

CULTURE AND EDUCATION

Native American tribes
The District of Columbia was formerly home to the Conoy, Powhatan, and Shawnee tribes.

Religions, ethnicities, and languages
Generally speaking, Washington is home to two distinct groups: people connected with the federal administration (including politicians and their aides, lobbyists, and diplomats) who constitute a transient population and who usually live in the city's affluent suburbs; and the mainly black population of the inner city. Washington took in thousands of freed slaves after the Civil War, but did not receive much of the 19th- and 20th-century immigrations from Europe and Asia. Most of its churchgoing residents are Protestant; there are also substantial Roman Catholic and Jewish communities.

Major museums and libraries
Folger Shakespeare Library
Library of Congress
National Archives
Museum of African Art
Smithsonian Institution:
Freer Gallery of Art
Hirshhorn Museum and Sculpture
· Garden

Museum of History and Technology
National Air and Space Museum
National Collection of Fine Art
National Gallery of Art
National Museum of Natural History
National Portrait Gallery

Major arts organizations
Arena Stage
Ford's Theatre
National Symphony Orchestra
National Theater
US Air Force Symphony Orchestra
Washington Opera

Colleges and universities
Number public (1983-84) 2
Number private (1983-84) 17
Total enrollment, in full-time equivalent students (1985) 60,400

Public elementary and secondary schools
Expenditure per pupil in average daily attendance (1983-84) $4,116
Pupil-teacher ratio (1983-84) 16.9
Average teacher salary (1983-84) $27,659

Major league sports teams
Basketball: Washington Bullets
Football: Washington Redskins
Hockey: Washington Capitals

THE DISTRICT OF COLUMBIA IN LITERATURE

Henry Adams *Democracy: An American Novel* (1880)
Novel about politics during Grant's second term, 1873–1877. The authorship of the work, inspired by Adams's intimate knowledge of politics, was not revealed until after his death in 1918.

Samuel Hopkins Adams *Revelry* (1926)
Fictional account of the corruption of the Harding administration.

————. *The Gorgeous Hussy* (1934)
Humorous novel of social and political life in Washington from 1812 to the Civil War.

Bill Adler (comp.) *Washington: A Reader; the National Capital As Seen through the Eyes of Thomas Jefferson and Others* (1967)

Louisa May Alcott *Hospital Sketches* (1863)
Letters written by the author as a nurse in a Union hospital during the Civil War.

Mary Clemmer Ames *Ten Years in Washington* 2 vols. (1874, 1882)
Memoirs of a journalist, novelist, and poet, chiefly drawn from her weekly columns in the *Independent*.

Marietta Minnigerode Andrews *My Studio Window: Sketches of the Pageant of Washington Life* (1928)
Reminiscences of famous and obscure people.

Frank G. Carpenter (ed. Frances Carpenter) *Carp's Washington* (1960)
Memoirs of a Cleveland journalist who was a Washington correspondent during the administrations of Arthur, Cleveland, and Harrison.

Marquis Childs *Washington Calling* (1937)
Novel of pre-war Washington politics.

Virginia Clay-Clopton (ed. Ada Sterling) *A Belle of the Fifties: Memoirs of Mrs. Clay of Alabama, Covering Social and Political Life in Washington and the South, 1853–1866* (1904, rpt. 1969)
Memoirs of congressional society before the Civil War.

Edna M. Colman *Seventy-Five Years of White House Gossip* (1926); *White House Gossip; from Andrew Johnson to Calvin Coolidge* (1927)
The domestic and social lives of presidents.

William H. Crook *Memories of the White House* (1911)
Personal recollections of the domestic life of presidents from Lincoln to Roosevelt.

George William Curtis *Trumps* (1861)
Novel of New York society and Washington politics.

Jonathan Daniels *The Time between the War; Armistice to Pearl Harbor* (1966)
Chronicle of the personalities and incidents in the "boom and bust" period of the administrations of Harding, Coolidge, Hoover, and Roosevelt.

John William De Forest *Honest John Vane* (1875); *Playing the Mischief* (1875)
Political novels set in the corrupt Washington of Grant's administration.

John Dos Passos *District of Columbia* (1952)
Edition of a trilogy published 1939–1949 made up of *Adventures of a Young Man, Number One,* and *The Grand Design,* set in Washington during the 1930s and '40s.

Allen Drury *Advise and Consent* (1959)
Political machinations in the Senate during the confirmation of a secretary of state.

Harvey Fergusson *Capitol Hill* (1923)
Novel set during the Taft administration.

Louis J. Hallé *Spring in Washington* (1947, rpt. 1988)
A naturalist's philosophical reflections on the city, written by a State Department official during World War II.

Irwin H. Hoover *Forty-Two Years in the White House* (1934)
Gossip about ten presidents by a member of the White House domestic staff.

Ward Just *The Congressman Who Loved Flaubert, and Other Washington Stories* (1973); *Nicholson at Large* (1975); *In the City of Fear* (1982); *Jack Gance* (1989)
Novels and stories of modern political intrigue.

Frances Parkinson Keyes *Letters from a Senator's Wife* (1924)
The wife of a New Hampshire senator describes Washington during the Harding administration.

Fletcher Knebel and **Charles W. Bailey, II** *Seven Days in May* (1962)
Novel of suspense about an attempt to overthrow the government in 1974.

Margaret Kernochan Leech *Reveille in Washington* (1941)
Pulitzer prize–winning documentary novel about Washington during the Civil War.

Francis Ellington Leupp *Walks about Washington* (1915)
Anecdotal and historical account of social and political life.

Elizabeth Lindsay Lomax (ed. Lindsay Lomax Wood) *Leaves from an Old Washington Diary* (1943)
Account of Washington 1854–1863.

Alice Longworth *Crowded Hours: Reminiscences* (1933)
Memoirs of Teddy Roosevelt's daughter.

Earle Looker *The White House Gang* (1929)
Memoirs of a playmate of Quentin Roosevelt, son of the president.

Dolly Madison *Memoirs and Letters* (1886, rpt. 1971)
Social and political life in the time of Jefferson and Madison.

Norman Mailer *The Armies of the Night* (1968)
The author's experiences during the four days of the peace march on the Pentagon in October, 1967.

Benjamin Poore *Reminiscences of 60 Years in the National Metropolis* (1886)
The author was Washington correspondent of the *Boston Journal,* 1854–1884.

William Safire *Full Disclosure* (1977)
Novel about a president's attempts to stay in office by a former speechwriter to Nixon.

Arthur Schlesinger *A Thousand Days* (1965)
The Kennedy presidential years as seen by an aide.

Ellen M. Slaydon *Washington Wife: Journal of Ellen Maury Slaydon from 1897–1919* (1963)
Political events as seen by a congressman's wife.

Harriet Prescott Spofford *Old Washington* (1906)
Stories of Washington life at the end of the Civil War.

William Osborn Stoddard *Inside the White House in War Times* (1890)
Memoirs of Lincoln's secretary.

Michael Teague (ed.) *Mrs. L.: Conversations with Alice Roosevelt Longworth* (1981)
Tape-recorded conversations with Theodore Roosevelt's daughter, who died in 1980.

Gore Vidal *Washington, D.C.* (1967)
Political ambitions and intrigues in Washington society, 1937–1952.
———. *Lincoln* (1984)
Biographical novel of the president's last years, depicting Washington during the Civil War.

Theodore H. White *Breach of Faith* (1975)
Journalist's account of the fall of Nixon.

GUIDES TO RESOURCES

American Institute of Architects. Washington Metropolitan Chapter *Washington Architecture, 1791–1957* (1957)

Congressional Quarterly, Inc. *Washington Information Directory, 1988–89* (1988)

Davis, Deering *Georgetown Houses of the Federal Period, Washington, D.C., 1780–1830* (1944)

Donaldson, Frances G. *The President's Square; the Cosmos Club and Other Historic Homes on Lafayette Square* (1968)

Evans, Henry *Old Georgetown on the Potomac; a Historical Sketch, with a Bibliography of Source Material* (1933)

Federal Writers' Project *Washington, D.C.; a Guide to the Nation's Capital* (1942, rev. ed. 1968)
———. *Our Washington: A Comprehensive Album . . .* (1939)

Fish, Lydia M. *The Last Firebase: A Guide to the Vietnam Veterans Memorial* (1987)

Jacobsen, Hugh Newell (ed.) *A Guide to the Architecture of Washington, D.C.* (1965)

Kennon, Donald R. and **Richard Striner** *Washington Past and Present: A Guide to the Nation's Capital* (2d ed. 1983)

Kerwood, John R. (comp. and ed.) *The United States Capitol; an Annotated Bibliography* (1973)

Lee, Richard M. *Mr. Lincoln's City: An Illustrated Guide to the Civil War Sites of Washington* (1981)

Meglis, Anne Llewellyn (comp.) *A Bibliographic Tour of Washington, D.C.* (1974)

Moore, Derry *Washington, Houses of the Capital* (1982)

National Capital Planning Commission *Downtown Urban Renewal Area Landmarks: Washington, D.C.* (1970)

National Park Service *The Lincoln Memorial: A Guide to the Lincoln Memorial, District of Columbia* (1986)

Schreyer, Alice D. *The History of Books: A Guide to Selected Resources in the Library of Congress* (1987)

Sclar, Charlotte L. *The Smithsonian: A Guide to Its National Public Facilities in Washington, D.C.* (1985)

United States Architect of the Capitol *Art in the United States Capitol* (1976)

White House Historical Association *The White House: An Historic Guide* (15th ed. 1982)

SELECTED NONFICTION SOURCES

Aikman, Lonnelle *The Living White House* (1970)
——. *We, the People: The Story of the United States Capitol, Its Past and Its Promise* (13th ed. 1985)

Alsop, Stewart *The Center; People and Power in Political Washington* (1968)

Beale, Marie *Decatur House and Its Inhabitants* (1954)

Best, Judith *National Representation for the District of Columbia* (1984)

Borchert, James *Alley Life in Washington: Family, Community, Religion, and Folklife in the City, 1850–1970* (1982)

Brown, George Rothwell *Washington: A Not Too Serious History* (1930)

Brown, Glenn *History of the United States Capitol* 2 vols. (1901–1903, rpt. 1970)

Brown, Letitia W. and Elsie M. Lewis *Washington from Banneker to Douglass, 1791–1870* (1971)
—— and Elsie M. Lewis *Washington in the New Era, 1870–1970* (1972)

Chappell, Gordon *East and West Potomac Parks: A History* (1973)

Congressional Quarterly, Inc. *Washington Information Directory, 1987–88* (1987)

Cosentino, Andrew J. and Henry H. Glassie *The Capital Image: Painters in Washington, 1800–1915* (1983)

Cowdrey, Albert E. *A City for the Nation: The Army Engineers and the Building of Washington, D.C., 1790–1967* (1979)

Cross, Wilbur and Ann Novotny *White House Weddings* (1967)

Daniels, Jonathan *Frontier on the Potomac* (1946, rpt. 1972)
——. *Washington Quadrille; the Dance Beside the Documents* (1968)

Derthick, Martha *City Politics in Washington, D.C.* (1972)

Ecker, Grace Dunlop *A Portrait of Old George Town* (2d ed. 1951)

Frary, Ihna Thayer *They Built the Capitol* (1940, rpt. 1969)

Furer, Howard B. *Washington, a Chronological and Documentary History, 1790–1970* (1975)

Furman, Bess *White House Profile; a Social History of the White House, Its Occupants and Its Festivities* (1951)

Gatchel, Theodore Dodge *Rambling Through Washington, an Account of Old and New Landmarks in Our Capital City* (1932)

Gilbert, Ben W. et al. *Ten Blocks from the White House; Anatomy of the Washington Riots of 1968* (1968)

Goode, James M. *The Outdoor Sculpture of Washington* (1974)
——. *Capital Losses: A Cultural History of Washington's Destroyed Buildings* (1979)

Green, Constance M. *Washington: Capital City, 1879–1950* (1976)
——. *Washington: Village and Capital, 1800–1878* (1963)
——. *The Secret City, a History of Race Relations in the Nation's Capital* (1967)

Grier, Eunice S. *People and Government: Changing Needs in the District of Columbia, 1950–1970* (1973)

Gurney, George *Sculpture and the Federal Triangle* (1985)

Gutheim, Frederick *The Potomac* (Rivers of America series) (1949, rpt. 1974)

Hamlin, Talbot *Benjamin Henry Latrobe* (1955)

Hart, Scott *Washington at War: 1941–1945* (1970)

Hatertepe, Kenneth *America's Castle: The Evolution of the Smithsonian Building and Its Institution, 1840–1878* (1984)

Heine, Cornelius W. *A History of National Capital Parks* (1953)

Herron, Paul *The Story of Capitol Hill* (1963)

Hinkel, John V. *Arlington: Monument to Heroes* (rev. ed. 1970)

Hunt-Jones, Conover *Dolly and the "Great Little Madison"* (1977)

Jeffries, Ona *In and Out of the White House* (1960)

Johnson, Haynes *Dusk at the Mountain: The Negro, the Nation, and the Capital* (1963)

Kelly, Charles Suddarth *Washington, D.C., Then and Now: 69 Sites Photographed in the Past and Present* (1984)

Kelly, Tom *The Imperial Post: The Meyers, the Grahams, and the Paper That Rules Washington* (1983)

Kilian, Michael and Arnold Sawislak *Who Runs Washington?* (1982)

Kimmel, Stanley Preston *Mr. Lincoln's Washington* (1957)

Kiplinger, Austin *Washington Now* (1975)

Kite, Elizabeth *L'Enfant and Washington, 1791–92* (1929, rpt. 1970)

Klapthor, Margaret Brown *The First Ladies* (3d ed. 1981)

Kutner, Nanette *The White House Saga* (1962)

Leish, Kenneth W. et al. *The White House* (1972)

Lewis, David L. *District of Columbia: A Bicentennial History* (States and the Nation series) (1976)

Lisio, Donald J. *The President and Protest; Hoover, Conspiracy, and the Bonus Riot* (1974)

Llewellyn, Robert *Washington, the Capital* (1981)

Logan, Rayford W. *Howard University, the First Hundred Years, 1867–1967* (1969)

Lombard, Helen C. *While They Fought: Behind the Scenes in Washington, 1941–1946* (1947)

McCabe, James D. *Behind the Scenes in Washington* (1873, rpt. 1974)

Miller, Hope Ridings *Embassy Row; the Life and Times of Diplomatic Washington* (1969)

Mitchell, Mary *Divided Town* (1968)
——. *Washington; Portrait of the Capital* (1972)
——. *Chronicles of Georgetown Life, 1865–1900* (1986)

National Archives and Records Service *Washington, Design of the Federal City* (1981)

National Park Service *The Pennsylvania Avenue District in United States History* . . . (1965)

Park, Edwards *Treasures of the Smithsonian* (1983)

Paxton, Annabel *Washington Doorways* (1940)

Philibert, Imogene *Saint Matthew's of Washington 1840–1940* (1940)

Proctor, John C. (ed.) *Washington Past and Present, a History* (1930, 1932)

Reed, Robert *Old Washington, D.C., in Early Photographs, 1846–1932* (1980)

Reps, John W. *Monumental Washington; the Planning and Development of the Capital Center* (1967)

Ryan, William and Desmond Guinness *The White House: An Architectural History* (1980)

Seale, William *The President's House: A History* 2 vols. (1986)

Severn, William *Democracy's Messengers: The Capitol Pages* (1975)

Singleton, Esther *The Story of the White House* 2 vols. (1907, rpt. 1969)

Smith, A. Merriman *The Good New Days: A Not Entirely Reverent Study of Native Habits and Customs in Modern Washington* (1962)

Smith, Margaret B. *The First Forty Years of Washington Society* (1906, rpt. 1965)

Smith, Sam *Captive Capital: Colonial Life in Modern Washington* (1947)

Smithsonian Institution *The Smithsonian Experience: Science, History, the Arts . . . the Treasures of the Nation* (1977)

Torres, Louis "To the Immortal Name and Memory of George Washington": The United States Army Corps of Engineers and the Construction of the Washington Monument (1985)

United States Congress *The Capitol: A Pictorial History of the Capitol and of the Congress* (8th ed. 1981)

Viola, Herman J. *Diplomats in Buckskin: A History of Indian Delegations in Washington, D.C.* (1981)

Washington Society of Engineers *Planning and Building the City of Washington* (1932)

Weller, Charles F. *Neglected Neighbors; Stories of Life in the Alleys, Tenements and Shanties of the National Capital* (1909)

Whitehill, Walter Muir *Dumbarton Oaks; the History of a Georgetown House and Garden, 1800–1966* (1967)

Wilroy, Mary Edith and Lucie Prinz *Inside Blair House* (1982)

Wirz, Hans and Richard Striner *Washington Deco: Art Deco Design in the Nation's Capital* (1984)

Wright, William *The Washington Game* (1974)

Young, James Sterling *The Washington Community, 1800–1828* (1966)

PUERTO RICO

Puerto Rico is the easternmost island in the Greater Antilles archipelago of the West Indies. To the north is the Atlantic Ocean; to the south, the Caribbean Sea. The nearest islands to the east are the US Virgin Islands; to the west, across the Canal de la Mona, is the island of Hispaniola (the location of Haiti and the Dominican Republic).

FULL NAME Commonwealth of Puerto Rico (Estado Libre Asociado de Puerto Rico)
POSTAL ABBREVIATION PR
INHABITANT Puerto Rican
POPULATION (est. 1985) 3,279,231

CAPITAL CITY San Juan, the largest city in the commonwealth, located on the Atlantic coast in northeastern Puerto Rico; population 424,600 (1980). Founded in 1508 as the settlement of Caparra by Juan Ponce de León, it is the oldest city in any territory or state of the United States.

NAME AND NICKNAMES The original Arawak Indian name was Boriquen. The island was named San Juan by Christopher Columbus in 1493. The name Puerto Rico, Spanish for "rich harbor," was originally applied to the capital city. Eventually the two names were reversed.

SEAL On the central medallion, a lamb, symbol of St. John, holding a white banner and resting on the Book of Revelation; below it, the commonwealth's motto; above it, the crowned letters F and I (for King Ferdinand and Queen Isabella of Spain), with royal insignia. Around the border are symbols of the Kingdom of Spain.

MOTTO Joannes Est Nomen Ejus (John is his name)

SONG La Borinqueña

SYMBOLS
Flower maga
Tree ceiba
Bird reinita

FLAG Five horizontal stripes, alternating red and white, and at the left a blue triangle bearing a five-pointed white star.

GEOGRAPHY AND CLIMATE

Puerto Rico is dominated by the Cordillera Central, a mountain range of peaks rising more than 3,000 feet from the center of the island. The range slopes steeply to the southeast and more gently to the north, shading into a northern plateau where rain is abundant; the southern half of the island is drier. Bordering the island is a coastal plain with long stretches of sandy white beach. There are some 1,300 streams, including 50 rivers. The climate, dominated by the North Equatorial Current, is mild.

AREA 3,435 square miles (including three small adjacent islands, Vieques, Culebra, and Mona)

ELEVATIONS *Highest point:* Cerro de Punta, Ponce district, 4,389 feet. *Lowest point:* Atlantic Ocean, sea level

MAJOR RIVERS Grande de Arecibo, Cibuco, Grande de Loiza, Rio de la Plata

MAJOR LAKES Lago de Guajataca, Lago Dos Bocas, Lago Caonillas, Embalse de Loiza, Laguna de Guanica

LAND USE About one-third of Puerto Rico's land is suitable for agricultural use. Some 90,000 acres have been reserved for reforestation.

TEMPERATURES The highest recorded temperature in San Juan was 98° F, the lowest 60° F. The mean temperature is 77° F.

NATIONAL SITES

NATIONAL HISTORIC SITE San Juan

NATIONAL WILDLIFE REFUGES Culebra–Cabo Rojo/Desecheo/Green Cay

HISTORY

1493	*November 19.* Christopher Columbus anchors off Puerto Rico on his second visit to the New World. He names the island San Juan Bautista.
1508	*August 12.* Spanish begin settlement of the island at the city Caparra (San Juan) under Juan Ponce de León, who gives the city a new name, Ciudad de Puerto Rico (rich port).
1511	King Ferdinand of Spain formally recognizes the island by granting San Juan a coat of arms.
1515	Sugar cane is brought to the island from Santo Domingo.
1518	The first black slaves arrive.
1528	French attack and destroy San Germán.
1533	King Charles I of Spain authorizes Puerto Rico's first fort on the western shore of San Juan.
1550	Indians who have not been killed or enslaved by the Spanish flee into the interior mountains.
1570	About $4 million worth of gold ore has been mined by Spanish.
1589	Architects are sent from Spain to complete the fortress, El Morro, as a defense against pirates.
1595	Sir Francis Drake unsuccessfully attacks San Juan hoping to acquire treasure for the English.
1598	English Earl George Clifford captures San Juan and holds it for five months.
1625	Dutch lay siege to San Juan and burn many of the buildings but are eventually ousted.
1765	A wall is built around San Juan to protect it from pirates and marauding nations.
1797	English again attack the island but are defeated.
1804	Island ports are open to foreign trade.
1807	*La Gaceta* newspaper is founded.
1811	Spanish arrive from Venezuela after that country declares independence from Spain.
1848	The Spanish government (the Crown) rules that children of slaves can be granted freedom when they are baptized as Catholics and make a payment of 25 pesos each.
1873	*March 22.* Slavery is abolished.
1897	*November.* Puerto Rico is granted a Charter of Autonomy giving the island the status of a Spanish dominion.

1898	*July 25*. US troops land in Puerto Rico under leadership of General Nelson A. Miles.
	December 10. Puerto Rico is ceded to the US by Spain after the Spanish-American War.
1900	The first American civil governor and cabinet are appointed by William McKinley under the Foracker Act.
1900s	Coffee is the most valuable crop.
1903	The University of Puerto Rico is founded at Rio Piedras.
1904	Samuel Gompers, American labor leader, visits Puerto Rico and reports intolerable labor conditions.
1912	The Inter American University is founded first as a Presbyterian Mission enterprise.
1917	Puerto Rico contributes 12,000 soldiers and sailors to the American armed forces during World War I.
	March 2. Puerto Ricans are made citizens of the US but are exempt from federal taxes and do not vote in US presidential elections.
1920	Approximately 75 percent of the population is dependent on the sugar industry for its livelihood.
1925	Puerto Rico's white marble capitol building is erected in San Juan.
1927	Tobacco production reaches a high of 50,000,000 pounds.
1932	Puerto Rican women are granted suffrage.
1941–1945	World War II. Puerto Rican soldiers and sailors gain recognition in the US armed forces.
1947	US Congress amends the Jones Act, which permits Puerto Ricans to elect their own governor.
1948	The government assumes a direct role in improving the economy under Operation Bootstrap, which is responsible for the shift from agricultural to industrial production.
1949	Luis Muñoz Marin is inaugurated as the first elected governor. He is instrumental in securing commonwealth status for Puerto Rico.
1950	The governor begins promoting and assisting private enterprise in Operation Bootstrap.
1951	Industry starts mining small quantities of high-grade iron ore.
1952	*July 25*. Puerto Rico becomes a free commonwealth with a new constitution.
1955	San Juan opens a new international airport.
1957	The legislature passes a bill to subsidize the three political parties in Puerto Rico.
1963	*December 6*. Governor Marin is awarded the Presidential Medal of Freedom by President Lyndon B. Johnson in Washington, D.C.
1964	*November 3*. Robert Sanchez Vilella succeeds Marin as governor.
1965	Tourism industry continues to grow. New factories are opened on the island at the rate of two per week.
1967	*July 23*. Sixty percent of the island's voters insure the future status of Puerto Rico as a commonwealth. Proponents of Puerto Rico as an independent state are defeated.
1968	Visitors to the island number 930,000, about 120,000 more than the previous year.
1969	The sugar industry experiences a severe decline. A five-year modernization program, requiring a government subsidy, is launched to revive the industry.
1970	*October*. A week of uninterrupted rain creates floods in 34 towns. President Nixon declares the island a major disaster area.
1971	The 450th anniversary of the founding of San Juan, oldest city under the US flag, is observed.
1974	*November–December*. Some 20 bombs are placed in businesses owned by Americans, damaging much property.
1975	Unemployment, inflation, and industrial strife are results of the dire economic situation.
1976	*June*. At the invitation of President Gerald Ford, leaders of England, France, West Germany, Japan, Italy, and Canada meet in Puerto Rico to discuss and coordinate efforts to stimulate the island's economy.

1977	As a result of widespread drought in farming areas, agricultural production declines.
1978	Tourism, manufacturing, and construction register slight improvements. Opening of a new convention center attracts visitors.
1979	*July–September.* Three major tropical storms cause extensive damage.
1984	Government corruption and political kickbacks are disclosed.
1985	*October.* Approximately 180 people die in floods that sweep the island.
1986	*October.* Unemployment drops 17%, the lowest jobless rate in six years.
	December 31. Arson in San Juan's Dupont Plaza Hotel kills 96 people.
1987	*May.* King Juan Carlos and Queen Sofia of Spain arrive in San Juan. It is the first visit by Spanish monarchs since 1898.
1989	*January.* Governor Rafael Hernandez-Colon calls for a plebiscite on Puerto Rico's political status.

DEMOGRAPHY

Population (est. 1985) . . . 3,279,231
Population (1980) 3,196,520
Population density in persons
   per square mile (1980) . . . 924.1

POPULATION CHARACTERISTICS (1980)
Percent of commonwealth population
Hispanic 99.9
Urban 66.8
Rural 33.2

Per capita income (1985) $4,301
Median age (1980) 24.6
Marriage rate per 1,000
   residents (1983) 9.0
Divorce rate per 1,000
   residents (1983) 4.0

Birth rate per 1,000
   residents (1983) 20.1
Death rate per 1,000
   residents (1983) 6.5
Infant mortality rate per 1,000
   live births (1983) 17.2

MAJOR CITIES

	1980 population
Bayamon	185,087
Cagaus	87,214
Carolina	147,835
Guaynabo	65,075
Mayaguez	82,968
Ponce	161,739
San Juan	424,600

GOVERNMENT AND POLITICS

POLITICAL STATUS Since 1917, Puerto Ricans have been citizens of the United States, represented in Congress by a nonvoting resident commissioner. They do not vote in presidential elections or pay federal income tax on income earned in Puerto Rico. The federal government manages its foreign relations, defense, postal service, and customs service; eligible Puerto Ricans may be drafted into the federal armed forces.

CONSTITUTION Puerto Rico is using its original constitution, adopted in 1952. The constitution provides for the inhabitants' self-government in internal affairs and free, noncolonial association with the United States.

LEGISLATURE The Legislative Assembly is divided into the Senate (27 members, 4-year term, minimum age 30) and the House of Representatives (51 members,

4-year term, minimum age 25). The membership is increased, when necessary, to ensure that one-third of the legislators represent minority parties. In 1987, the annual salary was $20,000 plus $62-$72 per day.

JUDICIARY The highest court is the Supreme Court, with 8 judges serving until they reach the age of 70. In 1987, the annual salary was $60,000. Cases may be appealed to the US Supreme Court.

EXECUTIVE The governor serves a 4-year term; the minimum age for holding office is 35. In 1987, the annual salary was $45,000. There are no other elected officials for the commonwealth.

MILITARY INSTALLATIONS
Total number: 5
Major bases:
   Navy: 1

FINANCES

Total revenue
(1982) . . . . . . $5,877.5 million
Total expenditure
(1982) . . . . $5,695.6 million
Federal aid (1985) $2,347,583

ECONOMY

DESCRIPTION The island's traditional crops are sugarcane, coffee, and tobacco; other crops include plantains, bananas, yams, pineapples, pepper, pumpkins, lettuce, and tomatoes. There is a growing dairy, poultry, and egg industry. Commercial fishing accounted for $7.9 million in 1984. Since 1950, Puerto Rico, through an incentive program called "Operation Bootstrap," has made a dramatic shift from an agrarian economy to a diversified manufacturing economy. Its major products include chemicals, which accounted for $3,714 million in value added to manufacture in 1982; electric and electronic equipment, which accounted for $1,140 million in value added to manufacture the same year; petrochemicals and petroleum refining; instruments and machinery; clothing and furniture; metal, rubber, plastic, stone, clay, glass, leather, and paper products; and food and tobacco products, including the traditional rum, beer, and cigars. Mining, mainly of marble, limestone, and copper ore, was worth $122.2 million in 1985. Puerto Rico's exceptional beaches are a draw to tourism, which brings in an estimated net income of $234 million annually.

EMPLOYMENT (1984)

Thousands of persons

Total number of employed workers	434.4
Construction	23.9
Finance, insurance, and real estate	29.2
Manufacturing	144.4
Mining	0.5
Services	86.8
Transportation and utilities	19.5
Wholesale and retail trade	107.9
Percent of labor force unemployed (1985)	21.7

ENERGY SOURCES Most of Puerto Rico's energy needs are served by thermal plants that burn imported fuels. Hydroelectric plants account for about 3 percent of its electricity.

TRANSPORTATION

Motor vehicles registered (1975)	774,000
Miles of roads, streets, and highways	4,000
Miles of Class I railway operated	0
Major airports	4
Major ports, with gross tonnage (1985): San Juan	11,642

CULTURE AND EDUCATION

Religions, ethnicities, and languages
The dominant ethnic strains in Puerto Rico are Spanish, African, and Indian. During the 19th century, settlers came from Denmark, France, Corsica, and Italy. In the 20th century, Puerto Rico received substantial numbers of immigrants from Cuba and the Dominican Republic. Roman Catholicism is the dominant religion and Spanish the common language. There is considerable cross-migration to and from the continental United States, with some 2 million Puerto Ricans living there in 1980, mostly in New York City.

Major museums and libraries
Ateneo Puertorriqueno, San Juan
Museo de Arte de Ponce
Museo de Bellas Artes, Old San Juan
Museo de la Fundacion Arqueologica Antropologica e Historica de Puerto Rico, Old San Juan
Museo del Grabado Latinoamericano, Old San Juan
Museo Historico de Puerto Rico, Santurce
Museum of Anthropology, History and Art, University of Puerto Rico, Rio Piedras

Major arts organizations
Opera de Camara, Condado Puerto Rico
Symphony Orchestra, Santurce

Colleges and universities
Number public (1986-7) 14
Number private (1986-7) 28
Total enrollment (1983-4) 155,700

Public elementary and secondary schools
Average teacher salary (1985) $8,163

Holidays
Three Kings Day. January 6

Eugenio Maria de Hostos' Birthday.
  January 11
Abolition Day. March 22
De Diego's Birthday. April 16

Luis Munoz Rivera's Birthday. July 17
Constitution Day. July 25
Barbosa's Birthday. July 27
Discovery Day. November 19

PUERTO RICO IN LITERATURE

Ricardo Alegría *The Three Wishes: A Collection of Puerto Rican Folk Tales* (trans. of *Cuentos folklóricos de Puerto Rico*, 1967) (1969)
Stories and legends from the oral tradition.

Rafael Arán *All in the Past* (1955)
Author's boyhood memories of life in Mayagüez during the first quarter of the century.

Francisco Arriví *Vegigantes* (1958)
Drama of racial conflicts in Puerto Rican society.

Bailly K. Ashford *A Soldier in Science* (1934)
Famous army doctor's career in Puerto Rico.

María Teresa Babín and **Stan Steiner** *Borinquen: An Anthology of Puerto Rican Literature* (1974)
Representative authors from the island and the US.

Manuel Méndez Ballester *Isla cerrada* (1937)
Historical novel of the beginnings of the Spanish colonial era in the 16th century.

Emilio S. Belaval *Cuentos para fomentar el turismo* (1946)
Humorous short stories on the everyday problems of the Puerto Rican *campesino*.

Josefina R. De Alvarez *Dictionary of Puerto Rican Literature* 2 vols. (1979)

Rosario Ferré *Papeles de Pandora* (1976)
Stories of Puerto Rico's upper classes and the role of women in society.
———. *Maldito amor* (1986)
Novel tracing 100 years of US rule in the island.

Carmen Lugo Filippi and **Ana Lydia Vega** *Vírgenes y mártires (cuentos)* (1981)
Stories with an ironic look at contemporary urban culture and male/female relations.

Juan Flores *The Insular Vision: Pedreira's Interpretation of Puerto Rican Culture* (1980)
A revision of earlier interpretations of Puerto Rican national culture, in particular that of Antonio Pedreira.

David W. Foster *Puerto Rican Literature: A Bibliography of Secondary Sources* (1982)

Manuel Zeno Gandía *La Charca* (trans. of *La charca*, 1894) (1982)
Classic novel on the economic plight of the Puerto Rican peasant in the nineteenth century.

José Luis González *La llegada (Crónica con "ficción")* (1980)
Novel that takes place on the eve of the US occupation of the island in 1898.
———. *El país de cuatro pisos* (1980)
Essays on the development of Puerto Rican national culture.

César Andreu Iglesias (ed.) *Memoirs of Bernardo Vega: A Contribution to the History of the Puerto Rican Community in New York* (trans. of *Memorias de Bernardo Vega*, 1977) (1984)
A personal account of the collective experiences of Puerto Rican migrants in the early 20th century.

Edgardo Rodríguez Juliá *Las tribulaciones de Jonás* (1981)
Interview with Luis Muñoz Marín and essays on his impact as a major political figure in twentieth-century Puerto Rico.
———. *Una noche con Iris Chacón* (1986)
Essays on religion, politics, and popular culture.

Enrique A. Laguerre *La llamarada* (1935)
Novel based on the impact of the sugar industry in the island.
———. *La resaca* (1949)
Novel of the final years of Spanish domination of the island.

Oscar Lewis *La Vida: A Puerto Rican Family in the Culture of Poverty* (1966)
Anthropological study of a family in San Juan and New York.

René Marqués *Palm Sunday* (1956)
Drama based on the Nationalist Movement and the Palm Sunday Massacre of 1937.
———. *Mariana o El Alba* (1965)
Drama of the historical figure Mariana Bracetti and the 1868 revolt in Lares against the Spanish.
———. *The Oxcart* (trans. of *La carreta*, 1963) (1969)
Tragic drama of the Puerto Rican emigrant's move from the country to San Juan and New York.
———. *En una ciudad llamada San Juan* (3d ed. 1970)
Short stories reflecting social and political turmoil in contemporary Puerto Rico.
———. *The Docile Puerto Rican* (1976)
An important essay, much attacked, arguing that socialization under colonialism has made Puerto Rico a docile culture.

Julio Marzán *Inventing a Word: An Anthology of Twentieth-Century Puerto Rican Poetry* (1980)
Representative poets, many expressing national themes, in bilingual edition.

Alfredo Matilla and **Iván Silén** *The Puerto Rican Poets/Los poetas puertorriqueños* (1972)
Poetry expressing a range of experiences from the island to New York, in bilingual edition.

Manuel Alonso Pacheco *El G'íbaro* (1849)
The traditions and customs of a peasant in the 19th century.

Antonio Pedreira *Insularismo* (1934)
Classic essay on Puerto Rican national character from a geographical and biological perspective.

Magali García Rámis *Felices Días, Tío Sergio* (1986)
Novel of a young girl's coming of age in middle-class urban Puerto Rico.

Edward Rivera *Family Installments: Memories of Growing Up Hispanic* (1982)
Novel tracing a family's history from a small village in Puerto Rico to the experience of emigration to New York.

Guillermo Rivera *A Tentative Bibliography of the Belles-Lettres of Porto Rico* (1931)

Edith Roberta *A Candle in the Sun* (1937)
Novel written by a North American resident of the island who had occupied an important governmental position.

Nestor Rodríguez Escuder *Litoral: Short Stories of the Sea of Puerto Rico* (trans. of *Litoral*, 1962) (1969)
Sketches of Aguadilla in its days as an important fishing port.

Luis Rafael Sánchez *En cuerpo de camisa* (1966)
Short stories examining the problems of contemporary society, in particular its marginalized sectors.
———. *Macho Camacho's Beat* (trans. of *La guaracha del Macho Camacho*, 1976) (1980)
Acclaimed novel of present-day Puerto Rican "neocolonial" society.

Pedro Juan Soto *Hot Land, Cold Season* (trans. of *Ardiente suelo, fría estación*, 1961) (1973)
A young man journeys from Puerto Rico to find rejection both in New York and upon his return to the island.

Alejandro Tapia y Rivera *Cofresí* (1876)
Novel based on the adventures of the Puerto Rican pirate Roberto Cofresí.

Luis Lloréns Torres *El Grito de Lares* (1927)
Historical drama based on the separatist revolt against the Spanish in 1868.

Emilio Díaz Valvárcel *Mi mamá me ama* (1981)
Novel on the influence of North American values on upper-middle-class Puerto Ricans.

GUIDES TO RESOURCES

Bravo, Enrique R. *An Annotated Selected Puerto Rican Bibliography* (1972)

Cevallos, Elena E. *Puerto Rico (World Bibliographic Series: 52)* (1985)

Federal Writers' Project *Puerto Rico: A Guide to the Island of Borinquen* (1940)

Fernández Méndez, Eugenio *The Sources on Puerto Rico Cultural History: A Critical Appraisal* (1967)

Fowlie-Flores, Fay (comp.) *Index to Puerto Rican Collective Biography* (1987)

Griffin, A. P. C. *A List of Books (with References to Periodicals) on Puerto Rico* (1901)

Hooker, Marjorie *Bibliography and Index of the Geology of Puerto Rico and Vicinity, 1866–1968* (1969)

Pedreira, Antonio S. *Bibliografía puertorriqueña (1493–1930)* (Puerto Rican Bibliography, 1493–1930) (1932)

Ribes Tovar, Federico *Enciclopedia puertorriqueña illustrada--The Puerto Rican Heritage Encyclopedia* (1970)

United States—Puerto Rico Commission on the Status of Puerto Rico *Status of Puerto Rico: Report* (1966)

University of the State of New York, Albany *An Annotated Bibliography of Materials on the Puerto Rican and Mexican Cultures* (1982)

Vivó, Paquita *The Puerto Ricans: An Annotated Bibliography* (1973)

SELECTED NONFICTION SOURCES

Abbad y Lasierra, Fray Iñigo *Historia geográfica, civil y natural de la isla de San Juan Bautista de Puerto Rico* (Geographic, Civil and Natural History of the Island of San Juan Bautista of Puerto Rico) (1788)

Alegría, Ricardo *Discovery, Conquest and Colonization of Puerto Rico: 1493–1599* (1971)

American Geographical Society *Puerto Rico* (1968)

Babín, Maria Teresa *The Puerto Rican Spirit: Their History, Life and Culture* (1971)

Brameld, Theodore *The Remaking of a Culture: Life and Education in Puerto Rico* (1959)

Bryan, William S. *Our Islands and Their People As Seen with Camera and Pencil* v. 2 (1899)

Carr, Raymond *Puerto Rico: A Colonial Experiment* (1984)

Coll y Toste, Cayetano *Tradiciones y leyendas puertorriqueñas (Puerto Rican Traditions and Legends)* 3 vols. (1924–1925)

Dawson Flinter, George *An Account of the Present State of the Island of Puerto Rico* (1834)

Dinwiddie, William *Porto Rico: Its Conditions and Possibilities* (1899)

Fernández, José A. *The Architecture of Puerto Rico* (1965)

Fernández Méndez, Eugenio *The Sources of Puerto Rican Culture History: A Critical Appraisal* (1967)

Fewkes, Jesse W. *The Aborigines of Porto Rico and Neighboring Islands* (1970)

Figueroa, Loida *History of Puerto Rico* (1972)

Golding, Morton J. *A Short History of Puerto Rico* (1973)

Jopling, Carol F. *Puerto Rican Houses in Sociohistorical Perspective* (1988)

Lewis, Gordon K. *Puerto Rico: Freedom and Power in the Caribbean* (1963)

López, Adalberto and James Petras (eds.) *Puerto Rico and the Puerto Ricans: Studies in History and Society* (1974)

Maldonado-Denis, Manuel *Puerto Rico: A Socio-Historic Interpretation* (1972)

Manucy, Albert and Ricardo Torres-Reyes *Puerto Rico and the Forts of Old San Juan* (1973)

McKown, Robin *The Image of Puerto Rico: Its History and Its People; on the Island--on the Mainland* (1973)

Mintz, Sidney *Worker in the Cane: A Puerto Rico Life History* (1960)

Morales Carrión, Arturo *Puerto Rico and the Non-Hispanic Caribbean: A Study in the Decline of Spanish Exclusivism* (1952)
———. *Puerto Rico, a Political and Cultural History* (1983)

Nieves Falcón, Luis *Diagnóstico de Puerto Rico* (Diagnosis of Puerto Rico) (1971)

Ober, Frederick A. *Puerto Rico and Its Resources* (1899)

Picó, Rafael *The Geography of Puerto Rico* (1974)

Rainey, Froelich *Porto Rican Archeology* (1940)

Ribes Tovar, Federico *A Chronological History of Puerto Rico* (1973)

Steiner, Stan *The Islands: The Worlds of the Puerto Ricans* (1974)

Steward, Julian (ed.) *The People of Puerto Rico* (1956)

Tugwell, Rexford G. *The Stricken Land: The Story of Puerto Rico* (1947)

Tumin, Melvin and Arnold Feldman *Social Class and Social Change in Puerto Rico* (1961)

Van Middeldyk, R. A. *The History of Puerto Rico: From the Spanish Discovery to the American Occupation* (1903)

Vivas, José Luis and Gaetano Massa *The History of Puerto Rico* (1970)

Wagenheim, Kal *Puerto Rico: A Profile* (1970)
——— and Olga Jiménez de Wagenheim *The Puerto Ricans: A Documentary History* (1973)

Wells, Henry *The Modernization of Puerto Rico: A Political Study of Changing Values and Institutions* (1969)

White, Trumbull *Puerto Rico and Its People* (1938)

Woll, Allen L. *Puerto Rican Historiography* (1978)

Yurchenko, Henrietta *Hablemos: Puerto Ricans Speak* (1971)

COMPARATIVE TABLES

State	Area (*Square* (*miles*))	Rank	Population (*est. 1987*)	Rank
Alabama	51,705	29	4,083,000	22
Alaska	591,004	1	525,000	49
Arizona	114,000	6	3,386,000	25
Arkansas	53,187	27	2,388,000	32
California	158,706	3	27,663,000	1
Colorado	104,091	8	3,296,000	26
Connecticut	5,108	48	3,211,000	28
Delaware	2,044	49	644,000	47
Florida	58,664	22	12,023,000	4
Georgia	58,910	21	6,222,000	11
Hawaii	6,471	47	1,083,000	39
Idaho	83,564	13	998,000	42
Illinois	56,345	24	11,582,000	6
Indiana	36,185	38	5,531,000	14
Iowa	56,275	24	2,834,000	29
Kansas	82,277	14	2,376,000	33
Kentucky	40,909	37	3,727,000	23
Louisiana	47,751	31	4,461,000	20
Maine	33,265	39	1,187,000	38
Maryland	10,460	42	4,535,000	19
Massachusetts	8,284	45	5,855,000	13
Michigan	58,527	23	9,200,000	8
Minnesota	84,402	12	4,246,000	21
Mississippi	47,689	32	2,625,000	31
Missouri	69,697	19	5,103,000	15
Montana	147,046	4	809,000	44
Nebraska	77,355	15	1,594,000	36
Nevada	110,561	7	1,007,000	41
New Hampshire	9,279	44	1,057,000	40
New Jersey	7,787	46	7,672,000	9
New Mexico	121,593	5	1,500,000	37
New York	49,108	30	17,825,000	2
North Carolina	52,669	28	6,413,000	10
North Dakota	70,703	17	672,000	46
Ohio	41,330	35	10,784,000	7
Oklahoma	69,956	18	3,272,000	27
Oregon	97,073	10	2,724,000	30
Pennsylvania	45,308	33	11,936,000	5
Rhode Island	1,212	50	986,000	43
South Carolina	31,113	40	3,425,000	24
South Dakota	77,116	16	709,000	45
Tennessee	42,144	34	4,855,000	16
Texas	266,807	2	16,789,000	3
Utah	84,800	11	1,680,000	35
Vermont	9,614	43	548,000	48
Virginia	40,767	36	5,904,000	12
Washington	68,138	20	4,538,000	18
West Virginia	24,231	41	1,897,000	34
Wisconsin	56,153	26	4,807,000	17
Wyoming	97,809	9	490,000	50

State	Population	Rank	Population Density (*Persons per sq mile*)	Rank	Percent Urban	Rank
Alabama	3,893,978	22	75.3	26	47.3	46-47
Alaska	525,000	49	0.7	50	64.3	30
Arizona	2,178,425	29	23.8	40	79.6	12-13
Arkansas	2,286,419	33	43.0	35	51.6	41
California	23,667,837	1	149.1	14	91.3	1
Colorado	2,889,735	28	27.8	38	80.6	10
Connecticut	3,107,576	25	619.3	4	78.8	14
Delaware	594,317	47	290.8	7	70.6	19
Florida	9,746,342	7	166.1	11	84.3	7
Georgia	5,462,992	13	92.7	22	62.4	34
Hawaii	964,691	39	149.1	15	86.5	3
Idaho	944,038	41	11.3	43	54.0	38
Illinois	11,427,414	5	203.0	10	83.3	9
Indiana	5,490,260	12	151.7	13	64.2	31-32
Iowa	2,913,808	27	51.8	32	58.6	36
Kansas	2,364,236	32	28.7	37	66.7	27-28
Kentucky	3,726,000	23	90.6	23	50.9	42
Louisiana	4,206,098	19	88.1	21	68.6	22
Maine	1,125,030	38	33.8	36	47.5	45
Maryland	4,216,941	18	403.2	5	80.3	11
Massachusetts	5,737,081	11	692.5	3	83.8	8
Michigan	9,262,070	8	158.3	12	70.7	18
Minnesota	4,075,970	21	48.3	33	66.9	26
Mississippi	2,520,631	31	52.9	31	47.3	46-47
Missouri	4,916,759	15	70.5	27	68.1	23
Montana	786,690	44	5.3	48	52.9	39
Nebraska	1,569,825	35	20.3	41	66.7	27-28
Nevada	800,493	43	7.2	47	85.3	4
New Hampshire	920,610	42	99.2	20	52.2	40
New Jersey	7,365,011	9	945.8	1	69.3	20-21
New Mexico	1,479,445	37	10.7	44	72.1	17
New York	17,558,072	2	357.5	6	84.6	5
North Carolina	5,881,385	10	111.7	17	48.0	44
North Dakota	652,717	46	9.2	45	48.8	43
Ohio	10,797,624	6	261.3	9	73.3	16
Oklahoma	3,025,495	26	43.2	34	67.3	25
Oregon	2,633,149	30	27.1	39	67.9	24
Pennsylvania	11,864,751	4	261.9	8	69.3	20-21
Rhode Island	947,154	40	781.5	2	87.0	2
South Carolina	3,122,814	24	100.4	19	54.1	37
South Dakota	690,768	45	9.0	46	46.4	48
Tennessee	4,591,120	17	108.9	18	60.4	35
Texas	14,227,574	3	53.3	30	79.6	12-13
Utah	1,461,037	36	17.2	42	84.4	6
Vermont	511,456	48	53.2	29	33.8	50
Virginia	5,346,797	14	131.2	16	66.0	29
Washington	4,132,204	20	60.6	28	73.5	15
West Virginia	1,950,258	34	80.5	25	36.2	49
Wisconsin	4,705,642	16	83.8	24	64.2	31-32
Wyoming	469,557	50	4.8	49	62.7	33

ORDER OF SETTLEMENT AND ORDER OF STATEHOOD

States Listed in Order of Settlement		States Listed in Order of Admission to the Union	
Florida	1565	Delaware	Dec. 7, 1787
Virginia	1607	Pennsylvania	Dec. 12, 1787
New Mexico	1610	New Jersey	Dec. 18, 1787
New York	1614	Georgia	Jan. 2, 1788
Massachusetts	1620	Connecticut	Jan. 9, 1788
New Hampshire	1623	Massachusetts	Feb. 6, 1788
Connecticut	1624	Maryland	Apr. 28, 1788
Maine	1624	South Carolina	May 23, 1788
Maryland	1634	New Hampshire	June 21, 1788
Rhode Island	1636	Virginia	June 25, 1788
Delaware	1638	New York	July 26, 1788
North Carolina	1660	North Carolina	Nov. 21, 1789
New Jersey	1664	Rhode Island	May 29, 1790
Michigan	1668	Vermont	Mar. 4, 1791
South Carolina	1670	Kentucky	June 1, 1792
Pennsylvania	1682	Tennessee	June 1, 1796
Texas	1682	Ohio	Mar. 1, 1803
Arkansas	1686	Louisiana	Apr. 30, 1812
Louisiana	1699	Indiana	Dec. 11, 1816
Mississippi	1699	Mississippi	Dec. 10, 1817
Alabama	1702	Illinois	Dec. 3, 1818
Illinois	1720	Alabama	Dec. 14, 1819
Vermont	1724	Maine	Mar. 15, 1820
Kansas	1727	Missouri	Aug. 10, 1821
West Virginia	1727	Arkansas	June 15, 1836
Georgia	1733	Michigan	Jan. 26, 1837
Indiana	1733	Florida	Mar. 3, 1845
Missouri	1735	Texas	Dec. 29, 1845
Wisconsin	1766	Iowa	Dec. 28, 1846
Tennessee	1769	Wisconsin	May 29, 1848
Kentucky	1774	California	Sept. 9, 1850
Arizona	1776	Minnesota	May 11, 1858
Alaska	1784	Oregon	Feb. 14, 1859
Iowa	1788	Kansas	Jan. 29, 1861
Ohio	1788	West Virginia	June 20, 1863
California	1789	Nevada	Oct. 31, 1864
Minnesota	1805	Nebraska	Mar. 1, 1867
Montana	1809	Colorado	Aug. 1, 1876
Oregon	1811	North Dakota	Nov. 2, 1889
Washington	1811	South Dakota	Nov. 2, 1889
North Dakota	1812	Montana	Nov. 8, 1889
Hawaii	1820	Washington	Nov. 11, 1889
Nebraska	1823	Idaho	July 3, 1890
Wyoming	1834	Wyoming	July 10, 1890
Idaho	1842	Utah	Jan. 4, 1896
Utah	1847	Oklahoma	Nov. 16, 1907
Nevada	1849	New Mexico	Jan. 6, 1912
Colorado	1858	Arizona	Feb. 14, 1912
South Dakota	1859	Alaska	Jan. 3, 1959
Oklahoma	1889	Hawaii	Aug. 21, 1959

State	High	Low	Mean
Alabama	2,407	sea level	500
Alaska	20,230	sea level	1,900
Arizona	12,633	70	4,100
Arkansas	2,753	55	650
California	14,494	−282	2,900
Colorado	14,433	3,350	6,800
Connecticut	2,380	sea level	500
Delaware	442	sea level	60
Florida	345	sea level	100
Georgia	4,784	sea level	600
Hawaii	13,796	sea level	3,030
Idaho	12,662	710	5,000
Illinois	1,235	279	600
Indiana	1,257	320	700
Iowa	1,670	480	1,100
Kansas	4,039	680	2,000
Kentucky	4,145	257	750
Louisiana	535	−5	100
Maine	5,268	sea level	600
Maryland	3,360	sea level	3,190
Massachusetts	3,491	sea level	500
Michigan	1,980	572	900
Minnesota	2,301	602	1,200
Mississippi	806	sea level	300
Missouri	1,772	230	800
Montana	12,799	1,800	3,400
Nebraska	5,246	840	2,600
Nevada	13,143	470	5,500
New Hampshire	6,288	sea level	1,000
New Jersey	1,803	sea level	250
New Mexico	13,161	2,817	5,700
New York	5,344	sea level	1,000
North Carolina	6,684	sea level	700
North Dakota	3,506	750	1,900
Ohio	1,550	433	850
Oklahoma	4,973	287	1,300
Oregon	11,239	sea level	3,300
Pennsylvania	3,213	sea level	1,100
Rhode Island	812	sea level	200
South Carolina	3,560	sea level	350
South Dakota	7,242	962	2200
Tennessee	6,643	182	900
Texas	8,749	sea level	1,700
Utah	13,528	2,000	6,100
Vermont	4,393	95	1,000
Virginia	5,729	sea level	950
Washington	14,410	sea level	1,700
West Virginia	4,863	240	1,500
Wisconsin	1,951	581	1,050
Wyoming	13,804	3,100	6,700

State	Inland Water (square miles)	Tidal Shoreline (miles)	Temperature (Fahrenheit) Highest	Lowest
Alabama	938	607	112	−27
Alaska	20,171	31,383	100	−80
Arizona	492	0	127	−40
Arkansas	1,159	0	120	−29
California	2,407	3,427	134	−45
Colorado	496	0	118	−61
Connecticut	146	618	105	−32
Delaware	112	381	110	−17
Florida	4,511	8,426	109	−02
Georgia	854	2,344	113	−17
Hawaii	46	1,052	100	+12
Idaho	1,152	0	118	−60
Illinois	700	0	117	−35
Indiana	253	0	116	−35
Iowa	310	0	118	−47
Kansas	499	0	121	−40
Kentucky	740	0	114	−34
Louisiana	3,230	7,721	114	−16
Maine	2,270	3,478	105	−48
Maryland	623	3,190	109	−40
Massachusetts	460	1,519	107	−35
Michigan	1,573	0	112	−51
Minnesota	4,854	0	114	−59
Mississippi	456	359	115	−19
Missouri	752	0	118	−40
Montana	1,658	0	117	−70
Nebraska	711	0	118	−47
Nevada	667	0	122	−50
New Hampshire	286	131	106	−46
New Jersey	319	1,792	110	−34
New Mexico	258	0	116	−50
New York	1,731	1,850	108	−52
North Carolina	3,826	3,375	110	−34
North Dakota	1,403	0	121	−60
Ohio	326	0	113	−39
Oklahoma	1,301	0	120	−27
Oregon	889	1,410	119	−54
Pennsylvania	420	89	111	−42
Rhode Island	157	384	104	−23
South Carolina	910	2,876	111	−19
South Dakota	1,164	0	120	−58
Tennessee	989	0	113	−32
Texas	4,790	3,359	120	−23
Utah	2,826	0	117	−69
Vermont	341	0	105	−50
Virginia	1,063	3,315	110	−29
Washington	1,627	3,026	118	−48
West Virginia	112	0	112	−37
Wisconsin	1,727	0	114	−54
Wyoming	820	0	114	−63

State	Under Age 18	Age 65 or Older	College-Educated	* Families Below Poverty Line	Public-Assistance Recipients
Alabama	29.8	11.3	12.6	14.9	8.1
Alaska	32.5	2.9	22.4	8.6	4.6
Arizona	29.1	11.3	16.8	9.5	3.0
Arkansas	29.4	13.7	9.7	14.9	7.2
California	27.0	10.2	19.8	8.7	8.8
Colorado	28.0	8.6	23.0	7.4	3.7
Connecticut	26.5	11.7	21.2	6.2	5.2
Delaware	28.0	10.0	16.3	8.9	6.6
Florida	24.3	17.3	14.7	9.9	4.4
Georgia	30.1	9.5	15.3	13.2	6.9
Hawaii	28.6	7.9	20.3	7.8	7.3
Idaho	32.5	9.9	16.1	9.6	3.0
Illinois	28.4	11.0	14.5	8.4	7.0
Indiana	29.4	10.7	12.4	7.3	3.7
Iowa	28.3	13.3	14.1	7.0	4.6
Kansas	27.5	13.0	15.7	7.4	3.8
Kentucky	29.6	11.2	11.0	14.6	7.2
Louisiana	31.6	9.6	13.4	15.1	8.3
Maine	26.6	13.1	14.0	9.8	7.4
Maryland	27.7	9.4	19.8	7.5	6.1
Massachusetts	26.0	12.7	20.0	7.6	8.3
Michigan	29.7	9.8	15.2	8.2	8.9
Minnesota	28.7	11.8	16.7	7.0	4.2
Mississippi	32.3	11.5	13.0	18.7	11.4
Missouri	27.7	13.2	14.0	9.1	5.9
Montana	29.5	10.7	17.3	9.2	3.4
Nebraska	27.5	13.0	16.1	8.0	3.2
Nevada	26.9	8.2	15.1	6.3	2.3
New Hampshire	25.8	11.7	18.4	6.1	3.0
New Jersey	27.0	11.7	18.6	7.6	7.4
New Mexico	32.1	8.9	17.3	14.0	6.1
New York	26.7	12.3	18.7	10.8	8.4
North Carolina	28.1	10.3	13.4	11.6	5.8
North Dakota	29.3	12.3	15.2	9.8	3.0
Ohio	28.7	10.8	14.8	8.0	6.0
Oklahoma	28.2	12.4	15.7	10.3	5.2
Oregon	27.4	11.5	17.2	7.7	4.9
Pennsylvania	26.3	12.9	13.8	7.8	6.7
Rhode Island	25.7	13.4	15.3	7.7	7.2
South Carolina	30.1	9.2	14.2	13.1	7.6
South Dakota	29.8	13.2	14.2	13.1	4.2
Tennessee	28.3	11.3	1.9	13.1	6.4
Texas	30.2	9.6	16.0	11.1	4.0
Utah	37.0	7.5	20.3	7.7	3.2
Vermont	26.2	11.9	19.5	8.9	6.4
Virginia	27.5	9.5	19.2	9.2	4.6
Washington	27.6	10.4	18.8	7.2	4.9
West Virginia	28.7	12.2	10.5	11.7	6.0
Wisconsin	28.9	12.0	14.9	6.3	6.1
Wyoming	30.3	7.9	17.2	5.8	1.9

State	Average Life Expectancy years (*1980*)	Per Capita Personal Income dollars (*1986*)	Millionaires per *100,000* residents (*1982*)
Alabama	72.5	11,115	104.0
Alaska	72.3	17,744	270.3
Arizona	74.3	13,220	190.2
Arkansas	73.7	10,773	112.7
California	74.6	16,778	261.2
Colorado	75.3	15,113	224.8
Connecticut	75.1	19,208	300.7
Delaware	73.2	15,010	116.7
Florida	74.3	14,281	387.8
Georgia	72.2	13,224	102.6
Hawaii	77.0	14,691	80.2
Idaho	75.2	11,432	102.4
Illinois	73.4	15,420	126.5
Indiana	73.8	12,944	82.1
Iowa	75.8	13,222	113.5
Kansas	75.3	14,379	132.9
Kentucky	73.1	11,129	94.7
Louisiana	71.7	11,227	141.5
Maine	74.6	12,709	70.4
Maryland	73.3	16,588	178.1
Massachusetts	75.0	17,516	132.3
Michigan	73.4	14,064	80.1
Minnesota	76.2	14,737	425.9
Mississippi	72.0	9,552	77.9
Missouri	73.8	13,657	155.8
Montana	73.9	11,904	111.8
Nebraska	75.5	13,777	207.7
Nevada	72.6	15,074	170.8
New Hampshire	75.0	15,922	221.5
New Jersey	74.0	18,284	111.7
New Mexico	74.0	11,037	80.5
New York	73.7	17,118	175.9
North Carolina	73.0	12,245	59.9
North Dakota	75.7	12,284	565.5
Ohio	73.5	13,743	117.0
Oklahoma	73.7	12,368	139.3
Oregon	75.0	13,217	78.7
Pennsylvania	73.6	13,944	216.3
Rhode Island	74.8	14,670	83.9
South Carolina	71.9	11,096	68.2
South Dakota	75.0	11,850	172.9
Tennessee	73.3	11,831	113.8
Texas	73.6	13,523	257.3
Utah	75.8	10,743	273.7
Vermont	74.5	12,845	134.6
Virginia	73.4	15,734	89.3
Washington	75.1	14,498	243.2
West Virginia	72.9	10,530	30.6
Wisconsin	75.4	13,796	90.6
Wyoming	73.9	13,230	254.9

State	Marriages per 1,000 residents (1986)	Divorces per 1,000 residents (1986)	Births per 1,000 residents (1985)	Infant Mortality per 1,000 births[1] (1985)	Abortions per 1,000 live births[2] (1985)
Alabama	11.5	6.2	14.7	13.0	333
Alaska	11.1	7.2	24.1	10.0	283
Arizona	10.9	7.0	18.5	9.6	373
Arkansas	13.1	7.0	14.9	10.9	159
California	8.1	5.0	17.9	9.5	640
Colorado	10.0	6.0	17.1	10.6	438
Connecticut	8.2	2.9	11.6	11.2	550
Delaware	8.7	4.9	15.9	13.2	451
Florida	11.0	6.7	14.4	11.3	465
Georgia	11.8	5.4	16.7	10.8	397
Hawaii	15.3	4.3	17.3	9.1	611
Idaho	10.5	6.0	17.4	7.7	155
Illinois	8.3	4.0	15.4	11.2	372
Indiana	9.2	7.7	14.7	10.3	202
Iowa	8.2	3.5	14.6	8.5	248
Kansas	9.2	3.3	16.0	8.7	264
Kentucky	12.7	5.2	13.9	8.8	189
Louisiana	8.2	3.8	18.1	12.0	240
Maine	10.3	4.8	13.9	8.8	308
Maryland	10.3	3.5	13.7	9.6	480
Massachusetts	7.0	3.4	14.2	9.1	533
Michigan	8.6	4.1	14.8	11.0	486
Minnesota	8.3	3.3	15.9	9.6	257
Mississippi	9.2	5.4	16.2	13.3	142
Missouri	10.0	5.1	15.4	10.5	261
Montana	8.3	5.3	16.0	8.3	288
Nebraska	7.5	3.9	15.9	10.6	268
Nevada	114.2	14.0	16.4	8.6	641
New Hampshire	11.4	4.6	15.8	6.8	419
New Jersey	8.0	3.7	13.7	10.8	672
New Mexico	9.6	6.0	19.9	9.7	219
New York	9.9	3.3	14.4	11.0	746
North Carolina	7.9	5.0	14.4	12.1	379
North Dakota	7.6	13.3	18.6	9.9	230
Ohio	9.0	5.0	15.0	10.3	357
Oklahoma	10.1	7.5	15.7	11.6	269
Oregon	8.0	5.6	15.1	10.1	374
Pennsylvania	7.4	3.4	13.7	11.2	378
Rhode Island	8.2	3.7	14.0	9.5	572
South Carolina	16.0	4.0	14.7	14.0	228
South Dakota	10.5	3.6	17.3	8.4	140
Tennessee	12.2	6.1	14.8	12.4	315
Texas	12.2	6.0	19.2	9.8	320
Utah	10.1	5.1	23.4	10.3	116
Vermont	10.4	4.4	14.8	7.3	448
Virginia	11.5	4.3	14.6	11.1	412
Washington	9.9	5.8	17.3	10.2	458
West Virginia	7.1	5.1	13.2	10.5	185
Wisconsin	8.0	3.5	15.3	8.7	246
Wyoming	10.5	7.0	17.4	8.0	125

[1] Infant Mortality Rate refers to deaths of children from birth to one year. In New York State, for example, out of every 1,000 children born in 1985, 11.0 died within one year.

[2] Abortion Rate refers to pregnancies terminated medically before birth. In New York State, for every 1,000 children born alive in 1985, another 746 were aborted.

546

State	Violent Crime per 100,000 residents (1985)	Property Crime per 100,000 residents (1985)	Alcohol Consumption in gallons per capita (1985)	Deaths from Motor Vehicle Accidents per 100,000 residents (1985)
Alabama	558.0	3,730.3	31.3	22.0
Alaska	570.4	5,675.5	53.8	24.0
Arizona	658.3	6,663.1	50.9	27.0
Arkansas	394.8	3,529.9	29.6	22.6
California	920.5	5,842.3	44.3	18.3
Colorado	523.6	6,508.3	44.2	17.9
Connecticut	425.8	4,403.0	37.1	14.0
Delaware	427.0	4,404.6	45.0	9.6
Florida	1,036.5	7,191.9	46.4	24.2
Georgia	587.6	4,867.8	37.2	22.3
Hawaii	245.2	5,426.2	47.3	11.9
Idaho	222.5	3,984.2	40.5	25.5
Illinois	800.0	4,746.0	41.6	13.3
Indiana	307.7	3,547.1	36.5	17.7
Iowa	235.1	4,915.6	36.9	16.6
Kansas	368.8	4,453.8	33.1	19.8
Kentucky	334.4	2,757.8	31.1	19.1
Louisiana	758.2	5,319.8	40.6	20.7
Maine	147.0	3,314.0	38.0	17.6
Maryland	833.0	4,768.8	40.8	16.3
Massachusetts	556.9	4,166.5	42.0	12.7
Michigan	803.9	5,687.6	39.8	16.9
Minnesota	284.6	4,077.6	39.6	14.5
Mississippi	274.1	3,070.9	35.0	25.3
Missouri	578.5	4,075.5	38.7	18.4
Montana	157.4	4,321.5	46.8	27.5
Nebraska	262.6	3,593.1	40.4	14.8
Nevada	718.9	5,570.8	63.1	28.7
New Hampshire	139.5	3,190.5	62.3	18.8
New Jersey	572.5	4,668.8	38.3	12.7
New Mexico	725.6	5,900.3	50.4	36.9
New York	985.9	4,781.8	36.6	11.3
North Carolina	475.9	3,856.0	33.0	23.7
North Dakota	51.3	2,554.2	39.4	13.1
Ohio	420.9	3,937.8	39.3	15.3
Oklahoma	436.4	5,577.7	30.1	22.4
Oregon	549.7	6,531.0	38.9	20.8
Pennsylvania	358.6	3,994.6	32.0	23.1
Rhode Island	335.5	4,567.0	43.3	11.3
South Carolina	674.6	4,462.8	38.0	28.4
South Dakota	124.7	2,591.2	35.8	18.4
Tennessee	539.6	3,994.6	37.1	17.1
Texas	658.9	6,749.2	48.9	22.5
Utah	266.7	5,211.7	26.7	18.4
Vermont	149.2	3,827.7	46.7	21.7
Virginia	306.0	3,553.8	37.1	17.1
Washington	437.0	6,442.6	39.0	16.8
West Virginia	164.5	2,152.2	31.1	21.7
Wisconsin	257.9	3,838.9	53.2	15.6
Wyoming	293.0	4,064.1	45.6	29.9

State	American Indian/ Aleut/Eskimo	Asian/ Pacific Islander	Black
Alabama	7,561	9,695	995,623
Alaska	64,047	8,035	13,619
Arizona	152,857	22,098	75,034
Arkansas	9,411	6,732	373,192
California	201,311	1,253,987	1,819,282
Colorado	18,059	29,897	101,702
Connecticut	4,533	18,970	217,433
Delaware	1,330	4,132	95,971
Florida	19,316	56,756	1,342,478
Georgia	7,619	24,461	1,465,457
Hawaii	2,778	583,660	17,352
Idaho	10,521	5,948	2,716
Illinois	16,271	159,661	1,675,525
Indiana	7,835	21,488	414,732
Iowa	5,453	11,577	41,700
Kansas	15,371	15,078	126,127
Kentucky	3,610	9,971	259,490
Louisiana	12,064	23,771	1,237,263
Maine	4,087	2,947	3,128
Maryland	8,021	164,276	958,050
Massachusetts	7,743	49,501	221,279
Michigan	40,038	56,731	1,198,710
Minnesota	35,026	26,533	53,342
Mississippi	6,180	7,142	887,206
Missouri	12,319	23,108	514,274
Montana	37,270	2,503	1,786
Nebraska	9,197	6,996	48,389
Nevada	13,304	14,109	50,791
New Hampshire	1,352	2,929	3,990
New Jersey	8,394	103,842	924,786
New Mexico	104,777	6,816	24,042
New York	38,732	310,531	2,401,842
North Carolina	64,635	21,168	1,316,050
North Dakota	20,157	1,979	2,658
Ohio	12,240	47,813	1,076,734
Oklahoma	169,464	17,274	204,658
Oregon	27,309	34,767	37,059
Pennsylvania	8,459	64,381	1,047,609
Rhode Island	2,898	5,303	27,584
South Carolina	5,768	11,807	948,146
South Dakota	45,101	1,728	2,144
Tennessee	5,103	13,963	725,949
Texas	40,074	120,306	1,710,250
Utah	19,256	15,076	9,225
Vermont	874	1,355	1,135
Virginia	9,336	66,209	1,008,311
Washington	60,771	102,503	105,544
West Virginia	1,610	5,194	65,061
Wisconsin	29,497	18,165	182,593
Wyoming	7,125	1,969	3,364

State	Hispanic	White	Other
Alabama	33,100	2,869,688	7,494
Alaska	9,497	308,455	6,325
Arizona	440,915	2,240,033	227,844
Arkansas	17,873	1,890,002	6,176
California	5,543,770	18,031,689	2,362,293
Colorado	339,300	2,570,615	168,561
Connecticut	124,499	2,799,240	67,220
Delaware	9,671	488,543	5,249
Florida	857,898	8,178,387	143,055
Georgia	61,261	3,948,007	18,721
Hawaii	74,479	318,608	42,602
Idaho	36,615	901,641	23,109
Illinois	1,675,525	9,225,575	341,835
Indiana	87,000	5,004,567	42,557
Iowa	27,536	2,838,805	15,852
Kansas	63,333	2,167,752	38,880
Kentucky	27,403	3,379,648	8,714
Louisiana	99,105	2,911,243	19,631
Maine	5,005	1,109,850	4,648
Maryland	64,740	3,158,412	27,687
Massachusetts	141,043	5,362,836	95,678
Michigan	162,388	7,868,956	93,909
Minnesota	32,124	3,936,948	25,299
Mississippi	24,731	1,615,190	4,650
Missouri	51,667	4,346,267	21,476
Montana	9,974	740,148	4,983
Nebraska	28,020	1,490,569	14,855
Nevada	53,786	699,377	21,603
New Hampshire	5,587	910,099	2,240
New Jersey	491,867	6,127,090	200,046
New Mexico	476,089	976,465	187,868
New York	1,659,245	13,961,106	845,077
North Carolina	56,607	4,453,010	19,566
North Dakota	3,903	625,536	2,455
Ohio	119,880	9,597,226	63,366
Oklahoma	57,413	2,597,783	36,087
Oregon	65,833	2,490,192	43,336
Pennsylvania	154,004	10,654,325	90,954
Rhode Island	19,707	896,692	14,677
South Carolina	33,414	2,145,122	8,375
South Dakota	4,028	638,955	2,250
Tennessee	34,081	3,835,078	10,657
Texas	2,985,643	11,197,663	1,160,090
Utah	60,302	1,382,550	34,930
Vermont	3,304	506,736	1,246
Virginia	79,873	4,229,734	32,689
Washington	119,986	3,777,296	84,049
West Virginia	12,707	1,874,751	3,038
Wisconsin	62,981	4,442,598	32,482
Wyoming	24,499	447,716	10,642

PRESIDENTIAL ELECTIONS 1948-1988

State	How Often Democratic Candidate Won	How Often Republican Candidate Won	How Often Third-Party Candidate Won	How Often Voters Chose National Winner
Alabama	4	5	2	6
Alaska*	1	7	0	6
Arizona	1	10	0	8
Arkansas	6	4	1	8
California	2	9	0	9
Colorado	2	9	0	9
Connecticut	2	9	0	7
Delaware	3	8	0	10
Florida	3	8	0	10
Georgia	5	5	1	5
Hawaii*	5.5	2.5	0	4
Idaho	2	9	0	9
Illinois	3	8	0	10
Indiana	1	10	0	9
Iowa	3	8	0	8
Kansas	1	10	0	8
Kentucky	4	7	0	9
Louisiana	3	6	2	7
Maine	2	9	0	7
Maryland	5	6	0	8
Massachusetts	7	4	0	8
Michigan	3	8	0	8
Minnesota	8	3	0	7
Mississippi	3	5	3	5
Missouri	5	6	0	10
Montana	2	9	0	9
Nebraska	1	10	0	8
Nevada	3	8	0	0
New Hampshire	1	10	0	8
New Jersey	2	9	0	9
New Mexico	3	8	0	10
New York	5	6	0	8
North Carolina	6	5	0	9
North Dakota	1	10	0	8
Ohio	3	8	0	10
Oklahoma	2	9	0	9
Oregon	2	9	0	7
Pennsylvania	4	7	0	9
Rhode Island	7	4	0	8
South Carolina	4	6	1	7
South Dakota	1	10	0	8
Tennessee	3	8	0	10
Texas	5	6	0	10
Utah	2	9	0	9
Vermont	1	10	0	8
Virginia	3	8	0	10
Washington	3	8	0	8
West Virginia	8	3	0	7
Wisconsin	4	7	0	9
Wyoming	2	9	0	9

*Figures are reported for 11 elections (1948-1988) except for Alaska and Hawaii, whose voters participated in 8 elections (1960-1988). In 1960, Hawaiian voters were evenly split between the Democratic and Republican candidates.

FINANCE   Total Revenues, Expenditures, and Federal Aid in thousands of dollars, 1985

State	Total Revenues	Total Expenditures	Total Federal Aid
Alabama	5,535,054	5,544,133	1,719,040
Alaska	5,453,073	4,604,555	639,871
Arizona	4,292,969	4,251,280	1,121,528
Arkansas	2,924,952	2,797,251	1,013,635
California	46,046,986	45,774,836	10,558,790
Colorado	4,133,456	4,251,146	1,165,999
Connecticut	5,697,963	4,871,035	1,377,388
Delaware	1,541,758	1,251,097	318,028
Florida	11,882,029	12,147,670	3,121,681
Georgia	7,572,067	7,086,938	2,371,486
Hawaii	2,245,293	2,080,777	435,570
Idaho	1,298,527	1,258,047	444,926
Illinois	15,377,208	14,781,436	4,688,411
Indiana	7,102,450	6,624,083	1,825,318
Iowa	4,004,037	4,228,661	1,163,730
Kansas	3,141,972	3,001,923	855,971
Kentucky	5,396,063	4,982,194	1,763,550
Louisiana	6,961,177	6,562,216	1,785,154
Maine	1,847,770	1,705,482	659,419
Maryland	7,093,148	6,380,869	1,811,665
Massachusetts	10,417,026	10,171,442	2,842,210
Michigan	15,164,596	14,063,002	3,961,474
Minnesota	8,260,655	7,492,284	1,982,655
Mississippi	3,303,269	3,203,645	1,188,296
Missouri	5,786,786	5,441,768	1,935,316
Montana	1,388,045	1,317,682	583,689
Nebraska	2,003,297	2,066,871	675,346
Nevada	1,397,858	1,317,938	387,267
New Hampshire	1,067,753	1,011,885	419,964
New Jersey	13,244,732	11,858,056	2,945,210
New Mexico	3,123,960	2,861,087	891,071
New York	37,432,447	33,358,620	11,092,526
North Carolina	8,288,109	7,828,407	2,133,677
North Dakota	1,471,930	1,440,294	452,291
Ohio	14,775,850	14,071,365	4,158,358
Oklahoma	4,933,429	4,366,858	1,235,997
Oregon	4,079,361	3,986,054	1,449,139
Pennsylvania	16,662,092	15,088,135	4,963,560
Rhode Island	1,859,583	1,786,915	573,163
South Carolina	4,544,945	4,399,862	1,323,560
South Dakota	929,400	964,490	480,179
Tennessee	5,351,295	5,025,340	2,049,340
Texas	18,795,846	17,535,597	4,476,730
Utah	2,582,538	2,563,524	759,414
Vermont	984,361	953,729	336,386
Virginia	7,687,100	7,233,655	1,816,529
Washington	7,407,484	7,401,755	1,826,295
West Virginia	2,964,217	2,779,542	904,024
Wisconsin	8,185,352	7,993,884	2,111,744
Wyoming	1,704,131	1,364,564	503,437

State	Education	Public Welfare	Health	Hospitals
Alabama	2,427,464	659,853	172,950	383,486
Alaska	1,143,566	200,154	190,630	25,167
Arizona	1,915,896	466,608	97,618	57,052
Arkansas	1,232,669	461,509	91,230	125,027
California	17,904,476	11,000,955	1,778,090	1,331,274
Colorado	1,833,724	675,957	117,641	231,662
Connecticut	1,279,610	953,287	118,684	360,143
Delaware	481,488	117,386	40,347	40,697
Florida	4,976,742	1,546,774	694,783	255,672
Georgia	3,034,575	1,135,386	268,390	335,531
Hawaii	729,962	287,048	76,523	102,972
Idaho	539,240	139,564	44,049	22,312
Illinois	4,916,620	3,489,101	430,006	496,376
Indiana	2,908,024	1,009,370	182,607	263,390
Iowa	1,789,860	734,993	57,501	265,293
Kansas	1,352,679	457,307	53,378	187,866
Kentucky	2,015,844	862,512	134,944	153,233
Louisiana	2,361,362	1,098,273	167,710	534,317
Maine	547,113	436,295	50,240	41,160
Maryland	1,964,693	1,199,007	264,204	242,991
Massachusetts	2,546,465	2,459,568	424,446	552,842
Michigan	4,185,009	3,885,099	917,373	703,333
Minnesota	2,695,769	1,479,501	130,332	381,181
Mississippi	1,285,217	482,160	98,578	167,487
Missouri	2,200,860	937,252	179,119	294,105
Montana	435,947	183,879	48,020	31,192
Nebraska	692,501	328,762	62,375	114,349
Nevada	464,617	117,390	29,842	25,445
New Hampshire	200,806	185,046	55,604	43,864
New Jersey	3,472,447	2,127,951	267,762	517,713
New Mexico	1,263,590	252,481	96,574	131,845
New York	9,448,898	9,621,260	1,046,360	2,210,010
North Carolina	3,826,940	945,221	264,267	411,962
North Dakota	540,545	177,129	32,594	60,992
Ohio	5,431,414	3,134,228	389,796	737,236
Oklahoma	1,950,213	701,178	112,881	260,923
Oregon	1,264,086	501,820	101,538	187,511
Pennsylvania	4,840,697	3,927,081	433,175	790,851
Rhode Island	489,448	431,764	71,673	107,900
South Carolina	2,076,648	505,108	216,642	270,446
South Dakota	254,936	119,877	27,796	31,554
Tennessee	2,002,990	852,837	191,376	252,606
Texas	9,545,476	2,145,603	371,724	1,014,477
Utah	1,174,019	310,476	90,126	107,987
Vermont	314,291	171,530	37,352	20,748
Virginia	3,026,592	953,185	224,645	520,606
Washington	3,291,974	1,208,519	227,937	261,540
West Virginia	1,192,378	355,305	87,469	54,743
Wisconsin	2,716,007	1,794,896	311,477	233,185
Wyoming	418,049	89,584	32,444	27,753

State	Number of Registered Motor Vehicles (*1986*)	Miles of Roads, Streets, and Highways (*1986*)	Miles of Class I Railway Operated (*1986*)
Alabama	3,456,934	87,979	3,650
Alaska	362,679	13,639	N/A
Arizona	2,345,521	77,314	1,698
Arkansas	1,426,247	77,050	2,594
California	19,760,260	175,092	6,287
Colorado	2,672,962	76,318	3,369
Connecticut	2,562,349	19,688	466
Delaware	479,665	5,332	212
Florida	10,361,512	99,074	3,085
Georgia	4,840,848	106,607	5,031
Hawaii	689,034	4,040	N/A
Idaho	857,326	71,544	2,256
Illinois	7,419,535	134,778	7,960
Indiana	4,173,614	91,462	4,813
Iowa	2,638,176	112,498	3,503
Kansas	2,176,023	132,642	7,376
Kentucky	2,685,262	69,596	2,846
Louisiana	2,889,658	58,229	2,785
Maine	872,430	21,968	46
Maryland	3,683,394	27,738	849
Massachusetts	3,840,977	33,803	1,079
Michigan	6,831,762	117,664	3,451
Minnesota	3,086,980	132,644	5,092
Mississippi	1,769,773	71,818	1,510
Missouri	3,683,394	119,398	5,823
Montana	672,547	71,706	3,274
Nebraska	1,280,646	92,199	4,426
Nevada	769,076	44,438	1,451
New Hampshire	1,071,247	14,491	355
New Jersey	5,267,489	34,040	1,194
New Mexico	1,320,121	53,596	2,062
New York	9,515,375	110,136	3,453
North Carolina	4,738,956	93,630	3,217
North Dakota	647,663	86,173	4,472
Ohio	8,159,171	113,288	6,102
Oklahoma	2,902,391	111,001	4,024
Oregon	2,263,989	94,578	2,865
Pennsylvania	7,477,017	115,663	5,113
Rhode Island	631,818	5,997	N/A
South Carolina	2,304,208	63,296	2,533
South Dakota	664,060	73,468	1,277
Tennessee	3,932,220	83,851	2,537
Texas	12,406,608	285,962	12,802
Utah	1,110,633	49,938	1,483
Vermont	418,191	14,049	102
Virginia	4,531,780	65,802	3,729
Washington	3,752,242	80,478	3,562
West Virginia	1,170,138	35,143	3,156
Wisconsin	3,120,026	108,667	3,647
Wyoming	440,155	38,931	1,993

DEPARTMENT OF DEFENSE

State	Total Military Installations (1988)	Civilian Workers (1985)	Military Personnel (1985)	Contract Awards in $millions (1985)
Alabama	34	27,317	23,096	1,418
Alaska	47	5,005	20,375	550
Arizona	20	10,365	20,704	2,006
Arkansas	6	4,845	9,748	810
California	104	137,935	204,822	29,115
Colorado	13	14,125	36,914	1,563
Connecticut	6	4,954	6,526	5,543
Delaware	3	1,796	4,662	261
Florida	53	33,029	73,140	5,271
Georgia	21	40,356	64,390	3,520
Hawaii	47	21,259	46,973	626
Idaho	4	1,271	5,647	50
Illinois	15	22,664	40,874	1,693
Indiana	11	15,436	6,576	3,177
Iowa	5	1,545	399	590
Kansas	8	7,028	23,627	2,139
Kentucky	7	14,793	40,782	506
Louisiana	11	8,306	25,710	2,175
Maine	9	10,601	5,382	957
Maryland	26	43,292	35,687	4,608
Massachusetts	22	12,332	9,417	7,714
Michigan	13	12,198	8,773	2,789
Minnesota	5	2,840	859	2,298
Mississippi	13	11,558	16,029	1,310
Missouri	12	20,991	16,072	7,613
Montana	5	1,236	3,728	102
Nebraska	7	3,827	12,794	193
Nevada	12	2,077	9,744	128
New Hampshire	4	1,802	4,122	678
New Jersey	15	28,961	18,974	3,862
New Mexico	9	9,830	16,421	492
New York	36	18,804	21,982	10,033
North Carolina	18	16,312	98,702	1,029
North Dakota	8	1,805	11,274	207
Ohio	19	34,318	13,815	4,648
Oklahoma	13	26,840	31,115	602
Oregon	5	3,107	782	256
Pennsylvania	22	55,743	6,711	4,149
Rhode Island	8	4,715	4,037	431
South Carolina	19	20,545	44,373	490
South Dakota	2	1,404	5,854	78
Tennessee	13	7,300	10,991	793
Texas	45	66,649	127,176	10,562
Utah	13	23,641	6,172	789
Vermont	3	606	74	163
Virginia	37	107,247	96,588	6,167
Washington	23	29,509	43,669	3,559
West Virginia	2	1,599	441	90
Wisconsin	6	3,152	912	1,065
Wyoming	3	1,078	3,747	125

State	Number Public (1986–87)	Number Private (1986–87)	Total Enrollment in Full-Time Equivalent Students (1985)
Alabama	53	26	149,000
Alaska	12	3	14,100
Arizona	19	13	135,000
Arkansas	20	14	63,200
California	138	161	1,062,400
Colorado	29	23	121,800
Connecticut	24	25	107,900
Delaware	5	5	25,800
Florida	37	52	308,300
Georgia	36	45	162,000
Hawaii	9	5	37,000
Idaho	6	4	32,600
Illinois	59	104	450,500
Indiana	29	47	195,600
Iowa	21	40	128,500
Kansas	29	23	100,800
Kentucky	21	35	110,500
Louisiana	20	12	149,000
Maine	13	18	38,000
Maryland	32	24	148,100
Massachusetts	31	90	321,000
Michigan	44	47	354,700
Minnesota	33	40	171,000
Mississippi	25	17	86,800
Missouri	28	64	178,100
Montana	10	7	30,000
Nebraska	18	15	70,800
Nevada	6	3	23,100
New Hampshire	12	16	41,700
New Jersey	31	30	201,300
New Mexico	18	3	47,200
New York	86	222	763,600
North Carolina	74	51	249,900
North Dakota	14	5	32,500
Ohio	60	82	383,900
Oklahoma	29	18	126,700
Oregon	21	24	102,200
Pennsylvania	62	150	422,300
Rhode Island	3	10	53,000
South Carolina	33	29	109,300
South Dakota	8	10	27,000
Tennessee	24	58	153,000
Texas	100	63	566,700
Utah	9	5	84,100
Vermont	6	16	25,600
Virginia	39	36	204,900
Washington	32	20	170,700
West Virginia	16	13	58,400
Wisconsin	29	33	211,700
Wyoming	8	3	17,000

State	Expenditures Per Pupil in Average Daily Attendance (1986–87)	Average Teacher Salary (1986–1987)	Pupil-Teacher Ratio (1987)
Alabama	$2,610	$24,480	19.8
Alaska	8,842	46,082	16.7
Arizona	2,784	28,971	18.4
Arkansas	2,772	21,067	17.5
California	3,887	32,230	23.0
Colorado	4,107	28,400	18.2
Conncticut	5,552	30,193	13.7
Delaware	4,776	28,440	16.0
Florida	4,056	25,552	17.5
Georgia	3,167	26,500	18.9
Hawaii	4,372	27,646	22.6
Idaho	2,555	22,299	20.4
Illinois	3,980	29,399	17.4
Indiana	3,310	26,557	18.3
Iowa	3,740	23,434	15.5
Kansas	4,150	25,297	15.4
Kentucky	3,107	23,560	18.6
Louisiana	3,008	21,736	18.5
Maine	3,650	21,943	15.5
Maryland	4,660	29,940	17.1
Massachusetts	4,856	30,810	14.4
Michigan	3,967	32,800	20.2
Minnesota	4,239	30,190	17.4
Mississippi	2,534	20,050	19.0
Missouri	3,345	24,383	16.4
Montana	4,070	24,370	15.6
Nebraska	3,437	24,138	15.1
Nevada	3,548	27,340	20.4
New Hampshire	3,682	22,625	15.9
New Jersey	6,177	30,770	14.7
New Mexico	3,537	26,892	19.0
New York	6,224	33,500	15.4
North Carolina	3,473	24,395	18.7
North Dakota	3,174	22,533	15.3
Ohio	3,764	27,379	18.1
Oklahoma	3,082	22,770	16.9
Oregon	4,383	28,000	18.3
Pennsylvania	4,691	28,042	16.3
Rhode Island	4,574	32,026	15.0
South Carolina	3,096	24,043	17.3
South Dakota	3,190	19,518	15.6
Tennessee	2,842	23,231	19.9
Texas	3,551	26,255	17.3
Utah	2,455	26,908	23.4
Vermont	4,459	23,292	*14.1
Virgina	3,809	26,401	16.8
Washington	3,808	28,746	20.5
West Virginia	3,619	22,428	15.3
Wisconsin	4,607	29,000	16.3
Wyoming	6,253	28,230	14.0

estimated